2008 Multistate Guide to Estate Planning

JEFFREY A. SCHOENBLUM

CCH
a Wolters Kluwer business

ISBN: 978-0-8080-9141-7

4025 W. Peterson Ave.
Chicago, IL 60646-6085
1 800 248 3248
http://CCHGroup.com

Portions of this work were published in a previous edition.

Printed in the United States of America

Introduction

The *2008 Multistate Guide to Estate Planning* is designed as a comprehensive practical reference for estate planning professionals. It enables the practitioner to keep abreast of the increasingly complex state rules that govern important estate planning issues. Each chart provides citations with which to access current state statutes governing important estate planning issues.

This book explores a number of the vital differences distinguishing the laws of the states pertaining to the transfer of family wealth. At one time, the local practitioner could be proud of his or her provincialism. Today, too many factors make ignorance of other states' laws a dangerous proposition. In our mobile society, with its geographically scattered families, out-of-state vacation homes, retirees moving to sunnier climes, and individuals and trusts with far-flung investments, proper estate planning means planning that addresses the cosmopolitan nature of most clients' lives. In both the transfer tax and income tax contexts, different states impose often markedly different tax burdens. Some states are also willing to assert taxing jurisdiction in a far more aggressive manner than other states. Only by being alert to the differences among the states can the estate planning professional and probate lawyer successfully serve his or her client and safely fulfill professional obligations. This valuable desk reference provides a detailed, readily accessible tool for researching the differences in both the non-tax and tax areas, thereby facilitating inquiry into appropriate estate planning and probate administration.

The easy-to-use format of the *2008 Multistate Guide to Estate Planning* enables the reader to readily locate information concerning one state's treatment of a particular issue—or compare the treatment required by several states—all on the same table. There are 15 tables, each addressing a different topic. Each table is broken into detailed, separate analyses. The analyses consist of a series of detailed questions. The tables are designed for state-by-state comparison.

The answers to the questions posed are to the point, whenever possible. In almost every case, the answer is followed by a relevant statutory, and occasional case, cite. The reader is thus provided with both a brief, reliable response to the query and a further reference if he or she wishes to research the matter further. This approach is intended to save valuable time and reduce the cost of on-line research.

What are the typical scenarios in which this book would prove of considerable benefit to the user? A number of these situations can be readily anticipated:

1. *When a client's property is located in a number of states.* An initial analysis has to be made of such matters as:
   - Who can serve as personal representative?
   - What are the likely state death taxes?
   - If the assets are held in trust, which states will impose tax, and at what rates?

- What claims will a spouse and/or descendants have with regard to estate assets in each of the various states?
- Will ancillary probate be necessary, and what are some of the requirements in the particular states?
- If assets of relatively limited value are involved, will a small-estate procedure be available?
- Who can serve as trustee of a testamentary trust?
- Will the will be deemed valid even though not executed with the formalities required by the law of the other state?

2. *When a client is planning to establish a trust.* Serious consideration must be given to the risk of multiple state income taxation. By knowing the jurisdictional bases for and rates of trust income taxation, the client can not only anticipate the extent of the tax bill, but with the assistance of counsel, alter relevant connecting factors to minimize or even eliminate state income taxation.
3. *When a client wants to establish a dynastic trust or at least maximize the duration of a trust.* Precisely how long can a trust last? The great interest in dynastic trusts has led to the abolition or extension of the rule against perpetuities in some states, but still not in most. In a few states, the common law holds on, while the Uniform Statutory Rule Against Perpetuities prevails in many others, but with all sorts of variations from one state to the next.
4. *When the individual client or professional needs to be concerned with trust accounting.* What are the ins and outs of the rules of the state regarding trust principal and income? How far has the state gone in authorizing modification of net income trusts into total return trusts? Does the state have rules recognizing a trust that is a total return trust from its inception? What are the specific rules with respect to total return trusts?
5. *When a client has moved to your state, perhaps to retire or due to a change in employment.* Suppose he or she has left property, beneficiaries, or relatives behind. How do the former state's rules impact on the property and rights of relatives? What are the likely state income and death tax consequences?
6. *When a client has been named personal representative or fiduciary for an out-of-state relative.* Can he, she, or it serve? What formal steps must be taken?
7. *When a client or other member of the family is in need of a guardianship due to minority or incompetency.* If property is owned in another jurisdiction, who can serve as a guardian or conservator?
8. *When there is a desire to use a testamentary substitute in place of a will.* Which states will give effect to alternatives like P.O.D. and T.O.D. designations? How are joint tenancies, tenancies by the entirety and joint bank accounts treated? Can a writing dispose of tangible personal property? Are the doctrines of incorporation by reference and acts of independent significance recognized?
9. *When a client dies with property in other jurisdictions.* What steps need to be taken in particular states to pay off creditors and retrieve the property? Can all this be accomplished without an ancillary probate?
10. *When a client is concerned about creditor claims.* As the exposure to creditors and the amount of judgments increase, many clients are seeking whatever asset protection is available to them. Various states offer substantial protection for particular types of assets. Through location of the property or the situs of a trust in the state, potential creditors' claims that may be made in the future can be avoided. The client's concerns may also be with claims against trust beneficiaries. What are the positions of various states as to spendthrift and other protections? What claims will succeed?
11. *When a client is concerned about "dying with dignity."* The recent highly visible public controversies and evolving law have made this a focus of primary concern for clients. There are tremendous differences from one state to another. What is a state's position with regard to living wills and health care directives? Just how much can be authorized and what exposure do doctors and hospitals have? Will an out-of-state document be given effect?

These are just some of the questions addressed in this book on a topic-by-topic, state-by-state basis. Considerable emphasis has been placed on formal validity of wills, probate, state taxation, family protections, ancillary administration, nonresident fiduciary qualification, small and informal estate administration, testamentary substitutes, living wills, asset protection, and the rule against perpetuities. These are topics that raise day-to-day, commonly encountered problems in estate practice. Nevertheless, these topics often involve analysis of some of the most convoluted and incomprehensible statutes.

And the 2008 edition also includes an updated CD-ROM containing the Advance Directives for all fifty states.

There is a great deal of material contained in the tables found in this publication. Over the years, a number of former and present students have been of substantial assistance in helping me compile the raw material, confirm the answers to the questions, and proofread. I am very grateful to them. Thank you.

Jeffrey A. Schoenblum
August 2007

Dedication

To Renee Hawkins, an extraordinary professional

About the Author

JEFFREY A. SCHOENBLUM, Centennial Professor of Law at Vanderbilt University, is a graduate of the Johns Hopkins University and Harvard Law School, where he was a Note Editor of the Harvard Law Review. After law school, he served as a clerk for Judge J. Edward Lumbard of the U.S. Court of Appeals for the Second Circuit and then was an associate with the New York law firm of Willkie Farr & Gallagher. Professor Schoenblum is the author of a number of books and articles and has spoken at numerous seminars, including the University of Miami Annual Institute on Estate Planning and, most recently, the Southern Federal Tax Institute. He is an academician of the International Academy of Estate and Trust Law and a fellow of the American College of Estate and Trust Counsel. He has served as Chairman of the ABA Real Property, Probate, and Trust Law Section's Committee on International Property, Estate and Trust Law.

Multistate Guide to Estate Planning
Table of Contents

NONTAX

TAX

Table 1
Formal Will Requirements
(current through 5/1/07)

A very large percentage of clients will have property located in another state. Most typically, this will be in the nature of a summer or winter home, or, perhaps, a farm or apartment inherited from a parent or grandparent. In other cases, the client may have moved due to employment considerations to another state. Property may have been left behind, possibly with the expectation of an eventual return to the prior state of residence. Still other cases may involve an elderly client, who has moved in with relatives or to a nursing home in a different state than the one in which she has previously resided.

In all of these cases, as well as numerous others, one question that the lawyer must address is the formal validity of the will. In other words, to be given effect, a will must comply with the formal execution requirements found in the state's statute of wills. Some attorneys assume that formalities are a collection of antiquated technicalities that have no practical effect and will certainly not be cited in invalidating a will. This is a grave misconception. A review of recent case law demonstrates that well-drafted wills can founder on the shoals of formal requirements. All the effort put into the estate plan may be wasted by this neglect. Additionally, lawyers may well be creating an exposure to malpractice liability.

Certain attorneys are careful to observe their own state's technical formalities. However, they fail to take account of other states' formalities. In the present-day world, this is a dangerous oversight. As noted, many clients have some assets linked to another state. There should be no blithe assumption that the local formalities with which the lawyer is familiar govern the disposition of these assets as well.

The common law rule is that the law of the domicile of the decedent at the time of his death governs a will disposing of personal property. The law of the state in which the real property is situated governs wills disposing of real property. Several jurisdictions, such as North Carolina and the District of Columbia, still follow this approach.

Clearly, separate wills are not typically drafted for personal property and each parcel of real property located in a different state. Thus, careful attention must be paid to the identification and situation of assets of the client. Once this has been accomplished, care must be taken to assure that the formalities of the *single* will of the testator and its execution be in accordance with the law of *all* relevant jurisdictions. The formalities of each of the

50 states and the District of Columbia are set out in Table 1 on a state-by-state basis for easy reference.

There is wide diversity among the states. Not all states adhere to the common law rule. Many have adopted statutes that provide for the formal validity of a will if it is valid under the law of any of a number of states. For example, the Uniform Probate Code approach validates a will if it is valid under the law of the state in which the will was executed, or the state in which the testator was domiciled or has his place of abode at *either* the time of his death or of will execution. In addition, if the will is valid under the local law where it is being probated, it will be given effect. This means that if there is local property, a locally valid will should work, even though the will is invalid, for example, at the testator's domicile, place of abode, or the place of execution. Note also that this approach abandons the separate common law rules for personal and real property.[1]

Not all states have gone as far as the Uniform Probate Code. Thus, again, no assumptions can be made as to whether a will validly executed elsewhere will be given effect locally or whether a will valid locally will be valid where certain estate assets are located.

Obviously, the concerns addressed by this table would not be of importance if all states had the same formal requirements for a valid will. They simply do not! Accordingly, careful review of the relevant state's formal requirements for execution of a will is unavoidable.

1. The Uniform Probate Code also validates a will that is valid under the law of the country of which the person is a national.

Alabama
Formal Will Requirements

Minimum age for executing will	The uniform age for real and personal property is 18. (§ 43-8-130)
Number of witnesses required	Two. (§ 43-8-131)
Holographic wills	No. (§ 43-8-131)
Wills admitted to probate if valid under the law of:	Alabama presently (§ 43-8-131) or if its execution complies with the law of the place where the will is executed, or the place where, at the time of execution or death, the testator is domiciled, has a place of abode, or is a national. (§ 43-8-135)
Does the signing by the testator and/or witnesses just of the self-proving affidavit constitute the execution of the will?	Yes. (§ 43-8-132(c))
Can self-proving affidavit be signed later by testator and/or witnesses?	Yes. At any time after execution, the will may be self-proved by the testator's acknowledgment of the will and the witnesses' affidavits attached or annexed to the will in substantially the form provided for in the statute. (§ 43-8-132(b))
If a witness is a devisee, does this result in the disqualification to serve as a witness or the invalidation of the devise?	No. (§ 43-8-134) (commentary)
Can any other person sign the will?	Yes, if in testator's presence and at his direction. (§ 43-8-131)
When must witnesses sign?	At signing of will by testator or his later acknowledgment of his signature or of the will. (§ 43-8-131)
Must they sign in the presence of the testator?	No, if later acknowledgment of signature or will by the testator in presence of the witness. (§ 43-8-131 commentary)
Must they sign in the presence of each other?	No. (Fulks v. Green, 20 So. 2d 787 (1945)) See also § 43-8-131 commentary.
Must the testator publish the will?	No. (§ 43-8-131 commentary)
Must the will be signed in a particular place?	No. (§ 43-8-131 commentary)
Must the required number of witnesses be present at the same time for the signing or acknowledgment by the testator?	No. (§ 43-8-131)
May the testator acknowledge either his will or his signature?	Yes. (§ 43-8-131)
Requirements to be witness	Any person generally competent to be a witness. (§ 43-8-134(a)) This means at the time of execution a person competent to testify in court as to the facts of execution. (*Id.* commentary)

Alaska
Formal Will Requirements

Minimum age for executing will	Real Property—18 years. (§ 13.12.501) Personal Property—18 years. (§ 13.12.501)
Number of witnesses required	Two. (§ 13.12.502(a)(3))
Holographic wills	Yes. (§ 13.12.502(b))
Wills admitted to probate if valid under the law of:	Alaska; place of execution at time of execution; place where, at time of execution or death, the testator is domiciled, has a place of abode, or is a national. (§ 13.12.506) But see § 13.06.068(c), which omits place of abode and where the testator is a national. § 13.12.506 applies "except as provided" in § 13.06.068. Quaere whether this means that these two bases for will validity are no longer applicable. Why are both of these choice of law sections, that is, §§ 13.12.506 and 13.06.068(c), in effect with regard to formal validity? An "international will" is also valid. (§ 13.12.912)
Does the signing by the testator and/or witnesses just of the self-proving affidavit constitute the execution of the will?	Yes. (§ 13.12.504(c))
Can self-proving affidavit be signed later by testator and/or witnesses?	Yes. At any time after execution, the will may be self-proved by the testator's acknowledgment of the will and the witnesses' affidavits attached or annexed to the will in substantially the form provided for in the statute. (§ 13.12.504(b))
If a witness is a devisee, does this result in the disqualification to serve as a witness or the invalidation of the devise?	No. (§ 13.12.505(b))
Can any other person sign the will?	Yes, if in testator's "conscious presence" and by the testator's direction. (§ 13.12.502(a)(2))
When must witnesses sign?	Within a "reasonable time" after witnessing the signing of the will or testator's acknowledgment of the signature or of the will. (§ 13.12.502(a)(3))
Must they sign in the presence of the testator?	No. (§ 13.12.502(a)(3))
Must they sign in the presence of each other?	No. (§ 13.12.502(a)(3))
Must the testator publish the will?[2]	No. (U.P.C. § 2-502 cmt.)
Must the will be signed in a particular place?	No. (U.P.C. § 2-502 cmt.[3])
Must the required number of witnesses be present at the same time for the signing or acknowledgment by the testator?	No. (§ 13.12.502(a)(3))
May the testator acknowledge either his will or his signature?	Yes. (§ 13.12.502(a)(3))

Requirements to be witness	An individual generally competent to be a witness (§ 13.12.505(a)), that is, the person would probably need to be age 18, as is required in the self-proving affidavit recommended form. (§ 13.12.504(a))

2. Although adopting the Uniform Probate Code, the editorial board comments of the U.P.C. have not been included in Alaska Statutes. Nonetheless, the assumption is that they would be relied upon in construing the statutory provisions.
3. *Id.*

Arizona
Formal Will Requirements

Minimum age for executing will	Real Property—18 years. (§ 14-2501) Personal Property—18 years. (§ 14-2501)
Number of witnesses required	Two. (§ 14-2502(A)(3))
Holographic wills	Yes. (§ 14-2503)
Wills admitted to probate if valid under the law of:	Arizona; place of execution at time of execution; place where, at the time of execution or death, the testator is domiciled, has a place of abode, or is a national. (§ 14-2506)
Does the signing by the testator and/or witnesses just of the self-proving affidavit constitute the execution of the will?	Yes. (§ 14-2504(C); In re Estate of McCay, 802 P.2d 443, 445 (Ct. App. 1990))
Can self-proving affidavit be signed later by testator and/or witnesses?	Yes. At any time after execution, the will may be self-proved by the testator's acknowledgment of the will and the witnesses' affidavits attached or annexed to the will in substantially the form provided for in the statute. (§ 14-2504(B))
If a witness is a devisee, does this result in the disqualification to serve as a witness or the invalidation of the devise?	No. (§ 14-2505(B))
Can any other person sign the will?	Yes, if in testator's "conscious presence" and by the testator's direction. (§ 14-2502(A)(2))
When must witnesses sign?	Within a "reasonable time" after witnessing the signing of the will or testator's acknowledgment of the signature or of the will. (§ 14-2502(A)(3))
Must they sign in the presence of the testator?	No. (§ 14-2502(A)(3))
Must they sign in the presence of each other?	No. (§ 14-2502(A)(3))
Must the testator publish the will?	No. (In re Harber's Estate, 428 P.2d 662, 670 (1967))
Must the will be signed in a particular place?	No. (In re Harris' Estate, 296 P. 267, 269 (1931))
Must the required number of witnesses be present at the same time for the signing or acknowledgment by the testator?	No. (§ 14-2502(A)(3))
May the testator acknowledge either his will or his signature?	Yes. (§ 14-2502(A)(3))
Requirements to be witness	A person who is generally competent to be a witness. (§ 14-2505(A)) Under § 12-2202, persons of unsound mind and children under age 10, who appear incapable of receiving just impressions of the facts respecting which they testify, or of relating them truly, may not be witnesses in a civil action.

Arkansas
Formal Will Requirements

Minimum age for executing will	Real Property—18 years. (§ 28-25-101) Personal Property—18 years. (§ 28-25-101)
Number of witnesses required	Two. (§ 28-25-103(a)); three "credible disinterested witnesses to the handwriting and signature" of the testator in the case of a holographic will without attesting witnesses
Holographic wills	Yes. (§ 28-25-104)
Wills admitted to probate if valid under the law of:	Arkansas; place of execution; place of testator's domicile at the time of execution. (§ 28-25-105)
Does the signing by the testator and/or witnesses just of the self-proving affidavit constitute the execution of the will?	Probably not. The affidavit must be written on the "will." "[I]f that is impracticable," then it must be "securely affixed to the will or to a true copy of the will by the officer administering the oath." (§ 28-25-106; Shamoon v. Tombridge, 723 S.W.2d 827 (1987))
Can self-proving affidavit be signed later by testator and/or witnesses?	Yes, "at any time," even after the testator's death, and even if not requested by an interested person. There is no provision for a testator signing. (§ 28-25-106(b))
If a witness is a devisee, does this result in the disqualification to serve as a witness or the invalidation of the devise?	There is no disqualification of the witness. The devise is invalid, at least in part, if there are not two disinterested witnesses. The portion in excess of the witness's intestate share is for feited. (§ 28-25-102(b))
Can any other person sign the will?	Yes, at testator's "discretion and in his or her presence." (§ 28-25-103(b)(1)(D)) The person must write his own name and state that he signed the testator's name at the request of the testator. (*Id.*)
When must witnesses sign?	Apparently, can sign it at any time if other requirements are fulfilled. (Upton v. Upton, 759 S.W.2d 811 (1988)) For example, the testator may declare his will and acknowledge his signature already made. (§ 28-25-103(b)(1)(B))
Must they sign in the presence of the testator?	Yes. Furthermore, it must be at his request. (§ 28-25-103(c))
Must they sign in the presence of each other?	Apparently not, as long as at testator's request and in his presence. See *Must they sign in the presence of the testator?* (Upton v. Upton, 759 S.W.2d 811, 812 (1988))
Must the testator publish the will?	Yes. He must declare to the attesting witnesses that the instrument is his will. (§ 28-25-103(b)(1))
Must the will be signed in a particular place?	At the end. (§ 28-25-103(b)(2)(A)) However, superfluous or administrative language can follow. (Clark v. National Bank, 802 S.W.2d 452 (1991))
Must the required number of witnesses be present at the same time for the signing or acknowledgment by the testator?	Yes. (§ 28-25-103(b)(2)(B))

May the testator acknowledge either his will or his signature?	No. Provision is made only for the acknowledgment of the testator's signature. (§ 28-25-103(b)(1)(B))
Requirements to be witness	18 years or older and generally competent to be a witness in the state. (§ 28-25-102(a))

California
Formal Will Requirements

Minimum age for executing will	Real Property—18 years. (Prob. § 6100) Personal Property—18 years. (Prob. § 6100) An emancipated minor can make a will. See Family Code §§ 7002 and 7050(e)(6).
Number of witnesses required	Two. (Prob. § 6110(c))
Holographic wills	Yes. (Prob. § 6111)
Wills admitted to probate if valid under the law of:	California; place where executed at time of execution; place at time of execution or death of testator's domicile, abode, or nationality. (Prob. § 6113) An "international will" is also valid. (Prob. § 6381)
Does the signing by the testator and/or witnesses just of the self-proving affidavit constitute the execution of the will?	Possibly so, since one form of evidence of execution is "an affidavit in the original will that includes or incorporates the attestation clause." (Prob. § 8220(b)) The result might be different with the alternative form of permitted affidavit, "to which there is attached a photographic copy of the will." (*Id.*)
Can self-proving affidavit be signed later by testator and/or witnesses?	No. (Prob. §§ 8220(b), 8221(b)(1)) However, provision is made for a separate affidavit by a person with personal knowledge of the circumstances of the execution. (Prob. § 8221(b)(2)) See also Prob. § 8220, which provides for an affidavit, with a photographic copy of the will attached.
If a witness is a devisee, does this result in the disqualification to serve as a witness or the invalidation of the devise?	There is no disqualification of the witness. (Prob. § 6112(b)) The devise is invalid, at least in part, if there are not two disinterested witnesses. The interested witness is entitled to "take such proportion of the devise made to the witness in the will as does not exceed the share of the estate which would be distributed to the witness if the will were not established." (Prob. § 6112(d)) Nevertheless, there is only a presumption of duress, menace, or fraud, or undue influence, which can be rebutted by the witness, except if the witness is a fiduciary. (Prob. § 6112(c))
Can any other person sign the will?	Yes, in the testator's name by a person in testator's presence and by testator's direction. (Prob. § 6110(b)(2)) Alternatively, by a conservator pursuant to a court order to make a will. (Prob. § 6110(b)(3))
When must witnesses sign?	No provision. The witnesses are simply required to sign the will. (Prob. § 6110 comment) Although modeled after U.P.C. § 2-502, there is no requirement that the witnesses sign within a "reasonable time" after the testator's signing or acknowledgment. Nevertheless, the will has to be witnessed prior to the testator's death. In re Estate of Sauressig, 38 Cal. 4th 1045, 44 Cal. Rptr. 3d 672 (Cal. 2006)).
Must they sign in the presence of the testator?	No. The new law repealed the former requirement to this effect. (Prob. § 6110 comment)

Must they sign in the presence of each other?	Yes. (Prob. § 6110 cmt.)
Must the testator publish the will?	No, but witnesses must understand that the instrument they sign is testator's will. (Prob. § 6110(c)(2))
Must the will be signed in a particular place?	No. The new law repealed the former requirement to this effect. (Prob. § 6110)
Must the required number of witnesses be present at the same time for the signing or acknowledgment by the testator?	Yes. (Prob. § 6110(c)(1))
May the testator acknowledge either his will or his signature?	Yes. (Prob. § 6110(c)(1))
Requirements to be witness	Any person generally competent to be a witness. (Prob. § 6112(a)) Under § 700 of the Evidence Code, age, per se, does not bar a person from being a competent witness.

Colorado
Formal Will Requirements

Minimum age for executing will	Real Property—18 years. (§ 15-11-501) Personal Property—18 years. (§ 15-11-501)
Number of witnesses required	Two. (§ 15-11-502(1)(c))
Holographic wills	Yes. (§ 15-11-502(2))
Wills admitted to probate if valid under the law of:	Colorado; place of execution at time of execution; place where, at the time of execution or death, the testator is domiciled, has a place of abode, or is a national. (§ 15-11-506) An "international will" is also valid. (§ 15-11-1003)
Does the signing by the testator and/or witnesses just of the self-proving affidavit constitute the execution of the will?	Yes. (§ 15-11-504(3))
Can self-proving affidavit be signed later by testator and/or witnesses?	At any time after execution, the will may be self-proved by the testator's acknowledgment of the will and the witnesses' affidavits attached or annexed to the will in substantially the form provided for in the statute. (§ 15-11-504(2))
If a witness is a devisee, does this result in the disqualification to serve as a witness or the invalidation of the devise?	No. (§ 15-11-505(2))
Can any other person sign the will?	Yes, if in testator's "conscious presence" and by the testator's direction. (§ 15-11-502(1)(b)) "Conscious presence" means physical proximity. (§ 15-11-502(4))
When must witnesses sign?	Within a "reasonable time" after witnessing the signing of the will or testator's acknowledgment of the signature or of the will. (§ 15-11-502(c)) The witnesses may sign after the death of the testator, if the "reasonable time" requirement is met.
Must they sign in the presence of the testator?	No. (§ 15-11-502(c))
Must they sign in the presence of each other?	No. (U.P.C. § 2-502 cmt.[4])
Must the testator publish the will?	No. (U.P.C. § 2-502 cmt.[5])
Must the will be signed in a particular place?	No. (U.P.C. § 2-502 cmt.[6])
Must the required number of witnesses be present at the same time for the signing or acknowledgment by the testator?	No. (§ 15-11-502(c))
May the testator acknowledge either his will or his signature?	Yes. (§ 15-11-502(c))

Requirements to be witness	A person who is generally competent to be a witness. (§ 15-11-505(1)) Under § 13-90-106, persons of unsound mind and certain children under age 10 may not be witnesses.

4. Although adopting the Uniform Probate Code, the editorial board of the U.P.C. has not been included in Colorado Revised Statutes. Nonetheless, the assumption is that they would be relied upon in construing the statutory provisions.
5. *Id.*
6. *Id.*

Connecticut
Formal Will Requirements

Minimum age for executing will	Real Property—18 years. (§ 45a-250) Personal Property—18 years. (§ 45a-250)
Number of witnesses required	Two. (§ 45a-251)
Holographic wills	No. (§ 45a-251)
Wills admitted to probate if valid under the law of:	Connecticut; place of execution. (§ 45a-251) An "international will" is also valid. (§ 50a-2)
Does the signing by the testator and/or witnesses just of the self-proving affidavit constitute the execution of the will?	The issue would probably not arise regarding the testator, since only the witnesses, and not the testator, sign the affidavits. Moreover, the witnesses must state in the affidavits "such facts as they would be required to testify to in court to prove [the] will," which would presumably include that the testator signed the will or acknowledged his signature in their presence. (§ 45a-285)
Can self-proving affidavit be signed later by testator and/or witnesses?	Yes, at any time, including after the testator's death, any or both of the witnesses may sign an affidavit. However, it must be at the testator's request or, if the testator is deceased, at the request of the executor or any person "interested" in the will. (§ 45a-285)
If a witness is a devisee, does this result in the disqualification to serve as a witness or the invalidation of the devise?	There is no disqualification of the witness. Unless there are sufficient other witnesses, a devise to the witness or the spouse of the witness is void. A person may be a witness without voiding the devise to a community, church, society, association, or corporation in which the witness has an interest. (§ 45a-258)
Can any other person sign the will?	No provision or reported case specifically authorizes this.
When must witnesses sign?	No provision, other than that they must subscribe in testator's presence. (§ 45a-251)
Must they sign in the presence of the testator?	Yes. (§ 45a-251)
Must they sign in the presence of each other?	No. (Wheat v. Wheat, 244 A.2d 359 (1968))
Must the testator publish the will?	No. (In re Simmons' Will, 132 N.Y.S.2d 795, 796 (Sur. Ct. 1954), construing the predecessor of § 45a-256)
Must the will be signed in a particular place?	It must be subscribed, that is, to "write underneath." However, this does not bar it from following certain nondispositive clauses. (Gardner v. Balboni, 588 A.2d 634, 638 (1991))
Must the required number of witnesses be present at the same time for the signing or acknowledgment by the testator?	Apparently, there is no requirement that the witnesses be present at all at the signing or that there be an acknowledgment. (Wheat v. Wheat, 244 A.2d 359 (1968))
May the testator acknowledge either his will or his signature?	No acknowledgment at all is required. (Wheat v. Wheat, 244 A.2d 359 (1968))
Requirements to be witness	No provision or reported case specifically addresses this.

Delaware
Formal Will Requirements

Minimum age for executing will	Real Property—18 years. (12 § 201) Personal Property—18 years. (12 § 201)
Number of witnesses required	Two. (12 § 202)
Holographic wills	No. (12 § 202)
Wills admitted to probate if valid under the law of:	Delaware; place of execution at time of execution; place where, at the time of execution or death, the testator is domiciled, has a place of abode, or is a national. (12 § 1306) An "international will" is also valid. (12 § 252)
Does the signing by the testator and/or witnesses just of the self-proving affidavit constitute the execution of the will?	Although the will can be made self-proved by acknowledgment of testator and affidavits of witnesses if "attached or annexed to the will in form and content substantially as [provided herein]." (12 § 1305) The signature on the affidavit alone suffices under the doctrine of integration. (In re Will of Carter, 565 A.2d 933, 936 (1989))
Can self-proving affidavit be signed later by testator and/or witnesses?	Yes, by later acknowledgment of testator and affidavits of witnesses attached or annexed to the will in substantially the form provided for in the statute. (12 § 1305)
If a witness is a devisee, does this result in the disqualification to serve as a witness or the invalidation of the devise?	There is no disqualification of the witness. (12 § 203(a)) There is no invalidation of the devise either. (12 § 203(b))
Can any other person sign the will?	Yes, in the testator's presence and by the testator's express direction. (12 § 202(a)(1))
When must witnesses sign?	At any time. The witnesses need not even have seen testator sign, nor need they know the instrument is testator's will. (In re Kemp's Will, 186 A. 890, 894 (Super. Ct. 1936))
Must they sign in the presence of the testator?	Yes. (12 § 202(a)(2))
Must they sign in the presence of each other?	No. (In re Estate of Hallett, 295 A.2d 755, 756 (Ch. 1972))
Must the testator publish the will?	No. (In re Kemp's Will, 186 A. 890, 894 (Super. Ct. 1936))
Must the will be signed in a particular place?	Yes. Despite no requirement in the statute, the case law requires that the witnesses subscribe their names below the dispositive provisions, even though this is not required of the testator. Owens v. Bennett, 5 Del. 367 (Super. Ct. 1852); In re Will of Panousseris, 52 Del. 21, 31, 151 A.2d 518, 523-24 (Orph. Ct. 1959).
Must the required number of witnesses be present at the same time for the signing or acknowledgment by the testator?	Apparently not. (In re Kemp's Will, 186 A. 890, 894 (Super. Ct. 1936))

May the testator acknowledge either his will or his signature?	Probably yes. It suffices for the testator to request that the witnesses subscribe their names as witnesses to his signature in his presence. (In re Kemp's Will, 186 A. 890, 894 (Super. Ct. 1936))
Requirements to be witness	Any person generally competent to be a witness. (12 § 203 (a)) The requirement, however, of 12 § 202 is that "credible" witnesses sign. Credible is construed to mean "competent," as provided in 12 § 203. (Hudson v. Flood, 94 A. 760 (Super. Ct. 1915)) To be credible and competent, the person must be capable of testifying in court. (*Id.*)

District of Columbia
Formal Will Requirements

Minimum age for executing will	Real Property—18 years. (§ 18-102) Personal Property—18 years. (§ 18-102)
Number of witnesses required	Two. (§ 18-103)
Holographic wills	No. (§ 18-103)
Wills admitted to probate if valid under the law of:	There is no statutory provision. The common law rule is in effect. Thus, the law of the situs governs real property. (Greenwood v. Page, 138 F.2d 921, 923 (D.C. Cir. 1943); Farrar v. Bingham, 93 F.2d 252, 254 (D.C. Cir. 1937)) The law of the domicile at death of the testator governs personal property. (In re Kerr's Estate, 433 F.2d 479, 481 n.10 (D.C. Cir. 1970))
Does the signing by the testator and/or witnesses just of the self-proving affidavit constitute the execution of the will?	There is no provision for a self-proving affidavit. A will can be admitted to abbreviated probate pursuant to which "due execution of the will shall be presumed." The will should have a recital by the attesting witnesses of facts constituting due execution. Alternatively, a verified statement of any person with personal knowledge of the circumstances of the execution may be used. (§ 20-312(b))
Can self-proving affidavit be signed later by testator and/or witnesses?	There is no provision for a self-proving affidavit.
If a witness is a devisee, does this result in the disqualification to serve as a witness or the invalidation of the devise?	There is no disqualification of the witness. (§ 18-104(d)) The devise is void to the extent it exceeds the amount that would be taken as an intestate share if there was no will. (§ 18-104 (b)) A creditor for whom there is a charge in the will can serve as a witness without diminishing the charge for the creditor's benefit. (§ 18-106) Interestingly, the statute does not provide for the interested witness taking if there are two other disinterested witnesses. This, however, is suggested by In re Estate of Pye, 325 F. Supp. 321 (D.D.C. 1971).
Can any other person sign the will?	Yes, if in his presence and by his express direction. (§ 18-103(1))
When must witnesses sign?	No statute or case authority directly on point.
Must they sign in the presence of the testator?	Yes. (§ 18-103(2))
Must they sign in the presence of each other?	No statute or case authority directly on point.
Must the testator publish the will?	Maybe. (Homovich v. Chapman, 191 F.2d 761 (D.C. App. 1951) (considering publication of the will as a factor in determining validity.))
Must the will be signed in a particular place?	No. (In re Estate of Hall, 328 F. Supp. 1305 (D.D.C. 1971), *aff'd*, 466 F.2d 340 (D.C. Cir. 1972))

Must the required number of witnesses be present at the same time for the signing or acknowledgment by the testator?	No. (Davis v. Davis, 471 A.2d 1008 (Ct. App. 1984))
May the testator acknowledge either his will or his signature?	Document must be acknowledged by the testator to be his or her will. (Davis v. Davis, 471 A.2d 1008 (Ct. App. 1984))
Requirements to be witness	The witnesses must be "credible." (§ 18-103(2))

Florida
Formal Will Requirements

Minimum age for executing will	Real Property—18 years. (§ 732.501) Personal Property—18 years. (§ 732.501). An emancipated minor can execute a will as well.
Number of witnesses required	Two. (§ 732.502(1)(b))
Holographic wills	No. (§ 732.502(2)); In re Estate of Salathe, 703 So. 2d 1167, 1168 (Fl. App. 1997))
Wills admitted to probate if valid under the law of:	In the case of a resident, the Florida law as to execution requirements must be observed. There is no choice of law statute for the benefit of residents. In the case of a will "executed by a nonresident of Florida" effective prior to 2002 the will must be validly executed under the law of the place "where the testator was at the time of execution." Effective for wills executed in 2002 or in subsequent years, as well as for any wills executed in prior years, the will shall be valid if valid "under the laws of the state or country where the will was executed." (§ 732.502(2)) This rule does not, however, allow for a holographic or nuncupative will even though allowed at the place of execution. See also In re Estate of Swanson, 397 So. 2d 465, 466 (Fl. App. 1981).
Does the signing by the testator and/or witnesses just of the self-proving affidavit constitute the execution of the will?	One court agrees for witnesses (In re Estate of Charry, 359 So. 2d 544 (Dist. Ct. App. 1978)), since there is no requirement as to where witnesses sign. The decision distinguishes the witnesses from the testator in this regard. As for the testator, it may also be acceptable, since a testator's signature in the attestation clause has been approved. (In re Schiele's Estate, 51 So. 2d 287 (1951)) However, each case would, with regard to the testator, turn on the particular facts. As for the statute, the implication is that it would not treat this as a proper execution of the will, since the self-proving form must be attached *to* or *follow* the will, it requires the testator's signature in addition to the signature in the will, and the affidavit must be attached to or follow *the* will in substantially the prescribed form. (§ 732.503)
Can self-proving affidavit be signed later by testator and/or witnesses?	Yes, by later acknowledgment of will by testator, affidavits of the witnesses, and officer's certificate "attached to or following the will, in substantially the [statutory] form. . . ." (§ 732.503)
If a witness is a devisee, does this result in the disqualification to serve as a witness or the invalidation of the devise?	There is no disqualification of the witness. (§ 732.504(2)) There is no reference to voiding the devise to an interested witness. The provision is intended to parallel U.P.C. § 2-504 and, thus, the devise to the witness probably is not invalid.
Can any other person sign the will?	Yes, in the testator's presence and at his direction. (§ 732.502(1)(a)(2))
When must witnesses sign?	No time specified. (§ 732.502(1)(c))

Must they sign in the presence of the testator?	Yes. (§ 732.502(1)(c))
Must they sign in the presence of each other?	Yes. (§ 732.502(1)(c))
Must the testator publish the will?	No. (York v. Smith, 385 So. 2d 1110, 1111 (Ct. App. 1980); In re Beakes' Estate, 306 So. 2d 99, 101 (1974))
Must the will be signed in a particular place?	Yes, the testator, but not the witnesses, must sign at the end. (§ 732.502(1)(a)(1)) However, if the testator signs, for example, in the attestation clause, this may be permissible if testamentary intent is established. (In re Schiele's Estate, 51 So. 2d 287, 289 (1951))
Must the required number of witnesses be present at the same time for the signing or acknowledgment by the testator?	No. (§ 732.502(1)(b)(2))
May the testator acknowledge either his will or his signature?	The acknowledgment may be either of the fact that he has previously signed the will or that another person subscribed his name to it. (§ 732.502(1)(b)(2)(a)-(b))
Requirements to be witness	Any person competent to be a witness. (§ 732.504(1))

Georgia[7]
Formal Will Requirements

Minimum age for executing will	Real Property—14 years. (§ 53-4-10) Personal Property—14 years. (§ 53-4-10)
Number of witnesses required	Two. (§ 53-4-20)
Holographic wills	No. (§ 53-4-20)
Wills admitted to probate if valid under the law of:	In the case of a domiciliary of Georgia at death, Georgia law determines the validity of the will. (Carr v. Kupfer, 296 S.E.2d 560, 562 (1968)) In the case of any other testator, the law of his domicile. (Arrington v. Hosemann, 163 S.E.2d 722, 723 (1982)) In the case of real property, the law of the situs controls. (Veach v. Veach, 53 S.E.2d 98, 101 (1949)) A statute now restates, at least in part, the common law. If a will is a "foreign will" or an "out-of-state will," and is "valid under the laws of this state," it can be offered for original probate under certain conditions. (§ 53-5-31) A "foreign will" is a will of a nondomiciliary who dies while domiciled in a jurisdiction that is not a state or territory governed by the Constitution of the United States and who at death owns property located in this state or a cause of action the venue of which lies in this state. (§ 53-5-30(2)) An "out-of-state will" is the will of a nondomiciliary who dies while domiciled in a state or territory that is governed by the Constitution of the United States and who at death owns property located in this state or a cause of action the venue of which lies in this state. (§ 53-5-30(4)) Quaere whether it is a foreign will if the person later becomes a resident (i.e., domiciliary) of Georgia and is one at the time of death.
Does the signing by the testator and/or witnesses just of the self-proving affidavit constitute the execution of the will?	Probably yes. (Westmoreland v. Tallent, 549 S.E.2d 113, 116 (2001))
Can self-proving affidavit be signed later by testator and/or witnesses?	Yes, at any time during "the lifetime of the testator and the witnesses." The testator and witnesses can sign an affidavit that is to be attached or annexed to the will in the form and contents substantially as provided in the statute. (§ 53-4-24(a) & (b))
If a witness is a devisee, does this result in the disqualification to serve as a witness or the invalidation of the devise?	There is no disqualification of the witness. However, unless there are two other subscribing witnesses who are not devisees, the devise to witness is void. (§ 53-4-23(a)) The fact that a spouse of a witness receives a devise under the will simply is a "fact going only to the credibility of the witness." (§ 53-4-23(b))
Can any other person sign the will?	Yes, if in the testator's presence and by his express direction. (§ 53-4-20(a))
When must witnesses sign?	Either at the testator's execution of the will or at a later acknowledgment of his signature. See In re Estate of Brannon, 441 S.E.2d 248, 248-49 (1994); Thornton v. Hulme, 128 S.E.2d 744, 745 (1962). § 53-4-20, which addresses witnessing in general, "carries forward" its predecessor, § 53-2-40. See Comment to § 53-4-20. The cited cases were decided under § 53-2-40.

Must they sign in the presence of the testator?	Yes. (§ 53-4-20(b)) A "line-of-vision" test under the current law: " 'it is not necessary for the testator to have watched the witnesses sign, as long as the testator could have watched them sign.' " (McCarmik v. Jeffers, 637 S.E.2d 666, 669 (Ga. 2006), citing to Restatement (Third) of Property § 3.1 at 177)) In addition, no special request of the witnesses to attest the will is required, since this is implied from the act itself of witnessing. (Whitfield v. Pitts, 53 S.E.2d 549 (1949)) Note also that one witness must not sign for the other. (§ 53-4-20(b))
Must they sign in the presence of each other?	No. (In re Estate of Brannon, 441 S.E.2d 248, 249 (Ga. 1994); Whitfield v. Pitts, 53 S.E.2d 549 (1949))
Must the testator publish the will?	No, as long as the witnesses are "requested by the testator to subscribe the memorandum of attestation" or are otherwise requested to attest his signature. (Slade v. Slade, 118 S.E. 645, 648 (1923))
Must the will be signed in a particular place?	Apparently not. (In re Estate of Brannon, 441 S.E.2d 248, 249 (1994) ("Where all of the signature pages are physically connected as part of the will, the fact that a testator's signature and the signatures of witnesses do not appear on the same page does not in itself invalidate the execution of the will"; the court points out that nothing in the statute requires signing on the same page; the implication is that there is no rule as to placement of signatures, although the decision's language leaves open the possibility of a different result under certain circumstances))
Must the required number of witnesses be present at the same time for the signing or acknowledgment by the testator?	No. See *May the testator acknowledge either his will or his signature?*
May the testator acknowledge either his will or his signature?	The testator must acknowledge his signature. (Norton v. Georgia R.R. Bank & Tr., 285 S.E.2d 910, 912 (1982), *aff'd*, 322 S.E.2d 870 (1984)) The acknowledgment may be implied. (Thornton v. Hulme, 128 S.E.2d 744, 745 (1962); Glenn v. Mann, 214 S.E.2d 911, 914 (1975))
Requirements to be witness	The witnesses must be competent to be a witness and at least be 14 years old. (§ 53-4-22)

7. Note that the references herein are to the Probate Code for estates of decedents dying on or after January 1, 1998.

Hawaii
Formal Will Requirements

Minimum age for executing will	Real Property—18 years. (§ 560:2-501) Personal Property—18 years. (§ 560:2-501)
Number of witnesses required	Two. (§ 560:2-502(a)(3))
Holographic wills	Yes. (§ 560:2-502(b))
Wills admitted to probate if valid under the law of:	Hawaii; place of execution at time of execution; place where, at the time of execution or death, the testator is domiciled, has a place of abode, or is a national. (§ 560:2-506)
Does the signing by the testator and/or witnesses just of the self-proving affidavit constitute the execution of the will?	Yes. (§ 560:2-504(c))
Can self-proving affidavit be signed later by testator and/or witnesses?	At any time after execution, the will may be self-proved by the testator's acknowledgment of the will and the witnesses' affidavits attached or annexed to the will in substantially the form provided for in the statute. (§ 560:2-504(b))
If a witness is a devisee, does this result in the disqualification to serve as a witness or the invalidation of the devise?	No. (§ 560:2-505(b))
Can any other person sign the will?	Yes, if in testator's "conscious presence" and by the testator's direction. (§ 560:2-502(a)(2))
When must witnesses sign?	Within a "reasonable time" after witnessing the signing of the will or testator's acknowledgment of the signature or of the will. (§ 560:2-502(a)(3))
Must they sign in the presence of the testator?	No. (§ 560:2-502(a)(3))
Must they sign in the presence of each other?	No. (§ 560:2-502(a)(3))
Must the testator publish the will?	No. (U.P.C. § 2-502 cmt.[8])
Must the will be signed in a particular place?	No. (U.P.C. § 2-502 cmt.[9])
Must the required number of witnesses be present at the same time for the signing or acknowledgment by the testator?	No. (§ 560:2-502 & U.P.C. § 2-502 cmt.[10])
May the testator acknowledge either his will or his signature?	Yes, as long as each witness signs within a "reasonable time" after the testator's acknowledgment. (§ 560:2-502 & U.P.C. § 2-502 cmt.[11])

Requirements to be witness	An individual generally competent to be a witness. (§ 560:2-505(a))

8. Although adopting the Uniform Probate Code, the editorial comments of the U.P.C. have not been included in Hawaii Code Annoted. Nonetheless, the assumption is that they would be relied upon in construing the statutory provisions.
9. *Id.*
10. *Id.*
11. *Id.*

Idaho
Formal Will Requirements

Minimum age for executing will	Any person 18 years old or an emancipated minor under age 18 who is of sound mind may also execute a will. (§ 15-2-501)
Number of witnesses required	Two. (§ 15-2-502)
Holographic wills	Yes. (§ 15-2-503)
Wills admitted to probate if valid under the law of:	Idaho; place of execution at time of execution; place where, at the time of execution or death, the testator is domiciled, has a place of abode, or is a national. (§ 15-2-506)
Does the signing by the testator and/or witnesses just of the self-proving affidavit constitute the execution of the will?	Yes. (§ 15-2-504(a))
Can self-proving affidavit be signed later by testator and/or witnesses?	Yes, at any time after execution, the will may be self-proved by the testator's acknowledgment of the will and the witnesses' affidavits attached or annexed to the will in substantially the form provided for in the statute. (§ 15-2-504(b))
If a witness is a devisee, does this result in the disqualification to serve as a witness or the invalidation of the devise?	No. (§ 15-2-505(b))
Can any other person sign the will?	Yes, if in the testator's presence and by his direction. (§ 15-2-502)
When must witnesses sign?	No time limit specified. (§ 15-2-502)
Must they sign in the presence of the testator?	No. (§ 15-2-502 cmt.)
Must they sign in the presence of each other?	No. (§ 15-2-502 cmt.)
Must the testator publish the will?	No. (§ 15-2-502 cmt.)
Must the will be signed in a particular place?	No. (§ 15-2-502 cmt.)
Must the required number of witnesses be present at the same time for the signing or acknowledgment by the testator?	No. (§ 15-2-502 cmt.)
May the testator acknowledge either his will or his signature?	Yes. (§ 15-2-502 cmt.)
Requirements to be witness	Any person 18 or older who is generally competent to be a witness. (§ 15-2-505(a))

Illinois
Formal Will Requirements

Minimum age for executing will	Real Property—18 years. (755 ILCS § 5/4-1) Personal Property—18 years. (755 ILCS § 5/4-1)
Number of witnesses required	Two. (755 ILCS § 5/4-3)
Holographic wills	No. (755 ILCS § 5/4-3)
Wills admitted to probate if valid under the law of:	Illinois; place where executed; place where testator domiciled at the time of execution. (755 ILCS § 5/7-1) An "international will" is also valid. (755 ILCS § 10/2)
Does the signing by the testator and/or witnesses just of the self-proving affidavit constitute the execution of the will?	Unlikely that testator would even sign, since the testator's signature is not required on affidavit. (755 ILCS § 5/6-4) However, since will can be signed anywhere and affidavit forms a part of or is attached to will, signing of affidavit by testator might well suffice.
Can self-proving affidavit be signed later by testator and/or witnesses?	Yes, by an affidavit signed after attestation and forming part of the will or attached to will or accurate facsimile. (755 ILCS 5/6-4(b))
If a witness is a devisee, does this result in the disqualification to serve as a witness or the invalidation of the devise?	There is no disqualification of the witness. Unless the will can be proved without the witness, the witness cannot take the excess over what the witness would have taken by intestate succession. (755 ILCS § 5/4-6(a))
Can any other person sign the will?	Yes, in the testator's presence and by his direction. (755 ILCS 5/4-3(a))
When must witnesses sign?	No time limit. Each can sign at a later date than testator, as long as signed in presence of testator by each witness and following acknowledgment of testator that the instrument was his act or deed, even if not revealing it is his will. (Martin v. Martin, 165 N.E. 644, 649-50 (1929))
Must they sign in the presence of the testator?	Yes. (755 ILCS 5/4-3(a))
Must they sign in the presence of each other?	No. (Heavner v. Heavner, 174 N.E. 413, 414 (1930)) However, this case precedes the current statute. The statute's language could be read as requiring both witnesses there at the same time, since it requires the will to be "attested in the presence of the testator by two or more credible witnesses." (755 ILCS § 5/4-3(a))
Must the testator publish the will?	No. (In re Estate of Carroll, 548 N.E.2d 650, 653 (1989))
Must the will be signed in a particular place?	No. (In re Estate of Carroll, 548 N.E.2d 650, 653 (1989))
Must the required number of witnesses be present at the same time for the signing or acknowledgment by the testator?	No. (755 ILCS § 5/4-3)

May the testator acknowledge either his will or his signature?	The testator would have to acknowledge before the witness signs that the instrument is his act or deed. (In re Estate of Carroll, 548 N.E.2d 650, 653 (1989))
Requirements to be witness	The witness must be "credible" (755 ILCS 5/4-3(a)), which means legally competent to testify to the facts attested at the time the will is subscribed. (Smith v. Goodell, 101 N.E. 255 (1913))

Indiana
Formal Will Requirements

Minimum age for executing will	Real Property—18 years. (§ 29-1-5-1) Personal Property—18 years. (§ 29-1-5-1) In both instances, if a member of the armed forces or merchant marines, a person younger than 18 may make a will.
Number of witnesses required	Two. (§ 29-1-5-3)
Holographic wills	No. (§ 29-1-5-3)
Wills admitted to probate if valid under the law of:	Under law in force at time of execution or death in Indiana, place of execution, domicile of testator at the time of execution or death. (§ 29-1-5-5)
Does the signing by the testator and/or witnesses just of the self-proving affidavit constitute the execution of the will?	No. The acknowledgment of the will by the testator and verifications of the witnesses must be evidenced by their signatures "attached or annexed to the will in form and content substantially as [provided in the statute]." (§ 29-1-5-3 (cmt.)) Unlike, for example, Delaware, Indiana does not recognize the doctrine of integration, which might make the self-proving affidavit part of the "will." (Keener v. Archibald, 533 N.E.2d 1268, 1270 (Ct. App. 1989))
Can self-proving affidavit be signed later by testator and/or witnesses?	Yes. (§ 29-1-5-3(b)(1)(B))
If a witness is a devisee, does this result in the disqualification to serve as a witness or the invalidation of the devise?	There is no disqualification of the witness. Unless the will can be proved without the witness, the witness cannot take the excess over what the witness would have taken by intestate succession. (§ 29-1-5-2(c))
Can any other person sign the will?	Yes, at the testator's direction and in the testator's presence. (§ 29-1-5-3(b)(1)(C))
When must witnesses sign?	No time specified, as long as other requirements in *Can self-proving affidavit be signed later by testator and/or witnesses?* and *May the testator acknowledge either his will or his signature?* are met. (§ 29-1-5-3(b))
Must they sign in the presence of the testator?	Yes. (§ 29-1-5-3(b)(2))
Must they sign in the presence of each other?	Yes. (§ 29-1-5-3(b)(2))
Must the testator publish the will?	Yes. (§ 29-1-5-3(b)(1))
Must the will be signed in a particular place?	No. There is no statutory provision. Earlier case law did not require a signature in a particular place. (Thrift Tr. Co. v. White, 167 N.E. 141, 168 N.E. 250, 251 (1929))
Must the required number of witnesses be present at the same time for the signing or acknowledgment by the testator?	Yes. (§ 29-1-5-3(a)(1))

May the testator acknowledge either his will or his signature?	The testator must signify in the presence of at least two witnesses that the will is his and acknowledge his signature if already made. (§ § 29-1-5-3(b)(1), 29-1-5-3(b)(1)(B))
Requirements to be witness	Any person competent to be a witness generally in Indiana. (§ 29-1-5-2(b))

Iowa
Formal Will Requirements

Minimum age for executing will	"Any person of full age and sound mind may dispose by will of all the person's property. . . ." (§ 633.264) Generally, full age would be 18, except if married at an earlier age. (§ 599.1)
Number of witnesses required	Two. (§ 633.279)
Holographic wills	No. (§ 633.279)
Wills admitted to probate if valid under the law of:	Iowa; place where executed; place where testator domiciled. (§ 633.283)
Does the signing by the testator and/or witnesses just of the self-proving affidavit constitute the execution of the will?	No. The acknowledgment of the will by the testator and verifications of the witnesses must be evidenced by their signatures "attached or annexed to the will, in form and content substantially as [provided in the statute]." (§ 633.279(2)) But see Delaware, *Does the signing by the testator and/or witnesses just of the self-proving affidavit constitute the execution of the will?*
Can self-proving affidavit be signed later by testator and/or witnesses?	Yes. (§ 633.279(2))
If a witness is a devisee, does this result in the disqualification to serve as a witness or the invalidation of the devise?	There is no disqualification of the witness. (§ 633.281) Unless there are two other disinterested witnesses, the witness cannot take the excess over what the witness would have taken by intestate succession. (§ 633.281)
Can any other person sign the will?	Yes, in the testator's presence and by the testator's express direction. (§ 633.279(1))
When must witnesses sign?	No time limit specified.
Must they sign in the presence of the testator?	Yes. (§ 633.279(1))
Must they sign in the presence of each other?	Yes. (§ 633.279(1))
Must the testator publish the will?	Yes. (§ 633.279(1))
Must the will be signed in a particular place?	No statute or case authority directly on point.
Must the required number of witnesses be present at the same time for the signing or acknowledgment by the testator?	No. (In re McElderry's Estate, 251 N.W. 610, 612 (1933) (decided under the former law))
May the testator acknowledge either his will or his signature?	The later acknowledgment of the signature is an alternative, but must, apparently, be done in the presence of the two witnesses. (In re McElderry's Estate, 251 N.W. 610, 612 (1933) (decided under the former law))
Requirements to be witness	Any person who is at least 16 and who is competent to be a witness generally in the state. (§ 633.280)

Kansas
Formal Will Requirements

Minimum age for executing will	"Age of majority." (§ 59-601) This is generally 18 years (§ 38-101). However, it is age 16, if married.
Number of witnesses required	Two. (§ 59-606)
Holographic wills	No. (§ 59-606)
Wills admitted to probate if valid under the law of:	Kansas; place where executed; place of testator's residence at the time of execution or death. (§ 59-609)
Does the signing by the testator and/or witnesses just of the self-proving affidavit constitute the execution of the will?	Yes, with respect to witnesses signing the affidavit and not the will itself. (§ 59-606) There is no similar reference to the testator, who also must sign the affidavit. However, In re Estate of Petty, 608 P.2d 987, 992 (1980), though involving witnesses, would appear to support the result that a will is duly executed even if the testator signs the self-proving affidavit.
Can self-proving affidavit be signed later by testator and/or witnesses?	Yes, by affidavits of testator and witnesses "in form and contents substantially as [provided by statute]." (§ 59-606)
If a witness is a devisee, does this result in the disqualification to serve as a witness or the invalidation of the devise?	Devise is void, unless there are two other disinterested witnesses or to the extent the witness would take by intestate succession. (§ 59-604)
Can any other person sign the will?	Yes, in the presence of the testator and by the testator's express direction. (§ 59-606)
When must witnesses sign?	No time specified.
Must they sign in the presence of the testator?	Yes. (§ 59-606) This may occur after the witness "saw" testator's signing or "heard" later acknowledgment of the same. (§ 59-606)
Must they sign in the presence of each other?	No. (In re Perkins' Estate, 504 P.2d 564, 568-69 (Kan. 1972)) However, the self-proving affidavit form has an express provision stating that the witnesses stated that "they did sign the will as witnesses in the presence of each other and in the presence of the testator and at the testator's request." To be valid, the self-proving affidavit must be in "form and contents substantially" as specified in the statute. (§ 59-606)
Must the testator publish the will?	No. (In re Estate of Koellen, 176 P.2d 544, 549 (1947))
Must the will be signed in a particular place?	At the end. (§ 59-606)
Must the required number of witnesses be present at the same time for the signing or acknowledgment by the testator?	No. (§ 59-606) The statute states that the will "shall be attested and subscribed in the presence of such party by two or more competent witnesses. . . ." In Humphrey v. Wallace, 216 P.2d 781, 783 (1950), presence at the same time was not required.
May the testator acknowledge either his will or his signature?	The acknowledgment must be of the signature, since the law describes two or more witnesses who "saw the testator subscribe or heard the testator acknowledge the same." (§ 59-606)
Requirements to be witness	Competency. (§ 59-607)

Kentucky
Formal Will Requirements

Minimum age for executing will	Real Property—18 years. (§ 394.020) Personal Property—18 years. (§ 394.020)
Number of witnesses required	Two. (§ 394.040)
Holographic wills	Yes. (§ 394.040)
Wills admitted to probate if valid under the law of:	Place where testator is domiciled, if he is not domiciled in Kentucky at the time of his death. (§ 394.120)
Does the signing by the testator and/or witnesses just of the self-proving affidavit constitute the execution of the will?	No. The acknowledgment of the will by the testator and verifications of the witnesses must be evidenced by their signatures "attached or annexed to the will in form and content substantially as [provided in the statute]." (§ 394.225(2)) But see Delaware, *Does the signing by the testator and/or witnesses just of the self-proving affidavit constitute the execution of the will?*
Can self-proving affidavit be signed later by testator and/or witnesses?	Yes, by the acknowledgment by testator of will and the affidavits of witnesses before "an officer authorized to administer oaths." (§ 394.225(2))
If a witness is a devisee, does this result in the disqualification to serve as a witness or the invalidation of the devise?	No. (§ 394.210) However, if the will cannot otherwise be proved without the witness, and the witness *or the witness' spouse* is a devisee, then the witness or witness' spouse cannot take more than the witness would take by intestate succession. (§ 394.210(2))
Can any other person sign the will?	Yes, in testator's presence and by his direction. (§ 394.040)
When must witnesses sign?	At either testator's execution or later acknowledgment. (§ 394.040)
Must they sign in the presence of the testator?	Yes. (§ 394.040)
Must they sign in the presence of each other?	Yes. (§ 394.040)
Must the testator publish the will?	No. (Wroblewski v. Yeager, 361 S.W.2d 108, 110 (Ct. App. 1962))
Must the will be signed in a particular place?	At the end or close of the writing. (§ 446.060(1)) This requirement is met in the case of a holographic will even if signature precedes date. (Fairweather v. Nord, 388 S.W.2d 122 (Ky. 1965))
Must the required number of witnesses be present at the same time for the signing or acknowledgment by the testator?	Yes. (§ 394.040)
May the testator acknowledge either his will or his signature?	The *will* must be acknowledged. (§ 394.040)
Requirements to be witness	No specific provision. Statute simply notes that subsequent incompetency does not invalidate attestation. (§ 394.210(1))

Louisiana[12]
Formal Will Requirements

Minimum age for executing will	Real Property—16 years. (Civ. Code art. 1476) Personal Property—16 years. (Civ. Code art. 1476)
Number of witnesses required	Two, plus a notary for a notarial or sealed testament. (Civ. Code art. 1577(1))
Holographic wills	Yes. (Civ. Code art. 1575)
Wills admitted to probate if valid under the law of:	Louisiana; place of execution; place where testator domiciled at the time of execution. (Rev. Stat. § 9:2401)

12. **Note:** Great caution should be exercised with regard to execution of a will because, while Louisiana allows for two types of wills, neither is precisely identical to those recognized in the other states or under the common law. These are holographic and notarial testaments. (Civ. Code art. 1574)

Maine
Formal Will Requirements

Minimum age for executing will	Real Property—18 years. (18A § 2-501) Personal Property—18 years. (18A § 2-501)
Number of witnesses required	Two. (18A § 2-502)
Holographic wills	Yes. (18A § 2-503)
Wills admitted to probate if valid under the law of:	Maine; place of execution at the time of execution; place where, at time of execution or death, testator is domiciled, has a place of abode, or is a national. (18A § 2-506)
Does the signing by the testator and/or witnesses just of the self-proving affidavit constitute the execution of the will?	Yes. (18-A § 2-504(a) & cmt.)
Can self-proving affidavit be signed later by testator and/or witnesses?	Yes, if acknowledgment of will by testator and affidavits of witnesses before notary attached or annexed to will in substantially the [prescribed statutory] form. (18-A § 2-504(b))
If a witness is a devisee, does this result in the disqualification to serve as a witness or the invalidation of the devise?	There is no disqualification of the witness. (18-A § 2-505 cmt.) The devise is not invalidated. (18-A § 2-505(b))
Can any other person sign the will?	Yes, if in the testator's presence and by his direction. (18-A § 2-502)
When must witnesses sign?	Either (1) at the time the will is signed; (2) the acknowledgment that the document is the testator's will; or (3) the acknowledgment by the testator that the signature is the testator's. (18-A § 2-502 & cmt.)
Must they sign in the presence of the testator?	No. (18-A § 2-502 cmt.)
Must they sign in the presence of each other?	No. (18-A § 2-502 cmt.)
Must the testator publish the will?	No. (18-A § 2-502 cmt.)
Must the will be signed in a particular place?	No. (18-A § 2-502 cmt.)
Must the required number of witnesses be present at the same time for the signing or acknowledgment by the testator?	No. (18-A § 2-502 cmt.)
May the testator acknowledge either his will or his signature?	Yes. (18-A § 2-502 cmt.)
Requirements to be witness	Any person generally competent to be a witness. (18-A § 2-505(a))

Maryland
Formal Will Requirements

Minimum age for executing will	Real Property—18 years. (Est. & Trusts § 4-101) Personal Property—18 years. (Est. & Trusts § 4-101)
Number of witnesses required	Two. (Est. & Trusts § 4-102)
Holographic wills	Yes, if entirely in the handwriting of a testator serving in the U.S. armed forces, who signs it outside the United States and its territories. The will is void one year after discharge of testator from the armed services. (Est. & Trusts § 4-103)
Wills admitted to probate if valid under the law of:	Maryland; place where executed; place where testator domiciled. (Est. & Trusts § 4-104)
Does the signing by the testator and/or witnesses just of the self-proving affidavit constitute the execution of the will?	There is no provision for self-proving a will.
Can self-proving affidavit be signed later by testator and/or witnesses?	There is no provision for self-proving a will.
If a witness is a devisee, does this result in the disqualification to serve as a witness or the invalidation of the devise?	No. (Leitch v. Leitch, 79 A. 600, 602-03 (1911))
Can any other person sign the will?	Yes, in his presence and by his express direction. (Est. & Trusts § 4-102)
When must witnesses sign?	No provision. (Casson v. Swogell, 500 A.2d 1031 (1985))
Must they sign in the presence of the testator?	Yes. (Est. & Trusts § 4-102)
Must they sign in the presence of each other?	No. (O'Neal v. Jennings, 455 A.2d 66, 67 (Md. App. 1983))
Must the testator publish the will?	No. (Casson v. Swogell, 500 A.2d 1031, 1032 (1985))
Must the will be signed in a particular place?	Uncertain. There is some language in Greenhawk v. Quimby, 184 A. 485, 487 (1936), about the signature being affixed "in the appropriate place for his signature."
Must the required number of witnesses be present at the same time for the signing or acknowledgment by the testator?	Apparently no. (Van Meter v. Van Meter, 183 Md. 614, 39 A.2d 752, 754 (1944))
May the testator acknowledge either his will or his signature?	Apparently, the will must be acknowledged. (Van Meter v. Van Meter, 183 Md. 614, 39 A.2d 752, 754 (1944))
Requirements to be witness	Must be "credible," which means competent. This in turn is determined under the common law which bars insane, those so young as to want discretion, and those guilty of an infamous crime. (McGarvey v. McGarvey, 405 A.2d 250, 253 (1979))

Massachusetts
Formal Will Requirements

Minimum age for executing will	Real Property—18 years. (191 § 1) Personal Property—18 years. (191 § 1)
Number of witnesses required	Two. (191 § 1)
Holographic wills	No. (191 § 1)
Wills admitted to probate if valid under the law of:	Massachusetts; place where executed; place where testator domiciled. (191 § 5)
Does the signing by the testator and/or witnesses just of the self-proving affidavit constitute the execution of the will?	Yes, if the form and content is substantially as provided by the statute. (192 § 2(iii))
Can self-proving affidavit be signed later by testator and/or witnesses?	There does not appear to be any prohibition in this regard, if the testator and witnesses sign affidavits. (192 § 2)
If a witness is a devisee, does this result in the disqualification to serve as a witness or the invalidation of the devise?	There is no disqualification of the witness. (191 § 2) However, the devise to the witness, or to the witness' spouse, is void, in the absence of two other disinterested witnesses. (191 § 2)
Can any other person sign the will?	Yes, in testator's presence and by his express direction. (191 § 1)
When must witnesses sign?	No specific time requirement, but definitely after testator signs. (Barnes v. Chase, 94 N.E. 694 (1911))
Must they sign in the presence of the testator?	Yes. (191 § 1)
Must they sign in the presence of each other?	No. (Ela v. Edwards, 82 Mass. 91, 92 (1860))
Must the testator publish the will?	No. (Genovese v. Genovese, 153 N.E.2d 662, 663 (1958); Barber v. Henderson, 22 N.E.2d 620, 622 (1939))
Must the will be signed in a particular place?	No. (Porter v. Ballou, 21 N.E.2d 237 (1939))
Must the required number of witnesses be present at the same time for the signing or acknowledgment by the testator?	No. (In re Dunham, 134 N.E.2d 915, 916 (1956))
May the testator acknowledge either his will or his signature?	If an acknowledgment of a signature is involved, the witnesses must actually see the signature, unless concealment was unintentional. (In re Dunham, 134 N.E.2d 915, 916 (1956))
Requirements to be witness	Any person of "sufficient understanding ... notwithstanding any common law disqualification for interest or otherwise...." (191 § 2)

Michigan
Formal Will Requirements

Minimum age for executing will	Real Property—18 years. (§ 700.2501) Personal Property—18 years. (§ 700.2501)
Number of witnesses required	Two. (§ 700.2502(1)(c))
Holographic wills	Yes. (§ 700.2502(2))
Wills admitted to probate if valid under the law of:	Michigan; place of execution at time of execution; or place where at the time of execution or death, the testator is domiciled, has a place of abode, or is a national. (§ 700.2506)
Does the signing by the testator and/or witnesses just of the self-proving affidavit constitute the execution of the will?	Yes. (§ 700.2504(1))
Can self-proving affidavit be signed later by testator and/or witnesses?	Yes. (§ 700.2504(2))
If a witness is a devisee, does this result in the disqualification to serve as a witness or the invalidation of the devise?	The signing of a will by an interested witness does not invalidate the will or any provision of it. (§ 700.2505(2))
Can any other person sign the will?	Yes, in the testator's "conscious" presence and by the testator's direction. (§ 700.2502(1)(b))
When must witnesses sign?	A reasonable time after witnessing the signing or the acknowledgment by the testator. (§ 700.2502(1)(c)) However, the signatures must be before the testator's death. (In re Estate of Mikeska, 362 N.W.2d 906, 910-11 (Ct. App. 1985))
Must they sign in the presence of the testator?	No specific requirement. (§ 700.2502)
Must they sign in the presence of each other?	No specific requirement. (§ 700.2502)
Must the testator publish the will?	No. (In re Estate of Clark, 603 N.W.2d 290, 293 (Ct. App. 1999); In re Balk's Estate, 298 N.W. 779, 780 (1941))
Must the will be signed in a particular place?	No, under prior law. (In re Thomas' Estate, 220 N.W. 764 (1928) (former statute); In re Norris' Estate, 191 N.W. 238, 239 (1922) (former statute))
Must the required number of witnesses be present at the same time for the signing or acknowledgment by the testator?	No specific requirement. (§ 700.2502; In re Estate of Allen, 2002 WL 31951319 (Ct. App. Dec. 6, 2002))
May the testator acknowledge either his will or his signature?	Yes. (§ 700.2502(1)(c))
Requirements to be witness	Competency. (§ 700.2505(1))

Minnesota
Formal Will Requirements

Minimum age for executing will	Real Property—18 years. (§ 524.2-501) Personal Property—18 years. (§ 524.2-501)
Number of witnesses required	Two. (§ 524.2-502(3))
Holographic wills	No. (§ 524.2-502)
Wills admitted to probate if valid under the law of:	Minnesota; place of execution at time of execution; place where, at the time of execution or death, the testator is domiciled, has a place of abode, or is a national. (§ 524.2-506) An "international will" is also valid. (§ 524.2-1002)
Does the signing by the testator and/or witnesses just of the self-proving affidavit constitute the execution of the will?	Yes. (§§ 524.2-504(c), 524.2-502)
Can self-proving affidavit be signed later by testator and/or witnesses?	Yes, if acknowledgment of will by testator and affidavits of witnesses before notary attached or annexed to will in substantially the [prescribed statutory] form. (§ 524.2-504(b))
If a witness is a devisee, does this result in the disqualification to serve as a witness or the invalidation of the devise?	No. (§ 524.2-505(b))
Can any other person sign the will?	Yes, if in the testator's conscious presence and by his direction. (§ 524.2-502(2))
When must witnesses sign?	Either within a reasonable time after the will is signed, the acknowledgment that the document is the testator's will, or the acknowledgment by the testator that the signature is his. (524.2-502 & U.P.C. § 2-502 cmt.[13])
Must they sign in the presence of the testator?	No. (U.P.C. § 2-502 cmt.[14])
Must they sign in the presence of each other?	No. (U.P.C. § 2-502 cmt.[15])
Must the testator publish the will?	No. (U.P.C. § 2-502 cmt.[16])
Must the will be signed in a particular place?	No. (U.P.C. § 2-502 cmt.[17])
Must the required number of witnesses be present at the same time for the signing or acknowledgment by the testator?	No. (U.P.C. § 2-502 cmt.[18])
May the testator acknowledge either his will or his signature?	Yes. (U.P.C. § 2-502 cmt.[19])

Requirements to be witness	Any person generally competent to be a witness. (§ 524.2-505(a))

---

13. Although adopting the Uniform Probate Code, the editorial board comments of the U.P.C. have not been included in Minnesota Statutes. Nonetheless, the assumption is that they would be relied upon in construing the statutory provisions.
14. *Id.*
15. *Id.*
16. *Id.*
17. *Id.*
18. *Id.*
19. *Id.*

Mississippi
Formal Will Requirements

Minimum age for executing will	Real Property—18 years. (§ 91-5-1) Personal Property—18 years. (§ 91-5-1)
Number of witnesses required	Two. (§ 91-5-1)
Holographic wills	Yes. (§ 91-7-10)
Wills admitted to probate if valid under the law of:	There is no statutory prohibition.
Does the signing by the testator and/or witnesses just of the self-proving affidavit constitute the execution of the will?	No support for this. However, there is no decision stating that it does not constitute due execution (e.g., through use of doctrine of integration). See Delaware, *Does the signing by the testator and/or witnesses just of the self-proving affidavit constitute the execution of the will?*
Can self-proving affidavit be signed later by testator and/or witnesses?	The statute provides for only witness affidavits. Although it only states that the witness affidavits "may" be signed at the will execution, this is not required. (§ § 91-7-7, 91-7-9)
If a witness is a devisee, does this result in the disqualification to serve as a witness or the invalidation of the devise?	There is no disqualification of the witness. The devise is void to the extent it exceeds what the witness would have received by intestate succession and there are not two other credible witnesses. (§ 91-5-9) A creditor is a competent witness, but any provision for payment or preference in the will is void. (§ 91-5-13)
Can any other person sign the will?	Yes, if in testator's presence and by testator's express direction. (§ 91-5-1)
When must witnesses sign?	There is no specific time requirement. But see *Can self-proving affidavit be signed later by testator and/or witnesses?*
Must they sign in the presence of the testator?	Yes. (§ 91-5-1)
Must they sign in the presence of each other?	No. (Phifer v. McCarter, 76 So. 2d 258, 259 (1954))
Must the testator publish the will?	Yes, but may be construed by testator's actions, rather than words. (Green v. Pearson, 110 So. 862, 864 (1927))
Must the will be signed in a particular place?	No. (In re Estate of McKellar, 380 So. 2d 1273, 1275 (Miss. 1980) (name of testator may be written any place on the instrument, so long as it is declared to be his signature))
Must the required number of witnesses be present at the same time for the signing or acknowledgment by the testator?	No. (Phifer v. McCarter (above) noted that the statute did not require the testator to sign in the presence of witnesses.)
May the testator acknowledge either his will or his signature?	Uncertain. One case holds that the testator needs to acknowledge both his signature and his will. (Austin v. Patrick, 176 So. 714, 716 (1937)) A later case refers to the need to "acknowledge signing the document." (In re Estate of McKellar, 380 So. 2d 1273, 1274 (1980))

Requirements to be witness	They must be "credible," which means competent. (Wallace v. Harrison, 65 So. 2d 456, 459 (1953))

Missouri
Formal Will Requirements

Minimum age for executing will	Real Property—18 years. (§ 474.310) Personal Property—18 years. (§ 474.310) Any minor emancipated by adjudication, marriage or entry into active military duty is also able to execute a valid will.
Number of witnesses required	Two. (§ 474.320)
Holographic wills	No.
Wills admitted to probate if valid under the law of:	Missouri; place of execution at time of execution; place where, at time of execution or death, the testator is domiciled, has a place of abode, or is a national. (§ 474.360)
Does the signing by the testator and/or witnesses just of the self-proving affidavit constitute the execution of the will?	No support for this. However, there is no decision stating that it does not constitute due execution (e.g., through use of doctrine of integration). See Delaware, *Does the signing by the testator and/or witnesses just of the self-proving affidavit constitute the execution of the will?*
Can self-proving affidavit be signed later by testator and/or witnesses?	Yes, "at any subsequent date," by "acknowledgment" of the testator and witnesses attached or annexed to the will in form and content substantially as provided in the statute. (§ 474.337(1))
If a witness is a devisee, does this result in the disqualification to serve as a witness or the invalidation of the devise?	There is no disqualification of the witness. In the event there are not sufficient disinterested witnesses, the devise is void to the extent it exceeds the share the witness would take by intestate succession. (§ 474.330(2))
Can any other person sign the will?	Yes, if by the direction of the testator and in his presence. (§ 474.320)
When must witnesses sign?	No time constraint, but must do so in the presence of the testator. See *Can self-proving affidavit be signed later by testator and/or witnesses?*
Must they sign in the presence of the testator?	Yes. (§ 474.320)
Must they sign in the presence of each other?	No. (Grimm v. Tittmann, 20 S.W. 664, 665 (1892))
Must the testator publish the will?	Yes, but need not be done by express words, as opposed to acts. (Hughes v. Dwyer, 546 S.W.2d 733, 736 (Ct. App. 1977))
Must the will be signed in a particular place?	No. (Potter v. Richardson, 230 S.W.2d 672 (1950))
Must the required number of witnesses be present at the same time for the signing or acknowledgment by the testator?	No. The prospect of acknowledgment itself was confirmed only recently. (Lopiccolo v. Semar, 890 S.W.2d 754, 759 (Ct. App. 1995))
May the testator acknowledge either his will or his signature?	No. The testator must make known to witnesses that he has signed the instrument as his will. (Grimm v. Tittman, 20 S.W. 664, 665 (1892))

Requirements to be witness	Any person who is competent to be a witness generally. (§ 474.330(1))

Montana
Formal Will Requirements

Minimum age for executing will	Real Property—18 years. (§ 72-2-521) Personal Property—18 years. (§ 72-2-521)
Number of witnesses required	Two. (§ 72-2-522(1)(c))
Holographic wills	Yes. (§ 72-2-522(2))
Wills admitted to probate if valid under the law of:	Montana; place of execution at time of execution; place where, at the time of execution or death, the testator is domiciled, has a place of abode, or is a national. (§ 72-2-526) An "international will" is also valid. (§ 72-2-902)
Does the signing by the testator and/or witnesses just of the self-proving affidavit constitute the execution of the will?	Yes. (§ 72-2-524(3))
Can self-proving affidavit be signed later by testator and/or witnesses?	At any time after execution, the will may be self-proved by the testator's acknowledgment of the will and the witnesses' affidavits attached or annexed to the will in substantially the form provided for in the statute. (§ 72-2-524(2))
If a witness is a devisee, does this result in the disqualification to serve as a witness or the invalidation of the devise?	No. (§ 72-2-525(2))
Can any other person sign the will?	Yes, if in the testator's conscious presence and by the testator's direction. (§ 72-2-522(1)(b))
When must witnesses sign?	Within a reasonable time after having witnessed either the signing of the will or the testator's acknowledgment of the signature or of the will. (§ 72-2-522(1)(c))
Must they sign in the presence of the testator?	No. (U.P.C. § 2-502 cmt.[20])
Must they sign in the presence of each other?	No. (U.P.C. § 2-502 cmt.[21])
Must the testator publish the will?	No. (U.P.C. § 2-502 cmt.[22])
Must the will be signed in a particular place?	No. (U.P.C. § 2-502 cmt.[23])
Must the required number of witnesses be present at the same time for the signing or acknowledgment by the testator?	No. (U.P.C. § 2-502 cmt.[24])
May the testator acknowledge either his will or his signature?	Yes. (U.P.C. § 2-502 cmt.[25])

Requirements to be witness	An individual must be generally competent to be a witness. (§ 72-2-525(1))

20. Although adopting the Uniform Probate Code, the editorial board comments of the U.P.C. have not been included in Montana Code Annotated. Nonetheless, the assumption is that they would be relied upon in construing the statutory provisions.
21. *Id.*
22. *Id.*
23. *Id.*
24. *Id.*
25. *Id.*

Nebraska
Formal Will Requirements

Minimum age for executing will	Real Property—18 years. (§ 30-2326) Personal Property—18 years. (§ 30-2326)
Number of witnesses required	Two. (§ 30-2327)
Holographic wills	Yes. (§ 30-2328)
Wills admitted to probate if valid under the law of:	Nebraska, place of execution at the time of execution; place where, at the time of execution or death, the testator is domiciled, has a place of abode, or is a national. (§ 30-2331)
Does the signing by the testator and/or witnesses just of the self-proving affidavit constitute the execution of the will?	The following language would appear to allow this: "Any will may be simultaneously executed, attested, and made self-proved by the acknowledgment thereof by the testator and the affidavits of the witnesses. . . ." (§ 30-2329(1))
Can self-proving affidavit be signed later by testator and/or witnesses?	Yes. "An attested will may at any time subsequent to its execution be made self-proved, by the acknowledgment thereof by the testator and the affidavits of the witnesses . . . in form and content substantially as [provided in the statute]." (§ 30-2329(2))
If a witness is a devisee, does this result in the disqualification to serve as a witness or the invalidation of the devise?	There is no disqualification of the witness. However, unless there is at least one disinterested witness, the devise is void to the extent it exceeds the share the interested witness would take by intestate succession. (§ 30-2330(b))
Can any other person sign the will?	Yes, if in the testator's presence and by his direction. (§ 30-2327)
When must witnesses sign?	No time constraint, although it must be after either the signing of the will or the testator's acknowledgment of the signature or of the will. (§ 30-2327)
Must they sign in the presence of the testator?	No. (U.P.C. § 2-502 cmt.[26])
Must they sign in the presence of each other?	No. (U.P.C. § 2-502 cmt.[27])
Must the testator publish the will?	No. (U.P.C. § 2-502 cmt.[28])
Must the will be signed in a particular place?	No. (U.P.C. § 2-502 cmt.[29])
Must the required number of witnesses be present at the same time for the signing or acknowledgment by the testator?	No. (U.P.C. § 2-502 cmt.[30])
May the testator acknowledge either his will or his signature?	Yes. (U.P.C. § 2-502 cmt.[31])

Requirements to be witness	Any individual generally competent to be a witness. (§ 30-2330(a))

26. Although adopting the Uniform Probate Code, the editorial comments of the U.P.C. have not been included in Revised Statutes of Nebraska Annotated. Nonetheless, the assumption is that they would be relied upon in construing the statutory provisions.
27. *Id.*
28. *Id.*
29. *Id.*
30. *Id.*
31. *Id.*

Nevada
Formal Will Requirements

Minimum age for executing will	Real Property—18 years. (§ 133.020) Personal Property—18 years. (§ 133.020)
Number of witnesses required	Two. (§ 133.040)
Holographic wills	Yes. (§ 133.090) See also approval of electronic wills. (§§ 133.040 & 133.085)
Wills admitted to probate if valid under the law of:	Nevada; place of execution; testator's domicile. (§ 133.080) See also approval of electronic wills. (§ 133.040)
Does the signing by the testator and/or witnesses just of the self-proving affidavit constitute the execution of the will?	Yes. (§ 133.055: A signature affixed to a self-proving affidavit attached to a will and executed at the same time as the will is a signature affixed to the will if necessary to prove the execution of the will.)
Can self-proving affidavit be signed later by testator and/or witnesses?	Yes, if made at the request of the testator. Thus, it could not be made after his death. (§ 133.050(3))
If a witness is a devisee, does this result in the disqualification to serve as a witness or the invalidation of the devise?	There is no disqualification of the witness. However, the devise is void unless there are two other competent witnesses. (§ 133.060) A mere charge on the estate does not make a creditor incompetent to serve as a witness. (§ 133.070)
Can any other person sign the will?	Yes, if in the testator's presence and at the testator's express direction. (§ 133.040)
When must witnesses sign?	No statute or case authority directly on point.
Must they sign in the presence of the testator?	Yes. (§ 133.040)
Must they sign in the presence of each other?	No statute or case authority directly on point.
Must the testator publish the will?	No statute or case authority directly on point.
Must the will be signed in a particular place?	No statute or case authority directly on point.
Must the required number of witnesses be present at the same time for the signing or acknowledgment by the testator?	No statute or case authority directly on point.
May the testator acknowledge either his will or his signature?	No statute or case authority directly on point.
Requirements to be witness	The witness must be "competent." (§ 133.040)

New Hampshire
Formal Will Requirements

Minimum age for executing will	Real Property—18 years. (§ 551:1) Personal Property—18 years. (§ 551:1) Married persons under 18 may make a will. (§ 551:1)
Number of witnesses required	Two. (§ 551:2 (IV)) Two witnesses are required (for wills executed on or after January 1, 1993).
Holographic wills	No. (§ 551:2)
Wills admitted to probate if valid under the law of:	New Hampshire; place of execution. (§ 551:5)
Does the signing by the testator and/or witnesses just of the self-proving affidavit constitute the execution of the will?	Probably not. (§ 551:2-I & II.)
Can self-proving affidavit be signed later by testator and/or witnesses?	No restriction if signatures of testator and witnesses are followed by a sworn acknowledgment by the testator and witnesses as provided in the statute. (§ 551:2-a) The language conspicuously omits a statement that the form can be in "substantially" the form and content set forth in the statute. Rather, the self-proving document must be "as follows." Furthermore, it must be notarized by an officer authorized "in the place of execution" of the will.
If a witness is a devisee, does this result in the disqualification to serve as a witness or the invalidation of the devise?	There is no disqualification of the witness. However, the devise to the witness or the witness' spouse is void unless there are two other disinterested witnesses. A provision for payment of a debt does not disqualify a creditor. (§ 551:3)
Can any other person sign the will?	Yes, if at the testator's express direction in the testator's presence. (§ 551:2(III))
When must witnesses sign?	There is no time constraint. But see *Must they sign in the presence of the testator?*
Must they sign in the presence of the testator?	Yes. (§ 551:2(IV))
Must they sign in the presence of each other?	Apparently not. Each witness must see the signature on the will and subscribe his name. (Welch v. Adams 1 A. 1 (1885))
Must the testator publish the will?	No. (Welch v. Adams, 1 A. 1 (1885))
Must the will be signed in a particular place?	No statute or case authority directly on point.
Must the required number of witnesses be present at the same time for the signing or acknowledgment by the testator?	No. (Welch v. Adams, 1 A. 1 (1885))
May the testator acknowledge either his will or his signature?	Yes. (Welch v. Adams, 1 A. 1 (1885))

Requirements to be witness	The witness must be "credible." (§ 551:2(IV)) This term is intended to mean "competent." (Ross v. Carlino, 417 A.2d 13 (1980)) A person under age 14 is presumed incompetent, but this presumption can be rebutted. (Carlton v. Carlton, 40 N.H. 14 (1859))

New Jersey
Formal Will Requirements

Minimum age for executing will	Real Property—18 years. (§ 3B:3-1) Personal Property—18 years. (§ 3B:3-1)
Number of witnesses required	Two. (§ 3B:3-2)
Holographic wills	Yes. (§ 3B:3-3)
Wills admitted to probate if valid under the law of:	New Jersey; place where executed; place where, at time of execution or death, testator was domiciled, had a place of abode, or was a national. (§ 3B:3-9)
Does the signing by the testator and/or witnesses just of the self-proving affidavit constitute the execution of the will?	Yes. (§ 3B:3-4)
Can self-proving affidavit be signed later by testator and/or witnesses?	No restriction if acknowledgment of will by testator and affidavits of witnesses attached or annexed to the will in substantially the statutory form. (§ 3B:3-5)
If a witness is a devisee, does this result in the disqualification to serve as a witness or the invalidation of the devise?	No. (§ 3B:3-8)
Can any other person sign the will?	Yes, if in the testator's presence and at his direction. (§ 3B:3-2)
When must witnesses sign?	At the testator's signing or acknowledgment. (§ 3B:3-2)
Must they sign in the presence of the testator?	No. (§ 3B:3-2; U.P.C. § 2-502 cmt.[32])
Must they sign in the presence of each other?	No. (U.P.C. § 2-502 cmt.[33])
Must the testator publish the will?	No. (U.P.C. § 2-502 cmt.[34])
Must the will be signed in a particular place?	No. (U.P.C. § 2-502 cmt.) *Cf.* In re Will of Ranney, 573 A.2d 467, 471 (Ct. App. 1990), *aff'd,* 589 A.2d 1339 (1991). Under former law, see In re Potts' Estate, 61 A.2d 649 (Co. Ct. 1948); In re Phelan's Estate, 87 A. 625 (1913), *aff'd,* 91 A. 1070 (1914).
Must the required number of witnesses be present at the same time for the signing or acknowledgment by the testator?	No. (U.P.C. § 2-502 cmt.[35])
May the testator acknowledge either his will or his signature?	Yes. (3B:3-2). See also U.P.C. § 2-502 cmt.[36]
Requirements to be witness	Any person who is generally competent to be a witness. (§ 3B:3-7)

32. Although adopting the Uniform Probate Code, the editorial comments of the U.P.C. have not been included in New Jersey Statutes. Nonetheless, the assumption is that they would be relied upon in construing the statutory provisions.
33. *Id.*
34. *Id.*
35. *Id.*
36. *Id.*

New Mexico
Formal Will Requirements

Minimum age for executing will	Real Property—18 years. (§ 45-2-501) Personal Property—18 years. (§ 45-2-501)
Number of witnesses required	Two. (§ 45-2-502(c))
Holographic wills	No. (§ 45-2-502)
Wills admitted to probate if valid under the law of:	A will is valid if executed in compliance with New Mexico law (§ 45-2-502) or if the will complies with the laws of the place of execution at the time of execution or the place where, at the time of execution or death, the testator is domiciled or is a national (§ 45-2-506). An "international will" is also valid. (§ 45-2-1002)
Does the signing by the testator and/or witnesses just of the self-proving affidavit constitute the execution of the will?	Yes, based on language that "will may be simultaneously executed, attested and made self-proved by acknowledgment thereof by the testator and affidavits of the witnesses." (§ 45-2-504(A))
Can self-proving affidavit be signed later by testator and/or witnesses?	No restriction if acknowledgment of will by testator and affidavits of witnesses attached or annexed to the will in substantially the statutory form. (§ 45-2-504(B))
If a witness is a devisee, does this result in the disqualification to serve as a witness or the invalidation of the devise?	No. (§ 45-2-505(B))
Can any other person sign the will?	Yes, if in the testator's conscious presence and by the testator's direction. (§ 45-2-502(B))
When must witnesses sign?	Uncertain. Provision states: "after each [witness] witnessed the signing of the will. . . ." (§ 45-2-502(C))
Must they sign in the presence of the testator?	Yes. (§ 45-2-502(C))
Must they sign in the presence of each other?	Yes. (§ 45-2-502(C))
Must the testator publish the will?	Yes. Even though § 45-2-502 is derived from the U.P.C., which does not require publication, publication is still required under New Mexico law. (In re Kelly's Estate, 660 P.2d 124, 129-30 (Ct. App. 1983))
Must the will be signed in a particular place?	No. (U.P.C. § 2-502 cmt.[37]
Must the required number of witnesses be present at the same time for the signing or acknowledgment by the testator?	Yes. Implied from requirement that witnesses must sign will "after each witnessed the signing of the will. . . ." (§ 45-2-502(C))
May the testator acknowledge either his will or his signature?	Yes. Implied from requirement that witnesses must sign will "after each witnessed the signing of the will. . . ." (§ 45-2-502(C) and publication requirements as set forth in In re Kelly's Estate, 660 P.2d 124, 129-30 (Ct. App. 1983))

Requirements to be witness	An individual who is generally competent to be a witness. (§ 45-2-505(A))

37. *Id.*

New York
Formal Will Requirements

Minimum age for executing will	Real Property—18 years. (Est., Powers & Tr. Law § 3-1.1) Personal Property—18 years. (Est., Powers & Tr. Law § 3-1.1)
Number of witnesses required	Two. (Est., Powers & Tr. Law § 3-2.1(a)(4))
Holographic wills	Yes, but only for members of the military while serving in armed conflict or for a person serving with or accompanying the armed services under these circumstances, or a mariner while at sea. (Est., Powers & Tr. Law §§ 3-2.2(a)(2), (b)) A holographic will made by a member of the armed services becomes invalid one year after his discharge from the armed services. It becomes invalid for a person serving with or accompanying the armed services one year after ceasing to do so. It becomes invalid for a mariner three years after the making of the will. (Est., Powers & Tr. Law § 3-2.2)
Wills admitted to probate if valid under the law of:	New York; place of execution at time of execution; place where testator is domiciled at the time of execution or death; applies to will of personal property located anywhere or real property in the state. (Est., Powers & Tr. Law § 3-5.1(c))
Does the signing by the testator and/or witnesses just of the self-proving affidavit constitute the execution of the will?	Probably not, since only the witnesses, and not the testator, sign the affidavits. Moreover, the witnesses must state in the affidavits "such facts as would if uncontradicted establish the . . . validity of its execution," which would presumably include that the testator signed the will or acknowledged his signature in their presence. (Sur. Ct. Proc. Act § 1406(1)) Notwithstanding the foregoing, one lower court has held witnesses validly executed the will when they signed the self-proving affidavit. (In re Will of Zuracino, 561 N.Y.S.2d 397 (Sur. Ct. 1990)) Unlike witnesses, the testator must sign in a particular place, so a different rule may apply to the testator. See Florida.
Can self-proving affidavit be signed later by testator and/or witnesses?	Yes, at any time, including after the testator's death, any or both of the witnesses may sign an affidavit. However, it must be at the testator's request or, if the testator is deceased, at the request of the executor, the proponent, the attorney of the proponent, or any person "interested" in the will. (Sur. Ct. Proc. Act § 1406(1))
If a witness is a devisee, does this result in the disqualification to serve as a witness or the invalidation of the devise?	There is no disqualification of the witness. (Est., Powers & Tr. Law § 3-3.2(a)) However, the devise is void if there are not sufficient other disinterested witnesses, in which case the witness is denied the excess over the share he would take by intestate succession. (Est., Powers & Tr. Law § 3-3.2(a)(3))
Can any other person sign the will?	Yes, if in the presence of the testator and by his direction. (Est., Powers & Tr. Law § 3-2.1(a)(1)) The person must also sign his own name and "affix his residence address," although this latter requirement will not invalidate the will. (Est., Powers & Tr. Law § 3-2.1(a)(1)(C))

When must witnesses sign?	Both must sign within a 30-day period. (Est., Powers & Tr. Law § 3-2.1(a)(4)) There is a rebuttable presumption that the 30-day requirement has been met. (*Id.*) The signatures must follow a request to do this by the testator. (*Id.*)
Must they sign in the presence of the testator?	No, as long as *When must witnesses sign?* above is satisfied.
Must they sign in the presence of each other?	No. (Est., Powers & Tr. Law § 3-2.1(a)(2))
Must the testator publish the will?	Yes. (Est., Powers & Tr. Law § 3-2.1(a)(3))
Must the will be signed in a particular place?	Yes, at the end. (Est., Powers & Tr. Law § 3-2.1(a)(1)(A)) However, if it comes before the end, preceding material may be given effect. (*Id.*) Material that follows the signature, other than the attestation clause, will not be given effect. (Est., Powers & Tr. Law § 3-2.1(a)(1)(B))
Must the required number of witnesses be present at the same time for the signing or acknowledgment by the testator?	No. (Est., Powers & Tr. Law § 3-2.1(a)(4))
May the testator acknowledge either his will or his signature?	No. The signature must be acknowledged in the presence of the witnesses. (Est., Powers & Tr. Law § 3-2.1(a)(4))
Requirements to be witness	The general rule of evidence applies. If the statute, as with respect to probate, does not specify a minimum age, there is none. As was stated in connection with a sworn deposition of a child below age 12 in a matter governed by the Family Court Act: "Although age is a relevant factor in determining the capacity of a person to make a statement under oath, the Family Court Act does not contain any age limitations. . . ." (In re Nelson R., 683 N.E.2d 329, 331, 660 N.Y.S.2d 707, 708-09 (Ct. App. 1997))

North Carolina
Formal Will Requirements

Minimum age for executing will	Real Property—18 years. (§ 31-1) Personal Property—18 years. (§ 31-1)
Number of witnesses required	Two. (§ 31-3.3(a))
Holographic wills	Yes. (§ 31-3.4)
Wills admitted to probate if valid under the law of:	There is no general statutory provision. In the case of a citizen or subject of another state or country, a will is valid if valid under the laws of North Carolina. (§ 31-27(b)) However, even if the law of North Carolina has not been complied with, the clerk of the court may take proof and the will may be adjudged duly proved. (§ 31-27(c)) The will would be effective to dispose of North Carolina real property. (§ 31-27(d)) In the case of a North Carolina domiciliary, as well as a nondomiciliary who did not avail himself of § 31-27(b)–(d), the common law rule would probably apply. That is, the will must comply with the law of the domicile for personal property and the law of the situs with respect to real property. (McEwan v. Brown, 97 S.E. 20, 22 (1918), overruled on other grounds)
Does the signing by the testator and/or witnesses just of the self-proving affidavit constitute the execution of the will?	Yes, based on language that "will may be simultaneously executed, attested and made self-proved by acknowledgment thereof by the testator and affidavits of the witnesses." (§ 31-11.6(a)) However, if the witnesses sign the self-proving affidavit after the execution, there may be a problem, since in this case the affidavit can be made only if the will has been properly attested already. One court has recognized this problem but decided to adhere to a substantial compliance approach. See New Jersey and In re Will of Ranney, 573 A.2d 467 (Ct. App. 1990). North Carolina courts might not do so.
Can self-proving affidavit be signed later by testator and/or witnesses?	No restriction if acknowledgment of will by testator and affidavits of witnesses attached or annexed to the will in substantially the statutory form. (§ 31-11.6(b))
If a witness is a devisee, does this result in the disqualification to serve as a witness or the invalidation of the devise?	There is no disqualification of the witness. A devise to the witness, the witness' spouse, or "anyone claiming under him" is void, unless there are at least two other disinterested witnesses. (§ 31-10(a))
Can any other person sign the will?	Yes, if in the testator's presence and at his direction. (§ 31-3.3(b))
When must witnesses sign?	After the testator's signature or acknowledgment, but no specific time period is prescribed. The witness cannot sign before the testator, at least not on a prior day. (In re McDonald's Will, 13 S.E.2d 239 (1941) although there may be an exception if they signed at "practically" the same time.)
Must they sign in the presence of the testator?	Yes. (§ 31-3.3(d))

Must they sign in the presence of each other?	No. (§ 31-3.3(d))
Must the testator publish the will?	Not technically, but he must signify that the "instrument is his instrument by signing it in their presence or by acknowledging to them his signature previously affixed thereto." (§ 31-3.3(c))
Must the will be signed in a particular place?	No. (In re Roberts' Will, 112 S.E.2d 505, 510 (1960))
Must the required number of witnesses be present at the same time for the signing or acknowledgment by the testator?	No. (§ 31-3.3(c))
May the testator acknowledge either his will or his signature?	The testator must acknowledge the signature. (§ 31-3.3(c))
Requirements to be witness	The witness must be competent. (§ 31-10(a)) The question of competency is one of law. (McLean v. Elliott, 72 N.C. 70 (1875))

North Dakota
Formal Will Requirements

Minimum age for executing will	Real Property—18 years. (§ 30.1-08-01) Personal Property—18 years. (§ 30.1-08-01)
Number of witnesses required	Two. (§ 30.1-08-02(1)(c))
Holographic wills	Yes. (§ 30.1-08-02(2))
Wills admitted to probate if valid under the law of:	North Dakota; place of execution at time of execution; place where, at time of execution or death, testator is domiciled, has a place of abode, or is a national. (§ 30.1-08-06) An "international will" is also valid. (§ 30.1-08.2-02)
Does the signing by the testator and/or witnesses just of the self-proving affidavit constitute the execution of the will?	Yes. (§ 30.1-08-04(3))
Can self-proving affidavit be signed later by testator and/or witnesses?	No restriction if acknowledgment of will by testator and affidavits of witnesses attached or annexed to the will in substantially the statutory form. (§ 30.1-08-04(2))
If a witness is a devisee, does this result in the disqualification to serve as a witness or the invalidation of the devise?	No. (§ 30.1-08-05(2))
Can any other person sign the will?	Yes, if in the testator's conscious presence and by the testator's direction. (§ 30.1-08-02(1)(b))
When must witnesses sign?	Within a reasonable time after witnessing either the signing of the will or the testator's acknowledgment of the signature or of the will. (§ 30.1-08-02(1)(c))
Must they sign in the presence of the testator?	No. (§ 30.1-08-02 cmt.)
Must they sign in the presence of each other?	No. (§ 30.1-08-02 cmt.)
Must the testator publish the will?	No. (§ 30.1-08-02 cmt.; In re Estate of Polda, 349 N.W.2d 11, 16 (1984))
Must the will be signed in a particular place?	No. (§ 30.1-08-02 cmt.)
Must the required number of witnesses be present at the same time for the signing or acknowledgment by the testator?	No. (§ 30.1-08-02 cmt.)
May the testator acknowledge either his will or his signature?	Yes. (§ 30.1-08-02 cmt.)
Requirements to be witness	Any person who is generally competent to be a witness. (§ 30.1-08-05(1))

Ohio
Formal Will Requirements

Minimum age for executing will	Real Property—18 years. (§ 2107.02) Personal Property—18 years. (§ 2107.02)
Number of witnesses required	Two. (§ 2107.03)
Holographic wills	No. (§ 2107.03)
Wills admitted to probate if valid under the law of:	Ohio; place of execution at the time of execution; or domicile at the time of death. (§ 2107.18)
Does the signing by the testator and/or witnesses just of the self-proving affidavit constitute the execution of the will?	There is no provision for a self-proved will. A probate court is required to admit a will to probate "if it appears from the face of the will . . . that the execution of the will complies with the law. . . ." (§ 2107.18)
Can self-proving affidavit be signed later by testator and/or witnesses?	There is no provision for a self-proved will. A probate court is required to admit a will to probate "if it appears from the face of the will . . . that the execution of the will complies with the law. . . ." (§ 2107.18)
If a witness is a devisee, does this result in the disqualification to serve as a witness or the invalidation of the devise?	There is no disqualification of the witness. However, the devise is void if there are not two other disinterested witnesses, to the extent the devise exceeds the share that the witness would take by intestate succession. The share is contributed to by devisees as if the witness was an absent or afterborn child. (§ 2107.15)
Can any other person sign the will?	Yes, if in the testator's presence and at his express direction. (§ 2107.03)
When must witnesses sign?	No time restriction, but must be after the witnesses saw the testator sign or "heard him acknowledge his signature." (§ 2107.03) Acknowledgment of the paper as testator's will may suffice. (In re Pittis' Will, 29 Ohio N.P. (NS) 41 (Prob. 1930))
Must they sign in the presence of the testator?	Yes. (§ 2107.03)
Must they sign in the presence of each other?	No. (McFadden v. Thomas, 96 N.E.2d 254, 257 (1951))
Must the testator publish the will?	The answer is uncertain. Probably no. Underwood v. Rutan, 101 Oh. St. 306, 128 N.E. 78 (1920) (no declaration required). See also In re Maurer, 31 Ohio N.P. (N.S.) 247 (Prob. Ct. 1933) (unlike in *Underwood*, the witnesses did not know the document was a will). But see Shinn v. Phillips, 197 N.E.2d 564, 566-67 (Ohio Ct. App. 1964), citing Collins v. Collins, 110 Ohio St. 105, 112-28, 143 N.E. 561, 565-67 (1924) (publication required for revival of will on the basis that it was required when the will was originally executed).
Must the will be signed in a particular place?	At the end. (§ 2107.03)

Must the required number of witnesses be present at the same time for the signing or acknowledgment by the testator?	No. (§ 2107.03)
May the testator acknowledge either his will or his signature?	No. The testator must acknowledge the signature. (§ 2107.03)
Requirements to be witness	The witnesses must be competent. Competency is determined under § 2317.01. (Rogers v. Helmes, 432 N.E.2d 186, 188 (1982)) § 2317.01 provides that all persons are competent witnesses except those of unsound mind and children under 10 years of age "who appear incapable of receiving just impressions of the facts and transactions respecting which they are examined, or of relating them truly."

Oklahoma
Formal Will Requirements

Minimum age for executing will	Real Property—18 years. (84 § 41) Personal Property—18 years. (84 § 41)
Number of witnesses required	Two. (84 § 55(4))
Holographic wills	Yes. (84 § 54)
Wills admitted to probate if valid under the law of:	Oklahoma; place of execution; place where testator is domiciled at execution. (84 § 71)
Does the signing by the testator and/or witnesses just of the self-proving affidavit constitute the execution of the will?	From the statutory language, it would appear not, since the affidavit must be attached or annexed to the "testamentary instrument." (84 § 55(5)(a)) Even the alternative declaration that is allowed, see 84 § 55(5)(b), refers to a "will." But see In re Estate of Cutsinger, 445 P.2d 778, 782 (1968), holding to contrary and validating a witness' signatures appearing only on the affidavit. The court deemed the sworn attestation statement to be part of the will and in "substantial compliance" with the statute. But see also Delaware.
Can self-proving affidavit be signed later by testator and/or witnesses?	No restriction if acknowledgment of will by testator and affidavits of witnesses "during the lifetimes of the testator and witnesses" attached or annexed to the will in substantially the statutory form. (84 § 55(5)(a)) The notary must be authorized to act in Oklahoma. (*Id.*) A written declaration in place of the notarized acknowledgment and affidavits is also allowed, but it must be in substantially the form provided for by statute. (84 § 55(5)(b))
If a witness is a devisee, does this result in the disqualification to serve as a witness or the invalidation of the devise?	There is no disqualification of the witness. However, the devise is void if there are not two other competent witnesses. (84 § 143) If void, the witness is still entitled to the devise to the extent it does not exceed the witness' share under intestate succession. (84 § 144) The other devisees contribute based on the proportion of the amount and parts devised to them. (84 § 144) A creditor is a competent witness despite a charge on the estate for the payment of debts. (84 § 143)
Can any other person sign the will?	Yes, if in the testator's presence and by his direction. (84 § 55(1))
When must witnesses sign?	At the time of the testator's subscription or at a later acknowledgment of the subscription by the testator. (84 § 55(2))
Must they sign in the presence of the testator?	Yes, and sign at the testator's request and at the end of the will. (84 § 55(4)) They should also write their places of residence, although failure to do does not invalidate the will. (84 § 56)
Must they sign in the presence of each other?	No provision, although there does not appear to be any such requirement as long as there is a proper acknowledgment by the testator before each of the witnesses signs.

Must the testator publish the will?	Yes. (84 § 55(3))
Must the will be signed in a particular place?	Yes, at the end. (84 § 55(1))
Must the required number of witnesses be present at the same time for the signing or acknowledgment by the testator?	No. (84 § 55(2))
May the testator acknowledge either his will or his signature?	No. The testator must acknowledge his subscription in the presence of the witnesses. (84 § 55(2)) He must also declare to them that the instrument is his will. (84 § 55(3))
Requirements to be witness	84 § 55, which sets forth the "formal requisites in execution" of a will, refers only to the "attesting witnesses." However, 84 § 145 states that if the witnesses "are competent at the time of attesting its execution, their subsequent incompetency, from whatever cause it may arise, does not prevent the probate and allowance of the will, if it is otherwise satisfactorily proved." On the other hand, 58 § 82 requires the proof of two "credible" witnesses in the case of a lost or destroyed will.

Oregon
Formal Will Requirements

Minimum age for executing will	Real Property—18 years. (§ 112.225) Personal Property—18 years. (§ 112.225) A married person under 18 may make a will. (§ 112.225)
Number of witnesses required	Two. (§ 112.235(3))
Holographic wills	No. (§ 112.235)
Wills admitted to probate if valid under the law of:	The will must be in writing and signed by the testator or at his direction. Then, it is valid if it is valid under the law of Oregon, at time of execution or death; domicile of testator at execution or death; place of execution at time of execution. (§ 112.255) An "international will" is also valid. (§ 112.255)
Does the signing by the testator and/or witnesses just of the self-proving affidavit constitute the execution of the will?	No, since the affidavit is submitted by each witness and not by the testator. As to the witnesses, no specific form of affidavit is provided. However, the language of the statute strongly suggests that there would have to be a will already signed by the testator and witnesses, since the affidavit is intended to give evidence of the execution of the will. (§ 113.055(1))
Can self-proving affidavit be signed later by testator and/or witnesses?	At the time of will execution or any time thereafter, presumably including after the testator's death, since the witness submits the affidavit. (§ 113.055(1))
If a witness is a devisee, does this result in the disqualification to serve as a witness or the invalidation of the devise?	There is no disqualification of the witness. (§ 112.245) The provision does not specifically address whether the devise is void, and there is no direct case authority on point. Curiously, the statute proceeds to define an "interested witness" after stating that the will is not "invalidated" though attested by an interested witness.
Can any other person sign the will?	Yes, if at the direction of the testator. (§ 112.235(1)(b)) A witness can sign for the testator. Whoever signs for the testator must sign his own name and write on the will that "the signer signed the name of the testator at the direction of the testator." (§ 112.235(2))
When must witnesses sign?	After witnessing the testator's signature or after each "hear[s] the testator acknowledge the signature on the will," but there is no specific time constraint. (§ 112.235(3)(a) & (b))
Must they sign in the presence of the testator?	No. This result is implied, since the statute simply states that the two witnesses shall each "attest the will by signing the witness' name to it." (§ 112.235(3)(c))
Must they sign in the presence of each other?	No. This result is implied, since the statute simply states that the two witnesses shall each "attest the will by signing the witness' name to it." (§ 112.235(3)(c); Wishard v. Turner, 478 P.2d 438, 440 (1970) (former statute))

Must the testator publish the will?	Uncertain. Although there is no specific requirement, the witnesses must "[s]ee the testator sign the will" or "[h]ear the testator acknowledge the signature on the will." (§ 112.235(3)) Under a prior statute requring that the will be "attested by two or more competent witnesses, subscribing their name to the will, in the presence of the testator," the Oregon Supreme Court held that "nor is it necessary that the testator should declare the instrument to be his last will and testament." In re Neill's Estate, 111 Or. 282, 293, 226 P. 439, 442 (1924).
Must the will be signed in a particular place?	There is no statutory provision or definite case authority on point.
Must the required number of witnesses be present at the same time for the signing or acknowledgment by the testator?	No. (§ 112.235(3))
May the testator acknowledge either his will or his signature?	No. The testator must acknowledge to each witness that the "signature on the will" is the testator's. (§ 112.235(3)(b))
Requirements to be witness	There is no statutory provision relating to the requirements for serving as a witness. Presumably, general competency requirements apply. The statute states that "any person who, having organs of sense can perceive, and perceiving can make known the perception to others, may be a witness." (§ 40.310, Rule 601)

Pennsylvania
Formal Will Requirements

Minimum age for executing will	Real Property—18 years. (20 § 2501) Personal Property—18 years. (20 § 2501)
Number of witnesses required	Two. (20 § 3132)
Holographic wills	There is no statutory provision but holographs are recognized by case law. (In re Sidlow's Estate, 543 A.2d 1143, 1144 (Super. Ct. 1988); In re Young's Estate, 58 Pa. D.&C.2d 659 (1972))
Wills admitted to probate if valid under the law of:	Pennsylvania; place where testator domiciled at time of execution or death. (20 § 2504.1)
Does the signing by the testator and/or witnesses just of the self-proving affidavit constitute the execution of the will?	The acknowledgment of the testator and affidavits of the witnesses can be "substantially as set forth in the Uniform Probate Code" or as set forth in the statute. The provision is not precise on which version of the Uniform Probate Code is determinative. Certain forms in the Code would support the conclusion that the will had been validly executed. If the Pennsylvania form were followed, there might be a problem since the testator acknowledges that his "name is signed to the attached or foregoing instrument." (20 § 3132.1)
Can self-proving affidavit be signed later by testator and/or witnesses?	Yes, by testator and witnesses, although the witnesses can submit separate affidavits if not done at same time as the required acknowledgment by the testator. The self-proving documents can be executed before an officer authorized in Pennsylvania or where executed, or before "an attorney at law," who must be "a member of the bar of the Supreme Court of Pennsylvania or of the highest court of the state in which execution of the will occurs . . ." and who then must certify to the officer authorized to take oaths that the acknowledgment and affidavit was made before him. (20 § 3132.1(c))
If a witness is a devisee, does this result in the disqualification to serve as a witness or the invalidation of the devise?	No statutory provision. However, the case law indicates that a witness could not take a devise (In re Umble's Estate, 186 A. 75, 76 (1936)), although the permutations, such as if the witness is supernumerary, have not been adequately addressed.
Can any other person sign the will?	Yes, if in the testator's presence and by his express direction. (20 § 2502(3))
When must witnesses sign?	There is no specific time constraint, although it must be after the testator signs or acknowledges his signature.
Must they sign in the presence of the testator?	Yes (20 § 2502(3)), at the execution, but only if someone else is signing for the testator. If the testator signs himself, the witnesses can sign alternatively at acknowledgment of signature.

Must they sign in the presence of each other?	Apparently not, if based on *acknowledgment* of the signature. (McClure v. Redman, 107 A. 25 (1919); In re Hoffmann's Estate, 15 Pa. D.&C. 2d 331 (1959), *aff'd,* 160 A.2d 237 (1960); In re Norton's Estate, 16 Erie 329 (1934); In re Kovel's Will, 24 Fid. 304 (1974))
Must the testator publish the will?	Yes, if subscribed by another for the testator. Otherwise, publication of the will is not required. (In re Brantlinger's Estate, 210 A.2d 246, 250 (1965); In re Lillibridge's Estate, 69 A. 1121 (1908); (20 § 2502(3))
Must the will be signed in a particular place?	At the end. (20 § 2502) Although the presence of subsequent writing will not, in and of itself, invalidate the will (20 § 2502 (1)), the entire will is invalidated if any dispositive provisions follow the signature (Evan's Appeal, 58 Pa. 238 (1868)).
Must the required number of witnesses be present at the same time for the signing or acknowledgment by the testator?	No. The testator may acknowledge his signature to the witnesses. There is no requirement that they both be present at the same time. (Leckey v. Cunningham, 56 Pa. 370 (1868)) Indeed, the statute itself does not mention the possibility of acknowledgment. Moreover, if the testator simply makes his mark, the statute requires that it be made in the presence of the two witnesses. (20 § 2502(2))
May the testator acknowledge either his will or his signature?	Apparently, the signature must be acknowledged. (Leckey v. Cunningham, 56 Pa. 370 (1868))
Requirements to be witness	Competency. 20 § 3132 requires that "[a]ll wills shall be proved by the oaths or affirmations of two competent witnesses." See also In re Goodwin's Estate, 12 Pa. D.&C. 77 (1928).

Rhode Island
Formal Will Requirements

Minimum age for executing will	Real Property—18 years. (§ 33-5-2) Personal Property—18 years. (§ 33-5-2)
Number of witnesses required	Two. (§ 33-5-5)
Holographic wills	No. (§ 33-5-5)
Wills admitted to probate if valid under the law of:	Rhode Island; place of execution or domicile. (§ 33-5-7)
Does the signing by the testator and/or witnesses just of the self-proving affidavit constitute the execution of the will?	No, since the affidavit does not provide for the testator's signature, but only that of the witnesses. (§ 33-7-26) It might still be integrated into will if the testator signed there. See Delaware, *Does the signing by the testator and/or witnesses just of the self-proving affidavit constitute the execution of the will?*
Can self-proving affidavit be signed later by testator and/or witnesses?	Yes. The witnesses alone are required to sign affidavits, and they can do this even after the testator's death. (§ 33-7-26 (2)) An affidavit "substantially in the form" set forth in the statute meets the requirements. (§ 33-7-26(3)) Note that this does not preclude other forms. Also, unlike other states, the statute only refers to the "form" of the affidavit and not its contents. Was this inadvertent?
If a witness is a devisee, does this result in the disqualification to serve as a witness or the invalidation of the devise?	There is no disqualification of the witness. The will is still valid, but the devise is void to the witness "or any person claiming under that person." Apparently, the presence of two other disinterested witnesses does not alter this result. (§ 33-6-1) The rule does not apply to a creditor where the will provides for a charge or a direction to pay any debts. (*Id.*)
Can any other person sign the will?	Yes, if in the testator's presence and by the testator's express direction. (§ 33-5-5)
When must witnesses sign?	No specific time, but testator must be present then. (§ 33-5-5)
Must they sign in the presence of the testator?	Yes. (§ 33-5-5)
Must they sign in the presence of each other?	Yes. (§ 33-5-5)
Must the testator publish the will?	"No other publication shall be necessary" other than signature or acknowledgment of signature by the testator. (§ 33-5-5)
Must the will be signed in a particular place?	There is no statutory provision or definite case authority on point.
Must the required number of witnesses be present at the same time for the signing or acknowledgment by the testator?	Yes. (§ 33-5-5)
May the testator acknowledge either his will or his signature?	No. The *signature* must be acknowledged. (§ 33-5-5)

Requirements to be witness	There are no specific requirements. The statute simply refers to "witnesses." Presumably, they would have to be competent to testify. See also § 33-7-10, which requires that the witnesses to the signature of the testator be "credible" when at least one of the original witnesses is not available.

South Carolina
Formal Will Requirements

Minimum age for executing will	Real Property—18 years. (§ 62-2-501) Personal Property—18 years. (§ 62-2-501) A married person under 18 may also make a will, as may an emancipated minor. (§ 62-1-201(24))
Number of witnesses required	Two. (§ 62-2-502)
Holographic wills	No. (§ 62-2-502)
Wills admitted to probate if valid under the law of:	South Carolina; place of execution; place where the testator is domiciled at the time of execution or at the time of death. (§ 62-2-505)
Does the signing by the testator and/or witnesses just of the self-proving affidavit constitute the execution of the will?	The following language would appear to allow this: "Any will may be simultaneously executed, attested, and made self-proved . . . acknowledgment by the testator and the affidavits of at least one witness. . . ." (§ 62-2-503(a))
Can self-proving affidavit be signed later by testator and/or witnesses?	Yes. "An attested will may at any time subsequent to its execution be made self-proved, by the acknowledgment thereof of the testator and the affidavit of at least one witness . . . in the following form or in a similar form showing the same intent." (§ 62-2-503(b))
If a witness is a devisee, does this result in the disqualification to serve as a witness or the invalidation of the devise?	There is no disqualification of the witness. However, the devise to the witness or the witness' spouse is void to the extent it exceeds the share that the witness or the spouse would be entitled under intestate succession. (§ 62-2-504) No reference is made in the statute to the validity of the devise in the event of two other disinterested witnesses. A creditor is a competent witness despite a charge of any debts to the estate. (*Id.*)
Can any other person sign the will?	Yes, if in the testator's presence and by the testator's direction. (§ 62-2-502)
When must witnesses sign?	There is no specific time constraint.
Must they sign in the presence of the testator?	Probably not. See § 62-2-502 cmt., stating that the prior law was like the current law but it "further required that three witnesses sign and that they do so in the presence of the testator and of each other."
Must they sign in the presence of each other?	Probably not. See § 62-2-502 cmt., stating that the prior law was like the current law but it "further required that three witnesses sign and that they do so in the presence of the testator and of each other."
Must the testator publish the will?	No. (§ 62-2-502 cmt.)
Must the will be signed in a particular place?	No. (§ 62-2-502 cmt.)

Must the required number of witnesses be present at the same time for the signing or acknowledgment by the testator?	No. (§ 62-2-502)
May the testator acknowledge either his will or his signature?	Yes. (§ 62-2-502)
Requirements to be witness	The witness must be "competent and able to testify." (§§ 62-3-406, 62-2-504 cmt.)

South Dakota
Formal Will Requirements

Minimum age for executing will	Real Property—18 years. (§ 29A-2-501) Personal Property—18 years. (§ 29A-2-501)
Number of witnesses required	Two. (§ 29A-2-502)
Holographic wills	Yes. (§ 29A-2-502)
Wills admitted to probate if valid under the law of:	South Dakota; place of execution at time of execution; place where, at time of execution or death, testator is domiciled, has a place of abode, or is a national. (§ 29A-2-506)
Does the signing by the testator and/or witnesses just of the self-proving affidavit constitute the execution of the will?	Yes. (§ 29A-2-504(c))
Can self-proving affidavit be signed later by testator and/or witnesses?	No restriction if acknowledgment of will by testator and affidavits of witnesses attached or annexed to the will in substantially the statutory form. (§ 29A-2-504(b))
If a witness is a devisee, does this result in the disqualification to serve as a witness or the invalidation of the devise?	No. (§ 29A-2-505(b))
Can any other person sign the will?	Yes, if in the testator's conscious presence and by the testator's direction. (§ 29A-2-502(b)(2))
When must witnesses sign?	There is no time constraint. However, it must occur after the testator signs or acknowledges his signature. (U.P.C. § 2-502 cmt.[38])
Must they sign in the presence of the testator?	Yes, but sufficient if in the "conscious presence" of the testator. (§ 29A-2-502(b)(3))
Must they sign in the presence of each other?	No. (U.P.C. § 2-502 cmt.[39])
Must the testator publish the will?	No. (U.P.C. § 2-502 cmt.[40])
Must the will be signed in a particular place?	No. (U.P.C. § 2-502 cmt.[41])
Must the required number of witnesses be present at the same time for the signing or acknowledgment by the testator?	No. (§ 29A-2-502(b)(3))
May the testator acknowledge either his will or his signature?	There is provision for acknowledgment of the signature. (§ 29A-2-502(b)(3)) No provision is made for the acknowledgment of the will itself, even though the U.P.C., from which this provision is derived, so provides. Compare U.P.C. § 2-502.

Requirements to be witness	An individual generally competent to be a witness. (§ 29A-2-505(a))

38. Although adopting the Uniform Probate Code, the editorial comments of the U.P.C. have not been included in South Dakota Codified Laws. Nonetheless, the assumption is that they would be relied upon in construing the statutory provisions.
39. *Id.*
40. *Id.*
41. *Id.*

Tennessee
Formal Will Requirements

Minimum age for executing will	Real Property—18 years. (§ 32-1-102) Personal Property—18 years. (§ 32-1-102)
Number of witnesses required	Two. (§ 32-1-104)
Holographic wills	Yes. (§ 32-1-105)
Wills admitted to probate if valid under the law of:	Tennessee; place of execution; place of testator's domicile at the time of execution. (§ 32-1-107)
Does the signing by the testator and/or witnesses just of the self-proving affidavit constitute the execution of the will?	Probably not, since only the witnesses, and not the testator, sign the affidavits. Moreover, the witnesses must state in the affidavits "such facts as they would be required to testify to in court to prove the will," which would presumably include that the testator signed the will or acknowledged his signature in their presence. (§ 32-2-110) But see Delaware.
Can self-proving affidavit be signed later by testator and/or witnesses?	Yes, at any time, including after the testator's death, any or both of the witnesses may sign an affidavit. However, it must be at the testator's request or, if the testator is deceased, at the request of the executor or any person "interested" in the will. (§ 32-2-110)
If a witness is a devisee, does this result in the disqualification to serve as a witness or the invalidation of the devise?	There is no disqualification of the witness. However, if there are not two other disinterested witnesses, the devise is void to the extent that the aggregate value exceeds the share the witnesses would take by intestate succession. (§ 32-1-103 (b)) A creditor would not be an interested witness, since a witness is interested only if the witness is given "some personal and beneficial interest." (§ 32-1-103(c))
Can any other person sign the will?	Yes, if at the testator's discretion and in the testator's presence. (§ 32-1-104(1)(c))
When must witnesses sign?	No precise time is specified. However, the witnesses must "sign: (A) In the presence of the testator; and (B) In the presence of each other." (§ 32-1-104(2))
Must they sign in the presence of the testator?	Yes. (§ 32-1-104(2)(A))
Must they sign in the presence of each other?	Yes. (§ 32-1-104(2)(B))
Must the testator publish the will?	Yes (§ 32-1-104(1)), but need not be express signification that the document is testator's will if it can be implied from the facts and circumstances. (Hale v. Bradley, 817 S.W.2d 320 (Ct. App. 1991))
Must the will be signed in a particular place?	Probably not. There is no statutory provision or definite case authority on point.
Must the required number of witnesses be present at the same time for the signing or acknowledgment by the testator?	Yes. (§ 32-1-104(1)(D))

May the testator acknowledge either his will or his signature?	The testator must acknowledge his signature. (§ 32-1-104(1)(B))
Requirements to be witness	Any person competent to be a witness. (§ 32-1-103(a))

Texas
Formal Will Requirements

Minimum age for executing will	Real Property—18 years. (Prob. § 57) Personal Property—18 years. (Prob. § 57) Prob. § 57 also provides that persons who are married or have been married or are members of armed forces or the auxiliaries thereof may execute wills, even though under age 18.
Number of witnesses required	Two. (Prob. § 59)(a))
Holographic wills	Yes. (Prob. § 60)
Wills admitted to probate if valid under the law of:	Texas; where testator domiciled at death. (Prob. §§ 95(B)(1), 103)
Does the signing by the testator and/or witnesses just of the self-proving affidavit constitute the execution of the will?	Yes. (Prob. § 59(b)) However, the will is not considered self-proved, since the signature is deemed on the will and missing instead from the self-proving affidavit.
Can self-proving affidavit be signed later by testator and/or witnesses?	Yes, by affidavits of the testator and witnesses "at any subsequent date during the lifetime of the testator and the witnesses. . . ." (Prob. § 59(a))
If a witness is a devisee, does this result in the disqualification to serve as a witness or the invalidation of the devise?	There is no disqualification of the witness. However, if there are not two other competent witnesses, the devise is void to the extent it exceeds the share that the witness would take by intestate succession. (Prob. § 61)
Can any other person sign the will?	Yes, by the testator's direction and in his presence. (Prob. § 59(a))
When must witnesses sign?	There is no time constraint in the statute. Obviously, it must be before the testator's death, since it must be in his presence.
Must they sign in the presence of the testator?	Yes (Prob. § 59(a)), but it may be "conscious" presence (i.e., even if testator did not actually see), the testator could have with slight physical exertion. (Nichols v. Rowan, 422 S.W.2d 21, 24 (Ct. Civ. App. 1967))
Must they sign in the presence of each other?	No. (Venner v. Layton, 244 S.W.2d 852, 856 (Ct. Civ. App. 1951))
Must the testator publish the will?	Uncertain, although attestation clause constitutes evidence where witnesses are uncertain. (Reese v. Franzheim, 381 S.W.2d 329 (Harris Co. Ct. Civ. App. 1974); but see Brown v. Traylor, 2006 WL 1098265, * 10-11 (Ct. Civ. App. Apr. 27, 2006)).
Must the will be signed in a particular place?	Although there is no statutory requirement, the older case law does not require the testator to sign at the end. (Lawson v. Dawson's Estate, 53 S.W. 64 (1899); In re Brown's Estate, 507 S.W.2d 801 (Ct. Civ. App. 1974))

Must the required number of witnesses be present at the same time for the signing or acknowledgment by the testator?	While the testator is not required to sign in the witnesses' presence, there is no provision relating to acknowledgment, and there are few cases. Moreover, the self-proving affidavit recommended form indicates that the testator *signed* in the presence of the witnesses. Since the affidavit used must have "contents substantially" as set forth in the statute, this would seem to support the conclusion that the witnesses must be present when the testator "executed" the will.
May the testator acknowledge either his will or his signature?	See *Must the required number of witnesses be present at the same time for the signing or acknowledgment by the testator?*
Requirements to be witness	They must be "credible" and "above the age of 14." (Prob. § 59(a)) A "credible" witness is a competent witness, that is, one competent to testify to the fact of will execution. (Moos v. First State Bank, 60 S.W.2d 888, 889 (Ct. Civ. App. 1933))

Utah
Formal Will Requirements

Minimum age for executing will	Real Property—18 years. (§ 75-2-501) Personal Property—18 years. (§ 75-2-501)
Number of witnesses required	Two. (§ 75-2-502)
Holographic wills	Yes. (§ 75-2-502)
Wills admitted to probate if valid under the law of:	Utah; place of execution at time of execution; place where domiciled, abode, or national at time of execution or death. (§ 75-2-506)
Does the signing by the testator and/or witnesses just of the self-proving affidavit constitute the execution of the will?	The following language would appear to allow this: "A will may be simultaneously executed, attested, and made self-proved by acknowledgment thereof by the testator and affidavits of the witnesses. . . ." (§ 75-2-504(1))
Can self-proving affidavit be signed later by testator and/or witnesses?	Yes. "An attested will may be made self-proved at any time after its execution by the acknowledgment thereof by the testator and the affidavits of the witnesses . . . [in form and content] substantially [as provided in the statute]." (§ 75-2-504(2))
If a witness is a devisee, does this result in the disqualification to serve as a witness or the invalidation of the devise?	No. (§ 75-2-505(2))
Can any other person sign the will?	Yes, if in the testator's conscious presence and by his direction. (§ 75-2-502)
When must witnesses sign?	There is no time constraint. However, it must occur within a reasonable time either after the testator executes the will or he acknowledges his signature or the will. (§ 75-2-502)
Must they sign in the presence of the testator?	No. (§ 75-2-502 cmt.)
Must they sign in the presence of each other?	No. (§ 75-2-502 cmt.)
Must the testator publish the will?	No. (§ 75-2-502 cmt.)
Must the will be signed in a particular place?	No. (§ 75-2-502 cmt.)
Must the required number of witnesses be present at the same time for the signing or acknowledgment by the testator?	No. (§ 75-2-502 & cmt.)
May the testator acknowledge either his will or his signature?	Yes. (§ 75-2-502 & cmt.)
Requirements to be witness	A person who is generally competent. (§ 75-2-505(1)) Utah imposes a very low bar for competency. (§ 78-24-1; Ut. R. Evid. 601; State v. Calliham, 57 P.3d 220, 226 (Sup. Ct. 2002))

Vermont
Formal Will Requirements

Minimum age for executing will	"A person of age and sound mind may devise, bequeath and dispose of his estate, real and personal. . . ." (14 § 1) A person of 18 years of age is considered of age. See 1 § 173.
Number of witnesses required	Two. (14 § 5)
Holographic wills	No. (14 § 5)
Wills admitted to probate if valid under the law of:	Vermont; place of execution or domicile. (14 § 112)
Does the signing by the testator and/or witnesses just of the self-proving affidavit constitute the execution of the will?	There is no provision.
Can self-proving affidavit be signed later by testator and/or witnesses?	There is no provision.
If a witness is a devisee, does this result in the disqualification to serve as a witness or the invalidation of the devise?	There is no disqualification of the witness. However, if there are not three other competent witnesses, a devise to the witness, the witness' spouse, or "one claiming under such person" (i.e., the witness) is void in full. On the other hand, regardless of its amount, the devise is valid, if the witness is an heir at law. (14 § 10) A charge for the payment of debts does not prevent creditors from bringing competent witnesses to the testator's will. (*Id.*)
Can any other person sign the will?	Yes, if in the testator's presence and by the testator's express direction. (14 § 5)
When must witnesses sign?	Although they do not have to sign when the testator executes the will, they do have to sign in his presence and the other two witnesses' presence. (14 § 5)
Must they sign in the presence of the testator?	Yes. (14 § 5)
Must they sign in the presence of each other?	Yes. (14 § 5) They need not actually look at each other signing. (In re Claflin's Will, 52 A. 1053, 1057 (1902))
Must the testator publish the will?	No. (In re Claflin's Will, 50 A. 815 (1901), *aff'd,* 52 A. 1053, 1054 (1902))
Must the will be signed in a particular place?	There is no statutory provision or definite case authority on point. Nevertheless, the key is the testator's intent in signing and not the actual location of the signature. (Adams v. Field, 21 Vt. 256 (1849))
Must the required number of witnesses be present at the same time for the signing or acknowledgment by the testator?	No. (In re Claflin's Will, 50 A. 815 (1901))

May the testator acknowledge either his will or his signature?	The testator may acknowledge signature, and this need not be in terms of express words. (In re Claflin's Will, 50 A. 815, 816 (1901))
Requirements to be witness	The witnesses must be "credible." (14 § 5) Credible means competent. (In re Potter's Will, 95 A. 646 (1915))

Virginia
Formal Will Requirements

Minimum age for executing will	Real Property—18 years. (§ 64.1-47) Personal Property—18 years. (§ 64.1-47) An emancipated minor may also execute a legally valid will. (§ 16.1-331)
Number of witnesses required	Two. (§ 64.1-49)
Holographic wills	Yes. (§ 64.1-49)
Wills admitted to probate if valid under the law of:	Place where domiciled if not domiciled in Virginia at time of death (limited to personal property). (§ 64.1-53) An "international will" is also valid. (§ 64.1-96.3)
Does the signing by the testator and/or witnesses just of the self-proving affidavit constitute the execution of the will?	Technically, the self-proving forms state that the will has already been signed. There are two types of forms, one which the testator and witnesses sign (§ 64.1-87.1) and another which the notary alone signs (§ 64.1-87.1). There is no authority on whether a signature on the first type would substitute for signing the will. The theory of integration arguably could be used. See Delaware.
Can self-proving affidavit be signed later by testator and/or witnesses?	The will may be made self-proved at any subsequent date by the acknowledgment of the testator and affidavits of the witnesses (§ 64.1-87.1) or "by the acknowledgment thereof by the testator and the attesting witnesses." It must be attached or annexed to the will, and is required to be substantially in form and content as provided in the statute. (§ 64.1-87.2) However, the certifying officer need not be a notary in Virginia if authorized to administer oaths under the law of the state where the acknowledgment occurred or an appropriate person authorized by the U.S. State Department. (*Id.*)
If a witness is a devisee, does this result in the disqualification to serve as a witness or the invalidation of the devise?	There is no disqualification of the witness. (§ 64.1-51) The provision does not address whether a devise is void. Presumably, the devise is allowed.
Can any other person sign the will?	Yes, if in the testator's presence and by his direction. (§ 64.1-49) It must be done in manner to make it manifest that the name is intended as a signature. (*Id.*)
When must witnesses sign?	At the time of the execution or later acknowledgment of will when the testator and witnesses are present. (§ 64.1-49)
Must they sign in the presence of the testator?	Yes. (§ 64.1-49)
Must they sign in the presence of each other?	Yes. (§ 64.1-49)
Must the testator publish the will?	There is nothing in the statute as to the original execution, although the testator must acknowledge his "will." (§ 64.1-49) Still, there is an old case that states that the will must be published, but that the testator has published the will even if he acknowledges it by referring to it as a deed. (Beane v. Yerby, 53 Va. (12 Gratt.) 239 (1855))

Must the will be signed in a particular place?	No, but it must be done in a manner to make it manifest that the name is intended as a signature. (§ 64.1-49; Slate v. Titmus, 385 S.E.2d 590, 591 (1989); Hamlet v. Hamlet, 32 S.E.2d 729, 731 (1945); McElroy v. Rolston, 34 S.E.2d 241, 242 (1945)) Whereas the testator must "sign," the witnesses must "subscribe," which has been interpreted to mean signing "underneath." (French v. Beville, 62 S.E.2d 883, 886 (1951))
Must the required number of witnesses be present at the same time for the signing or acknowledgment by the testator?	Yes. (§ 64.1-49)
May the testator acknowledge either his will or his signature?	No. "The will" must be acknowledged. (§ 64.1-49)
Requirements to be witness	The witnesses must be competent. (§ 64.1-49) A competent witness is one competent to testify in court. (Ferguson v. Ferguson, 47 S.E.2d 346, 351 (1948))

Washington
Formal Will Requirements

Minimum age for executing will	Real Property—18 years. (§ 11.12.010) Personal Property—18 years. (§ 11.12.010)
Number of witnesses required	Two. (§ 11.12.020)
Holographic wills	No. (§ 11.12.020)
Wills admitted to probate if valid under the law of:	Washington; place where executed; place where testator is domiciled either at the time of the will's execution or at the time of the testator's death. (§ 11-12-020)
Does the signing by the testator and/or witnesses just of the self-proving affidavit constitute the execution of the will?	In the case of the witnesses, this is recognized as an alternative to signing the will. (§ 11.12.020(1)) Since the testator does not sign the affidavit, and the affidavit states all facts necessary to prove the will in court, including the signature of the testator on the will, the testator's signature on the affidavit instead of the will itself probably would not be valid. Indeed, this was the position taken in invalidating witness signatures on the affidavit before § 11-12.020(1) was revised in 1990 to allow this with regard to witnesses. (Wa. S.B. No. 6392, approv. Mar. 15, 1990, 1990 Wash. Legis. Serv. 79.) No similar language authorizes a testator to sign only the self-proving affidavit and the rationale of *Ricketts*, though at times it only involved witnesses, would probably result in finding the instrument invalid. Even though the statute cited above appears to allow this, the statute only mentions the possibility of the witness signature on the affidavit qualifying as a *due attestation* of the will. (In re Estate of Ricketts, 773 P.2d 93, 95 (Ct. App. 1989)).
Can self-proving affidavit be signed later by testator and/or witnesses?	Yes. At any time, including after the testator's death, any or both of the witnesses may sign an affidavit. However, it must be at the testator's request or, if the testator is deceased, at the request of the executor or any person "interested" in the will. (§ 11.20.020(2)) However, § 11.12.020 deems to require the affidavit be signed "while in the presence of the testator and at the testator's direction or request. . . ."
If a witness is a devisee, does this result in the disqualification to serve as a witness or the invalidation of the devise?	There is no disqualification of the witness. (§ 11.12.160(2)) If there are not two other competent witnesses, a rebuttable presumption is created that the devise was obtained by duress, menace, fraud, or undue influence. (§ 11.12.160(2)) If the presumption is not rebutted, the witness can take only to the extent of the share the witness would have taken by intestate succession. (§ 11.12.160(3))
Can any other person sign the will?	Yes, if under the testator's direction and in the testator's presence. (§ 11.12.020) Such person must also subscribe his own name and state that he subscribed the testator's name at the testator's request. However, the signing and statement are not required if the testator evidences approval of the signature made at his request by making his mark on the will. (§ 11.12.030))

When must witnesses sign?	See *Must the required number of witnesses be present at the same time for the signing or acknowledgment by the testator?*, indicating the uncertain status of the law as to a later acknowledgment. (In re Gardner's Estate, 417 P.2d 948, 952 (1966))
Must they sign in the presence of the testator?	Yes, and "at the testator's direction or request." (§ 11.12.020)
Must they sign in the presence of each other?	No. (In re Gardner's Estate, 417 P.2d 948, 952 (1966))
Must the testator publish the will?	No. (In re Chambers' Estate, 60 P.2d 41, 42 (1936))
Must the will be signed in a particular place?	Probably not. (In re Estate of Price, 871 P.2d 1079, 1083 (1994) (formalities reduced to a minimum))
Must the required number of witnesses be present at the same time for the signing or acknowledgment by the testator?	There is conflicting authority on this point. The most recent decision does not require that the testator sign in the presence of the witnesses. (In re Gardner's Estate, 417 P.2d 948 (1966)) However, there is no statutory authority for post-execution acknowledgment and no definite case authority. Earlier cases indicate that the witnesses actually have to see the testator sign. (In re Conquist's Estate, 274 P.2d 585 (1954))
May the testator acknowledge either his will or his signature?	See *Must the required number of witnesses be present at the same time for the signing or acknowledgment by the testator?*
Requirements to be witness	The witnesses must be competent. (§ 11.12.020)

West Virginia
Formal Will Requirements

Minimum age for executing will	Real Property—18 years. (§ 41-1-2) Personal Property—18 years. (§ 41-1-2)
Number of witnesses required	Two. (§ 41-1-3)
Holographic wills	Yes. (§ 41-1-3)
Wills admitted to probate if valid under the law of:	Domiciliary state at death (limited to personal property). (§ 41-1-5)
Does the signing by the testator and/or witnesses just of the self-proving affidavit constitute the execution of the will?	The production of the will itself appears to suffice for ex parte probate. (§ 41-5-10)
Can self-proving affidavit be signed later by testator and/or witnesses?	Yes. (§ 41-5-15)
If a witness is a devisee, does this result in the disqualification to serve as a witness or the invalidation of the devise?	There is no disqualification of the witness. The devise to the witness or the witness' spouse is void if there are not other competent witnesses, except an intestate share is given to the witness, to the extent he would be entitled to one if the will were not established, but not in excess of the devise. (§ 41-2-1) A creditor can be a competent witness, as can a spouse of a creditor, despite the will being charged with the debt owed the creditor. (§ 41-2-2)
Can any other person sign the will?	Yes, in the testator's presence and by the testator's direction. (§ 41-1-3)
When must witnesses sign?	The statute does not provide when they must sign, though they are required to sign in the presence of the testator and of each other. Stevens v. Casdorph, 203 W. Va. 450, 508 S.E.2d 610 (1998) (also rejecting the argument of "substantial compliance" with the formalities of will execution). (§ 41-1-3)
Must they sign in the presence of the testator?	Yes. (§ 41-1-3) Technically, the testator must request that they act as witnesses, although the testator's agent can do this, if the testator hears and understands and does not dissent. (Cheatham v. Hatcher, 30 Grat. (71 Va.) 56 (1878))
Must they sign in the presence of each other?	Yes. (§ 41-1-3)
Must the testator publish the will?	Yes. (Freeman v. Freeman, 76 S.E. 657 (1912), overruled on other grounds) However, the testator need not declare it is his will if, for example, the witnesses read the attestation clause, which states that it is the will of the person whose signature they have been asked to witness.
Must the will be signed in a particular place?	No. (Black v. Maxwell, 46 S.E.2d 804, 809 (1948))
Must the required number of witnesses be present at the same time for the signing or acknowledgment by the testator?	Yes. The testator must sign or acknowledge the will "in the presence of at least two competent witnesses." (§ 41-1-3)

May the testator acknowledge either his will or his signature?	No. The will must be acknowledged. (§ 41-1-3)
Requirements to be witness	They must be competent. (§ 41-1-3)

Wisconsin
Formal Will Requirements

Minimum age for executing will	Real Property—18 years. (§ 853.01) Personal Property—18 years. (§ 853.01)
Number of witnesses required	Two. (§ 853.03(2))
Holographic wills	No. (§ 853.03)
Wills admitted to probate if valid under the law of:	Wisconsin; place of execution; place where testator resided, was domiciled or was a national at time of execution or death. (§ 853.05)
Does the signing by the testator and/or witnesses just of the self-proving affidavit constitute the execution of the will?	Yes. (§ 853.04(3))
Can self-proving affidavit be signed later by testator and/or witnesses?	Yes. (§ 853.04(2))
If a witness is a devisee, does this result in the disqualification to serve as a witness or the invalidation of the devise?	There is no disqualification of the witness. If there are not two other disinterested witnesses, the devise to the witness or to the witness' spouse is void to the extent it exceeds the share the witness would take by intestate succession. (§ 853.07 (2)) A person is not an "interested" witness subject to the foregoing provisions, if the witness or witness' spouse is devised an interest which is personal and beneficial. Thus, a provision for employment at the usual rate is not a problem (§ 853.07(3)(a)); nor is a "provision which would have conferred no benefit if the testator had died immediately following execution of the will." (§ 853.07(3)(b)) Thus, executors, trustees, and contingent remaindermen or discretionary trust beneficiaries would appear to be among those who are not "interested" witnesses.
Can any other person sign the will?	Yes, if by the testator's direction and in the testator's presence. (§ 853.03(1)) A witness can sign for the testator. This proxy signing must be in the presence of the witnesses or later acknowledged by the testator in the presence of the witnesses. (*Id.*)
When must witnesses sign?	Within a reasonable time after witnessing testator's signing or acknowledgment of the will. (§ 853.03(2))
Must they sign in the presence of the testator?	Yes. (§ 853.03(2))
Must they sign in the presence of each other?	Yes. (§ 853.03(2))
Must the testator publish the will?	No. (§ 853.03 cmt.)
Must the will be signed in a particular place?	No. (§ 853.03 cmt.)
Must the required number of witnesses be present at the same time for the signing or acknowledgment by the testator?	No. (§ 853.03 cmt.) Attestation appears to mean nothing more than "signed" by the witnesses. (§ 853.03(2) & cmt.)

May the testator acknowledge either his will or his signature?	Yes. (§ 853.03 cmt.) Attestation appears to mean nothing more than "signed" by the witnesses. (§ 853.03(2) & cmt.)
Requirements to be witness	Any person competent to testify as a witness in court to the facts relating to execution. (§ 853.07(1))

Wyoming
Formal Will Requirements

Minimum age for executing will	Real Property—18 years. (§ 2-6-101) Personal Property—18 years. (§ 2-6-101)
Number of witnesses required	Two. (§ 2-6-112)
Holographic wills	Yes. (§ 2-6-113)
Wills admitted to probate if valid under the law of:	Wyoming; place of execution at time of execution; place where, at time of execution or death, testator is domiciled, has a place of abode, or is a national. (§ 2-6-116)
Does the signing by the testator and/or witnesses just of the self-proving affidavit constitute the execution of the will?	Yes. (§ 2-6-114(b))
Can self-proving affidavit be signed later by testator and/or witnesses?	Yes. "An attested will may . . . at any subsequent date [to its execution] be made self-proven by the acknowledgment thereof by the testator and the affidavits of the witnesses . . . in form and contents substantially as [provided in the statute]." (§ 2-6-114(c))
If a witness is a devisee, does this result in the disqualification to serve as a witness or the invalidation of the devise?	There is no disqualification of the witness. If there are not two other disinterested and competent witnesses, the witness can only take a portion of the estate to the extent it does not exceed the amount the witness would take by intestate succession. (§ 2-6-112)
Can any other person sign the will?	Yes, in the testator's presence and by his express direction. (§ 2-6-112)
When must witnesses sign?	There is no time constraint. The statute simply requires that the "will" be "witnessed." (§ 2-6-112)
Must they sign in the presence of the testator?	There is no statutory provision or direct case authority on point.
Must they sign in the presence of each other?	There is no statutory provision or direct case authority on point.
Must the testator publish the will?	No. (In re Estate of Carey, 504 P.2d 793, 801 (1972))
Must the will be signed in a particular place?	There is no statutory provision or direct case authority on point.
Must the required number of witnesses be present at the same time for the signing or acknowledgment by the testator?	Since the witnesses must "attest" the "will" (§ 2-6-112), they, presumably, must see its execution or have it acknowledged. However, there is no specific statutory provision or direct case authority on point.
May the testator acknowledge either his will or his signature?	Since the witnesses must "attest" the "will" (§ 2-6-112), they, presumably, must see its execution or have it acknowledged. However, there is no specific statutory provision or direct case authority on point.
Requirements to be witness	They must be competent. (§ § 2-6-112, 2-6-115)

Table 2
Proving Foreign Wills
(current through 5/1/07)

Whenever assets of the estate of an individual are situated outside the state of domicile at death, the personal representative will face the quandary of how to proceed in the other state or states to prove that the will should be given effect with regard to those nondomicile assets and to establish the personal representative's own authority to act on behalf of the estate. Since each state has plenary power over the property within its physical or regulatory control, careful attention must be paid to this matter in order to unify the estate and avoid splintering probate and administration into a number of mini-estates scattered around the country.

Although a very commonplace problem, there has been very little attention paid to this matter. The statutes that do exist are incomplete and often border on, if not cross over into, the incomprehensible. There is little case law, and what there is, tends to consist of very old, highly particularized decisions.

Tables 2.01 and 2.02 detail the governing principles embodied in each state's law. Where appropriate, inferences have been drawn from the statutory language. Some questions, however, simply have no clear-cut answer. Undoubtedly, these questions are handled based on local county custom and practice.

The emphasis of this table is not on the requirements for original probate of the will in the domiciliary state. The assumption is that the attorney knows or can readily inquire as to how to accomplish this. Rather, the chapter addresses exclusively the situation of what each nondomicile state requires with regard to probate of the out-of-state decedent's will. It explores important aspects of the subject, such as proper venue for local probate, the possibilities of original probate locally of a nondomiciliary's will, the prerequisites to ancillary probate following probate at the domicile, special notice requirements in the state of ancillary probate, and the qualification locally to act on behalf of the estate of the domiciliary personal representative or the person designated in the will, if other than the domiciliary representative. As to which persons from out-of-state can qualify to serve as a personal representative, see Table 3.

Ultimately, the question of ancillary probate is crucial because it bears on the transfer of assets of the estate to the primary personal representative in the domiciliary state. The chapter, thus, considers, among other questions, whether and when assets may be transferred to the domiciliary personal representative from the local jurisdiction.

Table 2.01, Part 1
Proof of a Foreign Will

	What Proof is Required to Establish a Will Already Proved in Another State?	*Are There Special Rules For a Will Proved Outside the U.S.?*	*Is There a Special Rule For Local Property?*	*Can a Will Be Proved If Not Established at the Domicile?*		
				That Is, Is Original Probate Permitted?	*If So, What Are the Circumstances?*	*What About Original Probate After Probate in Another Jurisdiction?*
Alabama	An authenticated and certified copy of the will and its probate. (§ 43-8-175) This assumes that the testator, at the time of his death, was not an inhabitant of Alabama. (*Id.*) Inhabitant means domiciliary. (Ambrose v. Vandeford, 167 So. 2d 149 (Ala. 1969))	Yes. It must be probated as an original proceedings with respect to local real and personal property. (§ 43-8-175)	No, except for a will probated outside the U.S. (See § 43-8-175)	Prior probate in state of testator's domicile is not necessary for probate of a foreign will in Alabama. (Kelley v. Sutliff, 80 So. 2d 636 (1955))	Yes, if assets in state; assets later come into state; or designated in will and property owned in state at death. (§ 43-8-162(3), (4) & (5))	No. When a will, which has already been probated in another U.S. state where testator is an inhabitant at time of death, is presented for probate in Alabama, the only inquiries the court can make are whether granting court had jurisdiction and whether will properly authenticated. Duty of the court is then ministerial. (Carter v. Davis, 154 So. 2d 9 (1963))
Alaska	A final order of a court in a proceeding determining testacy, validity, or construction, there was notice and opportunity to contest by all interested parties, and there is a finding or it is based upon a finding of domicile of the decedent at death. (§ 13.16.175 & U.P.C. § 3-408 cmt[1].)	Yes. If the will comes from a place that does not provide for probate, it may be proved by a duly authenticated certificate of its legal custodian that the copy introduced is a true copy and that the will has become effective under the law of the	No.	Yes, at least under two circumstances: (i) if the will is from a place that does not provide for probate of a will after death (§13.16.090(e)); (ii) there is also a suggestion in the cmt. to U.P.C. §3-408, on which the statute is based, that a local proceeding is not	If proceedings are "concluded" in this state before they are concluded at the domicile. (U.P.C. cmt. to § 3-408,[2] which parallels § 13.16.175) Also, if only informal proceeding at the domicile, this does not block a local probate. (U.P.C.	No, if there is a final order of the domicile state. (§ 13.16.175) But this prohibition does not apply if *informal* proceedings. (U.P.C. cmt. to § 3-408,[4] which parallels § 13.16.175) See also § 13.16.090(d) and § 13.16.090(e).

		other place. (§ 13.16.180)		barred, even if (i) does not apply. Thus, the cmt. states: "Hence, if a local proceeding is concluded before formal proceedings at domicile have concluded, local law will control."	cmt. to § 3-408,[3] which parallels § 13.16.175)	
Arizona	A final order of a court in a proceeding determining testacy, validity, or construction, there was notice and opportunity to contest by all interested parties and there is a finding or it is based upon a finding of domicile of the decedent at death. (§ 14-3408[5])	Yes. If the will comes from a place that does not provide for probate, it may be proved by a duly authenticated certificate of its legal custodian that the copy introduced is a true copy and that the will has become effective under the law of the other place. (§ 14-3409)	No.	Yes, at least under two circumstances: (i) if the will is from a place that does not provide for probate of a will after death (§14-3409); (ii) there is also a suggestion in the cmt. to U.P.C. §3-408, on which the statute is based, that a local proceeding is not barred, even if (i) does not apply. Thus, the cmt. states: "Hence, if a local proceeding is concluded before formal proceedings at domicile have concluded, local law will control."	If proceedings are "concluded" in this state before they are concluded at the domicile. (U.P.C. cmt. to § 3-408,[6] which section parallels § 14-3408) Also, if only informal proceeding at the domicile, this does not block a local probate. (U.P.C. cmt. to § 3408,[7] which parallels § 14-3408)	No, if there is a final order of the domicile state. (§ 14-3408) But this prohibition does not apply if *informal* proceedings. (U.P.C. cmt. to § 3-408,[8] which parallels § 14-3408)
Arkansas	When a will of a nonresedent has been admitted to probate in another appropriate jurisdiction, an authenticated copy thereof, and an authenticated copy of the order admitting the will to probate must be filed. Court will then admit the *(cont'd)*	No.	No.	Yes. (McPherson v. McKay, 172 S.W.2d 911 (1943))	If the testator owned property in Arkansas that might be the subject of administration in Arkansas, or where there was a debt or demand due the testator that requires *(cont'd)*	No provision.

Table 2.01, Part 1
Proof of a Foreign Will *(continued)*

				Can a Will Be Proved If Not Established at the Domicile?		
	What Proof is Required to Establish a Will Already Proved in Another State?	*Are There Special Rules For a Will Proved Outside the U.S.?*	*Is There a Special Rule For Local Property?*	*That Is, Is Original Probate Permitted?*	*If So, What Are the Circumstances?*	*What About Original Probate After Probate in Another Jurisdiction?*
Arkansas *(cont'd)*	will if it appears the will was executed and proved in the manner prescribed by the law of its place of execution, laws of the testator's domicile at the time of execution, or by the laws of Arkansas. (§ 28-40-120(a) & (b))				administration to collect. (McPherson v. McKay, 172 S.W.2d 911 (1943))	
California	The will or an authenticated copy of the will, an authenticated copy of the order admitting the will to probate, or other evidence of the establishment or proof of the will. (Prob. § 12521(a)) See also Prob. §§ 12522 and 12523, indicating the will is not admissible to probate in California if there was no finding in the sister state or foreign country that the decedent was domiciled there at the time of death, an interested party was not given notice or opportunity to contest, the determination was not final, and in the case of a foreign nation, the judicial system does not provide impartial tribunals or procedures compatible with due process.	Yes. (Prob. §§ 12520(a), 12523)	No.	Yes. (Cmt. to Prob. § 12520(b))	If it has not been probated elsewhere or it fails to qualify for ancillary administration under Prob. § 12520.	Yes, if it fails to qualify for ancillary administration under Prob. § 12520 et seq. (Prob. § 12520(b))

Colorado	A final order of a court in a proceeding determining testacy, validity, or construction, there was notice and opportunity to contest by all interested parties, and there is a finding or it is based upon a finding of domicile of the decedent at death (§ 15-12-408 & U.P.C. § 3-408 cmt.[9])	Yes. If the will comes from a place that does not provide for probate, it may be proved by a duly authenticated certificate of its legal custodian that the copy introduced is a true copy and that the will has become effective under the law of the place. (§ 15-12-409)	No. However, Wimbush v. Wimbush, 587 P.2d 796 (1978), may allow for separate determination of validity of will for purposes of local real property.	Yes, at least under two circumstances: (i) if the will is from a place that does not provide for probate of a will after death (§§ 15-12-408, 15-12-409); (ii) there is also a suggestion in the cmt. to U.P.C. § 3-408, on which the statute is based, that a local proceeding is not barred, even if (i) does not apply. Thus, the cmt. states: "Hence, if a local proceeding is concluded before formal proceedings at domicile have concluded, local law will control."	If proceedings are "concluded" in this state before they are concluded at the domicile. (U.P.C. cmt. to § 3-408,[10] which section parallels § 15-12-408) Also, if only informal proceeding at the domicile, this does not block a local probate. (U.P.C. cmt. to § 3-408,[11] which section parallels § 15-12-408)	No. See Corrigan v. Jones, 23 P. 913 (1890); Estate of Vilm v. Vilm, 299 P.2d 513 (1956). Colorado has conspicuously not enacted a relevant provision, U.P.C. § 3-408.
Connecticut	An authenticated and exemplified copy of will and record of proceedings proving and establishing will. (§ 45a-288)	No.	No.	Yes. (§ 45a-287(b))	If denial of probate or "establishment" in the domicile state is for a cause which is not grounds for rejection of a will in this state. (§ 45a-287(b))	There is no statute or case authority.
Delaware	A verified copy of will and a verified copy of record admitting the same to probate. (12 § 1307(a)) To be verified, it must be certified by the proper officer under the officer's hand and seal of office and certificate stating that copy is certified in due form. (12 § 1307(b))				If not offered for prior probate in domiciliary jurisdiction or if rejected for a cause which is not grounds for rejection of a will in this state. (12§ 1307(a))	There is no statute or case authority.

Table 2.01, Part 1
Proof of a Foreign Will *(continued)*

				Can a Will Be Proved If Not Established at the Domicile?		
	What Proof is Required to Establish a Will Already Proved in Another State?	*Are There Special Rules For a Will Proved Outside the U.S.?*	*Is There a Special Rule For Local Property?*	*That Is, Is Original Probate Permitted?*	*If So, What Are the Circumstances?*	*What About Original Probate After Probate in Another Jurisdiction?*
District of Columbia	A duly certified copy or transcript of record of proceedings admitting will. (§ 14-504)	No.	No.	There is no statute or case authority.	There is no statute or case authority.	There is no statute or case authority.
Florida	Authenticated copy of probated will that is determined to comply with the order execution for malities or those of some other permissible jurisdiction under § 732.502(1) or § 732.502(2). (§ 734.102 (3)) A special procedure is provided for estates with less than $50,000 in value in Florida. (§ 734.1025)	A will in a foreign language must be accompanied by a true and complete English translation. (§ 733.204)	Yes as to real property. (§ 734.104) It requires authenticated copies of the will, the petition for probate, and the order admitting the will to probate. If a petition is not required, then there must be proof by affidavit or certificate that a petition is not required. The order admitting the will to probate must state that no petition was required in the foreign jurisdiction. Note that § 734.104 (2) could be read as applying to other property as well.	Yes. (§§ 731.106, 733.103)	Not specified. Presumably like any other will.	Unclear, but may be allowed. (§ 733.103 (2)) Only bars collateral attack with respect to "the probate of a will in Florida." On the other hand, § 733.103 pro vides that until a will is admitted "in this state or in the state where the decedent was domiciled," the will is ineffective. The implication is that, if proved at the domicile, it is effective.
Georgia	A properly certified copy of the will and a properly authenticated copy of the final probate proceedings at the domicile, certified	Yes. The same proof is required as in the prior question, but serves merely as prima facie evidence of due	No. See § 53-5-33 cmt., which notes extension of provision to real property.	Yes. (§ 53-5-36)	Upon proof that the will is valid under the laws of this state and has not been offered for probate in the	No.

	in accordance with § 24-7-24. (§ 53-5-33(b))	execution. (§ 53-5-33(c))			domiciliary jurisdiction or that it has been offered for probate but no timely objection was filed or the grounds of a pending objection would not, if proved, cause the denial of probate. (§§ 53-5-31, 53-5-32).	
Hawaii	A final order of a court in a proceeding determining testacy, validity, or construction, there was notice and opportunity to contest by all interested parties, and there is a finding or it is based upon a finding of domicile of the decedent at death. (§ 560:3-408 & U.P.C. § 3-408 cmt.)	Yes. If the will comes from a place that does not provide for probate, it may be proved by a duly authenticated certificate of its legal custodian that the copy introduced is a true copy and that the will has become effective under the law of the place. (§ 560:3-409)	No.	Yes, at least under two circumstances: (i) if the will is from a place that does not provide for probate of a will after death (§ 560:3-408); (ii) there is also a suggestion in the cmt. to U.P.C. § 3-408, on which the statute is based, that a local proceeding is not barred, even if (i) does not apply. Thus, the cmt. states: "Hence, if a local proceeding is concluded before formal proceedings at domicile have concluded, local law will control."	If proceedings are "concluded" in this state before they are concluded at the domicile. (U.P.C. cmt. to § 3-408,[13] which section parallels § 560:3-408) Also, if only informal proceed ing at the domicile, this does not block a local probate. (U.P.C. cmt. to § 3-408,[14] which section parallels § 560:3-408)	No, if there is a final order of the domicile state. (§ 560:3-408) But this prohibition does not apply if *informal* proceedings. (U.P.C. cmt. to § 3-408,[15] which section parallels § 560:3-408)
Idaho	A final order of a court in a proceeding determining testacy, validity, or construction, there was notice and opportunity to contest by all interested parties, and there is a finding or it is based upon a finding of domicile of the decedent at death. (§ 15-3-408 & cmt.)	Yes. If the will comes from a place that does not provide for probate, it may be proved by a duly authenticated certificate of its legal custodian that the copy introduced is a true copy and that the will has become effective *(cont'd)*	No.	Yes, at least under two circumstances: (i) if the will is from a place that does not provide for probate of a will after death (§ 15-3-408 cmt.); (ii) there is also a suggestion in the cmt. to U.P.C. §3-408, on which the statute is based, that a local *(cont'd)*	If proceedings are "concluded" in this state before they are concluded at the domicile. (§ 15-3-408 cmt.) Also, if only informal proceeding at the domicile, this does not block a local probate. (§ 15-3-408 cmt.)	No, if there is a final order of the domicile state. (§ 15-3-408) But this prohibition does not apply if *informal* proceedings. (§ 15-3-408 cmt.)

Table 2.01, Part 1
Proof of a Foreign Will *(continued)*

				Can a Will Be Proved If Not Established at the Domicile?		
	What Proof is Required to Establish a Will Already Proved in Another State?	*Are There Special Rules For a Will Proved Outside the U.S.?*	*Is There a Special Rule For Local Property?*	*That Is, Is Original Probate Permitted?*	*If So, What Are the Circumstances?*	*What About Original Probate After Probate in Another Jurisdiction?*
Idaho *(cont'd)*		under the law of the place. (§ 15-3-409)		proceeding is not barred, even if (i) does not apply. Thus, the cmt. states: "Hence, if a local proceeding is concluded before formal proceedings at domicile have concluded, local law will control."		
Illinois	An authenticated copy of the will and the probate thereof. (755 ILCS § 5/7-3(a))	No. (755 ILCS § 5/7-3(b))	No.	Yes. (755 ILCS § 5/7-4(a), (b), (c))	If the will can be proved under the laws of Illinois, place of execution, or place of domicile at the time of execution. (755 ILCS § 5/7-4(a), (b), (c))	No provision.
Indiana	Certified will or a certified copy of the will and probate of the will. In all cases, the documents must be attested as to authenticity. (§ 29-1-7-26)	No.	No.	No provision.	No provision.	No provision.
Iowa	Copy of the will and of the original probate record, both of which must be properly authenticated and certified. (§ 633.496)	No. (§ 633.496)	No. (§ 633.495)	Yes. (§ 633.495)	Only if not probated in another state; only in a county where either real or personal property of the deceased non-	No provision.

					resident is located. (§ 633.495)	
Kansas	Copy of will and the probate of it, both authenticated. (§ 59-2229) Court will then have a hearing to determine if the will was probated and that the will was executed in accordance with the laws of the testator's residence, the laws of the state in which it was executed, or the laws of Kansas. (§ 59-2230)	No. (§ 59-2229)	No.	All probate proceedings are original, not ancillary. (§ 59-804)	N/A	All probate proceedings are original, not ancillary. (§ 59-804)
Kentucky	Authenticated copy and certificate of probate. (§ 394.150)	No. (§ 394.150)	No.	No, except under peculiar circumstances. (Payne v. Payne, 39 S.W.2d 205 (Ct. App. 1931))	N/A	No.
Louisiana	"A will duly proved, allowed, and admitted to probate outside of this state, may be allowed and recorded in the proper court of any parish in this state, in which the testator shall have left any estate." (§ 9:2421)	No. (§ 9:2422)	No.	Yes. (Code Civ. Pro. §§ 2888, 3401)	It must be in a form that is valid in either the decedent's domicile or place of execution. Evidence must be provided proving the will's validity. (Code Civ. Pro. §§ 2888, 3401)	Not specified.
Maine	A final order of a court in a proceeding determining testacy, validity, or construction, there was notice and opportunity to contest by all interested parties, and there is a finding or it is based upon a finding of domicile of the decedent at death. (18-A § 3-408 & cmt.)	Yes. If the will comes from a place that does not provide for probate, it may be proved by a duly authenticated certificate of its legal custodian that the copy introduced is a true copy and that the will has become effective under the law of the *(cont'd)*	No.	Yes, at least under two circumstances: (i) if the will is from a place that does not provide for probate of a will after death (18-A § 3-408); (ii) there is also a suggestion in the cmt. to U.P.C. § 3-408, on which the statute is based, that a local proceeding is not barred, even if (i) does *(cont'd)*	If proceedings are "concluded" in this state before they are concluded at the domicile. (18-A § 3-408 cmt.) Also, if only informal proceeding at the domicile, this does not block a local probate. (18-A § 3-408 cmt.)	No, if there is a final order of the domicile state. (18-A § 3-408) But this prohibition does not apply if *informal* proceedings. (18-A § 3-408 cmt.)

Table 2.01, Part 1
Proof of a Foreign Will *(continued)*

				Can a Will Be Proved If Not Established at the Domicile?		
	What Proof is Required to Establish a Will Already Proved in Another State?	*Are There Special Rules For a Will Proved Outside the U.S.?*	*Is There a Special Rule For Local Property?*	*That Is, Is Original Probate Permitted?*	*If So, What Are the Circumstances?*	*What About Original Probate After Probate in Another Jurisdiction?*
Maine *(cont'd)*		place. (§ 18A § 3-409)		not apply. Thus, the cmt. states: "Hence, if a local proceeding is concluded before formal proceedings at domicile have concluded, local law will control."		
Maryland	An authenticated will and its probate. (Roach v. Jurchak, 35 A.2d 817 (1944); Est. & Trusts § 4-104)	Not specified.	No.	Yes. (Est. & Trusts § 4-104(3))	A will executed out side this state is properly executed if it is (1) in writing; (2) signed by the testator; and (3) executed in conformity with the provisions of Est. & Trusts § 4-102, the law of the domicile of the testator, or the place where the will is executed. (Est. & Trusts § 4-104)	
Massachusetts	An authenticated copy of the will and its probate, and an affidavit of the names and residences of known heirs and next-of-kin and their relationship to the testator must be produced to the probate and family court in any	No. (192 § 9)	No.	Yes. (191 § 5)	It must be in a form that is valid in either the decedent's domicile or place of execution, in writing, and signed by the testator. (191 § 5).	Not specified.

	county where there is property. (192 § 9)					
Michigan	A final order of a court in a proceeding determining testacy, validity, or construction, there was notice and opportunity to contest by all interested parties, and there is a finding or it is based upon a finding of domicile of the decedent at death. (§ 700.3408 & U.P.C. 3-408 cmt.)	Yes. If the will comes from a place that does not provide for probate, it may be proved by a duly authenticated certificate of its legal custodian that the copy introduced is a true copy and that the will has become effective under the law of the place. (§ 700.3409)	No.	Yes, at least under two circumstances: (i) if the will is from a place that does not provide for probate of a will after death (§700.3408); (ii) there is also a suggestion in the cmt. to U.P.C. § 3-408, on which the statute is based, that a local proceeding is not barred, even if (i) does not apply. Thus, the cmt. states: "Hence, if a local proceeding is concluded before formal proceedings at domicile have concluded, local law will control."	If proceedings are "concluded" in this state before they are concluded at the domicile. (U.P.C. cmt. to § 3-408, which section parallels § 700.3408)	No, if there is a final order of the domicile state. (§ 700.3408) But this prohibition does not apply if *informal* proceedings. (U.P.C. cmt. to § 3-408, which section parallels § 700.3408)
Minnesota	A final order of a court in a proceeding determining testacy, validity, or construction, there was notice and opportunity to contest by all interested parties, and there is a finding or it is based upon a finding of domicile of the decedent at death. (§ 524.3-408 & U.P.C. 3-408 cmt.[16])	Yes. If the will comes from a place that does not provide for probate, it may be proved by a duly authenticated certificate of its legal custodian that the copy introduced is a true copy and that the will has *(cont'd)*	No.	Yes, at least under two circumstances: (i) if the will is from a place that does not provide for probate of a will after death (§ 524.3-408); (ii) there is also a suggestion in the cmt. to U.P.C. § 3-408, on which the statute is based, that a local *(cont'd)*	If proceedings are "concluded" in this state before they are concluded at the domicile. (U.P.C. cmt. to § 3-408,[17] which section parallels § 524.3-408) Also, if only informal proceeding at the domicile, this does *(cont'd)*	No, if there is a final order of the domicile state. (§ 524.3-408) But this prohibition does not apply if *informal* proceedings. (U.P.C. cmt. to § 3-408,[19] which section parallels § 524.3-408)

Table 2.01, Part 1
Proof of a Foreign Will *(continued)*

				Can a Will Be Proved If Not Established at the Domicile?		
	What Proof is Required to Establish a Will Already Proved in Another State?	*Are There Special Rules For a Will Proved Outside the U.S.?*	*Is There a Special Rule For Local Property?*	*That Is, Is Original Probate Permitted?*	*If So, What Are the Circumstances?*	*What About Original Probate After Probate in Another Jurisdiction?*
Minnesota *(cont'd)*		become effective under the law of the place. (§ 524.3-409)		proceeding is not barred, even if (i) does not apply. Thus, the cmt. states: "Hence, if a local proceeding is concluded before formal proceedings at domicile have concluded, local law will control."	not block a local probate. (U.P.C. cmt. to § 3-408,[18] which section parallels § 524.3-408)	
Mississippi	*There is no ancillary probate in Mississippi. (§ 91-1-1; Carroll v. McPike, 53 Miss. 569 (1876))*					
Missouri	*There is no ancillary probate in Missouri. (§ 473.668; Yonke v. Alber's Estate, 351 S.W.2d 794 (Ct. App. 1961))*					
Montana	A final order of a court in a proceeding determining testacy, validity, or construction, there was notice and opportunity to contest by all interested parties, and there is a finding or it is based upon a finding of domicile of the decedent at death. (§ 72-3-312 & U.P.C. § 3-408 cmt.[20])	Yes. If the will comes from a place that does not provide for probate, it may be proved by a duly authenticated certificate of its legal custodian that the copy introduced is a true copy and that the will has become effective under the law of the place. (§ 72-3-313)	No.	Yes, at least under two circumstances: (i) if the will is from a place that does not provide for probate of a will after death (§ 72-3-312); (ii) there is also a suggestion in the cmt. to U.P.C. § 3-408, on which the statute is based, that a local proceeding is not barred, even if (i) does not apply. Thus, the cmt. states: "Hence, if a local proceeding is concluded before formal proceedings	If proceedings are "concluded" in this state before they are concluded at the domicile. (U.P.C. cmt. to § 3-408,[21] which section parallels § 72-3-312) Also, if only informal proceeding at the domicile, this does not block a local probate. (U.P.C. cmt. to § 3-408,[22] which section parallels § 72-3-312)	No, if there is a final order of the domicile state. (§ 72-3-312) But this prohibition does not apply if *informal* proceedings. (U.P.C. cmt. to § 3-408,[23] which section parallels § 72-3-312)

				at domicile have concluded, local law will control."		
Nebraska	A final order of a court in a proceeding determining testacy, validity, or construction, there was notice and opportunity to contest by all interested parties, and there is a finding or it is based upon a finding of domicile of the decedent at death. (§ 30-2432 & U.P.C. § 3-408 cmt.[24]) See also In re Estate of Hannan, 523 N.W.2d 672 (1994) (conditioning the recognition of foreign-proved will on reciprocity in the law as to decisions of Nebraska courts in probate proceedings).	Yes. If the will comes from a place that does not provide for probate, it may be proved by a duly authenticated certificate of its legal custodian that the copy introduced is a true copy and that the will has become effective under the law of the place. (§ 30-2433)	No.	Yes. (U.P.C. cmt. to § 3-408, which section parallels § 30-2411)	If proceedings are "concluded" in this state before they are concluded at the domicile. (U.P.C. cmt. to § 3-408,[25] which section parallels § 30-2411) Also, if only informal proceeding at the domicile, this does not block a local probate. (U.P.C. cmt. to § 3-408,[26] which section parallels § 30-2432)	No, if there is a final order of the domicile state. (§ 30-2432) But this prohibition does not apply if *informal* proceedings. (U.P.C. cmt. to § 3-408,[27] which section parallels § 30-2432)
Nevada	A certified copy of the will and a certified copy of the will's probate, along with a petition. There is a hearing on this petition. It must be established that (a) the will has been "duly proved and admitted to probate" outside of Nevada and (b) it was executed in accordance with the laws of the state of execution, decedent's domicile, or Nevada. (§ 136.260(2) & (3))	No. (§ 136.260 (2) & (3))	No.	Yes. (§ 136.070(1))	None, must simply petition the court. (§ 136.070(1))	Not specified.
New Hampshire	Authenticated copy of will and its probate. (§ 552:13)	No. (§ 552:13)	No.	Implied yes. (§ 552:1; Barstow v. Sprague, 40 N.H. 27 (1859))	Not specified.	Not specified.

Table 2.01, Part 1
Proof of a Foreign Will *(continued)*

				Can a Will Be Proved If Not Established at the Domicile?		
	What Proof is Required to Establish a Will Already Proved in Another State?	*Are There Special Rules For a Will Proved Outside the U.S.?*	*Is There a Special Rule For Local Property?*	*That Is, Is Original Probate Permitted?*	*If So, What Are the Circumstances?*	*What About Original Probate After Probate in Another Jurisdiction?*
New Jersey	A copy of the will or record of the will and the certificate/judgment for probate and, if real estate being transferred, the record of the grant of testamentary letters. The will shall be admitted to probate if valid under New Jersey laws. (§ 3B:3-27)	No. (§ 3B:3-27)	No.	Yes. (§ 3B:3-28)	No proceeding is pending at domicile. (§ 3B:3-28)	Not specified.
New Mexico	A final order of a court in a proceeding determining testacy, validity, or construction, there was notice and opportunity to contest by all interested parties, and there is a finding or it is based upon a finding of domicile of the decedent at death. (§ 45-3-408 & U.P.C. § 3-408 & cmt.[28])	Yes. If the will comes from a place that does not provide for probate, it may be proved by a duly authenticated certificate of its legal custodian that the copy introduced is a true copy and that the will has become effective under the law of the place. (§ 45-3-409)	No.	Yes, at least under two circumstances: (i) if the will is from a place that does not provide for probate of a will after death (§ 45-3-408); (ii) there is also a suggestion in the cmt. to U.P.C. § 3-408, on which the statute is based, that a local proceeding is not barred, even if (i) does not apply. Thus, the cmt. states: "Hence, if a local proceeding is concluded before formal proceedings at domicile have concluded, local law will control."	If proceedings are "concluded" in this state before they are concluded at the domicile. (U.P.C. cmt. to § 3-408,[29] which section parallels § 45-3-408) Also, if only informal proceeding at the domicile, this does not block a local probate. (U.P.C. cmt. to § 3-408,[30] which section parallels § 45-3-408)	No, if there is a final order of the domicile state. (§ 45-3-408) But this prohibition does not apply if *informal* proceedings. (U.P.C. cmt. to § 3-408,[31] which section parallels § 45-3-408)

New York	Proof that the will has been admitted to probate at the testator's domicile or has been established by the laws of the jurisdiction and, if it remains subject to contest at domicile, proof that it is not being contested. (Surr. Ct. Proc. Act § 1602(1))	No. (Surr. Ct. Proc. Act § 1602)	No.	Yes. (Surr. Ct. Proc. Act § 1605)	It must have been validly executed for probate in New York. (Surr. Ct. Proc. Act § 1605 (1)) Otherwise, if it has been denied probate or establishment at the testator's domicile, it may only be probated in New York if the denial of probate is not grounds for denial in New York. (Surr. Ct. Proc. Act § 1605(3))	Only if (1) the New York court is satisfied that ancillary probate would be unduly expensive, inconvenient, or impossible; (2) the testator has directed that the will be offered for probate in New York; or (3) laws of testator's domicile discriminate against domiciliaries of New York either as a beneficiary or a fiduciary. (Surr. Ct. Proc. Act § 1605(2))
North Carolina	A certified or exemplified copy of letters of appointment enables ancillary letters to be issued. (§ 28A-26-3)	No.	Only implied, since North Carolina does not require domiciliary probate regarding real estate subject to ancillary administration in another jurisdiction. (§ 28A-26-1)	Probably not, on reciprocity grounds, since North Carolina requires the original probate of the will of a North Carolina domiciliary to be in North Carolina and any other probate is deemed ancillary. (§ 28A-26-1)	No provision.	No provision.
North Dakota	A final order of a court in a proceeding determining testacy, validity, or construction, there was notice and opportunity to contest by all interested parties, and there is a finding or it is based upon a finding of domicile of the decedent at death. (§ 30.1-15-08 & cmt.)	Yes. If the will comes from a place that does not provide for probate, it may be proved by a duly authenticated certificate of its legal custodian that the copy introduced is a true copy and *(cont'd)*	No.	Yes, at least under two circumstances: (i) if the will is from a place that does not provide for probate of a will after death (§ 30.1-15-08); (ii) there is also a suggestion in the cmt. to U.P.C. § 3-408, on *(cont'd)*	If proceedings are "concluded" in this state before they are concluded at the domicile. (§ 30.1-15-08 cmt.) Also, if only informal proceeding at the domicile, this does not block a local *(cont'd)*	No, if there is a final order of the domicile state. (§ 30.1-15-08) But this prohibition does not apply if *informal* proceedings. (§ 30.1-15-08 cmt.)

Table 2.01, Part 1
Proof of a Foreign Will *(continued)*

				Can a Will Be Proved If Not Established at the Domicile?		
	What Proof is Required to Establish a Will Already Proved in Another State?	*Are There Special Rules For a Will Proved Outside the U.S.?*	*Is There a Special Rule For Local Property?*	*That Is, Is Original Probate Permitted?*	*If So, What Are the Circumstances?*	*What About Original Probate After Probate in Another Jurisdiction?*
North Dakota *(cont'd)*		that the will has become effective under the law of the place. (§ 30.1-15-09)		which the statute is based, that a local proceeding is not barred, even if (i) does not apply. Thus, the cmt. states: "Hence, if a local proceeding is concluded before formal proceedings at domicile have concluded, local law will control."	probate. (§ 30.1-15-08 cmt.)	
Ohio	An authenticated copy of the will, executed and proved under the laws of any other state, territory, or country. (§§ 2129.05, 2129.07(A))	Yes. (§ 2129.07)	No.	Yes. (§ 2129.11)	If no domiciliary administration has been commenced, the ancillary administrator shall proceed with administration in Ohio as though the decedent had been a resident of Ohio. (§ 2129.11)	Implied no. (§ 2129.11)
Oklahoma	Authenticated copy of the will and the order or decree admitting it to probate. (58 § 52(A))	No. (58 § 51)	No.	Yes. (58 § 22)	None, must simply petition the court (58 § 22)	Not specified, but after it is admitted to probate, the will has the same force and effect as a will first admitted to probate in Oklahoma. (58 § 53)
Oregon	Certified copy of the will and a certified copy of the	No. (§ 113.065(1))	No.	Yes. (§ 113.035)		Yes, the language of the statute appears

	order admitting the will to probate or establishment. (§ 113.065(1))				None, must simply petition the court (§ 113.035)	only to allow original probate. (§ 113.065(1))
Pennsylvania	An authenticated copy of the will and its probate. It is then entitled to be probated in Pennsylvania. (20 § 3136)	Yes. (20 § 3136)	No.	Yes. (20 § 3136)	Not specified.	Yes. (20 § 3136)
Rhode Island	Authenticated copy of the will and its probate. (§ 33-7-18)	No. (§ 33-7-18)	No.	Yes. (§ 33-7-25)	If it complies with the laws of execution in Rhode Island. (§ 33-7-25(a)) Otherwise, if it has been denied probate or establishment of the testator's domicile it may not be admitted to Original probate in Rhode Island unless the denial was for a cause that is not grounds for rejection in Rhode Island. (§ 33-7-25(c))	Only if (1) the ancillary probate would be unduly expensive, inconvenient, or impossible; (2) testator directed in the will that probate be offered in Rhode Island; or (3) laws of testator's domicile discriminate against domiciliaries of Rhode Island either as a beneficiary or as a fiduciary. (§ 33-7-25(b))
South Carolina	A final order of a court in a proceeding determining testacy, validity, or construction, there was notice and opportunity to contest by all interested parties, and there is a finding or it is based upon a finding of domicile of the decedent at death. (§ 62-3-408 & cmt.)	Yes. If the will comes from a place that does not provide for probate, it may be proved by a duly authenticated certificate of its legal custodian that the copy introduced is a true copy and that the will has *(cont'd)*	No.	Yes, at least under two circumstances: (i) if the will is from a place that does not provide for probate of a will after death (§62-3-408 cmt.); (ii) there is also a suggestion in the cmt. to U.P.C. § 3-408, on which the statute is based, that a local proceeding is not barred, *(cont'd)*	If proceedings are "concluded" in this state before they are concluded at the domicile. (§ 62-3-408 cmt.) Also, if only informal proceeding at the domicile, this does not block a local probate. (§ 62-3-408 cmt.)	No, if there is a final order of the domicile state. (§ 62-3-408) But this prohibition does not apply if *informal* proceedings. (§ 62-3-408 cmt.)

Table 2.01, Part 1
Proof of a Foreign Will *(continued)*

				Can a Will Be Proved If Not Established at the Domicile?		
	What Proof is Required to Establish a Will Already Proved in Another State?	*Are There Special Rules For a Will Proved Outside the U.S.?*	*Is There a Special Rule For Local Property?*	*That Is, Is Original Probate Permitted?*	*If So, What Are the Circumstances?*	*What About Original Probate After Probate in Another Jurisdiction?*
South Carolina *(cont'd)*		become effective under the law of the place. (§ 62-3-409)		even if (i) does not apply. Thus, the cmt. states: "Hence, if a local proceeding is concluded before formal proceedings at domicile have concluded, local law will control."		
South Dakota	A final order of a court in a proceeding determining testacy, validity, or construction, there was notice and opportunity to contest by all interested parties, and there is a finding or it is based upon a finding of domicile of the decedent at death. (§ 29A-3-408 & U.P.C. § 3-408 cmt.[32])	Yes. If the will comes from a place that does not provide for probate, it may be proved by a duly authenticated certificate of its legal custodian that the copy introduced is a true copy and that the will has become effective under the law of the place.(29A-3-409)	No.	Yes, at least under two circumstances: (i) if the will is from a place that does not provide for probate of a will after death (§ 29A-3-408); (ii) there is also a suggestion in the cmt. to U.P.C. § 3-408, on which the statute is based, that a local proceeding is not barred, even if (i) does not apply. Thus, the cmt. states: "Hence, if a local proceeding is concluded before formal proceedings at domicile have concluded, local law will control."	If proceedings are "concluded" in this state before they are concluded at the domicile. (U.P.C. § 3-408 cmt.) Also, if only informal proceeding at the domicile, this does not block a local probate. (U.P.C. § 3-408 cmt.)	No, if there is a final order of the domicile state. (§ 29A-3-408) But this prohibition does not apply if *informal* proceedings. (U.P.C. § 3-408 cmt., which section parallels § 29A-3-408[33])
Tennessee	An authenticated copy of the will, its probate,	Yes. (§§ 32-5-104, 32-5-105) A hearing is required. If it is	No.	Yes, with respect to local real property if the will has not been	The petition must state the death of the testator, the	Implied no, since § 32-5-110 allows original probate for

and a petition for probate. (§ 32-5-103)	established that the will was duly proved, allowed, and admitted to probate, as well as executed according to the law of the place in which made, or in which the testator was domiciled, or in conformity with the laws of Tennessee, then it must be admitted to probate as if an original probate. (§ 32-5-104) However, if probate "is not required" in the other jurisdiction, then two steps are involved. First, a duly authenticated copy of the will and a duly authenticated certificate of the legal custodian of the original will that the same is a true copy and that the will has become operable must be presented by an executor or interested person. If the will is a notarial will in the possession of a notary and must remain in the custody of a notary, then the will must *(cont'd)*		probated elsewhere. (§ 32-5-110) Although § 32-5-106 appears to allow a contest of a foreign probated will, this has been held not to be the case. (First Christian Church v. Moneypenny, 439 S.W.2d 620 (Tenn. Ct. App. 1968)).	testator's ownership in lands in the county, the facts of testacy. Then the court shall authorize the taking of proof necessary to prove the will in accordance with the laws of Tennessee. (§ 32-5-110)	wills that have not been probated elsewhere.

Table 2.01, Part 1
Proof of a Foreign Will *(continued)*

				Can a Will Be Proved If Not Established at the Domicile?		
	What Proof is Required to Establish a Will Already Proved in Another State?	*Are There Special Rules For a Will Proved Outside the U.S.?*	*Is There a Special Rule For Local Property?*	*That Is, Is Original Probate Permitted?*	*If So, What Are the Circumstances?*	*What About Original Probate After Probate in Another Jurisdiction?*
Tennessee *(cont'd)*		be duly authenticated by the notary. The second step is a hearing and notice as in the case of an original will presented for probate. (§ 32-5-105)				
Texas	A copy of the will and judgment, order, or decree by which it was admitted to probate or otherwise established, attested by the clerk or other person who has custody of the will or is in charge of probate records, with the seal of the court if one exists, and a certificate of the judge attesting to the form. If the will was probated in a state other than decedent's domicile, the application must also state the names and addresses of each devisee and heir. (Prob. § 95(b) & (c))	No. (Prob. § 95(a))	Yes, the will shall be effective irrespective of whether the will complies with Texas law. (Prob. § 95(e))	Yes. (Prob. § 103)	Original probate is permitted as long as the will is valid under Texas laws. However, if probate was rejected elsewhere, it must be for a cause that is not grounds for rejection in Texas. Otherwise, it cannot be originally probated in Texas. (Prob. § 103)	Not specified.
Utah	A final order of a court in a proceeding determining testacy, validity, or construction, there was notice and opportunity to contest	Yes. If the will comes from a place that does not provide for probate, it may be proved	No.	Yes, at least under two circumstances: (i) if the will is from a place that does not provide for probate of a will	If proceedings are "concluded" in this state before they are concluded at the domicile.	No, if there is a final order of the domicile state. (§ 75-3-408) But this prohibition does not apply if

	by all interested parties, and there is a finding or it is based upon a finding of domicile of the decedent at death. (§ 75-3-408 & cmt.)	by a duly authenticated certificate of its legal custodian that the copy introduced is a true copy and that the will has become effective under the law of the place. (75-3-409)		after death (§ 75-3-408 cmt.); (ii) there is also a suggestion in the cmt. to U.P.C. § 3-408, on which the statute is based, that a local proceeding is not barred, even if (i) does not apply. Thus, the cmt. states: "Hence, if a local proceeding is concluded before formal proceedings at domicile have concluded, local law will control."	(§ 75-3-408 cmt.) Also, if only informal proceeding at the domicile, this does not block a local probate. (§ 75-3-408 cmt.)	*informal* proceedings. (§ 75-3-408 cmt.)
Vermont	A duly authenticated copy of the will and its allowance, or a certificate of the legal custodian of the will that it is a true copy and has become operative by the laws of the state, or a copy of a notarial will which has been duly authenticated by such notary if the laws require that the notary retain custody of the will. (14 § 114(a))	No. (14 § 114(a))	No.	Yes. (14 § 112)	In writing and signed by the testator. (14 § 112)	No.
Virginia	Authenticated copy of the will and certificate of probate. If real estate is in Virginia, then the will must be valid under Virginia laws. (§ 64.1-92)	No. (§ 64.1-92)	If real estate is in Virginia, then the will must be valid under Virginia laws. (§ 64.1-92)	Yes. (§§ 64.1-75, 64.1-92; French v. Short, 151 S.E.2d 354 (1966))	Not specified.	For personal property, the will is pre sumed valid, in the absence of evidence to the contrary, and admitted to probate. For real property, the will is only to be admitted to probate

(cont'd)

Table 2.01, Part 1
Proof of a Foreign Will *(continued)*

				Can a Will Be Proved If Not Established at the Domicile?		
	What Proof is Required to Establish a Will Already Proved in Another State?	*Are There Special Rules For a Will Proved Outside the U.S.?*	*Is There a Special Rule For Local Property?*	*That Is, Is Original Probate Permitted?*	*If So, What Are the Circumstances?*	*What About Original Probate After Probate in Another Jurisdiction?*
Virginia *(cont'd)*						after the court determines the will com plies with the laws of Virginia, implying original probate applies to real property. (§ 64.1-92)
Washington	Copy of the will and the original probate record certified by the clerk, or if there is no clerk, certified by the judge and by the seal of the officers if they have a seal. (§ 11.20.090)	No. (§ 11.20.090)	No.	Yes. (§ 11.12.020(2))	Will complies with laws of the state where it is executed or decedent's domicile. (§ 11.12.020(1))	Not specified.
West Virginia	An authenticated copy and the certificate of probate. (§ 41-5-13)	No. (§ 41-5-13)	No.	Yes. (§§ 41-5-4(c) & (d), 41-5-5)	Not specified.	No. (§ 41-5-13)
Wisconsin	Will with proof that it has been probated or established in testator's domicile and not being contested there. (§ 868.01(1))	No. (§ 868.01(1))	No.	Yes. (§ 868.01(5))	If the will has not been rejected from probate or establish ment at the testator's domicile, and if so, it was for a reason which is notgrounds for rejection of a will in Wisconsin. (§ 868.01(5))	No.
Wyoming	Satisfaction of the court that the will has been duly proved, allowed, and admitted to	No. (§ 2-11-103)	No.	Yes. (§ 2-11-201)	It is required except where the estate does not exceed	It is required except where the estate does not exceed

probate outside of this state and executed according to the place where made or where the testator was domiciled at the time, or in conformity with the law of Wyoming. (§§ 2-11-102, 2-11-104) Also note that there are special rules for estates not exceeding $150,000, effective July 1, 2002. The rules allow for the dispensing of probate proceedings. (§§ 2-11-103, 2-11-201) A petition under oath must be filed with the district judge in the proper county, showing the facts in the case together with certified copies of the petition, order of appointment of personal representative, inventory, and final decree of distribution as well as a full showing that debts have been paid. (§ 2-11-201) Provision also made for the sale or other disposition of local property relating to estate being probated and settled elsewhere. (§ 2-11-202)			$150,000 in value, effective July 1, 2002. (§ 2-11-201)	$150,000 in value, effective July 1, 2002. (§ 2-11-201)

1. Although adopting the Uniform Probate Code, the editorial board comments of the U.P.C. have not been included in Alaska Statutes. Nonetheless, the assumption is that they would be relied upon in construing the statutory provisions.
2. *Id*
3. *Id.*
4. *Id.*

5. Although adopting the Uniform Probate Code, the editorial board comments of the U.P.C. have not been included in Arizona Revised Statutes. Nonetheless, the assumption is that they would be relied upon in construing the statutory provisions.
6. *Id.*
7. *Id.*
8. *Id.*
9. Although adopting the Uniform Probate Code, the editorial board comments of the U.P.C. have not been included in Colorado Revised Statutes. Nonetheless, the assumption is that they would be relied upon in construing the statutory provisions.
10. *Id.*
11. *Id.*
12. Although adopting the Uniform Probate Code, the editorial comments of the U.P.C. have not been included in Hawaii Code Annotated. Nonetheless, the assumption is that they would be relied upon in construing the statutory provisions.
13. *Id.*
14. *Id.*
15. *Id.*
16. Although adopting the Uniform Probate Code, the editorial board comments of the U.P.C. have not been included in Minnesota Statutes. Nonetheless, the assumption is that they would be relied upon in construing the statutory provisions.
17. *Id.*
18. *Id.*
19. *Id.*
20. Although adopting the Uniform Probate Code, the editorial board comments of the U.P.C. have not been included in Montana Code Annotated. Nonetheless, the assumption is that they would be relied upon in construing the statutory provisions.
21. *Id.*
22. *Id.*
23. *Id.*
24. Although adopting the Uniform Probate Code, the editorial comments of the U.P.C. have not been included in Revised Statutes of Nebraska Annotated. Nonetheless, the assumption is that they would be relied upon in construing the statutory provisions.
25. *Id.*
26. *Id.*
27. *Id.*
28. Although adopting the Uniform Probate Code, the editorial comments of the U.P.C. have not been included in New Mexico Statutes Annotated. Nonetheless, the assumption is that they would be relied upon in construing the statutory provisions.
29. *Id.*
30. *Id.*
31. *Id.*
32. Although adopting the Uniform Probate Code, the editorial comments of the U.P.C. have not been included in South Dakota Codified Laws. Nonetheless, the assumption is that they would be relied upon in construing the statutory provisions.
33. *Id.*

Table 2.01, Part 2
Proof of a Foreign Will

	Are There Special Notice Requirements?			
	What If Decedent Was Not a U.S. Citizen?	*What If a Beneficiary Is Not a U.S. Citizen?*	*What If Decedent Was a Domiciliary of Another State?*	*What If a Beneficiary Is a domiciliary of Another State?*
Alabama	No, but notice must be given. (§ 43-8-175)	No.	No, no notice requirement. (§ 43-8-175)	No.
Alaska	A provision requires notice to be given to spouse, children, heirs, devisees, and executors "named in any will that is . . . known by the petitioner to have been probated or offered for informal or formal probate elsewhere; and . . . any personal representative of the decedent whose appointment has not been terminated." This requirement is based on knowledge of petitioner, whereas there is a mandatory notice requirement, regardless of knowledge, in the case of wills that have been or are being probated in the local county. (§ 13.16.150(a)) It is unclear whether persons named in known, but *unprobated*, wills need to be notified. (U.P.C. § 3-403(a) cmt.)[1]			
Arizona	A provision requires notice to be given to spouse, children, heirs, devisees, and executors "named in any will that is . . . known by the petitioner to have been probated, or offered for informal or formal probate in another jurisdiction, and any personal representative of the decedent whose appointment has not been terminated." This requirement is based on knowledge of petitioner, whereas there is a mandatory notice requirement, regardless of knowledge, in the case of wills that have been or are being probated in the local county. (§ 14-3403(A)) It is unclear whether persons named in known but unprobated wills need to be notified. (§ 14-4301 & U.P.C. § 3-403(a) cmt.[2]; § 14-4203)			
Arkansas	No.			
California	No. (Prob. § 12512)			
Colorado	A provision requires notice to be given to spouse, children, heirs, devisees, and executors "named in any will that is . . . known by the petitioner to have been probated, or offered for informal or formal probate elsewhere, and any personal representative of the decedent whose appointment has not been terminated." This requirement is based on knowledge of petitioner, whereas there is a mandatory notice requirement, regardless of knowledge, in the case of wills that have been or are being probated in the local county. (§ 15-12-403(b)) It is unclear whether persons named in known but unprobated wills need to be notified. (U.P.C. § 3-403 cmt.[3])			
Connecticut	No.			
Delaware	No.			
District of Columbia	See Table 2.02, Part 2.			

Table 2.01, Part 2
Proof of a Foreign Will *(continued)*

	Are There Special Notice Requirements?			
	What If Decedent Was Not a U.S. Citizen?	*What If a Beneficiary Is Not a U.S. Citizen?*	*What If Decedent Was a Domiciliary of Another State?*	*What If a Beneficiary Is a domiciliary of Another State?*
Florida	No special notice requirements. The general requirements are set forth in § 733.212.			
Georgia	No provision.	No provision.	Yes. Notice is to be given by an ancillary personal representa tive in Georgia to all Georgia-domiciled creditors in the manner required for decedents who die domiciled in Georgia. (§ 53-5-40)	No provision.
Hawaii	A provision requires notice to be given to spouse, children, heirs, devisees, and executors "named in any will . . . that is known by the petitioner to have been probated, or offered for informal or formal probate elsewhere, and any personal representative of the decedent whose appointment has not been terminated." This requirement is based on knowledge of petitioner, whereas there is a mandatory notice requirement, regardless of knowledge, in the case of wills that have been or are being probated in the local county. (§ 560:3-403(a) & (b)) It is unclear whether persons named in known but unprobated wills need to be notified. (U.P.C. § 3-403 cmt.[4])			
Idaho	A provision requires notice to be given to spouse, children, heirs, devisees, and executors "named in any will . . . that is known by the petitioner to have been probated, or offered for informal or formal probate elsewhere, and any personal representative of the decedent whose appointment has not been terminated." This requirement is based on knowledge of petitioner, whereas there is a mandatory notice requirement, regardless of knowledge, in the case of wills that have been or are being probated in the local county. (§ 15-3-403(a)) It is unclear whether persons named in known but unprobated wills need to be notified. (*Id.* cmt.)			
Illinois	No.			
Indiana	No.			
Iowa	No. (§ 633.498)			
Kansas	The manner of notification is at the court's discretion. (§ 59-2229)	No.	The manner of notification is at the court's discretion. (§ 59-2229)	No.

Kentucky	No.			
Louisiana	No. (Code Civ. Pro. § 3401)			
Maine	A provision requires notice to be given to spouse, children, heirs, devisees, and executors "named in any will . . . that is known by the petitioner to have been probated or offered for informal or formal probate elsewhere, and any personal representative of the decedent whose appointment has not been terminated." This requirement is based on knowledge of petitioner, whereas there is a mandatory notice requirement, regardless of knowledge, in the case of wills that have been or are being probated in the local county. (18A § 3-403(a)) It is unclear whether persons named in known but unprobated wills need to be notified. (*Id.* cmt.)			
Maryland	Yes, but only for real and lease hold property. (Est. & Trusts § 5-503(b)(1))	No.	Yes, but only for real and lease hold property. (Est. & Trusts § 5-503(b)(1))	No.
Massachusetts	Notice in publication at such times and in such newspapers as the court orders, said publication to be 30 days at least before the time assigned for hearing. (192 § 9)	No.	Notice by publication at such times and in such newspapers as the court orders, said publication to be 30 days at least before the time assigned for hearing. (192 § 9)	No.
Michigan	A provision requires notice to be given to the decedent's heirs, devisees, and personal representatives named in the will that is known by petitioner to have been probated or offered for informal or formal probate "elsewhere," and any personal representative of the decedent whose appointment has not been terminated, the trustee of a trust, and notice by publication to known and unknown persons with an interest. (§ 700.3403)			
Minnesota	A provision requires notice to be given to spouse, children, heirs, devisees, and executors "named in any will . . . that is known by the petitioner to have been probated, or offered for informal or formal probate elsewhere, and any personal representative of the decedent whose appointment has not been terminated." This requirement is based on knowledge of petitioner, whereas there is a mandatory notice requirement, regardless of knowledge, in the case of wills that have been or are being probated in the local county. (§ 524.3-403(a)) It is unclear whether persons named in known but *unprobated* wills need to be notified. (U.P.C. cmt. to § 3-403(a),[5] which section parallels § 524.3-403(a))			
Mississippi	*There is no ancillary probate in Mississippi. (§ 91-1-1; Carroll v. McPike, 53 Miss. 569 (1876))*			
Missouri	*There is no ancillary probate in Missouri. (§ 473.668; Yonke v. Alber's Estate, 351 S.W.2d 794 (Ct. App. 1961))*			
Montana	A provision requires notice to be given to spouse, children, heirs, devisees, and executors "named in any will . . . that is known by the petitioner to have been probated or offered for informal or formal probate elsewhere; and any personal representative of the decedent whose appointment has not been terminated." This requirement is based on knowledge of petitioner, whereas there is a mandatory notice requirement, regardless of knowledge, in the case of wills that have been or are being probated in the local county. (§ 72-3-305(2)(b)) It is unclear whether persons named in known, but *unprobated*, wills need to be notified. (U.P.C. cmt. to § 3-403(a),[6] which section parallels § 72-3-305(3))			

Table 2.01, Part 2
Proof of a Foreign Will *(continued)*

	Are There Special Notice Requirements?			
	What If Decedent Was Not a U.S. Citizen?	*What If a Beneficiary Is Not a U.S. Citizen?*	*What If Decedent Was a Domiciliary of Another State?*	*What If a Beneficiary Is a domiciliary of Another State?*
Nebraska	A provision requires notice to be given to spouse, children, heirs, devisees, and executors "named in any will . . . that is known by the petitioner to have been probated, or offered for informal or formal probate elsewhere, and any personal representative of the decedent whose appointment has not been terminated." This requirement is based on knowledge of petitioner, whereas there is a mandatory notice requirement, regardless of knowledge, in the case of wills that have been or are being probated in the local county. (§ 30-2427(a)) It is unclear whether persons named in known but *unprobated* wills need to be notified. (U.P.C. § 3-403 cmt.[7])			
Nevada	No. (§ 136.260(2))			
New Hampshire	No. (§ 552:15)			
New Jersey	No.			
New Mexico	A provision requires notice to be given to spouse, children, heirs, devisees, and executors "named in any will . . . that is known by the petitioner to have been probated, or offered for informal or formal probate elsewhere; and any personal representative of the decedent whose appointment has not been terminated." This requirement is based on knowledge of petitioner, whereas there is a mandatory notice requirement, regardless of knowledge, in the case of wills that have been or are being probated in the local county. (§ 45-3-403(B)) It is unclear whether persons named in known but unprobated wills need to be notified. (U.P.C. § 3-403 cmt.[8])			
New York	No.			
North Carolina	No.			
North Dakota	A provision requires notice to be given to spouse, children, heirs, devisees, and executors "named in any will . . . that is known by the petitioner to have been probated, or offered for informal or formal probate elsewhere; and any personal representative of the decedent whose appointment has not been terminated." This requirement is based on knowledge of petitioner, whereas there is a mandatory notice requirement, regardless of knowledge, in the case of wills that have been or are being probated in the local county. (§ 30.1-15-03(1)) It is unclear whether persons named in known but *unprobated* wills need to be notified. (*Id.* cmt.)			
Ohio	No, but there are special notice requirements if the will was	No.	No.	No.

	probated in a foreign country or U.S. territory. (§ 2129.07(A))			
Oklahoma	No.			
Oregon	No.			
Pennsylvania	No.			
Rhode Island	No. (§ 33-7-19)			
South Carolina	A provision requires notice to be given to spouse, children, heirs, devisees, and executors "named in any will . . . that is known by the petitioner to have been probated, or offered for informal or formal probate elsewhere, and any personal representative of the decedent whose appointment has not been terminated." This requirement is based on knowledge of petitioner, whereas there is a mandatory notice requirement, regardless of knowledge, in the case of wills that have been or are being probated in the local county. (§ 62-3-403(a)) It is unclear whether persons named in known but *unprobated* wills need to be notified. (*Id.* cmt.)			
South Dakota	A provision requires notice to be given to spouse, children, heirs, devisees, and executors "named in any will . . . that is known by the petitioner to have been probated, or offered for informal or formal probate elsewhere, and any personal representative of the decedent whose appointment has not been terminated." This requirement is based on knowledge of petitioner, whereas there is a mandatory notice requirement, regardless of knowledge, in the case of wills that have been or are being probated in the local county. (§ 29A-3-403(b)) It is unclear whether persons named in known but *unprobated* wills need to be notified. (U.P.C. § 3-403 cmt.[9])			
Tennessee	No. (§ 32-5-103)			
Texas	Only that notice to devisees and heirs should be through registered or certified mail. (Prob. § 95(b)(2))	No.	Only that notice to devisees and heirs shall be through registered or certified mail. (Prob. § 95(b)(2))	No.
Utah	A provision requires notice to be given to spouse, children, heirs, devisees, and executors "named in any will . . . that is known by the petitioner to have been probated, or offered, for informal or formal probate elsewhere, and any personal representative of the decedent whose appointment has not been terminated." This requirement is based on knowledge of petitioner, whereas there is a mandatory notice requirement, regardless of knowledge, in the case of wills that have been or are being probated in the local county. (§ 75-3-403(1)) It is unclear whether persons named in known but *unprobated* wills need to be notified. (*Id.* cmt.)			
Vermont	No. (14 § 114(b))			
Virginia	No.			
Washington	No.			

Table 2.01, Part 2
Proof of a Foreign Will *(continued)*

	Are There Special Notice Requirements?			
	What If Decedent Was Not a U.S. Citizen?	*What If a Beneficiary Is Not a U.S. Citizen?*	*What If Decedent Was a Domiciliary of Another State?*	*What If a Beneficiary Is a domiciliary of Another State?*
West Virginia	No. (§ 41-5-13)			
Wisconsin	No.	Yes. (§ 879.03(3))	No.	No.
Wyoming	No.			

1. Although adopting the Uniform Probate Code, the editorial board comments of the U.P.C. have not been included in Alaska Statutes. Nonetheless, the assumption is that they would be relied upon in construing the statutory provisions.
2. Although adopting the Uniform Probate Code, the editorial board comments of the U.P.C. have not been included in Arizona Revised Statutes. Nonetheless, the assumption is that they would be relied upon in construing the statutory provisions.
3. Although adopting the Uniform Probate Code, the editorial board comments of the U.P.C. have not been included in Colorado Revised Statutes. Nonetheless, the assumption is that they would be relied upon in construing the statutory provisions.
4. Although adopting the Uniform Probate Code, the editorial comments of the U.P.C. have not been included in Hawaii Code Annotated. Nonetheless, the assumption is that they would be relied upon in construing the statutory provisions.
5. Although adopting the Uniform Probate Code, the editorial board comments of the U.P.C. have not been included in Minnesota Statutes. Nonetheless, the assumption is that they would be relied upon in construing the statutory provisions.
6. Although adopting the Uniform Probate Code, the editorial board comments of the U.P.C. have not been included in Montana Code Annotated. Nonetheless, the assumption is that they would be relied upon in construing the statutory provisions.
7. Although adopting the Uniform Probate Code, the editorial comments of the U.P.C. have not been included in Revised Statutes of Nebraska Annotated. Nonetheless, the assumption is that they would be relied upon in construing the statutory provisions.
8. Although adopting the Uniform Probate Code, the editorial comments of the U.P.C. have not been included in New Mexico Statutes Annotated. Nonetheless, the assumption is that they would be relied upon in construing the statutory provisions.
9. Although adopting the Uniform Probate Code, the editorial comments of the U.P.C. have not been included in South Dakota Codified Laws. Nonetheless, the assumption is that they would be relied upon in construing the statutory provisions.

Table 2.02, Part 1
Ancillary Probate

	For Ancillary Probate, Must:				
	There Be Proof of No Pending Contest at Domicile?	*There Be Proof That Period for Contesting Will at the Domicile Has Expired?*	*There Be Proof That Decedent Was Domiciled in Other Jurisdiction?*	*All Interested Parties Be Notified?*	*Other Considerations?*
Alabama	No.	No.	No.	No. (§ 43-8-175)	No.
Alaska	Implied, since the provision requires giving effect to an order of testacy elsewhere if there is a "final order" in a proceeding where interested persons were notified and given an opportunity to contest. (§ 13.16.175)	Implied. (§ 13.16.175)	Implied. (§ 13.16.175)	Yes, during the original probate at the domicile state. (§ 13.16.175)	After the time for notice has expired, but before the termination of the statute of limitations, the domicile of the testator may be reviewed. (§ 13.16.180)
Arizona	Implied, since the provision requires giving effect to an order of testacy elsewhere if there is a "final order" in a proceeding where interested persons were notified and given an opportunity to contest. (§ 14-3408)	Implied. (§ 14-3408)	Implied. (§ 14-3408)	Yes, during the original probate at the domicile state. (§ 14-3408)	After the time for notice has expired, but before the termination of the statute of limitations, the domicile of the testator may be reviewed. (§ 14-3409)
Arkansas	No.	No.	Petition for probate shall state the time and place of execution, testator's domicile at execution, and testator's domicile at the time of death. (§ 28-40-120(c))	Yes. (§ 28-40-111(a)(4))	No. Except where special provision is made otherwise, the law and procedure relating to the administration of estates of resident decedents shall apply to the ancillary administration of estates of nonresident decedents. (§ 28-42-101)

Table 2.02, Part 1
Ancillary Probate *(continued)*

	For Ancillary Probate, Must:				
	There Be Proof of No Pending Contest at Domicile?	*There Be Proof That Period for Contesting Will at the Domicile Has Expired?*	*There Be Proof That Decedent Was Domiciled in Other Jurisdiction?*	*All Interested Parties Be Notified?*	*Other Considerations?*
California	No.	No.	No.	Yes. (Prob. § 12512)	No.
Colorado	Implied, since the provision requires giving effect to an order of testacy elsewhere if there is a "final order" in a proceeding where interested persons were notified and given an opportunity to contest. (§ 15-12-408)	Implied. (§ 15-12-408)	Implied. (§ 15-12-408)	Yes, during the original probate at the domicile state. (§ 15-12-408)	After the time for notice has expired, but before the termination of the statute of limitations, the domicile of the testator may be reviewed. (15-12-409)
Connecticut	No. Only "proved and established" will required. (§ 45a-288)	No.	At least a claim of domicile out of state. (§ 45a-288)	Yes. (§ 45a-288)	No.
Delaware	No.	No.	No.	No.	No.
District of Columbia[1]	No provision.	No provision.	No provision.	Although there is no ancillary probate, a foreign personal representative must afford notice through publication in D.C. as provided in § 20-343(a).	No.
Florida	Implied, since will has no effect unless actually *admitted* to probate in Florida or where the	Implied. See the prior question.	No, but foreign probate can be challenged on this ground. See Table 2.02, Part 2.	Yes. See Table 2.02, Part 2.	If a foreign notarial will is in the possession of the notary pursuant to foreign law, a copy will suffice only

	decedent was domiciled. (§ 733.103(1)) Note that any collateral action or proceeding of a will in Florida shall be conclusive with respect to execution, competency of the testator, free of fraud, duress, mistake, and undue influence, and that the will was unrevoked on the testator's death. (§ 733.103(2))				if duly authenticated by the notary, whose position, signature, and seal of office are authenticated by a U.S. consular officer in jurisdiction of notary's residence (i.e., domicile). (§ 733.205)
Georgia	Yes, based on requirement of a copy of "final proceedings" of domicile for jurisdiction, but this does not bar will contest in ancillary proceeding. (§ 53-5-33(c))	Yes, based on requirement of a copy of "final proceedings" of domicile for jurisdiction, but this does not bar will contest in ancillary proceeding. (§ 53-5-33(c))	Yes, based on requirement of copy of "final proceedings" of domiciliary jurisdiction. (§ 53-5-33(c))	Yes. Statute provides particularly for notice to be given to all creditors of the nondomiciliary decedent who are domiciled in Georgia as is required for Georgia-domiciled decedents. (§ 53-5-40)	Ancillary probate can only be accomplished in solemn form. Also, it is not avail able until the proof is presented that the "will has not been offered for probate in this state in proceedings in which a caveat to such probate has been finally sustained or is pending." (§ 53-5-33(a)) This provision is necessary due to the possibility of original probate of a foreign will in Georgia. See Table 2.01, Part 1.
Hawaii	Implied, since the provision requires giving effect to an order of testacy elsewhere if there is a "final order" in a proceeding where interested persons were notified and given an opportunity to contest. (§ 560:3-408)	Implied. (§ 560:3-408)	Implied. (§ 560:3-408)	Yes, during the original probate at the domicile state. (§ 560:3-408)	After the time for notice has expired, but before the termination of the statute of limitations, the domicile of the testator may be reviewed. (§ 560:3-409)

Table 2.02, Part 1
Ancillary Probate *(continued)*

	For Ancillary Probate, Must:				
	There Be Proof of No Pending Contest at Domicile?	*There Be Proof That Period for Contesting Will at the Domicile Has Expired?*	*There Be Proof That Decedent Was Domiciled in Other Jurisdiction?*	*All Interested Parties Be Notified?*	*Other Considerations?*
Idaho	Implied, since the provision requires giving effect to an order of testacy elsewhere if there is a "final order" in a proceeding where interested persons were notified and given an opportunity to contest. (§ 15-3-408)	Implied. (§ 15-3-408)	Implied. (§ 15-3-408)	Yes, during original probate at the domicile state. (§ 15-3-408)	After the time for notice has expired, but before the termination of the statute of limitations, the domicile of the testator may be reviewed. (§ 15-3-409)
Illinois	No.	No.	No.	Yes. (755 ILCS §§ 5/7-2, 5/6-10)	No.
Indiana	No.	No.	No.	No.	No.
Iowa	No.	No.	No.	No. (In re Capper's Will, 52 N.W. 6 (1892))	No.
Kansas	N/A	N/A	N/A	During Kansas probate of a will executed outside the state, the court directs notice. (§ 59-2229)	N/A
Kentucky	No.	No.	Implied yes. Says any will offered for probate must contain a statement of the residence of the testator in the probate application. (§ 394.145; see also § 394.150)	Not specified for ancillary. For normal will, notice to all interested parties is not essential to give court jurisdiction of application to probate or set aside probate of a will. (Miller v. Hill, 168 S.W.2d 769 (1943))	No.

Louisiana	No.	No.	Yes. (Code Civ. Pro. §§ 2821, 3401)	Procedure for notice shall be the same as for a Louisiana domiciliary. (Code Civ. Pro. § 3401)	No.
Maine	Implied, since the provision requires giving effect to an order of testacy elsewhere if there is a "final order" in a proceeding where interested persons were notified and given an opportunity to contest. (18A § 3-408)	Implied. (18A § 3-408)	Implied. (18A § 3-408)	Yes, during the original probate at the domicile state. (18A § 3-408)	After the time for notice has expired, but before the termination of the statute of limitations, the domicile of the testator may be reviewed. (18A § 3-409)
Maryland	No.	No.	No.	Yes, but only for real and leasehold property. (Est. & Trusts § 5-503(b)(1))	No.
Massachusetts	No.	No.	No.	Yes. (192 §§ 9, 12)	No.
Michigan	Implied, since the provision requires giving effect to an order of testacy elsewhere if there is a "final order" in a proceeding where interested persons were notified and given an opportunity to contest. (§ 700.3408)	Implied. (§ 700.3408)	Implied. (§ 700.3408)	Yes, during the original probate at the domicile state. (§ 700.3408)	After the time for notice has expired, but before the termination of the statute of limitations, the domicile of the testator may be reviewed. (§ 700.3409)
Minnesota	Implied, since the provision requires giving effect to an order of testacy elsewhere if there is a "final order" in a proceeding where interested persons were notified and given an opportunity to contest. (§ 524.3-408)	Implied. (§ 524.3-408)	Implied. (§ 524.3-408)	Yes, during the original probate at the domicile state. (§ 524.3-408) Failure to notify, based on *Minnesota* standards, may result in denial of full faith and credit. (In re Estate of Farley, 397 N.W.2d 409 (Ct. App. 1986))	No. After the time for notice has expired, but before the termination of the statute of limitations, the domicile of the testator may be reviewed. (§ 524.3-409)
Mississippi	*There is no ancillary probate in Mississippi. (§ 91-1-1; Carroll v. McPike, 53 Miss. 569 (1876))*				

Table 2.02, Part 1
Ancillary Probate *(continued)*

	For Ancillary Probate, Must:				
	There Be Proof of No Pending Contest at Domicile?	*There Be Proof That Period for Contesting Will at the Domicile Has Expired?*	*There Be Proof That Decedent Was Domiciled in Other Jurisdiction?*	*All Interested Parties Be Notified?*	*Other Considerations?*
Missouri	*There is no ancillary probate in Missouri. (§ 473.668; Yonke v. Alber's Estate, 351 S.W.2d 794 (Ct. App. 1961))*				
Montana	Implied, since the provision requires giving effect to an order of testacy elsewhere if there is a "final order" in a proceeding where interested persons were notified and given an opportunity to contest. (§ 72-3-312)	Implied. (§ 72-3-312)	Implied. (§ 72-3-312)	Yes, during the original probate at the domicile state. (§ 72-3-312)	No. After the time for notice has expired, but before the termination of the statute of limitations, the domicile of the testator may be reviewed. (§ 72-3-313)
Nebraska	Implied, since the provision requires giving effect to an order of testacy elsewhere if there is a "final order" in a proceeding where interested persons were notified and given an opportunity to contest. (§ 30-2432)	Implied. (§ 30-2432)	Implied. (§ 30-2432)	Yes, during the original probate at the domicile state. (§ 30-2432)	After the time for notice has expired, but before the termination of the statute of limitations, the domicile of the testator may be reviewed. (§ 30-2433)
Nevada	No.	No.	Implied yes because the court examines the will to ensure that it was executed in accordance with the laws of the state of execution, decedent's domicile, or Nevada. (§ 136.260(3))	Yes. (§ 136.260(2))	No.
New Hampshire	No.	No.	No.	Yes. (§ 552:15)	No.

New Jersey	No.	No.	Implied yes, because a resident must prove domicile and ancillary probate of a resident is without effect in New Jersey. Therefore, it appears the question of domicile will be examined. (In re Estate of Kortvellessy, 245 A.2d 757 (A.D. 1968))	No.	No.
New Mexico	Implied, since the provision requires giving effect to an order of testacy else where if a "final order" in a proceeding where interested persons were notified and given an opportunity to contest. (§ 45-3-408)	Implied. (§ 45-3-408)	Implied. (§ 45-3-408)	Yes, during the original probate at the domicile state (§ 45-3-408)	After the time for notice has expired, but before the termination of the statute of limitations, the domicile of the testator may be reviewed. (§ 45-3-409)
New York	Yes. (Surr. Ct. Proc. Act § 1603(1)(b)) Can institute ancillary probate but may not transfer property. (Surr. Ct. Proc. Act § 1603(1))	Yes, if one year has elapsed since the will was admitted into ancillary probate in New York. (Surr. Ct. Proc. Act § 1603(1)(c)) Can institute ancillary probate but may not transfer property. (Surr. Ct. Proc. Act § 1603(1))	Yes. (Surr. Ct. Proc. Act § 1602(1))	Implied yes because New York allows for contesting in ancillary proceedings. (Surr. Ct. Proc. Act § 1602(2))	No.
North Carolina	No.	No.	If challenged, may have to prove, since there is requirement that for a North Carolina domiciliary, North Carolina has exclusive domiciliary probate. (§ 28A-26-1)	No special provision.	No.

Table 2.02, Part 1
Ancillary Probate *(continued)*

	For Ancillary Probate, Must:				
	There Be Proof of No Pending Contest at Domicile?	*There Be Proof That Period for Contesting Will at the Domicile Has Expired?*	*There Be Proof That Decedent Was Domiciled in Other Jurisdiction?*	*All Interested Parties Be Notified?*	*Other Considerations?*
North Dakota	Implied, since the provision requires giving effect to order of testacy elsewhere if a "final order" in a proceeding where interested persons were notified and given an opportunity to contest. (§ 30.1-15-08)	Implied. (§ 30.1-15-08)	Implied. (§ 30.1-15-08)	Yes, during the original probate at the domicile state. (§ 30.1-15-08)	After the time for notice has expired, but before the termination of the statute of limitations, the domicile of the testator may be reviewed. (§ 30.1-15-09)
Ohio	No.	No.	No.	Only if the will was probated in a U.S. territory or foreign country. (§ 2129.07)	No.
Oklahoma	No.	No.	No.	Yes. (58 § 52(A))	No.
Oregon	No.	No.	Yes. (§ 113.065(1))	Yes. (§ 113.075(3)(b))	No.
Pennsylvania	No.	No.	No.	Yes, since only original probate appears to be allowed. (20 § 3136)	No.
Rhode Island	No.	No.	No.	Yes. (§ 33-7-19)	No.
South Carolina	Implied, since the provision requires giving effect to order of testacy elsewhere if a "final order" in a proceeding where interested persons were notified and given an opportunity to contest. (§ 62-3-408)	Implied. (§ 62-3-408)	Implied. (§ 62-3-408)	Yes, during the original probate at the domicile state. (§ 62-3-408)	After the time for notice has expired, but before the termination of the statute of limitations, the domicile of the testator may be reviewed. (§ 62-3-409)

South Dakota	Implied, since the provision requires giving effect to order of testacy elsewhere if a "final order" in a proceeding where interested persons were notified and given an opportunity to contest. (§ 29A-3-408)	Implied. (§ 29A-3-408)	Implied. (§ 29A-3-408)	Yes, during the original probate at the domicile state. (§ 29A-3-409, §29A-3-408)	After the time for notice has expired, but before the termination of the statute of limitations, the domicile of the testator may be reviewed. (29A-3-409)
Tennessee	No.	No.	No.	Yes. (§ 32-5-103)	No.
Texas	If Texas court receives notice of proceeding to contest the will, probate shall cease until those proceedings have terminated or proof that such proceedings were never actually instituted. (Prob. § 101)	No.	Implied yes. (Prob. § 95(b))	Yes, if will was previously probated in nondomiciliary jurisdiction. (Prob. § 95(b)(2))	No.
Utah	Implied, since the provision requires giving effect to order of testacy elsewhere if a "final order" in a proceeding where interested persons were notified and given an opportunity to contest. (§ 75-3-408)	Implied. (§ 75-3-408)	Implied. (§ 75-3-408)	Yes, during the original probate at the domicile state. (§ 75-3-408)	After the time for notice has expired, but before the termination of the statute of limitations, the domicile of the testator may be reviewed. (§ 75-3-409)
Vermont	No.	No.	No.	Yes. (14 § 114(b))	No.
Virginia	No.	No.	Yes. (French v. Short, 151 S.E.2d 354 (1966))	Personalty: Although no notice requirement is specified, the statute presumes the validity of the foreign will "in the absence of evidence to the contrary." Thus,	No.

(cont'd)

Table 2.02, Part 1
Ancillary Probate *(continued)*

	For Ancillary Probate, Must:				
	There Be Proof of No Pending Contest at Domicile?	*There Be Proof That Period for Contesting Will at the Domicile Has Expired?*	*There Be Proof That Decedent Was Domiciled in Other Jurisdiction?*	*All Interested Parties Be Notified?*	*Other Considerations?*
Virginia *(cont'd)*				notification is implied. (§ 64.1-92) Real Property: The implication that notification is required is even stronger than with personalty, since there is no presumption of validity. (§ 64.1-92)	
Washington	No.	No.	No.	No, even though such persons would be allowed to contest following probate. (§§ 11.20.100, 11.24.010)	No.
West Virginia	No.	No.	No.	Yes. (§ 41-5-13)	No.
Wisconsin	Yes. (§ 868.01(1))	No.	Yes. (§ 868.01(1) & (6))	Implied yes, since the will may be contested. (§ 868.01(2) & (8))	No.
Wyoming	No.	No.	No.	Yes. (§§ 2-11-104, 2-7-201)	No.

1. Note: No ancillary probate is necessary. No letters are required to be obtained. If Table 2.01, *What proof is required to establish a will already proved in another estate?*, is complied with, foreign personal representative can act just like a local personal representative who has been duly appointed. (§ 20-341)

Table 2.02, Part 2
Ancillary Probate

	Can a Will Be Contested in the Ancillary Proceeding?	*At What Point in Ancillary Proceedings Can Property Be Transmitted to the Domiciliary Personal Representative?*	*Will Letters Be Issued to Person Named in Will, Although That Person Is Not the Domiciliary Personal Representative?*	*If No Other Person is Named in the Will, is the Domiciliary Personal Representative Entitled to Letters in the Ancillary Probate Jurisdiction?*
Alabama	Yes, except if already probated elsewhere. (§ 43-8-175; Carter v. Davis, 154 So. 2d 9 (1963))	No provision.	Implied yes, if an entitled relative or an entitled creditor makes no application for letters of administration. (§§ 43-2-192, 43-2-193)	Yes, if an entitled relative or an entitled creditor makes no application for letters of administration. (§§ 43-2-192, 43-2-193)
Alaska	Yes. (§§ 13.06.060, 13.16.025, 13.16.055)	After payment of claims locally. (§ 13.16.520(c)) With regard to debts, personal property, or instrument evidencing debt, obligation, stock, or chose in action, payment or transfer can be made directly to domiciliary personal representative after 60 days following death, if proof of appointment of domiciliary personal representative and affidavit stating: date of death, that no local administration is pending or has been applied for, and that domiciliary personal representative is entitled to payment or delivery. Transfer of securities is covered by § 3 of Uniform Act for Simplification of Fiduciary Security Transfers. (§ 13.21.015 & U.P.C. § 4201 cmt.[1]) However, cannot make any of these transfers if notified not to do so by local creditors of decedent. (§ 13.21.025)	Yes, if the will so specifies. (§ 13.16.065(g))	Yes. (§ 13.16.065(g))

Table 2.02, Part 2
Ancillary Probate *(continued)*

	Can a Will Be Contested in the Ancillary Proceeding?	*At What Point in Ancillary Proceedings Can Property Be Transmitted to the Domiciliary Personal Representative?*	*Will Letters Be Issued to Person Named in Will, Although That Person Is Not the Domiciliary Personal Representative?*	*If No Other Person is Named in the Will, is the Domiciliary Personal Representative Entitled to Letters in the Ancillary Probate Jurisdiction?*
Arizona	Yes. (§§ 14-1301, 14-3105, 14-3201)	After payment of claims locally. (§ 14-3815(C)) With regard to debts, personal property, or instrument evidencing debt, obligation, stock, or chose in action, payment or transfer can be made directly to domiciliary personal representative after 60 days following death, if proof of appointment of domiciliary personal representative and affidavit stating: date of death, that no local administration is pending or has been applied for, and that domiciliary personal representative is entitled to payment or delivery. Transfer of securities is covered by § 3 of Uniform Act for Simplification of Fiduciary Security Transfers. (§ 14-4201 & U.P.C. § 4201 cmt.[2]) However, cannot make any of these transfers if notified not to do so by local creditors of decedent. (§ 14-4203)	Yes. (§ 14-3203(G))	Yes. (§ 14-3203(G))
Arkansas	Yes, but only when the grounds of objection are filed within the specified time periods. (§ 28-40-113(b); Schweitzer v. Bean, 242 S.W. 63 (1922))	Prior to the final disposition of the ancillary estate, the domiciliary personal representative may apply to remove assets from Arkansas. An issuance of a bond	No specific provision, but any interested person may apply. It is in the court's discretion as to what is in the best interest of the estate. Domiciliary personal	Any interested person may apply. Domiciliary personal representative will be notified and can object. Preference is given to the domiciliary personal representative.

		may be required. The application may or may not be granted at the court's discretion. (§§ 28-42-106, 28-42-109)	representative will be notified and can object. (§§ 28-42-102(b) & (c), 28-42-105(a))	(§§ 28-42-102(b) & (c), 28-42-105(a))
California	Only if the sister state did not find the decedent domiciled in the sister state, one or more interested parties were not given notice and an opportunity to contest in the sister state, or the determination of the sister state is not final. (Prob. § 12522)	Representative may petition court for preliminary or final distribution of all or a part of decedent's personal property. (Prob. §§ 11600, 12540(a)) Preliminary distribution may not be made unless two months have elapsed, there is no injury to interested parties, and bond required by the court is filed. (Prob. §§ 11620, 11621) Final distribution may not be ordered unless the estate is in a condition to be closed. (Prob. § 11640) In all cases, the judge must determine the distribution is in the best interest of the estate or interested persons. (Prob. § 12540(a))	Yes. (Prob. § 12513)	Yes, the domiciliary personal representative has priority over all other persons, except where the decedent's will nominates a different person to be the personal representative for California. (Prob. § 12513)
Colorado	Yes. (§§ 15-10-301, 15-12-105, 15-12-201)	After payment of claims locally. (§ 15-12-815(3)) With regard to debts, personal property, or instrument evidencing debt, obligation, stock, or chose in action, payment or transfer can be made directly to domiciliary personal representative after 60 days following death, if proof of appointment of domiciliary personal representative and affidavit stating: date of death; that no local administration is pending or has been applied for; and that domiciliary personal representative is entitled to payment or delivery. Transfer of securities is	Yes. (§ 15-12-203(7))	Yes. (§ 15-12-203(7))

(cont'd)

Table 2.02, Part 2
Ancillary Probate *(continued)*

	Can a Will Be Contested in the Ancillary Proceeding?	*At What Point in Ancillary Proceedings Can Property Be Transmitted to the Domiciliary Personal Representative?*	*Will Letters Be Issued to Person Named in Will, Although That Person Is Not the Domiciliary Personal Representative?*	*If No Other Person is Named in the Will, is the Domiciliary Personal Representative Entitled to Letters in the Ancillary Probate Jurisdiction?*
Colorado *(cont'd)*		covered by § 3 of Uniform Act for Simplification of Fiduciary Security Transfers. (§ 15-13-201 & U.P.C. § 4-201 cmt.[3]) However, cannot make any of these transfers if notified not to do so by local creditors of decedent. (§ 15-13-203)		
Connecticut	Yes. (§ 45a-288(a) & (c))	No provision.	No provision.	No provision.
Delaware	Yes, at least where will is not already probated in another state. (12 § 1307)	No provision.	Implied yes. (12 § 1502(a))	Implied yes. (12 § 1502(a))
District of Columbia	No prohibition.	Personal or leasehold property may be removed, leased, or transferred if: (a) after the first publication of notice such representative holds letters from (1) a jurisdiction within the metropolitan area, (2) a jurisdiction outside the metropolitan area and such representative posts a bond; or (b) six months after the first publication of notice (1) no claims are filed or (2) all claims have been released or finally determined in favor of the personal representative. (§ 20-343(b)) Real property may be leased or transferred if the personal	A foreign personal representative needs no letters. (§ 20-341(a)) The information set forth in Table 2.01, Part 1 must be filed.	No letters are needed. (§ 20-341 (a)) The information set forth in Table 2.01, Part 1 must be filed.

		representative: (a) posts bond or, (b) allows six months to pass after the first publication and either no claims are filed or all claims have been released or finally determined in favor of the personal representative. (§ 20-343(c)) In the event of a failure of the personal representative to transfer the real or leasehold property in a reasonable time, the Court may order this if (a) the will or an authenticated copy is filed in the Register's Office, (b) notice has been published as specified indicating the property the decedent owned, and (c) all claims of creditors have been satisfied. (§ 20-344)		
Florida	Not by an interested person who was notified or appeared in proceeding in another state and did not challenge its domiciliary status. If a person was not bound by earlier proceeding, however, he could claim the decedent had a Florida domicile. See Lowenthal v. Mandell, 170 So. 169 (1936). If the person is shown to be a Florida domiciliary, the will can be challenged locally as if it were admitted for original probate in Florida. (§ 733.206(3))	After the payment of expenses of administration and claims against the estate. (§ 734.102(6))	Yes. (§ 734.102(1)) But see § 733.304 as to which nonresidents qualify.	Yes. (§ 734.102(1)) However, if not qualified to act, then an alternate or successor named in will and qualified to act is entitled to letters. If there are no such persons, then "those entitled to a majority interest of the Florida property may have letters issued to a personal representative selected by them and who is qualified to act in Florida." A special rule applies to cases of intestacy. See also § 733.304 as to which nonresidents qualify.

Table 2.02, Part 2
Ancillary Probate *(continued)*

	Can a Will Be Contested in the Ancillary Proceeding?	*At What Point in Ancillary Proceedings Can Property Be Transmitted to the Domiciliary Personal Representative?*	*Will Letters Be Issued to Person Named in Will, Although That Person Is Not the Domiciliary Personal Representative?*	*If No Other Person is Named in the Will, is the Domiciliary Personal Representative Entitled to Letters in the Ancillary Probate Jurisdiction?*
Georgia	Yes. (§ 53-5-33(b) & (c))	The general rules for a domiciliary personal representative apply, although a court may order after notice to heirs, beneficiaries, and creditors that distribution may only be made after payment to heirs, beneficiaries, and creditors "residing or situated" in Georgia. (§ 53-5-41)	Yes. (§ 53-5-37)	Yes, "in the absence of an objection," or failure to qualify within a "reasonable time." If "good cause" to the objection is found, then an administrator c.t.a. who qualifies under Georgia law will be appointed. (§ 53-5-37)
Hawaii	Yes. (§§ 560:1-301, 560:3-105, 560:3-201)	After payment of claims locally. (§ 560:3-815(c)) With regard to debts, personal property, or instrument evidencing debt, obligation, stock, or chose in action, payment or transfer can be made directly to domiciliary personal representative after 60 days following death, if proof of appointment of domiciliary personal representative and affidavit stating: date of death, that no local administration is pending or has been applied for, and that domiciliary personal representative is entitled to payment or delivery. Transfer of securities is covered by § 3 of Uniform Act for Simplification of Fiduciary Security Transfers. (§ 560:4-201 & U.P.C. § 4-201 cmt.[4]) However, cannot make any of these transfers if	Yes. (§ 560:3-203(g))	Yes. (§ 560:3-203(g))

		notified not to do so by local creditors of decedent. (§ 560:4-203)		
Idaho	Yes. (§§ 15-1-301, 15-3-105, 15-3-201)	After payment of claims locally. (§ 15-3-815(c)) With regard to debts, personal property, or instrument evidencing debt, obligation, stock, or chose in action, payment or transfer can be made directly to domiciliary personal representative after 60 days following death, if proof of appointment of domiciliary personal representative and affidavit stating: date of death, that no local administration is pending or has been applied for, and that domiciliary personal representative is entitled to payment or delivery. Transfer of securities is covered by § 3 of Uniform Act for Simplification of Fiduciary Security Transfers. (§ 15-4-201 & cmt.) However, cannot make any of these transfers if notified not to do so by local creditors of decedent. (§ 15-4-203)	Yes. (§ 15-3-203(g))	Yes. (§ 15-3-203(g))
Illinois	Yes. (755 ILCS § 5/8-1(a))	No provision.	Yes. (755 ILCS §§ 5/6-8, 5/7-5)	Yes. (755 ILCS §§ 5/6-8, 5/7-5)
Indiana	Yes. (§ 29-1-7-29)	No provision.	Yes. (§ 29-1-10-1(a)(1))	Yes. (§ 29-1-10-1(a)(1))
Iowa	Yes. (§ 633.310) However, this may not be the case if the will has already been probated elsewhere. (§ 633.496)	The court may require payment of all claims filed and allowed belonging to residents of Iowa, and all legacies and distributive shares payable to residents of Iowa, before allowing the property to be removed. (§ 633.504)	No provision. § 633.502 only applies to the duly qualified domiciliary personal representative.	Yes, and a resident personal representative will also be appointed to serve with the domiciliary personal representative unless good cause is shown that the domiciliary personal representative should act alone. (§ 633.502)

Table 2.02, Part 2
Ancillary Probate *(continued)*

	Can a Will Be Contested in the Ancillary Proceeding?	*At What Point in Ancillary Proceedings Can Property Be Transmitted to the Domiciliary Personal Representative?*	*Will Letters Be Issued to Person Named in Will, Although That Person Is Not the Domiciliary Personal Representative?*	*If No Other Person is Named in the Will, is the Domiciliary Personal Representative Entitled to Letters in the Ancillary Probate Jurisdiction?*
Kansas	Yes, because proceeding is considered original, not ancillary. (§§ 59-804, 59-2224)	All probate proceedings are original, not ancillary. (§ 59-804)	Yes. (§ 59-701)	Yes. (§§ 59-701, 59-1707)
Kentucky	Implied yes. The court presumes validity of will in the absence of evidence to the contrary. Therefore, it appears evidence may be brought in to contest the will. (§ 394.150)	After the payment of debts to Kentucky citizens. (§ 395.260)	Yes; however, any nonresident must be related by consanguinity, marriage, or adoption or be the spouse of such person so related to the decedent, ward, or incompetent. (§§ 395.020, 395.005(2))	Yes; however, any nonresident must be related by consanguinity, marriage, or adoption or be the spouse of such person so related to the decedent, ward, or incompetent. (§§ 395.020, 395.005(2))
Louisiana	Yes, except form and mode of execution. These persons may not have been parties to the foreign probate. (Shimshak v. Cox, 116 So. 714 (1928))	Not specified.	Not specified.	Yes, after qualifying with the court. (Code Civ. Pro. § 3402)
Maine	Yes. (18-A §§ 1-301, 3-105, 3-201)	After payment of claims locally. (18-A § 3-815(c)) With regard to debts, personal property, or instrument evidencing debt, obligation, stock, or chose in action, payment or transfer can be made directly to domiciliary personal representative after 60 days following death, if proof of appointment of domiciliary personal representative and affidavit stating: date of death, that no local administration is pending or has been applied for, and that	Yes. (18-A § 3-203(g))	Yes. (18-A § 3-203(g))

		domiciliary personal representative is entitled to payment or delivery. Transfer of securities is covered by § 3 of Uniform Act for Simplification of Fiduciary Security Transfers. (18-A § 4-201 & cmt.) However, cannot make any of these transfers if notified not to do so by local creditors of decedent. (18-A § 4-203)		
Maryland	No, because Maryland has effectively dispensed with ancillary proceedings since the personal representative may act without prior court authorization. (Est. & Trusts § 5-501)	At any point presumably, since there are no ancillary proceedings and the foreign representative may act without prior court authorization. (Est. & Trusts § 5-501)	A foreign representative is not required to take out letters in Maryland. (Est. & Trusts § 5-501)	A foreign representative is not required to take out letters in Maryland. (Est. & Trusts § 5-501)
Massachusetts	Yes, unless admitted to probate in another jurisdiction. (192 §§ 9, 10; Lee v. Monks, 62 N.E.2d 657 (1945))	After payment of debts, the estate is disposed of according to the last will. If no will, the real property will descend according to Massachusetts's laws. The personal property will be distributed according to the laws of the state or county of which decedent was an inhabitant. (199 §§ 1, 2)	Not specified.	Yes. (199A §§ 5, 6)
Michigan	Yes. (§§ 700.1301, 700.3105, 700.3201)	After payment of claims locally. (§ 700.3815(3)) With regard to debts, personal property, or instrument evidencing debt, obligation, stock, or chose in action, payment or transfer can be made directly to domiciliary personal representative after 63 days following death, if proof of appointment of domiciliary personal representative and affidavit stating: date of death, that no local	Yes. (§ 700.3203(1)(a))	Yes. (§ 700.3203(1)(a))

(cont'd)

Table 2.02, Part 2
Ancillary Probate *(continued)*

	Can a Will Be Contested in the Ancillary Proceeding?	*At What Point in Ancillary Proceedings Can Property Be Transmitted to the Domiciliary Personal Representative?*	*Will Letters Be Issued to Person Named in Will, Although That Person Is Not the Domiciliary Personal Representative?*	*If No Other Person is Named in the Will, is the Domiciliary Personal Representative Entitled to Letters in the Ancillary Probate Jurisdiction?*
Michigan *(cont'd)*		administration is pending or has been applied for, and that domiciliary personal representative is entitled to payment or delivery. (§ 700.4201 & U.P.C. § 4-201 cmt.[5])		
Minnesota	Yes. (§§ 524.1-301, 524.3-105, 524.3-201)	After payment of claims locally. (§ 524.3-815(c)) With regard to debts, personal property, or instrument evidencing debt, obligation, stock, or chose in action, payment or transfer can be made directly to domiciliary personal representative after 60 days following death, if proof of appointment of domiciliary personal representative and affidavit stating: date of death, that no local administration is pending or has been applied for, and that domiciliary personal representative is entitled to payment or delivery. Transfer of securities is covered by § 3 of Uniform Act for Simplification of Fiduciary Security Transfers. (§ 524.4-201 & U.P.C. § 4-201 cmt.[6]) However, cannot make any of these transfers if notified not to do so by local creditors of decedent. (§ 524.4-203)	Yes. (§ 524.3-203(g))	Yes. (§ 524.3-203(g))

Mississippi	*There is no ancillary probate in Mississippi. (§ 91-1-1; Carroll v. McPike, 53 Miss. 569 (1876))*			
Missouri	*There is no ancillary probate in Missouri. (§ 473.668; Yonke v. Alber's Estate, 351 S.W.2d 794 (Ct. App. 1961))*			
Montana	Yes. (§§ 72-1-201(2), 72-3-112, 72-3-105)	After payment of claims locally. (§ 72-3-821(3)) With regard to debts, personal property, or instrument evidencing debt, obligation, stock, or chose in action, payment or transfer can be made directly to domiciliary personal representative after 60 days following death, if proof of appointment of domiciliary personal representative and affidavit stating: date of death, that no local administration is pending or has been applied for, and that domiciliary personal representative is entitled to payment or delivery. Transfer of securities is covered by § 3 of Uniform Act for Simplification of Fiduciary Security Transfers. (§ 72-4-306 & U.P.C. § 4-201 cmt.) However, cannot make any of these transfers if notified not to do so by local creditors of decedent. (§ 72-4-308)	Yes. (§ 72-3-506)	Yes. (§ 72-3-506)
Nebraska	Yes. (§§ 30-2210(2), 30-2405, 30-2410)	After payment of claims locally. (§ 30-2497(c)) With regard to debts, personal property, or instrument evidencing debt, obligation, stock, or chose in action, payment or transfer can be made directly to domiciliary personal representative after 60 days following death, if proof of appointment of domiciliary personal representative and affidavit	Yes. (§ 30-2412(g))	Yes. (§ 30-2412(g))

(cont'd)

Table 2.02, Part 2
Ancillary Probate *(continued)*

	Can a Will Be Contested in the Ancillary Proceeding?	*At What Point in Ancillary Proceedings Can Property Be Transmitted to the Domiciliary Personal Representative?*	*Will Letters Be Issued to Person Named in Will, Although That Person Is Not the Domiciliary Personal Representative?*	*If No Other Person is Named in the Will, is the Domiciliary Personal Representative Entitled to Letters in the Ancillary Probate Jurisdiction?*
Nebraska *(cont'd)*		stating: date of death; that no local administration is pending or has been applied for; and that domiciliary personal representative is entitled to payment or delivery. (§ 30-2502) Transfer of securities is covered elsewhere. (U.P.C. § 4-201 & cmt.[7]) However, cannot make any of these transfers if notified not to do so by local creditors of decedent. (§ 30-2504)		
Nevada	Yes. (§ 136.010)	Not specified.	Yes. (§§ 138.010(1), 138.040)	Yes. (§§ 138.010(1), 138.040)
New Hampshire	Yes, implied. (§ 552:14)	Not specified.	Yes. (§ 553:2)	Yes, if the domiciliary personal representative was named in the will. (§ 553:2)
New Jersey	Yes. (§ 3B:3-28)	Not specified. (§ 3B:23-42)	Not specified.	Yes, provided letters have not been issued in New Jersey or an action for letters is not pending in New Jersey. (§§ 3B:14-28, 3B:14-29)
New Mexico	Yes. (§ § 45-1-301(B), 45-3-105, 45-3-201)	After payment of claims locally. (§ 45-3-815(C)) With regard to debts, personal property, or instrument evidencing debt, obligation, stock, or chose in action, payment or transfer can be made directly to domiciliary personal representative after 60 days	Yes. (§ 45-3-203(G))	Yes. (§ 45-3-203(G))

		following death, if proof of appointment of domiciliary personal representative and affidavit stating: date of death, that no local administration is pending or has been applied for, and that domiciliary personal representative is entitled to payment or delivery. Transfer of securities is covered by § 3 of Uniform Act for Simplification of Fiduciary Security Transfers. (§ 45-4-201 & U.P.C. § 4-201 cmt.[8]) However, cannot make any of these transfers if notified not to do so by local creditors of decedent. (§ 45-4-203)		
New York	Yes, but only on the grounds that the foreign proof requirements have not been satisfied or that the will has been denied probate in New York. (Surr. Ct. Proc. Act § 1602(2))	It is at the court's discretion. (Surr. Ct. Proc. Act § 1610)	Yes. (Surr. Ct. Proc. Act § 1604(1)(a))	Yes. (Surr. Ct. Proc. Act § 1604(1)(b) & (c))
North Carolina	Yes. § 28A-3-1(2) affords the jurisdiction. A decision under the prior law anticipates availability of caveat procedure. (See In re Mark's Will, 259 N.C. 326, 331-32, 130 S.E.2d 673, 677 (1963))	With regard to debts, personal property, or instrument evidencing debt, obligation, stock, or chose in action, payment or transfer can be made directly to domiciliary personal representative after 60 days following death, if proof of appointment of domiciliary personal representative and affidavit stating: date of death, that no local administration is pending or has been applied for, and that domiciliary personal representative is entitled to payment or delivery. (§ 28A-26-2(a)) However, cannot make any of these transfers if *(cont'd)*	Yes. (§ 28A-26-3(a))	Yes. (§ 28A-26-3(a)) Note that domiciliary personal representative may be substituted once appointed, even though local representative was previously serving. (§ 28A-26-3(b)) A local representative can be appointed if application for local appointment is not made by the domiciliary personal representative within 60 days of issuance of domiciliary letters or, if shorter, 90 days after the death of the decedent. (*Id.*) To be appointed, the domiciliary personal representative must present a certified or exemplified copy of letters to the county clerk *(cont'd)*

Table 2.02, Part 2
Ancillary Probate *(continued)*

	Can a Will Be Contested in the Ancillary Proceeding?	*At What Point in Ancillary Proceedings Can Property Be Transmitted to the Domiciliary Personal Representative?*	*Will Letters Be Issued to Person Named in Will, Although That Person Is Not the Domiciliary Personal Representative?*	*If No Other Person is Named in the Will, is the Domiciliary Personal Representative Entitled to Letters in the Ancillary Probate Jurisdiction?*
North Carolina *(cont'd)*		notified not to do so bylocal creditors of decedent. (§ 28A-26-2(c)) Payment of claims must be made before the property can be transferred to the domiciliary personal representative. (§ 28A-26-9)		of the superior court. (§ 28A-26-3(a))
North Dakota	Yes. (§§ 30.1-02-01, 30.1-12-05, 30.1-13-01)	After payment of claims locally. (§ 30.1-19-15(3)) With regard to debts, personal property, or instrument evidencing debt, obligation, stock, or chose in action, payment or transfer can be made directly to domiciliary personal representative after 60 days following death, if proof of appointment of domiciliary personal representative and affidavit stating: date of death, that no local administration is pending or has been applied for, and that domiciliary personal representative is entitled to payment or delivery. Transfer of securities is covered by § 3 of Uniform Act for Simplification of Fiduciary Security Transfers. (§ 30.1-24-02 & cmt.) However, cannot make any of these transfers if notified not to do so by local creditors of decedent. (§ 30.1-24-04)	Yes. (§ 30.1-13-03(7))	Yes. (§ 30.1-13-03(7))

Ohio	No, if probated in another state. (§ 2129.05; Jones v. Robinson, 17 Ohio St. 171 (1867)); yes, if not proved elsewhere and involving Ohio real property (Thomas v. Taylor, 2001 WL 992086 (Ct. App. Aug. 31, 2001)).	Not specified, but prior to filing a final account, the ancillary administrator shall file an application for a certificate of transfer for real estate. (§ 2129.19)	Yes, provided that person meets the Ohio qualifications in § 2109.21(B)(2).	Yes, provided that person meets the Ohio qualifications in § 2109.21(B)(2).
Oklahoma	Implied yes because admitting a foreign will to probate has the same force and effect as a will first admitted to probate in Oklahoma, and Oklahoma allows for contest of wills of the probate. (58 §§ 53, 61)	After final settlement of the administrative accounts, an application must be filed and the court determines whether it is in the best interest of the estate. (58 § 633)	Yes. (58 § 101)	Yes. (58 § 101)
Oregon	Yes, if it would be grounds for rejection in Oregon. (§ 113.065(2))	When administration has been completed and the estate is in a condition to be distributed. (§ 116.163)	Yes. (§ 113.085(1)(a))	Yes. (§ 113.085(1)(a))
Pennsylvania	Yes, even with respect to wills already probated outside the U.S. (20 § 3136) As for domestic wills, the issue is unresolved. See, e.g., In re Salwaroski's Estate, 37 Northam. 18 (1963))	Not specified.	Yes. (20 § 3155)	Yes. (20 § 3155)
Rhode Island	Yes, by showing cause why the will should not be filed and recorded. (§ 33-7-19)	Not specified.	May issue letters to the named executor. (§ 33-7-21)	May issue letters to the named executor. (§ 33-7-21)
South Carolina	Yes. (§§ 62-1-301, 62-3-105, 62-3-201)	After payment of claims locally. (§ 62-3-815(c)) With regard to debts, personal property, or instrument evidencing debt, obligation, stock, or chose in action, payment or transfer can be made directly to domiciliary personal representative after 60 days following death, if proof of	Yes. (§ 62-3-203(f))	Yes. (§ 62-3-203(f))

(cont'd)

Table 2.02, Part 2
Ancillary Probate *(continued)*

	Can a Will Be Contested in the Ancillary Proceeding?	*At What Point in Ancillary Proceedings Can Property Be Transmitted to the Domiciliary Personal Representative?*	*Will Letters Be Issued to Person Named in Will, Although That Person Is Not the Domiciliary Personal Representative?*	*If No Other Person is Named in the Will, is the Domiciliary Personal Representative Entitled to Letters in the Ancillary Probate Jurisdiction?*
South Carolina *(cont'd)*		appointment of domiciliary personal representative and affidavit stating: date of death, that no local administration is pending or has been applied for, and that domiciliary personal representative is entitled to payment or delivery. Transfer of securities is covered by § 3 of Uniform Act for Simplification of Fiduciary Security Transfers. (§ 62-4-201 & cmt.) However, cannot make any of these transfers if notified not to do so by local creditors of decedent. (§ 62-4-203)		
South Dakota	Yes. (§§ 29A-1-301, 29A-3-105, 29A-3-201)	After payment of claims locally. (§ 29A-3-815(c)) With regard to debts, personal property, or instrument evidencing debt, obligation, stock, or chose in action, payment or transfer can be made directly to domiciliary personal representative after 60 days following death, if proof of appointment of domiciliary personal representative and affidavit stating: date of death, that no local administration is pending or has been applied for, and that domiciliary personal representative is entitled to payment or	Yes. (§ 29A-3-203(g))	Yes. (§ 29A-3-203(g))

		delivery. Transfer of securities is covered by § 3 of Uniform Act for Simplification of Fiduciary Security Transfers. (§ 29A-4-201 & U.P.C. § 4-201 cmt.[9]) However, cannot make any of these transfers if notified not to do so by local creditors of decedent. (§ 29A-4-203)		
Tennessee	Yes, but not for personal property and not on the issue of devisavit vel non for real property outside the state. (§§ 32-5-103, 32-5-106)	Not specified.	Not specified.	Yes. (§ 32-5-102)
Texas	Yes. (Prob. § 96) However, if it has been probated in decedent's domicile, the only grounds for contest are: (a) that the foreign proceedings were not duly authenticated or recorded in the deed records; (b) will has been finally rejected for probate in Texas; or (c) probate has been set aside in decedent's domicile. (Prob. § 100(a))	There is no specific provision relating to ancillary probate; it appears the original probate laws of Texas govern distribution.	The executor named in the will is entitled to letters. (Prob. § 105)	The executor named in the will is entitled to letters. (Prob. § 105)
Utah	Yes. (§§ 75-1-301, 75-3-105, 75-3-201)	After payment of claims locally. (§ 75-3-815(3)) With regard to debts, personal property, or instrument evidencing debt, obligation, stock, or chose in action, payment or transfer can be made directly to domiciliary personal representative after 60 days following death, if proof of appointment of domicilliary personal representative and affidavit stating: date of death, that no local administration is pending or has been applied for, and that	Yes. (§ 75-3-203(7))	Yes. (§ 75-3-203(7))

(cont'd)

Table 2.02, Part 2
Ancillary Probate *(continued)*

	Can a Will Be Contested in the Ancillary Proceeding?	*At What Point in Ancillary Proceedings Can Property Be Transmitted to the Domiciliary Personal Representative?*	*Will Letters Be Issued to Person Named in Will, Although That Person Is Not the Domiciliary Personal Representative?*	*If No Other Person is Named in the Will, is the Domiciliary Personal Representative Entitled to Letters in the Ancillary Probate Jurisdiction?*
Utah *(cont'd)*		domiciliary personal representative is entitled to payment or delivery. Transfer of securities is covered by § 3 of Uniform Act for Simplification of Fiduciary Security Transfers. (§ 75-4-201 & cmt.) However, cannot make any of these transfers if notified not to do so by local creditors of decedent. (§ 75-4-203)		
Vermont	Not specified. Only states that there is a hearing and notice as to whether the will shall be allowed as the will of the decedent. Whether will can be contested is not addressed. (14 §§ 114(b), 115)	Not specified. Only states that after the payment of debts and administration the estate will be disposed of according to the will and the residue will be disposed of as provided in case of estates in Vermont belonging to persons who are not inhabitants of Vermont. (14 § 116)	Yes. (14 § 902)	Yes. (14 § 902)
Virginia	Yes. See Table 2.01, Part 1.	Not specified.	Yes. (§ 64.1-116)	Yes. (§ 64.1-116)
Washington	Yes. (§§ 11.20.100, 11.24.010)	Not specified.	Implied yes. (§ 11.28.120) However, anyone can object and a hearing will be held to determine whether the person should receive the letters. (§ 11.28.020)	Implied yes. (§ 11.28.120) However, anyone can object and a hearing will be held to determine whether the person should receive the letters. (§ 11.28.020)

West Virginia	Yes, but only if contesting whether it is a true copy of the will, that the probate of the will was set aside by the original probate court, or that such probate was improperly made. (§ 41-5-13)	Not specified.	Yes. (§ 44-1-1)	Yes. (§ 44-1-1)
Wisconsin	Yes, but only that the proof required for ancillary probate has not been met or that the will has been finally rejected from probate in Wisconsin. (§ 868.01(2))	Prior to the final disposition of the ancillary estate but after notice, acceptance of service of process, and the posting of a bond. (§ 868.03(7))	Yes. (§ 868.03(2)(a))	Yes, domiciliary personal represen tative is given preference unless the court determines it is not in the best interest of the estate. (§ 868.03(2)(a))
Wyoming	Yes. (§§ 2-2-103, 2-6-301)	Not specified.	Yes. (§ 2-6-202)	Yes. (§ 2-6-202)

1. Although adopting the Uniform Probate Code, the editorial board comments of the U.P.C. have not been included in Alaska Statutes. Nonetheless, the assumption is that they would be relied upon in construing the statutory provisions.
2. Although adopting the Uniform Probate Code, the editorial board comments of the U.P.C. have not been included in Arizona Revised Statutes. Nonetheless, the assumption is that they would be relied upon in construing the statutory provisions.
3. Although adopting the Uniform Probate Code, the editorial board comments of the U.P.C. have not been included in Colorado Revised Statutes. Nonetheless, the assumption is that they would be relied upon in construing the statutory provisions.
4. Although adopting the Uniform Probate Code, the editorial comments of the U.P.C. have not been included in Hawaii Code Annotated. Nonetheless, the assumption is that they would be relied upon in construing the statutory provisions.
5. Although adopting the provision from the Uniform Probate Code, the editorial board comments of the U.P.C. have not been included in the Michigan Statutes. Nonetheless, the assumption is that they would be relied upon in construing the statutory provision.
6. Although adopting the Uniform Probate Code, the editorial board comments of the U.P.C. have not been included in Minnesota Statutes. Nonetheless, the assumption is that they would be relied upon in construing the statutory provisions.
7. Although adopting the Uniform Probate Code, the editorial comments of the U.P.C. have not been included in Revised Statutes of Nebraska Annotated. Nonetheless, the assumption is that they would be relied upon in construing the statutory provision.
8. Although adopting the Uniform Probate Code, the editorial comments of the U.P.C. have not been included in New Mexico Statutes Annotated. Nonetheless, the assumption is that they would be relied upon in construing the statutory provisions.
9. Although adopting the Uniform Probate Code, the editorial comments of the U.P.C. have not been included in South Dakota Codified Laws. Nonetheless, the assumption is that they would be relied upon in construing the statutory provisions.

Table 2.02, Part 3
Ancillary Probate

	Is Provision Made for Cases Where the Foreign Domiciliary Jurisdiction Does Not Issue Letters?	*May Creditors File a Local Probate Petition?*	*The Proper Venue in the State for Ancillary Probate Is . . .*
Alabama	No.	Yes. (Nashville Trust Co. v. Cleage, 21 So. 2d 441 (1945); §§ 43-8-160, 43-8-190)	when the testator, not an inhabitant of the state, dies in a county in Alabama in which the testator owns assets, that county's probate court. If the testator dies outside the county, then the county where such assets are located. If the testator designates a county in which he/she owns property, then that county's probate court. (§ 43-8-162)
Alaska	Yes. Need duly authenticated certificate of legal custodian that copy is a true copy and that will has become effective under the law of the foreign place. (§ 13.16.180)	Yes, subject to the other rules described herein, such as the prior appointment of a personal representative. (§ 13.16.020)	if not domiciled in state, in any county in state where property at decedent's death. Note that a debt is located where the debtor resides or has its principal office, if not an individual. Commercial paper, investment paper, and other instruments are located where the instrument is. An interest in trust is located where the trustee may be sued. Note, as well, that if there is a challenge to venue, it must be brought in same court having exclusive jurisdiction. As for conflicting determination of domicile, the first determination of domicile is controlling. (§ 13.16.055)
Arizona	Yes. Need duly authenticated certificate of legal custodian that copy is a true copy and that will has become effective under the law of the foreign place. (§ 14-3409)	Yes, subject to the other rules described herein, such as the prior appointment of a personal representative. (§ 14-3104)	if not domiciled in state, in any county in state where property at decedent's death. Note that a debt is located where the debtor resides or has its principal office, if not an individual. Commercial paper, investment paper, and other instruments are located where the instrument is. An interest in trust is located where the trustee may be sued. Note, as well, that if there is a challenge to venue, it must be brought in same court having exclusive jurisdiction. As for conflicting determination of

			domicile, the first determination of domicile is controlling. (§ 14-3201)
Arkansas	No.	Any interested person may petition the court. (§ 28-40-107(a)(1))	the county where property with the greatest value is located; if there is no property, the county of death if the testator died in Arkansas; if the testator died out of state with no property in Arkansas, then in any county where a cause of action may be maintained by the personal representative. (§ 28-40-102(a)(2)–(4))
California	Only states that if the will is admitted to probate or established or proved in accordance with the laws of the foreign jurisdiction, then the will is to be admitted into probate in California. (Prob. § 12521(a))	Yes, any interested person may file. (Prob. § 12510)	in the county where the nonresident decedent died if the decedent had property there; if no property of the nonresident decedent is located in the country where the decedent died, or if the decedent did not die in the state, then any county where the decedent's property is located; if property of the nonresident decedent is located in more than one county, then proper venue is the county in which a petition for ancillary administration is first filed, and the court in that county has jurisdiction of the administration of the estate. (Prob. § 12511, § 7052(a), (b))
Colorado	Yes. Need duly authenticated certificate of legal custodian that copy is a true copy and that will has become effective under the law of the foreign place. (§ 15-12-409)	Yes, subject to the other rules described herein, such as the prior appointment of a personal representative. (§ 15-12-104)	if not domiciled in state, in any county in state where property at decedent's death. Note that a debt is located where the debtor resides or has its principal office, if not an individual. Commercial paper, investment paper, and other instruments are located where the instrument is. An interest in trust is located where the trustee may be sued. Note, as well, that if there is a challenge to venue, it must be brought in same court having exclusive jurisdiction. As for conflicting determination of domicile, the first determination of domicile is controlling. (§ 15-12-201)

Table 2.02, Part 3
Ancillary Probate *(continued)*

	Is Provision Made for Cases Where the Foreign Domiciliary Jurisdiction Does Not Issue Letters?	*May Creditors File a Local Probate Petition?*	*The Proper Venue in the State for Ancillary Probate Is . . .*
Connecticut	No.	Any person interested in such property may file. (§ 45a-288(a))	any of the following districts in which: (a) the testator last resided; (b) any of the testator's real or tangible property is situated; (c) any of the testator's intangible property is situated; (d) the executor or trustee named in the will resides; or (e) any cause of action in favor of the testator arose or any debtor of the testator resides or has an office. If more than one applies, the court which first assumes jurisdiction is to retain jurisdiction. (§ 45a-287(a))
Delaware	No.	Implied yes. (12 § 1307(a))	any county in Delaware where there are any goods or chattels, rights or credits, or lands or tenements of the deceased. (12 § 1302(a))
District of Columbia	No.	No provision. However, a creditor may file a claim in a book known as "Claims Against Nonresident Decedents." Until the claim is resolved, it constitutes a lien on decedent's D.C. real property and proceeds of an authorized sale. (§ 20-343(d))	No provision presumably since there are not several counties in D.C.
Florida	No.	Creditors as a category are not among those who are named as possible appointees as personal representative. (§ 733.301) However, they can petition the court for the appointment of a personal representative. See, e.g., In re Bush's Estate, 80 So. 2d 673 (1955).	if not domiciled in state, in any county in state where property at decedent's death; if no property in the state, then where any debtor of decedent is domiciled. (§ 733.101) Also, a statute recognizes that a married woman may have a Florida domicile even if her husband is a nonresident of Florida. (§ 733.101(2))
Georgia	Yes. Ancillary probate may be granted, even though a will has not been probated at the domicile, if it has been "established" there, provided it has not been offered for probate and successfully caveated in Georgia. (§ 53-5-33) See above for proof of establishment of will at the domicile.	Yes. (§ 53-5-44)	probate court of any county in which property owned by decedent or "any cause of action of which the decedent was possessed at death the venue of which lies in this state." (§ 53-5-36)

Hawaii	Yes. Need duly authenticated certificate of legal custodian that copy is a true copy and that will has become effective under the law of the for eign place. (§ 560:3-409)	Yes, subject to the other rules described herein, such as the prior appointment of a personal representative. (§ 560:3-104)	if not domiciled in state, in any county in state where property at decedent's death. Note that a debt is located where the debtor resides or has its principal office, if not an individual. Commercial paper, investment paper, and other instruments are located where the instrument is. An interest in trust is located where the trustee may be sued. Note, as well, that if there is a challenge to venue, it must be brought in same court having exclusive jurisdiction. As for conflicting determination of domicile, the first determination of domicile is controlling. (§ 560:3-201)
Idaho	Yes. Need duly authenticated certificate of legal custodian that copy is a true copy and that will has become effective under the law of the foreign place. (§ 15-3-409)	Yes, subject to the other rules described herein, such as the prior appointment of a personal representative. (§ 15-3-104)	if not domiciled in state, in any county in state where property at decedent's death. Note that a debt is located where the debtor resides or has its principal office, if not an individual. Commercial paper, investment paper, and other instruments are located where the instrument is. An interest in trust is located where the trustee may be sued. Note, as well, that if there is a challenge to venue, it must be brought in same court having exclusive jurisdiction. As for conflicting determination of domicile, the first determination of domicile is controlling. (§ 15-3-201)
Illinois	Yes, need an authenticated certificate of the legal custodian of the will that the copy is a true copy and that the will has become operative by the laws of that state or country. (755 ILCS § 5/7-3(b))	Yes. (755 ILCS §§ 5/7-2, 5/6-2)	the county in which the greater part of real estate is located or, if no real estate, where the greater part of his personal estate is located. (755 ILCS § 5/5-1(a), (b), & (c))
Indiana	No.	Any interested person may petition. (§§ 29-1-7-4(a), 29-1-7-27)	any county in Indiana where decedent's property resides. If more than one county commences a proceeding, the county that first commences probate proceedings shall determine venue. (§ 29-1-7-1(a) & (b))

Table 2.02, Part 3
Ancillary Probate *(continued)*

	Is Provision Made for Cases Where the Foreign Domiciliary Jurisdiction Does Not Issue Letters?	*May Creditors File a Local Probate Petition?*	*The Proper Venue in the State for Ancillary Probate Is . . .*
Iowa	No.	Implied yes. (§ 633.496)	in a county where real or personal property of testator is located. (Brown v. Monticello State Bank of Monticello, 360 N.W.2d 81 (1984); (§§ 633.12, 633.495)
Kansas	No.	Yes, may be made by any person interested in the will. (§ 59-2229)	any county where the decedent left any estate to be administered. (§ 59-2203)
Kentucky	No.	Yes, it is implied that any person may file. (§ 394.150)	where any part of the estate is located, or where there is a debt or demand owing to the decedent. (§ 394.140)
Louisiana	Yes. (§ 9:2424)	Yes, any person interested in the will may file. (§ 9:2422)	any parish where immovable property of the deceased is located or movable property of the deceased is located if the deceased owned no immovable property in Louisiana at death. (Code Civ. Pro. §§ 2811, 3401)
Maine	Yes. Need duly authenticated certificate of legal custodian that copy is a true copy and that will has become effective under the law of the foreign place. (18-A § 3-409)	Yes, subject to the other rules described herein, such as the prior appointment of a personal representative. (18-A § 3-104).	if not domiciled in state, in any county in state where property at decedent's death. Note that a debt is located where the debtor resides or has its principal office, if not an individual. Commercial paper, investment paper, and other instruments are located where the instrument is. An interest in trust is located where the trustee may be sued. Note, as well, that if there is a challenge to venue, it must be brought in same court having exclusive jurisdiction. As for conflicting determination of domicile, the first determination of domicile is controlling. (18-A § 3-201)
Maryland	A foreign representative is not required to take out letters in Maryland. (Est. & Trusts § 5-501)	Not specified.	the county where the largest part, in value, of decedent's property at death is located. (Est. & Trusts § 5-103(a))

Massachusetts	No.	Yes, any person interested in the will may file. (192 § 9)	a county where there is any property on which such will may operate. (192 § 9)
Michigan	Yes. Need duly authenticated certificate of legal custodian that copy is a true copy and that will has become effective under the law of the foreign place. (§ 700.3409(2))	Yes, subject to the other rules described herein, such as the prior appointment of a personal representative. (§ 700.3104)	if not domiciled in state, in any county in state where property at decedent's death. Note that a debt is located where the debtor resides or where the debtor has its principal office, if not an individual. Commercial paper, investment paper, and other instruments are located where the instrument is. An interest in trust is located where the trustee may be sued. Note, as well, that if there is a challenge to venue, it must be brought in same court having exclusive jurisdiction. As for conflicting determination of domicile, the first determination of domicile is controlling. (§ 700.3201)
Minnesota	Yes. Need duly authenticated certificate of legal custodian that copy is a true copy and that will has become effective under the law of the foreign place. (§ 524.3-409)	Yes, subject to the other rules described herein, such as the prior appointment of a personal representative. (§ 524.3-104)	if not domiciled in state, in any county in state where property at decedent's death. Note that a debt is located where the debtor resides or has its principal office, if not an individual. Commercial paper, investment paper, and other instruments are located where the instrument is. An interest in trust is located where the trustee may be sued. Note, as well, that if there is a challenge to venue, it must be brought in same court having exclusive jurisdiction. As for conflicting determination of domicile, the first determination of domicile is controlling. (§ 524.3-201)
Mississippi	*There is no ancillary probate in Mississippi. (§ 91-1-1; Carroll v. McPike, 53 Miss. 569 (1876))*		
Missouri	*There is no ancillary probate in Missouri. (§ 473.668; Yonke v. Alber's Estate, 351 S.W.2d 794 (Ct. App. 1961))*		

Table 2.02, Part 3
Ancillary Probate *(continued)*

	Is Provision Made for Cases Where the Foreign Domiciliary Jurisdiction Does Not Issue Letters?	*May Creditors File a Local Probate Petition?*	*The Proper Venue in the State for Ancillary Probate Is . . .*
Montana	Yes. Need duly authenticated certificate of legal custodian that copy is a true copy and that will has become effective under the law of the foreign place. (§ 72-3-316)	Yes, subject to the other rules described herein, such as the prior appointment of a personal representative. (§ 72-3-104)	if not domiciled in state, in any county in state where property at decedent's death. (§ 72-3-112) Note that a debt is located where the debtor resides or has its principal office, if not an individual. Commercial paper, investment paper, and other instruments are located where the instrument is. An interest in trust is located where the trustee may be sued. Note, as well, that if there is a challenge to venue, it must be brought in same court having exclusive jurisdiction. As for conflicting determination of domicile, the first determination of domicile is controlling. (§ 72-3-113)
Nebraska	Yes. Need duly authenticated certificate of legal custodian that copy is a true copy and that will has become effective under the law of the foreign place. (§ 30-2433)	Yes, subject to the other rules described herein, such as the prior appointment of a personal representative. (§ 30-2404)	if not domiciled in state, in any county in state where property at decedent's death. Note that a debt is located where the debtor resides or has its principal office, if not an individual. Commercial paper, investment paper, and other instruments are located where the instrument is. An interest in trust is located where the trustee may be sued. Note, as well, that if there is a challenge to venue, it must be brought in same court having exclusive jurisdiction. As for conflicting determination of domicile, the first determination of domicile is controlling. (§ 30-2410)
Nevada	Yes. If the foreign jurisdiction does not require probate, a duly certified copy of the will is filed with a certificate of the legal custodian of the original that the copy is a true copy and that the will has become operative in the foreign jurisdiction. If the will is a national will in the possession of a foreign notary, and the original cannot be released, then a copy must be certified by the notary. The copy of the foreign will is handled in	Any person interested in the will may file. (§ 136.260(2))	any county in which the testator left any estate. (§ 136.260(1))

	the same way as in the case of an original probate. (§ 136.260(4))		
New Hampshire	No.	Yes, any party in interest may file. (§ 552:13)	any county where there is an estate on which the will operates. (§ 552:14)
New Jersey	No provision.	Implied yes. (§§ 3B:3-26, 3B:3-27)	the surrogate's court of any county. (§ 3B:3-26)
New Mexico	Yes. Need duly authenticated certificate of legal custodian that copy is a true copy and that will has become effective under the law of the foreign place. (§ 45-3-409(B))	Yes, subject to the other rules described herein, such as the prior appointment of a personal representative. (§ 45-3-104(A))	if not domiciled in state, in any county in state where property at decedent's death. Note that a debt is located where the debtor resides or has its principal office, if not an individual. Commercial paper, investment paper, and other instruments are located where the instrument is. An interest in trust is located where the trustee may be sued. Note, as well, that if there is a challenge to venue, it must be brought in same court having exclusive jurisdiction. As for conflicting determination of domicile, the first determination of domicile is controlling. (§ 45-3-201)
New York	Yes. (Surr. Ct. Proc. Act § 1607(1))	Yes. (Surr. Ct. Proc. Act § 1609(1))	the court having jurisdiction over the property. (Surr. Ct. Proc. Act § 1602(1))
North Carolina	No.	If executor has not applied for probate within 60 days after the testator's death, a creditor, as a "person interested in the estate, may make such application, upon 10 days' notice thereof to the executor." (§ 31-13)	if not domiciled in North Carolina, then any county where left property or assets or into which they may have come (§ 28A-3-1(2)); if more than one county in which property or assets, then county where proceedings first commenced (§ 28A-3-1(2)); if nondomiciliary motorist who died in North Carolina, then any county in North Carolina. (§ 28A-3-1(3))
North Dakota	Yes. Need duly authenticated certificate of legal custodian that copy is a true copy and that will has become effective under the law of the foreign place. (§ 30.1-15-09)	Yes, subject to the other rules described herein, such as the prior appointment of a personal representative. (§ 30.1-12-04)	if not domiciled in state, in any county in state where property at decedent's death. Note that a debt is located where the debtor resides or has its principal office, if not an individual. Commercial paper, investment paper, and other instruments are located where the

(cont'd)

Table 2.02, Part 3
Ancillary Probate *(continued)*

	Is Provision Made for Cases Where the Foreign Domiciliary Jurisdiction Does Not Issue Letters?	*May Creditors File a Local Probate Petition?*	*The Proper Venue in the State for Ancillary Probate Is . . .*
North Dakota *(cont'd)*			instrument is. An interest in trust is located where the trustee may be sued. Note, as well, that if there is a challenge to venue, it must be brought in same court having exclusive jurisdiction. As for conflicting determination of domicile, the first determination of domicile is controlling. (§ 30.1-13-01)
Ohio	No.	Yes. (§ 2129.04)	where property of the decedent is located or where a debtor of the decedent resides. (§ 2129.04)
Oklahoma	No.	Yes, any person interested in the will may file. (58 § 52(A))	where any portion of the estate is left, or any portion of the estate for which claim is made. (58 § 51)
Oregon	No.	Yes, any interested person may file. (§ 113.035)	where property is located. (§ 113.015)
Pennsylvania	No.	Not specified. (20 § 3136)	any county where any of the property is located. (20 § 3131)
Rhode Island	No.	Yes, any person interested in the will may file. (§ 33-7-18)	any town or city where the testator had property upon which the will may operate. (§ 33-7-18)
South Carolina	Yes. Need duly authenticated certificate of legal custodian that copy is a true copy and that will has become effective under the law of the foreign place. (§ 62-3-409)	Yes, subject to the other rules described herein, such as the prior appointment of a personal representative. (§ 62-3-104).	if not domiciled in state, in any county in state where property at decedent's death. Note that a debt is located where the debtor resides or has its principal office, if not an individual. Commercial paper, investment paper, and other instruments are located where the instrument is. An interest in trust is located where the trustee may be sued. Note, as well, that if there is a challenge to venue, it must be brought in same court having exclusive jurisdiction. As for conflicting determination of

			domicile, the first determination of domicile is controlling. (§ 62-3-201)
South Dakota	Yes. Need duly authenticated certificate of legal custodian that copy is a true copy and that will has become effective under the law of the foreign place. (§ 29A-3-409)	Yes, subject to the other rules described herein, such as the prior appointment of a personal representative. (§ 29A-3-104)	if not domiciled in state, in any county in state where property at decedent's death. Note that a debt is located where the debtor resides or has its principal office, if not an individual. Commercial paper, investment paper, and other instruments are located where the instrument is. An interest in trust is located where the trustee may be sued. Note, as well, that if there is a challenge to venue, it must be brought in same court having exclusive jurisdiction. As for conflicting determination of domicile, the first determination of domicile is controlling. (§ 29A-3-201)
Tennessee	Yes. Need duly authenticated certificate of legal custodian that copy is a true copy and that will has become effective under the law of the foreign place. (§ 32-5-105(a))	Yes, any interested person may file. (§ 32-5-103)	where any part of the estate is left. (§ 32-5-101)
Texas	No.	Yes, any person interested may file (Prob. §§ 76(a), 95)	if testator died in state, either county where testator died or where the principal part of the estate was located at death. If testator did not die in the state, in the county where the near est of kin resides. If there is no kindred, in the county where the principal part of the estate was located at death. (Prob. § 6)
Utah	Yes. Need duly authenticated certificate of legal custodian that copy is a true copy and that will has become effective under the law of the foreign place. (§ 75-3-409)	Yes, subject to the other rules described herein, such as the prior appointment of a personal representative. (§ 75-3-104).	if not domiciled in state, in any county in state where property at decedent's death. Note that a debt is located where the debtor resides or has its principal office, if not an individual. Commercial paper, investment paper, and other instruments are located where the instrument is. An interest in trust is located where the trustee may be sued. Note, as well, that if there is a challenge to venue, it must be brought in same court having exclusive

(cont'd)

Table 2.02, Part 3
Ancillary Probate *(continued)*

	Is Provision Made for Cases Where the Foreign Domiciliary Jurisdiction Does Not Issue Letters?	*May Creditors File a Local Probate Petition?*	*The Proper Venue in the State for Ancillary Probate Is . . .*
Utah *(cont'd)*			jurisdiction. As for conflicting determination of domicile, the first determination of domicile is controlling. (§ 75-3-201)
Vermont	No.	Yes, any person interested may file. (14 § 114(a))	any district where testator left an estate. (4 § 311a(2))
Virginia	No.	Not specified as to whom may file. (§ 64.1-92)	in the county or city where any real estate lies that is devised or was owned by the decedent. If there be no such real estate, then in the county or city of death or where there is estate. (§ 64.1-75)
Washington	No.	Not specified.	in any county in which any part of probate estate is situated. (§ 11.96A.050(3)(b)(i)) If there are no assets in the state, any county where a nonprobate asset might be. (§ 11.96A.050 (3)(b)(ii)) Alternatively, proper venue for probate is the county in which the decedent died. (§ 11.96A.050(3)(b)(iii)); see also § 11.96A.040(1)(b) & (1)(c))
West Virginia	No.	Not specified as to whom may file for ancillary probate. (§ 41-5-13)	where any real estate devised is located, or if there be none, the county where the testator died, or where any property is located. (§ 41-5-4)
Wisconsin	No.	Yes, any interested person may file. (§ 856.07(1))	in any county where property of the decedent is located. The court that first exercises jurisdiction shall retain jurisdiction. (§ 856.01(2))
Wyoming	Yes, where will is required to be in the custody of a notary. (§ 2-11-105(a))	Yes, any interested person may file. (§ 2-11-103)	where any estate is left. (§ 2-11-102)

Table 3
Nonresident Qualification as a Fiduciary (current through 5/1/07)

Often a relative or bank from another state has the relationship and has engendered trust to manage affairs of an individual or administer an estate or trust. Quite commonly, the individual has retired to a state other than the one in which the most trusted individuals or bank are resident. In other cases, the individual has remained, but other members of the family or close friends have moved out of state. When naming fiduciaries in a will or a trust, or seeking qualification of a personal representative, trustee, or guardian,[1] careful consideration must be given to whether such person can qualify. In many instances, states draw distinctions between residents (usually meaning more precisely domiciliaries) and nonresidents (usually meaning more precisely nondomiciliaries). In some situations, nonresidents may serve, but only with the joint appointment of a resident or the designation of a resident agent.

The rules regarding fiduciaries vary widely, even within a state, based on the particular category of fiduciary involved. The rules also tend to vary, depending whether a domiciliary or ancillary estate, trust, or guardianship administration is involved. There are even distinct rules often for executors, as opposed to administrators. Finally, sharp differences exist in the treatment of nonresident individuals on the one hand and nonresident corporate entities on the other hand. With regard to the former, there may be a further differentiation between certain nonresident relatives, who are permitted to serve as fiduciaries locally, and other relatives and unrelated individuals, who do not qualify to serve under local law.

The ensuing tables address these issues. Table 3.01 is specifically concerned with the appointment of nonresident executors, administrators, and testamentary trustees. The table considers both nonresidents appointed in cases of domiciliary administration as well as in cases of ancillary administration. Thus, if a nonresident is seeking approval to serve in a state where some of the decedent's property is located, but the decedent was not domiciled (ancillary administration), the rules as to qualification may differ from the case where the nonresident is seeking to serve in a fiduciary capacity at the decedent's domicile. If the same person is seeking to serve in both places, he may be a resident in one state and a nonresident in the other state, thus requiring a review of the law of more than one state.

1. The table uses the term "guardian" generally, although in a particular state a different term, such as conservator or curator, may be used when referring, for example, to the party charged with responsibility for an incompetent adult or his assets.

Table 3.02 follows the same analysis, but with respect to individuals serving as domiciliary and ancillary guardians of minor and incompetent persons. Table 3.03 shifts the focus to nonindividual banks[2] serving as executors, administrators, and testamentary trustees. Table 3.04 considers the same issues from the standpoint of institutions serving as guardians of the property of minors and incompetents.

Because fiduciaries may, in fact, be required to qualify in a number of foreign states, careful consideration must be given to the requirements imposed by any number of several states in which qualification will be sought. The failure to satisfy the relevant state requirements can have dire consequences. The local court may appoint a local attorney or institution completely unknown to the family. Alternatively, a local member of the family may be appointed, even though not one preferred by the testator, settlor, or ward, as the case may be. Nevertheless, this person may exercise considerable control over family wealth and have tremendous impact on the futures of members of the family. Especially if appointed by the court, this person may be entitled to substantial fees that otherwise would not have been paid. Routine supervision by the court may also complicate and delay matters.

2. Similar rules would typically apply to trust companies and other institutions authorized to serve in a fiduciary capacity.

Table 3.01
Nonresident Individual as Executor, Administrator, and Testamentary Trustee

	Nonresident Individual as Executor	*Nonresident Individual as Administrator*	*Nonresident Individual as Testamentary Trustee*	*Nonresident Individual as Ancillary Executor*	*Nonresident Individual as Ancillary Administrator*	*Nonresident Individual as Ancillary Testamentary Trustee*
Alabama	Yes. (§ 43-2-191)	No. (§ 43-2-193) § 43-2-193 indicates that it is permissible to have a nonresident administrator for a non-resident decedent leaving property in Alabama if that admin istrator is also the administrator of the decedent's estate in another state.	Yes, by inference (Ingalls v. Ingalls, 81 So. 2d 610, 613–14 (1955))	Yes. (§ 43-2-191)	§ 43-2-193 indicates that it is permissible to have a nonresident administrator for a nonresident decedent leaving property in Alabama if that administrator is also the administrator of the decedent's estate at his domcile.	Yes, by inference (Ingalls v. Ingalls, 81 So. 2d 610, 613-14 (1955))
Alaska	Yes, if appointed at the domicile, if named in the will, or if nominated by the domiciliary personal representative. (§ 13.16.065(g))	Yes. § 13.16.065 does not condition appointment on domicile or residence in-state. Furthermore, § 13.16.065(g) recognizes a personal representative appointed at the domicile or if nominated by the domiciliary personal representative.	Yes. (§ 13.36.025(a))	Yes, same requirements as in the first column. (§13.16.065) If no local administration is pending, a foreign domiciliary personal representative can act locally after filing proof of appoitnment and of any bond given. §§ 13.21.035, 13.21.045)	Yes, same requirements as in the prior column. (§ 13.16.065(g))	Yes. (§ 13.36.025(a))
Arizona	Yes, if appointed at the domicile, if named in the will, or if nominated by the domiciliary personal representative. (§ 14-3203(G))	Yes. § 14-3203 does not condition appointment on domicile or residence in-state. Furthermore, §14-3203(G) recognizes a personal *(cont'd)*	Yes. (§§ 14-7202, 14-7205, 14-7305)	Yes, same requirements as in the first column. If no local administration is pending, a foreign domiciliary personal representative can *(cont'd)*	Yes, same requirements as in the prior column. (§ 14-3203(G))	Yes. (§§ 14-7202, 14-7205, 14-7305)

Table 3.01
Nonresident Individual as Executor, Administrator, and Testamentary Trustee *(continued)*

	Nonresident Individual as Executor	*Nonresident Individual as Administrator*	*Nonresident Individual as Testamentary Trustee*	*Nonresident Individual as Ancillary Executor*	*Nonresident Individual as Ancillary Administrator*	*Nonresident Individual as Ancillary Testamentary Trustee*
Arizona *(cont'd)*		representative appointed at the domicile or if nominated by the domiciliary personal representative.		act locally after filing proof of appointment and of any bond given. (§§ 14-4204 – 14-4207)		
Arkansas	Yes, if resident agent is appointed. (§ 28-48-101(b)(6)(A))	Yes, if resident agent is appointed. (§ 28-48-101(b)(6)(A))	No specific authorization or prohibition.	Yes, if the person is a personal representa tive in the domiciliary state and a resident agent is appointed. (§§ 28-42-102, 28-42-104) Alternatively, the same as Executor, as long as the domiciliary representative is given notice and is not appointed instead. (§ 28-42-102(c)) In any event, all ancillary appointments of non residents appear to be discretionary with the courts. See Phillips v. Sherrod Estate, 453 S.W.2d 60 (1970).	Yes, if the person is a personal representative in the domiciliary state and a resident agent is appointed. (§§ 28-42-102, 28-42-104) Alternatively, the same as Executor, as long as the domiciliary representative is given notice and is not appointed instead. (§ 28-42-102(c)) In any event, all ancillary appointments of non residents appear to be discretionary with the courts. See Phillips v. Sherrod Estate, 453 S.W.2d 60 (1970).	No specific authorization or prohibition.
California	Yes. (Prob. §§ 8570, 8572)	Yes, but only if the individual is a resident	There are no specific provisions that	Yes. (Prob. §§ 12540, 12541) Distribution	Yes. (Prob. §§ 12540, 12541) Distribution	There are no specific provisions on point.

		of the United States. (Prob. § 8402(a)(4) and in the priority listed in Prob. § 8461(a)-(r))	directly address this. But see § 15600(a): "The person named as trustee may accept the trust." See also § 17003(a) by accepting trusteeship of a trust with principal place of administration in California trustee submits personally to jurisdiction of court. See also § 17452(b), if the petition requests that only a nonresident of this state be appointed trustee, the petition shall be filed in the court of the country where either (1) any beneficiary resides or (2) a substantial portion of the trust property to be transferred is located or will be located.	to ancillary personal representative is approved only if court determines that it is in best interest of estate or interested persons. See Prob. § 12540(a) & official comment.	to ancillary personal representative is approved only if court determines that it is in best interest of estate or interested persons. See Prob. § 12540(a) & official comment.	(See § 15600(a)). Consideration should also be given to Estate of Knox, 126 P.2d 108, 343–344 (Cal. 1942) regarding exercise of jurisdiction over a nonresident trustee in an ancillary proceeding, and scope of jurisdiction.
Colorado	Yes, if appointed at the domicile, if named in the will, or if nominated by the domiciliary personal representative. (§ 15-12-203(b)(7))	Yes. § 15-12-203 does not condition appointment on domicile or residence in-state. Furthermore, §15-12-203(b)(7) recognizes a personal representative appointed at the domicile or if nominated by the domiciliary personal representative.	Yes. (§ 15-16-105)	Yes, same requirements as in the first column. If no local administration is pending, a foreign domiciliary personal representative can act locally after filing proof of appointment and of any bond given. (§ 15-12-203(b))	Yes, same requirements as in the prior column. (§ 15-12-203(b))	Yes. (§ 15-16-105)

Table 3.01
Nonresident Individual as Executor, Administrator, and Testamentary Trustee *(continued)*

	Nonresident Individual as Executor	*Nonresident Individual as Administrator*	*Nonresident Individual as Testamentary Trustee*	*Nonresident Individual as Ancillary Executor*	*Nonresident Individual as Ancillary Administrator*	*Nonresident Individual as Ancillary Testamentary Trustee*
Connecticut	Yes. (§ 52-60(a))	Yes. (§ 52-60(a))	Yes. (§ 52-60(a))	Yes. (§52-60(a) and notes)	Yes. (§52-60(a) and notes; interpretive commentary to ch. 802b)	Yes. (§52-60(a))
Delaware	Yes, after filing in the office of the Register of Wills an irrevocable power of attorney designating the Register as agent. (12 § 1506)	Yes, in the discretion of the Register if other individuals do not qualify. (12 § 1505) In addition, there must be filed in the Office of the Register of Wills an irrevocable power of attorney designating the Register as agent. (12 §§ 1505, 1506)	Yes, by implication. (12 § 3501 and notes)	Yes. (12 §§ 1506, 1566, 1568)	Yes. (12 §§ 1505, 1506, 1566, 1568)	Yes, by implication. (12 § 3501 and notes)
District of Columbia	Yes, after filing in the office of the Register of Wills an irrevocable power of attorney designating the Register as agent. (§ 20-303(b)(7)) Aliens who are not admitted as U.S. permanent residents may not serve. (§§ 20-303(b)(5), 20-303(b)(7))	Yes, after filing in the office of the Register of Wills an irrevocable power of attorney designating the Register as agent. (§ 20-303(b)(7)) Aliens not lawful permanent residents of U.S. may not serve. (§ 20-303(b)(5))	There is no direct authority. However, it is implied. See District of Columbia v. Chase Manhattan Bank, 689 A.2d 539 (Ct. App. 1997) (actually treating testamentary trust established by resident testator as "resident trust" for tax purposes, though nonresident trustee)	Yes, after filing in the office of the Register of Wills an irrevocable power of attorney designating the Register as agent. (§§ 20-303, 20-341, 20-342) A foreign personal representative of a nondomiciliary is not required to obtain letters in the District of Columbia. If a foreign personal representative is administering an estate that has property located in the	Yes, after filing in the office of the Register of Wills an irrevocable power of attorney designating the Register as agent. (§§ 20-303, 20-341, 20-342) A foreign personal representative of a nondomiciliary is not required to obtain letters in the District of Columbia. If a foreign personal representative is administering an estate that has property located in	There is no direct authority.

				District of Columbia, he must file with the Register a copy of the appointment as personal representative and a copy of the decedent's will, if any, authenticated pursuant to 28 U.S.C. § 1738.	the District of Columbia, he must file with the Register a copy of the appointment as personal representative and a copy of the decedent's will, if any, authenticated pursuant to 28 U.S.C. § 1738.	
Florida	No, unless he is a legally adoptive parent or adopted child, lineal relative, spouse, brother, sister, uncle, aunt, nephew, niece of decedent or lineal relative of such person, or spouse of a person otherwise qualified. (§ 733.304)	No, unless he is a legally adoptive parent or adopted child, lineal relative, spouse, brother, sister, uncle, aunt, nephew, niece of decedent or lineal relative of such person, or spouse of a person otherwise qualified. (§ 733.304)	Yes. (§ 736.0112)	Yes, if qualified to act in Florida. (§ 734.102) A nondomiciliary of Florida can only act if a legally adopted child or adoptive parent of the decedent; related by lineal consanguinity; a spouse or a brother, sister, uncle, aunt, nephew or niece of decedent, or someone related by lineal consanguinity to such person; or the spouse of a person otherwise qualified. (§ 733.304) Persons not qualified to serve are felons, those mentally or phys ically unable to perform duties, and those persons under the age of 18. (§ 733.303)	Yes. See prior column.	Yes. (§ 736.0112)

Table 3.01
Nonresident Individual as Executor, Administrator, and Testamentary Trustee *(continued)*

	Nonresident Individual as Executor	*Nonresident Individual as Administrator*	*Nonresident Individual as Testamentary Trustee*	*Nonresident Individual as Ancillary Executor*	*Nonresident Individual as Ancillary Administrator*	*Nonresident Individual as Ancillary Testamentary Trustee*
Georgia	Yes. (§§ 53-6-1, 53-6-50, 53-6-51) Unless waived by the will, a nonresident executor must post bond equal to double the amount of the estate.	Yes (§§ 53-6-1 and comment; 53-6-14 and comment; 53-6-51). A nonresident administrator must post bond equal to double the amount of the estate, unless waived by the unanimous consent of the heirs of the estate. (§ 53-6-50(c))	Yes. (§§ 53-12-350, 53-12-351)	Yes. (§ 53-5-37) However, ancillary proceedings may not be necessary. (§ 53-5-42)	Yes. (§ 53-5-37) However, ancillary proceedings may not be necessary. (§ 53-5-42)	Yes. (§§ 53-12-350, 53-12-351)
Hawaii	Yes, if appointed at the domicile, if named in the will, or if nominated by the domiciliary personal representative. (§ 560:3-203(g))	Yes. § 560:3-203 does not condition appointment on domicile or residence in-state. Furthermore, §560:3-203(g) recognizes a personal representative appointed at the domicile or if nominated by the domiciliary personal representative.	There is no direct authority. However, it appears to be recognized under the tax law, § 237-1.	Yes, same requirements as in the first column. If no local administration is pending, a foreign domiciliary personal representative can act locally after filing proof of appointment and of any bond given. (§§ 560:4-204–207)	Yes, same requirements as in the prior column. (§§ 560:4-205, 560:4-207, 560:3-203(g))	Recognition implied by § 560:7-203, which provides: The court will not entertain a proceeding pertaining to ancillary trusts, unless (1) all appropriate parties could not be bound by litigation in the courts of the principal state or (2) the interests of justice otherwise would seriously be impaired. See also tax law § 237-1, which impliedly recognizes this possibility.

Idaho	Yes, if appointed at the domicile, if named in the will, or if nominated by the domiciliary personal representative. (§ 15-3-203(g))	Yes. § 15-3-203 does not condition appointment on domicile or residence in-state. Furthermore, §15-3-203 recognizes a personal representative appointed at the domicile or if nominated by the domiciliary personal representative.	Yes. (§ 15-7-105)	Yes, same requirements as in the first column. If no local administration is pending, a foreign domiciliary personal representative can act locally after filing proof of appointment and of any bond given. (§§ 15-4-204–207)	Yes, same requirements as in the prior column. (§§ 15-3-203(g), 15-4-205, 15-4-207)	Yes. (§ 15-7-105)
Illinois	Yes, if a resident of the U.S., over 18 years old, of sound mind, not disabled, and not a convicted felon. The court has the discretion to require a nonresident executor to post a bond notwithstanding any contrary provision of the will. (755 ILCS § 5/6-13)	Yes, if a resident of the U.S., over 18 years old, of sound mind, not disabled, and not a convicted felon. (755 ILCS § 5/9-1)	Yes. (760 ILCS § 5/2(2))	Yes, if a resident of the U.S., over 18 years old, of sound mind, not disabled, and not a convicted felon. (755 ILCS § 5/6-13)	Yes,. if a resident of the U.S., over 18 years old, of sound mind, not disabled, and not a convicted felon. (755 ILCS § 5/9-1)	Yes. (760 ILCS § 5/2)
Indiana	Yes, if serving jointly with a resident (§ 29-1-10-1(c)); or by appointing a resident agent and posting a bond. (§ 29-1-10-1(d))	Yes, if serving jointly with a resident (§ 29-1-10-1(c)); or by appointing a resident agent and posting a bond. (§ 29-1-10-1(d))	Yes. (§ 30-4-2-11, Tr. Code Study Comm. Cmt. (a))	There is no statutory prohibition. However, § 29-2-1-1 states that a "local personal representative includes any personal representa tive appointed in this state pursuant to appointment proceedings described in article 1 of this title." That could include § 29-1-10-1(c), requiring joint *(cont'd)*	There is no statutory prohibition. However, § 29-2-1-1 states that a "local personal representative includes any personal representative appointed in this state pursuant to appointment proceedings described in article 1 of this title." That could include § 29-1-10-1(c), requiring joint *(cont'd)*	Yes. (§ 30-4-2-11; Tr. Code Study Comm. Cmt. (a))

Table 3.01
Nonresident Individual as Executor, Administrator, and Testamentary Trustee *(continued)*

	Nonresident Individual as Executor	*Nonresident Individual as Administrator*	*Nonresident Individual as Testamentary Trustee*	*Nonresident Individual as Ancillary Executor*	*Nonresident Individual as Ancillary Administrator*	*Nonresident Individual as Ancillary Testamentary Trustee*
Indiana *(cont'd)*				appointment of a resident. Note that if a domiciliary for eign personal representative has established his appointment the domiciliary personal representative can act like a local personal representative in Indiana. (§§ 29-2-1-5, 29-2-1-6)	appointment of a resident. Note that if a domiciliary for eign personal representative has established his appointment the domiciliary personal representative can act like a local personal representative in Indiana. (§§ 29-2-1-5, 29-2-1-6)	
Iowa	Yes, if a resident fiduciary is also appointed to serve with the nonresident or alone if good cause is shown. (§ 633.64)	Yes, if a resident fiduciary is also appointed to serve with the nonresident or alone if good cause is shown. (§ 633.64)	Yes, if a resident fiduciary is also appointed to serve with the nonresident or alone if good cause is shown. (§ 633.64)	Yes, if a resident is also appointed to serve with the nonresident or alone if good cause is shown. (§ 633.502)	Yes, if a resident is also appointed to serve with the nonresident or alone if good cause is shown. (§ 633.502)	Yes, if a resident is also appointed to serve with the nonresident or alone if good cause shown. (§ 633.502)
Kansas	Yes, if a resident agent is appointed. (§ 59-706(b))	Yes, if a resident agent is appointed. (§ 59-706(a))	Yes, if a resident agent is appointed. (§ 59-1706)	Yes, if a resident agent is appointed. (§§ 59-807, 59-1706) See also § 59-804.	Yes, at least if spouse or nominee of spouse of decedent, or one or more divisees or a nominee of such per son(s). (§ 59-807(b))	Yes, if a resident agent is appointed. (§ 59-1706)
Kentucky	Only if over 18 and related by consanguinity, marriage, adoption, or the spouse of such person so related. (§ 395.005)	Only if over 18 and related by consanguinity, marriage, adoption, or the spouse of such person so related. (§ 395.005)	Yes, 18 or legal age and related by consanguinity, marriage, adoption, or the spouse of such person so related. (§ 395.005)	Yes. (§§ 395.005, 395.170)	Yes. (§§ 395.005, 395.170)	Yes, if appointed and qualified according to the laws of the person's domicile. (§§ 386.170, 395.005)

Louisiana	Yes, if resident agent is appointed. (Code Civ. Pro. art. 3097(A)(4)) The rules of the next column apply if the appointment is of a dative testamentary executor. (*Id.*; § 3097(B))	Yes, if resident agent is appointed and if nonresident is the surviving spouse, heir, legatee, legal representative of an heir or legatee, the nominee of any of the above, or a creditor of the deceased, property with the deceased. (Code Civ. Pro. art. 3097(B))	Yes, but must be a citizen or resident of the U.S. with full capacity to contract. (§ 9:1783)	Yes, if resident agent is appointed. Also, a bond will have to be furnished on the application of an interested person for good cause shown. (Code Civ. Pro. arts. 3402, 3404, 3097) The rules of the next column apply if the appointment is of a dative testamentary executor. (*Id.*; § 3097(B))	Yes, if resident agent is appointed and if nonresident is the surviving spouse, heir, legatee, legal representative of an heir or legatee, the nominee of any of the above, or a creditor of the deceased, or a co-owner of immovable property with the deceased. (Code Civ. Pro. arts. 3402, 3404, 3097(B))	Yes, but must be a citizen or resident of the U.S. with full capacity to contract. (§ 9:1783)
Maine	Yes, if appointed at the domicile, if named in the will, or if nominated by the domiciliary personal representative. (18-A § 3-203(g))	Yes. 18-A § 3-203 does not condition appointment on domicile or residence instate. Furthermore, 18-A §3-203 recognizes a personal representative appointed at the domicile or if nominated by the domiciliary personal representative.	Yes. (18-A § 7-105)	Yes, same requirements as in the first column. If no local administration is pending, a foreign domiciliary personal representative can act locally after filing proof of appointment and of any bond given. (18-A §§ 4-204–4-207)	Yes, same requirements as in the prior column. (18-A §§ 4-205, 4-207, 3-203)	Yes. (18-A § 7-105)
Maryland	Yes, if resident agent is appointed. (Est. & Trusts § 5-105(b)(6))	Yes, if resident agent is appointed. (Est. & Trusts § 5-105(b)(6))	Yes. (Est. & Trusts § 14-110)	Yes, although a foreign personal representative is not required to take out letters in Maryland. *(cont'd)*	Yes, although a foreign personal representative is not required to take out letters in Maryland. *(cont'd)*	Yes. (Est. & Trusts § 14-110)

Table 3.01
Nonresident Individual as Executor, Administrator, and Testamentary Trustee *(continued)*

	Nonresident Individual as Executor	*Nonresident Individual as Administrator*	*Nonresident Individual as Testamentary Trustee*	*Nonresident Individual as Ancillary Executor*	*Nonresident Individual as Ancillary Administrator*	*Nonresident Individual as Ancillary Testamentary Trustee*
Maryland *(cont'd)*				(Est. & Trusts § 5-501)	(Est. & Trusts § 5-501)	
Massachusetts	Yes, if resident agent is appointed. (195 § 8)	Yes, if resident agent is appointed. (195 § 8)	Yes, if resident agent is appointed. (203 § 15)	Yes, if resident agent is appointed. (195 § 8; 199A §§ 6, 7; 202 § 32; 204 § 3)	Yes, if resident agent is appointed. (195 § 8; 199A §§ 6, 7; 202 § 32; 204 § 3)	Yes. (203 § 17A; 204 § 3)
Michigan	Yes. (§ 700.3203(3)).	Yes. (§ 700.3203(3)).	Yes. (§ 700.7105)	Yes. An out-of-state domiciliary personal representative can be appointed in Michigan if there is no local administration. (§ 700.4203) Without court approval, and after 63 days from a nonresident decedent's death, the afore said person can receive payment or delivery regarding personal property, a debt, obliga tion, stock, or chose in action. (§ 700.4201)	Yes. See prior column.	Yes. (§ 700.7105)
Minnesota	Yes, if appointed at the domicile, if named in the will, or if nominated by the domiciliary personal representative. (§ 524.3-203(g))	Yes. § 524.3-203 does not condition appointment on domicile or residence in-state. Furthermore, § 524.3-203(g) recognizes a personal	There is no specific provision. See generally § 501B.79.	Yes, same requirements as in the first column. If no local administration is pending, a foreign domiciliary personal representative can	Yes, same requirements as in the prior column. (§§ 524.4-203 et seq., 524.3-203(g))	There is no specific provision. See generally § 501B.79.

		representative appointed at the domicile or if nominated by the domiciliary personal representative.		act locally after filing proof of appointment and of any bond given. (§§ 524.4-204–524.4-207)		
Mississippi	There is no statutory prohibition. (§ 91-7-35)	There is no statutory prohibition. (§ 91-7-65)	There is no statutory prohibition. (§ 91-9-1 et seq.)	Yes, after appropriate filing in county where property located. (§ 91-7-259)	Yes, after appropriate filing in county where property located. (§ 91-7-259)	There is no statutory prohibition. (§ 91-9-1 et seq.)
Missouri	Yes, after designation of resident agent. (§ 473.117(3))	Yes, after designation of resident agent. (§ 473.117(3))	There is no statutory prohibition.	Yes, after appropriate filing in county where property located. (§§ 473.676, 473.677, 473.678)	Yes, after appropriate filing in county where property located. (§§ 473.676, 473.677, 473.678)	There is no statutory prohibition.
Montana	Yes, in that there is no specific prohibition. (§ 72-3-501)	Yes, in that there is no specific prohibition. (§ 72-3-501)	There is no statutory prohibition. (§ 72-35-503(2))	Yes. (§§ 72-4-201 et seq., 72-3-506)	Yes. (§§ 72-4-201 et seq., 72-3-506)	There is no statutory prohibition. (§ 72-35-503(2))
Nebraska	Yes, if appointed at the domicile, if named in the will, or if nominated by the domiciliary personal representative. (§ 30-2412(g))	Yes. § 30-2412 does not condition appointment on domicile or residence in-state. Furthermore, § 30-2412(g) recognizes a personal representative appointed at the domicile or if nominated by the domiciliary personal representative.	Yes, if reciprocal treat ment is accorded trustees resident in Nebraska. (§ 30-3820)	Yes, same requirements as in the first column. If no local administration is pending, a foreign domiciliary personal representative can act locally after filing proof of appointment and of any bond given. (§§ 30-2506–2508)	Yes, same requirements as in the prior column. (§§ 30-2506, 30-2508, 30-2412(g))	Yes, if reciprocal treat ment is accorded trustees resident in Nebraska. (§ 30-3820)

Table 3.01
Nonresident Individual as Executor, Administrator, and Testamentary Trustee *(continued)*

	Nonresident Individual as Executor	*Nonresident Individual as Administrator*	*Nonresident Individual as Testamentary Trustee*	*Nonresident Individual as Ancillary Executor*	*Nonresident Individual as Ancillary Administrator*	*Nonresident Individual as Ancillary Testamentary Trustee*
Nevada	Yes, in that there is no specific prohibition. (§ 138.020)	No, but may associate as co-administrator a resident of Nevada (§ 139.010(4))	Yes, since there is no statutory prohibition. (§ 163.020(4))	Yes, since there is no statutory prohibition. (§ 138.020)	No, but may associate as co-administrator a resident of Nevada. (§ 139.010(4))	Yes, since there is no statutory prohibition. (§ 163.020(4))
New Hampshire	No, unless judge deems proper. (§ 553:5)	No, unless judge deems proper. (§ 553:5)	Yes, after appointing a resident agent. (§ 564:12)	No, but in the court's discretion. (§ 553:5; see also § 554:28)	No, but in the court's discretion. (§ 553:5; see also § 554:28)	Yes, after appointing a resident agent. (§§ 554:28, 564:12)
New Jersey	Yes, after filing power of attorney with the surrogate of the county or clerk of the court. (§ 3B:14-47)	Yes, after filing power of attorney with the surrogate of the county or clerk of the court. (§§ 3B:14-47, 3B:10-2)	Yes, after filing power of attorney with the surrogate of the county or clerk of the court. (§ 3B:14-47)	Yes, after filing power of attorney with the surrogate of the county or clerk of the court. (§ 3B:14-47; see also § 3B:14-25 et seq.)	Yes, after filing power of attorney with the surrogate of the county or clerk of the court. (§ 3B:1447; see also §§ 3B:14-25 et seq., 3B:10-7)	Yes, after filing power of attorney with the surrogate of the county or clerk of the court. (§ 3B:14-47) see also § 3B:14-25 et seq.
New Mexico	Yes, if appointed at the domicile, if named in the will, or if nominated by the domiciliary personal representative. (§ 45-3-203(G))	Yes. § 45-3-203 does not condition appointment on domicile or residence in-state. Furthermore, § 45-3-203(G) recognizes a personal representative appointed at the domicile or if nominated by the domiciliary personal representative.	Yes. (§ 45-7-105)	Yes, same requirements as in the first column. If no local administration is pending, a foreign domiciliary personal representative can act locally after filing proof of appointment and of any bond given. (§§ 45-4-204–45-4-207)	Yes, same requirements as in the prior column. (§§ 45-3-203(g), 45-4-205, 45-4-207)	Yes. (§ 45-7-105)
New York	Yes. (Surr. Ct. Proc. Act §§ 707, 708) A nonresident alien	Yes. (Surr. Ct. Proc. Act §§ 707, 708) A nonresident alien	Yes. (Surr. Ct. Proc. Act §§ 707, 708) A nonresident alien	Yes, subject to the requirements of § 707 (Surr. Ct. Proc. Act	Yes, subject to the requirements of § 707 (Surr. Ct. Proc. Act	Yes. (Surr. Ct. Proc. Act §§ 707, 708) A nonresident alien

	can be an executor if he serves with one or more co-fiduciaries, at least one of whom must be a resident of New York. Any appointment of a resident or nonresident alien fiduciary is made in the court's discretion. No mention is made of a nonresident from another state. Also, the court may declare ineligible any fiduciary "unable to read and write the English language." (Surr. Ct. Proc. Act § 707(2))	can be an executor if he serves with one or more co-fiduciaries, at least one of whom must be a resident of New York. Any appointment of a resident or nonresident alien fiduciary is made in the court's discretion. No mention is made of a nonresident from another state. Also, the court may declare ineligible any fiduciary "unable to read and write the English language." (Surr. Ct. Proc. Act § 707(2))	can be an executor if he serves with one or more co-fiduciaries, at least one of whom must be a resident of New York. Any appointment of a resident or nonresident alien fiduciary is made in the court's discretion. No mention is made of a nonresident from another state. Also, the court may declare ineligible any fiduciary "unable to read and write the English language." (Surr. Ct. Proc. Act § 707(2))	§ 1608) See first column.	§ 1608) See first column.	can be an executor if he serves with one or more co-fiduciaries, at least one of whom must be a resident of New York. Any appointment of a residentor nonresident alien fiduciary is made in the court's discretion. No mention is made of a nonresident from another state. Also, the court may declare ineligible any fiduciary "unable to read and write the English language." (Surr. Ct. Proc. Act § 707(2))
North Carolina	Yes, if a resident agent is appointed. (§ 28A-4-2(4))	Yes, if a resident agent is appointed. (§ 28A-4-2(4))	Yes, after appointment of resident agent for service of process. (§ 28A-22-4)	Yes. (§ 28A-26-3)	Yes. (§ 28A-26-3)	Yes, after appointment of resident agent for service of process. (§28A-22-4)
North Dakota	Yes, if appointed at the domicile, if named in the will, or if nominated by the domiciliary personal representative. (§ 30.1-13-03(7))	Yes. § 30.1-13-03 does not condition appointment on domicile or residence in-state. Furthermore, §30.1-13-03 recognizes a personal representative appointed at the domicile or if nominated by the domiciliary personal representative.	Yes. (§ 30.1-32-05)	Yes, same requirements as in the first column. If no local administration is pending, a foreign domiciliary personal representative can act locally after filing proof of appointment and of any bond given. (§§ 30.1-24-06, 30.1-24-08, 30.1-13-03(7))	Yes, same requirements as in the prior column. (§§ 30.1-24-06, 30.1-24-08, 30.1-13-03(7))	Yes. (§ 30.1-32-05)

Table 3.01
Nonresident Individual as Executor, Administrator, and Testamentary Trustee *(continued)*

	Nonresident Individual as Executor	*Nonresident Individual as Administrator*	*Nonresident Individual as Testamentary Trustee*	*Nonresident Individual as Ancillary Executor*	*Nonresident Individual as Ancillary Administrator*	*Nonresident Individual as Ancillary Testamentary Trustee*
Ohio	Yes, in the court's discretion. (§ 2109.21(B)(1)) To qualify for appointment, a nonresident shall be either an individual who is related to the maker of the will by consanguinity or affinity or a person who resides in a state that allows appointment of a nonresident not related to the maker. See § 2109.21.	No. (§ 2109.21(A))	Yes, in the court's discretion. (§ 2109.21) To qualify for appointment, a nonresident shall be either an individual who is related to the maker of the will by consanguinity or affinity or a person who resides in a state that allows appointment of a nonresident not related to the maker. See § 2109.21(B)(1).	Yes, to qualify for appointment, a nonresident must be either an individual who is related to the maker of the will by consanguinity or affinity or a person who resides in a state that allows appointment of a nonresident not related to the maker. (§§ 2129.08, 2109.21(B)(2); see also § 2129.25)	Yes. To qualify for appointment, a person who is not a resident of this state shall be an individual who is related to the maker of the will by consanguinity or affinity, or a person who resides in a state that allows the appointment of a nonresident who is not related to the maker of the will. (§§ 2109.21(B)(2), 2129.08, 2129.25)	Likely. (§§ 2129.27-2129.30)
Oklahoma	Yes, after appointing resident agent. (58 § 162)	Yes, after appointing resident agent. (58 § 162)	There is no direct authority.	Yes. (58 § 262)	Yes. (58 § 262)	There is no direct authority.
Oregon	Yes, but pursuant to the discretion of the court. (§§ 113.085, 113.087)	Yes, but pursuant to the discretion of the court. (§§ 113.085, 113.087)	Yes. There is no statutory prohibition.	Yes, but ancillary appointment may not be necessary. (§§ 113.085, 113.087, 116.263)	Yes, but ancillary appointment may not be necessary. (§§ 113.085, 113.087, 116.263)	Yes. There is no statutory prohibition.

Pennsylvania	Yes, in that there is no specific prohibition. (20 § 3155)	Yes, at the discretion of the register. (20 §§ 3155, 3157)	Ther is no express limitation.	Yes. (20 §§ 3151, 3155, 4101 et seq.)	Yes, at the discretion of the register. (20 §§ 3151, 3155, 3157, 4101 et seq.)	Ther is no express limitation.
Rhode Island	Yes, if resident agent is appointed. (§ 33-18-9)	No, (§ 33-8-7) unless other circumstances, in the opinion of the court, render such appointment proper, and if resident agent is appointed. (§ 33-8-7)	Yes, there is no statutory prohibition.	Yes, if resident agent is appointed. (§§ 33-18-9, § 33-8-1)	No, (§ 33-8-7) unless other circumstances, in the opinion of the court, render such appointment proper, (§ 33-8-7) and if resident agent is appointed. (§ 33-18-9)	Yes, there is no statutory prohibition.
South Carolina	Yes, if appointed at the domicile, if named in the will, or if nominated by the domiciliary personal representative. (§ 62-3-203(e)(3))	Yes. § 62-3-203 does not condition appointment on domicile or residence in-state. Furthermore, § 62-3-203(e)(3) recognizes a personal representative appointed at the domicile or if nominated by the domiciliary personal representative.	Yes (§ 62-7-207) A resident agent for service of process must be appointed.	Yes, same requirements as in the first column. If no local administration is pending, a foreign domiciliary personal representative can act locally after filing proof of appointment and of any bond given. (§§ 62-4-204–62-4-207)	Yes, same requirements as in the prior column. (§§ 62-3-203, 62-3-603, 62-4-201, 62-4-203)	Yes. (§ 62-7-207) A resident agent for service of process must be appointed.
South Dakota	Yes, if appointed at the domicile, if named in the will, or if nominated by the domiciliary personal representative. (§ 29A-3-203(g))	Yes. § 29A-3-203 does not condition appointment on domicile or residence in-state. Furthermore, § 29A-3-203(g) recognizes a personal representative appointed at the domicile or if nominated by the domiciliary personal representative.	Yes. There is no statutory prohibition.	Yes, same requirements as in the first column. If no local administration is pending, a foreign domiciliary personal representative can act locally after filing proof of appointment and of any bond given. (§§ 29A-4-204–29A-4-207)	Yes, same requirements as in the prior column. (§ 29A-3-203)	Yes. There is no statutory prohibition.

Table 3.01
Nonresident Individual as Executor, Administrator, and Testamentary Trustee *(continued)*

	Nonresident Individual as Executor	*Nonresident Individual as Administrator*	*Nonresident Individual as Testamentary Trustee*	*Nonresident Individual as Ancillary Executor*	*Nonresident Individual as Ancillary Administrator*	*Nonresident Individual as Ancillary Testamentary Trustee*
Tennessee	Yes, any resident or nonresident person may serve.(§ 35-50-107(a)(2)(B)) A nonresident may also serve if a resident individual or a corporation authorized to do business in the state and maintaining an office there serves as cofiduciary. (§ 35-50-107(a)(1)) See also § 30-1-116.	Same as prior col. serve if a resident individual or a corporation authorized to do business in the state and maintaining an office there serves as cofiduciary. (§ 35-50-107(a)(1)) See also § 30-1-116.	Yes. (§ 35-50-107(a)(2)(D)) See also § 30-1-116.	Same as 1st col. serve if a resident individual or a corporation authorized to do business in the state and maintaining an office there serves as cofiduciary. (§ 35-50-107(a)(1)) See also § 30-1-116.	Same as 1st col. serve if a resident individual or a corporation authorized to do business in the state and maintaining an office there serves as cofiduciary. (§ 35-50-107(a)(1)) See also § 30-1-116.	Yes. (§ 35-50-107(a)(2)(D)) See also § 30-1-116.
Texas	Yes, if resident agent is appointed. (Prob. § 78)	Yes, if resident agent is appointed. (Prob. § 78)	Yes. There is no statutory provision directly authorizing, but see, e.g., Prob. § 107.	Yes. (Prob. § 78) If appointed at the domicile, the domiciliary executor is generally able to act in Texas. (Prob. § 105)	Questionable; Prob. § 105 only addresses a situation where a foreign executor is involved. But see Prob. § 107A, suggesting a foreign domiciliary administrator can recover debts in Texas.	Yes, there is no statutory provision directly authorizing, but see, e.g., Prob. § 107.
Utah	Yes, if appointed at the domicile, if named in the will, or if nominated by the domiciliary personal	Yes. § 75-3-203 does not condition appointment on domicile or residence in-state. Furthermore,	Yes. (§ 75-7-101)	Yes, same requirements as in the first column. If no local administration is pending, a foreign	Yes, same requirements as in the prior column. (§§ 75-4-205, 75-4-207, 75-3-203)	Yes. (§ 75-7-101)

	representative. (§ 75-3-203(7))	§ 75-3-203 recognizes a personal representative appointed at the domicile or if nominated by the domiciliary personal representative.		domiciliary personal representative can act locally after filing proof of appointment and of any bond given. (§§ 75-4-204–75-4-207)		
Vermont	Yes, in the court's discretion. (14 § 904(a)) Title 14 § 904(b) provides that where a nonresident executor is appointed, the executor must designate a resident agent. See also R. of Prob. P. 68.	Yes, in the court's discretion. However, the court is required to appoint a nonresident when requested to do so by the surviving spouse, surviving children, surviving parent, or guardian. (14 § 904(a)) Title 14 § 904(b) provides that where a nonresident administrator is appointed, the administrator must designate a resident agent. See also R. of Prob. P. 68.	Yes, if named in the will. Otherwise, the rules set forth with regard to *Nonresident Individual as Executor* apply. (14 § 904) Title 14, § 904(b) provides that where a nonresident trustee is appointed, the trustee must designate a resident agent. (14 § 904(b)) See also R. of Prob. P. 68.	Probably; there is no specific provision. Tit. 14 § 904 applies only when the principal administration is in Vermont; but see 14 §§ 1215, 1216.	Probably; there is no specific provision. Tit. 14 § 904 applies only when the principal administration is in Vermont; but see 14 §§ 1215, 1216.	Yes. (14 § 2311) See also R. of Prob. P. 68.
Virginia	Yes, after appointing a resident agent or accepting service upon clerk of court in which he is qualified/appointed. (§ 26-59)	Yes, after appointing a resident agent or accepting service upon clerk of court in which he is qualified/appointed. (§ 26-59)	Yes, after appointing a resident agent or accepting service upon clerk of court in which he is qualified/appointed. (§ 26-59)	Yes, after appointing a resident agent or accepting service upon clerk of court in which he is qualified/appointed. (§ 26-59)	Yes, after appointing a resident agent or accepting service upon clerk of court in which he is qualified/appointed. (§ 26-59)	Yes, after appointing a resident agent or accepting service upon clerk of court in which he is qualified/appointed. (§ 26-59)
Washington	Yes, after appointing a resident agent, or is the attorney of record of the estate. (§ 11.36.010)	Yes, after appointing a resident agent. (§ 11.36.010)	Yes, there is no statutory prohibition.	Yes, after appointing a resident agent. (§ 11.36.010)	Yes, after appointing a resident agent. (§ 11.36.010)	Yes, there is no statutory prohibition.

Table 3.01
Nonresident Individual as Executor, Administrator, and Testamentary Trustee *(continued)*

	Nonresident Individual as Executor	*Nonresident Individual as Administrator*	*Nonresident Individual as Testamentary Trustee*	*Nonresident Individual as Ancillary Executor*	*Nonresident Individual as Ancillary Administrator*	*Nonresident Individual as Ancillary Testamentary Trustee*
West Virginia	Yes, if resident decedent names the individual executor. (§ 44-5-3(a)(4)) Appointment as executor constitutes that the clerk of the county commission when appointment is made is attorney-in-fact for service of notice and process. (§ 44-5-3(c))	Yes, if distributees apply in the county court that would have jurisdiction as to the probate of his will, if there were one. Preference is given to husband or wife and persons applying within 30 days of death of the intestate (§§ 44-5-3(a)(5), 44-1-4)) Appointment as administrator constitutes that the clerk of the county commission wherein appointment was made is attorney-in-fact for service of notice and process. (§ 44-5-3(c))	There is no statutory prohibition. However, §44-11-7 assumes the possibility of a nonresident trustee.	Yes, but only if serving as such in decedent's state of domicile. (§ 44-5-3(a)(1))	Yes, but only if serving as such in decedent's state of domicile. (§ 44-5-3(a)(1), (a)(2))	There is no statutory prohibition. However, §44-11-7 assumes the possibility of a nonresident trustee.
Wisconsin	Yes, after appointment of a resident agent. (§ 856.23) However, nonresidency may be a sufficient cause for non-appointment or removal, in the court's discretion. (§ 856.23(2))	Yes, after appointment of a resident agent. (§ 856.23) However, nonresidency may be a sufficient cause for non-appointment or removal, in the court's discretion. (§ 856.23(2))	There is no specific statutory prohibition. (§§ 701.16(1)(a), 856.29)	Yes. (§ 868.03(2)(a)) See also § 877.16.	Yes. (§ 868.03(2)(a)) See also § 877.16.	Yes. (§§ 701.16(1)(a)&(d), 856.29)

Wyoming	Yes, after appointment of a resident agent. (§ 2-11-301)	No, unless a resident of Wyoming is appointed co-administrator. (§ 2-4-203)	Yes, after appointment of a resident agent. (§ 2-11-301) But see Ashley v. Read Const. Co., 195 F. Supp. 727 (D. Wyo. 1961).	Yes, after appointment of a resident agent and if property in state has a value of less than $150,000. (§§ 2-11-301, 2-11-201)	No, unless a resident of Wyoming is appointed co-administrator. (§§ 2-4-203, 2-11-201)	Yes, after appointment of a resident agent. (§ 2-11-301)

Table 3.02
Nonresident Individual as Guardian of Minor's or Incompetent's Property

	Nonresident Individual as Guardian of Minor's Property	*Nonresident Individual as Guardian of Incompetent's Property*	*Nonresident Individual as Ancillary Guardian of Minor's Property*	*Nonresident Individual as Ancillary Guardian of Incompetent's Property*
Alabama	Yes. (§§ 26-2A-76, 26-2A-138)	Yes. (§§ 26-2A-104, 26-2A-138)	Yes. (§§ 26-2A-138, 26-2A-160)	Yes. (§§ 26-2A-138, 26-2A-160)
Alaska	Yes. (§§ 13.26.035, 13.26.055, 13.26.210, 13.26.320)	Yes. (§§ 13.26.095, 13.26.145, 13.26.210, 13.26.320)	Yes. (§§ 13.26.035, 13.26.055, 13.26.210, 13.26.320)	Yes. (§§ 13.26.095, 13.26.145, 13.26.210, 13.26.320)
Arizona	Yes. (§§ 14-5202, 14-5206, 14-5410, 14-5432)	Yes. (§§ 14-5301, 14-5311, 14-5410, 14-5432)	Yes. (§§ 14-5202, 14-5206, 14-5410, 14-5432)	Yes. (§§ 14-5301, 14-5311, 14-5410, 14-5432)
Arkansas	Yes; resident agent must be appointed. (§ 28-65-203(e))	Yes; resident agent must be appointed. (§ 28-65-203(e))	Yes; resident agent must be appointed. (§ 28-65-203(e)) However, a guardian appointed in the state of the minor's residence may serve upon petition. (§ 28-65-601)	Yes; resident agent must be appointed. (§ 28-65-203(e)) However, a guardian appointed in the state of the incompetent's residence may serve upon petition. (§ 28-65-601)
California	Yes. (Prob. §§ 1514 & note 22, 1812)	Yes. (Prob. §§ 1514 & note 22, 1812)	Yes. (Prob. §§ 2801, 3800)	Yes. (Prob. §§ 2801, 3800)
Colorado	Yes.[1] (§§ 15-14-202, 15-14-206, 15-14-413, 15-14-433)	Yes.[2] (§§ 15-14-301, 15-14-310, 15-14-413, 15-14-433)	Yes. (§§ 15-14-202, 15-14-206, 15-14-413, 15-14-433)	Yes. (§§ 15-14-301, 15-14-310, 15-14-413, 15-14-433)
Connecticut	Yes, so long as judge is appointed as local agent. (§§ 45a-629, 52-60)	Yes. (§§ 45a-645, 45a-650, 52-60)	Yes. (§§ 45a-629, 45a-632, 52-60)	Yes. (§§ 45a-659, 52-60)
Delaware	Yes. (12 §§ 3901, 3902)	Yes. (12 § 3901)	Yes. (12 §§ 3901, 3902, 3904)	Yes. (12 §§ 3901, 3904)
District of Columbia	Yes, after filing in the office of the Register of Wills an irrevocable power of attorney designating the Register as agent. (§ 21-110) See also § 21-106.	There is no direct authority.	Yes, after filing in the office of the Register of Wills an irrevocable power of attorney designating the Register as agent. (§ 21-110) See also §§ 21-106, 21-111, 21-112.	There is no direct authority. However, see also § 21-2077, allowing person appointed in the domicile to serve if no conservator has been appointed locally, if authenticated copies of the appointment and bond, if any, are filed with the court.

Florida	Yes, if lineal relative, legally adopted child or adoptive parent, spouse, brother, sister, uncle, aunt, niece or nephew of ward, or lineal relative of such person, or spouse of a person otherwise qualified. (§ 744.309)	Yes, if lineal relative, legally adopted child or adoptive parent, spouse, brother, sister, uncle, aunt, niece or nephew of ward, or lineal relative of such person, or spouse of a person otherwise qualified. (§ 744.309)	Yes, if a resident agent is designated. (§§ 744.306, 744.307)	Yes, if a resident agent is designated. (§§ 744.306, 744.307)
Georgia	Implied. (§ 29-7-6)	Implied. (§ 29-7-6)	Yes. (§§ 29-7-1, 29-7-6)	Yes. (§§ 29-7-1, 29-7-6)
Hawaii	No, unless recognized by the appropriate court of some other jurisdiction where the protected person resides as a guardian of protected person's property, or nominated by the will of a parent to serve as guardian. (§§ 560:5-410(a)(1), 560:5-401)	No, unless recognized by the appropriate court of some other jurisdiction where the protected person resides as a guardian of protected person's property, or nominated by the will of a parent to serve as guardian. (§§ 560:5-410(a)(1), 560:5-401)	Yes, if nonresident is spouse, parent, or child of nonresident decedent who is otherwise qualified to serve as a personal representative. (§§ 560:5-410(a)(1), 560:5-401)	No, unless recognized by the appropriate court of some other jurisdiction where the protected person resides as a guardian of protected person's property, or nominated by the will of a parent to serve as guardian. (§§ 560:5-410(a)(1), 560:5-401)
Idaho	Yes. (§§ 15-5-202, 15-5-206, 15-5-410) (a)(4), 15-9-101)	Yes. (§§ 15-5-301, 15-5-311, 15-5-410) (a)(4), 15-9-101)	Yes. (§§ 15-5-202, 15-5-206, 15-5-410(a)(4), 15-9-101) But see § 15-11-101, referring only to a "temporary" appoinment.	Yes. (§§ 15-5-301(c), 15-5-311, 15-5-410(a)(4), 15-9-101) But see § 15-11-101, referring only to a "temporary" appoinment.
Illinois	Yes, if a resident of the U.S. and who court finds capable of providing an active and suitable program of guardianship for the minor. (755 ILCS § 5/11-3)	Yes, if a resident of the U.S. and who court finds capable of providing an active and suitable program of guardianship for the minor. (755 ILCS § 5/11a-5)	Yes, if a resident of the U.S. (755 ILCS § 5/11-3) There does not seem to be a specific provision as to ancillary guardians.	Yes, if a resident of the U.S. (755 ILCS § 5/11a-5) There does not seem to be a specific provision as to ancillary guardians.
Indiana	Yes. (§ 29-3-5-5) There is no prohibition. Furthermore, if no one is appointed locally, a guardian appointed at the protected person's domicile may prove his foreign appointment and then act as a guardian appointed in Indiana. (§ 29-3-13-2)	Yes. (§ 29-3-5-5) There is no prohibition. Furthermore, if no one is appointed locally, a guardian appointed at the protected person's domicile may prove his foreign appointment and then act as a guardian appointed in Indiana. (§ 29-3-13-2)	Yes, after the guardian proves his foreign appointment. (§ 29-3-13-2)	Yes, after the guardian proves his foreign appointment. (§ 29-3-13-2)

Table 3.02
Nonresident Individual as Guardian of Minor's or Incompetent's Property *(continued)*

	Nonresident Individual as Guardian of Minor's Property	*Nonresident Individual as Guardian of Incompetent's Property*	*Nonresident Individual as Ancillary Guardian of Minor's Property*	*Nonresident Individual as Ancillary Guardian of Incompetent's Property*
Iowa	Yes, if a resident is also appointed to serve with the non-resident or alone if good cause is shown. (§ 633.64)	Yes, if a resident is also appointed to serve with the non-resident or alone if good cause is shown. (§ 633.64)	Yes, if a resident is also appointed to serve with the non-resident or alone if good cause shown. (§§ 633.502, 633.64)	Yes, if a resident is also appointed to serve with the nonres ident or alone if good cause shown. (§§ 633.502, 633.64)
Kansas	Yes, if a resident agent is appointed. (§§ 59-1706, 59-3068)	Yes, if a resident agent is appointed. (§§ 59-1706, 59-3068)	Yes, if a resident agent is appointed. (§§ 59-1706, 59-3068)	Yes, if a resident agent is appointed. (§§ 59-1706, 59-3068)
Kentucky	Only if over 18 and related by consanguinity, marriage, adoption, or the spouse of such person so related. (§ 395.005)	Only if over 18 and related by consanguinity, marriage, adoption, or the spouse of such person so related. (§ 395.005)	Yes, if appointed and qualified according to the laws of the ward's domicile. (§§ 387.185, 395.005)	Yes, if appointed and qualified according to the laws of the ward's domicile. (§§ 387.185, 395.005; notes on the applicability of § 387.185 to incompetents)
Louisiana	Yes, if resident agent is appointed. (Code Civ. Pro. art. 4273; § 9:751)	Yes, if resident agent is appointed for service of process. (Code Civ. Pro. arts. 4273, 4556, 4561)	Yes. (Code Civ. Pro. art. 4431; see Caveat to Summary of Procedural Change in ch. 11)	Yes. (Code Civ. Pro. arts. 4556, 4561(B)(1)(c))
Maine	Yes. (18-A §§ 5-202, 5-206 and note 1, 5-410, 5-432)	Yes. (18-A §§ 5-301, 5-311, 5-410, 5-432)	Yes. (18-A §§ 5-202, 5-206 and note 1, 5-410, 5-432)	Yes. (18-A §§ 5-301, 5-311, 5-410, 5-432)
Maryland	Yes, if resident agent is appointed. (Est. & Trusts § 13-207)	Yes, if resident agent is appointed. (Est. & Trusts § 13-207)	Yes, although a foreign guardian or other fiduciary is not required to qualify as an ancillary. (Est. & Trusts §§ 13-222, 13-207)	Yes, although a foreign guardian or other fiduciary is not required to qualify as an ancillary. (Est. & Trusts §§ 13-222, 13-207)
Massachusetts	Yes, if resident agent is appointed. (201 § 49; 195 §§ 8-10)	Yes, if resident agent is appointed. (201 § 49; 195 §§ 8-10)	Yes. (201 § 27 et seq.; 202 § 33; 204 § 3)	Yes. (201 § 27 et seq.; 202 § 33; 204 § 3)

Michigan	There seems to be no statutory prohibition. (§§ 700.5212, 700.5201, 700.5409)	There seems to be no prohibition. (§§ 700.5313, 700.5301, 700.5409)	There seems to be no prohibition. (§§ 700.5409, 700.5432, 700.5433)	There seems to be no prohibition. (§§ 700.5409, 700.5432, 700.5433)
Minnesota	Yes. (§§ 524.5-202, 524.5-206, 524.5-413, 524.5-433).	Yes, by implication, since there is no statutory prohibition. (§§ 524.5-301, 524.5-309(1)), 524.5-413, 524.5-433).	Yes. (§§ 524.5-202, 524.5-206, 524.5-413, 524.5-433).	Yes, by implication, since there is no statutory prohibition. (§§ 524.5-301, 524.5-309(1)), 524.5-413, 524.5-433).
Mississippi	The parties may appoint a nonresident as a testamentary guardian. (§§ 93-13-7, 93-13-13)	There is no statutory prohibition. (§ 93-13-121 et seq.)	Yes. (§§ 93-13-181 et seq.)	Yes. (§ 93-13-181 et seq.)
Missouri	Yes, (§§ 475.055.1(1), 475.055(.3), 475.055(.4), after designation of resident agent (§ 473.117.1(3)).	Yes, (§§ 475.055.1(1), 475.055(.3), 475.055(.4) after designation of resident agent (§ 473.117.1(3)).	Yes. (§§ 475.055(.3), 475.339)	Yes. (§§ 475.055(.3), 475.339)
Montana	Yes. (§§ 72-5-211, 72-5-223, 72-5-410)	Yes. (§§ 72-5-312, 72-5-410)	Yes. (§§ 72-5-211, 72-5-223)	Yes. (§ 72-5-312)
Nebraska	Yes. (§§ 30-2606, 30-2610, 30-2639(2), 30-2661)	Yes. (§§ 30-2617, 30-2627, 30-2639, 30-2661)	Yes. (§§ 30-2606, 30-2610, 30-2639(2), 30-2661)	Yes. (§§ 30-2617, 30-2627, 30-2639(2), 30-2661)
Nevada	Yes, if the nonresident has associated a resident individual or banking corporation whose principal place of business is in the state as a co-guardian. The nonresident must have caused the appointment to be filed in the guardian ship proceeding. (§ 159.059(5)) See also § 159.0487(4) recognizing guardian appointed by the court of another state.	Yes, if the nonresident has associated a resident individual or banking corporation whose principal place of business is in the state as a co-guardian. The nonresident must have caused the appointment to be filed in the guardian ship proceeding. (§ 159.059(5)) See also § 159.0487(4) recognizing guardian appointed by the court of another state.	Yes, if the nonresident has associated a resident individual or bank ing corporation whose principal place of business is in the state as a co-guardian. The nonresident must have caused the appointment to be filed in the guardian ship proceeding. (§ 159.059(5)) See also § 159.0487(4) recognizing guardian appointed by the court of another state.	Yes, if the nonresident has associated a resident individual or bank ing corporation whose principal place of business is in the state as a co-guardian. The nonresident must have caused the appointment to be filed in the guardian ship proceeding. (§ 159.059(5)) See also § 159.0487(4) recognizing guardian appointed by the court of another state.

Table 3.02
Nonresident Individual as Guardian of Minor's or Incompetent's Property *(continued)*

	Nonresident Individual as Guardian of Minor's Property	*Nonresident Individual as Guardian of Incompetent's Property*	*Nonresident Individual as Ancillary Guardian of Minor's Property*	*Nonresident Individual as Ancillary Guardian of Incompetent's Property*
New Hampshire	Yes. (§ 463:10)	Yes. (§ 464-A:10)	Yes. (§§ 463:10, 463:30, 554:28)	Yes. (§§ 464-A:10, 464-A:44, 554:28)
New Jersey	Yes, after filing power of attorney with the surrogate of the county or clerk of the court. (§§ 3B:14-47, 3B:12-21)	Yes, after filing power of attorney with the surrogate of the county or clerk of the court. (§ 3B:14-47)	Yes, after filing power of attorney with the surrogate of the county or clerk of the court. (§§ 3B:14-47, 3B:12-21) See also § 3B:12-19 requiring supervision of surrogate.	Yes, after filing power of attorney with the surrogate of the county or clerk of the court. (§§ 3B:14-47, 3B:12-29)
New Mexico	Yes. (§§ 45-5-202, 45-5-206, 45-5-410, 45-5-432)	Yes. (§§ 45-1-201(7), 45-5-301, 45-5-311, 45-5-410)	Yes. (§§ 45-5-202(C), 45-5-206, 45-5-410(A)(1), 45-5-432)	Yes. (§§ 45-5-301(C), 45-5-311, 45-5-410(A)(1), 45-5-432)
New York	There seems to be no prohibition. (Surr. Ct. Proc. Act § 1707)	There does not seem to be a prohibition. (Men. Hyg. §§ 81.01, 81.19)	Yes. (Surr. Ct. Proc. Act § 1716 (4)) However, ancillary proceedings may not be necessary. (Surr. Ct. Proc. Act § 1716.1)	Yes, in court's discretion. (Men. Hyg. § 81.18)
North Carolina	Possibly under § 35A-1224(b), but nonresidency appears to be grounds for removal. (§ 35A-1290(b)(4))	Yes, if a resident agent is appointed and the nonresident agrees in a writing to the jurisdic tion of North Carolina. (§§ 35A-1213(b), 35A-1290(b)(4))	Possibly. § 35A-1280 states that the clerk *may* appoint an ancillary guardian if it is established that: 1. Nonresident has property in North Carolina. 2. Nonresident is a minor or incompetent; and 3. Nonresident has no guardian in North Carolina. However, ancillary proceedings may not be necessary. (§ 35A-1281)	Possibly. § 35A-1280 states that the clerk *may* appoint an ancillary guardian if it is established that: 1. Nonresident has property in North Carolina. 2. Nonresident is a minor or incompetent; and 3. Nonresident has no guardian in North Carolina. However, ancillary proceedings may not be necessary. (§ 35A-1281)

North Dakota	Yes. (§§ 30.1-27-06, 30.1-29-10)	Yes. (§§ 30.1-28-01, 30.1-28-11, 30.1-29-10, 30.1-29-32)	Yes. (§§ 30.1-27-06, 30.1-29-10(3)(a), 30.1-29-32)	Yes. (§§ 30.1-28-01, 30.1-28-11, 30.1-29-10(3)(a), 30.1-29-32)
Ohio	Yes, if named in a will by a parent of the minor, or selected by a minor over 14 years old (§ 2111.12) or appointed, after being nominated in or pursuant to a durable power of attorney as described in § 1337.08 or § 2111.121. See § 2109.21(c).	No. (§§ 2109.21(D), 2111.02(A))	No. (§ 2111.37)	No. (§ 2111.37)
Oklahoma	No, although a nonresident may be appointed guardian of his or her own spouse, child, children, grandchild, grandchildren, parent, grandparent, brother, sister, aunt, uncle, niece, or nephew and may also be appointed upon the written request of the father, mother, or next of kin, (30 § 4-104) after appointing resident agent (58 § 162).	No, although a nonresident may be appointed guardian of his or her own spouse, child, children, grandchild, grandchildren, parent, grandparent, brother, sister, aunt, uncle, niece, or nephew and may also be appointed upon the written request of the father, mother, or next of kin, (30 § 4-104) after appointing resident agent (58 § 162).	No, although a nonresident may be appointed guardian of his or her own spouse, child, children, grandchild, grandchildren, parent, grandparent, brother, sister, aunt, uncle, niece, or nephew and may also be appointed upon the written request of the father, mother, or next of kin. (30 § 4-104) However, if the incompetent ward and domiciliary guardian are both nonresidents, then no appointment of the guardian may even be required, since, pursuant to court approval, the ward's estate can be removed from the state. (30 §§ 4-605, 4-607)	No, although a nonresident may be appointed guardian of his or her own spouse, child, children, grandchild, grandchildren, parent, grandparent, brother, sister, aunt, uncle, niece, or nephew and may also be appointed upon the written request of the father, mother, or next of kin. (30 § 4-104) However, if the incompetent ward and domiciliary guardian are both nonresidents, then no appointment of the guardian may even be required, since, pursuant to court approval, the ward's estate can be removed from the state. (30 §§ 4-605, 4-607)
Oregon	Yes. (§ 125.200)	Yes. (§ 125.200)	Yes. (§ 125.200)	Yes. (§ 125.200)
Pennsylvania	Yes. (20 §§ 5112, 5147)	Yes. (20 §§ 5515, 5512)	Yes. (20 §§ 5111, 4101 et seq.)	Yes. (20 §§ 4101 et seq., 5512, 5511(b))

Table 3.02
Nonresident Individual as Guardian of Minor's or Incompetent's Property *(continued)*

	Nonresident Individual as Guardian of Minor's Property	*Nonresident Individual as Guardian of Incompetent's Property*	*Nonresident Individual as Ancillary Guardian of Minor's Property*	*Nonresident Individual as Ancillary Guardian of Incompetent's Property*
Rhode Island	Yes, if it is a testamentary appointment, (§ 33-15.1-8) and if a resident agent is appointed (§ 33-18-9).	Yes, there is no statutory prohibition, as long as a resident agent is appointed. (§ 33-18-9)	Yes. (§ 33-15.1-9) Moreover, the guardian may be able to remove property without local appointment. (§ 33-15-42)	Yes. There is no statutory prohibition. Moreover, the guardian may be able to remove property without local appointment. (§ 33-15-42)
South Carolina	Yes. (§§ 62-5-301, 62-5-410, 62-5-311, 62-5-432)	Yes. (§§ 62-5-301, 62-5-410, 62-5-311, 62-5-432)	Yes. (§§ 62-4-204, 62-5-431, 62-5-432, 62-5-301(c), 62-5-410(a)(1))	Yes. (§§ 62-5-301 et seq., 62-5-410(a)(1)), 62-5-311, 62-5-432
South Dakota	Yes. (§ 29A-5-110) A resident agent must be designated. (§ 29A-5-113)	Yes. (§ 29A-5-110) A resident agent must be designated. (§ 29A-5-113)	Yes. (§ 29A-5-114) However, ancillary proceedings may not be necessary. (§ 29A-5-115)	Yes. (§ 29A-5-114) However, ancillary proceedings may not be necessary. (§ 29A-5-115)
Tennessee	Yes, any person may serve as the guardian. (§ 35-50-107(a)(2)(E)) There is no statutory provision for guardian of the property. This would require resident cofiduciary. (§ 35-50-107(a)(1)) But see Brimhall v. Simmons, 338 F.2d 702, 707 (6th Cir. 1964), which construes Tennessee law as permitting nonresident guardian of incompetent appointed in another state to serve in Tennessee with respect to a nonresident ward in absence of statute and without requiring resident cofiduciary.	Yes,,any person may serve as guardian, referred to in statute as "conservator." (§ 35-50-107(a)(2)(F)) See also § 30-1-116. There is no statutory provision for guardian of the property. This would require resident cofiduciary. (§ 35-50-107(a)(1)) But see Brimhall v. Simmons, 338 F.2d 702, 707 (6th Cir. 1964), which construes Tennessee law as permitting nonresident guardian of incompetent appointed in another state to serve in Tennessee with respect to a nonresident ward in absence of statute and without requiring resident cofiduciary.	See first column.	Same as 2d col.
Texas	Yes, if resident agent is appointed. (Prob. § 681 (10))	Yes, if resident agent is appointed. (Prob. § 681 (10))	Yes, but the guardian must have been appointed where the ward resides, the guardian is qualified	Yes, but the guardian must have been appointed where the ward resides, the guardian is qualified as

			as a fiduciary in that jurisdiction, and a complete transcript is filed of the proceedings in which the appointment took place. (Prob. § 881)	a fiduciary in that jurisdiction, and a complete transcript is filed of the proceedings in which the appointment took place. (Prob. § 881) However, ancillary proceedings may not be necessary. (Prob. § 881A)
Utah	Yes. (§§ 75-5-202, 75-5-206, 75-5-410, 75-5-432)	Yes. (§§ 75-5-301, 75-5-311, 75-5-410, 75-5-432)	Yes. (§§ 75-5-202, 75-5-206, 75-5-410(1)(a), 75-5-432)	Yes. (§§ 75-5-301, 75-5-311, 75-5-410(1)(a), 75-5-432)
Vermont	Yes, in the court's discretion if the guardian is named in a will or is a relative of the ward. (14 § 2603) A nonresident guardian of a minor's property must appoint a resident agent. See R. Prob. P. Rule 68(b).	Yes, in the court's discretion if the guardian is named in a will or is a relative of the ward. (14 § 2603) A nonresident guardian of an incom petent's property must appoint a resident agent. (R. Prob. P. Rule 68(b)).	Yes, in the court's discretion if the guardian is named in a will or is a relative of the ward. (14 § 2603) A nonresident guardian of a minor's property must appoint a resident agent. See also 14 § 2649; R. Prob. P. Rule 68(b).	Yes, in the court's discretion if the guardian is named in a will or is a relative of the ward. (14 § 2603) A nonresident guardian of an incompetent's property must appoint a resident agent. See also 14 § 2649; R. Prob. P. Rule 68(b).
Virginia	Yes, after appointing a resident agent. (§ 26-59(A))	Yes, after appointing a resident agent. (§ 26-59(A))	Yes, after appointing a resident agent. (§ 26-59) However, ancillary proceedings may not be necessary. (§ 26-60)	Yes, after appointing a resident agent. (§ 26-59) However, ancillary proceedings may not be necessary. (§ 26-60)
Washington	Yes, after appointing a resident agent. (§§ 11.36.010, 11.88.020(1)(d))	Yes, after appointing a resident agent. (§§ 11.36.010, 11.88.020(1)(d))	Yes, after appointing a resident agent. (§§ 11.36.010, 11.88.020(1)(d))	Yes, after appointing a resident agent. (§§ 11.36.010, 11.88.020(1)(d))
West Virginia	Yes, for resident infants if appointed by infant's father or mother by last will and testament. (§§ 44-5-3(a)(6), 44-10-1) Appointment as testamentary guardian constitutes the clerk of the county commission where appointment is made as attorney-in-fact for service of notice and process. (§ 44-5-3(c))	Yes. (§§ 44-5-3(a)(7), 44-10-1)	Yes, as testamentary guardian if serving as such in minor's state of domicile. (§ 44-5-3(a)(3)) Appointment as testamentary guardian constitutes the clerk of the county commission where appointment is made as attorney-in-fact for service of notice and process. (§ 44-5-3(c))	Yes. (§§ 44-5-3(a)(7), 44-10-1)

Table 3.02
Nonresident Individual as Guardian of Minor's or Incompetent's Property *(continued)*

	Nonresident Individual as Guardian of Minor's Property	*Nonresident Individual as Guardian of Incompetent's Property*	*Nonresident Individual as Ancillary Guardian of Minor's Property*	*Nonresident Individual as Ancillary Guardian of Incompetent's Property*
Wisconsin	There is no statutory prohibition. (§ 54.15)	Yes. There is no statutory prohibition. (§ 54.15)	Yes. There is no statutory prohibition. (§ 54.15)	Yes, there is no statutory prohibition. (§ 54.15)
Wyoming	Yes. There is no statutory prohibition. (§§ 3-2-101, 3-2-107)	Yes. There is no statutory prohibition. (§ 3-2-101)	Yes. There is no statutory prohibition. (§§ 3-2-101, 3-2-107, 3-3-401)	Yes. There is no statutory prohibition. (§§ 3-2-101, 3-3-401)

1. § 15-14-410(1)(a) gives highest priority to the appointment of a person recognized by the appropriate court of the foreign jurisdiction in which the protected person "resides." The provision, however, does not specifically address the appointment of a foreign person when the protected person resides in Colorado. Presumably, no limitation is placed on such person serving, if the person otherwise complies with the statute.

2. *Id.*

Table 3.03
Nonresident Bank as Executor, Administrator, or Testamentary Trustee

	Nonresident Bank as Executor	*Nonresident Bank as Administrator*	*Nonresident Bank as Testamentary Trustee*	*Nonresident Bank as Ancillary Executor*	*Nonresident Bank as Ancillary Administrator*	*Nonresident Bank as Ancillary Testamentary Trustee*
Alabama	Yes, if reciprocal treatment is accorded Alabama banks. (§ 10-2B-15.41(a)(2)) Nonresident bank must file a verified statement with the Commissioner of Revenue. (§ 10-2B-15.42)	Yes, if reciprocal treatment is accorded Alabama banks. (§ 10-2B-15.41(a)(2)) Nonresident bank must file a verified statement with the Commissioner of Revenue. (§ 10-2B-15.42)	Yes, if reciprocal treatment is accorded Alabama banks. (§ 10-2B-15.41(a)(2)) Nonresident bank must file a verified statement with the Commissioner of Revenue. (§ 10-2B-15.42)	Yes, if reciprocal treatment is accorded Alabama banks. (§ 10-2B-15.41(a)(2)) Nonresident bank must file a verified statement with the Commissioner of Revenue. (§ 10-2B-15.42)	Yes, if reciprocal treatment is accorded Alabama banks. (§ 10-2B-15.41(a)(2)) Nonresident bank must file a verified statement with the Commissioner of Revenue. (§ 10-2B-15.42)	Yes, if reciprocal treatment is accorded Alabama banks. (§ 10-2B-15.41(a)(2)) Nonresident bank must file a verified statement with the Commissioner of Revenue. (§ 10-2B-15.42)
Alaska	Yes, if qualified doing business in Alaska under § 06.26.010(8) or otherwise as indicated in § 43.31.300 that a nonresident may serve as executor for a nonresident decedent if that executor is also the executor of the decedent's estate in the state of decedent's domicile. The provision, however, does not specifically address the appointment of a foreign executor when the decedent is an Alaska resident.	No specific authorization. But see § 13.16.110 for informal appointment. See also §§ 13.21.030 and 13.21.035 allowing the duly authorized personal representative to serve in Alaska if there is no local administration or application for one.	Is required to qualify as a foreign corporation doing business in the state if it maintains the principal place of administration of any trust in the state. (§ 13.36.025)	Yes. (§§ 06.26.010(8), 43.31.300) See also §§ 13.21.030 and 13.21.035 allowing the duly authorized personal representative to serve in Alaska if there is no local administration or application for one.	No specific author ization. But see § 13.16.110 for informal appointment. See also §§ 13.21.030 and 13.21.035 allowing the duly authorized personal representative to serve in Alaska if there is no local administration or application for one.	Is required to qualify as a foreign corporation doing business inthe state if it maintains the principal place of administration of any trust in the state. (§ 13.36.025)

Table 3.03
Nonresident Bank as Executor, Administrator, or Testamentary Trustee *(continued)*

	Nonresident Bank as Executor	*Nonresident Bank as Administrator*	*Nonresident Bank as Testamentary Trustee*	*Nonresident Bank as Ancillary Executor*	*Nonresident Bank as Ancillary Administrator*	*Nonresident Bank as Ancillary Testamentary Trustee*
Arizona	No. (§ 14-3203(F)(3))	No. (§ 14-3203(F)(3))	Yes. (§§ 14-7202, 14-7205, 14-7305)	No. (§ 14-3203(F)(3))	No. (§ 14-3203(F)(3))	Yes. (§§ 14-7202, 14-7205, 14-7305)
Arkansas	Yes, if authorized to act as a fiduciary in the state. (§ 28-48-101(b)(4))	Yes, if authorized to act as a fiduciary in the state. (§ 28-48-101(b)(4))	Yes. (§ 4-31-303)	Yes, if the person is a personal representative in the domiciliary state and a resident agent is appointed. (§§ 28-42-102, 28-42-104) Alternatively, the same as Executor, as long as the domiciliary representative is given notice and is not appointed instead. (§ 28-42-102(c)) In any event, all ancillary appointments of nonresidents appear to be discretionary with the courts. See Phillips v. Sherrod Estate, 453 S.W.2d 60 (1970). The bank, if a corporation, does not have to be authorized to do business in the state. (§ 28-42-102(a)(2))	Yes, if the person is a personal representative in the domiciliary state and a resident agent is appointed. (§§ 28-42-102, 28-42-104) Alternatively, the same as Executor, as long as the domiciliary representative is given notice and is not appointed instead. (§ 28-42-102(c)) In any event, all ancillary appointments of nonresidents appear to be discretionary with the courts. See Phillips v. Sherrod Estate, 453 S.W.2d 60 (1970). The bank, if a corporation, does not have to be authorized to do business in the state. (§ 28-42-102(a)(2))	Yes, reciprocal treatment. (§ 4-31-303)

California	Yes, if authorized to conduct business of a trust company in the state. (Prob. §§ 83 and notes, 300, 8572)	Yes, if authorized to conduct business of a trust company in the state. (Prob. §§ 83 and notes, 300, 8461(r), 8402)	Yes, if authorized to conduct business of a trust company in the state. (Prob. §§ 83 and notes, 300, 15642; Fin. § 1503)	Yes, if authorized to conduct business of a trust company in the state. (Prob. §§ 83 and notes, 300, 12540, 12541)	Yes, if authorized to conduct business of a trust company in the state. (Prob. §§ 83 and notes, 300, 12540, 12541)	Yes, if authorized to conduct business of a trust company in the state. (Prob. §§ 83 and notes, 300, 15642: Fin. § 1503)
Colorado	Yes, but may first be required to obtain a certificate of authority to transact business. (§§ 15-10-201(38), 15-12-203) The relevant provision is found at § 7-115-101 etseq.	Yes, but may first be required to obtain a certificate of authority to transact business. (§§ 15-12-203, 15-10-201(38)) The relevant provision is found at § 7-115-101 et seq.	Yes, but first may be required to obtain a certificate of authority to transact business or qualify as a foreign corporation doing business. (§ 15-16-105) The relevant provision is found at § 7-115-101 et seq.	Yes, but may first be required to obtain a certificate of authority to transact business. (§§ 15-12-203, 15-13-205) The relevant provision is found at § 7-115-101 etseq.	Yes, but may first be required to obtain a certificate of authority to transact business. (§§ 15-12-203, 15-13-205) The relevant provision is found at § 7-115-101 et seq.	Yes, but first may be required to obtain a certificate of authority to transact business or qualify as a foreign corporation doing business. (§ 15-16-105) The relevant provision is found at § 7-115-101 et seq.
Connecticut	Yes, if reciprocal treatment is accorded Connecticut banks. (§ 45a-206)	Uncertain	Yes, if reciprocal treatment accorded Connecticut banks. (§ 45a-206)	Yes, if reciprocal treatment is accorded Connecticut banks. (§ 45a-206)	Uncertain	Yes, if reciprocal treatment accorded Connecticut banks. (§ 45a-206)
Delaware	Yes, if reciprocal treatment accorded Delaware corporations, (8 § 380) and after filing in the office of the Register of Wills an irrevocable power of attorney designating the Register an agent (12 § 1506)	Yes, if reciprocal treatment accorded Delaware corporations, (8 § 380) and after filing in the office of the Register of Wills an irrevocable power of attorney designating the Register an agent (12 § 1506)	Yes, if reciprocal treatment accorded Delaware corporations. (8 § 380)	Yes, if reciprocal treatment accorded Delaware corporations. (8 § 380)	Yes, if reciprocal treatment accorded Delaware corporations. (8 § 380)	Yes, if reciprocal treatment accorded Delaware corporations. (8 § 380)

Table 3.03
Nonresident Bank as Executor, Administrator, or Testamentary Trustee *(continued)*

	Nonresident Bank as Executor	*Nonresident Bank as Administrator*	*Nonresident Bank as Testamentary Trustee*	*Nonresident Bank as Ancillary Executor*	*Nonresident Bank as Ancillary Administrator*	*Nonresident Bank as Ancillary Testamentary Trustee*
District of Columbia	Yes. (§§ 26-1301, 26-1309, 26-1310, 26-1335)	Yes. (§§ 26-1301, 26-1309, 26-1310, 26-1335)	Yes. (§§ 26-1301, 26-1309, 26-1310, 26-1335)	Yes. (§§ 26-1301, 26-1309, 26-1310, 26-1335, 20-341, 20-342)	Yes. (§§ 26-1301, 26-1309, 26-1310, 26-1335, 20-341, 20-342)	Yes. (§§ 26-1301, 26-1309, 26-1310, 26-1335)
Florida	No. (§ 660.41(1))	No. (§ 660.41(1))	No. (§ 660.41(2))	Yes. (§ 660.41(1))	Yes. (§ 660.41(1))	Yes. (§ 660.41(1)) If personal representative of the estate of nonresident decedent is a corporation duly authorized and qualified as personal representative in jurisdiction of decedent's domicile, it may maintain actions in Florida courts, etc. (§ 734.101)
Georgia	Yes, if it is a bank organized under or a national banking association having its principal place of business in state bordering on Georgia (Alabama, Florida, North Carolina, South Carolina, Tennessee) and that state gives reciprocal treatment to Georgia banks. (§§ 53-12-390, 53-12-391)	Yes, if it is a bank organized under or a national banking association having its principal place of business in state bordering on Georgia (Alabama, Florida, North Carolina, South Carolina, Tennessee) and that state gives reciprocal treatment to Georgia banks. (§§ 53-12-390, 53-12-391)	Yes, if it is a bank organized under or a national banking association having its principal place of business in state bordering on Georgia (Alabama, Florida, North Carolina, South Carolina, Tennessee) and that state gives reciprocal treatment to Georgia banks. (§§ 53-12-390, 53-12-391)	Yes, if it is a bank organized under or a national banking association having its principal place of business in state bordering on Georgia (Alabama, Florida, North Carolina, South Carolina, Tennessee) and that state gives reciprocal treatment to Georgia banks. (§§ 53-12-390, 53-12-391)	Yes, if it is a bank organized under or a national banking association having its principal place of business in state bordering on Georgia (Alabama, Florida, North Carolina, South Carolina, Tennessee) and that state gives reciprocal treatment to Georgia banks. (§§ 53-12-390, 53-12-391)	Yes, if it is a bank organized under or a national banking association having its principal place of business in state bordering on Georgia (Alabama, Florida, North Carolina, South Carolina, Tennessee) and that state gives reciprocal treatment to Georgia banks. (§§ 53-12-390, 53-12-391)

Hawaii	Yes, if named in will. (§ 560:3-203(a)(1)) Any bank, after having obtained approval (§ 412:5-205), can serve as a trust company. A trust company can serve as a personal representative or trustee. (§ 412:8-201)	Identical to prior column, except a court appointment of an administrator would only occur if persons with priority under the statute could not serve or were objected to by persons with a right to object. (§ 560:3-203)	Yes, if named in will. (§ 560:3-203(a)(1)) Any bank, after having obtained approval (§ 412:5-205), can serve as a trust company. A trust company can serve as a personal representative or trustee. (§ 412:8-201)	Same as first column. If appointed at domicile, a foreign personal representative may exercise all powers of a local representative.	Same as second column. If appointed at domicile, a foreign personal representative may exercise all powers of a local representative.	Yes, there is no statutory prohibition. (See § 560:7-203 concerning foreign trusts in general)
Idaho	Yes, but may first be required to procure a certificate of authority to transact business. (§§ 15-3-203, 30-1-1501, 30-1-1505(1))	Yes, but may first be required to procure a certificate of authority to transact business. (§§ 15-3-203, 30-1-1501, 30-1-1505(1))	Yes, but first may be required to procure a certificate of authority to transact business or qualify as a foreign corporation doing business. (§§ 15-7-105, 30-1-1501)	Yes, but may first be required to procure a certificate of authority to transact business. (§§ 15-3-203, 30-1-1501, 30-1-1505(1))	Yes, but may first be required to procure a certificate of authority to transact business. (§§ 15-3-203, 30-1-1501, 30-1-1505(1))	Yes, but first may be required to procure a certificate of authority to transact business or qualify as a foreign corporation doing business. (§§ 15-7-105, 30-1-1501)
Illinois	Yes, if the corporation is authorized by the laws of the state of its organization or domicile to act as a fiduciary in that state and reciprocal treatment is accorded Illinois banks. (205 ILCS § 620/4-2) Prior to the time any corporation can act, it must obtain from the Commissioner of Banks and Real Estate a certificate of authority. (205 ILCS § 620/4-5)	Yes, if the corporation is authorized by the laws of the state of its organization or domicile to act as a fiduciary in that state and reciprocal treatment is accorded Illinois banks. (205 ILCS § 620/4-2) Prior to the time any corporation can act, it must obtain from the Commissioner of Banks and Real Estate a certificate of authority. (205 ILCS § 620/4-5)	Yes, if the corporation is authorized by the laws of the state of its organization or domicile to act as a fiduciary in that state and reciprocal treatment is accorded Illinois banks. (205 ILCS § 620/4-2) Prior to the time any corporation can act, it must obtain from the Commissioner of Banks and Real Estate a certificate of authority. (205 ILCS § 620/4-5)	Yes, if the corporation is authorized by the laws of the state of its organization or domicile to act as a fiduciary in that state and reciprocal treatment is accorded Illinois banks. (205 ILCS § 620/4-2) Prior to the time any corporation can act, it must obtain from the Commissioner of Banks and Real Estate a certificate of authority. (205 ILCS § 620/4-5)	Yes, if the corporation is authorized by the laws of the state of its organization or domicile to act as a fiduciary in that state and reciprocal treatment is accorded Illinois banks. (205 ILCS § 620/4-2) Prior to the time any corporation can act, it must obtain from the Commissioner of Banks and Real Estate a cer tificate of authority. (205 ILCS § 620/4-5)	Yes, if the corporation is authorized by the laws of the state of its organization or domicile to act as a fiduciary in that state and reciprocal treatment is accorded Illinois banks. (205 ILCS § 620/4-2) Prior to the time any corporation can act, it must obtain from the Commissioner of Banks and Real Estate a certificate of authority. (205 ILCS § 620/4-5)

Table 3.03
Nonresident Bank as Executor, Administrator, or Testamentary Trustee *(continued)*

	Nonresident Bank as Executor	*Nonresident Bank as Administrator*	*Nonresident Bank as Testamentary Trustee*	*Nonresident Bank as Ancillary Executor*	*Nonresident Bank as Ancillary Administrator*	*Nonresident Bank as Ancillary Testamentary Trustee*
Indiana	Yes, if serving jointly with a resident. (§ 29-1-10-1(c))	Yes, if serving jointly with a resident. (§ 29-1-10-1(c))	Yes. The corporation "must have the power to take, hold, and deal with property for its own benefit and have the power to act as a trustee." Specifically, a national bank can serve if its principal place of business is in Indiana or a state or territory, or D.C., if the latter state grants Indiana banks and trust companies authority to act in similar fiduciary capacities. (§ 28-1-12-1(b)(2)(B)) See also § 30-4-2-11(b).	There is no statutory prohibition. However, § 29-2-1-1 states that a "local personal representative includes any personal representative appointed in this state pursuant to appointment proceedings described in article 1 of this title." That could include § 29-1-10-1(c), requiring joint appointment of a resident. Note that if a domiciliary foreign personal representative has established his appointment the domiciliary personal repre sentative can act like a local personal representative in Indiana. (§§ 29-2-1-5, 29-2-1-6)	There is no statutory prohibition. However, § 29-2-1-1 states that a "local personal representative includes any personal representative appointed in this state pursuant to appointment proceedings described in article 1 of this title." That could include § 29-1-10-1(c), requiring joint appointment of a resident. Note that if a domiciliary foreign personal representative has established his appointment the domiciliary personal repre sentative can act like a local personal representative in Indiana. (§§ 29-2-1-5, 29-2-1-6)	Yes. The corporation "must have the power to take, hold, and deal with property for its own benefit and have the power to act as a trustee." Specifically, a national bank can serve if its principal place of business is in Indiana or a state or territory, or D.C., if the latter state grants Indiana banks and trust companies authority to act in similar fiduciary capacities. (§ 28-1-12-1(b)(2)(B)) See also § 30-4-2-11(b).
Iowa	Yes, if reciprocal treatment is accorded Iowa banks. (§ 633.64)	Yes, if reciprocal treatment is accorded Iowa banks. (§ 633.64)	Yes, if reciprocal treatment is accorded Iowa banks. (§ 633.64)	Yes, if reciprocal treatment is accorded Iowa banks. (§§ 633.64, 633.502)	Yes, if reciprocal treatment is accorded Iowa banks. (§§ 633.64, 633.502)	Yes, if reciprocal treatment is accorded Iowa banks. (§§ 633.64, 633.502)

Kansas	Yes, if it is organized under the laws of, and has a principal place of business in, another state that permits a bank or other corporation that is similarly organized in Kansas to act in a like fiduciary capacity in the other state under similar conditions (§ 59-1701 (a)(3)) and a resident agent is appointed (§ 59-1706). An officer, employee, or agent of a bank or corporation which is not authorized to act as a fiduciary in Kansas may himself or herself not act as a fiduciary in Kansas, whether a resident or nonresi dent of Kansas, if such person is acting as a fiduciary on behalf of such bank or corporation. (§ 59-1701(b))	Yes, if it is organized under the laws of, and has a principal place of business in, another state that permits a bank or other corporation that is similarly organized in Kansas to act in a like fiduciary capacity in the other state under similar conditions (§ 59-1701 (a)(3)) and a resident agent is appointed (§ 59-1706). An officer, employee, or agent of a bank or corporation which is not authorized to act as a fiduciary in Kansas may himself or herself not act as a fiduciary in Kansas, whether a resident or nonresi dent of Kansas, if such person is acting as a fiduciary on behalf of such bank or corporation. (§ 59-1701(b))	Yes, if it is organized under the laws of, and has a principal place of business in, another state that permits a bank or other corporation that is similarly organized in Kansas to act in a like fiduciary capacity in the other state under similar conditions (§ 59-1701(a)(3)) and a resident agent is appointed (§ 59-1706). An officer, employee, or agent of a bank or corporation which is not authorized to act as a fiduciary in Kansas may himself or herself not act as a fiduciary in Kansas, whether a resident or nonresident of Kansas, if such person is acting as a fiduciary on behalf of such bank or corporation. (§ 59-1701(b))	Yes, if it is organized under the laws of, and has a principal place of business in, another state that permits a bank or other corporation that is similarly organized in Kansas to act in a like fiduciary capacity in the other state under similar conditions (§ 59-1701(a)(3)) and a resident agent is appointed (§ 59-1706). An officer, employee, or agent of a bank or corporation which is not authorized to act as a fiduciary in Kansas may himself or herself not act as a fiduciary in Kansas, whether a resident or nonresident of Kansas, if such person is acting as a fiduciary on behalf of such bank or corporation. (§ 59-1701(b))	Yes, if it is organized under the laws of, and has a principal place of business in, another state that permits a bank or other corporation that is similarly organized in Kansas to act in a like fiduciary capacity in the other state under similar conditions (§ 59-1701(a)(3)) and a resident agent is appointed (§ 59-1706). An officer, employee, or agent of a bank or corporation which is not authorized to act as a fiduciary in Kansas may himself or herself not act as a fiduciary in Kansas, whether a resident or nonresident of Kansas, if such person is acting as a fiduciary on behalf of such bank or corporation. (§ 59-1701(b))	Yes, if it is organized under the laws of, and has a principal place of business in, another state that permits a bank or other corporation that is similarly organized in Kansas to act in a like fiduciary capacity in the other state under similar conditions (§ 59-1701(a)(3)) and a resident agent is appointed (§ 59-1706). An officer, employee, or agent of a bank or cor poration which is not authorized to act as a fiduciary in Kansas may himself or herself not act as a fiduciary in Kansas, whether a resident or nonresident of Kansas, if such person is acting as a fiduciary on behalf of such bank or corporation. (§ 59-1701(b))
Kentucky	No. (§ 395.005)	No. (§ 395.005)	Yes. (§ 395.005, notes)	No. (§ 395.005)	No. (§ 395.005)	Yes. (§ 395.005, notes)
Louisiana	Yes; resident agent must be appointed. (Civ. Code Pro. arts. 3097, 5251(11); § 12:308)	Yes; resident agent must be appointed. (Civ. Code Pro. arts. 3097, 5251(11); § 12:308)	Yes. (§§ 9:1783, 12:308)	Yes; resident agent must be appointed. (Civ. Code Pro. arts. 3097, 5251(11), 3402, 3404; § 12:308)	Yes; resident agent must be appointed. (Civ. Code Pro. arts. 3097, 5251(11), 3402, 3404; § 12:308)	Yes. (§§ 9:1783, 12:308

Table 3.03
Nonresident Bank as Executor, Administrator, or Testamentary Trustee *(continued)*

	Nonresident Bank as Executor	*Nonresident Bank as Administrator*	*Nonresident Bank as Testamentary Trustee*	*Nonresident Bank as Ancillary Executor*	*Nonresident Bank as Ancillary Administrator*	*Nonresident Bank as Ancillary Testamentary Trustee*
Maine	Yes, if reciprocal treatment is accorded Maine banks. (18 § 4161)	Yes, if reciprocal treatment is accorded Maine banks. (18 § 4161)	Yes, if reciprocal treatment is accorded Maine banks. (18 § 4161)	Yes, if reciprocal treatment is accorded Maine banks. (18 § 4161)	Yes, if reciprocal treatment is accorded Maine banks. (18 § 4161)	Yes, if reciprocal treatment is accorded Maine banks. (18 § 4161)
Maryland	Yes. (Est. & Trusts § 5-105)	Yes. (Est. & Trusts § 5-105)	Yes, if resident agent is appointed and if reciprocal treatment is accorded Maryland banks. (Est. & Trusts § 14-110)	Yes, although a foreign personal representative is not required to take out letters in Maryland. (Est. & Trusts § 5-501)	Yes, although a foreign personal representative is not required to take out letters in Maryland. (Est. & Trusts § 5-501)	Yes, if resident agent is appointed and if reciprocal treatment is accorded Maryland banks. (Est. & Trusts § 14-110)
Massachusetts	Yes, if reciprocal treatment is accorded Massachusetts banks. (167 § 43)	Yes, if reciprocal treatment is accorded Massachusetts banks. (167 § 43)	Yes, if reciprocal treatment is accorded Massachusetts banks. (167 § 43)	Yes, if reciprocal treatment is accorded Massachusetts banks. (167 § 43)	Yes, if reciprocal treatment is accorded Massachusetts banks. (167 § 43)	Yes, if reciprocal treatment is accorded Massachusetts banks. (167 § 43)
Michigan	There is no specific prohibition (§ 700.3601, § 700.4201)	See previous column.	There is no specific mention of banks or corporations. (§ 700.7105)	There is no specific mention of banks or corporations. See § 700.4201 indicating that ancillary proceedings may not even be necessary.	See previous column.	There is no specific mention of banks or corporations. (§ 700.7105)
Minnesota	The bank must have its principal office in a state that accords reciprocal treatment	The bank must have its principal office in a state that accords reciprocal treatment	The bank must have its principal office in a state that accords reciprocal treatment	The bank must have its principal office in a state that accords reciprocal treatment	The bank must have its principal office in a state that accords reciprocal treatment	The bank must have its principal office in a state that accords reciprocal treatment to Minnesota

	to Minnesota banks and must designate Secretary of State as attorney for service of process. (§ 303.25)	to Minnesota banks and must designate Secretary of State as attorney for service of process. (§ 303.25)	to Minnesota banks and must designate Secretary of State as attorney for service of process. (§ 303.25)	to Minnesota banks and must designate Secretary of State as attorney for service of process. (§ 303.25)	to Minnesota banks and must designate Secretary of State as attorney for service of process. (§ 303.25)	banks and must designate Secretary of State as attorney for service of process. (§ 303.25)
Mississippi	Yes, if reciprocal treatment is accorded Mississippi banks and must appoint Secretary of State as service agent. (§ 81-5-43)	Yes, if reciprocal treatment is accorded Mississippi banks and must appoint Secretary of State as service agent. (§ 81-5-43)	Yes, if reciprocal treatment is accorded Mississippi banks and must appoint Secretary of State as service agent. (§ 81-5-43)	Yes, if reciprocal treatment is accorded Mississippi banks and must appoint Secretary of State as service agent. (§ 81-5-43)	Yes, if reciprocal treatment is accorded Mississippi banks and must appoint Secretary of State as service agent. (§ 81-5-43)	Yes, if reciprocal treatment is accorded Mississippi banks and must appoint Secretary of State as service agent. (§ 81-5-43)
Missouri	Yes, if reciprocal treatment is accorded Missouri banks and (a) if the bank is organized under another state's laws, or (b) if the bank is a national bank. (§§ 362.600, 473.117)	Yes, if reciprocal treatment is accorded Missouri banks and (a) if the bank is organized under another state's laws, or (b) if the bank is a national bank. (§§ 362.600, 473.117)	Yes, if reciprocal treatment is accorded Missouri banks and (a) if the bank is organized under another state's laws, or (b) if the bank is a national bank. (§§ 362.600, 473.117)	Yes, if reciprocal treatment is accorded Missouri banks and (a) if the bank is organized under another state's laws, or (b) if the bank is a national bank. (§§ 362.600, 473.117)	Yes, if reciprocal treatment is accorded Missouri banks and (a) if the bank is organized under another state's laws, or (b) if the bank is a national bank. (§§ 362.600, 473.117)	Yes, if reciprocal treatment is accorded Missouri banks and (a) if the bank is organized under another state's laws, or (b) if the bank is a national bank. (§§ 362.600, 473.117)
Montana	Yes, (§ 72-3-501) though may have to qualify to do business (§ 35-1-1026).	Yes, (§ 72-3-501) though may have to qualify to do business (§ 35-1-1026).	This possibility is recognized. (§ 72-35-503(2))	Yes, (§§ 72-3-506, 72-4-201) though may have to qualify to do business (§ 35-1-1026).	Yes (§§ 72-4-201 etseq., 72-3-506) though may have to qualify to do business (§ 35-1-1026).	This possibility is recognized. (§ 72-35-503(2))
Nebraska	Yes. (§ 30-2412, 8-158)	Yes. (§ 30-2412, 8-158))	Yes, though may have to qualify to do business. (§ 30-2805, renumbered § 30-3820, eff. Jan. 1, 2005)	Yes. (§§ 30-2412(g), 30-2505, 30-2506, 30-2508, 8158)	Yes. (§§ 30-2412(g), 30-2505, 30-2506, 30-2508, 8-158)	Yes, though may have to qualify to do business. (§ 30-2805, renumbered § 30-3820, eff. Jan. 1, 2005)
Nevada	§ 138.020 provides that a banking corporation, the principal place of business of	§ 139.010 provides that a banking corporation, the principal place of business of	Yes, since there is no statutory prohibition. (§ 163.020(4))	§ 138.020 provides that a banking corporation, the principal place of business of	§ 139.010 provides that a banking corporation, the principal place of business of	Yes, since there is no statutory prohibition. (§ 163.020(4))
	(cont'd)	*(cont'd)*		*(cont'd)*	*(cont'd)*	

Table 3.03
Nonresident Bank as Executor, Administrator, or Testamentary Trustee *(continued)*

	Nonresident Bank as Executor	*Nonresident Bank as Administrator*	*Nonresident Bank as Testamentary Trustee*	*Nonresident Bank as Ancillary Executor*	*Nonresident Bank as Ancillary Administrator*	*Nonresident Bank as Ancillary Testamentary Trustee*
Nevada *(cont'd)*	which is not Nevada, may serve as an executor, but only if it associates as co-executor a banking corporation the principal place of business of which is Nevada.	which is not Nevada, may serve as an administrator, but only if it associates as co-administrator a banking corporation the principal place of business of which is Nevada.		which is not Nevada, may serve as an executor, but only if it associates as co-executor a banking corporation the principal place of business of which is Nevada.	which is not Nevada, may serve as an administrator, but only if it associates as co-administrator a banking corporation the principal place of business of which is Nevada.	
New Hampshire	Yes, if the state in which such bank has its principal place of business accords reciprocal treatment to New Hampshire banks. (§§ 390:13, 390:15)	Yes, if the state in which such bank has its principal place of business accords reciprocal treatment to New Hampshire banks. (§§ 390:13, 390:15)	Yes, if the state in which such bank has its principal place of business accords reciprocal treatment to New Hampshire banks. (§§ 390:13, 390:15)	Yes, if the state in which such bank has its principal place of business accords reciprocal treatment to New Hampshire banks. (§§ 390:13, 390:15)	Yes, if the state in which such bank has its principal place of business accords reciprocal treatment to New Hampshire banks. (§§ 390:13, 390:15)	Yes, if the state in which such bank has its principal place of business accords reciprocal treatment to New Hampshire banks. (§§ 390:13, 390:15)
New Jersey	Yes, if named in a decedent's will or codicil, and if the state in which such bank has its principal office accords reciprocal treatment to New Jersey banks. (§ 17:9A-316) There may also be a basis if the bank is operating an office in New Jersey. (*Id.*; § 17:9A-418 et seq.)	No. (§ 17:9A-316) But there may be a basis if the bank is operating an office in New Jersey. (*Id.*; § 17:9A-418 et seq.)	Yes, if named in a decedent's will or codicil, if named in a dece dent's will or codicil, and if the state in which such bank has its principal office accords reciprocal treatment to New Jersey banks. (§ 17:9A-316) There may also be a basis if the bank is operating an office in New Jersey. (*Id.*; § 17:9A-418 et seq.)	Yes, if named in a decedent's will or codicil, if named in a dece dent's will or codicil, and if the state in which such bank has its principal office accords reciprocal treatment to New Jersey banks. (§ 17:9A-316) There may also be a basis if the bank is operating an office in New Jersey. (*Id.*; § 17:9A-418 et seq.)	No. (§ 17:9A-316) But there may be a basis if the bank is operating an office in New Jersey. (*Id.*; § 17:9A-418 et seq.)	Yes, if named in a decedent's will or codicil, if named in a dece dent's will or codicil, and if the state in which such bank has its principal office accords reciprocal treatment to New Jersey banks. (§ 17:9A-316) There may also be a basis if the bank is operating an office in New Jersey. (*Id.*; § 17:9A-418 et seq.)

New Mexico	Yes, if qualified to do business in New Mexico. (§§ 45-3-203, 53-17-1)	Yes, if qualified to do business in New Mexico. (§§ 45-3-203, 53-17-1	Yes, though may have to qualify to do business. (§§ 45-7-105, 53-17-1)	Yes. (§§ 45-4-204, 45-4-207, 45-3-203, 53-17-1)	Yes. (§§ 45-4-204, 45-4-207, 53-17-1, 45-3-203)	Yes, though may have to qualify to do business. (§§ 45-7-105, 53-17-1)
New York	Yes, if reciprocal treatment is accorded New York banks. (Banking Law § 131(3))	Yes, if reciprocal treatment is accorded New York banks. (Banking Law § 131(3))	Yes, if reciprocal treatment is accorded New York banks. (Banking Law § 131(3))	Yes, if reciprocal treatment is accorded New York banks, (Banking Law § 131 (3)) or according to the court's discretion (Surr. Ct. Proc. Act § 1608(6)).	Yes, if reciprocal treatment is accorded New York banks, (Banking Law § 131 (3)) or according to the court's discretion (Surr. Ct. Proc. Act § 1608(6)).	Yes, if reciprocal treatment is accorded New York banks. (Banking Law § 131(3))
North Carolina	Yes, if under will and a resident agent is appointed. (§§ 55-15-05, 28A-4-2(4))	Yes, if under will. (§ 55-15-05)	Yes, if under will and a resident agent is appointed. (§§ 55-15-05, 28A-4-2(4))	Yes. (§ 28A-26-3)	Yes. (§ 28A-26-3)	Although there is provi sion for appointing ancillary trustees where assets of a North Carolina trust will be present in other states, there is no provision covering the converse situation. (§§ 35A-1280, 1281)
North Dakota	Yes, after filing copy of charter and power of attorney with Secretary of State if reciprocal treatment is accorded North Dakota banks. (§§ 6-08-25, 6-08-26) There is a $50 filing fee and a $25 fee for the for warding of notice or service of process by the Secretary of State to the foreign bank.	Yes, after filing copy of charter and power of attorney with Secretary of State if reciprocal treatment is accorded North Dakota banks. (§§ 6-08-25, 6-08-26) There is a $50 filing fee and a $25 fee for the for warding of notice or service of process by the Secretary of State to the foreign bank.	Yes, but may have to qualify to do business in the state. (§ 30.1-32-05) See also § 6-08-25 (includes foreign L.L.C.).	Yes, after filing copy of charter and power of attorney with Secretary of State if reciprocal treatment is accorded North Dakota banks. (§§ 6-08-25, 6-08-26) There is a $50 filing fee and a $25 fee for the for warding of notice or service of process by the Secretary of State to the foreign bank.	Yes, after filing copy of charter and power of attorney with Secretary of State if reciprocal treatment is accorded North Dakota banks. (§§ 6-08-25, 6-08-26) There is a $50 filing fee and a $25 fee for the for warding of notice or service of process by the Secretary of State to the foreign bank.	Yes, but may have to qualify to do business in the state. (§ 30.1-32-05) See also § 6-08-25 (includes foreign L.L.C.).

Table 3.03
Nonresident Bank as Executor, Administrator, or Testamentary Trustee *(continued)*

	Nonresident Bank as Executor	*Nonresident Bank as Administrator*	*Nonresident Bank as Testamentary Trustee*	*Nonresident Bank as Ancillary Executor*	*Nonresident Bank as Ancillary Administrator*	*Nonresident Bank as Ancillary Testamentary Trustee*
Ohio	A foreign corporation may be licensed to do business in Ohio as a trust company for one year after meeting extensive filing and fee requirements. (§§ 1119.08, 1119.17, 2109.21 note 3)	A foreign corporation may be licensed to do business in Ohio as a trust company for one year after meeting extensive filing and fee requirements. (§§ 1119.08, 1119.17)	A foreign corporation may be licensed to do business in Ohio as a trust company for one year after meeting extensive filing and fee requirements. (§§ 1119.08, 1119.17)	Yes, if the other state in which the person resides has statutes or rules that authorize the appointment of a nonresident person who is not related to the maker of a will by consanguinity or affinity. (§ 2109.21(B)(1))	Yes, if reciprocal treatment is accorded Ohio banks. (§ 1109.02)	A foreign corporation may be licensed to do business in Ohio as a trust company for one year after meeting extensive filing and fee requirements. (§§ 1119.08, 1119.17)
Oklahoma	Yes, if reciprocal treatment is accorded Oklahoma banks. (6 § 1002)	Yes, if reciprocal treatment is accorded Oklahoma banks. (6 § 1002)	Yes, if reciprocal treatment is accorded Oklahoma banks. (6 § 1002)	Yes, if reciprocal treatment is accorded Oklahoma banks. (6 § 1002)	Yes, if reciprocal treatment is accorded Oklahoma banks. (6 § 1002)	Yes, if reciprocal treatment is accorded Oklahoma banks. (6 § 1002)
Oregon	Yes. (§§ 113.085, 113.087)	Yes. (§§ 113.085, 113.087)	Yes, there is no statutory prohibition.	Yes. (§§ 113.085, 113.087)	Yes. (§§ 113.085, 113.087)	Yes, there is no statutory prohibition.
Pennsylvania	Yes, if reciprocal treatment is accorded Pennsylvania banks. (7 § 106) In addition, there must be compliance withs minimal capital requirements. (7 § 106(b)(ii))	Yes, if reciprocal treatment is accorded Pennsylvania banks. (7 § 106) In addition, there must be compliance with minimal capital requirements. (7 § 106(b)(ii))	Yes, if reciprocal treatment is accorded Pennsylvania banks. (7 § 106) In addition, there must be compliance with minimal capital requirements. (7 § 106(b)(ii))	Yes, if reciprocal treatment is accorded Pennsylvania banks. (7 § 106) In addition, there must be compliance with minimal capital requirements. (7 § 106(b)(ii))	Yes, if reciprocal treatment is accorded Pennsylvania banks. (7 § 106) In addition, there must be compliance with minimal capital requirements. (7 § 106(b)(ii))	Yes, if reciprocal treatment is accorded Pennsylvania banks. (7 § 106) In addition, there must be compliance with minimal capital requirements. (7 § 106(b)(ii))
Rhode Island	Yes, if appointment of state official as true and lawful attorney for receipt of process. (§ 19-3.1-6)	Yes, if appointment of state official as true and lawful attorney for receipt of process. (§ 19-3.1-6)	Yes, if appointment of state official as true and lawful attorney for receipt of process. (§ 19-3.1-6)	Yes, if appointment of state official as true and lawful attorney for receipt of process. (§ 19-3.1-6)	Yes, if appointment of state official as true and lawful attorney for receipt of process. (§ 19-3.1-6)	Yes, if appointment of state official as true and lawful attorney for receipt of process. (§ 19-3.1-6)

South Carolina	No and neither may officers, employees, or agents of such corporations if acting onbehalf of the corporation. (§ 62-3-203 (e)(3))	No and neither may officers, employees, or agents of such corporations if acting onbehalf of the corporation. (§ 62-3-203 (e)(3))	Yes. Implied. (§ 15-9-450)	Yes. (§ 62-3-203) Applies only to estates of nonresident decedents. (§ 62-3-203(f))	Yes. (§ 62-3-203) Applies only to estates of nonresident decedents. (§ 62-3-203(f))	Yes. Implied. (§ 15-9-450)
South Dakota	Yes, if reciprocal treatment is accorded South Dakota banks and if filing provisions are met, especially naming the office of the Secretary of State as agent for the receipt of process. (§§ 51A-5-7–51A-5-10)	Yes, if reciprocal treatment is accorded South Dakota banks and if filing provisions are met, especially naming the office of the Secretary of State as agent for the receipt of process. (§§ 51A-5-7–51A-5-10)	Yes, if reciprocal treatment is accorded South Dakota banks and if filing provisions are met, especially naming the office of the Secretary of State as agent for the receipt of process. (§§ 51A-5-7–51A-5-10)	Yes, if reciprocal treatment is accorded South Dakota banks and if filing provisions are met, especially naming the office of the Secretary of State as agent for the receipt of process. (§§ 51A-5-7–51A-5-10)	Yes, if reciprocal treatment is accorded South Dakota banks and if filing provisions are met, especially naming the office of the Secretary of State as agent for the receipt of process. (§§ 51A-5-7–51A-5-10)	Yes, if reciprocal treatment is accorded South Dakota banks and if filing provisions are met, especially naming the office of the Secretary of State as agent for the receipt of process. (§§ 51A-5-7–51A-5-10)
Tennessee	Yes, if reciprocal treatment is accorded Tennessee banks. (§ 35-50-107(a)(2)(A)) The secretary of state must be appointed as agent for service of process. (§ 35-50-107(b)(2)) See also § 30-1-116.	Yes, if reciprocal treatment is accorded Tennessee banks. (§ 35-50-107(a)(2)(A)) The secretary of state must be appointed as agent for service of process. (§ 35-50-107(b)(2)) See also § 30-1-116.	Yes, if reciprocal treatment is accorded Tennessee banks. (§ 35-50-107(a)(2)(A)) The secretary of state must be appointed as agent for service of process. (§ 35-50-107(b)(2)) See also § 30-1-116.	Yes, if reciprocal treatment is accorded Tennessee banks. (§ 35-50-107(a)(2)(A)) The secretary of state must be appointed as agent for service of process. (§ 35-50-107(b)(2)) See also § 30-1-116.	Yes, if reciprocal treatment is accorded Tennessee banks. (§ 35-50-107(a)(2)(A)) The secretary of state must be appointed as agent for service of process. (§ 35-50-107(b)(2)) See also § 30-1-116.	Yes, if reciprocal treatment is accorded Tennessee banks. (§ 35-50-107(a)(2)(A)) The secretary of state must be appointed as agent for service of process. (§ 35-50-107(b)(2)) See also § 30-1-116.
Texas	Yes, if reciprocal treatment is accorded Texas banks and if filing provisions are met. (Prob. § 105A)	Yes, if reciprocal treatment is accorded Texas banks and if filing provisions are met. (Prob. § 105A)	Yes, if reciprocal treatment is accorded Texas banks and if filing provisions are met. (Prob. § 105A)	Yes, if reciprocal treatment is accorded Texas banks and if filing provisions are met. (Prob. § 105A)	Yes, if reciprocal treatment is accorded Texas banks and if filing provisions are met. (Prob. § 105A)	Yes, if reciprocal treatment is accorded Texas banks and if filling provisions are met. (Prob. § 105A)

Table 3.03
Nonresident Bank as Executor, Administrator, or Testamentary Trustee *(continued)*

	Nonresident Bank as Executor	*Nonresident Bank as Administrator*	*Nonresident Bank as Testamentary Trustee*	*Nonresident Bank as Ancillary Executor*	*Nonresident Bank as Ancillary Administrator*	*Nonresident Bank as Ancillary Testamentary Trustee*
Utah	No, unless all requirements are met, such as being subject to court-supervised administration. (§§ 7-18a-302, 7-5-1(c)(viii)(A))	No, unless all requirements are met, such as being subject to court-supervised administration. (§§ 7-18a-302, 7-5-1(c)(viii)(A))	Yes, (§§ 7-18a-302, 7-5-1, 75-7-101(1)) but only if the principal place of business of the foreign corporate trustee provides sub stantially similar provi sions applicable to trustees from Utah. It must also qualify as a foreign corporation doing business in the state if it maintains the principal place of Administration of any trust in the state. However, if the bank is simply engaged in trust activities in Utah to fulfill its duties as a trustee of the trust cre ated and administered in another state, it will not be regarded as engaged in trust business and will not be covered by the statute. (§ 7-5-1-(3))	No, unless all requirements are met, such as being subject to court-supervised administration. (§§ 7-18a-302, 7-5-1)	No, unless all requirements are met, such as being subject to court-supervised administration. (§§ 71-8a-302, 7-5-1(c)(viii)(A))	Yes. (§§ 7-18a-302, 7-5-1, 75-7-101(1), 75-7-101(c)(viii)(A))
Vermont	Yes. To qualify, the nonresident's domicili ary state must permit Vermont banks and trust companies to act as executors and trustees within its borders, and the nonresident	Tit. 11A § 15.01 can be interpreted two ways. Since it only mentions executors and trustees, it can be read as not imposing the requirements set forth in *Nonresident*	Yes. To qualify, the nonresident's domicili ary state must permit Vermont banks and trust companies to act as executors and trustees within its borders, and the	Yes. To qualify, the nonresident's domicili ary state must permit Vermont banks and trust companies to act as executors and trustees within its borders, and the	Tit. 11A § 15.01 can be interpreted two ways. Since it only mentions executors and trustees, it can be read as not imposing the requirements set forth in *Nonresident*	Yes. To qualify, the nonresident's domicili ary state must permit Vermont banks and trust companies to act as executors and trustees within its borders, and the nonresident

	bank must obtain a certificate of authority from the Vermont Secretary of State. (11A § 15.01(d)) See also R. of Prob. P. 68.	*Bank as Executor* for other types of nonresi dent fiduciaries. How ever, it could also be read as not allowing certification of nonresi dent banks acting in their other fiduciary roles.	nonresident bank must obtain a certificate of authority from the Vermont Secretary of State. (11A § 15.01(d)) See also R. of Prob. P. 68.	nonresident bank must obtain a certificate of authority from the Vermont Secretary of State. (11A § 15.01(d)) See also R. of Prob. P. 68.	*Bank as Executor* for other types of nonresi dent fiduciaries. How ever, it could also be read as not allowing certification of nonresident banks acting in their other fiduciary roles.	bank must obtain a certificate of authority from the Vermont Secretary of State. (11A § 15.01 (d)) See also R. of Prob. P. 68.
Virginia	No, unless authorized to do business in the state. (§ 26-59(B))	No, unless authorized to do business in the state. (§ 26-59(B))	No, unless authorized to do business in the state. (§ 26-59(B))	No, unless authorized to do business in the state. (§ 26-59(B))	No, unless authorized to do business in the state. (§ 26-59(B))	No, unless authorized to do business in the state. (§ 26-59(B))
Washington	Yes, if appoints an agent who is a resident of the county where the estate is being probated or is an attorney of record of the estate. Otherwise, no, except if a national bank authorized to so act, if upon petition of a person having a right to such appoint. The bank must not have drawn a will appointing it to the position. (§ 11.36.010)	Yes, if appoints an agent who is a resident of the county where the estate is being probated or is an attorney of record of the estate. Otherwise, no, except if a national bank authorized to so act, if upon petition of a person having a right to such appoint. The bank must not have drawn a will appointing it to the position. (§ 11.36.010)	No, except if a national bank authorized to so act, if upon petition of a person having a right to such appoint. The bank must not have drawn a will appoint ing it to the position. (§ 11.36.021)	Yes, if appoints an agent who is a resident of the county where the estate is being probated or is an attorney of record of the estate. Otherwise, no, except if a national bank authorized to so act, if upon petition of a person having a right to such appoint. The bank must not have drawn a will appointing it to the position. (§ 11.36.010)	Yes, if appoints an agent who is a resident of the county where the estate is being probated or is an attorney of record of the estate. Otherwise, no, except if a national bank authorized to so act, if upon petition of a person having a right to such appoint. The bank must not have drawn a will appointing it to the position. (§ 11.36.010)	No. (§ 11.36.021)
West Virginia	No, unless a main or branch office in the state. However, the provision then states that a nonresident corporation cannot have its principal office or place of business outside the state. (§ 44-5-3)	No, unless a main or branch office in the state. However, the provision then states that a nonresident corporation cannot have its principal office or place of business outside the state. (§ 44-5-3)	Yes. There is no statutory prohibition.	No, unless a main or branch office in the state. However, the provision then states that a nonresident cor poration cannot have its principal office or place of business outside the state. (§ 44-5-3)	No, unless a main or branch office in the state. However, the provision then states that a nonresident corporation cannot have its principal office or place of business outside the state. (§ 44-5-3)	Yes. There is no statutory prohibition.

Table 3.03
Nonresident Bank as Executor, Administrator, or Testamentary Trustee *(continued)*

	Nonresident Bank as Executor	*Nonresident Bank as Administrator*	*Nonresident Bank as Testamentary Trustee*	*Nonresident Bank as Ancillary Executor*	*Nonresident Bank as Ancillary Administrator*	*Nonresident Bank as Ancillary Testamentary Trustee*
Wisconsin	Yes, if (a) authorized to act as a fiduciary in its state of organization, and (b) the law of that state allows the following to act as a fiduciary "not unduly restrictive when compared with the laws of this state:" a corporation organized in Wisconsin, a national banking association having its principal place of business in Wisconsin, and a federal savings association or a federal savings bank having its principal place of business in Wisconsin and authorized to act as a fiduciary in Wisconsin. (§ 223.12)	Yes, if (a) authorized to act as a fiduciary in its state of organization, and (b) the law of that state allows the following to act as a fiduciary "not unduly restrictive when compared with the laws of this state:" a corporation organized in Wisconsin, a national banking association having its principal place of business in Wisconsin, and a federal savings association or a federal savings bank having its principal place of business in Wisconsin and authorized to act as a fiduciary in Wisconsin. (§ 223.12)	Yes, if acting under a will admitted to probate in another state. (§ 701.16(d))	Yes, if (a) authorized to act as a fiduciary in its state of organization, and (b) the law of that state allows the following to act as a fiduciary "not unduly restrictive when compared with the laws of this state:" a corporation organized in Wisconsin, a national banking association having its principal place of business in Wisconsin, and a federal savings association or a federal savings bank having its principal place of business in Wisconsin and authorized to act as a fiduciary in Wisconsin. (§ 223.12) If the bank bank has been appointed at the domicile, it qualifies without satisfying § 223.12. See also § 877.16.	Yes, if (a) authorized to act as a fiduciary in its state of organization, and (b) the law of that state allows the following to act as a fiduciary "not unduly restrictive when compared with the laws of this state:" a corporation organized in Wisconsin, a national banking association having its principal place of business in Wisconsin, and a federal savings association or a federal savings bank having its principal place of business in Wisconsin and authorized to act as a fiduciary in Wisconsin. (§ 223.12) If the bank bank has been appointed at the domicile, it qualifies without satisfying § 223.12. See also § 877.16.	Yes, if acting under a will admitted to probate in another state. (§ 701.16(d)) Yes, if (a) authorized to act as a fiduciary in its state of organization, and (b) the law of that state allows the following to act as a fiduciary "not unduly restrictive when compared with the laws of this state:" a corporation organized in Wisconsin, a national banking association having its principal place of business in Wisconsin, and a federal savings association or a federal savings bank having its principal place of business in Wisconsin and authorized to act as a fiduciary in Wisconsin. (§ 223.12) If the bank has been appointed at the domicile, it qualifies with out satisfying § 223.12.
Wyoming	Yes, after appointment of a resident agent if not doing business in the state. (§ 2-11-301)	No, unless a resident of Wyoming is appointed co-administrator. (§ 2-4-203)	Yes, after appointment of a resident agent if not doing business in the state. (§ 2-11-301)	Yes, after appointment of a resident agent if not doing business in the state. (§§ 2-11-301, 2-11-201)	Yes, likely requires a Wyoming resident to be appointed as co-administrator. (§ 2-4-203) See also § 2-11-201.	Yes, after appointment of a resident agent if not doing business in the state. (§ 2-11-301)

Table 3.04
Nonresident Bank as Guardian of Minor's or Incompetent's Property

	Nonresident Bank as Guardian of Minor's Property	*Nonresident Bank as Guardian of Incompetent's Property*	*Nonresident Bank as Ancillary Guardian of Minor's Property*	*Nonresident Bank as Ancillary Guardian of Incompetent's Property*
Alabama	Yes, if reciprocal treatment is accorded Alabama banks. (§ 10-2B-15.41(a)(2)) Nonresident banks must file a verified statement with the Commissioner of Revenue. (§ 10-2B-15.42)	Yes, if reciprocal treatment is accorded Alabama banks. (§ 10-2B-15.41(a)(2)) Nonresident banks must file a verified statement with the Commissioner of Revenue. (§ 10-2B-15.42)	Yes, if reciprocal treatment is accorded Alabama banks. (§ 10-2B-15.41(a)(2)) Nonresident banks must file a verified statement with the Commissioner of Revenue. (§ 10-2B-15.42)	Yes, if reciprocal treatment is accorded Alabama banks. (§ 10-2B-15.41(a)(2)) Nonresident banks must file a verified statement with the Commissioner of Revenue. (§ 10-2B-15.42)
Alaska	Yes. (§§ 06.26.010, 43.31.300, 13.26.035, 13.26.055, 13.26.210, 13.26.320)	Yes. (§§ 06.26.010, 43.31.300, 13.26.095, 13.26.145, 13.26.210, 13.26.320)	Yes. (§§ 06.26.010, 43.31.300, 13.26.035, 13.26.055, 13.26.210, 13.26.320)	Yes. (§§ 06.26.010, 43.31.300, 13.26.095, 13.26.145, 13.26.210, 13.26.320)
Arizona	Yes. (§§ 14-5206, 14-5410, 14-5432)	Yes. (§§ 14-5301, 14-5311, 14-5401, 14-5432)	Yes. (§§ 14-5206, 14-5410, 14-5432)	Yes. (§§ 14-5301, 14-5311, 14-5401, 14-5432)
Arkansas	Yes, if authorized to do business in the state and properly empowered by its charter to serve as guardian. (§ 28-65-203(d)(1)) A separate provision states that a bank may serve if it has trust powers. (§ 28-65-203(d)(2)) The provision is unclear as to whether the requirements of § 28-48-101(b)(6) must also be satisfied.	Yes, if authorized to do business in the state and properly empowered by its charter to serve as guardian. (§ 28-65-203(d)(1)) A separate provision states that a bank may serve if it has trust powers. (§ 28-65-203(d)(2)) The provision is unclear as to whether the requirements of § 28-48-101(b)(6) must also be satisfied.	Generally, the same standards apply as for personal representatives. (§ 28-65-103) Moreover, a guardian appointed in the state of the incompetent's residence may serve upon petition. (§ 28-65-601) The bank, if a corporation, does not have to be authorized to do business in the state. (§ 28-65-603)	Generally, the same rules apply for conservators of a disabled person as for guardians of minors. (§ 28-67-106)
California	Yes, if authorized to conduct business of a trust company in the state and in the best interest of the ward. (Prob. §§ 83, 300, 1514 & note 22)	Yes, if authorized to conduct business of a trust company in the state. The court has sole discretion in the selection. (Prob. §§ 83, 300, 1514 & note 22)	Yes, if authorized to conduct business of a trust company in the state. (Prob. §§ 83, 300, 2801) Domiciliary proceedings in California may not be necessary. (Prob. 3800)	Yes, if authorized to conduct business of a trust company in the state. (Prob. §§ 83, 300, 1812, 2801) Domiciliary proceedings in California may not be necessary. (Prob. 3800)
Colorado	Yes, but first may be required to obtain a certificate of authority to transact business.[1] (§§ 15-14-202, 15-14-206, 15-14-413) See also § 7-115-101 et seq.	Yes, but first may be required to obtain a certificate of authority to transact business.[2] (§§ 15-14-301(4), 15-14-311, 15-14-413) See also § 7-115-101 et seq.	Yes, but first may be required to obtain a certificate of authority to transact business.[3] (§§ 15-14-202, 15-14-206, 15-14-413, 15-14-433) See also § 7-115-101 et seq.	Yes, but first may be required to obtain a certificate of authority to transact business.[4] (§§ 15-14-301, 15-14-311, 15-14-413, 15-14-433) See also § 7-115-101 et seq.

Table 3.04
Nonresident Bank as Guardian of Minor's or Incompetent's Property *(continued)*

	Nonresident Bank as Guardian of Minor's Property	*Nonresident Bank as Guardian of Incompetent's Property*	*Nonresident Bank as Ancillary Guardian of Minor's Property*	*Nonresident Bank as Ancillary Guardian of Incompetent's Property*
Connecticut	There is no statutory prohibition. (§ 45a-629)	No general statutory prohibition against foreign corporation as conservator. (§ 45a-659) Only nonprofit Connecticut corporations can be guardians of mentally retarded wards. (§ 45a-669)	No statutory prohibitions. See § 45a-635 for right of foreign guardian to removal personal property. See also § 45a-632 providing that a guardian may be appointed in ancillary proceeding.	No statutory prohibition against foreign corporation as conservator. (§ 45a-659) Only nonprofit Connecticut corporations can be guardians of mentally retarded wards. (§ 45a-669)
Delaware	Yes, if reciprocal treatment accorded Delaware corporations. (8 § 380; 12 §§ 3901, 3902)	Yes, if reciprocal treatment accorded Delaware corporations. (8 § 380; 12 § 3901)	Yes, if reciprocal treatment accorded Delaware corporations. (8 § 380; 12 §§ 3901, 3902, 3904) If the minor is resident out of state, then it is the court's discretion. (12 § 3902(d))	Yes, if reciprocal treatment accorded Delaware corporations. (8 § 380; 12 § 3901, 3904)
District of Columbia	Yes. (§§ 26-1309, 26-1310, 26-1335)	Yes, there is no statutory prohibition. (§§ 26-1309(5), 26-1310, 26-1335)	Yes. (§§ 26-1309, 26-1310, 26-1335, 21-111, 21-112)	Yes. (§ 21-2057(a)(1)) See also §§ 26-1309, 26-1310, 26-1335. §§ 21-2076-21-2077 indicate that ancillary proceedings may not be necessary. The cited section relates to foreign *conservators*. See definition in § 21-2011(3).
Florida	There is no specific prohibition. (§ 744.309(4)) If the ward moves to Florida, the foreign guardian can act after filing its appointment papers. (§ 744.306) A foreign guardian can maintain or defend lawsuits locally. (§ 744.306(2))	There is no specific prohibition. (§ 744.309(4)) If the ward moves to Florida, the foreign guardian can act after filing its appointment papers. (§ 744.306) A foreign guardian can maintain or defend lawsuits locally. (§ 744.306(2))	A guardian of nonresident ward, if duly appointed in court of another state, may manage property in Florida. (§ 744.307) A foreign guardian may also maintain or defend an action. (§ 744.306(2)) If the ward moves to Florida, the foreign guardian can act locally after filing its appointment papers. (§ 744.306(1))	A guardian of nonresident ward, if duly appointed in court of another state, may manage property in Florida. (§ 744.307) A foreign guardian may also maintain or defend an action. (§ 744.306(2)) If the ward moves to Florida, the foreign guardian can act locally after filing its appointment papers. (§ 744.306(1))

Georgia	Yes, if it is a bank organized under or a national banking association having its principal place of business in state bordering on Georgia (Alabama, Florida, North Carolina, South Carolina, Tennessee) and that state gives reciprocal treatment to Georgia banks. (§§ 53-12-390, 53-12-391)	Yes, if it is a bank organized under or a national banking association having its principal place of business in state bordering on Georgia (Alabama, Florida, North Carolina, South Carolina, Tennessee) and that state gives reciprocal treatment to Georgia banks. (§§ 53-12-390, 53-12-391)	Yes, if it is a bank organized under or a national banking association having its principal place of business in state bordering on Georgia (Alabama, Florida, North Carolina, South Carolina, Tennessee) and that state gives reciprocal treatment to Georgia banks. (§§ 53-12-390, 53-12-391)	Yes, if it is a bank organized under or a national banking association having its principal place of business in state bordering on Georgia (Alabama, Florida, North Carolina, South Carolina, Tennessee) and that state gives reciprocal treatment to Georgia banks. (§§ 53-12-390, 53-12-391)
Hawaii	No, unless recognized by the appropriate court of some other jurisdiction where the protected person resides as a guardian of the protected person's property. (§ 560:5-410(a)(1))	No, unless recognized by the appropriate court of some other jurisdiction where the protected person resides as a guardian of the protected person's property. (§ 560:5-410(a)(1))	No, unless recognized by the appropriate court of some other jurisdiction where the protected person resides as a guardian of the protected person's property. (§ 560:5-410(a)(1))	No, unless recognized by the appropriate court of some other jurisdiction where the protected person resides as a guardian of the protected person's property. (§ 560:5-410(a)(1))
Idaho	Yes, but first may be required to procure a certificate of authority to transact business. (§§ 15-5-202, 15-5-206, 15-5-410, 15-9-101, 30-1-1501)	Yes, but first may be required to procure a certificate of authority to transact business. (§§ 15-5-301, 15-5-311, 15-5-410, 15-9-101, 30-1-1501)	Yes, but first may be required to procure a certificate of authority to transact business. (§§ 15-5-202, 15-5-206, 15-5-410, 15-9-101, 30-1-1501)	Yes, but first may be required to procure a certificate of authority to transact business. (§§ 15-5-301, 15-5-311, 15-5-410, 15-9-101, 30-1-1501)
Illinois	Yes, if the corporation is authorized by the laws of the state of its organization or domicile to act as a fiduciary in that state and reciprocal treatment is accorded Illinois banks. (205 ILCS § 620/4-2) Prior to the time any corporation can act, it must obtain from the Commissioner of Banks and Real Estate a certificate of authority. (205 ILCS § 620/4-5)	Yes, (755 ILCS § 5/11a-5(c)) if the corporation is authorized by the laws of the state of its organization or domicile to act as a fiduciary in that state and reciprocal treatment is accorded Illinois banks. (205 ILCS § 620/4-2) Prior to the time any corporation can act, it must obtain from the Commissioner of Banks and Real Estate a certificate of authority. (205 ILCS § 620/4-5)	Yes, if the corporation is authorized by the laws of the state of its organization or domicile to act as a fiduciary in that state and reciprocal treatment is accorded Illinois banks. (205 ILCS § 620/ 4-2) Prior to the time any corporation can act, it must obtain from the Commissioner of Banks and Real Estate a certificate of authority. (205 ILCS § 620/4-5)	Yes, (755 ILCS § 5/11a-5(c)) if the corporation is authorized by the laws of the state of its organization or domicile to act as a fiduciary in that state and reciprocal treatment is accorded Illinois banks. (205 ILCS § 620/4-2) Prior to the time any corporation can act, it must obtain from the Commissioner of Banks and Real Estate a certificate of authority. (205 ILCS § 620/4-5)
Indiana	Yes. There is no prohibition. Furthermore, if no one is appointed locally, a guardian appointed at the protected person's domicile may prove his foreign appointment and then act as a guardian appointed in	Yes. There is no prohibition. Furthermore, if no one is appointed locally, a guardian appointed at the protected person's domicile may prove his foreign appointment and then act as a guardian appointed in	Yes. There is no prohibition. Furthermore, if no one is appointed locally, a guardian appointed at the protected person's domicile may prove his foreign appointment and then act as a guardian appointed in	Yes. There is no prohibition. Furthermore, if no one is appointed locally, a guardian appointed at the protected person's domicile may prove his foreign appointment and then act as a guardian appointed in Indiana.
	(cont'd)	*(cont'd)*	*(cont'd)*	*(cont'd)*

Table 3.04
Nonresident Bank as Guardian of Minor's or Incompetent's Property *(continued)*

	Nonresident Bank as Guardian of Minor's Property	*Nonresident Bank as Guardian of Incompetent's Property*	*Nonresident Bank as Ancillary Guardian of Minor's Property*	*Nonresident Bank as Ancillary Guardian of Incompetent's Property*
Indiana (*cont'd*)	Indiana. (§ 29-3-13-2) A bank or trust company can also act if the state in which it has its principal place of business gives reciprocal treatment. (§ 28-1-12-1(b)(2)(B) & (3)(C))	Indiana. (§ 29-3-13-2) A bank or trust company can also act if the state in which it has its principal place of business gives reciprocal treatment. (§ 28-1-12-1(b)(2)(B) & (3)(C))	Indiana. (§ 29-3-13-2) A bank or trust company can also act if the state in which it has its principal place of business gives reciprocal treatment. (§ 28-1-12-1(b)(2)(B) & (3)(C))	(§ 29-3-13-2) A bank or trust company can also act if the state in which it has its principal place of business gives reciprocal treatment. (§ 28-1-12-1(b)(2)(B) & (3)(C))
Iowa	Yes, if reciprocal treatment is accorded Iowa banks. (§ 633.64)	Yes, if reciprocal treatment is accorded Iowa banks. (§ 633.64)	Yes, if reciprocal treatment is accorded Iowa banks. (§§ 633.64, 633.502)	Yes, if reciprocal treatment is accorded Iowa banks. (§§ 633.64, 633.502)
Kansas	Yes, if it is organized under the laws of, and has a principal place of business in, another state that permits a bank or other corporation that is similarly organized in Kansas to act in a like fiduciary capacity in the other state under-similar conditions (§ 59-1701(a)(3)) and a resident agent is appointed (§ 59-1706). An officer, employee, or agent of a bank or corporation which is not authorized to act as a fiduciary in Kansas may himself or herself not act as a fiduciary in Kansas, whether a resident or nonresident of Kansas, if such person is acting as a fiduciary on behalf of such bank or corporation. (§ 59-1701(b))	Yes, if it is organized under the laws of, and has a principal place of business in, another state that permits a bank or other corporation that is similarly organized in Kansas to act in a like fiduciary capacity in the other state under-similar conditions (§ 59-1701(a)(3)) and a resident agent is appointed (§ 59-1706). An officer, employee, or agent of a bank or corporation which is not authorized to act as a fiduciary in Kansas may himself or herself not act as a fiduciary in Kansas, whether a resident or nonresident of Kansas, if such person is acting as a fiduciary on behalf of such bank or corporation. (§ 59-1701(b))	Yes, if it is organized under the laws of, and has a principal place of business in, another state that permits a bank or other corporation that is similarly organized in Kansas to act in a like fiduciary capacity in the other state undersimilar conditions (§ 59-1701(a)(3)) and a resident agent is appointed (§ 59-1706). An officer, employee, or agent of a bank or corporation which is not authorized to act as a fiduciary in Kansas may himself or herself not act as a fiduciary in Kansas, whether a resident or nonresident of Kansas, if such person is acting as a fiduciary on behalf of such bank or corporation. (§ 59-1701(b))	Yes, if it is organized under the laws of, and has a principal place of business in, another state that permits a bank or other corporation that is similarly organized inKansas to act in a like fiduciary capacity in the other state undersimilar conditions (§ 59-1701(a)(3)) and a resident agent is appointed (§ 59-1706). An officer, employee, or agent of a bank or corporation which is not authorized to act as a fiduciary in Kansas may himself or herself not act as a fiduciary in Kansas, whether a resident or nonresident of Kansas, if such person is acting as a fiduciary on behalf of such bank or corporation. (§ 59-1701(b))
Kentucky	No. (§ 395.005)	No. (§ 395.005)	Yes. (§§ 387.010(3), 387.185)	Yes. (§§ 387.010(3), 387.185)

Louisiana	Yes, if resident agent is appointed. (Code Civ. Pro. arts. 4273, 5251 (11))	Yes, if resident agent is appointed for service of process. (Code Civ. Pro. 4273, 4556, 5251(11))	Yes. (Code Civ. Pro. art. 4431)	Yes, if resident agent is appointed for service of process. (Code Civ. Pro. arts. 4431, 4556, 5251(11))
Maine	Yes, if reciprocal treatment is accorded Maine banks. (18 § 4161)	Yes, if reciprocal treatment is accorded Maine banks. (18 § 4161)	Yes, if reciprocal treatment is accorded Maine banks. (18 § 4161)	Yes, if reciprocal treatment is accorded Maine banks. (18 § 4161)
Maryland	Yes, if resident agent is appointed. (Est. & Trusts § 13-207)	Yes, if resident agent is appointed. (Est. & Trusts § 13-207)	Yes, although a foreign guardian or other fiduciary is not required to qualify as an ancillary. (Est. & Trusts §§ 13-222, 13-207)	Yes, although a foreign guardian or other fiduciary is not required to qualify as an ancillary. (Est. & Trusts §§ 13-222, 13-207)
Massachusetts		Yes, if reciprocal treatment is accorded Massachusetts banks. (167 § 43)	Yes, if reciprocal treatment is accorded Massachusetts banks. (167 § 43)	Yes, if reciprocal treatment is accorded Massachusetts banks. (167 § 43) Yes, if reciprocal treatment is accorded Massachusetts banks. (167 § 43)
Michigan	Yes, no specific prohibition. (§ 700.5409)	Yes, no specific prohibition. (§ 700.5409)	Yes. (§ 700.5409(1)(a))	Yes. (§ 700.5409(1)(a))
Minnesota	The bank must have its principal office in a state that accords reciprocal treatment to Minnesota banks. (§ 303.25)	The bank must have its principal office in a state that accords reciprocal treatment to Minnesota banks. (§ 303.25)	The bank must have its principal office in a state that accords reciprocal treatment to Minnesota banks. (§ 303.25)	The bank must have its principal office in a state that accords reciprocal treatment to Minnesota banks. (§ 303.25)
Mississippi	Yes, if reciprocal treatment is accorded Mississippi banks. (§ 81-5-43)	Yes, if reciprocal treatment is accorded Mississippi banks. (§ 81-5-43)	Yes, if reciprocal treatment is accorded Mississippi banks. (§ 81-5-43)	Yes, if reciprocal treatment is accorded Mississippi banks. (§ 81-5-43)
Missouri	Yes, if reciprocal treatment is accorded Missouri banks and (a) if the bank is organized under another state's laws, or (b) if the bank is a national bank, after designation of a resident agent. (§§ 362.600, 473.117, 475.055(4))	Yes, if reciprocal treatment is accorded Missouri banks and (a) if the bank is organized under another state's laws, or (b) if the bank is a national bank, after designation of a resident agent. (§§ 362.600, 473.117, 475.055(4))	Yes, if reciprocal treatment is accorded Missouri banks and (a) if the bank is organized under another state's laws, or (b) if the bank is a national bank. (§§ 362.600, 473.117, 475.055(4), 475.095, 475.339)	Yes, if reciprocal treatment is accorded Missouri banks and (a) if the bank is organized under another state's laws, or (b) if the bank is a national bank. (§§ 362.600, 473.117, 475.055(4), 475.095, 475.339)
Montana	Yes, (§§ 72-5-211, 72-5-223, 72-5-410) though may have to qual ify to do business (§ 35-1-1026).	Yes, (§ 72-5-312) though may have to qualify to do business (§ 35-1-1026).	Yes, (§§ 72-5-312) though may have to qualify to do business (§ 35-1-1026).	Yes, (§§ 72-5-312, 72-5-410(1)(a)) though may have to qualify to do business (§ 35-1-1026).

Table 3.04
Nonresident Bank as Guardian of Minor's or Incompetent's Property *(continued)*

	Nonresident Bank as Guardian of Minor's Property	*Nonresident Bank as Guardian of Incompetent's Property*	*Nonresident Bank as Ancillary Guardian of Minor's Property*	*Nonresident Bank as Ancillary Guardian of Incompetent's Property*
Nebraska	Yes. (§§ 30-2639, 30-2606, 30-2610, 30-2661)	Yes. (§§ 30-2639, 30-2661, 30-2620)	Yes. (§§ 30-2639, 30-2606, 30-2610, 30-2661)	Yes. (§§ 30-2639, 30-2661, 30-2620)
Nevada	Yes, if the nonresident has associated a resident individual or banking corporation whose princi pal place of business is in the state as a co-guardian. The non-resident must have caused the appointment to be filed in the guardianship proceeding. (§ 159.059(5))	Yes, if the nonresident has associated a resident individual or banking corporation whose princi pal place of business is in the state as a co-guardian. The non-resident must have caused the appointment to be filed in the guardianship proceeding. (§ 159.059(5))	Yes, if the nonresident has associated a resident individual or banking corporation whose princi pal place of business is in the state as a co-guardian. The non-resident must have caused the appointment to be filed in the guardianship proceeding. (§ 159.059(5))	Yes, if the nonresident has associated a resident individual or banking cor-poration whose principal place of business is in the state as a co-guar-dian. The nonresident must have caused the appointment to be filed in the guardianship proceeding. (§ 159.059(5))
New Hampshire	Yes, if the bank has trust powers (§ 463:10) and if the state in which the bank has its principal place of business accords reciprocal treat-ment to New Hampshire banks (§§ 390:13, 390:15).	Yes, if the bank has trust powers (§ 464-A:10) and if the state in which the bank has its principal place of business accords recipro-cal treatment to New Hampshire banks (§§ 390:13, 390:15).	Yes, if the bank has trust powers (§ 463:10) and if the state in which the bank has its principal place of business accords reciprocal treat-ment to New Hampshire banks (§§ 390:13, 390:15).	Yes, if the bank has trust powers (§ 464-A:10) and if the state in which the bank has its principal place of business accords reciprocal treat-ment to New Hampshire banks (§§ 390:13, 390:15).
New Jersey	Yes, if named in a decedent's will or codicil, if the state in which such bank has its principal office accords reciprocal treatment to New Jersey banks, and if the nonresident bank has secured from the commissioner a certificate to transact trust business. (§ 17:9A-316) There may also be a basis if the bank is operating an office in New Jersey. (*Id.*; § 17:9A-418 et seq.)	Yes, if named in a decedent's will or codicil, if the state in which such bank has its principal office accords reciprocal treatment to New Jersey banks, and if the nonresident bank has secured from the commissioner a certificate to transact trust business. (§ 17:9A-316) There may also be a basis if the bank is operating an office in New Jersey. (*Id.*; § 17:9A-418 et seq.)	Yes, if named in a decedent's will or codicil, if the state in which such bank has its principal office accords reciprocal treatment to New Jersey banks, and if the nonresident bank has secured from the commissioner a certificate to transact trust business. (§ 17:9A-316) There may also be a basis if the bank is operating an office in New Jersey. (*Id.*; § 17:9A-418 et seq.)	Yes, if named in a decedent's will or codicil, if the state in which such bank has its principal office accords reciprocal treatment to New Jersey banks, and if the nonresident bank has secured from the commissioner a certificate to transact trust business. (§ 17:9A-316) There may also be a basis if the bank is operating an office in New Jersey. (*Id.*; § 17:9A-418 et seq.)

New Mexico	Yes, if qualified to do business in New Mexico. (§§ 45-5-202, 45-5-206, 45-5-410, 45-5-432, 53-17-1) If no local guardian has been appointed or there is no petition pending in New Mexico, a foreign guardian may file with the district court in the county in which the incapacitated person resides authenticated copies of his appointment and of any official bond he has given and a statement of his address and telephone number. (§ 45-5-301.2)	Yes, if qualified to do business in New Mexico. (§§ 45-5-301, 45-5-311, 45-5-410, 45-5-432, 53-17-1) If no local guardian has been appointed or there is no petition pending in New Mexico, a foreign guardian may file with the district court in the county in which the incapacitated person resides authenticated copies of his appointment and of any official bond he has given and a statement of his address and telephone number. (§ 45-5-301.2)	Yes. (§§ 45-5-202, 45-5-206, 45-5-410, 45-5-432, 53-17-1) If no local guardian has been appointed or there is no petition pending in New Mexico, a foreign guardian may file with the district court in the county in which the incapacitated person resides authenticated copies of his appointment and of any official bond he has given and a statement of his address and telephone number. (§ 45-5-301.2)	Yes, if qualified to do business in New Mexico. (§§ 45-5-301, 45-5-311, 45-5-410, 45-5-432, 53-17-1) If no local guardian has been appointed or there is no petition pending in New Mexico, a foreign guardian may file with the district court in the county in which the incapacitated person resides authenticated copies of his appointment and of any official bond he has given and a statement of his address and telephone number. (§ 45-5-301.2)
New York	Yes, if reciprocal treatment is accorded New York banks. (Banking Law § 131(3))	Yes, if reciprocal treatment is accorded New York banks. (Banking Law § 131(3))	Yes, if reciprocal treatment is accorded New York banks, (Banking Law § 131(3)) or according to the court's discretion (Surr. Ct. Proc. Act § 1716(3) & (4)).	Yes, if reciprocal treatment is accorded New York banks, (Banking Law § 131(3)) or according to the court's discretion (Men Hyg § 81.18).
North Carolina	Yes, if authorized to exercise fiduciary power in North Carolina. (§§ 55-15-05, 35A-1224(c))	Yes, if authorized to exercise fiduciary power in North Carolina. (§§ 55-15-05, 35A-1213(c))	§ 35A-1280 states that clerk *may* appoint an ancillary guardian if it is established that: 1. Nonresident has property in North Carolina; 2. Nonresident is a minor or incompetent; and 3. Nonresident has no guardian in North Carolina. However, ancillary proceedings may not be necessary. (§ 35A-1281(c))	§ 35A-1280 states that clerk *may* appoint an ancillary guardian if it is established that: 1. Nonresident has property in North Carolina; 2. Nonresident is a minor or incompetent; and 3. Nonresident has no guardian in North Carolina. However, ancillary proceedings may not be necessary. (§ 35A-1281(c))
North Dakota	Yes, after filing copy of charter and power of attorney with Secretary of State if reciprocal treatment is accorded North Dakota banks. (§§ 6-08-25, 6-08-26) There is a $50 filing fee and a $25 fee for the forwarding of notice or service of process by the Secretary of State to the foreign bank.	Yes, after filing copy of charter and power of attorney with Secretary of State if reciprocal treatment is accorded North Dakota banks. (§§ 6-08-25, 6-08-26) There is a $50 filing fee and a $25 fee for the forwarding of notice or service of process by the Secretary of State to the foreign bank.	Yes, after filing copy of charter and power of attorney with Secretary of State if reciprocal treatment is accorded North Dakota banks. (§§ 6-08-25, 6-08-26) There is a $50 filing fee and a $25 fee for the forwarding of notice or service of process by the Secretary of State to the foreign bank.	Yes, after filing copy of charter and power of attorney with Secretary of State if reciprocal treatment is accorded North Dakota banks. (§§ 6-08-25, 6-08-26) There is a $50 filing fee and a $25 fee for the forwarding of notice or service of process by the Secretary of State to the foreign bank.

Table 3.04
Nonresident Bank as Guardian of Minor's or Incompetent's Property *(continued)*

	Nonresident Bank as Guardian of Minor's Property	*Nonresident Bank as Guardian of Incompetent's Property*	*Nonresident Bank as Ancillary Guardian of Minor's Property*	*Nonresident Bank as Ancillary Guardian of Incompetent's Property*
Ohio	A foreign corporation may be licensed to do business in Ohio as a trust company for one year after meeting extensive filing and fee requirements. (§§ 1111.01(G) (defining "trust business" as including serving as a guardian or conservator), 1111.02(A)(1)(b)&(c), (A)(2), 1109.02)	A foreign corporation may be licensed to do business in Ohio as a trust company for one year after meeting extensive filing and fee requirements. (§§ 1111.01(G) (defining "trust business" as including serving as a guardian or conservator), 1111.02(A)(1)(b)&(c), 1109.02)	A foreign corporation may be licensed to do business in Ohio as a trust company for one year after meeting extensive filing and fee requirements. (§§ 1111.01(G) (defining "trust business" as including serving as a guardian or conservator), 1111.02(A)(1)(b)&(c), 1109.02)	A foreign corporation may be licensed to do business in Ohio as a trust company for one year after meeting extensive filing and fee requirements. (§§ 1111.01(G) (defining "trust business" as including serving as a guardian or conservator), 1111.02(A)(1)(b)&(c), 1109.02)
Oklahoma	No, although a nonresident may be appointed guardian of his or her own relatives and may also be appointed upon the written request of the father, mother, or next of kin. (30 § 4-104)	No, although a nonresident may be appointed guardian of his or her own relatives and may also be appointed upon the written request of the father, mother, or next of kin. (30 § 4-104)	No, although a nonresident may be appointed guardian of his or her own relatives and may also be appointed upon the written request of the father, mother, or next of kin. (30 § 4-104) However, if the incompetent ward and domiciliary guardian are both nonresidents, then no appoint ment of the guardian may be required, since pursuant to court approval, the ward's estate can be removed from the state. (30 §§ 4-605, 4-607)	No, although a nonresident may be appointed guardian of his or her own relatives and may also be appointed upon the written request of the father, mother, or next of kin. (30 § 4-104) However, if the incompetent ward and domiciliary guardian are both nonresidents, then no appoint ment of the guardian may be required, since pursuant to court approval, the ward's estate can be removed from the state. (30 §§ 4-605, 4-607)
Oregon	Yes. (§ 125.200)	Yes. (§ 125.200)	Yes. (§ 125.200)	Yes. (§ 125.200)
Pennsylvania	Yes, if reciprocal treatment is accorded Pennsylvania banks. (7 § 106) Any bank must meet minimum capital requirements. (7 § 106(b)(ii))	Yes, if reciprocal treatment is accorded Pennsylvania banks. (7 § 106) Any bank must meet minimum capital requirements. (7 § 106(b)(ii))	Yes, if reciprocal treatment is accorded Pennsylvania banks. (7 § 106) Any bank must meet minimum capital requirements. (7 § 106(b)(ii))	Yes, if reciprocal treatment is accorded Pennsylvania banks. (7 § 106) Any bank must meet minimum capital requirements. (7 § 106(b)(ii))
Rhode Island	Yes, if appointment of state official as true and lawful attorney for receipt of process. (§ 19-3.1-6)	Yes, if appointment of state official as true and lawful attorney for receipt of process. (§ 19-3.1-6)	Yes, if appointment of state official as true and lawful attorney for receipt of process. (§ 19-3.1-6) Moreover, the guardian may be able to remove property without local appointment. (§ 33-15-42)	Yes, if appointment of state official as true and lawful attorney for receipt of process. (§ 19-3.1-6) Moreover, the guardian may be able to remove property without local appointment. (§ 33-15-42)

South Carolina	Yes. (§§ 62-5-311, 62-5-410)	Yes. (§§ 62-5-311, 62-5-410)	Yes. (§§ 62-4-204, 62-5-431, 62-5-432, 62-5-410)	Yes. (§§ 62-4-204, 62-5-431, 62-5-432, 62-5-410)
South Dakota	Yes, if reciprocal treatment is accorded South Dakota banks and if filing provisions are met, especially naming the office of the Secretary of State as agent for the receipt of process. (§§ 51A-5-7-51A-5-10, 29A-5-110)	Yes, if reciprocal treatment is accorded South Dakota banks and if filing provisions are met, especially naming the office of the Secretary of State as agent for the receipt of process. (§§ 51A-5-7-51A-5-10, 29A-5-110)	Yes, if reciprocal treatment is accorded South Dakota banks and if filing provisions are met, especially naming the office of the Secretary of State as agent for the receipt of process. (§§ 51A-5-7-51A-5-10, 29A-5-110)	Yes, if reciprocal treatment is accorded South Dakota banks and if filing provisions are met, especially naming the office of the Secretary of State as agent for the receipt of process. (§§ 51A-5-7-51A-5-10, 29A-5-110)
Tennessee	Yes, if reciprocal treatment is accorded Tennessee banks. (§ 35-50-107(a)(2)(A)) The secretary of state must be appointed as agent for service of process. (§ 35-50-107(b)(2)) See also § 30-11-16.	Yes, if reciprocal treatment is accorded Tennessee banks. (§ 35-50-107(a)(2)(A)) The secretary of state must be appointed as agent for service of process. (§ 35-50-107(b)(2)) See also § 30-1-116.	Yes, if reciprocal treatment is accorded Tennessee banks. (§ 35-50-107(a)(2)(A)) The secretary of state must be appointed as agent for service of process. (§ 35-50-107(b)(2)) See also § 30-1-116.	Yes, if reciprocal treatment is accorded Tennessee banks. (§ 35-50-107(a)(2)(A)) The secretary of state must be appointed as agent for service of process. (§ 35-50-107 (b)(2)) See also § 30-1-116.
Texas	Yes, if reciprocal treatment is accorded Texas banks and if filing provisions are met. (Prob. § 105A)	Yes, if reciprocal treatment is accorded Texas banks and if filing provisions are met. (Prob. § 105A)	Yes, if reciprocal treatment is accorded Texas banks and if filing provisions are met. (Prob. § 105A)	Yes, if reciprocal treatment is accorded Texas banks and if filing provisions are met. (Prob. § 105A)
Utah	No, unless all requirements are met. (§§ 7-18a-302, 7-5-1)	No, unless all requirements are met. (§§ 7-18a-302, 7-5-1)	No, unless all requirements are met. (§§ 7-18a-302, 7-5-1)	No, unless all requirements are met. (§§ 7-18a-302, 7-5-1)
Vermont	Tit. 11A § 15.01 can be interpreted two ways. Since it only mentions executors and trustees, it can be read as not imposing the requirements set forth in *Nonresident Bank as Executor* for other types of nonresident fiduciaries. However, it could also be read as not allowing certification of nonresident banks acting in their other fiduciary roles.	Tit. 11A § 15.01 can be interpreted two ways. Since it only mentions executors and trustees, it can be read as not imposing the requirements set forth in *Nonresident Bank as Executor* for other types of nonresident fiduciaries. However, it could also be read as not allowing certification of nonresident banks acting in their other fiduciary roles.	Tit. 11A § 15.01 can be interpreted two ways. Since it only mentions executors and trustees, it can be read as not imposing the requirements set forth in *Nonresident Bank as Executor* for other types of nonresident fiduciaries. However, it could also be read as not allowing certification of nonresident banks acting in their other fiduciary roles.	Tit. 11A § 15.01 can be interpreted two ways. Since it only mentions executors and trustees, it can be read as not imposing the requirements set forth in *Nonresident Bank as Executor* for other types of nonresident fiduciaries. However, it could also be read as not allowing certification of nonresident banks acting in their other fiduciary roles.
Virginia	No, unless authorized to do business in the state. (§ 26-59(B))	No, unless authorized to do business in the state. (§ 26-59(B))	No, unless authorized to do business in the state. (§ 26-59) Ancillary proceedings may not be necessary. (§ 26-60)	No, unless authorized to do business in the state. (§ 26-59) Ancillary proceedings may not be necessary. (§ 26-60)

Table 3.04
Nonresident Bank as Guardian of Minor's or Incompetent's Property *(continued)*

	Nonresident Bank as Guardian of Minor's Property	*Nonresident Bank as Guardian of Incompetent's Property*	*Nonresident Bank as Ancillary Guardian of Minor's Property*	*Nonresident Bank as Ancillary Guardian of Incompetent's Property*
Washington	Yes, if appoints an agent who is a resident of the county where the estate is being probated or is an attorney of record of the estate. Otherwise, no, except if a national bank authorized to so act, if upon petition of a person having a right to such appoint. The bank must not have drawn a will appointing it to the position. (§ 11.36.010)	Yes, if appoints an agent who is a resident of the county where the estate is being probated or is an attorney of record of the estate. Otherwise, no, except if a national bank authorized to so act, if upon petition of a person having a right to such appoint. The bank must not have drawn a will appointing it to the position. (§ 11.36.010)	Yes, if appoints an agent who is a resident of the county where the estate is being probated or is an attorney of record of the estate. Otherwise, no, except if a national bank authorized to so act, if upon petition of a person having a right to such appoint. The bank must not have drawn a will appointing it to the position. (§ 11.36.010)	Yes, if appoints an agent who is a resident of the county where the estate is being probated or is an attorney of record of the estate. Otherwise, no, except if a national bank authorized to so act, if upon petition of a person having a right to such appoint. The bank must not have drawn a will appointing it to the position. (§ 11.36.010)
West Virginia	No, unless a main or branch office in the state. However, the provision then states that a nonresident corporation cannot have its principal office or place of business outside the state. (§ 44-5-3)	No, unless a main or branch office in the state. However, the provision then states that a nonresident corporation cannot have its principal office or place of business outside the state. (§ 44-5-3)	No, unless a main or branch office in the state. However, the provision then states that a nonresident corporation cannot have its principal office or place of business outside the state. (§ 44-5-3)	No, unless a main or branch office in the state. However, the provision then states that a nonresident corporation cannot have its principal office or place of business outside the state. (§ 44-5-3)
Wisconsin	Yes, if (a) authorized to act as a fiduciary in its state of organization, and (b) the law of that state allows the following to act as a fiduciary "not unduly restrictive when compared with the laws of this state:" a corporation organized in Wisconsin, a national banking association having its principal place of business in Wisconsin, and a federal savings association or a federal savings bank having its principal place of business in Wisconsin and authorized to act as a fiduciary in Wisconsin. (§ 223.12)	Yes, if (a) authorized to act as a fiduciary in its state of organization, and (b) the law of that state allows the following to act as a fiduciary "not unduly restrictive when compared with the laws of this state:" a corporation organized in Wisconsin, a national banking association having its principal place of business in Wisconsin, and a federal savings association or a federal savings bank having its principal place of business in Wisconsin and authorized to act as a fiduciary in Wisconsin. (§ 223.12)	Yes, if (a) authorized to act as a fiduciary in its state of organization, and (b) the law of that state allows the following to act as a fiduciary "not unduly restrictive when compared with the laws of this state:" a corporation organized in Wisconsin, a national banking association having its principal place of business in Wisconsin, and a federal savings association or a federal savings bank having its principal place of business in Wisconsin and authorized to act as a fiduciary in Wisconsin. (§ 223.12) If the bank has been appointed at the domicile, it qualifies without satisfying § 223.12. See also § 54.64(6).	Yes, if (a) authorized to act as a fiduciary in its state of organization, and (b) the law of that state allows the following to act as a fiduciary "not unduly restrictive when compared with the laws of this state:" a corporation organized in Wisconsin, a national banking association having its principal place of business in Wisconsin, and a federal savings association or a federal savings bank having its principal place of business in Wisconsin and authorized to act as a fiduciary in Wisconsin. (§ 223.12) If the bank has been appointed at the domicile, it qualifies without satisfying § 223.12. See also § 54.64(6).

Wyoming	Section 13-5-101(b)(i) provides that a trust company may ''act or be appointed by any court to act in like manner as an individual, as executor, administrator, guardian or conservator.''	Section 13-5-101(b)(i) provides that a trust company may ''act or be appointed by any court to act in like manner as an individual, as executor, administrator, guardian or conservator.''	Section 13-5-101(b)(i) provides that a trust company may ''act or be appointed by any court to act in like manner as an individual, as executor, administrator, guardian or conservator.''	Section 13-5-101(b)(i) provides that a trust company may ''act or be appointed by any court to act in like manner as an individual, as executor, administrator, guardian or conservator.''

1. § 15-14-410(1)(a) gives highest priority to the appointment of a person recognized by the appropriate court of the foreign jurisdiction in which the protected person ''resides.'' The provision, however, does not specifically address the appointment of a foreign person when the protected person resides in Colorado. Presumably, no limitation is placed on such person serving, if the person otherwise complies with the statute.

2. *Id.*

3. *Id.*

4. *Id.*

Table 4
Small Estates Procedure
(current through 5/1/07)

Almost every state has a simplified procedure for small estates. This table considers the option, which may be of particular relevance in the case of a decedent who dies domiciled in one state, but leaves a small amount of property in another state or states. By use of the small estates procedure, considerable expense, delay, conflicting decisions, and multiple will contests can be avoided. This table should be considered in conjunction with Table 2, which deals with ancillary or original probate in a state other than the domiciliary state, when the local assets are too substantial to qualify for the use of the small estate procedure.

There are several crucial issues that must be confronted before the small estates procedure can be utilized. First, the procedure may not necessarily be available to nonresidents at all. Second, if it is, there may be precise requirements for obtaining the benefit. For example, in some states, a hearing may be required. In others, a simple affidavit may be prepared and submitted to those in possession of the decedent's property. This table provides details as to the required contents of the petition and/or affidavit. It also indicates what notice requirements must be observed.

The small estates procedure is not available for all assets. Moreover, certain assets, such as automobiles, may have to be handled specially. Regardless of the nature of the assets allowed, each state also imposes a maximum dollar amount. If the "estate" exceeds this amount, the small estates procedure cannot be employed.

Difficult questions often arise as to authority to deal with the property. At what point can the assets be disposed of and by whom? In other words, there may be creditors, whose rights have to be addressed first. There is also the question whether an executor or administrator appointed in another state might seek to act and have priority. Alternatively, a nonresident fiduciary may be barred from acting in that capacity locally. Finally, a transferor of assets, who delivers the property upon presentation of an affidavit or petition, may want to be assured that there will be no liability if later someone else claims a right to the property. All of these matters are dissected and addressed, along with statutory references for further inquiry, if deemed necessary by the reader.

Lastly, each state table is headed with the title or type of small estate procedure. In some states, only a procedure for collection of assets by presentation of an affidavit to the holder is in effect. In other states, the statute only addresses the procedure for prompt probate of a will through summary administration. In a large number of states, the statute provides for both procedures.

Alabama
Summary Distribution of Small Estates

Who can initiate process?	The surviving spouse, if there is one; otherwise distributees of an estate of personal property only. (§§ 43-2-692(a), 43-2-691(1))
Can it be used if claims outstanding?	No, payments or arrangements for payment of all claims against the estate must be made. (§ 43-2-692(b)(9))
Different rules if die testate or intestate?	If the decedent dies intestate, the awards due under Alabama law to the surviving spouse and children must be certified by a probate judge and transmitted to the surviving spouse and children via certified copy of such determination. If the decedent died testate, the will must be filed in the probate judge's office. (§ 43-2-692(b)(6) & (7))
Notice?	Notice of filing must be published once a week for three successive weeks in a newspaper of general circulation in the county of decedent's domicile. If no such newspaper exists, notice must be posted at county courthouse for three weeks. (§ 43-2-692(b)(8))
heirs	No provision.
creditors	No provision.
others	No provision.
Which of the following must be observed?	
hearing	No provision.
affidavit, petition, other	Petition. (§ 43-2-692(a)) Can use an affidavit/order to claim decedent's property from another party in possession. (§ 43-2-694)
bond	No provision.
What are basic contents of petition or affidavit?	Petition shall describe the estate of decedent. (§ 43-2-692(a))
Is procedure available in the case of nonresident decedents?	No. (§ 43-2-692(b)(2))
Maximum allowable value of estate	$3,000 (entire estate). (§ 43-2-692(b)(1))
What property can be transferred by this means?	Personal property. (§ 43-2-692(b))
Special rules for certain assets (e.g., automobile)	No provision.
Can the spouse or other person take summarily if under certain amount?	Yes. The surviving spouse or distributee has a defeasible right if the entire estate is less than $3,000 and certain other criteria are satisfied. (§ 43-2-692(b))

Minimum period before filing allowed	Can file any time, but cannot recover until 45 days after filing and 21 days after first notice. (§ 43-2-692(b)(4))
Rights/obligations of party with affidavit	May have property transferred. (§ 43-2-694) Liable to personal representative of estate, surviving spouse, or minor children, or anyone with a superior right to the property. (§ 43-2-696)
Are some creditors given special privileges/ preference (e.g., medical expenses, funeral expenses)?	Yes, there is a priority imposed. In rank order: funeral expenses, probate fees, last illness expenses, state and municipality taxes, secured creditors, unsecured lienholders, unsecured creditors, and distributees or devisees. (§ 43-2-692(b)(9))
Creditors' rights, if insufficient assets	If there are insufficient assets to pay debts, and other arrangements are not made, summary distribution is not available. (§ 43-2-692(b)(9))
May the distribution of the estate proceed without appointment of personal representative?	Yes. (§ 43-2-692(b))
Must court approve affidavit?	No. Must be executed by a person with knowledge of compliance with the requirements of summary distribution. (§ 43-2-694)
Waiting period before authority to act	45 days after filing, 21 days after first notice. (§ 43-2-692(b)(4))
With whom do you file petition or affidavit?	Probate judge's office in county of decedent's domicile at death. (§ 43-2-692(a))
Is there an informal procedure for appointment of executor or administrator?	No provision.
Can a nonresident serve?	The power to utilize summary distribution is subject to any pre-existing right to administer. (§ 43-2-695)
Can the nonresident act locally based on appointment in another state?	Yes. (§§ 43-2-192 (executor), 43-2-193 (administrator))
What does a transferor need so as to be relieved of liability if challenged by another person later on who claims the particular property (e.g., copy of affidavit)?	Payor is relieved upon payment to same extent as if payment made to a personal representative. The payor need not investigate the truthfulness of the affidavit. (§ 43-2-696)

Alaska
Collection of Personal Property by Affidavit; Summary Administration

Who can initiate process?	There are two different procedures, depending on whether or not there is a personal representative. If there is no personal representative, the procedure is collection of personal property by affidavit and can be initiated by a person claiming to be the successor of the decedent. (§ 13.16.680(a)) If there is a personal representative, then the personal representative may initiate the procedure called summary administration. (§§ 13.16.690, 13.16.695(a))
Can it be used if claims outstanding?	*Affidavit.* No provision. *Summary Administration.* Yes. (§ 13.16.690)
Different rules if die testate or intestate?	No provision.
Notice?	
heirs	*Affidavit.* No provision. *Summary Administration.* Must send closing statement to distributees. (§ 13.16.695(a)(3))
creditors	*Affidavit.* No provision. *Summary Administration.* No notice is required to distribute the estate, but a closing statement must be sent. (§§ 13.16.690, 13.16.695(a)(3))
others	*Affidavit.* No provision. *Summary Administration.* All distributees and claimants of whom personal representative is aware and whose claims are neither paid nor barred must be sent a copy of the closing statement. (§ 13.16.695(a)(3))
Which of the following must be observed?	
hearing	No provision.
affidavit, petition, other	*Affidavit.* Affidavit. (§ 13.16.680(a)) *Summary Administration.* A verified statement. (§ 13.16.695(a))
bond	No provision.
What are basic contents of petition or affidavit?	*Affidavit.* Must show that the estate less liens and encumbrances does not exceed $15,000; 30 days have elapsed since death; no personal representative; party using is entitled to property. (§ 13.16.680) *Summary Administration.* Closing statement must show that value of estate did not exceed certain allowances and expenses; that estate is fully administered; and that a closing statement was sent to all distributees and claimants. (§ 13.16.695(a))

Is procedure available in the case of nonresident decedents?	No provision.
Maximum allowable value of estate	*Affidavit.* Value of entire estate, wherever located, less liens and encumbrances, must not exceed $15,000. (§ 13.16.680(a)(1)) *Summary Administration.* Value of entire estate, less liens and encumbrances, cannot exceed homestead, exempt property, family allowance, administration costs, funeral expenses, and medical expenses for last illness. (§ 13.16.690)
What property can be transferred by this means?	*Affidavit.* Personal property. (§ 13.16.680) *Summary Administration.* Entire estate. (§ 13.16.690)
Special rules for certain assets (e.g., automobile)	Stock in corporations organized under the Alaska Natives Claims Settlement Act is not to be considered under this section for distribution or estate valuation purposes. (§ 13.16.705(a))
Can the spouse or other person take summarily if under certain amount?	*Affidavit.* Yes, if the value of the entire estate, less liens and encumbrances, does not exceed $15,000. (§ 13.16.680(a)(1)) *Summary Administration.* No provision.
Minimum period before filing allowed	*Affidavit.* 30 days after death. (§ 13.16.680(a)(2)) *Summary Administration.* Any time after disbursement and distribution of estate. (§ 13.16.695(a))
Rights/obligations of party with affidavit	*Affidavit.* Accountable to anyone with a superior right or a personal representative. (§ 13.16.685) *Summary Administration.* No provision.
Are some creditors given special privileges/ preference (e.g., medical expenses, funeral expenses)?	*Affidavit.* No provision. *Summary Administration.* Yes, administration expenses, funeral expenses, and last illness medical expenses. (§ 13.16.690)
Creditors' rights, if insufficient assets	*Affidavit.* See *Rights/obligations of party with affidavit* above. *Summary Administration.* No right beyond a right to a closing statement. (§ 13.16.695)
May the distribution of the estate proceed without appointment of personal representative?	*Affidavit.* Yes. (§ 13.16.680) *Summary Administration.* No provision.
Must court approve affidavit?	No. (§ 13.16.680)
Waiting period before authority to act	*Affidavit.* 30 days after death. (§ 13.16.680(a)(2)) *Summary Administration.* No provision.

With whom do you file petition or affidavit?	*Affidavit.* With those in possession of property or transfer agent of any security. (§ 13.16.680(a), (b)) *Summary Administration.* File with the court. (§ 13.16.695)
Is there an informal procedure for appointment of executor or administrator?	Yes, if no qualified person has come forward to take charge of the assets and estate is $15,000 or less. (§ 13.16.700)
Can a nonresident serve?	Under the court-directed procedures of § 13.16.700, there is no language regarding foreign appointment. But a nonresident can be a personal representative. (§§ 13.21.015–13.21.040)
Can the nonresident act locally based on appointment in another state?	Yes. (§§ 13.21.015–13.21.040)
What does a transferor need so as to be relieved of liability if challenged by another person later on who claims the particular property (e.g., copy of affidavit)?	Payor is released from liability upon payment. No need to inquire into the truth of the affidavit. (§ 13.16.685)

Arizona
Transfer of Title to Small Estates by Affidavit and Summary Administration

Who can initiate process?	There are two procedures: (1) collection of personal/real property by affidavit, and (2) summary administration. *Personal and Real Property by Affidavit* (§ 14-3971). This procedure has three components—one for compensation owing to the decedent by the employer (§ 14-3971(A)), one for the collection of personal property (§ 14-3971(B)), and one for real property (§ 14-3971(E)). Under § 14-3971(A), the surviving spouse or someone acting on behalf of the surviving spouse may initiate. Under § 14-3971(B) & (E), a person claiming to be a successor may initiate. *Summary Administration.* (§ 14-3973) The personal representative. (§ 14-3973)
Can it be used if claims outstanding?	*Affidavit.* The affidavit procedure for real property requires unsecured debt, funeral expenses, expenses of last illness, and taxes to be paid. (§ 14-3971(E)(3) & (6)) *Summary Administration.* No provision.
Different rules if die testate or intestate?	No provision.
Notice?	*Affidavit.* Once the affidavit is filed and the registrar determines that it is complete, the registrar shall cause the affidavit to be recorded in the county where real property is located. (§ 14-3971(F)) *Summary Administration.* No general provision, but see below.
heirs	*Affidavit.* No provision. *Summary Administration.* A copy of the closing statement must be sent to all known distributees whose claims are neither paid nor barred. (§ 14-3974(A)(3))
creditors	*Affidavit.* No provision. *Summary Administration.* A copy of the closing statement must be sent to all known creditors whose claims are neither paid nor barred. (§ 14-3974(A)(3))
others	*Affidavit.* No provision. *Summary Administration.* A copy of the closing statement must be sent to other claimants of whom the personal representative is aware and whose claims are neither paid nor barred. (§ 14-3974(A)(3)).
Which of the following must be observed?	
hearing	No provision.
affidavit, petition, other	*Affidavit.* All types of collection by affidavit require the collector to present an affidavit that states the necessary information for that type of collection. (§ 14-3971) *Summary Administration.* Must have a closing statement. (§ 14-3974)
bond	No provision.

What are basic contents of petition or affidavit?	*Affidavit:* A. With regard to an employer owing compensation of no more than $5,000, the affidavit must state that: (1) affiant is surviving spouse or is authorized to act on the spouse's behalf; and (2) no application for the appointment of a personal representative pending or granted in Arizona. (§ 14-3971(A)) B. With regard to personal property, the affidavit must state that: (1) the entire estate, less liens and encumbrances, does not exceed $50,000; (2) 30 days have lapsed since decedent's death; (3) no application or petition for a personal representative is pending and a personal representative has not been appointed in any jurisdiction, or the personal representative has been discharged or more than one year has lapsed since a closing statement has been filed; and (4) successor is entitled to the property. (§ 14-3971(B)) C. With respect to real property, the affidavit may be filed in the county court of the decedent's domicile, or if not a domiciliary, the county in which the property is situated: (1) describing the real property and decedent's interest; (2) value of real property in Arizona, less liens and encumberances, does not exceed $50,000; (3) six months have lapsed since death; (4) no application or petition for personal representative is pending in any jurisdiction and no personal representative has been appointed in any jurisdiction, or the personal representative has been discharged or more than one year has elapsed since a closing statement has been filed; (5) funeral, last illness, and unsecured debts have been paid; (6) why the affiant is entitled to the property; (7) no other person has a right to the property; (8) no federal or Arizona estate taxes due on decedent's estate; and (9) an affirmation that the information is true. (§ 14-3971(E)) *Summary Administration.* Closing statement must state that to the best of personal representative's knowledge the estate value does not exceed the homestead, exempt property, and family allowances, plus reasonable administrative, funeral, and medical expenses. It must state that the personal representative has fully administered the estate by disbursing and distributing it to the persons entitled thereto. The closing statement must also state that the personal representative has distributed the assets and that copies of the closing statement have been sent to the required parties. (§ 14-3974(A))
Is procedure available in the case of nonresident decedents?	Yes. (§§ 14-4201, 14-4207)
Maximum allowable value of estate	*Affidavit.* $5,000 in compensation. (§ 14-3971(A)) $50,000 for personal property, less liens and encumbrances. (§ 14-3971(B)) $50,000 real property, less liens and encumbrances. (§ 14-3971(E)) *Summary Administration.* Entire estate, less liens and encumbrances, does not exceed homestead, family allowance, administration costs, and funeral/last illness expenses. (§ 14-3973)

What property can be transferred by this means?	*Affidavit.* Wages, personal property, and real property. (§ 14-3971) *Summary Administration.* Entire estate. (§ 14-3973)
Special rules for certain assets (e.g., automobile)	Registered ownership of any securities shall be changed by a tranfer agent. (§ 14-3971(C)) Automobile must be transferred through the motor vehicle division. (§ 14-3971(D))
Can the spouse or other person take summarily if under certain amount?	Yes, if the entire estate, less liens and encumbrances, does not exceed allowance in lieu of homestead, exempt property, family allowance, costs and expenses of administration, reasonable funeral expenses, and reasonable and necessary medical and hospital expenses of the last illness of the decedent, the personal representative may do so. (§ 14-3973)
Minimum period before filing allowed	*Affidavit.* For personal property, must wait 30 days after the death of decedent. (§ 14-3971(B)). For real property, must wait 6 months after the death of decedent. (§ 14-3971(E) *Summary Administration.* No minimum period. (§ 14-3973)
Rights/obligations of party with affidavit	Accountable to personal representative or anyone with a superior right. (§ 14-3972(A))
Are some creditors given special privileges/ preference (e.g., medical expenses, funeral expenses)?	*Affidavit.* For real property, funeral expenses, last illness expenses, unsecured debts, and federal or Arizona estate taxes must be paid first. (§ 14-3971(E)(3), (6)) *Summary Administration.* Administration expenses, funeral expenses, and last illness expenses have priority. (§ 14-3973)
Creditors' rights, if insufficient assets	No provision beyond the right to receive closing statement in summary administration. (§ 14-3974)
May the distribution of the estate proceed without appointment of personal representative?	*Affidavit.* Must proceed without personal representative. (§ 14-3971) *Summary Administration.* Personal representative required. (§ 14-3973)
Must court approve affidavit?	Only for real property. (§ 14-3971(E), (F))
Waiting period before authority to act	See *minimum period before filing allowed* above.
With whom do you file petition or affidavit?	For real property, an affidavit must be filed in the court in the county of decedent's domicile at time of death or, if decedent was not domiciled in Arizona, then in any county in which real property of the decedent is located. (§ 14-3971(E))
Is there an informal procedure for appointment of executor or administrator?	Yes. (§§ 14-3301, 14-3307 to -3311)
Can a nonresident serve?	Yes. (§ 14-3203(G))
Can the nonresident act locally based on appointment in another state?	Yes, if there is no local administration and the appropriate documentation is filed with local courts. (§§ 14-4205, 14-4204).
What does a transferor need so as to be relieved of liability if challenged by another person later on who claims the particular property (e.g., copy of affidavit)?	The transferor is discharged upon payment without need to investigate truth of affidavit. (§ 14-3972(A))

Arkansas
Distribution Without Administration

Who can initiate process?	In Arkansas, distributees can collect small estates by engaging in an affidavit procedure. (§ 28-41-101) If the court determines that the value of the estate does not exceed certain statutory allowances to which the widow or minor children are entitled free of debt, the affidavit procedure is not necessary and the court will vest the estate in the widow or minor children. (§ 28-41-103) *Affidavit.* Distributees of an estate. (§ 28-41-101) *No Administration.* Interested person. (§ 28-41-103)
Can it be used if claims outstanding?	*Affidavit.* No. (§ 28-41-101(a)(4)(A)) *No Administration.* Yes. (§ 28-41-103)
Different rules if die testate or intestate?	No provision.
Notice?	*Affidavit.* If real property is involved, notice shall contain (1) the name of the decedent and last known address, (2) the date of death, (3) a statement that an affidavit was filed, date of filing, a legal description of all real property, (4) a statement requiring all persons having claims against the estate to exhibit them, properly verified, within 3 months from the date of the first publication of the notice, (5) the name and mailing address of the distributee or attorney, and (6) the date the notice was first published. (§§ 28-41-101(b)(2)(B)) *No Administration.* Court discretion. (§ 28-41-103(c))
heirs	*Affidavit.* If the estate contains real property, notice shall be published in accordance with § 28-1-112(b) (listing several methods). In addition, within one month of first notice by publication, notice must be served upon all heirs whose names and addresses are known. (§§ 28-41-101(b)(2)(C), 28-40-111(a)(4)) *No Administration.* Court discretion. (§ 28-41-103(c))
creditors	*Affidavit.* If the estate contains real property, notice shall be published in accordance with § 28-1-112(b) (listing several methods). In addition, within one month of first notice by publication, notice must be served upon all unpaid creditors whose names, status as creditors, and addresses are known or reasonably ascertainable. (§§ 28-41-101(b)(2)(C), 28-40-111(a)(4)) *No Administration.* Court discretion. (§ 28-41-103(c))
others	*Affidavit.* If the estate contains real property. notice shall be published in accordance with §§ 28-1-112(b), 28-1-112(b)(4) and 28-40-111(a)(4) (§§ 28-41-101(b)(2)(C)) *No Administration.* Court discretion. (§ 28-41-103(c))
Which of the following must be observed?	
hearing	No provision.
affidavit, petition, other	*Affidavit.* Affidavit. (§ 28-41-101) *No Administration.* Petition. (§ 28-41-103(c))

bond	No provision.
What are basic contents of petition or affidavit?	*Affidavit.* Affidavit must set forth (1) that there are no unpaid claims, and the Department of Human Services has provided no state or federal benefits or has been reimbursed; (2) an itemized description and valuation of real and personal property; (3) the names and addresses of those in possession of real or personal property; and (4) the names, addresses, and relationship to decedent of persons entitled to property. (§ 28-41-101(a)(4)(A)–(D)) *No Administration.* Petition must establish that value of estate (personal property) does not exceed amounts that the widow or minor children are entitled to under dower, curtesy, or statutory allowance. (§ 28-41-103(a))
Is procedure available in the case of nonresident decedents?	Except where special provisions apply, same for nonresident decedents as resident decedents. (§ 28-42-101)
Maximum allowable value of estate	*Affidavit.* All property, less encumberances, excluding homestead and statutory allowances, must not exceed $100,000. (§ 28-41-101(a)(3)) *No Administration.* See *contents of petition* in § 28-41-103(a).
What property can be transferred by this means?	*Affidavit.* Entire estate. (§ 28-41-101(a)) *No Administration.* Personal property. (§ 28-41-103(a))
Special rules for certain assets (e.g., automobile)	No provision.
Can the spouse or other person take summarily if under certain amount?	No provision.
Minimum period before filing allowed	*Affidavit.* 45 days after death. (§ 28-41-101(a)(2)) *No Administration.* No provision.
Rights/obligations of party with affidavit	Distributee will be treated like a trustee who is answerable to anyone with a prior right or any personal representative. (§ 28-41-102(b))
Are some creditors given special privileges/ preference (e.g., medical expenses, funeral expenses)?	*Affidavit.* Department of Health and Human Services (''DHHS'') is given specific attention—Affidavit must indicate whether DHHS furnished benefits to the decedent and, if so, whether those funds were reimbursed. (§ 28-41-101(a)(4)(A)) *No Administration.* No provision.
Creditors' rights, if insufficient assets	*Affidavit.* Cannot use affidavit procedure if there are unpaid claims. (§ 28-41-101(a)(4)(A)) *No Administration.* No provision.
May the distribution of the estate proceed without appointment of personal representative?	Yes. (§§ 28-41-101(a), 28-41-103)
Must court approve affidavit?	No. Affidavit must simply be filed by probate clerk. (§ 28-41-101(b)(1))

Waiting period before authority to act	*Affidavit.* 45 days have elapsed since the death of the decedent. (§ 28-41-101(a)(2)) *No Administration.* None. (§ 28-41-103)
With whom do you file petition or affidavit?	Clerk of the Probate Court. (§ 28-41-101(a)(4) & (b)(1))
Is there an informal procedure for appointment of executor or administrator?	No provision.
Can a nonresident serve?	Yes, if appointed an agent to accept service of process and notice. (§ 28-48-101(b)(6))
Can the nonresident act locally based on appointment in another state?	Yes, after filing an authenticated copy of domiciliary letters in the proper venue. (§ 28-42-102(a)(1))
What does a transferor need so as to be relieved of liability if challenged by another person later on who claims the particular property (e.g., copy of affidavit)?	The person making payment is discharged to the same extent as if payment made to a personal representative. Such person is not required to examine truthfulness of the affidavit. (§ 28-41-102(a))

California
Small Estate Set Aside/Disposition of Estate Without Administration

Who can initiate process?	There are two procedures: small estate set aside ("Set Aside") (Prob. § 6600 et seq.) and disposition of estate without administration ("No Administration") (Prob. § 13000 et seq.). *Set Aside.* The following may initiate the process: (1) person named as executor in will; (2) surviving spouse; (3) guardian of minor child; (4) child who was a minor at time of death; or (5) personal representative. (Prob. § 6606(a)) *No Administration.* The successor of decedent may initiate the process. (Prob. § 13100) A successor is a person who is entitled to succeed to a particular item of property under a will or under the laws of intestate succession. (Prob. § 13006) The "No Administration" procedure is divided into a personal property procedure (Prob. §§ 13100-13116) and real property procedure. (Prob. §§ 13200-13210)
Can it be used if claims outstanding?	*Set Aside.* Discretionary. (Prob. § 6609(b)) *No Administration.* Under personal property procedure, yes, but the successor remains liable for unsecured debt of decedent. (Prob. §§ 13101, 13109) Under real property procedure, affiant must swear that funeral expenses, last illness expenses, and unsecured debts are paid. (Prob. § 13200(a)(8)) Successor remains liable for unsecured debt. (Prob. § 13204)
Different rules if die testate or intestate?	*Set Aside.* No provision. *No Administration.* Only to the extent that testacy/intestacy determines the successor. (Prob. §§ 13100, 13006)
Notice?	*Set Aside.* If administration proceedings are not pending, notice shall be mailed at least 15 days in advance of hearing to (1) each person named as executor in a will; (2) each heir and devisee known to petitioner; and (3) copy of petition to the surviving spouse, each child, and each devisee who is not petitioning. (Prob. §§ 6607(a), 1220) If proceedings are pending, notice must be mailed to each known heir and each devisee, executor, and alternate executor in the will at least 15 days in advance of hearing. (Prob. §§ 6607(c), 8110) Published notice is also required in a newspaper of general circulation in the city of decedent's domicile at death. The notice must be published three times at least once a week, with the first notice appearing at least 15 days before the hearing. (Prob. §§ 6607, 8121) *No Administration.* No notice required for personal property unless there is a hearing for a court order to determine succession. If there is such a hearing, notice of the hearing is to be mailed to each known heir, devisee, and guardian or conservator of the decedent. (Prob. §§ 13153, 13152) For real property, the succession hearing rules are the same, and a copy of the affidavit must be mailed to each known guardian/conservator. (Prob. § 13200(f))
heirs	See *Notice?* above.

creditors	See *Notice?* above.
others	See *Notice?* above.
Which of the following must be observed?	
hearing	*Set Aside.* Yes. (Prob. § 6607) *No Administration.* No provision.
affidavit, petition, other	*Set Aside.* Petition. (Prob. § 6602) *No Administration.* Affidavit or "declaration." (Prob. §§ 13101, 13200) For the real property procedure there is a $35 fee. (Prob. § 13201)
bond	No provision.
What are basic contents of petition or affidavit?	*Set Aside.* Petition shall allege that chapter applies and request for an order for set aside and shall include: (1) for administration not pending, facts necessary to determine the county in which the estate of the decedent may be administered; (2) name, address, relation of each known heir/devisee; (3) description and estimated value of decedent's estate and a list of all liens and encumbrances; (4) description and estimated value of real property outside of California that passed to surviving spouse/minor child; (5) description and estimated value of any joint property or multiple party accounts that passed to the surviving spouse/minor child; (6) any property outside of estate by virtue of homestead; (7) unpaid funeral, last illness, administration expenses; (8) requested disposition of estate and the considerations that support such a disposition. (Prob. § 6604) An inventory and appraisal must accompany the petition. (Prob. § 6608) *No Administration.* For personal property: (1) name of decedent; (2) date and place of decedent's death; (3) statement that 40 days have passed since death; (4) statement that either no administration proceeding is pending in California or that the personal representa tive has consented to this procedure; (5) gross fair market value of decedent's real and personal property in California (less exclusions of Prob. § 13050) does not exceed $100,000; (6) description of the property to be given to affiant; (7) name of the successor to the property; (8) statement that affiant is the successor or authorized to act on successor's behalf; (9) statement that no person has a superior right in the described property; (10) request for delivery; (11) affirmation as to truth; (12) death certificate; and (13) personal representative's consent if appropriate. (Prob. § 13101) Also required: in some cases, evidence of ownership (Prob. § 13102); inventory and appraisal of California real property (Prob. § 13103); proof of affiant's identity (Prob. § 13104). For real property: (1) name of decedent; (2) date and place of death; (3) legal description of property; (4) name/address of known guardians/conservators of estate; (5) statement that gross value of California real property (less exclusions) does not exceed $20,000; (6) statement that six months have passed since death; (7) no administration proceeding has been conducted, or the decedent's personal representative has

	consented to this procedure; (8) statement that funeral expenses, last illness expenses, and unsecured debt have been paid; (9) statement that affiant is successor and no person has a superior right; (10) affirmation of truth of affidavit; (11) notarized; (12) inventory/appraisal of non-excluded California real property; (13) if affiant is claiming under a will and there is no estate proceeding, a copy of the will must also be attached; and (14) certified copy of death certificate or personal representative's consent to use of affidavit procedure. (Prob. § 13200)
Is procedure available in the case of nonresident decedents?	No provision.
Maximum allowable value of estate	*Set Aside.* Net value less liens, encumbrances, and homestead interest must not exceed $20,000. (Prob. §§ 6602, 6600) *No Administration.* Personal property—current gross fair market value of real and personal property must not exceed $100,000 less certain exclusions. (Prob. §§ 13101(a)(5), 13050) Real property—gross value of California real property less exclusions must not exceed $20,000. (Prob. §§ 13200(a)(5), 13050)
What property can be transferred by this means?	*Set Aside.* Entire estate. (Prob. § 6602) *No Administration.* Personal property—personal only. (Prob. § 13101(a)) Real property—real only. (Prob. § 13200(a))
Special rules for certain assets (e.g., automobile)	Under all procedures, certain property does not count for valuation purposes. (Prob. §§ 6600, 13050)
Can the spouse or other person take summarily if under certain amount?	Yes, the surviving spouse can take property that passes by will or intestate succession without administration. (Prob. § 13500 et seq.)
Minimum period before filing allowed	*Set Aside.* Any time before order for final distribution. (Prob. § 6605(c)) *No Administration.* Personal property—40 days after death. (Prob. § 13101(a)(3)) Real property—six months after death. (Prob. § 13200(a)(6))
Rights/obligations of party with affidavit	*Set Aside.* Not applicable. *No Administration.* Personal property—liable for (1) unsecured debt (Prob. § 13109); (2) liable to those with superior claims (Prob. § 13110); (3) liable for treble damages if fraudulent (Prob. § 13110); (4) liable to personal representative if administration proceedings later commenced or if personal representative revokes consent to use of this procedure. (Prob. § 13111) Real property—same.
Are some creditors given special privileges/ preference (e.g., medical expenses, funeral expenses)?	*Set Aside.* If an order is made to set aside the small estate, the court will make an additional order requiring that unpaid last illness expenses, funeral charges, and administration expenses be paid. (§ 6609(d)) *No Administration.* Real property—the affiant must swear that funeral expenses, last illness expenses, and unsecured debts have been paid. (Prob. § 13200(a)(8))

Creditors' rights, if insufficient assets	*Set Aside.* No provision. *No Administration.* For personal property, affiants are liable for unsecured debt to the extent provided in § 13112. (§ 13109) For real property, affiants are liable for unsecured debt to the extent provided in § 13207. (Prob. § 13204)
May the distribution of the estate proceed without appointment of personal representative?	*Set Aside.* Yes. (Prob. § 6606) *No Administration.* Yes. (Prob. §§ 13108, 13210)
Must court approve affidavit?	*Set Aside.* While there is no affidavit, the court must approve a petition to assign the whole of the decedent's estate to the surviving spouse and the minor children. (Prob. § 6609) *No Administration.* For personal property, no court involvement is necessary. (Prob. § 13101) For real property, the affidavit must be filed in the Superior Court in the county of decedent's domicile at time of death, or if decedent was not domiciled in California, then in the any county in which real property of the decedent is located. (Prob. § 13200(a))
Waiting period before authority to act	*Set Aside.* None. (Prob. § 6605) *No Administration.* Personal property—40 days. (Prob. § 13101) Real property—six months. (Prob. § 13200)
With whom do you file petition or affidavit?	*Set Aside.* Petition shall be filed in the superior court of a county in which the estate may be administered. (Prob. § 6603) *No Administration.* Real property—Superior court in county of decedent's domicile at death. (Prob. § 13200(a)); Personal property—with holder of decedent's property (Prob. § 13101)
Is there an informal procedure for appointment of executor or administrator?	No provision.
Can a nonresident serve?	No provision.
Can the nonresident act locally based on appointment in another state?	No provision.
What does a transferor need so as to be relieved of liability if challenged by another person later on who claims the particular property (e.g., copy of affidavit)?	*Set Aside.* No provision. *No Administration.* Transferor is released from liability under personal property procedures. (Prob. § 13106(a)) No provision for real property procedures.

Colorado
Collection of Personal Property by Affidavit/ Summary Administration Procedure for Small Estates

Who can initiate process?	*Affidavit.* Successor. (§ 15-12-1201) *Summary Administration.* Personal representative. (§ 15-12-1203)
Can it be used if claims outstanding?	*Affidavit.* Yes. (§ 15-12-1201) *Summary Administration.* Yes. (§ 15-12-1203)
Different rules if die testate or intestate?	*Affidavit.* Same rules. (§ 15-12-1201) *Summary Administration.* Same rules. (§ 15-12-1203)
Notice?	*Affidavit.* No provision. *Summary Administration.* Closing statement must be sent to all distributees of the estate and to known creditors and other claimants of whom the personal representative is aware and whose claims are neither paid nor barred. (§ 15-12-1204(1)(c))
heirs	*Summary Administration.* Closing statement must be sent to all distributees of the estate. (§ 15-12-1204(1)(c))
creditors	*Summary Administration.* If the net value of the estate does not exceed the value of the personal property held by the decedent as fiduciary or trustee, exempt property allowance, family allowance, cost of administration, reasonable funeral and medical/hospital expenses of the last illness of the decedent, the representative may distribute the property without giving notice to creditors. (§ 15-12-1203) But a closing statement must be sent to known creditors whose claims are neither paid nor barred. (§ 15-12-1204(1)(c))
others	*Summary Administration.* Closing statement must be sent to all other claimants of whom the personal representative is aware and whose claims are neither paid nor barred. (§ 12-15-1204(1)(c))
Which of the following must be observed?	
Hearing	No provision.
affidavit, petition, other	Affidavit. (§ 15-12-1201) *Summary Administration.* Closing statement. (§ 15-12-1204)
Bond	No provision.
What are basic contents of petition or affidavit?	*Affidavit.* The affidavit must assert that (1) the fair market value of property at time of death, wherever located, less liens and encumbrances, does not exceed \$50,000; (2) 10 days have lapsed since death; (3) no application/petition for a personal representative is pending or has been granted in any jurisdiction; and (4) that the claimant is entitled to the property in the proportion set forth. (§ 15-12-1201(1)(a)–(d)) *Summary Administration.* Closing statement must assert that (1) to the best of personal representative's knowledge, the value of the entire estate did not exceed the value of personal

	property held by the decedent or in the decedent's possession as fiduciary or trustee, exempt property, family allowance, costs of administration, funeral/last illness expenses; (2) the estate has been disbursed to entitled persons by the personal representative; and (3) copies of the closing statement were sent to all distributees and creditors whose claims are neither paid nor barred, along with an accounting to those whose interests are affected. (§ 15-12-1204)
Is procedure available in the case of nonresident decedents?	Yes. (§ 15-13-201, 15-13-207)
Maximum allowable value of estate	*Affidavit.* Fair market value of all property at the time of death, less liens and encumbrances, must not exceed $50,000. (§ 15-12-1201(1)(a)) *Summary Administration.* Value of entire estate must not exceed the value of personal property held by the decedent or in possession of decedent as fiduciary/trustee, exempt property, family allowance, costs and expenses of administration, funeral/last illness expenses. (§ 15-12-1203)
What property can be transferred by this means?	*Affidavit.* Personal. (§ 15-12-1201) *Summary Administration.* All. (§ 15-12-1203)
Special rules for certain assets (e.g., automobile)	Registered ownership of any securities shall be changed by a tranfer agent upon presentation of the affidavit. (§ 15-12-1201(2)) A public official that is aware of any registered title of the decedent shall change the registered ownership from the decedent to the successor(s) upon presentation of the affidavit. (§ 15-12-1201(3))
Can the spouse or other person take summarily if under certain amount?	No provision.
Minimum period before filing allowed	*Affidavit.* 10 days after death. (§ 15-12-1201(1)(b)) *Summary Administration.* Any time after disbursement and distribution of estate. (§ 15-12-1204(1))
Rights/obligations of party with affidavit	Answerable and accountable to any personal representative or person with superior right. (§ 15-12-1202)
Are some creditors given special privileges/ preference (e.g., medical expenses, funeral expenses)?	*Affidavit.* No provision. *Summary Administration.* Funeral/last illness expenses. (§ 15-12-1203)
Creditors' rights, if insufficient assets	No provisions. Must be sent a closing statement. (§ 15-12-1204(1)(c))
May the distribution of the estate proceed without appointment of personal representative?	*Affidavit.* May proceed without personal representative. (§ 15-12-1201) *Summary Administration.* Must proceed with personal representative. (§ 15-12-1203)
Must court approve affidavit?	No. (§ 15-12-1201)
Waiting period before authority to act	*Affidavit.* 10 days after death. (§ 15-12-1201) *Summary Administration.* No waiting period. (§ 15-12-1203)

With whom do you file petition or affidavit?	*Affidavit.* Need not file. (§ 15-12-1201) *Summary Administration.* Closing statement filed with the court. (§ 15-12-1204)
Is there an informal procedure for appointment of executor or administrator?	Yes. (§§ 15-12-301, 15-12-307 to -11)
Can a nonresident serve?	Yes. (§ 15-13-205)
Can the nonresident act locally based on appointment in another state?	Yes, if there is no local administration and the appropriate documentation is filed with local courts. (§ 15-13-206)
What does a transferor need so as to be relieved of liability if challenged by another person later on who claims the particular property (e.g., copy of affidavit)?	Transferor is released to the same extent as if payor dealt with a personal representative, without any need to inquire into the truth of the affidavit. (§ 15-12-1202)

Connecticut
Settlement of Certain Small Estates Without Letters of Administration or Probate of Will

Who can initiate process?	(1) Surviving spouse; (2) if no surviving spouse, next of kin; or (3) if no next of kin or if surviving spouse and next of kin refuse, any person the court deems to have a sufficient interest. (§ 45a-273(a))
Can it be used if claims outstanding?	No. (§ 45a-273(a))
Different rules if die testate or intestate?	Yes. If a party seeks to use and qualifies for this procedure and the fair market value of estate exceeds claims and family allowances of § 45a-320, the court will proceed as follows: (1) if no will, court will order distribution per law of intestate succession; (2) if will provides for distribution which is the same as intestate succession, court will order distribution per law of intestate succession; (3) if will provides for method other than intestate succession and heirs sign a waiver, court will order excess to be paid in accordance with will; (4) if will provides for method other than intestate succession and no waiver is signed by heirs, will shall be offered for probate. (§ 45a-273(e))
Notice?	No provision, except for court-given notice to the commissioner of revenue of any decree. (§ 45a-273(j)(2))
heirs	No provision.
creditors	No provision.
others	No provision.
Which of the following must be observed?	
hearing	No provision.
affidavit, petition, other	Affidavit. (§ 45a-273(a))
bond	As a condition to a transfer under § 45a-273(e), the holder may require the execution of a bond of indemnity. (§ 45a-273(g))
What are basic contents of petition or affidavit?	Affidavit stating: (1) all debts have been paid; (2) the aggregate value of specified property does not exceed $20,000; and (3) whether decedent received state aid or aid from department of veteran affairs. (§ 45a-273(a))
Is procedure available in the case of nonresident decedents?	Yes, may use another state's procedures as a matter of comity if that state grants same privilege to Connecticut. (§ 45a-276(a))
Maximum allowable value of estate	The sum of the following property cannot exceed $20,000: (1) deposits in banks; (2) equity in shares in any savings and loan, credit union, or federal savings and loan doing business in Connecticut; (3) corporate stock or bonds; (4) unpaid wages from Connecticut sources; (5) death benefit payable from any fraternal order or shop society or under any insurance policy for which the decedent failed to name a beneficiary under the bylaws or regulations of such order or society; (6) other

	tangible/intangible personal property including motor vehicles/boats registered in decedent's name; or (7) an unreleased interest in a mortgage. (§ 45a-273(a) & (b))
What property can be transferred by this means?	After claims have been satisfied, all excess property. (§ 45a-273(e))
Special rules for certain assets (e.g., automobile)	No provision, except for nominal fees for transfers of motor vehicles and boats. (§ 45a-273(h))
Can the spouse or other person take summarily if under certain amount?	No provision.
Minimum period before filing allowed	This procedure is available only if no will is presented for probate within 30 days of death. (§ 45a-275)
Rights/obligations of party with affidavit	Liable to commissioner of revenue for any succession or transfer tax. (§ 45a-273(j)(1))
Are some creditors given special privileges/preference (e.g., medical expenses, funeral expenses)?	Yes: funeral expenses, last illness expenses, state aid. (§ 45a-273(c) & (d))
Creditors' rights, if insufficient assets	Creditors must have been paid in order to use the procedure. (§ 45a-273(a))
May the distribution of the estate proceed without appointment of personal representative?	Yes. (§ 45a-273(a))
Must court approve affidavit?	Yes. (§ 45a-273(c) & (e))
Waiting period before authority to act	30 days after death. (§ 45a-275)
With whom do you file petition or affidavit?	Court of probate in district where decedent resided. (§ 45a-273(a))
Is there an informal procedure forappointment of executor or administrator?	No provision.
Can a nonresident serve?	No provision.
Can the nonresident act locally based on appointment in another state?	No provision.
What does a transferor need so as to be relieved of liability if challenged by another person later on who claims the particular property (e.g., copy of affidavit)?	Payor may require the filing of waivers, the execution of a bond or indemnity, and a receipt for such transfer or payment. (§ 45a-273(g))

Delaware
Distribution of Decedent's Property Without Grant of Letters

Who can initiate process?	Spouse, grandparent, lineal descendant of a grandparent, the personal representative of any of the foregoing who may be deceased, or the guardian or trustee of any of the foregoing who may be incapacitated, or a trustee of a trust created by the decedent, or a funeral director licensed in the state. (12 § 2306(a)) Preference is given in the following order: (1) spouse; (2) child; (3) parent; (4) sibling; (5) grandchild or grandparent; (6) funeral director licensed in the state. (12 § 2306(b))
Can it be used if claims outstanding?	Only if "all known debts of the decedent are paid or provided for." (12 § 2306(a)(4))
Different rules if die testate or intestate?	Yes. If testate, the person receiving the estate must distribute per the will. If intestate, per intestate succession. (12 § 2306(a))
Notice?	No provision.
heirs	No provision.
creditors	No provision.
others	No provision.
Which of the following must be observed?	
hearing	No provision.
affidavit, petition, other	Affidavit. (12 § 2306)
bond	No provision.
What are basic contents of petition or affidavit?	Affidavit must state the following: (1) no petition for appointment of a personal representative pending or granted; (2) 30 days have elapsed since death; (3) value of personal estate (less jointly owned property, family Bible, clothes of decedent, family stores laid in before the death, insurance policy, pensions, bonds, stock options or other employee benefits payable to someone other than the decedent) does not exceed $30,000; (4) all known debts paid or provided for; (5) surviving spouse allowance paid, waived, or lapsed; (6) decedent did not own solely owned real estate located in Delaware; (7) the right of affiant to receive the money or property. (12 § 2306(a)(1)-(7))
Is procedure available in the case of nonresident decedents?	No provision.
Maximum allowable value of estate	Other than either property described in § 1901(b) & (c) or jointly owned property, $30,000. (12 § 2306(a)(3))
What property can be transferred by this means?	Personal estate. (12 § 2306(a))
Special rules for certain assets (e.g., automobile)	Property described in § 1901(b) & (c), such as family Bible, decedent's clothes, family stores laid in before death, property or death benefit, employee or incentive plan, and jointly owned

	property excluded from maximum allowed value. (12 § 2306(a)(3)) Next of kin has a right to take possession of the decedent's motor vehicle(s) and can enter any premises to remove clothing for the burial. (12 § 2306(c))
Can the spouse or other person take summarily if under certain amount?	No provision.
Minimum period before filing allowed	No filing required, but must wait until 30 days after death. (12 § 2306(a)(2))
Rights/obligations of party with affidavit	Answerable to anyone with a prior right, accountable to any intestate distributee or any personal representative thereafter appointed. (12 § 2307(a))
Are some creditors given special privileges/preference (e.g., medical expenses, funeral expenses)?	No provision. All known debts must be paid or provided for. (12 § 2306(a)(4))
Creditors' rights, if insufficient assets	No provision. All known debts must be paid or provided for. (12 § 2306(a)(4))
May the distribution of the estate proceed without appointment of personal representative?	Must proceed without personal representative. (12 § 2306(a)(1))
Must court approve affidavit?	No. (12 § 2306)
Waiting period before authority to act	30 days after death. (12 § 2306(a)(2))
With whom do you file petition or affidavit?	No filing required. (12 § 2306)
Is there an informal procedure for appointment of executor or administrator?	No provision.
Can a nonresident serve?	No provision.
Can the nonresident act locally based on appointment in another state?	No provision.
What does a transferor need so as to be relieved of liability if challenged by another person later on who claims the particular property (e.g., copy of affidavit)?	Transferor is released as if payment made to a personal representative. No need to inquire into the truthfulness of the affidavit. (12 § 2307(a))

District of Columbia
Small Estates

Who can initiate process?	Any person eligible for appointment as personal representative to an estate. (§§ 20-352, 20-303)
Can it be used if claims outstanding?	Yes. (§§ 20-352, 20-353)
Different rules if die testate or intestate?	No provision.
Notice?	All notice is at the discretion of the court. If the court provides notice, claims or objections must be made within 30 days of its publication. (§ 20-353(b))
heirs	No provision.
creditors	No provision.
others	No provision.
Which of the following must be observed?	
hearing	No provision.
affidavit, petition, other	Verified petition. (§ 20-352)
bond	No. (§ 20-354(a))
What are basic contents of petition or affidavit?	In addition to information required for standard probate petition under § 20-304, petition must include a statement that petitioner has made a diligent search to discover all property and debts of the decedent; a list of the known creditors of the decedent, with the amount of each claim, including contingent and disputed claims; and a statement of any legal proceedings pending in which decedent was a party. (§ 20-352)
Is procedure available in the case of nonresident decedents?	No provision.
Maximum allowable value of estate	$40,000. (§ 20-351)
What property can be transferred by this means?	Property subject to administration. (§ 20-351)
Special rules for certain assets (e.g., automobile)	If the only property of decedent is two or fewer automobiles, the Mayor may transfer title to the motor vehicles in accordance with § 50-1501.02(d). If title is so transferred, administration of decedent's estate is unnecessary. (§ 20-357)
Can the spouse or other person take summarily if under certain amount?	No provision.
Minimum period before filing allowed	No provision.
Rights/obligations of party with affidavit	There is no affidavit for the small estate procedure.
Are some creditors given special privileges/preference (e.g., medical expenses, funeral expenses)?	Funeral expenses. (§ 20-353(a)(4))

Creditors' rights, if insufficient assets	Right to file objection to small estates proceeding pursuant to notice. (§ 20-354(b))
May the distribution of the estate proceed without appointment of personal representative?	No. (§ 20-353(a)(1))
Must court approve affidavit?	Court must approve petition. (§ 20-353(a))
Waiting period before authority to act	No provision.
With whom do you file petition or affidavit?	Court. (§ 20-303)
Is there an informal procedure for appointment of executor or administrator?	No provision.
Can a nonresident serve?	Yes. Court appoints personal representatives after filing of a petition (§ 20-353), and any person eligible for appointment as a personal representative under § 20-303 may file a petition. Under § 20-303(b)(7), to qualify for appointment as a personal representative, a nonresident must file an irrevocable power of attorney with the Register designating the Register and the Register's successors in office as the person upon whom all notices and process issued by a competent court in the District of Columbia may be served with the same effect as personal service, in relation to all suits or matters pertaining to the estate in which the letters are to be issued.
Can the nonresident act locally based on appointment in another state?	No provision.
What does a transferor need so as to be relieved of liability if challenged by another person later on who claims the particular property (e.g., copy of affidavit)?	No provision.

Florida
Summary Administration, Disposition of Personal Property Without Administration

Who can initiate process?	*Summary Administration.* Any beneficiary or personal representative. (§ 735.203) *Disposition Without Administration.* Any interested party. (§ 735.301(2))
Can it be used if claims outstanding?	*Summary Administration.* Yes, if provision for payment of debts has been made. (§ 735.206) *Disposition Without Administration.* Disposition without administration can proceed where decedent leaves only personal property exempt under § 732.402, personal property exempt under the Constitution of Florida, and nonexempt personal property which does not exceed funeral expenses and medical/ hospital expenses of the last 60 days of last illness. (§ 735.301)
Different rules if die testate or intestate?	*Summary Administration.* If testate, decedent's will must not direct administration as required by Chapter 733. (§ 735.201(1)) *Disposition Without Administration.* No provision.
Notice?	*Summary Administration.* Any person who has received an order of summary administration may publish notice. If notice to creditors is published once per week for two consecutive weeks in the county in which the Order of Summary Administration was entered, creditors must file claims with court within three months from first publication, or be forever barred. (§§ 735.2063, 733.2121) *Disposition Without Administration.* No provision.
heirs	No provision.
creditors	*Summary Administration.* Prior to entry of the order of summary administration, petitioner shall make a diligent search and reasonable inquiry for known or reasonably ascertained creditors, serve a copy of the petition on them, and make provision for payment to the extent that assets are available. (§ 735.206(2))
others	*Summary Administration.* Any beneficiary who does not join the order for summary administration must receive notice. (§ 735.203(3))
Which of the following must be observed?	
hearing	*Summary Administration.* No provision *Disposition Without Administration.* No provision.
affidavit, petition, other	*Summary Administration.* Petition. (§ 735.203) *Disposition Without Administration.* Informal application required. May take the form of letter, affidavit, or other form. (§ 735.301(2))
bond	No provision.

What are basic contents of petition or affidavit?	*Summary Administration.* Must be signed and verified by the surviving spouse, if any, and any beneficiaries. (§ 735.203) Any beneficiary who does not join must receive formal notice. (*Id.*) *Disposition Without Administration.* No provision.
Is procedure available in the case of nonresident decedents?	*Summary Administration.* Yes. (§ 735.201) *Disposition Without Administration.* No provision.
Maximum allowable value of estate	*Summary Administration.* Value of estate less value of exempt property must not exceed $75,000 or decedent must have been dead for more than two years. (§ 735.201) *Disposition Without Administration.* Nonexempt personal property value must not exceed sum of preferred funeral expenses and reasonable and necessary medical and hospital expenses of the last 60 days of the illness. (§ 735.301)
What property can be transferred by this means?	*Summary Administration.* Entire estate (§ 735.201) *Disposition Without Administration.* Personal property. (§ 735.301)
Special rules for certain assets (e.g., automobile)	No provision.
Can the spouse or other person take summarily if under certain amount?	No provision.
Minimum period before filing allowed	*Summary Administration.* May be filed at any stage of administration of the estate if it currently appears to qualify. (§ 735.2055) *Disposition Without Administration.* No provision.
Rights/obligations of party with affidavit	No provision.
Are some creditors given special privileges/preference (e.g., medical expenses, funeral expenses)?	*Summary Administration.* No provision. *Disposition Without Administration.* Funeral and medical expenses. (§ 735.301(1))
Creditors' rights, if insufficient assets	*Summary Administration.* Beneficiaries or heirs remain liable on creditors' claims for up to two years after decedent's death. (§ 735.206(4)(d)(f)) Any known or reasonably ascertainable creditor who did not receive notice and for whom provision for payment was not made may enforce the claim and, if successful, shall be awarded reasonable attorney's fees. (*Id.*) *Disposition Without Administration.* No provision.
May the distribution of the estate proceed without appointment of personal representative?	*Summary Administration.* Yes. (§ 735.206) *Disposition Without Administration.* Yes. (§ 735.301)
Must court approve affidavit?	*Summary Administration.* No provision. *Disposition Without Administration.* Yes. (§ 735.301(2))
Waiting period before authority to act	*Summary Administration*: No waiting period. (§ 735.2055) *Disposition Without Administration.* No provision.
With whom do you file petition or affidavit?	*Summary Administration.* Court. (§ 735.206) *Disposition Without Administration.* Court. (§ 735.301)

Is there an informal procedure for appointment of executor or administrator?	*Summary Administration.* No provision. *Disposition Without Administration.* No. (§ 735.301)
Can a nonresident serve?	*Summary Administration.* No provision, but an opinion from the Florida Attorney General states: "A personal representative of a nonresident decedent must proceed through ancillary administration in the absence of an order of family administration or an order of summary administration or a letter or other writing under the seal of the court." (Op. Atty. Gen., 84-59, June 21, 1984) *Disposition Without Administration.* No provision.
Can the nonresident act locally based on appointment in another state?	No provision.
What does a transferor need so as to be relieved of liability if challenged by another person later on who claims the particular property (e.g., copy of affidavit)?	*Summary Administration.* Entered Order of Summary Administration. (§ 735.206(4)(b)) *Disposition Without Administration.* Court authorization. (§ 735.301)

Georgia
Order Dispensing with Administration

Who can initiate process?	Any heir at law of the deceased. (§ 53-2-40(a))
Can it be used if claims outstanding?	Only if all of the known creditors have consented or will be served. (§ 53-2-40(b))
Different rules if die testate or intestate?	Only applicable to the estate of a person dying intestate. (§ 53-2-40(a))
Notice?	If a petition is filed that states there are known creditors, a citation is issued, and the known creditors are served (§ 53-2-41(a)), typically by the sheriff. (§ 53-11-3(b))
heirs	The court is required to "ascertain the heirs." (§ 53-2-41(c)) Heirs must agree upon a division of the estate among themselves. (§ 53-2-40(b))
creditors	See above.
others	No provision.
Which of the following must be observed?	
hearing	No provision.
affidavit, petition, other	Need to file a petition to obtain an order dispensing with administration. (§ 53-2-40)
bond	No provision.
What are basic contents of petition or affidavit?	The petition must list the name and domicile of the decedent, the names, ages, majority status, and domicile of the heirs of the decedent; the description of the property in this state owned by the deceased owner; and a statement that the decedent owes no debts or that there are known debts and all creditors have consented or will be served, and that the heirs have agreed upon a division of the estate among themselves. (§ 53-2-40(b))
Is procedure available in the case of nonresident decedents?	The petition is available to nonresident decedents, if there is real property located in this state. (§ 53-2-40(a))
Maximum allowable value of estate	No provision.
What property can be transferred by this means?	Real and personal property. (§ 53-2-40(a))
Special rules for certain assets (e.g., automobile)	No provision.
Can the spouse or other person take summarily if under certain amount?	No provision.
Minimum period before filing allowed	No provision.
Rights/obligations of party with affidavit	No provision.
Are some creditors given special privileges/preference (e.g., medical expenses, funeral expenses)?	No provision.

Creditors' rights, if insufficient assets	After the granting of an order that no administration was necessary, any creditor has a right of action on the unsatisfied debts against the heirs to the extent of value of property received by the heirs. (§ 53-2-42) In addition, a creditor may object to the order prior to the grant and the order will not be issued as long as the objection is not withdrawn. (§ 53-2-41(b))
May the distribution of the estate proceed without appointment of personal representative?	Yes. (§ 53-2-40(a))
Must court approve affidavit?	Yes. If no objections to the order are filed and the court finds that the estate owes no debts or that all creditors have consented or withdrawn any objections and that the heirs are of age and under no disabilities or are represented by a guardian or a personal representative, the court must enter an order finding that no administration is necessary. (§ 53-2-41(c))
Waiting period before authority to act	No provision.
With whom do you file petition or affidavit?	The petition must be filed with the Probate Court of the county of domicile of the decedent, if the decedent was a resident of Georgia; if the decedent was not a Georgia resident, the petition must be filed in the county in which the real property is located. (§ 53-2-40(a))
Is there an informal procedure for appointment of executor or administrator?	No provision.
Can a nonresident serve?	No provision.
Can the nonresident act locally based on appointment in another state?	No provision.
What does a transferor need so as to be relieved of liability if challenged by another person later on who claims the particular property (e.g., copy of affidavit)?	No provision.

Hawaii
Collection of Personal Property by Affidavit and Summary Administration Procedure for Small Estates

Who can initiate process?	*By Affidavit.* A person claiming to be the successor of the decedent, or the Department of Human Services if it has a claim against the estate pursuant to § 346-15 or 346-37. (§ 560:3-1201(a)) *Summary Administration.* Personal representative. (§ 560:3-1203) *Clerk Administration.* Clerk of court of residence or domicile, or any interested person. (§ 560:3-1205)
Can it be used if claims outstanding?	*By Affidavit.* No provision. *Summary Administration.* Yes. (§ 560:3-1203) *Clerk Administration.* Yes. (§ 560:3-1206(a))
Different rules if die testate or intestate?	No provision.
Notice?	*By Affidavit.* No provision. *Summary Administration.* A copy of the closing statement must be sent to all distributees of the estate. (§ 560:3-1204(a)(3)) *Clerk Administration.* If the estate has a total value of $10,000 or less, the clerk is to publish the fact by posting a notice thereof at the front entrance of the court house of the judicial circuit and by advertising the notice in the English language at least once in a newspaper of general circulation in the judicial circuit. Notice must state that all creditors of the deceased must file with the clerk duly verified claims within 60 days from the date of publication, and that all persons claiming to be heirs of the estate must also file their claims with the clerk in that 60-day period. (§ 560:3-1206(a)) If the estate has a total value in excess of $10,000, the content and method of giving notice shall be as provided for informal probates in § 560:3-306. (§ 560:3-1206(b))
heirs	No provision.
creditors	*Summary Administration.* The distribution of the estate may be accomplished without notice being given to creditors. (§ 560:3-1203)
others	No provision.
Which of the following must be observed?	
hearing	No provision.
affidavit, petition, other	*By Affidavit.* Affidavit. (§ 560:3-1201) *Summary Administration.* Closing statement. (§ 560:3-1204) *Clerk Administration.* Petition. (§ 560:3-1205)
bond	No provision.
What are basic contents of petition or affidavit?	*By Affidavit.* Statements affirming the following: the gross value of the decedent's estate does not exceed $100,000, except that any motor vehicles registered in the decedent's name may be transferred regardless of value; no application or petition for the

	appointment of a personal representative is pending or has been granted in this state; and the claimed successor or successors are entitled to the property, or the Department of Human Services has paid for the decedent's burial. (§ 560:3-1201(a)) *Summary Administration.* After distribution, a verified statement must be filed which states that the value of entire estate, less liens and encumbrances, did not exceed homestead and family allowances, exempt property, administration expenses, and funeral and last illness expenses; the estate has been fully administered and distributed; and the closing statement sent to all known distributees and claimants. (§ 560:3-1204(a)) *Clerk Administration.* No provision.
Is procedure available in the case of nonresident decedents?	No provision.
Maximum allowable value of estate	*By Affidavit.* $100,000, apart from the value of any motor vehicle registered in decedent's name. (§ 560:3-1201(a)(1)) *Summary Administration.* Value of the entire estate, less liens and encumbrances, does not exceed homestead allowance, exempt property, family allowance, costs and expenses of administration, reasonable funeral expenses, and reasonable and necessary medical and hospital expenses of the last illness of the decedent. (§ 560:3-1203) *Clerk Administration.* $100,000. (§ 560:3-1205)
What property can be transferred by this means?	*By Affidavit.* Personal property. (§ 560:3-1201) *Summary Administration.* Entire estate. (§ 560:3-1203) *Clerk Administration.* Entire estate. (§ 560:3-1205)
Special rules for certain assets (e.g., automobile)	*By Affidavit.* Any motor vehicles registered in the decedent's name may be transferred by affidavit regardless of value. (§ 560:3-1201(a)(1)) *Summary Administration.* No provision. *Clerk Administration.* No provision.
Can the spouse or other person take summarily if under certain amount?	No provision.
Minimum period before filing allowed	No provision.
Rights/obligations of party with affidavit	*By Affidavit.* Rights: to compel transfer of property in a proceeding. Obligations: is answerable and accountable to any personal representative of the estate or to any other person having a superior right. (§ 560:3-1202) *Summary Administration.* No provision. *Clerk Administration.* No provision.
Are some creditors given special privileges/preference (e.g., medical expenses, funeral expenses)?	*By Affidavit.* The Department of Human Services, if it has paid for the decedent's burial, will have priority over those of other successors. (§ 560:3-1201(a)(3)(b)) *Summary Administration.* Funeral and last illness medical expenses. (§ 560:3-1204(a)(1)) *Clerk Administration.* No provision.

Creditors' rights, if insufficient assets	*By Affidavit.* Payee is accountable to the personal representative, or any person having a superior right in the property. (§ 560:3-1202) *Summary Administration.* No provision. *Clerk Administration.* No provision.
May the distribution of the estate proceed without appointment of personal representative?	*By Affidavit.* Yes. (§ 560:3-1201) *Summary Administration.* No. (§ 560:3-1203) *Clerk Administration.* Yes. (§ 560:3-1205)
Must court approve affidavit?	*By Affidavit.* No, but a death certificate must be presented with the affidavit. (§ 560:3-1201(a)) *Summary Administration.* No provision. *Clerk Administration.* No provision.
Waiting period before authority to act	*By Affidavit.* No provision. *Summary Administration.* No provision. *Clerk Administration.* The clerk is to, after the expiration of four months after the first publication, in the case of an estate valued in excess of $10,000, or after 60 days in the case of an estate valued at $10,000 or less, pay or distribute the money, funds, or property of the estate. (§ 560:3-1209)
With whom do you file petition or affidavit?	*By Affidavit.* No provision. *Summary Administration.* Closing statement must be filed with court. (§ 560:3-1204(a)) *Clerk Administration.* Petition must be filed with court. (§ 560:3-1205)
Is there an informal procedure for appointment of executor or administrator?	Yes. (§§ 560:3-301, 560:3-307 to 311)
Can a nonresident serve?	Yes. (§§ 560:3-301, 560:3-203)
Can the nonresident act locally based on appointment in another state?	Yes. If there is no local administration, and the domiciliary foreign personal representative has filed in a local court, the foreign personal representative may exercise with regard to assets in Hawaii all powers of a local personal representative, subject to conditions imposed upon nonresidents generally. (§ 560:4-205)
What does a transferor need so as to be relieved of liability if challenged by another person later on who claims the particular property (e.g., copy of affidavit)?	*By Affidavit.* Payor is discharged and released to the same extent as if that person dealt with a personal representative of the decedent. (§ 560:3-1202) *Summary Administration.* No provision. *Clerk Administration.* No provision.

Idaho
Collection of Personal Property by Affidavit and Summary Administration Procedure for Small Estates

Who can initiate process?	*By Affidavit.* The person claiming to be the successor. (§ 15-3-1201) *Summary Administration.* Personal representative or surviving spouse (i.e., sole beneficiary). (§§ 15-3-1203, 15-3-1205)
Can it be used if claims outstanding?	*By Affidavit.* No provision. *Summary Administration.* Yes. (§ 15-3-1204)
Different rules if die testate or intestate?	*By Affidavit.* No provision. *Summary Administration.* If surviving spouse is sole beneficiary and decedent died testate, original will must accompany petition. (§ 15-3-1205(a))
Notice?	
heirs	*By Affidavit.* No provision. *Summary Administration.* A copy of the closing statement must be sent to all distributees of the estate. (§ 15-3-1204(a)(3))
creditors	*By Affidavit.* No provision. *Summary Administration.* The distribution of the estate may be accomplished without giving notice to creditors. (§ 15-3-1203 and Comment)
others	No provision.
Which of the following must be observed?	
hearing	*By Affidavit.* No provision. *Summary Administration.* If the spouse is the sole beneficiary/devisee, there is a hearing to determine that the person was married to the decedent and was the sole beneficiary. (§ 15-3-1205)
affidavit, petition, other	*By Affidavit.* Affidavit. (§ 15-3-1201) *Summary Administration.* Closing statement. (§ 15-3-1203) If spouse is sole beneficiary/devisee, must file a petition. (§ 15-3-1205)
bond	No provision.
What are basic contents of petition or affidavit?	*By Affidavit.* Statements affirming the following: the fair market value of the estate which is subject to probate, less liens and encumbrances, does not exceed $100,000; 30 days have elapsed since death of decedent; no application or petition for the appointment of a personal representative or for summary administration is pending or has been granted in any jurisdiction; and the claiming successor is entitled to payment or delivery of the property. (§ 15-3-1201(a)(1)) *Summary Administration.* Closing statement must state that the estate value, less liens and encumbrances, did not exceed homestead and family allowances, exempt property, and funeral and medical expenses; that estate has been administered and

	distributed; and that closing statement has been sent to all distributees and claimants. (§ 15-3-1204(a)) If decedent leaves surviving spouse as sole devisee or beneficiary, the petition must set out marriage and the death of a person leaving a surviving spouse. If decedent died testate, the original of the last will and testament must accompany the petition. (§ 15-3-1205)
Is procedure available in the case of nonresident decedents?	No provision.
Maximum allowable value of estate	*By Affidavit.* For the use of an affidavit the fair market value of the entire estate, less liens, and encumbrances, cannot exceed $100,000. (§ 15-3-1201(a)(1)) *Summary Administration.* The value of the entire estate, less liens and encumbrances, cannot exceed homestead allowance, exempt property, family allowance, costs and expenses of administration, reasonable funeral expenses, and reasonable and necessary medical and hospital expenses of the last illness of the decedent. (§ 15-3-1203)
What property can be transferred by this means?	*By Affidavit.* Personal property. (§§ 15-3-1201, 15-3-1202 Comment) *Summary Administration.* Entire estate. (§ 15-3-1203)
Special rules for certain assets (e.g., automobile)	*By Affidavit.* Transfer agent of any security shall change the registered ownership on the books of a corporation upon presentation of an affidavit. (§ 15-3-1201(b)) *Summary Administration.* No provision.
Can the spouse or other person take summarily if under certain amount?	Yes. Surviving spouse who is sole beneficiary may take summarily. (§ 15-3-1205)
Minimum period before filing allowed	*By Affidavit.* 30 days after death of decedent must pass before offering affidavit. (§ 15-3-1201(a)) *Summary Administration.* Estate must be fully administered and distributed before closing statement may be filed. (§ 15-3-1204(a)(2))
Rights/obligations of party with affidavit	*By Affidavit.* Rights: to bring a proceeding to compel adherence to affidavit. Obligations: is answerable and accountable to any personal representative of the estate or to any other person having a superior right. (§ 15-3-1202) *Summary Administration.* No provision.
Are some creditors given special privileges/preference (e.g., medical expenses, funeral expenses)?	*By Affidavit.* No provision. *Summary Administration.* Funeral and last illness medical expenses. (§ 15-3-1204(a)(1))
Creditors' rights, if insufficient assets	*By Affidavit.* Payee is answerable to any person with a superior right in the property. (§ 15-3-1202) *Summary Administration.* No provision.
May the distribution of the estate proceed without appointment of personal representative?	*By Affidavit.* Yes. (Comment to § 15-3-1201) *Summary Administration.* Generally there must be a personal representative, but if surviving spouse is the sole beneficiary, she/he may petition. (§ 15-3-1205(a))

Must court approve affidavit?	*By Affidavit.* No provision. *Summary Administration.* If spouse proceeds as sole beneficiary, court must approve. (§ 15-3-1205)
Waiting period before authority to act	*By Affidavit.* 30 days must pass before the presentation of an affidavit. (§ 15-3-1201) *Summary Administration.* No provision.
With whom do you file petition or affidavit?	*By Affidavit.* No provision. *Summary Administration.* Closing statement and any petition by surviving spouse are filed with court. (§§ 15-3-1204, 15-3-1205)
Is there an informal procedure for appointment of executor or administrator?	Yes. (§§ 15-3-301, 15-3-307 to 311)
Can a nonresident serve?	Yes. (§§ 15-3-203, 15-3-301)
Can the nonresident act locally based on appointment in another state?	Yes. If there is no local administration, and the domiciliary foreign personal representative has filed in a local court, the foreign personal repressentative may exercise with respect to assets in Idaho all powers of a local personal representative, subject to conditions imposed upon nonresidents generally. (§§ 15-4-205, 15-4-204)
What does a transferor need so as to be relieved of liability if challenged by another person later on who claims the particular property (e.g., copy of affidavit)?	*By Affidavit.* Payor is discharged and released to the same extent as if he dealt with a personal representative of the decedent. (§ 15-3-1202) *Summary Administration.* No provision.

Illinois
Small Estates

Who can initiate process?	Distributees or their agents. (755 ILCS § 5/25-1(a))
Can it be used if claims outstanding?	The only kind of unpaid or contested claims allowed are the decedent's funeral expenses and such expenses must be listed on the affidavit. (755 ILCS § 5/25-1(b)(7)(a))
Different rules if die testate or intestate?	If decedent dies intestate, the names, addresses, and relationships of decedent's heirs, and the portion of the estate to which each heir is entitled must be listed in the affidavit. (755 § ILCS 5/25-1(b)(10)(a)) If decedent dies testate, affiant must attach certified copy of will to affidavit. (755 ILCS § 5/25-1(b)(10)(b))
Notice?	No provision.
heirs	No provision.
creditors	No provision.
others	No provision.
Which of the following must be observed?	
hearing	No provision.
affidavit, petition, other	Affidavit. (755 ILCS § 5/25-1)
bond	No provision.
What are basic contents of petition or affidavit?	Name of the affiant, his address; information about the decedent including: name, date of death, place of residency before death; statements affirming the following: no letters of office are now outstanding on the decedent's estate and no petition for letters is contemplated or pending in Illinois or in any other jurisdiction, gross value of the personal estate does not exceed $100,000, all decedent's funeral expenses have been paid or list the amounts and the person entitled thereto; the award allowable to the surviving spouse or child of a decedent who was an Illinois resident; the affiant is unaware of any dispute or potential conflict as to the heirship or will of the decedent; a description of how the property should be distributed. (755 ILCS § 5/25-1(b))
Is procedure available in the case of nonresident decedents?	No provision.
Maximum allowable value of estate	$100,000. (755 ILCS § 5/25-1(b)(6))
What property can be transferred by this means?	Personal property. (755 ILCS § 5/25-1(a))
Special rules for certain assets (e.g., automobile)	If a vehicle is part of the estate, the transferee is to mail or deliver to the Secretary of State, within 120 days, the last certificate of title, if available, the documentation required under the provisions of the Probate Act of 1975, and an application for certificate of title. (The small estate affidavit is to be furnished by the Secretary of State.) (625 ILCS § 5/3-114(b))

Can the spouse or other person take summarily if under certain amount?	No provision.
Minimum period before filing allowed	No provision.
Rights/obligations of party with affidavit	Rights: to recover the personal estate in a civil action, if someone refuses to transfer the property. (755 ILCS § 5/25-3) Obligations: indemnify and hold harmless all creditors and heirs of the decedent and other persons relying upon the affidavit who incur loss because of such reliance. (755 ILCS § 5/25-1(e))
Are some creditors given special privileges/preference (e.g., medical expenses, funeral expenses)?	All claims but funeral expenses must be paid. If funeral expenses have not been paid, they must be listed on the affidavit. (755 ILCS § 5/25-1(b)(7)(a))
Creditors' rights, if insufficient assets	Payee is answerable to any representative of the estate, or person having a prior right. (755 ILCS § 5/25-1(d))
May the distribution of the estate proceed without appointment of personal representative?	Administration must proceed without personal representative. (755 ILCS § 5/25-1)
Must court approve affidavit?	No provision.
Waiting period before authority to act	No provision.
With whom do you file petition or affidavit?	No provision.
Is there an informal procedure for appointment of executor or administrator?	No provision.
Can a nonresident serve?	A nonresident may be an affiant. The nonresident affiant shall provide contact information for agent as service of process within jurisdiction; if no non resident affiant, then court clerk in decedent's residence of death serves as agent. (755 ILCS § 5/25-1(f))
Can the nonresident act locally based on appointment in another state?	Yes, since there will be a designated agent for service of process. (755 ILCS § 5/25-1(f))
What does a transferor need so as to be relieved of liability if challenged by another person later on who claims the particular property (e.g., copy of affidavit)?	Payor is released to the same extent as if payment had been made to the representative of the estate. (755 ILCS § 5/25-1(d))

Indiana
Dispensing with Administration

Who can initiate process?	*By Affidavit.* Person claiming to be entitled to payment or delivery of property of decedent. (§ 29-1-8-1(a)) *Summary Distribution.* Personal representative or person acting on behalf of distributees. (§ 29-1-8-3(a))
Can it be used if claims outstanding?	*By Affidavit.* No provision. *Summary Distribution.* Yes. (§ 29-1-8-4(a)(3))
Different rules if die testate or intestate?	No provision.
Notice?	
heirs	*By Affidavit.* No provision. *Summary Distribution.* A copy of the closing statement must be sent to all distributees of the estate. (§ 29-1-8-4(a)(3))
creditors	*By Affidavit.* No provision. *Summary Distribution.* The distribution of the estate may be accomplished without notice being given to creditors. (§ 29-1-8-3(a) and Comment)
others	No provision.
Which of the following must be observed?	
hearing	No provision.
affidavit, petition, other	*By Affidavit.* Affidavit. (§ 29-1-8-1) *Summary Distribution.* Closing statement. (§ 29-1-8-4)
bond	No provision.
What are basic contents of petition or affidavit?	*By Affidavit.* Statements affirming the following: value of the gross probate estate does not exceed $50,000; 45 days have elapsed since the death of the decedent; no application or petition of a personal representative is pending or has been granted in any jurisdiction; and the claimant is entitled to payment or delivery of the property. (§ 29-1-8-1(b)) *Summary Distribution.* Closing statement must state that the value of the gross estate, less liens and encumbrances and reasonable funeral expenses, does not exceed sum of family allowance and funeral and administrative expenses; that estate is fully distributed; and that the closing statement was sent to all claimants and distributees. (§ 29-1-8-4(a))
Is procedure available in the case of nonresident decedents?	No provision.
Maximum allowable value of estate	*By Affidavit.* $50,000. (§ 29-1-8-1) *Summary Distribution.* The gross value of the estate cannot exceed the sum of: $25,000, the costs and expenses of administration, and reasonable funeral expenses. (§ 29-1-8-3(a)(1))
What property can be transferred by this means?	*By Affidavit.* Personal property. (§ 29-1-8-1) *Summary Distribution.* Entire estate. (§ 29-1-8-3)

Special rules for certain assets (e.g., automobile)	*By Affidavit.* If a motor vehicle or a watercraft is part of the estate, transfer of the certificate of title can take place five days after the death of the decedent, if the appointment of a personal representative is not contemplated. The transfer will be made by the bureau of motor vehicles upon receipt of an affidavit duly executed by the distributees of the estate. (§ 29-1-8-1(c)) A transfer agent of a security shall change the registered ownership on the books of a corporation upon presentation of an affidavit. (§ 29-1-8-1(d)) *Summary Distribution.* For real property, affiant must record affidavit in the office of the recorder in the county in which the real property is located. (§ 29-1-8-3(b))
Can the spouse or other person take summarily if under certain amount?	No provision.
Minimum period before filing allowed	*By Affidavit.* An affidavit can only be presented 45 days after the death of the decedent. (§ 29-1-8-1(b)(2)) *Summary Distribution.* Estate must be fully administered and distributed before filing closing statement. (§ 29-1-8-4(a))
Rights/obligations of party with affidavit	*By Affidavit.* Rights: to bring a proceeding to compel adherence to affidavit, after proving their right to the property. Obligations: are answerable and accountable to any personal representative of the estate or to any other person having a superior right. (§ 29-1-8-2) *Summary Distribution.* No provision.
Are some creditors given special privileges/preference (e.g., medical expenses, funeral expenses)?	Last illness medical and funeral expenses must be paid in full. (§ 29-1-8-9)
Creditors' rights, if insufficient assets	*By Affidavit.* Payee is accountable to any person having a superior right. (§ 29-1-8-2) *Summary Distribution.* No provision.
May the distribution of the estate proceed without appointment of personal representative?	*By Affidavit.* Yes. (1975 Comment to § 29-1-8-1) *Summary Distribution.* Yes. (§ 29-1-8-3(a))
Must court approve affidavit?	No provision.
Waiting period before authority to act	*By Affidavit.* An affidavit can only be presented 45 days after the death of the decedent. (§ 29-1-8-1(b)(2)) *Summary Distribution.* No provision.
With whom do you file petition or affidavit?	*By Affidavit.* No provision. *Summary Distribution.* Must file closing statement with court. (§ 29-1-8-4) If estate includes real property, must record affidavit with recorder in county where real property is located. (§ 29-1-8-3(b))
Is there an informal procedure for appointment of executor or administrator?	No provision.
Can a nonresident serve?	No provision.

Can the nonresident act locally based on appointment in another state?	No provision.
What does a transferor need so as to be relieved of liability if challenged by another person later on who claims the particular property (e.g., copy of affidavit)?	*By Affidavit*. Payor is discharged and released to the same extent as if he dealt with a personal representative. (§ 29-1-8-2) *Summary Distribution*. No provision.

Iowa
Administration of Small Estates

Who can initiate process?	Spouse or child of the decedent.[1] Parent or grandchild.[2] A person related within the fourth degree of consanguinity to the decedent.[3] (§ 635.1)
Can it be used if claims outstanding?	Yes. (§ 635.8)
Different rules if die testate or intestate?	Yes. (§ 635.1) (See *Who can initiate process?*)
Notice?	Administrator or executor must publish notice once a week for two consecutive weeks in a daily or weekly newspaper of general circulation published in the county in which the estate is pending and must mail notice to all claimants which may not be paid during administration. (§§ 635.13, 633.230, 633.304)
heirs	A copy of the closing statement must be sent to all distributees of the estate and a full account in writing of the administration of the estate must be furnished to the distributees whose interests are affected. (§ 635.8(2)(c))
creditors	A copy of the closing statement must be sent to all known creditors. (§ 635.8(2)(c))
others	No provision.
Which of the following must be observed?	
hearing	No provision.
affidavit, petition, other	Petition. (§ 635.1)
bond	No provision.
What are basic contents of petition or affidavit?	Petition requirements: aggregate gross value of estate must not be greater than that permitted under § 635.1; must list the name, domicile, and date of death of the decedent; the name and address of the surviving spouse, name and address of each parent, if the parent is an heir or beneficiary, each child, each grandchild, each relative within the fourth degree of consanguinity, who is an heir or beneficiary of the decedent, unless none are beneficiaries under the will of the decedent; must describe whether the decedent died intestate or testate, and must list the name and address of the proposed executor or administrator. (§ 635.2)
Is procedure available in the case of nonresident decedents?	No provision.
Maximum allowable value of estate	Gross value of the probate and nonprobate property cannot exceed $50,000, $15,000, or $10,000, depending upon who files the petition. (§ 635.1) See *Who can initiate process?*
What property can be transferred by this means?	Any property of the estate. (§ 635.3)

Special rules for certain assets (e.g., automobile)	Letters of appointment grant authority for the transfer of securities to persons entitled. (§ 635.5) Personal property that is of a perishable nature and for which there is a regularly established market can be sold by the executor or administrator without order of the court. (§ 635.6)
Can the spouse or other person take summarily if under certain amount?	No, but at any time within four months after letters of administration are issued for a small estate, any interested person may petition for administration of the estate other than as a small estate. (§ 635.9)
Minimum period before filing allowed	No provision.
Rights/obligations of party with affidavit	The executor or administrator is required to file the report and inventory for which provision is made in § 633.361. (§ 635.7) The executor or administrator is personally liable for the payment of debts and charges against the estate to the extent the assets would be subject to payment of those debts under administration other than small estate administration. (§ 635.8(1)) The executor or administrator must also file a closing statement within six months of issuance of the letters of appointment. (§ 635.8(2))
Are some creditors given special privileges/preference (e.g., medical expenses, funeral expenses)?	No provision.
Creditors' rights, if insufficient assets	Creditors may file claims against the estate within four months of second publication of notice. (§ 635.13)
May the distribution of the estate proceed without appointment of personal representative?	No. (§ 635.1)
Must court approve affidavit?	No provision.
Waiting period before authority to act	The executor or administrator shall not distribute property of the estate nor exempt from execution, prior to four months after the issuance of the letters of appointment. (§ 635.14)
With whom do you file petition or affidavit?	Clerk of Probate Court. (§ 635.1)
Is there an informal procedure for appointment of executor or administrator?	No provision.
Can a nonresident serve?	No, a resident of the state of Iowa must be appointed to act locally. (§ 635.1)
Can the nonresident act locally based on appointment in another state?	No. (§ 635.1)

What does a transferor need so as to be relieved of liability if challenged by another person later on who claims the particular property (e.g., copy of affidavit)?	Payor is exonerated from any liability. (§ 635.4)

---

1. If the total of the gross value of the estate is $50,000 and either of the following occurs: the decedent dies intestate and is survived by a spouse, or child, or both; the decedent leaves a last will and testament and the only beneficiaries are a spouse, or children, or both. (§ 635.1(1))
2. If the total of the gross value of the estate is $15,000 and either of the following occurs: the decedent dies intestate without a surviving spouse or children but with a surviving parent or parents or surviving grandchild or grandchildren; the decedent dies without a surviving spouse or children and leaves a last will and testament and the only beneficiaries are a surviving parent or parents or surviving grandchild or grandchildren. (§ 635.1(2))
3. If the total of the gross value of the estate is $10,000 and either of the following occurs: the decedent dies intestate without a surviving spouse, issue, or parent, but with heirs that are within the fourth degree of consanguinity; the decedent dies without a surviving spouse, issue, or parent, and leaves a last will and testament and the only beneficiaries are surviving persons related to the decedent within the fourth degree of consanguinity. (§ 635.1(3))

Kansas
Summary Proceedings and Payment of Certain Benefits to Certain Relatives

Who can initiate process?	*By Affidavit.* Surviving spouse or other relative who is the successor of the decedent. (§ 59-1507a(a)) *Summary Proceedings.* Executor or administrator. (§ 59-1507)
Can it be used if claims outstanding?	*By Affidavit.* Yes, with respect to personal property (§ 59-1507b); the affidavit must state that all claims have been or will be paid. *Summary Proceedings.* Yes. (§ 59-1507)
Different rules if die testate or intestate?	*By Affidavit.* No. (§ 59-1507b) *Summary Proceedings.* No provision.
Notice?	*By Affidavit.* No provision. *Summary Proceedings.* The court with or without notice may adjust, correct, settle, allow, or disallow account of the executor and administrator, and if the account is allowed, summarily determine the heirs, legatees, and devisees, and close the administration. (§ 59-1507)
heirs	No provision.
creditors	No provision.
others	No provision.
Which of the following must be observed?	
hearing	No provision.
affidavit, petition, other	*By Affidavit.* Affidavit. (§§ 59-1507a, 59-1507b) *Summary Proceedings.* Executor or administrator can present his or her account with an application for the settlement and allowance thereof. (§ 59-1507)
bond	No provision.
What are basic contents of petition or affidavit?	*By Affidavit.* Affidavit for certain benefits must list: (1) date of death of the deceased, (2) the relationship of the affiant to the deceased, (3) that no executor or administrator for the deceased has qualified or been appointed, and (4) that to the affiant's knowledge, there exists at the time of the filing of such affidavit, no relative of a closer degree or kindred to the deceased than the affiant. (§ 59-1507a(b)) In addition, the affidavit must comply with the form set forth by the judicial counsel. (§ 59-1507b) *Summary Proceedings.* No provision.
Is procedure available in the case of nonresident decedents?	*By Affidavit.* Not available for payment of certain personal property. (§ 59-1507b) *Summary Proceedings.* No provision.

Maximum allowable value of estate	*By Affidavit.* For the use of the affidavit for certain personal property, $20,000. (§ 59-1507b) *Summary Proceedings.* The estate, exclusive of the homestead and allowances to the spouse and minor children, cannot exceed the amounts required for funeral expenses, expenses of last sickness, wages of servants during the last sickness, costs of administration, debts having preference under the laws of the United States or Kansas, and taxes. (§ 59-1507)
What property can be transferred by this means?	*By Affidavit.* Monthly benefits (e.g., under title II of Social Security Act) or under any veterans administration program or public or private retirement or annuity plan. (§ 59-1507a(a)) Personal property in the form of moneys, stock, evidence of indebtedness, interest or any right transferable to decedent's estate by any corporation or person. (§ 59-1507b) *Summary Proceedings.* Entire estate. (§ 59-1507)
Special rules for certain assets (e.g., automobile)	No provision beyond §§ 59-1507a and 59-1507b. See *What property can be transferred by this means?*
Can the spouse or other person take summarily if under certain amount?	*By Affidavit.* If certain benefits do not exceed totally $5,000, spouse and certain other recipient relatives can take summarily based on prescribed affidavit. (§ 59-1507a) *Summary Proceedings.* No provision.
Minimum period before filing allowed	No provision.
Rights/obligations of party with affidavit	*By Affidavit.* No provision. *Summary Proceedings.* No provision.
Are some creditors given special privileges/preference (e.g., medical expenses, funeral expenses)?	*By Affidavit.* No provision. *Summary Proceedings.* Funeral expenses, expenses of last sickness, costs of administration, debts having preference under laws of U.S. or Kansas, and taxes. (§ 59-1507)
Creditors' rights, if insufficient assets	No provision.
May the distribution of the estate proceed without appointment of personal representative?	*By Affidavit.* Yes. (§§ 59-1507a, 59-1507b) *Summary Proceedings.* No. (§ 59-1507)
Must court approve affidavit?	No provision.
Waiting period before authority to act	*By Affidavit.* Certain benefits to decedent must be paid to relatives at least 180 days after decedent's death. (§ 59-1507a(a)) *Summary Proceedings.* No provision.
With whom do you file petition or affidavit?	*By Affidavit.* With the appropriate governmental office or private company or person. (§§ 59-1507a(b), 59-1507b) *Summary Proceedings.* Court. (§ 59-1507)
Is there an informal procedure for appointment of executor or administrator?	No provision.

Can a nonresident serve?	Yes. (§§ 59-1706 through -1708)
Can the nonresident act locally based on appointment in another state?	A nonresident fiduciary may assign, extend, release, satisfy or foreclose any mortgage, judgment or lien, or collect any debts secured thereby. (§ 59-1707) A nonresident fiduciary may also sue or be sued in any court in Kansas. (§ 59-1708)
What does a transferor need so as to be relieved of liability if challenged by another person later on who claims the particular property (e.g., copy of affidavit)?	*By Affidavit.* Transferor must have been furnished an affidavit. (§§ 59-1507a, 59-1507b) *Summary Proceedings.* No provision.

Kentucky
Dispensing with Administration by Agreement

Who can initiate process?	All persons beneficially entitled to the personal estate must have agreed in writing that there shall be no administration. (§ 395.470(1))
Can it be used if claims outstanding?	Yes, but only if the written agreement to dispense with administration designates a trustee with power to collect claims and demands. (§ 395.470(1))
Different rules if die testate or intestate?	Only available to the estate of a person dying intestate. (§ 395.470(1))
Notice?	
heirs	See *Who can initiate process?*
creditors	The persons applying for an order dispensing with administration shall advertise for creditors of the intestate to appear and present their claims.[4] The advertisement shall be posted at the courthouse door for six weeks, and published pursuant to § 424. (§ 395.470(4))
others	No provision.
Which of the following must be observed?	
hearing	No provision.
affidavit, petition, other	Need to file a petition to obtain an order dispensing with administration. (§ 395.470(2)) Must also file an affidavit showing that advertisement for creditors have been made. (§ 395.470(4))
bond	Give bond before the order is granted with surety in the amount of the personal estate. (§ 395.470(5))
What are basic contents of petition or affidavit?	All persons beneficially entitled to the personal estate have agreed in writing that there shall be no administration; and either there are no claims or demands due the estate, or the written agreement to dispense with the administration designates a trustee with power to collect claims and demands. (§ 395.470(1))
Is procedure available in the case of nonresident decedents?	No provision.
Maximum allowable value of estate	No provision.
What property can be transferred by this means?	All property contained in the personal estate. (§ 395.470(1))
Special rules for certain assets (e.g., automobile)	No provision.
Can the spouse or other person take summarily if under certain amount?	Yes, where the exemption of the surviving spouse alone, or together with preferred claims paid by a widow or by the widower where the wife's estate is legally liable for payment, equals or exceeds the amount of probatable assets. This provision does not distinguish between testate and intestate decedents' estates. (§ 395.455(1))

Minimum period before filing allowed	No provision.
Rights/obligations of party with affidavit	No provision.
Are some creditors given special privileges/preference (e.g., medical expenses, funeral expenses)?	No provision.
Creditors' rights, if insufficient assets	Bond provided by the persons applying for the order dispensing with administration for the benefit of creditors who, within six months form the order dispensing with administration, file their claims with the court. (§ 395.470(5))
May the distribution of the estate proceed without appointment of personal representative?	Yes. (§§ 395.455, 395.470)
Must court approve affidavit?	The court must approve the written agreement. (§ 395.470(2))
Waiting period before authority to act	No provision.
With whom do you file petition or affidavit?	The written agreement with a motion for an order dispensing with administration must be filed in district court. (§ 395.470(2))
Is there an informal procedure for appointment of executor or administrator?	No provision.
Can a nonresident serve?	Yes. (§ 395.170)
Can the nonresident act locally based on appointment in another state?	Yes, if there is no local administration. (§ 395.170)
What does a transferor need so as to be relieved of liability if challenged by another person later on who claims the particular property (e.g., copy of affidavit)?	No provision.

4. The person and place shall be designated in the advertisement. The advertisement shall also give notice when, where, and by whom the order dispensing with administration will be applied for. (§ 395.470)

Louisiana
Small Successions

Who can initiate process?	Competent major heirs and surviving spouse. (Code Civ. Pro. Art. 3432)
Can it be used if claims outstanding?	Yes. (Code Civ. Pro. Art. 3431(C))
Different rules if die testate or intestate?	Testate decedents do not qualify for small successions administration. Intestate decedents may qualify for small successions administration, depending on the survival of certain heirs and the value of the estate. (Code Civ. Pro. Arts. 3421, 3431, 3441)
Notice?	No notice required, unless decedent dies single and without an heir in Louisiana and a public administrator takes possession of the estate. In that case, the public administrator must advertise one time in the official journal of the parish. (Code Civ. Pro. Art. 3431(B))
heirs	Notice given pursuant to Art. 3431(B) shall read: "Notice is hereby given to any heirs or creditor . . ." (Code Civ. Pro. Art. 3431(C))
creditors	Notice given pursuant to Art. 3431(B) shall read: "Notice is hereby given to any heirs or creditor . . ." (Code Civ. Pro. Art. 3431(C))
others	No provision.
Which of the following must be observed?	
hearing	No provision.
affidavit, petition, other	Affidavit. (Code Civ. Pro. Art. 3432)
bond	No provision.
What are basic contents of petition or affidavit?	Decedent's date of death and domicile at death; statement that decedent died intestate and left no immovable property; marital status of deceased; names and addresses of any surviving spouse and heirs and their relationship to decedent; brief description of decedent's movable property. (Code Civ. Pro. Art. 3432)
Is procedure available in the case of nonresident decedents?	No. (Code Civ. Pro. Art. 3421, Official Revision Comments)
Maximum allowable value of estate	$50,000. (Code Civ. Pro. Art. 3421)
What property can be transferred by this means?	The estate must consist exclusively of movable property. (Code Civ. Pro. Art. 3431(A))
Special rules for certain assets (e.g., automobile)	No provision.
Can the spouse or other person take summarily if under certain amount?	Yes, if decedent died intestate with less than $50,000 in movable property and without immovable property, provided decedent's sole heirs are his descendants, his ascendants, his brothers or sisters or descendants thereof, and a surviving spouse. (Code Civ. Pro. Arts. 3421, 3431)

Minimum period before filing allowed	No provision.
Rights/obligations of party with affidavit	A copy of an affidavit endorsed by the inheritance tax collector is full authority for the delivery of property. (Code Civ. Pro. Art. 3434)
Are some creditors given special privileges/preference (e.g., medical expenses, funeral expenses)?	No provision.
Creditors' rights, if insufficient assets	If a public administrator takes possession of the estate, creditors are entitled to notice and have the right to object. (Code Civ. Pro. Art. 3431(C))
May the distribution of the estate proceed without appointment of personal representative?	Yes. (Code Civ. Pro. Art. 3431)
Must court approve affidavit?	Inheritance tax collector must approve affidavit. (Code Civ. Pro. Art. 3433)
Waiting period before authority to act	No provision.
With whom do you file petition or affidavit?	Inheritance tax collector. (Code Civ. Pro. Art. 3432)
Is there an informal procedure for appointment of executor or administrator?	No provision.
Can a nonresident serve?	No provision.
Can the nonresident act locally based on appointment in another state?	No provision.
What does a transferor need so as to be relieved of liability if challenged by another person later on who claims the particular property (e.g., copy of affidavit)?	Endorsed copy of affidavit. (Code Civ. Pro. Art. 3434)

Maine
Collection of Personal Property by Affidavit; Summary Administration for Small Estates

Who can initiate process?	*Affidavit.* Persons claiming to be successors. (18-A § 3-1201(a)) *Summary Administration.* Personal representative. (18-A § 3-1204(a))
Can it be used if claims outstanding?	*Affidavit.* Yes. (18-A § 3-1201(a)(1)) *Summary Administration.* Yes. (18-A § 3-1204(a)(3))
Different rules if die testate or intestate?	No provision.
Notice?	*Affidavit.* No provision. *Summary Administration.* All distributees and claimants must receive a copy of the closing statement. (18-A § 3-1204(a)(3))
heirs	No provision.
creditors	*Summary Administration.* If the net value of the estate does not exceed homestead allowance, exempt property, family allowance, administration expenses, funeral expenses, and medical/hospital expenses of last illness, then no notice to creditors is necessary. (18A § 3-1203)
others	No provision.
Which of the following must be observed?	
hearing	No provision.
affidavit, petition, other	*Affidavit.* Affidavit. (18-A § 3-1201(a)) *Summary Administration.* Closing statement. (18-A § 3-1204(a))
bond	No provision.
What are basic contents of petition or affidavit?	*Affidavit.* Statement that value of entire estate, wherever located, less liens and encumbrances, does not exceed $10,000; statement that 30 days elapsed since death of decedent; statement that no application or petition for the appointment of a personal representative is pending or has been granted in any jurisdiction; statement that claiming successor is entitled to payment or delivery of the property. (18-A § 3-1201(a)) *Summary Administration.* Closing statement must state: to the best of the personal representative's knowledge, the value of the entire estate, less liens and encumbrances, did not exceed homestead allowance, exempt property, family allowance, costs and expenses of administration, reasonable funeral expenses, and reasonable and necessary hospital expenses of the last illness of the decedent; the personal representative has fully administered the estate by disbursing and distributing it to the persons entitled thereto; and the personal representative has sent a copy of the closing statement to all distributees of the estate and to all creditors or other claimants of whom he is aware whose claims are neither paid nor barred and has furnished a full account in writing of his administration to the distributees whose interests are affected. (18-A § 3-1204(a))

Is procedure available in the case of nonresident decedents?	No provision.
Maximum allowable value of estate	*Affidavit.* Value of entire estate, wherever located, less liens and encumbrances, may not exceed $10,000. (18-A § 3-1201(a)(1)) *Summary Administration.* The value of the entire estate, less liens and encumbrances, must not exceed homestead allowance, exempt property, family allowance, costs and expenses of administration, reasonable funeral expenses, and reasonable and necessary hospital expenses of the last illness of the decedent. (18-A § 3-1204(a)(1))
What property can be transferred by this means?	*Affidavit.* Tangible personal property or an instrument evidencing a debt, obligation, stock, or chose in action. (18-A § 3-1201(a)) *Summary Administration.* Entire estate. (18-A § 3-1204(a))
Special rules for certain assets (e.g., automobile)	*Affidavit.* Within 30 days of death of Maine resident, the surviving spouse, deceased's child/grandchild, father/mother, or brother/sister may request deceased's Social Security owed if less than $1,000. (18A § 3-1205)
Can the spouse or other person take summarily if under certain amount?	*Affidavit.* Social Security. (18A § 3-1205)
Minimum period before filing allowed	*Affidavit.* There is no filing for this procedure. See *Waiting period before authority to act.* *Summary Administration.* Estate must be fully administered and distributed before a closing statement can be filed. (18-A § 3-1204(a)(2))
Rights/obligations of party with affidavit	*Affidavit.* Successor with affidavit is entitled to payment of indebtedness or delivery of property, but is accountable to those with superior rights. (18-A §§ 3-1201(a), 3-1202) *Summary Administration.* No provision.
Are some creditors given special privileges/preference (e.g., medical expenses, funeral expenses)?	*Affidavit.* No provision. *Summary Administration.* Funeral and last illness medical expenses. (18-A § 3-1204(a)(1))
Creditors' rights, if insufficient assets	*Affidavit.* Payees are accountable to persons with superior rights. (18-A § 3-1202) *Summary Administration.* No provision.
May the distribution of the estate proceed without appointment of personal representative?	*Affidavit.* Yes; absence of personal representative is required. (18-A § 3-1201(a)(3)) *Summary Administration.* No. (18-A § 3-1204(a))
Must court approve affidavit?	No provision.
Waiting period before authority to act	*Affidavit.* 30 days after death of decedent. (18-A § 3-1201(a)(2)) *Summary Administration.* No provision.
With whom do you file petition or affidavit?	*Affidavit.* No provision. *Summary Administration.* Court. (18-A § 3-1204(a))

Is there an informal procedure for appointment of executor or administrator?	Yes. (§§ 3-301, 3-307 to -311)
Can a nonresident serve?	Yes. (§§ 3-307, 3-203, 4-201 to -207)
Can the nonresident act locally based on appointment in another state?	If the foreign personal representative has complied with § 4-204, the foreign personal representative may exercise as to assets in Maine all powers of a local personal representative and may maintain actions and proceedings in Maine subject to any conditions imposed upon nonresident parties generally. (§ 4-205)
What does a transferor need so as to be relieved of liability if challenged by another person later on who claims the particular property (e.g., copy of affidavit)?	*Affidavit.* Payor is discharged and released to the same extent as if he dealt with a personal representative. (18-A § 3-1202) *Summary Administration.* No provision.

Maryland
Small Estates and Modified Administration

Who can initiate process?	*Small Estates.* Any person entitled to administration pursuant to § 5-104. (Est. & Trusts § 5-602) Under Est. & Trusts § 5-104, any person with a pecuniary interest in the estate's proper administration qualifies. *Modified Administration.* Personal representative. (Est. & Trusts § 5-702)
Can it be used if claims outstanding?	*Small Estates.* Yes. (Est. & Trusts § 5-602(c)) *Modified Administration.* No provision.
Different rules if die testate or intestate?	No provision.
Notice?	*Small Estates.* If it appears there will be property remaining after payments, allowances, and expenses, unless prior notice of appointment of personal representative has been published, the register shall publish notice of the appointment in a newspaper of general circulation in the county of appointment once a week in three successive weeks. (Est. & Trusts § 5-603(b)) *Modified Administration.* Personal representative must file election within three months of date of appointment, and must provide a copy of the verified final report to any interested person within 10 months of the date of appointment. (Est. & Trusts §§ 5-702, 5-706(5))
heirs	No provision.
creditors	No provision.
others	No provision.
Which of the following must be observed?	
hearing	No provision.
affidavit, petition, other	*Small Estates.* Petition. (Est. & Trusts § 5-602) *Modified Administration.* Election, final report. (Est. & Trusts § 5-702)
bond	*Small Estates.* Unless bond is expressly excused by the will or by written consent of all interested persons, personal representative must post bond if value of estate after payment of expenses and allowances is greater than $10,000. (Est. & Trusts § 5-604(a)(1)) *Modified Administration.* No provision.
What are basic contents of petition or affidavit?	*Small Estates.* In addition to information required by Est. & Trusts §§ 5-201 and 5-202, petition shall contain a statement that petitioner has made a diligent search to discover all property and debts of decedent; a list of known property and its value; a list of known creditors, and the amount of each claim; and a statement of any legal proceedings pending in which decedent was a party. (Est. & Trusts § 5-602) *Modified Administration.* There is no specific provision. Presumably, the petition would have to show all statutory

	prerequisites have been satisfied: (1) all residuary legatees of a testate decedent and heirs at law of an intestate decedent are limited to: the personal representative and individuals or entities exempt from an inheritance tax; (2) all trustees of each trust that is a residuary legatee are limited to the decedent's personal representative, surviving spouse, and children; (3) the estate is solvent and sufficient assets exist to satisfy all testamentary gifts; (4) a final report is filed within 10 months, (5) distribution can occur no later than 12 months from the date of appointment; and (6) all residuary legatees or heirs at law must consent to modified administration under the detailed procedures of Est. & Trusts § 5-706. (Est. & Trusts § 5-702) Final report shall include (1) a statement representing the continued qualification for modified administration; (2) an itemized schedule of property and the basis of its valuation; (3) an itemized schedule of liens, debts, taxes, and funeral expenses of the decedent and administration expenses of the estate; and (4) schedules setting forth distributive shares of the estate and the applicable inheritance tax. (Est. & Trusts § 5-707)
Is procedure available in the case of nonresident decedents?	No provision.
Maximum allowable value of estate	*Small Estates.* Fair market value of property less debts secured by the property is $30,000 or less. (Est. & Trusts § 5-601(a)) If the surviving spouse is the sole legatee or heir and before filing of an initial account in administration under Subtitle 3 or 4, fair market value of property less debts secured by the property must be $50,000 or less. (Est. & Trusts § 5-601(c)) *Modified Administration.* No provision.
What property can be transferred by this means?	*Small Estates.* Entire estate. (Est. & Trusts § 5-601(a)) *Modified Administration.* Entire estate. (Est. & Trusts § 5-702(3))
Special rules for certain assets (e.g., automobile)	No provision.
Can the spouse or other person take summarily if under certain amount?	No provision.
Minimum period before filing allowed	*Small Estates.* No provision. *Modified Administration.* Election for modified administration must be filed within 3 months of the date of appointment of a personal representative. (§ 5-702)
Rights/obligations of party with affidavit	No provision.
Are some creditors given special privileges/preference (e.g., medical expenses, funeral expenses)?	*Small Estates.* Immediate payment of allowable funeral expenses. (Est. & Trusts § 5-603(a)(2)) *Modified Administration.* No provision.
Creditors' rights, if insufficient assets	*Small Estates.* Right to object within 30 days of publication of notice. (Est. & Trusts § 5-603(b)) *Modified Administration.* Filing of written objection by an interested person revokes procedure. (Est. & Trusts § 5-708(a)(2))

May the distribution of the estate proceed without appointment of personal representative?	*Small Estates.* No. (Est. & Trusts § 5-603(a)(1)) *Modified Administration.* No. (Est. & Trusts § 5-702)
Must court approve affidavit?	*Small Estates.* Register must find that petition is accurate. (Est. & Trusts § 5-603(a)) *Modified Administration.* No provision.
Waiting period before authority to act	No provision.
With whom do you file petition or affidavit?	*Small Estates.* Register of wills. (Est. & Trusts § 5-603(a)) *Modified Administration.* Register of wills. (Est. & Trusts § 5-703)
Is there an informal procedure for appointment of executor or administrator?	*Small Estates.* If the register finds the petition is accurate, the petitioner shall serve as personal representative. (Est. & Trusts § 5-603(a)(1)) *Modified Administration.* No provision.
Can a nonresident serve?	Yes. (Est. & Trusts §§ 5-501 to -506)
Can the nonresident act locally based on appointment in another state?	Yes. (Est. & Trusts § 5-502)
What does a transferor need so as to be relieved of liability if challenged by another person later on who claims the particular property (e.g., copy of affidavit)?	No provision.

Massachusetts
Voluntary Informal Administration of Small Estates; Administration of Small Estates Where Executor Named in Will

Who can initiate process?	If intestate, or testate but no executor named in the will, surviving spouse, child, grandchild, parent, brother, sister, niece, nephew, aunt, or uncle. (195 § 16) The executor if so named in the will. (195 § 16A)
Can it be used if claims outstanding?	Yes. (195 §§ 16, 16A)
Different rules if die testate or intestate?	If intestate, or testate but no executor named in the will, family members can serve as voluntary administrator. If decedent names an executor in his/her will, that person serves as voluntary executor. (195 §§ 16, 16A)
Notice?	No provision.
heirs	No provision.
creditors	No provision.
others	No provision.
Which of the following must be observed?	
hearing	No provision.
affidavit, petition, other	Affidavit, accompanied by death certificate. (195 §§ 16, 16A)
bond	No provision.
What are basic contents of petition or affidavit?	(1) Name and address of affiant; (2) name, residence, and date of death of decedent; (3) relationship of affiant to decedent; (4) schedule showing value of assets of the estate; (5) statement that affiant has undertaken to act as voluntary administrator; (6) names and addresses of surviving joint owners of property with the deceased; and (7) names and addresses of those who would take under intestacy; and, (8) if an executor is named in the will, the names and addresses known to the affiant who would take under the provisions of the will. (195 §§ 16, 16A) Affidavit should be accompanied by death certificate. (195 § 16, 16A)
Is procedure available in the case of nonresident decedents?	Decedent must have been an inhabitant of the commonwealth. (195 §§ 16, 16A)
Maximum allowable value of estate	One motor vehicle plus $15,000 of other personal property. (195 §§ 16, 16A)
What property can be transferred by this means?	Any debt or obligation, chattel, or assets. (195 §§ 16, 16A)
Special rules for certain assets (e.g., automobile)	No provision.
Can the spouse or other person take summarily if under certain amount?	No provision.
Minimum period before filing allowed	30 days after death of decedent. (195 §§ 16, 16A)

Rights/obligations of party with affidavit	Right to receive payment of debt, obligation, or asset. (195 §§ 16 16A)
Are some creditors given special privileges/preference (e.g., medical expenses, funeral expenses)?	Voluntary administrator or voluntary executor shall first discharge funeral and last sickness expenses, then administration expenses, then pay the debts of decedent, then distribute the balance of the estate to the surviving spouse or, according to the terms of a will, if any; if none, to persons according to descent law. (195 §§ 16, 16A)
Creditors' rights, if insufficient assets	See *Are some creditors given special privileges/preference*? Voluntary administrator/executor is liable in his own wrong to all persons aggrieved by his administration. (195 §§ 16, 16A)
May the distribution of the estate proceed without appointment of personal representative?	Yes, administration may proceed with voluntary administrator if executor not named in the will. (195 § 16)
Must court approve affidavit?	No provision.
Waiting period before authority to act	30 days. (195 §§ 16, 16A)
With whom do you file petition or affidavit?	Probate Court. (195 §§ 16, 16A)
Is there an informal procedure for appointment of executor or administrator?	Yes, procedure for appointment of voluntary administrator if no executor named in a will. (195 § 16)
Can a nonresident serve?	No provision under 195 § 16A, where executor named in will. Under 195 § 16, where there is no will or no named executor, the surviving spouse, child, grandchild, parent, brother, sister, niece, nephew, aunt, or uncle must be a resident of the commonwealth.
Can the nonresident act locally based on appointment in another state?	No provision.
What does a transferor need so as to be relieved of liability if challenged by another person later on who claims the particular property (e.g., copy of affidavit)?	Receipt in writing. (195 §§ 16, 16A)

Michigan
Summary Administrative Proceedings

Who can initiate process?	*Sworn Statement.* Decedent's successor. (§ 700.3983(1)) *Summary Administrative Proceedings.* Personal representative. (§§ 700.3987, 700.3988(1))
Can it be used if claims outstanding?	*Sworn Statement.* Yes. (§ 700.3983(1)) *Summary Administrative Proceedings.* Yes. (§ 700.3988(1)(c))
Different rules if die testate or intestate?	*Sworn Statement.* No provision. *Summary Administrative Proceedings.* No. (§ 700.3988)
Notice?	*Sworn Statement.* No provision. *Summary Administrative Proceedings.* A copy of the closing statement must be sent to all distributees, creditors, and other claimants. (§ 700.3988(1))
heirs	No provision.
creditors	*Summary Administrative Proceedings.* Personal representative may disburse and distribute the estate without giving notice to creditors. (§ 700.3987)
others	No provision.
Which of the following must be observed?	
hearing	*Sworn Statement.* No. (§ 700.3983) *Summary Administrative Proceedings.* No. (§ 700.3988)
affidavit, petition, other	*Sworn Statement.* Affidavit, coupled with death certificate. (§ 700.3983(1)) *Summary Administrative Proceedings.* Closing statement. (§§ 700.3987, 700.3988)
bond	*Sworn Statement.* No provision. *Summary Administrative Proceedings.* No provision.
What are basic contents of petition or affidavit?	*Sworn Statement.* Sworn statement that (1) estate does not include real property and net of encumbrances and liens does not exceed $15,000; (2) 28 days have elapsed since decedent's death; (3) no application for appointment as personal representative is pending; (4) the claimant is entitled to property; and (5) the names and addresses of others entitled to property and their shares. (§ 700.3983) *Summary Administrative Proceedings.* The closing statement must indicate (1) that the value of the net estate, less liens and encumbrances, did not exceed reasonable administration, funeral, and last illness expenses; (2) all disbursements have been made to those entitled; and (3) a copy of the closing statement has been sent to all distributees, creditors, and other claimants. (§ 700.3988(1)) In addition to the foregoing, identification and a simple sworn statement can be provided by a decedent's spouse, child, or parent so as to collect $500 or less and wearing apparel from a hospital, convalescent or nursing home, morgue, or law enforcement agency. (§ 700.3981)

Is procedure available in the case of nonresident decedents?	No provision.
Maximum allowable value of estate	*Sworn Statement.* $15,000 net of liens, encumbrances, and real property. (§ 700.3983(1)(a)) *Summary Administrative Proceedings.* To the extent the entire estate, less encumbrances and liens, does not exceed administrative costs and expenses, reasonable funeral and burial expenses, homestead, family allowance, exempt property, and reasonable and necessary last illness medical and hospital expenses. (§ 700.3987)
What property can be transferred by this means?	*Sworn Statement.* Personal property. (§ 700.3983(1)) *Summary Administrative Proceedings.* Entire estate. (§ 700.3987)
Special rules for certain assets (e.g., automobile)	Hospital, convalescent or nursing home, morgue, or law enforcement agency holding cash less than $500 and wearing apparel of dece dent may deliver such property to a person furnishing identification and a sworn statement that the person is the decedent's spouse, child, or parent, and that no application is pending for administration of the estate. (§ 700.3981) Also, a transfer agent of a security shall change the registered ownership on the books of a corporation upon presentation of a sworn statement. (§ 700.3983(2))
Can the spouse or other person take summarily if under certain amount?	*Sworn Statement.* If funeral expenses have been paid and value of estate is less than $15,000, property is turned over to surviving spouse. If funeral expenses have not been paid and estate is less than $15,000, funeral expenses are paid first, and surviving spouse receives the balance. (§ 700.3982)
Minimum period before filing allowed	*Sworn Statement.* 28 days after death of decedent. (§ 700.3983(1)) *Summary Administrative Proceedings.* None, other than after review of inventory and appraisal. (§ 700.3987)
Rights/obligations of party with affidavit	Affiant who claims wearing apparel and petty cash is answerable to fiduciaries of the estate and to persons having a prior right to wearing apparel or cash. (§ 700.3981) *Sworn Statement.* The person holding the sworn statement has a right to collect from those holding property or owing the estate. (§ 700.3984(1)) The transferee is answerable and accountable for the property to a person having superior right. (§ 700.3984(2))
Are some creditors given special privileges/preference (e.g., medical expenses, funeral expenses)?	*Sworn Statement.* Not applicable since assumes a net estate after payment of debts and expenses. (§ 700.3983(1)(a)) *Summary Administrative Proceedings.* Funeral and burial expenses, and last illness medical expenses. (§ 700.3987)
Creditors' rights, if insufficient assets	*Sworn Statement.* The transferee is answerable and accountable for the property to a person having superior right. (§ 700.3984(2)) *Summary Administrative Proceedings.* No provision.

May the distribution of the estate proceed without appointment of personal representative?	*Sworn Statement.* Yes. (§ 700.3983) *Summary Administrative Proceedings.* No. (§ 700.3987)
Must court approve affidavit?	*Sworn Statement* . No. However, a standard form will be available for use. (§ 700.3983(3)) *Summary Administrative Proceedings.* No approval necessary. (§ 700.3987)
Waiting period before authority to act	*Sworn Statement.* Must be more than 28 days after decedent's death. (§ 700.3983) *Summary Administrative Proceedings.* No provision.
With whom do you file petition or affidavit?	*Sworn Statement.* Not required. (§ 700.3983) *Summary Administrative Proceedings.* Closing statement must be filed with court. (§ 700.3988(1))
Is there an informal procedure for appointment of executor or administrator?	Yes. (§§ 700.3301, 700.3307 to .3311)
Can a nonresident serve?	Yes. (§§ 700.4101 to .4205)
Can the nonresident act locally based on appointment in another state?	If domiciliary foreign personal representative files authenticated copies of appointment and official bond with the court, such person may exercise the power of a local representative subject to conditions imposed upon nonresidents generally. (§ 700.4203)
What does a transferor need so as to be relieved of liability if challenged by another person later on who claims the particular property (e.g., copy of affidavit)?	*Sworn Statement.* Payor is released and discharged simply by making the transfer under a sworn statement. (§ 700.3984(1)) *Summary Administrative Proceedings.* No provision.

Minnesota
Collection of Personal Property by Affidavit; Summary Administration Procedure for Small Estates

Who can initiate process?	*Affidavit.* Person claiming to be the successor of the decedent. (§ 524.3-1201(a)) *Summary Administration.* Any interested person. (§ 524.3-1203(1))
Can it be used if claims outstanding?	*Affidavit.* No provision. *Summary Administration.* No summary closing to distributees other than by family allowance is to be made without a showing that all claims have been paid. If the estate does not exceed $100,000 and is not exhausted by priority payments and exclusive of homestead, summary administration may proceed. (§ 524.3-1203(3), (5))
Different rules if die testate or intestate?	No provision.
Notice?	*Affidavit.* No provision. *Summary Administration.* All distributees and known claimants whose claims are neither paid nor barred must be sent a copy of the closing statement. (§ 524.3-1204(a)(3))
heirs	*Summary Administration.* All distributees must be sent a copy of the closing statement. (§ 524.3-1204(a)(3))
creditors	*Summary Administration.* All known claimants whose claims are neither paid nor barred must be sent a copy of the closing statement. (§ 524.3-1204(a)(3)).
others	No provision.
Which of the following must be observed?	
hearing	No provision.
affidavit, petition, other	*Affidavit.* Affidavit. (§ 524.3-1201(a)) *Summary Administration.* Petition & closing statement. (§§ 524.3-1203(1), 524.3-1204(a)(3))
bond	*Affidavit.* No provision. *Summary Administration.* If personal representative not appointed, court may require petitioner to file a corporate surety bond. If a personal representative is appointed, a representative's bond must be filed conditioned upon the fact that all exempt property, allowances, and claims listed in M.S.A. § 524.3-805(a)(1)-(6) have been paid. (§ 524.3-1203(4), (5))
What are basic contents of petition or affidavit?	*Affidavit.* (1) Value of estate, less liens and encumbrances, does not exceed $20,000; (2) 30 days have elapsed since death of decedent; (3) no application for appointment of personal representative is pending or granted; (4) amount of claim in multi-party financial accounts; and (5) claiming successor is entitled to payment or delivery of the property. (§ 524.3-1201(a)(1)-(5)) Certified death certificate must be presented with affidavit. (§ 524.3-1201(a))

	Summary Administration. Closing statement must state that (1) the value of the estate, less liens and encumbrances, did not exceed homestead and family allowances plus funeral and last illness expenses; (2) that the estate has been fully administered and distributed; and (3) that the closing statement has been sent to all distributees and claimants whose claims are neither paid nor barred. (§ 524.3-1204(a))
Is procedure available in the case of nonresident decedents?	No provision.
Maximum allowable value of estate	*Affidavit.* Value of estate less liens and encumbrances does not exceed $20,000. (§ 524.3-1201(a)(1)) *Summary Administration.* If the estate will not be exhausted in payment of the priority items enumerated in subdivisions 1 to 4, the estate may nevertheless be closed if the gross value of the estate exclusive of exempt homestead and any exempt property does not exceed $100,000. (§ 524.3-1203(5))
What property can be transferred by this means?	*Affidavit.* Payment of indebtedness; tangible personal property; instrument evidencing a debt, obligation, stock, or chose in action; and contents of safe deposit box. (§ 524.3-1201(a)) *Summary Administration.* Any real, personal, or other property in kind. (§ 524.3-1203(3))
Special rules for certain assets (e.g., automobile)	*Affidavit.* If presented with a proper affidavit, a motor vehicle registrar shall issue a new certificate of title. (§ 524.3-1201(d)) Also, in the case of a safe deposit box, payor need not deliver it if he has received an objection or if the key is not available. (§ 524.3-1201(e)) A transfer agent of any security shall change the registered ownership on the books of a corporation upon presentation of an affidavit. (§ 524.3-1201(b)) *Summary Administration.* No provision.
Can the spouse or other person take summarily if under certain amount?	*Affidavit.* No provision. *Summary Administration.* Court may summarily determine and assign shares. (§ 524.3-1203(1), (3))
Minimum period before filing allowed	*Affidavit.* There is no filing required under the affidavit procedure. See *Waiting period before authority to act.* (§ 524.3-1201(a)) *Summary Administration.* No provision.
Rights/obligations of party with affidavit	*Affidavit.* (1) Party can compel recovery of property upon proof of their right in a proceeding; (2) party with affidavit is answerable to any personal representative of the estate or to any other person having a supreme right. (§ 524.3-1202) *Summary Administration.* No provision.
Are some creditors given special privileges/preference (e.g., medical expenses, funeral expenses)?	*Affidavit.* No provision. *Summary Administration.* Yes, funeral, last illness medical expenses, and the classification of claims in M.S.A. § 524.3-805. (§§ 524.3-1203(1), (3), 524.3-1204(a)(1))
Creditors' rights, if insufficient assets	*Affidavit.* Payees are answerable to those with superior rights. (§ 524.3-1202) *Summary Administration.* See *Can it be used if claims outstanding?*

May the distribution of the estate proceed without appointment of personal representative?	*Affidavit.* Must proceed without personal representative. (§ 524.3-1201(a)(3)) *Summary Administration.* May proceed without personal representative. (§ 524.3-1203(4))
Must court approve affidavit?	*Affidavit.* No provision. *Summary Administration.* Yes (petition). (§ 524.3-1203(1))
Waiting period before authority to act	*Affidavit.* 30 days. (§ 524.3-1201(a)(2)) *Summary Administration.* No provision.
With whom do you file petition or affidavit?	*Affidavit.* No provision. *Summary Administration.* Probate Court. (§ 524.3-1203(1))
Is there an informal procedure for appointment of executor or administrator?	Yes. (§§ 524.3-301, 524.3-307 to -311)
Can a nonresident serve?	Yes. (§§ 524.4-201 to -207)
Can the nonresident act locally based on appointment in another state?	60 days after filing authentication of appointment and notice of intent, a domiciliary foreign personal representative may exercise as to assets in Minnesota all powers of a local personal representative subject to any conditions imposed upon nonresident parties generally. (§§ 524.4-205, 524.4-204)
What does a transferor need so as to be relieved of liability if challenged by another person later on who claims the particular property (e.g., copy of affidavit)?	*Affidavit.* Payor is discharged and released after transferring property pursuant to the affidavit to the same extent as if he dealt with a personal representative. (§ 524.3-1202) *Summary Administration.* No provision.

Mississippi
Payment of Indebtedness or Delivery of Personal Property of Decedent to Decedent's Successor; Affidavit of Successor

Who can initiate process?	Persons claiming to be "successors" of decedent, defined as: (1) decedent's spouse; (2) if no spouse, then adult with whom minor children of decedent are residing; (3) if no minor children, any adult child of decedent; or (4) if no adult child, either parent of the decedent. (§ 91-7-322(1) & (2))
Can it be used if claims outstanding?	No provision.
Different rules if die testate or intestate?	No provision.
Notice?	No provision.
heirs	No provision.
creditors	No provision.
others	No provision.
Which of the following must be observed?	
hearing	No provision.
affidavit, petition, other	Affidavit. (§ 91-7-322(1))
bond	No provision.
What are basic contents of petition or affidavit?	(1) Value of estate, excluding liens and encumbrances, does not exceed $30,000; (2) 30 days elapsed since death of decedent; (3) no application or petition for appointment of personal representative can be pending or granted; and (4) facts of relationship establishing affiant as a successor of the decedent. (§ 91-7-322(1)(a)-(d))
Is procedure available in the case of nonresident decedents?	No provision.
Maximum allowable value of estate	Value of entire estate, less liens and encumbrances, cannot exceed $30,000. (§ 91-7-322(1)(a))
What property can be transferred by this means?	Payment of indebtedness, tangible personal property, instrument evidencing a debt, obligation, stock or chose in action. (§ 91-7-322(1))
Special rules for certain assets (e.g., automobile)	No provision.
Can the spouse or other person take summarily if under certain amount?	No provision.
Minimum period before filing allowed	No filing required. See *Waiting period before authority to act.*

Rights/obligations of party with affidavit	(1) Affiant can compel recovery of property upon proof of right in a proceeding brought in Chancery Court; (2) affiant is answerable to any personal representative of the estate or to any other person having a superior right. (§ 91-7-322(5)) Affiant is also empowered to negotiate, transfer ownership and exercise all other incidents of ownership with respect to the personal property and other instruments described in § 91-7-322(1). (§ 91-7-322(4))
Are some creditors given special privileges/preference (e.g., medical expenses, funeral expenses)?	No provision.
Creditors' rights, if insufficient assets	Payees are answerable to persons with superior rights. (§ 91-7-322(5))
May the distribution of the estate proceed without appointment of personal representative?	Must proceed without appointment of personal representative. (§ 91-7-322(1)(c))
Must court approve affidavit?	No provision.
Waiting period before authority to act	30 days after death of decedent. (§ 91-7-322(1)(b))
With whom do you file petition or affidavit?	No provision.
Is there an informal procedure for appointment of executor or administrator?	No provision.
Can a nonresident serve?	No provision.
Can the nonresident act locally based on appointment in another state?	No provision.
What does a transferor need so as to be relieved of liability if challenged by another person later on who claims the particular property (e.g., copy of affidavit)?	Payor is discharged and released to the same extent as if such person had dealt with a personal representative. (§ 91-7-322(5))

Missouri
Small Estates—Distribution of Assets Without Letters, When Affidavit; Procedure; Fee

Who can initiate process?	Personal representative under the will if a will has been presented for probate; otherwise, any distributee entitled to receive property of the decedent. (§ 473.097(2))
Can it be used if claims outstanding?	Yes, if claims will be paid. (§ 473.097(2)(2))
Different rules if die testate or intestate?	No provision beyond *Who can initiate process?*
Notice?	
heirs	No provision.
creditors	If value of property in affidavit is greater than $15,000, clerk must publish notice to creditors in the newspaper. (§ 473.097(5))
others	No provision.
Which of the following must be observed?	
hearing	No provision.
affidavit, petition, other	Affidavit and certificate of the clerk. (§ 473.097)
bond	Yes. (§ 473.097(1)(3))
What are basic contents of petition or affidavit?	Affidavit must set forth: (1) decedent left no will or will has been presented for probate; (2) all unpaid debts or demands against decedent's estate will be paid, up to value of the property received; (3) itemized description and valuation of the property of the decedent; (4) names and addresses of persons having possession of the property; (5) names, addresses, and relationship to decedent of persons who will receive items included in the affidavit; and (6) facts establishing the right to such specific items of property. (§ 473.097(2)(1)-(6))
Is procedure available in the case of nonresident decedents?	No provision.
Maximum allowable value of estate	Value of entire estate, less liens and encumbrances, cannot exceed $40,000. (§ 473.097(1)(1))
What property can be transferred by this means?	Real property and personal property. (§ 473.097(1))
Special rules for certain assets (e.g., automobile)	No provision.
Can the spouse or other person take summarily if under certain amount?	No provision.
Minimum period before filing allowed	30 days after death of decedent. (§ 473.097(1)(2))

Rights/obligations of party with affidavit	Affiant is liable for debts of the decedent's estate up to the value of the property received. Secured creditors retain their right to decedent's property. Affiant is entitled to collect property of decedent described in the affidavit and may liquidate property as necessary to pay debts. (§ 473.097(2)(2), (6) & (7)) Affiant is also answerable and accountable to anyone having a superior right. (§ 473.100)
Are some creditors given special privileges/preference (e.g., medical expenses, funeral expenses)?	Must file bond ensuring payment of all the debts of the decedent, including any debts to the state and any debts related to funeral and burial. (§ 473.097(1)(3))
Creditors' rights, if insufficient assets	Right to payment up to the value of the property received by the affiant. (§ 473.097(2)(2))
May the distribution of the estate proceed without appointment of personal representative?	Administration must proceed without application for or appointment of personal representative. (§ 473.097(1)(2))
Must court approve affidavit?	Certificate of clerk showing names and addresses of the persons entitled to the described property must be annexed to or endorsed on the affidavit. (§ 473.097(2)(6))
Waiting period before authority to act	30 days after death of decedent. (§ 473.097(1)(2))
With whom do you file petition or affidavit?	Office of the clerk of the probate division. If receiving real property, must file affidavit and certificate of the clerk in the office of the recorder of deeds of each county where the real property is situated. (§ 473.097(3) & (4))
Is there an informal procedure for appointment of executor or administrator?	No provision.
Can a nonresident serve?	No provision.
Can the nonresident act locally based on appointment in another state?	No provision.
What does a transferor need so as to be relieved of liability if challenged by another person later on who claims the particular property (e.g., copy of affidavit)?	Transferor is discharged and released to the same extent as if made to an executor or administrator of the decedent. Transferor need not inquire into the truth of the affidavit. (§ 473.100)

Montana
Collection of Personal Property by Affidavit; Summary Administration Procedure for Small Estates

Who can initiate process?	*Affidavit.* Person claiming to be the successor of the decedent. (§ 72-3-1101(1)) *Summary Administration.* Personal representative. (§ 72-3-1103)
Can it be used if claims outstanding?	*Affidavit.* Yes. (§ 72-3-1101(1)(a)) *Summary Administration.* Yes. (§ 72-3-1103)
Different rules if die testate or intestate?	No provision.
Notice?	
heirs	*Affidavit.* No provision. *Summary Administration.* All distributees of estate must get a copy of the closing statement. (§ 72-3-1104(1)(c))
creditors	*Affidavit.* No provision. *Summary Administration.* Must send copy of the closing statement to all creditors whose claims are neither paid nor barred. (§ 72-3-1104(1)(c))
others	No provision.
Which of the following must be observed?	
hearing	No provision.
affidavit, petition, other	*Affidavit.* Affidavit. (§ 72-3-1101) *Summary Administration.* Closing statement. (§ 72-3-1104)
bond	No provision.
What are basic contents of petition or affidavit?	*Affidavit.* (1) Value of estate, less liens and encumbrances, does not exceed $50,000; (2) 30 days elapsed since death of decedent; (3) no application for appointment of personal representative is pending or granted; and (4) claiming successor is entitled to payment or delivery of property. (§ 72-3-1101(1)(a)-(d)) *Summary Administration.* Verified closing statement filed with the court must state (1) value of the estate, less liens and encumbrances, do not exceed family and homestead allowances, exempt property, and funeral, last medical, and administrative expenses; (2) estate has been fully administered and all inheritance taxes have been paid; and (3) copy of the closing statement has been distributed to distributees and creditors. (§ 72-3-1104(1)(a)-(c))
Is procedure available in the case of nonresident decedents?	No provision.

Maximum allowable value of estate	*Affidavit.* Value of estate less liens and encumbrances cannot exceed $50,000. (§ 72-3-1101(1)(a)) *Summary Administration.* Value of the entire estate less liens and encumbrances does not exceed homestead allowance, exempt property, family allowance, costs and expenses of administration, reasonable funeral expenses, and necessary medical and hospital expenses of the last illness of the decedent. (§ 72-3-1103)
What property can be transferred by this means?	*Affidavit.* (1) Payment of indebtedness; (2) tangible personal property; or (3) instrument evidencing a debt, obligation, stock, or chose in action. (§ 72-3-1101(1)) *Summary Administration.* Entire estate may be distributed. (§ 72-3-1103)
Special rules for certain assets (e.g., automobile)	A transfer agent must change the registered ownership of a security upon presentation of an affidavit. (§ 72-3-1101(2))
Can the spouse or other person take summarily if under certain amount?	No provision.
Minimum period before filing allowed	*Affidavit.* No filing required for affidavit procedure. See *Waiting period before authority to act.* *Summary Administration.* No provision.
Rights/obligations of party with affidavit	*Affidavit.* (1) Party can compel recovery of property upon proof of right in a proceeding; (2) party with affidavit is answerable to any personal representative of the estate or to any other person having a superior right. (§ 72-3-1102(2) & (3)) *Summary Administration.* No provision.
Are some creditors given special privileges/preference (e.g., medical expenses, funeral expenses)?	*Affidavit.* No provision. *Summary Administration.* Funeral and last illness medical expenses. (§ 72-3-1103)
Creditors' rights, if insufficient assets	*Affidavit.* Payee is answerable to any person with a superior right. (§ 72-3-1102(3)) *Summary Administration.* No provision.
May the distribution of the estate proceed without appointment of personal representative?	*Affidavit.* Administration must proceed without application or appointment in any jurisdiction. (§ 72-3-1101(1)(c)) *Summary Administration.* No. (Must have personal representative.) (§ 72-3-1103)
Must court approve affidavit?	No provision.
Waiting period before authority to act	*Affidavit.* 30 days after death of decedent. (§ 72-3-1101(1)(b)) *Summary Administration.* No provision.
With whom do you file petition or affidavit?	*Affidavit.* No provision. *Summary Administration.* Must file verified closing statement with the court. (§ 72-3-1104(1))
Is there an informal procedure for appointment of executor or administrator?	Yes. (§§ 72-3-201 to -202, -221 to -225)

Can a nonresident serve?	Yes. (§§ 72-4-301 to -311)
Can the nonresident act locally based on appointment in another state?	If domiciliary foreign personal representative files authenticated copies of appointment and official bond with the court, such person may exercise as to assets in Montana all of the powers of a local representative subject to conditions imposed upon nonresidents generally. (§§ 72-4-310, 72-4-309)
What does a transferor need so as to be relieved of liability if challenged by another person later on who claims the particular property (e.g., copy of affidavit)?	*Affidavit.* Payor is discharged to the same extent as if he dealt with a personal representative of decedent after transferring property pursuant to the affidavit. (§ 72-3-1102(1)) *Summary Administration.* No provision.

Nebraska
Collection of Personal Property by Affidavit; Summary Administration Procedure for Small Estates

Who can initiate process?	*Affidavit.* Any person claiming to be the successor of the decedent. (§ 30-24, 125(a)) *Summary Administration.* Personal representative. (§ 30-24, 127)
Can it be used if claims outstanding?	*Affidavit.* Yes. (§ 30-24,125(a)) *Summary Administration.* Yes. (§ 30-24,127)
Different rules if die testate or intestate?	No provision.
Notice?	
heirs	*Affidavit.* No provision. *Summary Administration.* Must send copy of the closing statement to all distributees of estate. (§ 30-24,128(a)(3))
creditors	*Affidavit.* No provision. *Summary Administration.* Must send copy of the closing statement to all creditors whose claims are neither paid nor barred. (§ 30-24,128(a)(3))
others	No provision.
Which of the following must be observed?	
hearing	No provision.
affidavit, petition, other	*Affidavit.* Affidavit. (§ 30-24,125(a)) *Summary Administration.* Closing statement. (§ 30-24,128(a))
bond	No provision.
What are basic contents of petition or affidavit?	*Affidavit.* (1) Value of personal property, less liens and encumbrances, does not exceed $25,000; (2) 30 days elapsed since death of decedent; (3) claiming successor's relationship to decedent or basis of claim; (4) claiming successor affirms that all statements are true; (5) no application for appointment of personal representative is outstanding or granted; and (6) claiming successor is entitled to delivery of the property. (§ 30-24,125(a)(1)-(6)) A copy of decedent's death certificate must be attached to the affidavit. (§ 20-24,125(a)(2)) *Summary Administration.* Verified closing statement filed with the court must state: (1) value of the estate, less liens and encumbrances, did not exceed family and homestead allowances, exempt property, and funeral, last illness medical, and administrative expenses; (2) estate has been fully administered; and (3) copy of the closing statement has been distributed to distributees and claimants. (§ 30-24,128(a)(1)-(3))

Is procedure available in the case of nonresident decedents?	No provision.
Maximum allowable value of estate	*Affidavit.* Value of estate less liens and encumbrances did not exceed $25,000. (§ 30-24,125(a)(1)) *Summary Administration.* Value of the entire estate, less liens and encumbrances, does not exceed homestead allowance, exempt property, family allowance, costs and expenses of administration, reasonable funeral expenses, and reasonable and necessary medical and hospital expenses of the last illness of the decedent. (§ 30-24,127)
What property can be transferred by this means?	*Affidavit.* Tangible personal property, instruments evidencing a debt, obligation, stock or chose in action and payment of indebtedness. (§ 30-24,125(a)) *Summary Administration.* Entire estate. (§ 30-24,127)
Special rules for certain assets (e.g., automobile)	*Affidavit.* If seeking to transfer certificate of title to a motor vehicle, affiant must furnish to the department of motor vehicles a statement of the value of the vehicle. (§ 30-24,125(c)) Transfers of securities must change the registered ownership on the corporate books. (§ 30-24,125(b)) *Summary Administration.* No provision.
Can the spouse or other person take summarily if under certain amount?	No provision.
Minimum period before filing allowed	*Affidavit.* No filing required. See *Waiting period before authority to act.* *Summary Administration.* No provision.
Rights/obligations of party with affidavit	*Affidavit.* (1) Party can compel recovery of property upon proof of right in a proceeding; (2) party is answerable to any personal representative of the estate or to any other person having a superior right. (§ 30-24,126) *Summary Administration.* No provision.
Are some creditors given special privileges/preference (e.g., medical expenses, funeral expenses)?	*Affidavit.* No provision. *Summary Administration.* Funeral and last illness medical expenses. (§ 30-24,127)
Creditors' rights, if insufficient assets	*Affidavit.* Payee is answerable to persons having a superior right. (§ 30-24,126) *Summary Administration.* No provision.
May the distribution of the estate proceed without appointment of personal representative?	*Affidavit.* Yes. It *must* proceed without application for or appointment of a personal representative. (§ 30-24,125(a)(5)) *Summary Administration.* No. (§ 30-24,127)
Must court approve affidavit?	No provision.
Waiting period before authority to act	*Affidavit.* 30 days after death of decedent. (§ 30-24,125(a)(2)) *Summary Administration.* No provision.
With whom do you file petition or affidavit?	*Affidavit.* No provision. *Summary Administration.* Must file verified closing statement with the court. (§ 30-24,128(a))

Is there an informal procedure for appointment of executor or administrator?	Yes. (§§ 30-2414, 30-2420 to -2424)
Can a nonresident serve?	Yes. (§§ 30-2501 to -2508)
Can the nonresident act locally based on appointment in another state?	If domiciliary foreign personal representative files authenticated copies of appointment and official bond with the court, such person may exercise as to assets in Nebraska all of the powers of a local representative subject to conditions imposed upon nonresidents generally. (§§ 30-2506, 30-2505)
What does a transferor need so as to be relieved of liability if challenged by another person later on who claims the particular property (e.g., copy of affidavit)?	*Affidavit.* Payor is released and discharged to the same extent as if he had dealt with a personal representative after transferring property pursuant to affidavit. (§ 30-24,126) *Summary Administration.* No provision.

Nevada
Distribution of Small Estates

Who can initiate process?	*Estates Not Exceeding $75,000.* If deceased leaves a surviving spouse or minor child, procedure is automatic; if the deceased is not survived by a spouse or minor child, then "good cause" must be shown by the petitioner, who would be, presumably, an interested person entitled to file for probate. (§ 146.070(1) & (2)) *Local Estate Not Exceeding $20,000 and Not Involving an Interest in or Lien on Real Property.* (1) Person who has right to succeed to decedent's property; (2) Director of the Department of Human Services or public administrator. (§ 146.080(1))
Can it be used if claims outstanding?	*Estates Not Exceeding $75,000.* Yes. (§ 146.070(3)(d)) *Local Estates Not Exceeding $20,000 and Not Involving an Interest in or Lien on Real Property.* No. All debts of decedent must have been paid or provided for. (§ 146.080(2)(f))
Different rules if die testate or intestate?	No provision.
Notice?	
heirs	*Estates Not Exceeding $75,000.* Petitioner shall give notice to all heirs and devisees. (§ 146.070(4)) *Local Estates Not Exceeding $20,000 and Not Involving an Interest in or Lien on Real Property.* Notice must be provided to every person whose right to succeed to decedent's property is equal or superior to that of the affiant. (§ 146.080(2)(h))
creditors	No provision.
others	*Estates Not Exceeding $75,*000. Petitioner shall give notice to the Director of the Department of Human Resources. (§ 146.070(4)) *Local Estates Not Exceeding $20,000 and Not Involving an Interest in or Lien on Real Property.* No provision.
Which of the following must be observed?	
hearing	*Estates Not Exceeding $75,*000. Yes. (§ 146.070(4)) *Local Estates Not Exceeding $20,000 and Not Involving an Interest in or Lien on Real Property.* No provision.
affidavit, petition, other	*Estates Not Exceeding $75,000.* Petition. (§ 146.070(3)) *Local Estates Not Exceeding $20,000 and Not Involving an Interest in or Lien on Real Property.* Affidavit. (§ 146.080(1))
bond	No provision.
What are basic contents of petition or affidavit?	*Estates Not Exceeding $75,000.* (1) Description of all decedent's property; (2) list of all liens and mortgages at death; (3) estimate of value of the property; (4) statement of decedent's debts; (5) names, ages, and residences of decedent's heirs and devisees. (§ 146.070(3)(a)-(e)) *Local Estates Not Exceeding $20,000 and Not Involving an Interest in or Lien on Real Property.* The affidavit must contain: (1) affiant's name and address and statement that affiant is

	entitled by law to succeed to the property; (2) the date and place of death of decedent; (3) gross value of estate property in Nevada is less than $20,000, and that there is no real property or interest therein; (4) at least 40 days have elapsed since death of decedent; (5) no petition for appointment of personal representative is pending or granted; (6) all debts of decedent, including funeral and burial expenses and money owed to the department of human resources as result of Medicaid payments have been paid or provided for; (7) description of personal property and portion claimed; (8) 14 days' notice given to every person whose right to succeed to decedent's property is equal or superior to that of the affiant; (9) statement that affiant is personally entitled or the Director of the Department of Human Resources is entitled to delivery of the property; and (10) affiant acknowledges understanding that filing false affidavit is a felony in Nevada. (§ 146.080(2)(a)(j))
Is procedure available in the case of nonresident decedents?	No provision.
Maximum allowable value of estate	*Estates Not Exceeding $75,000.* Gross value of estate, less encumbrances, cannot exceed $75,000. (§ 146.070(1)) *Local Estates Not Exceeding $20,000 and Not Involving an Interest in or Lien on Real Property.* Must leave no real property, nor interest therein, nor lien thereon in the state and gross value of decedent's property *in the state* over and above amounts due to decedent for services in the U.S. armed forces does not exceed $20,000. (§ 146.080(1))
What property can be transferred by this means?	*Estates Not Exceeding $75,000.* Entire estate. (§ 146.070(1) &(2)) *Local Estates Not Exceeding $20,000 and Not Involving an Interest in or Lien on Real Property.* (1) Money due the decedent; (2) personal property of the decedent; and (3) evidence of interest, indebtedness, or right. (§ 146.080(1))
Special rules for certain assets (e.g., automobile)	*Estates Not Exceeding $75,000.* No provision. *Local Estates Not Exceeding $20,000 and Not Involving an Interest in or Lien on Real Property.* Upon receiving proof of death of decedent and affidavit, transfer agent of securities shall change the registered ownership; government agencies shall issue a new certificate of ownership or registration. (§ 146.080(5))
Can the spouse or other person take summarily if under certain amount?	Yes, spouse and/or minor children. (§ 146.070(1))
Minimum period before filing allowed	*Estates Not Exceeding $75,000.* 30 days after death of decedent. (§ 146.070(3)) *Local Estates Not Exceeding $20,000 and Not Involving an Interest in or Lien on Real Property.* No filing required. See *Waiting period before authority to act.* (§ 146.080(1))
Rights/obligations of party with affidavit	*Estates Not Exceeding $75,000.* No provision. *Local Estates Not Exceeding $20,000 and Not Involving an Interest in or Lien on Real Property.* Right to have property transferred. (§ 146.080(1))

Are some creditors given special privileges/preference (e.g., medical expenses, funeral expenses)?	*Estates Not Exceeding $75,000.* If no surviving spouse or minor child, estate is first used for payment of funeral expenses, expenses of last illness, and money owed to Medicaid and creditors. The remaining balance goes to claimants pursuant to the will, or intestate succession. (§ 146.070(2)) The priority of the various claimants is not set forth. *Local Estates Not Exceeding $20,000 and Not Involving an Interest in or Lien on Real Property.* All debts of decedent, including funeral and Medicaid expenses, must be provided for. (§ 146.080(2)(f))
Creditors' rights, if insufficient assets	No provision.
May the distribution of the estate proceed without appointment of personal representative?	*Estates Not Exceeding $75,000.* Yes. (§ 146.070(1)) *Local Estates Not Exceeding $20,000 and Not Involving an Interest in or Lien on Real Property.* Yes; must proceed without a personal representative. (§ 146.080(2)(e))
Must court approve affidavit?	No. However, a false affidavit constitutes a felony. (§ 146.080(2)(j))
Waiting period before authority to act	*Estates Not Exceeding $75,000.* 30 days after death of decedent. (§ 146.070(3)) *Local Estates Not Exceeding $20,000 and Not Involving an Interest in or Lien on Real Property.* 40 days after death of decedent. (§ 146.080(1))
With whom do you file petition or affidavit?	*Estates Not Exceeding $75,000.* Court. (§ 146.070(3)) *Local Estates Not Exceeding $20,000 and Not Involving an Interest in or Lien on Real Property.* No filing. Simply furnish decedent's debtor, custodian, or transfer agent with an affidavit. (§ 146.080(1))
Is there an informal procedure for appointment of executor or administrator?	No provision.
Can a nonresident serve?	No provision.
Can the nonresident act locally based on appointment in another state?	No provision.
What does a transferor need so as to be relieved of liability if challenged by another person later on who claims the particular property (e.g., copy of affidavit)?	*Estates Not Exceeding $75,000.* No provision, since the distribution occurs under the aegis of the court. *Estates Not Exceeding $20,000 and Not Involving an Interest in or Lien on Real Property.* If person who receives affidavit relies in good faith on that affidavit, such person is immune from civil liability resulting from that reliance. (§ 146.080(4))

New Hampshire
Waiver of Administration

Who can initiate process?	The administrator of the estate. Process can only be initiated if (1) decedent dies testate and the surviving spouse, or if no spouse there is an only child named as the sole beneficiary and is appointed to serve as administrator, or (2) decedent dies intestate and the surviving spouse, or if no spouse an only child is the sole heir and is appointed to serve as administrator. (§ 553:32(I))
Can it be used if claims outstanding?	No. (§ 553:32(I))
Different rules if die testate or intestate?	No. (§ 553:32)
Notice?	No provision.
heirs	No provision.
creditors	No provision.
others	No provision.
Which of the following must be observed?	
hearing	No provision.
affidavit, petition, other	Affidavit of administration. (§ 553:32(1))
bond	Bond not required. (§ 553:32(I))
What are basic contents of petition or affidavit?	Affidavit of administration shall (1) state that to the best of the knowledge and belief of the administrator, there are no outstanding debts or obligations attributable to the estate, and (2) list all real estate owned by decedent at the time of death, including location, book and page. (§ 553:32(1)) The administrator, if nonresident, must also appoint some person residing in New Hampshire as an agent pursuant to § 553:25.
Is procedure available in the case of nonresident decedents?	No provision.
Maximum allowable value of estate	No provision.
What property can be transferred by this means?	Entire estate. (§ 553:32(I))
Special rules for certain assets (e.g., automobile)	No provision.
Can the spouse or other person take summarily if under certain amount?	No provision.
Minimum period before filing allowed	Affidavit of administration must be filed no earlier than 6 months and no later than one year after decedent's death. (§ 553:32(I))
Rights/obligations of party with affidavit	Affiant does not need to do an inventory of the estate or account for assets. Administration of the estate is complete once the probate court approves of the affidavit. (§ 553:32(I))

Are some creditors given special privileges/preference (e.g., medical expenses, funeral expenses)?	No provision.
Creditors' rights, if insufficient assets	Not applicable; there are no outstanding debts allowed for this procedure. (§ 553:32(I)) Any interested person may petition for a full administration of the estate any time from the original grant of administration to the filing of the affidavit of administration. (§ 533:32(II))
May the distribution of the estate proceed without appointment of personal representative?	No. (§ 553:32(I))
Must court approve petition?	Yes. (§ 553:32(I))
Waiting period before authority to act	6 months from date of death. (§ 553:32(I))
With whom do you file petition or affidavit?	Probate court. (§ 553:32(I))
Is there an informal procedure for appointment of executor or administrator?	No provision.
Can a nonresident serve?	Yes, provided a New Hampshire resident is appointed as agent. (§ 553:25)
Can the nonresident act locally based on appointment in another state?	No, unless the judge believes it is proper based on other circumstances. (§ 553:5)
What does a transferor need so as to be relieved of liability if challenged by another person later on who claims the particular property (e.g., copy of affidavit)?	No provision.

New Jersey
Small Estate Administration

Who can initiate process?	Surviving spouse or domestic partner (§ 3B:10-3), or any heir if there is no surviving spouse or domestic partner (§ 3B:10-4).
Can it be used if claims outstanding?	Yes. (§§ 3B:10-3, 3B:10-4)
Different rules if die testate or intestate?	Both §§ 3B:10-3 and 3B:10-4 expressly apply only to estates of an intestate decedent.
Notice?	Spouse/Domestic Partner—No provision. Heirs—see below.
heirs	Heirs—Must notify other remaining heirs, obtain their consent in writing, and file the written consent with the affidavit. (§ 3B:10-4)
creditors	No provision.
others	No provision.
Which of the following must be observed?	
hearing	No provision.
affidavit, petition, other	Affidavit. (§§ 3B:10-3, 3B:10-4)
bond	No provision.
What are basic contents of petition or affidavit?	Spouse/Domestic Partner: (1) That the affiant is the surviving spouse or domestic partner of the intestate; (2) that the value of the intestate's real and personal assets will not exceed $20,000.00; (3) the residence of the intestate at his or her death; and (4) specifically the nature, location, and value of the intestate's real and personal assets. (§ 3B:10-3) Heirs: (1) Residence of the intestate at his or her death; (2) names, residences, and relationships of all of the heirs; (3) the specific nature, location, and value of the intestate's real and personal assets; and (4) statement that the value of the intestate's real and personal assets will not exceed $10,000.00 (§ 3B:10-4)
Is procedure available in the case of nonresident decedents?	Yes. Sections 3B:10-3 and 3B:10-4 specifically provide for nonresident decedents.
Maximum allowable value of estate	Spouse/Domestic Partner—$20,000. (§ 3B:10-3) Heirs—$10,000. (§ 3B:10-4)
What property can be transferred by this means?	Real and personal. (§§ 3B:10-3, 3B:10-4)
Special rules for certain assets (e.g., automobile)	No provision.
Can the spouse or other person take summarily if under certain amount?	No provision.
Minimum period before filing allowed	No provision.

Rights/obligations of party with affidavit	Spouse/Domestic Partner: Affiant (1) has the rights, powers and duties of an administrator duly appointed for the estate, (2) is entitled absolutely to all the real and personal assets without administration, (3) is entitled to assets of the estate up to $5,000.00 free from all debts of the intestate, and (4) may be sued and required to account as if he had been appointed administrator. (3B:10-3) Heirs: Affiant (1) has the rights, powers and duties of an administrator duly appointed for the estate; (2) is entitled to receive the assets of the benefit of all the heirs and creditors without administration or entering into a bond, and (3) may be sued and required to account as if he had been appointed administrator. (3B:10-4)
Are some creditors given special privileges/preference (e.g., medical expenses, funeral expenses)?	No provision.
Creditors' rights, if insufficient assets	May be sued and required to account as if appointed administrator. (§§ 3B:10-3, 3B:10-4)
May the distribution of the estate proceed without appointment of personal representative?	Yes. (§§ 3B:10-3, 3B:10-4)
Must court approve affidavit?	No provision.
Waiting period before authority to act	No provision.
With whom do you file petition or affidavit?	The office of the surrogate, or if proceeding before the superior court, then in the office of the clerk of that court. If affiant is a not a resident of New Jersey, the surrogate may authorize in writing the affidavit to be executed in the affiant's domicile. (§§ 3B:10-3, 3B:10-4)
Is there an informal procedure for appointment of executor or administrator?	No provision.
Can a nonresident serve?	An affiant may be a nonresident. (§§ 3B:10-3, 3B:10-4)
Can the nonresident act locally based on appointment in another state?	Yes.[5]
What does a transferor need so as to be relieved of liability if challenged by another person later on who claims the particular property (e.g., copy of affidavit)?	Payors are permanently discharged if they are presented a copy of the affidavit marked a true copy by the surrogate or the clerk of the Superior Court. (§ 3B:10-5)

5. Both §§ 3B:10-3 and 3B:10-4 provide that a nonresident affiant, with written authorization of the surrogate, may execute the affidavit in the affiant's domicile before certain officers authorized by §§ 46:14-7 and 46:14-8. However, §§ 46:14-7 and 46:14-8 have both been repealed, and §§ 3B:10-3 and 3B:10-4 have not been amended to reflect the repeals.

New Mexico
Summary Administration Procedure for Small Estates

Who can initiate process?	*By Affidavit.* Person claiming to be successor of the decedent, defined in § 45-1-201(A)(45) as "persons, other than creditors, who are entitled to property of a decedent under his will or the Uniform Probate Code." (§ 45-3-1201(A)) *Summary Administration.* Personal representative. (§ 45-3-1203)
Can it be used if claims outstanding?	*By Affidavit.* Yes. (§ 45-3-1201(A)) *Summary Administration.* Yes. (§ 45-3-1203)
Different rules if die testate or intestate?	*By Affidavit.* No provision. *Summary Administration.* No provision[6]
Notice?	*By Affidavit.* No provision. *Summary Administration.* Personal representative must send a copy of the closing statement to several parties (see below) and must also provide a full accout in writing of the administration to the distributees whose interests are affected. (§ 45-3-1204(A)(3))
heirs	*Summary Administration.* Must send a copy of the closing statement to all distributees of the estate. (§ 45-3-1204(A)(3))
creditors	*Summary Administration.* Must send a copy of the closing statement to all creditors of whom he is aware whose claims are neither paid or barred. (§ 45-3-1201(A)(3))
others	*Summary Administration.* Must send a copy of the closing statement to all "other claimants" of whom he is aware whose claims are neither paid or barred. (§ 45-3-1204(A)(3))
Which of the following must be observed?	
hearing	No provision.
affidavit, petition, other	*By Affidavit.* Affidavit. (§ 45-3-1201) *Summary Administration.* Closing statement. (§ 45-3-1203)
bond	No provision.
What are basic contents of petition or affidavit?	*By Affidavit.* Affidavit must state that (1) the value of entire estate, wherever located, less liens and encumbrances, does not exceed $30,000; (2) 30 days have elapsed since death of decedent; (3) no application or petition for appointment of a personal representative is pending or has been granted in any jurisdiction; and (4) the claiming successor is entitled to payment or delivery of the property. (§ 45-3-1201(A)) *Summary Administration.* Closing statement must state that (1) to the best knowledge of the personal representative, the value of the entire estate, less liens and encumbrances, did not exceed the family allowance, personal property, allowance, costs and expenses of administration, reasonably necessary medical and hospital expenses of the last illness of the decedent, and reasonable funeral expenses; (2) the personal representative has fully disbursed the estate to persons entitled thereto; and

	(3) the personal representative has sent a copy of closing statement to all distributees of the estate and to all creditors or other claimants of whom he is aware whose claims are neither paid nor barred and has furnished a full account in writing of his administration to the distributees whose interests are affected. (§ 45-3-1204(A))
Is procedure available in the case of nonresident decedents?	*By Affidavit.* No provision. *Summary Administration.* No provision.
Maximum allowable value of estate	*By Affidavit.* \$30,000. (§ 45-3-1201(A)(1)) *Summary Administration.* Value of the entire estate, less liens and encumbrances, cannot exceed the family allowance, personal property allowance, costs and expenses of administration, reasonable and necessary medical and hospital expenses of the last illness of the decedent, and reasonable funeral expenses. (§ 45-3-1204(A)(1))
What property can be transferred by this means?	*By Affidavit.* Payment of debts, tangible personal property or instruments evidencing a debt, obligation, stock or chose in action belonging to the decedent.[7] (§ 45-3-1201(A)) *Summary Administration.* Entire estate. (§ 45-3-1203)
Special rules for certain assets (e.g., automobile)	Homestead. (§ 45-3-1205)
Can the spouse or other person take summarily if under certain amount?	No provision.
Minimum period before filing allowed	*By Affidavit.* No filing required. See *Waiting period before authority to act.* *Summary Administration.* No provision.
Rights/obligations of party with affidavit	*By Affidavit.* The affiant is (1) entitled to payment of debts and delivery of certain assets upon presentation of affidavit (§ 45-3-1201(A)); (2) can bring a proceeding to recover property if the other party refuses to recognize the affidavit (§ 45-3-1202); and (3) after payment is made, is answerable to any personal representative of the estate or any other person having a superior right (§ 45-3-1202). *Summary Administration.* No provision.
Are some creditors given special privileges/preference (e.g., medical expenses, funeral expenses)?	*By Affidavit.* No provision. *Summary Administration.* Reasonable and necessary medical and hospital expenses of the last illness of the decedent and reasonable funeral expenses. (§ 45-3-1203)
Creditors' rights, if insufficient assets	*By Affidavit.* Payee is liable to any person with superior rights. (§ 45-3-1202) *Summary Administration.* No provision.
May the distribution of the estate proceed without appointment of personal representative?	*By Affidavit.* Yes. Affiant can only use procedure if no personal representative has been appointed. (§ 45-3-1201(A)(3)) *Summary Administration.* No. (§ 45-3-1203)
Must court approve affidavit?	*By Affidavit.* No provision. *Summary Administration.* No provision.

Waiting period before authority to act	*By Affidavit.* 30 days after date of death. (§ 45-3-1201(A)(2)) *Summary Administration.* No provision.
With whom do you file petition or affidavit?	*By Affidavit.* No provision. *Summary Administration.* Verified closing statement is filed with the court. (§ 45-3-1204(A))
Is there an informal procedure for appointment of executor or administrator?	Yes. (§§ 45-3-301, 45-3-307 to -311)
Can a nonresident serve?	Yes. (§§ 54-2-201 to -207)
Can the nonresident act locally based on appointment in another state?	If there is no local administration and the domiciliary foreign personal representative files authenticated copies of appointment and official bond with the court, such person may exercise as to assets in New Mexico all of the powers of a local representative subject to conditions imposed upon nonresidents generally. (§§ 45-4-205, 45-4-204)
What does a transferor need so as to be relieved of liability if challenged by another person later on who claims the particular property (e.g., copy of affidavit)?	*By Affidavit.* Payor is discharged and released to the same extent as if he or she dealt with a personal representative of the decedent when he or she pays after being presented the affidavit. (§ 45-3-1202) *Summary Administration.* No provision.

6. Although these statutes do not expressly limit themselves to testate estates, the statutes are located in Article 3 of Chapter 45, which is entitled "Probate of Wills and Administration." No such procedures are discussed in Part 1 of Article 2, which deals with intestate succession.
7. The affidavit may not be used to perfect title to real estate. (§ 45-3-1201(C))

New York
Settlement of Small Estates

Who can initiate process?	A voluntary administrator as defined in Surr. Ct. Proc. Act § 1301 (2). See also Surr. Ct. Proc. Act § 1303.
Can it be used if claims outstanding?	Yes.[8]
Different rules if die testate or intestate?	If the deceased dies intestate, the right to act as a voluntary administrator follows a line of succession based on the closeness of relation to the decedent, starting with a surviving adult spouse. (Surr. Ct. Proc. Act § 1303(a)) If the decedent dies testate, the named executor or alternate executor has the first right to act as voluntary administrator, and if this person renounces or fails to qualify, any adult person who would be entitled to petition for letters of administration may act as voluntary administrator. (Surr. Ct. Proc. Act § 1303(b))
Notice?	The clerk of the Surrogate's Court must mail to each distributee other than those who have renounced the right to act, and to beneficiaries listed in the affidavit, notice of the proceeding by postcard or letter. (Surr. Ct. Proc. Act § 1304(4))
heirs	No provision.
creditors	No provision.
others	No provision.
Which of the following must be observed?	
hearing	No provision.
affidavit, petition, other	Affidavit and certified copy of death certificate. (Surr. Ct. Proc. Act § 1304(3))
bond	No. (Surr. Ct. Proc. Act § 1304(2))
What are basic contents of petition or affidavit?	Affidavit is to be in the form of Official Form No. 5, which is appended to Article 13 of the Surrogate Court Procedure Act, and is filed with a certified copy of the death certificate. (Surr. Ct. Proc. Act § 1304(3))
Is procedure available in the case of nonresident decedents?	Yes. (Surr. Ct. Proc. Act § 1301(1))
Maximum allowable value of estate	Personal property with a gross value of $20,000. (Surr. Ct. Proc. Act § 1301(1))
What property can be transferred by this means?	Personal property only. (Surr. Ct. Proc. Act § 1302)
Special rules for certain assets (e.g., automobile)	No provision.
Can the spouse or other person take summarily if under certain amount?	No provision.
Minimum period before filing allowed	None. (Surr. Ct. Proc. Act § 1304(1))
Rights/obligations of party with affidavit	Rights: (1) may maintain an action to recover property if payor refuses to pay after presentation of a certificate and receipt

	(Surr. Ct. Proc. Act § 1306(1)); (2) may sell any personal property coming into his or her possession for reasonable value (Surr. Ct. Proc. Act § 1306(2)); (3) rights, powers, and duties with respect to personal property of an administrator duly appointed for the estate (Surr. Ct. Proc. Act § 1306(3)). Obligations: (1) deposit all money received in an estate bank account and pay expenses of the decedent before distributing balance to persons entitled (Surr. Ct. Proc. Act § 1307(1)); (2) account to the court for all personal property of the decedent received and disbursed (Surr. Ct. Proc. Act § 1307(2)).
Are some creditors given special privileges/preference (e.g., medical expenses, funeral expenses)?	Funeral expenses. (Surr. Ct. Proc. Act § 1307(1))
Creditors' rights, if insufficient assets	If an issue arises about sufficiency of the assets to satisfy all of the decedent's debts and administration expenses, claimants' priorities are determined under Surr. Ct. Proc. Act § 1811. (Surr. Ct. Proc. Act § 1307, Practice Commentaries)
May the distribution of the estate proceed without appointment of personal representative?	Yes. (Surr. Ct. Proc. Act §§ 1301(2), 1303, 1304)
Must court approve affidavit?	No provision.
Waiting period before authority to act	None. (Surr. Ct. Proc. Act § 1304(1))
With whom do you file petition or affidavit?	Clerk of the decedent's domicile or, if decedent is a nondomiciliary, of the county in which his personal property is located. (Surr. Ct. Proc. Act § 1304(3))
Is there an informal procedure for appointment of executor or administrator?	Yes, voluntary administrator. (Surr. Ct. Proc. Act §§ 1301(2), 1304(3))
Can a nonresident serve?	Yes. If a nominated executor requests preliminary letters and qualifies under Surr. Ct. Proc. Act § 708, the court must appoint him. (Surr. Ct. Proc. Act § 1412, Practice Commentaries) There is no residency requirement in Surr. Ct. Proc. Act § 708. With intestate decedents, Surr. Ct. Proc. Act § 1001 does not expressly disqualify nonresidents, but an example in the Practice Commentaries to Surr. Ct. Proc. Act § 1001 suggests nondomiciliary alien distributees are not eligible.
Can the nonresident act locally based on appointment in another state?	Yes, provided non-domiciliary debtors, transfer agents, safe deposit companies, banks, trust companies or persons holding personal property in the domiciliary state recognize and pay or transfer the personal property of a New York domiciliary, pursuant to a short certificate of court as made under the Surr. Ct. Proc. Act. (Surr. Ct. Proc. Act § 1309(2))
What does a transferor need so as to be relieved of liability if challenged by another person later on who claims the particular property (e.g., copy of affidavit)?	A receipt for money or property given to the voluntary administrator after presentation of the short form certificate of letters of voluntary administration. (Surr. Ct. Proc. Act § 1305, Practice Commentaries) See also Surr. Ct. Proc. Act § 1309(3), which relieves payor of liability even without such a receipt.

8. The voluntary administrator can settle claims against the estate up to $20,000. (Surr. Ct. Proc. Act § 1306)

North Carolina
Small Estates

Who can initiate process?	If decedent died intestate, the public administrator appointed pursuant to § 28A-12-1, or an heir or creditor of the decedent, not disqualified under § 28A-4-2. (§ 28A-25-1(a)) If decedent died testate, proceedings can be initiated by a public administrator, person named or designated as executor in the will, a devisee, an heir, or a creditor of the decedent if decedent died testate. (§ 28A-25-1.1(a)) Whether decedent died testate or intestate, there is a special provision if the affiant is a surviving spouse and the sole heir of the decedent. (§ 28A-25-1.1(a))
Can it be used if claims outstanding?	Yes. (§ 28A-25-3(a)(1)(b))
Different rules if die testate or intestate?	Yes. The differences relate only to who may initiate the process (see *Who can initiate process?*) and particular details required to be in the affidavit (see *What are basic contents of petition or affidavit?*).
Notice?	Prior to recovery of any assets of the decedent, the clerk of the superior court of the county where decedent had his domicile at the time of his death mails a copy of the affidavit to persons shown in the affidavit as entitled to the property. (§§ 28A-25-1(b), 28A-25-1.1(b))
heirs	No provision.
creditors	No provision.
others	No provision.
Which of the following must be observed?	
hearing	No provision.
affidavit, petition, other	Affidavit. (§§ 28A-25-1(a), 28A-25-1.1(a))
bond	No provision.
What are basic contents of petition or affidavit?	If decedent dies intestate: (1) name and address of the affiant and that he or she is a public administrator or an heir or creditor of the decedent; (2) the name of the decedent and his residence at time of death; (3) the date and place of death of the decedent; (4) that 30 days have elapsed since the death of the decedent; (5) that the value of all the personal property owned by the estate of the decedent, less liens and encumbrances thereon, does not exceed $10,000; (6) that no application or petition for appointment of a personal representative is pending or has been granted in any jurisdiction; (7) names and addresses of those persons who are entitled, under the provisions of the Intestate Succession Act, to the personal property of the decedent and their relationship, if any, to the decedent; and (8) a description sufficient to identify each tract of real property owned by the decedent at the time of his death. (§ 28A-25-1(a)) If decedent dies testate: (1) the name and address of the affiant and the fact that he or she is the public administrator, or a person named or designated as executor in the will, or devisee or an heir or creditor of the decedent; (2) the name of the decedent and his

	residence at time of death; (3) the date and place of death of the decedent; (4) that 30 days have elapsed since the death of the decedent; (5) that the decedent died testate leaving personal property, less liens and encumbrances thereon, not exceeding $10,000 in value; (6) that the decedent's will has been admitted to probate in the court of proper county and a duly certified copy of the will has been recorded in each county in which is located any real property owned by the decedent at the time of his death; (7) that a certified copy of the decedent's will is attached to the affidavit; (8) that no application or petition for appointment of a personal representative is pending or has been granted in any jurisdiction; (9) the names and addresses of those persons who are entitled, under the provisions of the Intestate Succession Act, to the personal property of the decedent and their relationship, if any, to the decedent; and (10) a description sufficient to identify each tract of real property owned by the decedent at the time of his death. (§ 28A-25-1.1(a)) If the affiant is a surviving spouse and sole heir of the decedent: (1) name and address of the affiant and the fact that he or she is the surviving spouse and is entitled, under the provisions of the Intestate Succession Act or under the provisons of the decedent's will, to all of the property of the decedent; (2) that the value of all of the personal property owned by the estate of the decedent, less liens and encumbrances thereon, does not exceed $20,000; and (3) the information required in subdivisions (2), (3), (4), (6), and (8) of N.C. Gen. Stat. § 28A-25-1(a), if the decedent died intestate, or the information required in subdivisions (2), (3), (4), (6), (7), (8), and (10) of N.C. Gen. Stat. Ann. § 28A-25-1.1(a), if the decedent died testate. (§§ 28A-25-1(a), 28A-25-1.1(a))
Is procedure available in the case of nonresident decedents?	No. (§§ 28A-25-1(b), 28A-25-1.1(b))
Maximum allowable value of estate	Personal property, less liens and encumbrances, valued at $10,000. (§§ 28A-25-1(a), 28A-25-1.1(a)) The maximum is $20,000 if the affiant is the surviving spouse and sole heir of the decedent. (§§ 28A-25-1(a), 28A-25-1.1(a))
What property can be transferred by this means?	Payment of indebtedness, tangible personal property or an instrument evidencing a debt, obligation, stock or chose in action. (§§ 28A-25-1(a), 28A-25-1.1(a))
Special rules for certain assets (e.g., automobile)	Motor vehicles, checking and savings accounts, and stocks or securities. (§§ 28A-25-1(c), 28A-25-1.1(c))
Can the spouse or other person take summarily if under certain amount?	No provision.
Minimum period before filing allowed	30 days from date of death. (§§ 28A-25-1(a)(4), 28A-25-1.1(a)(4))
Rights/obligations of party with affidavit	Affiant is entitled, upon presentation of the affidavit, to any property or contract right owned by decedent at the time of his death. (§§ 28A-25-1(c), 28A-25-1.1(c)) The affiant may bring an action to compel payment if a person to whom an affidavit is delivered refuses to pay. (§ 28A-25-2) The affiant must disburse and distribute collected personal property in the proper order (§ 28A-25-3(a)(1)), and file an affidavit with the clerk of superior

	court that he has collected the personal property of the decedent and describe the manner in which he has disbursed and distributed the personal property. (§ 28A-25-3(a)(2)) It it appears to be in the best interst of the estate to sell, lease, mortgage any real property, the affiant must petition the clerk of superior court for the appointment of a personal representative to conclude the administration of the decedent's estate pursuant to § 28A-25-5. (§ 28A-25-3(b))
Are some creditors given special privileges/preference (e.g., medical expenses, funeral expenses)?	Creditors must be paid in the order prescribed in § 28A-19-6. (§ 28A-25-3(a)(1)(b))
Creditors' rights, if insufficient assets	Payee is answerable to any person having an interest in the estate. (§ 28A-25-2)
May the distribution of the estate proceed without appointment of personal representative?	Yes. (§§ 28A-25-1(a), 28A-25-1.1(a))
Must court approve affidavit?	No provision.
Waiting period before authority to act	30 days after date of death. (§§ 28A-25-1(a)(4), 28A-25-1.1(a)(4))
With whom do you file petition or affidavit?	The office of the clerk of superior court of the county where the decedent had his domicile at the time of his death. (§§ 28A-25-1(b), 28A-25-1.1(b))
Is there an informal procedure for appointment of executor or administrator?	Yes.[9]
Can a nonresident serve?	Yes.[10]
Can the nonresident act locally based on appointment in another state?	No provision.
What does a transferor need so as to be relieved of liability if challenged by another person later on who claims the particular property (e.g., copy of affidavit)?	Payor is discharged and released to the same extent as if he dealt with a duly qualified personal representative of the decedent if presented with a proper affidavit. Payor need not inquire into the truth of the affidavit. (§ 28A-25-2)

9. Any interested person, including the affiant, can petition the clerk of superior court for the appointment of a personal representative or collector to conclude administration of the estate. (§ 28A-25-5)
10. The nonresident must appoint a resident agent to accept service of process in all actions or proceedings with respect to the estate and file such appointment with the court. (§ 28A-42(4))

North Dakota
Summary Administration Procedure for Small Estates

Who can initiate process?	*By Affidavit.* Any person claiming to be the successor of the decedent. (§ 30.1-23-01) *Summary Administration.* Personal representative. (§§ 30.1-23-03, 30.1-23-04)
Can it be used if claims outstanding?	*By Affidavit.* Yes. (§ 30.1-23-01(1)) *Summary Administration.* Yes. (§ 30.1-23-03)
Different rules if die testate or intestate?	*By Affidavit.* Although these statutes do not expressly limit themselves to testate estates, the statutes are located in Article 3, which is entitled ''Probate of Wills and Administration.'' No such procedures are discussed in Article 2, which deals with intestate succession. *Summary Administration.* Although these statutes do not expressly limit themselves to testate estates, the statutes are located in Article 3, which is entitled ''Probate of Wills and Administration.'' No such procedures are discussed in Article 2, which deals with intestate succession.
Notice?	*By Affidavit:* No provision.
heirs	*Summary Administration.* Must send copy of closing statement to all distributees of the estate. (§ 30.1-23-04(1)(c))
creditors	*Summary Administration.* Must send copy of closing statement to all creditors of whom the personal representative is aware whose claims are neither barred nor paid. (§ 30.1-23-04(1)(c))
others	*Summary Administration.* Must send copy of closing statement to all ''other claimants''. (§ 30.1-23-04(1)(c))
Which of the following must be observed?	
hearing	No provision.
affidavit, petition, other	*By Affidavit.* Affidavit. (§ 30.1-23-01(1)) *Summary Administration.* Closing statement. (§ 30.1-23-04(1))
bond	No provision.
What are basic contents of petition or affidavit?	*By Affidavit.* (1) That the value of the entire estate, wherever located, less liens and encumbrances, does not exceed $50,000; (2) that 30 days have elapsed since death of decedent; (3) that no application or petition for the appointment of a personal representative is pending or has been granted in any jurisdiction; and (4) that the claiming successor is entitled to payment or delivery of the property. (§ 30.1-23-01(1)) *Summary Administration.* Closing statement must state that (1) to the best knowledge of personal representative, the value of the entire estate, less liens and encumbrances, did not exceed the homestead plus exempt property, family allowance, costs and expenses of administration, reasonable funeral expenses, and reasonable and necessary medical and hospital expenses of the last illness of the decedent; (2) personal representative has fully administered the estate by disbursing and distributing it to the

	persons entitled thereto; and (3) personal representative has sent a copy of the closing statement to all distributees and to all creditors of whom the personal representative is aware whose claims are neither barred nor paid and has furnished a full account in writing of the administration to distributees whose interests are affected. (§ 30.1-23-04(1))
Is procedure available in the case of nonresident decedents?	*By Affidavit.* Yes. (§ 30.1-23-02, Editorial Board Comment) *Summary Administration.* No provision.
Maximum allowable value of estate	*By Affidavit.* $50,000. (§ 30.1-23-01(1)(a)) *Summary Administration.* The value of entire estate, less liens and encumbrances, must not exceed the homestead plus exempt property, family allowance, costs and expenses of administration, reasonable funeral expenses, and reasonable and necessary medical and hospital expenses of the last illness of the decedent. (§ 30.1-23-03)
What property can be transferred by this means?	*By Affidavit.* Payment of indebtedness, tangible personal property, or an instrument evidencing a debt, obligation, stock, or chose in action. (§ 30.1-23-01(1)) *Summary Administration.* Entire estate. (§ 30.1-23-04(1))
Special rules for certain assets (e.g., automobile)	*Affidavit.* Transfer agent of any security shall change the registered ownership on the books of a corporation upon presentation of an affidavit. (§ 30.1-23-01(2)) *Summary Administration.* No provision.
Can the spouse or other person take summarily if under certain amount?	No provision.
Minimum period before filing allowed	*By Affidavit.* No filing required under affidavit procedure. See *Waiting period before authority to act.* *Summary Administration.* Entire estate must have been inventoried and appraised. (§ 30.1-23-03)
Rights/obligations of party with affidavit	*By Affidavit.* Affiant is entitled to payment from person possessing property belonging to the decedent. (§ 30.1-23-01) The affiant can bring an action if a party refuses to pay upon presentation of the affidavit. Affiant is accountable to any person having a superior right. (§ 30.1-23-02) *Summary Administration.* No provision.
Are some creditors given special privileges/preference (e.g., medical expenses, funeral expenses)?	*By Affidavit.* No provision. *Summary Administration.* Reasonable funeral expenses and reasonable and necessary medical and hospital expenses of the last illness of the decedent. (§ 30.1-23-03)
Creditors' rights, if insufficient assets	*By Affidavit.* Payees are answerable to any person having a superior right. (§ 30.1-23-02) *Summary Administration.* No provision.
May the distribution of the estate proceed without appointment of personal representative?	*By Affidavit.* Yes. (§ 30.1-23-01(1)(c)) *Summary Administration.* No. (§ 30.1-23-03)
Must court approve affidavit?	*By Affidavit.* No provision. *Summary Administration.* No provision.

Waiting period before authority to act	*By Affidavit.* 30 days after date of death. (§ 30.1-23-01(1)(b)) *Summary Administration.* No provision.
With whom do you file petition or affidavit?	*By Affidavit.* No provision. *Summary Administration.* Verified closing statement is filed with the district court. (§ 30.1-23-04(1))
Is there an informal procedure for appointment of executor or administrator?	Yes. (§§ 30.1-14-01, 30.1-14-07 to -11)
Can a nonresident serve?	Yes. (§ 30.1-24-01 to -08)
Can the nonresident act locally based on appointment in another state?	Yes. If there is no local administration and the domiciliary foreign personal representative has filed in a local court, such person may exercise to assets in North Dakota all powers of a local personal representative, subject to conditions imposed upon nonresidents generally. (§§ 30.1-24-06, 30.1-24-05)
What does a transferor need so as to be relieved of liability if challenged by another person later on who claims the particular property (e.g., copy of affidavit)?	*By Affidavit.* Payor is discharged under § 30.1-23-02. *Summary Administration.* No provision.

Ohio
Release from Administration

Who can initiate process?	Any interested party. (§ 2113.03(B))
Can it be used if claims outstanding?	Yes. (§ 2113.03(C))
Different rules if die testate or intestate?	No provision.
Notice?	
heirs	Surviving spouse and heirs at law must be given notice in advance of filing application for release from administration. The length of time prior is set by the probate court. (§ 2113.03(B))
creditors	No provision.
others	All interested parties must be given notice by publication in a newspaper of general circulation in the county, unless notices are waived or found unnecessary (§ 2113.03(B))
Which of the following must be observed?	
hearing	No provision.
affidavit, petition, other	Application. (§ 2113.03(B))
bond	No provision.
What are basic contents of petition or affidavit?	Application must satisfy court that § 2113.03(A) requirement is met. (§ 2113.03(B)) See *Maximum allowable value of estate.*
Is procedure available in the case of nonresident decedents?	No provision.
Maximum allowable value of estate	(1) $35,000; or (2) $100,000 if: (a) decedent devised and bequeathed all assets to a person named in the will as a spouse and is survived by that person; or (b) decedent is survived by a spouse who married decedent in accordance with Chapter 3101 of the Ohio Code or a similar foreign law, decedent died without a valid will, and the spouse gets all assets under § 2105.06 or under a combination of §§ 2105.06 and 2106.13. (§ 2113.03(A))
What property can be transferred by this means?	Real and personal. (§ 2113.03(B))
Special rules for certain assets (e.g., automobile)	No provision.
Can the spouse or other person take summarily if under certain amount?	Yes. (§ 2113.031(B)(2))
Minimum period before filing allowed	An interested party can only apply after proper notice has been given. (§ 2113.03(B))
Rights/obligations of party with affidavit	No provision.
Are some creditors given special privileges/preference (e.g., medical expenses, funeral expenses)?	No provision.

Creditors' rights, if insufficient assets	No provision.
May the distribution of the estate proceed without appointment of personal representative?	Yes. (§ 2113.03(B))
Must court approve affidavit?	Court may approve after being satisfied that § 2113.03(A) is satisfied. (§ 2113.03(B))
Waiting period before authority to act	No provision. See *Maximum allowable value of estate.* (§ 2113.03(B))
With whom do you file petition or affidavit?	The court. (§ 2113.03(B))
Is there an informal procedure for appointment of executor or administrator?	If there is a delay in granting letters testamentary or of administration, the probate court may appoint a special administrator who functions until an executor or administrator is appointed. (§ 2113.15)
Can a nonresident serve?	A nonresident cannot administer an intestate estate. (§ 2113.06) If the decedent died testate, the probate court shall issue letters testamentary to the executor named in the will, nominated by holders of a power as described in § 2107.65, or to the executor named in the will and to a coexecutor nominated by holders of such a power. (§ 2113.05)
Can the nonresident act locally based on appointment in another state?	No provision.
What does a transferor need so as to be relieved of liability if challenged by another person later on who claims the particular property (e.g., copy of affidavit)?	No provision.

Oklahoma
Dispensing with Regular Proceedings; Petition for Summary Administration

Who can initiate process?	*Dispensing with Regular Proceedings.* Personal representative. (58 § 241(A)) *Petition for Summary Administration.* Any interested person. (58 § 245(A))
Can it be used if claims outstanding?	*Dispensing with Regular Proceedings.* Yes. (58 § 241(C)) *Petition for Summary Administration.* Yes. (58 § 245(B)(7))
Different rules if die testate or intestate?	*Dispensing with Regular Proceedings.* No provision.[16] *Petition for Summary Administration.* Yes. See *What are basic contents of petition or affidavit?*
Notice?	*Dispensing with Regular Proceedings.* Notice to creditors and all persons interested in the estate. (58 § 241(C)) *Petition for Summary Administration.* Notice of the petition, notice to creditors, and final notice of accounting, determination of heirship, distribution and discharge must be published once a week for two consecutive weeks in an authorized newspaper in the county where the petition is filed. (58 § 246(B)) If no newspaper, then it must be posted in three public places in the county, including the courthouse. *Id.*
heirs	*Dispensing with Regular Proceedings.* Notice must be mailed to all interested persons at their respective last-known addresses not less than ten days prior to date of hearing. (58 § 241(C)) *Petition for Summary Administration.* No provision.
creditors	*Dispensing with Regular Proceedings.* Notice of hearing must be published once each week for two consecutive weeks in a generally circulated newspaper published in filing county, or if there is no such newspaper, notice shall be published in an adjoining county having a legal newspaper. (58 § 241(C)) *Petition for Summary Administration.* "Combined notice" must be mailed to all creditors of the decedent. (58 § 246(B), (C))
others	*Dispensing with Regular Proceedings.* No provision. *Petition for Summary Administration.* "Combined notice" must be sent to all interested persons at their last known addresses at least 30 days before the hearing. (58 § 246(B), (C))
Which of the following must be observed?	
hearing	*Dispensing with Regular Proceedings.* Yes. (58 § 241(D)) *Petition for Summary Administration.* Yes. (58 §§ 246(D), 247)
affidavit, petition, other	*Dispensing with Regular Proceedings.* Petition for probate (58 § 241(A)) and application for summary administration (58 § 241(B)). *Petition for Summary Administration.* Petition (58 § 245)
bond	*Dispensing with Regular Proceedings.* Implied. (58 § 241(D)) *Petition for Summary Administration.* Discretion of the court. (58 § 235(D)(3))

What are basic contents of petition or affidavit?	*Dispensing with Regular Proceedings.* No provision. *Petition for Summary Administration.* Petition must state (1) interest of petitioner; (2) name, age, date of death of decedent, county of decedent's domicile at time of death; (3) names, ages, and last-known addresses of the administrators, executors, nonpetitioning conominees, heirs, legatees and devisees of the decedent; (4) names and last-known addresses of all known creditors of the decedent; (5) probable value and character of the property of the estate and the legal description of all real property owned by the decedent in Oklahoma; (6) whether an application or petition for the appointment of a personal representative is pending or has been granted in any jurisdiction; (7) a statement of the relief requested; and (8) that the petitioners diligently searched for and failed to find a will. (58 § 245(B)) In addition, if decedent died testate, (1) a copy of the will must be attached and petition must state (a) the petitioner, to the best of their knowledge, believes the will to have been validly executed and (b) the petitioner is unaware of any instrument revoking the will, and believes that the instrument attached to the application is the decedent's last will; and (2) the petition must state whether the attached will has been admitted to probate in any other jurisdiction. *Id.*
Is procedure available in the case of nonresident decedents?	*Dispensing with Regular Proceedings.* No provision. *Petition for Summary Administration.* No provision.
Maximum allowable value of estate	*Dispensing with Regular Proceedings.* $150,000 of real and personal property. (58 § 241(A)) *Petition for Summary Administration.* $175,000. (58 § 245(A)(1)) But if decedent died more than 5 years prior, or resided in a different jurisdiction at the time of death, there appears to be no limit. (58 § 245(A))
What property can be transferred by this means?	*Dispensing with Regular Proceedings.* Real and personal. (58 § 241(B)) *Petition for Summary Administration.* Entire estate. (58 § 247)
Special rules for certain assets (e.g., automobile)	*Dispensing with Regular Proceedings.* No provision. *Petition for Summary Administration.* No provision.
Can the spouse or other person take summarily if under certain amount?	*Dispensing with Regular Proceedings.* No provision. *Petition for Summary Administration.* No provision.
Minimum period before filing allowed	*Dispensing with Regular Proceedings.* Court must be satisfied with estate valuation before personal representative may apply for summary administration. (58 § 241(B)) *Petition for Summary Administration.* No provision for an estate valued under $175,000. See *Maximum allowable value of estate.*
Rights/obligations of party with affidavit	*Dispensing with Regular Proceedings.* No provision. *Petition for Summary Administration.* No provision.

Are some creditors given special privileges/preference (e.g., medical expenses, funeral expenses)?	*Dispensing with Regular Proceedings.* Funeral expenses, last illness medical expenses, administration expenses, and allowed claims. (58 § 241(D)) *Petition for Summary Administration.* Funeral expenses, last illness medical expenses, and administration expenses. (58 § 247(A))
Creditors' rights, if insufficient assets	*Dispensing with Regular Proceedings.* Liens upon property for estate or transfer taxes are fully protected (58 § 241(B)); otherwise, no provision. *Petition for Summary Administration.* Creditors can object at the hearing if they file in time. (58 § 247(A))
May the distribution of the estate proceed without appointment of personal representative?	*Dispensing with Regular Proceedings.* No. (58 § 241(A) & (B)) *Petition for Summary Administration.* Yes. (58 § 245(A))
Must court approve affidavit?	*Dispensing with Regular Proceedings.* No provision. *Petition for Summary Administration.* Court must approve petition. (58 § 247(A))
Waiting period before authority to act	*Dispensing with Regular Proceedings.* No waiting period stated following the hearing. Hearing must be at least 35 days after first publication of notice. (58 § 241(D)) *Petition for Summary Administration.* See *Minimum period before filing allowed.*
With whom do you file petition or affidavit?	*Dispensing with Regular Proceedings.* Petition and application are filed with court. (58 § 241(A) & (B)) *Petition for Summary Administration.* No provision.
Is there an informal procedure for appointment of executor or administrator?	*Dispensing with Regular Proceedings.* No provision. *Petition for Summary Administration.* No provision.
Can a nonresident serve?	*Dispensing with Regular Proceedings.* Yes, but nonresident must appoint an agent to accept service of legal process that resides in the county where the nonresident is appointed personal representative. (58 § 162) *Petition for Summary Administration.* Yes. (58 § 262)
Can the nonresident act locally based on appointment in another state?	*Dispensing with Regular Proceedings.* No provision. *Petition for Summary Administration.* Yes. (58 § 262)
What does a transferor need so as to be relieved of liability if challenged by another person later on who claims the particular property (e.g., copy of affidavit)?	*Dispensing with Regular Proceedings.* No provision. *Petition for Summary Administration.* No provision.

16. Although these statutes do not expressly limit themselves to testate estates, the statutes are located in Title 58, which is entitled "Probate Administration."

Oregon
Small Estates

can initiate process?	One or more of the claiming successors, as defined in Or. Rev. Stat. § 114.505, or, if decedent died testate, any person named as personal representative in the will. (§ 114.515(1)) A creditor may file an affidavit if a decedent dies intestate and without heirs. (§ 114.520(1))
Can it be used if claims outstanding?	Yes, but affiant must pay claims. (§ 114.545(1)(c))
Different rules if die testate or intestate?	Who can initiate the process is differerent depending on whether the decedent died testate or intestate. See *Who can initiate process?* "Claiming Successors" has different definitions if the decedent dies testate or intestate.
Notice?	The affiant must, within 30 days after filing, mail, deliver or cause to be recorded each instrument which the affidavit states will be mailed, delivered or recorded. (§ 114.545(1)(b))
heirs	See *Notice?*
creditors	See *Notice?*
others	See *Notice?*
Which of the following must be observed?	
hearing	No provision.
affidavit, petition, other	Affidavit. (§ 114.515)
bond	No provision.
What are basic contents of petition or affidavit?	(1) Name, age, domicile, address, and social security number of the decedent; (2) date and place of decedent's death, attaching a copy of the death certificate; (3) fair market value of all property of the estate, with a legal description of real property; (4) statement that no application or petition for the appointment of a personal representative has been granted in Oregon; (5) whether decedent died testate or intestate, and if testate, attached copy of the will (6) list of heirs and their interest in property described in the affidavit and that a copy of the affidavit will be delivered or mailed to each heir; (7) list of devisees if decedent died testate, and their interest in property described in the affidavit and state that a copy of the affidavit has been delivered or mailed to each devisee; (8) the interest in the property described in the affidavit to which each heir or devisee is entitled and the interest, if any, that will escheat; (9) statement that reasonable efforts have been made to ascertain creditors and estimated amounts of the claims; (10) list of persons known to assert a claim against the estate and estimated amount of the claims; (11) statement that a copy of the affidavit will be mailed or delivered to the Department of Human Services; (12) statement that claims not listed or disputed will be barred unless presented to affiant in four months or if a personal representative is appointed; and (13) if affiant lists one or more claims that affiant disputes, statement that such claim(s) are barred unless (a) petition for summary determination is filed within 4 months, or (b) a personal representative is appointed within the time allowed under ORS § 114.555. (§ 114.525)

Is procedure available in the case of nonresident decedents?	No provision.
Maximum allowable value of estate	Maximum fair market value of total estate of $200,000; maximum personal property fair market value of $50,000; and maximum real property fair market value of $150,000. (§ 114.515(2))
What property can be transferred by this means?	Personal and real property. (§ 114.545(1)(f))
Special rules for certain assets (e.g., automobile)	No provision.
Can the spouse or other person take summarily if under certain amount?	If, after four months from the first publication of notice to interested parties, it appears that reasonable provision for support of the spouse and/or dependent children of decedent warrants that the whole estate, after payment of claims, taxes, and expenses of administration, be set apart for such support, the court may so order. (§ 114.085)
Minimum period before filing allowed	30 days after date of death. (§ 114.515(3))
Rights/obligations of party with affidavit	Rights: (1) entitled to delivery of personal property of the decedent upon presenting a certified copy of the affidavit (§ 114.535(1)); (2) may bring an action to recover if a person to whom an affidavit is delivered refuses to pay (§ 114.535(3)). Duties: (1) take control of property of the estate (§ 114.545(1)(a)); (2) mail, deliver or cause to be recorded each instrument which the affidavit states will be mailed, delivered or recorded. (§ 114.545(1)(b)); (3) pay claims and expenses (§ 114.545(1)(c)); (4)record deeds executed by the affiant or claiming successor (§ 114.545(3)).
Are some creditors given special privileges/preference (e.g., medical expenses, funeral expenses)?	No provision.
Creditors' rights, if insufficient assets	Affiants are answerable to creditors whose claims must be paid. (§ 114.545(2))
May the distribution of the estate proceed without appointment of personal representative?	Yes. (§ 114.525(4))
Must court approve affidavit?	No provision.
Waiting period before authority to act	Affiant may not file affidavit until 30 days after the death of the decedent. (§ 114.515(3)) Affiant cannot collect personal property until 10 days after filing the affidavit. (§ 114.535(1)) Affiant may convey real or personal property with the consent of heir/devisee, any time within four months after affidavit is filed. (§ 114.545(1)(f)) If property has not been converyed by the end of four months after the affidavit has been filed, it is automatically conveyed to those entitled to it. (§ 114.555)
With whom do you file petition or affidavit?	Clerk of the probate court in any county where there is venue for a proceeding seeking the appointment of a personal representative for the estate. (§ 114.515(1))

Is there an informal procedure for appointment of executor or administrator?	No provision.
Can a nonresident serve?	Generally, a nonresident can be a personal representative. (§ 113.095) There is no exclusion in § 113.085, which lists the preferences in appointing the personal representative. Nonresident personal representatives also are not excluded in § 113.095, which lists qualifications for personal representatives.
Can the nonresident act locally based on appointment in another state?	No provision.
What does a transferor need so as to be relieved of liability if challenged by another person later on who claims the particular property (e.g., copy of affidavit)?	Discharged if delivered a certified copy of the affidavit. (§ 114.535(1))

Pennsylvania
Settlement of Small Estates on Petition

Who can initiate process?	Any party in interest. (20 § 3102)
Can it be used if claims outstanding?	No provision.
Different rules if die testate or intestate?	No provision.
Notice?	All notice is at the discretion of the court. (20 § 3102)
heirs	No provision.
creditors	No provision.
others	No provision.
Which of the following must be observed?	
hearing	No provision.
affidavit, petition, other	Petition. (20 § 3102)
bond	No provision.
What are basic contents of petition or affidavit?	No provision.
Is procedure available in the case of nonresident decedents?	Not available for nondomiciliaries. (20 § 3102)
Maximum allowable value of estate	$25,000, excluding real property and payments to family and funeral directors, but including personal property claimed as family exemption. (20 § 3102)
What property can be transferred by this means?	Personal property. (20 § 3102)
Special rules for certain assets (e.g., automobile)	No provision.
Can the spouse or other person take summarily if under certain amount?	No provision.
Minimum period before filing allowed	No provision.
Rights/obligations of party with affidavit	No provision.
Are some creditors given special privileges/preference (e.g., medical expenses, funeral expenses)?	Funeral expenses. (20 § 3102)
Creditors' rights, if insufficient assets	Any party in interest may petition court for improper distribution within one year of decree of distribution. (20 § 3102)
May the distribution of the estate proceed without appointment of personal representative?	Yes. (20 § 3102)
Must court approve affidavit?	After petition, court may direct property distribution at its discretion. (20 § 3102)

Waiting period before authority to act	No provision.
With whom do you file petition or affidavit?	Orphan's court division of county of domicile at death. (20 § 3102)
Is there an informal procedure for appointment of executor or administrator?	No provision.
Can a nonresident serve?	No provision.
Can the nonresident act locally based on appointment in another state?	No provision.
What does a transferor need so as to be relieved of liability if challenged by another person later on who claims the particular property (e.g., copy of affidavit)?	No provision.

Rhode Island
Payments in Small Estates

Who can initiate process?	Decedent's surviving spouse, child, grandchild, parent, sibling, niece, nephew, aunt, uncle or any interested party. (§ 33-24-1) If will exists, then named executor, otherwise an alternate is chosen in descending priority from the same list as in § 33-24-1. (§ 33-24-2)
Can it be used if claims outstanding?	Yes. (§ 33-24-1 & 33-24-2)
Different rules if die testate or intestate?	The small estate procedure is available even if there is a will. (§ 33-24-2) The only difference is who can initiate the process. See *Who can initiate the process?*
Notice?	The statute does not specify, but payors may receive a written demand for payment from a personal representative. (§§ 33-24-1 & 33-24-2))
heirs	No provision.
creditors	No provision.
others	No provision.
Which of the following must be observed?	
hearing	No hearing is required. (§§ 33-24-1 & 33-24-2)
affidavit, petition, other	Affidavit. (§§ 33-24-1 & 33-24-2)
bond	No provision.
What are basic contents of petition or affidavit?	In case of will naming executor, the affidavit must also contain: (a) name and address of affiant; (b) name, address, date of death of decedent, with death certificate attached; (c) relationship of affiant to the deceased; (d) schedule of decedent's assets, with estimated values; (e) statement that affiant has undertaken to act as voluntary administrator; and (f) names and addresses, known to affiant, of those who would take under § 33-1-10 in the case of intestacy. (§ 33-24-1(a)–(f)) In case of will naming executor, the affidavit must also contain: (g) names and addresses known to the affiant of persons who take under the will. (§ 33-24-2)
Is procedure available in the case of nonresident decedents?	No. (§§ 33-24-1 & 33-24-2)
Maximum allowable value of estate	$15,000, exclusive of "tangible personal property." (§§ 33-24-1 & 33-24-2)
What property can be transferred by this means?	Personal property. (§§ 33-24-1 & 33-24-2)
Special rules for certain assets (e.g., automobile)	No provision.
Can the spouse or other person take summarily if under certain amount?	No provision.

Minimum period before filing allowed	30 days from the death of the decedent. (§§ 33-24-1 & 33-24-2)
Rights/obligations of party with affidavit	Voluntary administrator/executor is liable as an executor to all persons aggrieved by his or her administration of the estate. (§§ 33-24-1 & 33-24-2)
Are some creditors given special privileges/preference (e.g., medical expenses, funeral expenses)?	Payment for funeral, last illness, administration, and then other debts in order specified under R.I. Gen. L. § 33-12-11. (§§ 33-24-1 & 33-24-2)
Creditors' rights, if insufficient assets	As per R.I. Gen. L. § 33-12-11. (§§ 33-24-1 & 33-24-2)
May the distribution of the estate proceed without appointment of personal representative?	Yes. (§§ 33-24-1 & 33-24-2)
Must court approve affidavit?	Yes. (§§ 33-24-1 & 33-24-2)
Waiting period before authority to act	30 days after death. (§§ 33-24-1 & 33-24-2)
With whom do you file petition or affidavit?	Court. (§§ 33-24-1 & 33-24-2)
Is there an informal procedure for appointment of executor or administrator?	Voluntary administrator, who can be a surviving spouse, child, grandchild, parent, sibling, niece, nephew, aunt, uncle or interested party. (§ 33-24-1)
Can a nonresident serve?	No (§ 33-24-1); however, if there is a will naming an executor, there is no specific restriction. (§ 33-24-2)
Can the nonresident act locally based on appointment in another state?	No. (§§ 33-24-1 & 33-24-2)
What does a transferor need so as to be relieved of liability if challenged by another person later on who claims the particular property (e.g., copy of affidavit)?	Payment and delivery. (§§ 33-24-1 & 33-24-2)

South Carolina
Collection of Personal Property by Affidavit; Summary Administration Procedure for Small Estates

Who can initiate process?	*By Affidavit.* Person claiming to be successor of decedent. (§ 62-3-1201(a)) *Small Estates.* Personal representative. (§ 62-3-1203(a))
Can it be used if claims outstanding?	*By Affidavit.* Yes. (§ 62-3-1201(a)) *Small Estates.* Yes. (§ 62-3-1203(a))
Different rules if die testate or intestate?	No provision.
Notice?	*By Affidavit.* No provision.
heirs	*Small Estates.* Closing statement must be sent to all distributees of the estate. (§ 62-3-1204(a)(3))
creditors	*Small Estates.* Yes, pursuant to § 62-3-801. (§ 62-3-1203(a)) Closing statement must be sent to all creditors of whom the affiant is aware whose claims are neither paid nor barred. (§ 62-3-1204(a)(3))
others	*Small Estates.* Closing statement must be sent to all "other claimants" of whom the affiant is aware whose claims are neither paid nor barred. (§ 62-3-1204(a)(3))
Which of the following must be observed?	
hearing	No provision.
affidavit, petition, other	*By Affidavit.* Affidavit. (§ 62-3-1201(a)) *Small Estates.* Closing statement. (§ 62-3-1204(a))
bond	No provision.
What are basic contents of petition or affidavit?	*By Affidavit.* Affidavit must state (1) the value of the entire probate estate, less liens and encumbrances, does not exceed $10,000; (2) 30 days have elapsed since death of decedent; (3) no petition has been filed/granted for personal representative; and (4) a statement that the claiming successor is entitled to payment/delivery. (§ 62-3-1201(a)) *Small Estates.* Closing statement must provide (1) that the value of the entire estate, less liens and encumbrances, did not exceed $10,000 and exempt property and administrative, funeral, and medical expenses, or, alternatively, that summary administration was available under § 62-3-1203(b); (2) that the estate is fully administered; and (3) that a copy of the closing statement was sent to distributees, creditors, and other claimants. (§ 62-3-1204(a))
Is procedure available in the case of nonresident decedents?	No provision.
Maximum allowable value of estate	*By Affidavit.* $10,000, less liens and encumbrances. (§ 62-3-1201(a)(1)) *Small Estates.* See *What are basic contents of petition or affidavit?*

What property can be transferred by this means?	*By Affidavit.* Tangible personal property or instrument evidencing debt, obligation, stock, or chose in action belonging to decedent. (§ 62-3-1201(a)) *Small Estates.* Entire estate. (§ 62-3-1203(a))
Special rules for certain assets (e.g., automobile)	*By Affidavit.* A transfer agent of any security shall change registered ownership. (§ 62-3-1201(b)) *Small Estates.* No provision.
Can the spouse or other person take summarily if under certain amount?	Yes. If personal representative(s) is/are the sole devisee(s) or heir(s), the personal representative may immediately disburse after giving notice to creditors and must file a closing statement afterward. (§ 62-3-1203(b))
Minimum period before filing allowed	*By Affidavit.* 30 days after decedent's death. (§ 62-3-1201(a)) *Small Estates.* No provision.
Rights/obligations of party with affidavit	*By Affidavit.* Right to collect personal property. (§ 62-3-1201(a)(2)) Right to hearing on refusal of estate debtor to transfer asset. Transferee/affiant liable to personal representative or any person with superior right. (§ 62-3-1202) *Small Estates.* No provision.
Are some creditors given special privileges/preference (e.g., medical expenses, funeral expenses)?	*By Affidavit.* No provision. *Small Estates.* Funeral and last illness medical expenses. (§ 62-3-1204(a)(1)(i))
Creditors' rights, if insufficient assets	*By Affidavit.* Affiants are answerable to any person with a superior right. (§ 62-3-1202) *Small Estates.* No provision.
May the distribution of the estate proceed without appointment of personal representative?	*By Affidavit.* Yes. (§ 62-3-1201(a)(3)) *Small Estates.* No. (§ 62-3-1203(a))
Must court approve affidavit?	*By Affidavit.* Yes. (§ 62-3-1201(a)(5)) *Small Estates.* Not applicable.
Waiting period before authority to act	*By Affidavit.* 30 days after decedent's death. (§ 62-3-1201(a)) *Small Estates.* No provision.
With whom do you file petition or affidavit?	*By Affidavit.* Probate court. (§ 62-3-1201(a)(6)) *Small Estates.* Closing statement must be filed with court. (§ 62-3-1204(a))
Is there an informal procedure for appointment of executor or administrator?	Yes. (§§ 62-3-301 to -311)
Can a nonresident serve?	Yes. (§§ 62-4-201 to -207)
Can the nonresident act locally based on appointment in another state?	Yes. If there is no local administration, and the domiciliary foreign personal representative has filed in a local court, such person may exercise with respect to assets in South Carolina all powers of a local personal representative, subject to conditions imposed upon nonresidents generally. (§§ 62-4-205, 62-4-204)

What does a transferor need so as to be relieved of liability if challenged by another person later on who claims the particular property (e.g., copy of affidavit)?	*By Affidavit.* Payor is discharged and released to the same extent as if he dealt with a personal representative. (§ 62-3-1202)

South Dakota
Collection of Personal Property by Affidavit; Summary Administration Procedure for Small Estates

Who can initiate process?	Person claiming to be successor of decedent. (§ 29A-3-1201(a))
Can it be used if claims outstanding?	Yes, but affiant must pay secured claims. (§ 29A-3-1202(d))
Different rules if die testate or intestate?	No provision.
Notice?	No provision.
heirs	No provision.
creditors	No provision.
others	No provision.
Which of the following must be observed?	
hearing	No provision.
affidavit, petition, other	Affidavit. (§ 29A-3-1201(a))
bond	No provision.
What are basic contents of petition or affidavit?	Affidavit must state that (1) the value of estate, less liens and encumbrances, does not exceed $50,000; (2) 30 days have elapsed since death of decedent; (3) no application for personal representative has been filed/granted; (4) decedent incurred no debt to Department of Social Services for medical care/nursing home; and (5) the claiming successor is entitled to payment/delivery of property. (§ 29A-3-1201(a)(1)-(5))
Is procedure available in the case of nonresident decedents?	No provision.
Maximum allowable value of estate	$50,000 less liens and encumbrances. (§ 29A-3-1201(a)(1))
What property can be transferred by this means?	Tangible personal property or an instrument evidencing a debt, obligation, stock, or chose in action belonging to decedent. (§ 29A-3-1201(a))
Special rules for certain assets (e.g., automobile)	Transfer agent of any security shall change registered ownership upon presenting the affidavit. (§ 29A-3-1201(b))
Can the spouse or other person take summarily if under certain amount?	No provision.
Minimum period before filing allowed	No filing required. See *Waiting period before authority to act.*
Rights/obligations of affiant	Entitled to collect personal property (§ 29A-3-1201(a)); right to hearing on refusal of estate debtor to transfer asset (§ 29A-3-1202(b)); liable to personal representative or any person with superior right (§ 29A-3-1202(c)); duty to distribute property to creditors and eligible distributees (§ 29A-3-1202(d)); submits to jurisdiction of probate court (§ 29A-3-1202(e)).
Are some creditors given special privileges/preference (e.g., medical expenses, funeral expenses)?	Any affiant receiving payment or delivery of personal property must ensure that property is applied to funeral and administrative expenses, among other things. (§ 29A-3-1202(d))

Creditors' rights, if insufficient assets	Affiant is liable to persons having a superior right. (§ 29A-3-1202(c))
May the distribution of the estate proceed without appointment of personal representative?	Yes. It *must* proceed without a personal representative. (§ 29A-3-1201(a)(3))
Must court approve affidavit?	No provision.
Waiting period before authority to act	30 days after death of decedent. (§ 29A-3-1201(a))
With whom do you file petition or affidavit?	No provision.
Is there an informal procedure for appointment of executor or administrator?	Yes. (§§ 29A-3-301, 29A-3-307 to -311)
Can a nonresident serve?	Yes. (§§ 29A-4-201 to -207)
Can the nonresident act locally based on appointment in another state?	Yes. If there is no local administration, and the domiciliary foreign personal representative has filed in a local court, such person may exercise with respect to assets in South Dakota all powers of a local personal representative, subject to conditions imposed upon nonresidents generally. (§§ 29A-4-205, 29A-4-204)
What does a transferor need so as to be relieved of liability if challenged by another person later on who claims the particular property (e.g., copy of affidavit)?	Transferor is discharged and released as if he had dealt with a personal representative. (§ 29A-3-1202(a))

Tennessee
Small Estates

Who can initiate process?	One or more of decedent's competent, adult legatees/devisees (if testate), or heirs or next of kin (if intestate), or any creditor. (§ 30-4-103(1))
Can it be used if claims outstanding?	Yes. (§ 30-4-104(c))
Different rules if die testate or intestate?	If testate, distribute according to will; if intestate, distribute by intestate succession. (§ 30-4-104(c))
Notice?	
heirs	No provision.
creditors	Affiant may elect to give notice to creditors. (§ 30-4-103(1)(E))
others	No provision.
Which of the following must be observed?	
hearing	No provision.
affidavit, petition, other	Affidavit. (§ 30-4-103)
bond	Bond payable to state, with two or more sureties or one corporate surety, in amount equal to value of decedent's estate. (§ 30-4-103(5))
What are basic contents of petition or affidavit?	Affidavit must (1) state whether decedent left a will; (2) list decedent's unpaid debts, amounts due, creditors; (3) describe decedent's property and known possessors at time of death, and insurance payments to decedent's estate; (4) provide the name, age, address, and relationship of each devisee/legatee/heir entitled to receive property; and (5) whether or not the affiant elects to give notice to creditors. (§ 30-4-103(1))
Is procedure available in the case of nonresident decedents?	No provision.
Maximum allowable value of estate	Value of personal property does not exceed $25,000. (§ 30-4-102(5))
What property can be transferred by this means?	Personal property; life insurance on decedent payable to estate; any stock, bond, note or other evidence of ownership, indebtedness; right belonging to decedent's estate. (§§ 30-4-102(4), 30-4-104(a))
Special rules for certain assets (e.g., automobile)	No provision.
Can the spouse or other person take summarily if under certain amount?	No provision.
Minimum period before filing allowed	45 days from date of decedent's death, subject to court's discretion to shorten period on motion. (§ 30-4-103(1))

Rights/obligations of party with affidavit	Right to collect property. (§ 30-4-104(a)) Obligation to provide no false/misleading statement in affidavit. (§ 30-4-103(1)) Affiant liable to unpaid creditors/other valid claimants or later-appointed personal representative. (§ 30-4-104(c)) Affiant must pay tax on estate property. (§ 30-4-104(d)) Affiant may have hearing for debtor's refusal to honor payment/transfer under affidavit. (§ 30-4-104(e))
Are some creditors given special privileges/preference (e.g., medical expenses, funeral expenses)?	No provision, other than any creditor's right to file and present an affidavit. (§ 30-4-103(1))
Creditors' rights, if insufficient assets	Bond. (§ 30-4-103(5)) Affiant remains liable to unpaid creditors of estate. (§ 30-4-104(c))
May the distribution of the estate proceed without appointment of personal representative?	Yes. (§ 30-4-103(1))
Must court approve affidavit?	Court must file the affidavit, but no provision explicity requires approval. (§ 30-4-103(2))
Waiting period before authority to act	45 days from date of decedent's death. (§ 30-4-103(1))
With whom do you file petition or affidavit?	Court exercising probate jurisdiction in county of decedent's legal residence on date of death. (§§ 30-4-103(1), 30-4-102(2))
Is there an informal procedure for appointment of executor or administrator?	No provision.
Can a nonresident serve?	No provision.
Can the nonresident act locally based on appointment in another state?	No provision.
What does a transferor need so as to be relieved of liability if challenged by another person later on who claims the particular property (e.g., copy of affidavit)?	Payor is discharged and released as if he had dealt with a personal representative. (§ 30-4-104(b))

Texas
Small Estates

Who can initiate process?	Distributees of decedent's estate. (Prob. § 137(a))
Can it be used if claims outstanding?	Yes. (Prob. § 137(a))
Different rules if die testate or intestate?	Available only to distributees of intestates. (Prob. § 137(a))
Notice?	A copy of the affidavit must be furnished to the person(s) owing money to the estate, having custody or possession of property of the estate, or acting as a registrar/fiduciary/transfer agent for an interest beloning to the estate. (Prob. § 137(1)(7))
heirs	No provision.
creditors	No provision.
others	No provision.
Which of the following must be observed?	
hearing	Upon petition for no administration. (Prob. § 140) (See *Can the spouse or other person take summarily if under certain amount?*)
affidavit, petition, other	Affidavit. (Prob. § 137)
bond	No provision.
What are basic contents of petition or affidavit?	Affidavit must state that (1) no petition for personal representative granted/pending; (2) 30 days have elapsed since death of decedent; (3) the value of the estate, excluding homestead and exempt property, does not exceed $50,000; (4) must list all known assets/liabilities of estate; and (5) must list other relevant family history facts. (Prob. § 137(a)(1)-(5))
Is procedure available in the case of nonresident decedents?	No provision.
Maximum allowable value of estate	$50,000, not including homestead allowance and exempt property. (Prob. § 137(a)(3))
What property can be transferred by this means?	Decedent's entire estate. (Prob. § 137(a)) If a homestead is the only real property in decedent's estate, this procedure is also available for the homestead. (Prob. § 137(c))
Special rules for certain assets (e.g., automobile)	Homestead is real property subject to affidavit if it is the only real property of the estate. (Prob. § 137(c))
Can the spouse or other person take summarily if under certain amount?	Yes, upon petition for order that no administration is necessary. (Prob. § 139) In certain cases, the court may order summary distribution. (Prob. § 143)
Minimum period before filing allowed	30 days since death of decedent. (Prob. § 137(a)(2))
Rights/obligations of party with affidavit	Right to collect property. (Prob. § 137(a)) Right to hearing on refusal of estate debtor to transfer asset. Transferee/affiant liable to personal representative or any person with prior right. (Prob. § 138)

Are some creditors given special privileges/preference (e.g., medical expenses, funeral expenses)?	No provision.
Creditors' rights, if insufficient assets	Affiant is answerable to any person having a prior right. (Prob. § 138)
May the distribution of the estate proceed without appointment of personal representative?	Yes. It *must* proceed without a personal representative. (Prob. § 137(a)(1))
Must court approve affidavit?	Yes. (Prob. § 137(a)(4) & (6))
Waiting period before authority to act	30 days since death of decedent. (Prob. § 137(a)(2))
With whom do you file petition or affidavit?	Clerk of court with jurisdiction and venue. (Prob. § 137(a)(4))
Is there an informal procedure for appointment of executor or administrator?	No provision.
Can a nonresident serve?	No provision.
Can the nonresident act locally based on appointment in another state?	No provision.
What does a transferor need so as to be relieved of liability if challenged by another person later on who claims the particular property (e.g., copy of affidavit)?	Transferor of property needs merely to have been presented with valid affidavit to be discharged. (Prob. § 138)

Utah
Collection of Personal Property by Affidavit; Summary Administration Procedure for Small Estates

Who can initiate process?	*By Affidavit.* Person claiming to be successor of decedent. (§ 75-3-1201) *Summary Administration.* Personal representative. (§ 75-3-1203)
Can it be used if claims outstanding?	*By Affidavit.* Yes. (§ 75-3-1201(1)) *Summary Administration.* Yes. (§ 75-3-1203)
Different rules if die testate or intestate?	No provision.
Notice?	
heirs	*By Affidavit.* No provision. *Summary Administration.* Closing statement must be sent to all distributees of the estate. (§ 75-3-1204(1)(d))
creditors	*By Affidavit.* No provision. *Summary Administration.* Closing statement must be sent to all creditors of whom the personal representative is aware and whose claims are neither paid nor barred. (§ 75-3-1204(1)(d))
others	*By Affidavit.* No provision. *Summary Administration.* Closing statement must be sent to all "other claimants" of whom the affiant is aware and whose claims are neither paid nor barred.
Which of the following must be observed?	
hearing	No provision.
affidavit, petition, other	*By Affidavit.* Affidavit. (§ 75-3-1201) *Summary Administration.* Closing statement. (§ 75-3-1203)
bond	No provision.
What are basic contents of petition or affidavit?	*By Affidavit.* Statement including (1) value of entire estate less administration costs, liens and encumbrances, does not exceed $100,000; (2) 30 days elapsed since decedent's death; (3) no application/petition for appointment of personal representative is pending/has been granted; and (4) claiming successor entitled to payment/delivery of property. (§ 75-3-1201(1)) *Summary Administration.* Closing statement must state (1) the nature and value of estate assets; (2) that the value of the estate, less liens and encumbrances, did not exceed the value of exempt property, the homestead and family allowances, and administrative, funeral, and medical expenses; (3) that the estate is fully administered; and (4) that a copy of the closing statement has been sent to all distributees and claimants. (§ 75-3-1204(1))
Is procedure available in the case of nonresident decedents?	*By Affidavit.* Yes. (Comment to § 75-3-1202) *Summary Administration.* No provision.

Maximum allowable value of estate	*By Affidavit.* $100,000, less administration costs, liens, and encumbrances. (§ 75-3-1201) *Summary Administration.* See *What are basic contents of petition or affidavit?*
What property can be transferred by this means?	*By Affidavit.* Tangible personal property or an instrument evidencing a debt, obligation, stock, or chose in action belonging to decedent. (§ 75-3-1201(1)) *Summary Administration.* Entire estate. (§ 75-3-1203)
Special rules for certain assets (e.g., automobile)	*By Affidavit.* Not more than four boats, motor vehicles, trailers, or semi-trailers are exempt from calculation of estate value. (§ 75-3-1201(3)) Also, transferors of securities shall change registered ownership. (§ 75-3-1201(2)) *Summary Administration.* No provision.
Can the spouse or other person take summarily if under certain amount?	No provision.
Minimum period before filing allowed	*By Affidavit.* No filing required. See *Waiting period before authority to act.* *Summary Administration.* Estate must be fully administered before closing statement can be filed. (§ 75-3-1204(1)(c))
Rights/obligations of party with affidavit	*By Affidavit.* Right to collect property. (§ 75-3-1201) Right to hearing on refusal of estate debtor to transfer asset. Transferee/affiant liable to personal representative or any person with superior right. (§ 75-3-1202) *Summary Administration.* No provision.
Are some creditors given special privileges/preference (e.g., medical expenses, funeral expenses)?	*By Affidavit.* No provision. *Summary Administration.* Reasonable funeral expenses, reasonable and necessary medical/hospital expenses of last illness. (§ 75-3-1204(b))
Creditors' rights, if insufficient assets	*By Affidavit.* Affiant is liable to any person having a superior right. (§ 75-3-1202) *Summary Administration.* Right to file action against personal representative is implied. (§ 75-3-1204(2))
May the distribution of the estate proceed without appointment of personal representative?	*By Affidavit.* Yes. (§ 75-3-1201(1)(c)) *Summary Administration.* No. (§ 75-3-1203)
Must court approve affidavit?	No provision.
Waiting period before authority to act	*By Affidavit.* 30 days after decedent's death. (§ 75-3-1201(1)(b)) *Summary Administration.* No provision.
With whom do you file petition or affidavit?	*By Affidavit.* No provision. *Summary Administration.* Closing statement is to be filed with the court. (§ 75-3-1204(1))
Is there an informal procedure for appointment of executor or administrator?	Yes. (§§ 75-3-301 to -311)

Can a nonresident serve?	Yes. (§§ 75-4-201 to -207)
Can the nonresident act locally based on appointment in another state?	Yes. If there is no local administration, and the domiciliary foreign personal representative has filed in a local court, such person may exercise with respect to assets in Utah all powers of a local personal representative, subject to conditions imposed upon nonresidents generally. (§§ 75-4-205, 75-4-204)
What does a transferor need so as to be relieved of liability if challenged by another person later on who claims the particular property (e.g., copy of affidavit)?	*By Affidavit.* Transferor of property needs merely to have been presented with valid affidavit to be fully discharged. (§ 75-3-1202) *Summary Administration.* No provision.

Vermont
Small Estates

Who can initiate process?	Any petitioner or some other suitable person. No specific persons are listed. (14 § 1902)
Can it be used if claims outstanding?	Yes (14 § 1901(2)); funeral expenses are acceptable if appropriate bonds are posted.
Different rules if die testate or intestate?	Yes, but only for discharge. If dies intestate, 14 § 1903(a). If dies testate, 14 § 1903(b).
Notice?	No provision.
heirs	No provision.
creditors	No provision.
others	No provision.
Which of the following must be observed?	
hearing	No provision.
affidavit, petition, other	Petition. (14 § 1901)
bond	Bond of at least $300. (14 § 1901(2))
What are basic contents of petition or affidavit?	Inventory of estate; verification of bond; will (if any). (14 § 1901)
Is procedure available in the case of nonresident decedents?	No provision.
Maximum allowable value of estate	$10,000 (personal property only). (14 § 1902)
What property can be transferred by this means?	Decedent's personal estate. If estate contains real property, small estates procedure cannot be used. (14 § 1902)
Special rules for certain assets (e.g., automobile)	No provision.
Can the spouse or other person take summarily if under certain amount?	No provision.
Minimum period before filing allowed	No provision.
Rights/obligations of party with affidavit	No provision.
Are some creditors given special privileges/preference (e.g., medical expenses, funeral expenses)?	Funeral expenses guaranteed by bond. (14 § 1901(2))
Creditors' rights, if insufficient assets	No provision.
May the distribution of the estate proceed without appointment of personal representative?	Yes. (14 § 1902)
Must court approve affidavit?	Yes. (14 § 1902)

Waiting period before authority to act	Petitioner must wait for court approval before being allowed to administer estate. But no waiting period before filing with court. (14 § 1902)
With whom do you file petition or affidavit?	Probate court. (14 § 1902)
Is there an informal procedure for appointment of executor or administrator?	Court may grant administration to "petitioner or some other suitable person." (14 § 1902)
Can a nonresident serve?	No provision.
Can the nonresident act locally based on appointment in another state?	No provision.
What does a transferor need so as to be relieved of liability if challenged by another person later on who claims the particular property (e.g., copy of affidavit)?	No provision.

Virginia
Payments, Settlements or Administration Without Appointment of Representative

Who can initiate process?	Person claiming to be successor of decedent. (§ 64.1-132.2(A))
Can it be used if claims outstanding?	No provision.
Different rules if die testate or intestate?	No provision.
Notice?	
heirs	No provision.
creditors	No provision.
others	No provision.
Which of the following must be observed?	
hearing	No provision.
affidavit, petition, other	Affidavit. (§ 64.1-132.2(A))
bond	No provision.
What are basic contents of petition or affidavit?	Affidavit must state (1) that the value of the personal estate does not exceed $50,000; (2) 60 days have elapsed since decedent's death; (3) that no application granted/pending for personal representative; (4) will, if any, was duly probated and list of heirs filed; and (5) that claiming successor entitled to payment/delivery property. (§ 64.1-132.2(A))
Is procedure available in the case of nonresident decedents?	No provision.
Maximum allowable value of estate	$50,000. (§ 64.1-132.2(A)(1))
What property can be transferred by this means?	Tangible personal property or instrument evidencing debt, obligation, stock, or chose in action belonging to decedent. (§ 64.1-132.2(A))
Special rules for certain assets (e.g., automobile)	Transferor of security shall change registered ownership from decedent to successor. (§ 64.1-132.2(B))
Can the spouse or other person take summarily if under certain amount?	No provision.
Minimum period before filing allowed	No filing required. See *Waiting period before authority to act.*
Rights/obligations of party with affidavit	Right to collect property. (§ 64.1-132.2(A)) Right to hearing on refusal of estate debtor to transfer asset. Transferee/affiant liable to personal representative or any person with superior right. (§ 64.1-132.3)
Are some creditors given special privileges/preference (e.g., medical expenses, funeral expenses)?	No provision.
Creditors' rights, if insufficient assets	Affiant is liable to persons having a superior right. (§ 64.1-132.3)

May the distribution of the estate proceed without appointment of personal representative?	Yes. (§ 64.1-132.2(A)(3))
Must court approve affidavit?	No provision.
Waiting period before authority to act	60 days after death of decedent. (§ 64.1-132.2(A)(2))
With whom do you file petition or affidavit?	No provision.
Is there an informal procedure for appointment of executor or administrator?	No provision.
Can a nonresident serve?	No provision.
Can the nonresident act locally based on appointment in another state?	No provision.
What does a transferor need so as to be relieved of liability if challenged by another person later on who claims the particular property (e.g., copy of affidavit)?	Transferor of property needs merely to have been presented with valid affidavit for discharge/release. (§ 64.1-132.3)

Washington
Estates Under $60,000—Disposition of Property

Who can initiate process?	Person claiming to be successor of decedent, excluding creditors but including persons entitled to take under will/by intestate succession, surviving spouse to extent entitled to one-half interest in property, department of social and health services to extent funds were extended, the state in case of escheat property. (§§ 11.62.005(2)(a) & (b), 11.62.010(1))
Can it be used if claims outstanding?	No. All debts must have been satisfied or provided for. (§ 11.62.010(2)(f))
Different rules if die testate or intestate?	No provision.
Notice?	
heirs	Claiming successor must provide written notice to all other successors. (§ 11.62.010(2)(h))
creditors	No provision.
others	No provision.
Which of the following must be observed?	
hearing	Provided where estate debtor refuses to transfer property. (§ 11.62.020)
affidavit, petition, other	Affidavit. (§ 11.62.010)
bond	No provision.
What are basic contents of petition or affidavit?	Affidavit must state (1) names and addresses of claiming successor; (2) decedent was a state resident; (3) value of estate, less liens and encumbrances, is under $100,000; (4) 40 days have elapsed since decedent's death; (5) no petition filed/granted for appointment of personal representative; (6) all debts, including funeral expenses, paid or provided for; (7) description of personal property; (7) notice has been given to all successors, and that a minimum of ten days have elapsed since the service or mailing of the notice; and (8) that the successor is entitled to property or to the delivery of the property. (§ 11.62.010(2))
Is procedure available in the case of nonresident decedents?	No. (§ 11.62.010(2)(b))
Maximum allowable value of estate	$100,000, less spouse's community property interest, liens, and encumbrances. (§ 11.62.010(2)(c))
What property can be transferred by this means?	Tangible and intangible personal property beloning to decedent and decedent's surviving spouse as community property, including any instrument of debt, obligation, stock, chose in action, license or ownership. (§§ 11.62.005(1), 11.62.010(1)) Up to $1,000 from decedent's credit union account. (§ 11.62.030)
Special rules for certain assets (e.g., automobile)	Up to $1,000 from decedent's credit union account may be summarily transferred to surviving spouse. (§ 11.62.030)

Can the spouse or other person take summarily if under certain amount?	See *Special rules for certain assets.*
Minimum period before filing allowed	No filing is required. See *Waiting period before authority to act.*
Rights/obligations of party with affidavit	Right to collect property. (§ 11.62.010) Right to hearing on refusal of estate debtor to transfer asset. Transferee/affiant liable to personal representative or any person with superior right. (§ 11.62.020)
Are some creditors given special privileges/preference (e.g., medical expenses, funeral expenses)?	Department of Social and Health Services and state may qualify as "successor." (§ 11.62.005) All debts must be paid or provided for. (§ 11.62.010(2)(f))
Creditors' rights, if insufficient assets	All debts must be paid or provided for. (§ 11.62.010(2)(f))
May the distribution of the estate proceed without appointment of personal representative?	Yes. (§ 11.62.010(2)(e))
Must court approve affidavit?	No provision.
Waiting period before authority to act	40 days from date of decedent's death. (§ 11.62.010(1)) Also, 10 days must have elapsed since notice given to distributees. (§ 11.62.010(2)(h))
With whom do you file petition or affidavit?	Must mail copy along with decedent's social security number to department of social and health services, office of financial recovery. (§ 11.62.010(5))
Is there an informal procedure for appointment of executor or administrator?	No provision.
Can a nonresident serve?	No provision.
Can the nonresident act locally based on appointment in another state?	No provision.
What does a transferor need so as to be relieved of liability if challenged by another person later on who claims the particular property (e.g., copy of affidavit)?	Transferor of property needs merely to have been presented with valid affidavit for discharge/release. Transferor must not have had actual knowledge of the falsity of any statement required to be in the affidavit. (§ 11.62.020)

West Virginia

There are no provisions.

Wisconsin
Transfer by Affidavit; Summary Assignment of Small Estates; Summary Settlement of Small Estates

Who can initiate process?	*Affidavit.* Any heir. (§ 867.03(1g)) *Summary Assignment.* Personal representative or any interested person. If 30 days after decedent's death, nobody has petitioned the court, anyone with an interest in the property of the estate may petition. (§§ 867.02(2) & 856.07) *Summary Settlement.* Personal representative or any interested person. If 30 days after decedent's death, nobody has petitioned the court, anyone with an interest in the property of the estate may petition. (§§ 867.01(3) & 856.07)
Can it be used if claims outstanding?	*Affidavit.* Yes. (§ 867.03(1g)) *Summary Assignment.* Yes. (§ 867.02(1)) *Summary Settlement.* Yes. (§ 867.01(1))
Different rules if die testate or intestate?	No provision.
Notice?	*Affidavit.* Department of health and family services entitled to notice if decedent or spouse ever received certain state aid. (§ 867.03(1m)) *Summary Assignment.* All notice is at the discretion of the court. (§ 867.02(2)(d)) Petitioner must mail/deliver a copy of the order to all interested persons whose addresses are known by the petitioner. (§ 867.02) *Summary Settlement.* All notice is at the discretion of the court. (§ 867.01(3)(d))
heirs	No provision.
creditors	No provision.
others	No provision.
Which of the following must be observed?	
hearing	No provision.
affidavit, petition, other	*Affidavit.* Affidavit. (§ 867.03(1g)) *Summary Assignment.* Petition (§ 867.02(2)(am)). Order (§ 867.02(2)(g)). *Summary Settlement.* Petition (§ 867.01(3)(am)) Order. (§ 867.01(3)(f))
bond	*Affidavit.* No provision. *Summary Assignment.* Court may require as it sees fit. (§ 867.02(2)(c)) *Summary Settlement.* Court may require as it sees fit. (§ 867.01(3)(c))
What are basic contents of petition or affidavit?	*Affidavit.* (1) Description and value of property to be transferred, (2) total value of decedent's property in the state at date of death, and (3) whether decedent or spouse ever received certain state aid. (§ 867.03(1g)(a)–(c))

	Summary Assignment. (1) Statement that the estate does not exceed $50,000 in value and cannot be summarily settled under § 867.01; (2) statement as to whether petitioner has been able to locate decedent's will; (3) statement of property in which decedent had an interest; (4) names and addresses of all of decedent's creditors known by petitioner and the amount claimed by each; (5) names and addresses of all persons interested; and (6) whether the decedent or decedent's spouse received family care, medical assistance, long-term community support services, or other aid as listed in the statute. (§ 867.02(2)) *Summary Settlement.* (1) Statement that the value of the estate, less the amount of debts for which any property in the estate is security, does not exceed in value all allowed claims, OR that the estate, less secured debts, does not exceed $50,000 in value, and that decedent is survived by a spouse or at least one minor child or both; (2) detailed statement of property in which decedent had an interest; (3) names and addresses of all persons interested, ascertained by petitioner with reasonable diligence; and (4) whether the decedent's spouse received statutory family care benefit, medical assistance, long-term community support services or aid relating to cystic fibrosis, treatment of kidney disease, or hemophilia treatment services. (§ 867.01(3)(am))
Is procedure available in the case of nonresident decedents?	No provision.
Maximum allowable value of estate	*Affidavit.* $50,000 of solely owned, in-state property. (§ 867.03(1g)) *Summary Assignment.* $50,000, exclusive of secured debts. (§ 867.02(1)) *Summary Settlement.* Value of the estate, less the amount of debts for which any property in the estate is security, must not exceed in value all allowed claims, OR estate, less secured debts, must not exceed $50,000 in value, and decedent is survived by a spouse or at least one minor child or both. (§ 867.01(1))
What property can be transferred by this means?	*Affidavit.* Property owned solely by decedent. (§ 867.03(1g)) *Summary Assignment.* Entire estate. (§ 867.02(1)) *Summary Settlement.* Entire estate. (§ 867.01(1))
Special rules for certain assets (e.g., automobile)	No provision.
Can the spouse or other person take summarily if under certain amount?	No provision.
Minimum period before filing allowed	No provision.
Rights/obligations of party with affidavit	*Affidavit.* Right to property upon presentation of affidavit to person owing estate. (§ 867.03(1g)) *Summary Assignment.* See *Creditors' rights, if insufficient assets.* *Summary Settlement.* No provision.

Are some creditors given special privileges/preference (e.g., medical expenses, funeral expenses)?	*Affidavit.* No provision. *Summary Assignment.* Secured creditors. (§ 867.02(1)) *Summary Settlement.* Secured creditors. (§ 867.01(1)(b))
Creditors' rights, if insufficient assets	*Affidavit.* No provision. *Summary Assignment.* Unsatisfied creditors may recover from assignees. (§ 867.02(4)) *Summary Settlement.* Court may order notice to unsatisfied creditors. (§ 867.01(3)(g))
May the distribution of the estate proceed without appointment of personal representative?	*Affidavit.* No provision. *Summary Assignment.* Yes. (§ 867.02(1)) *Summary Settlement.* Yes. (§ 867.01(1))
Must court approve affidavit?	No provision.
Waiting period before authority to act	No provision.
With whom do you file petition or affidavit?	*Affidavit.* No provision. *Summary Assignment.* Court. (§ 867.02) *Summary Settlement.* Court. (§ 867.01)
Is there an informal procedure for appointment of executor or administrator?	*Affidavit.* No provision. *Summary Assignment.* Court may appoint special administrator. (§ 867.02(2)(f)) *Summary Settlement.* Court may appoint special administrator. (§ 867.01(3)(b))
Can a nonresident serve?	No provision.
Can the nonresident act locally based on appointment in another state?	No provision.
What does a transferor need so as to be relieved of liability if challenged by another person later on who claims the particular property (e.g., copy of affidavit)?	*Affidavit.* Upon transfer to affiant, transferor is released to the same extent as if the transfer had been made to a personal representative of the estate. (§ 867.03(2)) *Summary Assignment.* Transferors are released to the same extent as if the same had been made to a personal representative of the estate. (§ 867.02(3)) *Summary Settlement.* Transferors are released to the same extent as if the same had been made to a personal representative of the estate. (§ 867.01(4))

Wyoming
Distribution by Affidavit and Summary Procedure

Who can initiate process?	Person or persons claiming to be distributees. (§§ 2-1-201, 2-1-205) Under certain circumstances, government may initiate process. (§ 2-1-204)
Can it be used if claims outstanding?	*Personal Property.* Yes. (§ 2-1-201(a)) *Real Property.* Yes. (§ 2-1-205(b))
Different rules if die testate or intestate?	No provision.
Notice?	*Personal Property.* No provision. *Real Property.* Notice must be published once per week for two consecutive weeks in a newspaper of general circulation in the county where the real property is located. (§ 2-1-205(c))
heirs	No provision.
creditors	No provision.
others	No provision.
Which of the following must be observed?	
hearing	No provision.
affidavit, petition, other	*Personal Property.* Affidavit. (§ 2-1-201(a)) *Real Property.* Application for decree. (§ 2-1-205(a))
bond	No provision.
What are basic contents of petition or affidavit?	*Personal Property.* (1) Statement that value of entire estate less liens and encumbrances does not exceed $150,000; (2) statement that 30 days has elapsed since decedent's death; (3) statement that no application is pending or has been granted in any jurisdiction; (4) statement that claiming distributee is entitled to payment or delivery of property, including facts concerning distributee's relationship to decedent; and (5) statement that there are no other distributees having a right to succeed the property under probate. (§ 2-1-201(a)(i)–(iv)) *Real Property.* Same as personal property, but application must also include a description and valuation of the real property. (§ 2-1-205(b))
Is procedure available in the case of nonresident decedents?	No provision.
Maximum allowable value of estate	*Personal Property.* $150,000 less liens and encumbrances. (§ 2-1-201(a)(i)) *Real Property.* $150,000. (§ 2-1-205(a))
What property can be transferred by this means?	*Personal Property.* Personal property. (§ 2-1-201(a)) *Real Property.* Real and personal property. (§ 2-1-205(e))

Special rules for certain assets (e.g., automobile)	Clerk shall transfer title of vehicle from decedent to distributee upon presentation of affidavit. (§ 2-1-201(c)) Upon presentation of an affidavit, any bank, savings, or loan institution or credit union shall pay any deposit in the sole name of the decedent, with interest and dividends thereon, to the distributee(s). (§ 2-1-201(d))
Can the spouse or other person take summarily if under certain amount?	No provision.
Minimum period before filing allowed	30 days after death of decedent. (§§ 2-1-201(a)(ii), 2-1-205(a))
Rights/obligations of party with affidavit	*Personal Property.* Right to payment or delivery from persons indebted to decedent or in possession of property belonging to decedent. Must also file affidavit, and remains liable to those with superior rights. (§§ 2-1-201, 2-1-202) *Real Property.* No provision.
Are some creditors given special privileges/preference (e.g., medical expenses, funeral expenses)?	Governments. (§ 2-1-204)
Creditors' rights, if insufficient assets	*Personal Property.* Affiant is liable to persons having a superior right. (§ 2-1-202) *Real Property.* No provision.
May the distribution of the estate proceed without appointment of personal representative?	*Personal Property.* Yes. (§ 2-1-201(a)) *Real Property.* Yes. (§ 2-1-205(c))
Must court approve affidavit?	*Personal Property.* No provision. *Real Property.* Court must approve application. (§ 2-1-205(c))
Waiting period before authority to act	30 days after death of decedent. (§§ 2-1-201(a), 2-1-205(a))
With whom do you file petition or affidavit?	*Personal Property.* County clerk. (§ 2-1-201(c)) *Real Property.* District court of county where property is located (§ 2-1-205(a)).
Is there an informal procedure for appointment of executor or administrator?	No provision.
Can a nonresident serve?	No provision.
Can the nonresident act locally based on appointment in another state?	No provision.
What does a transferor need so as to be relieved of liability if challenged by another person later on who claims the particular property (e.g., copy of affidavit)?	*Personal Property.* Payor is discharged and released to the same extent as if he dealt with a personal representative. (§ 2-1-202) *Real Property.* No provision.

Table 5
Will Substitutes
(current through 5/1/07)

Increasingly, clients' assets are held in forms that pass outside the probate process. Oftentimes, planners advise their clients to use these ownership vehicles and techniques in order to avoid probate, simplify planning, and defeat or at least frustrate creditor's claims.

Despite the remarkable shift of individual wealth to these will substitutes, states disagree on which ones should be recognized and which ones should remain governed by the formal requirements of the wills law. The major categories reviewed in this table are:

Revocable Trusts: The settlor keeps control during life, but probate is avoided. Property is administered after the settlor's death or incompetency pursuant to the terms of the trust instrument.

Deeds: The grantor ordinarily provides for real property to pass at his death to a designated grantee. The key question seems to be whether the execution of the deed creates a present interest in the grantee, so that no interest passes at the time of the grantor's death.

Joint Tenancies: These create a right of survivorship in the other joint tenant(s). The joint tenancy serves as a valid substitute for a will, but is subject to severe deficiencies. It restricts flexibility in terms of tax planning and requires surrender of economic control of a pro rata share during life and complete control of the whole to the surviving joint tenant upon the death of the other joint tenant (s). Some states require specific language to create a joint tenancy or limit its availability to either personal or real property.

Tenancies by the Entirety: Similar to a joint tenancy in almost every respect, except that it can only be created between husband and wife. Unlike a joint tenancy, there is no right of partition available to a single joint tenant. Although it originally developed to protect the wife, it has been supplanted by other spousal protections in many states. In certain states, the status of this testamentary substitute is in limbo.

Totten Trusts: A technique approved of in a famous New York case, this form of ownership of a bank account as "A in trust for B," is essentially an implied revocable trust. Not all states recognize this form of account and, if they do, that is a valid testamentary substitute that need not comply with will formalities.

Joint-Name Bank Accounts: In many situations, a bank account will be in joint name, but there will be no reference to survivorship. An important question is whether the account will be deemed to create a right of survivorship or whether an interest is created that will pass under a will or, if no will, by intestate succession.

Payable on Death (P.O.D.) Bank Accounts: A bank account may indicate that at the death of the depositor, the account is to pass to a designated person. This designation will not typically comply with will formalities. The question is, therefore, whether it is a valid substitute that need not comply with those formalities. There is a considerable amount of ferment in this area and much disagreement among the states. The fact that a bank permits this designation does not mean that the designation is valid under the particular state's law.

Transfer on Death (T.O.D.) Securities Accounts: The T.O.D. designation is essentially the securities analogue to the P.O.D. bank account. However, there has been less acceptance of the T.O.D. as a valid testamentary substitute.

Life Insurance Proceeds: The life insurance designation seems almost wholly uncontroversial as a valid testamentary substitute. The beneficiary receives the life insurance proceeds as a third-party beneficiary of the contract between the owner of the policy and the insurance company.

Gifts: Many of the other testamentary substitutes that are recognized rest on the assumption that a lifetime transfer of an interest has occurred, so that no attempt at death-time transfer is deemed to have occurred. Certainly, this is true of a completed outright gift. However, different states set forth their own requirements for finding that a gift has been completed. While the requirements from state to state are often similar, there are nuances that need to be carefully observed. Otherwise, the property will be deemed still owned by the owner and pass pursuant to his will or by intestacy, as the case may be.

A Writing Disposing of Tangible Personal Property: In order to facilitate the disposition of personal effects and the like, a number of states allow for the disposition of items by a simple writing. In most cases, the writing does not have to be completely in the decedent's hand, as is true of a holographic will; nor need it be attested by witnesses or comply with the other requirements of a formally executed will. Many states have resisted the adoption of this streamlined mechanism. Concerns include potential for fraud, disruptive effect on and conflict with other dispositive instruments, and the lack of any limitation on the value of tangible assets that can be disposed of by this method.

In addition to the foregoing, consideration is given by Table 5.02 to the doctrines of incorporation by reference and facts of independent significance. In many cases, these doctrines obviate the need for repeated codicils or a new will, and allow for simplification of the content of the will. Thus, incorporation by reference allows for the inclusion of a pre-existing independent document, such as a list of assets, as part of the will. Facts of independent significance allow reference in a will to the disposition of assets acquired later on or even consistent with the terms of a subsequently executed instrument, such as a trust. An example might be: "I devise the stock owned at my death to Sally." Another example would be: "I leave the contents of my safe deposit box at my death to Bill." Still another example would be: "I leave my residuary estate in accord with the terms of the revocable trust of my wife, as she may amend it from time to time, both before and after my death." However, not all states recognize both incorporation by reference and facts of independent significance. Moreover, some states have statutory enactments acknowledging these doctrines and setting forth their parameters, while other states' enforcement of these doctrines is based on decisional law that is exemplified by contradictory holdings and/or ambiguities.

Since property is commonly situated in more than one jurisdiction and some of the aforementioned will substitutes may be subject to regulation by several states, careful review of the law of any potentially interested state is warranted. This is particularly true since this area of the law is currently in a state of considerable flux. If a particular will substitute is not, in fact, recognized by a state, the consequence could well be intestacy or the transmission of property by will to persons and in a form of ownership not intended by the decedent.

A vital planning dimension is also implicated as a result of differences among states with result to bank accounts and securities. This area of law is in a state of uncertainty, so that great care must be exercised. Opportunities, however, are available. For example, to the extent that the simple vehicle of a p.o.d. designation is preferred, opening an account in one neighboring state rather than another may be a winning strategy. Thus, in the New York metropolitan area, New York will not recognize such an account as a valid testamentary substitute. However, New Jersey will do so. The situation in Connecticut and Pennsylvania is unsettled, so these jurisdictions would not be as appealing as New Jersey.

Table 5.01, Part 1
Principal Will Substitutes

Which of the Following Are Valid to Pass Property at Death without Complying with Wills Formalities?

	Revocable Trust?	*Transfer by Deed Effective at Death, Assuming Intent to Make Present Conveyance of Title?*	*Joint Tenancy?*	*Tenancy by the Entirety?*	*Totten Trust Bank Account?*	*Joint-Name Bank Account with No Reference to Right of Survivorship?*
Alabama	No direct authority, although almost certainly not testamentary. (Tierce v. Macedonia United Methodist Church of Newport, 519 So. 2d 451 (1987) (transfer to inter vivos trust with a retained life income interest; however, court emphasized that the remainder was not revocable or contingent))	Yes. (Stephens v. Stephens, 193 So. 2d 755 (1967) (instrument executed by husband and wife conveying certain land to son and providing that deed should become effective at end of natural life of one of grantors who had life estate was deed with reservation of life estate and not a will))	Yes, if right of survivorship mentioned. (§ 35-4-7)	There is debate as to whether Alabama recognizes a tenancy by the entirety. (§ 8-9A-1 cmt.)	Yes. (§ 5-5A-40)	Yes. (§ 5-5A-41)
Alaska	Yes. (§ 13.33.101)	Yes. (§ 13.33.101)	Generally No, with an exception for interests in, if personalty. There is no joint tenancy in real property. (§ 34.15.130)	Yes. (§ 34.15.140) Note that spouses who acquire real property hold the estate as tenants by the entirety unless they specify otherwise. (§ 34.15.110)	This account has been incorporated into the P.O.D. type account. (§ 13.33.203)	Yes, except if terms of account specify otherwise. (§§ 13.33.212, 13.33.214)
Arizona	Yes. (§ 14-6101)	Yes. (§ 14-6101)	Yes. Must expressly state the devise or grant vests the estate in the survivor. (§ 33-431)	No statute or cases, since not recognized in state. However, there is an analogous form of ownership described as community property with right of survivorship. (§ 33-431(C))	Yes. (§ 6-236)	Yes, except if terms of account specify otherwise. (§§ 14-6212, 14-6214)

Arkansas	Yes. (Gall v. Union Nat. Bank of Little Rock, 159 S.W.2d 757 (1942))	Yes. (Smith v. Smith, 235 S.W.2d 886 (1951) (where deed was delivered to grantees by the grantor during his lifetime and deed contained a provision that it was not to become effective until death of grantor, deed was a valid warranty deed reserving a life estate in grantor and was not testamentary in character))	Yes. (§ 1812106)	Yes. (See Weir v. Brigham, 236 S.W.2d 435 (Ark. 1951); § 23-47-204)	Yes. (§ 23-47-204)	Yes. (§ 23-47-204)
California	Yes. (Prob. § 5000)	Yes. (Prob. § 5000)	Yes (Civ. § 683, see also Estate of Petersen, 34 Cal. Rptr. 2d 449 (1994))	No. (Civ. §§ 682, 683; Hannon v. Southern Pac. R. Co., 107 P. 335 (1909))	Yes. (Prob. §§ 5203, 5404, 80 (definition))	Yes. (Prob. § 5203) Potentially different result for community property account of spouses. (Prob. § 5203(a)(5))
Colorado	Yes. (§ 15-15-101)	Yes. (§ 15-15-101)	Yes. (§ 38-11-101)	Not recognized in state. (§ 38-31-201(1))	No. Now it is a P.O.D. account. (§ 15-15-203(1))	Yes. (§§ 15-15-212, 15-15-214)
Connecticut	Yes. (Cramer v. Hartford-Connecticut Trust Co., 147 A. 139 (1929) (instrument transferring property to trustee, in which settlor reserved life use and power of revocation and provided for payment to others on her death, created valid trust))	Depends. If intent is to defer transfer until death, then must comply with wills law. However, can have transfer as a present one, even though possession and enjoyment deferred until after death. Transferor's	Yes. (§ 47-14a)	No. (§ 47-14a)	Yes. (§ 36a-296)	Yes. (§ 36a-290)

(cont'd)

Table 5.01, Part 1
Principal Will Substitutes *(continued)*

Which of the Following Are Valid to Pass Property at Death without Complying with Wills Formalities?

	Revocable Trust?	*Transfer by Deed Effective at Death, Assuming Intent to Make Present Conveyance of Title?*	*Joint Tenancy?*	*Tenancy by the Entirety?*	*Totten Trust Bank Account?*	*Joint-Name Bank Account with No Reference to Right of Survivorship?*
Connecticut *(cont'd)*		intent is key. (Smith v. Trinity United Meth. Church, 821 A.2d 291, 294 (Ct. Super. 2002), aff'd, 819 A.2d 225 (Ct. 2003)				
Delaware	Yes. (Hanson v. Wilmington Trust Co., 119 A.2d 901 (1955))	No statute or cases on point.	Yes. (25 § 311)	Yes. (25 § 309)	Yes. (5 § 924)	Yes. (5 § 923)
District of Columbia	Yes. (§ 19-601.01 (a))	Yes. (§ 19-601.01(a))	Yes, but it must be "expressly declared to be a joint tenancy." (§ 42-516)	Yes. (Settle v. Settle, 8F.2d 911 (D.C. Cir. 1925); § 42-516)	Yes. (Schilt v. Duvall, 479 F.2d 1228, 1230 (D.C. Cir. 1978) ("Totten trust" is tentative trust, revocable at will and beneficiary has no right or title to deposit until death of trustee and while trustee lives he has full control over the deposit))	Yes. (§ 26-804)
Florida	Yes, as to written trusts. (§ 689.075(1)) See generally (Alter v. Zuckerman, 585 So. 2d 303 (1991))	Yes. (Williams v. Williams, 6 So. 2d 275 (1942))	Yes. Instrument must expressly provide for survivorship. (§ 689.15)	Yes. (§ 689.15; see also Knapp v. Fredricksen, 4 So. 2d 251 (1941))	Yes. See Litsey v. First Federal Sav. & Loan Ass'n of Tampa, App. 2	Yes. (§ 655.78)

					Dist., 243 So. 2d 239 (1971) (trust deposit accounts established by decedent during his lifetime constituted Totten Trusts; and the Totten Trust doctrine, despite claim that it should be overruled or receded from, remains a firmly established rule of law in Florida) See also § 655.82.	
Georgia	Yes, but involving trust with retained life estate. (Jennings v. Jennings, 160 S.E. 405 (1931))	Yes. (Harris v. Neely, 359 S.E.2d 885 (1987))	Yes, but only if the instrument expressly refers to the takers as ''joint tenants,'' ''joint tenants and not as tenants in common,'' ''joint tenants with survivorship,'' or as taking ''jointly with survivorship.'' (§ 44-6-190 (a)) If these words are not used, a tenancy in common is created. (*Id.*) The foregoing does not apply to securities or bank accounts. (§ 44-6-190(b))	Yes, if expressly created. (State v. Jackson, 399 S.E.2d 88 (1991); Sams v. McDonald, 160 S.E.2d 594 (1968) (recognized, but with suggestion it might just be treated as joint tenancy))	Yes. (§ 7-1-813(c))	Yes, rights of survivorship are recognized, unless there is clear and convincing evidence of a contrary intention at the time the account was created. (§§ 7-1-813(a), 7-1-815)

Table 5.01, Part 1
Principal Will Substitutes *(continued)*

	Which of the Following Are Valid to Pass Property at Death without Complying with Wills Formalities?					
	Revocable Trust?	*Transfer by Deed Effective at Death, Assuming Intent to Make Present Conveyance of Title?*	*Joint Tenancy?*	*Tenancy by the Entirety?*	*Totten Trust Bank Account?*	*Joint-Name Bank Account with No Reference to Right of Survivorship?*
Hawaii	No statute or cases on point.	No statute or cases on point.	No, unless "it manifestly appears from the tenor of the instrument that it was intended. . . ." (§ 509-1)	No, unless "it manifestly appears from the tenor of the instrument that it was intended. . . ." (§ 509-1)	Yes. (§§ 560: 6-104(c), 560: 6-106)	Yes. (§§ 560:6-104, 560:6-106)
Idaho	Yes. (§ 15-6-201)	Yes, if delivery of instrument during grantor's lifetime and intent thereby to divest himself of title. (McLaws v. Casey, 400 P.2d 386, 389 (1965))	No, unless declared in its creation to be a joint interest. (§ 55-104)	No statute or cases directly on point.	Yes. (§§ 15-6-104 (c), 15-6-106)	Yes. (§§ 15-6-104(a), 15-6-106)
Illinois	Yes. (Merchants Nat. Bank of Aurora v. Weinold, 138 N.E.2d 840 (1956))	No, at least where deed not delivered or recorded. (Oliver v. Oliver, 36 N.E. 955 (1894))	Yes. (765 ILCS § 1005/1), but must be expressly declared	Yes. (765 ILCS § 1005/1c)	Yes. (205 ILCS § 625/3)	No. (765 ILCS 1005/2)
Indiana	Yes. (§ 29-1-5-9)	Yes, if intent of grantor is to confer title presently, but simply postpone enjoyment. (VanOrman v. VanOrman, 41 N.E.2d 693 (1942))	Yes. (§§ 32-17-2-4 (disclaimer); 32-21-10-2, 32-21-10-3 (real property conveyances); Robison v. Fickle, 340 N.E.2d 824 (Ct. App. 1976)) But see last column for bank accounts.	Yes. (Baker v. Cailor, 186 N.E. 769 (1933)) See also § 32-21-10-2(c)(3).	Yes. (First Federal Sav. & Loan Assoc., 310 N.E.2d 101 (Ct. App. 1974)) See also §§ 32-17-11-1 et seq.)	Yes. (§§ 32-17-11-4, 32-17-11-5, 32-17-11-18)
Iowa	Yes, if the instrument passes a present interest, even though possession	Yes, if duly executed and recorded, even if recordation occurs after	Yes. (In re Murdoch's Estate, 29 N.W.2d 177 (1947))	Yes, with respect to securities. (§ 633D.3)	Yes. (In re Podhajsky's	Notwithstanding general prescription in favor of

	and enjoyment are postponed. (Trustees of Synod v. Horel, 16 N.W.2d 209, 212 (1944))	the grantor's death. In the latter case there is a visible presumption of an intent to pass immediate title. (Avery v. Lillie, 148 N.W.2d 474, 477 (1967))		Otherwise, this form of ownership is likely not recognized. See Fay v. Smiley, 207 N.W. 369, 371 (1926). However, §557.15 indicates that a conveyance to two or more persons creates a tenancy in common "unless a contrary intent is expressed."	Estate, 115 N.W. 590, 592 (1908))	tenancy in common, in the case of bank accounts, there is a presumption in favor of a joint tenancy. (In re Estate of Kokjohn, 531 N.W.2d 99 (Iowa 1995))
Kansas	Yes. (Moore v. Hayes, 26 P.2d 254 (1933))	Yes. § 59-3501 expressly allows this for real estate.	Yes. Devise must make clear that joint tenancy was intended to be created. (§ 58-501)	No. (Stewart v. Thomas, 68 P. 70 (1902) & Laws of 1891, Ch. 203) See also Shubert v. Hager, 796 P.2d 564 (Kan. Ct. App. 1990) (a grant to the spouses as tenants by the entirety creates a joint tenancy).	Yes. (In re Estate of Morton, 769 P.2d 616 (1987) (Totten trust valid in Kansas; need not comply with statute of wills))	Yes. (§ 9-1205)
Kentucky	Yes. (§ 391.360)	Yes, even if reserved life estate and power to revoke retained. (Commonwealth v. McCauley's Ex'r, 179 S.W. 411 (1915))	Yes. Must expressly provide for a right of survivorship. (§ 381.120)	Yes. (§ 381.050) Must expressly create a mutual right to the entirety by survivorship.	Yes. (§§ 391.315 (3), 391.325)	Yes. (§§ 391.315, 391.325)
Louisiana[1]	Yes. (Rev. Stat. §§ 9:2011, 9:2013, 9:2046)	Yes. (Succession of Lanata, 18 So. 2d 500 (1944); McKnight v. Cornet, 143 So. 726 (Ct. App. 1932))	Joint tenancy is not recognized. (Gathright v. Smith, 352 So. 2d 282 (1977)) However, this form of ownership is recognized for bank accounts if written agreement with bank provides for survivorship. (Rev. Stat. § 6:1255)	Tenancy by the entirety is not recognized. (Civ. Code Art. 3526, revision cmt. (h))	Yes, but limited to case where beneficiary is spouse, child, grandchild, parent, or sibling. (Rev. Stat. § 6:314(A))	No. Written agreement must provide for survivorship. (Rev. Stat. § 6:1255)

Table 5.01, Part 1
Principal Will Substitutes *(continued)*

Which of the Following Are Valid to Pass Property at Death without Complying with Wills Formalities?

	Revocable Trust?	*Transfer by Deed Effective at Death, Assuming Intent to Make Present Conveyance of Title?*	*Joint Tenancy?*	*Tenancy by the Entirety?*	*Totten Trust Bank Account?*	*Joint-Name Bank Account with No Reference to Right of Survivorship?*
Maine	Yes. (18A § 6201)	Not valid if, for example, kept by grantor's attorney, from whom grantor might demand its return at any time. Therefore, it depends on intent. (Eddy v. Pinder, 159 A. 727 (1932))	Yes. (33 § 159)	No. (19A § 801; Palmer v. Flint, 161 A.2d 837 (1960))	Yes. (18A §§ 6-104(c), 6-106)	Yes. (18A §§ 6-104, 6-106)
Maryland	Yes. (Brown v. Mercantile Tr. & Deposit Co., 40 A. 256 (1898))	Yes. (Register of Wills v. Blackway, 141 A.2d 713 (1958))	Yes. To create a joint tenancy, the deed, will, or other written instrument must expressly provide that the property granted is to be held in joint tenancy. (§ 2-117)	Yes. (McManus v. Summers, 430 A.2d 80 (1981))	Yes. (Financial Institutions Code § 1-204; Estates & Trusts Code § 1-401)	Yes. (Financial Institutions Code § 1-204; Estates & Trusts Code § 1-401)
Massachusetts	Yes. (Ascher v. Cohen, 131 N.E.2d 198 (1956))	Yes. (Kelley v. Snow, 70 N.E. 89 (1904))	Yes. (184 § 7)	Yes. (184 § 7)	Yes. (167D § 6)	Yes. (167D § 5)
Michigan	Yes. (Soltis v. First American Bank Muskegon, 513 N.W.2d 148, *appeal*	Problem when grantor retains possession of deed and the grantee	Yes. To be relied on, must be an express	Yes. (In re Selle's Estate, 292 N.W.2d	Yes. (§ 487.702)	Yes. (§ 490.56)

	denied, 522 N.W.2d 639 (1994))	lacks knowledge of it, even if it was recorded. (Havens v. Schoen, 310 N.W.2d 870, 871 (1981))	declared joint tenancy. (§ 554.44)	147 (1980)) See also § 557.71		
Minnesota	Yes. (Connecticut General Life Ins. Co. v. First Nat. Bank of Minneapolis, 262 N.W.2d 403 (1977))	Yes. (Hagen v. Hagen, 161 N.W. 380 (1917))	Yes. (Irvine v. Helvering, 99 F.2d 265 (1938)) See also § 500.19(2) (addressing joint tenancies in land)	No. (Wilson v. Wilson, 45 N.W. 710 (1890))	Yes. (In re Estate of Kroyer, 385 N.W.2d 31 (1986))	Yes. (§§ 524.6-204(a), 524.6-206)
Mississippi	No statute or cases on point.	No. Testamentary in nature, even if in form of deed, if the donor's intention was for it to take effect only after the grantor's death. (Simpson v. McGee, 73 So. 55 (1916))	Yes. Must appear from tenor of instru ment that it intended to create an estate in joint tenancy. (§ 89-1-7)	Yes. Must appear from tenor of instrument that it intended to create an estate in entirety with right of survivorship. (§ 89-1-7)	Yes. (§ 81-5-62)	Yes. (§ 81-5-63)
Missouri	Yes. (§§ 461.001, 461.009)	Yes. (§ 461.025)	Yes, if expressly declared. (§ 442.450) See also § 442.025; Neagle v. Johnson, 261 F.Supp. 634, *aff'd*, 381 F.2d 9 (1966)	Yes. (Jones v. Cox, 629 S.W.2d 511 (1981)) See also § 442.025	Yes. (§ 362.475)	Yes. (§ 362.470)
Montana	Yes. (§ 72-6-111)	Yes. (§ 72-6-111)	Yes. (§ 70-20-310)	No. (Clark v. Clark, 387 P.2d 907 (1963))	Yes. (§§ 72-6-212, 72-6-214)	Yes. (§§ 72-6-212, 72-6-214)
Nebraska	Yes. (§ 30-2715(a))	Yes. (§ 30-2715(a))	Yes. (§ 76-118)	No statute or cases on point. But see § 67-410(3)(a), which refers to a tenancy by the entireties not "by itself" establishing or creating a partnership.	Possibly recognized under § 30-2719(b). See also Comment § 30-2209.	If right of survivorship is not indicated, then intent to have survivorship may still be shown. (§ 30-2719(b))

Table 5.01, Part 1
Principal Will Substitutes *(continued)*

Which of the Following Are Valid to Pass Property at Death without Complying with Wills Formalities?

	Revocable Trust?	*Transfer by Deed Effective at Death, Assuming Intent to Make Present Conveyance of Title?*	*Joint Tenancy?*	*Tenancy by the Entirety?*	*Totten Trust Bank Account?*	*Joint-Name Bank Account with No Reference to Right of Survivorship?*
Nevada	Yes. (Coleman v. First Nat'l Bank, 506 P.2d 86 (Nev. 1973))	Yes. (§ 111.109(1))	Yes. The grant or devise must expressly declare the joint tenancy. (§ 111.060)	No statute—community property state.	Yes. (§ 663.025) (See also Byrd v. Lanahan, 783 P.2d 426, 428-29 (1989).)	Yes. (§ 100.085)
New Hampshire	Yes. (York's Estate, 65 A.2d 282 (1949))	Yes. ''In the normal course of events persons will use a deed, mortgage, note or contract as a substitute for accomplishing the same purpose by will. When a will is employed we require compliance with the statute of wills. But when a contractual undertaking is employed we do not declare it invalid because it accomplished in part what could have been accomplished by the use of a will.'' (McGrath v. McGrath, 220 A.2d 760, 762 (1966))	Yes. Must clearly express intention to execute a joint tenancy with rights of survivorship. (§ 477:18)	Yes. Must clearly express intention to create an estate as tenants by the entirety. (§ 477:18)	Yes. (§ 384-D:1)	Yes. (§ 384:28)
New Jersey	Yes, in case where settlor intends to create a present beneficial interest in favor of the named beneficiary,	Maybe. The key is that there be an intention to part with the deed, even if not actually delivered	Yes. (§§ 46:3-17, 46:3-17.1, 46:3-17.5)	Yes. (§§ 46:3-17, 46:3-17.2, 46:3-17.4, 46:3-17.5)	Yes. (§§ 17:16I-5(c), 17:16I-14)	Yes. (§§ 17:16I-5, 17:16I-14)

	while postponing his enjoyment thereof until the settlor's death. (In re Kovalyshyn's Estate, 343 A.2d 852 (1975))	and to pass title. (Rommell v. Happe, 115 A. 906, 908 (Ch. 1921)) There must be an intention to make deed presently effective. Held, intention not present in case in which grantors believed transfer would become effective on their deaths. (Montgomery v. Varley, 144 A. 183, 185 (1929))				
New Mexico	Yes. (§ 45-6-101)	Yes. (§ 45-6-101)	Yes. (§ 40-3-2); Menger v. Otera County State Bank, 98 P.2d 834 (1940) (title is not important, but rather the intent of the transferor)	No, since community property state. (Swink v. Fingado, 850 P.2d 978, 983 n.9 (1993); McDonald v. Senn, 204 P.2d 990, 995 (1949))	Yes. (§§ 45-6-212, 45-6-214) Modeled after U.P.C., which treats Totten trusts as P.O.D. designation. See § 45-6-201 cmts.	Yes. (§§ 45-6-212, 45-6-214)
New York	Yes. (In re Plotkin's Estate, 290 N.Y.S.2d 46 (1968))	Yes, if deed is absolute. (Slowey v. Hunt, 177 N.Y.S. 505 (1919))	Yes. (Est. Powers & Trusts § 6-2.1)	Yes, with respect to real property. It is permitted as well in the case of shares of stock of a cooperative apartment corporation allocated to an apartment or unit together with the appurtenant proprietary lease. (Est. Powers & Trusts § 6-2.1(4))	Yes. (Banking Law § 675)	No. (Banking Law § 675; In re Estate of Timoshevich, 521 N.Y.S.2d 311, 313 (App. Div. 1987))

Table 5.01, Part 1
Principal Will Substitutes *(continued)*

Which of the Following Are Valid to Pass Property at Death without Complying with Wills Formalities?

	Revocable Trust?	*Transfer by Deed Effective at Death, Assuming Intent to Make Present Conveyance of Title?*	*Joint Tenancy?*	*Tenancy by the Entirety?*	*Totten Trust Bank Account?*	*Joint-Name Bank Account with No Reference to Right of Survivorship?*
North Carolina	Yes. (Ridge v. Bright, 93 S.E.2d 607 (1956))	Yes, if grantor intends title to pass on its execution, despite the fact that enjoyment will be postponed until after grantor's death. (Phifer v. Mullis, 83 S.E. 582 (1908))	Yes, if "the instrument creating the joint tenancy expressly provides for a right of survivorship." (§ 41-2)	Yes. (§ 39-13.6; Bank of Greenville v. Gornto, 77 S.E. 222 (1913)) However, it only exists pursuant to contract. Also, it does not exist for personal property. (Bowling v. Bowling, 91 S.E.2d 176 (1956))	Yes. (§ 53-146.2)	No. (§ 41-2.1)
North Dakota	Yes. (§ 30.1-31-01)	Yes. (§ 30.1-31-01)	Yes. (§ 47-10-23)	No. (Renz v. Renz, 256 N.W.2d 883 (1977))	No. Replaced by P.O.D. account. (§ 30.1-31.04(2))	Yes, if a multiple party account. (§§ 30.1-31-09, 30.1-31-11) See also §30.1-31-02(8)(b)
Ohio	Yes. (Central Trust Co. v. McCarthy, 57 N.E.2d 126 (1943))	Yes, if intent is not to pass title only upon death, in which case the deed will be testamentary in character. (Tucker v. Morey, 143 N.E.2d 627, 629 (1956))	Yes. Joint tenancy with right of survivorship does not exist at common law in Ohio but is a matter of contract. See, e.g., Spitz v. Rapport 604 N.E.2d 801 (Ct. App. 1992); § 5302.20)	No. Instead, effective Apr. 4, 1985, a tenancy of survivorship, akin to a joint tenancy, is the replacement. (§§ 5302.17; 5302.21)	Yes. (§ 1109.06)	Yes. (§ 1109.07)

Oklahoma	Yes. (Limb v. Aldridge, 978 P.2d 365, 367 (Okla. Ct. Civ. App. 1998))	May not be, especially where grantor keeps control of property during his lifetime and acts as if he still owns it. (Thomas v. Bank of Oklahoma, 684 P.2d 553, 555 (1984))	Yes. (60 Okla. St. § 74)	Yes. (60 Okla. St. § 74)	Yes. (6 Okla. St. § 902)	Yes. (6 Okla. St. § 901)
Oregon	Yes, but care must be exercised. There is some authority that questions the trust's nontestamentary character when the grantor retains secret control over the trust assets and seeks to dispose of the trust assets by will, and the result might be the defeat of creditors. Each case turns on its facts. (Coston v. Portland Tr. Co., 282 P. 442 (1929))	There is a risk it will be considered testamentary if the deed is not delivered or if it only takes effect at the grantor's death and conveys all of his property. (Witham v. Witham, 66 P.2d 281 (1937); In re Neil's Estate, 226 P. 439 (1924))	Yes. The right of survivorship must be clearly and expressly declared in the conveyance. (§ 93.180)	Yes. (Gorger v. Gorger, 555 P.2d 1 (1976)) § 93.180 does not alter this result. See Noblitt v. Beebe, 35 P. 248 (1882).	Yes. (§§ 708A.470(3), 708A.480)	Yes. (§§ 708A.470, 708A.480)
Pennsylvania	Yes. (In re Huested's Estate, 169 A.2d 57 (1961))	Yes. (Damiani v. Lobasco, 79 A.2d 268 (1951))	Yes, but only if right of survivorship is clearly expressed. (68 § 110; Margarite v. Ewald, 381 A.2d 480 (1977)) Although this statute seems to be addressing real property, it applies as well to personal property. (Teacher v. Kijurina, 76 A.2d 197 (1950))	Yes. (In re Michael's Estate, 218 A.2d 338 (1966))	Yes. (20 §§ 6304(b), 6306)	Yes. (20 §§ 6304(a), 6306)

Table 5.01, Part 1
Principal Will Substitutes *(continued)*

	Which of the Following Are Valid to Pass Property at Death without Complying with Wills Formalities?					
	Revocable Trust?	*Transfer by Deed Effective at Death, Assuming Intent to Make Present Conveyance of Title?*	*Joint Tenancy?*	*Tenancy by the Entirety?*	*Totten Trust Bank Account?*	*Joint-Name Bank Account with No Reference to Right of Survivorship?*
Rhode Island	Yes. (Green v. Green, 559 A.2d 1047 (1989)) Also implied by pourover provision. (§ 33-6-33)	Yes. However, even if grantee is in possession of deed, it is not valid as a testamentary substitute if the grantor intended that it not take effect until death. (Lambert v. Lambert, 77 A.2d 325 (1950))	Yes, but must declare that tenancy is joint or is to those persons and the survivors or survivor of them. (§ 34-3-1)	Yes. § 34-3-1, which creates a presumption in favor of tenancy in common rather than joint tenancy, does not prohibit an estate by the entirety nor did the legislature intend to circumvent the common law as to such estates. (Bloomfield v. Brown, 25 A.2d 354 (1942))	Yes. (§ 19-9-12)	No. (§ 19-9-14) If a joint bank account does not provide for survivorship rights, that absence will be conclusive evidence of an intent not to transfer any right of ownership to the survivor, absent evidence of mistake or fraud. (Robinson v. Delfino, 710 A.2d 154 (R.I. 1998))
South Carolina	Yes. (§ 62-6-201)	Yes. (§ 62-6-201) See also Hydrick v. Hydrick, 141 S.E. 156 (1927)	Yes, but instrument creating joint tenancy must expressly provide for a right of survivorship. (§ 62-2-804)	This estate no longer exists. (Davis v. Davis, 75 S.E.2d 46 (1953))	Yes. (§§ 62-6-104(c), 62-6-106)	Yes. (§§ 62-6-104, 62-6-106)
South Dakota	Yes. (§ 29A-6-113)	Yes. (§ 29A-6-113)	Yes. (§§ 43-2-14; 25-2-3 (with respect to husband and wife); In re Hanson's Estate, 93 N.W.2d 606 (1958))	No. (Schimke v. Karlstad, 208 N.W.2d 710 (1973))	Yes. (§ 51A-10-4)	Yes. (§§ 29A-6-104, 29A-6-106)

Tennessee	Yes. (§ 35-15-601)	Yes, if duly acknowledged and legally delivered. (Johnson v. Mitchell, 20 Tenn. 168 (1839); Stamper v. Venable, 97 S.W. 812 (1906))	No. A joint tenancy with survivorship is cut down to a tenancy in common. (§ 66-1-107) However, it can be created if there is an express intention. (McLeroy v. McLeroy, 40 S.W.2d 1027 (1931))	Yes. (§§ 31-1-108, 36-3-505)	Yes. (§ 45-2-704)	Yes. (§ 45-2-703 (e)(4))
Texas	Yes. (Prob. § 450(a))	Yes. (Prob. § 450(a))	Yes, only if agree in writing that the interest of any joint owner who dies shall survive to the surviving joint owner or owners. (Prob. § 46) See also Prob. §§ 451, 454 (pertaining to creation of survivorship right in community property and in agreement between persons, such as cohabitants)	No statute or cases since community property state.	Yes. (Prob. §§ 439, 441, 447)	No. (Prob. §§ 439, 441)
Utah	Yes. (§ 75-6-201)	Yes. (Controlled Receivables, Inc. v. Harman, 413 P. 2d 807 (1966)) This is an interesting case, because the Utah Supreme Court viewed father's comments that he did not intend to pass title to his children until death as ''self-serving'' and inconsistent with *(cont'd)*	Yes. (§ 57-1-5)	Implied by fact that survivor can disclaim interest devolving by right of survivorship. (§ 75-2-801)	Yes. (§§ 75-6-104(3), 75-6-106)	Yes. (§§ 75-6-104, 75-6-106)

Table 5.01, Part 1
Principal Will Substitutes *(continued)*

Which of the Following Are Valid to Pass Property at Death without Complying with Wills Formalities?

	Revocable Trust?	*Transfer by Deed Effective at Death, Assuming Intent to Make Present Conveyance of Title?*	*Joint Tenancy?*	*Tenancy by the Entirety?*	*Totten Trust Bank Account?*	*Joint-Name Bank Account with No Reference to Right of Survivorship?*
Utah (*cont'd*)		his actions. He argued that in light of his purpose to avoid testamentary formalities, the deed was invalid. The court also emphasized that that purpose does not undermine the validity of the deed.				
Vermont	Yes, but burden is on the beneficiary to prove a completed trust for his benefit. (Reynolds v. Shambeau, 437 A.2d 1101, 1103 (1981))	Yes, if intent to transfer present interest, even if not present enjoyment. (Blair v. Blair, 10 A.2d 188 (1940); Straw v. Mower, 130 A. 687 (1925)) See also Scott v. Beland, 45 A.2d 641 (1946).	Yes. Conveyance and devises of land must express therein that the grantees or devisees shall take the lands jointly or in joint tenancy or to them and the survivors of them. (27 § 2)	Yes. (Buzzell v. Edward H. Everett Co., 180 F. Supp. 893 (1960))	Yes. (In re Estate of Adams, 587 A.2d 958 (1990))	Yes. (8 § 14204)
Virginia	Yes, as long as an interest or estate was intended to pass under the instrument to the trustee or beneficiaries prior to the grantor's death. (Bickers v. Shenandoah Valley Nat'l Bank of Winchester, 90 S.E.2d 865 (1956)) Also implied from pourover statute. (§ 64.1-73(C))	Yes, even when there is wording to effect that postponement of enjoyment until grantor's death "is testamentary in nature." (Short v. A. H. Still Inv. Corp., 147 S.E.2d 99 (1966))	Yes, but right of survivorship can only be conferred by the instrument conveying the property. (§§ 55-20, 55-21)	Yes. Must be manifest from wording of the conveyance that grantor wants to establish a tenancy by entirety. (§§ 55-20, 55-21)	Yes. (§§ 6.1-125.5 (C), 6.1-125.7)	Yes. (§§ 6.1-125.5, 6.1-125.7)

Washington	Yes. (In re Estate of Overmire, 794 P.2d 518 (1996); § 11.02.091)	Yes. (In re Estate of Mary O'Brien, 749 P.2d 154 (1988); § 11.02.091)	Yes. (§ 64.28.010)	No. This statute abolishes the right of survivorship as an incident of tenancy by the entireties. (§ 11.04.071)	Yes. (§ 30.22.100)	The statute is ambiguous. (§ 30.22.100) There is a rebuttable presumption that a joint account with right of survivorship has been created. See In re Haden, 2004 WL 2095641 (Wash. Ct. App. Sept. 20, 2004)
West Virginia	Yes. (Davis v. KB & T Co., 309 S.E.2d 45, 49 (1983))	Yes. (Spangler v. Vermillion, 92 S.E. 449 (1917); Lauck v. Logan, 31 S.E. 986 (1898))	No. (§ 36-1-19) However, § 36-1-20 opens a major exception allowing joint tenancies, based on "the tenor of the instrument" or the use of the disjunctive "or" where it links up multiple owners. (Lieving v. Hadley, 423 S.E.2d 600 (1992))	No. It is treated as a tenancy in common. (§ 36-1-19)	Yes. (§ 31A-4-33)	Yes. (§ 31A-4-33)
Wisconsin	Yes. (§ 705.10)	Yes. (§ 705.10)	Yes. (§§ 700.17, 700.19)	No. (Aaby v. Kaupanger, 221 N.W. 417, 418 (1928))	Yes. (§§ 705.01(8) & 705.04)	Yes. (§ 705.04)
Wyoming	Apparently so. This is implication of Briggs v. Wyoming Nat'l Bank, 836 P.2d 263 (1992).	Yes, if transfer is one of a present interest. (Forbes v. Volk, 358 P.2d 942 (1961))	Yes. (§ 34-1-140)	Yes. (§ 34-1-140)	Yes. (§ 2-1-203(c))	Yes. (§ 2-1-203(c))

1. *Caution:* A civil law system with very different concepts is followed. Even though common-law concepts like the trust have been recognized statutorily, they may be approached very differently.

Table 5.01, Part 2
Principal Will Substitutes

Which of the Following Are Valid to Pass Property at Death without Complying with Wills Formalities?

	Payable on Death (P.O.D.) Bank Account?	*Transfer on Death (T.O.D.) Security Registration?*	*Life Insurance Proceeds?*	*Gift?*	*A Writing Disposing of Tangible Personal Property Even If Not Entirely in the Testator's Handwriting?*
Alabama	Yes. (§§ 5-24-12, 5-24-14)	Yes. (§§ 8-6-146, 8-6-148)	Yes. (Williams v. Williams, 438 So. 2d 735 (1983) (designation of the beneficiary of a life insurance policy is governed by the provisions of the policy; such provisions are not testamentary))	Yes. The elements of a valid gift are: (a) an intention to give and surrender title to, and dominion over, the property; (b) delivery of the property to the donee; and (c) acceptance by the donee. (Dial v. Dial, 603 So. 2d 1020, 1022 (1992))	No statute or cases on point. There would appear to be no authority in support of this being given effect.
Alaska	Yes. (§§ 13.33.212, 13.33.214)	Yes. (§§ 13.33.307, 13.33.309)	Yes. (§ 13.33.101)	Yes. The donor cannot intend to retain control and ownership, and there must be delivery. (In re Estate of Evanco, 955 P.2d 525, 527 (Alaska 1998))	Yes. Writing must be signed by testator and describe items "other than money," with reasonable certainty. The writing may be referred to as one to be in existence at the time of the testator's death; it may be prepared before or after the execution of the will; it may be altered by the testator after its preparation; and it may be a writing that does not have significance apart from its effect in the dispositions made by the will. (§ 13.12.513)
Arizona	Yes. (§§ 14-6212(A)–(B), 14-6214)	Yes. (§§ 14-6307-6309)	Yes. (§ 14-6101)	Yes. A gift of goods or chat tel is not valid unless the gift is in writing, duly	Yes. Writing must be either in handwriting of or signed by testator and describe the

				acknowledged and recorded or by will, duly proved and recorded, or unless actual possession of the gift is passed to and remains with the donee or someone claiming under him. (§ 33-601)	items and devisees with reasonable certainty. The writing may be referred to as one to be in existence at the time of the testator's death, prepared before or after the execution of the will, or altered by the testator after its preparation. The writing may have no significance apart from its effect on the dispositions made by the will. (§ 14-2513)
Arkansas	Yes. (§ 23-47-204)	Yes. (§§ 28-14-107, 28-14-109)	Yes. (Slavik v. Estate of Slavik, 880 S.W.2d 524 (1994))	Yes, if proven by clear and convincing evidence that: (a) the donor was of sound mind; (b) an actual delivery of the property took place; (c) the donor clearly intended to make an immediate, present and final gift; (d) the donor unconditionally released all future dominion and control over the property; and (e) the donee accepted the gift. (Wright v. Union Nat. Bank of Arkansas, Little Rock, Ark., 819 S.W.2d 698, 700 (1991))	Yes. Writing must either be in the handwriting of or signed by testator and describe the items and devisees with reasonable certainty. The writing may be referred to as one to be in existence at the time of the testator's death, prepared before or after the execution of the will, or altered by the testator after its preparation. The writing may have no significance apart from its effect on the dispositions made by the will. (§ 28-25-107(b))
California	Yes. (Prob. § 5203)	Yes. (Prob. §§ 5000, 5500 etseq.)	Yes. (Prob. § 5000)	Yes. However, a verbal gift is not valid unless the means of obtaining posses sion and control of the thing are given nor if it is capable of delivery until there is actual and symbolic delivery of the thing to the donee. (Civ. § 1147)	Yes. (Prob. § 5000 (b)(3))

Table 5.01, Part 2
Principal Will Substitutes *(continued)*

Which of the Following Are Valid to Pass Property at Death without Complying with Wills Formalities?

	Payable on Death (P.O.D.) Bank Account?	*Transfer on Death (T.O.D.) Security Registration?*	*Life Insurance Proceeds?*	*Gift?*	*A Writing Disposing of Tangible Personal Property Even If Not Entirely in the Testator's Handwriting?*
Colorado	Yes. (§§ 15-15-212, 15-15-214)	Yes. (§§ 15-15-307, 15-15-309)	Yes. (§ 15-15-101)	Yes, the gift is valid if there is a clear and unmistakable intention to make a gift and a complete parting of possession and surrender by the donor of all control and dominion over the same to the donee. (Goemmer v. Hartman, 791P.2d 1238 (1990))	Yes. Writing must be either in the handwriting of or signed by testator and describe items and devisees with reasonable certainty. The writing may be referred to as one to be in existence at the time of the testator's death; it may be prepared before or after the execution of the will; it may be altered by the testator after its preparation; and it may be a writing that has no significance apart from its effect on the dispositions made by the will. (§ 15-11-513)
Connecticut	Yes. (§§ 45a-468e; 45a-468)	Yes. (§ 45a-468e-g)	Yes. (Dubno v. Colby, 458 A.2d 396 (1982))	Yes, if valid delivery accompanied by intent that title "pass immediately." (Bergen v. Bergen, 411 A.2d 22, 24 (1979))	No statute or cases on point. There would appear to be no authority in support of this being given effect.
Delaware	Yes. (12 §§ 804-805, 809)	Yes. (12 §§ 804-805, 809)	No statute or cases on point. Implied by 12 § 1901(c), which provides that if someone other than	Yes, if intent and "actual or constructive delivery of the gift during [the donor's] lifetime." The fact that	Yes. Writing must either be in the handwriting of or signed by testator and must identify the items and the

			the decedent or decedent's personal representative is designated as beneficiary, insurance proceeds are not included in decedent's estate and such person is entitled to the proceeds.	legal title to shares is not to be transferred until after the donor's death "does not make the gift testamentary," at least if the sole purpose of the arrangement was to enable the donor to retain dividend income during her lifetime. (Inre Estate of Surian, Civ. A. No. 9754, 1990 WL 100794 (Ch. 1990); Bothe v. Dennie, 324 A.2d 784, 786 (Super. 1974))	legatees with reasonable certainty. The writing may be one referred to as in existence at the time of the testator's death; it may be prepared before or after the execution of the will; it may be altered by the testator after the preparation; and it may be a writing which has no significance apart from its effect upon the dispositions made by the will. (12 § 212)
District of Columbia	Yes. (§ 19-602.12)	Yes. (§ 19-603.07)	Yes. (§ 19-601.01(a))	Yes. If donor has died must prove by clear and convincing evidence that there was delivery, intention on the part of the donor to make the gift, and absolute disposition of the subject of the gift. (Uckele v. Jewett, 642 A.2d 119 (1994))	No statute or cases on point. There would appear to be no authority in support of this being given effect.
Florida	Yes. (§ 655.82)	Yes. (§§ 711.507, 711.509)	Yes. (Gartley v. Gartley, 622 So. 2d 77 (1993))	Yes. (Canova v. Florida Nat'l Bank, 60 So. 2d 627 (1952) (in case of oral gift, need delivery, surrender by donor, intent to pass title))	Yes. Writing must be signed by testator and must describe the items with reasonable certainty. Testator may alter it after its preparation, and it may be a writing that has no significance apart from its effect on the dispositions made by the will. (§ 732.515)

Table 5.01, Part 2
Principal Will Substitutes *(continued)*

Which of the Following Are Valid to Pass Property at Death without Complying with Wills Formalities?

	Payable on Death (P.O.D.) Bank Account?	*Transfer on Death (T.O.D.) Security Registration?*	*Life Insurance Proceeds?*	*Gift?*	*A Writing Disposing of Tangible Personal Property Even If Not Entirely in the Testator's Handwriting?*
Georgia	Yes. (§§ 7-1-813(b), 7-1-815)	Yes. (§ 53-5-67)	Yes. (§ 33-25-11; National Life & Acc. Ins. Co. v. Thornton, 188 S.E.2d 435 (1972))	Yes, if the following requirements are satisfied: (a) the donor must intend to give the gift; (b) the donee must accept the gift; and (c) the gift must be delivered or some act which under the law is accepted as a substitute for delivery must be done. (§ 44-5-80)	No statute or cases on point. There would appear to be no authority in support of this being given effect.
Hawaii	Yes. (§§ 560:6-104(b), 560:6-106, 412:10-308)	Yes. (§§ 539-7, 539-9(a))	No statute or cases on point. But see § 431: 10D-114, pertaining to payment of premiums paid in advance and certain dividends to those the insurer deems "to be equitably entitled to such payment . . . ")	Yes, if delivery, acceptance, and intention to make a gift. (Welton v. Gallagher, 630 P.2d 1077 (1981))	Yes. Writing must be signed by testator and must describe the items and the devisees with reasonable certainty. The writing may be referred to as one to be in existence at the time of the testator's death; it may be prepared before or after the execution of the will; it may be altered by the testator after its preparation; and it may be a writing that has no significance apart from its effect on the dispositions made by the will. (§ 560:2-513)

Idaho	Yes. (§§ 15-6-104(b), 15-6-106)	Yes. (§§ 15-6-307, 15-6-309(1))	Yes. (§ 15-6-201)	Yes, if donor competent to contract, freedom of donor's will, a gift that is complete with nothing left undone, the property is delivered and accepted, and the gift goes into immediate and absolute effect. (Goggins v. Herndon, 249 P.2d 203 (1952))	Yes. Must either be in the handwriting of or signed by testator and must describe the items and the devisees with reasonable certainty. The writing may be referred to as one to be in existence at the time of the testator's death; it may be prepared before or after the execution of the will; it may be altered by the testator after its preparation; and it may be a writing which has no significance apart from its effect upon the dispositions made by the will. (§ 15-2-513)
Illinois	Yes. (205 ILCS § 625/4)	Yes. (815 ILCS §§ 10/7, 10/9(a))	Yes. (§ 755 ILCS § 30/1)	Yes, if show donative intent, delivery and acceptance. (Estate of Poliquin, 617 N.E.2d 40, 42-43 (1993))	No statute or cases on point. There would appear to be no authority in support of this being given effect.
Indiana	Yes. (§ 32-17-11-18)	Yes. (§§ 32-17-9-12, 32-17-9-14(a))	Yes. (§ 32-17-11-28)	Yes, if (a) donor is competent to contract, (b) there is freedom of will, (c) the gift is completed with nothing left undone, (d) there must be delivery, unless already in possession of donee, and acceptance, and (e) the gift must go into immediate and absolute effect. (Lewis v. Burke, 226 N.E.2d 332 (1967))	Yes, as long as referred to in a will (§ 29-1-6-1(m)) or in a revocable trust. (§ 30-4-2.1-11)

Table 5.01, Part 2
Principal Will Substitutes *(continued)*

Which of the Following Are Valid to Pass Property at Death without Complying with Wills Formalities?

	Payable on Death (P.O.D.) Bank Account?	*Transfer on Death (T.O.D.) Security Registration?*	*Life Insurance Proceeds?*	*Gift?*	*A Writing Disposing of Tangible Personal Property Even If Not Entirely in the Testator's Handwriting?*
Iowa	Yes. (§§ 633D.6, 633D.11)	Yes. (§§633D.5, 633D.6, 633D.11)	Yes. (§ 633.5)	Yes, if donative intent, delivery, and acceptance (Raim v. Stancel, 339 N.W.2d 621 (1983)); need present intent to make gift and divesting of all control and dominion over the property which is the subject of the gift (In re Estate of Crabtree, 550 N.W.2d 168, 170 (1996)).	Yes. Must either be in testator's handwriting or signed by testator. Must also be dated and must describe items and distributees with reasonable certainty. (§ 633.276)
Kansas	Yes. (§ 9-1215)	Yes. (§§ 17-49a07, 17-49a09)	Yes. (§ 59-3513(a)(1))	The prerequisites for an intervivos gift are (a) an intent to make a gift; (b) a delivery by the donor to the donee; and (c) an acceptance by the donee. (In re Estate of Button, 830 P.2d 1216, 1218 (1992))	Yes. Writing must be in handwriting of testator or be signed by testator and must describe the items with reasonable certainty. The writing may be referred to as in existence at the time of the testator's death; it may be prepared before or after the execution of the will; and the testator may alter it after its preparation. (§ 59-623)
Kentucky	Yes. (§§ 391.315, 391.325)	Yes. (§§ 292.6507, 292.6509)	Yes. (§ 391.360)	A valid gift must include: (a) a donor competent to make gift; (b) a donee capable of taking it; (c) an intent on the part of the	No statute or cases on point. There would appear to be no authority in support of this being given effect.

				donor to absolutely and irrevocably divest himself of title, dominion, and control of gift in praesentia; (d) irrevocable transfer of legal title and dominion to donee; and (e) delivery by donor to donee, and an acceptance by donee. (Bryant's Adm'r v. Bryant, 269 S.W.2d 219, 221 (1954))	
Louisiana[1]	Yes, but limited to case where beneficiary is spouse, child, grandchild, parent, or sibling. (Rev. Stat. § 6:766.1)	No, although this is under study.	Yes. For example, the law affords the opportunity to make proceeds payable to a trustee and this trust is deemed inter vivos and not testamentary. (Rev. Stat. App. 9:1816)	Yes, if simultaneous occurrence of donor's intent to give and actual possession by delivery. (Adams v. Sec. Ins. Co., 533 So. 2d 140 (Ct. App. 1988); Montet v. Lyles, 638 So. 2d 727 (Ct. App. 1994)) No formalities are required. (Civ. Code Art. 1539)	No statute or cases on point. There would appear to be no authority in support of this being given effect.
Maine	Yes. (18A §§ 6-104(b), 6-106)	Yes. (18A §§ 6-308, 6-310)	Yes. (18-A § 6-201)	To constitute a valid gift inter vivos, donor must part with all present and future dominion over the property given. There must be a delivery to the donee or to someone for the donee, and gift must be absolute and irrevocable, without any reference to its taking effect at some future period. (Rose v. Osborne, 180 A. 315, 317 (1935))	Yes. Writing must either be in the handwriting of or signed by testator and must describe items and devisees with reasonable certainty. Writing may be referred to as one to be in existence at time of testator's death; it may be prepared before or after the execution of the will; it may be altered by the testator after its preparation; it may be a writing which has no significance apart from its effect upon the dispositions made by the will. (18A § 2-513)

Table 5.01, Part 2
Principal Will Substitutes *(continued)*

Which of the Following Are Valid to Pass Property at Death without Complying with Wills Formalities?

	Payable on Death (P.O.D.) Bank Account?	*Transfer on Death (T.O.D.) Security Registration?*	*Life Insurance Proceeds?*	*Gift?*	*A Writing Disposing of Tangible Personal Property Even If Not Entirely in the Testator's Handwriting?*
Maryland	Yes. (Fin. Inst. Code § 1-204, Tr. & Est. Code § 1-401)	Yes. (Tr. & Est. Code §§ 16-107, 16-109)	Yes, as to contracts generally. (Reece v. Reece, 212 A.2d 468 (1965))	For valid gift, five factors are needed: a clear intent on the part of the donor; a gratuitous, unconditional transfer of possession; an immediate transfer of title; a delivery of title to the donee; an acceptance of the gift by the donee. (Dulany v. Taylor, 660 A.2d 1046, 1052 (1995))	No statute or cases on point. There would appear to be no authority in support of this being given effect.
Massachusetts	No statute or cases on point.	Yes. (201E §§ 201, 302)	Yes. (Stiles v. Stiles, 487 N.E.2d 874 (1986))	Can even have parol gift, if donor has intent, delivery that is actual or symbolic, all done in manner to transfer during life complete dominion and control. (Kobrosky v. Crystal, 125 N.E.2d 385 (1957))	No statute or cases on point. There would appear to be no authority in support of this being given effect.
Michigan	Yes. (§§ 700.6304, 700.6305, 700.6309)	Yes. (§§ 700.6304, 700.6305, 700.6309)	Yes. (§ 700.6101(1))	There must be intent to pass title to donee, there must be actual or constructive delivery, and there must be acceptance by the donee. (In re Munsinger Estate, 506 N.W.2d 238 (1993))	Yes. Testator must sign writing, and it must describe items and devisees with reasonable certainty. Writing may be referred to as one in existence at time of testator's death, may be prepared before or after the execution

					of the will, may be altered by the testator after its incorporation, and may be a writing which has no significance apart from dispositions made by will. (§ 700.2513)
Minnesota	Yes. (§§ 524.6-204(b), 524.6-206)	Yes. (§§ 524.6-307, 524.6-309)	No statute or cases on point.	Key elements are donative intent; delivery of gift; and absolute disposition of the property. (Cooke v. Belzer, 413 N.W.2d 623 (1987))	Yes. Writing must be in hand writing of the testator or be signed by the testator and must describe the items and devisees with reasonable certainty. Writing may be referred to as one in existence at the time of testator's death, prepared before execution of the will, altered by the testator after preparation, and may be a writing which has no significance apart from its effect on dispositions made by will. (§ 524.2-513)
Mississippi	Yes. (§§ 81-5-63, 81-5-62)	Yes. (§§ 91-21-15, 91-21-19)	Yes. (Jones v. Patty, 18 So. 794 (1895))	Property must have been transferred so that the donor surrendered all dominion over it during lifetime; alternatively, the gift must have been made in contemplation of death in the case of a gift cause mortis. (Gilder v. First Nat'l Bank, 214 So. 2d 681, 683 (1968))	No statute or cases on point. There would appear to be no authority in support of this being given effect.

Table 5.01, Part 2
Principal Will Substitutes *(continued)*

Which of the Following Are Valid to Pass Property at Death without Complying with Wills Formalities?

	Payable on Death (P.O.D.) Bank Account?	*Transfer on Death (T.O.D.) Security Registration?*	*Life Insurance Proceeds?*	*Gift?*	*A Writing Disposing of Tangible Personal Property Even If Not Entirely in the Testator's Handwriting?*
Missouri	Yes. (§ 362.471)	Yes. (§§ 461.028, 461.031)	Yes. (§§ 461.001, 461.009)	Yes, if present intention to make gift on part of donor to donee, acceptance by donee, and ownership takes effect immediately and absolutely. (Kennedy v. Milligan, 915 S.W.2d 784 (1996))	Yes. (§ 461.026)
Montana	Yes. (§§ 72-6-212, 72-6-214)	Yes. (§§ 72-6-307, 72-6-309)	Yes. (§ 72-6-111)	Yes, if intention to make gift, delivery, and acceptance. (Patterson v. Halterman, 505 P.2d 905 (1973))	Yes. Writing must be signed by testator and must describe the items and the devisees with reasonable certainty. The writing may be: referred to as one to be in existence at the time of the testator's death; prepared before or after the execution of the will; altered by the testator after its preparation; it may be a writing that has no significance apart from its effect upon the dispositions made by the will. (§ 72-2-533)
Nebraska	Yes. (§§ 30-2723(b), 30-2725)	Yes. (§§ 30-2715, 30-2742)	Yes. (§ 30-2715)	Yes, if intention to transfer title, delivery, and	Yes. Writing must have an indication of the date of the writing or signing and, in the

				acceptance. (Ralston v. Marget, 293 N.W. 124 (1940))	absence of such indication of date, be the only such writing or contain no inconsistency with any other old writing or permit determination of such date of writing or signing from the content of such writing, from extrinsic circumstances, or from other evidence, must either be in the handwriting of the testator or be signed by him, and must describe the items and the devisees with reasonable certainty. (§ 30-2338)
Nevada	Yes. (§§ 111.590–111.620)	Yes. (§§ 111.590–111.620)	No statute or cases on point.	Yes, if intent to make gift, actual constructive or symbolic delivery of the property in the donor's lifetime to be given without power of revocation. (Edmonds v. Perry, 140 P.2d 566 (1943))	Yes. Writing must have title indicating purpose, date of execution, reference to will to which it relates, reasonable description of items to be disposed of and the legatees, and must have testator's handwritten or electronic signature. The writing may be referred to as a writing in existence at the time of the testator's death, prepared before or after the execution of the will, altered by testator after its preparation, be a writing which has no significance apart from its effect upon the dispositions made by the will. (§ 133.045)

Table 5.01, Part 2
Principal Will Substitutes *(continued)*

	Which of the Following Are Valid to Pass Property at Death without Complying with Wills Formalities?				
	Payable on Death (P.O.D.) Bank Account?	*Transfer on Death (T.O.D.) Security Registration?*	*Life Insurance Proceeds?*	*Gift?*	*A Writing Disposing of Tangible Personal Property Even If Not Entirely in the Testator's Handwriting?*
New Hampshire	Yes. (§§ 563-C:5, 563-C:6, 563-C:10)	Yes. (§§ 563-C:5, 563-C:6, 563-C:10)	Yes. "In the normal course of events persons will use a deed, mortgage, note or contract as a substitute for accomplishing the same purpose by will. When a will is employed we require compliance with the statute of wills. But when a contractual undertaking is employed we do not declare it invalid because it accomplished in part what could have been accomplished by the use of a will." (McGrath v. McGrath, 220 A.2d 760, 762 (1966))	Yes. (Abbott v. Watson, 202 A.2d 476 (1967)) The requirements for a valid gift are: a manifestation of the donor to give, and an unconditional deliver and acceptance of the gift. (Nashua Tr. Co. v. Mosgovian, 79 A.2d 636, 637 (1951)) Other requirements stated are a voluntary transfer, no consideration, and perfected delivery of either the property or a deed. (Curriden v. Chandler, 108 A. 296 (1919)) Gifts causa mortis not valid unless actual delivery proved by two indifferent witnesses, upon petition of donee to the judge to establish the gift, filed within 60 days of death of donor. (§ 551:17)	No statute or cases on point. There would appear to be no authority in support of this being given effect.
New Jersey	Yes. (§17:16I-5(b)) P.O.D. account is defined in § 17:16I-2(j).	Yes. (§§ 3B:30-5, 3B:30-6, 3B:30-8, 3B:30-10)	Yes. (In re Posey's Estate, 214 A.2d 713, 718 (1965))	Yes, if there is donative intention, delivery, and to the extent an intangible is involved, the donor's	Yes. Writing must either be in the handwriting of or signed by testator and must describe the items and the

				stripping himself of all dominion over the property. (In re Posey's Estate, 214 A.2d 713, 719 (1965))	devisees with reasonable certainty. The writing may be referred to as one in existence at the time of the testator's death; it may be prepared before or after the execution of the will; it may be altered by the testator after its preparation; and it may be a writing which has no significance apart from its effect upon the dispositions made by the will. (§ 3B:3-11)
New Mexico	Yes. (§§ 45-6-212, 45-6-214)	Yes. (§§ 45-6-307, 45-6-309)	Yes. (§ 45-6-101)	Yes. Elements of gift are: property subject to gift; a donor competent to make a gift; donative intent not induced by force or fraud; delivery; acceptance by a competent donee; and a present gift fully executed. (Espinoza v. Petritis, 373 P.2d 820 (1962))	Yes. Writing must be signed by testator and describe items with reasonable certainty. The writing may be referred to as in existence at time of testator's death, it may be prepared either before or after execution of will, the writing can be altered by testator after preparation, or can be a writing that has no significance apart from dispositions made by will. (§ 45-2-513)
New York	No. (In re Peno's Estate, 221 N.Y.S. 205, 217 (Sur. Ct. 1927))	Yes. (In re Estate of Crystal, 348 N.Y.S.2d 717, 719 (Sur. Ct. 1973), *aff'd*, 363 N.Y.S.2d 311 (1974))	Yes. (In re Alvord's Estate, 416 N.Y.S.2d 196 (1979))	Yes, if intent to make an immediate gift, a delivery of the thing given, and an acceptance of the gift, which involves renunciation by donor and acquisition by donee of interest in	No. (In re Eldridge's Will, 64 N.Y.S.2d 234 (1946))

(cont'd)

Table 5.01, Part 2
Principal Will Substitutes *(continued)*

Which of the Following Are Valid to Pass Property at Death without Complying with Wills Formalities?

	Payable on Death (P.O.D.) Bank Account?	*Transfer on Death (T.O.D.) Security Registration?*	*Life Insurance Proceeds?*	*Gift?*	*A Writing Disposing of Tangible Personal Property Even If Not Entirely in the Testator's Handwriting?*
New York *(cont'd)*				and title to subject of gift. (In re Peno's Estate, 221 N.Y.S. 205, 217 (Sur. Ct. 1927))	
North Carolina	Yes. § 53-146.2	Yes. (§ 41-2.2(b)(2)(i))	Yes. Implied in Ballard v. Lance, 169 S.E.2d 199, 202 (Ct. App. 1969). See also Janet McLamb & Lisa K. Vira, Edwards' N.C. Prob. Handbook, § 18:4 (updated 2003)	Yes, if two key elements are present, donative intent and actual or constructive delivery. (Creekmore v. Creekmore, 485 S.E.2d 68 (1997))	No statute or cases on point. There would appear to be no authority in support of this being given effect.
North Dakota	Yes. (§§ 30.1-31-09, 30.1-31-11)	Yes. (§§ 30.1-31-24, 30.1-31-27)	Yes. (§ 30.1-31-01)	Yes, if the following elements are satisfied: donative intent; delivery, actual or constructive; and acceptance of the gift by donee. (In re Paulson's Estate, 219 N.W.2d 132 (1974))	Yes. Writing must be signed by testator and must describe the items and devisees with reasonable certainty. Writing may be referred to as one in existence at the time of the testator's death; it may be prepared before or after the execution of the will; it may be altered by the testator after preparation; and it may be a writing that has no significance apart from its effect on the dispositions made by the will. (§ 30.1-08-13)

Ohio	Yes. (§ 1109.07)	Yes. (§§ 1709.07, 1709.09)	Yes. (In re Gilger's Estate, 109 N.E.2d 333 (1952))	Yes, if (a) intention to transfer title and right to possession, (b) delivery of property to donee along with relinquishment of ownership, dominion and control over it. (Lauerman v. Destocki, 622 N.E.2d 1122 (1993))	No statute or cases on point. There would appear to be no authority in support of this being given effect.
Oklahoma	Yes. (6 Okla. St. § 901)	Yes. (71 Okla. St. §§ 905, 906, 908, 910)	No statute or cases directly on point, although implied by Graham v. Farmers New World Life Ins. Co., 841 P.2d 1165, 1167-68 (Ct. App. 1992) (insurance contracts are governed by contract law).	A valid gift is one in which the following elements are satisfied: intention to give, complete delivery of the property given, and acceptance by the donee. (McSpadden v. Mahoney, 431 P.2d 432 (1961)) There is not a gift if the donor retains "right of complete control and dominion, and especially the right to take back the 'gift' at any time." (Thomas v. Bank of Oklahoma, 684 P.2d 553, 554 (1984))	No statute or cases on point. There would appear to be no authority in support of this being given effect.
Oregon	Yes. (§§ 708A.470, 708A.480)	Yes. (§§ 59.565, 59.575)	Yes. (Gordon v. Portland Tr. Co., 271 P.2d 653, 655 (1954))	Yes, a gift is valid if there is (a) donative intent, (b) delivery of the property to the donee, (c) intent that the donee have a present interest in it, and (d) acceptance by the donee. (Kesterson v. Cronan, 806 P.2d 134, 136 (1991))	No statute or cases on point. There would appear to be no authority in support of this being given effect.

Table 5.01, Part 2
Principal Will Substitutes *(continued)*

Which of the Following Are Valid to Pass Property at Death without Complying with Wills Formalities?

	Payable on Death (P.O.D.) Bank Account?	*Transfer on Death (T.O.D.) Security Registration?*	*Life Insurance Proceeds?*	*Gift?*	*A Writing Disposing of Tangible Personal Property Even If Not Entirely in the Testator's Handwriting?*
Pennsylvania	No. However, court may seek to convert it to inter vivos gift creating joint survivorship account. (Nemcek v. Central City Nat. Bank, 149 A.2d 533 (1959))	Yes. (20 §§ 6407, 6409)	Yes. (20 § 6108)	Yes, if donative intent and delivery. (In re Estate of Petro, 694 A.2d 627 (1997))	No statute or cases on point. There would appear to be no authority in support of this being given effect.
Rhode Island	No statute or cases on point.	Yes. (§§ 7-11.1-8, 7-11.1-10)	Yes. (§ 27-4-11; Murino v. Reynolds, 550 A.2d 1058 (1988)) Note, however, that the same may not be true for other contracts. (Combined Ins. Co. v. Salisbury, 224 A.2d 383 (1966))	Yes. (People's Savings Bank v. Webb, 42 A. 874 (1899); Barrett v. Barrett, 894 A.2d 891 (2006))	No statute or cases on point. There would appear to be no authority in support of this being given effect.
South Carolina	Yes. (§§ 62-6-104(b), 62-6-106)	Yes. (§§ 35-6-70, 35-6-90(A))	Yes. (§ 62-6-201)	Yes. See Worrell v. Lathan, 478 S.E.2d 287, 288 (1996) ("gifts inter vivos and cause mortis must be fully and completely executed, that is, there must be a donative intent to transfer title to the property, a delivery by the donor, and an acceptance by the donee").	Yes. Must either be in the handwriting of or signed by testator and describe items and devisees with reasonable certainty. The writing may be referred to as one to be in existence at the time of the testator's death; it may be prepared before or after the execution of the will; it may be altered by the testator after its preparation; and it may be a writing which has no significance

					apart from its effect upon the disposition made by the will. (§ 62-2-512)
South Dakota	Yes. (§§ 29A-6-104(2), 29A-6-106)	Yes. (§§ 29A-6-307, 29A-6-309)	Yes. (§ 29A-6-113)	Yes, if intention, delivery, and acceptance. (Bunt v. Fairbanks, 134 N.W.2d 1 (1965))	Yes. Writing must be signed by the testator and must describe the items and the devisees with reasonable certainty. The writing may be referred to as in existence at the time of the testator's death; it may be prepared before or after the execution of the will; it may be altered by the testator after its preparation; and it may be a writing that has no significance apart from its effect on the dispositions made by the will. (§ 29A-2-513)
Tennessee	Yes. (§ 45-2-704) However, this refers to deposits in trust, so that §§ 35-12-108, 35-12-110 may be more pertinent in certain circumstances.	Yes. (§§ 35-12-108, 35-12-110)	Yes. (Cook v. Cook, 521 S.W.2d 808 (1975))	Yes, if there is (a) an intention on the part of the donor to make a gift and (b) the intent must be accompanied by delivery of the property. (Estate of Bowlin v. Ables, 766 S. W.2d 193 (1988))	No statute or cases on point. There would appear to be no authority in support of this being given effect.
Texas	Yes. (Prob. §§ 439, 441, 446)	Yes. (Prob. § 450(a)) However, this provision has been interpreted as not allowing "testamentary disposition of a person's entire estate, including real property, without the requirements of a will or	Yes. (Prob. § 450)	Yes, if intention of donor to make gift, the delivery of the gift to the donee, and the acceptance by the donee of the property. (Dorman v. Arnold, 932 S.W.2d 225 (1996))	No statute or cases on point. There would appear to be no authority in support of this being given effect.

(cont'd)

Table 5.01, Part 2
Principal Will Substitutes *(continued)*

Which of the Following Are Valid to Pass Property at Death without Complying with Wills Formalities?

	Payable on Death (P.O.D.) Bank Account?	*Transfer on Death (T.O.D.) Security Registration?*	*Life Insurance Proceeds?*	*Gift?*	*A Writing Disposing of Tangible Personal Property Even If Not Entirely in the Testator's Handwriting?*
Texas *(cont'd)*		the formalities of will execution." The section allows nontestamentary transfers of "property," "money," or "other benefits," but does not allow nontestamentary transfers of a person's entire estate. In the case, a document attempted in the form of an antenuptial agreement to give the drafter's estate to his wife if they were not separated or divorced at his death.			
Utah	Yes. (§§ 75-6-104(2), 75-6-106)	Yes. (§§ 75-6-308, 75-6-310)	Yes. (§ 75-6-201)	Yes, if it enters into immediate and absolute effect. It involves the donor divesting himself and the donee investing himself with the right of property in the subject of the gift. It must be absolute, irrevocable, and without any reference to its taking place at some future period. The donor has to deliver the property, and part with all present and	Yes. Writing must be signed by testator and must describe the devisees with reasonable certainty. The writing may be referred to as one to be in existence at the time of the testator's death; it may be prepared before or after the execution of the will; it may be altered by the testator after its preparation; and it may be a writing which has no significance

				future dominion over it. (Helper State Bank v. Crus, 81 P.2d 359 (1938))	apart from its effect upon the dispositions made by the will. (§ 75-2-513)
Vermont	Yes. (8 § 14205)	Yes. (9 §§ 4357, 4359)	No statute or cases on point.	The elements of a valid inter vivos gift are: (a) manifest intention to create in the donee a present interest during the joint lives of the donor and donee; (b) an unconditional delivery or divestiture of the thing transferred; and (c) acceptance by the donee. Acceptance is presumed if the first two elements are established. (In re Estate of Adams, 587 A.2d 958, 960 (1990))	No statute or cases on point. There would appear to be no authority in support of this being given effect.
Virginia	Yes. (§§ 6.1-125.5(B), 6.1-125.7)	Yes. (§§ 64.1-206.5, 64.1-206.7)	Yes. (Abbott v. Willey, 479 S.E.2d 528, 529 (1997) (treating policy as nontestamentary instrument); Short v. A. H. Still Inv. Corp., 147 S.E.2d 99 (1966) (relating generally to contracts))	Yes. However, in order for there to be a valid gift, there must be an intention to make a present gift accompanied by a delivery of the thing given or the means of obtaining it. A gift cannot be made to take effect in possession in the future. That would be only a promise to make a gift, and being without consideration is invalid. (Payne v. Tobacco Trading Corp., 18 S.E.2d 281 (1942))	Yes. Writing must be signed by testator and must describe items with reasonable certainty. (§ 64.1-45.1)

Table 5.01, Part 2
Principal Will Substitutes *(continued)*

Which of the Following Are Valid to Pass Property at Death without Complying with Wills Formalities?

	Payable on Death (P.O.D.) Bank Account?	*Transfer on Death (T.O.D.) Security Registration?*	*Life Insurance Proceeds?*	*Gift?*	*A Writing Disposing of Tangible Personal Property Even If Not Entirely in the Testator's Handwriting?*
Washington	Yes. (§ 30.22.100)	Yes. (§ 21.35.045)	Yes. (§ 11.02.091)	Yes, but only if: (a) an intention of the donor to presently give; (b) a subject matter capable of passing by delivery; (c) an actual delivery; and (d) an acceptance by the donee. (Brin v. Stutzman, 951 P.2d 291, 300 (Ct. App. 1998))	Yes. Will refers to the writing; writing is in handwriting of or signed by testator; and writing describes the items and recipients of property with reasonable certainty. (§ 11.12.260)
West Virginia	Yes. (§ 31A-4-33(a))	Yes. (§§ 36-10-7, 36-10-9)	Yes. (Equitable Trust Co. v. Epling, 167 S.E. 820 (1933); Transamerica Occidental Life Ins. Co. v. Burke, 368 S.E.2d 301, 304 (1988))	Yes, but valid only if made by a writing, signed by donor or his agent, or unless actual possession shall have come to and remained with donee or some person holding for or under him. (§ 36-1-5) However, apart from the statute, case law provides that three requirements must be satisfied: (a) an intention on the part of the donor to make a gift; (b) a delivery or transfer of the subject matter of the gift; and (c) acceptance. Sleigh v. Sleigh, 445 S.E.2d 509, 513 (1994))	No statute or cases on point. There would appear to be no authority in support of this being given effect.

Wisconsin	Yes. (§ 705.04)	Yes. (§§ 705.27, 705.29)	Yes. (§ 705.20)	Yes, if there is: (a) an intention to give on the part of the donor; (b) delivery, actual or constructive, to the donee; (c) termination of the donor's dominion over the subject of the gift; and (d) dominion in the donee. (In re Reist's Estate, 281 N.W.2d 86 (1979))	Yes. It must be signed and dated by the decedent. (§ 853.32(2))
Wyoming	Yes. (§ 2-1-203(d))	Yes. (§§ 2-16-108, 2-16-110)	No statute or cases on point.	Yes, if: (a) there is a present intention of the donor to make an immediate gift; (b) actual or constructive delivery of the gift that divests the donor of dominion and control; and (c) acceptance of the gift. (Rose v. Rose, 849 P.2d 1321 (1993))	Writing must be dated, be signed by testator, and include a description of the items and devisees with reasonable certainty. (§ 2-6-124)

1. *Caution:* A civil law system with very different concepts is followed. Even though common-law concepts like the trust have been recognized statutorily, they may be approached very differently.

Table 5.02
Incorporation by Reference and Facts of Independent Significance

	Incorporation by Reference?	*Facts of Independent Significance?*
Alabama	Yes. Writing must be in existence when will is executed. Will must describe writing sufficiently to identify it. Language of will must manifest intent to incorporate existing writing. (§ 43-8-139)	Yes. (§ 43-8-141)
Alaska	Yes. Language of will must manifest intent to incorporate existing writing. Will must contain sufficient description to identify writing. (§ 13.12.510)	Yes. (§ 13.12.512)
Arizona	Yes. Writing must exist at time testator executes will, will must manifest intent to incorporate document, and will must identify document with sufficient specificity to allow its identification. (§ 14-25-10)	Yes. (§ 14-2512)
Arkansas	Yes. Writing must be in existence when will is executed. Language of will must manifest intent to incorporate and writing must be sufficiently described to permit its identification. (§ 28-25-107)	No statute or case on point.
California	Yes. Writing must be in existence when will is executed. Will must describe writing sufficiently to identify it. Language of will must manifest intent to incorporate existing writing. (Prob. § 6130)	Yes. (Prob. § 6131)
Colorado	Yes. Writing must exist when will is executed, as language of will manifests intent to incorporate it and writing is sufficiently described to identify it. (§ 15-11-510)	Yes. (§ 15-11-512)
Connecticut	Yes. "Essential that it be in existence at the time the will is executed, and that it be so clearly and precisely described and referred to therein, as an existing document, as to be readily identified as the one, particular paper intended by the testator." The letter in this case was not sufficient to be an incorporation by reference. (Appeal of Bryan, 58 A. 748 (1904))	No statute or case on point.
Delaware	Yes. (Walsh v. St. Joseph's Home for Aged, 303 A.2d 691, 694 (Ch. 1973))	Yes. (Walsh v. St. Joseph's Home for Aged, 303 A.2d 691, 694 (Ch. 1973))
District of Columbia	Yes. (Vestry of St. John's Parish v. Bostwick, 8 App. D.C. 452 (1896))	No statute or case on point.

Florida	Yes. Writing in existence when will executed, will manifests intent to incorporate writing, writing is sufficiently identified by will. (§ 732.512(1))	Yes. (§ 732.512(2))
Georgia	No statute or case on point.	No statute or case on point.
Hawaii	Yes. (§ 560:2-510)	Yes. (§ 560:2-512)
Idaho	Yes. Writing in existence at will execution, language of will manifests intent to incorporate document, and will sufficiently describes document. (§ 15-2-510)	Yes. (§ 15-2-512)
Illinois	Yes. (In re Meskimen's Estate, 235 N.E.2d 619 (1968))	Yes. (In re Meskimen's Estate, 235 N.E.2d 619 (1968))
Indiana	Yes. (§ 29-1-6-1(h))	Yes. (§ 29-1-6-1(i))
Iowa	Yes. (In re Cameron's Estate, 241 N.W. 458 (1932))	No statute or case on point.
Kansas	Yes. (Shulsky v. Shulsky, 157 P. 407, 408 (1916))	No statute or case on point. Mentioned but not ruled on in In re Trusteeship of Will of Daniels, 247 Kan. 349, 350, 799 P.2d 479, 483 (Kan. 1990).
Kentucky	Yes. It is a ''well-recognized principle.'' (Scott v. Gastright, 204 S.W.2d 367)	Although mentioned favorably, it has not been explicitly endorsed. (Strouse v. First Nat'l Bank, 245 S.W.2d 914, 920 (1952))
Louisiana	Uncertain. A will can refer to another writing for the purpose of making certain the object referred to is in the will, but not for incorporating the writing into the will. (Hessner v. Edenborn, 199 So. 647, 650-51 (1940); Hall v. Hill, 6 La. Ann. 745 (1851)) It is allowed for trusts. (Rev. Stat. 9:1755)	No statute or case on point.
Maine	Yes. Writing must be in existence when will is executed, will must have language of intent to incorporate writing, and must describe writing sufficiently to permit its identification. (18A § 2-510)	Yes. (18A § 2-512)
Maryland	Yes. Writing must be in existence when a will or trust is executed. Writing may be incorporated to extent language of will manifests an intent to do so; describes the writing sufficiently to permit its identification. (§ 4-107)	No statute or case on point.
Massachusetts	Yes. (Taft v. Stearns, 125 N.E. 570 (1920))	No statute or case on point.
Michigan	Yes. Writing must be in existence when will is executed, will must manifest intent to incorporate writing, and must identify it sufficiently. (§ 700.2510)	Yes. (§ 700.2512)

Table 5.02
Incorporation by Reference and Facts of Independent Significance *(continued)*

	Incorporation by Reference?	*Facts of Independent Significance?*
Minnesota	Yes. (§ 524.2-510)	Yes. (§ 524.2-512)
Mississippi	Yes. However, note negative consequences if incorporation into an otherwise holographic will. (Hewes v. Hewes, 71 So. 4 (1916))	No statute or case on point.
Missouri	Yes. (Rosenblum v. Gibbons, 685 S.W.2d 924, 929 (Ct. App. 1984))	Yes. (Rosenblum v. Gibbons, 685 S.W.2d 924, 929 (Ct. App. 1984))
Montana	Yes. Writing in existence when will is executed, language of will manifests intent to incorporate, and will describes writing sufficiently. (§ 72-2-530)	Yes. (§ 72-2-532)
Nebraska	Yes. Writing must be in existence when will is executed, language in willmanifests intent to incorporate writing, and will describes writing sufficiently. (§ 30-2335)	Yes. (§ 30-2337)
Nevada	No statute or case on point.	No statute or case on point.
New Hampshire	Yes. (In re Estate of Came, 529 A.2d 962, 964–65 (N.H. 1987))	No statute or case on point.
New Jersey	Yes. Any writing in existence when will is executed may be incorporated by reference if the language of the will manifests this intent and describes the writing sufficiently. (§ 3B:3-10)	Yes. (§ 3B:3-12)
New Mexico	Yes. A will may incorporate by reference the provisions of the Uniform Statutory Will Act. (§ 45-2A-4) Writing in existence, intent to incorporate in language of will, reason ably identified writings. (§ 45-2-510)	Yes. (§ 45-2-512)
New York	Generally, the doctrine is not recognized in New York. (Booth v. Baptist Church, 28 N.E. 238 (Ct. App. 1891); In re Estate of O'Brien, 649 N.Y.S.2d 220 (App. Div. 1996)) There are exceptions, such as for pourovers to certain trusts. (Est. Powers & Trusts § 3-3.7))	No statute or case on point.

North Carolina	Yes. (In re Estate of Norton, 410 S.E.2d 487 (1991))	No statute or case on point.
North Dakota	Yes. Writing must be in existence when will executed. Language of will must manifest intent to incorporate writing and must sufficiently identify it. (§ 30.1-08-10)	Yes. (§ 30.1-08-12)
Ohio	Yes. An existing document, book, record, or memorandum may be incorporated in a will by reference if referred to as being in existence at time the will is executed. (§ 2107.05)	Yes. While the theory is recognized, it may not be applied. For example, it would not save a pour over to a trust that is unfunded at the testator's death. (Hageman v. Cleveland Tr. Co., 343 N.E.2d 121, 123-24 (1976))
Oklahoma	Yes. (Miller v. First Nat'l Bank & Trust Co., 637 P.2d 75 (1981))	No statute or case on point. In In re Estate of Richardson, 50 P.3d 584, 588 n.9 (Ct. App. 2002) the court stated that the facts of independent significance doctrine has not been applied in any Oklahoma case. It declined to apply it to overcome a pretermitted heirship statute where the testator explicitly omitted a son in an amendment to an inter vivos trust previously incorporated by reference into a will.
Oregon	Yes. The intention to incorporate, and not mere mention of preexisting document, must clearly appear from the will. (Witham v. Witham, 66 P.2d 281 (1937))	No statute or case on point.
Pennsylvania	Yes. (Estate of Pew, 655 A.2d 521, 547 (1994))	No statute or case on point.
Rhode Island	Yes. (Ind. Nat'l Bank v. R.I. Hosp., 207 A.2d 286, 293 (R.I. 1965))	No statute or case on point.
South Carolina	Yes. Writing must be in existence when will is executed and language of will must manifest intent to incorporate; will must describe writing sufficiently to identify it. (§ 62-2-509)	Yes. (§ 62-2-511)
South Dakota	Yes. Writing must be in existence when will is executed, language of will manifests intent to incorporate writing, will describes the writing sufficiently to permit its identification. (§ 29A-2-510)	Yes. (§ 29A-2-512)
Tennessee	Yes. (Goodwin v. Naveil, 912 S.W.2d 719 (Ct. App. 1995))	Yes. (In re Will of Tipler, 105 S.W.3d 244, 245 (Ct. App. 1998))
Texas	Yes. (Brooker v. Brooker, 106 S.W.2d 247 (1937))	Yes. (Welch v. Trustees of Robt. A. Welch Foundation, 465 S.W.2d 195, 200–01 (1971))

Table 5.02
Incorporation by Reference and Facts of Independent Significance *(continued)*

	Incorporation by Reference?	*Facts of Independent Significance?*
Utah	Yes. Writing must be in existence at time will is executed and language of will manifests intent and describes writing sufficiently to permit its identification. (§ 75-2-510)	Yes. (§ 75-2-512)
Vermont	Possibly, but the law as to incorporation by reference in a will ''remains undeveloped.'' (In re Will of Norris, 183 A.2d 519, 521 (1962))	No statute or case on point.
Virginia	Yes. (Thrasher v. Thrasher, 118 S.E.2d 820 (1961))	No statute or case on point.
Washington	Yes. Writing in existence when will is executed, will manifests intent to incorporate writing, and describes writing sufficiently. If conflict between writing and will, the will controls. (§ 11.12.255)	No statute or case on point.
West Virginia	Yes. (Wible v. Ashcroft, 178 S.E. 516 (1935))	No statute or case on point.
Wisconsin	Yes. (In re Erbach's Estate, 164 N.W.2d 238 (1969))	No statute or case on point.
Wyoming	Generally, no statute or case on point. It is expressly allowed in some circumstances, such as gifts for religious and educational uses. (§ 34-5-115)	No statute or case on point.

Table 6
The Rights of a Spouse
(current through 5/1/07)

A client may choose not to leave his entire estate or even a substantial portion of it to his surviving spouse. He may place the interest in trust or impose other restrictions that the surviving spouse finds unappealing. Under the law of states that do not have community property regimes, the surviving spouse may be entitled to elect to take a statutory share rather than be governed by the terms of the will.

Tables 6.01–6.04 explore various aspects of rights accorded a surviving spouse. Table 6.01 inquires into whether the state continues to give recognition to the common law rights of dower and curtesy. It also inventories other measures protective of the family afforded by the state, including homestead, exempt property, and family allowance. However, as this table makes clear, the elective share and these other benefits cannot be viewed in isolation. The availability of one may reduce another.

With particular regard to the statutory right to elect against the will, technical requirements must, typically, be satisfied in order to obtain a share of the estate. These requirements, addressed in Table 6.02, relate to when, what, and with whom must a filing be made. Also, the spouse may not survive long enough or may be incapable to make the election. The table considers who, if anyone, can make the election for the spouse.

In addition to these and other technical matters, the actual calculation of the elective share is examined in Table 6.03. One aspect of this inquiry is the often-complex computation of the base against which the percentage or fractional share of the surviving spouse is multiplied. The base itself may not be limited to the probate estate, but may include various testamentary substitutes, often described as the augmented estate. It may also hinge on the number of years the spouses have been married. Knowledge of the constitutive elements of the base are critical from a planning standpoint to the client who wishes to limit the surviving spouse's elective share claims against the estate. Moreover, the surviving spouse's obligation in some states to take account of her own estate in calculating her elective share and to satisfy any right first from property left to her in the will is also a critical issue. To the extent the surviving spouse is not so constrained, the exercise of any statutory right may have a dire impact on the decedent's dispositive plan. The table explores who bears the burden of satisfying the elective share claim in this situation.

The table also considers how the elective share is calculated and the degree to which it is even available when there is property in more than one state or one or both of the spouses was domiciled outside of the state in which the claim for an elective share has been made. To date, these highly intricate matters have received little attention, although the issues are present in many estates. Much as with multijurisdictional taxation, the possibility of either minimizing or oversatisfying the elective share claim exists, thus requiring proper planning on the part of the client who wishes to minimize the surviving spouse's claim, and careful strategizing on the part of a surviving spouse, who wishes to maximize the election, by taking a share of the estate in as many states as possible. Regardless of the actual burden, it may well have to be satisfied with assets under the control of a foreign jurisdiction. The table also explores how this issue is handled.

Of course, the client may seek to obtain a waiver of any statutory claims before or after marriage. This often takes place in the context of a prenuptial or postnuptial agreement. The general parameters of what is required for a valid waiver are detailed in Table 6.04.

Table 6.01
Rights Available in Addition to the Elective Share

	Is There Still a Right to Common Law Dower?	*Is There Still a Right to Common Law Curtesy?*	*What Are The Alternative Protective Rights Afforded the Surviving Spouse? Can They Be Asserted in Addition to the Elective Share?*
Alabama	No. (§ 43-8-57)	No. (§ 43-8-57)	Homestead, exempt property, and family allowance are in addition to elective share. (§ 43-8-74)
Alaska	No provision.	No provision.	Homestead, exempt property, and family allowance are in addition to elective share. (§ 13.12.202(c))
Arizona	*Community property—no quasi-community property*		Any community and separate property shares are subject to rights to allowance in lieu of homestead, exempt property, and family allowance. (*§* 14-3101(A))
Arkansas	Yes. (§ 28-11-101 et seq.)	Yes. (§ 28-11-101 et seq.)	Statutory allowances and homestead are in addition to dower and curtesy. (§ 28-39-401(b)(1), (2))
California *[Community property state with quasi-community property]*	No, except to the extent provided in Probate Code § 120. (Prob. § 6412)	No, except to extent provided in Probate Code § 120. (Prob. § 6412)	Right to one-half of quasi-community property. (Prob. § 101) In addition, there is a right to a family allowance (Prob. § 6540(a)(1)), exempt property (Prob. § 6510(a)), and a probate home stead (also available to the minor children) (Prob. §§ 6520, 6521(a)).
Colorado	No. (§ 15-11-112)	No. (§ 15-11-112)	Family allowance and exempt property arein addition to elective share. (§§ 15-11-202(2)(a), 15-11-201(3))
Connecticut	No. *See* Public Acts of 1877, ch. 114. *See generally* Hartford Connecticut Trust Co. v. Lawrence, 138 A. 159, 161 (Conn. 1927).	No. (§ 45a-436)	The statutory share is only available once a support allowance has stopped. (§ 45a-436(c) & (d)) The support allowance is provided for in § 45a-436 and defined in

(cont'd)

Table 6.01
Rights Available in Addition to the Elective Share *(continued)*

	Is There Still a Right to Common Law Dower?	*Is There Still a Right to Common Law Curtesy?*	*What Are The Alternative Protective Rights Afforded the Surviving Spouse? Can They Be Asserted in Addition to the Elective Share?*
Connecticut *(cont'd)*			§ 45a-320. There is also a homestead right and an exemp tion for household goods and possibly certain other personal property as provided for in § 45a-435. (§ 45a-321)
Delaware	No. (12 § 511)	No. (12 § 511)	Surviving spouse allowance is in addition to elective share. (12 § 2308(a)) There is also a provision for the family Bible, apparel, as well as certain other items. (12 § 1901(b))
District of Columbia	No. (§ 19-102)	No. (§ 19-102)	There are exemptions for certain assets not exceeding certain values (§§ 20-904, 15-501, 15-503) and homestead, exempt property, and family allowance. (§ 19-101.01–19-101.04)
Florida	No. (§ 732.111)	No. (§ 732.111)	Exempt property (§ 732.402) homestead (§ 732.4015) and family allowance (§ 732.403) are in addition to elective share. The elective share is in addition to homestead, exempt property, and allowances. (§732.2105)
Georgia *Georgia Year's Support—No elective share, however, the year's support is like the elective share because if the decedent makes provision for the spouse in lieu of year's support in the will, then the spouse must make an election to take the year's support rather than the provision under the will. (§ 53-3-3)*	No. (§ 53-1-3)	No. (§ 53-1-3)	There is no elective share right at all, but there is a right in the surviving spouse and minor children to a year's support. (§ 53-3-1) Certain property is also exempt in the case of an intestate insolvent estate. (§ 44-13-100)

Hawaii	No. (§ 560:2-112)	No. (§ 560:2-112)	Homestead allowance, exempt property, and family allowance are in addition to elective share. (§ 560:2-202(c))
Idaho *Community property state—with quasi-community property*	No. (§ 32-914)	No. (§ 32-914)	Homestead allowance, exempt property, and family allowance are in addition to elective share. (§ 15-2-206(b))
Illinois	No. (755 ILCS § 5/2-9)	No. (755 ILCS § 5/2-9)	Spouse's award for support for 9 months, (755 ILCS § 5/15-1(a)) as well as a child's award if a minor or adult dependent child does not reside with the surviving spouse. (755 ILCS § 5/15-2(a)) The elective share is calculated on the basis of the estate after payment of just claims and so does not reduce spouse's or child's award, which would not be "just claims."
Indiana	No. (§ 29-1-2-11)	No. (§ 29-1-2-11)	Survivor's allowance of $25,000, whether in the form of personal property or a residence. (§ 29-1-4-1) It can be asserted in addition to the elective share.
Iowa	No. (§ 633.236) (Common-law dower and curtesy abolished by § 2440, Code of 1873; see In re Finch's Estate, 32 N.W.2d 819, 829 (1948))	No. (§ 633.236) (Common-law dower and curtesy abolished by § 2440, Code of 1873; see In re Finch's Estate, 32 N.W.2d 819, 829 (1948))	12-month support and exempt personal property in addition to elective share. (§§ 633.332, 633.374) There is also a homestead right which is available "in lieu of" the elective share (§ 633.240) in legal and equitable estates in real property possessed by the decedent. (§ 633.238(1))
Kansas	No. (Abolished by Rev. Stat. 22-127; see generally Bates v. State Sav. Bank, 18 P.2d 143, 144 (Kan. 1933))	No. (Abolished by Rev. Stat. 22-127; see generally Bates v. State Sav. Bank, 18 P.2d 143, 144 (Kan. 1933))	Homestead and family allowance are in addition to elective share. (§ 59-6a202(c)) There is also an exempt property provision. (§ 59-403)
Kentucky	Yes. (§ 392.020)	Yes. (§ 392.020)	There is statutory dower and curtesy, which includes personal property. (§ 392.020) Dower and homestead are alternative rights. (In re Gibson, 33 F. Supp. 838 (1940); § 427.070) There is also a right to exempt property (§ 391.030) in addition to the statutory share (Opin. Att'y Gen. 81-256).

Table 6.01
Rights Available in Addition to the Elective Share *(continued)*

	Is There Still a Right to Common Law Dower?	*Is There Still a Right to Common Law Curtesy?*	*What Are The Alternative Protective Rights Afforded the Surviving Spouse? Can They Be Asserted in Addition to the Elective Share?*
Louisiana	*Community property state—no quasi-community property*		There is a homestead allowance (Rev. Stat. § 20:1) and a family allowance during administration if the court concludes that it is necessary. (Code Civ. Pro. Art. 3321).
Maine	No. (18-A § 2-113)	No. (18-A § 2-113)	Homestead, exempt property, and family allowance are in addition to the elective share. (18-A § 2-206)
Maryland	No. (Est. & Trusts § 3–202)	No. (Est. & Trusts § 3-202)	Family allowance of $5,000 (Est. & Trusts § 3-201) is in addition to the elective share.
Massachusetts	Yes, but wife is not entitled to her dower in addition to the provisions of her hus band's will, unless such plainly appears by the will to have been the intention of the testator. (191 § 17)	Yes, but husband is not entitled to his curtesy in addition to the provisions of his wife's will, unless such plainly appears by the will to have been the intention of the testator. (191 § 17)	Apparel, necessaries, and six months occupancy of house. (196 §§ 1–2) These are in addition to elective share.
Michigan	Yes. A widow can still elect her dower rights under § 558.1 to § 558.29. (§ 700.2202(1)(b) & (2)(c))	No. (See, e.g., Rockwell v. Estate of Rockwell, 180 N.W.2d 498, 501 (Mich.Ct. App. 1970). Moreover, § 700.2202(2)(c) suggests only dower for a ''widow'' is recognized.)	Spouse must choose between statutory share, the terms of the will, *or* dower. (§ 700.2202(2)(a)–(c)) There is additionally a provision for exempt property (§ 700.2404), a family allowance (§ 700.2403) and a homestead allowance of $15,000, all in addition to the elective share. (§ 700.2402)
Minnesota	Repealed by 1925 Minn. Laws C.174 § 2.	Repealed by 1925 Minn. Laws C.174 § 2.	Homestead, exempt property, and family allowance are in addition to elective share. (§§ 524.2-202, 524.2-204)
Mississippi	No. (§ 93-3-5)	No. (§ 93-3-5)	Exempt property, homestead (§ 91-1-19) and a year's support set aside (§ 91-7-135) are allowed in addition to the elective share.

Missouri	No, if vested after 1955 revisions. (§ 474.110)	No, if vested after 1955 revisions. (§ 474.110)	Exempt property, one-year support allowance, and the homestead exemption are in addition to the elective share. (§§ 474.160(1)(1), 474.250, 474.260, 474.290)
Montana	No. (§ 72-2-122)	No. (§ 72-2-122)	Homestead, exempt property, and family allowance are in addition to the elective share. (§§ 72-2-226, 72-2-221(3))
Nebraska	No. (§ 30-104)	No. (§ 30-104)	Homestead, exempt property, and family allowance are in addition to elective share. (§§ 30-2318(b), 30-2314(a))
Nevada	*Community property state—no quasi-community property* See also §123.020 (curtesy and dower not allowed)		Family allowance (§ 146.030(1)) and certain exempt property are allowed (§ 21.090).
New Hampshire	No. (§ 560:3)	No. (§ 560:3)	Homestead, exempt property, family allowance and elective share. To receive the elective share, the spouse must waive homestead. (§ 560:10) Exempt property (§§ 554:4, 554:5) and a family allowance (§ 560:1) are allowed in addition to the elective share.
New Jersey	Yes, if real property of which decedent was seized of an estate of inheritance prior to May 28, 1980. (§ 3B:28-1) Otherwise, no. (§ 3B:28-2)	Yes, if real property of which decedent was seized of an estate of inheritance prior to May 28, 1980. (§ 3B:28-1) Otherwise, no. (§ 3B:28-2)	Family allowance during will contest (§ 3B:3-30) and apparel-personal property exemption up to $5,000 (§ 3B:16-5) are in addition to the elective share.
New Mexico	Dower and curtesy are expressly abolished.	(§ 45-2-112)	Family allowance of $30,000 (§ 45-2-402) and specified exempt property up to $15,000 (§ 45-2-403). They are all in addition to the elective share. (§ 45-2-403)
New York[1]	Only if parties married before September 1, 1930. (Real Prop. § 190)	Only if wife dies by August 31, 1930. (Real Prop. § 189)	Exempt property (Est. Powers & Trusts § 5-3.1) and homestead (CPLR § 5206(b)) can be taken as well. A personal property exemption from creditors claims may also be available (CPLR § 5205). (Power v. Loonam, 266 N.Y.S.2d 865, 866-87 (Sup. Ct. 1966))

Table 6.01
Rights Available in Addition to the Elective Share *(continued)*

	Is There Still a Right to Common Law Dower?	*Is There Still a Right to Common Law Curtesy?*	*What Are The Alternative Protective Rights Afforded the Surviving Spouse? Can They Be Asserted in Addition to the Elective Share?*
North Carolina	No. (§ 29-4)	No. (§ 29-4)	A spousal allowance of $10,000 for one year (§ 30-15) and a year's allowance of $2,000 for minors and certain other children (§ 30-17). The homestead exemption (§ 1C-1602) and Const. Art. X, § 2(1) are homestead protections only available during life (Johnson v. Cross, 66 N.C. 167, 170 (1882)).
North Dakota	No. (§ 30.1-04-13) See also §14-07-09.	No. (§ 30.1-04-13) See also §14-07-09.	Family allowance (§ 30.1-07-02), exempt property not to exceed $10,000 (§ 30.1-07-01), and homestead exemption, not to exceed $80,000 (§ 47-18-01) are additional protections. (§ 30.1-05-01)
Ohio	Yes. (§ 2103.02)	No. (§ 2103.09)	Surviving spouse cannot take dower and elective share. (§ 2103.02(B)) There is a right to exempt property in the nature of as many as two automobiles, not to exceed $40,000, in addition to any vehicles other wise passing to the surviving spouse, such as by joint tenancy or will and one watercraft and one outboard motor (§§ 2106.18, 2106.19), family allowance, not to exceed $40,000, but reduced if the surviving spouse chose two automobiles under § 2106.18, by the value of the less valuable automobile (§ 2106.13), and a year's stay in the house (§ 2106.15).
Oklahoma	No. (84 § 214)	No. (84 § 214)	Yes—homestead (58 § 311), family allowance (58 § 314), and also exempt property (58 §§ 311, 312).

Oregon	No, unless decedent died before July 1, 1970. (§ 112.685)	No, unless decedent died before July 1, 1970. (§ 112.685)	Homestead (§ 114.005) and family allowance (§ 114.015) are additional protections.
Pennsylvania	No. (20 § 2105(A))	No. (20 § 2105(B))	Family exemption up to $3,500 in value (20 § 3121) and a separate exemption of real and/or personal property up to $3,500 (20 § 3121) are additional rights.
Rhode Island	No. (§ 33-25-1)	No. (§ 33-25-1)	Family allowance (§ 33-10-3) and exempt property (§ 33-10-1) are additional protections.
South Carolina	No. (Boan v. Watson, 316 S.E.2d 401, 402 (1984), prospectively abolished dower, holding it unconstitutional)	No. (Abolished, as reflected in Code 1976, § 21-5-10; see generally Boan v. Watson, 316 S.E.2d 401, 402 (1984))	Exempt property up to $5,000 in value (§ 62-2-401) is also available.
South Dakota	No. (§ 29A-2-112)	No. (§ 29A-2-112)	Homestead, exempt property, and family allowance are in addition to elective share. (§ 29A-2-202(c))
Tennessee	No. The right to dower is abolished except to the extent that the right vested before April 1, 1977. (§ 31-2-102)	No. The right to curtesy is abolished except to the extent that the right vested before April 1, 1977. (§ 31-2-102)	Homestead, exempt property, and year's support are in addition to elective share. (§ 31-4-101(b))
Texas	*Community property state; no quasi-community property*		Homestead (Prob. § 270), exempt property limited to $ 5,000 (Prob. §§ 271, 273), and an allowance in lieu of exempt property limited to $ 15,000 (Prob. § 273) are afforded.
Utah	No. (§ 75-2-112)	No. (§ 75-2-112)	Homestead allowance up to $15,000 (§ 75-2-402), exempt property up to $10,000 (§ 75-2-403), and family allowance (§ 75-2-404) are permitted, but chargeable against the elective share.
Vermont	No. However, there is a right to a one-third fee simple in real estate of the deceased spouse. This is increased to one-half if the decedent left only one heir, who is also the heir of the surviving spouse. (14 § 461)	Same as dower right (14 § 474)	The surviving spouse can elect a statutory share of personal and real property. (14 §§ 401, 461) In addition, the spouse is eligible for the household goods and family allowance (14 §§ 403, 404), along with a homestead exemption (27 § 105).

Table 6.01
Rights Available in Addition to the Elective Share *(continued)*

	Is There Still a Right to Common Law Dower?	*Is There Still a Right to Common Law Curtesy?*	*What Are The Alternative Protective Rights Afforded the Surviving Spouse? Can They Be Asserted in Addition to the Elective Share?*
Virginia	A spouse's interest in common-law dower has been abolished except where the interest vested prior to January 1, 1991, or, where a creditor or other third party in any real estate holds the interest. (§ 64.1-19.2)	A spouse's interest in common-law curtesy has been abolished except where the interest vested prior to January 1, 1991, or, where a creditor or other third party in any real estate holds the interest. (§ 64.1-19.2)	Homestead (maximum of $15,000) and elective share are alternative rights. (§ 64.1-151.3) However, family allowance and exempt property up to $15,000 are in addition to elective share. (§§ 64.1-151.1, 64.1-151.2)
Washington	*Community property state; no quasi-community property*		There is provision for homestead (§ 11.54.020), family allowance (§ 11.54.010), and exempt property (§ 11.54.080). The homestead is the lesser of total net value of (a) lands, mobile home, improve ments, and certain appurtenant personal property, (b) $40,000 in real property, or (c) $15,000 in personal property. *See* § 11.54.020, cross-reference § 6.13.030. In addition, all of the amounts described above can be adjusted as noted to meet basic maintenance and support. (§ 11.54.040) They can also be reduced. (§ 11.54.050) If the total exempt from creditors under § 6.13.030 is less than the minimum $40,000 specified therein with respect to lands, then other property can be substituted.
West Virginia	No. (§ 43-1-1)	No. (§ 43-1-1)	A homestead exemption of $5,000 and a personal property exemption of $1,000 is provided. (Const. Art. VI, § 48) See also § 38-9-1 which deals with the homestead exemption.

Wisconsin	*Community property state; quasi-community property known as deferred marital property estate is available to the surviving spouse (§ 861.02)*		There is provision for family allowance (§ 861.31), an additional discretionary amount in preference to creditors of as much as $10,000 (§ 861.41), and exempt property (§ 861.33).
Wyoming	No. (§ 2-4-101)	No. (§ 2-4-101)	Homestead allowance, exempt property, and family allowance are in addition to elective share. (§ 2-5-103)

[1] These answers assume that the decedent died after September 1, 1992.

Table 6.02
How Is the Elective Share Obtained?

	By When Must an Election to Take Against the Will Be Made?	*What Must Be Filed?*	*With Whom?*	*Who Can Make the Election? E.g., Guardian, Executor of Surviving Spouse after Her Death?*
Alabama	Within six months after death or six months after probate, whichever limitation last expires. (§ 43-8-73(a))	Petition. (§ 43-8-73(a))	With court and mailing or delivery to the personal representative, if any. (§ 43-8-73(a))	Personal to spouse during lifetime. Guardian can only upon petition to court if necessary to provide adequate support. (§ 43-8-71)
Alaska	Nine months after death or six months after probate, whichever is later. (§ 13.12.211(a))	Petition. (§ 13.12.211(a))	Court and mailing or delivering to the personal representative, if any. (§ 13.12.211(a))	Spouse personally or guardian, conservator, or agent with power of attorney. (§ 13.12.212(a))
Arizona	*Community property—no quasi-community property*			
Arkansas	Within one month after the period for making claims. The period for making claims is six months after the first publication of notice. See § 28-50-101 for specified requirements. If at the end of this period litigation is pending concerning the will, the period is extended further to an additional one month after the final order in this litigation. (§§ 28-39-403(b), 28-50-101)	A writing following the form set out in § 28-39-404(a)(2).	Office of the probate clerk of the circuit court. (§ 28-39-404(a)(1))	Personal to surviving spouse. Guardian of incompetent surviving spouse on permission of the court. (§ 28-39-405)
California	*Community property and quasi-community property (giving surviving spouse same rights in this property as if community property)*			

Colorado	Within nine months of death or six months of admission to probate, whichever is later. (§ 15-11-205(1)) Within nine months after the decedent's death, the surviving spouse may petition the court for an extension of time for making an election. (§ 15-11-205(2))	Petition. (§ 15-11-205(1))	Court and mailing or delivering to the personal representative, if any. (§ 15-11-205(1))	Spouse or her conservator, guardian, or agent under power of attorney. The surviving spouse must be living at the time of election. (§ 15-11-206(1))
Connecticut	Within 150 days from the date of appointment of the first fiduciary. (§ 45-a-436(c))	Written notice. (§ 45a-436(c))	Probate court. (§ 45a-436(c))	Spouse, conservator, guardian. (§ 45a-436(c))
Delaware	Six months after grant of letters. (12 § 906(a))	Petition. (12 § 906(a))	Court of Chancery and personal representative. (12 § 906(a))	Spouse, personal representative if spouse elected before death, or court if a protected person. The election may only be exercised during surviving spouse's lifetime. (12 § 904)
District of Columbia	Within six months after will is admitted to probate. (§ 19-113)	Written renunciation following the form set out in § 19-113(a)	Probate Court at D.C. Superior Court. (§§ 19-113, 19-115)	Surviving spouse, or if approved by the court, a guardian or other fiduciary. (§ 19-113(c))
Florida	Within the earlier of six months from date of first publication of notice of administration or two years after the decedent's death. Within the specified period, surviving spouse or attorney or guardian may petition the court for an extenion. (§ 732.2135(1))	An election. (§ 732.2135(1))	Court having jurisdiction of probate proceeding. (§ 732.2125(2))	Surviving spouse, with the approval of the court, by an attorney in fact or guardian of the property. (§ 732.2125)
Georgia *[Georgia Year's Support—No elective share. However, the year's support is like the elective share to the extent that if* *(cont'd)*	Within 24 months of the date of death of the decedent. (§ 53-3-5(c))	Petition for year's support. (§ 53-3-5)	The probate court having jurisdiction over the decedent's estate. (§ 53-3-5)	Surviving spouse, guardian, or other person acting on behalf of the spouse or on behalf of minor child. (§ 53-3-5(a))

Table 6.02
How Is the Elective Share Obtained? *(continued)*

	By When Must an Election to Take Against the Will Be Made?	*What Must Be Filed?*	*With Whom?*	*Who Can Make the Election? E.g., Guardian, Executor of Surviving Spouse after Her Death?*
Georgia *(cont'd)* *the decedent makes a provision in lieu of year's support in the will, then the spouse may elect to take the year's support rather than the provision under the will. (§ 53-3-3)]*				
Hawaii	Within nine months after the date of the decedent's death, or within six months after the probate of the decedent's will, whichever limitation later expires. (§ 560:2-211) Within nine months after the decedent's death, the spouse or reciprocal beneficiary may petition the court for an extension of time for making an election. (§ 560:2-211)	Petition. (§ 560:2-211)	The Probate Court. The petition for the elective share must also be mailed or delivered to the personal representative, if any. (§ 560:2-211)	Surviving spouse or reciprocal beneficiary who is living when the petition is filed. It may also be exercised by the surviving spouse's or reciprocal's conservator, guardian, or agent under a power of attorney. (§ 560:2.212(a)) If exercised by any such persons the surviving spouse or reciprocal is preumed incapacitated, may be required to be placed in a custodial trust. (§ 560:2-212(b))
Idaho *[Community property state—with quasi-community property]*	Within nine months after death of decedent or within six months after the date of filing of the petition for probate, whichever is later. (§ 15-2-205) The court may extend the time for election as it sees fit for cause shown by the surviving spouse before the time for election has expired. (§ 15-2-205)	A petition for the elective share. (§ 15-2-205)	The court and mailed or delivered to the personal representative. (§ 15-2-205)	Surviving spouse during lifetime or by court if protected person. (§ 15-2-204)

Illinois	Within seven months after the admission of the will to probate or within such further time as may be allowed by the court if, within seven months after the admi sion of the will to probate or before the expiration of any extended period, the surviving spouse files a petition stating that litigation is pending that affects the share of the surviving spouse in the estate. (755 ILCS § 5/2-8)	A written instrument signed by the surviving spouse and declaring the renunciation. (755 ILCS § 5/2-8(b))	The court in which the will was admitted to probate. (755 ILCS § 5/2-8(b))	Surviving spouse. If incompetent, conservator, guard ian ad litem, or next friend. (In re Klekunas' Estate, 205 N.E.2d 497, 500 (App. Ct. 1965))
Indiana	Claims must be filed within three months after the date admitting to probate the will against which the election is made. If litigation is pending as to the validity, the effect or construction of the will, the existence of issue surviving the decedent, or other matters affecting the share of the spouse, then the period is extended until 30 days after the final determination of the litigation. (§ 29-1-3-2)	An election in writing, signed and acknowledged by the surviving spouse or by the guardian of his estate. It may be in the form of that shown in § 29-1-3-3(a). (§ 29-1-3-3(a))	Clerk of the Probate Court. (§ 29-1-33(a))	The surviving spouse or the guardian of the surviving spouse's estate may make the election if the spouse is a protected person; otherwise the right to elect is not transferable and cannot be exercised subsequent to the spouse's death. (§ 29-1-3-4)
Iowa	If spouse is not personal representative of the decedent's estate, within four months after service of notice, the spouse must file an election in writing with the clerk of court electing the share as set forth in §633.236 and §§633.238 through 633.246. Otherwise, the spouse shall be deemed to take under the will or to receive the intestate share. (§ 633.237 (1)) If the spouse is a personal representative of the estate and	An election in writing to take against the will. (§ 633.237)	The clerk of the Probate Court. (§ 633.237)	Only the surviving spouse or her conservator may elect to take against the will because the right to elect is personal and not transferable. It cannot be exercised for the spouse subsequent to the spouse's death. (§§ 633.242, 633.236)

(cont'd)

Table 6.02
How Is the Elective Share Obtained? *(continued)*

	By When Must an Election to Take Against the Will Be Made?	*What Must Be Filed?*	*With Whom?*	*Who Can Make the Election? E.g., Guardian, Executor of Surviving Spouse after Her Death?*
Iowa *(cont'd)*	fails to file an election under this section within four months of the decedent's death, it shall be conclusively presumed that the surviving spouse elects to take under the will, receive the intestate share, or take under the revocable trust. (§ 633.237(4))			
Kansas	Six months after the date of the decedent's death, or within six months after the notice of the right to the elective share pursuant to § 59-2233, whichever limitation later expires. (§ 59-6a211(a)) The surviving spouse must give notice of the time and place set for hearing, pursuant to court orders, to persons interested in the estate and to the distributees and recipients of portions of the augmented estate whose interests will be adversely affected by the taking of the elective share. (§ 59-6a211(a))	Petition. (§ 59-6a211(a))	The Probate Court and delivered to the personal representative, if any. (§ 59-6a211)	Surviving spouse or personal representative if spouse is disabled or deceased. (§ 59-6a212(a))
Kentucky	Within six months after the probate, unless an action contesting the will is brought, then the surviving spouse need not make such relinquishment until six months succeeding the time	A statement relinquishing the will. (§ 392.080(1))	County clerk or his authorized deputy in the county where probate was made or acknowledged before a subscribing witness and proved before and left with the county clerk or his	Surviving spouse. (§ 392.080)

	when the action is disposed of. (§ 392.080(1))		authorized deputy. A copy of such relinquishment shall be filed with the clerk of the court in which probate was made. (§ 392.080)	
Louisiana	*Community property state—no quasi-community property*			
Maine	The later of within nine months after the date of death or within six months after probate of decedent's will, whichever expires latest. (18-A § 2-205(A))	Petition for elective share. (18-A § 2-205(A))	Court and any personal representative, if any. (18-A § 2-205(A))	Surviving spouse only; and in the case of a protected person, court order only. (18-A § 2-203)
Maryland	The election by a surviving spouse shall be made not later than the later of nine months, after the deceased spouse's death or six months after the date of the first appointment of a personal representative under a will. (Est. & Trusts § 3-206(a)(1)) This period may also be extended up to an additional three months before its expiration, with notice and if good cause is shown. (Est. & Trusts § 3-206(a)(2))	Must file a writing that may be in conformity with § 3-207 (b) and which is signed by the surviving spouse or other person entitled to make the election. (Est. & Trusts § 3-207)	The election must be filed in the court in which the personal representative of the decedent was appointed. (Est. & Trusts § 3-207(a))	Surviving spouse. The right to make an election is personal to him, not transferable, and can not be exercised after death. If the surviving spouse is under-18 years of age or under disability, the election may be exercised by order of the court having jurisdiction of the person or property of the spouse or person under disability. (Est. & Trusts § 3-204)
Massachusetts	Within six months after the probate of the deceased's will. (191 § 15) If, after probate of such will, legal proceedings have been instituted wherein its validity or effect is drawn in question, the probate court may, within said six months, on petition and after such notice as it orders, extend the time for filing the aforesaid claim and waiver until the expiration of six months from the termination of such proceedings. (191 § 15)	A writing signed by the surviving spouse, waiving any provisions that may have been made for the spouse in the testator's will, or claiming the spouses elective share. (191§ 15)	Registry of probate. (191§ 15)	The right to an election is purely a personal right and can only be exercised during the life of the surviving spouse. In addition, any election by a guardian or conservator must be approved by the probate court. Friedman v. Andrews, 200 N.E. 575, 576 (1936); Old Colony Trust Co. v. Coffman, 172 N.E.2d 609 (1961))

Table 6.02
How Is the Elective Share Obtained? *(continued)*

	By When Must an Election to Take Against the Will Be Made?	*What Must Be Filed?*	*With Whom?*	*Who Can Make the Election? E.g., Guardian, Executor of Surviving Spouse after Her Death?*
Michigan	The election must be made during the life of the surviving spouse and within 63 days after the date for presentment of claims, or within 63 days after filing proof of service of the inventory upon the spouse, whichever is later. (§ 700.2202(3))	Election in writing filed with the court that the spouse elects one of the choices specified in § 700.2202(1)(a)–(b) (intestate) or § 700.2202(2)(a)–(c) (testate). (§ 700.2202(1))	The court. (§ 700.2202(1))	The spouse can only exercise election during the lifetime of the spouse. In the case of a legally incapacitated person, the right of election may only be exercised by order of the court in which a proceeding as to that person's property is pending. Guardians generally do not have the right or duty to elect, at least not without the knowldge, consent, and approval of the probate court. (§ 700.2202(3) & (5); Huntington College v. Moore, 5 F. Supp. 541, 546–47 (D.C. 1933))
Minnesota	Election must be made within nine months after the date of death or within six months after the probate of the decedent's will, whichever time limitation last expires. (§ 524.2-211(a))	Must file a petition claiming the elective share. In addition, the surviving spouse must give notice of the time and place set for hearing to persons interested in the estate and to the distributees and recipients of portions of the augmented estate whose interests will be adversely affected by the taking of the elective share. (§ 524.2-211(a))	The court and mailed or delivered to the personal representative, if any. (§ 524.2-211(a))	The right of election of the surviving spouse may be exercised only during the surviving spouse's lifetime. In the case of a protected person, the right of election may be exercised only by order of the court in which protective proceedings as to the protected person's property are pending. (§ 524.2-212)

Mississippi	Within 90 days after the probate of the will. (§ 91-5-25)	A renunciation of the deceased's will and an election to take spouse's legal share. (§ 91-5-25)	The court office where the will was probated. (§ 91-5-25)	The elective share right is personal to the surviving spouse and may not be elected by his or her administrator after death. (Shattuck v. Estate of Tyson, 508 So. 2d 1077, 1080-81 (1987)) The right to renounce may be exercised by a guardian in the case of an incompetent surviving spouse. (§ 91-5-25; Estate of Mullins v. Estate of Mullins, 125 So. 2d 93, 95–96 (1960))
Missouri	The election by a surviving spouse must be made within 10 days after the expiration of the time limited for contesting the will of the decedent. If liti gation is pending concerning the will, 90 days after the termination of litigation. (§ 474.180)	Form of election must be in writing, signed and acknowledged by the surviving spouse or by the guardian ad litem or conservator of his estate. It may be filed in accordance with the form of § 474.190. (§ 474.190)	The office of the clerk of the court. (§ 474.190)	The right of election of the surviving spouse is personal to the spouse and cannot be exercised after the surviving spouse's death. But, if the surviving spouse is disabled or a minor, his guardian ad litem or conservator may elect for him with the approval of the court. (§ 474.200)
Montana	Within nine months after the date of death or within six months after the probate of the decedent's will, whichever time limitation last expires. (§ 72-2-225(1))	Must file a petition claiming the elective share. In addition, the surviving spouse must give notice of the time and place set for hearing to persons interested in the estate and to the distributees and recipients of portions of the augmented estate whose interests will be adversely affected by the taking of the elective share. (§ 72-2-225(1))	The court and mailed or delivered to the personal representative, if any. (§ 72-2-225(1))	A surviving spouse who is living when the petition for the elective share is filed with the court may only exercise the right of election. The surviving spouse's conservator, guardian or agent under the authority of a power of attorney may also exercise the election on the surviving spouse's behalf. (§ 72-2-223(1))
Nebraska	Within nine months after the date of death or within six *(cont'd)*	A petition for the elective share in any designated *(cont'd)*	Petition must be filed in the court and mailed or delivered to *(cont'd)*	Right of election of the surviving spouse may only be *(cont'd)*

Table 6.02
How Is the Elective Share Obtained? *(continued)*

	By When Must an Election to Take Against the Will Be Made?	*What Must Be Filed?*	*With Whom?*	*Who Can Make the Election? E.g., Guardian, Executor of Surviving Spouse after Her Death?*
Nebraska *(cont'd)*	months after the probate of the decedent's will, whichever time limitation last expires. (§ 30-2317(a)) The court may extend the time for election as it sees fit for cause shown by the surviving spouse before the time for election has expired. (§ 30-2317(a))	fraction not in excess of one-half of the augmented estate or, in the absence of any such designation, of one-half of the augmented estate. In addition, the surviving spouse must give notice of the time and place set for hearing to persons interested in the estate and to the distributees and recipients of portions of the augmented estate whose interests will be adversely affected by the taking of the elective share. (§ 30-2317(a) & (b))	the personal representative, if any. (§ 30-2317(a))	exercised by the spouse during the spouse's lifetime. In the case of a protected person, the court in which the protective proceedings as to his or her property are pending may only exercise the election. (§ 30-2315)
Nevada	*Community property state—no quasi-community property*			
New Hampshire	Within six months after appointment of executor or administrator, unless the judge of the probate court grants an extension for good cause shown. (§ 560:14)	Written waiver of will. (§ 560:14)	Probate office. (§ 560:14)	If a ward is insane, a guardian may waive testate distribution. (Wentworth v. Waldron, 172 A. 247, 251 (1934)) Otherwise, the right to the elective share is personal and cannot be exercised by surviving spouse's representatives. (Gowing v. Laing, 77 A.2d 32, 34 (1950); § 560:10)
New Jersey	Within 6 months after the appointment of a personal	A complaint. (§ 3B:8-12)	Superior Court. (§ 3B:8-12)	Surviving spouse or domestic partner during his lifetime. In

	representative of the decedent's estate. The court may, before the time for election has expired and upon good cause shown by the surviving spouse or domestic partner, extend the time for election upon notice to persons interested in the estate and to distributees and recipients of portions of the augmented estate whose interests will be adversely affected by the taking of the elective share. (§ 3B:8-12)			the case of a surviving spouse or domestic partner for whom the court has appointed a guardian to manage his estate, the right of election may be exercised only by order of the court making the appointment and only if election is necessary to provide adequate support of the surviving spouse or domestic partner during his probable life expectancy. (§ 3B:8-11)
New Mexico	*Community property state with quasi-community property* [Quasi-community property is defined in § 40-3-8(C). It is treated as community property for purposes of division of property incident to a dissolution of marriage or a legal separation if both parties are New Mexico domiciliaries at the time of the dissolution or legal separation. (§ 40-3-8(D)) It is not mentioned in any provision dealing with distribution of an estate.]			
New York[1]	Within six months from date of issuance of letters testamentary or of administration, but not more than two years after decedent's death. (Est. Powers & Trusts § 5-1.1-A(d)(1))	Written notice. (Est. Powers & Trusts § 5-1.1-A(d)(1))	Surrogate's court in which letters testamentary of administration were issued and upon personal representative or executor. (Est. Powers & Trusts § 5-1.1-A(d)(1))	Surviving spouse, an authorized guardian of the property of an infant spouse, an authorized committee of an incompetent spouse, an authorized conservator of a conservatee spouse, an authorized guardian ad litem for the surviving spouse, or an authorized guardian appointed under the mental hygiene law. (Est. Powers & Trusts § 5-1.1-A(c)(3))
North Carolina	Within six months after the issuance of letters testamentary or of administration in connection with the will or intestate proceeding. (See § 30-3.4(b))	A petition. (§ 30-3.4(b))	The clerk of the county superior court of primary administration and mailing or delivering petition to personal representative. (§ 30-3.4(b)(i) & (ii))	Surviving spouse or his or her agent under a power of attorney, or guardian of surviving spouse's estate. If the surviving spouse dies before the claim is settled his/her personal representative succeeds to the claim. (§ 30-3.4(a))

Table 6.02
How Is the Elective Share Obtained? *(continued)*

	By When Must an Election to Take Against the Will Be Made?	*What Must Be Filed?*	*With Whom?*	*Who Can Make the Election? E.g., Guardian, Executor of Surviving Spouse after Her Death?*
North Dakota	Within nine months of decedent's death, or within six months after probate of decedent's will, whichever expires later. (§ 30.1-05-05(1)) The surviving spouse shall serve a copy of the petition for the elective share on, and shall give written notice of the time and place set for hearing to persons interested in the estate and to the distributees and recipients of portions of the augmented estate whose interests may be adversely affected by the taking of the elective share. (§ 30.1-05-05(1)) The surviving spouse can petition for an extension (§ 30.1-05-05(2))	A petition for the elective share. (§ 30.1-05-05)	The filing in probate court and mailing or delivering to the personal representative, if any. (§ 30.1-05-05)	Surviving spouse or surviving spouse's conservator, guardian, or agent under the authority of a power of attorney, but only if surviving spouse is alive when the petition is filed. (§ 30.1-05-06(1))
Ohio	Anytime after death of decedent but not later than five months from the initial appointment of an administrator or executor of the estate. Court may allow more time for good cause if a motion is filed before the expiration of the five-month period. If proceedings for advice or to contest the validity of the will are begun within the time allowed for election, election	Election must be made in person. (§ 2106.06)	Must be before the probate judge or a deputy clerk who has been appointed to act as a referee. (§ 2106.06)	Surviving spouse or any suitable person to whom the probate court, upon the filing of an application on behalf of the surviving spouse, has issued a commission to take the election. (§ 2106.07) If the surviving spouse is unable to make an election because of a legal disability, the court may elect for the spouse. (§ 2106.08)

	may be made within three months after the final disposition of the proceedings, if the will is not set aside. (§ 2106.01(E))			
Oklahoma	On or before the final date for hearing of the petition for final distribution of the estate. (84 § 44(B)(3))	A writing. (84 § 44(B)(3))	District court in which the estate of the decedent is being administered. (84 § 44(B)(3))	Surviving spouse; if the surviving spouse is incompetent, a guardian or conservator may make the election with court approval. The surviving spouse must be alive when the election is made. (84 § 44(B)(4))
Oregon	Within 90 days after the date of the admission of the will to probate or 30 days after the date of the filing of the inven tory, whichever is later. (§ 114.145)	A statement served on personal representative or attorney of personal representative that the surviving spouse elects to take against the will. (§ 114.145)	In the estate proceeding and on the personal representa tive. (§ 114.145)	Surviving spouse. (§ 114.145) If the surviving spouse is financially incapable, the court or a conservator can file for the election. (§ 114.155)
Pennsylvania	Within six months after decedent's death or before expiration of six months after date of probate, whichever is later. (20 § 2210(B)) The court may extend the time for election for such period and upon such terms and conditions as the court shall deem proper under the circumstances on application of the surviving spouse filed with the clerk within the foregoing time limit. (20 § 2210(B))	Written signed election. (20§ 2210(A))	Clerk of the orphan's court division of the county where decedent died domiciled. Notice of election must be given to the decedent's personal representative, if any. (20 § 2210)	Surviving spouse or attorney-in-fact, only during spouse's lifetime. Minor spouse's right of election may be exercised only by spouse's guardians, and incapacitated spouse's right of election may be exercised by spouse's guardians or spouse's attorneys-in-fact. (20 § 2206)
Rhode Island	Within six months after date of first publication of the qualifications of the fiduciary of the estate. (§ 33-25-4)	Written statement waiving and renouncing devise and bequest, and claiming his or her share in life estate in decedent's real estate. (§ 33-25-4)	Probate court granting probate. The waiver and claim shall also be filed in the records of deeds in each city and town where any real estate is located, if located in any city other than that in which the will is probated. (§ 33-25-4)	Surviving spouse. (§ 33-25-4)

Table 6.02
How Is the Elective Share Obtained? *(continued)*

	By When Must an Election to Take Against the Will Be Made?	*What Must Be Filed?*	*With Whom?*	*Who Can Make the Election? E.g., Guardian, Executor of Surviving Spouse after Her Death?*
South Carolina	The surviving spouse must make his or her election within eight months after the date of death of the decedent or within six months after the probate of the decedent's will, whichever limitation last expires. (§ 62-2-205(a))	A petition for the elective share. (§ 62-2-205(a))	The petition must be filed with the court and also mailed or delivered to the personal representative, if any. The petitioning spouse must also give notice of the time and place set for hearing to the personal representative and to distributees and recipients of portions of the probate estate whose interests will be adversely affected by the taking of the elective share. (§ 62-2-205(a) & (b))	The right of election may be exercised by the surviving spouse only during his lifetime, or by his or her duly appointed attorney in fact, or, in the case of a "protected person," only by order of the court in which protective proceedings as to the protected person's property are pending. A "protected person" includes a minor or incapaci tated person for whom a con servator has been appointed or other protective order has been made. (§§ 62-2-203, 62-5-101(3))
South Dakota	The right of election must be exercised within nine months after the date of death of the decedent or within four months after the admission to either formal or informal probate of the decedent's will, whichever limitation later expires. The decedent's nonprobate transfers to others are not included within the augmented estate if the petition for the elective share is filed more than nine months after the decedent's death or	A petition for the elective share. (§ 29A-2-211(a))	The petition must be filed with the court and also mailed or delivered to the personal representative, if any. Notice of hearing must be given to persons interested in the estate and to the distributees and recipients of portions of the augmented estate whose interests will be adversely affected by the taking of the elective share. (§ 29A-2-211(a))	The right of election may be exercised either by the surviving spouse or by his or her conservator or agent under the authority of a power of attorney, or, if the surviving spouse dies prior to the expiration of the time for making an election, by the surviving spouse's personal representative. (§ 29A-2-212)

	beyond the time extended by the court. (§ 29A-2-211(a))			
Tennessee	Within nine months after the date of death or within six months after the appointment of the personal representative, whichever limitation last expires. (§ 31-4-102(a)(1)) However, when the title of the surviving spouse to property devised or bequeathed by the will is involved in litigation so that an election cannot be made, the surviving spouse shall have an additional year from the date of the probate of the will, as well as any additional time deemed necessary by the court, within which to elect. (§ 31-4-102(a)(2))	A petition for the elective share. (§ 31-4-102(a)(1))	The court and also mailed or delivered to the personal representative, if any. (§ 31-4-102(a)(1))	The surviving spouse may exercise the right of election, or,in the event the surviving spouse dies after the decedent spouse but before the time of election expires, by the personal representative of the decedent's surviving spouse. (§§ 31-4-101, 31-4-105) If surviving spouse is a minor or mentally incompetent, a guardian, conservator, or next friend can make the election. (§ 31-4-104)
Texas	*Community property state; no quasi-community property*			
Utah	Within nine months after the date of the decedent's death or within six months after the probate of the decedent's will, whichever limitation later expires. (§ 75-2-211(1)) Nonprobate transfers to others not included within the augmented estate for the purpose of com puting elective share if the petition is filed more than nine months after decedent's death. Within nine months after the decedent's death, the surviving spouse may petition the court for an extension of time for	A petition for the elective share. (§ 75-2-211(1))	The court and also mailed or delivered to the personal representative, if any. The petitioning spouse must also give notice of the time and place set for hearing to persons interested in the estate and to the distributees and recipients of portions of the augmented net estate whose interests will be adversely affected by the taking of the elective share. (§ 75-2-211(1) & (2))	The right of election may be exercised by the surviving spouse who is living when a petition for the elective share is filed in court, or on the surviving spouse's behalf by his conservator, guardian, or agent under the authority of a power of attorney. (§ 75-2-212)

(cont'd)

Table 6.02
How Is the Elective Share Obtained? *(continued)*

	By When Must an Election to Take Against the Will Be Made?	*What Must Be Filed?*	*With Whom?*	*Who Can Make the Election? E.g., Guardian, Executor of Surviving Spouse after Her Death?*
Utah *(cont'd)*	making an election. If, within nine months after the decedent's death, the spouse gives notice of the petition to all persons interested in the decedent's nonprobate transfers to others, the court for cause shown by the surviving spouse may extend the time for election. (§ 75-2-211(2))			
Vermont	Within eight months, unless extended by the probate court, after the decedent's will is proved or letters of administration are granted. (R. of Prob. Proc. 13(b)) See also 14 § 465.	The election must be filed on the official form given in the rules. (R. of Prob. Proc. 13 (b)) See also 14 § 465.	The probate court. (R. of Prob. Proc. 13(b)) See also 14 § 465.	The surviving spouse is entitled to make the election. (R. of Prob. Proc. 13(b)) The rules do not authorize anyone else. See also 14 § 465.
Virginia	Within six months from the later of (a) the time of the admission of the will to probate or (b) the qualification of an administrator on the intestate estate. (§ 64.1-13(A))	The surviving spouse must file a claim, in person or in writing, for the elective share. The claim will be recorded by the court and must conform to the requirements listed in § 55-106. (§ 64.1-13(A))	The court or clerk's office having jurisdiction over the administration of the decedent's estate. (§ 64.1-13(A))	The surviving spouse may exercise the right of election. (§ 64.1-13(A)) If the widow is incompetent, the court must choose whether to renounce the will. (First Nat'l Exch. Bank v. Hughson, 74 S.E.2d 797 (1953); § 64.1-13)
Washington	*Community property state; no quasi-community property*			
West Virginia	Within nine months after the date of the decedent's death or within six months after the probate of the decedent's will,	A petition for the elective share. (§ 42-3-4(a))	The court and also mailed or delivered to the personal representative, if any. The petitioning spouse must also	Surviving spouse, conservator, guardian, or agent under the authority of attorney. The

	whichever limitation later expires. (§ 42-3-4(a)) The surviving spouse may petition for an extension within nine months of the decedent's death. (§ 42-3-4(b))		serve a copy of the petition and a written notice of the time and place set for hearing on persons interested in the estate and on the distributees and recipients of portions of the augmented estate whose interests may be adversely affected by the taking of the elective share. (§ 42-3-4(a))	surviving spouse must be living. (§ 42-3-3(a))
Wisconsin	*Community property state; quasi-community property known as deferred marital property estate is available to the surviving spouse (§ 851.055)*			
Wyoming	Within three months after admission of will to probate or within 30 days after being advised by court of right to election, whichever is later. (§ 2-5-105(a)) Court must advise surviving spouse of right to election within three months after admission of will to probate. (§ 2-5-104)	Petition for elective share. (§ 2-5-105(a))	Court and any personal representative, if any. (§ 2-5-105(a))	Right is personal to surviving spouse. If spouse of a domiciliary decedent dies or becomes incompetent within three months after will is admitted to probate or before the court advises spouse of right to election, a personal representative or guardian of the estate of the deceased or incompetent surviving spouse has the same right of election as the surviving spouse would have had if living or competent. (§ 2-5-101(c))

1. These answers assume that the decedent died after September 1, 1992.

Table 6.03, Part 1
Calculation of Elective Share

	What Percentage Right?	*What Is the Right Based On?*	*Is the Share Based on the Estate Before Subtraction of All Debts, After Subtraction of Some Debts, After Subtraction of All Debts?*	*Is Foreign Real Property Taken Into Account?*	*Is Foreign Personal Property Taken Into Account?*
Alabama	Lesser of all of the estate less the surviving spouse's separate estate, or one-third of the estate. (§ 43-8-70(a)(1) & (2)) Separate estate is: (1) all property which immediately after death the surviving spouse owns outright or in fee simple absolute; (2) all legal/equitable interests in property acquired by surviving the decedent; and (3) all income and other beneficial interests (a) under a trust, (b) in proceeds of life insurance on the life of decedent, (c) under any broad-based nondiscriminatory pension, stock bonus, deferred compensation, disability, death benefit, or other such plan established by an employer. (§ 43-8-70(b))	Depends on which election spouse is entitled to—one-third or full estate less separate estate. If one-third election, the right is based on the probate estate. (§ 43-8-70) If full estate less separate estate, other sources of income to surviving spouse and property held by surviving spouse are considered. (§ 43-8-70(b)) See prior column.	No reference to creditors. However, the now abolished right to dower was superior to creditor claims, devisees, and legatees. (Steele v. Steele, 64 Ala. 438, 462 (1879); § 43-8-70)	Simply refers to "estate." (§ 43-8-70(a)(1) & (2))	Simply refers to "estate." (§ 43-8-70(a)(1) & (2))
Alaska	One-third of augmented estate. (§ 13.12.202(a))	Augmented estate. (§§ 13.12.202(a), 13.12.203) The augmented estate is a complicated calculation, the particulars of which should be checked	See Table 6.03, Part 2. Subtract funeral and administrative expenses, homestead, family allowance, exempt property, and	Yes. (§ 13.12.203)	Yes. (§ 13.12.203)

		specifically. (§ 13.12.204–207) In general terms, the augmented estate consists of: (a) decedent's net probate estate; (b) decedent's nonprobate transfers to others (e.g., joint tenancy, insurance, irrevocable transfers in which decedent retained rights to property, transfers which decedent retained power over the income of property) § 13.12.205); (c) decedent's nonprobate transfers to surviving spouse; (e) surviving spouse's property; and (f)surviving spouse's non probate transfers to others. (§ 13.12.203)	enforceable claims. (§ 13.12.204)		
Arizona			*Community property—no quasi-community property*		
Arkansas	With children: Land—one-third life estate in property in which the decedent was seized. (§ 28-11-301(a)) Personalty—one–third of property which decedent possessed/seized. (§ 28-11-305) Without children: Land—one–half in fee simple of the land that is newly acquired and not an ancestral estate; one-third as against creditors. (§ 28-11-307(a)) If an ancestral estate, one-half; one-third as against creditors. (§ 28-11-307(b)) Personalty—one-half absolutely; one-third as	Real property—that which was seized. (§§ 28-11-301, 28-11-307) Personal—that which was possessed or seized. (§ 28-11-305)	No deduction. (§ 28-11-305; Dolton v. Allen, 167 S.W.2d 893, 894 (1943); § 28-11-301; Tate v. Jay, 31 Ark. 576, 579 (1876))	No apparent distinction made between domestic and foreign property.	Same as prior column.

(cont'd)

Table 6.03, Part 1
Calculation of Elective Share *(continued)*

	What Percentage Right?	*What Is the Right Based On?*	*Is the Share Based on the Estate Before Subtraction of All Debts, After Subtraction of Some Debts, After Subtraction of All Debts?*	*Is Foreign Real Property Taken Into Account?*	*Is Foreign Personal Property Taken Into Account?*
Arkansas *(cont'd)*	against creditors. (§ 28-11-307(a))				
California[1]	One-half quasi-community property. (Prob. § 101)	Quasi-community property. (Prob. § 101) See second column to the right.	The surviving spouse remains liable for debts chargeable against quasi-community property equal to the percent of community property of the surviving spouse and the community property of the decedent that the surviving spouse takes. (Prob. §§ 13550, 13551) Other general debts can be allocated between surviving spouse and estate property. (Prob. § 11440 et seq.)	Quasi-community property is all property that is not community property and is: (a) all personal property wherever situated and all real property situated in California acquired by the decedent while domiciled elsewhere that would have been community property if the decedent had been domiciled in California at the time of acquisition; and (b) all personal wherever situated and real property in California acquired in exchange for real and personal property that would have been com munity property if the decedent had been domiciled in California at the time the property	See prior columns.

				so exchanged was acquired. (Prob. § 66)	
Colorado	Varies depending on length of marriage, maximum one-half of augmented estate. (§ 15-11-201(1)) If the amount of the surviving spouse's property and the property that passes to spouse by intestate or testate succession and the amount payable from the decedent's probate estate and nonprobate transfers is less than $50,000, the surviving spouse is entitled to a supplemental elective share of $50,000 less the above-described amounts. (§ 15-11-201(2))	Augmented estate is a complicated calculation, and the statute should be carefully checked before computation. Generally, it includes: (a) decedent's net probate estate; (b)nonprobate transfers to others (e.g., joint tenancy, multiple party accounts, certain life insurance, irrevocable transfers in which decedent reserved rights, any transfer creating a power in decedent over the income or principal of the property); (c) nonprobate transfers to surviving spouse; (d) spouse's property (§ 15-11-202(2)); and (e) spouse's nonprobate transfers to others (§ 15-11-202(2)(d)(II)).	Based on augmented estate, which calls for subtraction from probate estate of funeral and administrative expenses, family allowance, exempt property, and enforceable claims. (§ 15-11-202(2)(a))	Yes. (§ 1511202(1)(a)(VIII) & 15-11-202(2)(b))	Yes. (§§ 15-11-202(1)(a)(VIII) & 15-11-202(2)(b))
Connecticut	One-third life estate in value of all property passing under will, real and personal, legally or equitably owned by the decedent at the time of death. (§ 45a-436(a))	Refers only to property passing under will—estate property. (§ 45a-436(a))	Net estate (e.g., subtract all debts and charges against estate). (§ 45a–436(a))	Refers to all property. (§ 45a-436(a)) But see Banker's Trust Co. v. Greims, 147 A. 290, 292 (1929), indicating that foreign real property will not be counted in determining statutory share.	See prior column.
Delaware	One-third of "elective estate," less all transfers to surviving spouse. (12 § 901(a))	The "elective estate," less all transfers to surviving spouse valued at date of distribution. (12 § 901(a))	The elective estate is based on the federal gross estate less transfers to surviving spouse and I.R.C. §§ 2053 and 2054 deductions. (12 §§ 901(a), 902(a))	Only mentions "gross estate" and "elective estate." (12 § 902(a))	Only mentions "gross estate" and "elective estate." (12 § 902(a))

Table 6.03, Part 1
Calculation of Elective Share *(continued)*

	What Percentage Right?	*What Is the Right Based On?*	*Is the Share Based on the Estate Before Subtraction of All Debts, After Subtraction of Some Debts, After Subtraction of All Debts?*	*Is Foreign Real Property Taken Into Account?*	*Is Foreign Personal Property Taken Into Account?*
District of Columbia	Spouse is entitled to "legal share." The legal share is the share or interest in the real or personal property of the deceased spouse, as he would have taken if the deceased spouse had died intestate, not to exceed one-half of the net estate bequeathed and devised by the will. (§ 19-113(e))	The "legal share" includes real estate and surplus or the personal estate. (§ 19-301)	The "surplus personal estate" is not defined, but presumably is what remains after expenses of administration.	There is no specific limitation.	There is no specific limitation.
Florida	30% of the elective estate (§ 732.2065) as defined broadly in § 732.2035. For the definition of "values" of property interests that make up the elective estate, see § 732.2055.	Elective estate (§ 732.2035) that consists of the sum of values of the following property interests: decedent's probate estate if it is subject to administration in the U.S. (§ 732.2025(7)); P.O.D.s, T.O.D.s, "In Trust For"; joint tenancy with right of survivorship or in tenancy by the entirety; revocable transfers; property in which the decedent retained an income interest; or person other than surviving spouse had discretion to distribute or appoint the principal for the benefit of the decedent.	Probate estate reduced by all valid claims against the estate and all mortgages, liens, or security interests on the assets. (§ 732.2055(5))	Probably not if outside the U.S. (§ 732.2025(7))	Probably yes, if decedent was domiciled in the U.S. so that there is an administration in the U.S. (§ 732.2025(7))

Georgia[2]	The surviving spouse is entitled to a year's support in the form of property, including money. (§ 53-3-1) Personal and real property can be chosen for the year's support. (§§ 53-3-10, 53-3-11)	Property from the estate can be chosen. (§§ 53-3-1, 53-3-5)	The year's support is to be preferred before all other expenses since it is among the necessary expenses of administration. (§ 53-3-1(b))	There is a description of awarding an interest in real property located in Georgia for the year's support. (§ 53-3-11)	There is only a description of awarding an interest in property located inside or outside the county where the decedent was domiciled at the time of death for the year's support. (§ 53-3-10)
Hawaii	The percentage share is determined by the length of time the spouse and the decedent were married to each other, or the reciprocal beneficiary and the decedent were in a reciprocal beneficiary relationship, maximum of 50% of augmented estate. (§ 560:2-202) See § 560:2-201 for definition of "reciprocal beneficiary."	Augmented estate (§§ 560:2-202,560:2-203), which is composed of: decedent's net probate estate (§ 560:2-204), the decedent's nonprobate transfers to others (§ 560:2-205), the decedent's nonprobate transfers to the surviving spouse or reciprocal beneficiary (§ 560:2-206), and the surviving spouse's or reciprocal beneficiary property and nonprobate transfers to others (§ 560:2-207).	The value of the augmented estate includes the decedent's probate estate, reduced by funeral and administrative expenses, homestead allowance, family allowances, exempt property, and enforceable claims. (§ 560:2-204)	Yes, all real property wherever situated. (§ 560:2-203)	Yes, all personal property wherever situated. (§ 560:2-203)
Idaho[3]	One-half of quasi community property, unless not devised by will; then all goes to surviving spouse. (§ 15-2-201)	Augmented quasi-community property estate composed of: quasi-community property (all personal property, wherever situated, and all real property situated in this state which is acquired by the decedent while domiciled elsewhere and which would have been the community property of the decedent and the surviving spouse had the decedent been domiciled in this state at the time of its acquisition (§ 15-2-201(b)) and the *(cont'd)*	Before the subtraction of all debts, since the elective share is reduced by an allocable portion of: general administration expenses, homestead allowance, family allowance, exempt property and enforceable claims. (§ 15-2-203(b))	Yes. (§ 15-2-201(b))	Yes. (§ 15-2-201(b))

Table 6.03, Part 1
Calculation of Elective Share *(continued)*

	What Percentage Right?	*What Is the Right Based On?*	*Is the Share Based on the Estate Before Subtraction of All Debts, After Subtraction of Some Debts, After Subtraction of All Debts?*	*Is Foreign Real Property Taken Into Account?*	*Is Foreign Personal Property Taken Into Account?*
Idaho *(cont'd)*		augmented estate (transfers of quasi-community property to a person other than the surviving spouse without adequate consideration and without the consent of the surviving spouse (§§ 15-2-202, 15-2-203))			
Illinois	One-third of the estate if the testator leaves a descendant or one-half of the estate if the testator leaves no descendant. (755 ILCS § 5/2-8(a))	Probate estate. Inter vivos transfers can be made to defeat the elective share. (Estate of Mocny, 630 N.E.2d 87,93 (App. Ct. 1993)) Assets transferred into joint tenancy, where the transfer was made solely to establish a convenience account. (Estate of Mocny, 630 N.E.2d 87, 93 (App. Ct. 1993)) Life insurance policies are not vulnerable to being challenged in a cause of action for illegally defeating a marital right. (Id.)	Entire estate after payment of all just claims. (755 ILCS § 5/2-8; In re Grant's Estate, 415 N.E.2d 416 (1980))	Real property in another state is not part of the "entire estate." The law of the states where the real estate is located governs the surviving spouse's rights. (In re Estate of Pericles, 641 N.E.2d 10 (App. Ct. 1994))	There is no specific limitation.
Indiana	One-half of the net personal and real estate of the decedent, unless the surviving spouse is a second or other subsequent	Not only probate estate. Also, inter vivos trusts where the deceased settlor retains so much control over disposition and	Although the term "net personal and real estate" is used, the closest defined term is "net estate." "Net estate" is real and personal	Only property as would have passed under the laws of descent and distribution. (§ 29-1-3-1(a))	Only mentions net personal estate of testator. (§ 29-1-3-1)

	spouse who did not at any time have children by the decedent and the decedent left surviving a child or children or descendants of a child or children by a previous spouse, then one-third of the net personal estate of the decedent plus 25% of the fair market value of the lands of the decedent. (§ 29-1-3-1(a))	management of property in trust that trustee possesses only a naked or nominal title which does not impair full ownership of cestui que trust or beneficiary. (Leazenby v. Clinton County Bank & Trust Co., 355 N.E.2d 861, 864 (1976))	property exclusive of the family allowance provided for by § 29-1-4-1 and enforceable claims against the estate. (§§ 29-1-3-1, 29-1-1-3)		
Iowa	If the surviving spouse elects to take against the will, the share of the surviving spouse will be: (a) one-third in value of all the legal or equitable estates in real property possessed by the decedent at the time during the marriage, which have not been sold on execution or other judicial sale, and to which the surviving spouse has made no relinquishment of right; (b)all personal property that, at the time of death, was in the hands of the decedent as the head of a family, exempt from execution; and (c) one-third of all other personal property of the decedent that is not necessary for the payment of debts and charges. (§ 633.238)	See prior column. (§ 633.238)	One-third of all other personal property of the decedent after the subtraction of all debts. (§ 633.238; In re Estate of Thompson, 512 N.W.2d 560, 564 (1994))	All real property possessed by decedent at any time during marriage. (§ 633.238(1))	All personal property. (§ 633.238(1))
Kansas	Varies depending on length of marriage, maximum of *(cont'd)*	Augmented estate (§§ 59-6a202, 59-6a203), *(cont'd)*	The value of the augmented estate includes the *(cont'd)*	There is no specific limitation. (§ 59-6a203)	There is no specific limitation. (§ 59-6a203)

Table 6.03, Part 1
Calculation of Elective Share *(continued)*

	What Percentage Right?	*What Is the Right Based On?*	*Is the Share Based on the Estate Before Subtraction of All Debts, After Subtraction of Some Debts, After Subtraction of All Debts?*	*Is Foreign Real Property Taken Into Account?*	*Is Foreign Personal Property Taken Into Account?*
Kansas *(cont'd)*	one-half of augmented estate. (§ 59-6a202)	which is composed of: decedent's net probate estate (§ 59-6a204), the decedent's non-probate transfers to others (§ 59-6a205) (e.g., joint tenancy, insurance, irrevocable transfers in which decedent retained rights to property, transfers which decedent retained power over the income or property), the decedent's nonprobate transfers to the surviving spouse (§ 596a206), and the surviving spouse's property and nonprobate transfers to others (§ 59-6a207).	decedent's probate estate, reduced by funeral and administrative expenses, homestead or homestead allowance, family allow ances, and enforceable demands. (§ 596-a204)		
Kentucky	One-half of the surplus real estate of which the other spouse or anyone for the use of the other spouse was seized of an estate in fee simple at the time of death, and shall have an estate for his or her life in one-third of any real estate which the other spouse or anyone for the use of the other spouse, was seized	Not only probate estate. All property transferred with the intent to defeat the surviving spouse's claims to dower. (Harris v. Rock, 799 S.W.2d 10 (1990); § 392.020)	Dower is provided from the absolute one-half interest in the surplus personalty of a deceased spouse and is based on the personalty remaining after the pay ment of the debts, funeral expenses, charges of administration, and widow's exemptions have been deducted from the gross personalty possessed by the	There is no specific limitation.	There is no specific limitation.

	of in fee simple during the coverture but not at the time of death. The surviving spouse shall also have an absolute estate in one-half of the surplus personalty left by the decedent. (§ 392.020)		decedent at the time of his death. After subtraction of funeral expenses, charges of administration and debts. (§ 392.020; Harris v. Rock, 799 S.W.2d 10 (Sup. Ct. 1990); Mattingly v. Gentry, 419 S.W.2d 745 (Sup. Ct. 1967); Talbott's Ex'r v. Goetz, 151 S.W.2d 369 (1941))		
Louisiana	*Community property state—no quasi-community property*				
Maine	One-third of augmented estate. (18-A § 2-201(a))	Augmented estate: probate estate minus funeral and administration expenses, homestead, family allowance, exemptions, and enforceable claims augmented by surviving spouse's property and nonprobate transfers by surviving spouse and decedent. (18-A § 2-202)	Probate estate minus funeral and administrative expenses, homestead allowance, family allowances and exemptions, and enforceable claims. (18-A § 2-202)	There is no specific limitation.	There is no specific limitation.
Maryland	The surviving spouse may elect to take a one-third share of the net estate if there is surviving issue of the deceased, or a one-half share of the net estate if there is no surviving issue. (Est. & Trusts § 3-203(b))	Net estate, that is, property passing by testate succession. (Est. & Trusts § 3-203(a))	The property passing by testate succession is reduced by funeral and administration expenses, family allowance, and enforceable claims and debts against the estate. (Est. & Trusts § 3-203(a)(1)-(3))	Only mentions net estate. (Est. & Trusts § 3-203(a))	Only mentions net estate. (Est. & Trusts § 3-203(a))
Massachusetts	If the testator left issue, spouse takes one-third of the personal and one-third of the real property; if the deceased left kindred but no issue, spouse takes $25,000 and one-half of *(cont'd)*	Probate estate. (191 § 15)	There appears to be no provision for subtraction.	There is no specific limitation.	There is no specific limitation.

Table 6.03, Part 1
Calculation of Elective Share *(continued)*

	What Percentage Right?	*What Is the Right Based On?*	*Is the Share Based on the Estate Before Subtraction of All Debts, After Subtraction of Some Debts, After Subtraction of All Debts?*	*Is Foreign Real Property Taken Into Account?*	*Is Foreign Personal Property Taken Into Account?*
Massachusetts *(cont'd)*	the remaining personal and real property; except that in either case if the spouse would take real and personal property in an amount exceeding $25,000 in value, the spouse receives, in addition to that amount, only the income during the spouse's life of the excess of the spouse's share of such estate above that amount. If the testator left no issue or kindred, the surviving spouse takes $25,000 and one-half of the remaining real and personal property absolutely. (191 § 15)				
Michigan	Spouse has two choices if the decedent dies intestate—her intestate share under § 700.2102 or her dower right under § 558.1 et seq. If the decedent dies testate, the spouse has three choices—abiding by the terms of the will, if a "widow" that she will take dower rights, or the spouse	See prior column.	The reductions in the share are taken into account in arriving at the intestate estate, which serves as the base for calculating the elective share. See first column. The intestate share of the spouse is determined under § 700.2102.	There is no specific limitation. The key is that the decedent was domiciled in Michigan. (§ 700.2202(1)) If the decedent was not domiciled in Michigan, then the law of the place of domicile determines the surviving spouse's rights. (§ 700.2202(6))	There is no specific limitation. See prior column.

	can take one-half of the sum or share that would have passed to the spouse had the testator died intestate, reduced by one-half of the value of all property "derived by the spouse from the decedent" by any means other than testate or intestate succession upon the decedent's death. Such property "derived by the spouse from the decedent" includes all the following transfers: (a) a transfer made within two years of the decedent's death to the extent that the transfer is subject to federal gift or estate taxes; (b) a transfer made before the date of death subject to a power retained by the decedent which would make the property, or a portion of the property, subject to federal estate tax; and (c) a transfer effectuated by the death of the decedent through joint ownership, tenancy by the entireties, insurance beneficiary, or similar means. (§ 700.2202(1), (2), (7))				
Minnesota	Varies depending on length of marriage, maximum of one-half of augmented estate. (§ 524.2-202(a))	Augmented estate consists of the sum of: (a) the value of the decedent's probate estate, reduced by funeral and administrative	See prior column.	Yes. (§ 524.2-203) There is no specific limitation.	Yes. (§ 524.2-203) There is no specific limitation.

(cont'd)

Table 6.03, Part 1
Calculation of Elective Share *(continued)*

	What Percentage Right?	*What Is the Right Based On?*	*Is the Share Based on the Estate Before Subtraction of All Debts, After Subtraction of Some Debts, After Subtraction of All Debts?*	*Is Foreign Real Property Taken Into Account?*	*Is Foreign Personal Property Taken Into Account?*
Minnesota *(cont'd)*		expenses, homestead allowance, family allowances and exemptions, liens, mortgages and enforceable claims; (b) the value of the decedent's nonprobate transfers to others, other than the homestead, as listed in § 524.2-205(1) to (3); (c) the value of the decedent's nonprobate transfers to the surviving spouse, other than homestead and property passing to the spouse under the federal Social Security System, which is composed of all property that passed outside probate at the decedent's death; (d) property, other than the homestead, owned by the surviving spouse at the decedent's death; (e) property that would have been included in the surviving spouse's nonprobate transfers to others had the spouse been the decedent. Property is excluded from the			

		decedent's nonprobate transfers to others if: (a) the decedent received adequate and full consideration for the property; or (b)the surviving spouse consented in writing to the transfer. (§§ 524.2-203, 524.2-204, 524.2-205, 524.2-206, 524.2-207, 524.2-208)			
Mississippi	Surviving spouse is entitled to such part of the decedent's estate, real and personal, as the spouse would have been entitled if the decedent had died intestate, except that, even if the decedent left no child or descendant of such, the spouse is entitled to only one-half of the real and personal estate of the deceased. (§ 91-5-25)	The calculation for the elective share is based on the estate of the decedent had the decedent died intestate. (§ 91-5-25) The estate of the decedent should be reduced for the debts of the decedent, administrative expenses and funeral expenses. (Banks v. Junk, 264 So. 2d 387, 392 (1972)) Also, the separate estate of the surviving spouse, if any, must be calculated. The surviving spouse is only entitled to an elective share to the extent that the elective share exceeds the value of the surviving spouse's separate estate. (§§ 91-5-25, 91-5-29)	See prior column.	There is no specific limitation.	There is no specific limitation.
Missouri	The surviving spouse, upon election to take against the will, shall receive one-half of the estate, subject to the payment of claims, if there are no lineal descendants of the *(cont'd)*	The estate consists of all the money and property owned by the decedent at death, reduced by funeral and administration expenses, exempt property, family allowance and *(cont'd)*	See prior column.	Yes, to the extent of the surviving spouse's interest in community property in any other state. (§ 474.163(2)(6))	Yes, to the extent of the surviving spouse's interest in community property in any other state. (§ 474.163(2)(6))

Table 6.03, Part 1
Calculation of Elective Share *(continued)*

	What Percentage Right?	*What Is the Right Based On?*	*Is the Share Based on the Estate Before Subtraction of All Debts, After Subtraction of Some Debts, After Subtraction of All Debts?*	*Is Foreign Real Property Taken Into Account?*	*Is Foreign Personal Property Taken Into Account?*
Missouri *(cont'd)*	testator; or, if there are lineal descendants of the testator, the surviving spouse shall receive one-third of the estate subject to the payment of claims. (§ 474.160(1)(1))	enforceable claims, and increased by the aggregate value of all money and property derived by the surviving spouse from the decedent by any means other than testate or intestate succession, exempt property or family allowance without full consideration. See § 474.163 subdivision 2 (1)-(6) for examples of property derived from the decedent. (§ 474.163)			
Montana	Varies depending on length of marriage; maximum of one-half of augmented estate. (§ 72-2-221(1))	Augmented estate consists of the sum of: (a) the value of the decedent's probate estate, reduced by funeral and administrative expenses, homestead allowance, family allowances and exemptions, and enforceable claims; (b) the value of the decedent's non-probate transfers to others, which are composed of all property, whether real or personal, wherever situated, not included in the decedent's estate, of the types	See prior column.	Yes. (§ 72-2-222(1)(a)(vii))	Yes. (§ 72-2-222(1)(a)(vii))

listed in § 72-2-222(2)(b)(i) to (iii); (c) the value of the decedent's nonprobate transfers to the surviving spouse, which are composed of all property that passed outside probate at the decedent's death, including that property listed in § 72-2-222(2)(c)(i) to (iv); (d) except to the extent included in the augmented estate under (a) or (c), the value of property transferred to the spouse by reason of the decedent's death; and owned by the surviving spouse at the decedent's death, including (e)property that would have been included in the surviving spouse's nonprobate transfers to others had the spouse been the decedent. Property is excluded from the decedent's nonprobate transfers to others if: (a) the decedent received adequate and full consideration for the property; or (b) the surviving spouse consented in writing to the transfer; or (c) the property is life insurance, accident insurance, pension, profit sharing, retirement and other benefit plans payable to persons other than the surviving spouse or the decedent's estate. (§ 72-2-222(2) & (3))

Table 6.03, Part 1
Calculation of Elective Share *(continued)*

	What Percentage Right?	*What Is the Right Based On?*	*Is the Share Based on the Estate Before Subtraction of All Debts, After Subtraction of Some Debts, After Subtraction of All Debts?*	*Is Foreign Real Property Taken Into Account?*	*Is Foreign Personal Property Taken Into Account?*
Nebraska	Spouse has the right of election to take an elective share in any fraction not in excess of one-half of the augmented estate. (§ 30-2313(a))	Augmented estate is the estate, first, reduced by the aggregate amount of funeral and administrative expenses, homestead allowance, family allowances and exemptions, and enforceable claims and second, increased by the amount of the following items: (1) the value of property transferred by the decedent at any time during marriage to the surviving spouse to or for the benefit of any person other than a bonafide purchaser or the surviving spouse (see § 30-2314(a)(1)(i)–(iv) for examples of such transfers); and (2) the value of property owned by the surviving spouse at the death of the decedent and the value of property transferred by the surviving spouse at any time during marriage to the decedent to or for the benefit of any person other than the decedent, but exclusive	See prior column.	There is no specific limitation.	There is no specific limitation.

		of all income earned thereby before the death of the decedent. (§ 30-2314(a)) The augmented estate does not include the following, otherwise includable, items: (a) accident or life insurance proceeds, joint annuity or pension, any of which are payable to any person other than the surviving spouse; (b) property transferred by the decedent to any person other than the surviving spouse, where the surviving spouse consents to the transfer; and (c) property transferred by the decedent by any means other than intestate succession or testamentary disposition if an elective share petition is not filed within nine months of the death of the decedent. (§ 30-2314(c))			
Nevada	*Community property state—no quasi-community property*				
New Hampshire	Three alternative percentages under § 560:10, as follows: if any children of decedent survive, or any issue of deceased children survive, one-third of personalty and one-third of real estate. If there are no children of deceased and no issue of any deceased children, but the mother, father, brother, or sister of decedent survive, $10,000 of personalty, $10,000 of	Probate estate. (§ 560:10)	The probate estate, after subtracting payment of debts and administrative expenses. (§ 560:10) Decedent's inter vivos transfers are not taken into account, if made in good faith and not for the purpose of defeating the widow's statutory rights. (Hanke v. Hanke, 459 A.2d 246, 248 (1983))	There is no specific limitation.	There is no specific limitation.

(cont'd)

Table 6.03, Part 1
Calculation of Elective Share *(continued)*

	What Percentage Right?	*What Is the Right Based On?*	*Is the Share Based on the Estate Before Subtraction of All Debts, After Subtraction of Some Debts, After Subtraction of All Debts?*	*Is Foreign Real Property Taken Into Account?*	*Is Foreign Personal Property Taken Into Account?*
New Hampshire *(cont'd)*	realty, and one-half of the remainder above $10,000 in each category. If none of the above relations survive, $10,000 of value, plus $2,000 for each full year from date of marriage to date of death, and one-half of the remainder above the said sum, in personalty, and the same in real estate.				
New Jersey	One-third of the augmented estate. (§ 3B:8-1)	Based on the augmented estate. (§ 3B:8-3) Augmented estate includes: (a) decedent's net probate estate; (b) decedent's nonprobate transfers to others made after May 28, 1980 (i.e., joint tenancy, irrevocable transfers in which decedent retained possession or enjoyment, transfers in which decedent retained right to income, revocable transfers, and transfers within two years of death if amount to any one donee exceeds $3,000.00 in either of the years)	The "estate" minus funeral and administrative expenses and enforceable claims. (§ 3B:8-3)	There is no specific limitation.	There is no specific limitation.

		(§ 3B:8-3); (c) decedent's nonprobate transfers to surviving spouse or domestic partner (§ 3B:8-6(a)); and (d) surviving spouse's nonprobate transfer to others (§ 3B:8-6(b)). Augmented estate does not include: (a) transfers of property under § 3B:8-3 if made with the written consent or joinder of surviving spouse or domestic partner (§ 3B:8-5); and (b) life insurance, accident insurance, joint annuity or pension payable to a person other than the surviving spouse or domestic partner (§ 3B:8-5).			
New Mexico	*Community property state with quasi-community property.* [Quasi-community property is defined in § 4038(C). It is treated as community property for purposes of division of property incident to a dissolution of marriage or a legal separation if both parties are New Mexico domiciliaries at the time of the dissolution or legal separation. (§ 4038(D)) It is not mentioned in any provision dealing with distribution of an estate.]				
New York[4]	Capital value of net estate up to $50,000 or one-third of net estate, whichever is greater. (Est. Powers & Trusts § 5-1.1A(a)(2))	Net probate estate includes: (a) decedent's net probate estate (Est. Powers & Trusts § 5-1.1A(a)); (b) decedent's nonprobate transfers to other (i.e., gifts causa mortis) (Est. Powers & Trusts § 5-1.1A(b)(1)(A)); joint tenancy (Est. Powers & Trusts § 5-1.1A(b)(1)(E)); transfers to trusts where decedent retained right to income, right to revoke, or right to invade principle (Est. Powers & Trusts § 5-1.1A(b)(1)(F)); transfers of property over which	Net probate estate less debts, administrative expenses and reasonable funeral expenses. (Est. Powers & Trusts § 5-1.1A(a)(2))	Yes. (Est. Powers & Trusts § 5-1.1A(c)(7))	Yes. (Est. Powers & Trusts § 5-1.1A(c)(7))

(cont'd)

Table 6.03, Part 1
Calculation of Elective Share *(continued)*

	What Percentage Right?	*What Is the Right Based On?*	*Is the Share Based on the Estate Before Subtraction of All Debts, After Subtraction of Some Debts, After Subtraction of All Debts?*	*Is Foreign Real Property Taken Into Account?*	*Is Foreign Personal Property Taken Into Account?*
New York *(cont'd)*		decedent had a presently exercisable general power of appointment or if the power was released in the last year of his life or if he exercised the power in favor of someone other than himself or his estate (Est. Powers & Trusts § 5-1.1A(b)(1)(H)); property given away in last year of life (Est. Powers & Trusts § 5-1.1A(b)(1)(B)); money deposited, along with dividends and interest thereon, in the name of the decedent in trust for another person in a bank or savings and loan association (Est. Powers & Trusts § 5-1.1A(b)(1)(C)); money deposited, along with dividends and interest thereon, in the name of the decedent and another person and payable on death to the survivor and remaining on deposit in a bank or savings and loan association at the date of decedent's death. (Est. Powers & Trusts § 5-1.1A(b)(1)(D)); any money, securities or other			

		property payable under various plans/accounts, such as savings, retirement, deferred compensation, stock bonus or profit sharing plan, subject to certain limitations and exceptions (Est. Powers & Trusts § 5-1.1A(b)(1)(G))			
North Carolina	The "applicable share" of the Total Net Assets. (§ 30-3.1(a)) The applicable share is one-half if the decedent is not survived by lineal descendants or is survived by one child or a lineal descendant of a deceased child; one-third if the decedent is survived by two or more children, or by lineal descendants of one or more of such children. (Id.) The surviving spouse's share is halved if there are any lin eal descendants of a prior marriage surviving and the surviving spouse and the decedent have no surviving lineal descendants. (§ 30-3.1(b))	Total Net Assets less assets passing to the surviving spouse. Total Net "Assets" is essentially the net amount, after payment of funeral and administration expenses, a year's allowances to persons other than the surviving spouse, debts, and claims against the estate, of (i) the probate estate, (ii) one-half of property with right of survivorship with spouse, (iii) the entire value of survivorship property with others unless contribution can be established, (iv) property forming part of federal taxable estate under sections 2033, 2035–2040, (v) certain donative transfers within six months of death, (vi) retirement account proceeds where the decedent controlled designation of the beneficiary, (vii) any other property passing to the surviving spouse and not already taken into account.	See prior column.	There is no limitation as to situs in calculating Total Net Assets. (§ 30-3.1)	See prior column.

(cont'd)

Table 6.03, Part 1
Calculation of Elective Share *(continued)*

	What Percentage Right?	*What Is the Right Based On?*	*Is the Share Based on the Estate Before Subtraction of All Debts, After Subtraction of Some Debts, After Subtraction of All Debts?*	*Is Foreign Real Property Taken Into Account?*	*Is Foreign Personal Property Taken Into Account?*
North Carolina *(cont'd)*		(§ 30-3.2(4)(a)-(h)) Wrongful death proceeds and Social Security proceeds are not included. (§ 30-3.2(4)(b) & (g)) Death taxes are treated as a claim against the estate to the extent property passing to the surviving spouse does not qualify for the marital deduction. (§ 30-3.1(c)) Property passing to the surviving spouse is defined in § 30-3.3.			
North Dakota	One-half of the augmented estate. (§ 30.1-05-01(1))	The augmented estate (§30.1-05-02) is a complex calculation, the particulars of which should be checked specifically. Augmented estate consists of: (a) net probate estate (§ 30.1-05-02(2)(a)); (b) nonprobate transfers to others (i.e., property over which decedent alone held presently exercisable general power of appointment (§ 30.1-05-02(2)(b)(1)(a)); property held in joint tenancy (§ 30.1-05-02(2)(b)(1)(b) & (c)); transfers in	The net probate estate is arrived at by subtracting from the probate estate funeral and administration expenses, homestead allowance, family allowances, exempt property, and enforceable claims. (§ 30.1-05-02(2)(a))	Yes. (§ 30.1-05-02(1)(a)(7))	Yes. (§ 30.1-0-502(1)(a)(7))

		which decedent retained right to possession, enjoyment, or income (§ 30.1-05-02(2)(b)(2)(a)); transfers in which decedent could exercise control over the income or principal of transferred property (§ 30.1-05-02(2)(b)(2)(b)); any transfer of property to a person other than surviving spouse in last two years of decedent's life (§ 30.1-05-02(2)(b)(3)(a) & (b)); (c) nonprobate transfers to surviving spouse (§ 30.1-05-02 (2)(c)); (d) surviving spouse's property (§ 30.1-05-02 (2)(d)(1)); and (e) surviving spouse's nonprobate transfers to others (§ 30.1-05-02 (2)(d)(2)).			
Ohio	What surviving spouse would have received under § 2105.06 if decedent died intestate. (§ 2106.01(A)) This is not to exceed one-half of the net estate, unless two or more of decedent's children or their lineal descendants survive, in which case it is not to exceed one-third of the net estate. (§ 2106.01(C))	"Net estate." (§ 2106.01(C)) The net estate is what remains of the probate estate after satisfaction of indebtedness of the decedent and the obligations of the estate. (Winkelfoos v. Mann, 475 N.E.2d 509, 514 (Ct. App. 1984); Weeks v. Vandeveer, 233 N.E.2d 502, 506 (Sup. Ct. 1968))	Net estate before payment of federal estate tax, state estate taxes or any other tax that is subject to apportionment. (§ 2106.01(C)) The net estate is defined in court decisions as "what was left after the costs of administration, unpaid debts of the decedent, and other obligations of the estate." (In re Estate of McVicker, 492 N.E.2d 491 (1985); Campbell v. Lloyd, 122 N.E.2d 695, 696 (1954))	There is no specific limitation.	There is no specific limitation.

Table 6.03, Part 1
Calculation of Elective Share *(continued)*

	What Percentage Right?	*What Is the Right Based On?*	*Is the Share Based on the Estate Before Subtraction of All Debts, After Subtraction of Some Debts, After Subtraction of All Debts?*	*Is Foreign Real Property Taken Into Account?*	*Is Foreign Personal Property Taken Into Account?*
Oklahoma	Undivided one-half interest in the property acquired by the joint industry during coverture. (84 § 44(B)(1) & (2))	Property acquired by the joint industry of the spouses during coverture. (84 § 44(B)(1) & (2)) Thus, property acquired before marriage and gifts or devises from others to one spouse would not be covered. (In re Estate of Hardaway, 872 P.2d 395, 397, 398 (1994)) The same is true of exchanges of separate property between spouses, the purchase by one spouse of separate property with separate funds, and compensation received by one spouse for personal injury. *Id.* Commingling of property that is separate results in a loss of separate property classification. (Catron v. First Nat'l Bank & Trust Co., 434 P.2d 263, 271 (Sup. Ct. 1967))	Not liable for the payment of estate taxes. (In re Estate of Hardesty, 708 P.2d 596, 598 (1985))	Yes, so long as it was acquired by joint industry during coverture. (84 § 44(B)(1) & (2))	Yes, so long as it was acquired by joint industry during coverture. (84 § 44(B)(1) & (2))
Oregon	One-quarter of the net estate minus the value of the following given to the surviving spouse under the will of the decedent: (a)	The right is based on net estate. (§ 114.105)	The net estate is defined as "the real and personal property of a decedent, except property used for the support of the surviving spouse	There is no specific limitation.	There is no specific limitation.

property given outright; (b) present value of legal life estates; and (c) present value of the right of the surviving spouse to income or an annuity, or a right of withdrawal from any property transferred in trust by the will that is capable of valuation with reasonable certainty. (§ 114.105(1)) The surviving spouse may also not receive by election under ORS § 114.105 any amount which, together with any of the following property received by the surviving spouse, exceeds one-half of the total of the following property, such property to be reduced by the federal estate tax payable by reason of the property: (a) the property passing under the will; (b) joint annuities; (c) proceeds of insurance; (d) transfers by the decedent within three years before death where the decedent did not receive full compensation; (e) transfers by the decedent to which the decedent retained power; (f) payments from the employer excluding workers' compensation and Social Security; (g) property appointed by the decedent by will or deed within three years of death in favor of

(cont'd)

and children and for the payment of expenses of administration, funeral expenses, claims and taxes.'' (§ 111.005(23))

Table 6.03, Part 1
Calculation of Elective Share *(continued)*

	What Percentage Right?	*What Is the Right Based On?*	*Is the Share Based on the Estate Before Subtraction of All Debts, After Subtraction of Some Debts, After Subtraction of All Debts?*	*Is Foreign Real Property Taken Into Account?*	*Is Foreign Personal Property Taken Into Account?*
Oregon *(cont'd)*	the surviving spouse; and (h) property in joint names of the decedent and one or more other persons. (§ 114.125(1)) This is a complicated calculation; the statute should be consulted carefully before computation.				
Pennsylvania	One-third of the property described in the next column. (20 § 2203)	Property passing by will or intestacy; income or use of remaining life of spouse of property conveyed by decedent during marriage, to the extent that decedent had use of property or an interest in or power to withdraw the income; property conveyed during life where decedent had at his death the power to revoke the conveyance or to consume, invade, or dispose of the principal for his own benefit; property conveyed during marriage by decedent to himself and other(s) with right of survivorship where decedent had power at death to unilaterally convey property	The calculation in the prior column is limited in that it does not include the following: any conveyance made with express consent or joinder of the spouse; life insurance proceeds; interests in any ''broad-based nondiscriminatory''pension, profit-sharing, stock bonus, deferred compensation, disability, death benefit, or other employer-established plan for employees and their beneficiaries; property passing by decedent's exercise or nonexercise of a power given to him by someone else. (20 § 2203(b)(1)–(4)) No transferee of or holder of a lien against property	There is no specific limitation.	There is no specific limitation.

		absolutely or in fee; survivorship rights conveyed to a beneficiary of an annuity contract to the extent it was purchased by decedent during marriage and decedent was receiving annuity payments therefrom at the time of his death; property conveyed by the decedent during marriage and within one year of death, to the extent that the aggregate amount so conveyed to each donee exceeds $3,000, valued at the time of the conveyance. (20 § 2203(a)(1)–(6))	subject to a spouse's election is liable to a surviving spouse if the transferee or lienholder has given a bona fide consideration, unless there is an order or decree of court providing otherwise. (20 § 2211(f))		
Rhode Island	Life estate in all real estate owned in fee simple by decedent at death. (§ 33-25-2(a))	Real estate. (§ 33-25-2(a))	Life estate is subject to any encumbrances existing at decedent's death. Liability of decedent to discharge encumbrances shall not be impaired. (§ 33-25-2(a)) Also, life estate takes precedence over any claims of decedent's creditors, except claims secured by a lien or any form of encumbrance on the real estate. (§ 33-25-3)	Possibly. There is provision for filing the waiver and claim in any other city or town than where the will is being probated. (§ 33-25-4) On the other hand, Rhode Island courts could not exercise authority over out-of-state realty.	N/A
South Carolina	One-third of the decedent's probate estate computed under § 62-2-202. (§ 62-2-201(a))	The decedent's probate estate includes the decedent's property passing by will and by intestacy, reduced by funeral and administration expenses and by enforceable claims. A trust declared void as illusory may be included in the decedent's estate for the	The calculation is based on the decedent's probate estate after the subtraction of funeral and administration expenses and of enforceable claims. (§ 62-2-202)	Probate estate includes property passing by will or intestacy. (§ 62-2-202)	Probate estate includes property passing by will or intestacy. (§ 62-2-202)

(cont'd)

Table 6.03, Part 1
Calculation of Elective Share *(continued)*

	What Percentage Right?	*What Is the Right Based On?*	*Is the Share Based on the Estate Before Subtraction of All Debts, After Subtraction of Some Debts, After Subtraction of All Debts?*	*Is Foreign Real Property Taken Into Account?*	*Is Foreign Personal Property Taken Into Account?*
South Carolina *(cont'd)*		purpose of calculating a surviving spouse's elective share. The trust is illusory if the settler retained substantial control as in the case of a revocable trust. (§ 67-7-112; Dreher v. Dreher, 634 S.E.2d 646 (S.C. 2006)) But see Smith v. McCall, 477 S.E.2d 475 (Ct. App. 1996), which rejected attempt to extend *Seifert* to a joint tenancy account since the joint accounts are valid and are authorized by statute. (§§ 62-6-101 to -113)			
South Dakota	Varies depending on length of marriage, maximum of one-half of augmented estate. If the total is less than $50,000, the surviving spouse is entitled to take a supplemental elective share amount equal to $50,000 minus the sum of certain other amounts. (§ 29A-2-202(a) & (b))	The augmented estate (§ 29A-2-203) is a complex calculation, the particulars of which should be checked specifically. In general terms, the augmented estate consists of: (1) the decedent's net probate estate (decedent's probate estate reduced by funeral and administration expenses, by homestead, family, and exempt property	See prior column.	Yes. (§ 29A-2-203)	Yes. (§ 29A-2-203)

allowances, and by enforceable claims) (§ 29A-2-204); (2) the decedent's nonprobate transfers to others (property over which the decedent held a power of appointment; property held by joint tenancy with right of survivorship; property or accounts held in POD, TOD, or co-ownership with right of survivorship; proceeds of insurance; property over which decedent retained right to possession, enjoyment, or income) (§ 29A-2-205); (3) the decedent's nonprobate transfers to the surviving spouse (property held by joint tenancy with right of survivorship; property or accounts held in co-ownership registration with right of survivorship) along with property passing to the spouse that would have been included in the augmented estate if it has passed to a person other than the spouse (§ 29A-2-206); and (4) the surviving spouse's property and nonprobate transfers to others (property held in joint tenancy with right of survivorship; property or accounts held in co-ownership registration with right of survivorship; property that passed to surviving spouse by reason of

(cont'd)

Table 6.03, Part 1
Calculation of Elective Share *(continued)*

	What Percentage Right?	*What Is the Right Based On?*	*Is the Share Based on the Estate Before Subtraction of All Debts, After Subtraction of Some Debts, After Subtraction of All Debts?*	*Is Foreign Real Property Taken Into Account?*	*Is Foreign Personal Property Taken Into Account?*
South Dakota *(cont'd)*		decedent's death, but not including hometead allowance, family allowance, exempt property, or Social Security payments; property that would have been included in surviving spouse's nonprobate transfers to others had he or she been the decedent). (§ 29A2-207)			
Tennessee	Varies depending on length of marriage, maximum of 40% of net estate. (§ 31-4-101(a)) The elective share is available in the case of intestate decedents as well. (§ 31-4-101(a))	The calculation of the elective share is based on the application of the appropriate percentage right to the decedent's "net estate." The result is then reduced by the value of all assets includable in the decedent's gross estate which were transferred, or deemed transferred, to, or for the benefit of, the surviving spouse. The term "gross estate" has the meaning it has for inheritance tax purposes pursuant to § 67-8-301 et seq. (§ 31-4-101(c)) Those sections include items in addition to the probate estate,	The "net estate," which includes the decedent's real and personal property subject to disposition under the provisions of the decedent's will or the laws of intestate succession, reduced by (1) secured debts to the extent that secured creditors are entitled to realize on the applicable collateral, (2) funeral and administrative expenses, and (3) awards of exempt property, homestead allowance and year's support allowance. (§ 31-4-101(b))	There is no specific limitation.	There is no specific limitation.

		but are not coextensive with the federal gross estate concept.			
Texas		*Community property state; no quasi-community property*			
Utah	The calculation is based on one-third of the augmented estate. (§ 75-2-202(1)) A supplemental elective share that increases the total to as much as a fixed amount of $25,000 is afforded as special relief. (§ 75-2-202(2))	The augmented estate (§ 75-2-203) is a complex calculation, the particulars of which should be checked specifically. In general terms, the augmented estate consists of: (1) the net probate estate (the estate reduced by funeral and administrative expenses, homestead allowance, family allowances and exempt property (§ 75-2-202(3)) and enforceable claims); (2) the decedent's nonprobate transfers to others (property in which decedent held, immediately before death, a general power exercisable immediately before death, or joint tenancy with right of survivorship; P.O.D. accounts, T.O.D. accounts or co-ownership registration; life insurance owned by the decedent or over which he had a general power of appointment, if payable at his death to a person other than the spouse; (3) property transferred by the decedent during marriage, specifically where an income interest was	Yes, in that the net probate estate, a component of the augmented estate, is the probate estate reduced by funeral and administration expenses, homestead allowance, family allowances, exempt property and enforceable claims. (§ 75-2-204)	Yes. (§ 75-2-203)	Yes. (§ 75-2-203)

(cont'd)

Table 6.03, Part 1
Calculation of Elective Share *(continued)*

	What Percentage Right?	*What Is the Right Based On?*	*Is the Share Based on the Estate Before Subtraction of All Debts, After Subtraction of Some Debts, After Subtraction of All Debts?*	*Is Foreign Real Property Taken Into Account?*	*Is Foreign Personal Property Taken Into Account?*
Utah *(cont'd)*		retained, a transfer in which decedent created a general power of appointment; (4) property that passed during marriage and during the two-year period prior to the decedent's death if an interest terminated in property that otherwise would have been included in (1)-(3) above, with special provisions for life insurance; and any other transfers made to or for the benefit of a person other than the surviving spouse, not otherwise included in the augmented estate to the extent of aggregate transfers to a donee in excess of $10,000 in either of the two years (§ 75-2-205); (5) various transfers to surviving spouse (§ 75-2-206); (6) the surviving spouse's property and the surviving spouse's nonprobate transfers to others. (§ 75-2-207)			

Vermont	Not less than one-third of personalty and one-third of realty. (14 §§ 401, 461)	See Table 6.03, Part 2. Note that intervivos transfers with intent to defeat wife's dower claim, with control by husband during life, was deemed fraudulent and set aside. Same theory might apply under present substitute for dower. (Thayer v. Thayer, 14 Vt. 107, 118-119 (1842))	The decedent's estate after the payment of debts, funeral charges and expenses of administration. (14 §§ 401, 461) The surviving spouse's share is based on gross value of real property and cannot be used for payment.	"[A]ll the real estate." (14 § 461)	No limitation. (14 § 401)
Virginia	One-third of the decedent's augmented estate, or, if no children or their descendants survive, the percentage right is one-half of the decedent's augmented estate. (§ 64.1-16)	The augmented estate is a complex calculation, the particulars of which should be checked specifically. In general terms, the augmented estate consists of: (1) the decedent's net probate estate (estate passing by testate or intestate succession, real and personal, after payment of elected allowances and exemptions, expenses, and debts); (2) the value of property, other than tangible personal property received by gift and the proceeds thereof, owned or acquired by the surviving spouse at the decedent's death, to the extent that the property is derived from the decedent, by any means other than testate or intestate succession, without a full consideration in money or money's work; (3) the decedent's nonprobate transfers to the surviving spouse transferred by the	The net probate estate is reduced by allowances, exemptions, funeral expenses, charges of administration, other than federal and state transfer taxes, and debts. (§ 64.1-16.1(A)) In addition, the following are excluded from the augmented estate: property transferred during marriage with the written consent or joinder of the surviving spouse; property, or its income or proceeds received by gift, will, intestate succession, before or during marriage by the decedent spouse, from a person other than the surviving spouse, and maintained as separate property; any transfers made irrevocably prior to Jan. 1, 1991, to the extent that such transfer is irrevocable on that date. (§ 64.1-16.1(B))	There is no specific limitation.	There is no specific limitation.

(cont'd)

Table 6.03, Part 1
Calculation of Elective Share *(continued)*

	What Percentage Right?	*What Is the Right Based On?*	*Is the Share Based on the Estate Before Subtraction of All Debts, After Subtraction of Some Debts, After Subtraction of All Debts?*	*Is Foreign Real Property Taken Into Account?*	*Is Foreign Personal Property Taken Into Account?*
Virginia *(cont'd)*		surviving spouse during the marriage to a person other than the decedent which would have been includable in the surviving spouse's augmented estate had he or she predeceased the decedent; (4) the decedent's transfers to any person during the marriage for which the decedent did not receive adequate and full consideration (transfers in which the decedent retained rights over the whole property, its principal, or its income; transfers in which the decedent retained a right of survivorship; transfers within the five years preceding death which, in aggregate, exceed $10,000). (§ 64.1-16.1(A)) "Estate" and "property" that are part of the augmented estate include insurance policies, retirement benefits exclusive of Social Security, annuities, pension plans, deferred compensation arrangements, and			

		employee benefit plans, owned by, vested in or subject to the decedent's control at death or at the time of an irrevocable transfer during life. (§ 64.1-16.1(D))			
Washington	*Community property state; no quasi-community property*				
West Virginia	Varies depending on length of marriage, maximum of one-half of augmented estate. (§ 42-3-1(a))	The augmented estate is a complex calculation, the particulars of which should be checked specifically. In general terms, the augmented estate consists of: (1) the decedent's net probate estate (probate estate reduced by funeral and administrative expenses, homestead exemption, exempt property, and enforceable claims); (2) the decedent's nonprobate transfers to others (property in which the decedent held a power of appointment, a right of survivorship, a right to income, possession, or enjoyment; property transferred to a donee within the two years before death that exceeds $10,000); (3) the decedent's nonprobate transfers to the surviving spouse (proceeds from insurance, death benefits, or retirement plan); and (4) the surviving spouse's property. (§ 42-3-2(b))	See prior column.	Yes. (§ 42-3-2(b)(2))	Yes. (§ 42-3-2(b)(2))

Table 6.03, Part 1
Calculation of Elective Share *(continued)*

	What Percentage Right?	*What Is the Right Based On?*	*Is the Share Based on the Estate Before Subtraction of All Debts, After Subtraction of Some Debts, After Subtraction of All Debts?*	*Is Foreign Real Property Taken Into Account?*	*Is Foreign Personal Property Taken Into Account?*
Wisconsin		*Community property state; quasi-community property known as deferred marital property estate is available to the surviving spouse (§§ 851.055, 861.02)*			
Wyoming	One-half of probate estate if there is no surviving issue of decedent, or if surviving spouse is also a parent of any surviving issue of the decedent; or one-quarter of probate estate if surviving spouse is not the parent of any surviving issue of decedent. (§ 2-5-101(a)(i)(ii))	Property subject to disposition under the will. (§ 2-5-101)	Probate estate reduced by funeral and administrative expenses, homestead allowance, family allowances and exemption, and enforceable claims. (§ 2-5-101)	Elective share applies to property subject to disposition under the will. (§ 2-5-101(a))	Elective share applies to property subject to disposition under the will. (§ 2-5-101(a))

1. Community property state with quasi-community property.
2. Georgia Year's Support—No elective share, however, the year's support is like the elective share because if the decedent makes a provision in lieu of year's support in the will, then the spouse may elect.
3. Community property state with quasi-community property.
4. These answers assume that the decedent died after September 1, 1992.

Table 6.03, Part 2
Calculation of Elective Share

	Is the Election Allowed If Benefits Are Taken Under the Will?	*If the Elective Share Is Taken, Are Other Benefits, Like Family Allowance, Reduced, or Vice Versa?*	*Is the Elective Share Denied If a Surviving Spouse Was Not Living With the Decedent, Abandoned Him, Was Guilty of Adultery, One of the Spouses Had Filed for Divorce, and Similar Circumstances? If So, Which Ones?*	*Is a Nondomiciliary Spouse of a Domiciliary Decedent Entitled to an Elective Share If the Decedent Died Domiciled in the State?*	*Is a Spouse Entitled to an Elective Share If the Decedent Was Not a Domiciliary, e.g., Spouse Moves to State After Decedent's Death to Claim Share in Local Real Property?*
Alabama	Yes. (§ 43-8-74 commentary) Under the old law, she could not. See, e.g., Adams v. Adams, 39 Ala. 274 (Ala. 1864); Dorsey v. Dorsey, 140 So. 540 (1932) (if taken, she could restore the fund and, thus, preserve her elective share right)	Vice versa. (§§ 43-8-70; 43-8-74; Garrard v. Lang, 514 So. 2d 933, 934 (Ala. 1987)) Gross estate reduced by homestead and exempt property before elective share determined and also reduced by claims by creditors of the estate. (Brakefield v. Hocutt, 779 So. 2d 1165 (Sup. Ct. 2000))	Surviving spouse does not include: (a) person who obtains a final decree of divorce or an annulment unless the couple subsequently remarries; or (b) individual who was a party to a valid proceeding concluded by an order ter minating marital property rights. A decree of separation which does not terminate the status of husband and wife is not a divorce for purposes of this section. (§ 43-8-252)	The domiciliary status of the decedent controls. (§ 43-8-70(a) & (c))	Governed by law of decedent's domicile at death. (§ 43-8-70(c))
Alaska	Yes, but will be used first to satisfy the elective share. (§ 13.12.209)	Vice versa. Homestead, family allowance, exempt property are paid before calculation of elective share. (§ 13.12.202(c))	A person who obtains or consents to a final decree of divorce/annulment is not a spouse unless by a subsequent marriage, the person is married to the decedent at the time of his death. A decree of separation that does not terminate the status of husband and wife is not a divorce for purposes of this section. (§ 13.12.802)	Decedent's domicile controls. (§ 13.12.202)	Law of decedent's domicile controls. (§ 13.12.202)

Table 6.03, Part 2
Calculation of Elective Share *(continued)*

	Is the Election Allowed If Benefits Are Taken Under the Will?	*If the Elective Share Is Taken, Are Other Benefits, Like Family Allowance, Reduced, or Vice Versa?*	*Is the Elective Share Denied If a Surviving Spouse Was Not Living With the Decedent, Abandoned Him, Was Guilty of Adultery, One of the Spouses Had Filed for Divorce, and Similar Circumstances? If So, Which Ones?*	*Is a Nondomiciliary Spouse of a Domiciliary Decedent Entitled to an Elective Share If the Decedent Died Domiciled in the State?*	*Is a Spouse Entitled to an Elective Share If the Decedent Was Not a Domiciliary, e.g., Spouse Moves to State After Decedent's Death to Claim Share in Local Real Property?*
Arizona			*Community property—no quasi-community property*		
Arkansas	No, unless will expressly states that it is not in lieu of dower. (§§ 28-11-404, 28-11-405, 28-39-401; Gathright v. Gathright, 1 S.W.2d 809, 810 (1928); Chambless v. Gentry, 11 S.W.2d 460 (1928) (property given "in lieu of dower" means offer to widow to accept property under will or take dower))	The right to dower is in addition to family allowances and homestead. (§ 28-39-401(b)(1))	Divorce only. (Grober v. Clements, 76 S.W. 555, 557 (1903))	Yes, as there is no specific provision restricting the right. (§§ 28-39-401(a), 28-11-301(a))	Yes. (§ 28-39-401) There is a specific provision to the effect that the surviving spouse "of an alien shall be entitled to dower in the estate of the deceased spouse in the same manner as if the alien had been a native-born citizen of the state." (§ 28-11-202) Presumably, the same benefit would be accorded a domiciliary of another state who is not an alien.
California	No elective share due to community (Prob. § 100) and quasi-community property (Prob. § 101).	There is no express provision; however, it would seem that the family allowance, which is payable during administration out of estate assets, should not affect quasi-community	No provision.	With respect to quasi-community property, decedent's domicile controls. If a domiciliary of California, one-half of decedent's quasi-community property	If California real property was not community property, surviving spouse has same elective share rights as under the law of decedent's domicile. (Prob. § 120)

		property which vests upon death. (Prob. §§ 101, 6540)		belongs to the surviving spouse. (Prob. § 101)	
Colorado	Yes, but these benefits will be used first to satisfy elective share. (§ 15-11-203(1)(a))	Vice versa. (§§ 15-11-201(3), 15-11-202(2)(a))	Only divorce, annulment, and proceedings that terminate marital property rights. A decree of separation that does not terminate the status of husband and wife is not a divorce for purposes of this section. (§ 15-11-802)	Surviving spouse of domiciliary entitled to elective share. (§ 15-11-201(1))	Governed by law of decedent's domicile. (§ 15-11-201(4))
Connecticut	No, unless contrary is expressly stated in will or clearly appears therein. (§ 45a-436(b))	Cannot take statutory share until period of support has expired. (§ 45a-436(d))	Abandonment without sufficient cause and continued abandonment until death. (§ 45a-436(g))	The statute applies with respect to "the death of a spouse" and does not expressly require the decedent to have been a domiciliary of Connecticut. Moreover, there is no provision requiring the surviving spouse to be a domiciliary of the state. (§ 45a436(a))	The section provides that the surviving spouse is entitled to statutory share for any property passing under will. (§ 45a-436) If local real property passes under a foreign will, it is likely that such document will need to be proven in Connecticut and any rights of the spouse in such property will be governed by Connecticut elective share law. (§ 45a-287)
Delaware	Yes. (12 § 907(a))	Not reduced. Allowance is a claim against decedent's estate. (12 § 2308(c)) But if allowance is taken, the estate is necessarily reduced, which in turn would reduce the elective share. The elective share is one-third of the elective estate. (12 § 901)	A complete property settlement entered into, after or in anticipation of separation or divorce is a waiver of all rights to the elective share by each spouse in the property of the other. (12 § 905)	The domiciliary status of the decedent controls. If the decedent is a domiciliary, the surviving spouse is entitled to elective share of estate as per this state's law. (12 § 901(a) & (b)) If the decedent was not a domiciliary, see next question.	Governed by law of decedent's domicile. If the decedent is not domiciled in the State, the right of the surviving spouse to take an elective share in real or tangible personal property is governed by the law of the situs of such property). (12§ 901(b))
District of Columbia	No. (§§ 19-112, 19-113)	Not reduced. (§ 19-101.02)	No provision. Section 19-103, which provided for forfeiture due to desertion or adultery, was repealed.	No provision.	No provision for dower election. Decedent must be a D.C. resident for legal share election. (§ 19301 et seq.)

Table 6.03, Part 2
Calculation of Elective Share *(continued)*

	Is the Election Allowed If Benefits Are Taken Under the Will?	*If the Elective Share Is Taken, Are Other Benefits, Like Family Allowance, Reduced, or Vice Versa?*	*Is the Elective Share Denied If a Surviving Spouse Was Not Living With the Decedent, Abandoned Him, Was Guilty of Adultery, One of the Spouses Had Filed for Divorce, and Similar Circumstances? If So, Which Ones?*	*Is a Nondomiciliary Spouse of a Domiciliary Decedent Entitled to an Elective Share If the Decedent Died Domiciled in the State?*	*Is a Spouse Entitled to an Elective Share If the Decedent Was Not a Domiciliary, e.g., Spouse Moves to State After Decedent's Death to Claim Share in Local Real Property?*
Florida	No, but accomplished indirectly by satisfying spouse's share in part out of property that has passed to him. (§ 732.2075)	Not reduced. (§ 732.2105)	No provision.	The domiciliary status of the decedent controls. If the decedent is a domiciliary, the surviving spouse is entitled to elective share of estate as per this state's law. (§ 732.201)	See answer to prior question.
Georgia[1]	Yes, as long as the bene fits taken under the will were not provided for the spouse in lieu of the year's support, in which case she would have to elect to take either under the will or to take the year's support. (§ 53-3-3)	No, because a family allowance in addition to the year's support does not exist. (§ 53-3-1)	The surviving spouse's right to the year's support is only barred by the marriage or death of the spouse prior to the filing of the petition for year's support. (§ 53-3-2(a))	Yes. (Farris v. Battle 7 S.E. 262, 264 (Sup. Ct. 1887))	No. (Farris v. Battle 7 S.E. 262, 264 (Sup. Ct. 1887))
Hawaii	No, but accomplished indi rectly by satisfying spouse's share in part out of property that has passed to her.	No, the homestead allowance, exempt property, and family allowance are not charged against but are in addition to the elective-	Divorce and annulment seem to deny the elective share to the surviving spouse; a decree of separation that does not terminate	The domiciliary status of the decedent controls. If the decedent is a domicili ary, the surviving spouse is entitled to	Governed by the law of the decedent's domicile at death. (§ 560:2-202(d))

	(§§ 560:2-209(a)(1), 560:2-202))	share and supplemental share amounts. (§ 560:2-202(c))	the status of husband and wife is not a divorce for purposes of this section (§§ 560:2-201, 560:2-802) the former spouse is not considered a surviving spouse. (§ 560:2-802); Magoon v. Magoon, 780 P.2d 80 (1989) (divorced person is not surviving spouse) The same is true for a person ''who has terminated'' a reciprocal beneficiary relationship with the decedent. That person is not deemed a surviving reciprocal beneficiary. (§ 560: 2-802)	elective share of estate as per this state's law. (§ 560:2-202(a))	
Idaho	Yes. (§ 15-2-206(a))	No. If the elective share is taken other benefits are not reduced (§ 15-2-206(b)); however, since these benefits are paid out of the quasi-community estate, the elective share will be reduced. (§ 15-2-203(b))	Only divorce or annulment or valid order terminating marital property rights. A decree of separation which does not terminate the status of husband and wife is not a divorce for purposes of this section. (§ 15-2-802 and Comment to Official Text)	Yes. The sole prerequisite is that the deceased spouse was domiciled in the state at death. (§§ 15-2-201, 15-2-202)	Yes. (§ 15-2-209)
Illinois	No. (755 ILCS § 5/2-8(a))	Other benefits are not reduced. The surviving spouse takes one-third of the ''entire estate,'' which has been held to be net of claims. (In re Estate of Murphy, 464 N.E.2d 1057 (Sup. Ct. 1984); 755 ILCS § 5/2-8)	No provision.	The domiciliary status of the decedent controls. If the decedent is a domiciliary, the surviving spouse is entitled to elective share of estate as per this state's law. (755 ILCS § 5/2-8) If the decedent was not a domiciliary, see next question.	Governed by the law of the domicile of the deceased at the time of death. (Johnson v. LaGrange State Bank, 365 N.E.2d 1056, 1059 (1977); 755 ILCS § 5/2-8)
Indiana	No, the election is not allowed if benefits are *(cont'd)*	No, the elective share will not reduce the ''family *(cont'd)*	If a person shall abandon his or her spouse without just *(cont'd)*	Only mentions ''surviving spouse,'' without *(cont'd)*	Only mentions deceased married individual. (§ 29-1-3-1)

Table 6.03, Part 2
Calculation of Elective Share *(continued)*

	Is the Election Allowed If Benefits Are Taken Under the Will?	*If the Elective Share Is Taken, Are Other Benefits, Like Family Allowance, Reduced, or Vice Versa?*	*Is the Elective Share Denied If a Surviving Spouse Was Not Living With the Decedent, Abandoned Him, Was Guilty of Adultery, One of the Spouses Had Filed for Divorce, and Similar Circumstances? If So, Which Ones?*	*Is a Nondomiciliary Spouse of a Domiciliary Decedent Entitled to an Elective Share If the Decedent Died Domiciled in the State?*	*Is a Spouse Entitled to an Elective Share If the Decedent Was Not a Domiciliary, e.g., Spouse Moves to State After Decedent's Death to Claim Share in Local Real Property?*
Indiana *(cont'd)*	taken under the will, unless the value of the property given the surviving spouse under the will is less than the amount the surviving spouse would receive by electing to take against the will, then she may elect to retain any or all specific bequests or devises in the will and receive the balance due in cash or property. (§ 29-1-3-1)	allowance.'' The survivor's allowance (''family allowance'') is not chargeable against the distributive share due a spouse when the spouse elects against a will. (Estate of Calcutt v. Calcutt, 576 N.E.2d 1288 (1991); §§ 29-1-3-1, § 29-1-4-1)	cause, or if the husband or wife shall have left the other and shall be living at the time of his or her death in adultery, he or she shall take no part of the estate of the decedent husband or wife. (§§ 29-1-2-14, 29-1-2-15)	any requirement as to domicile or residence. (§ 29-1-3-1)	
Iowa	No. (§ 633.236)	The share of the surviving spouse in real estate is set off to include the homestead, or so much there of as will be equal to the share allotted to the spouse by § 633.238. See § 633.239. The spouse is eligible for 12 months' support. The court considers the estate in making this determination. (§ 633.374)	No provision.	Only mentions ''surviving spouse,'' without any requirement as to domicile or residence. (§ 633.236)	Only mentions death of a married person domiciled in Iowa at the time of death. (§ 633.236)

Kansas	Yes, but the benefits under the will are applied first to satisfy the elective share. (§ 59-6a209)	No, the homestead allowance and family allowance are not charged against but are in addition to the elective-share and supplemental share amounts. (§ 59-6a202(c))	No provision.	Only mentions "surviving spouse," without any requirement as to domicile or residence. (§ 59-6a202)	Uncertain. § 59-6a202(d) refers the issue to art. 8 of ch. 59 and § 59-806(a) makes clear that the dispositions of Kansas property of a nondomiciliary generally is subject to the same substantive provisions as would be a domiciliary. However, § 59-806(a)(2) states that the provision shall not be deemed to affect "(2) The rights of a surviving spouse electing to accept or take against the will of a nonresident [i.e., nondomiciliary] decedent, or the method of such election. . . ." Quaere whether this language is referring to the domiciliary state's elective share provision or Kansas' own elective share provision.
Kentucky	No. (Hannah v. Hannah, 824 S.W.2d 866, 867 (1992); § 392.080)	Must elect between dower (one-third of real estate) and homestead. (In re Gibson, 33 F. Supp. 838, 841 (1940); § 427.070)	Absolute divorce bars all claims; (§ 392.090) however, the spouse is entitled to her share when her separation from the decedent is intended as permanent. (Meyers' Adm'r v. Meyers, 50 S.W.2d 81, 82 (1932)) If either spouse voluntarily leaves the other and lives in adultery, the offending party forfeits all right and interest in and to the property and estate of the other unless they afterward become reconciled and live together as husband and wife. (§ 392.090)	Only mentions "survivor," without any requirement as to domicile or residence. (§ 392.020)	Only mentions decedent. (§ 392.020)

Table 6.03, Part 2
Calculation of Elective Share *(continued)*

	Is the Election Allowed If Benefits Are Taken Under the Will?	*If the Elective Share Is Taken, Are Other Benefits, Like Family Allowance, Reduced, or Vice Versa?*	*Is the Elective Share Denied If a Surviving Spouse Was Not Living With the Decedent, Abandoned Him, Was Guilty of Adultery, One of the Spouses Had Filed for Divorce, and Similar Circumstances? If So, Which Ones?*	*Is a Nondomiciliary Spouse of a Domiciliary Decedent Entitled to an Elective Share If the Decedent Died Domiciled in the State?*	*Is a Spouse Entitled to an Elective Share If the Decedent Was Not a Domiciliary, e.g., Spouse Moves to State After Decedent's Death to Claim Share in Local Real Property?*
Louisiana	*Community property state—no quasi-community property*				
Maine	No. (U.S. Trust Co. of N.Y. v. Douglass, 56 A.2d 633, 636 (1948); 18-A § 2-201)	Not reduced. (18-A § 2-206)	No provision.	Only mentions ''surviving spouse,'' without any requirement as to domicile or residence. (18-A § 2-201)	Governed by the law of decedent's domicile at death. (18A § 2-201(b))
Maryland	If spouse takes an elective share, all property that would have passed to the spouse under the decedent's will shall be treated as if the surviving spouse died before the execution of the will. The surviving spouse may not receive property under the will. (Est. & Trusts § 3-208(a))	No provision.	No provision.	Only mentions ''surviving spouse,'' without any requirement as to domicile or residence. (Est. & Trusts § 3-203 (a))	Yes, but only with respect to Maryland real property. (Bish v. Bish, 181 Md. 621, 628 (1943))
Massachusetts	No. To elect against the will, the surviving spouse must waive all provisions of the testator's will. The waiver of the will must be absolute. (191 § 15; Kramer v. Crosby, 165 N.E. 686, 687 (1929))	No provision.	No provision.	Only mentions surviving husband or wife. (191 § 15)	Only mentions deceased person. (191 § 15)

Michigan	Spouse must choose to take under the will or by elective share, unless the contrary plainly appears by the will to be intended by the testator. (§ 700.2202(3))	No provision.	No provision.	Only mentions "surviving spouse," without any requirement as to domicile or residence. (§ 700.2202(1) & (2))	Governed by the law of decedent's domicile at death. (§ 700.2202(6))
Minnesota	Spouse may make election and also take under the provisions of the decedent's will or intestate succession; but property which is part of the augmented estate which passes to the spouse by testate or intestate succession is applied first to satisfy the elective share. (§ 524.2-209(a)(1))	The surviving spouse's homestead allowance, exempt property and family allowance are not charged against, but are in addition to, the elective share. But, the augmented estate is reduced by homestead allowance, exempt property and family allowance. (§§ 524.2-202(c), 524.2-204)	No provision.	Only mentions "surviving spouse," without any requirement as to domicile or residence. (§ 524.2-202(a))	Governed by the law of the decedent's domicile at death. (§ 524.2-202(d))
Mississippi	No. (§ 91-5-25)	Homestead right is not to be considered part of the surviving spouse's separate estate for purposes of determining and reducing the value of the spouse's elective share. (§ 91-5-25; Matter of Estate of Hollaway, 631 So. 2d 127, 137 (1993))	Where wife living separate and apart from her husband through husband's fault (evidence sustained finding that wife was justified in living separate and apart from husband at the time of his death), at his death she was entitled to renounce his will. (§ 91-5-25; Stringer v. Arrington, 32 So. 2d 879, 880 (1947))	Presumably. Since a surviving spouse of a nondomiciliary decedent spouse can claim a share of property in Mississippi, the same should be true of the surviving spouse of a domiciliary decedent spouse. (Bolton v. Barnett, 95 So. 721 (Sup. Ct. 1923))	Husband may renounce wife's will and take child's share, although domicile of the deceased was a foreign state. The right to take the property was governed by the law of the state and not by the law of the decedent's domicile. (§ 91-5-25; Bolton v. Barnett, 95 So. 721, 726 (Sup. Ct. 1923))
Missouri	No. If surviving spouse elects against the will, the spouse shall take nothing under the will. (§ 474.160 (1) & (2))	An election is received in addition to exempt property and family allowance. How ever, any homestead allow ance made to the surviving spouse shall be offset against the elective share. (§ 474.160(1)(1) & (2))	Yes, if adultery or abandonment under certain circumstances. (§ 474.140)	Only mentions married testator. (§ 474.160) However, case law indicates that if decedent was a domiciliary, the surviving spouse is entitled to the elective share. (Colvin v. *(cont'd)*	Only mentions married testator. (§ 474.160) However, case law indicates that the elective share is available with regard to local real estate, at least if there has also not been an acceptance of benefits under the will at *(cont'd)*

Table 6.03, Part 2
Calculation of Elective Share *(continued)*

	Is the Election Allowed If Benefits Are Taken Under the Will?	*If the Elective Share Is Taken, Are Other Benefits, Like Family Allowance, Reduced, or Vice Versa?*	*Is the Elective Share Denied If a Surviving Spouse Was Not Living With the Decedent, Abandoned Him, Was Guilty of Adultery, One of the Spouses Had Filed for Divorce, and Similar Circumstances? If So, Which Ones?*	*Is a Nondomiciliary Spouse of a Domiciliary Decedent Entitled to an Elective Share If the Decedent Died Domiciled in the State?*	*Is a Spouse Entitled to an Elective Share If the Decedent Was Not a Domiciliary, e.g., Spouse Moves to State After Decedent's Death to Claim Share in Local Real Property?*
Missouri *(cont'd)*				Hutchison, 92 S.W.2d 667 (Sup. Ct. 1936))	the decedent's domicile. (Colvin v. Hutchison, 92 S.W.2d 667 (Sup. Ct. 1936))
Montana	Spouse's election does not affect the surviving spouse's share under the provisions of the decedent's will or intestate succession. But, property which is part of the augmented estate that passes to the spouse by testate or intestate succession is applied first to satisfy the elective share. (§§ 72-2-222(2)(a), 72-2-227(1)(a))	The surviving spouse's homestead allowance, exempt property and family allowance are not charged against, but are in addition to, the elective share. But, the augmented estate is reduced by homestead allowance, exempt property and family allowance. (§§ 72-2-221(3), 72-2-222(2)(a), 72-2-226)	No provision.	The domiciliary status of the decedent controls. If the decedent is a domiciliary, the surviving spouse is entitled to elective share of estate as per this state's law. (§ 72-2-221) If the decedent was not a domiciliary, see next question.	Governed by the law of the decedent's domicile at death. (§ 72-2-221(4))
Nebraska	Spouse's election does not affect the share of the surviving spouse under the provisions of the decedent's will or intestate succession. But, property which is part of the augmented estate, which	Spouse is entitled to homestead allowance, exempt property and family allowance whether or not an elective share is taken. But, the augmented estate is reduced by homestead allowance, exempt property	An individual who is divorced from the decedent or whose marriage to the decedent has been dissolved or annulled by a decree that has become final is not a surviving spouse unless, by virtue of a subsequent	The domiciliary status of the decedent controls. If the decedent is a domiciliary, the surviving spouse is entitled to elective share of estate as per this state's law. (§ 30-2313) If the	Governed by the law of the decedent's domicile at death. (§ 30-2313(b))

	passes to thespouse by testate or intestate succession, is applied first to satisfy the elective share. (§§ 30-2318(a), 30-2319(a))	and family allowance. (§§ 30-2318(b), 30-2314(a))	marriage, he is married to the decedent at the time of death. Note that a decree of separation which does not terminate the status of husband and wife does not bar the surviving spouse from claiming the elective share. (§ 30-2353); See 30-2353(b) for more specifications as to who is a "surviving spouse")	decedent was not a domiciliary, see next question.	
Nevada	*Community property state—no quasi-community property*				
New Hampshire	No, unless it appears by will "that such was not the intention." (§ 560:17)	Elective share is reduced by family allowance. (§ 560:1) On the other hand, the homestead allowance may have to be waived if the election is made, although the statutory language is ambiguous. (§ 560.10)	Elective share is denied if husband has abandoned or willfully neglected wife for three years before wife's death, although in that case the husband may still take under any provisions of wife's will. This provision, however, does not apply where the spouses are separated by agreement. (§ 560:18; Foote v. Nicker son, 48 A. 1088 (1900)) In addition, the elective share is denied if, at the time of decedent's death, decedent was justifiably living apart from surviving spouse because surviving spouse was or had been guilty of conduct which constitutes cause for divorce. (§ 560:19) The surviving spouse is still entitled to such as may be given by the will of the deceased. (Id.)	Only mentions "surviving spouse," without any requirement as to domicile or residence. (§ 560:10)	No provision.

Table 6.03, Part 2
Calculation of Elective Share *(continued)*

	Is the Election Allowed If Benefits Are Taken Under the Will?	*If the Elective Share Is Taken, Are Other Benefits, Like Family Allowance, Reduced, or Vice Versa?*	*Is the Elective Share Denied If a Surviving Spouse Was Not Living With the Decedent, Abandoned Him, Was Guilty of Adultery, One of the Spouses Had Filed for Divorce, and Similar Circumstances? If So, Which Ones?*	*Is a Nondomiciliary Spouse of a Domiciliary Decedent Entitled to an Elective Share If the Decedent Died Domiciled in the State?*	*Is a Spouse Entitled to an Elective Share If the Decedent Was Not a Domiciliary, e.g., Spouse Moves to State After Decedent's Death to Claim Share in Local Real Property?*
New Jersey	Yes, but the "value of all property, estate or interest therein . . . succeeded to by the surviving spouse or domestic partner as a result of decedent's death" will be first applied to the amount of the surviving spouse's or domestic partner's elective share. (§ 3B:8-18)	Presumably no (no provision).	Yes, if at time of death, decedent and surviving spouse were living separate and apart in different habitations or had ceased to cohabit as man and wife, either as a result of judgment of divorce or under circumstances which would have given rise to a cause of action for divorce or nullity of marriage to decedent prior to his death. (§ 3B:8-1) With respect to jointure, dower, and curtesy, if a spouse "goes away and continues with his par amour in adultery," these benefits will be denied, unless there is a reconciliation and the deserted spouse lives with the deserting spouse. (§§ 3A:37-2; 3B:28-15)	Since surviving spouse must live with a decedent domiciled in New Jersey to be eligible under § 3B:8-1, if spouse is nondomiciliary and decedent is domiciled in New Jersey, there is no elective share.	Governed by the law of decedent's domicile at death. (§ 3B:8-2)
New Mexico	*Quasi-community property is defined in § 40-3-8(C).*				

	[It is treated as community property for purposes of division of property incident to a dissolution of marriage or a legal separation if both parties are New Mexico domiciliaries at the time of the dissolution or legal separation. (§ 40-3-8(D)) It is not mentioned in any provision dealing with distribution of an estate.]				
New York[2]	Not unless decedent has provided otherwise. (Est. Powers & Trusts § 51.1-A (a)(4)(A))	The other benefits are not reduced. (Est. Powers & Trusts §§ 5-1.1-A, Practice Commentaries; 53.1) The elective share, though, is based on the "net estate." (Est. Powers & Trusts § 5-1.1-A(a)(2))	Divorce, annulment, separation, abandonment, incest, bigamy, provisions all determine whether the husband or wife is a "surviving spouse" within the meaning of the statutes. (Est. Powers & Trusts §§ 5-1.2(a))	Only mentions "surviving spouse," without any requirement as to domicile or residence. (Est. Powers & Trusts § 5-1.1-A)	Not unless nondomiciliary decedent elected to have the disposition of his or her property in New York be governed by New York law. (Est. Powers & Trusts § 5-1.1-A(c)(6))
North Carolina	The base for calculating the elective share is reduced for property pass ing to the surviving spouse under the will and other wise. (§ 30-3.3(a)(2))	The other benefits are not reduced. (§ 30-15) However, the other benefits would reduce the elective share. (§§ 30-3.1(a), 30-3.2(4), 30-3.3(a)(2))	Yes. In the event of a spouse who voluntarily separates from the other spouse and lives in adultery and such has not been condoned; a spouse who willfully and without just cause abandons and refuses to live with the other spouse and is not living with the other spouse at the time of the other spouse's death; a spouse who obtains a divorce not recognized in the state; and a spouse who knowingly contracts a bigamous relationship.(§ 31A-1)	Only mentions "surviving spouse," without any requirement as to domicile or residence. (§ 30-3.1(a))	No. The decedent must have died domiciled in the state. (§ 30-3.1(a))
North Dakota	Yes, but they are included in the augmented estate. (§ 30.1-05-02(2)(d)(1)(c))	No. (§ 30.1-05-02(2)(d)(1)(c))	No provision. Mere voluntary separation or living apart is not enough. (In re Zimmerman, 579 N.W.2d 591 (Sup. Ct. 1998))	Only mentions "surviving spouse," without any requirement as to domicile or residence. (§ 30.1-05-01)	Governed by law of decedent's domicile at death. (§ 30.1-05-01(4))
Ohio	No. (Jones v. Lloyd, 33 Ohio St. 572, 577-578 (1878) (where a widow elects not to take under the will, she can take *(cont'd)*	No. (In re Green's Estate, 410 N.E.2d 812, 814-815 (Com. Pl. 1980); § 2106.01)	Adultery is a bar to dower in real property. (§ 2103.05)	Only mentions surviving spouse. (§ 2106.01)	No provision.

Table 6.03, Part 2
Calculation of Elective Share *(continued)*

	Is the Election Allowed If Benefits Are Taken Under the Will?	*If the Elective Share Is Taken, Are Other Benefits, Like Family Allowance, Reduced, or Vice Versa?*	*Is the Elective Share Denied If a Surviving Spouse Was Not Living With the Decedent, Abandoned Him, Was Guilty of Adultery, One of the Spouses Had Filed for Divorce, and Similar Circumstances? If So, Which Ones?*	*Is a Nondomiciliary Spouse of a Domiciliary Decedent Entitled to an Elective Share If the Decedent Died Domiciled in the State?*	*Is a Spouse Entitled to an Elective Share If the Decedent Was Not a Domiciliary, e.g., Spouse Moves to State After Decedent's Death to Claim Share in Local Real Property?*
Ohio *(cont'd)*	nothing in virtue of the bequests, made to her by the will in lieu of dower); § 2106.01)				
Oklahoma	No. (84 § 44(B)(2); Turner v. First National Bank & Trust Co., 262 P.2d 897, 900 (1953) (surviving spouse may elect to take under will or as heir at law))	Homestead (84 § 44(B)(1); 58 § 311), other exempt property (58 § 311), and additional allowance (58 § 314) whether or not elective share is sought, are available. See also Oden v. Russell, 371 P.2d 489, 495 (Sup. Ct. 1962). The elective share is a one-half interest "in the property acquired by the joint industry of the husband and wife during coverture." (84 § 44 (B)(1)) Thus, the elective share would not seem to be affected by these allowances.	No provision.	Yes. (In re Estate of Miller, 768 P.2d 373, 377 (1988))	Yes, with respect to property, such as Oklahoma real property, subject to local ancillary administration. (In re Estate of Miller, 768 P.2d 373, 377-78 (1988))
Oregon	No. (§§ 114.105(2), 114.145)	The homestead is an absolute right, but the court shall make a reasonable family allowance. Thus, the	Possibly. If the decedent and surviving spouse were living apart at the time of death, the court has	Only mentions "surviving spouse," without any requirement as to	No. (§ 114.105(1))

		elective share probably reduces family allowance. (§§ 114.005, 114.015)	discretion to deny the election, reduce the elective share, or grant the elective share in full. (§ 114.135)	domicile or residence. (§ 114.105)	
Pennsylvania	No. (20 § 2204)	No provision.	No provision.	Only mentions ''surviving spouse,'' without any requirement as to domicile or residence. (20 § 2203)	Governed by the laws of decedent's domicile at death, subject to rights of fiduciaries, custodians, and obligors in Pennsylvania, as well as transferees for value and holders of liens for value on real estate or tangible personal property located in Pennsylvania. (20 § 2202)
Rhode Island	No. (§ 33-25-4)	At least with respect to real estate set aside for the support of the surviving spouse (§ 33-10-4), this right is in addition to the statutory estate. (Id.) There is no provision as to any other benefits.	No provision.	Probably. The statute simply refers to a surviving spouse of a person who dies, with rights granted in ''the real estate owned by the decedent.'' (§ 33-25-2)	Probably. The statute simply refers to a surviving spouse of a person who dies, with rights granted in ''the real estate owned by the decedent.'' (§ 33-25-2)
South Carolina	Yes. However, the amounts of benefits taken under the will be applied first to sat isfy the surviving spouse's right to the elective share. (§§ 62-2-206, 62-2-207(a))	No, but other benefits accruing to the surviving spouse, including property passed to him or her by will, by intestacy, by homestead allowance, or by exempt property, will be applied first to satisfy the elective share. (§ 62-2-207(a))	Yes. A person is not considered a ''surviving spouse'' for the purposes of any right to an elective share if there exists a final, valid decree of divorce, annulment, or valid proceeding terminating marital property rights. (§ 62-2-802)	Only mentions ''surviving spouse,'' without any requirement as to domicile or residence. (§ 62-2-201)	Governed by the law of the decedent's domicile at death. (§ 62-2-201(b))
South Dakota	No provision. However, ''amounts which pass or have passed to the surviving spouse by testate . . . succession'' are first applied to satisfy the elective share. (§ 29A-2-209)	If the right of election is exercised by or on behalf of a surviving spouse, the surviving spouse's homestead allowance, exempt property, and family allowance, if any, are not charged to against	No provision.	Only mentions ''surviving spouse,'' without any requirement as to their domicile or residence. (§ 29A-2-202(a))	Governed by the law of the decedent's domicile at death. (§ 29A-2-202(d))

(cont'd)

Table 6.03, Part 2
Calculation of Elective Share *(continued)*

	Is the Election Allowed If Benefits Are Taken Under the Will?	*If the Elective Share Is Taken, Are Other Benefits, Like Family Allowance, Reduced, or Vice Versa?*	*Is the Elective Share Denied If a Surviving Spouse Was Not Living With the Decedent, Abandoned Him, Was Guilty of Adultery, One of the Spouses Had Filed for Divorce, and Similar Circumstances? If So, Which Ones?*	*Is a Nondomiciliary Spouse of a Domiciliary Decedent Entitled to an Elective Share If the Decedent Died Domiciled in the State?*	*Is a Spouse Entitled to an Elective Share If the Decedent Was Not a Domiciliary, e.g., Spouse Moves to State After Decedent's Death to Claim Share in Local Real Property?*
South Dakota *(cont'd)*		but are in addition to the elective share and supplemental elective share amounts. (§ 29A-2-202(c))			
Tennessee	Yes, but the elective share is reduced by the transfers and deemed transfers to the surviving spouse. (§ 31-4-101(c))	Vice versa. Homestead, exempt property, and year's support allowance reduce net estate. (§ 31-4-101(b))	The misconduct of a widow will not bar her from making an election. (Fogo v. Griffin, 551 S.W.2d 677, 679 (1977) (''all that is required is a valid marriage and survival of widow''); § 31-4-101)	Only mentions ''surviving spouse,'' without any requirement as to domicile or residence. (§ 31-4-101)	Only mentions decedent. (§ 31-4-101)
Texas	*Community property state; no quasi-community property*				
Utah	Yes, but benefits received under the will are charged against the elective share. (§ 75-2-209(1)(a))	The surviving spouse is entitled to homestead allowance, exempt property, and family allowance whether or not he or she elects to take the elective share. However, unless specified in the will or governing instrument, the homestead (§ 75-2-402), exempt property allowance (§ 75-2-403), and the family	No provision.	Only mentions ''surviving spouse,'' without any requirement as to domicile or residence. (§ 75-2-202(1))	Governed by the law of the decedent's domicile at death. (§ 75-2-202(4))

		allowance (§ 75-2-404(2)) are all chargeable against the spouse's elective share. (See also § 75-2-202(3))			
Vermont	Yes, if testator so intends. (In re O'Rourke's Estate, 175 A. 24, 26 (1934); 14 § 401)	Surviving spouse's eligibility to receive household items, temporary support, and other rights like home stead are in addition to the statutory share (14 §§ 403, 404) (In re O'Rourke's Estate, 175 A. 24, 26 (1934))	Statutory share of the dece dent's personal property may by denied where surviving spouse is not the decedent's first wife under certain circumstances. (R. of Prob. P. 13, Reporter's Note (6); 14 § 402) Also, separation because of family discord does not waive spouse's share; likewise, spouse's indiscretion or desertion with out justifiable cause does not forfeit her rights. (Thayer v. Thayer, 14 Vt. 107, 123 (1842); 14 § 461)	Only mentions "surviving spouse," without any requirement as to domicile or residence. (14 §§ 402, 461, 474)	Only mentions decedent without any requirement as to domicile or residence. (14 §§ 402, 461, 474)
Virginia	No. (First Nat'l Exch. Bank v. Hughson, 74 S.E.2d 797, 804 (1953); § 64.1-16)	The right to an elective share is in addition to a right to family allowance and exempt property. (§§ 64.1-151.1, 64.1-151.2) If the surviving spouse exercises the right to the elective share, he or she sacrifices any homestead allowance (the homestead allowance is in lieu of any share passing to the surviving spouse by intestate succession. (§ 64.1-151.3)	A spouse who willfully deserts or abandons the decedent spouse is barred from all interest in the elective share. (§ 64.1-16.3)	Only mentions "surviving spouse," without any requirement as to domicile or residence. (§ 64.1-16)	Governed by the law of the decedent's domicile at death. (§ 64.1-13(B))
Washington			*Community property state; no quasi-community property*		
West Virginia	This section does not expressly require the surviving spouse to elect *(cont'd)*	No provision.	No provision.	Only mentions "surviving spouse," without any requirement as to *(cont'd)*	Governed by the law of the decedent's domicile at death. (§ 42-3-1(c))

Table 6.03, Part 2
Calculation of Elective Share *(continued)*

	Is the Election Allowed If Benefits Are Taken Under the Will?	*If the Elective Share Is Taken, Are Other Benefits, Like Family Allowance, Reduced, or Vice Versa?*	*Is the Elective Share Denied If a Surviving Spouse Was Not Living With the Decedent, Abandoned Him, Was Guilty of Adultery, One of the Spouses Had Filed for Divorce, and Similar Circumstances? If So, Which Ones?*	*Is a Nondomiciliary Spouse of a Domiciliary Decedent Entitled to an Elective Share If the Decedent Died Domiciled in the State?*	*Is a Spouse Entitled to an Elective Share If the Decedent Was Not a Domiciliary, e.g., Spouse Moves to State After Decedent's Death to Claim Share in Local Real Property?*
West Virginia *(cont'd)*	between rights under the will and under general law, but such is within the plain spirit and intention of the statute. (Beard v. Callison, 54 S.E.2d 568 (1949); § 42-3-1)			domicile or residence. (§ 42-3-1)	
Wisconsin	*Community property state; quasi-community property known as deferred marital property estate is available to the surviving spouse (§ 851.055)*				
Wyoming	Yes. The surviving spouse has a right of election whenever the will deprives the surviving spouse of more than the elective share. This clearly anticipates situations in which a spouse is devised some amount under the will, but, nevertheless, makes the election. Note that there does not appear to be offset for the amount devised by will. (§ 2-5-101)	No, unless will expressly provides otherwise. (§ 2-5-103)	No provision.	Only mentions "surviving spouse," without any requirement as to domicile or residence. (§ 2-5-101(a))	Governed by the law of decedent's domicile at death. (§ 2-5-101(b))

1. Georgia Year's Support—No elective share, however, the year's support is like the elective share because if the decedent makes a provision in lieu of year's support in the will, then the spouse may elect to take the year's support rather than the provision under the will. (§ 5333)
2. These answers assume that the decedent died after September 1, 1992.

Table 6.03, Part 3
Calculation of Elective Share

	Are Amounts That Pass to the Surviving Spouse or Owned by the Surviving Spouse Used to Satisfy the Elective Share?	*Are These Interests Valued in a Special Way, e.g., Life Income Interest at One-Half Value of Trust Property in Which the Surviving Spouse has an Interest?*	*How is the Burden of the Elective Share Apportioned Among Estate and/or Nonprobate Beneficiaries?*
Alabama	When satisfying the elective share, values in the estate which have passed to surviving spouse or would have passed to surviving spouse but were renounced are applied first to satisfy the elective share. (§ 43-8-75(a))	The special valuation does not pertain to determining the value of the elective share (§ 43-8-70 (b)), but when determining how the share is satisfied, beneficial interests in life estates and trusts are valued at one-half. (§ 43-8-75(a))	Equitably apportioned among recipients of the estate in proportion to the value of their interests therein. (§ 43-8-75(b))
Alaska	Yes. First, amounts included in the augmented estate that pass or have passed to spouse under will, intestate succession or covered nonprobate transfers to the spouse; next, the portion of the augmented estate consisting of the surviving spouse's property, and covered nonprobate transfers, but no more than two-thirds of the augmented estate. If these are insufficient, then the decedent's probate estate transfers and nonprobate transfers to others are reached. (§ 13-12-209)	Commuted value is to be used for present and future interests, life insurance settlement option, annuity contract, pensions, disability compensation, or similar arrangement. The calculation method is not specified. If there is an overlap under various provisions, only one of the values is relied upon, but it is the highest one. (§ 13.12.208(b)&(c)) The value of community property is not included in the augmented estate. (§ 13.12.208(d))	After taking account of values in the first column, liability is equitably apportioned among recipients of the amounts transferred by decedent's probate estate and by decedent's nonprobate transfers to others. If the elective share is still not fully satisfied, the remaining portion of the decedent's nonprobate transfers to others is applied so that the liability is equitably apportioned among recipients of decedent's nonprobate transfers. (§ 13.12.209(b)&(c))
Arizona		*Community Property—no quasi-community property*	
Arkansas	No provision.	No provision.	No provision.
California[1]	No provision.	No provision.	No provision.
Colorado	Yes. First, amounts which pass or have passed to the surviving spouse by testate or intestate succession, as well as amounts otherwise included in the augmented estate and passing to the surviving spouse; then amounts included in the augmented estate, but which were disclaimed by the surviving spouse; then property included in the augmented estate which was owned by the surviving spouse and property that *(cont'd)*	Commuted value is used with regard to any present/future interest, trust, life insurance settlement option, annuity, pension, disability compensation, retirement plan, death benefit, or similar arrangement "exclusive of social security." The statute does not specify how to determine commuted value or what value to use if different provisions apply but dictate different values. (§ 15-11-202(4))	After taking account of values in the first column, liability is equitably apportioned among recipients of the amounts transferred by decedent's probate estate and by decedent's nonprobate transfers to others. If the elective share is still not fully satisfied, the remaining portion of the decedent's nonprobate transfers to others is applied so that the liability is equitably *(cont'd)*

Table 6.03, Part 3
Calculation of Elective Share *(continued)*

	Are Amounts That Pass to the Surviving Spouse or Owned by the Surviving Spouse Used to Satisfy the Elective Share?	*Are These Interests Valued in a Special Way, e.g., Life Income Interest at One-Half Value of Trust Property in Which the Surviving Spouse has an Interest?*	*How is the Burden of the Elective Share Apportioned Among Estate and/or Nonprobate Beneficiaries?*
Colorado *(cont'd)*	passed to the surviving spouse from the decedent, with certain exceptions, and certain nonprobate transfers to others by the surviving spouse that would have been included in her augmented estate if she had died, but not more than the "applicable percentage, which is twice the elective share percentage." (§ 15-11-203(1))		apportioned among recipients of decedent's nonprobate transfers. (§ 15-11-203(2)&(3))
Connecticut	No provision.	No provision.	Shall be set out by the fiduciary or the distributors appointed by the court and shall be determined according to the judgment of the fiduciary or distributors as to personal or real property or both of them. (§ 45a-436(e))
Delaware	Yes, transfers to the spouse will reduce the amount of elective share. (12 § 901) Transfers to the spouse which are counted in this calculation include property passing to spouse by will or intestate succession, property transferred to spouse by decedent during decedent's lifetime and includible in decedent's gross estate under 26 U.S.C. § 2036, joint tenancies, any other beneficial interests in a trust created by the decedent during his lifetime, property appointed to the spouse by decedent's exercise of general or special power of appointment, insurance on the life decedent including accidental death benefits attributable to premiums paid by the decedent, any lump sums and the commuted	Yes, property owned by the spouse at the decedent's death is valued as of date it is valued for purposes of computing the elective estate. Income earned by included property prior to decedent's death is not treated as property derived from the decedent. (12 § 903(2))	After application of the amounts described in the first column, liability is apportioned among recipients of the "contributing estate." The "contributing estate" consists of the portion of the "elective estate" that was not transferred or deemed transferred to the surviving spouse. The contributing estate does not include joint tenancy property of the decedent, insurance proceeds payable to a beneficiary other than an estate, or any property held in trust. (12 § 908 (b)) The "elective estate" is the federal gross estate less deductions allowable under I.R.C. §§ 2053 & 2054 and transfers by the decedent during life that were made with the written consent or joinder of the surviving spouse.

	value of proceeds of annuity contracts of which the decedent was the primary annuitant attributable to premiums paid by the decedent, the commuted value of amounts payable of the decedent's death under a public or private pension, disability compensation, death benefit or retirement plan, exclusive of the federal Social Security System, by reason of service performed or disabilities incurred by the decedent, and the value of the share of the surviving spouse resulting from rights in property formerly owned by the decedent. (12 § 903)		(12 § 902(a)) The apportionment will be made in the proportion that the value of each recipient's property bears to the total value of all recipients' property, although this does not include a temporary interest. The amount is due from the corpus. (12 § 908(a))
District of Columbia	No provision.	No provision.	No provision.
Florida	Yes. Account is taken in the following priority of amounts paid to or for the benefit of the spouse: life insurance on the life of decedent paid to or for the benefit of the surviving spouse and not owned by the surviving spouse; any pension, retirement, or deferred compensation plan and the like paid to or for the benefit of the surviving spouse; joint tenancy interest of the decedent paid to or for the benefit of the surviving spouse; property in a qualifying property in a special needs trust for the benefit of the surviving spouse; property forming part of the elective estate; property interests that would have satisfied the elective share as part of the "elective estate," but which were disclaimed. The "elective estate" is essentially a broad augmented estate concept. (§ 732.2035)	Value is determined at decedent's death, except if there has been an earlier irrevocable transfer within one year of death, in which case the date of transfer is utilized. (§ 732.2055)	After taking into account values in the first column, liability is first satisfied by recipients of decedent's probate estate and revocable trusts; then P.O.D., T.O.D., and Totten Trust accounts, as well as joint tenancy and tenancy by the entirety property and net cash surrender value immediately before death of insurance on decedent's life; then property subject to a retained income or principal interest of the decedent or a power in a third person to appoint property to decedent, as well as amounts payable under decedent's retirement or similar plan; then all other property interests other than protected charitable lead interests included in the elective share; and then protected charitable lead interests, as long as doing so does not jeopardize charitable deductions under the federal gift tax laws. (§ 732.2075(2)) Within a class of recipients, liability is apportioned based on proportional value received. In the case of the recipient of trust or probate estate principal, the amount distributed is multiplied by the contribution percentage, which is essentially the trust's or estate's portion of the elective share liability. (§ 732.2085)

Table 6.03, Part 3
Calculation of Elective Share *(continued)*

	Are Amounts That Pass to the Surviving Spouse or Owned by the Surviving Spouse Used to Satisfy the Elective Share?	*Are These Interests Valued in a Special Way, e.g., Life Income Interest at One-Half Value of Trust Property in Which the Surviving Spouse has an Interest?*	*How is the Burden of the Elective Share Apportioned Among Estate and/or Nonprobate Beneficiaries?*
Georgia[2]	If there is no objection, the court will enter an order setting aside year's support. (§ 53-3-7(a)) If an objection is made to the amount or nature of the property proposed to be set aside as year's support, then the court shall set apart an amount taking into consideration the support available to the individual for whom the property is to be set apart from sources other than year's support, including but not limited to the principal of any separate estate and the income and earning capacity of that individual, the solvency of the estate and such other criteria as the court deems equitable. (§ 53-3-7(c))	No provision.	No provision.
Hawaii	First, amounts which pass or have passed to the surviving spouse by testate or intestate succession, as well as amounts otherwise included in the augmented estate and passing to the surviving spouse; then amounts included in the augmented estate, but which were disclaimed by the surviving spouse; then property included in the augmented estate which was owned by the surviving spouse and property that passed to the surviving spouse from the decedent, with certain exceptions, and certain nonprobate transfers to others by the surviving spouse that would have been included in her augmented estate if she had died, but not more than the "applicable percentage, which is twice the elective share percentage." (§ 560:2-209)	Commuted value is to be used for present and future interests, payable under any trust, life insurance settlement option, annuity contract, pensions, disability compensation, death benefit, retirement plan, or similar arrangement. The calculation method is not specified. If there is an overlap under various provisions, only one of the values is relied upon, but it is the highest one. (§ 560:2-208(b)&(c))	After taking account of values in the first column, liability is equitably apportioned among recipients of the amounts transferred by decedent's probate estate and by decedent's nonprobate transfers to others. If the elective share is still not fully satisfied, the remaining portion of the decedent's nonprobate transfers to others is applied so that the liability is equitably apportioned among recipients of decedent's nonprobate transfers. (§ 560:2-209(b)&(c))

Idaho[3]	The property which passes or has passed to the surviving spouse by testate or intestate succession and property included in the augmented estate which has not been renounced is applied first to satisfy the elective share. (§ 15-2-207(a))	No provision.	If amounts described in the first column are not sufficient to satisfy the elective share, then the remaining amount of the elective share is equitably apportioned among beneficiaries of the will and transferees of the augmented estate in proportion to the value of their interest therein. (§ 15-2-207(b))
Illinois	No provision.	No provision.	Proportionate reductions. (755 ILCS § 5/2-8 (d); Kane v. Schofield, 76 N.E.2d 216, 221-222 (App. Ct. 1947))
Indiana	No. (§ 29-1-3-1(a))	No. (§ 29-1-3-1)	The shares of the distributees abate, for the payment of the share of the surviving spouse who elects to take against the will, without any preference or priority between real and personal property, in the following order: property not disposed of by the will, property devised to the residuary devisee, property disposed of by the will but not specifically devised and not devised to the residu ary devisee, and property specifically devised, (§ 29-1-17-3(a)) unless otherwise necessary "to give effect to the intention of the testator." (§ 29-1-17-3(b))
Iowa	No. (§ 633.238)	No. (§ 633.238)	By mutual consent or by referees appointed by the court after an application in writing submitted to the court. (§ 633.247)
Kansas	First, amounts which pass or have passed to the surviving spouse by testate or intestate succession, as well as amounts otherwise included in the augmented estate and passing to the surviving spouse; then amounts included in the augmented estate, but which were disclaimed by the surviving spouse; then property included in the augmented estate which was owned by the surviving spouse and property that passed to the surviving spouse from the decedent, with certain exceptions, and certain nonprobate transfers to others by the surviving spouse that would have been included in her augmented estate if she had *(cont'd)*	Commuted value is to be used for present and future interests, life insurance settlement option, annuity contract, pensions, disability compensation, or similar arrangement exclusive of social security. The calculation method is not specified. If there is an overlap under various provisions, only one of the values is relied upon, but it is the highest one. (§ 59-6a208(b)(2)&(c))	After taking account of values in the first column, liability equitably apportioned among recipients of the amounts transferred by decedent's probate estate and by decedent's nonprobate transfers to others. If the elective share is still not fully satisfied, the remaining portion of the decedent's nonprobate transfers to others is applied so that the liability is equitably apportioned among recipients of decedent's nonprobate transfers. (§ 59-6a209(b)&(c))

Table 6.03, Part 3
Calculation of Elective Share *(continued)*

	Are Amounts That Pass to the Surviving Spouse or Owned by the Surviving Spouse Used to Satisfy the Elective Share?	*Are These Interests Valued in a Special Way, e.g., Life Income Interest at One-Half Value of Trust Property in Which the Surviving Spouse has an Interest?*	*How is the Burden of the Elective Share Apportioned Among Estate and/or Nonprobate Beneficiaries?*
Kansas *(cont'd)*	died, but not more than the "applicable percentage, which is twice the elective share percentage." (§ 59-6a209)		
Kentucky	No. (§ 392.020)	No. (§ 392.020)	No provision.
Louisiana	*Community Property state—no quasi-community property*		
Maine	Yes. "... Values included in the augmented estate which pass or have passed to the surviving spouse, or which would have passed to the spouse but were renounced, are applied first to satisfy the elective share." (18-A § 2-207(a))	Spouse's interest in life estate or trust is to be valued at one-half of total value of the property in which surviving spouse has interest, unless higher or lower values are established by proof. (18-A § 2-207(a))	After taking into account values in first column, remaining property of augmented estate is so applied that liability for the balance of the elective share is equitably apportioned among recipients of augmented estate in proportion to the value of their interests. (18-A § 2-207(b))
Maryland	Yes, apparently to the extent of postmortem distributions to the surviving spouse. (Est. & Trusts § 3-203(e))	No provision.	Contribution to the payment of the elective share shall be prorated among all legatees. Instead of contributing an interest in specific property, a legatee may pay the surviving spouse in cash or other property acceptable to the surviving spouse. (Est. & Trusts § 3-208(b))
Massachusetts	No provision.	No. (191 § 15)	Losses to particular legatees resulting because of a spouse's election against the testator's will should be apportioned as nearly equally as may be upon other legatees, unless a different intention is established in the testator's will. (191 § 15; Crocker v. Crocker, 120 N.E. 110, 112 (1918))
Michigan	Spouse takes one-half of the sum or share that would have passed to the spouse had the tes tator died intestate, reduced by one-half of the	No provision.	"It is the duty of courts to accomplish as near as may be done equitably the same result between the beneficiaries as would have resulted from

	value of all property derived by the spouse from the decedent by any means other than testate or intestate succession. (§ 700.2202(2)(b))		distribution of the estate in accordance with the terms of the will.'' Thus, a residuary devise is reduced before a specific devise. (In re Povey's Estate, 261 N.W. 98, 100 (Sup. Ct. 1935))
Minnesota	Yes. Amounts which have passed or pass to the spouse by testate and intestate succession are applied first to satisfy the elective share, along with nonprobate transfers to the spouse that constitute part of the augmented estate. (§ 524.2-209(a)(1)) Then, amounts included in the augmented estate which are disclaimed by the spouse are taken into account (§ 524.2-209 (a)(2)); then property owned by the surviving spouse or which would have been taken into account if she had died, up to the applicable percentage, which is twice the elective share percentage set forth in § 524.2-202. (§ 524.2-209(a)(3))	Commuted value of spouse's interest in a life estate or interest ''in any trust'' is valued at one-half the total property that is subject to the life estate or trust estate, unless higher or lower values for these interests are established by proof. (§ 524.2-208(c)(2))	After satisfying the claim out of amounts passing or regarded as passing to the spouse (see first column), liability for property of the augmented estate due to the surviving spouse is equitably apportioned among the recipients of the decedent's probate estate and the recipients of the decedent's nonprobate transfers in proportion to the value of their interests therein. (§ 524.2-209(b))
Mississippi	Yes. If the surviving spouse's ''separate estate'' is equal to the elective share she is not entitled to dissent from the will. If it is less, then she is only entitled to the difference. However, the surviving spouse is entitled to the entire elective share if separate property is no greater than one-fifth of the elective share value. As to the ''separate estate,'' it includes such items as beneficiary of life insurance on decedent spouse's life, as well as bank accounts in the names of both spouses. (§ 91-5-29; Matter of Estate of Mason 616 So. 2d 322. (Miss. 1993)	In order to value the lawful elective share and the surviving spouse's separate estate, the court ''may'' appoint three commissioners to make the determinations and report to the court. (§ 91-5-29)	If, for example, the surviving spouse has a separate estate that is only two-thirds of the elective share, then she is entitled to one-third of the realty and one-third of the personalty. (§ 91-5-29) Note the right to a percentage of realty *and* personalty.
Missouri	Homestead offsets the elective share. (§ 474.160(2)) Furthermore, the elective share is reduced by funeral and administration expenses, exempt property, family allowance and enforceable claims, and increased by the aggregate value of all money and property derived by the surviving spouse from the decedent by any means other than testate or *(cont'd)*	Commuted value is used for annuity contract proceeds under which the decedent was the primary annuitant, attributable to premiums paid by him. (§ 474.163 at 2.(4)) Also, commuted value is utilized for amounts payable after decedent's death under pensions, disability compensation, death benefit or retirement plans, exclusive of the federal Social Security System, by reason of *(cont'd)*	Apparently, the traditional abatement by the residuary devisee, then the general and specific would occur. (§§ 473.620; 473.623)

Table 6.03, Part 3
Calculation of Elective Share *(continued)*

	Are Amounts That Pass to the Surviving Spouse or Owned by the Surviving Spouse Used to Satisfy the Elective Share?	*Are These Interests Valued in a Special Way, e.g., Life Income Interest at One-Half Value of Trust Property in Which the Surviving Spouse has an Interest?*	*How is the Burden of the Elective Share Apportioned Among Estate and/or Nonprobate Beneficiaries?*
Missouri *(cont'd)*	intestate succession. (§ 474.163(1)) The meaning of "derived from the decedent" is set forth in § 474.163(2) and includes a beneficial interest in a trust created by the decedent during his lifetime, property appointed by the decedent, insurance proceeds, annuity proceeds, pension, disability, death benefit or retirement plan benefits of decedent, and the value of the surviving spouse's own share of community property formerly owned by the decedent.	services performed, or dis abilities incurred by the decedent. (*Id.* at 2.(5)) Income earned prior to decedent's death by included property owned or transferred by surviving spouse is not taken into account. (§ 474.163(4)) Premiums paid by decedent's employer, partner, or creditor are deemed paid by decedent. (§ 474.163(2), flush language at end of section) If surviving spouse was a cotenant or remainderman, she includes whole value of property at decedent's death, except the proportion of value based on what she or ascendant or collateral relatives of the surviving spouse, other than the decedent contributes to acquire, create or establish the money, property, fund or account.	
Montana	First, amounts included in the augmented estate that pass or have passed to the surviv ing spouse by testate or intestate succession; then nonprobate transfers to spouse included in the augmented estate; then amounts that would have passed to the surviving spouse but were disclaimed; then property owned by the surviving spouse or which would have been included in her augmented estate up to the applicable percentage, which is twice the elective share percentage. (§ 72-2-227)	Yes. Commuted values of life and term interests are determined in accordance with U.S. Treasury Regulations. (§ 72-2-222(4))	After taking account of values in the first column, liability is equitably apportioned among recipients of the amounts transferred by decedent's probate estate and by decedent's nonprobate transfers to others. If the elective share is still not fully satisfied, the remaining portion of the decedent's nonprobate transfers to others is applied so that the liability is equitably apportioned among recipients of decedent's nonprobate transfers. (§ 72-2-227(2)&(3))
Nebraska	Property which is part of the augmented estate which passes or has passed to the surviving spouse by testate or intestate succession or by other means and which has not been renounced is applied first. (§ 30-2319(a))	No provision.	After taking account of values in the first column, liability is equitably apportioned among the recipients of the augmented estate in proportion to the value of their interests therein. A person liable to contribution to the surviving

			spouse may choose to give up the property transferred to him or to pay its value. (§ 30-2319(b)&(c))
Nevada	*community property state—no quasi-community property*		
New Hampshire	No provision.	No provision.	No provision.
New Jersey	Yes. Value of all property, estate or interest therein, owned by the surviving spouse or domestic partner in his own right at the time of death of decedent from whatever source acquired or succeeded to by surviving spouse or domestic partner as a result of decedent's death, even if such property has been renounced by surviving spouse; in addition, any property derived from decedent by means other than testate or intestate succession; also, property described in the preceding clause which was transferred by the surviving spouse or domestic partner during marriage or domestic partnership without full consideration and which would have been included in his augmented estate had he died. (§§ 3B:8-18; 3B:8-6)	Electing spouse's total or proportional beneficial interest in any life estate in real or personal property or in any trust is valued at one half of the total value of the property or trust or the portion of the property or trust subject to the life estate. (§ 3B:8-17) There is no provision to prove a different value.	If the amount of elective share is not satisfied by property in § 3B:8-18(a) and (b), the remaining property is so applied that liability for the balance of the elective share is equitably apportioned among recipients of augmented estates in proportion to the value of their interests therein. (§ 3B:8-18(c))
New Mexico	Community property state with quasi-community property. Quasi-community property is defined in § 40-3-8(C). It is treated as community property for purposes of division of property incident to a dissolution of marriage or a legal separation if both parties are New Mexico domi ciliaries at the time of the dissolution or legal separation. (§ 40-3-8(D)) It is not mentioned in any provision dealing with distribution of an estate.	Community property state with quasi-community property. Quasi-community property is defined in § 40-3-8(C). It is treated as community property for purposes of division of property incident to a dissolution of marriage or a legal separation if both parties are New Mexico domiciliaries at the time of the dissolution or legal separation. (§ 40-3-8(D)) It is not men tioned in any provision dealing with distribution of an estate.	Community property state with quasi-community property. Quasi-community property is defined in § 40-3-8(C). It is treated as community property for purposes of division of property incident to a dissolution of marriage or a legal separation if both parties are New Mexico domiciliaries at the time of the dissolution or legal separation. (§ 40-3-8(D)) It is not mentioned in any provision dealing with distribution of an estate.
New York[4]	Yes. The elective share is reduced by capital value of any interest passing absolutely from decedent to the spouse, or which would have passed, but was renounced. Interests in trust and interests of less than the entire property are not deemed to pass "absolutely." (Est. Powers & Trusts § 5-1.1-A(a)(4))	No provision.	Pro rata among estate and nonprobate beneficiaries. (Est. Powers & Trusts § 5-1.1-A(c)(2))

Table 6.03, Part 3
Calculation of Elective Share *(continued)*

	Are Amounts That Pass to the Surviving Spouse or Owned by the Surviving Spouse Used to Satisfy the Elective Share?	*Are These Interests Valued in a Special Way, e.g., Life Income Interest at One-Half Value of Trust Property in Which the Surviving Spouse has an Interest?*	*How is the Burden of the Elective Share Apportioned Among Estate and/or Nonprobate Beneficiaries?*
North Carolina	Yes. The elective share is reduced by one-half of joint tenancy property and tenancy by the entirety property with the spouse; then any benefits, other than social security, passing to the surviving spouse outright, in trust, or by power of appointment or default of exercise of power by devise, intestacy, or by beneficiary, designation or testamentary exercise or default of power; then year's allowance; then the value of property renounced by surviving spouse; then the value of surviving spouse's interest in life insurance proceeds on the decedent's life; certain gifts to the surviving spouse during the decedent's life; then trusts involving a non adverse trustee that require principal and income to be used. (§§ 30-3.1(a), 30-3.3)	Partial and contingent interests are based on mortuary and annuity tables set forth in §§ 8-46 and 8-47, and upon 6% of the gross value of the underlying property. In the case of interests of the surviving spouse, the following rules apply: if there is fiduciary discretion, the value is zero unless the spouse is the fiduciary or a nonadverse party is required to use income and principal exclusively for the spouse; if the interest hinges on a contingency not addressed in the tables referred to under §§ 8-46 and 8-47, then the contingency will be conclusively presumed to result in the lowest possible value to the surviving spouse; but if the contingency is death or remarriage then remarriage will be ignored; if the contingency is dependent on life expectancy, it shall be presumed to be no less than 10 years regardless of the surviving spouse's actual age at the decedent's death. (§ 30-3.4(e))	Pro rata. (§ 30-3.5(c))
North Dakota	First, the net probate estate passing to the surviving spouse; then the nonprobate assets in the augmented estate passing to the surviving spouse; then the assets that would have been included in the surviving spouse's augmented estate if the surviving spouse had died. (§ 30.1-05-03(1)(a)-(b))	Reference is made to commuted values of any present or future interests and amounts payable under a trust, life insurance settlement option, annuity contract, pensions, or any similar arrangement, exclusive of Social Security. (§ 30.1-05-02(4)) ''Commuted value'' is not defined.	After taking account of values in the first column, liability is equitably apportioned among recipients of the amounts transferred by decedent's probate estate and by decedent's nonprobate transfers to others. If the elective share is still not fully satisfied, the remaining portion of the decedent's nonprobate transfers to others is applied so that the liability is equitably apportioned among recipients of decedent's nonprobate transfers. (§ 30.1-05-03(2)&(3))
Ohio	No provision.	No provision.	No provision.

Oklahoma	Yes, in that the decedent cannot devise to others so that the surviving spouse receives less in value that a one-half interest in the property acquired by the joint industry of husband and wife during coverture. (84 § 44(B)(1))	No provision.	Election by widow to take under statute rather than will does not invalidate will in its entirety. Its provisions shall be carried out as far as possible in the distribution of the remaining property. (Long v. Drumright, 375 P.2d 953, 955 (1962); 84 § 44)
Oregon	Yes. ". . . the elective share shall be reduced by the value of the following property given to the surviving spouse under the will of the decedent: (a) property given outright; (b) present value of legal life estates; and (c) present value of the right of the surviving spouse to income or an annuity . . ." (§ 114.105)	No provision.	Estate property is applied in satisfaction of the elective share in the following order, unless the will provides otherwise: (a) any intestate property; (b) after the intestate property has been exhausted, each devisee shall contribute ratably to the elective share out of the portion of the estate passing to the devisee under the will, except that in abating the interests of the devisees the character of the testamentary plan adopted by the testator shall be preserved so far as possible. (§ 114.165)
Pennsylvania	Any beneficial interest in § 2204(a) property which is owned outright by the surviving spouse immediately after decedent's death is chargeable against the elective share. (20 § 2204(c)) "Beneficial interest" refers to typical probate and augmented estate interests and includes any power of appointment or consumption and any benefit arising from a direction of the decedent regarding the source of payment of inheritance or estate taxes. (20 § 2204(d))	No provision.	Generally, property which otherwise would pass by intestacy is first applied toward satisfaction of elective share. Balance of elective share is charged separately against each conveyance subject to the election, providing spouse a fractional interest in each conveyance. Items of property within each conveyance are then allocated between elective and nonelective share property to give maximum effect to decedent's intentions with respect to dispositions of particular items or kinds of property. (20 § 2211(b)(1))
Rhode Island	No provision.	No provision.	No provision.
South Carolina	Yes. All property, including beneficial interests, which pass or have passed to the surviving spouse under the decedent's will, by intestacy, by any homestead allowance, by exempt property allowance, or which would have passed to the spouse but was renounced, is applied first to satisfy the elective share and to reduce any contributions due from other recipients of *(cont'd)*	Yes. The value of the electing spouse's beneficial interest in any property which would qualify for the federal estate tax marital deduction pursuant to I.R.C. § 2056 is computed at the full value of the qualifying property. (§ 62-2-207(a))	After property passing or that was passed to the surviving spouse, or that has been renounced, see first column, then liability for the balance of the elective share will be satisfied by the decedent's devises which will abate in accordance with the general abatement provision, § 62-3-902, that is, without preference or priority as between real and personal property, in the *(cont'd)*

Table 6.03, Part 3
Calculation of Elective Share *(continued)*

	Are Amounts That Pass to the Surviving Spouse or Owned by the Surviving Spouse Used to Satisfy the Elective Share?	*Are These Interests Valued in a Special Way, e.g., Life Income Interest at One-Half Value of Trust Property in Which the Surviving Spouse has an Interest?*	*How is the Burden of the Elective Share Apportioned Among Estate and/or Nonprobate Beneficiaries?*
South Carolina *(cont'd)*	transfers included in the probate estate. (§ 62-2-207(a))		following order: (1) property not disposed of by will; (2) residuary devises; (3) general devises; (4) specific devises, unless contrary to the testator's intention. (§ 62-2-207(b))
South Dakota	First, amounts which pass or have passed to the surviving spouse by testate or intestate succession, as well as amounts otherwise included in the augmented estate and passing to the surviving spouse; then amounts included in the augmented estate, but which were disclaimed by the surviving spouse; then property included in the augmented estate which was owned by the surviving spouse and property that passed to the surviving spouse from the decedent, with certain exceptions, and certain nonprobate transfers to others by the surviving spouse that would have been included in her augmented estate if she had died, but not more than the "applicable percentage, which is twice the elective share percentage." (§ 29A-2-209)	Commuted value is to be used for present and future interests, life insurance settlement option, annuity contract, pensions, disability compensation, or similar arrangement, exclusive of federal Social Security. The calculation method is not specified. If there is an overlap under various provisions, only one of the values is relied upon, but it is the highest one. (§ 29A-2-208(b)&(c))	After taking account of values in the first column, liability is equitably apportioned among recipients of the amounts transferred by decedent's probate estate and by decedent's nonprobate transfers to others. If the elective share is still not fully satisfied, the remaining portion of the decedent's nonprobate transfers to others is applied so that the liability is equitably apportioned among recipients of decedent's nonprobate transfers. (§ 29A-2-209(b)&(c))
Tennessee	The amount of the surviving spouse's elective share shall be reduced by the value of the assets within the decedent's gross estate which were transferred, or deemed transferred, to or for the benefit of the surviving spouse. (§ 31-4-101(c))	Yes. The value of the decedent's gross estate is determined by the court in the same manner as for inheritance tax purposes pursuant to T.C.A. §§ 67-8-301, et seq., except that the value of any life estate or trust for the lifetime benefit of the surviving spouse shall be actuarially determined. (§ 31-4-101(c))	Persons to whom property from the decedent's net estate was distributed may be liable for contribution to satisfy the elective share. The action for contribution may be maintained against fewer than all persons against whom relief could be sought, but no person is subject to contribution in any greater amount than the person would have been if relief had been secured against all persons subject to contribution. (§ 31-4-102(d))

Texas	*community property state—no quasi-community property*		
Utah	Yes. First, amounts included in the augmented estate that pass or have passed by intestate or testate succession to the surviving spouse, other than the decedent's "separate property" (see next column); then decedent's nonprobate transfers to the spouse; then the surviving spouse's property and nonprobate transfers to others; then the value of the decedent's "separate property" that passes to the surviving spouse; then the surviving spouse's homestead allowance, exempt property, and family allowance. (§ 75-2-209(1))	"Separate property," such as premarital property owned by one of the spouses, gifts or inheritance from a third party, certain personal injury property, and separate property created by waiver, as well as appreciation or income thereon during marriage, are not taken into account in determining the augmented estate. (§ 75-2-208(1)-(4)) Commuted value is used for present or future interests. (§ 75-2-208(7)(b)) Commuted value is to be used for present and future interests, life insurance settlement option, annuity contract, pensions, disability compensation, or similar arrangement. The calculation method is not specified, exclusive of federal Social Security. If there is an overlap under various provisions, only one of the values is relied upon, but it is the highest one. (§ 75-2-208(7)(b)&(8))	After taking account of values in the first column, liability is equitably apportioned among recipients of the amounts transferred by decedent's probate estate and by decedent's nonprobate transfers to others. If the elective share is still not fully satisfied, the remaining portion of the decedent's nonprobate transfers to others is applied so that the liability is equitably apportioned among recipients of decedent's nonprobate transfers. (§ 75-2-209(2)&(3))
Vermont	No. (14 §§ 401, 402, 461, 474)	No provision.	No provision.
Virginia	The value of property included in the augmented estate which passes or has passed to the surviving spouse, or which would have passed to the spouse but was disclaimed, is applied first to satisfy the elective share. (§ 64.1-16.2)	"Property" included in the augmented estate is valued as of the decedent's death, except that property transferred irrevocably during the lifetime of the decedent is valued as of the date the transfer came into possession or enjoyment if that event occurs first. Life estates and remainder interests are valued according to § 55-269.1, and deferred payments and estates for years are discounted to present value using the interest rate specified in § 55-269.1. Life insurance and other benefits exempt from creditors are, nevertheless, part of the estate subject to the elective share claim. (§ 64.1-16.1)	After taking account of values in the first column, liability is apportioned equitably among the recipients of the augmented estate in proportion to the value of their interests therein. (§ 64.1-16.2(B))
Washington	*Community Property state—no quasi-community property*		
West Virginia	First, amounts which pass or have passed to the surviving spouse by testate or intestate succession, as well as amounts otherwise included in *(cont'd)*	Commuted value is used with regard to any present/future interest, trust, life insurance settlement option, annuity, pension, retirement plan, *(cont'd)*	After taking account of values in the first column, liability is equitably apportioned among recipients of the amounts transferred by *(cont'd)*

Table 6.03, Part 3
Calculation of Elective Share *(continued)*

	Are Amounts That Pass to the Surviving Spouse or Owned by the Surviving Spouse Used to Satisfy the Elective Share?	*Are These Interests Valued in a Special Way, e.g., Life Income Interest at One-Half Value of Trust Property in Which the Surviving Spouse has an Interest?*	*How is the Burden of the Elective Share Apportioned Among Estate and/or Nonprobate Beneficiaries?*
West Virginia *(cont'd)*	the augmented estate and passing to the surviving spouse; then amounts included in the augmented estate, but which were disclaimed by the surviving spouse; then property included in the augmented estate which was owned by the surviving spouse and property that passed to the surviving spouse from the decedent, with certain exceptions, and certain nonprobate transfers to others by the surviving spouse that would have been included in her augmented estate if she had died, but not more than the "applicable percentage, which is twice the elective share percentage." (§ 42-3-6(a))	death benefit, or similar arrangement, exclusive of federal Social Security. The statute does not specify how to determine commuted value or what value to use if different provisions apply but dictate different values. (§ 42-3-2(a)(1)(vi))	decedent's probate estate and by decedent's nonprobate transfers to others except for property irrevocably transferred within two years before death. If the elective share is still not fully satisfied, the remaining portion of the decedent's eligible nonprobate transfers to others is applied so that the liability is equitably apportioned among recipients of decedent's nonprobate transfers. (§ 42-3-6(b)&(c))
Wisconsin	*Community Property state—quasi-community property known as deferred marital property estate is available to the surviving spouse*		
Wyoming	No provision.	No provision.	Court discretion. (§ 2-5-105)

1. Community property state with quasi-community property.
2. Georgia Year's Support—No elective share, however, the year's support is like the elective share because if the decedent makes a provision in lieu of year's support in the will, then the spouse may elect to take the year's support rather than the provision under the will. (§ 53-3-3)
3. Community property state with quasi-community property.
4. These answers assume that the decedent died after September 1, 1992.

Table 6.04
Waiver of Spousal Rights, Including Antenuptial Agreements

	Can Rights of Surviving Spouse Be Waived:		*Special Conditions of Any Waiver*			
	Before Marriage?	*During Marriage?*	*Writing*	*Express Reference to Rights*	*Full Disclosure of Financial Status*	*Partial Waiver Allowed*
Alabama	Yes. (§ 43-8-72)	Yes. (§ 43-8-72)	Yes. (§ 43-8-72)	Waiver of "all rights" or a property settlement (divorce) will constitute such a waiver. (§ 43-8-72)	Only requires "fair" disclosure. (§ 43-8-72)	Yes. (§ 43-8-72)
Alaska	Yes. (§ 13.12.213(a))	Yes. (§ 13.12.213(a))	Yes—contract, agreement, waiver signed by surviving spouse. (§ 13.12.213(a))	Waiver of "all rights" or property settlement (divorce) will suffice. (§ 13.12.213(d))	A fair and reasonable disclosure of the property or financial obligations of the decedent is necessary, unless the person voluntarily and expressly waived, in writing, any right to disclosure of the property or financial obligations of the decedent beyond the disclosure provided. Also if the person had, or reason ably could have had, an adequate knowledge of the property or financial obligations of the decedent, no disclosure is necessary. (§ 13.12.213(b)(2))	Yes. (§ 13.12.213(a))
Arizona	*Community Property—no quasi-community property. Note, prenuptial agreements are enforced with respect to divorce.*					
Arkansas	Yes.[1]	Yes.[2]	Yes.[3]	"In lieu of all rights" will waive rights.[4]	Yes.[5]	Yes.[6]

Table 6.04
Waiver of Spousal Rights, Including Antenuptial Agreements *(continued)*

	Can Rights of Surviving Spouse Be Waived:		*Special Conditions of Any Waiver*			
	Before Marriage?	*During Marriage?*	*Writing*	*Express Reference to Rights*	*Full Disclosure of Financial Status*	*Partial Waiver Allowed*
California[7]	Yes. (Prob. §§ 140, 141(a)(7))	Yes. (Prob. §§ 140, 141(a)(7))	Yes. (Prob. § 142(a))	Is advisable (Prob. §§ 144, 145) but not necessary (Prob. § 143).	Fair and reasonable disclosure or a waiver of such disclosure, or knowledge of such statutes. (Prob. §§ 143, 144)	Yes. (Prob. § 141)
Colorado	Yes. (§ 15-11-207(1))	Yes. (§ 15-11-207(1))	Yes. (§ 15-11-207(1))	Yes. Can say ''all-rights.'' (§ 15-11-207 (1))	Fair and reasonable disclosure required. (§§ 15-11-207(1) & (2), 14-2-307(1)(b)) ''Unconscionability,'' though not in statute, appears relevant and is considered at the time the agreement was entered into. (In re Lebsock's Estate, 618 P.2d 683 (Ct. App. 1980))	Yes. (§ 15-11-207(1))
Connecticut	Yes. (§ 46b-36d)	Yes, if provision is made in the agree ment for the spouse. (§ 45a-436(f)) Also, a postnuptial agreement may be approved if ''fair and equitable'' in accordance with § 46b-66 and in compliance with its other terms. See Oliver v. Oliver, 1999 Conn. Super.	Yes. (§§ 45a-436(f), 46b-36c)	No provision. However, it must not be unconscionable and the person must be afforded a reasonable opportunity to consult with independent counsel. (§ 46b-36g(a)(2)&(4))	Fair and reasonable disclosure required. (§ 46b-36g(a)(3))	Yes. (§ 46b-36d)

		Lexis 457, at 10-11 (Feb. 17, 1999).				
Delaware	Yes. (12 § 905)	Yes. (12 § 905)	Yes, written contract, agreement, or waiver signed by the party waiving. (12 § 905)	Not required, but recommended. A reference to "all rights" or to "property settlement" in the event of divorce will suffice. The waiver cannot be unconscionable. (12 § 905, 13 § 326)	Fair and reasonable disclosure required. (13 § 326)	Yes. (12 § 905)
District of Columbia	Yes. (§ 19-113(f))	Yes. (§ 19-113(f))	Valid agreement. (§ 19-113(f))	No provision.	Yes. See Burtoff v. Burtoff, 418 A.2d 1085, 1089 (1980).	No provision, but implied. (§ 19-113(f))
Florida	Yes. (§ 732.702(1))	Yes. (§ 732.702(1))	Yes, written contract, agreement, or waiver signed by the waiving party in the presence of two subscribing witnesses. (§ 732.702(1))	Waiver of "all rights" or equivalent language. (§ 732.702(1))	Before marriage—no disclosure. After marriage—fair disclosure. (§ 732.702(2))	Yes. (§ 732.702(1))
Georgia[8]	Yes. (§ 19-3-63)	Yes, but not statutory authority. See, e.g., Sanders v. Colwell, 283 S.E.2d 461 (Sup. Ct. 1981): "Agreements in contemplation of divorce settling issues of . . . property division . . . are not invalid."	Required, and the writing must be attested by two witnesses. (§ 19-3-63)	No technical expression required. Construed liberally to carry out intent of parties. (§ 19-3-63)	No provision.	No provision.
Hawaii	Yes. (§ 560:2-213(a))	Yes. (§ 560:2-213(a))	Yes, written contract, agreement, or waiver signed by the surviving spouse or reciprocal *(cont'd)*	An express reference to rights is not necessary; a waiver of "all rights" is sufficient to imply a waiver of all *(cont'd)*	A fair and reasonable disclosure of the property or financial obligations of the decedent is necessary, unless the *(cont'd)*	Yes. (§ 560:2-213(a))

Table 6.04
Waiver of Spousal Rights, Including Antenuptial Agreements *(continued)*

	Can Rights of Surviving Spouse Be Waived:		*Special Conditions of Any Waiver*			
	Before Marriage?	*During Marriage?*	*Writing*	*Express Reference to Rights*	*Full Disclosure of Financial Status*	*Partial Waiver Allowed*
Hawaii *(cont'd)*			beneficiary. (§ 560:2-213(a))	rights of elective share. (§ 560:2-213(d))	person voluntarily and expressly waived, in writing, any right to disclosure of the property or financial obligation of the decedent beyond the disclosure provided. Also if the person had, or reasonably could have had, an adequate knowledge of the property or financial obligations of the decedent, no disclosure is necessary. (§ 560: 2-213(b)(2)(A)(C))	
Idaho[9]	Yes. (§ 15-2-208)	Yes. (§ 15-2-208)	Yes, written contract, agreement, or waiver signed by the party waiving. (§ 15-2-208)	A waiver of "all rights" (or equivalent lan guage) is sufficient to waive the right of election. (§ 15-2-208)	Only fair disclosure is required. (§ 15-2-208)	Yes. (§ 15-2-208)
Illinois	Yes. (750 ILCS § 10/4(a)(3))	Yes. (In re Estate of Brosseau, 531 N.E.2d 158 (App. Ct. 1988); 755 ILCS § 5/2-8)	Must be in writing and signed by both parties. (750 ILCS § 10/3; In re Estate of Brosseau, 531 N.E.2d 158 (App. Ct. 1988))	Express reference to rights is necessary; however, exact language such as "surviving spouse's award" is not necessary. (In re Estate of Brosseau, 531 N.E.2d 158, 161 (App. Ct. 1988))	A fair and reasonable disclosure of the property or financial obligations of the decedent is necessary, unless, the person voluntarily and expressly waived, in writing, any right to disclosure of the property or financial obligation of the decedent beyond the	No provision.

					disclosure provided. Also if the person had, or rea- son ably could have had, an adequate knowledge of the property or finan- cial obligations of the decedent, no disclosure is necessary. (750 ILCS § 10/7(a)(i)-(iii))	
Indiana	Yes. (§§ 29-1-2-13, 29-1-3-6) See also § 31-11-3-8.	Yes. (§§ 29-1-2-13, 29-1-3-6)	Written contract is necessary and must be signed by party waiving. (§§ 29-1-2-13, 29-1-3-6(a)) See also § 31-11-3-4 (prenuptial agreement)	Even if the waiver includes a clause refer ring to the specific statutory provision entitling the spouse to elect to take against the will, the spouse still must be informed of the nature and extent of her statutory rights before signing the waiver. (Bohnke v. Estate of Bohnke, 454 N.E.2d 446, 449 (1983); §§ 29-1-2-13, 29-1-3-6); Boetsma v. Boetsma, 768 N.E.2d 1016, 1022 (2002) (distinguishing *Bohnke* on the grounds that the waiver was more precise in terms of rights being waived, and the spouse contacted an attorney who fully explained the agreement to her); See also § 31-11-3-8, 31-11-3-5 (prenuptial agreement).	Full disclosure of the nature and extent of the right is required. (§§ 29-1-2-13, 29-1-3-6) The agreement must also not be unconscionable when it was executed. (§ 31-11-3-8(a)(2)) (prenuptial agreement).	No provision.

Table 6.04
Waiver of Spousal Rights, Including Antenuptial Agreements *(continued)*

	Can Rights of Surviving Spouse Be Waived:		*Special Conditions of Any Waiver*			
	Before Marriage?	*During Marriage?*	*Writing*	*Express Reference to Rights*	*Full Disclosure of Financial Status*	*Partial Waiver Allowed*
Iowa	Yes. (§ 596.5)	No provision.	A premarital agreement must be signed by both prospective spouses. (§ 596.4)	No provision, but contract cannot be unconscionable. (§ 596.9)	The spouse must be provided a fair and reasonable disclosure of the property or financial obligations of the other spouse, unless the spouse has, or could reasonably have, an adequate knowledge of the property or financial obligations of the other spouse. (§ 596.8(3))	No provision.
Kansas	Yes. (§ 59-6a213(a))	Yes. (§ 59-6a213(a))	Yes, written contract, agreement, any instrument, or waiver signed by the surviving spouse. (§ 59-6a213(a))	An express reference to rights is not necessary; a waiver of ''all rights'' is sufficient to imply a waiver of all rights of elective share. (§ 59-6a213 (d)) How ever, the waiver cannot be unconscionable. (§ 59-6a213(b)(2)) On or after July 1, 2002, the homestead, the homestead allowance, the family allowance, or all of them must be referred to in the document as having been waived by the spouse	A fair and reasonable disclosure of the property or financial obligations of the decedent is necessary, unless, the person voluntarily and expressly waived, in writing, any right to disclosure of the property or financial obligation of the decedent beyond the disclosure provided. Also if the person had, or reasonably could have had, an adequate knowledge of the property or financial obligations of the decedent, no disclosure is necessary. (§ 59-6a213 (b)(2)(A)–(C))	Yes. (§ 59-6a213(a))

				understandably and knowledgeably. (Id.)		
Kentucky	Yes. (Gaines v. Gaines' Adm'r, 173 S. W. 774, 777 (1915); § 392.020)	Yes. (Campbell v. Campbell, 377 S. W.2d 93, 94 (1964); § 392.020)	No specific authority.	No provision.	A full disclosure of financial condition is necessary. (Lawson v. Loid, 896 S.W.2d 1, 7 (1995))	No provision.
Louisiana	*Community property state—no quasi-community property*					
Maine	Yes. (18-A § 2-204)	Yes. (18-A § 2-204)	Yes, written contract, agreement, or waiver signed by the party waiving. (18-A § 2-204)	''All rights'' or equivalent language is sufficient. (18-A § 2-204)	Fair disclosure. (18-A § 2-204) There is a probability of invalidity due to the agreement being so unreasonable, even with full disclosure. (Wilson v. Wilson, 170 A.2d 679, 686 (Me. 1961))	Yes. (18-A § 2-204)
Maryland	Yes. (Est. & Trusts § 3-205)	Yes. (Est. & Trusts § 3-205)	Yes, written contract, agreement, or waiver signed by the party waiving election. (Est. & Trusts § 3-205)	''All rights'' is sufficient as is the parties entering into a ''complete property settlement.'' (Est. & Trusts § 3-205)	Yes. See, e.g., Hartz v. Hartz, 234 A.2d 865, 870-71 (1967) (requiring ''frank, full and truthful disclosure of worth of property, real and personal, as to which there is wavier of rights in whole or in part'') Unconscionability, determined at the time the agreement is entered into, nevertheless, can invalidate it. (Martin v. Farber, 510 A.2d 608, 610 (Ct. App. 1986))	Yes, but it is implied. (Est. & Trusts § 3-205)
Massachusetts	Yes. (209 § 25) There are also special provisions regarding dower. (189 § 7)	Uncertain. The Massachusetts Supreme Judicial Court expressly put off deciding the issue. *(cont'd)*	Yes, written contract (209 § 25)	Schedule of affected property is required and must be recorded if protection desired against creditors, but *(cont'd)*	''Fair disclosure'' is required. See Osborne v. Osborne, 428 N.E.2d 810, 816 (Mass. 1981), citing to the rules in *(cont'd)*	Yes. (209 § 25) The statute refers to ''any designated part of the real or personal property. . . .''

Table 6.04
Waiver of Spousal Rights, Including Antenuptial Agreements *(continued)*

	Can Rights of Surviving Spouse Be Waived:		*Special Conditions of Any Waiver*			
	Before Marriage?	*During Marriage?*	*Writing*	*Express Reference to Rights*	*Full Disclosure of Financial Status*	*Partial Waiver Allowed*
Massachusetts *(cont'd)*		See Fogg v. Fogg, 567 N.E.2d 921, 922 N. 2 (1991).		the contract will still be valid as between the parties. (209 § 26)	Rosenberg v. Lipnick, 389 N.E.2d 385 (1979).	
Michigan	Yes. (§ 700.2205)	Yes. (§ 700.2205)	Yes, by a written contract, agreement or waiver signed by the party waiving. (§ 700.2205)	"All rights" is sufficient to waive every thing. (§ 700.2205)	"Fair disclosure" is required. (§ 700.2205)	Yes. (§ 700.2205)
Minnesota	Spouse may waive right to election prior to marriage, but waiver must be made pursuant to § 519.11. (§ 524.2-213)	Yes. (§§ 519.11(1)(a), 524.2-213)	Writing executed in the presence of two witnesses and acknowledged by the parties. (§ 519.11(2))	A waiver of "all rights" is only a waiver of the right to elective share. (§ 524.2-213)	"Full and fair disclosure." (§ 519.11(1)) But see § 524.2-213: "fair disclosure."	Yes. (§ 524.2-213)
Mississippi	Yes; agreement is enforceable like any other contract. See Smith v. Smith, 656 So. 2d 1143, 1147 (1995).	Yes; agreement is enforceable like any other contract. See Roberts v. Roberts, 381 So. 2d 1333, 1335 (1980).	Yes, to the extent required by the statute of frauds. (§ 15-3-1)	No provision.	Yes. See Smith v. Smith, 656 So. 2d 1143, 1147 (1995).	No provision.
Missouri	Yes. (§ 474.220) See also § 451.220.	Yes. (§ 474.220) See also § 451.220.	Yes, written contract, agreement, or waiver signed by the waiving party. (§ 474.220) See also § 451.220.	No provision.	Full disclosure of nature and extent of right with fair consideration. (§ 474.220) Nevertheless, the agreement can be invalidated on the grounds of unconscionability, but not certain	No provision.

					whether only at signing or at time of enforcement. (Darr v. Darr, 950 S.W.2d 867, 871 (Ct. App. 1997))	
Montana	Yes. (§ 72-2-224(1))	Yes. (§ 72-2-224(1))	Yes, written contract, agreement, or waiver, signed by the surviving spouse (§ 72-2-224(1))	A waiver of ''all rights'' or equivalent language waives everything. (§ 72-2-224(4)) However, the waiver cannot be unconscionable. ((§ 72-2-224(2)(b))	A fair and reasonable disclosure of the property or financial obligations of the decedent is necessary, unless the person voluntarily and expressly waived, in writing, any right to disclosure of the property or financial obligations of the decedent beyond the disclosure provided. Also if the person had, or reasonably could have had, an adequate knowl edge of the property or financial obligations of the decedent, no fair and reasonable disclosure is necessary. (§ 72-2-224(2)(b)(i)) The waiver must not be unconscionable at the time of execution.	Yes. (§ 72-2-224(1))
Nebraska	Yes. (§ 30-2316(a))	Yes. (§ 30-2316(a))	Yes, written contract, agreement, or waiver signed by the surviving spouse. (§ 30-2316(a))	A waiver of ''all rights'' or equivalent language waives elective share, homestead, exempt property, family allowance, and rights by testate or intestate succession. (§ 30-2316(d)) However, *(cont'd)*	A fair and reasonable disclosure of the property or financial obligations of the decedent is necessary, unless the person voluntarily and expressly waived, in writing, any right to disclosure of the property or financial obligations of *(cont'd)*	Yes. (§ 30-2316(a))

Table 6.04
Waiver of Spousal Rights, Including Antenuptial Agreements *(continued)*

	Can Rights of Surviving Spouse Be Waived:		*Special Conditions of Any Waiver*			
	Before Marriage?	*During Marriage?*	*Writing*	*Express Reference to Rights*	*Full Disclosure of Financial Status*	*Partial Waiver Allowed*
Nebraska *(cont'd)*				the waiver cannot be unconscionable, (§ 30-2316(b)(2))	the decedent beyond the disclosure provided. Also if the person had, or reasonably could have had, an adequate knowledge of the property or financial obligations of the decedent, no disclosure is necessary. (§ 30-2316(b)(2)(i))	
Nevada	Yes. See, e.g., Matley v. Matley, 701 P.2d 749 (1985).	Unsettled. See Cord v. Neuhoff, 573 P.2d 1170, 1172 (1978) (since the postnuptial agreement was viewed as integrated, an invalid limitation in it as to one spouse's support obligation had the result of invalidating the entire agreement).	Yes. A premarital agreement must be in writing and signed by both parties. (§ 123A.040) See also Matley v. Matley, 701 P.2d 749, 751 (1985).	No provision.	Yes. Where spouse has not voluntarily and expressly waived, in writing, any right to disclosure of the property or financial obligations of the other party beyond the disclosure provided and did not have, or reasonably could not have had, an adequate knowledge of the property or financial obligations of the other party, fair and reasonable disclosure of the property or financial obligations of the other party is necessary) (§123A.080) See also Matley v. Matley, 701 P.2d 749, 750-751 (1985).	Yes. See Jensen v. Jensen, 753 P.2d 342 (1988) (relating to modification of existing agreement).

New Hampshire	Yes. (§ 460:2-a)[10]	No provision.	Yes. (§ 460:2-a)	Yes. (§ 460:2-a)	Yes. See In re Yannalfo, 794 A.2d 795 (N.H. 2002) (dictum). The agreement can be invalidated on the ground of unconscionability at the time of execution or enforcement. Id. See also MacFarlane v. Rich, 567 A.2d 585, 616 (N.H. 1989)	Yes. Since may "be in lieu of homestead right, distributive share, or either of them . . ." (§ 560:15)
New Jersey	Yes. (§ 3B:8-10)	Yes. (§ 3B:8-10)	Written contract, agreement, or waiver signed by the party waiving. (§ 3B:8-10)	No, unless it provides to the contrary, a waiver of "all rights" (or equivalent language) waives everything. (§ 3B:8-10)	"Fair disclosure." (§ 3B:8-10)	Yes. (§ 3B:8-10)
New Mexico	Yes. (§ 45-2-407), but limited to family allowance and personal allowance. Other rights can be waived by contract. See also Lebeck v. Lebeck, 881 P.2d 727 (Ct. App. 1994).	Yes. (§ 45-2-407) See also Christiansen v. Christiansen, 666 P.2d 781 (1983).	Yes. Written contract, agreement or waiver signed by the surviving spouse. (§§ 45-2-407, 40-2-4) See also Lebeck v. Lebeck, 881 P.2d 727 (Ct. App. 1994).	Unless it provides to the contrary, a waiver of "all rights", or equivalent language, is a waiver of all rights of family allowance and personal property allowance by each spouse in the property of the other and a renunciation by each of all benefits that would otherwise pass to each from the other by intestate succession or by virtue of any will. (§ 45-2-407)	A fair and reasonable disclosure of the property or financial obligations of the decedent is necessary, unless the person voluntarily and expressly waived, in writing, any right to disclosure of the property or financial obligations of the decedent beyond the disclosure provided. Also if the person had, or reasonably could have had, an adequate knowledge of the property or financial obligations of the decedent, no disclosure is necessary. (§ 45-2-407(B)(2))	Yes. (§ 45-2-407) See also Lebeck v. Lebeck, 881 P.2d 727, 734 (Ct. App. 1994).

Table 6.04
Waiver of Spousal Rights, Including Antenuptial Agreements *(continued)*

	Can Rights of Surviving Spouse Be Waived:		*Special Conditions of Any Waiver*			
	Before Marriage?	*During Marriage?*	*Writing*	*Express Reference to Rights*	*Full Disclosure of Financial Status*	*Partial Waiver Allowed*
New York[11]	Yes. (Est. Powers &Trusts § 5-1.1-A(e)(3)(A) (waiver of right of election); Gen. Oblig. L. § 3-303 (antenuptial agreement))	Yes. (Est. Powers &Trusts § 5-1.1-A(e)(3)(A)) A postnuptial agreement is valid under case law, and not statute. See, e.g., Kosovsky v. Zahl, 684 N.Y.S.2d 524 (A.D. 1999)	Yes. (Est. Powers & Trusts § 5-1.1-A(e)(2) (waiver of elective share rights)) See, e.g., Dygert v. Remerschnider, 32 N.Y. 629 (1865) (antenuptial agreement).	No. (Est. Powers &Trusts § 5-1.1-A(e)(1)) However, In re Greif, 680 N.Y.S.2d 894 (1998), holds that if the surviving spouse shows "a fact-based particularlized inequality" between the parties, then the burden of going forward shifts to the proponent of the antenuptial agreement.	No, if in the form of antenuptial agreement and regardless of fairness and reasonableness. The signatories were not in a confidential relationship when they entered into the agreement (Eckstein v. Eckstein, 514 N.Y.S.2d 47, 49 (A.D. 1987))	Yes. (Est. Powers & Trusts § 5-1.1-A(e)(1)); no specific provision as to marital agreement.
North Carolina	Yes. (§ 52-10(a))	Yes. (§ 52-10(a))	A premarital agreement must be in writing and signed by both parties. (§ 52B-3) As to other waivers, the same requirements as for any other contract. See, e.g., Loftin v. Loftin, 208 S.E.2d 670 (1974). Under § 52-10(a) the contract or release must be in writing if entered into during coverture and affecting real estate of either spouse or the income there of for more than	No. (In re Estate of Tucci, 380 S.E.2d 782, 785, *cert. denied* as to additional issues, 384 S.E.2d 514 (1989), *aff'd,* 388 S.E.2d 768 (1990))	A fair and reasonable disclosure of the property or financial obligations of the decedent is necessary, unless the person voluntarily and expressly waived, in writing, any right to disclosure of the property or financial obligations of the decedent beyond the disclosure provided. Also if the person had, or reasonably could have had, an adequate knowledge of the property or financial obligations of the dece dent, no disclosure	No provision.

			three years next ensuring the making of the contract or release. (§ 52-10(a))		is necessary. (§ 52B-7) (for antenuptial agreements)	
North Dakota	Yes. (§ 30.1-05-07(1))	Yes. (§ 30.1-05-07(1))	Written contract, agreement, or waiver signed by surviving spouse. (§ 30.1-05-07(1))	No. Waiver of "all rights" or equivalent language waives everything. (§ 30.1-05-07(4))	A fair and reasonable disclosure of the property or financial obligations of the decedent is necessary, unless the person voluntarily and expressly waived, in writing, any right to disclosure of the property or financial obligations of the decedent beyond the disclosure provided. Also if the person had, or reasonably could have had, an adequate knowledge of the property or financial obligations of the decedent, no disclosure is necessary. (§ 30.1-05-07(1))	Yes. (§ 30.1-05-07(1))
Ohio	Yes. (Hook v. Hook, 431 N.E.2d 667 (1982); § 2106.01)	Yes. (Carnahan v. Carnahan, 159 N.E.2d 795 (1959) (contract after decedent's death made with other beneficiaries); § 2106.01)	No provision.	Yes. (In re Estate of Mowery, No. 10813, 1982 WL 5164 (Dist. Ct. App.); § 2106.01)	Full disclosure or full knowledge of effects. (Hook v. Hook, 431 N.E.2d 667 (1982); § 2106.01)	Seemingly so under In re Estate of Mowery, No. 10813, 1982 WL 5164 (Dist. Ct. App.); § 2106.01.
Oklahoma	Yes. (Washington and Lee University v. District Court of Oklahoma County, 492 P.2d 320 (1971); 84 § 44(B)(1))	No. A post-nuptial agreement of husband and wife waiving the right of survivor to take the other's estate under law of intestate succession, is not authorized by	Yes. (84 § 44(B)(1))	No provision.	Full and fair disclosure required. (In re Cobb's Estate, 305 P.2d 1028, 1032 (1957)	No provision.

(cont'd)

Table 6.04
Waiver of Spousal Rights, Including Antenuptial Agreements *(continued)*

	Can Rights of Surviving Spouse Be Waived:		*Special Conditions of Any Waiver*			
	Before Marriage?	*During Marriage?*	*Writing*	*Express Reference to Rights*	*Full Disclosure of Financial Status*	*Partial Waiver Allowed*
Oklahoma *(cont'd)*		statute and is invalid and unenforceable. (Atkinson v. Barr, 428 P.2d 316, 32021 (1967); 84 § 44)				
Oregon	Yes. (§ 114.115)	Yes. (§ 114.115)	Yes, written agreement signed by both spouses. (§ 114.115)	No provision.	A fair and reasonable disclosure of the property or financial obligations of the decedent is necessary, unless the person voluntarily and expressly waived, in writing, any right to disclosure of the property or financial obligations of the decedent beyond the disclosure provided. Also if the person had, or reasonably could have had, an adequate knowledge of the property or financial obligations of the decedent, no disclosure is necessary. (§ 108.725) (with respect to prenuptial agreement); (Day v. Vitus, 792 P.2d 1240, 1241 (1990) (post-nuptial agreement))	No provision.
Pennsylvania	Yes (20 § 2207 (waiver of right of	Yes, as to a waiver (20 § 2207); a	As required by contract law. (Stoner v.	No authority.	"Full and fair disclosure" for antenuptial and	Yes, for waiver. (20 § 2207) No apparent

	election)); antenuptial agreements are valid under common-law contracts. See, e.g., Simeone v. Simeone, 581 A.2d 162, 165 (1990).	postnuptial marital agree ment is valid. See, e.g., Stoner v, Stoner, 819 A.2d 529, 532 n.5 (Sup. Ct. 2003)	Stoner, 819 A.2d 529, 532 (Sup. Ct. 2003); Simeone v. Simeone, 581 A.2d 162, 165-66 (Sup. Ct. 1990))		postnuptial agreements. ((Simeone v. Simeone, 581 A.2d 162, 166-67 (Sup. Ct. 1990); Stoner v. Stoner, 819 A.2d 529, 533 (Sup. Ct. 2003) only refers to ''full disclosure''))	obstacle with regard to marital agreement.
Rhode Island	Yes. (§ 15-17-6)	No substantial statutory or case law.	Yes, if writing is signed by both parties (§ 15-17-2)	Yes. (Carr v. Carr, 1993 WL 8538075-6 (Super. Ct. Apr. 22, 1993)	A fair and reasonable disclosure of the property or financial obligations of the decedent is necessary, unless the person voluntarily and expressly waived, in writing, any right to disclosure of the property or financial obligations of the decedent beyond the disclosure provided. Also if the person had, or reasonably could have had, an adequate knowledge of the property or financial obligations of the decedent, no disclosure is necessary. (§ 15-17-6(a)(2)(i))	Yes. A waiver is allowed with regard to ''any of the property of either or both'' spouses. (§ 15-17-3(a))
South Carolina	Yes. (§ 62-2-204)	Yes. (§ 62-2-204)	Yes, written contract, agreement, or waiver, signed by the party waiving. (§ 62-2-204)	A waiver of all rights waives everything. (§ 62-2-204)	Required fair disclosure. (§ 62-2-204)	Yes. (§ 62-2-204)
South Dakota	Yes. (§ 29A-2-213(a))	Yes. (§ 29A-2-213(a))	Yes, written contract, agreement, or waiver signed by the surviving spouse. (§ 29A-2-213(a))	A waiver of ''all rights'' waives everything. (§ 29A-2-213(d))	A fair and reasonable disclosure of the property or financial obligations of the decedent is necessary, unless the person voluntarily and expressly waived, in	Yes. (§ 29A-2-213(a))

(cont'd)

Table 6.04
Waiver of Spousal Rights, Including Antenuptial Agreements *(continued)*

	Can Rights of Surviving Spouse Be Waived:		*Special Conditions of Any Waiver*			
	Before Marriage?	*During Marriage?*	*Writing*	*Express Reference to Rights*	*Full Disclosure of Financial Status*	*Partial Waiver Allowed*
South Dakota *(cont'd)*					writing, any right to disclosure of the property or financial obligations of the decedent beyond the disclosure provided. Also if the person had, or reasonably could have had, an adequate knowledge of the property or financial obligations of the decedent, no disclosure is necessary. (§ 29A-2-213(b)(2)(i))	
Tennessee	Yes. (§ 36-3-501)	Yes. (§ 36-3-501)	Required. (§ 36-3-501)	Required. (§ 36-3-501)	Required. (§§ 36-3-501, 31-4-103)	Allowed. (In re Estate of Gray, 729 S.W.2d 668 (Ct. App. 1987))
Texas	Yes. (Fam. Code § 4.002)	Yes. See Marsh v. Marsh, 949 S.W.2d 734, 739 n.4 (1997), but not by statute and higher standard than antenuptial agreement due to fiduciary duty of spouses. See also Fam. Code § 4.102 as to partition and exchange of community property.	Yes if signed by both parties. (Fam. Code § 4.002)	No provision.	Yes. See, e.g., Williams v. Williams, 569 S.W.2d 867, 870 (1978 (full disclosure of the nature and extent of the property interest involved)	Yes. (Fam. Code § 4.003)
Utah	Yes. (§ 75-2-213(1))	Yes. (§ 75-2-213(1))	Yes, written contract, agreement, or waiver signed by the	A waiver of "all rights" or equivalent language waives	A fair and reasonable disclosure of the property or financial	Yes. (§ 75-2-213(1))

			surviving spouse. (§ 75-2-213(1))	everything. (§ 75-2-213(4))	obligations of the decedent is necessary, unless the person voluntarily and expressly waived, in writing, any right to disclosure of the property or financial obligations of the decedent beyond the disclosure provided. Also if the person had, or reasonably could have had, an adequate knowledge of the property or financial obligations of the decedent, no disclosure is necessary. (§ 75-2-213(2)(b)(i))	
Vermont	Yes. (Bassler v. Bassler, 593 A.2d 82, 87 (1991))	Yes. (Bassler v. Bassler, 593 A.2d 82 (1991) (general holding based on contracts though no express approval of postnuptial agreements))	Yes, but part performance can remove a contract from the Statute of Frauds. (Bassler v. Bassler, 593 A.2d 82, 86 (1991))	Not required. (Bassler v. Bassler, 593 A.2d 82 (1991))	Fair and reasonable disclosure. (Bassler v. Bassler, 593 A.2d 82, 87 (1991)) The agreement must not be unconscionable. (Id.)	Yes. (Bassler v. Bassler, 593 A.2d 82, 84 (1991))
Virginia	Yes. (§ 20-150(3))	Yes. (§ 20-155)	Required. (§ 20-149)	Required. (§ 20-151)	Fair and reasonable disclosure assuming no voluntary and express waiver in writing of the right to disclosure. (§ 20-151(A)(2)(i))	Yes. (§ 20-150(3))
Washington	Yes. Although the Uniform Premarital Agreement Act has not been adopted, many of the considerations are relevant concerns in evaluating an agreement. See In *(cont'd)*	Yes, as to community property. (§ 26.16.120)	Yes, in accordance with the same process used for real estate deeds. (§§ 19.36.010(3) (separate property); 26.16.120 (community property))	No provision.	Yes. "Full disclosure" is required. See In re Estate of Crawford, 730 P.2d 675, 678 (1986) (en banc).	Yes. *Cf.* In re Marriage of Fox, 795 P.2d 1170 (Ct. App. 1990).

Table 6.04
Waiver of Spousal Rights, Including Antenuptial Agreements *(continued)*

	Can Rights of Surviving Spouse Be Waived:		*Special Conditions of Any Waiver*			
	Before Marriage?	*During Marriage?*	*Writing*	*Express Reference to Rights*	*Full Disclosure of Financial Status*	*Partial Waiver Allowed*
Washington *(cont'd)*	re Estate of Crawford, 730 P.2d 675, 678 (1986) (en banc).					
West Virginia	Yes. (§ 42-3-3a(a))	Yes. (§ 42-3-3a(a))	Yes, written contract, agreement, or waiver signed by surviving spouse. (§ 42-3-3a(a))	Waiver of ''all rights'' or equivalent language waives the elective share. (§ 42-3-3a(d))	A fair and reasonable disclosure of the property or financial obligations of the decedent is necessary, unless the person voluntarily and expressly waived, in writing, any right to disclosure of the property or financial obligations of the decedent beyond the disclosure provided. Also if the person had, or reasonably could have had, an adequate knowledge of the property or financial obligations of the decedent, no disclosure is necessary. (§ 42-3-3a(b)(2)(i))	Yes. (§ 42-3-3a(a))
Wisconsin	Yes. (§ 767.255(L))	Yes. (§ 767.255(L)) Rules of antenuptial apply as well to postnuptial. See In re Beat's Estate, 130 N.W.2d 739, 741 n.4 (1964).	Not always required. See, e.g., Bibelhausen v. Bibelhausen, 150 N.W. 516, 52021 (1915).	No provision. But see In re Paulson's Estate, 31 N.W.2d 182, 184 (1948). § 767.255(L) recognizes an agreement's effectiveness if it is in writing but does not	Full disclosure or knowledge is required, and second marriages where the parties have independent wealth may affect the necessity of disclosure. See, e.g., In re Beat's Estate, 130	Probably. The statute applies to ''any arrangement for property distribution . . .'' and this, presumably, does not require an arrangement for the

				specifically baroral agreements.	N.W.2d 739, 742-745 (1964). More generally, however, "the widow, in asserting fraud, has the burden of proving it. In meeting this burden she may be aided by a presumption of fraud that arises in those instances where she is not adequately provided for by the terms of the agreement and where there has not been a full and fair disclosure to her of the husband's worth" (footnotes omitted).	distribution of *all* property. (§ 767.255)
Wyoming	Yes. (§ 2-5-102)	Yes. (§ 2-5-102)	Yes, written contract, agreement, or waiver signed by the party waiving. (§ 2-5-102)	A waiver of "all rights" waives everything. (§ 2-5-102)	Fair disclosure. (§ 2-5-102)	Yes. (§ 2-5-102)

1. Taking land under will, will waive dower rights. (§ 28-11-404) Taking of other property that is expressly "in lieu of," will waive. (§ 28-11-403) If spouse joins decedent in conveying property, this will result in the waiving of dower rights with regard to that property. (§ 28-11-201(a)) Also rights and interests can be waived partially or wholly by antenuptial agreement in writing, with financial disclosure. (§§ 9-11-403, 9-11-406)
2. Id.
3. Id.
4. Id.
5. Id.
6. Id.
7. Community property state with quasi-community property.
8. Georgia Year's Support—No elective share. However, the year's support is like the elective share in that if the decedent makes a provision in lieu of year's support in the will, then the spouse may elect to take the year's support rather than the provision under the will. (§ 53-3-3)
9. Community property state with quasi-community property.
10. § 460:2-a authorizes the prenuptial; §560:15 relates to what rights can be waived; and § 560:16 makes § 560:15 applicable to waivers by husbands.
11. These answers assume that the decedent died after Sept. 1, 1966 (§ 5-1.1-A(e)(3)(B)).

Table 7
Living Will
(current through 5/1/07)

Virtually every state has a living will statute. However, because of its controversial nature, states have developed quite diverse legislative responses to the topic. Certain states still have no comprehensive statute. In these states, a patient's right to terminate life is determined by a patchwork of statutory provisions and/or decisional law.

Increasingly, estate planners and elder law specialists are drafting living wills that address a host of issues not always considered in the more widely disseminated standard forms. This chapter considers in considerable depth these issues under the laws of the various states. It also considers in Table 7.06 the question of whether a living will executed in one state will be valid in another state. This question is not insubstantial, since it is common for a person to be hospitalized in a state other than the one in which he or she executed the living will.

The living will is not the only document likely to come into play. In situations in which the individual is not terminally ill, but is incapable of making health care decisions for herself, a health care directive is provided for in many jurisdictions. In some jurisdictions, a single document suffices, but in other jurisdictions, separate instruments are required. Table 7.01 indicates this for each state, as well as those states that simply do not provide for a health care directive.

As for the living will itself, many technical coverage issues arise. For example, there are difficult questions as to when a terminal condition exists and what sort of life support can legally be and not be withdrawn. These are addressed in Table 7.01. Table 7.02, on the other hand, is concerned with the formal requirements for executing a valid living will. For example, in some, but by no means the majority of states, a living will *must* be executed exactly like a testamentary instrument. A related question is the proper manner for revoking a living will. This matter is addressed on a state-by-state basis in Table 7.03. However, in numerous states, no clear consideration has been given to the question of the proper method to revoke a living will.

A major issue is the civil and criminal liability of medical personnel and hospitals if there is a failure to carry out the wishes expressed in the living will. These penalties serve as important leverage to compel observance of the living will. In this respect, the presence of a scienter requirement also has a considerable impact. In most cases, actual knowledge of the living will must have been present for liability to be imposed. These matters are explored in Table 7.04.

The presence of a living will can have an effect on the availability of insurance proceeds. First, with respect to health insurance, a person generally cannot be required to sign a living will in order to obtain health insurance. The state authority for this widespread position is set forth in Table 7.05. Second, state laws generally provide that the execution and giving effect to a living will is not suicide. Otherwise, life insurance proceeds could be denied under the terms of life insurance contracts.

Table 7.01, Part 1
Coverage of Living Will Statute

	Must There Be Separate Documents for Living Will and Health Care?	*What Is the Specific Title of the Living Will Instrument?*	*Is a Terminal Condition Sufficient to Justify Withdrawing Support?*	*Is a Persistent Vegetative State Sufficient to Justify Withdrawing Support?*	*If a Different Standard Is Used, What Is it Exactly?*	*Has a "Terminal Condition," Persistent Vegetative State, or Other Standard Used Been Defined by State or Case Law?*
Alabama	No. (§§ 22-8A-3(3), 22-8A-4(b))	Living Will. However, some provisions refer more generally to advance directive for health care which may also include a health care proxy. (§ 22-8A-3(3))	Yes. (§ 22-8A-4(d))	Yes, but the term "permanent unconsciousness" is used. (§ 22-8A-4(d))	An advance directive for health care becomes effective when a patient has a terminal illness or injury or a state of permanent unconsciousness. The declarant must also be unable to understand, appreciate, and direct his/her medical treatment. (§ 22-8A-4(d))	By statute "terminally ill" or injured patient (§ 22-8A-3(14)), and permanent unconsciousness has been defined. (§ 22-8A-3(10))
Alaska	Not specified, but probably no. However, an agent can make any health care decision the principal could have made while having capacity. (§ 13.52.010(b))	Advance health care directive, which is defined as a durable power of attorney for health care. (§§ 13.52.010; 13.52.390(1))	Yes. The existence of a "qualifying condition" is required to withdraw life-sustaining procedures. (§ 13.52.045) A qualifying condition under § 13.52.160 is determined by primary physician and one other. The term qualifying condition *(cont'd)*	No. However, permanent unconsciousness is a basis since it is a qualifying condition. (§ 13.52.390(36))	N/A	Yes, "terminal condition" has been defined by statute as "an incurable or irreversible illness or injury." (§ 13.52.390(42)) "Permanent unconsciousness" is defined more extensively in § 13.52.390(31).

Table 7.01, Part 1
Coverage of Living Will Statute *(continued)*

	Must There Be Separate Documents for Living Will and Health Care?	*What Is the Specific Title of the Living Will Instrument?*	*Is a Terminal Condition Sufficient to Justify Withdrawing Support?*	*Is a Persistent Vegetative State Sufficient to Justify Withdrawing Support?*	*If a Different Standard Is Used, What Is it Exactly?*	*Has a "Terminal Condition," Persistent Vegetative State, or Other Standard Used Been Defined by State or Case Law?*
Alaska *(cont'd)*			is defined as a terminal condition or permanent unconsciousness. (§ 13.52.390(36)) The optional statutory form in § 13.52.300 uses both terms, terminal condition and persistent vegetative state, as being sufficient to withdraw support.			
Arizona	A living will can be "attached" to the health care power of attorney. Also, any writing that complies with the living will requirements qualifies as a living will (id.), presumably even if it addresses other health care matters. (§§ 36-3262)	Living Will. (§ 36-3262)	Yes (as indicated in the statutory form). (§ 36-3262)	Yes (as indicated in the statutory form). (§ 36-3262)	N/A	No.

Arkansas	No. (§ 20-13-104(e))	Declaration. (§ 20-17-202)	Yes. (§ 20-17-202(b))	A "permanently unconscious" state will justify withdrawing support. (§ 20-17-202(c))	"Permanently unconscious" state means the condition is lasting, indefinitely without change, and thought, feeling, sensation and awareness of self/environment are all absent from the patient. (§ 20-17-201(6))	Yes. The statute defines "terminal condition" and"permanently unconscious." (§§ 20-17-201(11), 20-17-201(6))
California	No. (Prob. § 4670)	Individual health care instruction. (Prob. § 4670) A power of attorney for health care may be executed to give another person the authority to make health care decisions and may include individual health care instructions. (Prob. § 4671)	N/A	N/A	Either: (a) incurable and irreversible condition that will result in death within relatively short time; (b) unconsciousness, with reasonable degree of medical certainty that consciousness will not be regained; or (c) the likely risks of treatment will outweigh the expected benefits. (§ 4701, statutory form (2.1))	Same as prior column.
Colorado	Not specified.	Declaration as to Medical or Surgical Treatment. (§ 15-18-104(1))	Yes. (§ 15-18-104(1))	Yes, but the terms "unconscious" or "comatose" for seven or more days are used in the statutory form. (§ 15-18-104(3)(1)(b))	"Unconscious" or "comatose" for seven or more days. (§ 15-18-104(3)(1)(b))	Yes, "terminal condition" has been defined by statute. (§ 15-18-103(10))

Table 7.01, Part 1
Coverage of Living Will Statute *(continued)*

	Must There Be Separate Documents for Living Will and Health Care?	*What Is the Specific Title of the Living Will Instrument?*	*Is a Terminal Condition Sufficient to Justify Withdrawing Support?*	*Is a Persistent Vegetative State Sufficient to Justify Withdrawing Support?*	*If a Different Standard Is Used, What Is it Exactly?*	*Has a "Terminal Condition," Persistent Vegetative State, or Other Standard Used Been Defined by State or Case Law?*
Connecticut	No. An advance health care directive can be separate or part of a living will. There is also provision for a separate document ensuring the appointment of a health care representative, if not a part of the living will. (§ 19a-577) (§§ 19a-570(1) & (8), 19a-575, 19a-575a)	Document concerning health care and withholding or withdrawal of life support systems. (§ 19a-575)	Yes, as indicated in the statutory form. (§ 19-575)	Uses "permanently unconscious." (§§ 19a-575, 19a-571(a)(2))	Uses "permanently unconscious." (§§ 19a-575, 19a-571(a)(2))	Yes, by statute. Terminal condition: final stage of incurable/ irreversible condition that will result in death within relatively short time without life support system. (§ 19a-570(11)) Permanently unconscious: permanent coma and persistent vegetative state that is irreversible, patient unaware of self/environment, and no behavioral response to environment. (§ 19a-570(10))
Delaware	No. An "advance health-care directive" can either mean an individual instruction or a power of attorney for health care, or both. (16 § 2501(a))	Advance health-care directive. (16 §§ 2503, 2501(a))	Yes, as indicated in the optional form. (16 §§ 2505, 2501(r)(2))	Yes, as indicated in the optional form. (16 §§ 2505, 2501(r)(1))	In addition to having a "qualifying condition," the patient must lack capacity for an advance health-care directive to become effective. (16 § 2503(c))	Yes. (16 § 2501(r)(1)(2))

District of Columbia	No. (As indicated in statutory durable power of attorney for health care form) (§ 21-2207) Note that the attorney-in-fact is given very broad authority "to grant, refuse or withdraw consent to provision of any health care service, treatment, or procedure . . ." (§ 21-2206(a)(1))	Declaration. (§ 7-622)	Yes. (§ 7-622(a))	Not specified.	N/A	"Terminal condition" means an incurable condition which, regard less of the application of life-sustaining procedures, would produce death, and where the application of life-sustaining procedures would serve only to postpone the moment of death of the patient. (§ 7-621(6))
Florida	Yes. Health care surrogate (§ 765.203) and living will (§ 765.303). Note, however, that a health care surrogate may make decisions as to the withholding or withdrawing of life-prolonging procedures unless the designation of health care surrogate limits his authority to make such decisions. (§ 765.305(1))	Living will. (§ 765.303(1))	Yes. (§ 765.302)	Yes. (§§ 765.101(12), 765.302)	"End stage condition" also qualifies. (§ 765.302)	Yes, statute. Terminal condition: injury disease or illness from which there is no reasonable probability of recovery and will cause death without treatment. (§ 765.101 (17)) Persistent vegetative state: permanent/irreversible unconsciousness where there is no voluntary action/ cognitive behavior and no ability to interact/ communicate (§ 765.101(12)) End stage condition: irreversible condition that is caused by injury, disease, or illness which has resulted in

(cont'd)

Table 7.01, Part 1
Coverage of Living Will Statute *(continued)*

	Must There Be Separate Documents for Living Will and Health Care?	*What Is the Specific Title of the Living Will Instrument?*	*Is a Terminal Condition Sufficient to Justify Withdrawing Support?*	*Is a Persistent Vegetative State Sufficient to Justify Withdrawing Support?*	*If a Different Standard Is Used, What Is it Exactly?*	*Has a "Terminal Condition," Persistent Vegetative State, or Other Standard Used Been Defined by State or Case Law?*
Florida *(cont'd)*						progressively severe and permanent deterioration, and which, to a reasonable degree of medical probability, treatment of the condition would be ineffective. (§ 765.101(4))
Georgia	Alternative documents can be used, *e.g.*, living will (§ 31-36-11), a durable power of attorney for health care (§ 31-36-4) or statutory form power of attorney for health care (§ 31-36-10(a)). The living will takes precedence if there is more than one document addressing the matter of life-prolonging procedures. (§ 31-36-4)	"Declaration" is referred to in text of statute, but the sample "Declaration" in the statute is headed "Living Will," so either is almost certainly acceptable. (§ 31-32-3(b))	Yes. (§ 31-32-3(a))	Yes (as indicated in the statutory form). (§ 31-32-3(b))	A coma without reason able expectation of regaining consciousness will also satisfy if authorized by declarant (as indicated in the statutory form). (§ 31-32-3(b))	Yes, "terminal condition," "persistent vegetative state," and "coma" have been defined by statute. (§§ 31-32-2(13) ("terminal condition"), 31-32-2(9) ("persistent vegetative state"), 31-32-2(2) ("coma")).

Hawaii	No. (§ 327E-3 (a) & (b))	Advance health-care directive (§ 327E-3), which may be in the form of an individual instruction or a power of attorney for health care, or both. (§ 327E-3(a) & (b))	N/A	N/A	Either: (a) incurable and irreversible condition that will result in death within relatively short time; (b) unconsciousness, with reasonable degree of medical certainty that consciousness will not be regained; or (c) the likely risks of treatment will outweigh the expected benefits. (§ 327E-16, statutory form Pt. 2 (6))	Same as prior column.
Idaho	No, as indicated in the statutory living will and durable power of attorney for health care form. (§ 39-4510)	Living will and Durable Power of Attorney for Health Care. (§ 39-4510)	Yes (as indicated in the statutory form). (§ 39-4510)	Yes (as indicated in the statutory form). (§ 39-4510)	The statutory form additionally uses the term "injury, disease, illness or condition" to give the living will effect. (§ 39-4510)	No, but "terminal condition" is defined in § 39-4502(14) as an incurable or irreversible condition which, without the administration of life-sustaining procedures, will, in the opinion of a physician, result in death if it runs its usual course.

Table 7.01, Part 1
Coverage of Living Will Statute *(continued)*

	Must There Be Separate Documents for Living Will and Health Care?	*What Is the Specific Title of the Living Will Instrument?*	*Is a Terminal Condition Sufficient to Justify Withdrawing Support?*	*Is a Persistent Vegetative State Sufficient to Justify Withdrawing Support?*	*If a Different Standard Is Used, What Is it Exactly?*	*Has a "Terminal Condition," Persistent Vegetative State, or Other Standard Used Been Defined by State or Case Law?*
Illinois	No, as indicated in the statutory durable power of attorney for health care form. (755 ILCS § 45/4-10(a))	Declaration. (755 ILCS § 35/3(e))	Yes. (755 ILCS § 35/3(a))	Not specified.	Not specified.	Yes, statute. Terminal condition: "incurable/ and irreversible condition which is such that death is imminent and the application of death delaying procedures serves only to prolong the dying process." (755 ILCS § 35/2(h))
Indiana	Not specified, although there is an implication that the documents can be the same, since the Living Will Declaration can contain "additional directions." (§ 16-36-4-9)	Living Will Declaration. (§ 16-36-4-10) Note that a new form has been enacted, effective July 1, 2005, but with the same citation.	Yes. (§ 16-36-4-13(a)(1))	Not specified.	Not specified.	A "terminal condition" means a condition caused by injury, disease or illness from which, to a reasonable degree of medical certainty: (a) there can be no recovery; and (b) death will occur within a short period of time without the provision of life-prolonging procedures. (§ 16-36-4-5)
Iowa	Not specified, but implied by § 144B, Durable Power of	Declaration (relating to use of	Yes. (§ 144A.3(1))	Yes (only if accompanied by an incurable or irreversible condition	Not specified.	Yes, "terminal condition" has been defined

	Attorney for Health Care. Note that sample form (§ 144B.5) does not mention any provisions relating to use of life-sustaining procedures, although it does allow the individual to include specific instructions.	life-sustaining procedures). (§ 144A.3)		and the term used is "permanent unconsciousness") (as indicated in the definition of terminal condition and in the statutory form). (§ 144A.3(5))		by statute. (§ 144A.2(13))
Kansas	Not specified.	Declaration (directing the withholding/with drawal of life sustaining procedures). (§ 65-28,103(a))	Yes. (§ 65-28,103(a))	Not specified.	Incurable injury, disease, or illness certified to be a terminal condition (as indicated in the statutory form). (§ 65-28,103(c))	Yes, "terminal condition" has been defined in the statutory form. (§ 65-28,103(c))
Kentucky	No, as indicated in the statutory living will directive form. (§ 311.625)	Living Will Directive. (§ 311.625)	Yes (as indicated in the statutory form). (§ 311.625(1))	Yes. Kentucky uses the phrase "permanently unconscious" (as indicated in the statutory form). (§ 311.625(1))	Not specified.	"Terminal Condition" means a condition which, to a reasonable degree of medical probability, is incurable and irreversible and will result in death within a relatively short time, and where the application of life-prolonging treatment would serve only to artificially prolong the dying process. (§ 311.621(16)) "Permanently Unconscious" means a condition which, to a reasonable degree of medical probability, as

(cont'd)

Table 7.01, Part 1
Coverage of Living Will Statute *(continued)*

	Must There Be Separate Documents for Living Will and Health Care?	*What Is the Specific Title of the Living Will Instrument?*	*Is a Terminal Condition Sufficient to Justify Withdrawing Support?*	*Is a Persistent Vegetative State Sufficient to Justify Withdrawing Support?*	*If a Different Standard Is Used, What Is it Exactly?*	*Has a "Terminal Condition," Persistent Vegetative State, or Other Standard Used Been Defined by State or Case Law?*
Kentucky *(cont'd)*						determined by the patient's attending physician and one other physician on clinical examination, is characterized by an absence of cerebral cortical functions indicative of consciousness or behavioral interaction with the environment. (§ 311.621(12))
Louisiana	Not specifically indicated, but the illustrative form allows the declaration as to a terminal condition to allow the designation of a person to make treatment decisions. (§ 40:1299.58.3 (c)(1))	Declaration. (§ 40:1299.58.3(C)(1))	Yes. (§ 40:1299.58.3 (A)(1))	Yes (but the term "pro found comatose state" is used). (§ 40:1299.58.3(C) (1))	Not specified.	Yes, "terminal and irreversible condition" has been defined by statute. (§ 40:1299.58.2(15))
Maine	No (as indicated in the statutory form). (18-A § 5-804)	Advance Health-Care Directive. (18-A § 5-802)	Yes. Statutory form uses the phrase "incurable and irreversible condition" that will result in death within a relatively short time. (18-A § 5-804)	Yes. Statutory form uses the phrase "unconsciousness that to a reasonable degree of a medical certainty will not end." (18-A § 5-804)	If the likely risks and burdens of treatment outweigh the expected benefits, the directive will take effect (as indicated in the statutory form). (18-A § 5-804)	Yes, both have been defined by statute. (18-A § 5-801(S) & (T))

Maryland	There is an "Advance Directive." It is optional and other forms are also valid. (Health-Gen. § 5-603)	Advance Directive (Health-Gen. § 5-603)	Yes (as indicated in the statutory form). (Health-Gen. § 5-603(II)(B))	Yes (as indicated in the statutory form). (Health-Gen. § 5-603(II)(C))	Not specified. (Health-Gen. § 5-603)	Yes, "terminal condition" and "persistent vegetative state" have been defined by statute. (Health-Gen. § 5-601(q) & (o))
Massachusetts[1]	No living will in Massachusetts.	Health care proxy. (201D § 2)	Not specified.	Not specified.	Not specified.	Not specified.
Michigan	[Note: § 333.5654 requires the physician to inform the patient or patient surrogate or patient advocate that there are alternatives to recommended treatments in the event of an "advanced illness". These treatments include withholding or withdrawing care under generally accepted standards of medical practice and not prohibited by law, and palliative care. The patient or his patient surrogate or patient advocate, upon being informed, can make an informed decision, whether to secure, receive, continue, discontinue, or refuse treatment (§ 333.5655). "Advanced illness" means the same as "terminal illness" in the medical community. (§ 333.5653(1)(a)) There is no living will law in Michigan.]					
Minnesota	No. (§ 145B.03)	Health Care Living Will. (§ 145B.04)	Yes (as indicated in the statutory form). (§ 145B.04(e))	Not specified. (§ 145B.04(e))	Not specified.	Yes, "terminal condition" has been defined by statute. (§ 145B.02 (Subd. 8))
Mississippi	No (as indicated in the statutory durable power of attorney for health care form) (§ 41-41-209)	Advanced health-care directive; if authority is given to an agent, that part is described as a power of attorney for health care. (§§ 41-41-205, 41-41-209, statutory form Pt. 1)	Yes, but statutory form uses the phrases (a) incurable and irreversible condition that will result in death within a relatively short time, (b) unconscious and "to a reasonable degree of medical uncertainty," consciousness will not be regained, or (c) the likely risks and burdens of treatment would outweigh the expected benefits. (§ 41-41-209, statutory form (6)(a))	Implied by use of language referring to "consciousness" not being regained. (§ 41-41-209 statutory form (6)(a))	A third basis is that the likely risks and burdens of treatment would outweigh the expected benefits. (§ 41-41-209, statutory form (6)(a)(iii))	No.

Table 7.01, Part 1
Coverage of Living Will Statute *(continued)*

	Must There Be Separate Documents for Living Will and Health Care?	*What Is the Specific Title of the Living Will Instrument?*	*Is a Terminal Condition Sufficient to Justify Withdrawing Support?*	*Is a Persistent Vegetative State Sufficient to Justify Withdrawing Support?*	*If a Different Standard Is Used, What Is it Exactly?*	*Has a "Terminal Condition," Persistent Vegetative State, or Other Standard Used Been Defined by State or Case Law?*
Missouri	Not specified, but Declaration may contain other specific directions. (§ 459.015(3))	Declaration. (§ 459.015)	Yes (as indicated in the statutory form). (§ 459.015(3))	No. (§ 459.015(3))	Not specified. (§ 459.015(3))	Yes, "terminal condition" has been defined by statute. (§ 459.010(6))
Montana	Yes. (§ 50-9-103(2) &(3))	Declaration. (§ 50-9-103(2))	Yes. (§ 50-9-105(1)(b))	Not specified.	N/A	"Terminal Condition" means an incurable or irreversible condition that, without the administration of life-sustaining treatment, will, in the opinion of the attending physician, result in death within a relatively short time. (§ 50-9-102(16))
Nebraska	No (as indicated in the health care power of attorney statutory form). (§ 30-3408)	Declaration. (§ 20-404)	Yes. (§ 20-405(2))	Yes. (§ 20-405(2))	Not specified.	Yes, statute. Terminal condition: incurable and irreversible condition that will result in death in a relatively short time without life-sustaining treatment. (§ 20-403(11)) Persistent vegetative state: to a reasonable degree of medical certainty in accordance with

						current medical standards is a total and irreversible loss of consciousness, no ability for cognitive interaction, and no reasonable hope for improvement. (§ 20-403(6))
Nevada	No (as indicated in the durable power of attorney for health care form). (§ 449.830(6) Statement of Desires)	Declaration. (§ 449.610)	Yes. (§ 449.617)	Not specified.	Not specified.	"Terminal condition" means an incurable and irreversible condition that, without the administration of life-sustaining treatment, will, in the opinion of the attending physician, result in death within a relatively short time. (§ 449.590)
New Hampshire	An advance directive can be a living will, a durable power of attorney for health care, a direction as to future medical care or designation of another person to make medical decisions. It can all be in one document or separate. (§§137-J:2(I); 137-J:20)	Living will or as part of an "Advance Directive" (§§ 137-J:2(I); 137-J:20)	Yes, where "death is imminent" or "near death" (§ 137-J:2(XVI)) and as indicated in the statutory form. (§ 137-J:20)	Yes, statutory form uses the term "permanently unconscious." (§ 137-J:20)	Not specified.	Yes, "permanently unconscious" has been defined by statute. (§§ 137-J:2 (XVII))
New Jersey	No. (§ 26:2H-55)	Advance Directive for Health Care. (§ 26:2H-56)	Yes. (§§ 26:2H-67(3), 26:2H-55)	Yes. (§§ 26:2H-67(2), 26:2H-55)	Permanently unconscious, life-sustaining treatment that is experimental, serious irreversible condition, or terminal condition. (§ 26:2H-67(a)(1)–(4))	Permanently unconscious: a medical condition diagnosed in accord with currently accepted medical standards and with reasonable medical certainty as total and irreversible

(cont'd)

Table 7.01, Part 1
Coverage of Living Will Statute *(continued)*

	Must There Be Separate Documents for Living Will and Health Care?	*What Is the Specific Title of the Living Will Instrument?*	*Is a Terminal Condition Sufficient to Justify Withdrawing Support?*	*Is a Persistent Vegetative State Sufficient to Justify Withdrawing Support?*	*If a Different Standard Is Used, What Is it Exactly?*	*Has a "Terminal Condition," Persistent Vegetative State, or Other Standard Used Been Defined by State or Case Law?*
New Jersey *(cont'd)*						loss of consciousness, no capacity for interaction with environment which includes persistent vegetative state and irreversible comas (§ 26:2H-55); experimental life-sustaining treatment: not proven, likely to be ineffective/ futile in prolonging life or will only serve to prolong the imminent dying process (§ 26:2H-67(a)(1)); irreversible illness/ condition: risks and burdens outweigh benefits to the patient or intervention would be inhumane but physician must consult with a reviewing body or get approval from a public agency set up for this purpose (§ 26:2H-67(a)(4)); terminal condition: terminal stage of an irreversibly fatal illness, disease or condition (§ 26:2H-55).

						Specific life expectancy is not a requirement, but a prognosis of a life expectancy of six months or less will constitute a terminal condition. (Id.)
New Mexico	No. (§§ 24-7A-2(A), 24-7A-4))	Advance Health-Care Directive. (§ 24-7A-2)	Yes, but the term "incurable or irreversible condition" is used (as indicated in the statutory form). (§ 24-7A-4, Pt. 2)	Yes, but the term unconscious" and "to a reasonable degree of medical certainty" will not regain consciousness is used (as indicated in the statutory form). (§ 24-7A-4, Pt. 2)	In addition to the standards in the prior two columns, support can be withdrawn if "the likely risks and burdens of treatment would outweigh the expected benefits." (§ 24-7A-4, Pt. 2)	Not defined, but described. (§ 24-7A-4, Pt. 2)
New York	No living will law in New York, but a health care proxy may include the principal's wishes or instructions as to health care and restrictions on the health care agent designated in the health care proxy. (Pub. Health § 2981(5)(b)) Specific instructions as to issues, such as artificial nutrition and hydrtion, may be provided to the agent, thereby limiting the agent's authority. (Pub. Health § 2981(5)(d) permissible form: Note)	Health care proxy. (Pub. Health §§ 2981(2), 2980 (8)). Note that there is also provision for orders not to resuscitate. However, the provisions governing health care proxies and agents take precedence. (Pub. Health § 2962(5)(a)) Under certain circumstances, the patient, or if not capable, a surrogate or agent, can consent to an order not to resuscitate. See, e.g., Pub. Health § 2965(c). See generally Pub. Health § 2961 et seq.	Not specified.	Not specified.	Decision-making standard should be, after consultation with principal's physicians, (a) in accordance with the principal's wishes, including the principal's religious and moral beliefs, or (b) if the principal's wishes are not reasonably known and cannot with reasonable diligence be ascertained, in accordance with the principal's best interests. (Pub. Health § 2982(2))	Not specified.

Table 7.01, Part 1
Coverage of Living Will Statute *(continued)*

	Must There Be Separate Documents for Living Will and Health Care?	*What Is the Specific Title of the Living Will Instrument?*	*Is a Terminal Condition Sufficient to Justify Withdrawing Support?*	*Is a Persistent Vegetative State Sufficient to Justify Withdrawing Support?*	*If a Different Standard Is Used, What Is it Exactly?*	*Has a "Terminal Condition," Persistent Vegetative State, or Other Standard Used Been Defined by State or Case Law?*
North Carolina	No. (§ 90-321(j))	Declaration Of A Desire For A Natural Death. (§ 90-321(d))	Yes (uses the term "terminal and incurable"). (§ 90-321(b)(1)(a))	Yes. (§ 90-321(b)(1)(c))	Not specified.	Yes, "brain death" and "persistent vegetative state" have been defined by statute. (§§ 90-323, 90-321(a)(4))
North Dakota	No (as indicated in the health care directive statutory form). (§ 23-06.5-17).	Health care directive. (§ 23-06.5-17)	No. Not specified. A health care directive, including the agent's authority, is in effect only when the principal lacks capacity to make health care decisions, as certified in writing by the principal's attending physician and filed in the principal's medical record. A health care directive is only effective while the principal lacks capacity. (§ 23-06.5-04)	No. Not specified.	Not specified.	Prior to its repeal by Laws 2005, ch. 232, § 19, § 23-06.4-02(7) provided, "terminal condition" means an incurable or irreversible condition that, without the administration of life-prolonging treatment, will result, in the opinion of the attending physician, in imminent death. The term does not include any form of senility, Alzheimer's disease, mental retardation, mental illness, or chronic mental or physical impairment, including comatose conditions that will not result in imminent death.

Ohio	No, in that the attorney in fact may also be authorized to make these decisions. However, if there are both a living will declaration and durable power of attorney for health care, the living will declaration supersedes a durable power of attorney declaration, even if the power of attorney was created after the declaration. (§§ 2133.03(b)(2); 1337.12 (D)(1)) However, the durable power of attorney supersedes a Do-Not-Resuscitate Order and Identification. (§ 1337.12(D)(1))	Declaration. (§ 2133.02(A1)) A person may also execute a declaration that authorizes the withholding or with drawal of CPR, known as a Do-Not-Resuscitate Order. (§ 2133.21)	Yes. (§ 2133.02(A2))	Use "permanently unconscious" state. (§ 2133.02(A2))	Permanently unconscious state. (§ 2133.02(A2))	Yes, statute. Terminal condition: irreversible, incurable, untreatable condition caused by disease, illness, or injury from which there can be no recovery and death will occur in a relatively short time without life-sustaining treatment. (§ 2133.01 (AA)) Permanently unconscious state: permanent unconsciousness where the declarant to a reasonable degree of medical certainty as determined in accordance with reasonable medical standards is irreversibly unaware of him self/environment and there is a total loss of cerebral cortex functioning such that the declarant cannot experience pain or suffering. (§ 2133.01(U))
Oklahoma	No. (63 § 3101.3)	Advance Directive for Health Care. (63 § 3101.4(B))	Yes, if authorized (as indicated in the statutory form). (63 § 3101.4(B)(I)(b)(1))	Yes, if authorized, but the term "persistently unconscious" is used (as indicated in the statutory form). (63 § 3101.4(B)(I)(b)(1))	"Persistently unconscious" is also satisfactory (as indicated in the statutory form). (63 § 3101.4 (B)(I)(b)(1))	Yes, "terminal condition" and "persistently unconscious" are defined by statute. (63 § 3101.3(7) & (12))

Table 7.01, Part 1
Coverage of Living Will Statute *(continued)*

	Must There Be Separate Documents for Living Will and Health Care?	*What Is the Specific Title of the Living Will Instrument?*	*Is a Terminal Condition Sufficient to Justify Withdrawing Support?*	*Is a Persistent Vegetative State Sufficient to Justify Withdrawing Support?*	*If a Different Standard Is Used, What Is it Exactly?*	*Has a "Terminal Condition," Persistent Vegetative State, or Other Standard Used Been Defined by State or Case Law?*
Oregon	No. (§ 127.531(2))	Advance Directive. (§ 127.531(2))	Yes. (§ 127.635(1)(a))	Use permanently unconscious. (§ 127.635(1)(b))	Statutory form indicates permanently unconscious, progressive illness, and extraordinary suffering. (§ 127.531(2)(C))	Yes, statute. Terminal condition: death is imminent irrespective of treatment and life-sustaining procedures or nutrition/hydration only postpone death. (§ 127.505(22)) Permanently unconscious: no awareness of self/environment, no reasonable possibility of returning to consciousness, and it has been confirmed by a neurological specialist. (§ 127.505(18)) Advanced progressive illness: fatal illness in its advanced stage where one cannot communicate, swallow food/water safely, care for oneself, recognize family, and unlikely condition will improve. (§ 127.531(2)(C)) Extraordinary suffering: life support does not help patient's condition

						and will only cause permanent and severe pain. (§ 127.531(2)(C))
Pennsylvania	No. (20 § 5447)	None. (20 § 5447) A proposed combined form is entitled "Durable Health Care Power of Attorney and Health Care Treatment Instructions (Living Will)," (20 § 5471)	An end-stage medical condition or permanent unconsciousness, combined with incompetence. (20 § 5443(a)(2))	Yes. See prior column.	See third column.	"End-stage medical condition" is "an incurable and irreversible medical condition in an advanced state caused by injury, disease or physical illness that will, in the opinion of the attending physician, to a reasonable degree of medical certainty, result in death, despite the introduction or continuation of medical treatment." (20 § 5422)
Rhode Island	No (as indicated in the durable power of attorney for health care statutory form). (§ 23-4.10-2(4)(a))	Declaration. (§ 23-4.11-3(d))	Yes. (§ 23-4.11-3(c)(2))	Not specified.	N/A	Yes, statute. Terminal condition: incurable/ irreversible condition that will cause death without life-sustaining procedures. (§ 23-4.11-2(13))
South Carolina	No. (§§ 44-77-40, 44-77-50)	Declaration of a Desire for a Natural Death. (§ 44-77-50)	Yes. (§ 44-77-40(1))	Yes. (§ 44-77-40(1))	"Permanently unconscious" is also satisfactory. (§ 44-77-40(1))	Yes, "terminal condition" and "permanent unconsciousness" are defined by statute. (§§ 44-77-20(4), 44-77-20(7))

Table 7.01, Part 1
Coverage of Living Will Statute *(continued)*

	Must There Be Separate Documents for Living Will and Health Care?	*What Is the Specific Title of the Living Will Instrument?*	*Is a Terminal Condition Sufficient to Justify Withdrawing Support?*	*Is a Persistent Vegetative State Sufficient to Justify Withdrawing Support?*	*If a Different Standard Is Used, What Is it Exactly?*	*Has a "Terminal Condition," Persistent Vegetative State, or Other Standard Used Been Defined by State or Case Law?*
South Dakota	A durable power of attorney may contain provisions as to medical procedures, intervention or treatment. (§ 59-7-2.1) If an individual has executed both a declaration and a durable power of attorney, the later executed document controls to the extent that the provisions conflict. (§ 34-12D-4)	Living Will Declaration. (§ 34-12D-3)	Yes, if death is imminent and the declarant is no longer able to communicate decisions about medical care. (§ 34-12D-5)	Uses coma or permanent unconsciousness. (§§ 34-12D-1(8), 34-12D-5)	Uses coma or permanent unconsciousness. (§§ 34-12D-1(8), 34-12D-5)	Yes, statute. Terminal condition: incurable/irreversible condition that will result in death shortly or a coma/other permanently unconscious condition which will indefinitely last without improvement, person unable to communicate, no purposeful movement or motor activity, and cannot interact with environmental stimuli. (§ 34-12D-1(8))
Tennessee	No. (§ 34-6-204(a)(1) & (b)) (unless limited by the power, the attorney-in-fact can make the same decisions as the principal could. Presumably, then, living will provisions can be addressed in the durable power of attorney for health care)	Living Will. (§ 32-11-105)	Yes (as indicated in the statutory form). (§ 32-11-105)	Yes, "persistent vegetative state" is included in definition of terminal condition. (§ 32-11-103(9))	Loss of competency causes living will to become effective. (§ 32-11-104(a))	Yes, "terminal condition" has been defined by statute. (§ 32-11-103(9))

Texas	No. (Health & Safety §§ 166.033, 166.032(c))	Directive to Physicians and Family or Surrogates. (Health & Safety § 166.033)	Yes (as indicated in the statutory form). (Health & Safety § 166.033)	Not specified.	Incurable/irreversible condition caused by injury, disease, or illness certified to be a terminal condition (as indicated in the statutory form). (Health & Safety § 166.033)	Yes, "terminal condition" has been defined by statute. (Health & Safety § 166.002(13))
Utah (2007)	Personal Choice and Living Will Act sets out different forms for directive and special power of attorney. (§§ 75-2-1104, 75-2-1106)	Directive to physicians and providers of medical services. (§ 75-2-1104)	Yes (as indicated in the statutory form). (§ 75-2-1104(4)(2))	Yes (as indicated in the statutory form). (§ 75-2-1104(4)(2))	Not specified. (§ 75-2-1104(4)(2))	Yes, "terminal condition" and "persistent vegetative state" are defined by statute. (§§ 75-2-1103(10), 75-2-1103(8))
Utah (2008) (The new law is effective Jan. 1, 2008. A health care directive executed prior to this date under the provisions then in effect, Ch. 2, pt. II, Personal Choice and Living Will, may, in good faith, be relied upon by a health care provider or health care facility. (§ 75-2a-1120(1)(b))	No. They can be combined in an advance health care directive. (§ 75-2a-1106(1)(a))	Advance Health Care Directive. (§ 75-2a-1106)	The term is not actually used (as indicated in the statutory form). (§ 75-2a-1116, Pt. II)	Yes (as indicated in the statutory form). (§ 75-2a-1116, Pt. II)	For example, an agent can stop care prolonging the declarant's life if a progressive illness will cause death, the declarant is close to death and unlikely to recover, the declarant cannot communicate and his condition is unlikely to improve, he does not recognize friends and family and his condition is unlikely to improve, or he is in a persistent vegetative state. (§ 75-2a-1116, Pt. II)	No.

Table 7.01, Part 1
Coverage of Living Will Statute *(continued)*

	Must There Be Separate Documents for Living Will and Health Care?	*What Is the Specific Title of the Living Will Instrument?*	*Is a Terminal Condition Sufficient to Justify Withdrawing Support?*	*Is a Persistent Vegetative State Sufficient to Justify Withdrawing Support?*	*If a Different Standard Is Used, What Is it Exactly?*	*Has a "Terminal Condition," Persistent Vegetative State, or Other Standard Used Been Defined by State or Case Law?*
Vermont	No. (18 § 9702)	Advance Directive. (18 § 9703)	Not specified. However, lack of capacity is required. (18 § 9706(a))	Not specified.	Not specified.	Yes, "capacity" is defined by statute. (18 § 9701(3))
Virginia	No. (§§ 54.1-2983, 54.1-2984)	Advance Medical Directive. (§ 54.1-2984)	Yes. (§ 54.1-2983)	Yes, "persistent vegetative state" is included in definition of terminal condition. (§ 54.1-2982)	Not specified.	Yes, "terminal condition" and "persistent vegetative state" are defined by statute. (§ 54.1-2982)
Washington	Not specified.	Health Care Directive. (§ 70.122.030(1))	Yes. (§ 70.122.030(1))	Yes. (§ 70.122.030(1))	"Permanent unconscious condition" is also satisfactory. (§ 70.122.030(1))	Yes, "terminal condition" and "permanent unconscious condition" are defined by statute. (§§ 70.122.020(9), 70.122.020(6))
West Virginia	No. (§ 16-30-4)	Living Will. (§ 16-30-4)	Yes (as indicated in the statutory form). (§ 16-30-4)	Yes (as indicated in the statutory form). (§ 16-30-4)	Not specified. (§ 16-30-4)	Yes, "terminal condition" and "persistent vegetative state" have been defined by statute. (§§ 16-30-3(s), 16-30-3(aa))
Wisconsin	No (as indicated in the durable power of attorney statutory form). (§ 155.30)	Declaration to physicians; Wisconsin living will. (§ 154.03(2))	Yes. (§ 154.03(1))	Yes. (§ 154.03(1))	Not specified.	Yes, statute. Persistent vegetative state: complete/irreversible loss of all cerebral cortex functions causing complete, chronic,

						irreversible loss of all cognitive functioning and consciousness and no behavioral responses indicating cognitive functioning although autonomic functioning persists. (§ 154.01(5m)) Terminal condition: incurable condition caused by injury/illness, death is imminent, and life-sustaining procedures only postpone death. (§ 154.01(8))
Wyoming	There is a single document. (§ 35-22-403)	Advance Health Care Directive. However, reference is also made to a power of attorney for health care. (§ 35-22-403)	No condition is required. An agent for a person who is incapacitated can simply refuse health care or artificial nutrition and hydration, just as an individual might for himself. (§ 35-22-402(a)(ix))	Condition not required. See prior column.	See third column.	See third column.

1. Only deals with health care proxies.

Table 7.01, Part 2
Coverage of Living Will Statute

	Who Determines the Condition of the Patient?	*What Sort of Medical Procedures Can Be Withheld or Withdrawn?*	*If "Life-Sustaining" Procedures or "Extraordinary Means," or Otherwise, Briefly What Does This Entail, If Defined?*	*Specifically, May Food and/or Hydration Be Withheld or Withdrawn?*	*Does the Statute Use "Artificially" or "Unnaturally" Prolonged in Describing When, e.g., Life-Sustaining Procedures or Extraordinary Means Can Be Withheld or Withdrawn?*
Alabama	Attending physician and one other physician. (§ 22-8A-4(d))	Life-sustaining treatment and artificial nutrition and hydration. (§ 22-8A-4(a))	Life-sustaining treatment includes any medical treatment, procedure, or intervention that, in the judgment of the attending physician, when applied to the patient, would serve only to prolong the dying process where the patient has a terminal illness or injury, or would serve only to maintain the patient in a condition of permanent unconsciousness. These procedures shall include, but are not limited to, assisted ventilation, cardiopulmonary resuscitation, renal dialysis, surgical procedures, blood transfusions, and the administration of drugs and antibiotics. Life-sustaining treatment shall not include the administration of medication or the performance of any medical treatment where, in the opinion of the attending physician, the medication or treatment is necessary to provide comfort or to alleviate pain. (§ 22-8A-3(8))	Yes, if specifically authorized in the living will. (§ 22-8A-4(a))	Not specified.

Alaska	Primary physician. (§ 13.52.300)	Life-sustaining procedures. (§ 13.52.045)	Life-sustaining procedure means any medical procedure or intervention that, when administered to a qualified patient, would serve only to prolong the dying process. (§ 13.52.390(26))	Yes, with respect to artificial nutrition and hydration. (§ 13.52.390(20)(C))	Neither term is used.
Arizona	The patient's surrogate. (§ 36-3203(c)) However, the patient has the option of providing for the continuation of all treatment until "my doctors reasonably conclude that my condition is terminal or is irreversible and incurable or I am in a persistent vegetative state" (as indicated in the statutory form). (§ 36-3262)	The patient can have the following treatment withheld: chest compressions, defibrillation, assisted ventilation, intubation, advanced life support medications, CPR, electric shock, artificial breathing, artificially administered food and drugs and all life-sustaining treatment generally. The patient can also add to this list of exclusions (as indicated in the statutory form). (§§ 36-3251, 36-3262)	Not defined.	Yes (as indicated in the statutory form). (§ 36-3262)	Artificially (as indicated in the statutory form). (§ 36-3262)
Arkansas	The attending physician and one other physician in the case of a "terminal condition" or "permanently unconscious state" determines whether a person is a "qualified person." However, the attending physician and another qualified physician are required to determine the declarant is in a terminal condition and no longer able to make decisions regarding administration of life-sustaining treatment *(cont'd)*	"Life-sustaining treatment." (§ 20-17-202(a))	"Life-sustaining treatment" is defined as any procedure or intervention that would only prolong death or keep the person in a permanently unconscious state. (§ 20-17-201(5))	Maybe. The person may authorize the withdrawal of hydration and/or nutrition (as indicated in the statutory form). (§ 20-17-202) The attending physician has the responsibility to provide nutrition and/or hydration, however, for the patient's comfort or the alleviation of pain. (§ 20-17-206(b))	Not specified.

Table 7.01, Part 2
Coverage of Living Will Statute *(continued)*

	Who Determines the Condition of the Patient?	*What Sort of Medical Procedures Can Be Withheld or Withdrawn?*	*If "Life-Sustaining" Procedures or "Extraordinary Means," or Otherwise, Briefly What Does This Entail, If Defined?*	*Specifically, May Food and/or Hydration Be Withheld or Withdrawn?*	*Does the Statute Use "Artificially" or "Unnaturally" Prolonged in Describing When, e.g., Life-Sustaining Procedures or Extraordinary Means Can Be Withheld or Withdrawn?*
Arkansas *(cont'd)*	or to be permanently unconscious before a declaration can become operative. (§ 20-17-203)				
California	Primary physician. (Prob. § 4732)	Any care. (Prob. § 4701, Explanation (a))	N/A	Yes (as indicated in the statutory form); uses "artificial." (Prob. § 4701, Explanation (d))	No, just the word "prolong." (Prob. § 4701, Pt. 2(2.1))
Colorado	Attending physician and one other qualified physician. (§ 15-18-107)	Life-sustaining procedures and artificial nourishment. (§ 15-18-104(1) &(2.5))	Life-sustaining procedure means any medical procedure or intervention that serves only to prolong the dying process. It does not include any procedure necessary to alleviate pain or provide nourishment. (§ 15-18-103(7))	Yes. (§ 15-18-104 (2.5)(a))	Not specified.
Connecticut	Incapacitation determined by attending physician. (§ 19a-579) Terminal condition determined by attending physician. (§ 19a-571(a)(2)) Permanently unconscious determined by attending physician and a physician qualified to make	Life support systems. (§ 19a-575)	"Life support system" means any medical procedure/intervention that would serve only to postpone death or keep patient permanently unconscious, including, but not limited to, mechanical or electronic devices, including artificial means of providing nutrition and hydration (§ 19a-570(7))	Yes. (§ 19a-570(1))	Yes. The word "artificial" is used. (§ 19a-570(7))

	neurological diagnosis after examining the patient. (§ 19a-571(a)(2))				
Delaware	A determination that an individual lacks capacity or has recovered capacity must be made by a physician. Decisions to with draw treatment from a patient must be made in consultation with a physician. (16 § 2503(e) & (f))	The patient can request that any medical procedures be withheld, including life-sustaining procedures and artificial nutrition and hydration (as indicated in the statutory form). (16 § 2505)	A "life-sustaining procedure" is any medical procedure that (a) utilizes mechanical or other artificial means to sustain, restore, or supplant a spontaneous vital function, or (b) does not afford the patient a reasonable chance of recovery from a terminal condition or permanent unconsciousness. (16§ 2501(l))	Yes (as indicated in the statutory form). (16 § 2505(e))	Yes. A life-sustaining procedure is one that "artificially sustains, restores, or supplants a spontaneous vital function." (16 § 2501(l))
District of Columbia	A terminal condition must be certified by two physicians, one of whom shall be the attending physician (as indicated in the statutory form). (§§ 7-622(c), 7-621(3))	All life-sustaining procedures may be withheld. (§ 7-622(a))	The term "life-sustaining procedure" means any medical procedure that would serve only to artificially prolong the dying process. The term shall not include the administration of medication or the performance of medical procedures deemed necessary to provide comfort to the patient. (§ 7-621(3))	Not specified.	Yes. A life-sustaining procedure is one that would seem only to artificially prolong the dying process. (§ 7-621(3))
Florida	Attending/treating physician and one other physician after an examination. (§ 765.306)	Life-prolonging procedures. (§ 765.302(1))	Life-prolonging procedures: any medical procedure, treatment, intervention which uses mechanical/artificial means for vital function and only prolongs the dying process including artificially provided food and hydration. (§ 765.101(10))	Yes, since included in the definition of life-prolonging procedures. (§ 765.101(10)) Also, it is implied (as indicated in the statutory form which says that provision may be made only to receive medication or procedures to alleviate pain or provide comfort care). (§ 765.303(1))	Legislative findings and intent section says "artificial prolongation of life" (§ 765.102(3)); sample living will says "procedures would serve only to prolong artificially the process of dying" (§ 765.303(1)).

Table 7.01, Part 2
Coverage of Living Will Statute *(continued)*

	Who Determines the Condition of the Patient?	*What Sort of Medical Procedures Can Be Withheld or Withdrawn?*	*If "Life-Sustaining" Procedures or "Extraordinary Means," or Otherwise, Briefly What Does This Entail, If Defined?*	*Specifically, May Food and/or Hydration Be Withheld or Withdrawn?*	*Does the Statute Use "Artificially" or "Unnaturally" Prolonged in Describing When, e.g., Life-Sustaining Procedures or Extraordinary Means Can Be Withheld or Withdrawn?*
Georgia	Two physicians, one of whom must be the attending physician, make the determination after personally examining the declarant. (§ 31-32-2(13))	Life-sustaining procedures. (§ 31-32-3(a))	Life-sustaining procedures are defined as any medical procedures or interventions, which, when applied to a patient in a terminal condition or in a coma or vegetative state (with no reasonable expectation of regaining consciousness or significant function) which only serves to prolong dying. This may include (at the declarant's option) the provision of nourishment and hydration, but does not include pain relief medications or procedures. (§ 31-32-2(6))	Yes, if authorized by the declarant. (§§ 31-32-3(a), 31-32-2(6))	Neither term is used. (§ 31-32-3(b))
Hawaii	Primary physician (unless otherwise specified in a written advance health-care directive) (§ 327E-3(f)) or supervising health care provider (§ 327E-7(c))	Any, including the with holding or removal of artificially provided nutrition and hydration. (§§ 327E-3, 327E-16, Explanation (a))	N/A	Yes. (§ 327E-16, Explanation (d))	No, just the word "prolong." (§ 327E-16, Pt.2(6)(a))
Idaho	One examining phycician. (§ 39-4510 recommended form)	All medical treatment, including withdrawal of artificial nutrition and hydration. (§ 39-4510 recommended form)	"Artificial life-sustaining procedure" means any medical procedure or intervention that utilizes mechanical means to sustain or supplant a vital function which when applied to a qualified patient, would serve only to	Yes. (§ 39-5410 recommended form)	Artificially. (§ 39-4509) The statutory form mentions the term "artificial life-sustaining." (§ 39-4510 recommended form

			artificially prolong life. "Artificial life-sustaining procedure" does not include the administration of medication or the performance of any medical procedure deemed necessary to alleviate pain. (§ 39-4509(1)) "Termination condition" means an incurable or irreversible condition which, without the administration of life-sustaining procedures, will, in the opinion of the physician, result in death if it runs its usual course. (§ 39-450(14)) "Persistent vegetative state means an irreversible state that has been medically confirmed by a neurological specialist who is an expert in the examination of nonresponsive individuals in which the person has intact brainstem function but no higher cortical function and no awareness of self or environment." (§ 39-4501(10))		which uses other standards as well)
Illinois	Attending physician. (755 ILCS §§ 35/2(a), 35/6)	"Death delaying procedures." (755 ILCS § 35/3(a))	"Death delaying procedures": any medical procedure/intervention that only postpones death. Does not include treatments for care/comfort. (755 ILCS § 35/2(d))	Yes, unless death would result solely from dehydration/starvation. (755 ILCS § 35/2(d))	Artificially (as indicated in the statutory form). (755 ILCS § 35/3(e))
Indiana	The attending physician must determine the condition of the patient. (§§ 16-36-4-10, 16-36-4-13)	All life prolonging procedures can be withheld. (§ 16-36-4-10)	"Life prolonging procedure" means any medical procedure, treatment, or intervention that (1) uses mechanical or other artificial means to sustain, restore, or support a vital function, and (2) serves to prolong the dying process. (§ 16-36-4-1)	Yes. (§ 16-36-4-10)	Artificial. (§ 16-36-4-1)

Table 7.01, Part 2
Coverage of Living Will Statute *(continued)*

	Who Determines the Condition of the Patient?	*What Sort of Medical Procedures Can Be Withheld or Withdrawn?*	*If "Life-Sustaining" Procedures or "Extraordinary Means," or Otherwise, Briefly What Does This Entail, If Defined?*	*Specifically, May Food and/or Hydration Be Withheld or Withdrawn?*	*Does the Statute Use "Artificially" or "Unnaturally" Prolonged in Describing When, e.g., Life-Sustaining Procedures or Extraordinary Means Can Be Withheld or Withdrawn?*
Iowa	Attending physician and another physician. (§ 144A.5)	Life-sustaining procedures. (§ 144A.3(1))	Life-sustaining procedures means any medical procedure, treatment, or intervention which utilizes mechanical or artificial means to sustain, restore, or supplant a vital function which only serves to prolong dying. This does not include the provision of nutrition or hydration or pain relief medications or procedures. (§ 144A.2(8))	No. (§ 144A.2(8) flush paragraph after (b))	Artificial. (§ 144A.2(8))
Kansas	Attending physician and one other physician (as indicated in the statutory form). (§ 65-28,103(c))	Life-sustaining procedures. (§ 65-28,103(a))	Life-prolonging procedure means any medical procedure or intervention that would serve only to prolong the dying process and where death would occur whether or not such procedures are used. This does not include pain relief medications or procedures. (§ 65-28,102(c))	Not specified.	Artificially (as indicated in the statutory form). (§ 65-28,103(c))
Kentucky	A terminal condition is determined by the patient's attending physician and one other physician. (§ 311.621 (16))	All life-prolonging treatment can be withheld (as indicated in the statutory form). (§ 311.625(1))	"Life-prolonging treatment" means any medical procedure which: (a) utilizes mechanical or other artificial means to sustain, prolong, restore, or supplant a spontaneous vital function; and (b) when administered to a patient would serve only to	Yes. (§§ 311.625(1), 311.623(1)(b))	Artificial. (§ 311.621(11))

			prolong the dying process. This does not include treatment or medication for pain. (§ 311.621(11))		
Louisiana	Attending physician and one other physician (as indicated in the statutory form). (§ 40:1299.58.3(C)(1))	Life-sustaining procedures. (§ 40:1299.58.3(A)(1))	Life-sustaining procedure means any medical procedure or intervention, such as the invasive administration of nutrition and hydration and administration of cardiopulmonary resuscitation which would serve only to prolong the dying process where the person has been diagnosed with a terminal and irreversible condition. This does not include pain relief medications or procedures. (§ 40:1299.58.2(9))	Yes (specifically the invasive administration of nutrition and hydration). (§§ 40:1299.58.3(A)(1), 40:1299.58.3(C)(1), 40:1299.58.2(9))	Artificially (as indicated in the statutory form). (§ 40:1299.58.3(C)(1))
Maine	Unless otherwise specified in a written advance health-care directive, a determination that a condition exists that affects the directive must be made by the primary physician or by a court of competent jurisdiction. (18-A § 5-802(D))	All life-sustaining treatment may be withheld (as indicated in the statutory form). (18-A § 5-804)	"Life-sustaining treatment" means any medical procedure that will only serve to prolong the process of dying. (18-A § 5-801(R))	Yes (as indicated in the statutory form). (18-A § 5-804)	Not specified.
Maryland	Attending physician and one other physician, unless otherwise provided in document. If patient is unconscious, only one doctor's determination is needed. (Health-Gen. § 5-602(e))	Life-sustaining procedures. (Health-Gen. § 5-602(a)&(d)(1))	Life-sustaining procedures means any medical procedure, treatment, or intervention which uses mechanical means to sustain or supplant a vital function which affords the patient no reasonable expectation of recovery. These procedures include artificially administered hydration and nutrition and cardiopulmonary resuscitation. (Health-Gen. § 5-601(m))	Yes, if authorized, artificially administered hydration and nutrition can be withheld/withdrawn. (Health-Gen. §§ 5-601(m)(2); 5-602(a)&(d)(1))	"Artificially" is used. (Health-Gen. §§ 5-601(m)(2))

Table 7.01, Part 2
Coverage of Living Will Statute *(continued)*

	Who Determines the Condition of the Patient?	*What Sort of Medical Procedures Can Be Withheld or Withdrawn?*	*If "Life-Sustaining" Procedures or "Extraordinary Means," or Otherwise, Briefly What Does This Entail, If Defined?*	*Specifically, May Food and/or Hydration Be Withheld or Withdrawn?*	*Does the Statute Use "Artificially" or "Unnaturally" Prolonged in Describing When, e.g., Life-Sustaining Procedures or Extraordinary Means Can Be Withheld or Withdrawn?*
Massachusetts[1]	Attending physician decides the patient lacks capacity for health care decisions. (201D § 6)	Not specified.	Not specified.	Implies that artificial oral feeding can be withheld/withdrawn. (201D § 13)	Not specified.
Michigan	Attending physician and one other physician or licensed psychologist determine if the patient can make medical decisions. (§ 700.5508(1))	Treatment. (§ 333.5655)	Not specified.	Not specified.	Not specified.
Minnesota	Attending physician. (§ 145B.13)	Life-sustaining procedures and artificially administered sustenance (as indicated in the statutory form). (§ 145B.04 (e)(5) & (6))	Not defined. (§ 145B.04(e)(6))	Yes, if specifically authorized. (§ 145B.03 (Subd. 2)(b)(1))	Not specified.
Mississippi	The primary physician unless otherwise specified. (§ 41-41-205(6))	Treatment that would prolong life. (§ 41-41-209, statutory form (6))	Not specified.	Yes. (§ 41-41-209, statutory form (7))	Neither term is used. (§ 41-41-209, statutory form (6))
Missouri	Attending physician. (§ 459.010(6))	Death-prolonging procedures (as indicated in the statutory form). (§ 459.015(3))	Death-prolonging procedures include any medical procedure or intervention that only serves to artificially prolong the dying process when death will occur within a short time whether or not such procedures are used. These procedures do not include	No. (§ 459.010(3))	Artificially. (§ 459.010(3))

			pain-alleviating medications or procedures or any procedures used to provide nutrition or hydration. (§ 459.010(3))		
Montana	The attending physician or attending advanced practice registered nurse. (§ 50-9-105(b))	All life-sustaining treatment can be withheld. (§ 50-9-103(1))	"Life-sustaining treatment" means any medical procedure or intervention that, when administered to a patient, serves only to prolong the dying process. (§ 50-9-102(9))	Yes, statutory form allows for this to extent not necessary for comfort or to alleviate pain. (§ 50-9-103)	Not specified.
Nebraska	Attending physician. (§ 20-405(2))	Life-sustaining treatment. (§ 20-404(1))	Life-sustaining treatment: any medical procedure/intervention that would prolong the dying process or keep the patient in a persistent vegetative state. (§ 20-403(5))	No. (§ 20-408(2))	Not specified.
Nevada	The attending physician. (§ 449.617)	All life-sustaining treatment can be withheld. (§ 449.600(1))	"Life-sustaining treatment" means a medical procedure/intervention that serves only to prolong the process of dying. (§ 449.570)	Yes. (§ 449.624(3))	Not specified.
New Hampshire	Attending physician or ARNP, or any other physician or ARNP aware of the principal's execution of an advance directive. (§ 137-J:7(c)) (§§ 137-J:20, 137-J:2)	Life-sustaining procedures. (§ 137-J:20)	"Life-sustaining procedures" means any medical procedure or intervention which uses mechanical or other medically administered means to sustain, restore, or supplant a vital function which when applied to a qualified patient would serve, in the written opinion of the attending physician or ARNP, only to artificially prolong the moment of death and where the	Yes, but only if there is a clear expression of intent in the directive, the principal objects, or it would actually hasten death. (§137-J:7(111))	Artificially. (§ 137-J:20)

(cont'd)

Table 7.01, Part 2
Coverage of Living Will Statute *(continued)*

	Who Determines the Condition of the Patient?	*What Sort of Medical Procedures Can Be Withheld or Withdrawn?*	*If "Life-Sustaining" Procedures or "Extraordinary Means," or Otherwise, Briefly What Does This Entail, If Defined?*	*Specifically, May Food and/or Hydration Be Withheld or Withdrawn?*	*Does the Statute Use "Artificially" or "Unnaturally" Prolonged in Describing When, e.g., Life-Sustaining Procedures or Extraordinary Means Can Be Withheld or Withdrawn?*
New Hampshire *(cont'd)*			person is near death or permanently unconscious. These procedures do not include medication, natural ingestion of food or fluids, or the performance of any medical procedure deemed necessary to provide comfort to the patient or to alleviate pain. (§ 137-J:2(XIII))		
New Jersey	Permanently unconscious and terminal condition decided by attending physician and one other physician. (§ 26:2H-67(a)(2) & (3)) Experimental life-sustaining treatment not specified; irreversible illness/condition: attending physician in consultation with either a reviewing body or a public agency set up for that purpose. (§ 26:2H-67(a)(4))	Any form of health care including life-sustaining treatment. (§ 26:2H-58(b))	Life-sustaining treatment: any medical device or procedure, artificially provided fluids and nutrition, drugs, surgery or therapy which uses mechanical/artificial means to sustain, restore, or supplant a vital bodily function and thereby increase the expected lifespan of a patient. (§ 26:2H-55)	Yes, specifically artificial. (§ 26:2H-55)	Yes, artificial means. (§ 26:2H-55)
New Mexico	Primary physician and one other qualified health-care professional. (§ 24-7A-11(C))	Life-sustaining treatment. (§ 24-7A-4)	Life-sustaining treatment means any medical treatment or procedure without which the individual is likely to die within a	Yes, artificially provided nutrition and hydration can be withdrawn, if authorized	Neither term is used. (§ 24-7A-4, Pt. 2)

	(See also § 24.7A-4, statutory form Pt. 2.)		relatively short time, as determined to a reasonable degree of medical certainty by the primary physician. (§ 24-7A-1(K))	(as indicated in the statutory form). (§ 24-7A-4, Pt. 2)	
New York	Attending physician and another physician for a decision to withdraw or withhold life-sustaining treatment. (Pub. Health § 2983(1))	Any treatment (Pub. Health § 2982(1)), including life-sustaining treatment (as indicated in Pub. Health § 2983(1)). But if the principal's wishes regarding the administration of artificial nutrition and hydration are not reasonably known and cannot with reasonable diligence be ascertained, the agent shall not have the authority to make decisions regarding these measures. (Pub. Health § 2982(2))	Not specified.	If the principal's wishes regarding the administration of artificial nutrition and hydration are not reasonably known and cannot with reasonable diligence be ascertained, the agent shall not have the authority to make decisions regarding these measures. (Pub. Health § 2982(2))	Not specified.
North Carolina	Attending physician and one other physician. (§ 90-321(b)(1) & (2))	Extraordinary means and artificial nutrition or hydration (if authorized by declarant). (§ 90-321(b)(2))	Extraordinary means includes any medical procedure or intervention that the attending physician determines would only serve to postpone death artificially by sustaining, restoring, or supplanting a vital function. (§ 90-321(a)(2))	Yes (if specifically authorized by declarant). (§ 90-321(b)(2))	Artificially. (§ 90-321(a)(2))
North Dakota	After consultation with the attending physician. (§ 23-06.5-03)	All treatment may be with held or withdrawn. (§ 23-06.5-02(4))	Not specified.	Yes. (§ 23-06.5-02(4))	Not specified.

Table 7.01, Part 2
Coverage of Living Will Statute *(continued)*

	Who Determines the Condition of the Patient?	*What Sort of Medical Procedures Can Be Withheld or Withdrawn?*	*If "Life-Sustaining" Procedures or "Extraordinary Means," or Otherwise, Briefly What Does This Entail, If Defined?*	*Specifically, May Food and/or Hydration Be Withheld or Withdrawn?*	*Does the Statute Use "Artificially" or "Unnaturally" Prolonged in Describing When, e.g., Life-Sustaining Procedures or Extraordinary Means Can Be Withheld or Withdrawn?*
Ohio	Attending physician and one other physician. In the case of permanent unconsciousness, the consulting physician must in some way be specifically qualified to make the assessment. (§ 2133.03(A))	Life-sustaining treatments. (§ 2133.02(A)(1))	Life-sustaining treatment: any medical procedure, treatment or intervention that will principally serve to prolong the dying process. (§ 2133.01(Q))	Yes, but only if the patient is in a permanently unconscious state. There are a number of requirements that the patient must meet in order to qualify which are too extensive and detailed to list, but which include obtaining an order from the county probate court. (§ 2133.09)	Not specified.
Oklahoma	Attending physician and one other physician (as indicated in the statutory form). (63 § 3101.4(B)(I)(a))	Life-sustaining treatment (as indicated in the statutory form). (63 § 3101.4(B)(I)(b)(1))	Life-sustaining treatment means any medical procedure or intervention, including artificially administered nutrition and hydration (if authorized), which would only serve to prolong dying. This does not include medications or treatments for pain relief nor the normal consumption of food and water. (63 § 3101.3(6))	Yes, artificially provided nutrition and hydration can be withdrawn, if authorized. (63 § 3101.4(B)(I)(b)(2))	Artificially (as indicated in the statutory form). (63 § 3101.4(B))

Oregon	Attending doctor and another knowledgeable doctor (as indicated in the statutory form). (§ 127.531(2)(C))	Tube feeding and life support procedures (as indicated in the statutory form). (§ 127.531(2)(C))	Tube feeding: artificial nutrition/hydration. (§ 127.505(23)) Life-sustaining procedures: any medical procedure, pharmaceutical, device, intervention that maintains life by sustaining, supporting, or supplanting a vital function; does not include care for cleanliness and comfort. (§ 127.505(16))	Yes, if artificial. (§§ 127.531(2)(C), 127.505(23))	Not specified.
Pennsylvania	Attending physician. (20 § 5408)	Life-sustaining treatment. (20 § 5404(a))	Life-sustaining treatment: any medical procedure/intervention that prolongs death or maintains one in a state of permanent unconsciousness; this includes nutrition and hydration if artificial or invasive so long as the declaration specifically states this. (20 § 5403)	Yes, if specifically stated in the declaration and is artificial/invasive. (20 § 5404)	Not specified.
Rhode Island	Attending physician. (§ 23-4.11-3(c)(2))	Life-sustaining procedures. (§ 23-4.11-3(a))	Life-sustaining procedure: any medical procedure/intervention that will only prolong the dying process but does not include anything that will provide comfort/care or alleviate pain. (§ 23-4.11-2(8))	Yes, if feeding is artificial (as indicated in the statutory form). (§ 23-4.11-3(d))	Not specified.
South Carolina	Attending physician and one other physician. (§ 44-77-30)	Life-sustaining procedures. (§ 44-77-30)	Life-sustaining procedures means any medical procedure or intervention, including nutrition and hydration administered by tubes (if authorized), which would only serve to prolong dying. This does not include medications or treatments for pain relief nor the normal consumption of food and water. (§ 44-77-20(2))	Yes, artificially provided nutrition and hydration can be withdrawn, if authorized. (§ 44-77-20(2))	Artificial is used. (§ 44-77-50)

Table 7.01, Part 2
Coverage of Living Will Statute *(continued)*

	Who Determines the Condition of the Patient?	*What Sort of Medical Procedures Can Be Withheld or Withdrawn?*	*If "Life-Sustaining" Procedures or "Extraordinary Means," or Otherwise, Briefly What Does This Entail, If Defined?*	*Specifically, May Food and/or Hydration Be Withheld or Withdrawn?*	*Does the Statute Use "Artificially" or "Unnaturally" Prolonged in Describing When, e.g., Life-Sustaining Procedures or Extraordinary Means Can Be Withheld or Withdrawn?*
South Dakota	Attending physician. (§ 34-12D-5)	"Life-sustaining treatment." (§ 34-12D-2)	Life-sustaining treatment: any medical procedure/intervention that will only postpone death or keep patient permanently unconscious. Does not include: care for comfort, hygiene, human dignity, or food/water/medication/medical procedures that are necessary for pain. (§ 34-12D-1(4))	Declarant may put in the living will no food/hydration (§ 34-12D-2), but it will be administered if necessary for pain/comfort/hygiene/human dignity regardless of the provisions in the living will. (§ 34-12D-9)	Not specified.
Tennessee	Attending physician. (§ 32-11-105)	Artificially provided nourishment and fluids and all medical care (not including pain relief medication or procedures). (§ 32-11-105 (in form of declaration))	Medical care: any procedure or treatment rendered by a physician or health care provider designed to diagnose, assess, or treat a disease, illness, or injury. This does not include the withholding of nourishment and fluids unless the living will clearly so indicates. (§ 32-11-103(5)) (in form of declaration)	Yes. (§§ 32-11-105; 32-11-103(5))	Not specified. "Artificially" describes only nourishment and fluids. (§ 32-11-105 (in form of declaration))
Texas	The attending physician (as indicated in the statutory form). (Health &	Life-sustaining treatment (as indicated in the	Life-sustaining treatment means treatment that, based on reasonable medical judgment,	Yes (as indicated in statutory form). (§ 166.033)	Artificially. § 166.002(10))

	Safety §§ 166.033, 166.038)	statutory form). (Health & Safety § 166.033)	sustains the life of a patient and without which the patient will die. This does not include pain relief medications or procedures. (Health & Safety § 166.002(10))		
Utah (2007)	Two physicians. (§ 75-2-1104(4)(2))	Life-sustaining procedures. (§ 75-2-1104(4)(2))	"Life-sustaining procedure" means any medical procedure or intervention, including artificially administered nutrition and hydration (unless declarant specifically instructs it to be excluded), which would only serve to prolong dying. This does not include medications or performances for pain, relief or comfort. (§ 75-2-1103(7))	Yes, unless excluded. (§ 75-2-1103(7))	Unnaturally (as indicated in the statutory form). (§ 75-2-1104(4)(2))
Utah (2008) The new law is effective Jan. 1, 2008. A health care directive executed prior to this date under the provisions then in effect, Ch. 2, pt. II, Personal Choice and Living Will, may, in good faith, be relied upon by a health care provider or health care facility. (§ 75-2a-1120(1)(b))	Not relevant. The agent can decide on all health care decisions, including withholding of life-sustaining procedures. (§ 75-2a-1106(1)(a)(iii))	All health care decisions. (§ 75-2a-1109(i))	Not relevant.	Yes. (§ 75-2a-1103(a)(iii))	Not relevant.

Table 7.01, Part 2
Coverage of Living Will Statute *(continued)*

	Who Determines the Condition of the Patient?	*What Sort of Medical Procedures Can Be Withheld or Withdrawn?*	*If "Life-Sustaining" Procedures or "Extraordinary Means," or Otherwise, Briefly What Does This Entail, If Defined?*	*Specifically, May Food and/or Hydration Be Withheld or Withdrawn?*	*Does the Statute Use "Artificially" or "Unnaturally" Prolonged in Describing When, e.g., Life-Sustaining Procedures or Extraordinary Means Can Be Withheld or Withdrawn?*
Vermont	Principal's clinician (18 § 9706(1))	Life-sustaining treatments (as indicated in the statutory form). (18 § 9702)	"Life-sustaining treatment" means any medical intervention, including nutrition and hydration administered by medical means and antibiotics, which is intended to extend life and without which the principal is likely to die. (18 § 9701(18))	Yes. (18 § 97202(7))	Not specified.
Virginia	Attending physician (as indicated in the statutory form). (§ 54.1-2984)	Life-prolonging procedures. (§ 54.1-2983)	Life-prolonging procedures means any medical procedure, treatment, or intervention which uses mechanical means to sustain or supplant a vital function which affords the patient no reasonable expectation of recovery and would only serve to prolong the dying process. These procedures include artificially administered hydration and nutrition, but not pain relieving medicines (even excessive dosages) or procedures done to provide physical comfort to the patient. (§ 54.1-2982)	Yes, artificially administered hydration and nutrition can be withheld/withdrawn. (§§ 54.1-2984, 54.1-2982)	Artificially (as indicated in the statutory form). (§ 54.1-2984)
Washington	Attending physician if terminal illness; two physicians if permanent unconscious state (as indicated	Life-sustaining treatment. (§ 70.122.030(1))	Life-sustaining treatment means any medical or surgical intervention that uses mechanical or other artificial means, including	Artificially provided nutrition and hydration can be withdrawn.	Artificially (as indicated in the statutory form). (§ 70.122.030(1))

	in the statutory form). (§ 70.122.030(1))		artificially provided nutrition and hydration, to sustain, restore, or replace a vital function that only serves to prolong dying. This does not include pain relief medications or pain relief surgical intervention. (§ 70.122.020(5))	(§§ 70.122.030(1), 70.122.020(5))	
West Virginia	One physician (as indicated in the statutory form). (§ 16-30-4)	Life-prolonging medical intervention. (§ 16-30-4)	Life-prolonging intervention means any medical procedure or intervention that would serve only to artificially prolong the dying process or maintain the person in a persistent vegetative state. This does include pain relief medications or procedures. (§ 16-30-3(m))	Yes. (§ 16-30-3(m))	Artificially. (§ 16-30-3(m))
Wisconsin	Attending physician and one other physician after both have examined the patient (as indicated in the statutory form). (§ 154.03(2))	Life-sustaining procedures or feeding tubes. (§ 154.03(1))	Life-sustaining procedures: any medical procedure/intervention that only prolongs death, but will not avert death. Does not include: medication or procedures to alleviate pain or nutrition/hydration. (§ 154.01(5))	Yes, unless it will cause pain/discomfort or is administered through some means other than a feeding tube (unless it is determined medically contraindicated). (§ 154.03(1))	Artificially (as indicated in the statutory form. (§ 154.03(2))
Wyoming	If not otherwise specified, the primary physician unless unavailable. (§ 35-22-403(e)) The physician merely determines if the patient is capable. If not, the surrogate is allowed to make health care decisions.	Any treatments or procedures, including withholding of artificial nutrition and hydration. (§ 35-22-402(a)(ix))	Not specified.	Yes. (§ 35-22-402(a)(ix))	No, since the surrogate can make all health care decisions. (§§ 35-22-402(a)(ix), 35-22-406)

1. Only deals with health care proxies.

Table 7.02, Part 1
Formal Requirements

		What Formalities Satisfy the Requirements?				
	Must the Living Will Be in Writing?	*Just Like a Will?*	*Writing?*	*Signed by the Person?*	*Signed By Someone (1) In His Presence and (2) At His Direction?*	*Signed Otherwise? Specify.*
Alabama	Yes. (§ 22-8A-4(c)(1))	Shall be "substantially" in the form of living will provided in § 22-8A-4(h). [Note: no specific requirement that living will be in exact form of a will.] Not specified. (§ 22-8A-4)	Yes. (§ 22-8A-3(9))	Yes. (§ 22-8A-4(c)(2))	(1) Yes. (§ 22-8A-4(c)(2)) (2)Yes. (§ 22-8A-4(c)(2))	Not specified. (§ 22-8A-4(c)(2))
Alaska	No. Can be oral or written. However, durable power of attorney for health care must be written. (§ 13.52.010(b))	Sample "Advance Health Care Directive" provided. (§ 13.52.300)	Yes. (§ 13.52.010(a))	Yes. (§ 13.52.010(a))	Yes. (§ 13.52.010(b)) Yes. (§ 13.52.300)	Statutory form indicates that the signatures of two witnesses or, alternatively the signature of a notary is required. (§ 13.52.300)
Arizona	Yes. (§§ 36-3201(9), 36-3261, 36-3262)	No. "Any writing" may be used to create a living will. (§ 36-3262)	Yes. (§§ 36-3261, 36-3262)	There are no specific requirements. But see the more specific requirements for pre-hospital medical care directives, which are distinct from living wills. (§ 36-3251)	See prior column.	Not specified. Sample form of living will calls for declarant to place initials next to his/her preferred health care options. (§ 36-3262)

Arkansas	Yes. (§§ 20-17-202(a), 20-17-201(2))	Not specified. (Sample declarations provided.) (§ 20-17-202(b))	Yes. (§§ 20-17-201(2), 20-17-202(a))	Yes, or by someone at his or her direction. (§ 20-17-202(a))	Presence is not specified but it must be at the declarant's direction if the declarant himself is not signing it. (§ 20-17-202(a))	Not specified.
California	No, individual instructions may be oral or written. (Probate § 4670)	Not specified. (Sample directive provided.) (Probate § 4701, Pt. 2)	Yes. (Probate §§ 4673, 4670)	Yes, if written. (Probate § 4673(b))	(1) Yes. (Probate § 4673(b)) (2) Yes. (Probate § 4673(b))	Must be either acknowledged by notary or signed by witnesses. (Probate § 4673(c))
Colorado	Yes. (§ 15-18-103(5))	Not specified. (§ 15-18-104) (Sample declaration provided.) (§ 15-18-104(3))	Yes. (§ 15-18-103(5))	Yes. (§§ 15-18-104(3), 15-18-106(1))	(1) Yes. (§ 15-18-105(1)) (2) Yes. (§ 15-18-105(1))	If declarant physically unable to sign, person signing for declarant cannot be a physician, employee of the health care facility, an attending physician, person with a claim against declarant's estate, or any person who believes he is an heir or beneficiary. (§ 15-18-105(1))
Connecticut	Yes. (§§ 19a-570(8), 19a-575)	Not specified. (Sample of living will provided.) (§ 19a-575a)	Yes. (§ 19a-575)	Yes. (§ 19a-575)	Not specified.	Not specified.
Delaware	Yes. (16 § 2503(b)(1)(a))	Not specified. (Optional form of advance health-care directive provided.) (16 § 2505)	Yes. (16 § 2503(b)(1)(a))	Yes. (16 § 2503(b)(1)(b))	(1) Yes. (16 § 2503(b)(1)(b)) (2) Yes. (16 § 2503(b)(1)(b))	Not specified.

Table 7.02, Part 1
Formal Requirements *(continued)*

		What Formalities Satisfy the Requirements?				
	Must the Living Will Be in Writing?	*Just Like a Will?*	*Writing?*	*Signed by the Person?*	*Signed By Someone (1) In His Presence and (2) At His Direction?*	*Signed Otherwise? Specify.*
District of Columbia	Yes. (§ 7-622(a)(1))	Not specified. (Sample declaration provided.) (§ 7-622(c))	Yes. (§ 7-622(a)(1))	Yes. (§ 7-622(a)(2))	(1) Yes. (§ 7-622(a)(2)) (2) Yes. (§ 7-622(a)(2))	Not specified.
Florida	No. (§ 765.101(11)(b))	Not specified. (Sample form of living will provided.) (§ 765.303)	Yes, or a witnessed oral statement but nothing further is provided regarding the oral statement. (§ 765.101(11)(a) &(b))	Yes. (§ 765.302(1))	(1) Yes, but must be one of the witnesses if declarant physically unable. (§ 765.302(1)) (2) Yes, but must be one of the witnesses if declarant physically unable. (§ 765.302(1))	Not specified.
Georgia	Yes. (§§ 31-32-2(7), 31-32-3(b))	No. Any declaration expressing declarant's intent shall be honored, regardless of form. (§ 31-32-3(b))	Yes. (§§ 31-32-2(7), 31-32-3(b))	Yes. (§ 31-32-3(a))	Not specified.	If declarant is a patient in hospital or skilled nursing facility, must be signed in presence of two witnesses and in presence of (i) chief of staff or medical director, (ii) any physician not participating in care, or (iii) other staff person not participating in care. (§ 31-32-4)

Hawaii	No. Instruction may be oral or written. (§ 327E-3(a))	Not specified. (Sample directive provided.) (§ 327E-16)	Yes. (§§ 327E-3(a), 327E-16)	Yes (as indicated in the statutory form). (§ 327E-16)	Not specified.	Not specified.
	[Note: Hawaii formal requirements specifically relate only to execution of power of attorney for health care.]					
Idaho	Presumably, since living will is described as a "document" containing elements included in the statutory form. (§ 39-4510)	Substantially the same form as provided form. (§ 39-4510)	Yes. (§ 39-4510)	Yes (as indicated in the statutory form). (§ 39-4510)	Not specified. (§ 39-4510)	Not specified. (§ 39-4510)
Illinois	Yes. (755 ILCS § 35/2(b))	Not specified. (Sample declaration provided.) (755 ILCS § 35/3(e))	Yes. (755 ILCS §§ 35/2(b), 35/3(a))	Yes. (755 ILCS § 35/3(b))	(1) Not specified. (2) Yes. (755 ILCS § 35/3(b))	Not specified.
Indiana	Yes. (§ 16-36-4-8(b)(2))	Not specified. (Form of living will declaration provided.) (§ 16-36-4-10)	Yes. (§ 16-36-4-8(b)(2))	Yes. (§ 16-36-4-8(b)(3))	(1) Yes. (§ 16-36-4-8(b)(3)) (2) Yes. (§ 16-36-4-8(b)(3))	Not specified.
Iowa	Yes. (§§ 144A. 2(3), 144A.3)	Not specified. (Sample declaration provided.) (§ 144A.3(5))	Yes. (§§ 144A.2(3), 144A.3)	Yes. (§ 144A.3(2))	(1) Not specified. (§ 144A.3(2)) (2) Yes. (§ 144A.3(2))	Not specified. (§ 144A.3(2))
Kansas	Yes. (§ 65-28, 103 (a)(1))	Not specified. (Sample declaration provided.) (§ 65-28, 103(c))	Yes. (§ 65-28,103(a)(1))	Yes. (§ 65-28,103(a)(2))	(1) Yes. (§ 65-28, 103(2)) (2) Yes. (§ 65-28, 103(2))	Not specified. (§ 65-28,103(a))
Kentucky	Yes. (§ 311.625(2))	Not specified. (Sample form of living will directive provided.) (§ 311.625(1))	Yes. (§ 311.625(2))	Yes. (§ 311.625(2))	(1) Not specified. (2) Yes. (§ 311.625(2))	Statutory form indicates that the signatures of two witnesses or, alternatively the signature of a notary is required. (§ 311-625(1))

Table 7.02, Part 1
Formal Requirements *(continued)*

		What Formalities Satisfy the Requirements?				
	Must the Living Will Be in Writing?	*Just Like a Will?*	*Writing?*	*Signed by the Person?*	*Signed By Someone (1) In His Presence and (2) At His Direction?*	*Signed Otherwise? Specify.*
Louisiana	No. An oral or nonverbal declaration can be made in the presence of two witnesses any time subsequent to the diagnosis of a terminal and irreversible condition. (§ 40:1299.58.3(A)(3))	Not specified. (Sample declaration provided.) (§ 40:1299.58.3(c)(1))	Yes. (§ 40:1299.58.3(A)(1))	Yes. (§ 40:1299.58.3(A)(2))	Not specified.	If patient cannot communicate, any person previously designated in a written instrument signed by the patient in the presence of at least two witnesses has authority to make a declaration for patient. (§ 40:1299.58.5(2)(a))
Maine	No. The directive can be oral, but an oral directive is only valid if made to a health care provider or to a surrogate. (18-A § 5-802(A))	Not specified. (Sample directive provided.) (18-A § 5-804)	Yes. (18-A § 5-802(A))	Yes (as indicated in the statutory form). (18-A § 5-804)	Not specified.	Not specified.
Maryland	No, can be written or oral. (Health-Gen. § 5-602(a) & (d))	No. Different forms may be used. (Health-Gen. § 5-603)	Yes. (Health-Gen. § 5-602(a))	Yes (if directive is written). (Health-Gen. § 5-602(c))	(1) Not specified. (2) Yes. (Health-Gen. § 5-602(c))	Documentation of oral directive shall be dated and signed by attending physician and a witness. (Health-Gen. § 5-602(d)(2))
Massachusetts[1]	Yes. (201D § 2)	Not specified.	Yes. (201D § 2)	Yes. (201D § 2)	(1) Not specified. (2) Yes. (201D § 2)	Not specified.

Michigan	[Note: § 333.5654 requires the physician to inform the patient or surrogate or advocate that there are alternatives to recommended treatments in the event of advanced illness. These treatments include discontinuing care and palliative care. "Advanced illness" means "a medical or surgical condition with significant functional impairment that is not reversible by curative therapies and that is anticipated to progress toward death despite attempts at curative therapies or modulation, the time course of which may or may not be determinable through reasonable medical prognostication." (§ 333.5653(1)(a))]					
Minnesota	Yes. (§§ 145B.03, 145B.02)	Not specified. (Sample living will provided.) (§ 145B.04)	Yes. (§§ 145B.03, 145B.02)	Yes. (§ 145B.03 (Subd. 2)(a))	(1) Not specified. (2) Yes, a witness cansign at the declarant's direction. (§ 145B.03 (Subd. 2)(c))	Must be signed by declarant and two witnesses or a notary public. (§ 145B.03 (Subd. 2)(a)) If declarant is physically unable to sign, one of the witnesses shall sign. (§ 145B.03 (Subd. 2)(c))
Mississippi	No. May be oral or written. (§ 41-41-205(1))	No. Statutory form may be modified partially or in full. (§ 41-41-209)	Yes. (§ 41-41-205(1))	Yes, if statutory form used. (§ 41-41-209)	Not specified; seemingly not, since all references are to the individual. (§§ 41-41-205, 41-41-209)	Not specified.
Missouri	Yes. (§ 459.015(1)(1))	Not specified. (Sample declaration provided.) (§ 459.015(3))	Yes. (§ 459.015(1)(1))	Yes. (§ 459.015(1)(2))	(1) Yes. (§ 459.015(1)(2)) (2) Yes. (§ 459.015(1)(2))	If not wholly in declarant's handwriting, must be signed in presence of two or more witnesses. (§ 459.015(1)(4))
Montana	Yes. (§ 50-9-103(1))	Not specified. (Sample declaration provided.) (§ 50-9-103(2))	Yes. (§ 50-9-103(1))	Yes. (§ 50-9-103(1))	(1) Not specified. (2) Yes. (§ 50-9-103(1))	Not specified.
Nebraska	Yes. (§§ 20-403(3), 20-404(1))	Not specified. (Sample declaration provided.) (§ 20-404(2))	Yes. (§§ 20-403(3), 20-404(1))	Yes. (§ 20-404(1))	(1) Not specified. (2) Yes. (§ 20-404(1))	Not specified.
Nevada	Yes. (§ 449.600(1))	Not specified. (Sample declaration provided.) (§ 449.610)	Yes. (§ 449.600(1))	Yes. (§ 449.600(1))	(1) Not specified. (2) Yes. (§ 449.600(1))	Not specified.

Table 7.02, Part 1
Formal Requirements *(continued)*

		What Formalities Satisfy the Requirements?				
	Must the Living Will Be in Writing?	*Just Like a Will?*	*Writing?*	*Signed by the Person?*	*Signed By Someone (1) In His Presence and (2) At His Direction?*	*Signed Otherwise? Specify.*
New Hampshire	Yes. (§§ 137-J:2(XIV), 137-J:14(I)(a))	District requirements (§ 137-J:14(I)(a))	Yes. (§§ 137-J:14(I)(a))	Yes (as indicated in the statutory form). (§ 137-J:14(I)(a)	(1) Yes. (2) Yes. (§ 137-J:14(II))	Not specified.
New Jersey	Yes. (§ 26:2H-55)	Not specified.	Yes. (§ 26:2H-55)	Yes. (§ 26:2H-56)	(1) Not specified. (2) Yes. (§ 26:2H-56)	Must be signed by or at direction of declarant and either two witnesses or a notary, attorney, or other person authorized to administer oaths. (§ 26:2H-56)
New Mexico	No, it can be oral or written. If oral, directive must be made by personally informing a health care provider. (§ 24-7A-2(A))	No. Statutory form is optional and may be modified partially or in full. (§ 24-7A-4)	Yes. (§ 24-7A-2(A))	Yes (as indicated in statutory form). (§ 24-7A-4)	Not specified.	Not specified.
New York[2]	Yes. (Pub. Health § 2981(2))	Not specified. (Statutory form provided. See Pub. Health § 2981(5))	Yes. (Pub. Health § 2981(2))	Yes. (Pub. Health § 2981(2))	(1) Yes. (2) Yes. (Pub. Health § 2981(2))	Not specified.
North Carolina	Yes. (§ 90-321(c))	Not specified. (Sample declaration provided.) (§ 90-321(d))	Yes. (§ 90-321(c))	Yes. (§ 90-321(c)(3))	Not specified.	Must also be "proved" before court clerk or notary who certified substantially as in form set forth in § 90-321(d). See § 90-321(c)(4).

North Dakota	Yes. Health care directive. (§ 23-06.5-05(1)(a))	Not specified. (Sample declaration provided.) (§ 23-06.5-05(1))	Yes. (§ 23-06.5-05(1)(a))	Yes. (§ 23-06.5-05(1)(d))	(1) Not specified. (2) Yes. (§ 23-06.5-05(1)(d))	Two witnesses at least 18 years old or a notary required to sign. (§ 23-06.5-05(2))
Ohio	Yes. (§§ 2133.02(A)(1), 2133.01(F))	Not specified.	Yes. (§§ 2133.02(A)(1), 2133.01(F))	Yes. (§ 2133.02(A)(1))	(1) Not specified. (2) Yes. (§ 2133.02(A)(1))	Statute requires that declaration be signed "at the end." (§ 2133.02(A)(1))
Oklahoma	Yes. (63 §§ 3101.3(1), 3101.4(B))	Not specified. (Sample directive provided.) (63 § 3101.4(B))	Yes. (63 § 3101.4(B))	Yes. (63 § 3101.4(A))	Not specified.	Witnessed by two individuals. (63 § 3101.4(A))
Oregon	Yes. (§ 127.531)	No. Must be in statutory form. (§ 127.531(1))	Yes. (§ 127.531)	Yes. (§ 127.515(4))	Not specified.	Not specified.
Pennsylvania	Yes. (20 §§ 5404(b), 5403)	Not specified. (Sample declaration provided.) (20 § 5404(b))	Yes. (20 §§ 5404(b), 5403)	Yes. (20 § 5404(a))	(1) Not specified. (2) Yes. (20 § 5404(a))	Not specified.
Rhode Island	Yes. (§§ 23-4.11-2(4), 23-4.11-3(a))	Not specified. (Sample declaration provided.) (§ 23-4.11-3(d))	Yes. (§§ 23-4.11-2(4), 23-4.11-3(a))	Yes. (§ 23-4.11-3(a))	(1) Not specified. (2) Yes. (§ 23-4.11-3(a))	Not specified.
South Carolina	Yes. (§ 44-77-50)	Not specified. (Sample declaration provided.) (§ 44-77-50)	Yes. (§ 44-77-50)	Yes. (§ 44-77-40(2))	Not specified.	Must be signed in the presence of an officer authorized to administer oaths under the laws of the state where the signing occurs and in the presence of two witnesses. (§ 44-77-40(2))
South Dakota	Yes. (§§ 34-12D-2, 34-12D-1(2))	Not specified. (Sample living will provided.) (§ 34-12D-3)	Yes. (§§ 34-12D-1(2), 34-12D-2)	Yes. (§ 34-12D-2)	(1) Not specified. (2) Yes. (§ 34-12D-2)	Not specified.

Table 7.02, Part 1
Formal Requirements *(continued)*

	Must the Living Will Be in Writing?	*What Formalities Satisfy the Requirements?* *Just Like a Will?*	*Writing?*	*Signed by the Person?*	*Signed By Someone (1) In His Presence and (2) At His Direction?*	*Signed Otherwise? Specify.*
Tennessee	Yes. (§§ 32-11-103(4), 32-11-105)	Not specified. (Sample living will provided.) (§ 32-11-105)	Yes. (§§ 32-11-103(4), 32-11-105)	Yes (can also be "a mark" by a declarant unable to fully sign). (§§ 32-11-104(a), 32-11-110(f), 1-3-105)	Not specified.	Not specified.
Texas	No, in addition to a written directive, the statute also allows a nonwritten directive to be made. (Health & Safety §§ 166.032(a), 166.034(a))	Not specified. (Sample written directive provided.) (§ 166.033)	Yes. (§ 166.032(a))	Yes (for written directives). (Health & Safety § 166.032(b))	Not specified.	The statute also allows for a nonwritten directive which must be issued in the presence of the attending physician and two witnesses. (Health & Safety § 166.034)
Utah (2007)	Yes. (§ 75-2-1104(2)(a))	Not specified. (Sample directive provided.) (§ 75-2-1104(4))	Yes. (§ 75-2-1104(2)(a))	Yes. (§ 75-2-1104(2)(b))	(1) Yes. (§ 75-2-1104 (2)(b)) (2) Yes. (§ 75-2-1104(2)(b))	Not specified.
Utah (2008) The new law is effective Jan. 1, 2008. A health care directive executed prior to this date under the provisions then in effect, Ch. 2, pt. II, Personal Choice and Living Will, may, in good faith, be relied upon by a health	A health care directive may be oral or in writing. (§ 75-2a-1106(1)(b))	Not specified. (§ 75-2a-1106(1)(b))	No. (§ 75-2a-1106(1)(b))	Not specified. (§ 75-2a-1106(1)(b))	Not specified. (§ 75-2a-1106(1)(b))	Regardless if oral or in writing, there must be one witness. (§ 75-2a-1106(1)(c))

care provider or health care facility. (§ 75-2a-1120(1)(b))						
Vermont	Yes. (18 § 9703(b)).	Not specified.	Yes. (18 § 9703)	Yes (18 § 9703(b))	(1) Yes. (18 § 9703(b)) (2) Yes. (18 § 9703(b))	Two or more witnesses. (18 § 9703(b)).
Virginia	No, it can be written or oral. (§ 54.1-2983)	Not specified. (Sample directive provided.) (§ 54.1-2984)	Yes. (§ 54.1-2983)	Yes (if directive is written). (§ 54.1-2983)	Not specified. (§ 54.1-2983)	If oral, it must be in front of the attending doctor and two witnesses. (§ 54.1-2983)
Washington	Yes. (§§ 70.122.020(3), 70.122.030(1))	Not specified. (Sample directive provided.) (§ 70.122.030(1))	Yes. (§ 70.122.030(1))	Yes. (§ 70.122.030(1))	Not specified.	Not specified.
West Virginia	Yes. (§ 16-30-4(a)(1))	Not specified. (Sample living will provided.) (§ 16-30-4(g))	Yes. (§ 16-30-4(a)(1))	Yes. (§ 16-30-4(a)(4))	(1) Yes. (§ 16-30-4(a)(2)) (2) Yes. (§ 16-30-4(a)(2))	Not specified.
Wisconsin	Yes. (§§ 154.02(1), 154.03(1))	Not specified. (Sample declaration provided.) (§ 154.03(2))	Yes. (§§ 154.02(1), 154.03(1))	Yes. (§ 154.03(1))	(1) Yes. (§ 154.03(1)) (2) Yes. (§ 154.03(1))	Declarant and witnesses must sign at the same time (as indicated in the statutory form). (§ 154.03(2))
Wyoming	An individual instruction may be oral or written (§ 35-22-403 (a)) A power of attorney for health care must be written. (§ 35-22-403(b))	Not specified. (§ 35-22-403) (Optional form provided.) (§ 35-22-405)	A power of attorney for health care must be in writing (§ 35-22-403 (b)), but a writing is not required for an individual instruction by an adult or emancipated minor regarding a health care decision for the individual. (§ 35-22-402(a)(xi) (§ 35-22-403(a))	Yes, a power of attorney for health care must be signed by the principal. (§ 35-22-403(b))	(1) Yes. (§ 35-22-403(b)) (2) Yes. (§ 35-22-403(b))	Not specified.

1. Only deals with health care proxies.
2. Only deals with Order Not to Resuscitate.

Table 7.02, Part 2
Formal Requirements

What Formalities Satisfy the Requirements?

	Dated?	*Number of Witnesses?*	*Age of Witnesses?*	*Other Witness Requirements? E.g., Is a Witness Statement Required?*
Alabama	Yes. (§ 22-8A-4(c)(3))	At least two witnesses. (§ 22-8A-4(c)(4))	At least 19 years old. (§ 22-8A-4(c)(4))	Witnesses must attest (as indicated in the statement in the statutory form) to statement on the statutory form. (§ 22-8A-4(h))
Alaska	Yes (as indicated in the optional statutory form). (§ 13.52.300)	Two qualified adult witnesses or a notary required. (Optional form, §§ 13.52.300(15)(A) & 13.52.010(b)(1))	Adult. (optional form § 13.52.300)	Not specified. (§ 13.52.300)
Arizona[1]	Yes. (§ 36-3251(B))	One witness and a licensed health care provider must sign the pre-hospital medical care directive. (§ 32-3251(B))	Not specified.	Statement on form of pre-hospital medical care directive indicates witness was present at signing and that declarant was of sound mind and free from duress. (§ 36-3251(B))
Arkansas	Yes (as indicated in the statutory form). (§ 20-17-202(b))	Two. (§ 20-17-202(a))	Not specified.	Statement that declarant voluntarily signed in the witness' presence (as indicated in the statutory form). (§ 20-17-202(b))
California	Yes. (Probate § 4673(a))	Two, if not acknowledged before notary. (Probate § 4673(c))	Adult. (Probate § 4674(a))	Witnesses declaration required. (Probate § 4674(d)) If declarant is a patient in a skilled nursing facility, a patient advocate or ombudsman must sign as a witness (Probate § 4675(a)) must sign as a witness. (Probate § 4675(a))
Colorado	Yes (as indicated in the statutory form). (§ 15-18-104(3))	Two. (§ 15-18-106(1))	Not specified. (§ 15-18-106)	Witnesses attest to statement on the statutory form (as indicated in the statutory form). (§ 15-18-104(3))

Connecticut	Yes. (§ 19a-575)	Two. (§ 19a-575)	Not specified.	Declarant must sign in presence of witnesses. They must declare that declarant appeared to be of age, sound mind, able to understand the consequences, and under no improper influence (as indicated in the statutory form). (§ 19a-575)
Delaware	Yes. (16 § 2503(b)(1)(c))	Two. (16 § 2503(b)(1)(d))	Witnesses must be adults. (16 § 2503(b)(1)(d))	Witness statement is required. (16 § 2503(b)(2))
District of Columbia	Yes. (§ 7-622(a)(3))	Two. (§ 7-622(4))	Witnesses must be 18 years of age. (§ 7-622(4))	Witness statement included on statutory form. (§ 7-622(c))
Florida	Yes (as indicated in the statutory form). (§ 765.303(1))	Two. (§ 765.302(1))	Not specified.	At least one witness cannot be a spouse or blood relative of declarant. (§ 765.302(1))
Georgia	Yes (as indicated in the statutory form). (§ 31-32-3(b))	Two. (§ 31-32-3(a))	18 or older. (§§ 31-32-3(a), 31-32-2(3))	Witnesses must be competent, meaning of sound mind. (§§ 31-32-3(a), 31-32-2(3)) If the living will is executed by a patient ina hospital or skilled nursing facility, a qualified health care worker must also witness the signing. (§ 31-32-4) Witness statement required, as indicated on statutory form. (§ 31-32-3(b))
Hawaii	Yes. (as indicated in the statutory form). (§ 327E-16)	Must be signed in the presence of two witnesses or acknowledged before notary (as indicated in the statutory form). (§ 327E-3(b)(1))	Witnesses must be adults (as indicated in the statutory form). (§ 327E-16)	Witness statement required (as indicated in the statutory form). (§ 327E-16)
Idaho	Yes (as indicated in the statutory form). (§ 39-4510)	Not specified. (§ 39-4510)	Not specified. (§ 39-4510)	Not specified. (§ 39-4510)
Illinois	Yes (as indicated in the statutory form). (755 ILCS § 35/3(e))	Two. (755 ILCS § 35/3(b))	18 or older. (755 ILCS § 35/3(b))	Witness statement required (as indicated in statutory form). (755 ILCS § 35/3(e))

Table 7.02, Part 2
Formal Requirements *(continued)*

	What Formalities Satisfy the Requirements?			
	Dated?	*Number of Witnesses?*	*Age of Witnesses?*	*Other Witness Requirements? E.g., Is a Witness Statement Required?*
Indiana	Yes. (§ 16-36-4-8(b)(4))	Two. (§ 16-36-4-8(b)(5))	18 or older. (§ 16-36-4-8(b)(5))	Witness statement required in the statutory form. (§ 16-36-4-10)
Iowa	Yes. (§ 144A.3(2))	Two (if not acknowledged before notary). (§ 144A.3(2))	At least 18 years old. (§ 144A.3(2)(a)(3))	Not specified. (§ 144A.3(2))
Kansas	Yes. (§ 65-28,103(a)(3))	Two (if not acknowledged before notary). (§ 65-28,103(4))	At least 18 years old. (§ 65-28,103(a)(4)(A))	Witness statement required (as indicated in statutory form). (§ 65-28,103(c))
Kentucky	Yes. (§ 311.625(2))	The directive must be signed before two witnesses or acknowledged before a notary public. (§ 311.625(2))	The witnesses must be 18 or over. (§§ 311.625(2), 311.621(1))	Witness cannot be: (a) a blood relative of the grantor; (b) a beneficiary of the grantor via descent or distribution; (c) an employee of the healthcare facility where the grantor is a patient; (d) an attending physician of the grantor; or (e) any person directly financially responsible for the grantor's health care. (§ 311.625(2)(a)–(e))
Louisiana	Yes (as indicated on the statutory form). (§ 40:1299.58.3(C)(1))	Two. (§ 40:1299.58.3(A)(2))	Adult. (§ 40:1299.58.2(16))	"Witness" defined as competent adult not related to declarant by blood or marriage and not entitled to any portion of declarant's estate. (§ 40:1299.58.2(16))
Maine[2]	Yes (as indicated in the statutory form). (18-A § 5-804)	Two witnesses required. (18-A § 5-802(b), also see statutory form explanation part in 18-A § 5-804) However, according to Uniform Health Care Decisions Act Comment, "the Act does not require witnessing, but to encourage the practice the form provides space	Not specified.	Not specified.

		for signatures of two witnesses." (18-A § 5-804)		
Maryland	Yes (if directive is written). (Health-Gen. § 5-602(c))	Two witnesses (if directive is written). (Health-Gen. § 5-602(c))	18 years of age. (Health-Gen. §§ 5-602(c)(2), 5-601(f))	Witnesses cannot include health care agent and at least one witness cannot be entitled to any portion of declarant's estate or entitled to any benefit by declarant's death. (Health-Gen. § 5-602(c)(2))
Massachusetts[3]	Not specified.	Two. (201D § 2)	Adult. (201D § 2)	Witnesses must sign that they believe the declarant to be 18, of sound mind, and not under constraint or undue influence. (201D § 2)
Michigan	[Note: No formal requirements. Patient, surrogate, or advocate simply responds to physician's information about alternative treatments, which include discontinuing care and solely palliative care. The physician must have informed the patient orally and in writing. (§ 333.5655)]			
Minnesota	Yes (as indicated in the statutory form). (§ 145B.04)	Two witnesses (or a notary public). (§ 145B.03(Subd. 2)(a))	Adult (as indicated in the statutory form). (§ 145B.04)	Witness statement required. (§ 145B.03(Subd.2)(d))
Mississippi	Yes (as indicated in the statutory form (12)). (§ 41-41-209)	At least two witnesses (as indicated in the statutory form (13)). (§ 41-41-209)	Adult (as indicated in the statutory form (13)). (§ 41-41-209)	Witnesses must declare under penalties of perjury (as indicated in the statement in the statutory form (13)) to statement on the statutory form. (§ 41-41-209)
Missouri	Yes. (§ 459.015(1)(3))	At least two (only if the declaration is not wholly in the declarant's handwriting). (§ 459.015(1)(4))	At least 18 years old. (§ 459.015(1)(4))	Witnesses cannot be person who signed declaration on declarant's behalf. (§ 459.015(1)(4)) Must also sign statement (as indicated in statutory form). (§ 459.015(3))
Montana	Yes (as indicated in the statutory form). (§ 50-9-103(2))	A declaration must be signed before two witnesses. (§ 50-9-103(1))	Not specified.	Not specified.
Nebraska	Yes (as indicated in the statutory form). (§ 20-404(2))	Two or a notary. (§ 20-404(1))	Adult for witness and not specified for notary. (§ 20-404(1)) Adult defined as: 19 or older or a person who is/has been married. (§ 20-403(1))	No witness can be an employee of the declarant's life/health insurance provider; no more than one witness can work for the declarant's health care provider. These restrictions do not apply to the notary. (§ 20-404(1))

Table 7.02, Part 2
Formal Requirements *(continued)*

	What Formalities Satisfy the Requirements?			
	Dated?	*Number of Witnesses?*	*Age of Witnesses?*	*Other Witness Requirements? E.g., Is a Witness Statement Required?*
Nevada	Yes (as indicated in the statutory form). (§ 449.610)	Two witnesses must attest the declaration. (§ 449.600(1))	Not specified.	Not specified.
New Hampshire	Not specified. (§ 137-J:14(I)) However, the advance directive must be "in substantially" the form specified, which includes a date. (§ 137-J:20)	At least two witnesses. (§ 137-J:14(I)(a))	Not specified.	Witnesses cannot be declarant's spouse, heir, attending physician, ARNP, person under control of attending physician or ARNP, or any person employed by any part of principal's estate, trust, or deed. No more than one witness may be the principal's health or residential care provider or such provider's employee. Instead of witnesses, a notary or justice of the peace shall acknowledge the witness's signature. (§ 137-J:14(I)(b))
New Jersey	Yes. (§ 26:2H-56)	Two or acknowledged by declarant before a notary, attorney, or another who can administer oaths. (§ 26:2H-56)	Adult, defined as 18 or older. (§§ 26:2H-55, 26:2H-56)	Must attest the declarant to be of sound mind and free of duress/undue influence. A designated health care representative cannot be a witness. (§ 26:2H-56)
New Mexico	Yes (as indicated in the statutory form). (§ 24-7A-4)	Two witnesses (implied by the statutory form). (§ 24-7A-4)	Not specified.	Not specified.
New York	Yes. (Pub. Health § 2981(2))	Two. (Pub. Health § 2981(2))	Adult (18 years and older), or is the parent of a child or has married. (Pub. Health §§ 2981(2), 2980(1))	Witness cannot be the person appointed as agent; witness statement is required. (Pub. Health § 2981(2))
North Carolina	Yes. (§ 90-321(c))	Two. (§ 90-321(c)(3))	Not specified.	Witness statement required. (§ 90-321(c)(3))
North Dakota	Yes (as indicated in the statutory form). (§ 23-06.5-17)		Adult (At least 18 years old). (§ 23-06.5-17)	At least one witness must not be a health care provider, providing

		A directive must be notarized or signed before two witnesses. (§ 23-06.5-17)		direct care to the declarant or an employee of such health care provider on the date of execution. No witness may be a spouse or related to the declarant by blood, marriage, or adoption; entitled to inherit any part of the estate of the declarant upon his or her death; a claimant against the estate of the declarant at the time of execution of the declaration. (§ 23-06.5-17)
Ohio	Yes. (§ 2133.02(A) & (1))	Two, or acknowledged before a notary public. (§§ 2133.02(B)(1) & (2))	Adults defined as 18 or older. (§§ 2133.02(B)(1), 2133.01(A))	Witnesses cannot be related to declarant by blood, marriage, or adoption, cannot be an attending physician, and cannot be administrator of nursing home providing care to declarant. (§ 2133.02(B)) Witness or notary must sign, after declarant's signature, that they believe the declarant to be of sound mind and not under duress, fraud, or undue influence. (§ 2133.02(B))
Oklahoma	Not specified (as indicated in the statutory form). (63 § 3101.4(B))	Two witnesses. (63 § 3101.4(A))	At least 18 years old. (63 § 3101.4(A))	No statement required, but witnesses cannot be legatees, devisees, or heirs of declarant. (63 § 3101.4(A))
Oregon	Yes. (§ 127.515(4))	Two. (§ 127.515(4))	Adult, defined as an individual 18 or older, who has been adjudicated as an emancipated minor, or who is married. (§§ 127.515(4), 127.505(1))	Witness statement is required. (§ 127.515(4)(b)) In addition, one witness shall be a person who is not: related by blood, marriage, or adoption to declarant; entitled to any portion of declarant's estate; or an owner or employee of facility where declarant is a patient. (§ 127.515(4)(c)) Attorney-in-fact for health care or attending physician may not be a witness. (§ 127.515(4)(d)) If declarant is patient at long-term facility, one

(cont'd)

Table 7.02, Part 2
Formal Requirements *(continued)*

	What Formalities Satisfy the Requirements?			
	Dated?	*Number of Witnesses?*	*Age of Witnesses?*	*Other Witness Requirements? E.g., Is a Witness Statement Required?*
Oregon *(cont'd)*				witness must be designated by facility and have qualifications specified by DHS. (§ 127.515(4)(e))
Pennsylvania	Yes (as indicated in the statutory form). (20 § 5404(b))	Two. (20 § 5404(a))	18 or older. (20 § 5404(a))	Must sign that the declarant knowingly/voluntarily signed in the presence of the witness (as indicated in the statutory form). (20 § 5404(b))
Rhode Island	Yes (as indicated in the statutory form). (§ 23-4.11-3(d))	Two. (§ 23-4.11-3(a))	Not specified.	Witness must sign that they know the declarant and the declarant signed the declaration voluntarily in their presence (as indicated in the statutory form). (§ 23-4.11-3(d))
South Carolina	Yes. (§ 44-77-40(2))	Two witnesses (one of whom may be the required officer authorized to administer oaths). (§ 44-77-40(2))	Not specified.	Witnesses must subscribe to affidavit, which must be sworn to by at least one witness. (§ 44-77-40(2) & (4)) If declarant is patient in hospital or resident of nursing home, one of the two witnesses must be an ombudsman, with the same qualities required of witnesses. (§ 44-77-40(3))
South Dakota	Yes (as indicated in the statutory form). (§ 34-12D-3)	Two. (§ 34-12D-2)	Adult. (§ 34-12D-2)	Witnesses sign under statement that declarant voluntarily signed in their presence (as indicated in the statutory form). (§ 34-12D-3)
Tennessee	Yes (as indicated in the statutory form). (§ 32-11-105)	Two witnesses. (§ 32-11-104(a))	Not specified.	Witness statement required. (§§ 32-11-104(a), 32-11-105)

Texas	Yes (for written directives) (as indicated in the statutory form). (Health & Safety § 166.033)	Two witnesses (for written directives). (Health & Safety § 166.032(b))	Adult. (Health & Safety §§ 166.032(b), 166.003(1))	At least one witness may not: be a person designated to make treatment decisions for the patient; be related to patient by blood or marriage; be entitled to or have a claim against any part of patient's estate; be the attending physician or his/her employee; be involved in direct patient care to the patient; or be an officer, director, or other senior employee of patient's health care facility or any parent organization. (Health & Safety §§ 166.032(b), 166.003(2), 166.033)
Utah (2007)	Yes. (§ 75-2-1104(2)(c))	At least two witnesses. (§ 75-2-1104(2)(d))	At least 18 years old. (§ 75-2-1104(2)(d))	Witness statement required (as indicated in the statutory form). (§ 75-2-1104(4))
Utah (2008) The new law is effective Jan. 1, 2008. A health care directive executed prior to this date under the provisions then in effect, Ch. 2, pt. II, Personal Choice and Living Will, may, in good faith, be relied upon by a health care provider or health care facility. (§ 75-2a-1120(1)(b))	Not specified.	One in the case of an oral declaration. (§ 75-2a-1103(11)(b)(ii))	Not specified.	No.

Table 7.02, Part 2
Formal Requirements *(continued)*

	What Formalities Satisfy the Requirements?			
	Dated?	*Number of Witnesses?*	*Age of Witnesses?*	*Other Witness Requirements? E.g., Is a Witness Statement Required?*
Vermont	Yes (as indicated in the included statutory form). (18 § 9703(b))	Two or more witnesses. (18 § 9703(b))	At least 18 years old. (18 § 9703(b))	Witness statement required. (18 § 9703(b))
Virginia	Yes (as indicated in the statutory form if written directive). (§ 54.1-2984)	Two witnesses. (§ 54.1-2983)	Not specified. (§ 54.1-2983)	Witness statement required (as indicated in statutory form). (§ 54.1-2984)
Washington	Yes (as indicated in the statutory form). (§ 70.122.030(1))	Two witnesses. (§ 70.122.030(1))	Not specified. (§ 70.122.030(1))	Witnesses must attest (as indicated in the statement in the statutory form) that the declarant is known to them and is capable of making health care decisions. (§ 70.122.030(1))
West Virginia	Yes. (§ 16-30-4(a)(3))	At least two witnesses. (§ 16-30-4(a)(4))	At least 18 years old. (§ 16-30-4(a)(4))	Witnesses must attest (as indicated in the statement in the statutory form) to statements on the statutory form. (§ 16-30-4(a)(5))
Wisconsin	Yes (as indicated in the statutory form). (§ 154.03(2))	Two. (§ 154.03(1))	Adult (as indicated in the statutory form). (§ 154.03(2))	Witness statement required (as indicated in the statutory form). (§ 154.03(2))
Wyoming	Not specified.	If a power of attorney for health care, notary or at least two witnesses. (§ 35-22-403(b))	Not specified.	No.

1. The information presented relates to pre-hospital medical care directives (applicable in the event of cardiac or respiratory arrest), and not the "living will" dealt with in §§ 36-3261 and 36-3262.
2. The information presented relates to pre-hospital medical care directives (applicable in the event of cardiac or respiratory arrest), and not the "living will" dealt with in §§ 36-3261 and 36-3262.
3. Only deals with health care proxies.

Table 7.02, Part 3
Formal Requirements

	What Formalities Satisfy the Requirements?						
	What are Impermissible Conflicts of Witnesses Specified in the Statute?	*Must Witnesses Affirm or Just Declare/Sign on the Basis of Knowledge and Belief?*	*Must Witnesses Sign the Document?*	*Must Attorney or Drafter Sign?*	*Capacity of Declarant: What Standard Is Used? E.g., Sound Mind, Sane?*	*Capacity of Declarant: Age Requirement?*	*Capacity of Declarant: Signed Before Notary?*
Alabama	Witnesses cannot be related to the declarant, entitled to any part of his/her estate, financially responsible for the declarant, the person who signed the advance directive, or appointed as the health care proxy therein. (§ 22-8A-4(c)(4))	Sign on knowledge/belief (as indicated in the statutory form). (§ 22-8A-4(h))	Not specified. However, sample form requires witness signatures. (§ 22-8A-4(c)(4) & (h))	Not specified.	Competent adult. (§§ 22-8A-4(a), 22-8A-3(5) [competent adult defined as alert, capable of under standing lay descriptions of medical procedures, and able to appreciate consequences of providing or withdrawing procedures])	At least 19 years old. (§§ 22-8A-4(a), 22-8A-3(1))	Not specified. (§ 22-8A-4)
Alaska	The witness must not be a health care provider at the health care institution or health care facility where the principal is receiving health care; an employee there, the agent, and at least one witness should not be related to the principal by blood, marriage, or adoption, and should not *(cont'd)*	No. The witnesses must sign and must personally know the principal. (§ 13.52.010(b)(1))	Yes. (§ 13.52.010(b))	Not specified.	Not specified, but rebuttably presumed to have capacity to make health care decision. (§ 13.52.100)	Adult, aged 18, subject to certain exceptions. (§ 13.52.010(a))	Not specified.

Table 7.02, Part 3
Formal Requirements *(continued)*

	What Formalities Satisfy the Requirements?						
	What are Impermissible Conflicts of Witnesses Specified in the Statute?	*Must Witnesses Affirm or Just Declare/Sign on the Basis of Knowledge and Belief?*	*Must Witnesses Sign the Document?*	*Must Attorney or Drafter Sign?*	*Capacity of Declarant: What Standard Is Used? E.g., Sound Mind, Sane?*	*Capacity of Declarant: Age Requirement?*	*Capacity of Declarant: Signed Before Notary?*
Alaska *(cont'd)*	be entitled to a portion of the estate of the principal upon the principal's death under a will or codicil of the principal existing at the time of execution of the durable power of attorney for health care or by operation of law then existing. (§ 13.52.010(d) & (e))						
Arizona	Not specified. Required form has witness's declaration stating declarant of sound mind, but no mention of conflicts. (§ 36-3251(B))	For pre-hospital medical care directive, sign only. (§ 36-3251(B)) For living will, not specified.	For pre-hospital medical care directive, statutory form requires signatures of witness and licensed health care provider. (§ 36-3251(B)) For living will, not specified.	Not specified.	The form requires a statement by the witness that "The patient then appeared to be of sound mind and free from duress." (§ 36-3251(B))	Not specified.	Not specified.
Arkansas	Not specified. Option form: witness signature, but attest to signing being voluntary.	Attest it was voluntarily signed by declarant in the witness's presence (as indicated in the	Yes (as indicated in the statutory form). (§ 20-17-202(b))	Not specified.	Sound mind. (§ 20-17-202(a))	18 or older. (§ 20-17-202(a))	Not specified.

		statutory form). (§ 20-17-202(b))					
California	Witnesses cannot be health care provider or employee of provider; operator or employee of community care facility; or operator or employee of residential care facility for elderly. At least one witness cannot be related to declarant by blood, marriage, or adoption, or entitled to any part of declarant's estate. (Probate § 4674(c)-(f)) Witness requirements do not apply to notary. (Probate § 4674(g)) Witnesses must declare that declarant is known to them, signed in their presence, and was of sound mind and free from duress or influence. (Probate § 4674(d))	Witnesses affirmatively state, under penalty of perjury. (Probate § 4701 in optional form)	Yes, if not acknowledged by notary. (Probate § 4673(c))	Not specified.	Capacity, meaning ability to understand nature, consequences, risks, benefits, and alternatives of health care decisions. (Probate §§ 4670, 4609)	Adult. (Probate § 4670)	Yes, if not signed by witnesses. (Probate § 4673(c))
Colorado	Witnesses cannot include any physician, an employee of the physician or the health care facility, a person that knows or believes he is entitled to part of or has a claim against the declarant's estate (including heirs) or any other patient in the *(cont'd)*	Sign and declare on knowledge/belief (as indicated in the statutory form). (§ 15-18-104(3))	Yes (as indicated in the statutory form). (§ 15-18-104(3))	Not specified. (§ 15-18-104)	Competent. (§ 15-18-104(1))	At least 18 years old. (§§ 15-18-104 (1), 15-18-103 (1) definition of adult)	Yes (as indicated in the statutory form). (§ 15-18-104(3))

Table 7.02, Part 3
Formal Requirements *(continued)*

	What Formalities Satisfy the Requirements?						
	What are Impermissible Conflicts of Witnesses Specified in the Statute?	*Must Witnesses Affirm or Just Declare/Sign on the Basis of Knowledge and Belief?*	*Must Witnesses Sign the Document?*	*Must Attorney or Drafter Sign?*	*Capacity of Declarant: What Standard Is Used? E.g., Sound Mind, Sane?*	*Capacity of Declarant: Age Requirement?*	*Capacity of Declarant: Signed Before Notary?*
Colorado *(cont'd)*	same health care facility. (§§ 15-18-106(1), 15-18-106(2))						
Connecticut	Not specified.	Sign in declarant's presence on basis of appearance of declarant (as indicated in the statutory form). (§ 19a-575) Witnesses may also swear to an affidavit before a duly authorized officer. The affidavit shall be written on the living will, or attached thereto. (§ 19a-578(a))	Yes (as indicated in the statutory form). (§ 19a-575)	Not specified.	Sound mind and after careful reflection (as indicated in the statutory form). (§ 19a-575)	18 or older. (§ 19a-575)	Not specified.
Delaware	Witness must satisfy the following, although there is no provision that it be in writing. The witness (a) is not related to the declarant; (b) is not entitled to any portion of	Not specified.	Not specified.	Not specified.	Mentally competent. (16 § 2503(a))	Adult. (16 § 2503(a))	Not specified.

	the estate of the declarant under any will or trust; (c) does not have a claim against the declarant's estate; (d) does not have direct financial responsibility for the declarant's medical care; and (e) does not have a controlling interest in or is an operator of or an employee of a health care institution at which the declarant is a patient. (16 § 2503(b) (1)(d) (1)–(5)) An optional form lists these above the line for the witnesses' signatures as well as a statement that the declarant is mentally competent and that the witnesses are not under age 18. (16 § 2505)						
District of Columbia	Witnesses cannot be: (a) the person who signed the declaration on behalf of and at the direction of the declarant; (b) related to the declarant by blood or marriage; (c) entitled to any portion of the estate of the declarant; (d) directly financially responsible for the declarant's medical *(cont'd)*	Sign on basis of belief that declarant is of sound mind. Witnesses must also declare they are of age and that there are no impermissible conflicts (as indicated in the statutory form). (§ 7-622(c))	Yes (as indicated in the statutory form). (§ 7-622(c))	Not specified.	Declarant must be of sound mind (as indicated in the statutory form). (§ 7-622(c))	18 years of age or older. (§ 7-622(a))	Not specified.

Table 7.02, Part 3
Formal Requirements *(continued)*

	What Formalities Satisfy the Requirements?						
	What are Impermissible Conflicts of Witnesses Specified in the Statute?	*Must Witnesses Affirm or Just Declare/Sign on the Basis of Knowledge and Belief?*	*Must Witnesses Sign the Document?*	*Must Attorney or Drafter Sign?*	*Capacity of Declarant: What Standard Is Used? E.g., Sound Mind, Sane?*	*Capacity of Declarant: Age Requirement?*	*Capacity of Declarant: Signed Before Notary?*
District of Columbia *(cont'd)*	care; or (e) an attending physician, employees of the attending physician, or employees of a health care facility where the declarant is a patient. (§ 7-622(a)(4)(A)–(E))						
Florida	No statement required, but at least one witness cannot be a spouse or blood relative of declarant. (§ 765.302(1))	Not specified, but implied that witness must simply sign (as indicated in the statutory form). (§ 765.303(1))	Yes (as indicated in the statutory form). (§ 765.303(1))	Not specified.	Competent. (§ 765.302(1))	Adult. (§ 765.302(1))	Not specified.
Georgia	A witness cannot be an attending physician, attending physician's employee, an employee of the declarant's health care facility, related by blood or marriage to the declarant, entitled to or have a claim against the declarant's estate, or financially responsible for the declarant's medical care.	Witnesses must be free of listed conflicts "to the best of their knowledge." (§ 31-32-3(a)) They must attest to the same on the statutory form. (§ 31-32-3(b))	Yes (as indicated in the statutory form). (§ 31-32-3(b)) When living will is signed in hospital or skilled nursing facility, it must also be signed by additional witness who is the chief/director, a physician not participating in care, or employee	Not specified.	Competent, meaning of sound mind. (§§ 31-32-3(a), 31-32-2(3)) Sound mind and competency. (§§ 31-32-3(a), 31-32-3(b))	18 or older. (§§ 31-32-3(a), 31-32-2(3))	Not specified.

	(§ 31-32-3(a)) However, there is no requirement that this be in the form.		not participating in care (as indicated in the statutory form). (§ 31-32-3(b))				
Hawaii	Although not required in writing, witnesses cannot berelated to the declarant; or entitled to any part of declarant's estate; an attending physician; employees of the attending physician, or employees of a health care facility where the declarant is a patient; or person appointed as agent (as indicated in statutory form). One of the witnesses *can* be related or entitled to a portion of the estate. (§ 327E-3(d)) There is a statement in the sample form, but the form is optional. (§§ 327E-16; 327E-3(c) & (d))	Witnesses affirmatively declare under penalty of false swearing (as indicated in the statutory form). (§ 327E-16)	Yes (as indicated in the statutory form). (§ 327E-16)	Not specified.	Sound mind (as indicated in the statutory form). (§ 327E-16)	Adult or emancipated minor. (§ 327E-3)	Yes, if not signed before witnesses (as indicated in the statutory form). (§ 327E-16)
Idaho	Not specified by the living will form. (§ 39-4510)	Not specified. (§ 39-4510)	Not specified. (§ 39-4510)	Not specified. (§ 39-4510)	"Competent person," that is, any emancipated minor or person eighteen or more years who is of sound mind. (§ 39-4508(4))	At least 18 years old or emancipated minor. (§ 39-4508(4))	Not specified.

Table 7.02, Part 3
Formal Requirements *(continued)*

What Formalities Satisfy the Requirements?

	What are Impermissible Conflicts of Witnesses Specified in the Statute?	*Must Witnesses Affirm or Just Declare/Sign on the Basis of Knowledge and Belief?*	*Must Witnesses Sign the Document?*	*Must Attorney or Drafter Sign?*	*Capacity of Declarant: What Standard Is Used? E.g., Sound Mind, Sane?*	*Capacity of Declarant: Age Requirement?*	*Capacity of Declarant: Signed Before Notary?*
Illinois	Witnesses must say they personally know declarant, believe him/her to be of sound mind, saw declarant sign, witness signed in the declarant's presence, did not sign it at the direction of the declarant, not entitled to anything through intestate and do not believe they are to receive anything under the will, and that they are not directly financially responsible for declarant's medical care. (755 ILCS § 35/3(e))	Witnesses sign under affirmative statement (as indicated in statutory form). (755 ILCS § 35/3(e))	Yes (as indicated in the statutory form). (755 ILCS § 35/3(e))	Not specified.	Sound mind. (755 ILCS § 35/3(a))	Age of majority or emancipated as a "mature minor." (755 ILCS § 35/3(a))	Not specified.
Indiana	Witness cannot be: (a) the person who signed the declaration on behalf of and at the direction of the declarant; (b) the parent, spouse, or child of the decedent; (c) entitled to	Witnesses affirmatively state lack of listed conflicts (as indicated in the statutory form). (§ 16-36-4-10)	Yes (as indicated in the statutory form). (§ 16-36-4-10)	Not specified.	Declarant must be of sound mind. (§ 16-36-4-8(a))	Declarant must have reached 18 years of age. (§ 16-36-4-8(a))	Not specified.

	any portion of the estate of the decedent; or (d) directly financially responsible for the declarant's medical care. (§ 16-36-4-8(c)(1)(4))						
Iowa	No statement required, but witnesses cannot be an attending health care provider, provider's employee, or a minor. Additionally, at least one witness cannot be related (by blood, marriage or adoption) to the declarant. (§ 144A.3(2)(a))	Presumably only have to sign on knowledge and belief. (§ 144A.3(2)(a))	Yes. (§ 144A.3(2)(a))	Not specified.	Competency. (§ 144A.3(1))	At least 18 years old. (§§ 144A.3(1), 144A.2(1))	Yes, if not signed before two witnesses. (§ 144A.3(2)(b))
Kansas	A witness cannot be the person signing on declarant's behalf, related by blood or marriage to the declarant, entitled to any portion of the declarant's estate (including under a will) or directly financially responsible for the declarant's medical care. (§ 65-28,103(a)(4)(A))	Witnesses affirmatively state lack of listed conflicts. (§ 65-28,103(c))	Yes (as indicated in the statutory form). (§ 65-28,103(c))	Not specified.	Sound mind (as indicated in the statutory form). (§ 65-28,103(c))	"Adult" (but not defined). (§ 65-28,103 (a))	Yes, if not signed before two witnesses. (§ 65-28, 103(a)(4)(B))
Kentucky	Conflicts not listed in witness statement. (§ 311.625(1))	Not specified.	Yes (as indicated in the statutory form). (§ 311.625(1))	Not specified.	Declarant must have decisional capacity. (§ 311.623(1))	Declarant must beat least 18 years old. (§§ 311.623(1), 311.621(1))	Notary can sign the document in lieu of two witnesses. (§ 311.625(2))

Table 7.02, Part 3
Formal Requirements *(continued)*

	What Formalities Satisfy the Requirements?						
	What are Impermissible Conflicts of Witnesses Specified in the Statute?	*Must Witnesses Affirm or Just Declare/Sign on the Basis of Knowledge and Belief?*	*Must Witnesses Sign the Document?*	*Must Attorney or Drafter Sign?*	*Capacity of Declarant: What Standard Is Used? E.g., Sound Mind, Sane?*	*Capacity of Declarant: Age Requirement?*	*Capacity of Declarant: Signed Before Notary?*
Louisiana	Conflicts not listed in witness statement. (§ 40:1299.58.3(C)(1)) Must be a competent adult not related to the declarant by blood or marriage and who would not be entitled to any portion of the declar-ant's estate. (§40:1299.58.2(16))	Sign on knowledge/ belief. (§ 40:1299.58.3 (C)(1))	Yes (as indicated on the statutory form). (§ 40:1299.58.3 (C)(1))	Not specified.	Sound mind (as indicated in the statutory form). (§ 40:1299.58.3 (C)(1))	Adult. (§§ 40: 1299.58.3 (A)(1), 40:1299. 58.2 (16))	Not specified.
Maine	No statement required. (18-A § 5-804)	Witnesses not required.	Two witnesses must sign. (18-A § 5-804(D))	Not specified.	The patient must have capacity, meaning ability to understand condition, risks and benefits of health care, and consequences of health care decisions. (18-A §§ 5-802 (b), 5-801(c))	The patient must be an adult or an emancipated minor. (18-A § 5-802(B))	Not specified.
Maryland	The witness cannot be a health care agent. At least one of the wit-nesses must be some-one who will not	No statement precedes witness signatures. (Health-Gen. § 5-603)	Yes (as indicated in the statutory form). (Health-Gen. § 5-603) Witness must sign documentation	Not specified.	Competency. (Health-Gen. §§ 5-602(a), 5-601(f))	At least 18 years old. (Health-Gen. §§ 5-602(a), 5-601(f))	Not specified.

	knowingly inherit anything from the decedent or otherwise knowingly gain a financial benefit from the decedent's death. (Health-Gen. § 5-603)		of oral declaration. (Health-Gen. § 5-602(d)(2))				
Massachusetts[1]	No witness can be the health care agent. (201D § 2)	Belief. (201D § 2)	Yes. (201D § 2)	Not specified.	Competent. (201D § 2)	18 years of age. (201D § 2)	Not specified.
Michigan	[Note: No formal requirements. Patient, surrogate, or advocate simply responds to physician's information about alternative treatments, which include discontinuing care and solely palliative care. The physician must have informed the patient orally and in writing. (§ 333.5655)]						
Minnesota	A witness cannot be named as a proxy by the living will or be entitled to any part of the declarant's estate. (§ 145B.03)	Witnesses must certify to statement on statutory form. (§§ 145B.03 (Subd. 2)(d), 145B.04)	Yes, unless signed by notary. (§ 145B.03 (Subd. 2)(a))	Not specified.	Competency and sound mind. (§§ 145B.03 (Subd. 1), 145B.04)	States "adult," but does not define. (§ 145B.03 (Subd. 1)	Notary must sign, unless signed instead by two witnesses. (§ 145B.03 (Subd. 2)(a))
Mississippi	One witness must not be appointed as agent by the document; not be a health care provider; not be an employee of a health care provider or facility; not be related by blood, marriage, or adoption; and to the best of his or her knowledge, not be entitled to any part of the estate "under a will now existing or by operation of law." In the case of the other witness, the familial connections are not barred. (§ 41-41-209, statutory form)	Acknowledge under penalties of perjury. (§ 41-41-209(2)(a), statutory form (13))	Yes or notary public (§ 41-41-209 statutory form (13))	Not specified.	Sound mind. (§ 41-41-209, statutory form (13))	The declarant must be at least 18 years old or anemancipated minor. (§§ 41-41-205(1), 41-41-203(e) 41-41-211(2))	Yes, as an alternative to witnesses. (§ 41-41-205(2)(b))

Table 7.02, Part 3
Formal Requirements *(continued)*

	What Formalities Satisfy the Requirements?						
	What are Impermissible Conflicts of Witnesses Specified in the Statute?	*Must Witnesses Affirm or Just Declare/Sign on the Basis of Knowledge and Belief?*	*Must Witnesses Sign the Document?*	*Must Attorney or Drafter Sign?*	*Capacity of Declarant: What Standard Is Used? E.g., Sound Mind, Sane?*	*Capacity of Declarant: Age Requirement?*	*Capacity of Declarant: Signed Before Notary?*
Missouri	Conflicts not listed in witness statement. (§ 459.015(3))	Witnesses sign under affirmative statement (as indicated in statutory form). (§ 459.015(3))	Yes (as indicated inthe statutory form). (§ 459.015(3))	Not specified. (§ 459.015(3))	Sound mind and competency. (§§ 459.015(1), 459.015(3))	At least 18 years old (as indicated in the statutory form). (§ 459.015(3))	Not specified.
Montana	Witnesses sign under statement that declarant signed voluntarily (as indicated in statutory form). (§ 50-9-103(2))	Not specified.	Yes (as indicated in the statutory form). (§ 50-9-103(2))	Not specified.	Patient must be of sound mind. (§ 50-9-103(1))	Patient must be at least 18 years of age. (§ 50-9-103(1))	Not specified.
Nebraska	Conflicts not listed in witness statement. Witnesses simply sign under statement that declarant signed voluntarily. (§ 20-404(2))	Attest it was voluntarily signed in witness' presence (as indicated in the statutory form). (§ 20-404(2))	Yes (as indicated in the statutory form). (§ 20-404(2))	Not specified.	Sound mind. (§ 20-404(1))	Adult: 19 or older or a person who is/has been married. (§§ 20-403(1), 20-404(1))	Not required, but if signed before a notary then no other witnesses are necessary. (§ 20-404(1))
Nevada	Witnesses attest to statement that declarant signed voluntarily. (§ 449.610)	Attest. (§ 449.600(1))	Yes (as indicated in the statutory form). (§ 449.610)	Not specified.	Declarant must be of sound mind. (§ 449.600(1))	Declarant must beat least 18 years old. (§ 449.600(1))	Not specified.
New Hampshire	See Table 7.02, Part 2.	Affirm that principal appeared to be of sound mind and free from duress at the time the advance directive was signed and that the principal	Yes. (§ 137-J:14(I)(a))	Not specified.	Sound mind. (§ 137-J:14(I)(a))	At least 18 years old. (§ 137-J:2(XIX))	Instead of a witness. (§ 137-J:14(I)(b))

		affirmed that he or she was aware of the nature of the document and signed it. (§ 137-J:14(I)(a))					
New Jersey	Not specified.	Must attest the declarant to be of sound mind, free of duress/undue influence and signed in witness' presence. (§ 26:2H-56)	Not specified.	No requirement, although attorney may sign in lieu of witnesses. (§ 26:2H-56)	Sound mind and free of duress/undue influence. (§ 26:2H-56)	Although witnesses must be "adults" (18 years or older), statute does not specify whether declarant must also be an adult. (§§ 26:2H-56, 26:2H-55)	Yes, if not signed before witnesses. (§ 26:2H-56)
New Mexico	Not specified.	Not specified.	Statutory form indicates that witnesses' signatures are optional. (§ 24-7A-4)	Not specified.	Capacity. (§§ 24-7A-2(A), 24-7A-11)	Adult or emancipated minor. (§§ 24-7A-2(A), 24-7A-1(D))	Not specified.
New York	The statement must include that the witness personally knows the principal and is not the person appointed as agent by this document (Pub. Health § 2981(2), see also statutory form. Pub. Health § 2981(5))	Yes. (Pub. Health § 2981(2) & (5))	Yes. (Pub. Health § 2981(2) & (5))	Not specified.	Competent. (Pub.Health § 2981(1)) Language "sound mind and acting willingly and free from duress" is used in witness statement (Pub. Health § 2981(5))	Adult (18 years and older), or married, or the parent of a child. (Pub. Health §§ 2980 (1), 2981(1))	Not specified.
North Carolina	A witness cannot be related to the declarant or the declarant's spouse within the third degree; cannot have a reasonable expectation *(cont'd)*	Affirm (as indicated in the statutory form). (§ 90-321(d))	Yes (as indicated in the statutory form). (§ 90-321(d))	Not specified.	Sound mind (as indicated in the statutory form). (§ 90-321(d))	Not specified.	Yes (or can instead be proved before a clerk or assistant clerk of a superior court). (§ 90-321(c)(4))

Table 7.02, Part 3
Formal Requirements *(continued)*

	What Formalities Satisfy the Requirements?						
	What are Impermissible Conflicts of Witnesses Specified in the Statute?	*Must Witnesses Affirm or Just Declare/Sign on the Basis of Knowledge and Belief?*	*Must Witnesses Sign the Document?*	*Must Attorney or Drafter Sign?*	*Capacity of Declarant: What Standard Is Used? E.g., Sound Mind, Sane?*	*Capacity of Declarant: Age Requirement?*	*Capacity of Declarant: Signed Before Notary?*
North Carolina *(cont'd)*	of being entitled to or currently have a claim against any portion of the declarant's estate; and cannot be the attending physician or his or the health facility's/nursing home's employee. (§ 90-321(c)(3))						
North Dakota	Witness cannot be: (a) the agent; (b) the spouse; (c) heir; (d) related to the declarant by blood or marriage or adoption; (e) entitled to any portion of the declarant's estate under a will or deed in existence or by operation of law; (f) claimants against any portion of the estate; (g) directly financially responsible for the declarant's medical care; or (h) the declarant's attending physician. In addition, at least one witness must not be a health care or	Witnesses must "verify" the principal's signature. (§ 23-06.5-05(2))	Yes. (§ 23-06.5-05(2))	Not specified.	Principal must have ability to understand and appreciate nature and consequences of health care decisions including the significant benefits and harms of and reasonable alternatives to any proposed health care, and have ability to communicate a decision. (§ 23-06.5-02	Declarant must be an adult at least 18 years of age. (§ 23-06.5-02(9)). Although not defined in Title 23, an adult is defined as age eighteen or older. (§ 14-10-02)	May be signed before notary in lieu of two witnesses. (§ 23-06.5-05 (1)(e))

	long term care provider providing direct care to the principal on the date of execution. (§ 23-06.5-05(2))				(3)) Principal is presumed to have capacity. (§ 23-06.5-13(3))		
Ohio	Conflicts not listed in witness statement. (§ 2133.02(B))	Witnesses must attest to belief as to sound mind and not under duress, fraud, or undue influence. (§ 2133.02(B))	Yes, unless signed by notary. (§ 2133.02(B))	Not specified.	Sound mind. (§ 2133.02(A)(1))	Adult defined as 18 or older. (§§ 2133.02(A)(1), 2133.01(A))	May be signed by notary in lieu of two witnesses. (§ 2133.02(A)(1) & (B)(2))
Oklahoma	No statement required.	Sign only, attesting that declarant signed in their presence (as indicated in the statutory form). (63 § 3101.4(B))	Yes (as indicated in the statutory form). (63 § 3101.4(B))	Not specified.	Sound mind. (63 § 3101.4(A))	At least 18 years old. (63 § 3101.4(A))	Not specified.
Oregon	Both witnesses must attest that the declarant: is personally known to them or has shown proof of ID; signed or acknowledged the declarant's signature in their presence; appears to be of sound mind and not under duress, fraud, or undue influence; has not appointed either as health care representative or alternative representative; and is not a patient whom they serve as the attending physician. Other impermissible conflicts listed in	Witnesses must affirm written declaration. (§ 127.531(2)(D))	Yes (as indicated in the statutory form). (§ 127.531(2)(D))	Not specified.	Sound mind (as indicated in the statutory form). (§ 127.531(2)(A))	Capable adult, defined as 18 or older, person adjudicated as an emancipated minor, or who is married. (§§ 127.510(2), 127.505(1))	Not specified.

(cont'd)

Table 7.02, Part 3
Formal Requirements *(continued)*

	What Formalities Satisfy the Requirements?						
	What are Impermissible Conflicts of Witnesses Specified in the Statute?	*Must Witnesses Affirm or Just Declare/Sign on the Basis of Knowledge and Belief?*	*Must Witnesses Sign the Document?*	*Must Attorney or Drafter Sign?*	*Capacity of Declarant: What Standard Is Used? E.g., Sound Mind, Sane?*	*Capacity of Declarant: Age Requirement?*	*Capacity of Declarant: Signed Before Notary?*
Oregon *(cont'd)*	statement below witness signatures (as indicated in statutory form). (§ 127.531(2)(D))						
Pennsylvania	No statement regarding conflicts required, but a witness cannot be the one who signs for the declarant. (20 § 5404(a))	Affirm that the declarant knowingly/voluntarily signed the declaration in the presence of the witness (as indicated in the statutory form). (20 § 5404(b))	Yes (as indicated in the statutory form). (20 § 5404(b))	Not specified.	Sound mind. (20 § 5404(a))	18 or older, high school graduate, or a person who has married. (20 § 5404(a))	Not specified.
Rhode Island	No statement regarding conflicts required, but witnesses cannot be related by blood or marriage to the declarant. (§ 23-4.11-3(a))	Affirm that they personally know declarant and that the declarant voluntarily signed in the presence of the witness (as indicated in the statutory form). (§ 23-4.11-3(d))	Yes (as indicated in the statutory form). (§ 23-4.11-3(d))	Not specified.	Competent. (§ 23-4.11-3(a))	18 or older. (§ 23-4.11-3(a))	Not specified.
South Carolina	A witness cannot be: related to the declarant by blood, marriage, or adoption; entitled to any portion of the declarant's estate presently or under a will; financially	Witnesses must affirm that they are qualified witnesses in required affidavit. Sign on "best information and belief" as to signing of	Yes. (§ 44-77-40(4))	Not specified.	Sound mind (as indicated in statutory form). (§ 44-77-50)	At least 18. (§ 44-77-30)	Yes. (§ 44-77-40(2))

	responsible for the declarant's medical care; a beneficiary of the declarant's life insurance policy; the attending physician or his employee; or a person with a claim against any portion of declarant's estate. Not more than one of the witnesses can be employed by the health care facility in which the declarant is presently a patient. (§ 44-77-40(2))	declaration by a known, declarant of sound mind. (§ 44-77-50)					
South Dakota	Not specified.	Witnessing is all that is required. (§ 34-12D-2)	The statute simply states that the written declaration should be "witnessed." (§ 34-12D-2)	Not specified.	Competent. (§ 34-12D-2)	Adult. (§ 34-12D-2)	The signing may be in the presence of a notary public. (§ 34-12D-2)
Tennessee	Witnesses must verify that they are not related to declarant by blood or marriage, that they are not entitled to and do not have a claim against any portion of declarant's estate, and that they are not an attending physician or an employee of the physician or health facility where declarant is a patient. (§ 32-11-104(a))	Witnesses affirmatively state lack of impermissible conflicts. (§ 32-11-105)	Yes (as indicated in the statutory form). (§ 32-11-105)	Not specified. (§ 32-11-105)	Sound mind and competency. (§§ 32-11-105, 32-11-104(a))	Only states "adult" (not defined). (§ 32-11-104(a))	Yes (as indicated in the statutory form). (§ 32-11-105)

Table 7.02, Part 3
Formal Requirements *(continued)*

	What Formalities Satisfy the Requirements?						
	What are Impermissible Conflicts of Witnesses Specified in the Statute?	*Must Witnesses Affirm or Just Declare/Sign on the Basis of Knowledge and Belief?*	*Must Witnesses Sign the Document?*	*Must Attorney or Drafter Sign?*	*Capacity of Declarant: What Standard Is Used? E.g., Sound Mind, Sane?*	*Capacity of Declarant: Age Requirement?*	*Capacity of Declarant: Signed Before Notary?*
Texas	No affirmative witness statement, but witnesses sign under list of impermissible conflicts (as indicated in the statutory form). (Health & Safety § 166.033)	Witnesses simply sign. (Health & Safety § 166.033)	Yes. (Health & Safety § 166.032(b))	Not specified.	Competent, meaning able to under stand the nature and consequences of treatment decisions. (Health & Safety §§ 166.032(a), 166.002(4))	Statute states "adult," but does not define. (Health & Safety § 166.032(a))	Directive specifically does not have to be notarized. (Health & Safety § 166.036)
Utah (2007)	A witness cannot be related to the declarant by blood or marriage; the person who signed on the behalf of the declarant; entitled to any portion of the declarant's estate presently or under a will; directly financially responsible for the declarant's medical care; or an agent of the health care facility in which the declarant is presently a patient. (§ 75-2-1104(3)(a)–(e))	Witnesses affirmatively certify lack of impermissible conflicts. (§ 75-2-1104(4))	Yes (as indicated in the statutory form). (§ 75-2-1104(4))	Not specified.	Sound mind (as indicated in the statutory form). (§ 75-2-1104(4))	At least 18 years old. (§ 75-2-1104(1))	Not specified.
Utah (2008) The new law is effective Jan. 1,	A witness cannot be related to the declarant by blood or marriage; the person who signed	No provision, except if oral directive then witness must state the circumstances	See prior column	Not specified.	The declarant is presumed to have the capacity to complete a	At least 18 years old, unless the declarant is an	Not specified.

2008. A health care directive executed prior to this date under the provisions then in effect, Ch. 2, pt. II, Personal Choice and Living Will, may, in good faith, be relied upon by a health care provider or health care facility. (§ 75-2a-1120(1)(b))	on the behalf of the declarant; entitled to any portion of the declarant's estate presently or under a will; directly financially responsible for the declarant's medical care; a health care provider to the declarant; or an administrator of the health care facility in which the declarant is receiving care; or the appointed agent. (§ 75-2a-1106(1)(c)(i)-(vi))	under which the directive was made. (§ 75-2a-1106(1)(d))			health care directive. (§§ 75-2a-1104(1), 1105(1) The standard is "health care decision making capacity." (§ 75-2a-1104(1))	emancipated minor as defined in § 78-3a-1001 -1105. (§ 75-2a-1103 (14)(a))	
Vermont	Statement not required but witnesses cannot be the declarant's agent, spouse, reciprocal beneficiary, parent, adult sibling, adult child, or adult grandchild. (18 § 9703(c))	Witnesses affirm. (18 § 9703(b))	Yes (as indicated in the statutory form). (18 § 9703(b))	Not specified.	"Capacity" means an individual's ability to make and communicate a decision regarding the issue that needs to be decided. (18 § 9701(3))	Adult. (18 § 9702(a))	Not specified.
Virginia	Must be 18 years or older. (§§ 54.1-2984, 54.1-2982)	Witnesses affirmatively state that declarant signed in their presence. (§ 54.1-2984)	Yes (as indicated in the statutory form). (§ 54.1-2984)	Not specified.	Competency. (§ 54.1-2983)	Only states "adult." (§ 54.1-2983)	Not specified.
Washington	Affirmative statement not required, but a witness cannot be: an attending physician or his/her or the health facility's employee; *(cont'd)*	Sign on knowledge/belief (as indicated in the statutory form). (§ 70.122.030(1))	Yes (as indicated in the statutory form). (§ 70.122.030(1))	Not specified.	"Capacity to make health care decisions" (as indicated in the statutory form). (§ 70.122.030(1))	Must be an "adult person." (§ 70.122.030 (1))	Not specified.

Table 7.02, Part 3
Formal Requirements *(continued)*

	What Formalities Satisfy the Requirements?						
	What are Impermissible Conflicts of Witnesses Specified in the Statute?	*Must Witnesses Affirm or Just Declare/Sign on the Basis of Knowledge and Belief?*	*Must Witnesses Sign the Document?*	*Must Attorney or Drafter Sign?*	*Capacity of Declarant: What Standard Is Used? E.g., Sound Mind, Sane?*	*Capacity of Declarant: Age Requirement?*	*Capacity of Declarant: Signed Before Notary?*
Washington *(cont'd)*	related by blood or marriage to the declarant; or entitled to or have a claim against the declarant's estate. (§ 70.122.030(1))						
West Virginia	A witness cannot be: an attending physician; related by blood or marriage to the declarant; entitled to any portion of the declarant's estate; directly financially responsible for the declarant's medical care; the person who signed the living will for the declarant on the behalf and direction of the declarant; or declarant's medical power of attorney representative. (§ 16-30-4(b))	Witnesses affirm lack of impermissible conflicts. (§ 16-30-4(a)(5))	Yes. (§ 16-30-4(a)(5))	Not specified.	Competency. (§ 16-30-4(a))	Adult, meaning a person 18 or older, an emancipated minor, or a mature minor. (§§ 16-30-4(a), 16-30-3(b))	Yes. (§ 16-30-4(a)(5))
Wisconsin	Cannot be related by blood, marriage or adoption; cannot have knowledge they are	Sign on belief as to declarant's sound mind. Witnesses affirmatively state	Yes. (§ 154.03(1))	Not specified.	Sound mind. (§ 154.03(1))	18 or older. (§ 154.03(1))	Not specified.

	entitled to, or have a claim against any part of the estate; cannot be directly responsible for the declarant's health care; and cannot be a health care provider, employee of the health care provider, or an employee of an inpatient health care facility serving the declarant (chaplains and social workers are allowed). (§ 154.03(1)(a)–(d))	that they are free of impermissible conflicts. (§ 154.03(2))					
Wyoming	A witness cannot be: a treating health care provider or an employee thereof; the attorney-in-fact nominated in the writing; the operator of a community care facility or employee thereof; the operator of a residential care facility or employee thereof. (§ 35-22-403(c))	Sign on penalty of perjury that the person signing is the principal, that the principal signed in his presence, that the principal was in sound mind, and the witness is free of the conflicts listed in the prior column. (§ 35-22-403(c)).	Yes, or sworn before a notary public. (§ 35-22-403(b))	Not specified.	"Capacity" means an individual's ability to understand the significant benefits, risks and alternatives to proposed health care and to make and communicate a health care decision.	Statute states "adult," but does not define, as well as emancipated minor. (§ 35-22-403(b))	Not specified.

1. Only deals with health care proxies.

Table 7.02, Part 4
Formal Requirements

	Effect of Pregnancy?	*Must Pregnancy Test Be Administered?*	*Is There a Requirement That a Notified Attending Physician Make the Declaration Part of the Medical Record?*	*Is There Automatic Severability of Defective Clauses or Does Entire Living Will Fail (Or No Provision)?*	*Must There Be a Registration of the Living Will?*	*Must You Follow the Living Will Form in the Statute or Is Something "Substantially" Equivalent a Satisfactory Alternative?*
Alabama	If pregnancy is known by the physician, the living will has no effect during the course of the pregnancy. (§ 22-8A-4(e))	Not specified. (§ 22-8A-4(e))	Yes. (§ 22-8A-4(f))	Automatic severability. (§ 22-8A-4(h))	Not specified.	Yes. (Language is: "shall be substantially in the following form, but in addition may include other specific directions.") (§ 22-8A-4(h))
Alaska	The supervising health care provider must determine if a woman of childbearing age is pregnant before implementing a health-care decision involving her. (§ 13.52.055(a)). The health-care directive may not be given effect if the patient is pregnant and lacks capacity; the directive or decision is to withhold or withdraw life-sustaining procedures; the withholding or withdrawal of the life-sustaining procedures would, in reasonable medical judgment, be likely to result in the death of the patient; and it is probable that the fetus could develop to the point of live birth if the life-sustaining procedures	Yes, if a woman of childbearing age, the supervising health care provider is required to take reasonable steps to determine whether the woman is pregnant. (§ 13.52.055(a))	Yes. (§ 13.52.060(b))	Yes. (§ 13.52.290)	Not specified.	No. May be, but "need not be" in the statutory form or substantially similar. (§ 13.52.300)

	were provided. However, the foregoing does not apply to emergency services in the field. (§ 13.52.055(b))					
Arizona	The patient can request that life-sustaining treatment not be removed, notwithstanding any directive to the contrary, if she is known to be pregnant (as indicated in the statutory form). (§ 36-3262)	Not specified.	Not specified.	Not specified.	Not specified.	A pre-hospital medical care directive must be in the form set forth in § 36-3251 (B). A living will can be in any form that complies with the requirements of § 36-3262.
Arkansas	If the physician knows the declarant is pregnant the declaration will not be given effect if there is a possibil ity "the fetus could develop to the point of live birth" by continuing to givethe declarant life-sustaining treatment. (§ 20-17-206(c))	Not specified.	Yes. (§§ 20-17-202(d), 20-17-205)	Severability. (§ 20-17-216)	Not specified.	Declaration "may, but need not" be in the statutory form. (§ 20-17-202(b))
California	Not specified, but statute does not authorize consent to abortion. (Probate § 4652(e))	Not specified.	Yes. (Probate § 4731(a))	Severability. (Probate § 11)	Registration is optional. (Probate §§ 4800, 4803)	Directive, may, but need not, follow statutory form, which may be modified partially or in full. (Probate §§ 4700, 4701)
Colorado	If the attending physician knows that the declarant is pregnant, a medical evaluation must be conducted to determine if the fetus is viable. If so, the declaration has no effect. (§ 15-18-104(2))	Not specified. (§ 15-18-104(2))	Yes. (§ 15-18-104(1))	Not specified.	Not specified.	Declaration "may, but need not" be in the statutory form. (§ 15-18-104(3))

Table 7.02, Part 4
Formal Requirements *(continued)*

	Effect of Pregnancy?	*Must Pregnancy Test Be Administered?*	*Is There a Requirement That a Notified Attending Physician Make the Declaration Part of the Medical Record?*	*Is There Automatic Severability of Defective Clauses or Does Entire Living Will Fail (Or No Provision)?*	*Must There Be a Registration of the Living Will?*	*Must You Follow the Living Will Form in the Statute or Is Something "Substantially" Equivalent a Satisfactory Alternative?*
Connecticut	Living will without effect if pregnant. (§ 19a-574)	Not specified.	Yes, as well as any oral communication made by the patient to the physician, other health care person or agent, legal guardian, conservator, or next of kin concerning health care. (§ 19a-578(b))	Not specified.	Not specified. The living will or appointment of health care representative becomes operative when furnished to the attending physician and the declarant is determined to be incapacitated. (§ 19a-579)	Living will may be "substantially" in statutory form. (§ 19a-575a)
Delaware	A life-sustaining procedure may not be withheld from a patient known to be pregnant so long as it is probable that the fetus will develop to be viable outside of the uterus. (16 § 2503(j))	Not specified.	Yes. (16 § 2508(b))	Not specified.	Not specified.	Statutory form "may, but need not" be used to create an advance health-care directive. Individuals may complete or modify all or any part of the following form. (16 § 2505)
District of Columbia	Not specified.	N/A	Yes. (§ 7-622(b))	Severability of additional specific directions found to be invalid. (§ 7-622(c))	Not specified.	A declaration must be substantially in the form set forth in § 7-622, but may include other specific directions of the declarant. (§ 7-622(c))

Florida	Surrogate/proxy cannot consent to the withdrawal of life-prolonging procedures prior to viability. (§ 765.113)	Not specified.	Yes. (§ 765.302(2))	Not specified.	Not specified.	May be in same form, but need not to be valid. (§ 765.303(1))
Georgia	If the attending physician determines that the declarant is pregnant, physician must determine that fetus is not viable and that living will specifically indicates that living will is to be carried out. Otherwise, the living will cannot be in effect. (§ 31-32-8(a)(1))	Not specified, but states that physician, to the best of his knowledge, shall determine if declarant is pregnant and if fetus is viable. (§ 31-32-8(a)(1))	Yes. (§ 31-32-8(a)(4))	Not specified.	Not specified.	"Any declaration" expressing declarant's intent shall be honored, regardless of form. Declarations "similar to" statutory form or "substantially" in form specified under prior law shall be presumed valid. (§ 31-32-3(b))
Hawaii	Not specified.	Not specified.	Yes. (§ 327E-7(b))	Not specified.	Not specified.	Statutory form is optional and may be modified in any way, or a different form that contains the substance of the optional form may be used. (§ 327E-16)
Idaho	If diagnosed as pregnant, living will has no force during course of pregnancy. (§ 39-4510)	Not specified. (§ 39-4510)	Not specified. (§ 39-4510)	Not specified.	No. (§ 39-4510(2)) The health care provider is not required to request a living will or durable power of attorney for health care from the registry. (§ 39-4513(4))	Living will shall be "substantially" in statutory form or another form that contains the same elements. (§ 39-4510)
Illinois	Void if attending physician believes the fetus could *(cont'd)*	Not specified.	Yes. (755 ILCS § 35/3(d))	Severability. (755 ILCS § 35/3(e))	Not specified.	Declaration "may, but need not" be in the statutory form, and may include *(cont'd)*

Table 7.02, Part 4
Formal Requirements *(continued)*

	Effect of Pregnancy?	*Must Pregnancy Test Be Administered?*	*Is There a Requirement That a Notified Attending Physician Make the Declaration Part of the Medical Record?*	*Is There Automatic Severability of Defective Clauses or Does Entire Living Will Fail (Or No Provision)?*	*Must There Be a Registration of the Living Will?*	*Must You Follow the Living Will Form in the Statute or Is Something "Substantially" Equivalent a Satisfactory Alternative?*
Illinois *(cont'd)*	develop to live birth. (755 ILCS § 35/3(c))					other specific directions. (755 ILCS § 35/3(e))
Indiana	A living will declaration of a person diagnosed as pregnant by the attending physician has no effect during the person's pregnancy. (§ 16-36-4-8(d))	Not specified.	Yes. (§ 16-36-4-8(e))	The invalidity of any additional specific directions does not affect the validity of the declaration. (§ 16-36-4-9)	Not specified.	A living will declaration must substantially follow the form set forth in § 16-36-4-10, but may also include additional specific directions of the declarant. (§ 16-36-4-9)
Iowa	If the attending physician knows patient is pregnant, the living will cannot be in effect as long as fetus could develop to live birth. (§ 144A.6(2))	Not specified. (§ 144A.6(2))	Not specified, but implied, since revocation of the directive *must* be made part of the declarant's medical record. (§ 144A.4(2))	Not specified.	Not specified.	Declaration may be, but "need not be" in the statutory form. (§ 144A.3(5))
Kansas	If the attending physician has diagnosed declarant as pregnant, the declaration is ineffective during the course of pregnancy. (§ 65-28,103(a))	Not specified. (§ 65-28,103(a))	Yes. (§ 65-28,103(b))	Automatic severability. (§ 65-28,103(c))	Not specified.	Must be in substantially the same form but may include other specific directions. (§ 65-28,103(c))
Kentucky	If the patient is diagnosed as pregnant the directive shall have no force during the course of the pregnancy unless the life-prolonging procedures will	Not specified.	Yes. (§ 311.633(1))	If any additional specific directions are held to be invalid, that invalidity shall not affect the	Not specified.	§ 311.625(1) states that a living will directive shall be substantially in the form set forth in that section and may include additional specific directions.

	not allow for the continuing develop ment and live birth of the unborn child, or will be physically harmful to the woman, or will prolong severe pain. (§ 311.629(4))			directive. (§ 311.625(1))		However, § 311.637(6) states that persons can make advance directives outside the provisions of § 311.625.
Louisiana	Not specified.	Not specified.	Yes (or a copy of the declaration). (§ 40:1299.58.3 (B)(3) & (4))	Automatic sever-ability. (§ 40:1299.58.3 (C)(2))	Declarant or attor-ney "may" register. (§ 40:1299.58.3 (D)(1))	Declaration may be, but "need not be" in the statu-tory form and can include other specific directions. (§ 40:1299.58.3(C)(1))
Maine	Not specified.	N/A	Yes. (18-A § 5-807(B))	Not specified.	Not specified.	The advance health-care directive form set forth in 18-A § 5-804 is optional and may be modified par-tially or in its entirety.
Maryland	Declarant can give specific instructions to be followed if she is pregnant as stated in the statutory form. (Health-Gen. § 5-603(II)(F))	Not specified. (Health-Gen. § 5-603)	Yes. (Health-Gen. § 5-602(f)(2))	Not specified.	Not specified.	Form is only suggested as a guide. Forms may be par-tially completed, and dif-ferent forms may be used. (Health-Gen. § 5-603)
Massachusetts[1]	Not specified.	Not specified.	Yes. (201D § 5)	Not specified.	Not specified.	No form provided, only specified what is provided in Table 7.02, Parts 1–3.
Michigan	N/A	N/A	N/A	N/A	N/A	N/A
Minnesota	If the attending physician knows that the declarant is pregnant, the living will cannot be in effect as long as the fetus can develop to the point of live birth if life-	Not specified.	Yes. (§ 145B.06 (Subd. 1)(a))	Not specified.	Not specified.	Must be substantially in the statutory form. (§ 145B.04)

(cont'd)

Table 7.02, Part 4
Formal Requirements *(continued)*

	Effect of Pregnancy?	*Must Pregnancy Test Be Administered?*	*Is There a Requirement That a Notified Attending Physician Make the Declaration Part of the Medical Record?*	*Is There Automatic Severability of Defective Clauses or Does Entire Living Will Fail (Or No Provision)?*	*Must There Be a Registration of the Living Will?*	*Must You Follow the Living Will Form in the Statute or Is Something "Substantially" Equivalent a Satisfactory Alternative?*
Minnesota *(cont'd)*	sustaining treatment is continued. (§ 145B.13(3))					
Mississippi	Not specified, except to extent the advanced health-care directive does not override the abortion laws. (§ 41-41-227(7))	Not specified.	Not specified.	Not specified.	No specified.	Yes. Although the form "may" be used, "any other writing" may also suffice. (§ 41-41-209)
Missouri	The declaration is not in effect during the declarant's pregnancy if the attending physician diagnosed the declarant as being pregnant. (§ 459.025)	Not specified. (§ 459.025)	Yes. (§ 459.015(2))	Automatic severability. (§ 459.015(3))	Not specified.	The declaration may be in the statutory form, but it is not necessary to use the sample form. In addition, the declaration may include other specific directions. (§ 459.015(3))
Montana	Life-sustaining treatment cannot be withheld from a person known to the attending physician to be pregnant so long as it is probable that the fetus will develop to the point of live birth with the continued application of life-sustaining treatment. (§§ 50-9-106(6), 50-9-202(3))	Not specified.	Yes. (§ 50-9-103(5))	Not specified.	Not specified.	The declaration may, but need not, be in the statutory form. (§ 50-9-103(2))
Nebraska	If physician knows of pregnancy and it is probable that the fetus can develop to live birth if life-sustaining	Not specified.	Yes. (§ 20-404(3))	No provision.	Not specified.	Need not be in the statutory form. (§ 20-404(2))

	treatment is administered, then the declaration will not be given effect. (§ 20-408(3))					
Nevada	Life-sustaining treatment may not be withheld from a patient known to the attending physician to be pregnant so long as it is probable that the fetus will develop to the point of live birth with the continued application of life-sustaining treatment. (§§ 449.624 (4), 449.626(6))	Not specified.	Yes. (§ 449.600 (2))	Not specified.	Not specified.	Declaration may, but need not, be in statutory form. (§ 449.610)
New Hampshire	Statute does not condone withdrawal of life-sustaining treatment, unless treatment will not permit continuing development and live birth of fetus or will be physically harmful to principal or prolong severe pain which cannot be alleviated by medication. (§§ 137-J:5(V)(c); 137-J:10(IV)(a))	Not specified.	Yes, upon request by the declarant. (§ 137-J:5)	Not specified.	No, but it must be made a part of medical record upon request of principal. (§ 137-J:7(I)(a))	Advance directive must be in substantially similar form). (§ 137-J:20)
New Jersey	Female declarants may include instructions to be followed in the event of pregnancy. (§ 26:2H-56)	Not specified.	Yes. (§ 26:2H-62(a))	Not specified.	Not specified.	Statutory form not provided.
New Mexico	Not specified.	Not specified.	Yes. (§ 24-7A-7(B))	Automatic severability. (§ 24-7A-18)	Not specified.	Directive may, but need not, follow statutory form. Form can be modified partially or in full. (§ 24-7A-4)
New York	Not specified.	Not specified.	Yes. (Pub. Health § 2984(1))	Not specified.	Not specified.	No, a health care proxy may, but need not, be in

(cont'd)

Table 7.02, Part 4
Formal Requirements *(continued)*

	Effect of Pregnancy?	*Must Pregnancy Test Be Administered?*	*Is There a Requirement That a Notified Attending Physician Make the Declaration Part of the Medical Record?*	*Is There Automatic Severability of Defective Clauses or Does Entire Living Will Fail (Or No Provision)?*	*Must There Be a Registration of the Living Will?*	*Must You Follow the Living Will Form in the Statute or Is Something "Substantially" Equivalent a Satisfactory Alternative?*
New York *(cont'd)*						the statutory form. (Pub. Health § 2981(5)(d))
North Carolina	Not specified.	Not specified.	Not specified.	Not specified.	No, optional. (§§ 90-321(c), 130A-467)	Sample form is "specifically determined to meet the requirements" of the statute. (§ 90-321(d))
North Dakota	Medical treatment must be provided to a pregnant patient with a terminal condition unless, to a reasonable degree of medical certainty, such medical treatment will not maintain the patient in such a way as to permit the continuing development and live birth of the unborn child or will prolong severe pain. (§ 23-06.5-09(5))	Not specified.	Yes, by implication in § 23-06.5-07(2).	Not specified.	Not specified.	No. The statutory form is an optional, but not a required, form. (§ 23-06.5-17)
Ohio	Declaration is ineffective if removing the treatments would terminate pregnancy, unless the fetus would not be born alive. (§ 2133.06(B))	Not specified.	Yes. (§ 2133.02(C))	Not specified.	Not specified.	No statutory form is provided. Must follow requirements for execution in § 2133.02. Section 2133.07 states that a printed form of a declaration may be sold or distributed for use by adults not advised by an attorney.
Oklahoma	If declarant has been diagnosed as pregnant and the	Yes (implied), where appropriate considering	Yes. (63 § 3101.4(C))	Not specified, but implied, since the	Not specified.	Advance directive shall be "substantially"

	attending physician knows it, the directive has no effect during the course of the pregnancy. (63 § 3101.8(C))	age and other factors. (63 § 3101.8(C))		directive may be revoked "in whole or part." (63 § 3101.6(A))		in the statutory form (63 § 3101.4(B))
Oregon	Not specified.	Not specified.	Yes. (§ 127.510(5))	If not in compliance with statutory form or formal requirements, the directive is not valid, but will consti tute evidence of the patient's desires. (§ 127.535(6))	Not specified.	Must be in the statutory form, although declarant may cross out or add words to express wishes better. (§ 127.531(1))
Pennsylvania	Life-sustaining treatment, nutrition and hydration must be provided unless, to a reasonable degree of medical certainty, they will not maintain the pregnant woman in a way as to permit continuing development and live birth of the unborn child, will be physically harmful to the pregnant woman, or will cause pain to the pregnant woman that cannot be alleviated by medication. (20 § 5429)	No provision.	Yes. (20 § 5443(b))	Not specified.	Not specified.	Declaration may, but need not, be in the statutory form, and may include other specific directions. (20 §§ 5447 (living will); 5465 (health care power of attorney); 5471 (combined form))
Rhode Island	Declaration is void as long as it is probable that the fetus could develop to live birth. (§ 23-4.11-6(c))	Not specified.	Yes. (§ 23-4.11-3(b))	Severability. (§ 23-4.11-15)	Not specified.	Declaration may, but need not, be in the statutory form. (§ 23-4.11-3(d))
South Carolina	If declarant has been diagnosed as pregnant, the declaration is not effective	Not specified. (§ 44-77-70)	Not specified.	Not specified.	Not specified.	Declaration must be substantially in statutory form, with revocation provisions
	(cont'd)					*(cont'd)*

Table 7.02, Part 4
Formal Requirements *(continued)*

	Effect of Pregnancy?	*Must Pregnancy Test Be Administered?*	*Is There a Requirement That a Notified Attending Physician Make the Declaration Part of the Medical Record?*	*Is There Automatic Severability of Defective Clauses or Does Entire Living Will Fail (Or No Provision)?*	*Must There Be a Registration of the Living Will?*	*Must You Follow the Living Will Form in the Statute or Is Something "Substantially" Equivalent a Satisfactory Alternative?*
South Carolina *(cont'd)*	during the course of the pregnancy. (§ 44-77-70)					appearing in upper case or boldface. (§ 44-77-50)
South Dakota	Pregnant woman will be given life-sustaining treatment and food/hydration unless these procedures will not result in live birth or will be harmful/painful to the female as decided by attending physician and one other physician. (§ 34-12D-10)	Not specified.	Yes. (§ 34-12D-7)	No provision.	Not specified.	May, but need not, be in the statutory form. (§ 34-12D-3)
Tennessee	Not specified.	Not specified.	Yes. (§ 32-11-104(b))	Automatic severability. (§ 32-11-110(g))	Not specified.	Declaration shall be "substantially" in the statutory form provided for in § 32-11-105. (§ 32-11-104 (a)) This is not to the exclusion of other written and clear expressions of intent to accept, refuse, or withdraw medical care. (§ 32-11-105)
Texas	A person may not withdraw/withhold life-sustaining procedures from a pregnant patient. (Health & Safety § 166.049)	Not specified. (Health & Safety § 166.049)	Yes. (Health & Safety §§ 166.032 (d) & 166.034(c) (for unwritten directive))	Not specified.	Not specified.	Only states that directive "may be" written in the statutory form, not specified otherwise. (Health & Safety § 166.033)

Utah (2007)	A directive has no effect during a declarant's pregnancy. (§ 75-2-1109)	Not specified. (§ 75-2-1109)	Yes. (§ 75-2-1110)	Not specified.	Not specified.	Directive shall be "substantially" in statutory form or substantially similar to form approved under prior Utah law. (§ 75-2-1104(4))
Utah (2008) The new law is effective Jan. 1, 2008. A health care directive executed prior to this date under the provisions then in effect, Ch. 2, pt. II, Personal Choice and Living Will, may, in good faith, be relied upon by a health care provider or health care facility. (§ 75-2a-1120(1)(b))	A directive has no force during a declarant's pregnancy. (§ 75-2a-1122)	Not specified. (§ 75-2a-1122)	Yes. (§ 75-2a-1114(b)(1))	Not specified.	Not specified.	A health care directive is presumed valid if in the optional form of the statute or a substantially similar form. (§ 75-2a-1116)
Vermont	Can direct which life sustaining procedures the principal would or would not desire if pregnant. (18 § 9702)	Not specified.	Yes, every health care provider must develop a system to ensure directive is available when services are rendered. (18 § 9709)	Severability. (18 § 9720)	Not specified.	No statutory form.
Virginia	Not specified.	Not specified.	Yes. (§ 54.1-2983)	Severability. (§ 54.1-2984)	Not specified.	Directive may, but need not, be in statutory form. (§ 54.1-2984)

Table 7.02, Part 4
Formal Requirements *(continued)*

	Effect of Pregnancy?	*Must Pregnancy Test Be Administered?*	*Is There a Requirement That a Notified Attending Physician Make the Declaration Part of the Medical Record?*	*Is There Automatic Severability of Defective Clauses or Does Entire Living Will Fail (Or No Provision)?*	*Must There Be a Registration of the Living Will?*	*Must You Follow the Living Will Form in the Statute or Is Something "Substantially" Equivalent a Satisfactory Alternative?*
Washington	If declarant has been diagnosed as pregnant and the physician knows it, the health-care directive has no effect during the pregnancy (as indicated in the statutory form). (§ 70.122.030(1)(d))	Not specified. (§ 70.122.030(1)(d))	Yes. (§ 70.122.030(1))	Automatic severability. (§§ 70.122.905, 70.122.920)	Not specified.	Directive may be in statutory form, but it may include other specific directions. (§ 70.122.030(1))
West Virginia	Not specified, but the statute expressly states that the common law doctrine of medical necessity is not abrogated. (§ 16-30-17)	Not specified.	Yes. (§ 16-30-4(d))	Automatic sever ability. (§ 16-30-4(g))	Not specified.	May but "need not be" in the statutory form and can include other specific directions. (§ 16-30-4(g))
Wisconsin	Declaration has no effect during pregnancy. (§ 154.07(2))	Not specified.	Yes. (§§ 154.03(1), 154.11(8))	No provision.	No, registration for a fee is optional. (§ 154.13(1))	No, not limited to the statutory form but declarations prepared and provided by department of health and family services shall be in statutory form. (§§ 154.02(1), 154.03(2))
Wyoming	Not specified. (§§ 35-22-403, 35-22-405)	Not specified. (§§ 35-22-403, 35-22-405)	Yes. (§ 35-33-408(c))	Not specified.	Not specified.	Not specified.

1. Only deals with health care proxies.

Table 7.03, Part 1
Revocation

			If a Writing, Is It Sufficient If:			
	What Physical Acts Accomplish This?	*By a Writing?*	*Signed by Declarant?*	*Signed by a Person (1) In His Presence and (2) At His Direction?*	*Dated?*	*Witnessed?*
Alabama	Burning, obliteration, tearing, destroying, or defacing in a manner showing intention to revoke. (§ 22-8A-5(a)(1))	Yes. (§ 22-8A-5(a)(2))	Can be signed by either declarant or person acting at his "direction." (§ 22-8A-5(a)(2))	(1) Not specified. (2) Yes. (§ 22-8A-5(a)(2))	Yes. (§ 22-8A-5(a)(2))	No. (§ 22-8A-5(a)(2))
Alaska	States any manner that communicates an intent to revoke. (§ 13.52.020(b))	Yes (implied, since any manner qualifies). (§ 13.52.020(b))	Not specified. (§ 13.52.020(b))	Not specified. (§ 13.52.020(b))	Not specified. (§ 13.52.020(b))	Not specified. (§ 13.52.020(b))
Arizona	Making a new health-care directive or any act that demonstrates a specific intent to revoke a directive. (§ 36-3202(3) & (4))	Yes. (§ 36-3202(1))	Not specified.	Not specified.	Not specified.	Not specified.
Arkansas	"Communication [in any manner] to the attending physician or other health care provider by the declarant or a witness to the revocation." (§ 20-17-204(a))	Yes, but presumably not required, since "communication" is used.	Not specified.	Not specified.	Not specified.	Not specified. But revocation can be "communicated" by a witness. (§ 20-17-204(a))
California	Patient having capacity can revoke at any time and in any manner that communicates an intent to revoke. (Probate § 4695(b))	Yes, presumably. (Probate § 4695(b))	Not specified.	Not specified.	Not specified.	Not specified.
Colorado	Burning, tearing, canceling, obliterating, or destroying. (§ 15-18-109)	Yes. (§ 15-18-109)	Not specified. (§ 15-18-109)	Not specified. (§ 15-18-109)	Not specified. (§ 15-18-109)	Not specified. (§ 15-18-109)

Table 7.03, Part 1
Revocation *(continued)*

			If a Writing, Is It Sufficient If:			
	What Physical Acts Accomplish This?	*By a Writing?*	*Signed by Declarant?*	*Signed by a Person (1) In His Presence and (2) At His Direction?*	*Dated?*	*Witnessed?*
Connecticut	Can be done in any manner by the declarant. (§ 19a-579a(a))	Yes (but not specifically required). (§ 19a-579a(a))	Not specified.	Not specified.	Not specified.	Not specified.
Delaware	A health-care directive may be revoked in any manner that communicates an intent to revoke. It must be done in the presence of two competent persons, one of whom is a health care provider. (16 § 2504(a)(2))	Yes. (16 § 2504(a)(1))	Written revocation must be signed by the declarant. (16 § 2504(a)(1))	Not specified.	Not specified.	A revocation must be witnessed only if it is not done by asigned writing. (16 § 2504(a)(2))
District of Columbia	A declaration may be revoked by being obliterated, burned, torn, or otherwise destroyed by the declarant or by some person in the declarant's presence and at the declarant's direction. (§ 7-624(a)(1))	Yes. (§ 7-624(a)(2))	Yes. (§ 7-624(a)(2))	(1) Not specified. (2) Yes. (§ 7-624(a)(2))	Yes. (§ 7-624(a)(2))	Not specified.
Florida	Physical cancellation/destruction by principal or by another in the principal's presence/direction. (§ 765.104(1)(b))	Yes. (§ 765.104(1)(a))	Yes. (§ 765.104(1)(a))	Not specified.	Yes. (§ 765.104(1)(a))	Not specified.
Georgia	Being defaced, obliterated, burned, canceled, torn, or destroyed by the declarant (or person in his presence at his direction). (§ 31-32-5(a)(1))	Yes. (§ 31-32-5(a)(2))	Yes. (§ 31-32-5(a)(2))	(1) Not specified. (§ 31-32-5(a)(2)) (2) Yes. (§ 31-32-5(a)(2))	Yes. (§ 31-32-5(a)(2))	Not specified. (§ 31-32-5(a)(2))

Hawaii	Can be revoked at any time and in any manner that communicates an intent to revoke. (§ 327E-4(b))	Yes, presumed. (§ 327E-4(b))	Not specified.	Not specified.	Not specified.	Not specified.
Idaho	Defacing, cancelling, burning, tearing, obliteration, or destroying by the declarant or another present person at the declarant's direction. (§ 39-4511(a) (see slip laws))	Yes. (§ 39-4511(b) (see slip laws))	Yes. (§ 39-4511(b) (see slip laws))	Can be revoked by destruction by some person in declarant's presence and by his direction. (§ 39-4511(a))	Not specified. (§ 39-4511)	Not specified. (§ 39-4511)
Illinois	Obliterating, burning, tearing, or otherwise destroying or defacing the declaration in a manner indicating an intent to cancel. (755 ILCS § 35/5(a)(1))	Yes. (755 ILCS § 35/5(a)(2))	Yes. (755 ILCS § 35/5(a)(2))	(1) Not specified. (2) Yes. (755 ILCS § 35/5(a)(2))	Yes. (755 ILCS § 35/5(a)(2))	Not specified. However, one witness is required if the revocation is oral, and then the declarant must sign and date a writing confirming that such expression of intent was made. (755 ILCS § 35/5(a)(3))
Indiana	A living will declaration can be revoked by physical cancellation or destruction of the declaration by the declarant or another person in the declarant's presence and at the declarant's direction. (§ 16-36-4-12(a)(2))	Yes. (§ 16-36-4-12(a)(1))	Yes. (§ 16-36-4-12(a)(1))	Not specified.	Yes. (§ 16-36-4-12(a) (1))	Not specified.
Iowa	Any manner by which the declarant is able to communicate his intent to revoke causes revocation. (§ 144A.4(1))	Yes (implied since any manner with intent satisfies). (§ 144A.4(1))	Not specified.	Not specified.	Not specified.	Not specified.

Table 7.03, Part 1
Revocation *(continued)*

			If a Writing, Is It Sufficient If:			
	What Physical Acts Accomplish This?	*By a Writing?*	*Signed by Declarant?*	*Signed by a Person (1) In His Presence and (2) At His Direction?*	*Dated?*	*Witnessed?*
Kansas	Being obliterated, burned, torn, or destroyed or defaced in a manner indicating intention to cancel. (§ 65-28,104(a)(1))	Yes. (§ 65-28, 104(a)(2))	Yes. (§ 65-28, 104(a)(2))	(1) Not specified. (§ 65-28,104(a)(2)) (2) Yes. (§ 65-28,104(a)(2))	Yes. (§ 65-28, 104(a)(2))	Not specified. (§ 65-28, 104(a)(2))
Kentucky	A directive may be revoked by destruction of the document by the grantor, or by some person in the grantor's presence and at the grantor's direction. (§ 311.627(1)(c))	Yes. (§ 311.627(1)(a))	Yes. (§ 311.627(1)(a))	Not specified.	Yes. (§ 311.627(1)(a))	Not specified.
Louisiana	Being defaced, canceled, obliterated, burned, torn, or destroyed by the declarant or someone in his presence and at his direction. (§ 40:1299.58.4(A)(1))	Yes. (§ 40:1299.58.4(A)(2))	Yes. (§ 40:1299.58.4(A)(2))	Not specified. (§ 40:1299.58.4(A)(2))	Yes. (§ 40:1299.58.4(A)(2))	Not specified. (§ 40:1299.58.4(A)(2))
Maine	An individual with capacity may revoke all or part of an advance health-care directive at any time and in any manner that communicates an intent to revoke. (18-A § 5-803(B))	Yes (presumed, since "any manner" is sufficient). (18-A § 5-803(B))	Not specified.	Not specified.	Not specified.	Not specified.

Maryland	"Physical cancellation" or destruction. (Health-Gen. § 5-604(a))	Yes. (Health-Gen. § 5-604(a))	Yes. (Health-Gen. § 5-604(a))	Not specified. (Health-Gen. § 5-604)	Yes. (Health-Gen. § 5-604(a))	Not specified. (Health-Gen. § 5-604)
Massachusetts[1]	Any act evidencing an intent to revoke. (201D § 7)	Yes. (201D § 7)	Not specified.	Not specified.	Not specified.	Not specified.
Michigan	N/A	N/A	N/A	N/A	N/A	N/A
Minnesota	Declaration can be revoked in any manner by the declarant. (§ 145B.09 (Subd. 1))	Yes (implied since can be revoked in any manner). (§ 145B.09 (Subd.1))	Not specified.	Not specified.	Not specified.	Not specified.
Mississippi	May be revoked "at any time and in any manner that communicates an intent to revoke." (§ 41-41-207(2))	Not specified.	No specified.	Not specified.	Not specified.	Not specified.
Missouri	Any manner by which the declarant is able to communicate his intent to revoke causes revocation. (§ 459.020(1))	Yes. (§§ 459.015(3), 459.020(1))	Yes (as indicated in the statutory form). (§ 459.015(3))	Not specified. (§ 459.015(3))	Yes (as indicated in the statutory form). (§ 459.015(3))	No (not required in the statutory form). (§ 459.015(3))
Montana	A declarant may revoke a declaration at any time and in any manner, without regard to mental or physical condition. Such declaration must be communicated to the attending physician. (§ 50-9-104(1))	Presumably, since any manner is sufficient. (§ 50-9-104(1))	Not specified.	Not specified.	Not specified.	Not specified.
Nebraska	Declaration may be revoked "at any time" and in "any manner." (§ 20-406(1))	Yes, presumably, since "any manner" is sufficient. (§ 20-406(1))	Not specified.	Not specified.	Not specified.	Not specified.

Table 7.03, Part 1
Revocation *(continued)*

			If a Writing, Is It Sufficient If:			
	What Physical Acts Accomplish This?	*By a Writing?*	*Signed by Declarant?*	*Signed by a Person (1) In His Presence*	*Dated?*	*Witnessed?*
Nevada	A declarant may revoke a declaration at any time and in any manner, without regard to mental or physical condition. Such declaration must be communicated to theattending physician or other health-care provider. (§ 449.620(1))	Yes, presumably, since "any manner" is sufficient. (§ 449.620(1))	Not specified.	Not specified.	Not specified.	Not specified.
New Hampshire	Burning, tearing, obliterating, or other act evidencing a specific intent to revoke or causing the same to be done by another person at the principal's direction and in the principal's presence. (§ 137-J:15(I)(a))	Yes. (§ 137-J:15(I)(a)-(b))	Yes. (§ 137-J:15(I)(a)-(b))	Not specified.	Yes, with respect to a written revocation but not necessarily by a subsequent executed advance directive. (§ 137-J:15(I)(a)-(b))	No, if written revocation. Yes, if by a subsequent executed advance directive, except if a notary is used. (§ 137-J:15(I)(a)-(b))
New Jersey	Oral or written notification to health care representative, physician, nurse/other health care person, or a reliable witness, execution of another advance directive, or any other act showing an intent to revoke. (§ 26:2H-57(b)(1) & (2))	Yes. (§ 26:2H-57(b)(1))	Not specified.	Not specified.	Not specified.	Not specified.
New Mexico	States any manner that communicates an intent to revoke. (§ 24-7A-3(B)) The statutory form	Yes (implied, since any manner qualifies). (§ 24-7A-3(B))	Not specified. (§ 24-7A-3(B))	Not specified. (§ 24-7A-3(B))	Not specified. (§ 24-7A-3(B))	Not specified. (§ 24-7A-3(B))

	allows for "personally informing the supervising healthcare provider." (§ 24-7A-4)					
New York	Any act evidencing a specific intent to revoke the proxy. (Pub. Health § 2985(1)(a))	Yes. (Pub. Health § 2985(1)(a))	Yes, presumably if in writing. (Pub. Health § 2985(1)(a))	Not specified.	Not specified.	Not specified.
North Carolina	Any manner by which the declarant is able to communicate his intent to revoke. (§ 90-321(e))	Yes (implied since any manner qualifies if intent is shown). (§ 90-321(e))	Not specified. (§ 90-321(e))	Not specified. (§ 90-321(e))	Not specified. (§ 90-321(e))	Not specified. (§ 90-321(e))
North Dakota	A health care directive is revoked by notification by the principal to the agent or a health care or long-term care services provider orally, or in writing, or by any other act evidencing a specific intent to revoke the directive; or by execution by the principal of a subsequent health care directive. (§23-06.5-07(1)(a) & (b))	Yes. (§ 23-06.5-07(1)(a)))	Not specified. (§ 23-06.5-07)	Not specified. (§ 23-06.5-07)	Not specified. (§ 23-06.5-07)	Not specified.
Ohio	Revocation can occur at any time and in any manner. (§ 2133.04(A))	Presumably yes since revocation can be done "in any manner." (§ 2133.04(A))	Not specified.	Not specified.	Not specified.	Not specified.
Oklahoma	Directive may be revoked in whole or in part at any time and in any manner by the declarant. (63 § 3101.6(A))	Yes (implied), since it can be revoked in any manner by the declarant. (63 § 3101.6(A))	Not specified.	Not specified. (63 § 3101.6(A))	Not specified. (63 § 3101.6(A))	Not specified. (63 § 3101.6(A))
Oregon	Revocation may occur at any time and in any manner that communicates the intent to revoke. (§ 127.545(1))	Presumably yes since "any manner." (§ 127.545(1))	Not specified but can be revoked at any time and in any manner by a	Not specified.	Not specified.	Not specified.

(cont'd)

Table 7.03, Part 1
Revocation *(continued)*

			If a Writing, Is It Sufficient If:			
	What Physical Acts Accomplish This?	*By a Writing?*	*Signed by Declarant?*	*Signed by a Person (1) In His Presence and (2) At His Direction?*	*Dated?*	*Witnessed?*
Oregon *(cont'd)*			capable principal. (§ 127.545(1)(b))			
Pennsylvania	Revocation may occur at any time and in any manner. (20 § 5444)	Presumably yes since "any manner" is sufficient. (20 § 5444)	Not specified.	Not specified.	Not specified.	Not specified.
Rhode Island	Any manner which communicates an intent to revoke. (§ 23-4.11-4(a)(1))	Presumably yes since "any manner." (§ 23-4.11-4(a)(1))	Not specified.	Not specified.	Not specified.	Not specified.
South Carolina	Being defaced, obliterated, torn, or otherwise destroyed in any manner indicating an intention to revoke. (§ 44-77-80(1))	Yes. (§ 44-77-80(2))	Yes. (§ 44-77-80(2))	Not specified, but can be revoked in writing by the declarant's designee. (§ 44-77-80(1) & (4))	Yes. (§ 44-77-80(2))	Not specified. (§ 44-77-80(2))
South Dakota	Declaration can be revoked at any time and in any manner. (§ 34-12D-8)	Presumably yes. (§ 34-12D-8)	Not specified.	Not specified.	Not specified.	Not specified.
Tennessee	Statute only refers to written or oral revocation. (§ 32-11-106)	Yes. (§ 32-11-106(1))	Yes. (§ 32-11-106(1))	Not specified. (§ 32-11-106(1))	Yes. (§ 32-11-106(1))	Not specified. (§ 32-11-106(1))
Texas	Being defaced, canceled, obliterated, burned, torn, or otherwise destroyed by the declarant or someone at his direction/presence. (Health & Safety § 166.042(a)(1))	Yes. (Health & Safety § 166.042(a)(2))	Yes. (Health & Safety § 166.042 (a)(2))	Not specified.	Yes. (Health & Safety § 166.042(a)(2))	Not specified.

Utah (2007)	Being obliterated, burned, torn, or otherwise destroyed or defaced in any manner indicating an intention to revoke. (§ 75-2-1111(1)(a))	Yes. (§ 75-2-1111(1)(b))	Yes. (§ 75-2-1111(1)(b))	(1) Not specified, but uses the term "on behalf." (§ 75-2-1111(1)(b)) (2) Yes. (§ 75-2-1111(1)(b))	Yes. (§ 75-2-1111(1)(b))	Not specified. (§ 75-2-1111(1)(b))
Utah (2008) The new law is effective Jan. 1, 2008. A health care directive executed prior to this date under the provisions then in effect, Ch. 2, pt. II, Personal Choice and Living Will, may, in good faith, be relied upon by a health care provider or health care facility. (§ 75-2a-1120(1)(b))	Being obliterated, burned, torn, or otherwise destroyed or defaced in any manner indicating an intention to revoke, including writing "void" across it. (§ 75-2a-1116)	Yes. (§ 75-2a-1116) Also by oral declaration. (Id.)	Yes. (§ 75-2a-1116)	Presence not specified. The person must be at the direction of the declarant. (§ 75-2a-1116)	Not specified.	Not specified. (§ 75-2a-1116)
Vermont	Burning, tearing, or obliterating by declarant or another in declarant's presence and at his direction. (18 § 9704 (b)(1)(C))	Yes. (18 § 9704(b)(1)(A))	Not specified.	Not specified.	Not specified	Not specified.
Virginia	"Physical cancellation" or destruction. (§ 54.1-2985)	Yes. (§ 54.1-2985)	Yes. (§ 54.1-2985)	Not specified. (§ 54.1-2985)	Yes. (§ 54.1-2985)	Not specified. (§ 54.1-2985)

Table 7.03, Part 1
Revocation *(continued)*

	What Physical Acts Accomplish This?	*By a Writing?*	*If a Writing, Is It Sufficient If:* *Signed by Declarant?*	*Signed by a Person (1) In His Presence and (2) At His Direction?*	*Dated?*	*Witnessed?*
Washington	Being defaced, canceled, obliterated, burned, torn, or otherwise destroyed by declarant or at his direction in his presence. (§ 70.122.040(1)(a))	Yes. (§ 70.122.040 (1)(b))	Yes. (§ 70.122.040(1) (b))	Not specified. (§ 70.122.040(1) (b))	Yes. (§ 70.122.040 (1)(b))	Not specified. (§ 70.122.040(1) (b))
West Virginia	By being destroyed by the declarant or someone at his direction *and* in his presence. (§ 16-30-18(a)(1))	Yes. (§ 16-30-18(a)(2))	Yes. (§ 16-30-18(a)(2))	(1) Not specified. (2) Yes. (§ 16-30-18(a)(2))	Yes. (§ 16-30-18(a)(2))	Not specified.
Wisconsin	By being cancelled, defaced, obliterated, burned, torn, or otherwise destroyed by declarant or another at declarant's direction and in declarant's presence. (§ 154.05(1)(a))	Yes. (§ 154.05(1)(b))	Yes. (§ 154.05(1)(b))	Not specified.	Yes. (§ 154.05(1)(b))	Not specified.
Wyoming	An individual with capacity may revoke all or part of an advance health care directive, other than the designation of an agent at any time and in any manner that communicates an intent to revoke. (§ 35-22-404(b) Revoking the designation of an agent must be in a signed writing. (§ 35-22-404(a))	Yes. (§ 35-22-404 (b)) Any oral revocation shall, as soon as possible, be documented in a writing signed and dated by the individual or a witness to the revocation. (§ 35-22-404(b))	Yes. (§ 35-22-404(b))	(1) Not specified. (§ 35-22-404) (2) Not specified. (§ 35-22-404)	Yes. (§ 35-22-404(b))	Not specified. (§ 35-22-404)

1. Only deals with health care proxies.

Table 7.03, Part 2
Revocation

	Verbally						
	Witnesses	*Capacity of Witnesses*	*Subsequent Confirmatory Writing by Witness Required*	*Requirement of Doctor Recording Notice of Revocation in Medical Record*	*Sufficient If Physician Sees Actual Confirmatory Writing Revoking Living Will?*	*Is Another Form of Notification Satisfactory?*	*If So, from Whom?*
Alabama	One witness is required for oral statement. (§ 22-8A-5(a)(3))	At least 19 years old. (§ 22-8A-5(a)(3))	Yes. (§ 22-8A-5(a)(3))	Yes. (§ 22-8A-5(a)(3))	Yes. A health care provider or attending physician must receive the writing. (§ 22-8A-5(a)(3))	Not specified. A health care provider or attending physician must receive the writing. (§ 22-8A-5(a)(3))	Not specified. (§ 22-8A-5(a)(3))
Alaska	Not specified, but implied that oral revocation satisfies since any manner qualifies. (§ 13.52.020(b), special rules apply to a principal suffering from mental illness (§ 13.52.020(c)). The communication is assumed likely to be given to a health care provider, agent, guardian, or surrogate, who is required to communicate it immediately to the supervising health care provider and any health care institution at which the patient is receiving care. (§ 13.52.020(d))	Not specified. See Col. 1.	Not specified. (§ 13.52.020(b))	Yes. (§ 13.52.020(c))	Not specified. (§ 13.52.020(c))	Yes. (§ 13.52.020(b))	Not specified. (§ 13.52.020)

Table 7.03, Part 2
Revocation *(continued)*

	Verbally						
	Witnesses	*Capacity of Witnesses*	*Subsequent Confirmatory Writing by Witness Required*	*Requirement of Doctor Recording Notice of*	*Sufficient If Physician Sees Actual Confirmatory*	*Is Another Form of Notification Satisfactory?*	*If So, from Whom?*
Arizona[1]	Not specified.	Not specified.	Not specified.	Not specified.	Not specified.	Not specified.	Not specified.
Arkansas[2]	Not specified.	Not specified.	Not specified.	Yes. (§ 20-17-204(b))	Not specified, but implied. (§ 20-17-204(a))	Yes, any communication from a witness to the revocation. (§ 20-17-204(a))	Yes, any communication from a witness to the revocation. (§ 20-17-204(a))
California	Not specified.	Not specified.	Not specified.	Yes. (Probate § 4731(a))	Not specified.	Revocation must be "communicated" to provider. (Probate § 4696)	Communication to provider can be from any provider, agent, conservator, or surrogate who is informed of revocation. (Probate § 4696)
Colorado	Oral revocation is permitted, but no witness requirement is specified. (§ 15-18-109)	Not specified. (§ 15-18-109)	Not specified. (§ 15-18-109)	Not specified. (§ 15-18-109)	Not specified.	Not specified. (§ 15-18-109)	Not specified. (§ 15-18-109)
Connecticut	Not specified, but statute refers to revocation "by the declarant." (§ 19a-579a(a))	Not specified.	Not specified.	Yes. (§ 19a-579a(b))	Not specified.	Revocation "at any time and in any manner" is satisfactory. (§ 19a-579a(a))	Not specified.

Delaware	A verbal revocation must be done in the presence of two competent persons, one of whom is a health care provider. (16 § 2504(a)(2))	Competent.	Yes. Witnesses must memorialize the revocation in writing. It must be signed and dated by both witnesses. (16 § 2504(b))	Yes. (16 § 2508(b))	Not specified, but presumed. (16 § 2504(b) & (c))	Any manner that communicates an intent to revoke is sufficient if done in the presence of two competent witnesses, one of whom is a health care provider. (16 § 2504(a)(2))	Not specified.
District of Columbia	Declarant must verbally revoke in the presence of a witness. (§ 7-624(a)(3))	Witness must be 18 years or older. (§ 7-624(a)(3))	Yes. (§ 7-624(a)(3))	Yes. (§ 7-624(a)(3))	Yes. (§ 7-624(a)(3))	Revocation effective upon "communication" to physician. (§ 7-624(a)(3))	Communication from declarant or person acting on his/her behalf. (§ 7-624(a)(3))
Florida[3]	Not specified.	Not specified.	Not specified.	Not specified, but implied in requirement that "advance directives shall travel with the patient as part of the patient's medical record." (§ 765.110(2))	Not specified.	Yes, effective when "communicated" to surrogate, health care provider or facility. (§ 765.104(3))	Yes, effective when "communicated" to surrogate, health care provider or facility. No specific party mentioned. (§ 765.104(3))
Georgia	Not specified, but communication to attending physician by declarant or at declarant's direction is required. (§ 31-32-5(a)(3))	Not specified.	Not specified.	Yes. (§ 31-32-5(a)(3))	Presumably. Sufficient if revocation is communicated to physician, by declarant or at declarant's direction. (§ 31-32-5(a)(3))	Yes. Revocation is effective upon "communication." (§ 31-32-5(a)(3))	A person acting at the direction of the declarant can notify the physician. (§ 31-32-5(a)(3))
Hawaii	Not specified.	Not specified.	Not specified.	Yes. (§ 327E-7(b))	Not specified.	Revocation shall be "communicated" to provider. (§ 327E-4(c))	Can be communicated by provider, agent, guardian, or surrogate who is informed of revocation. (§ 327E-4(c))

Table 7.03, Part 2
Revocation *(continued)*

	Verbally						
	Witnesses	*Capacity of Witnesses*	*Subsequent Confirmatory Writing by Witness Required*	*Requirement of Doctor Recording Notice of*	*Sufficient If Physician Sees Actual Confirmatory*	*Is Another Form of Notification Satisfactory?*	*If So, from Whom?*
Idaho	Not specified. (§ 39-4511)	Not specified. (§ 39-4511)	Not specified. (§ 39-4511)	Not specified. (§ 39-4511)	Not specified. (§ 39-4511)	Not specified. (§ 39-4511)	Not specified. (§ 39-4511)
Illinois[4]	One. (755 ILCS § 35/5(a)(3))	Not specified, but must be 18 or older. (755 ILCS § 35/5(a)(3))	Yes. (755 ILCS § 35/5(a)(3))	Yes. (755 ILCS § 35/5(b))	Yes. (755 ILCS § 35/5(b))	Revocation effective upon "communication" to physician, by declarant or witness. (755 ILCS § 35/5(b))	By a witness to the revocation. (755 ILCS § 35/5(b))
Indiana[5]	Not specified.	Not specified.	Not specified.	Not specified.	Revocation effective when "communicated" to physician (§ 16-36-4-12(b))	Not specified.	Not specified.
Iowa	Not specified. (§ 144A.4(1))	Not specified. (§ 144A.4(1))	Not specified. (§ 144A.4(1))	Yes. (§ 144A.4 (2))	Revocation effective only upon "communication" to attending physician. (§ 144A.4(1))	Revocation effective upon any communication. (§ 144A.4(1))	By declarant or by another to whom the revocation was communicated. (§ 144A.4(1))
Kansas	One witness. (§ 65-28,104(a) (3))	At least 18 years old. (§ 65-28, 104(a)(3))	Yes. (§ 65-28, 104(a)(3))	Yes. (§ 65-28, 104(a)(3))	Yes. (§ 65-28, 104(a)(3))	Not specified. (§ 65-28,104(a))	Not specified. (§ 65-28,104(a))
Kentucky	Must be revoked in the presence of two adults, one of whom shall be a health care provider. (§ 311.627(1)(b))	18 or older, and of sound mind. (§§ 311.627(1) (b), 311.621(1))	Not specified.	Yes. (§ 311.627(3))	Not specified.	Not specified.	Not specified.

Louisiana	Not specified, but can revoke verbally. (§ 40:1299.58.4 (A)(3)(a))	Not specified. (§ 40:1299.58.4 (A)(3)(a))	Not specified. (§ 40:1299.58.4 (A)(3)(a))	Yes. (§ 40:1299.58.4 (A)(3)(c))	Not specified. (§ 40:1299.58.4 (A)(3)(a))	Yes. Oral or non-verbal revocation effective upon "communication" to physician. (§ 40:1299.58.4 (A)(3)(b))	Not specified.
Maine[6]	Not specified.	Not specified.	Not specified.	Yes. (18-A § 5-807(B))	Not specified.	Any communication to physician or facility is presumably sufficient. (18-A § 5-803(C))	Revocation can be communicated by declarant, provider, agent, guardian, or surrogate. (18-A § 5-803(C))
Maryland	A health care practitioner and another witness are required to witness an oral revocation. (Health-Gen. § 5-604(b))	One witness must be a health care practitioner. (Health-Gen. § 5-604(a))	Yes. (Health-Gen. § 5-604(b))	Yes. (Health-Gen. § 5-604(b))	Not specified. (Health-Gen. § 5-604)	Not specified. (Health-Gen. § 5-604)	Not specified. (Health-Gen. § 5-604)
Massachusetts[7]	Not specified.	Not specified.	Not specified.	Yes. (201D § 7)	Presumably yes, since any act is used. (201D § 7)	Yes, by the principal informing the agent or nursing staff who then will tell the attending physician. (201D § 7)	By the principal informing the agent or nursing staff who then will tell the attending physician. (201D § 7)
Michigan	N/A	N/A	N/A	N/A	N/A	N/A	N/A
Minnesota	Not specified. (§ 145B.09 (Subd.1))	Not specified.	Not specified.	Yes. (§ 145B.09 (Subd. 1))	Presumably yes. (§ 145B.09 (Subd.1))	Yes, effective when declarant "communicates" revocation to physician. (§ 145B.09 (Subd.1))	None other than declarant specified. (§ 145B.09 (Subd.1))
Mississippi	Not specified, only states that the *(cont'd)*	Not specified.	Merely requires that health care *(cont'd)*	Yes, with respect to a supervising *(cont'd)*	Not specified.	Not specified.	Not specified.

Table 7.03, Part 2
Revocation *(continued)*

	Verbally						
	Witnesses	*Capacity of Witnesses*	*Subsequent Confirmatory Writing by Witness Required*	*Requirement of Doctor Recording Notice of*	*Sufficient If Physician Sees Actual Confirmatory*	*Is Another Form of Notification Satisfactory?*	*If So, from Whom?*
Mississippi *(cont'd)*	advance health-care directive may be revoked "at any time and in any manner that communicates an intent to revoke." (§ 41-41-207(2))		provider, agent, guardian, or surrogate "promptly communicate the fact of the revocation to the supervising health care provider and to any health care institution at which the patient is receiving care." (§ 41-41-207(3))	health care provider. (§ 41-41-215(2))			
Missouri	Not specified, but any manner by which the declarant is able to communicate his intent to revoke causes revocation. Statute does not specify number of witnesses, if any, needed. (§ 459.020(1))	Not specified. (§ 459.020(1))	Not specified. (§ 459.020(1))	Yes. (§ 459.020(2))	Not specified. (§ 459.020(2))	Not specified. (§ 459.020(2))	Not specified. (§ 459.020(2))
Montana[8]	Not specified.	Not specified.	Not specified.	Yes. (§ 50-9-104(2))	Yes, presumably. (§ 50-9-104(1))	Revocation is effective upon "communication" to physician or provider by declarant or witness. (§ 50-9-104(1))	Presumably, anyone can serve as a witness to a revocation as long as it is communicated to the physician. (§ 50-9-104(1))

Nebraska	Not specified, but communication to physician by a witness is sufficient. (§ 20-406(1))	Not specified.	Not specified.	Yes. (§ 20-406(2))	Yes, presumably. (§ 20-406(1))	Any communication from a witness to the revocation. (§ 20-406(1))	Presumably, any one can serve as a witness, as long as revocation is communicated tothe physician. (§ 20-406(1))
Nevada[9]	Not specified, but communication to physician by a witness is sufficient. (§ 449.620(1))	Not specified.	Not specified.	Yes, if unformed. (§ 449.620(2))	Yes, presumably. (§ 449.620(1))	Yes, any "communication" to physician. (§ 449.620(1))	By declarant or a witness. (§ 449.620(1))
New Hampshire	Yes, at least two witnesses. (§ 137-J:15(I)(a))	No witness can be the principal's spouse or heir at law. (§ 137-J:15(I)(a))	Not specified.	Yes, if unformed. (§ 137-J:15(II))	Yes, presumably, although statute only refers to duty of person to make physician or ARNP aware of revocation and does not explicitly require physician or ARNP to follow it. (§ 137-J:7(I)(b))	By filing of divorce, legal separation, annulment or protective order between principal and agent, except if there is another agent. Also by court order. (§ 137-J:15(I)(c))	See prior column.
New Jersey[10]	Written or oral notification of revocation to a witness is sufficient. (§ 26:2H-57(b)(1))	Notification of revocation can be made to health care representative, physician, nurse, or other reliable witness. (§ 26:2H-57(b)(1))	Not specified.	Yes. (§ 26:2H-62(a))	Yes, presumably. (§ 26:2H-57(e))	Revocation effective upon "communication" to any person capable of transmitting the information. (§ 26:2H-57(e))	Presumably, anyone who communicates the revocation. (§ 26:2H-57(e))
New Mexico	Not specified. (§ 24-7A-3(B))	Not specified. (§ 24-7A-3(B))	Not specified. (§ 24-7A-3(B))	Yes. (§ 24-7A-7(B))	Not specified. (§ 24-7A-3(B))	Communication of revocation is required. (§ 24-7A-3(C))	Communication to physician can be by health care provider, agent,

(cont'd)

Table 7.03, Part 2
Revocation *(continued)*

	Verbally						
	Witnesses	*Capacity of Witnesses*	*Subsequent Confirmatory Writing by Witness Required*	*Requirement of Doctor Recording Notice of*	*Sufficient If Physician Sees Actual Confirmatory*	*Is Another Form of Notification Satisfactory?*	*If So, from Whom?*
New Mexico *(cont'd)*							guardian, or surrogate. (§ 24-7A-3 (C))
New York	Not specified.	Not specified.	Not specified, except that a physician informed of or provided with a revocation must record it. (Pub. Health § 2985(2)(a)(i))	Yes, presumably. (Pub. Health § 2985(2)(a))	Yes. (Pub. Health § 2985(2)(a)(i))	It is satisfactory by notifying the agent or a health care provider orally or in writing or by any other act evidencing a specific intent to revoke the proxy. (Pub. Health § 2985(1)(a))	Health care agent. (Pub. Health § 2985(1)(a))
North Carolina	Not specified, but revocation is effective only upon communication to the attending physician by declarant or an individual acting on his behalf. (§ 90-321(e))	Not specified. (§ 90-321(e))	Not specified. (§ 90-321(e))	Not specified. (§ 90-321(e))	Yes, presumed. (§ 90-321(e)	Revocation effective upon "communication" to physician. (§ 90-321(e))	By declarant or an individual acting on his behalf. (§ 90-321(e))
North Dakota[11]	Not specified. (§ 23-06.5-07)	Not specified. (§ 23-06.5-07)	Not specified. (§ 23-06.5-07)	Yes. (§ 23-06.5-07(2))	Yes, presumed. (§ 23-06.5-07(1) (a))	Revocation effective upon "notification" to physician. (§ 23-06.5-07(1)(a))	Only principal is specified. (§ 23-06.5-07(2))
Ohio	Not specified.	Not specified.	Not specified.	Yes. (§ 2133.04(B))	Yes, presumed. (§ 2133.04(A))	Revocation effective upon its "communication" to attending	Communication can be from declarant, a witness to the revocation, or other health care

						physician. (§ 2133.04(A))	personnel to whom witness communicates the revocation. (§ 2133.04(A))
Oklahoma	Not specified.	Not specified. (63 § 3101.6(A))	Not specified. (63 § 3101.6(A))	Yes. (63 § 3101.6(B))	Yes, presumed. (63 § 3101.6(A))	Revocation is effective upon "communication" to attending physician. (63 § 3101.6(A))	Communication can be by declarant or a witness to the revocation. (63 § 3101.6(A))
Oregon[12]	Not specified.	Not specified.	Not specified.	Yes. (§ 127.545(3))	Presumably yes. (§ 127.545(2))	Revocation is effective upon "communication" by principal to attending physician, provider, or health care representative. If made to representative, the representative must inform physician or provider. (§ 127.545(2))	The health care representative who then notifies the attending or health care provider. (§ 127.545(2))
Pennsylvania[13]	Not specified.	Not specified.	Not specified.	Yes. (20 § 5444)	Presumably yes since "communication" used. (20 § 5444)	Revocation effective upon "communication" to physician or provider. (20 § 5444)	Communication can be by declarant or a witness to the revocation. (20 § 5444)
Rhode Island[14]	Not specified.	Not specified.	Not specified.	Yes. (§ 23-4.11-4(a)(2))	Presumably yes since "any communication" is effective. (§ 23-4.11-4(a)(1))	Revocation effective as to physician or provider upon "communication" to that physician or provider. (§ 23-4.11-4(a)(1))	Communication can be by declarant or another who witnessed the revocation. (§ 23-4.11-4(a)(1))
South Carolina	Not specified, but oral revocation is *(cont'd)*	Not specified.	No (revocation must only be "com- *(cont'd)*	Yes. (§ 44-77-80(3))	Presumably yes. (§ 44-77-80(3))	Revocation effective upon *(cont'd)*	Communication can be directly *(cont'd)*

Table 7.03, Part 2
Revocation *(continued)*

	Verbally						
	Witnesses	*Capacity of Witnesses*	*Subsequent Confirmatory*	*Requirement of Doctor Recording Notice of*	*Sufficient If Physician Sees Actual*	*Is Another Form of Notification Satisfactory?*	*If So, from Whom?*
South Carolina *(cont'd)*	effective if communicated to physician by a witness. (§ 44-77-80(3))		municated" to physician within a reasonable time). (§ 44-77-80(3))			"communication" to physician. (§ 44-77-80(3))	from declarant to the attending physician or from another witness if declarant is not capable of communicating. (§ 44-77-80(3))
South Dakota[15]	Not specified.	Not specified.	Not specified.	Yes. (§ 34-12D-8)	Presumably yes since communication used. (§ 34-12D-8)	Revocation effective upon "communication" to physician or provider. (§ 34-12D-8)	Not specified.
Tennessee	Oral revocation must be made "to the attending physician." (§ 32-11-106(2))	Not specified (only attending physician can witness). (§ 32-11-106(2))	N/A	Yes. (§ 32-11-106(2))	States only that oral statement or revocation is to be made "by the declarant to the attending physician." (§ 32-11-106(2))	Not specified. (§ 32-11-106(2))	Not specified. (§ 32-11-106(2))
Texas	Oral revocation is permitted, but unspecified if any witnesses needed. (Health & Safety § 166.042(a)(3))	Not specified.	Not specified.	Yes. Physician must also enter the word "void" on each page of the directive in the record. (Health & Safety § 166.042(c))	Yes, presumed, since any "notification" is sufficient. (Health & Safety § 166.042(c))	Revocation effec tive upon any "notification" of physician. (Health &Safety § 166.042(c))	Notification to the physician can be by the declarant or a person acting on his/her behalf. (Health & Safety § 166.042(c))

Utah (2007)	One witness. (§ 75-2-1111(1) (c))	At least 18 years old. (§ 75-2-1111 (1) (c))	Yes. (§ 75-2-1111(1) (c))	Yes. (§ 75-2-1111(2))	Yes, attending physician must see the writing. (§ 75-2-1111(2))	No. (§ 75-2-1111(2))	N/A
Utah (2008) The new law is effective Jan. 1, 2008. A health care directive executed prior to this date under the provisions then in effect, Ch. 2, pt. II, Personal Choice and Living Will, may, in good faith, be relied upon by a health care provider or health care facility. (§ 75-2a-1120(1)(b))	One witness in the case of an oral directive.(§ 75-2a-1113(1)(e))	At least 18 years old. (§ 75-2a-1113 (1)(e))	Not specified.	Yes. (§ 75-2a-1114(1)(b)(1))	The health care provider must be notified of the existence of the revocation. (§ 75-2a-1114(1))	No specific type of notifications specified. (§ 75-2a-1114(1))	N/A
Vermont	Not specified. (18 § 9704)	Not specified. (18 § 9704)	Not specified. (18 § 9704)	Yes. (18 § 9704 ((c)(1)(C))	Yes, presumably. (18 § 9704(c)(1) (A))	Yes, presumably. (18 § 9704(c)(1) (A))	Not specified. (18 § 9704)
Virginia	Not specified, only mentions oral expression of intent to revoke. (§ 54.1-2985)	Not specified. (§ 54.1-2985)	Not specified. (§ 54.1-2985)	Not specified. (§ 54.1-2985)	Not specified. (§ 54.1-2985)	Revocation effective when "communicated" to physician. (§ 54.1-2985)	Implied that any person can communicate the revoca tion to the attending physician. (§ 54.1-2985)
Washington	Not specified, but oral communication to the attending physician by the declarant or by a *(cont'd)*	Not specified. (§ 70.122.040(1) (c))	Not specified. (§ 70.122.040(1) (c))	Yes. (§ 70.122.040(1) (b) & (c))	Yes, presumed. (§ 70.122.040(1) (c))	Revocation effective upon "communication" to physician. *(cont'd)*	Communication can be by declarant or someone acting on his/ her behalf. *(cont'd)*

Table 7.03, Part 2
Revocation *(continued)*

	Verbally						
	Witnesses	*Capacity of Witnesses*	*Subsequent Confirmatory Writing by Witness Required*	*Requirement of Doctor Recording Notice of Revocation in Medical Record*	*Sufficient If Physician Sees Actual Confirmatory*	*Is Another Form of Notification Satisfactory?*	*If So, from Whom?*
Washington *(cont'd)*	person acting on the behalf of the declarant is required. (§ 70.122.040(1)(c))					(§ 70.122.040 (1)(c))	(§ 70.122.040 (1)(c))
West Virginia	One witness. (§ 16-30-18(a)(3))	At least 18 years old. (§ 16-30-18(a)(3))	Yes. (§ 16-30-18(a)(3))	Yes. (§ 16-30-18(a)(2) & (3))	Yes, presumed. (§ 16-30-18(a)(3))	Verbal revocation is effective only upon communication to physician. (§ 16-30-18(a)(3))	Communication to the physician can be by the declarant or a person acting on his behalf. (§ 16-30-18(a)(3))
Wisconsin	Not specified.	Not specified.	Not specified.	Yes. (§ 154.05(2))	Not specified, but presumed. (§ 154.05(1)(c))	Revocation effective only if physician is "notified." (§ 154.05(1)(c))	Notification can be by declarant or person acting on declarant's behalf. (§ 154.05(1)(c))
Wyoming	Witness to oral revocation can sign subsequent written document memorializing revocation in lieu of the individual. (§ 35-22-404(b))	Not specified.	Possibly. If individual does not sign subsequent written document memorializing revocation,	No, but must communicate the fact of the revocation to the primary health care provider and to any heath care	Yes, presumed. (§ 35-22-404)	Revocation effective when health care provider is "informed" of it. (§35-22-404(c).	Not specified. (§ 35-22-404)

witness must. (§ 35-22-404(b))	insitution at which the patient is receiving care. (§ 35-22-404(c))

1. The patient can make an oral revocation of a health-care directive by notifying the patient's guardian for health care or health care provider. (§36-3202(2)) Note also that the information as to Arizona relates to "health-care directives" and not to "living wills."
2. Generally any communication, so revocation can be verbal. (§20-17-204(a))
3. Can do it verbally. (§765.104(1)(c))
4. Oral revocation is authorized. (755 ILCS §35/5(a)(3))
5. A living will declaration can be revoked by an oral expression of intent to revoke. (§16-36-4-12(a)(3))
6. An individual with capacity may revoke all or part of an advance health-care directive at any time and in any manner that communicates an intent to revoke. (18-A §5-803(b))
7. Only deals with health care proxies. Revocation is automatic when a new health care proxy is executed or there is a divorce and the former spouse was the agent. (*Id.*) (201D §7)
8. A declarant may revoke a declaration at any time and in any manner, without regard to mental or physical condition. Such declaration must be communicated to the attending physician. (§50-9-104(1))
9. A declarant may revoke a declaration at any time and in any manner, without regard to mental or physical condition. Such declaration must be communicated to the attending physician or other health care provider. (§449.620(1))
10. Oral revocation is authorized. (§26:2H-57(b)(1))
11. A declaration may be revoked by an oral expression of intent to revoke. (§23-06.4-05(1)(c))
12. Presumably, verbal revocation is effective, since "any manner" is used. (§127.545(1))
13. Presumably, verbal revocation is effective, since "any manner" is used. (20 §5406(a))
14. Presumably, verbal revocation is effective, since "any manner" is used. (§23-4.11-4(a)(1))
15. Presumably, verbal revocation is effective, since "any manner" is used. (§34-12D-8)

Table 7.04
Civil or Criminal Liability for Failure to Act

	Is There Any Civil or Criminal Liability for Failing to Act Without Actual Knowledge?	*Is There Any Civil or Criminal Liability for Failing to Act With Actual Knowledge?*	*Is a Physician's Confirmation of a Terminal Condition in Writing Required Before the Living Will Can Be Given Effect?*	*Is the Physician Liable If There Is Mistaken Withholding or Withdrawing of Life Support?*	*Is There Criminal Liability for Destroying a Living Will?*	*Is There Criminal Liability for Forging a Living Will?*
Alabama	No. (§ 22-8A-5(b))	Yes. (§ 22-8A-5(b))	Yes, it must be "documented" in the medical record by two physicians. (§ 22-8A-4(d))	Physician not liable if acted in good faith, pursuant to reasonable medical standards and without actual knowledge of revocation. (§ 22-8A-7(c))	Yes, if destroyed without declarant's consent. (§ 22-8A-8(c))	Yes. (§ 22-8A-8(d))
Alaska	There is no liability without intent to violate the law or to intentionally falsify, forge, conceal, deface, or obliterate a health care directive or coerce an individual or fraudulently induce to give, revoke, or not give an advanced directive. (§ 13.52.090 (b))	See Col. 1. If there is the requisite intent, liability is the greater of $10,000 or actual damages. (§ 13.52.090(a))	No, but physician is required to make confirmation part of declarant's medical record. (§ 13.52.160)	No. (§ 13.52.080) The standard that must be met is "reasonable efforts, with a level of diligence appropriate to the seriousness and urgency of the situation . . ." In addition, the health care provider must act in good faith and in "accordance with generally accepted health care standards applicable to health care provider."	Although not specified in this chapter, it is recognized as a possibility. (§ 13.52.080(a))	Equitable relief may be available. (§ 13.52.140(a))

Arizona	Surrogates, guardians for health care and health care providers are not subject to civil or criminal liability if they act in good faith. (§§ 36-3203 (D), 36-3205(A)) A surrogate acts in good faith if the surrogate "acts [or refuses] to act based on [the] surrogate's reasonable belief of [the] patient's desires. . . . " (§ 36-3203(D)) A health care provider acts in good faith if the provider acts or refuses to act in reliance on the provisions of a health-care directive or directions of a surrogate. (§ 36-3205(B)) A health care provider is not subject to civil or criminal liability if the provider fails to comply with a direction that violates the provider's conscience, provided that the provider *(cont'd)*	Surrogates, guardians for health care and health care providers are not subject to civil or criminal liability if they act in good faith. (§§ 36-3203 (D), 36-3205(A)) A surrogate acts in good faith if the surrogate "acts [or refuses] to act based on [the] surrogate's reasonable belief of [the] patient's desires. . . . " (§ 36-3203(D)) A health care provider acts in good faith if the provider acts or refuses to act in reliance on the provisions of a health-care directive or directions of a surrogate. (§ 36-3205(B)) A health care provider is not subject to civil or criminal liability if the provider fails to comply with a direction that violates the provider's conscience, provided that the provider *(cont'd)*	Not specified.	Health care providers are not released from civil or criminal liability for the negligent treatment of a patient if the negligence is unrelated to the provider's reliance on a health care directive or directions from a surrogate. (§ 36-3205(D))	Not specified.	Not specified.

Table 7.04
Civil or Criminal Liability for Failure to Act *(continued)*

	Is There Any Civil or Criminal Liability for Failing to Act Without Actual Knowledge?	*Is There Any Civil or Criminal Liability for Failing to Act With Actual Knowledge?*	*Is a Physician's Confirmation of a Terminal Condition in Writing Required Before the Living*	*Is the Physician Liable If There Is Mistaken Withholding or Withdrawing of Life Support?*	*Is There Criminal Liability for Destroying a Living Will?*	*Is There Criminal Liability for Forging a Living Will?*
Arizona *(cont'd)*	transfer the patient to a health care provider who will comply with the patient's or guardian's directions. (§ 36-3205(C))	transfer the patient to a health care provider who will comply with the patient's or guardian's directions. (§ 36-3205(C))				
Arkansas	No. (§ 20-17-208 (a))	If the physician will not comply, then that person must transfer the patient to another physician. (§ 20-17-207) If the person fails to transfer the patient then that person is guilty of a Class A misdemeanor. (§ 20-17-209(a)) Any person who withholds personal knowledge of a revocation is guilty of a Class D felony. (§ 20-17-209(d))	Declaration becomes effective when (i) communicated to physician and (ii) attending physician and another physician in consultation determines that declarant is in terminal condition, unable to make medical decisions, or permanently unconscious. Although this determination must be entered in the declarant's medical record, a writing is not specifically required for effectiveness. (§ 20-17-203)	No, so long as the physician's actions comport with "reasonable medical standards." (§ 20-17-208(b))	Yes, if without the declarant's consent. (§ 20-17-209(c))	Yes. (§ 20-17-209(d))

California	No, so long as in good faith. (Probate § 4741)	Civilliability for any intentional violation. (Probate § 4742(a))	Yes. (Probate § 4732)	No. (Probate § 4740(c))	Yes. Only civil damages specified. (Probate § 4742(b))	Yes. (Probate § 4743)
Colorado	No. (§ 15-18-110)	Only states that it is unprofessional conduct, but physician can transfer care. (§ 15-18-113(5))	Yes. (§ 15-18-107)	No, with respect to an apparently valid declaration and in the absence of actual knowledge of revocation, fraud, or improper execution. (§ 15-18-110(1))	Yes, if destroyed without the declarant's knowledge and consent. (§ 15-18-113(1))	Yes. (§ 15-18-113 (2) &(3))
Connecticut	Not specified.	Affirmative duty to transfer patient but no mention of liability. (§ 19a-580a)	Living will becomes operative when (1) furnished to physician and (2) physician determines declarant to be incapacitated. Writing not specifically required. (§ 19a-579) However, within a reasonable time prior to withholding or causing the removal of any life support system, the attending physician must make reasonable efforts to notify the declarant's health care representative, next-of-kin, guardian, conservator, or other person designated for decision–making under § 1-56r. (§ 19a-580).	No. (§ 19a-579a(c))	Not specified.	Not specified.

Table 7.04
Civil or Criminal Liability for Failure to Act *(continued)*

	Is There Any Civil or Criminal Liability for Failing to Act Without Actual Knowledge?	*Is There Any Civil or Criminal Liability for Failing to Act With Actual Knowledge?*	*Is a Physician's Confirmation of a Terminal Condition in Writing Required Before the Living Will Can Be Given Effect?*	*Is the Physician Liable If There Is Mistaken Withholding or Withdrawing of Life Support?*	*Is There Criminal Liability for Destroying a Living Will?*	*Is There Criminal Liability for Forging a Living Will?*
Delaware	No liability for providing treatment in an emergency if existence of health-care directive is unknown. (16 § 2510(a)(4))	No liability for declining to comply with advance health-care directive because the instruction is contrary to conscious or good faith medical judgment of the provider or the written policies of the institution. (16 § 2510(a)(5)) See also 16 § 2508(e)-(g), which allows declining to comply if it is for reasons of conscience (e), or medically ineffective treatment or health care, although the patient must be promptly informed and the health care provider must provide continuing care, including continuing life sustaining care, to the patient until a transfer can be effected; and not	Advance health-care directive becomes effective after "determination" that declarant lacks capacity. Writing not specifically required. (16 § 2503(c))	No liability if, in good faith and according to generally accepted standards, advance health-care directive is complied with and lack of revocation or termination is assumed. (16 § 2510(a)(3))	Not specified.	Not specified.

		impede the transfer of the patient to another health care provider or institution identified by the patient, the patient's agent or the patient's surrogate (g).)				
District of Columbia	Not specified. (§ 7-627(a))	Physicians who cannot comply with declaration must effect a transfer of the patient. Failure to transfer shall constitute unprofessional conduct. Civil or criminal liability not specified. (§ 7-627(b))	Yes. (§ 7-625)	There is no civil or criminal liability for failure to act on a revocation of a declaration unless such person has actual knowledge of the revocation. (§ 7-624(b))	Yes, if without the declarant's consent. (§ 7-627(c))	Yes, if contrary to wishes of declarant and if it results in hastening of death. (§ 7-627(d))
Florida	No, with respect to an amendment or revocation. (§ 765.104(3))	Must transfer if refusal to comply based on moral or ethical beliefs, but no mention of liability. (§ 765.1105)	Yes, in the medical record. (§ 765.306)	No. (§ 765.104(3))	Yes, if without principal's consent. (§ 765.1115(1))	Yes. (§ 765.1115(2))
Georgia	Not specified, but probably no civil liability. (§ 31-32-8(b))	No civil liability for failing to comply with living will in good faith. Physician refusing to comply shall notify next of kin and either transfer patient or allow next of kin to obtain another physician. (§ 31-32-8(b))	Yes. (§ 31-32-8(a)(2))	No. (§ 31-32-5(b))	Yes, if destroyed without the declarant's consent. (§ 31-32-10)	Yes, if directly intends and causes life-sustaining procedures to be withdrawn/withheld contrary to the wishes of the declarant and, consequently, death is hastened. (§ 31-32-10)

Table 7.04
Civil or Criminal Liability for Failure to Act *(continued)*

	Is There Any Civil or Criminal Liability for Failing to Act Without Actual Knowledge?	*Is There Any Civil or Criminal Liability for Failing to Act With Actual Knowledge?*	*Is a Physician's Confirmation of a Terminal Condition in Writing Required Before the Living Will Can Be Given Effect?*	*Is the Physician Liable If There Is Mistaken Withholding or Withdrawing of Life Support?*	*Is There Criminal Liability for Destroying a Living Will?*	*Is There Criminal Liability for Forging a Living Will?*
Hawaii	No. (§ 327E-9(a)(3))	Not if based on good faith belief that person lacked authority. (§ 327E-9(a)(2))	Yes. (§ 327E-7(c))	No. (§ 327E-9(a)(3))	Only civil damages specified. (§ 327E-10)	Only civil damages specified. (§ 327E-10)
Idaho	No criminal or civil liability for acts in good faith. (§ 39-4513(1))	Physician who cannot comply for ethical or professional reasons may withdraw without incurring liability provided he/she makes a good faith effort to assist in obtaining another physician. (§ 39-4513(2) (see slip laws))	Not specified. (§ 39-4510)	No. (§ 39-4513)	Not specified.	Not specified.
Illinois	No (implied). (755 ILCS § 35/8(c))	Yes, if physician fails to notify patient of unwillingness to comply. (755 ILCS § 35/8(c)&(d))	Yes. (755 ILCS § 35/6)	No. (755 ILCS § 35/5(c))	No, civil liability only. (755 ILCS § 35/8(a))	Yes, if contrary to wishes of patient thereby hastening death. (755 ILCS § 35/8(b))
Indiana	Not specified.	Not specified, but physicians violating transfer provisions of § 16-36-4-13(e) are subject to	Yes. (§ 16-36-4-13)	There is no civil or criminal liability for failing to act upon a revocation unless the person	Yes, if without the declarant's consent. (§ 16-36-4-15)	Yes. (§ 16-36-4-16)

		disciplinary sanctions. (§ 16-36-4-21)		had actual knowledge of the revocation. (§ 16-36-4-12(c))		
Iowa	Not specified, but no liability for actions in accord with reasonable medical standards. (§ 144A.9(2))	Not specified, but no liability for actions in accord with reasonable medical standards. (§ 144A.9(2)) Compliance with statute is absolute defense. (§ 144A.9 (3)) If physician or provider cannot comply, transfer shall be effected. (§ 144A.8)	The physician is required to record determination of terminal condition in the declarant's record. It is unclear whether it is required before the living will can be given effect. (§ 144A.5)	No. (§ 144A.9(1)(a))	Yes, if destroyed without the declarant's consent. (§ 144A.10(1))	Yes. (§ 144A.10(2))
Kansas	Not specified.	Only states that it constitutes unprofessional conduct if physician does not comply with declaration and fails to transfer patient to another physician. (§ 65-28,107(a))	Yes. (§ 65-28,105)	No. (§ 65-28,104(b))	Yes, if destroyed without the declarant's consent. (§ 65-28,107(b))	Yes, if directly intends and causes life-sustaining procedures to be withdrawn/withheld contrary to the wishes of the declarant and, consequently, death is hastened. (§ 65-28,107(c))
Kentucky	Not specified.	Not specified, but physicians and facilities refusing to comply with living will directive shall notify patient (or responsible party) of *(cont'd)*	Not specified.	No health care provider shall be subject to any liability for acting in good faith upon the knowledge, or lack thereof, of the *(cont'd)*	Not specified. The destruction of a living will does result in civil liability. (§ 311.641(1))	Yes. (§ 311.641(2))

Table 7.04
Civil or Criminal Liability for Failure to Act *(continued)*

	Is There Any Civil or Criminal Liability for Failing to Act Without Actual Knowledge?	*Is There Any Civil or Criminal Liability for Failing to Act With Actual Knowledge?*	*Is a Physician's Confirmation of a Terminal Condition in Writing Required Before the Living Will Can Be Given Effect?*	*Is the Physician Liable If There Is Mistaken Withholding or Withdrawing of Life Support?*	*Is There Criminal Liability for Destroying a Living Will?*	*Is There Criminal Liability for Forging a Living Will?*
Kentucky *(cont'd)*		refusal and seek a transfer. (§ 311.633 (2)) If notification and transfer not carried out, physician or facility may be liable. (§ 311.635)		existence of a revocation of a living will directive. (§ 311.627(3))		
Louisiana	Not specified.	Not specified, but only states that if physician cannot comply, he shall transfer patient to another physician. (§ 40:1299.58.7(B))	Yes. (§ 40:1299.58.7(A))	Not specified, but states that health care worker can assume that the declaration is valid until notified of revocation. (§ 40:1299.58.4(B))	Not specified. Destruction without consent does result in civil liability. (§ 40:1299.58.9 (A))	Yes, if directly causes life-sustaining procedures to be withdrawn/withheld contrary to the wishes of the declarant and, consequently, death is hastened. (§ 40:1299.58.9(B))
Maine	Not specified.	No liability for declining to comply if based on belief that person lacked capacity or that decision did not comply with statute. (18-A § 5-809(A)(2)) Otherwise, a provider or institution intentionally	Physician is required to note condition in the patient's record. It is unclear whether it is required before the living will can be given effect. (18-A § 5-807(C))	A health care provider acting in good faith and in accordance with generally accepted health care standards is not subject to civil or criminal liability for complying with a health-care directive and assuming that	No. Person is subject to civilliability. (18-A § 5-810(B))	No. Person is subject to civilliability. (18-A § 5-810(B))

		violating the statute is liable for, including the notification and transfer requirements of 18-A § 5-807(G), damages. (18-A § 5-810(A))		the directive is valid and has not been revoked or terminated. (18-A § 5-809(A)(3))		
Maryland	Not specified, but the health care provider should make every reasonable effort to transfer the patient. Also, the statute does not authorize the provider to provide health care over the objection of competent individuals. (Health-Gen. § 5-613)	Not specified, but the health care provider should make every reasonable effort to transfer the patient. Also, the statute does not authorize the provider to provide health care over the objection of competent individuals. (Health-Gen. § 5-613)	Yes. (Health-Gen. § 5-606(b)(1))	Not specified, but generally, not if the physician acted in good faith. (Health-Gen. § 5-609(c))	Yes, if without the declarant's consent and thereby contravenes the intent of the patient. (Health-Gen. § 5-610(a))	Yes, if contravenes the intent of the patient and death is hastened. (Health-Gen. § 5-610(b))
Massachusetts[1]	Not specified.	Must transfer patient but no mention of liability. (201D § 14)	Not specified.	No (implied) if it is done in good faith. (201D § 8)	Not specified.	Not specified.
Michigan	[Note: By making available to the patient, surrogate, or advocate, a specified written summary of alternative treatments, the physician will have fulfilled the requirement of § 333.5655 to make such information known. If a physician also makes available a form indicating that required oral notice under § 333.5654 and written notice under § 333.5655, then the physician is also required to seek signature by the patient, surrogate, or advocate. Once signed, a copy of the form shall be placed in the patient's record. This will bar suit by the signer based on failure to obtain informed consent. (§ 333.5657)]					
Minnesota	Not specified.	Not specified, but states that if cannot comply, the declarant can be transferred. (§ 145B.06 (Subd. 1))	Not specified.	Not specified, only states physician's actions after diagnosis must be based on reasonable medical practice. (§ 145B.13)	Yes, if without the declarant's consent. (§ 145B.105, subdivision (1))	Yes. (§ 145B.105, subdivision (3))

Table 7.04
Civil or Criminal Liability for Failure to Act *(continued)*

	Is There Any Civil or Criminal Liability for Failing to Act Without Actual Knowledge?	*Is There Any Civil or Criminal Liability for Failing to Act With Actual Knowledge?*	*Is a Physician's Confirmation of a Terminal Condition in Writing Required Before the Living Will Can Be Given Effect?*	*Is the Physician Liable If There Is Mistaken Withholding or Withdrawing of Life Support?*	*Is There Criminal Liability for Destroying a Living Will?*	*Is There Criminal Liability for Forging a Living Will?*
Mississippi	No. (§§ 41-41-219, 41-41-221)	No, if decision is madein good faith. (§ 41-41-219(2))	Not specified.	No, if made in good faith or based on the belief that person lacked authority. (§ 41-41-219 (1)(b) &(2))	There is civilliability. (§ 41-41-221)	Not specified. There is civil liability. (§ 41-41-221)
Missouri	Not specified.	Only states that it constitutes unprofessional conduct if without serious reason. (§ 459.045(1)) Any person so failing to act, without serious reason, shall lose rights of inheritance under patient's will. (§ 459.045(2))	Yes. (§ 459.025)	No (unless revocation is in medical record or person has actual knowledge of revocation). (§ 459.020)	Yes, if destroyed without the declarant's consent. (§ 459.045(3))	Yes. (§ 459.045(4))
Montana	Not specified although no liability for withdrawal or withholding of life-sustaining treatment if the doctor or advanced	Yes, if physician will fully fails to comply with transfer provisions of § 50-9-203. (§ 50-9-206(1))	Physician is required to record the patient's terminal condition in the medical record. It is unclear whether this is necessary before the living will can be	No, unless there was actual notice of a revocation. (§ 50-9-204(1))	Yes, if without consent. (§ 50-9-206(3))	Yes. (§ 50-9-206(4))

	practice registered nurse acted consistent with the requirements of the law, especially the exercise of "reasonable medical judgment," per "reasonable medical standards," or "actions undertaken in good faith." (§ 50-9-204(1)-(4))		given effect. (§ 50-9-201)			
Nebraska	Not specified, but not if within "reasonable medical standards." (§ 20-410(2))	Yes, if physician will fully fails to comply with transfer provisions. (§ 20-411(1))	Yes. (§§ 20-405(2), 20-407)	No. (§ 20-410(1))	Yes, if without consent. (§ 20-411(3))	Yes. (§ 20-411(4))
Nevada	Not specified.	Yes, if physician willfully fails to comply with transfer provisions. (§ 449.660(1))	Physician is required to note the terminal condition in the patient's medical record. It is unclear whether this is required before the living will can be given effect. (§§ 449.617, 449.622)	No, in the absence of knowledge of revocation. (§ 449.630(1))	Yes, if without consent. (§ 449.660(3))	Yes, if contrary to declarant's wishes and death is hastened. (§ 449.660(4))
New Hampshire	Not specified.	There is immunity if there is a good-faith belief that a directive of an agent is in conflict with or	Yes. (§§ 137-J:7(I)(c); 137-J:10(I)(a)-(b))	There is liability for a failure to exercise due care. (§ 137-J:12(111))	Yes, if done knowingly and falsely. (§ 137-J:23)	Yes, if done knowingly and falsely. (§ 137-J:23)

(cont'd)

Table 7.04
Civil or Criminal Liability for Failure to Act *(continued)*

	Is There Any Civil or Criminal Liability for Failing to Act Without Actual Knowledge?	*Is There Any Civil or Criminal Liability for Failing to Act With Actual Knowledge?*	*Is a Physician's Confirmation of a Terminal Condition in Writing Required Before the Living Will Can Be Given Effect?*	*Is the Physician Liable If There Is Mistaken Withholding or Withdrawing of Life Support?*	*Is There Criminal Liability for Destroying a Living Will?*	*Is There Criminal Liability for Forging a Living Will?*
New Hampshire *(cont'd)*		exceeds the scope of the authority of the agent or the advance directive. (§ 137-J:12(II)(b)) There is also provision for transfer of a qualified patient of the physician or ARNP, who because of personal beliefs or conscience cannot comply with the advance directive. (§ 137-J:7(II))				
New Jersey	Not specified.	Yes, if in the absence of timely notification of unwillingness to act and arrange a transfer (§ 26:2H-62 (b)), professional misconduct and civil liability. (§ 26:2H-78(a) & (b))	Yes. (§ 26:2H-60)	No liability for any action if in good faith and in accord with the statute. (§ 26:2H-73)	Yes, if without consent. (§ 26:2H-78(c)(1))	Yes. (§ 26:2H-78(c)(2))
New Mexico	Not specified.	Civil damages or fine of $5,000 (whichever is greater) if done intentionally	Yes. (§ 24-7A-7(c))	No, if based on a good faith assumption that directive was valid and there	Not specified criminally (but alludes to the possibility), only specifies a fine/civil	Not specified criminally (but alludes to the possibility), only specifies a fine/civil

		and caused a violation. (§ 24-7A-10(A))		has been no revocation. (§ 24-7A-9(A)(3))	damages if done without the declarant's consent. (§ 24-7A-10(B) & (C))	damages if done without the declarant's consent. (§ 24-7A-10(B) & (C))
New York	No, so long as in good faith. (Pub. Health § 2986(1))	Not specified, but transfer is required if unwilling to act. (Pub. Health § 2984(4))	Not specified.	No, so long as in good faith. (Pub. Health § 2986(1))	Not specified.	Not specified.
North Carolina	Not specified.	Not specified.	Not specified. Confirmation is required, but a writing is not specified. (§ 90-321(b)(2))	Not specified.	Not specified.	Not specified.
North Dakota	No, so long as in good faith and ordinary care. (§ 23-06.5-12(2))	No, but notification and transfer required if unwilling to act. (§ 23-06.5-12(3))	Physician is required to record the condition in the patient's medical record. It is unclear whether this is required before the living will can be given effect. (§ 23-06.5-04)	No, in the absence of knowledge of a revocation. (§ 23-06.5-12)	Not specified.	Not specified.
Ohio	Not if actions are in good faith, using reasonable medical standards, and the person not acting outside the scope of authority. (§ 2133.11(A)(5) & (D))	Not if in good faith, person does not prevent or attempt to prevent or delay or attempt to delay the transfer of the patient and the person is not acting out side their authority. (§ 2133.11 (A)(4) & (D))	Yes. (§§ 2133.03 (A)(1), 2133.05(A))	No, if declaration is carried out in good faith and without actual knowledge of a revocation or defect. (§ 2133.11 (A)(1))	Not specified.	Not specified.

Table 7.04
Civil or Criminal Liability for Failure to Act *(continued)*

	Is There Any Civil or Criminal Liability for Failing to Act Without Actual Knowledge?	*Is There Any Civil or Criminal Liability for Failing to Act With Actual Knowledge?*	*Is a Physician's Confirmation of a Terminal Condition in Writing Required Before the Living Will Can Be Given Effect?*	*Is the Physician Liable If There Is Mistaken Withholding or Withdrawing of Life Support?*	*Is There Criminal Liability for Destroying a Living Will?*	*Is There Criminal Liability for Forging a Living Will?*
Oklahoma	Not specified.	Civil or criminal liability is not specified, but physician is guilty of unprofessional conduct if willfully fails to act without arranging for transfer to another physician/ health care worker. (63 §§ 3101.9, 3101.11(A))	Not required to give effect, but physician is required to make confirmation part of declarant's medical record. (63 § 3101.7)	No, in absence of knowledge of revocation. (63 § 3101.10(A))	Yes, if destroyed without the declarant's consent. (63 § 3101.11(C))	Yes. (63 § 3101.11 (D))
Oregon	Not specified.	No, unless failure to comply with discharge or transfer requirements. (§ 127.555(3))	Not specified.	No, there is liability only if the provider relied on a directive that he/she knew to be revoked. (§ 127.555(3)(d)(A))	Yes. (§ 127.995)	Yes. (§ 127.995)
Pennsylvania	No. (20 § 5431)	Not if attending physician or other health care provider cannot do so in good conscience. However, the attending physician or health care provider must make every reasonable	Yes. (20 § 5443)	No, so long as following, in good faith, declarant's previous wishes as outlined in the declaration. (20 § 5431(a))	Yes, if without consent. (20 § 5432)	Yes, if contrary to declarant's wishes and death is hastened. (20 § 5432)

		effort to assist the transfer to a physician or other health care provider who will comply. (20 § 5424(a) & (b))				
Rhode Island	No specific provision but generally no liability if actions are within reasonable medical standards. (§ 23-4.11-8(b))	Failure to transfer is unprofessional conduct and may result in civil liability. (§ 23-4.11-9(a) & (e))	Yes. (§§ 23-4.11-3 (c)(2), 23-4.11-5)	No. (§ 23-4.11-8(a)(1))	Yes. (§ 23-4.11-9(c))	Yes. (§ 23-4.11-9(d))
South Carolina	Not specified.	Civil or criminal liability is not specified, but physician is guilty of unprofessional conduct if willfully fails to act without transferring patient to another physician/facility. (§ 44-77-100)	Not specified, only states that condition must be "certified." (§ 44-77-30)	No, if relying on an apparently valid declaration without actual notice of revocation. (§ 44-77-90)	No, only civilliability for damages. (§ 44-77-160(C))	Yes, if declarant dies as a result. (§ 44-77-160(A))
South Dakota	Not specified.	Not specified.	Yes. (§§ 34-12D-5, 34-12D-7)	No, absent actual knowledge of revocation. (§ 34-12D-13)	Not specified.	Not specified.
Tennessee	No. (§ 32-11-108 (b))	Yes. Civil liability and professional disciplinary actions for failing to comply with notification and transfer provisions. (§ 32-11-108(a))	Not specified.	No, presumably, if action taken without notice of revocation. (§ 32-11-108(b)) Statute also states no liability if physician complies with reasonable medical standards. (§ 32-11-110(i))	Yes, if destroyed without the declarant's consent. (§ 32-11-109)	Yes. (§ 32-11-109)
Texas	No. (Health & Safety § 166.045(a))	Not specified, but physician refusing to comply is subject to *(cont'd)*	Yes. (Health & Safety § 166.040 (a))	Not specified, but generally no liability for failure to act on *(cont'd)*	Yes, if without the declarant's consent. *(cont'd)*	Yes if contrary to patient's desires and death is *(cont'd)*

Table 7.04
Civil or Criminal Liability for Failure to Act *(continued)*

	Is There Any Civil or Criminal Liability for Failing to Act Without Actual Knowledge?	*Is There Any Civil or Criminal Liability for Failing to Act With Actual Knowledge?*	*Is a Physician's Confirmation of a Terminal Condition in Writing Required Before the Living Will Can Be Given Effect?*	*Is the Physician Liable If There Is Mistaken Withholding or Withdrawing of Life Support?*	*Is There Criminal Liability for Destroying a Living Will?*	*Is There Criminal Liability for Forging a Living Will?*
Texas *(cont'd)*		review and disciplinary action by licensing board. (Health & Safety § 166.045(b)) No liability if physician complies with provisions of § 166.046. (Health & Safety § 166.045(d))		revocation without actual knowledge. (Health & Safety § 166.042(d))	(Health & Safety § 166.048(a))	hastened. (Health & Safety § 166.048(b))
Utah (2007)	Not specified.	Civil or criminal liability is not specified, but physician is guilty of unprofessional conduct if willfully fails to act and does not transfer patient to another attending physician or medical provider. (§ 75-2-1112(3))	Yes, (as indicated in the statutory form). (§ 75-2-1104(4))	No liability for failing to act on an unknown revocation. (§ 75-2-1111(3))	Yes, if destroyed without the declarant's consent. (§ 75-2-1115(1))	Yes, if contrary to declarant's wishes and death is hastened. (§ 75-2-1115(2))
Utah (2008) The new law is effective Jan. 1, 2008. A health care directive executed prior to this date under the provisions then in effect, Ch. 2, pt. II, Personal Choice and Living Will, may, in good faith, be relied upon by a health care	No. (§ 75-2a-1114 (2)(a))	Not if based on the belief that a surrogate ordering withholding or withdrawing of care had decision-making authority (§ 75-2a-1114(3)(b) & (4)(b)(i)) or the instructions are inconsistent with the patient's wishes (§ 75-2a-1114(4)(b)(i)(c) & (4)(e) or on	The key is acting in "good faith." (§ 75-2a-1114(3))	Yes. (§ 75-2a-1117 (1)(a))	Yes. (§ 75-2a-1117 (1)(b))	

provider or health care facility. (§ 75-2a-1120(1)(b))		account of reasons of conscience (§ 75-2a-1114(4)(b) (ii) 75-2a-1114(4) (b)-(c))				
Vermont	No, so long as acts in good faith. (18 § 9713(b))	No, so long as the provider informs the principal, assists the principal in the transfer of care to a provider who is willing to honor the instruction, provides care until a new provider has been found, and documents the conflict, the steps taken to resolve it, and its resolution in the principal's medical record. (18 §§ 9707(b)(3), 9714(a))	Not specified.	Not specified.	Not specified.	Not specified.
Virginia	Not specified.	Civil or criminal liability is not specified, but attending physician can transfer the patient to another physician if unwilling to comply. (§ 54.1-2987)	This is specified in the statutory form, but the form is optional. (§ 54.1-2984)	No, unless actual knowledge of a revocation. (§ 54.1-2985)	Yes, if caused life-prolonging procedures to be used in contravention of the declarant's intent. (§ 54.1-2989)	Yes, if contrary to declarant's wishes and death is hastened. (§ 54.1-2989)
Washington	Not specified.	No, if acting in good faith and in accordance with provisions for a written plan to control in cases of inability to act. (§ 70.122.060(3))	Yes. (§ 70.122.030(2))	No, unless actual or constructive knowledge of revocation. (§ 70.122.040(2))	Yes, if destroyed without the declarant's consent. (§ 70.122.090)	Yes, if contrary to declarant's wishes and death is hastened. (§ 70.122.090)
West Virginia	No. (§ 16-30-22(a))	Liability not specified, but subject to review and disciplinary action *(cont'd)*	Yes. (§§ 16-30-7(a) & (b), 16-30-19(a))	No, unless actual knowledge of a *(cont'd)*	Not specified.	Not specified.

Table 7.04
Civil or Criminal Liability for Failure to Act *(continued)*

	Is There Any Civil or Criminal Liability for Failing to Act Without Actual Knowledge?	*Is There Any Civil or Criminal Liability for Failing to Act With Actual Knowledge?*	*Is a Physician's Confirmation of a Terminal Condition in Writing Required Before the Living Will Can Be Given Effect?*	*Is the Physician Liable If There Is Mistaken Withholding or Withdrawing of Life Support?*	*Is There Criminal Liability for Destroying a Living Will?*	*Is There Criminal Liability for Forging a Living Will?*
West Virginia *(cont'd)*		by licensing board for failure to comply. (§ 16-30-22(b))		revocation. (§ 16-30-18(b))		
Wisconsin	Not specified.	No, only that it is unprofessional conduct if a physician fails to make good faith attempt to transfer. (§ 154.07 (1)(a)(3))	Yes. (§ 154.02(3))	No, if no actual knowledge of revocation. (§ 154.07(1)(a)(2))	Yes, if without consent. (§ 154.15(1))	Yes. (§ 154.15(2))
Wyoming	Not specified.	Not if acting in good faith (§35-22-410) or in good conscience (§35-22-408(e)). If acting on the basis of conscience, must inform and transfer patient to provider willing to comply with the instruction and provide life-sustaining care until such a transfer can be effected. (§ 35-22-408(g))	Not specified.	No, so long as acting in good faith and in accordance with generally accepted health care standard. (§ 35-22-410 (a)(iii))	Civil liability, if destroyed without the declarant's consent. (§ 35-22-411(b)). Criminal liability not specified.	Yes, civil liability. (§ 35-22-411(b)) Criminal liability not specified.

1. Only deals with health care proxies.

Table 7.05
Effect Regarding Insurance

	Are Persons Protected from Being Required to Sign a Living Will in Order to Be Given Health Insurance or Health Care?	*Is the Execution and Giving Effect to the Living Will Expressly Considered Not to Be Suicide for Life Insurance Contracts?*
Alabama	Yes. (§ 22-8A-9(c))	Yes (states not suicide for any purpose). (§ 22-8A-9(a))
Alaska	Yes. (§ 13.52.060(h))	Yes (states not suicide for any purpose). (§ 13.52.120(b))
Arizona	Yes. (§ 36-3207(A)) (relating to all health-care directives)	Yes. (§ 36-3207(C)) (relating to all health-care directives)
Arkansas	Yes. (§§ 20-17-210(c), 20-17-209(e))	Yes. (§§ 20-17-210(a) & (b))
California	Yes. (Probate § 4677)	Yes. (Probate § 4656)
Colorado	Yes. (§ 15-18-111)	Yes (states not suicide for any purpose). (§ 15-18-111)
Connecticut	Yes. (§ 19a-580b)	Not specified.
Delaware	Yes. (16 § 2512(c))	Yes. (16 § 2512(a))
District of Columbia	Yes. (§ 7-628(c))	Yes. (§ 7-628(a))
Florida	Yes. (§§ 765.108, 765.110(2))	Yes. (§§ 765.309(2), 765.108)
Georgia	Yes. (§ 31-32-9(c))	Yes (states not suicide for any purpose). (§ 31-32-9(a))
Hawaii	Yes. (§ 327E-7(h))	Yes. (§ 327E-13(b))
Idaho	Yes. (§ 39-4514(7))	Not specified, but states that no life insurance policy can be impaired or invalidated by withholding or withdrawal of artificial life-sustaining procedures. (§ 39-4514(7)(a))
Illinois	Yes. (755 ILCS §§ 35/8(e), 35/9(c))	Yes. (§ 755 ILCS § 35/9(a) & (b))
Indiana	Yes. (§ 16-36-4-17(d))	Yes. (§ 16-36-4-17(a)(c))
Iowa	Yes. (§ 144A.11(3))	Yes (states not suicide for any purpose). (§§ 144A.11(1), 144A.11(2))
Kansas	Yes. (§ 65-28,108(c))	Not specified, but states that no life insurance policy can be impaired or invalidated by withholding or withdrawal of artificial life-sustaining procedures. (§ 65-28,108(b))

Table 7.05
Effect Regarding Insurance *(continued)*

	Are Persons Protected from Being Required to Sign a Living Will in Order to Be Given Health Insurance or Health Care?	*Is the Execution and Giving Effect to the Living Will Expressly Considered Not to Be Suicide for Life Insurance Contracts?*
Kentucky	Yes. (§ 311.637(2))	Yes. (§ 311.637(1))
Louisiana	Yes. (§ 40:1299.58.10(B)(4))	Yes (states not suicide for any purpose). (§ 40:1299.58.10(B)(1))
Maine	Yes, as to health care. (18-A § 5-807(H))	Yes. (18-A § 5-813(B))
Maryland	Yes. (Health-Gen. § 5-614(c))	Yes (states not suicide for any purpose). (Health-Gen. § 5-614(a))
Massachusetts[1]	Yes. (201D § 10)	Not specified, but implied, since "nothing in this chapter shall be construed to constitute . . . suicide." (201D § 12)
Michigan	Yes. (§ 333.5659)	Yes. (§ 333.5659(e))
Minnesota	Yes. Requiring patient to sign is a misdemeanor. (§ 145B.105 (5))	Not specified, but states that no life insurance policy can be affected, impaired, or modified by the effectuation of a living will. (§ 145B.11)
Mississippi	Yes. (§ 41-41-215(8))	Yes (states not suicide for any purpose). (§ 41-41-227(2))
Missouri	Yes. (§ 459.050(2))	Not specified, but no life insurance policy can be impaired or invalidated by the withdrawal or withholding of death-prolonging procedures. (§ 459.050(1))
Montana	Yes. (§ 50-9-205(3))	Yes. (§ 50-9-205(1))
Nebraska	Yes. (§§ 20-411(5), 20-412(3))	Yes. (§ 20-412(1))
Nevada	Yes. (§ 449.650(3))	Yes. (§ 449.650(1) & (2))
New Hampshire	Yes. (§ 137-J:3(I))	Yes, not suicide. (§§ 137-J:10(III); 137-J:3(II))
New Jersey	Yes. (§§ 26:2H-75, 26:2H-78(c)(4))	Yes. (§§ 26:2H-75, 26:2H-77(a))
New Mexico	Yes. (§ 24-7A-2.1(A) & (B))	Yes (states not suicide for any purpose). (§ 24-7A-13(B))
New York	Yes. (Pub. Health § 2988)	N/A
North Carolina	Yes. (§ 90-321(g))	Yes (states not suicide for any purpose). (§ 90-321(f))
North Dakota	Yes. (§ 23-06.5-13(11))	Yes. (§ 23-06.5-13(9)) (states not suicide for any purpose)

Ohio	Yes. (§ 2133.12(B)(4))	Yes. (§§ 2133.12(A), 2133.12(B)(1) & (2))
Oklahoma	Yes. (63 § 3101.12(C))	Yes (states not suicide for any purpose). (63 § 3101.12(A))
Oregon	Yes. (§ 127.565(2))	Yes. (§§ 127.570(2), 127.565(3))
Pennsylvania	Yes. (20 § 5428(1))	Yes. (20 § 5426)
Rhode Island	Yes. (§ 23-4.11-10(c))	Yes. (§ 23-4.11-10(a) & (b))
South Carolina	Yes. (§ 44-77-120)	Yes (states not suicide for any purpose). (§ 44-77-110)
South Dakota	Yes. (§ 34-12D-16)	Yes. (§§ 34-12D-14, 34-12D-15)
Tennessee	Yes. (§ 32-11-110(c))	Yes. (§ 32-11-110(a) & (b))
Texas	Yes. (Health & Safety § 166.007)	Not specified, but states that no life insurance policy can be impaired or invalidated by withholding or withdrawal of artificial life-sustaining procedures. (Health & Safety § 166.006(b))
Utah (2007)	Yes. (§ 75-2-1117(3))	Yes (§§ 75-2-1116, 75-2-1117(1) & (2))
Utah (2008) The new law is effective Jan. 1, 2008. A health care directive executed prior to this date under the provisions then in effect, Ch. 2, pt. II, Personal Choice and Living Will, may, in good faith, be relied upon by a health care provider or health care facility. (§75-2a-1120(1)(b))	Yes. (§75-2a-1118(3)(a))	Yes (§§75-2-1116, 75-2a-1118)
Vermont	Yes. (18 § 9707(d))	Yes (states shall not be construed as suicide). (18 § 9715(a))

Table 7.05
Effect Regarding Insurance *(continued)*

	Are Persons Protected from Being Required to Sign a Living Will in Order to Be Given Health Insurance or Health Care?	*Is the Execution and Giving Effect to the Living Will Expressly Considered Not to Be Suicide for Life Insurance Contracts?*
Virginia	Yes. (§ 54.1-2991)	Yes (states not suicide for any purpose). (§ 54.1-2991)
Washington	Yes. (§ 70.122.070(3))	Yes (states not suicide for any purpose). (§ 70.122.070(1) & (2))
West Virginia	Yes. (§ 16-30-14(d))	Yes (states not suicide for any purpose). (§ 16-30-14(b))
Wisconsin	Yes. (§ 154.11(3))	Yes. (§ 154.11(1) & (2))
Wyoming	Yes. (§ 35-22-408(h))	Yes (states not suicide). (§ 35-22-414(b))

1. Only deals with health care proxies.

Table 7.06
Governing Law

	Will a Foreign-Executed Living Will Be Given Effect? (Note If Says "State" and Does Not Include Foreign Country)
Alabama	Yes, but not if it authorizes the administration, withholding/withdrawal of health care that is prohibited under Alabama law. Uses term "another state." (§ 22-8A-12) Does not include foreign countries.
Alaska	Declarations issued and authorized in compliance with laws of another state are effective in Alaska to the extent that it complies with Alaska law. (§ 13.52.010)
Arizona	A health-care directive prepared outside the state is valid in Arizona if it was valid in the place where and at the time when it was adopted and only to the extent that it does not conflict with Arizona's criminal laws. (§ 36-3208)
Arkansas	A declaration executed in another state in compliance with the law of that state or of Arkansas is validly executed. (§ 20-17-212) Does not include foreign countries.
California	Any instrument executed in another state or jurisdiction in compliance with the law of that state or jurisdiction or of California is valid in Cali fornia. (Probate § 4676(a))
Colorado	Not specified.
Connecticut	Yes, if not violative of Connecticut public policy. A health care provider can rely on health care instructions or appointment of a health care proxy from outside Connecticut if there is an order from a court of competent jurisdiction or there is a notarized statement from the patient or holder of the proxy that is valid where executed, not against Connecticut public policy, and is based as well on the health care provider's own good faith analysis. (Ct. P.A. 06-195, § 80-81 (June 7, 2006))
Delaware	Yes, a living will executed in another state in compliance with the laws of that state or of Delaware is valid. Does not include foreign countries. (16 § 2517)
District of Columbia	Not specified.
Florida	If executed in compliance with law of another state or of Florida, the directive is considered validly executed in Florida. (§ 765.112) Does not include foreign countries.
Georgia	Not specified.
Hawaii	Yes, a document executed in another state will be considered valid if the document complies with Hawaii law or with laws of the state where enacted. (§ 327E-3(j)) Does not include foreign countries.

Table 7.06
Governing Law *(continued)*

Will a Foreign-Executed Living Will Be Given Effect?
(Note If Says "State" and Does Not Include Foreign Country)

State	
Idaho	Not specified, but § 54-1142 states that a "Durable power of attorney for health care" means the document described in chapter 45, title 39, Idaho Code, or any similar document properly executed under the laws of another jurisdiction.
Illinois	A declaration executed in another state in compliance with the law of that state or Illinois is validly executed. (755 ILCS § 35/9(h)) Does not include foreign countries.
Indiana	Not specified.
Iowa	A document executed in another state or jurisdiction shall be deemed valid and enforceable in Iowa, to the extent the document is consistent with the laws of Iowa. (§ 144A.3(4))
Kansas	Not specified.
Kentucky	Not specified.
Louisiana	A declaration properly executed in another state is valid. (§ 40:1299.58.10(D)) Does not include foreign countries.
Maine	Yes, as long as it complies with Maine law, or if valid where executed. (18-A § 5-802(H))
Maryland	Yes, if in compliance with the laws of Maryland or the state in which it was executed. Uses the term "another state." (Health-Gen. § 5-617) Does not include foreign countries.
Massachusetts	A health care proxy executed in another state or jurisdiction is enforceable if it is in compliance with the laws of the other state or jurisdiction. (201D § 11)
Michigan	Not specified.
Minnesota	Yes, if it "substantially" complies with the Minnesota chapter on living wills. Uses the term "another state." (§ 145B.16) Does not include foreign countries.
Mississippi	Yes, if it complies with the local law. (§ 41-41-205(10))
Missouri	Not specified.
Montana	Yes, as long as meets the laws of the state where executed and substantially complies with Montana laws. (§ 50-9-111) Does not include foreign countries.

Nebraska	Yes, a declaration executed in another state in compliance with the law of that state or of Nebraska is valid. (§ 20-414) Does not include foreign countries.
Nevada	Yes, as long as it is in compliance with the laws of that state or with Nevada laws. (§ 449.690(1)) An instrument executed anywhere before July 1, 1977 is effective if it clearly expresses the declarant's voluntary intent to withhold treatment. (§ 449.690(2)) An instrument executed anywhere before October 1, 1991 is effective if in substantial compliance with current Nevada law and not revoked. (§ 449.690(2))
New Hampshire	Yes, but "any exercise of power" under a foreign living will must comply with the laws of New Hampshire. Uses the term "another state or jurisdiction." (§ 137-J:17)
New Jersey	Yes, if valid in that state, country, or New Jersey and if not contrary to New Jersey public policy. A living will valid under the law of another state or country is valid even if executed there, if not contrary to New Jersey public policy. (§ 26:2H-76)
New Mexico	Yes, directive from another state or jurisdiction is valid if it complies with the laws of the state where it was made. (§ 24-7A-16(C))
New York	A health care proxy or similar instrument executed in another state or jurisdiction in compliance with the law of that state or jurisdiction shall be considered validly executed. (Pub. Health § 2990)
North Carolina	Not specified.
North Dakota	Yes, directive or similar instrument from another state or jurisdiction is valid if it was executed in compliance with the laws of the other state or jurisdiction. (§ 23-06.5-11)
Ohio	Yes, as long as the declaration is in compliance with the laws of that state or in substantial compliance with Ohio law. (§ 2133.14) Does not include foreign countries.
Oklahoma	Yes, if complies with Oklahoma state law or another state's law that does not exceed authorizations permitted under Oklahoma state law. Uses the term "another state." (63 § 3101.14) Does not include foreign countries.
Oregon	An advance directive executed by an adult who at the time of execution resided in another state, in compliance with the laws of that state, the laws of the state where the person was located at the time, or Oregon laws, is validly executed. (§ 127.515(5)) Does not include foreign countries.
Pennsylvania	Not specified.
Rhode Island	A declaration executed in another state in compliance with the law of that state is valid. (§ 23-4.11-12) Does not include foreign countries.
South Carolina	Yes, if the law of the state of the declarant's domicile when the declaration was made expresses a substantially similar intent to applicable South Carolina law. Uses the term "state." (§ 44-77-30)
South Dakota	Statute states that declaration which meets the execution requirements of the jurisdiction where executed, where declarant was a resident, or of South Dakota is valid. (§ 34-12D-22)

Table 7.06
Governing Law *(continued)*

Will a Foreign-Executed Living Will Be Given Effect?
(Note If Says "State" and Does Not Include Foreign Country)

Tennessee	Yes, if in compliance with either the laws of Tennessee or of the state of the declarant's residence. (§ 32-11-111) Does not include foreign countries.
Texas	Directive or similar instrument validly executed in "another state or jurisdiction" shall be effective as long as it does not violate Texas law. (Health & Safety § 166.005)
Utah (2007)	Directive executed in another state shall be presumed to comply with Utah law, unless otherwise provided in the directive. (§ 75-2-1119) Does not include foreign countries.
Utah (2008) The new law is effective Jan. 1, 2008. A health care directive executed prior to this date under the provisions then in effect, Ch. 2, pt. II, Personal Choice and Living Will, may, in good faith, be relied upon by a health care provider or health care facility. (§75-2a-1120 (1)(b))	Directive executed in another state shall be presumed to comply with Utah law, unless otherwise provided in the directive and, in good faith, may be relied upon by health care provider or health care facility. (§75-2a-1120(1)) Does not include foreign countries.
Vermont	A declaration executed in another state in compliance with the law of that state is valid. (18 § 9716)
Virginia	Yes, if it complies with Virginia state law or the law of the state where the directive was made. Uses the term "another state." (§ 54.1-2993) Does not include foreign countries.

Washington	Yes, to the extent permitted by Washington state law and federal constitutional law. Uses the term "another political jurisdiction." (§ 70.122.030(3))
West Virginia	A declaration executed in another state is valid if it is in compliance with West Virginia law or the state law in which it was executed. Uses the term "another state." (§ 16-30-21) Does not include foreign countries.
Wisconsin	A valid document executed in another state or jurisdiction in compliance with the laws of that state or jurisdiction is valid in Wisconsin to the extent that the document is consistent with Wisconsin laws. (§ 154.11(9))
Wyoming	Not specified, although states "This act shall be applied and construed to effectuate its general purpose to make uniform the law with respect to the subject matter of this act among states enacting it." (§ 35-22-416)

Table 8
Intestate Succession
(current through 5/1/07)

Although the expectation is that all wealth of an individual will be properly disposed of, the situation may arise with respect to at least a portion of the estate, in which this is not, in fact, the case. In such situation, the particular state's rules of intestate succession will control the disposition of the property. Furthermore, the majority of individuals actually die without a will or other dipsositive instrument. A family member may seek an estate planner's advice as to whether he or she is entitled to a share of the deceased relative's estate.

Ordinarily, in the described situation, an attorney will be familiar with the parameters of the local law of descent and distribution. However, the estate at issue may also have real property situated in another state. Furthermore, the intestate may have died a domiciliary of another state, thus making its law pertinent to the disposition of all of the intestate's personal property. The analysis contained in this Table 8 details the intestacy laws of each of the states.

From an academic standpoint, this Table affords an up-to-date comparison of the way in which different states approach the topic of descent and distribution. Wide differences from state to state are readily apparent in terms of the share afforded a surviving spouse when there are no issue and also when there are issue, some of who are only the children or descendants of the surviving spouse or the intestate. Sharp distinctions in approach are also revealed on such matters as the precise order of succession with respect to collateral levels. Likewise, the cut-off of rights of inheritance due to remoteness is at the grandparent parentela in some states but in others is not so limited. Indeed, in certain states, escheat is avoided by granting rights to the heirs of a predeceasing spouse of the decedent.

One area of particular disagreement among the states relates to representation. When a person entitled to take is deceased, the descendants of such person may be entitled to take in his or her place. One issue that divides the states is the question when representation is available to the descendants at all. A second issue concerns what method should be employed in determining who should take. There are four principal approaches:

1. *Per capita at each generation*. The property subject to intestacy is divided into as many shares as there are descendants in the nearest degree living and deceased descendants in that degree who are survived by descendants. The living descendants take a single share. The shares of the deceased descendants are aggregated and the process is

repeated at the next generation level, while treating those who have already received shares, along with their descendants, as being deceased and as if that line does not exist. This approach is repeated at each generation level, until all the property is distributed.

2. *Per capita with representation.* The first generation level at which there are descendants surviving is identified. The property subject to intestacy is divided into as many shares as there are living descendants at that generation level and deceased descendants leaving descendants of their own. The share of each deceased descendant is distributed within his or her line by following the same procedure at the next generation level and so on.
3. *Per stirpes.* The property subject to intestacy is divided into as many shares as there are children of the intestate or other relevant person who are either alive or are deceased but are survived by descendants. The division occurs at the child level even if *no* children survive the intestate or other relevant person. The share allocated to a child's line is subdivided among grandchildren taking by representation. If a grandchild is also deceased but survived by children of his or her own, then they take by representation the grandchild's share. This procedure is repeated down the generations until the entire share is apportioned.
4. *Per capita if of equal degree, otherwise per stirpes.* In certain states, a per stirpital approach is ordinarily applied. However, if all of the takers are of the same degree they are treated equally by utilizing a per capita distributional scheme, notwithstanding that a per stirpital approach would have yielded a different outcome.

The foregoing approaches and their potentially different outcomes are revealed by the following example:

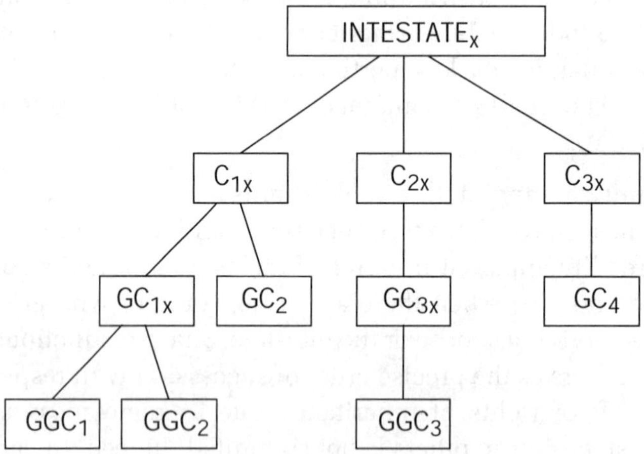

An x indicates that a person is deceased.

1. Per capita at each generation level: $GC_2 =$ $1/4$, $GC_4 = 1/4$, $GGC_1 = 1/6$, $GGC_2 = 1/6$, $GGC_3 = 1/6$
2. Per capita with representation: $GC_2 =$ $1/4$, $GC_4 = 1/4$, $GGC_1 = 1/8$, $GGC_2 = 1/8$, $GGC_3 = 1/4$
3. Per stirpes: $GC_2 = 1/6$, $GC_4 = 1/3$, $GGC_1 = 1/12$, $GGC_2 = 1/12$, $GGC_3 = 1/3$
4. Per capita if of equal degree, otherwise per stirpes. The result is the same as per stirpes, since the takers are not all of the same degree. If the example were changed so that GC_2 and GC_4 were also deceased and each were survived respectively by GGC_4 and GGC_5,

then all of the GGCs would take 1/5, even though a per stirpital distribution would result in GGC_1 and GGC_2 taking 1/12, GGC_3 taking 1/3, GGC_4 taking 1/6, and GGC_5 taking 1/3.

As the foregoing example indicates, a clear understanding of the divisional rules are of the utmost importance in determining what each heir takes. Care must also be exercised to assure that the descriptive words used in the statute, such as "per stirpes," really encompass the traditional meaning or are defined elsewhere in the law to mean a different divisional scheme, such as per capita if of equal degree, or even per capita with representation.

Alabama
Who Takes by Intestate Succession?

A. Surviving spouse takes:	
1. If no surviving issue or parent	100% (§ 43-8-41(1))
2. If no surviving issue, but parent or parents survive	$100,000, plus ½ of balance (§ 43-8-41(2))
3. If there are surviving issue all of whom are issue of the surviving spouse	$50,000, plus ½ of balance (§ 43-8-41(3))
4. If there are surviving issue, one of whom is not issue of the surviving spouse[1]	½ of the intestate estate (§ 43-8-41(4))
B. All the estate, or the surplus if there is a surviving spouse, passes to:	
1. Issue	100% equally if of same degree, and otherwise by representation (§ 43-8-42(1))
2. Parent, or parents equally, if no issue	100% (§ 43-8-42(2))
3. Issue of parents	100%, by representation[2] (§ 43-8-42(3))
4. Grandparents, if no issue of parents	50% to the paternal and 50% to the maternal side. The grandparents on either side share equally in the 50% share, and if only one, that grandparent takes the entire 50% share (§ 43-8-42(4))
5. Issue of grandparents, if no grandparents on one side	Issue take equally 50% share if of the same degree, or otherwise by representation (§ 43-8-42(4))
6. Grandparents and issue of grandparents on the other side, if no grandparents or issue of grandparents on one side	The 50% share is added to the other 50% share and distributed as per 4. and 5. above
7. State, if no grandparents or issue of grandparents	100% (§ 43-8-44)

1. If the estate is in 2 or more states, the amount in the aggregate cannot exceed the preceding amounts. See § 43-8-41(5).
2. "Representation" means per capita with representation.

Alaska
Who Takes by Intestate Succession?

A. Surviving spouse takes:	
1. If no surviving descendants or parents	100% (§ 13.12.102(a)(1)(A))
2. If all descendants are descendants of decedent and spouse	100% (§ 13.12.102(a)(1)(B))
3. If no surviving descendant but a parent(s) survives	$200,000 plus 75% of balance (§ 13.12.102(a)(2))
4. If surviving descendants are also those of spouse but spouse has at least one other descendant	$150,000 plus 50% of balance (§ 13.12.102(a)(3))
5. If a surviving descendant of the decedent is not also a descendant of surviving spouse	$100,000 plus 50% of balance (§ 13.12.102(a)(4))
6. Stock under Alaska Native Claims Settlement Act	If no surviving issue—100% If issue—50% (§§ 13.12.102(b)(1)&(2))
B. All the estate, or the surplus if there is a surviving spouse, passes to:	
1. Descendants by representation[3]	100% (§ 32.12.103(1))
2. Parents, or parents equally, if no descendants	100% (§ 13.12.103(2))
3. Descendants of parents by representation,[3] *if no parents*	100% (§ 13.12.103(3))
4. Grandparents or their descendants, if no descendants of parents	50% to paternal and 50% to maternal grandparents or their surviving descendants by representation[3] (§ 13.12.103(4))
5. State, if no grandparents or their descendants	100% (§ 13.12.105)

3. Representation: per capita at each generation level (§ 13.12.106).

Arizona
Who Takes by Intestate Succession?

A. Surviving spouse takes:	
1. If no surviving issue	100% (§ 14-2102(1))
2. If surviving issue but all are issue of surviving spouse as well	100% (§ 14-2102(1))
3. If any issue of decedent not also issue of surviving spouse	50% of separate property and none of decedent's portion of community property (§ 14-2102(2))
B. All the estate, or the surplus if there is a surviving spouse, passes to:	
1. Issue by representation:[4]	100% (§ 14-2103(1))
2. Parent, or parents equally, if no descendants	100% (§ 14-2103(2))
3. Descendants of parents, if no parents	100% (§ 14-2103(3))
4. Grandparents, if no issue of parents	50% to the paternal and 50% to the maternal side. The grandparents on either side share equally in the 50% share, and if only one, that grandparent takes the entire 50% share (§ 14-2103(4))
5. Issue of grandparents, if no grandparents on one side	Issue take equally 50% share if of the same degree, or otherwise by representation (§ 14-2103(4))
6. Grandparents and issue of grandparents on the other side, if no grandparents or issue of grandparents on one side	The 50% share is added to the other 50% share and distributed as per 4. and 5. above (§ 14-2103(4))
7. State, if no grandparents or their descendants	100% (§ 14-2105)

4. Representation: per capita at each generation level (§ 14-2106).

Arkansas
Who Takes by Intestate Succession?

1. *Children and descendants of a deceased child*	100%, per capita or per stirpes pursuant to §§ 28-9-204 and 28-9-205 (§ 28-9-214(1))
2. Surviving spouse, if no children or descendants:	
a. *If married continuously for at least 3 years prior to death*	100% (§ 28-9-214(2))
b. *If married less than 3 years prior to death*	50% (§ 28-9-214(2))
3. *Parent or parents, if no spouse or descendants*	100%, with parents taking equally if both survive (§ 28-9-214(3)); same result with respect to portion not passing to surviving spouse due to brevity of marriage (§ 28-9-214(4))
4. *Siblings and issue of predeceased siblings, if no parent*	100% of portion not passing to surviving spouse, per capita or per stirpes pursuant to §§ 28-9-204 and 28-9-205[5] (§ 28-9-214(5))
5. *Grandparents, uncles, and aunts, and issue of predeceasing uncles and aunts, with respect to amounts not covered by 1.–4. above*	100%, without regard to whether on the maternal or paternal side, whether any such deceased person is survived by descendants or whether a person is a grandparent, uncle, or aunt. If an uncle or aunt is deceased, the issue of such person takes per capita or per stirpes, pursuant to §§ 28-9-204 and 28-9-205 (§ 28-9-214(6))
6. *Great-grandparents, great-uncles, and great-aunts, if none of the persons in 5. above survive*	100%, without regard to whether on the maternal or paternal side, or any such person's descendants or whether a person is a great-grandparent, great-uncle, or great-aunt. However, if a great-uncle or great-aunt is deceased, the issue of such person takes per capita or per stirpes, pursuant to §§ 28-9-204 and 28-9-205[5] (§ 28-9-214(7))
7. *Surviving spouse, if married less than 3 years and if none of the persons in 6. survive*	100% (§ 28-9-215(1))
8. *Heirs of last spouse, if there is no spouse surviving and the marriage did not terminate in divorce*	100%, with pattern the same as if decedent's own heirs (§ 29-9-215(2))
9. *Escheat to county where decedent last "resided at death," if no other takers*[6]	100% (§ 28-9-215(3))

5. If of the same degree, the persons take per capita. If they are of different degree, they take "per stirpes," which, as defined in § 28-9-205(a)(3), actually is what is described generally as per capita with representation. In the case of 5. above, the living persons who qualify for the designated *relationships to the decedent* take per capita.
6. This could, presumably, be a county in another state.

California
Who Takes by Intestate Succession?

A. Surviving spouse or surviving domestic partner (as defined in Prob. Code § 37(a) and Fam. Code § 297) takes:	
1. Community property (Prob. Code § 100) and quasi-community property (Prob. Code § 101)	the decedent's 50% share (Prob. Code § 6401(a)&(b))
2. Separate property:	
a. if no surviving issue, parent, sibling, or issue of sibling	100% (Prob. Code § 6401(c)(1))
b. if one child or issue of that child	50% (Prob. Code § 6401(c)(2)(A))
c. If no child or issue, but parent or issue of parent	50% (Prob. Code § 6401(c)(2)(B))
d. If more than one child	33.33% (Prob. Code § 6401(c)(3)(A))
e. If one child and issue of more than one deceased child	33.33% (Prob. Code § 6401(c)(3)(B))
f. If issue of more than one child	33.33% (Prob. Code § 6401(c)(3)(C))
B. All the estate, or the surplus if there is a surviving spouse, passes to:	
1. Issue	100%, with issue of same degree taking equally and if not of same degree then per capita with representation under Prob. Code § 240 (Prob. Code § 6402(a))
2. Parent, or parents equally, if no issue	100% (Prob. Code § 6402(b))
3. Issue of parents, if no parent or parents	100% with issue of same degree taking equally and if not of same degree then per capita with representation under Prob. Code § 240 (Prob. Code § 6402(c))
4. Grandparents, or issue of grandparents if no surviving grandparents	100%, with no distinction as to paternal or maternal. If more than one grandparent, they take equally. If no grandparents, issue take. If all of same degree, they take equally, and if not of same degree then per capita with representation under Prob. Code § 240 (Prob. Code § 6402(d))
5. Issue of a predeceased spouse (as defined in Prob. Code § 6402.5), if no grandparents or issue of grandparents	100% and the issue take equally if of same degree and if not of same degree then per capita with representation under Prob. Code § 240 (Prob. Code § 6402(e))
6. Next of kin by degree, if no grandparents, no issue of grandparents, and no issue of a predeceased spouse	100% and the issue take equally if of same degree and if not of same degree then per capita with representation under Prob. Code § 240 (Prob. Code § 6402(f))

7. *Parent or parents of predeceased spouse, if no next of kin and no surviv ing issue of a predeceased spouse*	Parents take equally. If none survive decedent, issue take equally if of same degree, and if not of same degree, then per capita with representation under Prob. Code § 240 (Prob. Code § 6402(g))
8. *Escheat, if no other taker*	100%, as provided in Prob. Code § 6800 et seq.

Special Rule Regarding a Predeceasing Spouse For Purposes of Distributing Real Property: If predeceasing spouse died within last 15 years, and there is no surviving spouse or issue of decedent at decedent's death, then special rules apply for the portion of the estate attributable to the decedent's predeceased spouse. (Prob. Code § 6402.5)

Colorado
Who Takes by Intestate Succession?

A. Surviving spouse takes:	
1. If no descendant or parent	100% (§ 15-11-102(1)(a))
2. If all of decedent's descendants are also descendants of surviving spouse and the surviving spouse has no other descendants	100% (§ 15-11-102(1)(b))
3. If no descendant of decedent survives, but a parent survives	First $200,000, plus ¾ of the balance (§ 15-11-102(2))
4. If all of decedent's surviving descendants are also descendants of the surviving spouse and she has at least one descendant who is not a descendant of the decedent	First $150,000, plus ½ of the balance (§ 15-11-102(3))
5. If at least one of decedent's surviving descendants is not a surviving descendant of the surviving spouse and any such child is an adult	First $100,000, plus ½ of the balance (§ 15-11-102 (4))
6. If at least one of decedent's surviving descendants is not a surviving descendant of the surviving spouse and any such child is a minor	One-half (§ 15-11-102(5))
If two or more of the above situations apply, the one yielding the largest amount for the surviving spouse governs. (§ 15-11-102)	
B. All the estate, or the surplus if there is a surviving spouse, passes to:	
1. Descendants	100%, per capita at each generation (§ 15-11-103(1))
2. Parent or parents, if no descendants	100%, in equal shares if both survive (§ 15-11-103(2))
3. Descendants of parents, or either of them, if no parents	100%, per capita at each generation (§ 15-11-103(3))
4. Grandparents, if no descendants of parents	100%, in equal shares (§ 15-11-103(4))
5. Descendants of grandparents, if no grandparents	100%, per capita at each generation (§ 15-11-103(5))
6. Adopted-away children if no descendants of grandparents; a "birth child" must make a claim within 90 days of decedent's death	100%, per capita at each generation (§ 15-11-103(6))
7. Natural parent or parents of adopted child, if no claiming birth children; the same 90-day filing requirement as in B.6. above applies	100% to the parents equally, or to one if only one survives (§ 15-11-103(7))
8. State, if no other takers	100% (§ 15-11-105)

Connecticut
Who Takes by Intestate Succession?

A. Surviving spouse takes:	
1. If there are no surviving issue or parent of the decedent	100% (§ 45a-437(a)(1))
2. If there are no surviving issue of the decedent but the decedent is survived by a parent or parents	First one hundred thousand dollars plus 75% (§ 45a-437(a)(2))
3. If there are surviving issue of the decedent all of whom are also issue of the surviving spouse	First one hundred thousand dollars plus 50% (§ 45a-437(a)(3))
4. If there are surviving issue of the decedent one or more of whom are not issue of the surviving spouse	50% (§ 45a-437(a)(4))
B. All the estate, or the surplus if there is a surviving spouse, passes to:	
1. Descendants	100% (§ 45a-438(a))
2. Parent or parents equally, if there is no spouse or children	100% (§ 45a-439(a)(1))
3. Brothers or sisters of the intestate and those who legally represent them[7] equally, if there is no parent	100% (§ 45a-439(a)(2))
4. Next of kin in equal degree under the civil law rule (§ 45a-439(d)), if there are no brothers or sisters or those who legally represent them	100% (§ 45a-439(a)(3)) Limited to collaterals and not their representatives (Id.)
5. Stepchildren and those who legally represent them,[7] if there is no next of kin	100% (§ 45a-439(a)(4))
6. State, if no other takers	100% (§ 45a-452)

7. "Those who legally represent them" means a per stirpital distribution. See, e.g., Daniels v. Daniels, 115 Conn. 239, 161 A. 94 (1932).

Delaware
Who Takes by Intestate Succession?

A. Surviving spouse takes:	
1. *If there are no surviving issue or parents of the decedent*	100% (12 § 502(1))
2. *If there are no surviving issue but the decedent is survived by a parent or parents*	First $50,000.00 of the intestate personal estate, plus 50% of the balance of the intestate personal estate, plus a life estate in the intestate real estate (12 § 502(2))
3. *If there are surviving issue all of whom are issue of the surviving spouse also*	First $50,000.00 of the intestate personal estate, plus 50% of the balance of the intestate personal estate, plus a life estate in the intestate real estate (12 § 502(3))
4. *If there are surviving issue, one or more of whom are not issue of the surviving spouse*	50% of the intestate personal estate, plus a life estate in the intestate real estate (12 § 502(4))
B. All the estate, or the surplus if there is a surviving spouse, passes to:	
1. *Issue of the decedent*	100%, per stirpes[8] (12 § 503(1))
2. *Parents, if there is no surviving issue*	100% equally[8] (12 § 503(2))
3. *Brothers and sisters and the issue of each deceased brother or sister, if there is no surviving parent*	100% per stirpes[8] (12 § 503(3))
4. *Next of kin of the decedent, and to the issue of deceased next of kin, if there is no issue of a parent*	100% per stirpes[8] (12 § 503(4))
5. *State, if no next of kin*	(12 § 1101)

8. Any property passing under 12 § 503 to 2 or more persons passes to such persons as tenants in common.

District of Columbia
Who Takes by Intestate Succession?

A. *Surviving spouse or surviving domestic partner takes:*	
1. *If no descendant or parent of the decedent survives the decedent*	100% (§ 19-302(1))
2. *If the decedent's surviving descendants are also descendants of the surviving spouse and there is no other descendant of the surviving spouse who survives the decedent*	⅔ of any balance of the intestate estate (§ 19-302(2))
3. *If no descendant of the decedent survives the decedent, but a parent of the decedent survives the decedent*	¾ of any balance of the intestate estate (§ 19-302(3))
4. *If all of the decedent's surviving descendants are also descendants of the surviving spouse and the surviving spouse has one or more surviving descendants who are not descendants of the decedent*	One-half of any balance of the intestate estate (§ 19-302 (4))
5. *If one or more of the decedent's surviving descendants are not descendants of the surviving spouse*	One-half of any balance of the intestate estate (§ 19-302(5))
B. *All the estate, or the surplus if there is a surviving spouse or surviving domestic partner, passes to (§ 19-305):*	
1. *Children, if no other descendants*	100% divided equally (§ 19-306)
2. *Children and the children of deceased children, if not just living children*	100% divided equally among children, with children of deceased children taking their parent's share equally if of the degree (§ 19-307(a)&(b))
3. *Parents, if there is no surviving child or descendant*[9]	100% divided equally between the father and mother "or their survivor" (§ 19-308)
4. *Brother and sister or their descen dants, if no parent*	100% (§ 19-309) equally, with descendants "stand[ing] in the place"[10] of deceased parents (§ 19-310)
5. *Collaterals in closest equal degree only, if no siblings or descendants of siblings*	100%, with representation not allowed[11] (§ 19-311)
6. *Grandparents, if no collaterals*	100%, share alike (§ 19-312)
7. *District of Columbia, if no relations within fifth degree*	100% (§ 19-701)

9. The reference to descendant is confusing, because B2. above only anticipates inheritance as far down as grandchildren, but no further.

10. "Standing in the place" remains undefined.

11. Section 19-701 is also confusing because grandparents would take if there are no collaterals, see § 19-312, notwithstanding § 19-701, which provides for escheat if there are no descendants of a common ancestor of the decedent within the fifth degree.

Florida
Who Takes by Intestate Succession?

A. Surviving spouse takes:	
1. If there is no surviving lineal descendant of the decedent	100% (§ 732.102(1))
2. If there are surviving lineal descendants of the decedent, all of whom are also lineal descendants of the surviving spouse	First $60,000 of the intestate estate, plus 50% of the balance of the intestate estate. Property allocated to the surviving spouse to satisfy the $60,000 is valued at the fair market value on the date of distribution. (§ 732.102(2))
3. If there are surviving lineal descendants, one or more of whom are not lineal descendants of the surviving spouse	50% of the intestate estate (§ 732.102(3))
B. All the estate, or the surplus if there is a surviving spouse, passes to:	
1. Lineal descendants of the decedent	100% (§ 732.103(1))[12]
2. Parents equally, or to the survivor of them, if no lineal descendants survive	100% (§ 732.103(2))
3. Siblings and the descendants of a deceased sibling, if no lineal descendants	100% (§ 732.103(3))[12]
4. Grandparents	100%, with 50% share to the paternal side and 50% share to the maternal side. The grandparents on each side share equally, or if only one, that grandparent takes the entire 50% share. (§ 732.103(4)(a))
a. Uncles and aunts and descendants of deceased uncles and aunts of the decedent, if there are no grandparents on that side	100% (§ 732.103(4)(b))[12]
b. The kindred on the other side, if there is no kindred on one side	100% (§ 732.103(4)(c)) The one side's share is combined with the other side's share and distributed as in 4.a. and b. above[12]
5. The kindred of the last deceased spouse of the decedent, as if the deceased spouse had survived the decedent and then died intestate entitled to the estate, if there is no kindred of either side	100% (§ 732.103(5))[12]
6. Lineal descendants of the decedent's great grandparents, if any descendants of the decedent's great grandparents were Holocaust victims as defined in § 626.9543(3)(b). [Provision ceases to be effective for proceedings filed after December 31, 2004.] 732.103(b) incorrectly refers to 626.9543(3)(b)	100% (§ 732.103(6))
7. State, if there are no other takers	100% (§ 732.107(1))

12. Distributions are made per stripes. See § 732.104.

Georgia
Who Takes by Intestate Succession?

A. Surviving spouse or reciprocal beneficiary takes:	
1. If there are no children or other descendants	100% (§ 53-2-1(b)(1))
2. If there is any child or other descendant who survives the decedent	Equally with the children or descendants taking a deceased child's share, but no less than 1/3 (§ 53-2-1(b)(1))
B. All the estate, or the surplus if there is a surviving spouse, passes to:	
1. Children and descendants of deceased children	100%, with descendants of deceased children taking per stirpes (§ 53-2-1(b)(3))
2. Parent, or parents equally, if no child or other descendants	100% (§ 53-2-1(b)(4))
3. Siblings, if no parents	100%, equally (§ 53-2-1(b)(5))
4. Nieces and nephews or their descen dants, if no siblings	100%, equally with descendants of a niece or nephew taking per stirpes (§ 53-2-1(b)(5))
5. Grandparents, if no nieces, neph ews, or their descendants	100%, equally (§ 53-2-1(b)(6))
6. Uncles and aunts, and the descen dants of a deceased uncle or aunt	100%, equally, with descendants taking per stirpes (§ 53-2-1(b)(7))
7. First cousins, if no uncles and aunts, even if there are surviving other descendants of uncles and aunts	100%, equally (§ 53-2-1(b)(7))
8. Escheat, if no other taker	100% (§§ 53-2-50 & 53-2-51)[13]

13. If surviving spouse dies intestate and within 6 months, without heirs, undistributed property to which she was entitled from the first-to- die spouse, under intestacy, does not escheat but is distributed to the heirs of the first-to-die. (§ 53-2-8(a))

Hawaii
Who Takes by Intestate Succession?

A. Surviving spouse or reciprocal beneficiary takes:

1. *If no descendant or parent of the decedent survives the decedent*	100% (§ 560:2-102(1)(A))
2. *If all of the decedent's surviving descendants are also descendants of the surviving spouse or reciprocal beneficiary and there is no other descendant of the surviving spouse or reciprocal beneficiary who survives the decedent*	100% (§ 560:2-102(1)(B))
3. *If no descendant of the decedent survives the decedent, but a parent of the decedent survives the decedent*	First $200,000, plus ¾ of any balance of the intestate estate (§ 560:2-102(2))
4. *If all of the decedent's surviving descendants are also descendants of the surviving spouse or reciprocal beneficiary and the surviving spouse or reciprocal beneficiary has one or more surviving descendants who are not descendants of the decedent*	First $150,000, plus 50% of any balance of the intestate estate (§ 560:2-102(3))
5. *If one or more of the decedent's surviving descendants are not descendants of the surviving spouse or reciprocal beneficiary*	First $100,000.00, plus 50% of any balance of the intestate estate (§ 560:2-102(4))

B. All the estate, or the surplus if there is a surviving spouse, passes to:

1. *Descendants by representation*[14]	100% (§ 560:2-103(1))
2. *Decedent's parents if both survive, or to the surviving parent; provided, however, if the decedent is a minor, and if it is shown by clear and convincing evidence that any parent has deserted the child, failed to communicate with child for at least one year, or failed to provide for care or support for one year*	100% (§ 560:2-103(2)), but nothing if proviso not satisfied (§ 560:2-103(2)(A)–(C))
3. *Descendants of the decedent's parents or either of them by representation,*[14] *if there is no parent entitled to inherit*	100% (§ 560:2-103(3))
4. *Grandparents or their descendants, if there are no descendants of decedent's parents*	50% of the estate to the decedent's paternal grandparents equally if both survive, or to the surviving paternal grandparent, or to the descendants of the decedent's paternal grandparents or either of them if both are deceased, the descendants taking by representation, and the other 50% passes to the decedent's maternal relatives in the same manner; but if there is no surviving grandparent or descendant of a grandparent on either the paternal or the maternal side, the entire estate passes to the decedent's relatives on the other side in the same manner as the half. (§ 560:2-103(4))
5. *State, if no grandparents or their descendants*	100% (§ 560:2-105)

14. "Representation" means per capita at each generation. See § 560:2-106(b).

Idaho
Who Takes by Intestate Succession?

A. *Surviving spouse takes:*	
1. *Separate Property: If there is no surviving issue or parent of the decedent*	100% (§ 15-2-102(a)(1))
2. *Separate Property: If there is no surviving issue but the decedent is survived by a parent or parents*	50% of the estate (§ 15-2-102(a)(2))
3. *Separate Property: If there is surviving issue of the deceased spouse*	50% of the estate (§ 15-2-102(a)(3))
4. *Community property*	The decedent's portion passes 100% to the surviving spouse (§ 15-2-102(b)(1))
B. *All the estate, or the surplus if there is a surviving spouse, passes to:*	
1. *Issue*	100% if they are all of the same degree of kinship to the decedent they take equally, but if of unequal degree, then those of more remote degree take by representation[15] (§ 15-2-103(a))
2. *Parent, or parents equally, if there is no surviving issue*	100% (§ 15-2-103(b))
3. *Issue of the parents or either of them by representation, if there is no parent*	100% (§ 15-2-103(c))
4. *Grandparents or issue of grandparents, if there is no surviving issue, parent or issue of a parent*	50% to paternal grandparents and 50% to maternal grandparents, with the grandparents on one side sharing equally if they both survive. If neither grandparent on that side survives, to the issue of the grandparents or grandparent on that side by representation. If no issue survive on that side either, then the 50% share is added to the 50% share on the other side and the grandparents or their issue on the other side take the entire 100% in the manner described herein. (§ 15-2-103(d))
5. *State, if there are no other takers*	100% (§ 14-113) Note that the provision only refers to "moneys and effects." See also § 14-503, which addresses taking custody of intangible unclaimed property but not real property.

15. "Representation" means per capita with representation. See § 15-2-106.

Illinois
Who Takes by Intestate Succession?

A. Surviving spouse takes:	
1. If no descendant	100% (755 ILCS § 5/2-1(c))
2. If a descendant survives as well	50% (755 ILCS § 5/2-1(a))
B. All the estate, or the surplus if there is a surviving spouse, passes to:	
1. Descendant, if no surviving spouse	100% per stirpes (755 ILCS § 5/2-1(b))
2. Descendant and surviving spouse	50% to spouse and 50% to descendants per stirpes (755 ILCS § 5/2-1(a))
3. Parent, sibling, or descendants of a deceased sibling	100%, in equal parts, with descendants of deceased siblings taking per stirpes. If there is only one parent surviving, that parent takes a double portion. (755 ILCS § 5/2-1(d))
4. Grandparents, if no parents, siblings, or descendants of siblings	50% to the paternal side and 50% to the maternal side. The grandparents on one side share equally, and if only one survives, that grandparent takes the entire 50% share. (755 ILCS § 5/2-1(e))
5. Descendants of grandparents, if no grandparents on that side	The entire share is distributed per stirpes (755 ILCS § 5/2-1(e))
6. Grandparents or descendants of grandparents on one side, if no descendants of grandparents on the other side	The 50% share is combined with the other side's 50% share and the entire amount is distributed as per 4. and 5. above (755 ILCS § 5/2-1(e))
7. Greatgrandparents or their descendants, if no grandparents or their descendants on either the maternal or paternal side	50% share to paternal greatgrandparents and 50% to maternal greatgrandparents in equal parts of the 50% share on each side or to the descendants of a predeceased greatgrandparent per stirpes (755 ILCS § 5/2-1(f)) If no greatgrandparents or descendants of greatgrandparents on one side, then added to the share on the other side and distributed as described above in 7.
8. Nearest kindred, if no greatgrandparents or descendants of greatgrandparents	100%, in equal shares for those of nearest degree by civil law method of country and without representation (755 ILCS § 5/2-1(g))
9. Escheat, if no kindred	Real estate escheats to county in which it is physically located. Personal estate escheats to county in which it is physically located. If property is located outside state and is subject to Illinois administration and ancillary administration elsewhere, then it passes to county in which decedent "was a resident," and if not a resident, the county in which the property was located. All other personal property or proceeds therefrom, wherever situated, passes to state, specifically State Treasurer pursuant to Uniform Disposition of Unclaimed Property Act. (755 § 5/2-1(h))

Indiana
Who Takes by Intestate Succession?

A. Surviving spouse takes:	
1. If the intestate is survived by at least one child or by the issue of at least one deceased child	50% (§ 29-1-2-1(b)(1))
2. If there is no surviving issue but the intestate is survived by one or both of the intestate's parents	75% (§ 29-1-2-1(b)(2))
3. If there is no surviving issue or parent	100% (§ 29-1-2-1(b)(3))
4. If the surviving spouse is a second or other subsequent spouse who did not at any time have children by the decedent, and the decedent left surviving him a child or children or the descendants of a child or children by a previous spouse	Life estate in 25% of the lands of the deceased spouse, and the fee vests, at the decedent's death, at once in such child or children, or the descendants of such as may be dead, subject only to the life estate of the surviving spouse. Such second or subsequent childless spouse, however, receives the same share of the personal property of the decedent with respect to surviving spouses generally. (§ 29-1-2-1(c))
B. All the estate, or the surplus if there is a surviving spouse, passes to:	
1. Issue	Equally; or if of unequal degree, then those of more remote degree take by representation[16] (§ 29-1-2-1(d)(1))
2. Surviving parents, if there is a surviving spouse but no surviving issue of the decedent	100% (§ 29-1-2-1(d)(2))
3. Surviving parents, brothers, and sisters, and the issue of deceased brothers and sisters of the intestate, if there is no surviving spouse or issue of the intestate	Each living parent of the intestate is treated as of the same degree as a brother or sister and is entitled to the same share as a brother or sister. However, the share of each parent is not to be less than one-fourth of the net estate. Issue of deceased brothers and sisters take by representation.[16] (§ 29-1-2-1(d)(3))
4. Surviving grandparents, if there are no surviving issue, or parent of the intestate, or issue of a parent	100%, shared equally (§ 29-1-2-1(d)(5))
5. Aunts and uncles and issue of deceased aunts and uncles, if no grandparents	100%; one share passes to each of the aunts and uncles, as well as deceased aunts and uncles who leave issue. The latter take per stirpes. (§ 29-1-2-1(d)(6))
6. State, if no siblings of parents or no issue of deceased siblings	100% (§ 29-1-2-1(d)(8))

16. "Representation" means per stirpes. See, e.g., Brown v. Taylor, 62 Ind. 295 (1878).

Iowa
Who Takes by Intestate Succession?

A. Surviving spouse takes:	
1. If no issue or issue are also the issue of the surviving spouse	100% (§ 633.211)
2. If issue some of whom are not the issue of the surviving spouse	a. 50% real property possessed during marriage and regarding which surviving spouse did not relinquish rights (§ 633.212 (1)) b. 100% exempt personal property of decedent as "head of a family" (§ 633.212(2)) c. 50% of all other personal property not necessary for payment of debts and charges (§ 633.212(3)) d. if a.–c. is less than $50,000, additional homestead interest and other property subject to debts and charges is given to the surviving spouse (§ 633.212(4))
B. All the estate, or the surplus if there is a surviving spouse, passes to:	
1. Issue	100%, per stirpes (§ 633.219(1))
2. Parents, if there is no surviving issue	100% (§ 633.219(2))
3. Issue of decedent's parents, if no parents	50%, per stirpes, on the maternal and paternal side. If there are no surviving issue of one deceased parent, the entire estate passes to the issue of the other deceased parent per stirpes. (§ 633.219(3))
4. Grandparents, if no issue of decedent's parents	50% per stirpes on the maternal and paternal sides. The paternal or maternal share is further divided among issue if neither grandparent on the particular side survives. One share passes per stirpes to the issue of the grandfather and one share passes per stirpes to the issue of the grandmother. If there are no issue, then to the issue of the other grandparent per stirpes. If there are no issue of either grandparent, then both of these subshares pass to the grandparents or their issue on the other side and are distributed in the same manner described above. (§ 633.219(4))
5. Great grandparents or issue of great grandparents, if no grandparents or issue of grandparents	Estate passes equally to each set of great grandparents or their issue, per stirpes (§ 633.219(5))[17]
6. Issue of deceased spouse, if no great grandparents or their issue	100%, per stirpes (§ 633.219(6)) If there is more than one predeceasing former spouse, then the estate passes equally among issue per stirpes of all such spouses. (Id.)
7. State, if no issue former spouse	100% (§ 633.219(7))

17. Although the language of the statute is not clear, presumably a surviving great grandparent would take before issue of the other deceased great grandparent could take.

Kansas
Who Takes by Intestate Succession?

A. Surviving spouse takes:	
1. If no children or issue of children	100% (§ 59-504)
2. If a child or issue of a predeceased child	50% (§ 59-504)
B. All the estate, or the surplus if there is a surviving spouse, passes to:	
1. Children and issue of children	100%, with issue taking "collectively" what predeceasing child would have taken (§ 59-506)
2. Parents, or parents equally, if no children or issue	100% (§ 59-507)
3. Heirs (other than spouses) of parents, as if parents died at time of intestate's death, if no parents	100%, equally divided between paternal and maternal sides, but if no heirs on one side, then all to the heirs on the other side (§ 59-508)
4. Heirs of last spouse of intestate predeceasing intestate, if no heirs of parents	100% (§ 59-514)
5. State, if no heirs of last spouse who predeceased intestate	100% (§ 59-514)

Note: Pursuant to Section 59-505, the surviving spouse is entitled to 50% of all real estate decedent was "seized or possessed" at any time during the marriage if the surviving spouse did not consent to the disposition in writing, by will, or by election under the law. Exceptions exist for executions and judicial sales, and when the surviving spouse has not been a resident of Kansas during the marriage.

Kentucky
Who Takes by Intestate Succession?

1. *Children and descendants*	100% (§ 391.010(1))[18]
2. *Parents, or parents equally, if no children or descendants*	100% (§ 391.010(2)) If a parent has given real estate and is still alive, that parent inherits the real estate. (§ 391.020(1)) If a person under age 18 dies without issue, any real property received gratuitously from a parent passes to that parent or the parent's kindred, and if none, then to the other parent and that parent's kindred. The kindred of one parent are not to be excluded if the kindred of the other is more remote than grandparents or aunts and uncles or their descendants. (§ 391.020(2))
3. *Siblings and their descendants, if no parents*	100% (§ 391.010(3))
4. *Surviving spouse, if no siblings or descendants of them*	100% (§ 391.010(4))
5. *Grandparents, if no surviving spouse*	50% to the paternal side and 50% to the maternal side; with respect to each of these moieties, it is shared by grandfather and grandmother, or if only one survives, the entire moiety passes to that grandparent (§ 391.010(5)(a))
6. *Aunts and uncles, or their descendants, if no grandparents with respect to the moiety*	100% (§ 391.010(5)(b))[19]
7. *Great grandparents, if no aunts, uncles, or their descendants with respect to the moiety*	100%, in same manner as in 5. above (§ 391.010(5)(c))[19]
8. *Siblings of grandparents, or their descendants, if no great grandparents with respect to the moiety*	100% (§ 391.010(5)(d))[19]
9. *Nearest lineal ancestors and their descendants, if no siblings of grandparents or descendants of such siblings*	100% (§ 391.010(5)(d))[19]
10. *Kindred of the other side, if no kindred on the one side (either paternal or maternal) as divided in 5. above*	100% (§ 391.010(6))
11. *State, if no kindred on the other side either*	100% (§ 393.020)

18. Section 391.010 refers to real property. The same pattern of distribution with respect to personal property is adopted by section 391.030(1).
19. Section 391.040 provides for a per stirpital distribution.

Louisiana[20]
Who Takes by Intestate Succession?

A. Surviving spouse takes:	
1. If no descendants	100% of decedent's share of community property (Civ. Code art. 889)
2. If descendants	Usufruct in decedent's share of community property until death or remarriage (Civ. Code art. 890)
3. If no descendants, parents, siblings, or descendants, and the surviving spouse was not judicially separated from him	100% (Civ. Code art. 894)
B. All the estate, or the surplus if there is a surviving spouse, passes to:	
1. Descendants	100% (Civ. Code art. 888)
2. Parents and siblings or descendants of sibling	Siblings or their descendants by representation subject to usufruct in favor of surviving parent or parents, which is joint and successive if both parents survive (Civ. Code art. 891)
3. Siblings or descendants of sibling, if no parents	100%, equally to siblings and descendants of siblings by representation (Civ. Code art. 892) If born of different parents, then equal shares are created on paternal and maternal side (Civ. Code art. 893)
4. Parents, or sole surviving parent, if no siblings or descendants of sibling	100% (Civ. Code art. 892)
5. Grandparents, and if not, more removed ascendants, where no parents, siblings, or descendants of siblings	If ascendants in maternal and paternal lines are of same degree, then equal shares to maternal and paternal lines. Ascendants on each side divide their share per capita. If the ascendant on one line is of nearer degree all passes to that ascendant, even if this excludes the other line. (Civ. Code art. 895)
6. Collaterals, if no ascendants	100% to the one in the nearest degree. If more than one in that degree, then they take per capita. (Civ. Code art. 896)
7. State, if there are no other takers	100% (Civ. Code art. 902)

20. With respect to immovables, ascendants inherit real property originally given by them to their children. (Civ. Code art. 897) If property has been alienated, the ascendant is entitled to receive the remaining unpaid price as well as any right of reversion upon condition. (Id.)

Maine
Who Takes by Intestate Succession?

A. *Surviving spouse or registered domestic partner takes:*	
1. *If there is no surviving issue or parent of the decedent*	100% (18-A § 2-102(1))
2. *If there is no surviving issue but the decedent is survived by a parent or parents*	First $50,000, plus 50% (18-A § 2-102(2))
3. *If there are surviving issue all of whom are issue of the surviving spouse also*	First $50,000, plus 50% (18-A § 2-102(3))
4. *If there are surviving issue one or more of whom are not issue of the surviving spouse*	50% (18-A § 2-102(4))
B. *All the estate, or the surplus if there is a surviving spouse or surviving registered domestic partner, passes to:*	
1. *Issue*	100%, per capita, at each generation (18-A § 2-103(1))
2. *Parents, or parents equally, if no descendants*	100%, equally (18-A § 2-103(2))
3. *Issue of parents or either of them, if there is no surviving parent*	100%, per capita at each generation (18-A § 2-103(3))
4. *Grandparents or issue of grandparents, if there is no surviving issue of a parent*	50% paternal side, 50% maternal side (18-A § 2-103(4)) Grandparents share equally, or all to one if just one survives. If no grandparents on one side, then to the issue per capita at each generation. If no grandparents or issue of grandparents on one side, then 100% to the other side. Id.
5. *Great-grandparent or issue of great grandparent*	50% paternal, 50% maternal (18-A § 2-103(5)) If no great grandparents on one side, then to the issue per capita at each generation. If no great-grandparents or issue of great-grandparents on one side, then 100% to the other side. Id.
6. *State, if no great-grandparents or issue of great-grandparents*	100% (18-A § 2-105)

Maryland
Who Takes by Intestate Succession?

A. *Surviving spouse takes:*	
1. *If there is a surviving minor child*	50% (Est. & Trusts § 3-102(b))
2. *If there is no surviving child, but there is surviving issue*	First $15,000 plus 50% residue (Est. & Trusts § 3-102(c))
3. *If there is no surviving issue but a surviving parent*	First $15,000 plus 50% residue (Est. & Trusts § 3-102(d))
4. *If no surviving issue or parent*	100% (Est. & Trusts § 3-102(e))
B. *All the estate, or the surplus if there is a surviving spouse, passes to:*	
1. *Issue*	Divided equally by representation as defined in § 1-210 (Est. & Trusts § 3-103)
2. *Parents, or parents equally, if no issue*[21]	100% (Est. & Trusts § 3-104(b))
3. *Issue of parents, if no parents*	100%, by representation (Est. & Trusts § 3-104(b))
4. *Grandparents and their issue, if no surviving issue of a parent*	50% to surviving paternal grandparents equally or all to the survivor (or if neither survives then to their issue by representation); 50% likewise to surviving maternal grandparents equally or all to the survivor (or if neither survives then to their issue by representation). If there are no grandparents or issue of grandparents on one side, then the 50% share is added to the 50% share to the other side, and the entire amount is distributed as provided above. (Est. & Trusts § 3-104(c))
5. *Great-Grandparents and their issue, if no surviving issue of a grandparent*	25% to each pair of great-grandparents equally or all to the survivor, or if neither survives, all to the issue of either or of both of that pair of great-grandparents, by representation. In the event that neither member of a pair of great-grandparents nor any issue of either of that pair survives, the quarter share applicable is to be distributed equally among the remaining pairs of great-grandparents or the survivor of a pair or issue of either of a pair of great-grandparents, in the same manner as prescribed for a quarter share. (Est. & Trusts § 3-104(d))
6. *Stepchildren, if no surviving blood relative*	100% equally to surviving stepchildren and to issue of predeceasing stepchildren by representation (Est. & Trusts § 3-104(e))
7. *State, if no stepchildren*	100% (Est. & Trusts § 3-105(a))

21. Under § 3-112 the surviving parent's inheritance rights may be denied in the case of an abandonment or failure to support a minor child.

Massachusetts
Who Takes by Intestate Succession?

A. *Surviving spouse takes:*	
1. *If the deceased leaves kindred and no issue, and it appears on determination by the probate court that the whole estate does not exceed two hundred thousand dollars in value*	First $200,000; otherwise the surviving spouse takes $200,000 and 50% of the remaining personal and 50% of the remaining real property (190 § 1(1))
2. *If the deceased leaves issue*	50% of personal and 50% of real property (190 § 1(2))
3. *If no issue and no kindred*	100% (190 § 1(3))
B. *All the estate, or the surplus if there is a surviving spouse, passes to:*	
1. *Children and issue of deceased children*	100%, equally and to issue by representation[22] (190 § 3(1))
2. *Issue, if no children*	100%, equally if all issue in same degree, otherwise by representation[22] (190 § 3(1))
3. *Parents, or parents equally, if no issue*	100%, equally, or all to survivor (190 § 3(2)-(4))
4. *Siblings and issue of declared siblings*	100%, equally and to issue by representation[22] (190 § 3(5))
5. *Issue of siblings, if no siblings*	100%, equally if all issue in same degree, otherwise by representation[22] (190 § 3(5))
6. *Next of kin, if no issue of siblings*	100%, equally if of same degree; if claiming through different ancestors, then those claiming through nearest ancestor are preferred (190 § 3(6))
7. *State,*[23] *if no next of kin*	100% (190 § 3(7))

22. "Representation" means per stirpes. See 190 § 8.
23. If intestate was a member of Soldier's Home, then estate inures to legacy fund of relevant home.

Michigan
Who Takes by Intestate Succession?

A. *Surviving spouse takes:*	
1. *If no descendant or parent of decedent*	100% (§ 700.2102(1)(a))
2. *If all of the decedent's surviving descendants are also descendants of surviving spouse and there are no other descendants of the surviving spouse*	First $150,000*, plus ½ of the balance (§ 700.2102(1)(b))
3. *If no descendant of the decedent survives but a parent survives*	First $150,000*, plus ¾ of the balance (§ 700.2102(1)(c))
4. *If all of decedent's surviving descendants are also descendants of the surviving spouse and she has at least one descendant who is not a descendant of the decedent*	First $150,000*, plus ½ of the balance (§ 700.2102(1)(d))
5. *If at least one but not all of decedent's surviving descendants is not also descendant of surviving spouse*	First $150,000*, plus ½ of the balance (§ 700.2102(1)(e))
6. *If all of decedent's surviving descendants are not descendants of the surviving spouse*	First $100,000*, plus ½ of the balance (§ 700.2102(1)(f))
B. *All the estate, or the surplus if there is a surviving spouse, passes to:*	
1. *Descendants*	100%, by representation[24] (§ 700.2103(a))
2. *Parents, or parents equally, if no descendants*	100% (§ 700.2103(b))
3. *Descendants of parents, or either of them, if no parents*	100%, by representation[24] (§ 700.2103(c))
4. *Grandparents, if no descendants of parents*	50% to the paternal side and 50% to the maternal side. On each side, the grandparents share equally, and if only one, he or she takes the entire share (§ 700.2103(d))
5. *Descendants of grandparents, if no grandparents on one side*	The 50% share passes by representation[24] (§ 700.2103(d))
6. *The other side, if no descendants of grandparents on one side*	The 50% share is added to the 50% share passing to the grandparents or their descendants on the other side and the entire amount is distributed as per B.4. and B.5. above (§ 700.2103(d))
7. *State, if no grandparents or descendants of grandparents on either side*	100% (§ 700.2105)

24. "Representation" means per capita at each generation. See § 700.2106.

Minnesota
Who Takes by Intestate Succession?

A. Surviving spouse takes:	
1. If no descendant of decedent	100% (§ 524.2-102(1)(i))
2. If all of decedent's descendants are descendants of surviving spouse and the surviving spouse has no other descendants	100% (§ 524.2-102(1)(ii))
3. If one of the surviving spouse's descendants is not a descendant of the decedent or one of the decedent's descendants is not a descendant of the surviving spouse	First $150,000, plus ½ of balance (§ 524.2-102(2))
B. All the estate, or the surplus if there is a surviving spouse, passes to:	
1. Descendants	100%, by representation[25] (§ 524.2-103(1))
2. Parents, or parents equally, if no descendants	100% (§ 524.2-103(2))
3. Descendants of parents, or of either of them, if no parents	100%, by representation[25] (§ 524.2-103(3))
4. Grandparents, if no descendants of parents	50% to the paternal side and 50% to the maternal side. On each side, the grandparents share equally, and if only one, he or she takes the entire share (§ 524.2-103(4))
5. Descendants of grandparents, if no grandparents on one side	The 50% share passes by representation[25] (§ 524.2-103(4))
6. The other side, if no descendants of grandparents on one side	The 50% share is added to the 50% share passing to the grandparents or their descendants on the other side (§ 524.2-103(4))
7. Next of kin, if no descendants of grandparents on either side	100%, but if more than one, then equally if in equal degree. However, if in equal degree, but claiming through different ancestors, those claiming through the nearest ancestor take to the exclusion of those claiming through a more remote ancestor (§ 524.2-103(5))
8. State, if no grandparents or descendants of grandparents on either side and no next of kin	100% (§ 524.2-105)

25. "Representation" means in the case of descendants of decedent a per stirpital distribution. See § 524.2-106(b). However, in the case of descendants of parents and grandparents, it means per capita with representation. See § 524.2-106(c)(1)&(2).

Mississippi
Who Takes by Intestate Succession?

A. Surviving spouse takes:	
1. If no children or descendants of children	100% (§ 91-1-7)
2. If any children or descendants of children	A child's part (§ 91-1-7)
B. All the estate, or the surplus if there is a surviving spouse, passes to:	
1. Children and descendants of deceased children	100% equally, but with descendants of deceased children taking by representation (§ 91-1-3)[26]
2. Parents, siblings, and descendants of siblings, if no children or descendants of children	100% in equal parts, with the "descendants of a sister or brother of the intestate to have in equal parts among them their deceased parent's share" (§ 91-1-3)
3. Grandparents, uncles, and aunts, if no parents, siblings, or descendants of siblings	100% in equal parts (§ 91-1-3)
4. Next of kin, if no grandparents, uncles, and aunts	100% in equal shares to those of equal degree under the civil law method of counting, but without representation (§ 91-1-3)
5. State, if no other takers	100% (§ 89-11-1)

26. The statute refers only to real estate. However, § 91-1-11 applies the same rules to personal property. "Representation" is not defined, although there is some authority indicating that it means per stirpes. See, e.g., In re Griffin's Will, 411 So. 2d 766, 769-70 (1982).

Missouri
Who Takes by Intestate Succession?

A. *Surviving spouse takes:*	
1. *If there is no surviving issue of the decedent*	100% (§ 474.010(1)(a))
2. *If there are surviving issue, all of whom are also issue of the surviving spouse*	First $20,000.00, plus 50% (§ 474.010(1)(b))
3. *If there are surviving issue, one or more of whom are not issue of the surviving spouse*	50% (§ 474.010(1)(c))
B. *All the estate, or the surplus if there is a surviving spouse, passes to:*	
1. *Decedent's children or their descendants*	100%, in equal parts (§ 474.010(2)(a))
2. *Decedent's father, mother, brother and sisters or their descendants, if there are no children, or their descendants*	100%, in equal parts (§ 474.010(2)(b))
3. *Grandfathers, grandmothers, uncles and aunts or their descendants,*[27] *if no father, mother, brother or sister, or their descendants*[28]	100%, in equal parts (§ 474.010(2)(c))
4. *Great-grandfathers, great-grandmothers, or their descendants and so on passing to the nearest lineal ancestors and their children, or their descendants (provided, however, that collateral relatives, that is relatives who are neither ancestors nor descendants of the decedent, may not inherit unless they are related to the decedent at least as closely as the ninth degree), if there are no grandfather, grandmother, uncles, aunts, nor their descendants*	100%, in equal parts (§ 474.010(2)(d))
5. *Kindred of each predeceased spouse who was married to the decedent at the spouse's death, if there is no surviving spouse or kindred of the decedent entitled to inherit*	100%, in "equal shares" to the kindred of each predeceasing spouse. Each such share passes as described in B.1.-B.4. above. (§ 474.010(3))
6. *Escheat as provided by the law, if no other takers*	(§ 474.010(4))

27. Generally, if takers are of the same lineal degree they take per capita. Otherwise, they take per stirpes. See § 474.020.
28. There is no indication whether descendants of a deceased aunt or uncle take if there are surviving aunts or uncles. It would seem however, to be the case. Furthermore, the reference to descendants would appear to be referring to uncles and aunts, rather than grandparents. However, these matters are unresolved.

Montana
Who Takes by Intestate Succession?

A.	*Surviving spouse takes:*	
1.	*If no descendant or parent of the decedent survives the decedent*	100% (§ 72-2-112(1)(a))
2.	*If all of the decedent's surviving descendants are also descendants of the surviving spouse and there is no other descendant of the surviving spouse who survives the decedent*	100% (§ 72-2-112(1)(b))
3.	*If no descendant of the decedent survives the decedent but a parent of the decedent survives the decedent*	First $200,000.00, plus 75% of the balance (§ 72-2-112(2))
4.	*If all of decedent's descendants are also surviving spouse's descendants and one or more of the spouse's descendants are not decedent's descendants*	First $150,000, plus 50% (§ 72-2-112(3))
5.	*If one or more of the decedent's surviving descendants are not descendants of the surviving spouse*	First $100,000, plus 50% of the balance (§ 72-2-112(4))
B.	*All the estate, or the surplus if there is a surviving spouse, passes to:*	
1.	*Decedent's descendants*	100% by representation (§ 72-2-113(1)(a))
2.	*Decedent's parents equally if both survive or to the surviving parent, if there is no surviving descendant*	100% (§ 72-2-113(1)(b))
3.	*Descendants of the decedent's parents or either of them, if there is no surviving parent*	100%, by representation[29] (§ 72-2-113(1)(c))
4.	*Grandparents or descendants of grandparents, if there is no descendant of a parent*	One-half to the decedent's paternal/maternal grandparents or descendants of the decedent's paternal/maternal grandparents, with each surviving grandparent on that side taking an equal portion if both survive. If not survived by a grandparent, then to descendants of grandparents on either the paternal or the maternal side (§ 72-2-113(d)(i))
5.	*The other side if no grandparents or descendants of grandparents on the one side*	100%, in same manner as B.4. above (§ 72-2-113(d)(ii))
6.	*The person or persons of the closest degree of kinship with the decedent, if no grandparents or descendants of grandparents*	100% (§ 72-2-113(1)(e)); if persons are of same degree but have different common ancestors with the decedent, the one(s) with the nearest ancestor takes exclusively (§ 72-2-113(2))
7.	*State, if there is no other taker*	100% (§ 72-2-115)

29. "Representation" means per capita with representation. See § 72-2-116(2).

Nebraska
Who Takes by Intestate Succession?

A.	*Surviving spouse takes:*	
1.	*If there is no surviving issue or parent of the decedent*	100% (§ 30-2302(1))
2.	*If there is no surviving issue but the decedent is survived by a parent or parents*	First $50,000.00, plus 50% (§ 30-2302(2))
3.	*If there are surviving issue all of whom are issue of the surviving spouse also*	First $50,000.00, plus 50% (§ 30-2302(3))
4.	*If there are surviving issue one or more of whom are not issue of the surviving spouse*	50% (§ 30-2302(4))
B.	*All the estate, or the surplus if there is a surviving spouse, passes to:*	
1.	*Issue of the decedent*	If they are all of the same degree of kinship to the decedent they take equally, but if of unequal degree, then those of more remote degree take by representation[30] (§ 30-2303(1))
2.	*Parents, or parents equally, if no surviving issue*	100% (§ 30-2303(2))
3.	*Issue of the parents or either of them by representation, if there is no surviving issue or parent*	100% (§ 30-2303(3))
4.	*Grandparents, if there is no surviving issue of a parent*	50% paternal side to be shared equally if both grandparents survive or otherwise all to sole surviving grandparent; 50% share for maternal side to be distributed in same manner (§ 30-2303(4))
5.	*Issue of grandparents on one side, if there are no surviving grandparents on that side*	100%, taking equally if issue are of same degree or, otherwise, taking by representation[30] (§ 30-2303(4))
6.	*The other side if no grandparents or issue of grandparents on the one side*	100%, in same manner as B.4. above (§ 30-2303(4))
7.	*Next of kin, if there is no surviving grandparent or issue of any grandparent*	100% in equal degree, excepting that when there are two or more collateral kindred in equal degree, but claiming through different ancestors, those who claim through the nearest ancestor are preferred to those claiming through a more remote ancestor (§ 30-2303(5))
8.	*State, if no other taker*	100% (§ 30-2305)

30. "Representation" means per capita with representation.

Nevada
Who Takes by Intestate Succession?

A. *Surviving spouse takes:*	
1. *If the decedent leaves a surviving spouse and only one child, or the lawful issue of one child*	50% surviving spouse and 50% to the child or the issue of the child (§ 134.040(1))
2. *If the decedent leaves a surviving spouse and more than one child living, or a child and the lawful issue of one or more deceased children*	One-third to the surviving spouse and the remainder in equal shares to the children and the lawful issue of any deceased child by right of representation (§ 134.040(2))
3. *If the decedent leaves no issue nor parents*	50% of the separate property of the decedent goes to the surviving spouse and the other 50% goes in equal shares to the brothers and sisters of the decedent (§ 134.050(2))
4. *If the decedent leaves no issue*	50% to the surviving spouse, 25% to the father of the decedent and 25% to the mother of the decedent, if both are living. If both parents are not living, 50% to either the father or the mother then living (§ 134.050(1))
5. *If the decedent leaves children but no spouse*	100%, share and share alike (§ 134.090)
6. *If the decedent leaves no issue, parent, sibling, or children of issue*	100% of the separate property(§ 134.050(4))
B. *All the estate, or the surplus if there is a surviving spouse, passes to:*	
1. *Children and the issue of a deceased child*	100%, with the issue taking by representation[31] (§ 134.100)
2. *Issue of children but no children*	100%, by representation (§ 134.110)
3. *Parents, if there is no surviving issue or surviving spouse*	50% to the father of the decedent and 50% to the mother of the decedent, if both are living. If both parents are not living, 100% to either the father or the mother then living. (§ 134.050(3))
4. *Siblings and the children of deceased siblings, if no issue, parent, children of issue, of spouse*	100% by representation (§ 134.060)
5. *Next of kin if no issue, spouse, parent, or sibling*	100%, equally, if in equal degree, but if claiming through different ancestors, the one(s) claiming through the nearest ancestor takes (§ 134.070)
6. *State, if no kindred*	100% to state for educational purposes (§ 134.120)

Note: The decedent's share of community property with right of survivorship passes to the surviving spouse. (§ 134.010(1)) If there is no right of survivorship and it is not disposed of by will, it also passes to the surviving spouse. (§§ 134.010(2); 123.250(b)(1)) In the case of the death of a minor who has not been married and is childless and whose parents are deceased, the estate that came to the child by inheritance from the parent passes to the issue of the parent equally if they are of the same degree and otherwise they are entitled to take by representation. (§ 134.080)

31. "Representation" is not defined in the statute or case law.

New Hampshire
Who Takes by Intestate Succession?

A. *Surviving spouse takes:*	
1. *If there is no surviving issue or parent*	100% (§ 561:1(I)(a))
2. *If there is no surviving issue, but parent*	First $250,000, plus ¾ of the balance (§ 561:1(I)(c))
3. *If there are surviving issue all of whom are also issue of surviving spouse*	First $250,000, plus ¼ of the balance (§ 561:1(I)(b))
4. *If there is any surviving issue not also issue of surviving spouse*	$100,000 plus § of intestate estate (§ 561:1(I)(e))
B. *All the estate, or the surplus if there is a surviving spouse, passes to:*	
1. *Issue*	100%, equally if of same degree of kinship and if not, then by representation[32] (§ 561:1(II)(a))
2. *Parents, if no issue*	100% (§ 561:1(II)(b))
3. *Siblings, if no parents*	100%, equally (§ 561:1(II)(c))
4. *Issue of siblings, if no siblings*	100%, equally if of same degree, but if not, then by representation[32] (§ 561:1(II)(c))
5. *Grandparents, if no issue of siblings*	50% to the paternal grandparents or surviving grandparent and the same on the maternal side (§ 561:1(II)(d))
6. *Issue of grandparents, if no grandparents on that side*	100%, equally if of same degree of kinship, but if not, then those of more remote degree take by representation.[32] (§ 561:1(II)(e)) The issue of grandparents only take if they are not beyond the fourth degree of kinship to the decedent. If there are no issue within the fourth degree on either the paternal or maternal grandparent side, then those issue on the other side take in full.
7. *Grandparents or issue of grandparents on one side, if no grandparents or issue of grandparents on the other side*	Entire share added to the other side's 50% share and then distributed as in B.5. and B.6. above (§ 561:1(II)(d))
8. *State, if no other taker*	100% (§ 561:1(II)(g))

32. "Representation" means per capita with representation. See Colony v. Colony, 97 N.H. 386, 394-96, 89 A.2d 909, 914-15 (1952); Preston v. Cole, 64 N.H. 459, 13 A. 788 (1888); Merrow v. Merrow, 105 N.H. 103, 193 A.2d 19 (1963).

New Jersey
Who Takes by Intestate Succession?

A. *Surviving spouse or domestic partner takes:*	
1. *If no descendant or parent of the decedent survives the decedent*	100% (§ 3B:5-3(a)(1))
2. *If all of the decedent's surviving descendants are also descendants of the surviving spouse and there is no other descendant of the surviving spouse who survives the decedent*	100% (§ 3B:5-3(a)(2))
3. *If no descendant of the decedent survives the decedent, but a parent of the decedent survives the decedent*	The first 25% of the intestate estate, but not less than $50,000.00 nor more than $200,000.00, plus 3/4 of any balance of the intestate estate. (§ 3B:5-3(b))
4. *If all of the decedent's surviving descendants are also descendants of the surviving spouse and the surviving spouse has one or more surviving descendants who are not descendants of the decedent*	The first 25% of the intestate estate, but not less than $50,000.00 nor more than $200,000.00, plus 1/2 of the balance of the intestate estate. (§ 3B:5-3(c)(1))
5. *If one or more of the decedent's surviving descendants is not a descendant of the surviving spouse*	The first 25% of the intestate estate, but not less than $50,000.00 nor more than $200,000.00, plus one-half of the balance of the intestate estate. (§ 3B:5-3(c)(2))
B. *All the estate, or the surplus if there is a surviving spouse or domestic partner, passes to:*	
1. *Descendants of decedent*	100%, by representation.[33] (§ 3B:5-4(a))
2. *Parent, or parents equally, if no surviving descendant*	100% (§ 3B:5-4(b))
3. *Descendants of decedent's parents, if there are no surviving parents*	100%, descendants of parents or either of them taking by representation.[33] (§ 3B:5-4(c))
4. *Grandparents, if there is no surviving descendant, parent, or descendant of a parent*	50% of the estate passes to the paternal grandparents equally if both survive, or to the surviving paternal grandparent; the same is true of the maternal grandparents. If both are deceased, then to the descendants of the grandparents or either of them, the descendants taking equally if they are all of the same degree of kinship to the decedent, but if of unequal degree those of more remote degree take by representation.[33] (§ 3B:5-4(d)&(e))
5. *Grandparents, and descendants of grandparents on the other side, if there are no grandparents or descen dants of grandparents on one side*	100%, adding the 50% share on one side to the 50% share on the other side and then distributing the whole as in B.4. above. (§ 3B:5-4(d))
6. *Decedent's step-children or their descendants, if no surviving descendants of grandparents*	100%, taking by representation.[33] (§ 3B:5-4(f))

7. *State, if there are no other takers*	a. Use and custody by state in case of certain safe deposit contents constituting tangible personal property and most intangible personal property (§§ 46:30B-37.1; 46:30B-6(r) ("property" defined for purposes of Uniform Disposition of Unclaimed Property Act)) b. 100% escheat in the case of most tangible personal and real property (§ 2A:37-1; Van Kleek v. O' Hanlon, 21 N.J.L. 582 (1845); In re Mill's Estate, 212 A.2d 799 (Ch. 1965))

33. "Representation" means per capita at each generation level. See § 3B:1-2.

New Mexico
Who Takes by Intestate Succession?

A. Surviving spouse takes:	
1. If no surviving issue of the decedent	100%, as to separate property (§ 45-2-102(A)(1))
2. If there is surviving issue of the decedent	25%, as to separate property (§ 45-2-102(A)(2))
3. Community property as to which the decedent could have exercised the power of testamentary disposition	50% (§ 45-2-102)(B)
B. All the estate, or the surplus if there is a surviving spouse, passes to:	
1. Descendants, if there is no surviving spouse	100%, by representation (§ 45-2-103(A))
2. Parents, if there is no surviving descendant	100%, to the decedent's parents equally if both survive, or to the surviving parent (§ 45-2-103(B))
3. Descendants of the decedent's parents or either one of them, if there is no surviving descendant or parent	100%, by representation (§ 45-2-103(C))
4. Grandparents or descendants of the grandparents, if there is no descendant of a parent	50% of the estate to the decedent's paternal grandparents equally if both survive, or to the surviving paternal grandparent, or to the descendants of the decedent's paternal grandparents or either of them if both are deceased, the descendants taking by representation, and the other 50% passes to the decedent's maternal relatives in the same manner; but if there is no surviving grandparent or descendant of a grandparent on either the paternal or the maternal side, the entire estate passes to the decedent's relatives on the other side in the same manner as the half (§ 45-2-103(D))
5. State, if there is no other taker	100% (§ 45-2-105)

New York
Who Takes by Intestate Succession?

A.	*Surviving spouse takes:*	
	1. If there is issue	$50,000 and 50% of the residue (EPTL § 4-1.1(a)(1))
	2. If there is no issue	100% (EPTL § 4-1.1(a)(2))
B.	*All the estate, or the surplus if there is a surviving spouse, passes to:*	
	1. Issue, if there is no spouse	100%, by representation (EPTL § 4-1.1(a)(3))
	2. One or both parents, if there is no issue	100% (EPTL § 4-1.1(a)(4))
	3. Issue of parents, if there is no spouse, issue or parent	100%, by representation (EPTL § 4-1.1(a)(5))
	4. Grandparents or the issue of grandparents, but only so far as grandchildren, if no spouse, issue, parent or issue of parents	50% to the surviving paternal grandparent or grandparents, or if neither of them survives the decedent, to their issue, by representation, and the other 50% to the surviving maternal grandparent or grandparents, or if neither of them survives the decedent, to their issue, by representation; provided that if the decedent was not survived by a grandparent or grandparents on one side or by the issue of such grandparents, the whole to the surviving grandparent or grandparents on the other side, or if neither of them survives the decedent, to their issue, by representation, in the same manner as the one-half (EPTL § 4-1.1(a)(6))
	5. Great-grandchildren of grandparents, if no spouse, issue, parent, issue of parents, grandparent, children of grandparents or grandchildren of grandparents	50% to the great-grandchildren of the paternal grandparents, per capita, and the other 50% to the great-grandchildren of the maternal grandparents, per capita; provided that if the decedent was not survived by great-grandchildren of grandparents on one side, the whole to the great-grandchildren of grandparents on the other side, in the same manner as the one-half (EPTL § 4-1.1(a)(7))
	6. Escheat as abandoned property, if no other takers	100% (EPTL § 4-1.5)

North Carolina
Who Takes by Intestate Succession?

A. *Surviving spouse takes:*	
1. *real property: if the intestate is survived by only one child or by any lineal descendant of only one deceased child*	One-half undivided interest (§ 29-14(a)(1))
2. *real property: if the intestate is survived by two or more children, or by one child and any lineal descendant of one or more deceased children or by lineal descendants of two or more deceased children*	One-third undivided interest (§ 29-14(a)(2))
3. *real property: if the intestate is not survived by a child, children or any lineal descendant of a deceased child or children, but is survived by one or more parents*	One-half undivided interest (§ 29-14(a)(3))
4. *real property: if the intestate is not survived by a child, children or any lineal descendant of a deceased child or children, or by a parent*	100% (§ 29-14(a)(4))
5. *personal property: if the intestate is survived by only one child or by any lineal descendant of only one deceased child, and the net personal property does not exceed thirty thousand dollars in value*	100%; if the net personal property exceeds thirty thousand dollars in value, the sum of thirty thousand dollars plus one half of the balance of the personal property (§ 29-14(b)(1))
6. *personal property: if the intestate is survived by two or more children, or by one child and any lineal descendant of one or more deceased children or by lineal descendants of two or more deceased children*	100%; if the net personal property exceeds thirty thousand dollars in value, the sum of thirty thousand dollars plus one-third of the balance of the personal property (§ 29-14(b)(2))
7. *personal property: if the intestate is not survived by a child, children or any lineal descendant of a deceased child or children, but is survived by one or more parents*	100%; if the net personal property exceeds fifty thousand dollars in value, the sum of fifty thousand dollars plus 50% of the balance of the personal property (§ 29-14(b)(3))
8. *personal property: if the intestate is not survived by a child, children, or any lineal descendant of a deceased child or children, or by a parent*	100% (§ 29-14(b)(4))

Note: § 29-14(c) provides that the amount a surviving spouse receives under § 29-14(a)-(b) is offset by the net value of any equitable distribution awarded to the surviving spouse pursuant to § 50-20 subsequent to the death of the decedent spouse.

B. All the estate, or the surplus if there is a surviving spouse, passes to:	
1. If the intestate is survived by only one child or by only one lineal descendant of only one deceased child	100%, by representation[34] (§ 29-15(1))
2. If the intestate is survived by two or more children or by one child and any lineal descendant of one or more deceased children, or by lineal descendants of two or more deceased children	100%, by representation[34] (§ 29-15(2))
3. Parents, if the intestate is not survived by a child, children or any lineal descendant of a deceased child or children	100% to be shared equally if both survive and if only one, then the entire estate (§ 29-15(3))
4. Siblings of the intestate, and the lineal descendants of the deceased siblings, if the intestate is not survived by a parent	100%, by representation[34] (§ 29-15(4))
5. Paternal/maternal grandparents, if no siblings or lineal descendants of siblings	50% of the net estate in equal shares to each side. Within each side, each grandparent takes 50%, or, if either is dead, the survivor takes the entire 50% of the net estate, and if neither grandparent survives, the uncles and aunts of the decedent on that side or the descendants of an uncle or aunt by representation share in said 50%. If there is no grandparent and no uncle or aunt, or lineal descendant of a deceased uncle or aunt, on that side, then those of the other side who otherwise would be entitled to take 50% as hereinbefore provided take the whole. (§ 29-15(5)(a-d))

34. "Representation" means per capita at each generation. See § 29-16. In the case of descendants of siblings, no descendants removed beyond the fifth degree are entitled to take. See § 29-16(5).

North Dakota
Who Takes by Intestate Succession?

A. Surviving spouse takes:	
1. no descendant or parent of the decedent survives the decedent	100% (§ 30.1-04-02(1)(a))
2. all of the decedent's surviving descendants are also descendants of the surviving spouse and there is no other descendant of the surviving spouse who survives the decedent	100% (§ 30.1-04-02(1)(b))
3. If no descendant of the decedent survives the decedent, but a parent of the decedent survives the decedent	First two hundred thousand dollars, plus 75% of any balance of the intestate estate (§ 30.1-04-02(2))
4. If all of the decedent's surviving descendants are also descendants of the surviving spouse and the surviving spouse has one or more descendants who are not descendants of the decedent	First one hundred and fifty thousand dollars, plus one-half of any balance of the intestate estate (§ 30.1-04-02(3))
5. If one or more of the decedent's surviving descendants are not descendants of the surviving spouse	First one hundred thousand dollars, plus 50% of any balance of the intestate estate (§ 30.1-04-02(4))
B. All the estate, or the surplus if there is a surviving spouse, passes to:	
1. Decedent's descendants	100%, by representation (§ 30.1-04-03(1))
2. Decedent's parents, if there is no surviving descendant	100% divided equally, or all if only one survives the decedent (§ 30.1-04-03(2))
3. Descendants of the decedent's parents or either of them, if there is no surviving parent	100%, by representation (§ 30.1-04-03(3))
4. Decedent's grandparents, if there is no surviving descendant of a parent	50% of the net estate in equal shares to the paternal and maternal sides. On each side, the grandparents share equally, or if either is deceased, the survivor takes the entire 50% share. If neither grandparent survives, the descendants of the grandparents on that side or of either one share in said 50%. If there is no grandparent or the descendant of deceased grandparents, on that side, then those on the other side who otherwise would be entitled to take 50% as hereinbefore provided take the whole by the same rules. (§ 30.1-04-03(4))
5. State, if there is no other taker	100% (§ 30.1-04-05)

Ohio
Who Takes by Intestate Succession?

A. Surviving spouse takes:	
1. *If one or more children of the decedent or their lineal descendants are surviving and all of the decedent's children who survive or have lineal descendants surviving also are children of the surviving spouse*	100% (§ 2105.06(B))[35]
2. *If one child of the decedent or the child's lineal descendants survive and the surviving spouse is not the natural or adoptive parent of the decedent's child*	First twenty thousand dollars and 50% of the balance of the intestate estate if the spouse and the remainder to the child or the child's lineal descendants (§ 2105.06(C))[35]
3. *If more than one child or their lineal descendants survive and the spouse is the natural or adoptive parent of one, but not all, of the children*	First $60,000 plus / of the balance (§ 2105.06(D))[35]
4. *If more than one child or their lineal descendants surviving and the spouse is the natural or adoptive parent of none of the children*	$20,000 plus 33% of the balance (§ 2105.06(D))
5. *If there are no children or their lineal descendants*	100% (§ 2105.06(E))
B. All the estate, or the surplus if there is a surviving spouse, passes to:	
1. *Children or their lineal descendants*	100%, equally if only children, but if there are any lineal descendants of deceased children, then per stirpes (§§ 2105.06(A), 2105.11, 2105.13) However, if there are only lineal descendants all of the same degree, then they share equally per capita (§ 2105.12)
2. *Parents of the intestate share equally, or the whole to the surviving parent, if no sole children or their lineal descendants*	100% (§ 2105.06 (F))
3. *Brothers and sisters, whether of the whole or of the half blood of the intestate, or their lineal descendants*	100%, per stirpes (§ 2105.06 (G))
4. *Grandparents, if there are no brothers or sisters or their lineal descendants*	50% to the paternal grandparents of the intestate equally, or to the survivor of them, and 50% to the maternal grandparents of the intestate equally, or to the survivor of them (§ 2105.06 (H))
5. *Lineal descendants of the deceased grandparents, if there is no paternal grandparent or no maternal grandparent*	50% distributed among the lineal descendants on each side, per stirpes[36] (§ 2105.06 (I))

6. *The surviving grandparents on the other side or their lineal descendants, if there are no such lineal descendants on the other side*	100%, as per B.4. and B.5. above (§ 2105.06 (I))
7. *The next of kin of the intestate,*[37] *if there are no surviving grandparents or their lineal descendants*	100%, but without representation (§ 2105.06 (I))
8. *The stepchildren or their lineal descendants, if there are no next of kin*	100%, per stirpes (§ 2105.06 (J))
9. *State, if there are no stepchildren or their lineal descendants*	100% (§ 2105.06 (K))

35. Real property is made subject to the foregoing rules by § 2105.061 and passes in parcenary subject to the monetary charge of the surviving spouse.

36. Notwithstanding the use of the term "per stirpes" in § 2105.06, § 2105.13 provides for a distribution in this case per capita with representation.

37. Next of kin is determined by the civil degree method of counting. See § 2105.03. There does not appear to be any cut-off for laughing heirs.

Oklahoma
Who Takes by Intestate Succession?

A. Surviving spouse takes:	
1. If no surviving issue, parent, or sibling	100% (84 § 213(B)(1)(a))
2. If no surviving issue, but parent or parents, or siblings	100% of property acquired "by joint industry" of spouses during coverture (84 § 213(B)(1)(b)(1)), and an undivided ¾ interest in the balance (84 § 213(B)(1)(b)(2))
3. If there are issue who are all issue of surviving spouse	½ of the estate (84 § 213(B)(1)(c))
4. If there are surviving issue, one of whom is not issue of surviving spouse	An undivided ½ interest in property acquired "by joint industry" of spouses during coverture (84 § 213(B)(1)(d)(1)), and an undivided equal part with each of the living children of the decedent and the lawful issue of any deceased child by right of representation in the balance (84 § 213(B)(1)(d)(2))
B. All the estate, or the surplus if there is a surviving spouse, passes to:	
1. Issue and their descendants	100%, by representation[38] (84 § 213(B)(2)(a))
2. Parent or parents, if no issue and their descendants	100% in undivided equal shares (84 § 213(B)(2)(b))
3. Issue of parents, if no parents	100% in undivided equal shares by right of representation[38] (84 § 213(B)(2)(c))
4. Grandparents, if no issue of parents	50% to paternal grandparents and 50% to maternal grandparents, with the grandparents on each side taking equally if both survive; otherwise, the survivor takes the entire 50% share (84 § 213(B)(2)(d))
5. Issue of grandparent or grandparents if neither grandparent on one side survives	The 50% share is distributed to issue of same degree equally, and if not of equal degree, then by representation[38] (84 § 213(B)(2)(d))
6. Grandparents or issue of grandparents on the other side, if no issue of grandparents on one side	100%, as per B.4.–5. above (84 § 213(B)(2)(d))
7. Next of kin if no grandparent or issue on the other side	100% to next of kin in nearest equal degree (84 § 213(B)(2)(e))
8. State for support of common schools, if no next of kin	100% (84 § 213(B)(3))

38. "Representation" means per capita with representation. See In re Estate of Kendall, 968 P.2d 364 (1998).

Oregon
Who Takes by Intestate Succession?

A. Surviving spouse takes:	
1. If there are surviving issue of the decedent all of whom are issue of the surviving spouse also	100% (§ 112.025(1))
2. If there are surviving issue of the decedent one or more of whom are not issue of the surviving spouse	50% (§ 112.025(2))
3. If the decedent leaves a surviving spouse and no issue	100% (§ 112.035)
B. All the estate, or the surplus if there is a surviving spouse, passes to:	
1. Issue of the decedent	100%. If the issue are all of the same degree of kinship to the decedent, they take equally, but if of unequal degree, then those of more remote degrees take by representation.[39] (§ 112.045(1))
2. Surviving parents, if no issue of the decedent	100% (§ 112.045(2)) If, at the time of taking, surviving parents are married to each other, they take real property as tenants by the entirety and personal property as joint owners with the right of survivorship (§ 112.045(5))
3. Brothers and sisters of the decedent and the issue of any deceased brother or sister of the decedent, if no surviving parents	100%, equally if siblings only, and by representation[39] to the extent of any issue of deceased siblings of the decedent (§ 112.045(3))
4. Issue of brothers and sisters, if there is no surviving brother or sister	100%. If they are all of the same degree of kinship to the decedent, they take equally, but if of unequal degree, then those of more remote degree take by representation[39] (§ 112.045(3))
5. Grandparents of the decedent and the issue of any deceased grandparent of the decedent, if there is no surviving issue of a brother or sister of the decedent	100%, with the issue of a deceased grandparent taking by representation[39] (§ 112.045(4)) If, at the time of taking, surviving grandparents are married to each other, they take real property as tenants by the entirety and personal property as joint owners with the right of survivorship (§ 112.045(5))
6. Issue of grandparents, if there is no surviving grandparent	100%. If they are all of the same degree of kinship to the decedent, they take equally, but if of unequal degree, then those of more remote degrees take by representation[39] (§ 112.045(4))
7. State, if there are no other takers	100% (§ 112.055)

39. "Representation" means per capita with representation. See § 112.065.

Pennsylvania
Who Takes by Intestate Succession?

A. Surviving spouse takes:	
1. If there is no surviving issue or parent of the decedent	100% (20 § 2102(1))
2. If there is no surviving issue of the decedent but he is survived by a parent or parents	The first $30,000 plus 50% of the balance of the intestate estate (20 § 2102(2))
3. If there are surviving issue of the decedent all of whom are issue of the surviving spouse also	The first $30,000 plus 50% of the balance of the intestate estate (20 § 2102(3))
4. If there are surviving issue of the decedent one or more of whom are not issue of the surviving spouse	50% (20 § 2102(4))
B. All the estate, or the surplus if there is a surviving spouse, passes to:	
1. Issue	100% (20 § 2103(1))
2. Parents, if no issue survives	100% (20 § 2103(2))
3. Brothers, sisters, or their issue, if no parent survives	100% (20 § 2103(3))[40]
4. Grandparents, if no issue of either of the decedent's parents but at least one grandparent survives the decedent	50% to the paternal grandparents or grandparent, or if both are deceased, to the children of each of them and the children of the deceased children of each of them,[40] and 50% to the maternal grandparents or grandparent, or if both are deceased to the children of each of them and the children of the deceased children of each of them.[40] If both of the paternal grandparents or both of the maternal grandparents are deceased leaving no child or grandchild surviving the decedent, the half which would have passed to them or to their children and grandchildren are added to the half passing to the grandparents or grandparent or to their children and grandchildren on the other side (20 § 2103(4))
5. Uncles, aunts, their children, and grandchildren, if no grandparent survives the decedent	100% to uncles and aunts equally, and children or grandchildren of a deceased uncle or aunt. However, no share for any grandchild of an uncle or an aunt if there are any children of any other uncle or aunt, the latter taking exclusively. If there are no children, then grandchildren of uncles and aunts take, but no issue of a grandchild of an uncle or aunt is entitled to take under any circumstances. (20 §§ 2103(5) & 2104(1))
6. State, in default of all other persons	100% (20 § 2103(6))

40. "Representation" means per capita with representation. See 20 § 2104(1). However, if all takers are of the same degree, they take equally. See 20 § 2104(2).

Rhode Island
Who Takes by Intestate Succession?

A.	*Surviving spouse takes:*[41]	
1.	*If no issue*[41]	Real property: Life interest in real estate (§ 33-1-5)[42] Personal property: $50,000, plus ½ of the remainder (§ 33-1-10(1))
2.	*If issue*	/½ of the personal property (§ 33-1-10(2))
B.	*All the estate, or the surplus if there is a surviving spouse, passes to:*[43]	
1.	*Children or their descendants*	100% (§ 33-1-1(1))
2.	*Parents, equally, or the surviving parent of the intestate, if there are no children nor their descendants*	100%, in equal shares (§ 33-1-1(2))
3.	*Brothers and sisters of the intestate and their descendants, if there is no parent*	100% (§ 33-1-1(3))
4.	*Grandparents, if there is no brother, sister, nor their descendants*	50% to the paternal grandparents and 50% to the maternal grandparents, to be divided equally between the grandparents on each side, if they both survive (§ 33-1-2(1))
5.	*Uncles and aunts or their descendants, if there be no grandparents on that side*	100%, with representation[44] in the case of descendants of deceased uncles and aunts (§ 33-1-2(2))
6.	*Great grandparents, if no uncle, aunt, or their descendants on that side*	100%, in equal shares (§ 33-1-2(3))
7.	*Great uncles and great aunts or their descendants, if no great grandparent on that side*	100%, with descendants of deceased great aunts or great uncles taking by representation[44] (§ 33-1-2(4))
8.	*Nearest lineal ancestors and their descendants, if there are no great uncles, aunts, or descendants on that side*	100%, with descendants of deceased nearest lineal descendants taking by representation[44] (§ 33-1-2(4))
9.	*Grandparents or other kindred on the other side, if no lineal ancestors or their descendants on the one side*	The 50% share of the one side is added to the other side's moiety, and the entire estate is distributed as per B.4.-B.8. above (§ 33-1-3)
10.	*Surviving spouse, if no kindred of the intestate on either the paternal nor maternal sides*	100%, in like manner as per B.4.-B.9. above (§ 33-1-3)

41. The surviving spouse, or, if deceased, the kindred of the surviving spouse, take if there are no kindred of the intestate to take on the paternal or maternal sides, as set forth in B.10. below.

11.	*Treated as unclaimed property, belonging to state and with respect to real property, town council takes possession, if no other takers*	100% (§§ 33-21-1 et seq. (real property) & 33-21.1-2 et seq. (personal property) See also City of Providence v. Solomon, 444 A.2d 870 (1982)

42. The surviving spouse may also petition, if there are no issue, for a set-off of an amount not exceeding $75,000 in value of real estate, which may be allowed in the discretion of the court. (§ 33-1-6)

43. The personal property is distributed in accordance with the descent of real property, as set forth below. See § 33-1-10.

44. "Representation" means per stirpes. See, e.g., Daboll v. Field, 9 R.I. 266 (1869); Kelaghan v. Lewis, 98 R.I. 458, 466, 204 A.2d 633, 637 (1964). See also B.M.C. Durfee Trust Co. v. Franzheim, 349 Mass. 335, 207 N.E.2d 913, 916 (1965). See generally § 33-1-7, which is not particularly helpful.

South Carolina
Who Takes by Intestate Succession?

A. *Surviving spouse takes:*	
1. *If there is no surviving issue*	100% (§ 62-2-102(1))
2. *If there are surviving issue*	50% (§ 62-2-102(2))
B. *All the estate, or the surplus if there is a surviving spouse, passes to:*	
1. *Issue, if there is no surviving spouse*	100%; if they are all of the same degree of kinship to the decedent they take equally, but if of unequal degree then those of more remote degree take by representation[45] (§ 62-2-103(1))
2. *Parent, or parents equally, if there is no surviving issue*	100% (§ 62-2-103(2))
3. *Issue of the parents or either of them by representation, if there is no surviving parent*	100% (§ 62-2-103(3))
4. *Grandparents or issue of grandparents, if there is no surviving issue of a parent*	50% to the paternal grandparents if both survive, or to the surviving paternal grandparent, or to the issue of the paternal grandparents if both are deceased, the issue taking equally if they are all of the same degree of kinship to the decedent, but if of unequal degree those of more remote degree take by representation;[45] 50% to the maternal relatives in the same manner (§ 62-2-103(4))
5. *Relatives on the other side, if there be no surviving grandparent or issue of grandparent on one side*	In the same manner as B.4. above (§ 62-2-103(4))
6. *Greatgrandparents or issue of greatgrandparents, if there are no grandparents or issue of grandparents*	50% to the surviving paternal great grandparents in equal shares, or to the surviving paternal great grandparent if only one survives, or to the issue of the paternal great grandparents if none of the great grandparents survive, the issue taking equally if they are all of the same degree of kinship to the decedent, but if of unequal degree those of more remote degree take by representation;[45] 50% to the maternal relatives in the same manner (§ 62-2-103(5))
7. *Relatives on the other side, if there be no surviving greatgrandparent or issue of a greatgrandparent on either the paternal or the maternal side*	In the same manner as B.6. above (§ 62-2-103(5))
8. *Stepchildren or issue of stepchildren, if there are no greatgrandparents or issue of greatgrandparents*	100%; if they are all of the same degree of step-kinship to the decedent they take equally, but if of unequal degree then those of more remote degree take by representation (§ 62-2-103(6))
9. *State, if there is no other taker*	100% (§ 62-2-105)

45. "Representation" means per capita with representation. See § 62-2-106.

South Dakota
Who Takes by Intestate Succession?

A. Surviving spouse takes:	
1. If no descendant of the decedent survives the decedent	100% (§ 29A-2-102(1)(i))
2. If all of the decedent's surviving descendants are also descendants of the surviving spouse	100% (§ 29A-2-102(1)(ii))
3. If one or more of the decedent's surviving descendants are not descendants of the surviving spouse	The first $100,000, plus one-half of any balance of the intestate estate (§ 29A-2-102(2))
B. All the estate, or the surplus if there is a surviving spouse, passes to:	
1. Descendants	100% by representation[46] (§ 29A-2-103(1))
2. Parents equally if both survive, or the surviving parent, if there is no surviving descendant	100% (§ 29A-2-103(2))
3. Descendants of the decedent's parents or either of them by representation, if there is no surviving parent	100% (§ 29A-2-103(3))
4. Grandparents, if there is no surviving descendant of a parent	50% to the decedent's paternal grandparents equally if both survive, or the whole of the share to the surviving paternal grandparent, or by representation[46] to the descendants of the decedent's paternal grandparents or either of them if both paternal grandparents are deceased; 50% passes to the decedent's maternal relatives in the same manner (§ 29A-2-103(4))
5. Decedent's relatives on the other side, if there is no surviving grandparent or descendant of a grandparent on one side	In the same manner as B.4. above (§ 29A-2-103(4))
6. State, if there are no other takers	100% (§ 29A-2-105)

46. "Representation" means per capita with representation. See § 29A-2-106.

Tennessee
Who Takes by Intestate Succession?

A. *Surviving spouse takes:*	
1. *If there is no surviving issue of the decedent*	100% (§ 31-2-104(a)(1))
2. *If there are surviving issue of the decedent*	Greater of ¾ or a child's share of the entire intestate estate (§ 31-2-104(a)(2))
B. *All the estate, or the surplus if there is a surviving spouse, passes to:*	
1. *Issue*	100%; if the issue are all of the same degree of kinship to the decedent they take equally, but if of unequal degree, then those of more remote degree take by representation.[47] (§ 31-2-104(b)(1))
2. *Parent or parents equally, if there is no surviving issue*	100% (§ 31-2-104(b)(2))
3. *Brothers and sisters and the issue of each deceased brother and sister, if there is no parent*	100%, by representation[47] (§ 31-2-104(b)(3))
4. *Issue of brothers and sisters, if there is no surviving brother or sister*	100%, by representation[47] (§ 31-2-104(b)(3))
5. *Grandparents or issue of grandparents, if there is no surviving issue of a parent*	50% to the paternal grandparents if both survive, or to the surviving paternal grandparent or to the issue of the paternal grandparents if both are deceased, the issue taking equally if they are all of the same degree of kinship to the decedent, but if of unequal degree those of more remote degree take by representation;[47] 50% to the maternal relatives in the same manner; but if there are no surviving grandparent or issue of grandparent on either the paternal or maternal side, the entire estate passes to the relatives on the other side in the same manner as the half. (§ 31-2-104(b)(4))
6. *State, if there are no other takers*	100% (§ 31-2-110)

47. "Representation" means per stirpes. See § 31-2-106.

Texas
Who Takes by Intestate Succession?

A. Surviving spouse takes:	
1. If the deceased is survived by a child or children, or their descendants	33% of the personal estate and an estate for life, in one-third of the land of the intestate, with remainder to the child or children of the intestate and their descendants; the balance of the personal estate passes to the child or children of the deceased and their descendants (Prob. § 38(b)(1)); all of the decedent's community estate, but only if all surviving children and surviving descendants of children are also children and descendants of the surviving spouse (Prob. § 45(a)(2)); if a child or descendant of the deceased spouse is not a child or descendant of the surviving spouse, then the surviving spouse retains ½ of the community estate and the other ½ passes to the children or descendants of the deceased spouse. (Prob. § 45(b))
2. If the deceased is not survived by a child or children, or their descendants	100% of the personal estate and 50% of the lands of the intestate, without remainder to any person, and the other 50% passes according to the rules of descent and distribution; provided, however, that if the deceased has neither surviving father nor mother nor surviving brothers or sisters, or their descendants, then the surviving husband or wife is entitled to the whole of the estate of such intestate (Prob. § 38(b)(2)); all of the decedent's community estate (Prob. § 45(a)(1))
B. The children and their descendants, if no spouse	100% (Prob. § 38(a)(1))
C. Parents take, if there are no children nor their descendants:	
1. If both survive	50% each (Prob. § 38(a)(2))
2. If only the father or mother survive the intestate	50% to such survivor, and 50% to the brothers and sisters of the deceased parent, and to their descendants; but if there be none such, then the whole estate passes to the surviving father or mother (Prob. § 38(a)(2))
3. The brothers and sisters of the intestate and their descendants if there is neither father nor mother surviving	100% (Prob. § 38(a)(3))
4. Grandparents and descendants of deceased grandparents if no siblings or descendants of siblings	Divided into two moieties, one of which passes to the paternal and the other to the maternal kindred, in the following course: To the grandfather and grandmother in equal portions, but if only one of them survives, then the estate is divided into two equal parts, one of which goes to such survivor, and the other goes to the descendant or descendants of such deceased grandfather or grandmother. If the grandparent has no descendants then all of the moiety to the surviving grandparent or descendants of that grandparent (Prob. § 38(a)(4))

5. *Nearest lineal ancestors on the same side and their descendants, if neither grandparents or their descendants on either the paternal or maternal side fail to survive**	100% in like manner as with grandparents (Prob. § 38(a)(4))
6. *State, if there are no other takers*	100% (Prop. Code § 71.001(b))

Note: When persons are deceased and their descendants are entitled to take, they take the share of the deceased per stirpes if not all of the same degree. However, if of the same degree they take per capita. (Prob. § 43)

*If in the first degree, relatives take per capita. Otherwise, they take per stirpes. (Prob. § 43)

Utah
Who Takes by Intestate Succession?

A.	*Surviving spouse takes:*	
1.	*If no descendant of the decedent survives the decedent*	100% (§ 75-2-102(1)(a)(i))
2.	*If all of the decedent's surviving descendants are also descendants of the surviving spouse*	100% (§ 75-2-102(1)(a)(ii))
3.	*If one or more of the decedent's surviving descendants are not descendants of the surviving spouse*	$50,000 plus 50% of any balance of the intestate estate (§ 75-2-102(1)(b)) If the intestate estate passes to the surviving spouse and decedent's heirs, any nonprobate transfer received by the surviving spouse is chargeable against the surviving spouse's intestate share. (§ 75-2-102(2))
B.	*All the estate, or the surplus if there is a surviving spouse, passes to:*	
1.	*Decedent's descendants*	100%, per capita at each generation (§ 75-2-103(1)(a))
2.	*Parents equally if both survive, or all to the surviving parent, if there is no surviving descendant*	100% (§ 75-2-103(1)(b))
3.	*The descendants of the decedent's parents, if no surviving parent*	100% per capita at each generation (§ 75-2-103(1)(c))
4.	*Grandparents or descendants of grandparents, if no descendants of parents*	50% passes to the decedent's paternal grandparents equally if both survive, or to the surviving paternal grandparent, or to the descendants of the decedent's paternal grandparents or either of them if both are deceased, per capita at each generation; 50% to the decedent's maternal relatives in the same manner. If there is no surviving grandparent or descendant of a grandparent on one side, the entire estate passes to the decedent's relatives on the other side as is distributed in the same manner as the half (§ 75-2-103(1)(d))
5.	*State, if there are no other takers*	100% (§ 75-2-105)

Vermont
Who Takes by Intestate Succession?

A. The children of the decedent or the legal representatives of deceased children	100% (14 § 551(1))[48]
B. Surviving spouse takes	
1. If the decedent leaves no issue	100% if the estate does not exceed $25,000.00 and the surviving spouse does not elect to take a third in value of the real estate of which the decedent dies seised in his or her own right or waives the provisions of the will of such decedent; if the estate exceeds $25,000.00, then the surviving spouse is entitled to $25,000.00 and half the remainder (14 § 551(2))
2. If the decedent leaves no kindred who may inherit	100%, including the 50% of the remainder not otherwise passing to the surviving spouse as described in B.1.above (14 § 551(2))
C. Parents, if the decedent does not leave issue nor surviving spouse[49]	50% each; if the mother is not living and the father survives, the estate descends to the father; if the father is not living and the mother survives, the estate descends to the mother (14 § 551(3))
D. Brothers and sisters of decedent and the legal representatives of deceased brothers and sisters, if no parents[49]	100%[48] (14 § 551(4))
E. Next of kin, if no siblings or their legal representatives[49]	100%, in equal shares if in same degree; however, no right to take by representation (14 § 551(5))
F. Escheat, if there are no other takers	100%, with real property to town where located and personal property to last town decedent inhabited or, if none, where property located (14 §§ 681, 683)

48. While the statute itself does not address the matter, the case law makes clear that if those taking are of equal degree, they take equally, and if they are of unequal degree, they take by representation, per stirpes. See In re Martin's Estate, 96 Vt. 455, 120 A. 862 (1923).

49. The statute does not address a situation in which there is a surviving spouse but the surviving spouse is only entitled to 50% of the remainder of the estate in excess of $25,000. These provisions are all expressly conditioned on a case in which the decedent does not leave a surviving spouse. Presumably, the remaining 50% is distributed as if the surviving spouse is deceased, although there is no explicit statement in the statute to this effect.

Virginia
Who Takes by Intestate Succession?

A. Surviving spouse takes:	
1. If no children or all children are also children of the surviving spouse	100% (§ 64.1-1(First))
2. If the intestate is survived by children or their descendants, one or more of whom are not children or the descendants of the surviving spouse	33% (§ 64.1-1(First))
B. All the estate, or the surplus if there is a surviving spouse, passes to:	
1. Children and their descendants	100% (§ 64.1-1(Second))[50]
2. Parents, or parents equally, if no children or their descendants	100% (§ 64.1-1(Third))
3. Brothers and sisters and their descendants, if no parents	100% (§ 64.1-1(Fourth))[50]
4. Grandparents, if no siblings or descendants of siblings	50% shared between the grandparents on the paternal and 50% shared between the grandparents on the maternal side, or the entire 50% to a sole surviving grandparent on a side (§ 64.1-1(Sixth))
5. Aunts and uncles and their descendants, if no grandparents on the paternal or maternal side	100% of the 50% share (§ 64.1-1(Seventh))[50]
6. Great grandfathers and grandmothers, if no descendants of grandparents	50% shared between the great grandparents on the paternal and 50% shared between the great grandparents on the maternal side, or the entire 50% to a sole surviving great grandparent on a side (§ 64.1-1(Eighth))
7. Brothers and sisters of the grandfathers and grandmothers and their descendants, if no great grandparents on the paternal or maternal side	100% (§ 64.1-1(Ninth))[50]
8. The same procedure in B.6. and 7. above with respect to the identification of next nearest lineal ancestors and their descendants on the paternal and maternal sides without end, if no descendants of great grandparents	100% (§ 64.1-1(Tenth))[50]
9. Paternal, if no maternal kindred, and vice versa	100% (§ 64.1-1(Eleventh)[50]
10. The kindred of the husband or wife in a like course as above as if such husband or wife had died entitled to the estate, if neither maternal nor paternal kindred	100% (§ 64.1-1(Eleventh))[50]

11. State, if there are no other takers	100% (United States v. 198.73 Acres of Land, More or Less, 800 F.2d 434, 435 (4th Cir. 1986); McDonald v. Treasurer, 1991 WL 835330 (Cir. Ct. Dec. 2, 1991). See also § 55-210.2:1 et seq. with respect to unclaimed personal property and § 55-171 with respect to real property.

Note: Pursuant to § 64.1-11, the provisions of § 64.1-1, which apply to real property, are made applicable to personal property.

50. Pursuant to § 64.1-3, if those entitled to take are in the same degree, they take equally. If they are of unequal degree, they take per stirpes. In this regard, when one share is allocated to the paternal side and one share to the maternal side, the foregoing rules are applied to each share separately. See, e.g., Williams v. Knowles, 178 Va. 84, 16 S.E.2d 316 (1941).

Washington
Who Takes by Intestate Succession?

A. Surviving spouse takes:	
1. If no surviving issue or issue of parent	100% plus all of decedent's net community estate (§ 11.04.015(1)(a)&(d))
2. If surviving issue	½ net separate estate plus all of decedent's net community estate (§ 11.04.015(1)(a)&(b))
3. If no surviving issue but a parent survives or issue of parent survives	¾ of net separate estate plus all of decedent's net community estate (§ 11.04.015(1)(a)&(c))
B. All the estate, or the surplus if there is a surviving spouse, passes to:	
1. Issue if no surviving spouse	100% equally if in same degree, otherwise by representation[51] (§ 11.04.015(2)(a))
2. Parents, or parents equally, if no issue	100% (§ 11.04.015(2)(b))
3. Issue of parents, if no parents	100% equally if in same degree, otherwise by representation[51] (§ 11.04.015(2)(c))
4. Grandparents, if no issue of parents	50% to paternal and 50% to maternal grandparents. If both survive on one side they take equal portions of the 50% share, and if not the surviving one takes the whole 50% (§ 11.04.015(2)(d))
5. Issue of grandparents, if no grandparents on that side	100%, with those on the maternal grandparents' side and paternal grandparents' side taking 50% as a group. Within the group, those issue of the same degree of kinship take equally and those of more remote degree take by representation (§ 11.04.015(2)(e))[51] Implication, even though not explicitly set forth in the statute, that if there are no issue of grandparents on one side, the issue on the other side take 100%.[52]
6. State, if there is no other taker	100% (§ 11.08.140)

51. "Representation" means per capita with representation. (§ 11.02.005(3))

52. There does not appear to be any provision for adding the share of one side to the other side if there are no issue of grandparents on one side.

West Virginia
Who Takes by Intestate Succession?

A. *Surviving spouse takes:*	
1. *If no descendant of the decedent survives*	100% (§ 42-1-3(a)(1))
2. *If all of the decedent's surviving descendants are also descendants of the surviving spouse and the surviving spouse has one or more surviving descendants who are not descendants of the decedent*	100% (§ 42-1-3(a)(2))
3. *If any of the decedent's surviving descendants are not descendants of the surviving spouse*	½ (§ 42-1-3(c))
4. *If all the decedent's surviving descendants are also descendants of the surviving spouse and the surviving spouse has one or more surviving descendants who are not descendants of the decedent*	½ (§ 42-1-3(b)
B. *All the estate, or the surplus if there is a surviving spouse, passes to:*	
1. *Descendants*	100% by representation[53] (§ 42-1-3a(a))
2. *Parents, or parents equally, if no descendants*	100% (§ 42-1-3a(b))
3. *Descendants of parents, if no parents*	100% by representation[53] (§ 42-1-3a(c))
4. *Grandparents or their descendants, if no surviving descendant of a parent*	50% to paternal grandparents and 50% to maternal grandparents, with the grandparents on one side sharing equally if they both survive. If neither grandparent on that side survives, to the issue of the grandparents or grandparent on that side by representation. If no issue survive on that side either, then the 50% share is added to the 50% share on the other side and the grandparents or their issue on the other side take the entire 100% in the manner described herein. (§ 42-1-3a(d))
5. *State, if no surviving grandparents or their descendants*	100% (§ 42-1-3c) Real property passes to the state auditor and personal property passes to the state treaurer for disposition by public sale (*Id*).

53. "Representation" means per capita at each generation. See § 42-1-3d(b).

Wisconsin
Who Takes by Intestate Succession?

A. *Surviving spouse takes:*	
1. *If no surviving issue of the decedent*	100% (§ 852.01(1)(a)(1))
2. *If surviving issue are all issue of the surviving spouse*	100% (§ 852.01(1)(a)(1))
3. *If there are surviving issue one or more of whom are not issue of the surviving spouse*	50% of the decedent's property, other than marital property (§ 852.01(1)(a)(2))
B. *All the estate, or the surplus if there is a surviving spouse, passes to:*	
1. *Children, if no surviving spouse*	100% (§ 852.01(1)(b))
2. *Parents, if no surviving spouse or issue*	100% (§ 852.01(1)(c))
3. *Brothers and sisters and the issue of any deceased brother or sister if no surviving parent*	100%, with any issue taking per stirpes (§ 852.01(1)(d))
4. *Grandparents and their issue, if no parent or issue of a parent*	50% to paternal and 50% to maternal grandparents. If both grandparents on one side survive, they take equally. If only one survives, that one takes the entire 50% share. (§§ 852.01(1)(f)(1)&(2)) If both grandparents on one side are deceased, then to their issue per stirpes (§ 852.01(1)(f)(1))
5. *Grandparents and issue of grandparents on the other side, if no grandparents or their issue survive on one side*	The 50% share of the one side is added to the 50% share of the other side and the whole is distributed as set forth in B.4. and 5. above (§ 852.01(1)(f)(3))
6. *State, if no grandparents or their descendants*	100% (§ 852.01(3))

Note: If marital property is held as "survivorship marital property," it vests in the surviving spouse as a nontestamentary disposition at death. (§ 766.60(5)(a))

Wyoming
Who Takes by Intestate Succession?

A. *Surviving spouse takes:*	
1. *If no surviving children or descendants of any child*	100% (§ 2-4-101(a)(ii))
2. *If surviving children*	50% (§ 2-4-101(a)(i))
B. *All the estate, or the surplus if there is a surviving spouse, passes to:*	
1. *Children and the descendants of deceased children*	100% equally, and descendants of deceased child "collectively" taking that child's share (§ 2-4-101(c)(i))
2. *Mother, father, brothers, sisters, and the descendants of brothers and sisters who are deceased, if no children or their descendants*	100%, shared equally, with descendants of a deceased sibling taking "collectively"[54] the sibling's share (§ 2-4-101 (c)(ii))
3. *Grandfather, grandmother, uncles, aunts and their descendants, if no father, mother, brothers, sisters, or descendants of deceased brothers and sisters*	100%, shared equally, with descendants of one of the mentioned relatives taking "collectively"[54] the relative's share In equal parts (§ 2-4-101(c)(iii))
4. *State, if there are no other takers*	100% (§ 9-5-202) See also Kirby v. Royalties, Inc. v. Texaco, Inc., 458 P.2d 101 (1969)

54. "Collectively" appears to mean per stirpes. See Fosler v. Collins, 13 P.3d 686 (2000).

Table 9
Asset Protection
(current through 5/1/07)

The objectives of conserving, enhancing, and ultimately transmitting wealth cannot be accomplished if the owner of the property is subject to catastrophic judgments that deplete the estate. Many persons with substantial resources are standard prey for enterprising plaintiffs and their attorneys. Since successful persons are often in professions or businesses in which the potential for lawsuits and favorable jury verdicts is high, there has been much interest in insulating assets from these claims. The concern regarding exposure is not limited to the owner himself. In many instances, it will be one of assuring benefits or an interest reserved in a trust for a younger-generation beneficiary from possible future creditors. The need for protection may not be limited to the ordinary creditor. Often, concern may be focused on divorce or child support. While a state may afford protection against general creditors in many circumstances, it may not do so in the context of spousal or child support. State laws also play an important role in bankruptcy. There may be valuable exemptions accorded by certain states that are not given by others. Thus, a particular bankruptcy may not reach all assets that a bankruptcy in another jurisdiction may, in fact, reach.

Table 9 is subdivided into five subparts. Table 9.01 addresses life insurance. It explores initially whether the beneficiaries of proceeds have a superior claim to those proceeds than do creditors. The table then considers such vital issues as whether payments to the estate of the insured, an owner other than the insured, an owner retaining the right to change beneficiaries, and a spouse of the insured are insulated from creditors' claims. The table proceeds to detail the dollar amount of the protection, when available. It also includes coverage as to the exposure of the policy to creditors in the premortem period as well as to bankruptcy.

Table 9.02 takes a similar approach to annuities. In particular, an inquiry is made on a state-by-state comparative basis as to whether the annuitant's rights can be reached. This question is also considered in the context of bankruptcy. In addition, certain tax-exempt annuity trusts subject to I.R.C. § 403(b) are considered independently.

Table 9.03 looks more specifically at pension plans. A variety of questions are explored. To begin with, consideration is given to whether I.R.C. § 401 federally exempt retirement plans are insulated from the reach of creditors. The same is considered with regard to I.R.C. § 403(a) annuity plans. The analysis then proceeds to I.R.C. § 408 tax-sheltered IRAs.

The laws of certain states are likely to be affected by the Supreme Court's decision in Rousey v. Jacoway, 125 S. Ct. 1561 (April 4, 2005), which holds that IRAs are "similar plans" to exempt pension plans and that the right to receive payments under such plans are on account of "age," thus satisfying the other requirement for Bankruptcy Code exemption and state laws taking advantage of this exemption. Having addressed these mainstay tax-exempt retirement vehicles, the table then considers whether there is at least an income exemption for plans that are not tax-exempt. In some states, income may be regarded as deferred wage payments that are entitled to protections similar to those for garnishment of wages generally.

The final question considered concerns whether transfers to a plan shortly before bankruptcy can be brought back into the bankruptcy estate. Some states will not afford protection if the transfers are too close in time to the bankruptcy. Other states have no such restrictions, thereby affording certain debtors a major opportunity, subject, of course, to fraudulent conveyance laws and the like.

Table 9.04 deals with jointly owned property. The term is used in its broadest sense, so as to refer as well to tenancies in common. The first issue dealt with by the table is whether, in the use of a joint tenancy with a right of survivorship, the creditors of the first joint tenant to die can reach his interest. At common law, there was no such right, since on death, the interest of the surviving joint tenant(s) automatically became a whole interest, with the deceased's interest consumed. While most states maintain this position by statute or case law, this is not true in all states.

The second question considered in Table 9.04 is the form of ownership that will be presumed when there are interests of several persons. In other words, if ownership is in the form of "A or B" or "A and B," and no right of survivorship is indicated, will the presumption be that a joint tenancy or tenancy in common has been established?

Table 9.05 considers various creditors' rights with respect to spendthrift and related trusts. This area of asset protection law has received enormous attention recently, especially with developments in Alaska and Delaware. Those states have enacted legislation permitting self-settled spendthrift trusts. Arguably, this legislation permits protection from future creditors by placing assets in a properly drafted and administered Alaska or Delaware trust. Several other states have enacted their own versions of this sort of protective legislation.

Apart from consideration of the states that permit or disallow self-settled trusts, Table 9.05 engages in a careful analysis of other relevant issues. As a question of drafting, it considers whether a spendthrift trust will be presumed without the presence of a specific clause. It then addresses whether a judgment can be satisfied from the debtor's beneficial interest. Even if this is not ordinarily the case, it may be true in the event of a divorce settlement or a claim for child support. The table also explores the effectiveness of a spendthrift trust in the event of a claim for spousal or child support, taxes, tort claims, and necessaries. The comparable support trust as a vehicle for defeating creditor claims is also evaluated.

Another limitation that is recognized is in terms of amount. That is, a spendthrift trust provision may be enforced, but only up to a particular dollar figure. The table discloses, as well, whether states only protect trust income or principal.

In the typical Medicaid situation, the question is whether the state can reach assets held in trust. This is explored on a state-by-state basis, including situations where the debtor is a discretionary beneficiary or holds a special or general power of appointment. Finally, the table includes an analysis of access by a creditor to the trust corpus if the debtor has the power to designate the trustee, including himself, or can change the trustee and he is a discretionary beneficiary.

The function of this table is fourfold. First, it affords a quick answer to the protection from creditors afforded certain assets under certain circumstances. Second, it alerts the attorney to the exposure of assets and the need to alter the mix of investments, the ownership vehicle, or the ownership itself. Third, it affords a basis of comparison with "offshore" and "onshore" asset protection jurisdictions that may over-promise protection or provide it but at too great a risk. Fourth, it pinpoints those states outside the home state, the law of which would be more favorable. In some (but by no means all) cases, that favorable law can then be made to govern the outcome.

Table 9.01
Life Insurance

	Are Payments to Beneficiaries Other Than the Insured or Owner Protected?	*Are Payments to the Insured's Estate Protected?*	*Are Payments to the Owner If Not the Insured Protected?*	*What if Payments Are to Spouse of Person Where Proceeds Can Be Reached?*	*Is There a Limit on the Protection?*	*Can Policies Be Reached Prior to Death?*	*Does It Matter Whether the Debtor Is in Bankruptcy?*
Alabama	Yes. (§ 6-10-8)	No. (§ 6-10-8)	No, with respect to the person "effecting" the life insurance policy. (§ 6-10-8)	Yes. (§ 6-10-8)	No. (Shepard v. Morris, 30 Bankr. 392 (Bankr. N.D. Ala. 1983))	No, unless intent to defraud creditors, in which case premiums and interest there on can be reached. (§ 27-14-29(a))	No. (§ 27-14-29(a))
Alaska	Yes, if beneficiary is spouse or dependent of insured. (§ 09.38.030(e)(4))	No. (§ 09.38.030(e)(4))	No. Protection limited to spouse or dependent of insured. (§ 09.38.030(e)(4))	No. (§ 09.38.030(e)(4))	Yes, applies to unmatured life insurance. May reach accrued dividends in amount greater than $10,000. Section 09.38.115 periodically adjusts this for cost-of-living increases. (§ 09.38.025(a))	No. (§ 09.38.025(a))	No. (§ 09.38.055)
Arizona	Yes, if surviving spouse or child upon death of spouse, parent, or legal guardian but limited to $20,000. (§ 33-1126(A)(1))	Appears no. Exemption for payments to "surviving spouse or child." (§ 33-1126(A)(1))	No. Protection limited to surviving spouse or child. (§ 33-1126(A)(1))	There is no statutory provision or definite case authority on point.	$20,000 for life insurance proceeds. (§ 33-1126(A)(1))	No, if owned by debtor continuously for two years, and payable to spouse, child, parent, sibling, or dependent; only the portion designated to these	No, since exemption applies to any process issued from "any court." (§ 33-1126(A) & (A)(6))

						beneficiaries (if others exist) is exempt. § 33-1126(A)(6))	
Arkansas	Yes. (§ 23-79-131(a)(1))	No. (§ 23-79-131(a)(1))	No, with respect to the person "effecting" the life insurance policy. (§ 23-79-131(a)(1))	There is no statutory provision or definite case authority on point.	There is no statutory provision or definite case authority on point.	No, if insured or beneficiary debtor is a resident. All moneys paid or payable to any resident of the state as insured or beneficiary are exempt. (§ 16-66-209) No distinction is made as to when proceeds are actually paid. *See also* Lee v. Johnson, 85 B. R. 518 (Bankr. W. D. Ark. 1987)	No. (§ 16-66-209) In Federal Sav. & Loan Ins. Co. v. Holt, 894 F.2d 1005 (8th Cir. 1990), the court held that an unlimited exemption in § 16-66-209 did not apply to bankruptcy debtors in light of monetary limits in Art. 9 § 2 of the Arkansas Constitution. In response, the Arkansas legislature enacted § 16-66-209, allowing an individual to opt for the limited $500 exemption of the Arkansas Constitution or the unlimited federal exemption in 11 U.S.C. § 522(d)(7). This was held constitutional in In re Criswell, 152 B. R. 264 (Bankr. E. D. Ark. 1992)
California	Yes. (Civ. Proc. § 704.100(a) (unmatured policies) & (c) (matured *(cont'd)*	Yes. (Civ. Proc. § 704.100(c) (Legislative Comm. Comment))	Yes. (Civ. Proc. § 704.100(a)-(c)) "Judgment debtor" may be insured or the *(cont'd)*	Yes. (Civ. Proc. § 704.100(b) (Legislative Comm. Comment))	$9,700. (Civ. Proc. § 704.100(b)) Applies to loan value of unmatured life insurance. This *(cont'd)*	No. (Civ. Proc. Code § 704.100(a) (Legislative Comm. Comment)	Yes. A debtor may elect to exempt the following from the bankruptcy estate: (a) *(cont'd)*

Table 9.01
Life Insurance *(continued)*

	Are Payments to Beneficiaries Other Than the Insured or Owner Protected?	*Are Payments to the Insured's Estate Protected?*	*Are Payments to the Owner If Not the Insured Protected?*	*What if Payments Are to Spouse of Person Where Proceeds Can Be Reached?*	*Is There a Limit on the Protection?*	*Can Policies Be Reached Prior to Death?*	*Does It Matter Whether the Debtor Is in Bankruptcy?*
California *(cont'd)*	policies)) In the case of matured policies, they are only exempt to extent reasonably necessary for the support of debtor, debtor's spouse, and dependents. (Jackson v. Fisher, 363 P.2d 479 (1961); Holmes v. Marshall, 79 P. 534 (1905))		beneficiary. It also protects against creditors of the spouse and dependents of the insured. (§ 704.100(a)-(c) (Legislative Comm. Comment))		can be doubled if married, even if spouse has no interest in policy and is not a judgment debtor.		unmatured life insurance contract owned by debtor, other than credit life insurance (Civ. Proc. § 703.140(b)(7)); (b)debtor's interest, subject to $9,300 limitation, in accrued dividend or interest, or loan value, of unmatured life insurance contract where debtor is owner and insured, or where debtor owns and dependent is insured (Civ. Proc. § 703.140(b)(8)); and (c) debtor's right to receive payment of life insurance contract where debtor was dependent of insured, to the extent reasonably

							necessary for support of debtor and any dependent of debtor (Civ. Proc. § 703.140(b)(11)(C)).
Colorado	Yes. (§ 13-54-102(1)(l)(I)(B))	No. (§ 13-54-102(1)(l)(II) & (III))	Yes, if owner is a designated beneficiary. (§ 13-54-102(1)(l)(I)(B))	There is no direct statutory provision or definite case authority on point. But see generally § 10-7-106.	$50,000 (§ 13-5-4-102(1)(l)(I)(A)), unless contributed more than four years prior to writ of attachment (only applies to cash surrender value); if proceeds go to the designated beneficiary, no limit. (§ 13-5-4-102(1)(l)(I)(B))	Yes (cash surrender value up to $50,000). (§ 13-54-102(1)(l)(I)(A))	Yes. If debtor has right to cash surrender value in the event of default on policy, trustee (B.R.) may exercise the right. (Travellers' Ins. Co. v. Middlekamp, 185 P. 335 (1918))
Connecticut	Yes, unless there is intent to defraud. (§ 38a-453(a))	There is no statutory provision or definite case authority on point.	Yes. (§ 38a-453(a))	There is no statutory provision or definite case authority on point.	There is no statutory provision or definite case authority on point.	There is no statutory provision or definite case authority on point.	There is no statutory provision or definite case authority on point.
Delaware	Yes, except premiums paid with intent to defraud. (18 § 2725(a))	No. (18 § 2725(a))	No, with respect to the person "effecting" the life insurance policy. (18 § 2725(a))	Yes, i.e., spouse of person effecting the policy. (18 § 2725(a))	If made with intent to defraud creditors, they get premiums paid plus interest. (18 § 2725(a))	Yes. Rights vest in beneficiary as of insured's death. (18 §2725(a)) Prior to that time owner's interest can be reached. See column 3.	There is no statutory provision or definite case authority on point. 18 § 2725(a) says proceeds and avails with no limit.
District of Columbia	Yes. (§ 31-4716(a))	No. (§ 31-4716(a))	No, with respect to the person "effecting" the life insurance policy. (§ 31-4716(a))	Yes, i.e., spouse of person effecting the policy. (§ 31-4716(a))	If made with intent to defraud creditors, they get premiums paid plus interest. (§ 31-4716(a))	Yes. Rights vest in beneficiary as of insured's death. (§ 31-4716(a)) Prior to that time owner's interest can be reached. See column 3.	There is no statutory provision or definite case authority on point. § 31-4716 says proceeds and avails with no limit.

Table 9.01
Life Insurance *(continued)*

	Are Payments to Beneficiaries Other Than the Insured or Owner Protected?	*Are Payments to the Insured's Estate Protected?*	*Are Payments to the Owner If Not the Insured Protected?*	*What if Payments Are to Spouse of Person Where Proceeds Can Be Reached?*	*Is There a Limit on the Protection?*	*Can Policies Be Reached Prior to Death?*	*Does It Matter Whether the Debtor Is in Bankruptcy?*
Florida	Yes. (§ 222.13(1))	No—part of the estate. (§ 222.13(1))	Yes. (§ 222.13(1))	Maybe. (U.S. v. Gilmore, 222 F.2d 167 (1955) (spouse was beneficiary of life insurance and administratrix of estate and liable for decedent's unpaid federal taxes))	No. "The proceeds thereof shall be exempt." (§ 222.13(1))	No. (§ 222.14) Cash surrender value is exempt.	Not exempt if the debtor is the insured. (In re D.F. & C.P. Long, 282 F. 383 (S.D. Fla. 1918); Morgan v. McCaffrey, 286 F. 922 (5th Cir. 1923))
Georgia	Yes. (§ 33-25-11(a))	No. (§ 33-25-11(a))	There is no statutory provision or definite case authority on point.	Yes. (§ 33-25-11(a))	Yes. If intend to defraud creditors, get amount paid plus interest. (§ 33-25-11(b))	No. (§§ 33-25-11, 44-13-100(a)(8))	Yes, exempts unmatured life insurance contract owned by debtor other than credit life insurance contract. (§ 44-13-100(a)(8))
Hawaii[1]	Yes. (§ 431:10-232(a))	There is no statutory provision or definite case authority on point.	There is no statutory provision or definite case authority on point.	Yes. (§ 431:10-232(b))	Cannot defraud creditors. (§ 431:10-232(a))	There is no statutory provision or definite case authority on point.	There is no statutory provision or definite case authority on point.
Idaho	Yes. (§ 41-1833(1))	No. (§ 41-1833(1))	No, with respect to the person "effecting" the life insurance policy. (§ 41-1833(1))	Can keep what is necessary to support self and dependents. (§ 11-604(1)(d))	If made with intent to defraud creditors, they get premiums paid plus interest. (§ 41-1833)	There is no statutory provision or definite case authority on point.	There is no statutory provision or definite case authority on point.

Illinois	Yes, if beneficiaries are the spouse, child, parent, and/or dependent person. (735 ILCS § 5/12-1001(f))	No. (735 ILCS §5/ 12-1001(f))	Yes, if the owner is the spouse, child, parent, or dependent person of insured. (735 ILCS § 5/12-1001(f))	There is no statutory provision or definite case authority on point.	No. (735 ILCS § 5/12-1001(f))	No. (735 ILCS § 5/12-1001(f) (cash value))	If insurance acquired within six months of the filing for bankruptcy, presumed to have been acquired in contemplation of bankruptcy. (735 ILCS § 5/12-1001(i))
Indiana	Yes, if beneficiary is a spouse, child, dependent, or creditor. (§ 27-1-12-14(e))	No. (§ 27-1-12-14(e))	Depends on relationship to insured. (§ 27-1-12-14(e))	Proceeds or avails are exempt from debts of spouses. (§ 27-1-12-14(e))	No. The "proceeds" are "free and clear from all claims." (§ 27-1-12-14(e))	No. (§ 27-1-12-14(d))	Premiums must be paid one year prior to bankruptcy. (§ 27-1-12-14(f))
Iowa	Only to dependents, surviving spouse, or child. (§ 627.6(6))	No. (§ 627.6(6) An exception may exist for "reasonable costs, fees, and expenses of administration" out of life insurance proceeds paid to decedent's estate. These expenditures are distinguishable from "debts of a decedent." (In re Wilson's Estate, 202 N.W.2d 41, 43-44 (Iowa 1972))	There is no statutory provision or definite case authority on point.	$15,000 exempted from spouse's creditors. (§ 627.6(6))	Yes, $10,000 for interest acquired within two years of the date of execution is issued or exemptions are claimed, or for additions within the period for prior existing policies. (§ 627.6(6)) Matured policies are exempt only up to $15,000. (§ 627.6(6))	There is no statutory provision or definite case authority on point.	There is no statutory provision or definite case authority on point.
Kansas	Yes. (§ 40-414(a)(1))	No. (Shawnee State Bank v. Royal Union Life Ins. Co., 127 Kan. 456, 274 P. 132 (1929))	Yes, if owner has insurable interest in life of the insured. (§ 40-414(a))	There is no statutory provision or definite case authority on point.	There is no statutory provision or definite case authority on point.	No. (§ 40-414(a) & (b))	Yes, nonforfeiture value not exempt if policy purchased within one year of bankruptcy. (§ 40-414(b)(1))

Table 9.01
Life Insurance *(continued)*

	Are Payments to Beneficiaries Other Than the Insured or Owner Protected?	*Are Payments to the Insured's Estate Protected?*	*Are Payments to the Owner If Not the Insured Protected?*	*What if Payments Are to Spouse of Person Where Proceeds Can Be Reached?*	*Is There a Limit on the Protection?*	*Can Policies Be Reached Prior to Death?*	*Does It Matter Whether the Debtor Is in Bankruptcy?*
Kentucky	Yes. (§ 304.14-300(1))	No. (§ 304.14-300(1))	No, with respect to the person "effecting" the life insurance policy. (§ 304.14-300(1))	Yes, i.e., spouse of person effecting the policy. (§ 304.14-300(1))	No. (Proceeds and avails exempt) (§ 304.14-300(1))	Yes. Rights vest in beneficiaries as of insured's death. (Parks' Ex'rs v. Parks, 156 S.W.2d 480, 486 (Ky. 1941)) Prior to that time, owner's interest can be reached. See column 3.	No. (In re Daly, 2004 Bankr. LEXIS 803 (E.D. Ky. June 16, 2004))
Louisiana	Yes. (§ 22:647(A)(1))	Yes. (§ 22:647(A)(1))	There is no statutory provision or definite case authority on point.	There is no statutory provision or definite case authority on point.	Yes. Limited to $35,000 if policy was issued within nine months of the attempted seizure. (§ 22:647(A)(2))	Yes, if more than $35,000. Cash surrender value is exempt up to $35,000 if policy issued within nine months of the writ, mandate, or filing of a bankruptcy petition. (§ 22:647(A)(2))	Yes. Exemption limited to $35,000 if policy issued within nine months of bankruptcy. (§ 22:647(A)(2))
Maine	Yes. (24-A § 2428(2))	No. (24-A § 2428(2))	No, with respect to the person "effecting" the life insurance policy. (24-A § 2428(2))	There is no statutory provision or definite case authority on point.	If made with intent to defraud creditors, they get premiums paid plus interest. (24-A § 2428(2))	Unmatured life insurance contracts owned by the debtor, other than a credit life insurance contract, are exempt (14 § 4422(10))	There is no statutory provision or definite case authority on point.

						Debtor's interest, up to $4,000, in any accrued dividend or interest under any unmatured life insurance contract owned by the debtor under which the insured is the debtor or debtor's dependent is exempt. (14 § 4422(11))	
Maryland	Yes, as long as beneficiary is the spouse, child, or dependent relative. (Ins. § 16-111(a))	No. (Ins. § 16-111(a))	No. Protection limited to spouse, child, or dependent relative of insured. (Ins. § 16-111(a))	There is no statutory provision or definite case authority on point.	Creditors can reach proceeds if pledged as security of a debt. (Ins. § 16-111(C)) A change of beneficiary, assignment, or other transfer is not protected if intent to hinder, delay, or defraud creditors (Ins. § 16-111(d))	There is no statutory provision or definite case authority on point.	No. (In re Kleinman, 271 B.R. 171 (D. Md. 2002))
Massachusetts	Yes. (175 § 125)	No. (175 § 125)	No, with respect to the person "effecting" the life insurance policy. (175 § 125)	There is no statutory provision or definite case authority on point.	If made with intent to defraud creditors, they get premiums paid plus interest. (175 § 125)	No (proceeds). (175 § 125)	No. (175 § 125; In re Beach, 8 F. Supp. 910 (D. Mass. 1934))
Michigan	Yes, but only if beneficiaries are spouse or children. (§ 500.2207(1))	No. (§ 500.2207(2))	No. Protection limited to spouse and child of insured and their assigns. Where owner is an *(cont'd)*	There is no statutory provision or definite case authority on point.	If made with intent to defraud creditors, they get premiums paid plus *(cont'd)*	Yes. Cash value is exempt to same extent as proceeds. (§ 500.2207(1))	No. (In re Johnson, 274 B.R. 473 (E.D. Mich. 2002))

Table 9.01
Life Insurance *(continued)*

	Are Payments to Beneficiaries Other Than the Insured or Owner Protected?	*Are Payments to the Insured's Estate Protected?*	*Are Payments to the Owner If Not the Insured Protected?*	*What if Payments Are to Spouse of Person Where Proceeds Can Be Reached?*	*Is There a Limit on the Protection?*	*Can Policies Be Reached Prior to Death?*	*Does It Matter Whether the Debtor Is in Bankruptcy?*
Michigan *(cont'd)*			assignee of spouse and/or child, payments to owner may be protected. (§ 500.2207(2))		interest. (§ 500.2207(2))		
Minnesota	Yes. (§ 61A.12(1))	No. (§ 61A.12(1))	No, with respect to the person "effecting" the life insurance policy. (§ 61A.12(1))	There is no statutory provision or definite case authority on point.	If made with intent to defraud creditors, they get premiums paid plus interest. (§ 61A.12(1))	Yes, but only in excess of $4,000 of accrued dividend, interest, or loan value on contract owned by debtor where debtor is insured or insured is person of whom debtor is a dependent. (§ 550.37(23)) Fraternal contracts cannot be favored in this regard. (In re Haggerty, 448 N.W. 2d 363, 365-66 (Minn. 1989); In re Tveten, 402 N.W. 2d 551 (Minn. 1987))	Yes. All insurance proceeds to spouse or child up to $20,000 plus an additional $5,000 for each child will be shielded from creditors. (§ 550.37(10))
Mississippi	Yes (§ 85-3-11(1)), except the excess over $50,000 of cash surrender value as a result of	Yes. (§ 85-3-11 (1)) Up to $50,000 protected. (§ 85-3-13)	Yes. (§ 85-3-11(1)), as long as owner has insurable interest (§ 83-5-251)	Proceeds of life policy on husband's life, payable to wife, not exempted from	Yes. See the first two columns.	Yes. Any portion of cash surrender value or loan value of any life insurance policy which	Yes. Any portion of cash surrender value or loan value of any life insurance policy which

	premiums made within 12 months of issuance of writ of seizure, attachment, garnishment or other process on insured where someone else is owner and beneficiary. (§ 85-3-11 (2)(a)) Also, any premiums paid with intent to defraud creditors, plus interest (§ 85-3-11(2)(b)).			judgment against her on note signed by both. (Goza v. Provine, 140 Miss. 315, 105 So. 534 (1925))		exceeds the sum of $50,000 as a result of any payments made within 12 months of issuance of a writ of seizure, attachment garnishment, or other process, or the filing of a bankruptcy petition. (§ 85-3-11(2)(a))	exceeds the sum of $50,000 as a result of any payments made within 12 months of issuance of a writ of seizure, attachment garnishment, or other process, or the filing of a bankruptcy petition. (§ 85-3-11(2)(a))
Missouri	There is no statutory provision or definite case authority on point. See Judson v. Walker, 55 S.W. 1083 (1900) (proceeds protected if insured not insolvent at time premium payment made).	There is no statutory provision or definite case authority on point.	There is no statutory provision or definite case authority on point.	Protected if wife paid premiums. (§ 376.530)	If premiums are paid with intent to defraud, this cannot affect creditors. (Kansas City v. Helverson, 352 Mo. 1027, 1032 (1944))	No, except for any claim for child support. (§ 513.430(1)(8))	Yes. Exemption limited to $150,000 in any bankruptcy proceeding and exemption is limited to owner-insured or where owner-debtor is dependent of insured. (§ 513.430(1)(8)) If purchased within one year prior to commencement of proceedings, no exemption at all. (*Id.*)
Montana	Yes. (§ 33-15-511(1))	No. (§ 33-15-511(1))	No, with respect to the person "effecting" the life insurance policy. (§ 33-15-511(1))	There is no statutory provision or definite case authority on point.	If intent to defraud creditors, they get amount paid in premiums plus	Yes, unmatured life insurance is exempt up to $4,000. (§ 25-13-609(4))	Yes, it matters. If the debtor is in bankruptcy, the policy is not exempt.

(cont'd)

(cont'd)

Table 9.01
Life Insurance *(continued)*

	Are Payments to Beneficiaries Other Than the Insured or Owner Protected?	*Are Payments to the Insured's Estate Protected?*	*Are Payments to the Owner If Not the Insured Protected?*	*What if Payments Are to Spouse of Person Where Proceeds Can Be Reached?*	*Is There a Limit on the Protection?*	*Can Policies Be Reached Prior to Death?*	*Does It Matter Whether the Debtor Is in Bankruptcy?*
Montana *(cont'd)*					interest. (§ 33-15-511(1))		(§§ 31-2-106(1), 33-15-511(1))
Nebraska	Yes, if beneficiary is related by blood or marriage. (§ 44-371(1)(a))	No. (§ 44-371(1)(a), ("other than the estate of the insured"))	No. Protection limited to persons related by blood or marriage to insured. (§ 44-371(1))	There is no statutory provision or definite case authority on point.	No. But note that there is no exemption for a judgment against the beneficiary if the judgment was based on criminal conduct of the beneficiary for which the beneficiary was convicted and was punishable by death or life imprisonment. (§ 44-371(2)) Also, no exemption if "a written assignment to the contrary has been obtained by the claimant." (§ 44-371(1)(a)) Limited to aggregate value of $100,000. (§ 44-371(1)(b)(i))	Yes, for example cash values in a bankruptcy proceeding. (§ 44-371(b)(ii))	Protections "shall not apply to. . .proceeds, cash values, or benefits accruing . . . within three years prior to bankruptcy." (§ 44-371(b)(ii))
Nevada	Yes. (§ 687B.260(1))	No. (§ 687B.260(1))	No, with respect to the person "effecting" the life	There is no statutory provision or definite case authority on point.	Yes. Annual premium not to exceed $15,000. (§ 21.090(1)(k))	No, subject to some exceptions. See *Is There a*	No. (§ 21.090(3))

			insurance policy. (§ 687B.260(1))		If made with intent to defraud creditors, they get premiums paid plus interest. (§ 687B.260(1))	*Limit on the Protection?*	
New Hampshire	Yes, except if premiums paid in fraud of creditors. (§ 408:2)	No. (§ 408:2)	No, with respect to the person "effecting" the life insurance policy. (§ 408:2)	There is no statutory provision or definite case authority on point.	Yes. If, e.g., premiums paid with intent to defraud, creditors get premiums plus interest. (§§ 408:2, 408:3)	Yes, cash surrender value is not exempt. (In re Monahan, 171 B.R. 710 (D.N.H. 1994))	Yes. New Hampshire has opted out of federal bankruptcy exemptions. State exemption does not protect an owner insured, but only a third-party beneficiary. (Caron v. Farmington Nat'l Bank, 82 F.3d 7, 10-11 (1st Cir. 1996))
New Jersey	Yes. (§ 17B:24-6(a))	No. (§ 17B:24-6(a)(3))	No, with respect to the person "effecting" the life insurance policy. (§§ 17B:24-6(a), 17B:24-6(a)(2))	There is no statutory provision or definite case authority on point.	Yes. If made with intent to defraud, creditors get premiums plus interest. (§ 17B:24-6 (b)) Also subject to child support obligations of decedent. (Deceglia v. Estate of Colleti, 625 A.2d 590 (1993))	No. (§ 17B:24-6(a))	No. However, there is no protection to the extent of premiums paid with intent to defraud, and interest thereon. (§ 17B:24-6(b))
New Mexico	Yes, unless there is a special contract or arrangement to the contrary in writing. (§ 42-10-5)	Yes. (§ 42-10-5)	Yes. (§ 42-10-5)	Yes, unless special contact or written agreement say otherwise. (§ 42-10-5)	Yes, if special contract or agreement in writing. (§ 42-10-5)	No, unless made or assigned in writing for benefit of such creditor, even protected from garnishment. (§ 42-10-3)	No, unless fraudulent. (In re Zouhar, 10 Bankr. 154 (Bankr. D.N.M. 1981))

Table 9.01
Life Insurance *(continued)*

	Are Payments to Beneficiaries Other Than the Insured or Owner Protected?	*Are Payments to the Insured's Estate Protected?*	*Are Payments to the Owner If Not the Insured Protected?*	*What if Payments Are to Spouse of Person Where Proceeds Can Be Reached?*	*Is There a Limit on the Protection?*	*Can Policies Be Reached Prior to Death?*	*Does It Matter Whether the Debtor Is in Bankruptcy?*
New York	Yes. (Ins. § 3212(b))	No. (In re Will of Adas, 335 N.Y. S.2d 128 (1972))	Yes. (§ 3212(b)(1)-(2))	Only protected if spouse effected policy. (§ 3212(b)(2))	There is no statutory provision or definite case authority on point.	No, except to satisfy a judgment for unpaid alimony. (Rubenstein v. Rubenstein, 105 N.Y.S.2d 24 (1951))	No. (§ 3212(b))
North Carolina	Yes. (§ 58-58-95)	No. (§ 58-58-115)	No, with respect to the person "effecting" the life insurance policy. (§ 58-58-115)	There is no statutory provision or definite case authority on point.	If made with intent to defraud, creditors get premiums paid plus interest. (§ 58-58-115))	No. (§ 58-58-115)	No. (§ 58-58-115)
North Dakota	Yes. Payable to spouse, children, or any relative or insured who is dependent or likely to be dependent upon the insured for support, provided policies or plans have been in effect for a period of at least one year. (§ 28-22-03.1(3))	There is no statutory provision or definite case authority on point.	Yes if the owner is the spouse, child, or any relative of insured. (§ 28-22-03.1(3))	There is no statutory provision or definite case authority on point.	Yes. $100,000 limit individually, $200,000 in aggregate with pensions, IRAs, and retirement plans. (§ 28-22-03.1(3))	No. (§ 2822-03.1(3))	No, but exemption covers policy in effect for period of one year. (§ 28-22-03.1(3))
Ohio	Yes, if the beneficiary is a person or entity is within classes of beneficiaries named in	No, because insured's estate is not an exempted class of	Yes. (§ 3911.10)	There is no statutory provision or definite case authority on point.	If made with intent to defraud, creditors get premiums paid plus interest. (§ 3911.10)	No. Cash surrender value of unmatured life insurance policies cannot be garnished, as long	No. (§ 2329.66(A)(6)(b))

	§ 3911.9(B)(1)10 (spouse, child, dependent relative, any creditor, certain charities, or to trustee of such beneficiaries).	beneficiaries. (§ 3911.10)				as policy condition precedent to right of surrender value is unperformed. (Marquis v. New York Life Ins. Co., 92 Ohio App. 389, 108 N.E.2d 227 (1952))	
Oklahoma	Yes. (36 § 3631.1(A))	Yes. (36 § 3631.1)	Yes. (36 § 3631.1(D))	There is no statutory provision or definite case authority on point.	If made with intent to defraud, creditors get premiums paid plus interest. (36 § 3631.1(C)(1))	No, except for premium payments made infraud on creditors, fines imposed by violation of state or federal statutes, or a debt of the insured secured by a pledge of the policy. (36 § 3631.1(C)(1)-(3))	No. (36 § 3631.1(A)(4))
Oregon	Yes. (§ 743.046(1))	No. (§ 743.046(1))	No, with respect to the person "effecting" the life insurance policy. (§ 743.046(1))	N/A	Yes. If fraud, creditors get premiums and interest. (§ 743.046(4))	No, so long as the policy is payable to a beneficiary other than the estate of the insured. (§ 743.046(3))	No, so long as the policy is payable to a beneficiary other than the estate of the insured. (§ 743.046(3))
Pennsylvania	Yes, if beneficiary is the spouse, child, or dependent relative of insured. (42 § 8124(c)(6))	No. (42 § 8124(c)(6))	Yes if the owner is the spouse, child, or dependent relative of insured. (42 § 8124(c)(6))	There is no statutory provision or definite case authority on point.	Exemption will not apply if the judgment debtor is spouse, child, or dependent relative. (42 § 8124(c)(6))	There is no statutory provision or definite case authority on point.	There is no statutory provision or definite case authority on point.
Rhode Island	Yes, except in cases of intent to defraud. (§ 27-4-11)	No. (§ 27-4-11)	No, with respect to the person "effecting" the life insurance policy. (§ 27-4-11)	There is no statutory provision or definite case authority on point.	If made with intent to defraud, creditors get premiums paid plus interest. (§ 27-4-11)	There is no statutory provision or definite case authority on point.	There is no statutory provision or definite case authority on point.

Table 9.01
Life Insurance *(continued)*

	Are Payments to Beneficiaries Other Than the Insured or Owner Protected?	*Are Payments to the Insured's Estate Protected?*	*Are Payments to the Owner If Not the Insured Protected?*	*What if Payments Are to Spouse of Person Where Proceeds Can Be Reached?*	*Is There a Limit on the Protection?*	*Can Policies Be Reached Prior to Death?*	*Does It Matter Whether the Debtor Is in Bankruptcy?*
South Carolina	Yes, if beneficiaries are insured's spouse, child, or dependent. (§ 38-63-40(A))	No. (§ 38-63-40 (A))	Yes, if the owner is the spouse, child, or dependents of insured. (§ 38-63-40(A))	There is no statutory provision or definite case authority on point.	Yes, up to $4,000 in any unmatured life insurance dividend, interest or loan value. (§ 15-41-30(8)) Also, no exemption to the extent of premiums and interest if attempt to defraud creditors. (§ 38-63-40(A)(2))	No, unless credit life insurance contract. (§ 15-41-30(7))	Yes. Cash surrender value or payments are not exempt if insured has filed bankruptcy petition within two years of purchasing insurance. (§§ 38-63-40(A)(1), 15-41-30(7))
South Dakota	Yes, if beneficiary is surviving spouse or child. (§ 58-12-4)	Yes, if for use of surviving spouse or minor children. (§ 43-45-6)	Yes, in the absence of an agreement or assignment. (§ 58-12-4)	Yes, the proceeds are protected. (§ 58-12-4)	Yes, $20,000 if payments to beneficiaries, or $10,000 if payments to insured's estate. (§§ 58-12-4, 43-45-6)	Yes, to the extent over limits on protection. (§§ 58-12-4, 43-45-6)	There is no statutory provision or definite case authority on point.
Tennessee	Yes, if beneficiary is surviving spouse, child, or dependent relative for claims existing after January 1, 1932. (§ 56-7-203)	Yes, if for use of surviving spouse or children and debts are not specifically charged in the will. (§ 56-7-201)	Yes if the owner is the spouse, child, or dependent relative of insured. (§ 56-7-203)	There is no statutory provision or definite case authority on point.	No. (§ 56-7-203)	No, as long as the beneficiary is surviving spouse, child, or dependent relative. (§ 56-7-203; In re Thurman, 127 Bankr. 401 (M.D. Tenn. 1991))	No, as long as the beneficiary is the surviving spouse, a child, or a dependent relative. (§ 56-7-203; In re Thurman, 120 Bankr. 99 (Bankr. M.D. Tenn. 1990))

Texas	Yes. (Ins. Code § 1108.051(b)(2))	No. (Ins. Code § 1108.052(2))	No. Statute only provides protection for the "insured" or "beneficiary" (Ins. Code § 1108.051(a))	There is no statutory provision or definite case authority on point.	No. (Ins. Code § 1108.051)	No. (Ins. Code § 1108.051(a))	No. (Ins. Code § 1108.051(b)(2)(C))
Utah	Yes, but only if (1) decedent is the spouse or child of the debtor, OR the beneficiary is the spouse or child of the debtor; AND (2) the policy has been in existence for a continuous unexpired period of one year. (§ 78-23-5(1)(a)(xi)-(xii))	No. (§ 78-23-5(1)(a)(xi)-(xiii))	Yes, if owner is the spouse or children of insured. (§ 78-23-5(1)(a)(xi)-(xiii))	There is no statutory provision or definite case authority on point.	No. (§ 78-23-5(2)), unless the proceeds or avails were pledged as collateral. (§ 78-23-5(1)(a)(xi)-(xiii))	Yes, but only payments made on the contract during the one year immediately preceding a creditor's levy are reachable. (§ 78-23-5(1)(a)(xiii))	There is no statutory provision or definite case authority on point.
Vermont	Yes, except in cases of transfer with intent to defraud. (8 § 3706(a))	No. (8 § 3706(a))	No, with respect to the person "effecting" the life insurance policy. (8 § 3706(a))	Yes, assuming no intent to defraud. (8 § 3706(a))	No. However, if intent to defraud creditors, they are entitled to the amount of premiums paid plus interest thereon. (8 § 3706(a))	No, unless it is a credit life insurance contract. (12 § 2740(18))	No. (12 § 2740(18))
Virginia	Yes, except in cases of transfer with intent to defraud. (§ 38.2-3122(1))	No. (§ 38.2-3122(2))	No, with respect to the person "effecting" the life insurance policy. (§ 38.2-3122(2))	There is no statutory provision or definite case authority on point.	If made with intent to defraud, creditors get premiums paid plus interest. (§ 38.2-3122(5); White v. Pacific Mutual, 143 S.E. 340 (1928))	There is no statutory provision or definite case authority on point.	There is no statutory provision or definite case authority on point.

Table 9.01
Life Insurance *(continued)*

	Are Payments to Beneficiaries Other Than the Insured or Owner Protected?	*Are Payments to the Insured's Estate Protected?*	*Are Payments to the Owner If Not the Insured Protected?*	*What if Payments Are to Spouse of Person Where Proceeds Can Be Reached?*	*Is There a Limit on the Protection?*	*Can Policies Be Reached Prior to Death?*	*Does It Matter Whether the Debtor Is in Bankruptcy?*
Washington	Yes. (§ 48.18.410(1))	No. (Elsom v. Gadd, 93 Wash. 603, 93 Wa. 162 P. 867 (1917))	No. (§§ 48.18.410(1), 48.18.410(3)(a))	There is no statutory provision or definite case authority on point.	If there is intent to defraud creditors, they get amount remaining in the possession of the insurer at the time they are given notice of claim. (§§ 48.18.410(1), 48.18.410(3)(b)) Spouse is entitled to his half community property interest in the proceeds regardless of beneficiary designation. (In re Towey's Estate, 22 Wash. 2d 212, 155 P.2d 273, 275 (1945))	There is no statutory provision or definite case authority on point.	Probably not. See Turner v. Bovee, 92 F.2d 791 (9th Cir. 1937).
West Virginia	Yes, except in cases of transfer with intent to defraud. (§ 33-6-27(a))	No. (§ 33-6-27(a))	No, with respect to the person "effecting" the life insurance policy. (§ 33-6-27(a))	There is no statutory provision or definite case authority on point.	If made with intent to defraud, creditors get premiums paid plus interest. (§ 33-6-27(b))	There is no statutory provision or definite case authority on point.	Can exempt unmeasured life insurance contract owned by the debtor, other than a credit life insurance contract from bankruptcy estate (§ 38-10-4(g)), and debtor's interest, not in excess of $8,000, in dividend

							or interest under, or loan value in, any unmeasured life insurance contract owned by debtor where insured is the debtor or is an individual of whom the debtor is a dependent (§ 38-10-4(h)).
Wisconsin	Yes, if the beneficiary is a dependent of the insured on the date of the insured's death to the extent reasonably necessary for support of the dependent or dependents. (§ 815.18(3)(i)(1)(a))	No.	Yes, under circumstances set forth in the fifth column.	There is no statutory provision or definite case authority on point.	There is no limit where the beneficiary is the spouse. (§ 859.18(4)(a)(4)) In other cases, see first and sixth columns for whether policies can be reached prior to the death of the insured.	Unmatured life insurance contracts are exempt, but may be limited to as little as $4,000 if the policy was acquired or first funded 24 months or less before a cause of action is filed resulting in a judgment or an exemption claim is made. There is no exemption for credit insurance subject to the 24 month condition; protection is also limited to $150,000 in value of any accrued dividends, interest, or loan value on all unmatured policies owned by the debtor and insuring the debtor, the	No. (Cannon v. Lincoln Nat. Life Ins. Co., 243 N.W. 320 (1932))

(cont'd)

Table 9.01
Life Insurance *(continued)*

	Are Payments to Beneficiaries Other Than the Insured or Owner Protected?	*Are Payments to the Insured's Estate Protected?*	*Are Payments to the Owner If Not the Insured Protected?*	*What if Payments Are to Spouse of Person Where Proceeds Can Be Reached?*	*Is There a Limit on the Protection?*	*Can Policies Be Reached Prior to Death?*	*Does It Matter Whether the Debtor Is in Bankruptcy?*
Wisconsin *(cont'd)*						debtor's dependent, or an individual of whom the debtor is a dependent. (§ 815.18(3)(f)(2))	
Wyoming	Yes, except in cases of transfer with intent to defraud. (§ 26-15-129(a))	No. (§ 26-15-129(a))	No, with respect to the person "executing" the life insurance policy. (§ 26-15-129(a))	There is no statutory provision or definite case authority on point.	If made with intent to defraud, creditors get premiums paid plus interest. (§ 26-15-129(b))	No (§ 26-15-129(a)), including cash surrender value. But see In re Evans, 2000 U. S. Dist. LEXIS 21893 (D. Wyo. 2000), which suggests a different result in the case of bankruptcy.	Yes. At least benefits available at date of filing can be reached. (In re Evans, 2000 U.S. Dist. LEXIS 21893 (D. Wyo. 2000))

1. Exemptions are allowed to the extent they are established in the life insurance policy. (§ 431:10D-112)

Table 9.02
Annuities

	Can the Rights of the Annuitant Be Reached?	*Are Certain Annuity Trusts, e.g., § 403(b), Protected?*	*Does It Matter Whether the Debtor Is in Bankruptcy?*
Alabama	No, unless intent to defraud creditors or for amount over $250/month. (§ 27-14-32(a))	Yes. § 19-3B-508(e)(4).	No. (§ 19-3B-508(d))
Alaska	No, but subject to $10,000 dollar limit. (§ 09.38.025(a))	Yes. (§ 09.38.017(a) & (e)(3)).	No. (§ 09.38.055)
Arizona	No, so long as the annuity contract has been owned by the debtor for two years continuously and the beneficiary is the spouse, child, parent, sibling, or other dependent family member. (§ 33-1126(A)(7))	Yes. (§ 33-1126(B))	Yes. Amounts contributed to annuity trusts within 120 days before a debtor files for bankruptcy are not exempt. (§ 33-1126(B)(2)) Annuity contracts are not treated differently. (§ 33-1126(A))
Arkansas	No, unless payment to annuitant with intent to defraud creditors, or in excess of reasonable requirements of annuitant and dependent family members. (§ 23-79-134(a))	Yes. (§ 16-66-220(a))	No. § 23-79-134(a) speaks of creditors generally, yet does not specifically mention bankruptcy.
California	No. (Civ. Proc. § 704.100(a)-(c)) Subject to $9,700 limit. Must qualify as or function like life insurance. (In re Turner, 186 B.R. 108 (9th Cir. BAP 1995)) If matured, then exempt to the extent reasonably necessary for the support of the debtor and the spouse and dependents of the debtor. (In re Moffat, 959 F.2d 740,742 (9th Cir. 1992))	Yes. (Civ. Proc. § 704.115(3)(b))	No. (§ 703.140(b)(10)(E))
Colorado	No. (§§ 10-7-106; 13-54-102(1)(s))	Yes, and any benefits in ERISA-type plan or IRA. (§ 13-54-102(1)(s))	No. (§ 10-7-106)
Connecticut	No. Retirement annuities are exempt from the claims of creditors to the same extent as "ERISA qualified" retirement plans. (§§ 52-352b, 52-321a)	Yes. (§ 52-321a(a)(1))	There is no statutory provision or definite case authority on point.

Table 9.02
Annuities *(continued)*

	Can the Rights of the Annuitant Be Reached?	*Are Certain Annuity Trusts, e.g., § 403(b), Protected?*	*Does It Matter Whether the Debtor Is in Bankruptcy?*
Delaware	No, except premiums paid with intent to defraud. (18 § 2728(a)) If amount is greater than $350/month, it is subject to garnishment as wages and salary. (18 § 2728(a)(2))	See Table 9.03.	There is no statutory provision or definite case authority on point.
District of Columbia	Yes, if certain requirements are not met. (§ 15-501(a)(7)(E)) First $200/month exempt if principal supporter of family for two months preceding the issuance of a writ. (§ 15-503(a)) $60/month for the two months preceding the issuance of a writ for people who do not provide support for a family. (§ 15-503(b))	Yes. (§ 15-501(a)(9))	There is no statutory provision or definite case authority on point.
Florida	No, unless effected for the benefit of the creditor. (§ 222.14)	Yes (§ 222.21(2)(a)(1)), unless subject to qualified domestic relations order (§ 222.21(2)(d)).	Still exempt. (Matter of Rettemnier, 113 B.R. 757 (S.D. Fla. 1990))
Georgia	Yes, unless assigned to or effected for the benefit of the creditor or transfer is made with intent to defraud creditor. (§ 33-28-7)	Yes. Exempt from bankruptcy to the extent reasonably necessary for the support of the debtor and any dependent. (§ 44-13-100(a)(2)(E))	Yes, exemption for support of debtor or dependent, as an alternative to the § 44-13-100(a)(1) personal property exemption. (§ 44-13-100(a)(2)(E))
Hawaii	No, subject to qualified domestic relations order. (§ 651-124)	Yes, subject to qualified domestic relations order. (§ 651-124)	No, unless contribution is made within three years of filing. (§ 651-124)
Idaho	Yes, if (1) premium paid with intent to defraud, (2) total exemption benefits exceed $1,250/month, or (3) total exemption benefits exceed $1,250/month and the court ordered to pay creditors after taking account reasonable requirements of the judgment debtor and his family if dependent upon him. (§ 41-1836)	Yes, unless subject to qualified domestic relations order. (§ 55-1011)	There is no statutory provision or definite case authority on point.
Illinois	No. (735 ILCS § 5/12-1006(a) & (b)(3))	Yes. (735 ILCS § 5/12-1006(a) & (b)(3))	A debtor is not entitled to the federal exemptions provided by 11 U.S.C. 522(d)(10)(E) of the Bankruptcy Code. (735 ILCS § 5/12-1201)

Indiana	Yes, if annuitant is the person who provided consideration for the contract. (§ 27-2-5-1(b))	Yes, exempt from bankruptcy. (§§ 34-6-2-131, 34-55-10-2(c)(6))	Yes. Premiums paid not more than one year prior to bankruptcy are not exempt. (§ 27-2-5-1(c)(1))
Iowa	No. (§ 627.6(8)(e)) The rights can be reached if the annuity has its origin as an IRA on the assumption that IRAs are not exempt from bankruptcy. (In re Hupton, 287 B.R. 438 (N.D. Iowa 2000)) However, see the U.S. Supreme Court decision in Rousey v. Jacoway, 125 S. Ct. 1561 (2005) (IRAs do qualify for bankruptcy exemption).	Yes. (§ 627.6(8)(f))	Yes. Contribution must fall outside of one year of bankruptcy. (§ 627.6(8)(e))
Kansas	Only certain annuities are exempt. (§ 60-2308(b))	Yes. (§ 60-2308(b))	Not mentioned.
Kentucky	Yes, if (1) premium paid with intent to defraud, (2) total exemption benefits exceed $350/month, or (3) total exemption benefits exceed $350/month and the court ordered to pay creditors after taking account reasonable requirements of the judgment debtor and his family if dependent upon him. (§ 304.14-330(1)(b))	Yes, subject to court order for payment of "maintenance" or "child support." (§ 427.150(2)(f))	Funds contributed to the plan within 120 days of bankruptcy are not exempt. (§ 427.150(2)(f))
Louisiana	No. (§ 22:647(B))	Yes. (§ 20:33(1))	A maximum $35,000 is exempt if bankruptcy filed within nine months of policy issuance. (§ 22:647(A)(2))
Maine	Yes, if (1) premium paid with intent to defraud, (2) total exemption benefits exceed $450/month, or (3) total exemption benefits exceed $450/month and the court ordered to pay creditors after taking account reasonable requirements of the judgment debtor and his family if dependent upon him. (24-A § 2431(1))	Yes. (14 § 4422(13)(E)(3))	There is no statutory provision or definite case authority on point.
Maryland	No, if proceeds benefit spouse, child, or dependent relative. (Ins. § 16-111(a))	Yes. (Cts. & Jud. Proc. § 11-504(h)(1))	A debtor is not entitled to the federal exemptions provided by § 522(d)(10)(E) of the U.S. Bankruptcy Code. (Ct. & Jud. Proc. § 11-504(g))

Table 9.02
Annuities *(continued)*

	Can the Rights of the Annuitant Be Reached?	*Are Certain Annuity Trusts, e.g., § 403(b), Protected?*	*Does It Matter Whether the Debtor Is in Bankruptcy?*
Massachusetts	No, unless there is (1) divorce, separate maintenance or child support court order or (2) a court order requiring payment of monetary penalty or restitution in the case of a crime. (235 § 34A)	Yes. (235 § 34A)	There is also a limitation for non-rollover individual plans for sums deposited in the 5 years prior to a declaration of bankruptcy or entry of judgment in excess of 7% of the total income of the individual during the 5-year period.
Michigan	No, unless there is an order of divorce, separate maintenance, or child support. (§ 600.6023(1)(l))	Yes. (§ 600.6023(1)(l))	Yes, does not exempt contributions within 120 days before filing bankruptcy. (§ 600.6023(1)(l))
Minnesota	No, so long as the owner is different than beneficiary. (§§ 61A.12(1))	Yes, unless the debt is owed under a support order as defined in § 518.54(4a). (§ 550.37(24))	No. Protection is afforded. (In re Walsh, 19 F. Supp. 567 (D. Minn. 1937))
Mississippi	No, with respect to employee annuity or self-employed individual annuity if the purpose is to provide retirement benefits. (§ 85-3-1(c))	Yes. (§ 85-3-1(c) & (e))	No. Even though Mississippi has elected to "opt-out" of federal exemptions under § 522(d), state exemptions for annuities are essentially the same.
Missouri	No. Exempt to the extent reasonably necessary for the support of the debtor and any dependent of debtor. (§ 513.430(1)(10)(e))	Yes. (§ 513.430(1)(10)(e)(c))	Yes. Funds not exempt if fraudulent, and for three-year period prior to commencement of the proceedings. (§ 513.430(1)(10)(f))
Montana	Yes, if (1) premium paid with intent to defraud, (2) total exemption benefits exceed $350/month, or (3) total exemption benefits exceed $350/month and the court ordered to pay creditors after taking account reasonable requirements of the judgment debtor and his family if dependent upon him. (§ 33-15-514(1)).	Yes. (§ 31-2-106(3)(c))	Yes, contributions within one year before filing of bankruptcy which exceed 15% of individual's income for such year. (§ 31-2-106(3))
Nebraska	Yes. Funds are protected only if beneficiary is related by blood or marriage to insurer (§ 44-371(1)(a)) and only up to $100,000. (§ 44-371(1)(b))	Yes, to the extent reasonably necessary for the support of the debtor. (§ 25-1563.01)	Yes. The 403(b) annuity trust is not exempt if, within two years prior to bankruptcy, plan was established or amended to increase contribution. (§ 25-1563.01(1))

Nevada	Yes, if (1) premium paid with intent to defraud, (2) total exemption benefits exceed $350/month, or (3) total exemption benefits exceed $350/month and the court ordered to pay creditors after taking account reasonable requirements of the judgment debtor and his family if dependent upon him. (§ 687B.290(1))	Yes, up to $500,000. (§ 21.090(1)(q)(4))	No. (§§ 21.090(3), 21.090(1)(n))
New Hampshire	Retirement plan annuities are protected with respect to pre-1999 extensions of credits and the possibility of federal preemption, see De Carolis v. De Carolis, 259 B.R. 467, 471 n. 9 (1st Cir. Bankr. App. Panel (2001)). (§ 511:2(XIX))	Yes. (§ 511:2(XIX))	There is no statutory provision or definite case authority on point.
New Jersey	Yes, if (1) premium paid with intent to defraud, (2) total exemption benefits exceed $500/month, or (3) total exemption benefits exceed $500/month and the court ordered to pay creditors after taking account reasonable requirements of the judgment debtor and his family if dependent upon him. (§ 17B:24-7(a))	Yes, unless there is an order for child or spousal support. (§ 25:2-1(b)(2))	No. Only subject to "intent to defraud" exception preference or fraudulent conveyance. (§§ 17B:24-7(a)(1), 25:2-1(b)(1))
New Mexico	No. (§ 42-10-3)	Yes. (§§ 42-10-1, 42-10-2)	No. (§§ 42-10-1, 42-10-2).
New York	No. (N.Y. Civ. Pract. L&R § 5205(c)(3) & (d)(1))	Yes. (N.Y. Civ. Pract. L&R § 5205(c)(2) & (d)(1))	No (N.Y. Civ. Pract. L&R § 5205(c)(3) & (d)(1)), except that only $5,000 is exempt if purchased within six months of the petition. (NY Debt. & Cred. § 283(1))
North Carolina	No. (§ 1C-1601(a)(8) & (9)	Yes. (§ 1C-1601(a)(9).	No statutory provision or case authority on point.
North Dakota	No, so long as (1) beneficiary is the spouse, child, relative of the insured dependent, or likely to be dependent and (2) it has been in effect for at least one year. (§ 28-22-03.1(3))	Yes, up to $100,000 individually and $200,000 in combination with other accounts, pensions, IRAs, life insurance, and retirement plans. (§ 28-22-03.1(3))	No. Exemption covers plans in effect for a period of one year. (§ 28-22-03.1(3))
Ohio	No, as long as annuitant is a member of an exempted class under § 3911.10. (§ 2329.66(A)(6)(b))	Yes, to extent payments are reasonably necessary for support. (§ 2329.66(A)(10)(b))	No. (§ 2329.66(A)(6)(b))

Table 9.02
Annuities *(continued)*

	Can the Rights of the Annuitant Be Reached?	*Are Certain Annuity Trusts, e.g., § 403(b), Protected?*	*Does It Matter Whether the Debtor Is in Bankruptcy?*
Oklahoma	No, except for (1) premium payments made in fraud on creditors, (2) fines imposed by violation of state or federal statutes, or (3) a debt of the insured secured by a pledge of the policy. (36 § 3631.1(A) & (C))	Yes, to extent that contributions by or on behalf of a participant were not subject to federal income tax at the time of such contributions. (31 § 1(A)(20))	No. (36 § 3631.1(A)(4))
Oregon	Yes, if (1) premium paid with intent to defraud, (2) total exemption benefits exceed $500/month, or (3) total exemption benefits exceed $500/month and the court ordered to pay creditors after taking account reasonable requirements of the judgment debtor and his family if dependent upon him. (§ 743.049(1))	Yes, except for certain claims regarding fraudulent transfers and support. (§ 18.358)	No. (In re Thompson, 197 B.R. 326 (Bankr. D. Or. 1996))
Pennsylvania	Yes, $100/month is exempt. (42 § 8124(c)(3)). Proceeds to spouse, child, or dependent relative are wholly exempt. (42 § 8124(c)(6))	Yes. (42 § 8124(b)(1)(ix))	Will not protect amounts contributed within one year of bankruptcy. (42 § 8124(b)(1)(ix)(A))
Rhode Island	Yes, if not protected by ERISA or if there is an order of the court pursuant to spousal or child support. (§ 9-26-4(12))	Yes. (§ 9-26-4(12))	No. (§ 9-26-4(12))
South Carolina	No, unless certain limitations are not met. (§ 15-41-30(10)(E))	Yes. (§ 15-41-30(10)(E)(iii))	No. (§ 15-41-30(10)(E))
South Dakota	Yes, if total exemption exceeds $250 per month. (§ 58-12-8)	Yes, up to total of $250,000 principal and income and distributions related thereto, in aggregate for all employee benefit plans. (§§ 43-45-15 to 43-45-18)	No. (§§ 43-45-15 to 43-45-18)
Tennessee	No, if beneficiary is spouse, child, or dependent relative for claims arising after January 1, 1932. (§ 56-7-203)	Yes, except for claims of the state of Tennessee or claims under a qualified domestic relations order. (§ 26-2-111(1)(D)(iii))	No, as long as beneficiary is spouse, child, or dependent relative. (In re Thurman, 120 Bankr. 99 (Bankr. M.D. Tenn. 1990)
Texas	No. (Ins. Code § 1108.051(a)(2))	Yes. (Prop. § 42.0021; Ins. Code § 1108.051(a)(2)))	No. (Ins. Code § 1108.051(a)(2)); In re Shurley, 163 B.R. 286 (Bankr. W.D. Texas 1993)

Utah	No, if for disability or illness (§ 78-23-5(1)(a)(iii)(A)-(B)) or pursuant to certain types of qualified plans. (§ 78-23-5(1)(a)(xiv))	Yes, unless the creditor is an alternative payee under a domestic relations order. (§ 78-23-5(1)(a)(xiv) & (xv))	If it is a § 403(b) trust, amounts contributed or benefits accrued on or on behalf of a debtor, within one year before the debtor files for bankruptcy are not exempt. (§ 78-23-5(1)(b)(ii))
Vermont	Yes, if (1) premium paid with intent to defraud, (2) total exemption benefits exceed $350/month, or (3) total exemption benefits exceed $350/month and the court ordered to pay creditors after taking account reasonable requirements of the judgment debtor and his family if dependent upon him. (8 § 3709(a)(2))	Yes, to extent reasonably necessary for support (12 § 2740(19)(J)), but does not specifically cite I.R.C. § 403(b).	No. (12 § 2740(19)(J))
Virginia	There is no statutory provision or definite case authority on point. However, § 34-4 provides for a $5,000 general exemption.	Yes, up to $25,000 per year. (§ 34-34(B))	There is no statutory provision or definite case authority on point.
Washington	Yes, if (1) premium paid with intent to defraud, (2) total exemption benefits exceed $2,500/month, or (3) total exemption benefits exceed $2,500/month and the court ordered to pay creditors after taking account reasonable requirements of the judgment debtor and his family if dependent upon him. (§ 48.18.430(1)(b))	Yes. (§ 6.15.020(4))	No. (§ 6.15.020(3))
West Virginia	Yes, unless in bankruptcy, then exempt as reasonably necessary for support of the debtor or a dependent of the debtor. (§ 38-10-4(j)(5))	Yes, for amount reasonably necessary for support of debtor and dependents, but the provision only refers to bankruptcy proceedings. (§ 38-10-4(j)(5))	Can exempt payments to annuity to the extent reasonably necessary for support of the debtor and any dependents. (§ 38-10-4(j)(5))
Wisconsin	No, unless the annuity contract was issued less than 24 months prior, in which case the exemption must not exceed $4,000. (§ 815.18(3)(f))	Yes. (§ 815.18(3)(j)(1))	There is no statutory provision or definite case authority on point.
Wyoming	Yes, if (1) premium paid with intent to defraud, (2) total exemption benefits exceed $2500/month, or (3) total exemption benefits exceed $2500/month and the court ordered to pay creditors after taking account reasonable requirements of the judgment debtor and his family if dependent upon him. (§ 26-15-132(a))	Yes. (§ 1-20-110)	Yes, exempt to extent payment made to fund while solvent. (§ 1-20-110(a)(ii))

Table 9.03
Pension Plans

	Are Federally Qualified § 401 Pension Plans Exempt?	*Are § 403(a) Annuity Plans Exempt?*	*Are § 408 IRAs Exempt?* **	*Is There an Income Exemption for Payments Not Covered by the Pension Plan Exemption?*	*Are Contributions Within a Certain Period of Bankruptcy Exempt?*
Alabama	Yes, unless to satisfy a qualified domestic relations order. (§ 19-3B-508 (e)(4)).	There is no statutory provision or definite case authority on point.	Yes, exempt from bankruptcy. (§ 19-3B-508(d); In re Hyde, 200 B.R. 694 (Bankr. N.D. Ala. 1996))	There is no statutory provision or definite case authority on point.	Yes. (§ 19-3B-508(d)) Statute does not provide a time limit; In re Hyde exempts these plans from bankruptcy.
Alaska	Yes. (§ 09.38.017(e)(3))	Yes. (§ 09.38.017(e)(3))	Yes. (§ 09.38.017(e)(3))	No. § 09.38.030(e) treats the payments as earnings.	Yes, unless contribution is made within 120 days before filing for bankruptcy. (§ 09.38.017(b))
Arizona	Yes. (§ 33-1126(B))	Yes. (§ 33-1126(B))	Yes. (§ 33-1126(B))	No. § 12-1598(4) treats as earnings.	Yes. Contributions made before 120 days of filing for bankruptcy are excluded. (§ 33-1126(B)(2))
Arkansas	Yes. (§ 16-66-220(a))	Yes. (§ 16-66-220(a))	Yes, unless exceeding amount deductible under Internal Revenue Code. (§ 16-66-220(b)(1))	There is no statutory provision or definite case authority on point.	There is no statutory provision or definite case authority on point.
California[1]	Yes. (Civ. Proc. § 704.115 (a)(3))	Yes. (Civ. Proc. § 704.115 (a)(3))	Yes. (Civ. Proc. § 704.115 (a)(3))	Exempt from garnishment to the same extent as wages in private plans (Civ. Pro. § 704.115(f)), public plans (Civ. Pro. § 704.110(c)(2)).	The status of pension in bankruptcy is determined as of the date of bankruptcy filing. If non-exempt assets from an IRA are transferred into a retirement plan that is protected by a state bankruptcy exemption, and there was no fraudulent intent, then the IRA is protected, though

					transferred to protected status after the bankruptcy filing. (Gill v. Stern, 345 F.3d 1036 (9th Cir. 2003))
Colorado[1]	Yes. (§ 13-54-102(1)(s))	No, not expressly listed as exempt. (§ 13-54-102(1)(s))	Yes. (§ 13-54-102(1)(s))	No. (§ 13-54-102(1)(s))	There is no statutory provision or definite case authority on point.
Connecticut	Yes. (§ 52-321a(a)(1))	Yes. (§ 52-321a(a)(1))	Yes. (§ 52-321a(a)(2); Central Bank v. Hickey, 680 A.2d 298 (1996))	No. (§ 52-321a)	There is no statutory provision or definite case authority on point.
Delaware	N/A. Under Delaware law, only plans created by the state retirement system are exempt from the claims of employee's creditors. (9 § 4316; 29 § 5503)	N/A. Under Delaware law, only plans created by the state retirement system are exempt from the claims of employee's creditors. (9 § 4316; 29 § 5503)	N/A. Under Delaware law, only plans created by the state retirement system are exempt from the claims of employee's creditors. (9 § 4316; 29 § 5503)	N/A. Under Delaware law, only plans created by the state retirement system are exempt from the claims of employee's creditors. (9 § 4316; 29 § 5503)	N/A. Under Delaware law, only plans created by the state retirement system are exempt from the claims of employee's creditors. (9 § 4316; 29 § 5503)
District of Columbia[1]	Yes, if on account of illness, disability, death, age or length of service, to the extent reasonably necessary for the support of the debtor and any dependent of the debtor. (§ 15-501(a)(7)(E)(iii))	Yes. (§ 15-501(a)(9))	Yes. (§ 15-501(a)(9))	Yes. $200/month exempt if principal supporter of family for two months preceding the issuance of a writ. (§ 15-503(a)) $60/month for the two months preceding the issuance of a writ for people who do not provide support for a family. (§ 15-503(b))	There is no statutory provision or definite case authority on point.
Florida	Yes (§ 222.21(2)(a)), unless subject to qualified domestic relations order. (§ 222.21(2)(d))	Yes (§ 222.21(2)(a)), unless subject to qualified domestic relations order. (§ 222.21(2)(d))	Yes (§ 222.21(2)(a)), unless subject to qualified domestic relations order. (§ 222.21(2)(d))	Yes, if alternate payee under qualified domestic relations order. (§ 222.21(2)(d))	There is no statutory provision or definite case authority on point.
Georgia[1]	Yes. Exempt from bankruptcy to the extent reason ably necessary for *(cont'd)*	Yes. Exempt from bankruptcy to the extent reasonably necessary for the *(cont'd)*	Yes. Exempt from bankruptcy to the extent reasonably necessary for the *(cont'd)*	There is no statutory provision or definite case authority on point.	There is no statutory provision or definite case authority on point.

Table 9.03
Pension Plans *(continued)*

	Are Federally Qualified § 401 Pension Plans Exempt?	*Are § 403(a) Annuity Plans Exempt?*	*Are § 408 IRAs Exempt?* **	*Is There an Income Exemption for Payments Not Covered by the Pension Plan Exemption?*	*Are Contributions Within a Certain Period of Bankruptcy Exempt?*
Georgia *(cont'd)*	the support of the debtor and any dependent. (§ 44-13-100(a)(2)(E))	support of the debtor and any dependent. (§ 44-13-100(a)(2)(E))	support of the debtor and any dependent. (§ 44-13-100(a)(2)(F))		
Hawaii	Yes, unless subject to a qualified domestic relations order. (§ 651-124)	Yes, unless subject to a qualified domestic relations order. (§ 651-124)	Yes, unless subject to a qualified domestic relations order. (§ 651-124)	Yes, unless subject to a qualified domestic relations order. (§ 651-124)	Yes, three years within filing for bankruptcy is nonexempt. (§ 651-124)
Idaho	Yes, but subject to a qualified domestic relations order under 26 U.S.C. § 414(p) (§ 55-1011)	Yes, but subject to a qualified domestic relations order under 26 U.S.C. § 414(p) (§ 55-1011)	Yes, but subject to a qualified domestic relations order under 26 U.S.C. § 414(p) (§ 55-1011)	Exempt to the extent necessary for the support of the debtor and dependents. (§ 11-604(2))	There is no statutory provision or definite case authority on point.
Illinois[1]	Yes. Plans intended in good faith to be I.R.C.-exempt are also exempted. (735 ILCS § 5/12-1006(a))	Yes. (735 ILCS § 5/12-1006(a))	Yes. (735 ILCS § 5/12-1006(a))	There is no statutory provision or definite case authority on point.	No time limit as long as intended to qualify as retirement plans. (In re Tempklin, 146 B.R. 757 (Bankr. N.D. Ill. 1992))
Indiana	Yes, exempt from bankruptcy. (§§ 34-6-2-131, 34-55-10-2(c)(6))	Yes, exempt from bankruptcy. (§§ 34-6-2-131, 34-55-10-2(c)(6))	Yes, exempt from bankruptcy. (§§ 34-6-2-131, 34-55-10-2(c)(6)(A)(ii))	There is no statutory provision or definite case authority on point.	There is no statutory provision or definite case authority on point. One case has held, however, that an ERISA-qualified pension is a spendthrift trust under state law and not included in bankruptcy estate where the plan contains an absolute restriction on alienation of at least 70% of benefits. (In re LeFeber, 906 F.2d 330 (7th Cir. 1990))

Iowa	Yes. (§ 627.6(8)(f))	Yes, either all or a portion. (§ 627.6(8)(e))	Yes. (§ 627.6(8)(f))	There is no statutory provision or definite case authority on point.	Payments made before one year of bankruptcy exempt. (§ 627.6(8)(e))
Kansas	Yes. (§ 60-2308(b))	Yes. (§ 60-2308(b))	Yes. (§ 60-2308(b))	There is no statutory provision or definite case authority on point.	There is no statutory provision or definite case authority on point.
Kentucky[1]	Yes. (§ 427.150(2)(f))	Yes. (§ 427.150(2)(f))	Yes. (§ 427.150(2)(f))	There is no statutory provision or definite case authority on point.	Funds contributed 120 days before filing for bankruptcy are not exempt. (§§ 427.005(2), 427.150(2)(f))
Louisiana[1]	Yes, only to extent they are exempt from federal taxation. (R.S. § 20:33(1))	Yes, exempt only to extent they are exempt from federal taxation. (R.S. § 20:33(1))	Yes, exempt only to extent they are exempt from federal taxation. (R.S. § 20:33(1))	Yes. Gratuitous payments from an employer are exempt. (R.S. § 20:33(2))	Not exempt if made "less than one calendar year of the date of filing for bankruptcy whether voluntary or involuntary. . . ." (13:3881(D)(2))
Maine	Yes. (14 § 4422(13)(E)(3))	Yes. (14 § 4422(13)(E)(3))	Yes. (14 § 4422(13)(E)(3))	There is no statutory provision or definite case authority on point.	There is no statutory provision or definite case authority on point.
Maryland	Yes. (Cts. & Jud. Proc. § 11-504(h))	Yes. (Cts. & Jud. Proc. § 11-504(h))	Yes. (Cts. & Jud. Proc. § 11-504(h))	There is no statutory provision or definite case authority on point.	There is no statutory provision or definite case authority on point.
Massachusetts	Yes, except to enforce child or spousal support upon order of court. (235 § 34A)	Yes. (235 § 34A)	Yes. (235 § 34A)	There is no statutory provision or definite case authority on point.	Generally, yes. However, in the case of IRAs of a non-rolled over kind, only contributions in the 5 years prior to bankruptcy not in excess of the total income of the individual for this period is protected.
Michigan	Yes. (§ 600.6023(1)(l))	There is no statutory provision or definite case authority on point.	Yes. (§ 600.6023(1)(k)) Only up to deduction allowed by I.R.C. § 403. (§ 600.6023(1)(k))	There is no statutory provision or definite case authority on point.	Contributions are generally not exempt if made within 120 days of filing for bankruptcy by the debtor. (§ 600.6023(1)(k) & (l))

Table 9.03
Pension Plans *(continued)*

	Are Federally Qualified § 401 Pension Plans Exempt?	*Are § 403(a) Annuity Plans Exempt?*	*Are § 408 IRAs Exempt? ***	*Is There an Income Exemption for Payments Not Covered by the Pension Plan Exemption?*	*Are Contributions Within a Certain Period of Bankruptcy Exempt?*
Minnesota[1]	Yes, up to $30,000 (§ 550.37(24))	Yes, up to $30,000 (§ 550.37(24))	Yes, up to $30,000 (§ 550.37(24))	Yes. (§ 571.922)	There is no statutory provision or definite case authority on point.
Mississippi	Yes. (§ 85-3-1(e)(i))	Yes. (§ 85-3-1(e)(i))	Yes. (§ 85-3-1(e)(iii)) See also In re Henderson, 167 B.R. 67 (N.D. Miss. 1993), in which bankruptcy debtors' exemption claims in their SEP-IRAs extended only to amounts reasonably necessary for support of debtors as well as any dependents.	There is no statutory provision or definite case authority on point.	There is no statutory provision or definite case authority on point.
Missouri	Yes. (§ 513.430(1)(10)(e)(c))	Yes. (§ 513.430(1)(10)(e)(c))	Yes. (§ 513.430(1)(10)(e)(c))	There is no statutory provision or definite case authority on point.	Yes. Funds are not exempt for the three years period prior to commencement of the proceedings. (§ 513.430(10)(f))
Montana	Yes. (§ 31-2-106(3)(c))	Yes. (§ 31-2-106(3)(c))	Yes. (§ 31-2-106(3)(c))	There is no statutory provision or definite case authority on point.	Yes, contributions within one year before filing of bankruptcy which exceed 15% of individual's income for such year. (§ 31-2-106(3))
Nebraska	Yes, to extent reasonably necessary for the support of the debtor. (§ 25-1563.01(2))	Yes, to extent reasonably necessary for the support of the debtor. (§ 25-1563.01(2))	Yes, to extent reasonably necessary for the support of the debtor. (§ 25-1563.01(2))	There is no statutory provision or definite case authority on point.	Exempt unless within two years prior to bankruptcy, plan was established or amended to increase contributions. (§ 25-1563.01(1))
Nevada[1]	Yes, up to $500,000. (§ 21.090(1)(q)(4))	Yes, up to $500,000. (§ 21.090(1)(q)(3))	Yes, up to $500,000. (§ 21.090(1)(q)(1) & (2))	There is no statutory provision or definite case authority on point.	No. (§§ 21.090(3), 21.090(1)(n))

New Hampshire[1]	Yes. (§ 511:2(XIX))	Yes. (§ 511:2(XIX))	Yes. (§ 511:2(XIX))	Yes. (§ 512:21)	There is no statutory provision or definite case authority on point.
New Jersey	Yes, unless there is an order for child or spousal support. (§ 25:2-1(b)(2))	Yes, unless there is an order for child or spousal support. (§ 25:2-1(b)(2))	Yes, unless there is an order for child or spousal support. (§ 25:2-1(b)(2))	There is no statutory provision or definite case authority on point.	No, unless preference or fraudulent conveyance. (§ 25:2-1(b)(1))
New Mexico[1]	Yes. (§§ 42-10-1, 42-10-2)	Yes. (§§ 42-10-1, 42-10-2)	Yes. (§§ 42-10-1, 42-10-2)	There is no statutory provision or definite case authority on point.	Yes, except fraudulent contributions. (§ 42-10-2; Dona Ana S & L v. Dofflemeyer, 855 P.2d 1054 (1993))
New York	Yes. (N.Y. Civ. Pract. L&R § 5205(c)(2) & (d)(1))	Yes. (N.Y. Civ. Pract. L&R § 5205(c)(2) & (d)(1))	Yes. (N.Y. Civ. Pract. L&R § 5205(c)(2) & (d)(1))	There is no statutory provision or definite case authority on point.	There is no statutory provision or definite case authority on point.
North Carolina	Yes, as to individual retirement plans under the Internal Revenue Code, and any plan treated in the same manner as an individual retirement plan under the Code. (§ 1C-1601(a)(9))	Yes, as to individual retirement plans under the Internal Revenue Code, and any plan treated in the same manner as an individual retirem-ent plan under the Code. (§ 1C-1601(a)(9))	Yes. (§ 1C-1601(a)(9))	There is no statutory provision or definite case authority on point.	They may generally be exempt. (In re Hare, 32 B. R. 16 (1983))
North Dakota[1]	Yes, up to \$100,000 for each plan and \$200,000 for all plans, policies, and pensions combined; however, this can be increased to situations where this property "is reasonably necessary for the support of the resident and the resident's dependents." (§ 28-22-03.1(3))	Yes, up to \$100,000 for each plan and \$200,000 for all plans, policies, and pensions combined; however, this can be increased to situations where this property "is reasonably necessary for the support of the resident and the resident's dependents." (§ 28-22-03.1(3))	Yes, up to \$100,000 for each plan and \$200,000 for all plans, policies, and pensions combined; however, this can be increased to situations where this property "is reasonably necessary for the support of the resident and the resident's dependents." (§ 28-22-03.1(3))	There is no statutory provision or definite case authority on point.	Exemption covers plans in effect for a period of one year. (§ 28-22-03.1(3))
Ohio	Yes, to extent payments are reasonably necessary for support. (§ 2329.66 (A)(10)(b))	Yes, to extent payments are reasonably necessary for support. (§ 2329.66 (A)(10)(b))	Yes, except for any assets deposited for the purpose of evading debts and certain other exceptions. (§ 2329.66 (A)(10)(c) & (d))	There is no statutory provision or definite case authority on point.	There is no statutory provision or definite case authority on point.

Table 9.03
Pension Plans *(continued)*

	Are Federally Qualified § 401 Pension Plans Exempt?	*Are § 403(a) Annuity Plans Exempt?*	*Are § 408 IRAs Exempt? ***	*Is There an Income Exemption for Payments Not Covered by the Pension Plan Exemption?*	*Are Contributions Within a Certain Period of Bankruptcy Exempt?*
Oklahoma	Yes, to extent that contributions by or on behalf of a participant were not subject to federal income tax at the time of such contributions. (31 § 1(A)(20))	Yes, to extent that contribu tions by or on behalf of a participant were not subject to federal income tax at the time of such contributions. (31 § 1(A)(20))	Yes, to extent that contribu tions by or on behalf of a participant were not subject to federal income tax at the time of such contributions. (31 § 1(A)(20))	There is no statutory provision or definite case authority on point.	No time requirement. Section exempts all these accounts from attachment, execution or other forced sale in a bankruptcy proceeding. (31 § 1(A)(20))
Oregon	Yes, except for certain claims regarding fraudulent transfers and support. (§ 18.358)	Yes, except for certain claims regarding fraudulent transfers and support. (§ 18.358)	Yes, except for certain claims regarding fraudulent transfers and support. (§ 18.358)	There is no statutory provision or definite case authority on point.	There is no statutory provision or definite case authority on point.
Pennsylvania	Yes. (42 § 8124(b)(1)(ix))	Yes. (42 § 8124(b)(1)(ix))	Yes. (42 § 8124(b)(1)(ix))	Amounts over $15,000 contributed within a one year period are not exempt. (42 § 8124(b)(1)(ix)(B))	Won't protect amounts contributed within one year of bankruptcy. (42 § 8214(b)(1)(ix)(A))
Rhode Island[1]	Yes, but not to the extent subject to an order of divorce, separate maintenance or child support. (§ 9-26-4(12))	No, if it is not protected by ERISA. (§ 9-26-4(12))	Yes. (§ 9-26-4(11))	There is no statutory provision or definite case authority on point.	There is no statutory provision or definite case authority on point.
South Carolina	Yes. (§ 15-41-30(10)(E)(iii))	Yes. (§ 15-41-30(10)(E)(iii))	Yes. (§ 15-41-30(12))	There is no statutory provision or definite case authority on point.	There is no statutory provision or definite case authority on point.
South Dakota	Yes, up to total of $250,000 principal and income and distributions related thereto, in aggregate for all employee	Yes, up to total of $250,000 principal and income and distributions related thereto, in aggregate for all employee	Yes, up to total of $250,000 principal and income and distributions related thereto, in aggregate for all employee	Yes. (§§ 21-18-51 to 21-18-53)	"Absolute exemption." (§ 43-45-15)

	benefit plans. (§§ 43-45-15 to 43-45-18)	benefit plans. (§§ 43-45-15 to 43-45-18)	benefit plans. (§§ 43-45-15 to 43-45-18)		
Tennessee	Yes, in the case of a resident if payable on or after age 58, on a periodic basis and there is no option to accelerate so as to receive in a lump sum or over a period of 60 months or less. (§ 26-2-111(1)(D))	Yes, in the case of a resident if payable on or after age 58, on a periodic basis and there is no option to accelerate so as to receive in a lump sum or over a period of 60 months or less. (§ 26-2-111(1)(D))	Yes, in the case of a resident if payable on or after age 58, on a periodic basis and there is no option to accelerate so as to receive in a lump sum or over a period of 60 months or less. (§ 26-2-111(1)(D))	Yes. (§ 26-2-106)	There is no statutory provision or definite case authority on point.
Texas	Yes, to extent contributions are deductible and not subject to a child support lien. (Prop. 42.0021 (a), 42.005)	Yes, to extent contributions are deductible and not subject to a child support lien. (Prop. 42.0021 (a), 42.005)	Yes, to extent contributions are deductible and not subject to a child support lien. (Prop. 42.0021 (a), 42.005)	There is no statutory provision or definite case authority on point.	There is no statutory provision or definite case authority on point.
Utah	Yes, unless the creditor is an alternative payee under a domestic relations order. (§ 78-23-5(1)(a)(xiv))	Yes, unless the creditor is an alternative payee under a domestic relations order. (§ 78-23-5(1)(a)(xiv))	Yes, unless the creditor is an alternative payee under a domestic relations order. (§ 78-23-5(1)(a)(xiv))	There is no statutory provision or definite case authority on point.	Amounts contributed or benefits accrued by or on behalf of a debtor within one year before the debtor files bankruptcy are not exempt. (§ 78-23-5(1)(b)(ii))
Vermont	Yes, to extent reasonably necessary for support in the case of a debtor entitled to receive payments. (12 § 2740(16)) Otherwise, in the case of self-directed accounts, there is a general exemption requiring a debtor's interest in an account, but only to the extent of tax-deductible and exempt contributions, as well as interest, dividends or other earnings on these *(cont'd)*	Yes, to extent reasonably necessary for support. (12 § 2740(19)(J))	Yes, to extent reasonably necessary for support. (12 § 2740(16)) There is a general exemption regarding a debtor's interest in a Roth IRA, but only to extent of contribution limits under IRC § 408A and interest, dividends or other earnings on these contributions and all growth thereon. (12 § 2740(16)) In the case of attachment for child support, the *(cont'd)*	Yes. (12 § 2740(19)(J))	No protection for a contribution to a self-directed plan or account within one year before debtor files for bankruptcy. (12 § 2740(16))

Table 9.03
Pension Plans *(continued)*

	Are Federally Qualified § 401 Pension Plans Exempt?	*Are § 403(a) Annuity Plans Exempt?*	*Are § 408 IRAs Exempt?* *	*Is There an Income Exemption for Payments Not Covered by the Pension Plan Exemption?*	*Are Contributions Within a Certain Period of Bankruptcy Exempt?*
Vermont *(cont'd)*	contributions and all growth thereon. (12 § 2740(16)) In the case of attachment for child support, the exemption is limited to $5,000.		exemption is limited to $5,000.		
Virginia	Yes, to extent value of interest would pay a benefit of $25,000 per year for life beginning at age 65. (§ 34-34(B))	Yes, to extent value of interest would pay a benefit of $25,000 per year for life beginning at age 65. (§ 34-34(B))	Yes, to extent value of interest would pay a benefit of $25,000 per year for life beginning at age 65. (§ 34-34(B))	Yes. (§ 34-29)	Contributions within two years of year in which bankruptcy is declared are not exempt. (§ 34-34(D))
Washington	Yes. (§ 6.15.020(4))	Yes. (§ 6.15.020(4))	Yes. (§ 6.15.020(4))	There is no statutory provision or definite case authority on point.	There is no statutory provision or definite case authority on point.
West Virginia	Yes, for amount reasonably necessary for support of debtor and dependents if in bankruptcy. (§ 38-10-4(j)(5))	Yes, for amount reasonably necessary for support of debtor and dependents if in bankruptcy. (§ 38-10-4(j)(5))	Yes, for amount reasonably necessary for support of debtor and dependents if in bankruptcy. (§ 38-10-4(j)(5))	There is no statutory provision or definite case authority on point.	Yes, for amounts reasonably necessary for support of debtor and dependents. (§ 38-10-4(j)(5))
Wisconsin[1]	Yes. (§ 815.18(3)(j)(1))	Yes. (§ 815.18(3)(j)(1))	Yes. (§ 815.18(3)(j)(1))	There is no statutory provision or definite case authority on point.	There is no statutory provision or definite case authority on point.
Wyoming[1]	Yes. (§ 1-20-110(a)(ii))	Yes. (§ 1-20-110(a)(ii))	Yes. (§ 1-20-110(a)(iii))	There is no statutory provision or definite case authority on point.	Exempt to extent payment made to fund while solvent. (§ 1-20-110(a)(ii))

* A number of state statutes keyed non-exemption to the assumption that IRAs had no federal bankruptcy exemption. In Rousey v. Jacoway, 125 S. Ct. 1561 (April 4, 2005), the U.S. Supreme Court held that IRAs did qualify for federal bankruptcy exemption. This may alter the outcome in a number of states in affording more protection against creditor claims to IRAs.

1. The statute does not refer to specific provisions of the Internal Revenue Code, but affords a general exemption with respect to pension or retirement arrangements and annuity contracts.

Table 9.04
Jointly-Owned Property

	Upon the Death of Joint Tenant, Can Creditors Reach His Interest?	*If Not Specified, Is Joint Tenancy or Tenancy in Common Presumed?*
Alabama	No. (Johnson v. Keener, 425 So. 2d 1108 (1983))	Tenancy in common. (§ 35-4-7)
Alaska	§ 34.15.130 abolishes the joint tenancy in Alaska. § 34.15.110(b) allows spouses to create tenancy by entirety. In the tenancy by entirety, creditors may partition; also, the income is divisible. (Pilip v. U.S., 186 F.Supp. 397 (D. Alaska 1960))	Tenancy in common. (§ 34.15.110)
Arizona	No specific authority, although dictum that on death property is solely that of survivor. (Graham v. Allen, 463 P.2d 102, 103 (Ct. App. 1970))	Tenancy in common. (§ 33-431(A))
Arkansas	No, but can be reached after death of both tenants. (Lowe v. Morrison, 711 S.W.2d 833 (1986))	Tenancy in common. (§ 18-12-603)
California	No. (Ziegler v. Bonnell, 126 P.2d 118 (App. 1 Dist. 1942) (judgment debtor died prior to levy of execution))	Tenancy in common. (Civ. Code § 686)
Colorado	No explicit authority, but implied by First Nat'l Bank v. Energy Fuels Corp., 618 P.2d 1115, 1118-9 (Colo. 1980)	Personal property: Tenancy in common. (§ 38-11-101) Real property: Tenancy in common. (§ 38-11-101(1)) However, with respect to real property, a joint tenancy is preserved if a conveyance or devise is made to two or more personal representatives, trustees, or other fiduciaries. (§ 38-31-101(3)) An estate in joint tenancy in real property can only be created in natural persons and by instrument or in fiduciaries including ones who are not natural persons. (§ 38-31-101(4))
Connecticut	Yes. (§ 47-14f; In re Bernier, 176 B.R. 976 (Bankr. D. Conn. 1995))	Tenancy in common. (Dennen v. Searle, 176 A.2d 561, 565 (1961))
Delaware	There is no statutory provision or definite case authority on point.	Tenancy in common. (25 § 701)
District of Columbia	No. (Dist. of Columbia v. Riggs Nat'l Bank, 335 A.2d 238 (D.C. App. 1975))	Tenancy in common. (§ 42-516(a))
Florida	No if tenant by entirety; yes if solely right of survivorship. (Hurlbert v. Shackleton, 560 So. 2d 1276, 1279 (Fla. App. 1990))	Tenancy in common. (§ 689.15)
Georgia	No. (Taylor v. Taylor, 394 S.E.2d 628 (Ct. App. 1990))	Tenancy in common. (§ 44-6-120)
Hawaii	No. (U.S. v. Property Entitled in Hands of Alexander Mario Toki & Elizabeth Mile Toki, 779 F. Supp. 1272 (D. Hawaii 1991))	Tenancy in common. (§ 509-1)

Table 9.04
Jointly-Owned Property *(continued)*

	Upon the Death of Joint Tenant, Can Creditors Reach His Interest?	*If Not Specified, Is Joint Tenancy or Tenancy in Common Presumed?*
Idaho	No. (Ogilvie v. Idaho Bank & Trust Co., 99 Idaho 361, 582 P.2d 215 (1978))	Tenancy in common. (§§ 55-104, 55-508)
Illinois	No. (In re Alpert's Estate, 95 Ill. 2d 377, 447 N.E.2d 796 (1983))	Tenancy in common. (765 ILCS § 1005/3)
Indiana	No. (Richardson v. Richardson, 98 N.E.2d 190 (1951))	Tenancy in common. (§ 32-17-2-1)
Iowa	No. (Frederick v. Shorman, 147 N.W.2d 478 (1966))	Tenancy in common. (§ 557.15)
Kansas	No. (Matter of Laue's Estate, 225 Kan. 177, 589 P.2d 558 (1979))	Tenancy in common. (§ 58-501)
Kentucky	No. (Sanderson v. Saxon, 834 S.W.2d 676 (1992))	Tenancy in common. (§ 381.120)
Louisiana	N/A. Joint tenancy laws have no application in determining ownership of property. (Gathright v. Smith, 352 So. 2d 282 (2d Cir. 1977), *aff'd and remanded*, 368 So. 2d 679))	"Ownership of indivision" (Civil Code Arts. 480 & 797). Most like tenancy in common.
Maine	No. (Irvin L. Young Foundation v. Damrell, 511 A.2d 1069 (1936))	Tenancy in common. (33 § 159)
Maryland	No. (Eastern Shore Building & Loan Corp. v. Bank of Somerset, 253 Md. 525, 253 A.2d 367 (1969))	Tenancy in common. (Real Prop. § 2-117)
Massachusetts	No. (Weaver v. City of New Bedford, 335 Mass. 646, 140 N.E.2d 309 (1957))	Tenancy in common. (184 § 7)
Michigan	No. (Albro v. Allen, 454 N.W.2d 85 (1990))	Tenancy in common. (§§ 554.43-554.45)
Minnesota	No. (Irvine v. Helvering, 99 F.2d 265 (C.C.A. 8 1938))	Tenancy in common. (§ 500.19)
Mississippi	No. (Canter v. Sunray, 94 So. 2d 624 (1957))	Tenancy in common. (§ 89-1-7)
Missouri	No. (Heintz v. Hudkins, 824 S.W.2d 139 (Ct. App. 1992))	Tenancy in common. (§ 442.450)
Montana	No. (§ 72-6-111)	Tenancy in common (§ 70-1-313), except motor vehicles, which is joint tenancy (§ 61-3-202(4)).
Nebraska	No. (DeForge v. Patrick, 162 Neb. 568, 76 N.W.2d 733 (1956))	Tenancy in common. (§ 76-275.07)
Nevada	No. (McKissick v. McKissick, 93 Nev. 139, 560 P.2d 1366 (1977))	Tenancy in common. (§ 111.060)

New Hampshire	Maybe. (Sullivan v. Chapman, 117 N.H. 1060, 331 A.2d 749 (1977) (joint bank accounts upon death are property of surviving joint tenant))	Tenancy in common. (§ 477:18)
New Jersey	No. (Gauger v. Gauger, 376 A.2d 523 (1977))	Tenancy in common. (§ 46:3-17)
New Mexico	Yes. (§ 45-6-101)	Tenancy in common. (§ 47-1-15)
New York	No. (Matter of McKelway's Estate, 221 N.Y. 15, 116 N.E. 348 (1917); In re Cotter's Will, 159 Misc. 324, 287 N.Y.S. 670 (1936))	Tenancy in common. (Est., Powers & Tr. Law § 6-2.2(a))
North Carolina	No. (Wilson County v. Wooten, 111 S.E.2d 875, 877 (1960))	Tenancy in common. (§ 41-2)
North Dakota	No, except payment of estate taxes. (Schlichenmayer v. Luithle, 221 N.W.2d 77 (1974))	Tenancy in common. (§ 47-02-08)
Ohio	No. (In re Certificates of Deposit Issued by Hocking Valley Bank of Athens Co., 58 Ohio St. 3d 172, 569 N.E.2d 484 (1991))	Tenancy in common. (§ 5302.19)
Oklahoma	No. (Clovis v. Clovis, 460 P.2d 878 (1969))	Tenancy in common. (84 § 184 (when devise or legacy given to more than one person); Clinton v. Clinton, 101 P.2d 609 (1940))
Oregon	No. (Erickson v. Erickson, 115 P.2d 172 (1941))	Tenancy in common, unless between husband and wife, in which case treated as tenancy by entirety. (§ 93.180; Pfaffinger v. Seely, 134 Or. 542, 291 P. 1015 (1970))
Pennsylvania	Maybe. Joint bank accounts go to surviving joint tenant. (20 Pa. CSA § 6304)	Tenancy in common. (68 § 110)
Rhode Island	No. (Knibb v. Security Ins. Co. of New Haven, 121 R.I. 406, 399 A.2d 1214, 1216 (1979))	Tenancy in common. (§ 34-3-1)
South Carolina	No. (Ball v. Deas, 21 S.C. Eq. (2 Strob) 24 (1846))	Tenancy in common. (Telfair v. Howe, 24 S.C. Eq. (3 Rich.) 235 (1851); Free v. Sandifer, 126 S.E. 521 (1925))
South Dakota	Yes, to extent of the value of the amount contributed by deceased joint owner subject to all homestead and legal exemptions in such debtor's jointly owned property. (§§ 43-46-1 to 43-46-5)	Tenancy in common. (§ 43-2-17)
Tennessee	No provision. Survivorship in joint tenancy abolished (§ 66-1-107) except by express agreement (Lowry v. Lowry, 541 S.W.2d 128 (1996))	Tenancy in common. (§ 66-1-107)

Table 9.04
Jointly-Owned Property *(continued)*

	Upon the Death of Joint Tenant, Can Creditors Reach His Interest?	*If Not Specified, Is Joint Tenancy or Tenancy in Common Presumed?*
Texas	No. (Prob. §§ 46, 439, 450-52, 462)	Tenancy in common. (Prob. § 46)
Utah	No. (Matter of Breckon's Estate, 591 P.2d 442 (1979))	Tenancy in common, unless real property interest is between husband and wife, in which case a joint tenancy is presumed. (§ 57-1-5)
Vermont	No provision.	Tenancy in common. (27 § 2)
Virginia	No. (§ 34-8))	Tenancy in common. (§§ 55-20, 55-21)
Washington	Property held by the decedent and other joint tenants will be treated for the purposes of settling claims of creditors as specifically bequeathed property and subject to claims of creditors only to the extent that the decedent's intestate property, residuary estate, and general gifts are not sufficient to settle the claims. (§§ 11.10.040(2)(a), 11.10.010(1))	Tenancy in common unless acquired by them in partnership, for partnership purposes, unless declared in its creation to be a joint tenancy, or unless acquired by executors or trustees. (§ 64.28.020)
West Virginia	Maybe. (Timberlake v. Heflin, 180 W.Va. 644, 379 S.E.2d 149 (1989))	Tenancy in common. (§§ 36-1-19, 36-1-20)
Wisconsin	If unsecured, no. (§ 859.18(4)(a)(2)) If interest secured by a mortgage, security interest, or lien, the joint tenant takes the decedent's interest subject to the mortgage, security interest, or lien. (§ 700.24)	Tenancy in common. (§ 700.18)
Wyoming	No. (Wightman v. American Nat'l Bank, 591 P.2d 903 (1979), vacated by Supreme Court on rehearing, 610 P.2d 1001 (1980) (emphasizing a different result when there is a preexisting security interest held by the creditor)).	Tenancy in common. (In re Anselmi, 52 B.R. 479 (Bkrptcy. D. 1985))

Table 9.05, Part 1
Spendthrift and Related Trusts

	Is a Spendthrift Provision for the Benefit of the Grantor Recognized?	*Is a Spendthrift Clause Presumed Even If Not Expressly Included in the Trust?*	*Can Creditors Break the Trust to Satisfy a Judgment?*	*Can The Trust Interest Be Reached As Part of a Divorce Settlement?**	*Is There a Dollar Limit to the Protection?*	*Is There Protection If The Beneficiary Has the Right to Receive the Income?*
Alabama	No. (§ 19-3B-505)	The statute suggests language is required as to both voluntary and involuntary language or that reference be made to a "spendthrift trust." (§19-3B-501) But there does not appear to be an absolute requirement. The common law might be relevant. (§ 19-3B-501) Under the common law, the question is not addressed directly by the Trust Code, but the Code is based on the Uniform Trust Code, the comments of which allow reaching trust assets. Also, this is the result under common law.	No, with certain exceptions. (§§19-3B-502; 19-3B-503)	Yes. (§ 19-3B-503(b)(1)	There is no statutory provision or definite case authority on point.	Yes. (§ 19-3B-502)
Alaska	Yes, unless the trust requires that all or part of income, principal, or both must be distributed to the settlor. (§ 34.40.110(b)(3)) However, this *(cont'd)*	Apparently, there must be a specific provision. (§ 34.40.110(a)) On the other hand, if the trust complies with § 09.38.017 *(cont'd)*	No. (§ 34.40.110(a) & (b))	No. (§ 34.40.110(a) & (b))	There is no statutory provision or definite case authority on point.	Yes. (§ 34.40.110(b))

Table 9.05, Part 1
Spendthrift and Related Trusts *(continued)*

	Is a Spendthrift Provision for the Benefit of the Grantor Recognized?	*Is a Spendthrift Clause Presumed Even If Not Expressly Included in the Trust?*	*Can Creditors Break the Trust to Satisfy a Judgment?*	*Can The Trust Interest Be Reached As Part of a Divorce Settlement?**	*Is There a Dollar Limit to the Protection?*	*Is There Protection If The Beneficiary Has the Right to Receive the Income?*
Alaska *(cont'd)*	exception does not apply to the settlor's trust in a charitable remainder trust, an annual percentage distribution right as under a total return trust, an interest in a QPRT or a GRAT or a GRUT. (§§ 34.40.110(b)(3) (A)-(D))	(pension plans), it is presumed to be a spendthrift trust.				
Arizona	No. (§ 14-7705(A))	Yes. (§ 14-7702(A))	No, if the trust (1) is not subject to voluntary or involuntary transfer or (2) provides for the education and support of the beneficiary. (§§ 14-7702, 14-7703)	Yes. (§ 14-7707(1))	There is no statutory provision or definite case authority on point.	Yes. (§§ 14-7701(A), 14-7702(A)) Protected until it becomes a payment, then creditor may petition the court for that amount if it is not a spendthrift trust. (§ 14-7701(B))
Arkansas	No. (§ 28-73-505)	No. Instrument must place a restraint on transfer of trust interest. (§ 28-73-502; (Sanders v. Putman, 866 S.W.2d 827, 829 (1993)) However, a spendthrift	No. (§ 28-73-502(c))	There is no statutory provision or definite case authority on point.	There is no statutory provision or definite case authority on point.	Yes, until its receipt by the the beneficiary. (§ 28-73-502(c))

		clause is presumed if a retirement plan meets the qualifications of I.R.C. § 401 or 403. (§ 28-69-501)				
California	No. (Prob. § 15304(a)(b))	No. (Prob. § 15300)	No. (Prob. § 15300)	Yes. (Hardy v. Hardy, 181 Cal. App. 2d 317 (App. 3 Dist. 1960))	There is no statutory provision or definite case authority on point.	Yes, "until paid to the beneficiary." (Prob. § 15300)
Colorado	No, for existing creditors at the time of the transfer. However, the statute's reference to existing creditors indicates that a grantor may be protected from claims of future creditors. (§ 38-10-111)	No. Must be "clear and unequivocal" language. (Newell v. Tubbs, 84 P.2d 820 (1938))	No. (Brasser v. Hutchison, 549 P.2d 801 (Ct. App. 1976))	Yes. (Kaladic v. Kaladic, 41 Colo. App. 419, 421, 589 P.2d 502 (Ct. App. 1978))	There is no statutory provision or definite case authority on point.	Yes. (Snyder v. O'Connor, 102 Colo. 567, 569, 81 P.2d 773 (1938))
Connecticut	No. (Greenwich Trust Co. v. Tyson, 27 A.2d 166 (1942))	No. Trust instrument must include restrictions on payments. (Chandler v. Hale, 377 A.2d 318 (1977))	No, if trustee has right to withhold income or if given expressly for support. (§ 52-321(a))	No. (Cooley v. Cooley, 32 Conn. App. 152, 628 A.2d 608 (Ct. App. 1993))	There is no statutory provision or definite case authority on point.	Yes. (Hildreth Press Employees Fed. Cr. Union v. Connecticut Life Ins. Co., 30 Conn. Sup. 513, 517 (Com. P./A.D. 1972))
Delaware	If trustor also a beneficiary, then funds may be reached. (12 § 3536(c)) However, this provision does not apply to "qualified dispositions in trust." This trust involves a qualified disposition (12 § 3570(6)) to a *(cont'd)*	There is no statutory provision or definite case authority on point.	No. (12 § 3536(a))	Yes. (Wife, J.B.G. v. Husband, P.J.G., 286 A.2d 256 (Del. Ch. 1971) (against public policy))	There is no statutory provision or definite case authority on point.	Yes. (12 § 3536(a))

Table 9.05, Part 1
Spendthrift and Related Trusts *(continued)*

	Is a Spendthrift Provision for the Benefit of the Grantor Recognized?	*Is a Spendthrift Clause Presumed Even If Not Expressly Included in the Trust?*	*Can Creditors Break the Trust to Satisfy a Judgment?*	*Can The Trust Interest Be Reached As Part of a Divorce Settlement?**	*Is There a Dollar Limit to the Protection?*	*Is There Protection If The Beneficiary Has the Right to Receive the Income?*
Delaware *(cont'd)*	Delaware qualified trustee (12 § 3570 (9)) and a particular "trust instrument" that adopts Delaware law and is deemed irrevocable even if the grantor retains a variety of powers and the right to receive income. With certain exceptions, creditors cannot reach or avoid qualified dispositions by the grantor. (12 § 3572)					
District of Columbia	No. (§ 19-1305.05)	The statute suggests language is required as to both voluntary and involuntary language or that reference be made to a "spendthrift trust." (§ 19-1305.02) But there does not appear to be an absolute requirement. The common law might be relevant. (§ 19-1301.06)	No. (§ 19-1305.02(b))	The question is not addressed directly by the Trust Code, but the Code is based on the Uniform Trust Code, the comments of which allow reaching trust assets. Also, this is the result under common law. (Buchanan v. Nat'l Savings & Trust Co., 146 F.2d 13 (D.C. Cir. 1944))	There is no statutory provision or definite case authority on point.	Yes. (§ 19-1305.02)

		Under the common law, no special language is required, just need testator's intent. (Morrow v. Apple, 26 F.2d 543, 544 (D.C. 1928))				
Florida	No. (Govaert v. Strehlow, 84 B.R. 241 (S.D. Florida 1988))	Settlor must express intent to restrain beneficiary from alienating interest. (Nixon v. P. J. Pedone & Co., Inc., 42 B.R. 772 (M.D. Florida 1984))	There is no statutory provision or definite case authority on point.	Yes, for attorney fees. (Gilbert v. Gilbert, 463 So. 2d 223 (1985))	There is no statutory provision or definite case authority on point.	There is no statutory provision or definite case authority on point.
Georgia	No, except with regard to community trust trusts administered by nonprofit organizations for handicapped persons in accordance with § 30-10-2 et seq. (§ 53-12-28(c); Speed v. Speed, 430 S.E.2d 348 (1993))	There is no statutory provision or definite case authority on point.	No. (§ 53-12-28(c))	There is no statutory provision or definite case authority on point.	There is no statutory provision or definite case authority on point.	No, if the trust man dates the distribution of income. (Matter of Kinsler, 24 B.R. 962 (Bankr. N.D. Ga. 1982))
Hawaii	No. (Security Pacific Bank Washington v. Chang, 80 F.3d 1412 (9th Cir. 1996))	There is no statutory provision or definite case authority on point.	No. (Welsh v. Campbell, 41 Hawaii 106 (Hawaii Terr. 1955))	There is no statutory provision or definite case authority on point.	No. (Welsh v. Campbell, 41 Hawaii 106 (Hawaii Terr. 1955))	In Altman v. Commissioner, 83 B.R. 35, 37 (Bankr. Hawaii 1988), the trust income and principal were not protected from creditors and the IRS because the settlor was a potential and named beneficiary. There

(cont'd)

Table 9.05, Part 1
Spendthrift and Related Trusts *(continued)*

	Is a Spendthrift Provision for the Benefit of the Grantor Recognized?	*Is a Spendthrift Clause Presumed Even If Not Expressly Included in the Trust?*	*Can Creditors Break the Trust to Satisfy a Judgment?*	*Can The Trust Interest Be Reached As Part of a Divorce Settlement?**	*Is There a Dollar Limit to the Protection?*	*Is There Protection If The Beneficiary Has the Right to Receive the Income?*
Hawaii *(cont'd)*						appears to be an inference that, had the settlor not been a named beneficiary (entitled to the entire principal and income), the trust would have been protected.
Idaho	There is no statutory provision or definite case authority on point.	There is no statutory provision or definite case authority on point.	There is no statutory provision or definite case authority on point.	There is no statutory provision or definite case authority on point.	There is no statutory provision or definite case authority on point.	There is no statutory provision or definite case authority on point.
Illinois	No. (In re Simon, 170 B.R. 999 (Bankr. S.D. Ill. 1994); 735 ILCS § 5/2-1403)	There is no statutory provision or definite case authority on point.	No, if trust created in good faith by a person other than debtor. (735 ILCS § 5/2-1403)	Only if it involves child support in arrears. (Miller v. Miller, 643 N.E.2d 288 (App. 4 Dist. 1994))	There is no statutory provision or definite case authority on point.	Yes, except child support in arrears. (735 ILCS § 5/2-1403)
Indiana	No. (§ 30-4-3-2(b))	No particular words are necessary; settlor need only manifest intent that trust be a spendthrift trust. (§ 30-4-3-2 (Trust Code Study Comments))	There is no statutory provision or definite case authority on point.	There is no statutory provision or definite case authority on point.	There is no statutory provision or definite case authority on point.	Yes, if the trust agreement provides protection to the beneficiary. (§ 30-4-3-2(a))

Iowa	No. (§§ 633A.2302; 633A.2303)	The Iowa Trust Code does not expressly address the matter. (§ 633A.2301) In these situations, the common law applies. (§ 633A.1104) The case law indicates that a spendthrift trust will be given effect if the trust evidences intent to create spendthrift. (Standard Chemical Co. v. Weed, 285 N.W. 175 (1939))	Typically, no. Nevertheless, a mandatory distribution can be reached. (§ 633A.2301(2))	There is no statutory provision or definite case authority on point.	There is no statutory provision or definite case authority on point.	Yes. (§ 633.2301(1)); (In re Bucklin's Estate, 243 Iowa 312, 51 N.W.2d 412 (1952); In re Hupton, 287 B.R. 438 (N.D. Iowa 2002)
Kansas	No. (§ 58a-505)	The statute suggests language is required as to both voluntary and involuntary language or that reference be made to a "spendthrift trust." (§ 58a-502) But there does not appear to be an absolute requirement. The common law might be relevant. (§ 58a-106) Under the common law, the settlor must manifest intent to create a spendthrift trust. (Matter of Sowers' Estate, 1 Kan. App. 2d 675, 574	No. (§ 58a-502(c))	The Trust Code is silent. Under the common law, the answer is no. (In re Watts, 162 P.2d 82 (1945))	There is no statutory provision or definite case authority on point.	Yes, prior to payment. (§ 58a-502(e)) Yes. (Johnson v. Morawitz, 292 F.2d 341 (10th Cir. 1961); In re Watts, 162 P.2d 82 (1945))

(cont'd)

Table 9.05, Part 1
Spendthrift and Related Trusts *(continued)*

	Is a Spendthrift Provision for the Benefit of the Grantor Recognized?	*Is a Spendthrift Clause Presumed Even If Not Expressly Included in the Trust?*	*Can Creditors Break the Trust to Satisfy a Judgment?*	*Can The Trust Interest Be Reached As Part of a Divorce Settlement?**	*Is There a Dollar Limit to the Protection?*	*Is There Protection If The Beneficiary Has the Right to Receive the Income?*
Kansas *(cont'd)*		P.2d 224 (Ct. App. 1977))				
Kentucky	No. (§ 381.180(7))	Yes. (§ 381.180(3))	No. (§ 381.180)	Only alimony payments and support. (§ 381.180(6)(a))	There is no statutory provision or definite case authority on point.	Yes. (§ 381.180(4))
Louisiana	No. (§ 9:2004(2))	There is no statutory provision or definite case authority on point.	Yes, for necessary services rendered or supplies furnished. (§ 9:2005(2))	Yes, with respect to alimony payments and maintenance of person the beneficiary is obligated to support. (9:2005(1))	There is no statutory provision or definite case authority on point.	No. (§ 9:2005)
Maine	No. (18-B § 505)[1]	The statute suggests language is required as to both voluntary and involuntary language or that reference be made to a "spendthrift trust." (18-B § 502) But there does not appear to be an absolute requirement. The common law might be relevant. (18-B § 106) Under the common law, the testator must unequivocally express it. (Tilton v. Davidson, 98 Me. 55, 56 A. 215 (1903))	No. (18-B § 502(3))[1]	No. (18-B § 503)[1]	No. However, a mandatory distribution can be enforced. (18-B § 506)**	Yes, until payment is made. (18-B § 502(3))[1]

Maryland	No. (Watterson v. Edgerly, 40 Md. App. 230, 388 A.2d 934 (1978))	Yes, if intent manifested. (Jones v. Endslow, 23 Md. App. 578, 328 A.2d 339 (1974))	No, generally. (Hoffman Chevrolet, Inc. v. Washington County Nat. Sav. Bank, 297 Md. 691, 467 A.2d 758 (1983))	Yes, since spouses not creditors. (Prince George's County Pension Plan v. Burke, 321 Md. 699, 584 A.2d 702 (1991))	There is no statutory provision or definite case authority on point.	Yes, except in case of alimony and child support. (Safe Deposit & Trust Co. v. Robertson, 65 A.2d 292 (1949))
Massachusetts	No. (Ware v. Gulda, 117 N.E.2d 137 (1954))	Yes, as long as intent. (Perabo v. Gallagher, 135 N.E. 113 (1922))	Generally no. (Perabo v. Gallagher, 135 N.E. 113 (1922))	No. (Buckham v. Buckham, 200 N.E. 918 (1930))	There is no statutory provision or definite case authority on point.	Yes. (Perabo v. Gallagher, 135 N.E. 113 (1922))
Michigan	No. (§ 566.131; In re Johannes Trust, 479 N.W.2d 25 (1991))	Yes, as long as intent manifested. (Miller v. Dept. of Mental Health, 442 N.W.2d 617 (1989))	No. (Miller v. Dept. of Mental Health, 442 N.W.2d 617 (1989))	There is no statutory provision or definite case authority on point.	There is no statutory provision or definite case authority on point.	Yes. (In re Edgar, 389 N.W.2d 696 (1986))
Minnesota	No. (Morrison v. Doyle, 582 N.W.2d 237 (1998))	Yes, as long as intent to establish a spend thrift. (Morrison v. Doyle, 582 N.W.2d 237 (1998))	No. (Morrison v. Doyle, 582 N.W.2d 237 (1998))	There is no statutory provision or definite case authority on point.	There is no statutory provision or definite case authority on point.	Yes. (Erickson v. Erickson, 197 Minn. 71, 266 N.W. 161 (1936))
Mississippi	No, invaild as to past and future creditors. (Deposit Guar. Nat. Bank v. Walter E. Heller & Co., 204 So.2d 856 (1967)) Note, however, that § 91-9-503, enacted subsequently, simply refers to "a beneficiary's interest" and does not exclude the grantor's interest as a beneficiary.	There is no statutory provision or definite case authority on point.	No. (§ 91-9-503)	No. (§ 91-9-503)	No. (§ 91-9-503)	Yes. (Deposit Guaranty Nat. Bank v. Walter E. Heller & Co., 204 So. 2d 856 (1967))

Table 9.05, Part 1
Spendthrift and Related Trusts *(continued)*

	Is a Spendthrift Provision for the Benefit of the Grantor Recognized?	*Is a Spendthrift Clause Presumed Even If Not Expressly Included in the Trust?*	*Can Creditors Break the Trust to Satisfy a Judgment?*	*Can The Trust Interest Be Reached As Part of a Divorce Settlement?**	*Is There a Dollar Limit to the Protection?*	*Is There Protection If The Beneficiary Has the Right to Receive the Income?*
Missouri	No. (§ 456.5-505)	No. (§ 456.5-502(2)), although the Trust Code does not prevent the case law from so holding. (§ 456.1-106)	No. (§ 456.5-502)	Yes. (§ 456.5-503(2))	No, but mandatory distributions are reachable. (§ 456.5-506)	Yes, before payment. (§ 456.5-502)
Montana	No. (§ 72-33-305)	There is no statutory provision or definite case authority on point.	No. (§§ 72-33-301, 72-33-302, 72-33-303)	No, if only a contingent remainder (not vested). (In re Marriage of Meeks v. Meeks, 915 P.2d 831 (1996))	There is no statutory provision or definite case authority on point.	Yes, until paid to beneficiary. (§ 72-33-301)
Nebraska	No. (§ 30-3850)	The statute suggests language is required as to both voluntary and involuntary language or that reference be made to a "spendthrift trust." (§ 30-3847(b)) But there does not appear to be an absolute requirement. The common law might be relevant. (§ 30-3806) Under the common law, no particular form of words necessary. (Lancaster	No. (§ 30-3847(c))	Yes. (§ 30-3848(b))	No. However, creditors can reach mandatory distributions that the trustee has not made within a reasonable time. (§ 30-3851)	Yes, prior to payment. (§ 30-3847(c))

		County Bank v. Marshel, 264 N.W. 470 (1936))				
Nevada	Yes. One of the trustees must be a person who resides in the state or a company or bank that is organized or maintains an office in the state. (§ 166.015)	Yes. It is sufficient if the creator manifests an intention to create such a trust in the written terms of the trust. (§ 166.050)	No. (§ 166.120(3))	There is no statutory provision or definite case authority on point. § 166.120(3) implies no.	Silent on this issue. See § 166.120.	Yes, if beneficiary has benefit of all of the income from the trust estate without exception or deduction other than for administrative costs and fees and fines. (§ 166.100)
New Hampshire	No. (§ 564-B:5-505(a)(1))	No. (§ 564-B:5-502(a)) Spendthrift trusts were not valid under common law. E.g., Cadbury v. Parrish, 200 A. 791 (1938)	No. (§ 564-B:5-502(c))	Yes. (However, only if the judgment or order specified alimony "to the most basic food, shelter and medical needs." (§ 564-B:5-503(b)(2))	No. However, mandatory distributions can be reached if withheld beyond a reasonable time by the trustee. (§ 564-B:5-506)	Yes, if a statute so provides. (§ 564-B:5-503(c))
New Jersey	No (§ 25:2-1(a)), except retirement trusts. (§ 25:2-1(b))	Yes. (Moore v. Moore, 137 N.J. Eq. 314, 321, 44 A.2d 639, 642-43 (Ch. 1945))	No. (§ 25:2-1(b))	Yes. (§ 25:2-1(b)(2))	There is no statutory provision or definite case authority on point.	Yes. (In re Griswold, 354 A.2d 717 (1976))
New Mexico	No. (§ 46A-5-505(A)(1))	Probably not. (§ 46A-5-502)	No. (§ 46A-5-502(C))	Yes. (§ 46A-5-503(B))	No. However, mandatory distributions can be reached if held for more than a reason able time. (§ 46A-5-506)	Yes. (§ 46A-5-502(C))
New York	No. (Est., Powers & Tr. Law § 7-3.1(a); State v. Coyle, 171 A.D.2d 288, 575 N.Y. S.2d 975 (1991))	Yes with regard to income interest. (Est., Powers & Tr. Law § 7-1.5(b)) All New York trusts are spendthrift by statute with regard to	There is no statutory provision or definite case authority on point.	Yes, can reach the income interest for alimony obligation. (Matter of Knauth, 12 N.Y.2d 259, 238 N.Y.S.2d 942, 189	There is no statutory provision or definite case authority on point.	Yes, unless otherwise provided in trust. (Est., Powers & Tr. Law § 7-1.5(a)(1))
		(cont'd)		*(cont'd)*		

Table 9.05, Part 1
Spendthrift and Related Trusts *(continued)*

	Is a Spendthrift Provision for the Benefit of the Grantor Recognized?	*Is a Spendthrift Clause Presumed Even If Not Expressly Included in the Trust?*	*Can Creditors Break the Trust to Satisfy a Judgment?*	*Can The Trust Interest Be Reached As Part of a Divorce Settlement?**	*Is There a Dollar Limit to the Protection?*	*Is There Protection If The Beneficiary Has the Right to Receive the Income?*
New York *(cont'd)*		income interest, absent contrary provision.		N.E.2d 482, 484 (1963))		
North Carolina	No. (Pilkington v. West, 99 S.E.2d 798, 802 (1957))	The statute suggests language is required as to both voluntary and involuntary language or that reference be made to a "spendthrift trust." (§ 36C-5-502)	No. (§ 36C-5-502(c))	Yes. (Swink v. Swink, 169 S.E.2d 539 (Ct. App. 1969))	There is no statutory provision or definite case authority on point.	Yes. (§ 36C-5-502; Fowler & Lee v. Webster, 92 S.E. 157 (1917))
North Dakota	There is no statutory provision or definite case authority on point.	There is no statutory provision or definite case authority on point.	No, unless fraudulent transfer. (Bye v. Elvick, 336 N.W.2d 106 (1983))	Yes. (VanOosting v. VanOosting, 521 N.W.2d 93 (1994))	There is no statutory provision or definite case authority on point.	Yes. (Bye v. Elvick, 336 N.W.2d 106 (1983))
Ohio	No. (§ 5805.06(A)(1))	The statute suggests language is required as to both voluntary and involuntary language or that reference be made to a "spendthrift trust." (§ 5408.01) But there does not appear to be an absolute requirement. The common law might be relevant. (§ 5408.01) Under the common	No, with certain exceptions. (§ 5805.02)	Yes, (§ 5805.02(B) (1); but see § 5805.02(C) re former spouse).	There is no statutory provision or definite case authority on point.	Yes. (§ 5805.01(B) & (C))

		law, the question is not addressed directly by the Trust Code, but the Code is based on the Uniform Trust Code, the comments of which allow reaching trust assets. Also, this is the result under common law.				
Oklahoma	No. (60 § 175.25(H); In re Threet, 118 B.R. 805 (Bankr. N.D. Okla. 1990))	No, must provide specific words that beneficiaries' income interests are inalienable. (60 § 175.25(A))	No, but see limitations. (60 § 175.25)	Yes, to the extent of all *income* due or to accrue in the future to the trust beneficiary. With respect to other creditors, all income due or to accrue in the future in excess of $25,000 per calendar year. (60 §§ 175.25(B)(1)(a), (c) & (B)(2))	Yes, in the case of creditors other than a spouse or children, the first $25,000 in aggregate of income per beneficiary per calendar year is protected. (60 § 175.25(B)(2), (D))	Yes. (60 § 175.25(B))
Oregon	No. Creditors may reach trust to extent of grantor's interest. (Johnson v. Commercial Bk., 284 Or. 675, 680, 588 P.2d 1096, 1099 (1978))	Yes, if donor's intent would be frustrated if otherwise. (In re Shoup's Estate 31 Pa. Super 162 (1906))	No. (Johnson v. Commercial Bank, 588 P.2d 1096 (1978))	Yes. (Cogswell v. Cogswell, 167 P.2d 324 (1946) (even foreign decrees))	There is no statutory provision or definite case authority on point.	Yes. (Kirkpatrick v. U.S. Nat'l Bank, 502 P.2d 579 (1972))
Pennsylvania	No. (Schellentrager v. Tradesmen's Nat'l Bank, 370 Pa. 501, 88 A.2d 773, 775 (1952); In re Bowers Trust Estate, 346 Pa. 85, 29 A.2d 519, 521 (1943))	There is no statutory provision or definite case authority on point.	No. (Sproul-Bolton v. Sproul-Bolton, 117 A.2d 688, 690 (1955))	There is no statutory provision or definite case authority on point.	There is no statutory provision or definite case authority on point.	Yes. (Sproul-Bolton v. Sproul-Bolton, 117 A.2d 688, 690 (1955))

Table 9.05, Part 1
Spendthrift and Related Trusts *(continued)*

	Is a Spendthrift Provision for the Benefit of the Grantor Recognized?	*Is a Spendthrift Clause Presumed Even If Not Expressly Included in the Trust?*	*Can Creditors Break the Trust to Satisfy a Judgment?*	*Can The Trust Interest Be Reached As Part of a Divorce Settlement?**	*Is There a Dollar Limit to the Protection?*	*Is There Protection If The Beneficiary Has the Right to Receive the Income?*
Rhode Island	Yes, with respect to qualified dispositions. A qualified disposition is a disposition by a transferor to a trustee, with or without consideration, by means of a trust instrument. (§ 18-9.2-2(6)) If a qualified disposition is not involved, then generally, no protection is afforded. (§ 18-9.1-1) A "trust instrument" involves an irrevocable trust, incorporates Rhode Island law, and is unassignable, whether voluntarily or involuntarily, before the trustee distributes the property or income to the beneficiary. (§ 18-9.2-2(9))	Yes, in the case of a self-declared asset protection trust. (§ 18-9.2-2(9)) With respect to other trusts, there is no statutory provision or definite case authority on point.	Yes. See next column. Also true in the case of death, personal injury or property damage determined to be caused by the transferor or person for whom transferor is vicariously liable, if death, injury or damage occurred before "qualified disposition."	Yes, if the "qualified disposition" is made after an agreement or order of court. (§ 18-9.2-5)	There is no statutory provision or definite case authority on point.	Yes, with respect to a self-declared asset protection trust. (§ 18-9.2-3) No, with respect to other trusts. (Industrial Nat'l Bank v. Budlong, 106 R.I. 780, 264 A.2d 18 (1970))
South Carolina	No. (§ 62-7-505(a)(2))	The statute suggests language is required as to both voluntary and involuntary transfers or that	Creditors cannot reach the funds in trustee's hands, but a child can reach the funds if there is a	Yes, for child support. (§ 62-7-503(b))	No, but mandatory distributions are reachable if not distributed within a reasonable time after	Yes, until paid to beneficiary. (§ 62-7-502(c))

		reference be made to a "spendthrift trust." (§ 62-7-502) But there does not appear to be an absolute requirement. The common law might be relevant. (§ 62-7-106)	judgment for child support. (§§ 62-7-502, 62-7-503(b))		the designated distribution date. (§ 62-7-506)	
South Dakota	No, unless there is a reference to Chapter 55-16 and the transfer qualifies under chapter 55-16, relating to qualified dispositions in trust. (§ 55-1-19) The trust instrument must indicate South Dakota law governs, the trust is irrevocable, the transferor's interest cannot be assigned before distribution, and has a qualified trustee. A qualified trustee is a natural person who is a resident of the state other than the transferor or another person authorized to serve as a trustee in the state, is a federally regulated institution, and maintains or arranges for custody in the state of some or all of the property subject to the qualified disposition. (§§ 15-16-1–15-16-3) In addition, *(cont'd)*	Sufficient to have a declaration in a trust instrument that the interest of a beneficiary shall be held subject to a spendthrift trust. (§ 55-1-17)	Appears no. (Farmers State Bank v. Janish, 410 N.W.2d 188 (1987))	There is no statutory provision or definite case authority on point.	There is no statutory provision or definite case authority on point.	Yes, until payment or delivery of the interest. (§ 55-1-16)

Table 9.05, Part 1
Spendthrift and Related Trusts *(continued)*

	Is a Spendthrift Provision for the Benefit of the Grantor Recognized?	*Is a Spendthrift Clause Presumed Even If Not Expressly Included in the Trust?*	*Can Creditors Break the Trust to Satisfy a Judgment?*	*Can The Trust Interest Be Reached As Part of a Divorce Settlement?**	*Is There a Dollar Limit to the Protection?*	*Is There Protection If The Beneficiary Has the Right to Receive the Income?*
South Dakota *(cont'd)*	creditors cannot reach federal income tax reimbursements to the grantor of an irrevocable trust taxed as a grantor trust under the rules of I.R.C. §§ 671–679 as of Jan. 1, 2005.					
Tennessee	No. (§ 35-15-505) However, an exception exists for Investment Services Trusts, trusts that cannot be amended by the transferor and must have as trustee an individual resident of Tennessee or a corporate entity authorized to conduct business in Tennessee. The transferor must sign an affidavit establishing solvency and no pending creditor litigation. The transferor, though not able to serve as trustee, can reserve investment powers, receive income or an annuity not exceeding 5% of the unitrust amount,	The statute suggests language is required as to both voluntary and involuntary language or that reference be made to a "spendthrift trust." (§ 35-15-502) But there does not appear to be an absolute requirement. The common law might be relevant. (§ 35-15-106) Under the common law, the question is not addressed directly by the Trust Code, but the Code is based on the Uniform Trust Code, the comments of which allow reaching trust assets. Also, this is the result under common law.	No. (§ 35-15-502(b))	There is no statutory provision or definite case authority on point.	No, but mandatory distributions are reachable if not distributed within a reasonable time after the designated distribution date. (§ 35-15-506)	Yes, before payment. (§ 35-15-502(b))

	can place his home in the trust, receive discretionary distributions, veto distributions to others, direct distributions at his death to persons other than his creditors, and can appoint trustees and trust advisors, as well as successors, if not related or subordinate to the transferor. Note that asset protection is not effective until four years after the transfer. (§ 85-15-505)					
Texas	No, but see definition of "settlor" in the section. (Prop. § 112.035(d))	It is sufficient to declare in a trust instrument that the intent of a beneficiary shall be held subject to a "spendthrift trust." (Prop. § 112.035(b))	No. (Prop. § 112.035(b))	Yes, since the spouse is not treated as a creditor but the owner of a community interest in the trust. (Irving Firemen's Relief Fund v. Sears, 803 S.W.2d 747 (1990))	No. (Prop. § 112.035)	Yes, before payment. (Prop. § 112.035(a))
Utah	No. (§ 75-7-505)	The statute suggests language is required as to both voluntary and involuntary language or that reference be made to a "spendthrift trust." (§ 75-7-502) But there does not appear to be an absolute requirement. The common law might be relevant. (§ 75-7-106)	No. (§ 75-7-502(3))	Yes, for child support. (§ 75-7-503(2))	No, but there are special provisions as to the assessment, an order for child or spousal support will be enforced. (§ 75-7-504(3))	Yes, before payment. (§ 75-7-502(3))

(cont'd)

Table 9.05, Part 1
Spendthrift and Related Trusts *(continued)*

	Is a Spendthrift Provision for the Benefit of the Grantor Recognized?	*Is a Spendthrift Clause Presumed Even If Not Expressly Included in the Trust?*	*Can Creditors Break the Trust to Satisfy a Judgment?*	*Can The Trust Interest Be Reached As Part of a Divorce Settlement?**	*Is There a Dollar Limit to the Protection?*	*Is There Protection If The Beneficiary Has the Right to Receive the Income?*
Utah *(cont'd)*		Under the common law, settlor's intent must be clearly shown. (Cronquist v. Utah State Agr. College, 201 P.2d 280, 283 (1949))				
Vermont	There is no statutory provision or definite case authority on point.	Yes. (Huestis v. Manley, 110 Vt. 413, 419, 8 A.2d 644, 646 (1939))	No. (Huestis v. Manley, 110 Vt. 413, 419, 8 A.2d 644, 646 (1939))	There is no statutory provision or definite case authority on point.	There is no statutory provision or definite case authority on point.	Yes. (Huestis v. Manley, 110 Vt. 413, 419, 8 A.2d 644, 646 (1939))
Virginia	No. (§ 55-545.05(A))	The statute suggests language is required as to both voluntary and involuntary aspects or that reference be made to a "spendthrift trust." (§ 55-454.02(B)) But there does not appear to be an absolute requirement. The common law might be relevant. (§ 55-541.06) The question is not addressed directly by the Trust Code, but the state code is based on the Uniform Trust Code, the comments of which allow reaching trust	No. (§ 55-545.02(C))	Yes, for child support. (§ 55-545.03 (B))	No.	Yes, before payments. (§ 55-545.02)

		assets. Also, this is the result under common law.				
Washington	No. (§ 19.36.020)	There is no statutory provision or definite case authority on point.	No. (Milner v. Outcalt, 36 Wash. 2d 720, 219 P.2d 982 (1950))	There is no statutory provision or definite case authority on point.	There is no statutory provision or definite case authority on point.	Yes. (Seattle First Nat'l Bank v. Crosby, 254 P.2d 732, 739 (1953))
West Virginia	No. (§ 36-1-18(a)(1))	Only if the intent to create a spendthrift is clearly disclosed by the instrument as a whole. (Keller v. Keller, 169 W.Va. 372, 287 S.E.2d 508, 512 (1982))	There is no statutory provision or definite case authority on point.	There is no statutory provision or definite case authority on point.	There is no statutory provision or definite case authority on point.	Yes, if income is paid for support and maintenance of beneficiary. (§ 36-1-18)
Wisconsin	Not protected to the extent of the grantor's proportionate contribution to the trust. (§ 701.06(6)(a))	No, there must be express provision. (§ 701.06(1) & (2))	No. (§ 701.06)	No. (Friebel v. Friebel, 181 Wis. 2d 285, 510 N.W.2d 767, 771 (Ct. App. 1993))	No. (§ 701.06)	Yes, until paid to beneficiary. (§ 701.06(1))
Wyoming[1]	No. (§ 4-10-505))	The statute suggests language is required as to both voluntary and involuntary language or that reference be made to a "spendthrift trust." (§ 4-10-502) But there does not appear to be an absolute requirement. The common law might be relevant. (§ 4-10-106)	No. (4-10-502(c))	Yes, for child support. Unlike the Uniform Trust Code from which it is derived, this Code explicitly permits trust interest to be reached for child support claims. (§§ 4-10-503(b); 4-10-504(c))	No. (§ 4-10-502(c))	Yes, prior to payment. (4-10-502(c))

* Effective July 2005.

1. Caution: Even if a spendthrift trust beneficiary's interest can be reached pursuant to a court ordered or approved settlement, an out-of-court settlement may not be given the same effect.

Table 9.05, Part 2
Spendthrift and Related Trusts

	Is There Protection If the Beneficiary Has the Future Right to a Distribution of Principal?	*Can the Trust Be Invaded to Provide for Payment for Necessaries?*	*Can Federal* or State Tax Claims Be Satisfied?*	*Can the Trust Be Reached for Spousal** and Child Support?*	*Can the Trust Be Reached for the Benefit of Tort Creditors?*	*Under What Circumstances Can the State Reach the Property If the State Is Providing Assistance?*
Alabama	Yes. (§ 19-3B-502)	No. (§19-3B-503 & UTC cmt.)	Yes. (§ 19-3B-503(b)(3))	Yes. (§ 19-3B-503(b)(1))	No. (§ 19-3B-503)	To the extent a statute so provides. (§ 19-3B-503(b)(3))
Alaska	Yes. (§ 34.40.110 (b))	There is no statutory provision or definite case authority on point.	No, if these creditors are considered creditors under § 34.40.110(b); however, there is no statutory provision or definite case authority on point.	Yes, if settlor is in default by 30 or more days on child support. (§ 34.40.110(b)(4))	No. (§ 34.40.110(b)) No exception for tort creditors found in statutory provision or definite case authority.	There is no statutory provision or definite case authority on point.
Arizona	Yes. Protected until it becomes a payment, then creditor may petition the court for that amount if it is not a spendthrift trust. (§§ 14-7701(A), 14-7702(A))	Yes. (§ 14-7707(2))	Yes. (§ 14-7707(4))	Yes. (§ 14-7707(1))	No. (§ 14-7701(A))	If a state statute makes the beneficiary liable for reimbursement of pubic support, the court may require payment from the trust. (§ 14-7708)
Arkansas	Yes. (§ 28-73-502(c))	There is no statutory provision or definite case authority on point.	There is no statutory provision or definite case authority on point.	Yes. Income of spend thrift trust may be used for arrearage of alimony. (Council v. Owens, 770 S.W.2d 193 (Ct. App. 1989))	There is no statutory provision or definite case authority on point.	There is no statutory provision or definite case authority on point.

California	Yes, "until paid to the beneficiary," but if due and payable, creditor may reach upon petition to the court. (Prob. §§ 15300, 15301(a))	Yes. (Lackmann v. Dept. of Mental Hygiene, 156 Cal. App. 2d 674, 679 (App. 1 Dist. 1958))	Yes. (Leuschner v. First Western Bank & Trust Co., 261 F.2d 705 (9th Cir. 1958))	Yes, subject to court order. (Prob. § 15305(c))	There is no statutory provision or definite case authority on point.	Subject to a determination by the court ordering payment (considers equitable factors). (Prob. § 15305(c); Lackmann v. Dept. of Mental Hygiene, 156 Cal. App. 2d 674 (App. 1 Dist. 1958))
Colorado	Yes. (Snyder v. O'Connor, 102 Colo. 567, 569-70, 81 P.2d 773, 774 (1938))	There is no statutory provision or definite case authority on point.	There is no statutory provision or definite case authority on point.	There is no statutory provision or definite case authority on point.	There is no statutory provision or definite case authority on point.	There is no statutory provision or definite case authority on point.
Connecticut	Yes. (Greenwich Trust Co. v. Tyson, 27 A.2d 166 (1942))	There is no statutory provision or definite case authority on point.	Federal, no. (United States v. Cohn, 855 F. Supp. 572 (D. Conn. 1994)) Unclear on state tax liens.	There is no statutory provision or definite case authority on point.	There is no statutory provision or definite case authority on point.	None. (Bridgeport v. Reilly, 133 Conn. 31, 47 A.2d 865 (1946))
Delaware	Yes. (12 § 3536(a))	There is no statutory provision or definite case authority on point.	There is no statutory provision or definite case authority on point.	Yes. (Garretson v. Garretson, 306 A.2d 737 (Super. Ct. 1973))	No. (Gibson v. Speegle, 1984 Del. Ch. Lexis 475, at **56 (May 30, 1984))	There is no statutory provision or definite case authority on point.
District of Columbia	Yes. (§ 19-1305.02)	No specific provision. (§ 19-1305.03) However the Uniform Trust Code, on which the law is based, has a comment to § 106, stating that the Code is supplemented by the common law. Assuming the common law can be referenced, § 19-1301.06, the *(cont'd)*	Yes. (§ 19-1305.03(c)) This assumes a federal or state statute "so provides." The comment in the Uniform Trust Code § 503 is ambivalent as to federal tax claims. But see 26 U.S.C. § 6321. There is no specific D.C. *(cont'd)*	Yes, for child support. (§ 19-1305.03) As for alimony, this Trust Code is silent.	No particular provision. However, comment to Uniform Trust Code § 503, on which this Trust Code is based, rejects access to the trust for this purpose.	If there is a statute that so provides. (§ 19-1305.03(c))

Table 9.05, Part 2
Spendthrift and Related Trusts *(continued)*

	Is There Protection If the Beneficiary Has the Future Right to a Distribution of Principal?	*Can the Trust Be Invaded to Provide for Payment for Necessaries?*	*Can Federal* or State Tax Claims Be Satisfied?*	*Can the Trust Be Reached for Spousal** and Child Support?*	*Can the Trust Be Reached for the Benefit of Tort Creditors?*	*Under What Circumstances Can the State Reach the Property If the State Is Providing Assistance?*
District of Columbia *(cont'd)*		answer is yes for others as well. (American Security & Trust v. Utley, 382 F. 2d 451, 453 (D.C. Cir. 1967))	statute that "so provides."			
Florida	Yes, implied. (Philip v. Trainor, 100 So. 2d 181, 186 (Ct. App. 1958))	There is no statutory provision or definite case authority on point.	There is no statutory provision or definite case authority on point.	Yes for spousal support, but only after more traditional means of collection have been attempted. (Bacardi v. White, 463 So. 2d 218 (1985); Gilbert v. Gilbert, 463 So. 2d 223 (1985)) With child support, must take trust income into account. (Oxley v. Oxley, 695 So. 2d 364 (D.C. Ct. App. 1997))	There is no statutory provision or definite case authority on point.	There is no statutory provision or definite case authority on point.
Georgia	Yes. (§ 53-12-28(a))	Yes. (§ 53-12-28(c)(6))	Yes. (§ 53-12-28(c)(2))	Yes. (§ 53-12-28(c)(4) & (5))	Yes. (§ 53-12-28(c)(1))	If it is considered to be a "government claim." (§ 53-12-28(c)(3))
Hawaii	In Altman v. Commissioner, 83 B.R. 35, 37 (Bankr. Hawaii 1988), the trust income and principal were not protected	There is no statutory provision or definite case authority on point.	See prior two questions.	There is no statutory provision or definite case authority on point.	There is no statutory provision or definite case authority on point.	There is no statutory provision or definite case authority on point.

	from creditors and the IRS because the settlor was a potential and named beneficiary. There appears to be an inference that, had the settlor not been a named beneficiary (entitled to the entire principal and income), the trust would have been protected.					
Idaho	There is no statutory provision or definite case authority on point.	There is no statutory provision or definite case authority on point.	There is no statutory provision or definite case authority on point.	There is no statutory provision or definite case authority on point.	There is no statutory provision or definite case authority on point.	There is no statutory provision or definite case authority on point.
Illinois	Yes, except child support in arrears. (735 ILCS § 5/2-1403)	There is no statutory provision or definite case authority on point.	Yes, if federal tax lien exists. (LaSalle Nat. Bank v. U.S., 636 F. Supp. 874 (N.D. Ill. 1986))	Only for child support arrearages, not future payment. (In re Marriage of Stevens, 687 N.E.2d 165 (App. 4 Dist. 1997))	There is no statutory provision or definite case authority on point.	If state supplying services, such as medical care. (Department of Mental Health and Development Disabilities v. Phillips, 500 N.E.2d 29 (1986))
Indiana	Yes. (§ 30-4-3-2)	Yes, trustee can be held liable. (Sisters of Mercy Health Corp. v. First Bank of Whiting, 624 N.E.2d 520 (Ct. App. 1993))	Yes, federal. United States v. Grimm, 865 F. Supp. 1303 (N.D. Ind. 1974))	Yes, can be invaded for alimony claims. (Clay v. Hamilton, 116 Ind. App. 214, 63 N.E.2d 207 (Ct. App. 1945))	There is no statutory provision or definite case authority on point.	There is no statutory provision or definite case authority on point.
Iowa	Yes. (§ 633A.2301(1))	Not addressed by the Trust Code. As for the common law, which fills the gap (§ 633A.1104), yes, if consistent with settlor's intent. (In re Estate of Dodge, 281 N.W.2d 447 (1979))	There is no statutory provision or definite case authority on point.	Not addressed by the Trust Code. As for the common law, which fills the gap (§ 633.1104), no. (In re Estate of Dodge, 281 N.W.2d 447, 450 (1979)) There is a different *(cont'd)*	There is no statutory provision or definite case authority on point. However, In re Estate of Dodge, 281 N.W.2d 447 (1979), recognizes the right of a provider of necessaries to be *(cont'd)*	There is no statutory provision or definite case authority on point. However, In re Estate of Dodge, 281 N.W.2d 447 (1979), reargues the right of a provider of necessities to be reimbursed *(cont'd)*

Table 9.05, Part 2
Spendthrift and Related Trusts *(continued)*

	Is There Protection If the Beneficiary Has the Future Right to a Distribution of Principal?	*Can the Trust Be Invaded to Provide for Payment for Necessaries?*	*Can Federal[*] or State Tax Claims Be Satisfied?*	*Can the Trust Be Reached for Spousal[**] and Child Support?*	*Can the Trust Be Reached for the Benefit of Tort Creditors?*	*Under What Circumstances Can the State Reach the Property If the State Is Providing Assistance?*
Iowa *(cont'd)*				result, possibly, for a discretionary trust. (In re Marriage of Meredith, 394 N.W.2d 336, 339 (1986))	reimbursed from a spendthrift trust, although the decision turned on the intent of the testator. The issue was addressed, but not resolved in In re Estate of Tone, 39 N.W.2d 401 (1949).	from a spendthrift trust, although the decision focuses on the intent of the testator.
Kansas	Yes. (§ 58a-502(c))	There is no statutory provision or definite case authority on point.	There is no statutory provision or definite case authority on point.	There is no Trust Code provision. The answer is no under common law. (Watts v. Watts, 151 Kan. 125, 98 P.2d 125 (1940) (yes in some states mentioned in dicta, but not holding))	There is no statutory provision or definite case authority on point.	There is no Trust Code provision. Under the common law, the property can be reached. If state provides support, and income is available and must be distributed. (State exrel. Sec. of Social and Rehabilitation Services v. Jackson, 249 Kan. 635, 822 P.2d 1033 (1991) (income available to beneficiary, corpus discretionary, cannot be reached))

Kentucky	Yes. (§ 381.180(5))	Yes. (§ 381.180(6)(b))	Yes, both. (§ 381.180(6)(c))	Yes, both. (§ 381.180(6)(a))	There is no statutory provision or definite case authority on point.	There is no statutory provision or definite case authority on point.
Louisiana	No. (§ 9:2005)	Yes. (§ 9:2005(2))	Yes, for federal tax claims (Jackson v. D'Aubin, 316 So.2d 478 (Ct. App. 1975)), but not for state taxes, since no exception listed. (§§ 9:2004-2006)	Yes. (§ 9:2005(1))	No provision (prior provision repealed).	There is no statutory provision or definite case authority on point.
Maine	Yes. (18-B § 502(3))	No. (18-B § 503)	No. (18-B § 503)	No. (18-B § 503)	No. (18-B § 503)	None. (18-B § 503)
Maryland	Yes, except in case of spousal or child support. (Safe Deposit & Trust Co. v. Robertson, 65 A.2d 292 (1949))	Only if support trust. (First Nat. Bank of Maryland v. Dept. of Health & Mental Hygiene, 399 A.2d 891 (1979))	Yes, federal. (Mercantile Trust Co. v. Hofferbert, 58 F. Supp. 701 (Co. Md. 1944))	Yes. (Zouck v. Zouck, 104 A.2d 573 (1954))	There is no statutory provision or definite case authority on point.	There is no statutory provision or definite case authority on point.
Massachusetts	Yes. (Town of Randolph v. Roberts, 346 Mass. 578, 579-80, 195 N.E.2d 72, 73-74 (1964))	There is no statutory provision or definite case authority on point.	Yes, federal. (U.S. v. Rye, 550 F.2d 682 (1st Cir. Mass. 1977))	Yes. (Cooper v. Cooper, 680 N.E.2d 1173 (Ct. App. 1997))	There is no statutory provision or definite case authority on point.	Very difficult if not impossible. (Town of Randolph v. Roberts, 195 N.E.2d 72 (1964))
Michigan	Yes. (In re Edgar, 389 N.W.2d 696 (1986); Preminger v. Union Bank, 220 N.W.2d 795 (1974))	Yes. (Miller v. Dept. of Mental Health, 442 N.W.2d 617, 619 (1989))	Yes, both. (Miller v. Dept. of Mental Health, 432 Mich. 626, 442 N.W.2d 617, 619 (1989))	Yes. Alimony (Cover ston v. Kellogg, 136 Mich. App. 504, 357 N.W.2d 705 (1984)); child support (Miller v. Dept. of Mental Health, 442 N.W.2d 617, 619 (1989))	There is no statutory provision or definite case authority on point.	There is no statutory provision or definite case authority on point.
Minnesota	Yes. (Erickson v. Erickson, 197 Minn. 71, 266 N.W. 161 (1936))	There is no statutory provision or definite case authority on point.	There is no statutory provision or definite case authority on point.	No. (In Matter of Campbell's Trusts, 258 N.W.2d 856 (1977))	There is no statutory provision or definite case authority on point.	There is no statutory provision or definite case authority on point.

Table 9.05, Part 2
Spendthrift and Related Trusts *(continued)*

	Is There Protection If the Beneficiary Has the Future Right to a Distribution of Principal?	*Can the Trust Be Invaded to Provide for Payment for Necessaries?*	*Can Federal* or State Tax Claims Be Satisfied?*	*Can the Trust Be Reached for Spousal** and Child Support?*	*Can the Trust Be Reached for the Benefit of Tort Creditors?*	*Under What Circumstances Can the State Reach the Property If the State Is Providing Assistance?*
Mississippi	Yes. (§ 91-9-503)	No. (§ 91-9-503)	No. (§ 91-9-503)	No. (§ 91-9-503)	No. (§ 91-9-503)	None. (§ 91-9-503)
Missouri	Yes, before payment or delivery of interest. (§ 456.5-502)	The Trust Code does not directly address this. However, the common law fills the gap (§ 456.1-106) and the answer would be in the affirmative. See State ex rel. Nixon v. Turpin, 994 S.W.2d 53 (Ct. App. 1999) (but only if the distribution is required and the trustee has distributed the amount).	There is no statutory provision or definite case authority on point.	Yes. (§ 456.5-503(2))	There is no statutory provision or definite case authority on point.	To the extent a statute so provides. (§ 456.5-503(3))
Montana	Yes, until paid to beneficiary. (§ 72-33-302(1))	Yes. Where not to provide for necessaries, would be abuse of discretion. (In re Estate of Lundgren v. Hoglund, 711 P.2d 809 (1985))	No. (Justin W. Stark, *Montana's Spendthrift Trust Doctrine: Analysis and Recommendations,* 57 Mont. L. Rev. 211, 233 (1996))	No. (§ 72-33-301 (Official Comments))	No. (§ 72-33-301; Justin W. Stark, *Montana's Spendthrift Trust Doctrine: Analysis and Recommendations,* 57 Mont. L. Rev. 211, 233 (1996))	None. (§ 72-33-301 (Official Comments))
Nebraska	Yes. (§ 30-3847(c))	There is no statutory provision or definite case authority on point.	Only if statute so provides. (§ 30-3848(c))	Yes. (§ 30-3848(b))	There is no statutory provision or definite case authority on point.	To the extent a statute so provides. (§ 30-3848(c))

Nevada	Yes. A beneficiary of a spendthrift trust has a protected interest even if he is entitled to the corpus at some future time. (§ 166.130)	No (implied by § 166.120(3)). There is no statutory provision or definite case authority on point.	Yes. (§ 166.100)	See *Can the Trust Be Invaded to Provide for Payment for Necessaries?*	There is no statutory provision or definite case authority on point.	There is no statutory provision or definite case authority on point.
New Hampshire	Yes. (§ 564-B:5-502(c))	No, except for spouse or person protecting trust from creditors. (§ 564-B: 5-503(b)(2)-(3))	Yes, to the extent provided by statute. (§ 564-B: 5-503(b)(4))	Yes. (§ 564-B: 5-503(b)(1)-(2))	There is no provision.	To the extent a statute so provides. (§ 564-B: 5-503(b)(4))
New Jersey	Yes. (In re Griswold, 354 A.2d 717 (1976))	There is no statutory provision or definite case authority on point.	There is no statutory provision or definite case authority on point.	Yes. (§ 25:2-1(b)(2); Cleveland v. Board of Trustees, 550 A.2d 1287 (N.J. Super. Ct. 1988); Marsh v. Scott, 63 A.2d 275, 279 (1949))	There is no statutory provision or definite case authority on point.	A court may order the trustee of a spendthrift trust that allows discretionary distributions to pay claims of the state for the care of beneficiary. (Costanza v. Verona, 137 A.2d 614, 617 (1958))
New Mexico	Yes. (§ 46A-5-502(c))	Apparently not since it is not listed as an exception to enforcement of spendthrift trusts. (§ 46A-5-503)	Yes, if statute so provides. (§ 46A-5-503)(C))	Yes. (§§ 46A-5-503(B))	There is no statutory provision or definite case authority on point.	To the extent a statute so provides. (§ 46A-5-503(c))
New York	Assignments made prior to the vesting of the interests in the principal are unenforceable. In re Estate of Vought, 57 Misc. 2d 396, 293 N.Y.S.2d 34, 45 (1967), *aff'd,* 30 A.D.2d 805, 292 N.Y.S.2d 941 (1968))	No, but a creditor who furnishes necessities to a beneficiary can obtain a beneficiary's full name and address from a trustee by appropriate judicial process. (N.Y. Est., Powers & Tr. Law § 7-3.5(a))	Yes, if not discretionary trust. (Magavern v. U.S., 550 F.2d 797 (2d Cir. 1977), *cert. denied,* 434 U.S. 826)	Yes, income interest for child support. (Matter of Knauth, 12 N.Y.2d 259, 238 N.Y.S.2d 942, 189 N.E.2d 482, 484 (1963))	There is no statutory provision or definite case authority on point.	The state may not be able to recover sums expended for the care of an indigent patient who is beneficiary of a support trust. (Maul v. Fitzgerald, 78 A.D.2d 706, 432 N.Y.S.2d 282 (1980))

Table 9.05, Part 2
Spendthrift and Related Trusts *(continued)*

	Is There Protection If the Beneficiary Has the Future Right to a Distribution of Principal?	*Can the Trust Be Invaded to Provide for Payment for Necessaries?*	*Can Federal* or State Tax Claims Be Satisfied?*	*Can the Trust Be Reached for Spousal** and Child Support?*	*Can the Trust Be Reached for the Benefit of Tort Creditors?*	*Under What Circumstances Can the State Reach the Property If the State Is Providing Assistance?*
North Carolina	Yes, subject to judicial modification. (§ 36C-5-502(c); Davison v. Duke University, 194 S.E.2d 761 (1973))	Yes. (Davison v. Duke University, 194 S.E.2d 761 (1973) (principal or corpus may be invaded if necessary and no impairment to other beneficiaries' interest))	There is no statutory provision or definite case authority on point.	Yes, for child support (§ 36C-5-503(b)), no for spousal support (§ 36C-5-503, N.C. Comment),	There is no statutory provision or definite case authority on point.	There is no statutory provision or definite case authority on point.
North Dakota	Yes. (Bye v. Elvick, 336 N.W.2d 106 (1983))	Yes, if trust provides for support and maintenance. (Hecker v. Stark City Social Service Bd., 527 N.W.2d 226 (1995)). This should be contrasted with a discretionary trust. (Eckes v. Richland County Social Services, 621 N.W.2d 851 (N.D. 2001))	There is no statutory provision or definite case authority on point.	There is no statutory provision or definite case authority on point.	There is no statutory provision or definite case authority on point.	There is no statutory provision or definite case authority on point. Of course, trust can be interpreted liberally to establish intent of grantor to provide assistance by way of a support trust. (Kryzsko v. Ramsey County Social Serv. 607 N.W.2d 237 (N.D. 2000))
Ohio	Yes. (§ 5805.02(E))	Apparently not.	Yes. (§ 5805.02(B)(2))	Yes. (§ 5805.02(B)(1))	There is no statutory provision or definite case authority on point.	Spendthrift provisions do not apply to claims by the state. (§ 5805.02(B)(2))

Oklahoma	Yes, without limitation. (60 § 175.25 (E))	Yes. (60 § 175.25(B)(1)(b))	There is no statutory provision or definite case authority on point.	Yes. (60 § 175.25(B)(1)(a))	No, unless over the dollar limit of protection. (60 § 175.25 (B)(2))	The state can reach all the income, but not the principal. (60 § 175.25(B)(1)(b), (E))
Oregon	Yes. (Kirkpatrick v. U.S. Nat'l Bank, 502 P.2d 579 (1972))	There is no statutory provision or definite case authority on point.	There is no statutory provision or definite case authority on point.	Yes. (Kirkpatrick v. U.S. Nat'l Bank, 502 P.2d 579 (1972); Shelley v. Shelley, 354 P.2d 282 (1960))	No. (Kirk v. Kirk, 254 Or. 44, 456 P.2d 1009 (1969))	There is no statutory provision or definite case authority on point.
Pennsylvania	Yes. (20 § 7745(1) & (2))	No. (20 § 7743)	Yes. (20 § 7743(b)(4))	Yes. (§ 20 § 7743(b)(1) & (2))	No. (20 § 7743)	To the extent a statute so provides. (20 § 7743(4))
Rhode Island	Yes, if the trust is a "qualified disposition" as defined under § 18-9.2-2(6). (§ 18-9.2-4(a))	No, if this is a discretionary trust. (In re Gordon, 2000 WL 276829 (R.I. Super., 2000)	There is no statutory provision or definite case authority on point.	Yes. (Pansey v. Pansey, 115 R.I. 97, 340 A.2d 120 (1975))	Yes, if the tort damage occurred on or before the date the trust was created. (§ 18-9.2-5(B))	There is no statutory provision or definite case authority on point.
South Carolina	Yes. (§ 62-7-502(c)).	There is no statutory provision or definite case authority on point.	No. (§ 62-7-503, S.C. Comment).	Yes, for child support (§ 62-7-503(b)), no for spousal support (§ 62-7-503, N.C. Comment	No. (§ 62-7-503, N.C. Comment)	There is no statutory provision or definite case authority on point.
South Dakota	Yes. (§ 55-1-16)	There is no statutory provision or definite case authority on point.	There is no statutory provision or definite case authority on point.	There is no statutory provision or definite case authority on point.	There is no statutory provision or definite case authority on point.	There is no statutory provision or definite case authority on point.
Tennessee	Yes. (§ 35-15-502(c))	Apparently not. (§ 35-15-504 & cmt.)	Yes. (Howard v. United States, 566 S.W.2d 521 (1978) (federal tax claims); § 35-15-503 (state claims))	There is no statutory provision or definite case authority on point.	There is no statutory provision or definite case authority on point. The Uniform Trust Code does not approve of this. (UTC § 503 cmt.)	Spendthrift provisions do not apply to a claim of the state to the extent a statute of the state so provides. (§ 35-15-503)

Table 9.05, Part 2
Spendthrift and Related Trusts *(continued)*

	Is There Protection If the Beneficiary Has the Future Right to a Distribution of Principal?	*Can the Trust Be Invaded to Provide for Payment for Necessaries?*	*Can Federal* or State Tax Claims Be Satisfied?*	*Can the Trust Be Reached for Spousal** and Child Support?*	*Can the Trust Be Reached for the Benefit of Tort Creditors?*	*Under What Circumstances Can the State Reach the Property If the State Is Providing Assistance?*
Texas	Yes. (Prop. § 112.035(a))	There is no statutory provision or definite case authority on point.	Yes. (Dallas Nat'l Bk. v. U.S., 167 F.2d 468 (5th Cir. 1948) (federal tax liens))	Yes (child support). (Fam. Code Ann. § 154.005)	There is no statutory provision or definite case authority on point.	There is no statutory provision or definite case authority on point.
Utah	Yes. (§ 75-7-502(3))	The comment to § 75-7-503 indicates that no such right exists, except for services provided to protect a beneficiary's interest in the trust. (§ 75-7-503(2))	Yes, but only to the extent a federal or state statute so provides. (§ 75-7-503(3))	Yes. (§§ 75-7-503(2); 75-7-504(3))	Apparently not. (§ 75-7-503 cmt.)	To the extent a statute so provides. (§ 75-7-503(3))
Vermont	Yes. (Huestis v. Manley, 110 Vt. 413, 419, 8 A.2d 644, 646 (1939))	There is no statutory provision or definite case authority on point.	There is no statutory provision or definite case authority on point.	There is no statutory provision or definite case authority on point.	There is no statutory provision or definite case authority on point.	To the extent of a provision in trust for support and maintenance. (Shrewsbury v. Bucklin, 105 Vt. 188, 163 A. 626 (1933))
Virginia	Yes. (§ 55-545.02 (C)))	Apparently not. See comments to § 504 of the Uniform Trust Code.	Yes, both. (§ 55-545.03(C))	Yes, for child support. (§ 55-545.03(B))	There is no statutory provision or definite case authority on point.	State may recover to the extent that the beneficiary has a right to compel income or principal or, in fact, to the extent that the trustee in the future chooses to make payments to or for the benefit of the beneficiary in the

						trustee's discretion. However, a trust provision to make disbursements so as not to render the beneficiary ineligible for assistance is not a right possessed by the beneficiary. The trust will also not be subject to a court order if the beneficiary is a person who has a medically determined physical or mental disability that substantially impairs his ability to provide for his care or custody, and constitutes a substantial handicap. (§55-545.03:1(D))
Washington	There is no statutory provision or definite case authority on point.	Yes. (Erickson v. Bank of Calif., 97 Wash. 2d 246, 643 P.2d 670, 673 (1982))	There is no statutory provision or definite case authority on point.	Yes. (Knettle v. Knettle, 197 Wash. 225, 84 P.2d 996, 998 (1938))	There is no statutory provision or definite case authority on point.	There is no statutory provision or definite case authority on point.
West Virginia	There is protection only if (1) the income/principal may only be applied to health, education, support or maintenance of a beneficiary and (2) it is not subject to alienation by the beneficiaries. (§ 36-1-18(a))	There is no statutory provision or definite case authority on point.	There is no statutory provision or definite case authority on point.	There is no statutory provision or definite case authority on point.	There is no statutory provision or definite case authority on point.	There is no statutory provision or definite case authority on point.

Table 9.05, Part 2
Spendthrift and Related Trusts *(continued)*

	Is There Protection If the Beneficiary Has the Future Right to a Distribution of Principal?	*Can the Trust Be Invaded to Provide for Payment for Necessaries?*	*Can Federal* or State Tax Claims Be Satisfied?*	*Can the Trust Be Reached for Spousal** and Child Support?*	*Can the Trust Be Reached for the Benefit of Tort Creditors?*	*Under What Circumstances Can the State Reach the Property If the State Is Providing Assistance?*
Wisconsin	Yes, until payments have become due and payable, then creditor can reach money. (§ 701.06(2))	There is a possibility, if the creditor expects payment from the trustee. (In re Walker's Will, 266 Wis. 134, 149, 63 N.W.2d 78, 85 (1954))	There is no statutory provision or definite case authority on point.	Can order payment to beneficiary for child support. (§ 701.06 (4)) When they come due, can reach fund to support wife and minor children. (Dillon v. Dillon, 244 Wis. 122, 11 N.W.2d 628, 630–31 (1943))	There is no statutory provision or definite case authority on point.	Court may order payment. (§ 701.06(5))
Wyoming	Yes.(§ 4-10-502(c))	The only provision relates to providers of protection of the trust against creditors' claims. (§ 4-10-503(b))	There is no statutory provision or definite case authority on point.	The only mention is of child support. (§§ 4-10-503(b); 4-10-504(c))	There is no statutory provision or definite case authority on point.	There is no statutory provision or definite case authority on point.

* In United States v. Craft, 535 U.S. 274 (2002), the Supreme Court held that while state law determines the rights a person has in property, the question whether they are "property and rights to property" for purposes of the federal tax lien statute, 26 U.S.C. § 6321, is ultimately a question of federal law.

** Caution: A number of statutes use the word "alimony" and, thus, may not allow a spendthrift trust beneficiary's interest to be reached in the case of a property settlement.

Table 9.05, Part 3
Spendthrift and Related Trusts

	Does the State Recognize a Spendthrift Trust to the Extent It Is a Support Trust?	*If the Beneficiary Has an Interest As a Discretionary Beneficiary, Is It Protected?*	*If the Person Has a Special Power of Appointment, Is the Underlying Property Protected from the Donee's (i.e., Holder's) Creditors?*	*If the Person Has a General Power of Appointment, Is the Underlying Property Protected from the Donee's (i.e., Holder's) Creditors?*	*Same As the Prior Question, but the Power Is Exercised in Favor of Other Persons. Can the Creditors Recoup It?*	*Does The Beneficiary Have the Power to Replace the Trustee and Is the Trust a Discretionary Trust or, Alternatively, can the Beneficiary Appoint Himself As Trustee?*
Alabama	Yes. (§ 19-3B-504(b))	Yes. (§ 19-3B-504(b))	There is no statutory provision or definite case authority on point. If the trustee has the power, the property is protected. (§ 19-3B-504(e))	There is no statutory provision or definite case authority on point. If the trustee has the power, the property can be reached unless the power's exercise is limited by an ascertainable standard. (§ 19-3B-504(b))	Presumably Yes. See § 19-3B-504(b).	There is no statutory provision or definite case authority on point.
Alaska	Recognizes regardless of whether it is a support trust. (§ 34.40.110(a) & (b))	Yes. (§ 34.40.110(b)(2)) In the case of the settlor, this is true even if the settlor is a co-trustee or trust advisor, as long as the settlor does not have the trustee power over discretionary distributions. (§ 34.40.110(f))	Yes. (§ 34.40.110(b)(2))	No. (§ 34.40.110(b)(2)) Only protected if special power of appointment or similar power; general power is neither.	There is no statutory provision or definite case authority on point.	There is no statutory provision or definite case authority on point. The settlor's interest will be protected even if the settlor has the authority under the trust instrument to appoint a trust protector or advisor. (§ 34.40.110(h))

Table 9.05, Part 3
Spendthrift and Related Trusts *(continued)*

	Does the State Recognize a Spendthrift Trust to the Extent It Is a Support Trust?	*If the Beneficiary Has an Interest As a Discretionary Beneficiary, Is It Protected?*	*If the Person Has a Special Power of Appointment, Is the Underlying Property Protected from the Donee's (i.e., Holder's) Creditors?*	*If the Person Has a General Power of Appointment, Is the Underlying Property Protected from the Donee's (i.e., Holder's) Creditors?*	*Same As the Prior Question, but the Power Is Exercised in Favor of Other Persons. Can the Creditors Recoup It?*	*Does The Beneficiary Have the Power to Replace the Trustee and Is the Trust a Discretionary Trust or, Alternatively, Can the Beneficiary Appoint Himself As Trustee?*
Arizona	Yes. (§ 14-7703)	Yes. (§ 14-7704(A))	There is no statutory provision or definite case authority on point.	There is no statutory provision or definite case authority on point.	There is no statutory provision or definite case authority on point.	If the beneficiary is one of many, and is also one of multiple trustees, it is protected. (§ 14-7706(A). If sole beneficiary *and* sole trustee, no protection. (§ 14-7706(B) If beneficiary has the right to consult with/direct the trustee, it is still protected. (§ 14-7706(C))
Arkansas	The recently enacted provision does not specify. But prior case law implies such in its definition of "spendthrift trust." A spendthrift trust is one created to provide support for a designated beneficiary. (Pool, Trustee v. Cross County Bank, 133 S. W.2d 19 (1935))	Yes. (§ 28-73-504(a)) Is the discretion is in the form of standard distribution or is their discretion limited by an "ascertainable standard." (§ 28-73-504(c))	There is no statutory provision or definite case authority on point.	There is no statutory provision or definite case authority on point.	There is no statutory provision or definite case authority on point.	Yes. If beneficiary is the trustee, the interest is protected if their discretion is limited by an "ascertainable standard." (§ 28-73-504(c))

California	Money or property is protected to the level of support, then the overage is subject to judgment. (Prob. § 15307)	Yes, except court may order trustee to pay child support or spousal support as payments are made. (Prob. § 15305(b))	Yes. (Ammco Ornamental Iron, Inc. v. Wing, 26 Cal. App. 4th 409 (App. 2 Dist. 1994))	There is no statutory provision or definite case authority on point.	There is no statutory provision or definite case authority on point.	There is no statutory provision or definite case authority on point.
Colorado	Yes. Spendthrift trusts were established to provide for the maintenance of the beneficiary and secure against improvidence or incapacity. (Newell v. Tubbs, 84 P.2d 820 (1938)) Discretionary support trusts that are not spendthrift trusts are also protected. (In re Marriage of Rosenblum, 602 P.2d 892 (1979))	Yes. (In re Marriage of Jones, 812 P.2d 1152 (1991); In re Marriage of Rosenblum, 602 P.2d 892 (Ct. App. 1979))	There is no statutory provision or definite case authority on point.	Yes. (University Nat'l Bank v. Rhoadarmer, 827 P.2d 561 (Ct. App. 1991))	There is no statutory provision or definite case authority on point.	There is no statutory provision or definite case authority on point.
Connecticut	Yes, but excess over support needs of beneficiary and family, if not also spendthrift trust, can be directed by court, "as justice and equity require." (§ 52-321(d))	Yes, as long as trustee does not abuse discretion in withholding funds. (Bridgeport v. Reilly, 133 Conn. 31, 47 A.2d 865 (1946))	There is no statutory provision or definite case authority on point.	There is no statutory provision or definite case authority on point.	There is no statutory provision or definite case authority on point.	There is no statutory provision or definite case authority on point.
Delaware	May create a spendthrift trust with no mention of support. There is no specific authority regarding support trust. (12 § 3536(a))	Yes. (12 § 3536(a))	There is no statutory provision or definite case authority on point.	Yes. (12 § 3536(a))	There is no statutory provision or definite case authority on point.	There is no statutory provision or definite case authority on point.

Table 9.05, Part 3
Spendthrift and Related Trusts *(continued)*

	Does the State Recognize a Spendthrift Trust to the Extent It Is a Support Trust?	*If the Beneficiary Has an Interest As a Discretionary Beneficiary, Is It Protected?*	*If the Person Has a Special Power of Appointment, Is the Underlying Property Protected from the Donee's (i.e., Holder's) Creditors?*	*If the Person Has a General Power of Appointment, Is the Underlying Property Protected from the Donee's (i.e., Holder's) Creditors?*	*Same As the Prior Question, but the Power Is Exercised in Favor of Other Persons. Can the Creditors Recoup It?*	*Does The Beneficiary Have the Power to Replace the Trustee and Is the Trust a Discretionary Trust or, Alternatively, Can the Beneficiary Appoint Himself As Trustee?*
District of Columbia	Yes, as to support or maintenance order regarding a beneficiary's child. (§ 19-1305.03) To the extent the common law fills the gap (§ 19-1301.06), there is no definitive common law guidance.	The statutory provision from the Uniform Trust Code has not been enacted and there is a reservation in the Code. The common law protects a discretionary interest. (Morrow v. Apple, 26 F.2d 543, 544 (1928))	There is no statutory provision or definite case authority on point.	No, as to a power of withdrawal. In the event of a lapse, release or waiver, only the greater of the 5 or 5 or the federal gift tax annual exclusion is reachable by creditors. (§ 19-1305.05(b))	No, as to a power of withdrawal. In the event of a lapse, release or waiver, only the greater of the 5 or 5 or the federal gift tax annual exclusion is reachable by creditors. (§ 19-1305.05(b))	There is no statutory provision or definite case authority on point.
Florida	If a support trust qualifies as a spendthrift trust, the trust estate is protected. (Mason v. Mason, 798 So.2d 895, 897 (Ct. App. 2001), citing Bacardi v. White, 463 So.2d 218 (Sup. Ct. 1985))	Yes. (Philip v. Trainor, 100 So.2d 181, 183-84 (1958))	There is no statutory provision or definite case authority on point.	There is no statutory provision or definite case authority on point.	There is no statutory provision or definite case authority on point.	There is no statutory provision or definite case authority on point.
Georgia	Assets may not be reached to the extent they are necessary for the beneficiary's support and education. (In re McLoughlin, 507 F.2d 177, 185 (5th Cir. 1975))	Yes. (Henderson v. Collins, 245 Ga. 776, 778 (1980))	Yes. (Jordan v. Caswell, 450 S.E.2d 818 (1994))	Yes. (Avera v. Avera, 315 S.E.2d 883 (1984))	There is no statutory provision or definite case authority on point.	There is no statutory provision or definite case authority on point.

Hawaii	There is no statutory provision or definite case authority on point.	No. (Altman v. Commissioner, 83 B.R. 35 (Bankr. Hawaii 1988) (trust provision granting trustee discretion to distribute to settlor will render trust invalid))	There is no statutory provision or definite case authority on point.	There is no statutory provision or definite case authority on point.	There is no statutory provision or definite case authority on point.	There is no statutory provision or definite case authority on point.
Idaho	There is no statutory provision or definite case authority on point.	There is no statutory provision or definite case authority on point.	There is no statutory provision or definite case authority on point.	There is no statutory provision or definite case authority on point.	There is no statutory provision or definite case authority on point.	There is no statutory provision or definite case authority on point.
Illinois	Yes. Both spendthrift and support trusts are protected from general creditors of beneficiaries. (735 ILCS § 5/2-403; In re Estate of McInerny, 289 Ill. App. 3d 589, 599-600, 682 N.E.2d 284, 290 (Ct. App. 1997))	Yes. (In re Balay, 113 B.R. 429 (Bankr. N.D. Ill. 1990))	There is no statutory provision or definite case authority on point.	There is no statutory provision or definite case authority on point.	There is no statutory provision or definite case authority on point.	There is no statutory provision or definite case authority on point.
Indiana	Yes. (Clay v. Hamilton, 116 Ind. App. 214, 223-224, 63 N.E.2d 207, 210-11 (Ct. App. 1945))	Yes, generally. (Loeb v. Loeb, 261 Ind. 193, 201-205, 301 N.E.2d 349, 356-57 (1973))	There is no statutory provision or definite case authority on point.	Creditors may only reach assets if power actually exercised. (Irwin Union Bank v. Long, 312 N.E.2d 908 (1974))	Creditors may only reach assets if the debtor actually exercises the power. (Irwin Union Bank v. Long, 312 N.E.2d 908 (1974))	There is no statutory provision or definite case authority on point.
Iowa	Yes, but can reach amounts to reimburse providers of support services. (In re Estate of Dodge, 281 N.W.2d 447 (1979))	There is no statutory provision or definite case authority on point.	There is no statutory provision or definite case authority on point.	There is no statutory provision or definite case authority on point.	There is no statutory provision or definite case authority on point.	There is no statutory provision or definite case authority on point.

Table 9.05, Part 3
Spendthrift and Related Trusts *(continued)*

	Does the State Recognize a Spendthrift Trust to the Extent It Is a Support Trust?	*If the Beneficiary Has an Interest As a Discretionary Beneficiary, Is It Protected?*	*If the Person Has a Special Power of Appointment, Is the Underlying Property Protected from the Donee's (i.e., Holder's) Creditors?*	*If the Person Has a General Power of Appointment, Is the Underlying Property Protected from the Donee's (i.e., Holder's) Creditors?*	*Same As the Prior Question, but the Power Is Exercised in Favor of Other Persons. Can the Creditors Recoup It?*	*Does The Beneficiary Have the Power to Replace the Trustee and Is the Trust a Discretionary Trust or, Alternatively, Can the Beneficiary Appoint Himself As Trustee?*
Kansas	There is no Trust Code provision. Under the common law, the answer is no, at least with respect to Medicaid. (Miller v. Dept. Soc. & Rehab., 275 Kan. 349, 64 P.3d 295 (Kan. 2003)) See also Wilcox v. Gentry, 254 Kan. 411, 867 P.2d 281 (1994).	Yes. (§ 58.3a-502(d))	There is no statutory provision or definite case authority on point.	The statute suggests language is required as to both voluntary and involuntary language or that reference be made to a "spendthrift trust." (§ 58.3a-505(b)) But there does not appear to be an absolute requirement. The common law may be relevant.	The statute suggests language is required as to both voluntary and involuntary language or that reference be made to a "spendthrift trust." (§ 58.3a-505(b)) But there does not appear to be an absolute requirement. The common law may be relevant.	There is no statutory provision or definite case authority on point.
Kentucky	Support trust is not protected from direct claims by creditors of the beneficiaries unless it is also a spendthrift trust. (§§ 38.31.18.30(2); 38.31.18.30(6)(b); Goforth v. Gee, 975 S.W.2d 448 (Ky. 1998))	There is no statutory provision or definite case authority on point.	There is no statutory provision or definite case authority on point.	There is no statutory provision or definite case authority on point.	There is no statutory provision or definite case authority on point.	There is no statutory provision or definite case authority on point.
Louisiana	There is no statutory provision or definite case authority on point.	There is no statutory provision or definite case authority on point.	There is no statutory provision or definite case authority on point.	There is no statutory provision or definite case authority on point.	There is no statutory provision or definite case authority on point.	There is no statutory provision or definite case authority on point.

Maine	No. However, a mandatory distribution may be enforced. (18.3-B § 506)	Yes. (18.3-B § 504(1))	There is no statutory provision or definite case authority on point.	The statute suggests language is required as to both voluntary and involuntary language or that reference be made to a "spendthrift trust." (18.3-B § 505(2)) But there does not appear to be an absolute requirement. The common law may be relevant.	The statute suggests language is required as to both voluntary and involuntary language or that reference be made to a "spendthrift trust." (18.3-B § 505(2)) But there does not appear to be an absolute requirement. The common law may be relevant.	There is no statutory provision or definite case authority on point.
Maryland	Yes, implied. (Wenzel v. Powder, 100 Md.36, 59 A 194, 196 (1904))	Yes. (First Nat. Bank of Md. v. Department of Mental Health & Mental Hygiene, 284 Md. 720, 399 A.2d 891 (1979))	There is no statutory provision or definite case authority on point.	There is no statutory provision or definite case authority on point.	There is no statutory provision or definite case authority on point.	There is no statutory provision or definite case authority on point.
Massachusetts	There is no statutory provision or definite case authority on point.	Yes. (Pemberton v. Pemberton, 9 Mass. App. 9, 411 N.E.2d 1305 (1980))	There is no statutory provision or definite case authority on point.	There is no statutory provision or definite case authority on point.	There is no statutory provision or definite case authority on point.	There is no statutory provision or definite case authority on point.
Michigan	Support trust is not a spendthrift trust, but still is protected as well. (Miller v. Dept. of Mental Health, 442 N.W.2d 617, 619 (1989))	Yes. (In re Estate of Ferguson, 186 Mich. App. 409, 465 N.W.2d 357 (1990), *rev'd*, 483 N.W.2d 353 (1992))	There is no statutory provision or definite case authority on point.	There is no statutory provision or definite case authority on point.	There is no statutory provision or definite case authority on point.	There is no statutory provision or definite case authority on point.
Minnesota	Support trust can be reached. (U.S. v. O'Shaughnessy, 517 N.W.2d 574 (Sup. Ct. 1994))	Yes. (U.S. v. O'Shaughnessy, 517 N.W.2d 574 (1994))	Probably yes. (U.S. v. O'Shaughnessy, 517 N.W.2d 574 (Sup. Ct. 1994) (involving discretionary trust))	There is no statutory provision or definite case authority on point.	There is no statutory provision or definite case authority on point.	There is no statutory provision or definite case authority on point.

Table 9.05, Part 3
Spendthrift and Related Trusts *(continued)*

	Does the State Recognize a Spendthrift Trust to the Extent It Is a Support Trust?	*If the Beneficiary Has an Interest As a Discretionary Beneficiary, Is It Protected?*	*If the Person Has a Special Power of Appointment, Is the Underlying Property Protected from the Donee's (i.e., Holder's) Creditors?*	*If the Person Has a General Power of Appointment, Is the Underlying Property Protected from the Donee's (i.e., Holder's) Creditors?*	*Same As the Prior Question, but the Power Is Exercised in Favor of Other Persons. Can the Creditors Recoup It?*	*Does The Beneficiary Have the Power to Replace the Trustee and Is the Trust a Discretionary Trust or, Alternatively, Can the Beneficiary Appoint Himself As Trustee?*
Mississippi	Yes. (Leigh v. Harrison, 11 So. 604 (1892))	Yes. (§ 91-9-507; Mitchell v. Choctaw Bank, 65 So. 278 (1914) (money distributed equally among *living* children upon each one reach ing 21 years of age)). See also § 91-9-509, providing for no exceptions in the case of support trusts.	There is no statutory provision or definite case authority on point.	There is no statutory provision or definite case authority on point.	There is no statutory provision or definite case authority on point.	There is no statutory provision or definite case authority on point.
Missouri	No. (§ 456.5-503)(as to support or maintenance judgment of spouse, child or former spouse, and for judgment creditors for services for protection of beneficiary's interest).	Yes. (§ 456.5-504(1))	There is no statutory provision or definite case authority on point.	There is no statutory provision or definite case authority on point.	There is no statutory provision or definite case authority on point.	There is no statutory provision or definite case authority on point.
Montana	Yes. (§ 72-33-305(2)) See also § 72-33-303 (self-settled trust).	Yes. (§ 72-33-304)	There is no statutory provision or definite case authority on point.	Probably yes due to the broad nature of the Montana statute.	There is no statutory provision or definite case authority on point.	There is no statutory provision or definite case authority on point.

Nebraska	Apparently not under the Trust Code. Under the gap-filling common law (§ 30-38.306), however, true support trusts can be reached by creditors for support-related debts. (Smith v. Smith, 246 Neb. 193, 517 N.W.2d 394 (Sup. Ct. 1994))	Yes. (§ 30-38.349(b))	There is no statutory provision or definite case authority on point.	There is no statutory provision or definite case authority on point.	There is no statutory provision or definite case authority on point.	The interest is protected if the distributions are limited by an ascertainable standard. (§ 30-38.349(e))
Nevada	A trust must provide for the support, education, and maintenance of the beneficiary. (§ 166.090(1)) Without these provisions, the trust will not even be enforced as a spendthrift trust. (Ambrose v. First Nat'l Bank, 482 P.2d 828, 830 (Sup. Ct. 1971))	Yes. (§ 199.110)	There is no statutory provision or definite case authority on point.	There is no statutory provision or definite case authority on point.	There is no statutory provision or definite case authority on point.	There is no statutory provision or definite case authority on point.
New Hampshire	No, other than in the case of a child or spouse. (§§ 564-B: 5-503(b)(1) & (2)) The same result under the common law. (Athorne v. Athorne, 100 N.H. 413, 416–17, 128 A.2d 910, 912–13 (1957))	Yes, except regarding a claim by a spouse or child for support. (§ 564-B:5-504(c))	No. (§ 564-B:5-504)	Yes, unless exercise subject to ascertainable standard or consent of co-trustee or person with adverse intent. (§ 564-B:5-504)	Presumably Yes. (§ 564-B:5-504)	There is no provision.

Table 9.05, Part 3
Spendthrift and Related Trusts *(continued)*

	Does the State Recognize a Spendthrift Trust to the Extent It Is a Support Trust?	*If the Beneficiary Has an Interest As a Discretionary Beneficiary, Is It Protected?*	*If the Person Has a Special Power of Appointment, Is the Underlying Property Protected from the Donee's (i.e., Holder's) Creditors?*	*If the Person Has a General Power of Appointment, Is the Underlying Property Protected from the Donee's (i.e., Holder's) Creditors?*	*Same As the Prior Question, but the Power Is Exercised in Favor of Other Persons. Can the Creditors Recoup It?*	*Does The Beneficiary Have the Power to Replace the Trustee and Is the Trust a Discretionary Trust or, Alternatively, Can the Beneficiary Appoint Himself As Trustee?*
New Jersey	There is no statutory provision or definite case authority on point.	Yes. (In re Griswold, 354 A.2d 717 (1976) (general reference to spendthrift trusts))	There is no statutory provision or definite case authority on point.	There is no statutory provision or definite case authority on point.	There is no statutory provision or definite case authority on point.	There is no statutory provision or definite case authority on point.
New Mexico	A spendthrift trust is not protected where a spouse or child obtains a judgment for support or maintenance. (§ 46A-5-503(B))	Yes, except regarding a claim of a spouse or child. (§ 46A-5-504(B))	There is no statutory provision or definite case authority on point.	There is no statutory provision or definite case authority on point.	There is no statutory provision or definite case authority on point.	There is no statutory provision or definite case authority on point.
New York	If trust does not permit trust income to be accumulated, income in excess of sum necessary for education and support of beneficiary is subject to claims of his creditors. (N.Y. Est., Powers & Tr. Law § 7-3.4) This provision overrides § 7-1.5 which treats income interests as inalienable unless otherwise provided by the	Yes, a creditor may not reach trust income which is payable by the absolute discretion of the trustee until after such discretion has been exercised in favor of the debtor. (Hamilton v. Drogo, 241 N.Y. 401, 150 N.E. 496 (1926); Vanderbilt Credit Corp. v. Chase Manhattan Bank, 100 A. D.2d 544, 473 N.Y.	There is no statutory provision or definite case authority on point.	There is no statutory provision or definite case authority on point.	There is no statutory provision or definite case authority on point.	There is no statutory provision or definite case authority on point.

	grantor. Note also CPLR § 5205(d)(1), which allows a creditor to reach 10% of the income or other payments from a trust. If, in fact, some of the exempt 90% is "unnecessary for the reasonable requirements of the judgment debtor and his dependents, it too can be reached by creditors.	S.2d 242, 245 (1984))				
North Carolina	A spendthrift trust is not protected where their child obtains a judgment for support or maintenance. (§ 36C-5-503(b))	Yes. (§ 36C-5-504(b))	There is no statutory provision or definite case authority on point.	There is no statutory provision or definite case authority on point.	There is no statutory provision or definite case authority on point.	The interest is protected if the distributions are limited by an ascertainable standard. (§ 36C-5-504(f))
North Dakota	No. (Eckes v. Richland County Social Services, 621 N.W.2d 851, 855 (Sup. Ct. 2001); Hecker v. Stark County Social Services Board, 527 N.W.2d 226, 230 (Sup. Ct. 1994))	Yes. (Kryzsko v. Ramsey County Social Serv., 607 N.W.2d 237 (N.D. 2000); Hecker v. Stark City Social Service Bd., 527 N.W.2d 226 (1995))	There is no statutory provision or definite case authority on point.	There is no statutory provision or definite case authority on point.	There is no statutory provision or definite case authority on point.	There is no statutory provision or definite case authority on point.

Table 9.05, Part 3
Spendthrift and Related Trusts *(continued)*

	Does the State Recognize a Spendthrift Trust to the Extent It Is a Support Trust?	*If the Beneficiary Has an Interest As a Discretionary Beneficiary, Is It Protected?*	*If the Person Has a Special Power of Appointment, Is the Underlying Property Protected from the Donee's (i.e., Holder's) Creditors?*	*If the Person Has a General Power of Appointment, Is the Underlying Property Protected from the Donee's (i.e., Holder's) Creditors?*	*Same As the Prior Question, but the Power Is Exercised in Favor of Other Persons. Can the Creditors Recoup It?*	*Does The Beneficiary Have the Power to Replace the Trustee and Is the Trust a Discretionary Trust or, Alternatively, Can the Beneficiary Appoint Himself As Trustee?*
Ohio	Yes. (§ 5805.4 & cmt.)	Yes. (§ 5805.3, 5804 (B))	Not if person has dominion and control over trust. (In re Baldwin, 142 B.R. 210 (Bankr. S.D. Ohio 1992))	Not if person has dominion and control over trust. (In re Baldwin, 142 B.R. 210 (Bankr. S.D. Ohio 1992))	Not if person has dominion and control over trust. (In re Baldwin, 142 B.R. 210 (Bankr. S.D. Ohio 1992))	Not protected, since it is not treated as a spendthrift trust. (In re Baldwin, 142 B.R. 210 (Bankr. S.D. Ohio 1992))
Oklahoma	Yes, but not with regard to claims of support by a spouse or child of the beneficiary, or those of providers of necessary services or supplies, or on income due or to accrue in the calendar year in excess of $25,000. The beneficiary's rights under all spendthrift trusts are taken into account. (60 § 175.25(B)(1) & (2), (D))	Yes. (60 § 175.25(F))	There is no statutory provision or definite case authority on point.	There is no statutory provision or definite case authority on point.	There is no statutory provision or definite case authority on point.	There is no statutory provision or definite case authority on point.
Oregon	There is no statutory provision or definite case authority on point.	There is no statutory provision or definite case authority on point.	There is no statutory provision or definite case authority on point.	No. (Johnson v. Commercial Bk., 284 Or. 675, 680, 588 P.2d 1096, 1099 (1978))	There is no statutory provision or definite case authority on point.	There is no statutory provision or definite case authority on point.
Pennsylvania	Might prevent assign ment if incompatible with purpose of trust	Yes. (Kehr Estate, 2 Pa. D&C2d 633 (1955))	There is no statutory provision or definite	There is no statutory provision or definite	There is no statutory provision or definite	There is no statutory provision or definite

	since income not used for stipulated purpose. (Keeler's Estate, 334 Pa. 225, 3 A.2d 413, 415-16 (1930))		case authority on point.	case authority on point.	case authority on point.	case authority on point.
Rhode Island	There is no statutory provision or definite case authority on point.	Yes (§ 18.3-9.2-3)	There is no statutory provision or definite case authority on point.	If testamentary, not part of donee's estate and exempt from debts. (Hooker v. Drayton, 69 R.I. 290, 33 A.2d 206, 209 (1943))	There is no statutory provision or definite case authority on point.	There is no statutory provision or definite case authority on point.
South Carolina	Generally, a spendthrift trust is not protected where the beneficiary's child obtains a judgment for support or maintenance. But the child support judgment is unenforceable against a special needs, or similar, trust. (§ 62-7-503(b), (c))	Generally yes. But distribution from a discretionary trust can be compelled where the standards of distribution have been violated or where there has been an abuse of discretion. (§ 62-7-504(c))	There is no statutory provision or definite case authority on point.	There is no statutory provision or definite case authority on point.	There is no statutory provision or definite case authority on point.	The interest is protected if the distributions are limited by an ascertainable standard related to the beneficiary-trustee's health, education, maintenance, and support. (§ 62-7-505(b))
South Dakota	There is no statutory provision or definite case authority on point.	There is no statutory provision or definite case authority on point.	There is no statutory provision or definite case authority on point.	There is no statutory provision or definite case authority on point.	There is no statutory provision or definite case authority on point.	There is no statutory provision or definite case authority on point.
Tennessee	Yes. (§ 35-15-504)	Yes. (§ 35-15-504)	There is no statutory provision or definite case authority on point.	There is no statutory provision or definite case authority on point.	There is no statutory provision or definite case authority on point.	There is no Code provision. The common law fills the gap (§ 35-15-106). Under the common law the beneficiary is not protected. See generally McArthur v. Faw, 183 Tenn. 504, 193 S.W.2d 763 (1946).

Table 9.05, Part 3
Spendthrift and Related Trusts *(continued)*

	Does the State Recognize a Spendthrift Trust to the Extent It Is a Support Trust?	*If the Beneficiary Has an Interest As a Discretionary Beneficiary, Is It Protected?*	*If the Person Has a Special Power of Appointment, Is the Underlying Property Protected from the Donee's (i.e., Holder's) Creditors?*	*If the Person Has a General Power of Appointment, Is the Underlying Property Protected from the Donee's (i.e., Holder's) Creditors?*	*Same As the Prior Question, but the Power Is Exercised in Favor of Other Persons. Can the Creditors Recoup It?*	*Does The Beneficiary Have the Power to Replace the Trustee and Is the Trust a Discretionary Trust or, Alternatively, Can the Beneficiary Appoint Himself As Trustee?*
Texas	Yes. (Prop. 112.035) However, a creditor can reach the trust estate to the extent the beneficiary could compel distributions for support. (State v. Rubion, 308 S.W.2d 4 (1957))	Yes, implied. (Prop. 112.035(a); Kolpack v. Torres, 829 S.W.2d 913 (Ct. App. 1992))	There is no statutory provision or definite case authority on point.	If settlor has a general power of appointment, the underlying property is not protected. (Fewell v. Republic Nat'l Bk. of Dallas, 513 S.W.2d 596 (Ct. App. 1974))	There is no statutory provision or definite case authority on point.	There is no statutory provision or definite case authority on point.
Utah	Yes, except for child and spousal support. (§ 75-7-503(2))	Generally yes. But distribution from a discretionary trust can be compelled where the standards of distribution have been violated or where there has been an abuse of discretion. (75-7-504(2), (3))	There is no statutory provision or definite case authority on point.	The statute suggests language is required as to both voluntary and involuntary language or that reference be made to a "spendthrift trust." (§ 75-7-505(2)) But there does not appear to be an absolute requirement. The common law may be relevant.	The statute suggests language is required as to both voluntary and involuntary language or that reference be made to a "spendthrift trust." (§ 75-7-505(2)) But there does not appear to be an absolute requirement. The common law may be relevant.	There is no statutory provision or definite case authority on point.
Vermont	No exception for support trusts. (Huestis v. Manley, 110 Vt. 413, 419, 8 A.2d 644, 646 (1939))	There is no statutory provision or definite case authority on point.	There is no statutory provision or definite case authority on point.	There is no statutory provision or definite case authority on point.	There is no statutory provision or definite case authority on point.	There is no statutory provision or definite case authority on point.

Virginia	Yes. (§ 55-545.04(B) & Uniform Trust Code § 504 cmt.)	Yes. (§ 55-545.04(B))	There is no statutory provision or definite case authority on point.	There is no statutory provision or definite case authority on point.	There is no statutory provision or definite case authority on point.	There is no statutory provision or definite case authority on point.
Washington	There is no statutory provision or definite case authority on point.	There is no statutory provision or definite case authority on point.	There is no statutory provision or definite case authority on point.	There is no statutory provision or definite case authority on point.	There is no statutory provision or definite case authority on point.	There is no statutory provision or definite case authority on point.
West Virginia	A trust where income/principal is applied only to health, education, support or maintenance of the beneficiary is protected unless the trust is subject to alienation by the beneficiary. (§ 36-1-18(a)(1))	There is no statutory provision or definite case authority on point.	There is no statutory provision or definite case authority on point.	There is no statutory provision or definite case authority on point.	There is no statutory provision or definite case authority on point.	Where trustee is the beneficiary, the interest is still protected. (§ 36-1-18.3(b))
Wisconsin	Wisconsin recognizes spendthrift trusts. (§ 701.06) It also recognizes discretionary support trusts as unreachable by creditors until trustee exercises discretion in favor of beneficiary. (Grohmann v. Grohmann, 180 Wis. 2d 690, 511 N.W.2d 312 (1993), *aff'd* 189 Wis. 2d 532, 525 N.W.2d 261 (1995))	Future payments may be subject to claims. (§ 701.06(4), (5))	There is no statutory provision or definite case authority on point.	There is no statutory provision or definite case authority on point.	There is no statutory provision or definite case authority on point.	There is no statutory provision or definite case authority on point.

Table 9.05, Part 3
Spendthrift and Related Trusts *(continued)*

	Does the State Recognize a Spendthrift Trust to the Extent It Is a Support Trust?	*If the Beneficiary Has an Interest As a Discretionary Beneficiary, Is It Protected?*	*If the Person Has a Special Power of Appointment, Is the Underlying Property Protected from the Donee's (i.e., Holder's) Creditors?*	*If the Person Has a General Power of Appointment, Is the Underlying Property Protected from the Donee's (i.e., Holder's) Creditors?*	*Same As the Prior Question, but the Power Is Exercised in Favor of Other Persons. Can the Creditors Recoup It?*	*Does The Beneficiary Have the Power to Replace the Trustee and Is the Trust a Discretionary Trust or, Alternatively, Can the Beneficiary Appoint Himself As Trustee?*
Wyoming	Yes, except for child support. (§ 4-10-503(b))	Yes. (§ 4-10-504(b))	There is no statutory provision or definite case authority on point.	There is no statutory provision or definite case authority on point.	There is no statutory provision or definite case authority on point.	The interest is protected if the distributions are limited by an ascertainable standard. (§ 4-10-504(e))

Table 10
Rule Against Perpetuities
(current through 5/1/07)

The rule against perpetuities is in flux. In all, three camps have emerged: states adhering to the common law rule, states adopting the Uniform Statutory Rule Against Perpetuities, and states abolishing the rule altogether or adopting a perpetuities period several hundred years in length coupled with novel and flexible statutory provisions. Differences exist even among states within a particular camp, so that careful analysis of a relevant state's law is essential.

The question whether the rule applies and, if so, what are its components, is not simply an academic inquiry. The common law rule has serious, even severe consequences *ab initio* if violated. On the other hand, there are a number of valuable planning opportunities in states where the rule has been abolished. First, dead hand control can be perpetuated for many generations via a dynastic trust. Second, substantial tax advantages can be achieved in connection with generation-skipping transfer tax (GST) exemption. Property sheltered by the increasing GST exemption is not subject to tax. In addition, the appreciation experienced by such exempt property is sheltered as well. Ordinarily, when this exempt property is distributed, a beneficiary may receive an asset that has appreciated significantly over several decades and, thus, presents him with a severe estate planning/tax problem of his own. However, if the rule has been abolished, there is no requirement to ever make a major, final distribution to a younger generation beneficiary. By drafting for successive life interests, the death of any beneficiary does not trigger estate tax. Of course, the sheltered principal also remains exempt from generation-skipping transfer tax.

States that have enacted USRAP typically provide a variety of benefits as well, even if somewhat less dramatic. The centerpiece of USRAP is the wait-and-see rule, which eliminates the harshness of the common law rule's invalidating an interest solely on the hypothetical possibility that it may violate the perpetuities period in the future. In addition, through careful planning and the use of special powers of appointment, the perpetuities period can be extended well beyond the common law rule, albeit not in perpetuity.

The accompanying table analyzes in detail many of the critical questions associated with the rule against perpetuities through a series of 26 questions. It does so on a state-by-state basis. Since this is a volatile area, the reader should confirm that the authority cited in support of an answer to a particular question has not changed since the date indicated above. Care should also be exercised in simply adopting the law of a state that appears to take a favorable stance on the perpetuities issue. There are highly complex choice-of-law issues that may undermine the attempt to adopt the law of a particular state on this subject. See 1 Jeffrey A. Schoenblum, *Multistate And Multinational Estate Planning §13.03 (3d ed. 2006).*

Table 10
Rule Against Perpetuities

	ALABAMA	*ALASKA*	*ARIZONA*
1. *Which rule is in effect: the common law rule, the Uniform Statutory Rule Against Perpetuities (USRAP), other law, or none?*	Common Law Rule. (Ala. Code §§ 35-4-4 – 35-4-5)	Other. (Alaska Stat. § 34.27.051 – 34.27.054)	USRAP. (Ariz. Rev. Stat. §§ 14-2901 – 14-2906) However, see #2.b.(c), which allows the drafter effectively to opt out of the rule by providing for a power in a trustee to sell the trust assets, and at least one person alive when the trust is created has an unlimited power to terminate the interest in question.
2. a. *Is the common law rule relevant to any interests?*	Yes. (§ 35-4-4)	The common law is superseded and does not apply in the state. (§ 34.27.075) However, there is a 1,000 year limitation with respect to powers of appointment, largely intended to avoid the "Delaware Tax Trap." (§ 34.27.051)	Yes, but only as the starting point of the analysis. (§ 14-2901(A))
b. *What is the relevant rule?*	("[The] common law rule states that "no interest is good unless it must vest, if at all, not later than twenty-one years after some life in being at the creation of the interest.") Jones v. Ellis, 551 So. 2d 396, 400 (Ala. 1989)	See # 2a.	A nonvested property interest is invalid unless at least one of the following is true: 1. At the time the interest is created it is certain to vest or to terminate not later than twenty-one years after the death of a person who is then alive. 2. The interest either vests or terminates within ninety years after its creation. 3. The interest is under a trust whose trustee has the expressed

(cont'd)

Table 10
Rule Against Perpetuities *(continued)*

		ALABAMA	*ALASKA*	*ARIZONA*
	b. What is the relevant rule? (cont'd)			or implied power to sell the trust assets and at one or more times after the creation of the interest one or more persons who are living when the trust is created have an unlimited power to terminate the interest. (§ 14-2901(A))
3.	*Does the rule apply to other than private trusts?*	No. The rule does not apply to charitable trusts. Mastin v. First Nat'l Bank, 177 So. 2d 808, 816 (Ala. 1965).	N/A	Yes. The rule applies except to: 1. A nonvested property interest or a power of appointment arising out of a nondonative transfer, except for a nonvested property interest or a power of appointment arising out of any of the following: (a) A premarital or postmarital agreement. (b) A separation or divorce settlement. (c) A spouse's election. (d) A similar arrangement arising out of a prospective, existing or previous marital relationship between the parties.

(e) A contract to make or not to revoke a will or trust.

(f) A contract to exercise or not to exercise a power of appointment.

(g) A transfer in satisfaction of a duty of support.

(h) A reciprocal transfer.

2. A fiduciary's power relating to the administration or management of assets, including the power of a fiduciary to sell, lease or mortgage property, and the power of a fiduciary to determine principal and income.
3. A power to appoint a fiduciary.
4. A discretionary power of a trustee to distribute principal before termination of a trust to a beneficiary who has an indefeasibly vested interest in the income and principal.
5. A nonvested property interest held by a charity, government or governmental agency or subdivision, if the nonvested property interest is preceded by an interest held by another charity, government or governmental agency or subdivision.
6. A nonvested property interest in or a power of appointment with respect to a trust or any other property arrangement forming

(cont'd)

Table 10
Rule Against Perpetuities *(continued)*

	ALABAMA	*ALASKA*	*ARIZONA*
3. *Does the rule apply to other than private trusts? (cont'd)*			part of any pension, profit sharing, stock bonus, health, disability, death benefit, income deferral or other current or deferred benefit plan for one or more employees, independent contractors or their beneficiaries or spouses, to which contributions are made for the purpose of distributing to or for the benefit of the participants or their beneficiaries or spouses the property, income or principal in the trust or other property arrangement, except a nonvested property interest or a power of appointment that is created by an election of a participant or a beneficiary or spouse. 7. A property interest, power of appointment or arrangement that was not subject to the common law rule against perpetuities or is excluded by the laws of this state. (§ 14-2904)
4. *Does the rule invalidate the interest at its creation, or is the rule revised by a wait-and-see approach?*	At its creation. (See # 2a.)	There is no rule against perpetuities, but a wait-and-see approach applies to powers of appointment and certain	Wait-and-see. (§ 14-2901(A)(2))

		interests created by powers. (§ 34.27.051)	
5. *Can the trust be reformed?*	N/A	Yes, but only "[i]f a nonvested property interest or a power of appointment was created before January 1, 1996, and is determined in a judicial proceeding, commenced on or after that date, to violate this state's rule against perpetuities as that rule existed before January 1, 1996, or if a nonvested property interest or a power of appointment was created on or after January 1, 1996, but before April 2, 1997, and is determined in a judicial proceeding, commenced on or after that date, to violate this state's rule against perpetuities as that rule existed, on or after January 1, 1996, and before April 2, 1997." (§ 34.27.070(b))	Yes, but only if: 1. A nonvested property interest or a power of appointment becomes invalid under section 14-2901. (See 2b). 2. A class gift is not but might become invalid under section 14-2901 and the time has arrived when the share of any class member is to take effect in possession or enjoyment. 3. A nonvested property interest that is not validated by section 14-2901, subsection A, paragraph 1, that is, the traditional common rule, can vest but not within ninety years after its creation. (§14-2903)
6. *If yes to 5., under what theory?*	N/A	A court, upon the petition of an interested person, may reform the disposition in the manner that most closely approximates the transferor's manifested plan of distribution. (34.27.070(b))	A court, on the petition of an interested person, may reform the disposition in the manner that most closely approximates the transferor's manifested plan of distribution and that is within the ninety years allowed under section 14-2901. (§ 14-2903) *See also* § 14-2905(B) ("If a nonvested property interest or a power of appointment was created before December 31, 1994 and is

(cont'd)

Table 10
Rule Against Perpetuities *(continued)*

	ALABAMA	*ALASKA*	*ARIZONA*
6. *If yes to 5., under what theory? (cont'd)*			determined in a judicial proceeding, commenced on or after December 31, 1994, to violate this state's rule against perpetuities as that rule existed before December 31, 1994," a court may also make a reformation.)
7. *When is a general testamentary power of appointment invalid?*	*See* Unif. Statutory Rule Against Perpetuities § 1, 8B U.L.A. 248 (amended 1990) ("Under the Common-law Rule . . . a *nongeneral power* (whether or not presently exercisable) or a *general testamentary power* is invalid as of the time of its creation if it *might* not terminate (by irrevocable exercise or otherwise) within a life in being plus 21 years.")	A general or nongeneral power of appointment not presently exercisable because of a condition precedent is invalid unless, within a period of 1,000 years after its creation, either the power is irrevocably exercised or the power terminates. (§ 34.27.051(a))	A general testamentary power of appointment is invalid unless: 1. At the time the power is created it is certain to be irrevocably exercised or otherwise to terminate not later than twenty-one years after the death of a person who is then alive, or 2. The power is irrevocably exercised or otherwise terminates within ninety years after its creation. (§ 14-2901(C)) Note that the requirements set forth in # 9 also appear to apply to a general testamentary power. (§14-2901(B))
8. *Same, but nongeneral testamentary power.*	See # 7.	See # 7.	A nongeneral power of appointment . . . is invalid unless: 1. At the time the power is created it is certain to be irrevocably

			exercised or otherwise to terminate not later than twenty-one years after the death of a person who is then alive. 2. The power is irrevocably exercised or otherwise terminates within ninety years after its creation. (§ 14-2901(C))
9. *Same, but general inter vivos power.*	*See* Unif. Statutory Rule Against Perpetuities § 1, 8B U.L.A. 248 (amended 1990) ("Under the Common-law Rule, a *general power not presently exercisable because of a condition precedent* is invalid as of the time of its creation if the condition *might* neither be satisfied nor become impossible to satisfy with a life in being plus 21 years.")	See # 7.	A general power of appointment that is not presently exercisable because of a condition precedent is invalid unless either of the following is true: 1. At the time the power is created the condition precedent is certain to be satisfied or becomes impossible to satisfy no later than twenty-one years after the death of a person who is then alive. 2. The condition precedent either is satisfied or becomes impossible to satisfy within ninety years after its creation. (§ 14-2901(B))
10. *Same, but nongeneral inter vivos power.*	See # 7.	See # 7.	See # 8.
11. *Is a period of gestation added to the perpetuity period?*	Yes. First Alabama Bank v. Adams, 382 So. 2d 1104, 1107 (Ala. 1980) ("[The period of the rule] is twenty-one years after any reasonable number of lives in being at the creation of the *(cont'd)*	N/A	No. The possibility that a child will be born to a person after that person's death is disregarded. (§ 14-2901 (D)) *See also* Unif. Statutory Rule Against Perpetuities § 1, 8B U.L.A. 242-43 (amended 1990) *(cont'd)*

Table 10
Rule Against Perpetuities *(continued)*

	ALABAMA	*ALASKA*	*ARIZONA*
11. Is a period of gestation added to the perpetuity period? (cont'd)	interest, plus actual periods of gestation.'')		(''[T]he possibility that a child will be born to [a testator] after his death must be disregarded; and the possibility that a child will be born to any of [the testator's] descendants after their deaths must also be disregarded. Note, however, that the rule of subsection (d) does *not* apply to the question of the entitlement of an after-born child to take a beneficial interest in the trust'').
12. What is the treatment of a ''later of the traditional rule or 90 years'' clause? See UPC 2-901(e).	N/A	N/A	That language is inoperative to the extent that it produces a period of time that exceeds 21 years after the death of the survivor. (§ 14-2901(E))
13. When is an interest created by the exercise of a general testamentary power deemed created?	*See* comment to Unif. Probate Code § 2-902(a) (''general principles of property law determine that a nonvested property interest or power of appointment created by will is created at the decedent's death''); Unif. Statutory Rule Against Perpetuities § 2, 8B U.L.A. 268 (amended 1990) (stating the same).	No provision. However, if a nongeneral power is exercised to create a new presently exercisable general power, property interests subject to the new power either vest or terminate within 1,000 years of the creation of the new power. (§34.27.051(b))	Except as provided in subsections B and C of this section and section 14-2905, subsection A, the time of creation of a nonvested property interest or a power of appointment is determined under general principles of property law. (§ 14-2902(A)) The first two of the excepted provisions state that as long as a person with a general power to become the unqualified beneficial owner has that power, the nonvested interest is created when the power terminates. The third of the excepted provisions states that a nonvested property

			interest, which arises from a transfer to an existing trust, is created when the nonvested property interest in the trust was created. *See also* Unif. Statutory Rule Against Perpetuities § 2, 8B U.L.A. 268 (amended 1990) (explaining that "general principles of property law determine that the time . . . [of creation] is at the decedent's death.") *See generally* § 14-2905(C) ("a nonvested property interest or a power of appointment created by the exercise of a power of appointment is created when the power is irrevocably exercised or when a revocable exercise becomes irrevocable.")
14. Same, but nongeneral testamentary power.	See # 13.	No provision. However, if a nongeneral power is exercised to create a new or successive nongeneral or general testamentary power, all property interests created by the exercise of the new or successive power must vest or terminate within 1,000 years after the creation of the original instrument creating the nongeneral power. (§34.27.051(c))	See # 13.
15. Same, but general inter vivos power.	*See* comment to Unif. Probate Code § 2-902(a) ("With respect to an intervivos transfer, an interest or power is created on the date the transfer becomes *(cont'd)*	If the power is the original power creating an interest, there is no provision. If the power creating an interest is itself created by an *(cont'd)*	Except as provided in subsections B and C of this section and section 14-2905, subsection A, the time of creation of a nonvested property interest or a power of appointment is *(cont'd)*

Table 10
Rule Against Perpetuities *(continued)*

	ALABAMA	*ALASKA*	*ARIZONA*
15. *Same, but general inter vivos power. (cont'd)*	effective for purposes of property law generally, normally the date of delivery of the deed or funding of the trust.''); Unif. Statutory Rule Against Perpetuities § 2, 8B U.L.A. 268 (stating the same).	earlier nongeneral power's exercise, see # 13 or # 14.	determined under general principles of property law (§ 14-2902(A)) The first two of the excepted provisions states that as long as a person with a general power to become the unqualified beneficial owner has that power, the nonvested interest is created when the power terminates. The third of the excepted provisions states that a nonvested property interest, which arises from a transfer to an existing trust, is created when the nonvested property interest in the trust was created. *See also* Unif. Statutory Rule Against Perpetuities § 2, 8B U.L.A. 268 (amended 1990) (explaining that ''the time when the interest or power is created is the date the transfer becomes effective for purposes of property law generally, normally the date of delivery of the deed''); Comment to Unif. Probate Code § 2-902(a) (stating same and adding ''the funding of the trust'' as ''normally'' the time when the interest is created). *See generally* § 14-2905(C) (''For purposes of this section, a nonvested property interest or a power of appointment created by the exercise

			of a power of appointment is created when the power is irrevocably exercised or when a revocable exercise becomes irrevocable.'')
16. *Same, but nongeneral inter vivos power.*	See # 15.	If the power was the original power creating the interest, there is no provision. If the power created another power which then created an interest of if the power itself was created by an earlier nongeneral power's exercise, see # 13 or # 14.	See # 15.
17. *When is an interest created if the grantor of a trust has a power to revoke?*	*See* comment to Unif. Probate Code § 2-902(b) (noting that ''nonvested property interest and powers of appointment created in [a revocable inter-vivos trust] are created when the power to revoke expires, usually at the settlor's death''); Unif. Statutory Rule Against Perpetuities § 2, 8B U.L.A. 268 (amended 1990) (explaining that ''any nonvested property interest subject to [a power to revoke] is not created . . . until the power terminates (by release, expiration at the death of the donee, or otherwise'').	There is no statute or case law. Statutory provisions addressing the matter were repealed by § 9, Ch.17 SLA 2000. These previously appeared as sections 34.27.055–34.27.065.	If there is a person who alone can exercise a power created by a governing instrument to become the unqualified beneficial owner of a nonvested property interest or a property interest subject to a power of appointment described in section 14-2901, subsection B or C, the nonvested property interest or power of appointment is created when that *person's* power to become the unqualified beneficial owner terminates. (§ 14-2902(B)) *See also* Unif. Statutory Rule Against Perpetuities § 2, 8B U.L.A. 268 (amended 1990) (explaining that ''any nonvested property interest subject to [a power to revoke] is not created . . . until the power terminates (by release, expiration at the death of the donee, or otherwise'');

(cont'd)

Table 10
Rule Against Perpetuities *(continued)*

	ALABAMA	*ALASKA*	*ARIZONA*
17. When is an interest created if the grantor of a trust has a power to revoke? (cont'd)			Comment to Unif. Probate Code § 2-902(b) (noting that "nonvested property interest and powers of appointment created in [a revocable inter-vivos trust] are created when the power to revoke expires, usually at the settlor's death"). *See generally* § 14-2905(C) ("a nonvested property interest or a power of appointment created by the exercise of a power of appointment is created when the power is irrevocably exercised or when a revocable exercise becomes irrevocable.")
18. When does the period of the rule start re an interest contributed to an irrevocable trust?	*See comment* to Unif. Probate Code 2-902(c) ("Arguably, at common law, each transfer [to an existing irrevocable inter-vivos trust] starts the period of the Rule running anew as to each transfer.").	N/A	A nonvested property interest or a power of appointment arising from a transfer of property to a previously funded trust or any other existing property arrangement is created when the nonvested property interest or power of appointment in the original contribution was created. (§ 14-2902(C))
19. Is there a conclusive presumption of fertility, that is, the "fertile octogenarian" rule?	*See, e.g.*, Arkansas, question # 19.	N/A	No specific state case or statute.[1] *See* Unif. Statutory Rule Against Perpetuities § 1, 8B U.L.A. 256 (amended 1990) (holding that "[t]his principle is not superseded by this Act, and in view of new

			advances in medical science . . . [this] is not unrealistic.")); *but see* C. P. Jhong, Annotation, *Modern Status of Presumption of Possibility of Issue Being Extinct*, 98 A.L.R.2d 1285 (2003) (noting "a trend toward denying the conclusive or absolute nature of the presumption against the possibility of issue being extinct where there is competent evidence to the contrary has developed in the decisions, although some courts still adhere to the traditional view treating the presumption as conclusive or absolute").
20. *What is the earliest age a child is deemed capable of bearing a child? What is the impact of illegitimacy?*	Under the rule, courts must presume that living persons are capable of having or fathering children, no matter how young they are. *See* In re Graite's Will Trusts, [1949] 1 All E.R. 459, 460 (Ch.). Thus, the rule strikes down any interest whose vesting depends on the assertion that, for example, a toddler will not have children. (Keith L. Butler, Notes & Comments, *Long Live the Dead Hand: A Case for the Repeal of the Rule Against Perpetuities in Washington*, 75 Wash. L. Rev. 1237, 1246 n.78 (2000)).	N/A	Not specifically addressed by USRAP, but the reasoning is the same as set forth in the comment to section 1 of USRAP, 2, Comment, Technical Violations of the Common Law Rule. Wait and see will typically result in no violation. Nevertheless, the common law rule ordinarily will be applied initially. Under the rule, courts must presume that living persons are capable of having or fathering children, no matter how young they are. *See* In re Graite's Will Trusts, [1949] 1 All E.R. 459, 460 (Ch.). Thus, the rule strikes down any interest whose vesting depends on the assertion that, for example, a toddler will not have children. (Keith L. Butler, Notes & Comments, *Long Live the Dead Hand: A Case for the*

(cont'd)

Table 10
Rule Against Perpetuities *(continued)*

	ALABAMA	*ALASKA*	*ARIZONA*
20. What is the earliest age a child is deemed capable of bearing a child? What is the impact of illegitimacy? (cont'd)			*Repeal of the Rule Against Perpetuities in Washington*, 75 Wash. L. Rev. 1237, 1246 n.78 (2000)).
21. Is the "unborn widow" rule observed?	*See, e.g.*, Arkansas, question # 21.	N/A	No specific state statute or case. *See* Unif. Statutory Rule Against Perpetuities § 1, 8B U.L.A. 246 (amended 1990) (explaining that "[t]he chance that [an] interest will become invalid under the Statutory Rule is small" and so the unborn widow rule would rarely invalidate an interest); *see also* 61 Am Jur 2d *Perpetuities and Restraints on Alienation* § 40 (2003) (noting the same).
22. Does the "slothful executor" rule apply, i.e., an administrative contingency clause providing for a "distribution to, e.g., those issue living at the time of the satisfaction of the administrative condition precedent?"	*See, e.g.*, California, question # 22.	N/A	Unclear. *See* In re Estate of Johnson, 811 P.2d 360, 363 (Ariz. Ct. App. 1991) (holding that a clause in a will was not an "administrative contingency violation."); *see also* Unif. Statutory Rule Against Perpetuities § 1, 8B U.L.A. 245 (amended 1990) (Under USRAP an "interest becomes invalid only if it remains in existence and nonvested 90 years after [the testator's] death. Since it is almost certain that the final distribution of [an] estate will occur well within this 90-year period, the chance that [an]

			interest will be invalid is negligible.'')
23. *Does the all-or-nothing rule apply to class gifts?*	Yes. Crawford v. Carlisle, 89 So. 565, 572 (Ala. 1921) (applying the all-or-nothing rule).	N/A	No specific state case or statute. *See* Unif. Statutory Rule Against Perpetuities § 1, 8B U.L.A. 257 (amended 1990) (''Although this Act does not supersede the basic idea of the much-maligned 'all-or-nothing' rule, the evils sometimes attributed to it are substantially if not entirely eliminated by the wait-and-see feature of the Statutory Rule and by the availability of reformation under Section 3.'')
24. *Is there an exception to the all-or-nothing rule in the case of subclasses or specific sums to each member of the class?*	*See* Unif. Statutory Rule Against Perpetuities § 2, 8B U.L.A. 257 (''The common law also recognizes a doctrine called the specific-sum doctrine which is derived from Storrs v. Benbow, 3 De G.M. & G. 390, 43 Eng. Rep 153 (Ch. 1853), and states: If a specified sum of money is to be paid to each member of a class, the interest of each class member is entitled to separate treatment and is valid or invalid under the Rule on its own. The common law also recognizes a doctrine called the sub-class doctrine, which is derived from Cattlin v. Brown, 11 Hare 372, 68 Eng. Rep. 1318 (Ch. 1853), and states: If the ultimate *(cont'd)*	N/A	No specific case or statute. *See* Unif. Statutory Rule Against Perpetuities § 1, 8B U.L.A. 257 (amended 1990) (''The specific-sum and sub-class doctrines are not superseded by this Act.'')

Table 10
Rule Against Perpetuities *(continued)*

	ALABAMA	*ALASKA*	*ARIZONA*
24. Is there an exception to the all-or-nothing rule in the case of subclasses or specific sums to each member of the class? (cont'd)	takers are not described as a single class but rather as a group of separate subclasses, and if the share to which each separate subclass is entitled will finally be determined within the period of the Rule, the gifts to the different subclasses are separate for the purpose of the Rule.'').		
25. Is the infectious invalidity rule followed outside class gifts?	*See, e.g.*, Colorado, question # 25.	N/A	No specific state case or statute. *See* Unif. Statutory Rule Against Perpetuities § 1, 8B U.L.A. 256 (amended 1990) (explaining that ''[t]he doctrine of infectious invalidity is superseded by this Act by Section 3, under which courts . . . are required to *reform* the disposition to approximate as closely as possible the transferor's . . . plan of distribution.'')
26. Is there a rule against the suspension of the power of alienation? If so, how is it stated?	Prohibition against absolute restraint on alienation. Pritchett v. Turner, 437 So. 2d 104, 108 (Ala. 1983).	A future interest or trust is void if, as to property subject to the future interest or trust, (1) the future interest or trust suspends the power of alienation of the property, the suspension of the power of alienation is for a period of	No specific state statute. Case law unclear. See Tovrea v. Umphress, 556 P.2d 814 (Ariz. Ct. App. 1976) (holding that an option agreement that could be exercised up to one year after the death of one of the parties did not constitute a restraint on alienation).

at least 30 years after the death of an individual alive at the time of the creation of the future interest or trust, and the suspension of the power of alienation occurs in the document creating the future interest or trust;

(2) the future interest or trust suspends the power of alienation of the property and the suspension of the power of alienation is for a period of at least 30 years after the death of an individual alive at the time of the creation of the future interest or trust as computed from the time of the termination of a settlor's power to revoke the trust;

(3) the future interest or trust suspends the power of alienation of the property, the future interest or trust is created by the exercise of a presently exercisable general power of appointment, whether by will or otherwise, and the suspension of the power of alienation is for a period of at least 30 years after the death of an individual alive at the time of the creation of the future interest or trust as computed

(cont'd)

Table 10
Rule Against Perpetuities *(continued)*

	ALABAMA	*ALASKA*	*ARIZONA*
26. Is there a rule against the suspension of the power of alienation? If so, how is it stated? (cont'd)		from the time of creation of the presently exercisable power of appointment; or (4) the future interest or trust suspends the power of alienation of the property, the future interest or trust is created by the exercise of a nongeneral or testamentary general power of appointment, and the suspension of the power of alienation is for a period of at least 30 years after the death of an individual alive at the time of the creation of the future interest or trust as computed from the time of creation of the original instrument or conveyance creating the original power of appointment that was exercised to create a new or successive nongeneral or testamentary general power of appointment. (§ 34.27.100(a)) For exceptions to the rule, *see* § 34.27.100(c)	

27. *Effective date.*	N/A	April 2, 1997. Separate statutory provisions apply to nonvested interests and powers created on or after January 1, 1996 and before April 2, 1997. (§ 34.27.070) Prior interests and powers can be reformed. See # 5. (§ 34.27.070(b)) The 1,000 year rule of section 34.27.051, respecting powers of appointment, only applies to a trust instrument or conveyance executed on or after April 2, 1997, if the trust instrument or conveyance creates a contingent power of appointment or nonvested property interest subject to the exercise of a power of appointment creating a new or successive power of appointment. (§ 34.27.070(c))	January 1, 1995. See # 6.

1. For questions # 19–25, *see* § 14.906 (noting that the state's USRAP "applies notwithstanding the common law rule against perpetuities . . .").

Table 10
Rule Against Perpetuities *(continued)*

	ARKANSAS	*CALIFORNIA*	*COLORADO*
1. *Which rule is in effect: the common law rule, the Uniform Statutory Rule Against Perpetuities (USRAP), other law, or none?*	USRAP (§ 18-3-101)	USRAP. (Cal. Prob. Code §§ 21200 – 21225)	There are several rules in effect: 1. With respect to an interest or power created after May 31, 2001, (i) a nonvested property interest must vest or terminate within 1,000 years of its creation; (ii) in the case of a general power of appointment subject to a condition precedent, the condition precedent must be satisfied or be impossible to satisfy within 1,000 years after its creation; (iii) a nongeneral power of appointment or a general testamentary power must be irrevocably exercised or otherwise terminate within 1,000 years after its creation. (Colo. Rev. Stat. Ann. § 15-11-1102.5(1)(a)-(b)) 2. Interests and powers created on or after May 31, 1991, but before June 1, 2001, remain governed by a modified USRAP. (§ 15-11-1102.5(2)(a)-(b)) 3. Interests and powers created by the exercise of a nongeneral power over all or part of a trust that was irrevocable on September 25, 1985, do not qualify under 1. above, but will qualify

			under 2. above. (§ 15-11-1102.5(3)(c)(I)-(II)) 4. With respect to any interest or power of appointment created before July 1, 2006, the owner or holder of the interest or power may deliver a written notice that 1. above should not apply retroactively. If this is done then the modified USRAP explained below applies instead. (§ 15-11-1102 (6)) This provision is repealed effective July 1, 2008. However, a modified USRAP will be preserved for interests and powers created as specified in 2. above. CAUTION: The analysis below, ##1-27, pertains to the interests created post-May 31, 1991, and prior to June 1, 2001, in which the owner or holder has elected continued application of USRAP, except if indicated otherwise. USRAP. (Colo. Rev. Stat. §§ 15-11-1101–15-11-1107) However, see #2.b.(c), which allows the drafter effectively to opt out of the rule by providing for discretionary distributions of income or principal to a person living when the trust is created.
2. a. *Is the common law rule relevant to any interests?*	The common law rule is superseded (§ 18-3-109) but has to be taken into account all the same. *See* 2.b.(1).	Yes, but only as the starting point of the analysis.	Yes, but only as the starting point of the analysis.
b. *What is the relevant rule?*	A nonvested property interest is invalid unless: (1) When the interest is created, it is certain to vest or terminate no later than *(cont'd)*	A nonvested property interest is invalid unless one of the following conditions is satisfied: (a) When the interest is created, it is certain to vest *(cont'd)*	A nonvested property interest is invalid unless: (a) When the interest is created, it is certain to vest or terminate no later than twenty-one years *(cont'd)*

Table 10
Rule Against Perpetuities *(continued)*

	ARKANSAS	CALIFORNIA	COLORADO
b. *What is the relevant rule? (cont'd)*	21 years after the death of an individual then alive; or (2) The interest either vests or terminates within 90 years after its creation. (§ 18-3-101(a))	or terminate no later than 21 years after the death of an individual then alive. (b) The interest either vests or terminates within 90 years after its creation. (§ 21205)	after the death of an individual then alive; or (b) The interest either vests or terminates within ninety years after its creation. (c) The interest is in a trust and all or part of the income or principal of the trust may be distributed, in the discretion of the trustee, to a person who is living when the trust is created. (§ 15-11-1102(1))
3. *Does the rule apply to other than private trusts?*	Yes. The rule applies except to: (1) A nonvested property interest or a power of appointment arising out of a nondonative ransfer, except a nonvested property interest or a power of appointment arising out of any of the following: (A) A premarital or postmarital agreement; (B) A separation or divorce settlement; (C) A spouse's election; (D) A similar arrangement arising out of a prospective, an existing, or a previous marital relationship between the parties; (E) A contract to make or not to revoke a will or trust;	Yes. The rule applies except to: (a) A nonvested property interest or a power of appointment arising out of a nondonative transfer, except a nonvested property interest or a power of appointment arising out of (1) a premarital or postmarital agreement, (2) a separation or divorce settlement, (3) a spouse's election, (4) or a similar arrangement arising out of a prospective, existing, or previous marital relationship between the parties, (5) a contract to make or not to revoke a will or trust, (6) a contract to exercise or not to exercise a power of appointment, (7) a transfer in satisfaction of a duty of	Yes. The rule applies except to: (a) A nonvested property interest or a power of appointment arising out of a nondonative transfer, except a nonvested property interest or a power of appointment arising out of: (I) A premarital or postmarital agreement; (II) A separation or divorce settlement; (III) A spouse's election; (IV) A similar arrangement arising out of a prospective, existing, or previous marital relationship between the parties; (V) A contract to make or not to revoke a will or trust; (VI) A contract to exercise or not to exercise a power of appointment;

(F) A contract to exercise or not to exercise a power of appointment;

(G) A transfer in satisfaction of a duty of support;

(H) A reciprocal transfer.

(2) A fiduciary's power relating to the administration or management of assets, including the power of a fiduciary to sell, lease, or mortgage property, and the power of a fiduciary to determine principal and income.

(3) A power to appoint a fiduciary.

(4) A discretionary power of a trustee to distribute principal before termination of a trust to a beneficiary having an indefeasibly vested interest in the income and principal.

(5) A nonvested property interest held by a charity, government, or governmental agency or subdivision, if the nonvested property interest is preceded by an interest held by another charity, government, or governmental agency or subdivision.

(6) A nonvested property interest in or a power of appointment with respect to a trust

(cont'd)

support, or (8) a reciprocal transfer.

(b) A fiduciary's power relating to the administration or management of assets, including the power of a fiduciary to sell, lease, or mortgage property, and the power of a fiduciary to determine principal and income.

(c) A power to appoint a fiduciary.

(d) A discretionary power of a trustee to distribute principal before termination of a trust to a beneficiary having an indefeasibly vested interest in the income and principal.

(e) A nonvested property interest held by a charity, government, or governmental agency or subdivision, if the nonvested property interest is preceded by an interest held by another charity, government, or governmental agency or subdivision.

(f) A nonvested property interest in or a power of appointment with respect to a trust or other property arrangement forming part of a pension, profit-sharing, stock bonus, health, disability, death benefit, income deferral, or other current or deferred benefit plan for one or more

(cont'd)

(VII) A transfer in satisfaction of a duty of support; or

(VIII) A reciprocal transfer. Note this exception has been deleted, effective July 1, 2006.

(b) A fiduciary's power relating to the administration or management of assets, including the power of a fiduciary to sell, lease, or mortgage property, and the power of a fiduciary to determine principal and income;

(c) A power to appoint a fiduciary;

(d) A discretionary power of a trustee to distribute principal before termination of a trust to a beneficiary having an indefeasibly vested interest in the income and principal;

(e) A nonvested property interest held by a charity, government, or governmental agency or subdivision, if the nonvested property interest is preceded by an interest held by another charity, government, or governmental agency or subdivision;

(f) A nonvested property interest in or a power of appointment with respect to a trust or other property arrangement forming part of a pension, profit-sharing, stock bonus, health, disability, death benefit, income deferral, or other current or deferred benefit plan for one or more

(cont'd)

Table 10
Rule Against Perpetuities *(continued)*

	ARKANSAS	CALIFORNIA	COLORADO
3. *Does the rule apply to other than private trusts? (cont'd)*	with respect to a trust or other property arrangement forming part of a pension, a profit sharing, a stock bonus, a health, a disability, a death benefit, an income deferral, or other current or deferred benefit plan for one (1) or more employees, independent contractors, or their beneficiaries or spouses, to which contributions are made for the purpose of distributing to or for the benefit of the participants or their beneficiaries or spouses the property, income, or principal in the trust or other property arrangement, except a nonvested property interest or a power of appointment that is created by an election of a participant or a beneficiary or spouse. (7) A property interest, power of appointment, or arrangement that was not subject to the common law rule against perpetuities or is excluded by another Arkansas statute. (§18-3-104)	employees, independent contractors, or their beneficiaries or spouses, to which contributions are made for the purpose of distributing to or for the benefit of the participants or their beneficiaries or spouses the property, income, or principal in the trust or other property arrangement, except a nonvested property interest or a power of appointment that is created by an election of a participant or a beneficiary or spouse. (g) A property interest, power of appointment, or arrangement that was not subject to the common law rule against perpetuities or is excluded by another statute of this state. (h) A trust created for the purpose of providing for its beneficiaries under hospital service contracts, group life insurance, group disability insurance, group annuities, or any combination of such insurance, as defined in the Insurance Code. (§ 21225)	employees, independent contractors, or their beneficiaries or spouses, to which contributions are made for the purpose of distributing to or for the benefit of the participants or their beneficiaries or spouses the property, income, or principal in the trust or other property arrangement, except a nonvested property interest or a power of appointment that is created by an election of a participant or a beneficiary or spouse; or (g) A property interest, power of appointment, or arrangement that was not subject to the common law rule against perpetuities or is excluded by another statute of this state. (§ 15-11-1105)
4. *Does the rule invalidate the interest at its creation, or is the rule revised by a wait-and-see approach?*	Wait-and-see. (§18-3-103)	Wait-and-see. (§ 21205(b))	Wait-and-see. (§ 15-11-1102(1)(b))

5. *Can the trust be reformed?*	Yes, but only if one of the following conditions is met: (1) a nonvested property interest or a power of appointment becomes invalid under § 18-3-101; (2) a class gift is not but might become invalid under § 18-3-101 and the time has arrived when the share of any class member is to take effect in possession or enjoyment; or (3) a nonvested property interest that is not validated by § 18-3-101(a)(1), that is, the traditional common law rule, can vest but not within ninety (90) years after the interest's creation. (§ 18-3-103)	Yes, but only if any of the following conditions is satisfied: (a) A nonvested property inter est or a power of appointment becomes invalid under the statutory rule against perpetuities provided in Article 2 (commencing with Section 21205). (b) A class gift is not but might become invalid under the statutory rule against perpetuities provided in Article 2 (commencing with Section 21205), and the time has arrived when the share of any class member is to take effect in possession or enjoyment. (c) A nonvested property interest that is not validated by subdivision (a) of Section 21205, that is, the traditional common law rule, can vest but not within 90 years after its creation. (§ 21220) *See also* # 27.	Yes, but only if one of the following conditions is satisfied: (a) A nonvested property interest or a power of appointment becomes invalid under the statutory rule against perpetuities of section 15-11-1102; (b) A class gift is not but might become invalid under section 15-11-1102 and the time has arrived when the share of any class member is to take effect in possession or enjoyment; or (c) A nonvested property interest that is not validated by section 15-11-1102(1)(a), that is, the traditional common law rule, can vest but not within ninety years after its creation. (§ 15-11-1104) *See also* # 27. Note: This provision is repealed, effective July 1, 2008. It does not apply at all to interest and powers created on or after July 1, 2006. It does not apply to earlier created interests and powers unless the owner or holder elects its application in writing. In all other cases, a plan can be reformed so that there is a disposition within the 1000-year period. (§ 15-11-1104.5(1))
6. *If yes to 5., under what theory?*	A court shall reform a disposition in the manner that most closely preserves the transferor's plan of distribution and is within the ninety (90) years allowed by §§ 18-3-101(a)(2), 18-3-101(b)(2), or 18-3-101(c)(2). (§ 18-3-103) *See also* § 18-3-105(b) ("If a *(cont'd)*	A court shall reform a disposition in the manner that most closely approximates the transferor's manifested plan of distribution and is within the 90 years allowed by the applicable provision in Article 2 (commencing *(cont'd)*	A court shall reform a disposition in the manner that most closely approximates the transferor's manifested plan of distribution and is within the ninety years allowed by section 15-11-1102 (1)(b), (2)(b), or (3)(b). (§ 15-11-1104) *(cont'd)*

Table 10
Rule Against Perpetuities *(continued)*

	ARKANSAS	CALIFORNIA	COLORADO
6. *If yes to 5., under what theory? (cont'd)*	nonvested property interest or a power of appointment was created before the effective date of this chapter, and: (1) is determined in a judicial proceeding commenced on or after the effective date of this chapter, to violate this state's rule against perpetuities as that rule existed before the effective date of this chapter; or (2) may violate this state's rule against perpetuities as that rule existed before the effective date of this chapter; a court upon the petition of an interested person may reform the disposition by inserting a savings clause that most closely approximates the transferor's manifested plan of distribution and is within the limits of the rule against perpetuities applicable when the nonvested property interest or power of appointment was created.")	with Section 21205). (§ 21220)	*See also* § 15-11-1106(b) ("If a nonvested property interest or a power of appointment was created before May 31, 1991, and is determined in a judicial proceeding, commenced on or after May 31, 1991, to violate this state's rule against perpetuities as that rule existed before May 31, 1991, a court upon the petition of an interested person shall reform the disposition by inserting a savings clause that preserves most closely the transferor's manifested plan of distribution and that brings that plan within the limits of the rule against perpetuities applicable when the nonvested property interest or power of appointment was created.") See #4 above for applicability.
7. *When is a general testamentary power of appointment invalid?*	A general testamentary power of appointment is invalid unless one of the following conditions is satisfied:	A general testamentary power of appointment is invalid unless one of the following conditions is satisfied:	A general testamentary power of appointment is invalid unless one of the following conditions is satisfied:

	(1) When the power is created, it is certain to be irrevocably exercised or otherwise to terminate no later than 21 years after the death of an individual then alive; (2) The power is irrevocably exercised or otherwise terminates within 90 years after its creation. (§18-3-101(c))	(a) When the power is created, it is certain to be irrevocably exercised or otherwise to terminate no later than 21 years after the death of an individual then alive. (b) The power is irrevocably exercised or otherwise terminates within 90 years after its creation. (§ 21207)	(a) When the power is created, it is certain to be irrevocably exercised or otherwise to terminate no later than 21 years after the death of an individual then alive. (b) The power is irrevocably exercised or otherwise terminates within 90 years after its creation. (§ 15-11-1102(3))
8. *Same, but nongeneral testamentary power.*	A nongeneral power of appointment is invalid unless one of the following conditions is satisfied: (1) When the power is created, it is certain to be irrevocably exercised or otherwise to terminate no later than 21 years after the death of an individual then alive; (2) The power is irrevocably exercised or otherwise terminates within 90 years after its creation. (§ 18-3-101(c))	A nongeneral power of appointment . . . is invalid unless one of the following conditions is satisfied: (a) When the power is created, it is certain to be irrevocably exercised or otherwise to terminate no later than 21 years after the death of an individual then alive. (b) The power is irrevocably exercised or otherwise terminates within 90 years after its creation. (§ 21207)	A nongeneral power of appointment . . . is invalid unless one of the following conditions is satisfied: (a) When the power is created, it is certain to be irrevocably exercised or otherwise to terminate no later than 21 years after the death of an individual then alive. (b) The power is irrevocably exercised or otherwise terminates within 90 years after its creation. (§ 15-11-1102(3))
9. *Same, but general inter vivos power.*	A general power of appointment not presently exercisable because of a condition precedent is invalid unless one of the following conditions is satisfied: (1) When the power is created, the condition precedent is *(cont'd)*	A general power of appointment not presently exercisable because of a condition precedent is invalid unless one of the following conditions is satisfied: (a) When the power is created, the condition precedent is *(cont'd)*	A general power of appointment not presently exercisable because of a condition precedent is invalid unless one of the following conditions is satisfied: (a) When the power is created, the condition precedent is certain to *(cont'd)*

Table 10
Rule Against Perpetuities *(continued)*

	ARKANSAS	CALIFORNIA	COLORADO
9. *Same, but general inter vivos power. (cont'd)*	certain to be satisfied or become impossible to satisfy no later than 21 years after the death of an individual then alive; (2) The condition precedent either is satisfied or becomes impossible to satisfy within 90 years after its creation. (§ 18-3-101(b))	certain to be satisfied or become impossible to satisfy no later than 21 years after the death of an individual then alive. (b) The condition precedent either is satisfied or becomes impossible to satisfy within 90 years after its creation. (§ 21207)	be satisfied or become impossible to satisfy no later than 21 years after the death of an individual then alive. (b) The condition precedent either is satisfied or becomes impossible to satisfy within 90 years after its creation. (§ 15-11-1102(2))
10. *Same, but nongeneral inter vivos power.*	See # 7.	See # 8.	See # 8.
11. *Is a period of gestation added to the perpetuity period?*	No. The possibility that a child will be born to a person after that person's death is disregarded. (§ 18-3-101(d)) *See also* Unif. Statutory Rule Against Perpetuities § 1, 8B U.L.A. 242-43 (amended 1990) ("[T]he possibility that a child will be born to [a testator] after his death must be disregarded; and the possibility that a child will be born to any of [the testator's] descendants after their deaths must also be disregarded. Note, however, that the rule of subsection (d) does *not* apply to the question of the entitlement of an	No. The possibility that a child will be born to a person after that person's death is disregarded. (§ 21208) *See also* Unif. Statutory Rule Against Perpetuities § 1, 8B U.L.A. 242-43 (amended 1990) ("[T]he possibility that a child will be born to [a testator] after his death must be disregarded; and the possibility that a child will be born to any of [the testator's] descendants after their deaths must also be disregarded. Note, however, that the rule of subsection (d) does *not* apply to the question of the entitlement of an after-born child	No. The possibility that a child will be born to a person after that person's death is disregarded. (§15-11-1102(4)) *See also* Unif. Statutory Rule Against Perpetuities § 1, 8B U.L.A. 242-43 (amended 1990) ("[T]he possibility that a child will be born to [a testator] after his death must be disregarded; and the possibility that a child will be born to any of [the testator's] descendants after their deaths must also be disregarded. Note, however, that the rule of subsection (d) does *not* apply to the question of the entitlement of an after-born child to take a beneficial interest in the trust").

	after-born child to take a beneficial interest in the trust'').	to take a beneficial interest in the trust'').	
12. *What is the treatment of a ''later of the traditional rule or 90 years'' clause? See UPC 2-901(e).*	It is not allowed to extend the perpetuities period beyond the traditional rule. The language is inoperative. (§ 18-3-101(e))	That language is inoperative to the extent it produces a period of time that exceeds 21 years after the death of the survivor of the specified lives. (§ 21209)	That language is inoperative to the extent it produces a period of time that exceeds 21 years after the death of the survivor of the specified lives. (§ 15-11-1102(5))
13. *When is an interest created by the exercise of a general testamentary power deemed created?*	Except as provided in subsections (b) and (c) and in section 1 (a) of § 18-3-102 and in § 18-3-105, the time of creation of a nonvested property interest or a power of appointment is determined under general principles of property law. (§ 18-3-102(a)) The first two of the excepted provisions state that as long as a person with a general power to become the unqualified beneficial owner has that power, the nonvested interest is created when the power terminates. The third of the excepted provisions states that a nonvested property interest, which arises from a transfer to an existing trust, is created when the nonvested property interest in the trust was created. *See also* Unif. Statutory Rule Against Perpetuities § 2, 8B U.L.A. 268 (amended 1990) (explaining that ''general principles of property law determine *(cont'd)*	Except as provided in Sections 21211 and 21212, the time of creation of a nonvested property interest or a power of appointment is determined by other applicable statutes or, if none, under general principles of property law. (§ 21210) The first two of the excepted provisions states that as long as a person with a general power to become the unqualified beneficial owner has that power, the nonvested interest is created when the power terminates. The third of the excepted provisions states that a nonvested property interest, which arises from a transfer to an existing trust, is created when the nonvested property interest in the trust was created. *See also* Unif. Statutory Rule Against Perpetuities § 2, 8B U.L.A. 268 (amended 1990) (explaining that ''general principles of property law determine that the time . . . [of *(cont'd)*	Except as provided in subsections (2) and (3) of this section and in section 15-11-1106(1), the time of creation of a nonvested property interest or a power of appointment is determined under general principles of property law. (§ 15-11-1103(1)) The first two of the excepted provisions states that as long as a person with a general power to become the unqualified beneficial owner has that power, the nonvested interest is created when the power terminates. The third of the excepted provisions states that a nonvested property interest, which arises from a transfer to an existing trust, is created when the nonvested property interest in the trust was created. *See also* Unif. Statutory Rule Against Perpetuities § 2, 8B U.L.A. 268 (amended 1990) (explaining that ''general principles of property law determine that the time . . . [of creation] is at the decedent's death.'') *See generally* § 15-11-1106(1) (''a nonvested property interest or a *(cont'd)*

Table 10
Rule Against Perpetuities *(continued)*

	ARKANSAS	CALIFORNIA	COLORADO
13. When is an interest created by the exercise of a general testamentary power deemed created? (cont'd)	that the time. . .[of creation] is at the decedent's death.'') *See generally* §18-3-105(a) (''a nonvested property interest or a power of appointment created by the exercise of a power of appointment is created when the power is irrevocably exercised or when a revocable exercise becomes irrevocable.'')	creation] is at the decedent's death.'')	power of appointment created by the exercise of a power of appointment is created when the power is irrevocably exercised or when a revocable exercise becomes irrevocable.'')
14. Same, but nongeneral testamentary power.	See # 13.	See # 13.	See # 13.
15. Same, but general inter vivos power.	Except as provided in subsections (b) and (c) and in section 1 (a) of § 18-3-102 and in § 18-3-105, the time of creation of a nonvested property interest or a power of appointment is determined under general principles of property law. (§ 18-3-102(a)) The first two of the excepted provisions state that as long as a person with a general power to become the unqualified beneficial owner has that power, the nonvested interest is created when the power terminates. The third of the excepted provisions states that a nonvested property interest, which arises from a transfer to an existing trust, is	Except as provided in Sections 21211 and 21212, the time of creation of a nonvested property interest or a power of appointment is determined by other applicable statutes or, if none, under general principles of property law. (§ 21210) The first two of the excepted provisions states that as long as a person with a general power to become the unqualified beneficial owner has that power, the nonvested interest is created when the power terminates. The third of the excepted provisions states that a nonvested property interest, which from a transfer to an existing trust, is created	Except as provided in subsections (2) and (3) of this section and in section 15-11-1106(1), the time of creation of a nonvested property interest or a power of appointment is determined under general principles of property law.(§ 15-11-1103(1)) The first two of the excepted provisions states that as long as a person with a general power to become the unqualified beneficial owner has that power, the nonvested interest is created when the power terminates. The third of the excepted provisions states that a nonvested property interest, which arises from a transfer to an existing trust, is created when the nonvested property interest in the trust was created.

	created when the nonvested property interest in the trust was created. *See also* Unif. Statutory Rule Against Perpetuities § 2, 8B U.L.A. 268 (amended 1990) (explaining that "the time when the interest or power is created is the date the transfer becomes effective for purposes of property law generally, normally the date of delivery of the deed"); Comment to Unif. Probate Code § 2-902(a) (stating same and adding "the funding of the trust" as "normally" the time when the interest is created). *See generally* § 18-3-105(a) ("a nonvested property interest or a power of appointment created by the exercise of a power of appointment is created when the power is irrevocably exercised or when a revocable exercise becomes irrevocable.")	when the nonvested property interest in the trust was created. *See also* Unif. Statutory Rule Against Perpetuities § 2, 8B U.L.A. 268 (amended 1990) (explaining that "the time when the interest or power is created is the date the transfer becomes effective for purposes of property law generally, normally the date of delivery of the deed"); Comment to Unif. Probate Code § 2-902(a) (stating same and adding "the funding of the trust" as "normally" the time when the interest is created).	*See also* Unif. Statutory Rule Against Perpetuities § 2, 8B U.L.A. 268 (amended 1990) (explaining that "the time when the interest or power is created is the date the transfer becomes effective for purposes of property law generally, normally the date of delivery of the deed"); Comment to Unif. Probate Code § 2-902(a) (stating same and adding "the funding of the trust" as "normally" the time when the interest is created). *See generally* § 15-11-1106(1) ("a nonvested property interest or a power of appointment created by the exercise of a power of appointment is created when the power is irrevocably exercised or when a revocable exercise becomes irrevocable.")
16. *Same, but nongeneral inter vivos power.*	See # 15.	See # 15.	See # 15.
17. *When is an interest created if the grantor of a trust has a power to revoke?*	If there is a person who alone can exercise a power created by a governing instrument to become the unqualified beneficial owner of: (1) a nonvested property interest; or (2) a property interest subject to a power of appointment *(cont'd)*	If there is a person who alone can exercise a power created by a governing instrument to become the unqualified beneficial owner of (1) a nonvested property interest or (2) a property interest subject to a power of appointment described in Section 21206 or 21207, the nonvested property interest or *(cont'd)*	For purposes of this part 11, if there is a person who alone can exercise a power created by a governing instrument to become the unqualified beneficial owner of either a nonvested property interest or a property interest subject to a power of appointment described in section 15-11-1102 (2) or (3), the nonvested property interest or power of *(cont'd)*

Table 10
Rule Against Perpetuities *(continued)*

	ARKANSAS	CALIFORNIA	COLORADO
17. *When is an interest created if the grantor of a trust has a power to revoke? (cont'd)*	described in §18-3-101(b) or §18-3-101(c); the nonvested property interest or power of appointment is created when the power to become the unqualified beneficial owner terminates. (§ 18-3-102(b)) *See also* Unif. Statutory Rule Against Perpetuities § 2, 8B U.L.A. 268 (amended 1990) (explaining that "any nonvested property interest subject to [a power to revoke] is not created . . . until the power terminates (by release, expiration at the death of the donee, or otherwise"); Comment to Unif. Probate Code § 2-902(b) (noting that "nonvested property interest and powers of appointment created in [a revocable inter-vivos trust] are created when the power to revoke expires, usually at the settlor's death"). *See generally* § 18-3-105(a) [prospective application to nonvested property interest or a power of appointment created on or after the effective date]	power of appointment is created when the power to become the unqualified beneficial owner terminates. (§ 21211(a)). *See also* Unif. Statutory Rule Against Perpetuities § 2, 8B U.L.A. 268 (amended 1990) (explaining that "any nonvested property interest subject to [a power to revoke] is not created . . . until the power terminates (by release, expiration at the death of the donee, or otherwise"); Comment to Unif. Probate Code § 2-902(b) (noting that "nonvested property interest and powers of appointment created in [a revocable inter-vivos trust] are created when the power to revoke expires, usually at the settlor's death").	appointment is created when the power to become the unqualified beneficial owner terminates. (§ 15-11-1103(2)) *See also* Unif. Statutory Rule Against Perpetuities § 2, 8B U.L.A. 268 (amended 1990) (explaining that "any nonvested property interest subject to [a power to revoke] is not created . . . until the power terminates (by release, expiration at the death of the donee, or otherwise"); Comment to Unif. Probate Code § 2-902(b) (noting that "nonvested property interest and powers of appointment created in [a revocable inter-vivos trust] are created when the power to revoke expires, usually at the settlor's death"). *See generally* § 15-11-1106(1) ("a nonvested property interest or a power of appointment created by the exercise of a power of appointment is created when the power is irrevocably exercised or when a revocable exercise becomes irrevocable.")

	(''a nonvested property interest or a power of appointment created by the exercise of a power of appointment is created when the power is irrevocably exercised or when a revocable exercise becomes irrevocable.'')		
18. *When does the period of the rule start re an interest contributed to an irrevocable trust? See UPC 2-902(c).*	A nonvested property interest or a power of appointment arising from a transfer of property to a previously funded trust or other existing property arrangement is created when the nonvested property interest or power of appointment in the original contribution was created. (§ 18-3-102(c))	A nonvested property interest or a power of appointment arising from a transfer of property to a previously funded trust or other existing property arrangement is created when the nonvested property interest or power of appointment in the original contribution was created. (§ 21212)	A nonvested property interest or a power of appointment arising from a transfer of property to a previously funded trust or other existing property arrangement is created when the nonvested property interest or power of appointment in the original contribution was created. (§ 15-11-1103(3)) No specific state case or statute. [2]
19. *Is there a conclusive presumption of fertility, that is, the ''fertile octogenarian'' rule?*	Yes. (Love v. McDonald, 148 S.W.2d 170, 171 (Ark. 1941) ('''the presumption being that there may be issue so long as life continues''')) *See also* Unif. Statutory Rule Against Perpetuities §1, 8B U.L.A. 256 (amended 1990) (holding that ''[t]his principle is not superseded by this Act, and in view of new advances in medical science . . . [this] is not unrealistic.''); *but see* C. P. Jhong, Annotation, *Modern Status of Presumption of Possibility of Issue Being Extinct*, 98 A.L.R.2d *(cont'd)*	Yes. Fletcher v. Los Angeles T. & Sav. Bank, 187 P. 425, 428 (Cal. 1920); In re Sahlender's Estate 201 P. 2d 69, 81 (Cal. Ct. App. 1948).[1] *See also* Unif. Statutory Rule Against Perpetuities § 1, 8B U.L.A. 256 (amended 1990) (holding that ''[t]his principle is not superseded by this Act, and in view of new advances in medical science . . . [this] is not unrealistic.''); *but see* C. P. Jhong, Annotation, *Modern Status of Presumption of Possibility of Issue Being* *(cont'd)*	*See* Unif. Statutory Rule Against Perpetuities § 1, 8B U.L.A. 256 (amended 1990) (holding that ''[t]his principle is not superseded by this Act, and in view of new advances in medical science . . . [this] is not unrealistic.'')); *but see* C. P. Jhong, Annotation, *Modern Status of Presumption of Possibility of Issue Being Extinct*, 98 A.L.R.2d 1285 (2003) (noting ''a trend toward denying the conclusive or absolute nature of the presumption against the possibility of issue being extinct where there is competent evidence to the contrary has *(cont'd)*

Table 10
Rule Against Perpetuities *(continued)*

	ARKANSAS	*CALIFORNIA*	*COLORADO*
19. Is there a conclusive presumption of fertility, that is, the "fertile octogenarian" rule? (cont'd)	1285 (2003) (noting "a trend toward denying the conclusive or absolute nature of the presumption against the possibility of issue being extinct where there is competent evidence to the contrary has developed in the decisions, although some courts still adhere to the traditional view treating the presumption as conclusive or absolute").	*Extinct*, 98 A.L.R.2d 1285 (2003) (noting "a trend toward denying the conclusive or absolute nature of the presumption against the possibility of issue being extinct where there is competent evidence to the contrary has developed in the decisions, although some courts still adhere to the traditional view treating the presumption as conclusive or absolute").	developed in the decisions, although some courts still adhere to the traditional view treating the presumption as conclusive or absolute").
20. What is the earliest age a child is deemed capable of bearing a child? What is the impact of illegitimacy?	Not specifically addressed by USRAP, but the reasoning is the same as set forth in the comment to section 1 of USRAP, 2, Technical Violations of the Common Law Rule. Wait and see will typically result in no violation. Nevertheless, the common law rule ordinarily will be applied initially. Under the rule, courts must presume that living persons are capable of having or fathering children, no matter how young they are. *See* In re Graite's Will Trusts, [1949] 1 All E.R. 459, 460 (Ch.). Thus, the rule strikes down any interest	Not specifically addressed by USRAP, but the reasoning is the same as set forth in the comment to section 1 of USRAP, 2, Technical Violations of the Common Law Rule. Wait and see will typically result in no violation. Nevertheless, the common law rule ordinarily will be applied initially. Under the rule, courts must presume that living persons are capable of having or fathering children, no matter how young they are. *See* In re Graite's Will Trusts, [1949] 1 All E.R. 459, 460 (Ch.). Thus, the rule strikes	Not specifically addressed by USRAP, but the reasoning is the same as set forth in the comment to section 1 of USRAP, 2, Technical Violations of the Common Law Rule. Wait and see will typically result in no violation. Nevertheless, the common law rule ordinarily will be applied initially. Under the rule, courts must presume that living persons are capable of having or fathering children, no matter how young they are. *See* In re Graite's Will Trusts, [1949] 1 All E.R. 459, 460 (Ch.). Thus, the rule strikes down any interest whose vesting depends on the assertion that, for example, a

	whose vesting depends on the assertion that, for example, a toddler will not have children. (Keith L. Butler, Notes & Comments, *Long Live the Dead Hand: A Case for the Repeal of the Rule Against Perpetuities in Washington*, 75 Wash. L. Rev. 1237, 1246 n.78 (2000)).	down any interest whose vesting depends on the assertion that, for example, a toddler will not have children. (Keith L. Butler, Notes & Comments, *Long Live the Dead Hand: A Case for the Repeal of the Rule Against Perpetuities in Washington*, 75 Wash. L. Rev. 1237, 1246 n.78 (2000)).	toddler will not have children. (Keith L. Butler, Notes & Comments, *Long Live the Dead Hand: A Case for the Repeal of the Rule Against Perpetuities in Washington*, 75 Wash. L. Rev. 1237, 1246 n.78 (2000)).
21. *Is the "unborn widow" rule observed?*	Yes. (Dickerson v. Union Nat'l Bank, 595 S.W.2d 677, 680 (Ark. 1980) *See also* Unif. Statutory Rule Against Perpetuities §1, 8B U.L.A. 246 (amended 1990) (explaining that "[t]he chance that [an] interest will become invalid under the Statutory Rule is small" and so the unborn widow rule would rarely invalidate an interest); *see also* 61 Am Jur 2d *Perpetuities and Restraints on Alienation* §40 (2003) (noting the same).	No specific state case or statute. *See* Unif. Statutory Rule Against Perpetuities § 1, 8B U.L.A. 246 (amended 1990) (explaining that "[t]he chance that [an] interest will become invalid under the Statutory Rule is small" and so the unborn widow rule would rarely invalidate an interest); *see also* 61 Am Jur 2d *Perpetuities and Restraints on Alienation* § 40 (2003) (noting the same).	No specific state case or statute. *See* Unif. Statutory Rule Against Perpetuities § 1, 8B U.L.A. 246 (amended 1990) (explaining that "[t]he chance that [an] interest will become invalid under the Statutory Rule is small" and so the unborn widow rule would rarely invalidate an interest); *see also* 61 Am Jur 2d *Perpetuities and Restraints on Alienation* § 40 (2003) (noting the same).
22. *Does the "slothful executor" rule apply, i.e., an administrative contingency clause providing for a "distribution to, e.g., those issue living at the time of the satisfaction of the administrative condition precedent?"*	No specific state case or statute. *See* Unif. Statutory Rule Against Perpetuities §1, 8B U.L.A. 245 (amended 1990) (Under USRAP, an "interest becomes invalid only if it remains in existence and nonvested 90 years after [the testator's] death. Since it is almost certain that the final distribution *(cont'd)*	No. Estate of Taylor, 428 P. 2d 301, 303 (Cal. 1967) ("In the absence of any indication to the contrary a testator contemplates prompt distribution. His intention is substantially complied with if a beneficiary who is alive at the time distribution could and should have occurred *(cont'd)*	No. Miller v. Weston, 189 P. 610, 612-613 (Colo. 1920) (validating a will despite an administrative contingency clause). *See also* Unif. Statutory Rule Against Perpetuities § 1, 8B U.L.A. 245 (amended 1990) (Under USRAP an "interest becomes invalid only if it remains in existence and nonvested 90 years after [the *(cont'd)*

Table 10
Rule Against Perpetuities *(continued)*

	ARKANSAS	*CALIFORNIA*	*COLORADO*
22. *Does the "slothful executor" rule apply, i.e., an administrative contingency clause providing for a "distribution to, e.g., those issue living at the time of the satisfaction of the administrative condition precedent?" (cont'd)*	of [an] estate will occur well within this 90-year period, the chance that [an] interest will be invalid is negligible.")	is allowed to take under the will.") *See also* Unif. Statutory Rule Against Perpetuities § 1, 8B U.L.A. 245 (amended 1990) (Under USRAP an "interest becomes invalid only if it remains in existence and nonvested 90 years after [the testator's] death. Since it is almost certain that the final distribution of [an] estate will occur well within this 90-year period, the chance that [an] interest will be invalid is negligible.")	testator's] death. Since it is almost certain that the final distribution of [an] estate will occur well within this 90-year period, the chance that [an] interest will be invalid is negligible.")
23. *Does the all-or-nothing rule apply to class gifts?*	No specific state case or statute. *See* Unif. Statutory Rule Against Perpetuities §1, 8B U.L.A. 257 (amended 1990) ("Although this Act does not supersede the basic idea of the much-maligned 'all-or-nothing' rule, the evils sometimes attributed to it are substantially if not entirely eliminated by the wait-and-see feature of the Statutory	Sometimes. Estate of Ghiglia, 116 Cal. Rptr. 827, 832 (Cal. Ct. App. 1974) (citations omitted) (explaining that the test to sever an invalid part of a class gift from the valid "is 'whether the two [parts] are so parts of a single plan or scheme or otherwise so dependent one upon the other, that by avoiding the invalid provisions and allowing the valid to stand there will result a	No specific state case or statute. *See* Unif. Statutory Rule Against Perpetuities § 1, 8B U.L.A. 257 (amended 1990) ("Although this Act does not supersede the basic idea of the much-maligned 'all-or-nothing' rule, the evils sometimes attributed to it are substantially if not entirely eliminated by the wait-and-see feature of the Statutory Rule and by the availability of reformation under Section 3.")

	Rule and by the availability of reformation under Section 3.'').	disposition of the estate so different from what the testator contemplated or so unreasonable that it must be presumed that [he] would not have made the valid provisions if he had been aware of the invalidity of the others' ''). *See also* Unif. Statutory Rule Against Perpetuities § 1, 8B U.L.A. 257 (amended 1990) (''Although this Act does not supersede the basic idea of the much-maligned 'all-or-nothing' rule, the evils sometimes attributed to it are substantially if not entirely eliminated by the wait-and-see feature of the Statutory Rule and by the availability of reformation under Section 3.'')	
24. *Is there an exception to the all-or-nothing rule in the case of subclasses or specific sums to each member of the class?*	No specific state case or statute. *See* Unif. Statutory Rule Against Perpetuities § 1, 8B U.L.A. 257 (amended 1990) (''The specific-sum and sub-class doctrines are not superseded by this Act.'')	No specific state case or statute. *See* Unif. Statutory Rule Against Perpetuities § 1, 8B U.L.A. 257 (amended 1990) (''The specific-sum and sub-class doctrines are not superseded by this Act.'')	No specific state case or statute. *See* Unif. Statutory Rule Against Perpetuities § 1, 8B U.L.A. 257 (amended 1990) (''The specific-sum and sub-class doctrines are not superseded by this Act.'')
25. *Is the infectious invalidity rule followed outside class gifts?*	No specific state case or statute. *See* Unif. Statutory Rule Against Perpetuities §1, 8B U.L.A. 256 (amended 1990) (explaining that ''[t]he doctrine	No specific state case or statute. *See* Unif. Statutory Rule Against Perpetuities § 1, 8B U.L.A. 256 (amended 1990) (explaining that ''[t]he doctrine	Yes. Perry v. Brundage, 614 P. 2d 362, 366 (Colo. 1980); *But see* Unif. Statutory Rule Against Perpetuities § 1, 8B U.L.A. 256 (amended 1990) (explaining that ''[t]he doctrine of
	(cont'd)	*(cont'd)*	*(cont'd)*

Table 10
Rule Against Perpetuities *(continued)*

	ARKANSAS	CALIFORNIA	COLORADO
25. Is the infectious invalidity rule followed outside class gifts? (cont'd)	of infectious invalidity is superseded by this Act by Section 3, under which courts. . .are required to *reform* the disposition to approximate as closely as possible the transferor's. . .-plan of distribution.'')	of infectious invalidity is superseded by this Act by Section 3, under which courts . . . are required to *reform* the disposition to approximate as closely as possible the transferor's . . . plan of distribution.'')	infectious invalidity is superseded by this Act by Section 3, under which courts . . . are required to *reform* the disposition to approximate as closely as possible the transferor's . . . plan of distribution.'')
26. Is there a rule against the suspension of the power of alienation? If so, how is it stated?	Yes, as to restraints on alienation of property. Such restraints are void. *See* Casey v. Casey, 700 S.W.2d 46, 48 (Ark. 1985): Broach v. City of Hampton, 677 S.W.2d 851 (Ark. 1984).	Cal. Civ. Code § 715, which provided a rule against the suspension of the power of alienation was repealed in 1991. *See also* Cal. Civ. Code § 711 (''Conditions [of ownership] restraining alienation, when repugnant to the interest created, are void.'')	Reasonableness standard. Perry v. Brundage, 614 P. 2d 362, 366-67 (Colo. 1980) (''The common law doctrine of restraints on alienation is part of the common law in Colorado and prohibits 'unreasonable restraints.' '')
27. Effective date.	March 9, 2007. *See* Act 240, H.B. 1130, §5.	Effective for all interests and powers whenever created, except if validity determined in a judicial proceeding or settlement. (§ 21202)	May 31, 1991. (§ 15-11-1106(1)) The law is repealed effective July 1, 2008. Even prior to that date, an interest or power created after May 31, 1991 will be governed by the 1000-year rule against perpetuities and the 1000-year reform rule, as set

forth in §§ 15-11-1102.5 and 15-11-1104.5, unless a written election to preserve modified USRAP is delivered to the trustee prior to July 1, 2008. (§ 15-11-1106.5)

1. For questions # 19–25, *see also* § 21201 (noting that the state's USRAP supersedes the common law rule against perpetuities). This does not mean the common law is neglected, but only that it is the starting point in the analysis.

2. For questions # 19–25, *see also* § 15-11-1107(b) (noting that the state's USRAP supersedes the common law rule against perpetuities). This does not mean the common law is neglected, but only that it is the starting point in the analysis.

Table 10
Rule Against Perpetuities *(continued)*

	CONNECTICUT	*DELAWARE*	*DISTRICT OF COLUMBIA*
1. *Which rule is in effect: the common law rule, the Uniform Statutory Rule Against Perpetuities (USRAP), other law, or none?*	USRAP. (Conn. Gen. Stat. §§ 45a-490 – 45a-496; §§ 45a-502 – 45a-508)	Other. (25 §§ 501; 503)	USRAP. (D.C. Code Ann. §§ 19-901 – 19-907)
2. a. *Is the common law rule relevant to any interests?*	Yes, but only as the starting point of the analysis.	Yes, other than interests in trust. "The rule against perpetuities is defined in Taylor v. Crosson, 11 Del. Ch. 145, 98 A. 375 (1916) as follows: 'No interest is good unless it must vest, if at all, not later than twenty-one years after some life in being at the creation of the interest.'" In re Will of Greenwood, 268 A.2d 867, 868 (Del. 1970).	Yes, but only as the starting point of the analysis.
b. *What is the relevant rule?*	A nonvested property interest is invalid unless: (1) When the interest is created, it is certain to vest or terminate no later than twenty-one years after the death of an individual then alive; or (2) the interest either vests or terminates within ninety years after its creation. (§ 45a-491(a))	With respect to trusts, the rule is: (a) No interest created in real property held in trust shall be void by reason of the com mon law rule against perpetuities and no interest created in personal property held in trust shall be void by reason of any rule against perpetuities whether the common law rule or otherwise. (25 § 1503(a))	A nonvested property interest is invalid unless: (1) When the interest is created, it is certain to vest or terminate no later than twenty-one years after the death of an individual then alive; or (2) the interest either vests or terminates within ninety years after its creation. (§ 19-901(a))

(b) In this State, the rule against perpetuities for real property held in trust is that at the expiration of 110 years from the later of the date on which a parcel of real property or an interest in real property is added to or purchased by a trust or the date the trust became irrevocable, such parcel or interest, if still held in such trust, shall be distributed in accordance with the trust instrument regarding distribution of such property upon termination of the trust as though termination occur-red at that time, or if no such provisions exist, to the persons then entitled to receive the income of the trust in proportion to the amount of the income so receivable by such beneficiaries, or in equal shares if specific proportions are not specified in the trust instrument.

(25 § 503(b)) Note that real property does not include intangible personal property such as an interest in a corporation, limited liability company, partnership, statutory trust, business trust or other entity, regardless whether the entity owns real property or an interest therein. (25 § 503(d))

Table 10
Rule Against Perpetuities *(continued)*

	CONNECTICUT	DELAWARE	DISTRICT OF COLUMBIA
3. *Does the rule apply to other than private trusts?*	Yes. The rule applies except to: (1) A nonvested property interest or a power of appointment arising out of a nondonative transfer, except a nonvested property interest or a power of appointment arising out of (A) a premarital or postmarital agreement, (B) a spouse's election, (C) a similar arrangement arising out of a prospective, existing or previous marital relationship between the parties, (D) a contract to make or not to revoke a will or trust, (E) a contract to exercise or not to exercise a power of appointment, (F) a transfer in satisfaction of a duty of support, or (H) a reciprocal transfer; (2) A fiduciary's power relating to the administration or management of assets, including the power of a fiduciary to sell, lease or mortgage property, and the	The rule does not apply to the following trusts, all of which may be perpetual: (1) A trust for the benefit of 1 or more charitable organizations; (2) A trust created by an employer as part of a stock bonus plan, pension plan, disability or death benefit plan or profit sharing plan for the exclusive benefit of some or all of its employees, to which contributions are made by such employer or employees, or both, for the purpose of distributing to such employees the earnings or the principal, or both earnings and principal, of the fund held in trust; (3) A statutory trust formed under Chapter 38 of Title 12 for which a certificate of statutory trust (akin to a Massachusetts business trust) is on file in the office of the Secretary of State; or (4) A trust of real or personal property created for the perpetual care of cemeteries	The rule applies except to: (1) A nonvested property interest or a power of appointment arising out of a nondonative transfer, except a nonvested property interest or a power of appointment arising out of: (A) A premarital or postmarital agreement; (B) A separation or divorce settlement; (C) A spouse's election under section 19-113; (D) A similar arrangement arising out of a prospective, existing, or previous marital relationship between the parties; (E) A contract to make or not to revoke a will or trust; (F) A contract to exercise or not to exercise a power of appointment; (G) A transfer in satisfaction of a duty of support; or (H) A reciprocal transfer; (2) A fiduciary's power relating to the administration or management of assets, including the power of a fiduciary to sell, lease, or mortgage property, and

power of a fiduciary to determine principal and income;

(3) A power to appoint a fiduciary;

(4) A discretionary power of a trustee to distribute principal before termination of a trust to a beneficiary having an indefeasibly vested interest in the income and principal;

(5) A nonvested property interest held by a charity, government or governmental agency or subdivision, if the nonvested property interest is preceded by an interest held by another charity, government or governmental agency or subdivision;

(6) A nonvested property interest in or a power of appointment with respect to a trust or other property arrangement forming part of a pension, profit-sharing, stock bonus, health, disability, death benefit, income deferral or other current or deferred benefit plan for one or more employees, independent contractors or their beneficiaries or spouses, to which contributions are made for the purpose of

(cont'd)

pursuant to the provisions of subchapter IV of Chapter 35 of Title 12.

(25 § 503(b))

the power of a fiduciary to determine principal and income;

(3) A power to appoint a fiduciary;

(4) A discretionary power of a trustee to distribute principal before termination of a trust to a beneficiary having an indefeasibly vested interest in the income and principal;

(5) A nonvested property interest held by a charity, government, or governmental agency or subdivision;

(6) A nonvested property interest in or a power of appointment with respect to a trust or other property arrangement forming part of a pension, profit-sharing, stock bonus, health, disability, death benefit, income deferral, or other current or deferred benefit plan for one or more employees, independent contractors, or their beneficiaries or spouses, to which contributions are made for the purpose of distributing to or for the benefit of the participants or their beneficiaries or spouses the property, income, or principal in the trust or other property arrangement, except a nonvested property interest or a power of appointment that is created by an election of a participant or a beneficiary or spouse;

(cont'd)

Table 10
Rule Against Perpetuities *(continued)*

	CONNECTICUT	DELAWARE	DISTRICT OF COLUMBIA
3. *Does the rule apply to other than private trusts? (cont'd)*	distributing to or for the benefit of the participants or their beneficiaries or spouses the property, income or principal in the trust or other property arrangement, except a non-vested property interest or a power of appointment that is created by an election of a participant or a beneficiary or spouse; or (7) A property interest, power of appointment or arrangement that was not subject to the common-law rule against perpetuities or is excluded by another statute of this state. (45a-494)		(7) A property interest, power of appointment, or arrangement that was not subject to the common-law rule against perpetuities or is excluded by another statute of the District of Columbia; (8) A gift of a present interest or devise to charitable uses; (9) In accordance with section 43-113, a grant, donation, or bequest for the embellishment, preservation, renewal, or repair of any tomb, monument, gravestone, or other structure, fence, railing, or other enclosure in or around any cemetary lot, or for the planting and cultivation of any trees, shrubs, flowers, or plants in or around any cemetery lot, according to the terms of such grant, donation, or bequest; or (10) A trust in which the governing instrument states that the provisions of this chapter do not apply to the trust and under which the trustee, or other person to whom the power is properly granted or delegated, has the power under the governing

			instrument, applicable statute, or common law to hold, sell, lease, or mortgage property for any period of time beyond the period that is required for an interest created under the governing instrument to vest. (§ 19-904)
4. *Does the rule invalidate the interest at its creation, or is the rule revised by a wait-and-see approach?*	Wait-and-see. (§ 45a-491(a)(2))	Wait-and-see for real property held in trust (25 § 503) and for interests created by the exercise of a power of appointment (25 § 501). Otherwise, the rule does not apply at all for interests in trust. For provisions subject to the common law rule, there is no wait-and-see provision.	Wait-and-see. (§ 19-901(a)(2))
5. *Can the trust be reformed?*	Yes, but only if one of the following conditions is satisfied: (1) A nonvested property interest or a power of appointment becomes invalid under section 45a-491 (see # 2b); (2) A class gift is not but might become invalid under section 45a-491 and the time has arrived when the share of any class member is to take effect in possession or enjoyment; or (3) A nonvested property interest that is not validated by *(cont'd)*	No specific state case or statute.	Yes, but only if one of the following conditions is satisfied: (1) A nonvested property interest or a power of appointment becomes invalid under section 19-901; (see # 2b); (2) A class gift is not but might become invalid under section 19-901 and the time has arrived when the share of any class member is to take effect in possession or enjoyment; or (3) A nonvested property interest that is not validated by section 19-901(a)(1), that is, the *(cont'd)*

Table 10
Rule Against Perpetuities *(continued)*

	CONNECTICUT	*DELAWARE*	*DISTRICT OF COLUMBIA*
5. Can the trust be reformed? (cont'd)	subdivision (1) of subsection (a) of section 45a-491, that is, the traditional common law rule, can vest but not within ninety years after its creation. (§ 45a-493) *See also* # 27.		traditional common law rule, can vest but not within 90 years after its creation. (§ 19-903) *See also* # 27.
6. If yes to 5., under what theory?	A court shall reform a disposition in the manner that most closely approximates the transferor's manifested plan of distribution and is within the ninety years allowed by subdivision (2) of subsection (a), (b) or (c) of section 45a-491. (§ 45a-493) However, if a nonvested property interest or a power of appointment that was created before October 1, 1989, and is determined in a judicial proceeding, commenced on or after October 1, 1989, to violate this state's rule against perpetuities as that rule existed before October 1, 1989, a court upon the petition of an interested person may reform the disposition in the manner that most closely	See # 5.	A court shall reform a disposition in the manner that most closely approximates the transferor's manifested plan of distribution and is within the 90 years allowed by section 19-901(a)(2), (b)(2), or (c)(2). (§19-903) However, if a nonvested property interest or a power of appointment was created before the effective date of this [April 27, 2001] chapter and is determined in a judicial proceeding, commenced on or after the effective date of this chapter, to violate the District of Columbia's rule against perpetuities as that rule existed before the effective date of this chapter [April 27, 2001], a court, upon the petition of an interested person, may reform the disposition in the manner that

	approximates the transferor's manifested plan of distribution and is within the limits of the rule against perpetuities applicable when the nonvested property interest or power of appointment was created.		most closely approximates the transferor's manifested plan of distribution and is within the limits of the rule against perpetuities applicable when the nonvested property interest or power of appointment was created.
7. *When is a general testamentary power of appointment invalid?*	A general testamentary power of appointment is invalid unless: (1) When the power is created, it is certain to be irrevocably exercised or otherwise to terminate no later than 21 years after the death of an individual then alive. (2) The power is irrevocably exercised or otherwise terminates within 90 years after its creation. (§ 45a-491(c))	With respect to wills, *see* Unif. Statutory Rule Against Perpetuities § 1, 8B U.L.A. 248 (amended 1990) (''Under the Common-law Rule . . . a *nongeneral power* (whether or not presently exercisable) or a *general testamentary power* is invalid as of the time of its creation if it *might* not terminate (by irrevocable exercise or otherwise) within a life in being plus 21 years.'') With respect to trusts, *see* # 2b above.	A general testamentary power of appointment is invalid unless: (1) When the power is created, it is certain to be irrevocably exercised or otherwise to terminate no later than 21 years after the death of an individual then alive. (2) The power is irrevocably exercised or otherwise terminates within 90 years after its creation. (§ 19-901(c))
8. *Same, but nongeneral testamentary power.*	A nongeneral power of appointment . . . is invalid unless: (1) When the power is created, it is certain to be irrevocably exercised or otherwise to terminate no later than 21 years after the death of an individual then alive. (2) The power is irrevocably exercised or otherwise terminates within 90 years after its creation. (§ 45a-491(c))	See # 7.	A nongeneral power of appointment . . . is invalid unless: (1) When the power is created, it is certain to be irrevocably exercised or otherwise to terminate no later than 21 years after the death of an individual then alive. (2) The power is irrevocably exercised or otherwise terminates within 90 years after its creation. (19-901(c))

Table 10
Rule Against Perpetuities *(continued)*

	CONNECTICUT	DELAWARE	DISTRICT OF COLUMBIA
9. *Same, but general inter vivos power.*	A general power of appointment not presently exercisable because of a condition precedent is invalid unless: (1) When the power is created, the condition precedent is certain to be satisfied or become impossible to satisfy no later than 21 years after the death of an individual then alive. (2) The condition precedent either is satisfied or becomes impossible to satisfy within 90 years after its creation. (§ 45a-491(b))	With respect to wills, *see* Unif. Statutory Rule Against Perpetuities § 1, 8B U.L.A. 248 (amended 1990) (''Under the Common-law Rule, a *general power not presently exercisable because of a condition precedent* is invalid as of the time of its creation if the condition *might* neither be satisfied nor become impossible to satisfy with a life in being plus 21 years.'') With respect to trusts, *see* # 2b above.	A general power of appointment not presently exercisable because of a condition precedent is invalid unless: (1) When the power is created, the condition precedent is certain to be satisfied or become impossible to satisfy no later than 21 years after the death of an individual then alive. (2) The condition precedent either is satisfied or becomes impossible to satisfy within 90 years after its creation. (§ 19-901(b))
10. *Same, but nongeneral inter vivos power.*	See # 8.	See # 7.	See # 8.
11. *Is a period of gestation added to the perpetuity period?*	No. The possibility that a child will be born to a person after that person's death is disregarded. (§ 45a-491(d)) *See also* Unif. Statutory Rule Against Perpetuities § 1, 8B U.L.A. 242-43 (amended 1990) (''[T]he possibility that a child will be born to [a testator] after his death must be disregarded; and the	Yes. (*See* Wilmington Trust Co. v. Sloane, 54 A.2d 544, 548 (Del. 1947)).[1]	No. The possibility that a child will be born to a person after that person's death is disregarded. (§ 19-901(d)) *See also* Unif. Statutory Rule Against Perpetuities § 1, 8B U.L.A. 242-43 (amended 1990) (''[T]he pos sibility that a child will be born to [a testator] after his death must be disregarded; and the possibility that a child will be born to any of [the

	possibility that a child will be born to any of [the testator's] descendants after their deaths must also be disregarded. Note, however, that the rule of subsection (d) does *not* apply to the question of the entitlement of an after-born child to take a beneficial interest in the trust'').		testator's] descendants after their deaths must also be disregarded. Note, however, that the rule of subsection (d) does*not* apply to the question of the entitlement of an after-born child to take a beneficial interest in the trust'').
12. *What is the treatment of a ''later of the traditional rule or 90 years'' clause? See UPC 2-901(e).*	That language is inoperative to the extent it produces a period of time that exceeds 21 years after the death of the survivor. (§ 45a-491(e))	N/A	The language is inoperative to the extent it produces a period of time that exceeds 21 years after the death of the survivor. (§ 19-901(e))
13. *When is an interest created by the exercise of a general testamentary power deemed created?*	Except as provided in subsections (b) and (c) of this section and in subsection (a) of section 45a-495, the time of creation of a nonvested property interest or a power of appointment is determined under general principles of property law. (§ 45a-492(a)) The first two of the excepted provisions states that as long as a person with a general power to become the unqualified beneficial owner has that power, the nonvested interest is created when the power terminates. The third of the excepted provisions states that a nonvested property interest, which arises from a transfer to an existing trust, is created *(cont'd)*	Every estate or interest in property, real or personal, created through the exercise, by will, deed or other instrument, of a power of appointment . . . shall, for the purpose of any rule of law against perpetuities, remoteness in vesting, restraint upon the power of alienation or accumulations now in effect or hereafter enacted be deemed to have been created at the time of the exercise and not at the time of the creation of such power of appointment. (25 § 501)	Except as provided in subsections (b) and (c) of this section and in section 19-905(a), the time of creation of a nonvested property interest or a power of appointment is determined under general principles of property law. (§ 19-902(a)) The first two of the excepted provisions states that as long as a person with a general power to become the unqualified beneficial owner has that power, the nonvested interest is created when the power terminates. The third of the excepted provisions states that a nonvested property interest, which arises from a transfer to an existing trust, is created when the nonvested property interest in the trust was created. *(cont'd)*

Table 10
Rule Against Perpetuities *(continued)*

	CONNECTICUT	DELAWARE	DISTRICT OF COLUMBIA
13. *When is an interest created by the exercise of a general testamentary power deemed created? (cont'd)*	when the nonvested property interest in the trust was created. *See also* Unif. Statutory Rule Against Perpetuities § 2, 8B U.L.A. 268 (amended 1990) (explaining that "general principles of property law determine that the time . . . [of creation] is at the decedent's death.") *See generally* § 45a-495(a) ("a nonvested property interest or a power of appointment created by the exercise of a power of appointment is created when the power is irrevocably exercised or when a revocable exercise becomes irrevocable.")		*See also* Unif. Statutory Rule Against Perpetuities § 2, 8B U.L.A. 268 (amended 1990) (explaining that "general principles of property law determine that the time . . . [of creation] is at the decedent's death.") *See generally* § 19-905(a) ("[A] nonvested property interest or a power of appointment created by the exercise of a power of appointment is created when the power is irrevocably exercised or when a revocable exercise becomes irrevocable.")
14. *Same, but nongeneral testamentary power.*	See # 13.	See # 13. However, if the power is over a trust that is not subject to the generation-skipping transfer tax or has a zero inclusion ratio, then the estate or interest created by the exercise of the power is deemed created at the creation of the power and not at its exercise. As for any power created by the exercise of the initial power, said power and any estate or interest created by its exercise are deemed created	See # 13.

		at the creation of the initial power. (25 § 504)	
15. Same, but general inter vivos power.	Except as provided in subsections (b) and (c) of this section and in subsection (a) of section 45a-495, the time of creation of a nonvested property interest or a power of appointment is determined under general principles of property law. (§ 45a-492(a)) *See also* Unif. Statutory Rule Against Perpetuities § 2, 8B U.L.A. 268 (amended 1990) (explaining that "the time when the interest or power is created is the date the transfer becomes effective for purposes of property law generally, normally the date of delivery of the deed"); Comment to Unif. Probate Code § 2-902(a) (stating same and adding "the funding of the trust" as "normally" the time when the interest is created). *See generally* § 45a-495(a) ("a nonvested property interest or a power of appointment created by the exercise of a power of appointment is created when the power is irrevocably exercised or when a revocable exercise becomes irrevocable.")	See # 13.	Except as provided in subsections (b) and (c) of this section and in section 19-905(a), the time of creation of a nonvested property interest or a power of appointment is determined under general principles of property law. (§ 19-902(a)) *See also* Unif. Statutory Rule Against Perpetuities § 2, 8B U.L.A. 268 (amended 1990) (explaining that "the time when the interest or power is created is the date the transfer becomes effective for purposes of property law generally, normally the date of delivery of the deed"); Comment to Unif. Probate Code § 2-902(a) (stating same and adding "the funding of the trust" as "normally" the time when the interest is created). *See generally* § 19-905(a) ("[A] nonvested property interest or a power of appointment created by the exercise of a power of appointment is created when the power is irrevocably exercised or when a revocable exercise becomes irrevocable.")

Table 10
Rule Against Perpetuities *(continued)*

	CONNECTICUT	*DELAWARE*	*DISTRICT OF COLUMBIA*
16. *Same, but nongeneral inter vivos power.*	See # 15.	See # 13. However, if the power is over a trust that is not subject to the generation-skipping transfer tax or has a zero inclusion ratio, then the estate or interest created by the exercise of the power is deemed created at the creation of the power and not at its exercise. As for any power created by the exercise of the initial power, said power and any estate or interest created by its exercise are deemed created at the creation of the initial power. (25 § 504)	See # 15.
17. *When is an interest created if the grantor of a trust has a power to revoke?*	For purposes of sections 45a-490 to 45a-496, inclusive, if there is a person who alone can exercise a power created by a governing instrument to become the unqualified beneficial owner of (1) a nonvested property interest or (2) a property interest subject to a power of appointment described in subsection (b) or (c) of section 45a-491, the nonvested property interest or power of appointment is created when the power to	Trusts created by the exercise of a power of appointment, whether limited or general, and whether by will, deed or other instrument, shall be deemed to have become irrevocable by the trustor or testator on the date on which such exercise became irrevocable. (25 § 503(c)) The donors of nongeneral powers are deemed the settlor or testator and the donees of general powers are likewise deemed the settlors and testators. If a trust	For purposes of this chapter, if there is a person who alone can exercise a power created by a governing instrument to become the unqualified beneficial owner of a nonvested property interest or a property interest subject to a power of appointment described in section 19-901(b) or (c), the nonvested property interest or power of appointment is created when the power to become the unqualified beneficial owner terminates. (§ 19-902(b))

	become the unqualified beneficial owner terminates. (§ 45a-492(b)) *See also* Unif. Statutory Rule Against Perpetuities § 2, 8B U.L.A. 268 (amended 1990) (explaining that "any nonvested property interest subject to [a power to revoke] is not created . . . until the power terminates (by release, expiration at the death of the donee, or otherwise"); Comment to Unif. Probate Code § 2-902(b) (noting that "nonvested property interest and powers of appointment created in [a revocable inter-vivos trust] are created when the power to revoke expires, usually at the settlor's death.") *See generally* § 45a-495(a) ("a nonvested property interest or a power of appointment created by the exercise of a power of appointment is created when the power is irrevocably exercised or when a revocable exercise becomes irrevocable.")	is created by a nongeneral exercise of a power, the trust is deemed to have become irrevocable on the date the power was created. (25 § 503(c))	*See also* Unif. Statutory Rule Against Perpetuities § 2, 8B U.L.A. 268 (amended 1990) (explaining that "any nonvested property interest subject to [a power to revoke] is not created . . . until the power terminates (by release, expiration at the death of the donee, or otherwise"); Comment to Unif. Probate Code § 2-902(b) (noting that "nonvested property interest and powers of appointment created in [a revocable inter-vivos trust] are created when the power to revoke expires, usually at the settlor's death.") *See generally* § 19-905(a) ("[A] nonvested property interest or a power of appointment created by the exercise of a power of appointment is created when the power is irrevocably exercised or when a revocable exercise becomes irrevocable.")
18. *When does the period of the rule start re an interest contributed to an irrevocable trust? See UPC 2-902(c).*	A nonvested property interest or a power of appointment arising from a transfer of property to a previously funded trust or other existing property arrangement is created when the nonvested *(cont'd)*	No statute or case law generally. However, see questions # 13–17 with regard to powers of appointment.	A nonvested property interest or a power of appointment arising from a transfer of property to a previously funded trust or other existing property arrangement is created when the nonvested property interest or *(cont'd)*

Table 10
Rule Against Perpetuities *(continued)*

	CONNECTICUT	*DELAWARE*	*DISTRICT OF COLUMBIA*
18. *When does the period of the rule start re an interest contributed to an irrevocable trust? See UPC 2-902(c). (cont'd)*	property interest or power of appointment in the original contribution was created. (§ 45a-492(c))		power of appointment in the original contribution was created. (§ 19-902(c))
19. *Is there a conclusive presumption of fertility, that is, the "fertile octogenarian" rule?*	Yes. Willimantic Investors, Inc. v. Covell, 156 A.2d 473, 475 (Conn. 1959) ("The presumption that the possibility of issue is never extinct so long as a person lives is settled law in this country as it pertains to the validity of titles and the distribution of property.") *See* Unif. Statutory Rule Against Perpetuities § 1, 8B U.L.A. 256 (amended 1990) (holding that "[t]his principle is not superseded by this Act, and in view of new advances in medical science . . . [this] is not unrealistic."); *but see* C. P. Jhong, Annotation, *Modern Status of Presumption of Possibility of Issue Being Extinct*, 98 A.L.R.2d 1285 (2003) (noting "a trend toward denying the conclusive or absolute nature of the presumption against the possibility of issue being extinct where there is competent	Yes. P v. Wilmington Trust Co., 188 A.2d 361, 364 (Del. Ch. 1962) (noting the "common law doctrine, usually applied in determining questions of remoteness of vesting but nonetheless clearly recognized in Delaware, that human beings are presumed to be capable of getting and bearing children regardless of age").[2]	Apparently not, even under the common law. *See* Whitney v. Groo, 40 App. D.C. 496, 497 (D.C. Cir. 1913) (finding that a title did not have a defect nor was it not marketable because of the remote contingency that a widow may have children after 70 years of age).[3] *See also* Unif. Statutory Rule Against Perpetuities § 1, 8B U.L.A. 256 (amended 1990) (holding that "[t]his principle is not superseded by this Act, and in view of new advances in medical science. . . [this] is not unrealistic.")); *but see* C. P. Jhong, Annotation, *Modern Status of Presumption of Possibility of Issue Being Extinct*, 98 A.L.R.2d 1285 (2003) (noting "a trend toward denying the conclusive or absolute nature of the presumption against the possibility of issue being extinct where there is competent evidence to the contrary has developed in the decisions, although some courts still adhere to the

	evidence to the contrary has developed in the decisions, although some courts still adhere to the traditional view treating the presumption as conclusive or absolute'').		traditional view treating the presumption as conclusive or absolute'').
20. *What is the earliest age a child is deemed capable of bearing a child? What is the impact of illegitimacy?*	Not specifically addressed by USRAP, but the reasoning is the same as set forth in the comment to section 1 of USRAP, 2, Technical Violations of the Common Law Rule. Wait and see will typically result in no violation. Nevertheless, the common law rule ordinarily will be applied initially. Under the rule, courts must presume that living persons are capable of having or fathering children, no matter how young they are. See In re Graite's Will Trusts, [1949] 1 All E.R. 459, 460 (Ch.). Thus, the rule strikes down any interest whose vesting depends on the assertion that, for example, a toddler will not have children. (Keith L. Butler, Notes & Comments, *Long Live the Dead Hand: A Case for the Repeal of the Rule Against Perpetuities in Washington*, 75 Wash. L. Rev. 1237, 1246 n.78 (2000)).	Under the rule, courts must presume that living persons are capable of having or fathering children, no matter how young they are. See In re Graite's Will Trusts, [1949] 1 All E.R. 459, 460 (Ch.). Thus, the rule strikes down any interest whose vesting depends on the assertion that, for example, a toddler will not have children. (Keith L. Butler, Notes & Comments, *Long Live the Dead Hand: A Case for the Repeal of the Rule Against Perpetuities in Washington*, 75 Wash. L. Rev. 1237, 1246 n.78 (2000)).	Not specifically addressed by USRAP, but the reasoning is the same as set forth in the comment to section 1 of USRAP, 2, Technical Violations of the Common Law Rule. Wait and see will typically result in no violation. Nevertheless, the common law rule ordinarily will be applied initially. Under the rule, courts must presume that living persons are capable of having or fathering children, no matter how young they are. *See* In re Graite's Will Trusts, [1949] 1 All E.R. 459, 460 (Ch.). Thus, the rule strikes down any interest whose vesting depends on the assertion that, for example, a toddler will not have children. (Keith L. Butler, Notes & Comments, *Long Live the Dead Hand: A Case for the Repeal of the Rule Against Perpetuities in Washington*, 75 Wash. L. Rev. 1237, 1246 n.78 (2000)).
21. *Is the ''unborn widow'' rule observed?*	No specific state case or statute. *See* Unif. Statutory Rule	*See, e.g.*, Arkansas, question # 21.	No specific state case or statute. *See* Unif. Statutory Rule Against

(cont'd)

(cont'd)

Table 10
Rule Against Perpetuities *(continued)*

	CONNECTICUT	*DELAWARE*	*DISTRICT OF COLUMBIA*
21. Is the "unborn widow" rule observed? (cont'd)	Against Perpetuities § 1, 8B U.L.A. 246 (amended 1990) (explaining that "[t]he chance that [an] interest will become invalid under the Statutory Rule is small" and so the unborn widow rule would rarely invalidate an interest); *see also* 61 Am Jur 2d *Perpetuities and Restraints on Alienation* § 40 (2003) (noting the same).		Perpetuities § 1, 8B U.L.A. 246 (amended 1990) (explaining that " [t]he chance that [an] interest will become invalid under the Statutory Rule is small" and so the unborn widow rule would rarely invalidate an interest); *see also* 61 Am Jur 2d *Perpetuities and Restraints on Alienation* § 40 (2003) (noting the same).
22. Does the "slothful executor" rule apply, i.e., an administrative contingency clause providing for a "distribution to e.g., those issue living at the time of the satisfaction of the administrative condition precedent?"	No. Belfield v. Booth, 27 A. 585, 588 (1893) (validating a will despite an administrative contingency clause and noting that "wills are not defeated by informality in the expression of the testator's wishes, where his substantial intent is apparent, and the estate which he seeks to create is not an unlawful one"). *See also* Unif. Statutory Rule Against Perpetuities § 1, 8B U.L.A. 245 (amended 1990) (Under USRAP an "interest becomes invalid only if it remains in existence and nonvested 90 years after [the testator's]	No. Asche v. Asche, 216 A.2d 272, 279 (Del. Ch. 1966) (affirming the Restatement rule that "when a will directs distribution to be made to persons to be ascertained 'on the probate of this will,' or 'on the conclusion of the administration of this estate', it is reasonable to infer that the testator has merely envisioned those preliminaries required by law prior to the time when distribution first becomes practicable and that the quoted language was not intended to postpone the ascertainment of the distributees by the injecting of a period of indefinite length.")	*See* Unif. Statutory Rule Against Perpetuities § 1, 8B U.L.A. 245 (amended 1990) (Under USRAP an "interest becomes invalid only if it remains in existence and nonvested 90 years after [the testator's] death. Since it is almost certain that the final distribution of [an] estate will occur well within this 90-year period, the chance that [an] interest will be invalid is negligible.")

	death. Since it is almost certain that the final distribution of [an] estate will occur well within this 90-year period, the chance that [an] interest will be invalid is negligible.'')		
23. *Does the all-or-nothing rule apply to class gifts?*	Yes. Warren v. Duval, 200 A.804, 806 (Conn. 1938). *See also* Unif. Statutory Rule Against Perpetuities § 1, 8B U.L. A. 257 (amended 1990) (''Although this Act does not supersede the basic idea of the much-maligned 'all-or-nothing' rule, the evils sometimes attributed to it are substantially if not entirely eliminated by the wait-and-see feature of the Statutory Rule and by the availability of reformation under Section 3.'')	Yes. Stuart v. Stuart, 106 A.2d 771, 773 (Del. Ch. 1953) (''If the gift is bad as to the class, even though some of the class are within the rule or even though, as it may later develop, all of the class may be within the rule, the gift is still bad.'')	No specific case or statute. *See* Unif. Statutory Rule Against Perpetuities § 1, 8B U.L.A. 257 (amended 1990) (''Although this Act does not supersede the basic idea of the much-maligned 'all-or-nothing' rule, the evils sometimes attributed to it are substantially if not entirely eliminated by the wait-and-see feature of the Statutory Rule and by the availability of reformation under Section 3.'')
24. *Is there an exception to the all-or-nothing rule in the case of subclasses or specific sums to each member of the class?*	No specific state case or statute. *See* Unif. Statutory Rule Against Perpetuities § 1, 8B U.L. A. 257 (amended 1990) (''The specific-sum and sub-class doctrines are not superseded by this Act.'')	*See* Unif. Statutory Rule Against Perpetuities § 2, 8B U.L.A. 257 (''The common law also recognizes a doctrine called the specific-sum doctrine which is derived from Storrs v. Benbow, 3 De G.M. & G. 390, 43 Eng. Rep 153 (Ch. 1853), and states: If a specified sum of money is to be paid to each member of a class, the interest of each class member is entitled to separate treatment and is valid or invalid under the Rule on its own. The common law also recognizes a doctrine called the sub-class	No specific case or statute. *See* Unif. Statutory Rule Against Perpetuities § 1, 8B U.L.A. 257 (amended 1990) (''The specific-sum and sub-class doctrines are not superseded by this Act.'')

(cont'd)

Table 10
Rule Against Perpetuities *(continued)*

	CONNECTICUT	DELAWARE	DISTRICT OF COLUMBIA
24. Is there an exception to the all-or-nothing rule in the case of subclasses or specific sums to each member of the class? (cont'd)		doctrine, which is derived from Cattlin v. Brown, 11 Hare 372, 68 Eng. Rep. 1318 (Ch. 1853), and states: If the ultimate takers are not described as a single class but rather as a group of separate subclasses, and if the share to which each separate subclass is entitled will finally be determined within the period of the Rule, the gifts to the different subclasses are separate for the purpose of the Rule.").	
25. Is the infectious invalidity rule followed outside class gifts?	No specific state case or statute. *See* Unif. Statutory Rule Against Perpetuities § 1, 8B U.L.A. 256 (amended 1990) (explaining that "[t]he doctrine of infectious invalidity is superseded by this Act by Section 3, under which courts . . . are required to *reform* the disposition to approximate as closely as possible the transferor's . . . plan of distribution.")	*See, e.g.*, Colorado, question # 25.	No specific case or statute. *See* Unif. Statutory Rule Against Perpetuities § 1, 8B U.L.A. 256 (amended 1990) (explaining that "[t]he doctrine of infectious invalidity is superseded by this Act by Section 3, under which courts . . . are required to *reform* the disposition to approximate as closely as possible the transferor's . . . plan of distribution.")

26. Is there a rule against the suspension of the power of alienation? If so, how is it stated?	No specific state statute. Case law unclear. See Tappan's Appeal, 52 Conn. 412, 420 (1885) (stating that a statute at that time provided that "suspension may be made during any number of lives in being when the will is made creating the suspension, and during such a period afterwards as will leave it impossible for the estate to be carried by the terms of the will to parties not in being when the will was made and not the immediate issue of parties then in being").	No specific case on real property. *See* Tracey v. Franklin, 67 A.2d 56, 59 (Del. 1949) (explaining in the case of personal property, "arbitrary restraints on alienation are forbidden and unless restraints are imposed for purposes recognized as sufficient, they will be held invalid.") Note also that provisions directing or authorizing accumulations are valid. (25 § 506)	D.C. Code Ann. § 42-302, which provided a rule against the suspension of the power of alienation, was repealed in 2001.
27. Effective date.	October 1, 1989. (§ 45a-495(a)) *See also* # 6.	The exemption from the rule against perpetuities is effective with respect to trusts becoming irrevocable on or after July 7, 1995. The provisions relating to powers of appointment and the Delaware Tax Trap, *see* # 14 & 16, are effective with respect to powers exercised after July 6, 2000, regardless of when the power was created.	April 27, 2001. (§19-905(a)) *See also* # 6.

1. The USRAP provision stating that the common law rule against perpetuities has been superseded is omitted in the Connecticut law.

2. The answers to questions # 19–25 are not likely to apply in most cases because of the abolition of the rule with respect to the vast majority of trusts.

3. For questions, # 19–25, *see also* § 19-906 (noting that the state's USRAP supersedes the common law rule against perpetuities). This does not mean that the common law is neglected, only that it is the starting point in the analysis.

Table 10
Rule Against Perpetuities *(continued)*

	FLORIDA	GEORGIA	HAWAII
1. *Which rule is in effect: the common law rule, the Uniform Statutory Rule Against Perpetuities (USRAP), other law, or none?*	USRAP. (Fla. Stat. § 689.225)	USRAP. (Ga. Code Ann. §§ 44-6-200 – 44-6-206)	USRAP. (Haw. Rev. Stat. Ann. §§ 525-1 – 525-6)
2. a. *Is the common law rule relevant to any interests?*	Yes, but is only as the starting point of the analysis.	Yes, but is only as the starting point of the analysis.	Yes, but is only as the starting point of the analysis.
b. *What is the relevant rule?*	A nonvested property interest in real or personal property is invalid unless: (1) When the interest is created, it is certain to vest or terminate no later than 21 years after the death of an individual then alive; or (2) The interest either vests or terminates within 90 years after its creation. (§ 689.225(2)(a)) However, as to any trust created after December 31, 2003, 90 years is changed to 360 years. (§ 689.225(3)(b))	A nonvested property interest is invalid unless: (1) When the interest is created, it is certain either to vest or to terminate within the lifetime of an individual then alive or within 21 years after the death of that individual; or (2) The interest either vests or terminates within 90 years after its creation. (§ 44-6-201(a))	A nonvested property interest is invalid unless: (1) When the interest is created, it is certain to vest or terminate no later than 21 years after the death of an individual then alive; or (2) The interest either vests or terminates within 90 years after its creation. (§ 525-1(a))
3. *Does the rule apply to other than private trusts?*	Yes. The rule applies except to: (a) A nonvested property interest or a power of appointment arising out of a nondonative transfer, except a nonvested	Yes. The rule applies except to: (1) A nonvested property interest or a power of appointment arising out of a nondonative transfer, except a nonvested property	Yes. The rule applies except to: (1) A fiduciary's power to sell, lease, or mortgage property, and the power of a fiduciary to determine principal and income;

property interest or a power of appointment arising out of:

1. A premarital or postmarital agreement;
2. A separation or divorce settlement;
3. A spouse's election;
4. A similar arrangement arising out of a prospective, existing, or previous marital relationship between the parties;
5. A contract to make or not to revoke a will or trust;
6. A contract to exercise or not to exercise a power of appointment;
7. A transfer in satisfaction of a duty of support; or
8. A reciprocal transfer;

(b) A fiduciary's power relating to the administration or management of assets, including the power of a fiduciary to sell, lease, or mortgage property, and the power of a fiduciary to determine principal and income;

(c) A power to appoint a fiduciary;

(d) A discretionary power of a trustee to distribute principal before termination of a trust to a beneficiary having an

(cont'd)

interest or a power of appointment arising out of:

(A) A premarital or postmarital agreement;

(B) A separation or divorce settlement;

(C) A spouse's election;

(D) A similar arrangement arising out of a prospective, existing, or previous marital relationship between the parties;

(E) A contract to make or not to revoke a will or trust;

(F) A contract to exercise or not to exercise a power of appointment;

(G) A transfer in satisfaction of a duty of support; or

(H) A reciprocal transfer;

(2) A fiduciary's power relating to the administration or management of assets, including the power of a fiduciary to sell, lease, or mortgage property, and the power of a fiduciary to determine principal and income;

(3) A power to appoint a fiduciary;

(4) A discretionary power of a trustee to distribute

(cont'd)

(2) A discretionary power of a trustee to distribute principal before termination of a trust;

(3) A nonvested property interest held by a charity, government, or governmental agency or subdivision, if the nonvested property interest is preceded by an interest held by another charity, government, or governmental agency or subdivision;

(4) A property interest in or a power of appointment with respect to a pension, profit-sharing, stock bonus, health, disability, death benefit, income deferral, or other current or deferred benefit plan for one or more employees, independent contractors, or their beneficiaries or spouses; or

(5) A property interest, power of appointment, or arrangement that was not subject to the common-law rule against perpetuities or is excluded by any other applicable law.

(§ 525-4)

Table 10
Rule Against Perpetuities *(continued)*

	FLORIDA	*GEORGIA*	*HAWAII*
3. Does the rule apply to other than private trusts? (cont'd)	indefeasibly vested interest in the income and principal; (e) A nonvested property interest held by a charity, government, or governmental agency or subdivision, if the nonvested property interest is preceded by an interest held by another charity, government, or governmental agency or subdivision; (f) A nonvested property interest in, or a power of appointment with respect to, a trust or other property arrangement forming part of a pension, profit-sharing, stock bonus, health, disability, death benefit, income deferral, or other current or deferred benefit plan for one or more employees, independent contractors, or their beneficiaries or spouses, to which contributions are made for the purpose of distributing to or for the benefit of the participants, or their beneficiaries or spouses, the property, income, or principal in the trust or other	principal before termination of a trust to a beneficiary having an indefeasibly vested interest in the income and principal. Nothing contained in paragraphs (2) and (3) of this Code section and this paragraph shall be construed to permit the fiduciary to continue the administration or management of assets once the nonvested property interest becomes invalid as described in subsection (a) of 44-6-201 (5) A nonvested property interest held by a charity, government, or governmental agency or subdivision, if the nonvested property interest is preceded by an interest held by another charity, government, or governmental agency or subdivision; (6) A nonvested property interest in or a power of appointment with respect to a trust or other property arrangement forming part of a pension, profit-sharing, stock	

	property arrangement, except a nonvested property interest or a power of appointment that is created by an election of a participant or a beneficiary or spouse; or (g) A property interest, power of appointment, or arrangement that was not subject to the common-law rule against perpetuities or is excluded by another statute of this state. (§ 689.225(5))	bonus, health, disability, death benefit, income deferral, or other current or deferred benefit plan for one or more employees, independent contractors, or their beneficiaries or spouses, to which contributions are made for the purpose of distributing to or for the benefit of the participants or their beneficiaries or spouses the property, income, or principal in the trust or other property arrangement, except a nonvested property interest or a power of appointment that is created by an election of a participant or a beneficiary or spouse; or (7) A property interest, power of appointment, or arrangement that was not subject to the common-law rule against perpetuities or is excluded by another statute of this state. (§ 44-6-204)	
4. *Does the rule invalidate the interest at its creation, or is the rule revised by a wait-and-see approach?*	Wait-and-see. (§ 689.225(2)(a)(2))	Wait-and-see. (§ 44-6-201(a)(2))	Wait-and-see. (§ 525-1(a)(2))

Table 10
Rule Against Perpetuities *(continued)*

	FLORIDA	*GEORGIA*	*HAWAII*
5. *Can the trust be reformed?*	Yes, but only if one of the following conditions applies: (a) A nonvested property interest or a power of appointment becomes invalid under subsection (2) (see # 2b); (b) A class gift is not but might become invalid under subsection (2) and the time has arrived when the share of any class member is to take effect in possession or enjoyment; or (c) A nonvested property interest that is not validated by subparagraph (2)(a), that is, the traditional common law rule, can vest but not within 90 years after its creation. (§ 689.225(4)) *See also* # 27.	Yes, but only if one of the following conditions applies: (1) A nonvested property interest or a power of appointment becomes invalid under Code Section 44-6-201 (see # 2b); (2) A class gift is not but might still become invalid under Code Section 44-6-201 and the time has arrived when the share of any class member is to take effect in possession or enjoyment; or (3) A nonvested property interest that is not validated by paragraph (1) of subsection (a) of Code Section 44-6-201, that is, the traditional common law rule, can vest, but not within 90 years after its creation. (§ 44-6-203) *See also* # 27.	Yes, but only if one of the following conditions applies: (1) A nonvested property interest or a power of appointment becomes invalid under section 525-1 (see # 2b); (2) A class gift is not but might become invalid under section 525-1 and the time has arrived when the share of any class member is to take effect in possession or enjoyment; or (3) A nonvested property interest that is not validated by section 525-1(a)(1), that is, the traditional common law rule, can vest but not within 90 years after its creation. (§ 525-3) *See also* # 27.
6. *If yes to 5., under what theory?*	A court shall reform a disposition in the manner that most closely approximates the transferor's manifested plan of distribution and is within the 90 years	A court shall reform a disposition in the manner that most closely approximates the transferor's manifested plan of distribution and is within the 90 years	A court shall reform a disposition in the manner that most closely approximates the transferor's manifested plan of distribution and is within the ninety years allowed by

	allowed by subparagraph (2)(a)2., subparagraph (2)(b)2., or subparagraph (2)(c)2. (§ 689.225(4)) *See also* § 689.225(6)(c) ("If a nonvested property interest or a power of appointment was created before October 1, 1988, and is determined in a judicial proceeding commenced on or after October 1, 1988, to violate this state's rule against perpetuities as that rule existed before October 1, 1988, a court, upon the petition of an interested person, may reform the disposition in the manner that most closely approximates the transferor's manifested plan of distribution and is within the limits of the rule against perpetuities applicable when the nonvested property interest or power of appointment was created.")	allowed by paragraph (2) of subsection (a), paragraph (2) of subsection (b), or paragraph (2) of subsection (c) of Code Section 44-6-201. (§ 44-6-203) *See also* § 44-6-205(b) ("With respect to a nonvested property interest or a power of appointment that was created before May 1, 1990, and that violates this state's rule against perpetuities as that rule existed before May 1, 1990, a court upon the petition of an interested party may exercise its equitable power to reform the disposition in the manner that most closely approximates the transferor's manifested plan of distribution and is within the limits of the rule against perpetuities applicable when the nonvested property interest or power of appointment was created.")	section 525-1(a)(2), (b)(2), or (c)(2). (§ 525-3) *See also* § 525-5(b) ("If a nonvested property interest or a power of appointment was created before June 18, 1992, and is determined in a judicial proceeding, commenced on or after June 18, 1992, to violate this State's common law rule against perpetuities as that rule existed before June 18, 1992, a court upon the petition of an interested person may reform the disposition in the manner that most closely approximates the transferor's manifested plan of distribution and is within the limits of the rule against perpetuities applicable when the nonvested property interest or power of appointment [sic] was created.")
7. *When is a general testamentary power of appointment invalid?*	A general testamentary power of appointment is invalid unless one of the following conditions is satisfied: (1) When the power is created, it is certain to be irrevocably exercised or otherwise to terminate no later than 21 years after the death of an individual then alive.	A general testamentary power of appointment is invalid unless: (1) When the power is created, it is certain to be irrevocably exercised or otherwise to terminate within the lifetime of an individual then alive or within 21 years after the death of that individual; or	A general testamentary power of appointment is invalid unless one of the following conditions is satisfied: (1) When the power is created, it is certain to be irrevocably exercised or otherwise to terminate no later than 21 years after the death of an individual then alive. (2) The power is irrevocably exercised or otherwise terminates
	(cont'd)	*(cont'd)*	*(cont'd)*

Table 10
Rule Against Perpetuities *(continued)*

	FLORIDA	GEORGIA	HAWAII
7. *When is a general testamentary power of appointment invalid? (cont'd)*	(2) The power is irrevocably exercised or otherwise terminates within 90 years after its creation. (§ 689.225(2)(c))	(2) The power is irrevocably exercised or otherwise terminates within 90 years after its creation. (§ 44-6-201(c))	within 90 years after its creation. (§ 525-1(c))
8. *Same, but nongeneral testamentary power.*	A nongeneral power of appointment . . . is invalid unless one of the following conditions is satisfied: (1) When the power is created, it is certain to be irrevocably exercised or otherwise to terminate no later than 21 years after the death of an individual then alive. (2) The power is irrevocably exercised or otherwise terminates within 90 years after its creation. (§ 689.225(2)(c))	A nongeneral power of appointment . . . is invalid unless: (1) When the power is created, it is certain to be irrevocably exercised or otherwise to terminate within the lifetime of an individual then alive or within 21 years after the death of that individual; or (2) The power is irrevocably exercised or otherwise terminates within 90 years after its creation. (§ 44-6-201(c))	A nongeneral power of appointment . . . is invalid unless one of the following conditions is satisfied: (1) When the power is created, it is certain to be irrevocably exercised or otherwise to terminate no later than 21 years after the death of an individual then alive. (2) The power is irrevocably exercised or otherwise terminates within 90 years after its creation. (§ 525-1(c))
9. *Same, but general inter vivos power.*	A general power of appointment not presently exercisable because of a condition precedent is invalid unless one of the following conditions is satisfied: (1) When the power is created, the condition precedent is certain to be satisfied or	A general power of appointment not presently exercisable because of a condition precedent is invalid unless: (1) When the power is created, the condition precedent is certain either to be satisfied or to become impossible to	A general power of appointment not presently exercisable because of a condition precedent is invalid unless one of the following conditions is satisfied: (1) When the power is created, the condition precedent is certain to be satisfied or become

	become impossible to satisfy no later than 21 years after the death of an individual then alive. (2) The condition precedent either is satisfied or becomes impossible to satisfy within 90 years after its creation. (689.225(2)(b))	satisfy within the lifetime of an individual then alive or within 21 years after the death of that individual; or (2) The condition precedent either is satisfied or becomes impossible to satisfy within 90 years after its creation. (§ 44-6-201(b))	impossible to satisfy no later than 21 years after the death of an individual then alive. (2) The condition precedent either is satisfied or becomes impossible to satisfy within 90 years after its creation. (§ 525-1(b))
10. *Same, but nongeneral inter vivos power.*	See # 8.	See # 8.	See # 8.
11. *Is a period of gestation added to the perpetuity period?*	No. The possibility that a child will be born to a person after that person's death is disregarded. (§ 689.225(2)(d)) *See also* Unif. Statutory Rule Against Perpetuities § 1, 8B U.L. A. 242-43 (amended 1990) ("[T]he possibility that a child will be born to [a testator] after his death must be disregarded; and the possibility that a child will be born to any of [the testator's] descendants after their deaths must also be disregarded. Note, however, that the rule of subsection (d) does *not* apply to the question of the entitlement of an after-born child to take a beneficial interest in the trust").	No. The possibility that a child will be born to a person after that person's death is disregarded (§ 44-6-201(d)) *See also* Unif. Statutory Rule Against Perpetuities § 1, 8B U.L. A. 242-43 (amended 1990) ("[T]he possibility that a child will be born to [a testator] after his death must be disregarded; and the possibility that a child will be born to any of [the testator's] descendants after their deaths must also be disregarded. Note, however, that the rule of subsection (d) does *not* apply to the question of the entitlement of an after-born child to take a beneficial interest in the trust").	No. The possibility that a child will be born to a person after that person's death is disregarded (§ 525-1(d)) *See also* Unif. Statutory Rule Against Perpetuities § 1, 8B U.L.A. 242-43 (amended 1990) ("[T]he possibility that a child will be born to [a testator] after his death must be disregarded; and the possibility that a child will be born to any of [the testator's] descendants after their deaths must also be disregarded. Note, however, that the rule of subsection (d) does *not* apply to the question of the entitlement of an after-born child to take a beneficial interest in the trust").

Table 10
Rule Against Perpetuities *(continued)*

	FLORIDA	*GEORGIA*	*HAWAII*
12. *What is the treatment of a "later of the traditional rule or 90 years" clause? See UPC 2-901(e).*	The language is inoperative to the extent it produces a period of time that exceeds 21 years after the death of the survivor. (§ 689.225(2)(e))	Georgia's USRAP does not specify how it will treat "later of" clauses.	The language is inoperative to the extent it produces a period of time that exceeds 21 years after the death of the survivor of the specified lives. (§ 525-1(e))
13. *When is an interest created by the exercise of a general testamentary power deemed created?*	Except as provided in paragraphs (b), (d), and (e) of this subsection and in paragraph (a) of subsection (6), the time of creation of a nonvested property interest or a power of appointment is determined under general principles of property law. (§ 689.225(3)(a)) The first two of the excepted provisions states that as long as a person with a general power to become the unqualified beneficial owner has that power, the nonvested interest is created when the power terminates. The third of the excepted provisions states that a nonvested property interest, which arises from a transfer to an existing trust, is created when the nonvested property interest in the trust was created. *See also* Unif. Statutory Rule Against Perpetuities § 2, 88 U.L.A. 268 (amended 1990)	Except as provided in subsections (b) and (c) of this Code section and in subsection (a) of Code Section 44-6-205, the time of creation of a nonvested property interest or a power of appointment is determined under general principles of property law. (§ 44-6-202(a)) The first two of the excepted provisions states that as long as a person with a general power to become the unqualified beneficial owner has that power, the nonvested interest is created when the power terminates. The third of the excepted provisions states that a nonvested property interest, which arises from a transfer to an existing trust, is created when the nonvested property interest in the trust was created. *See also* Unif. Statutory Rule Against Perpetuities § 2, 8B U.L.	Except as provided in subsections (b) and (c) and in section 525-5(a), the time of creation of a nonvested property interest or a power of appointment is determined under general principles of property law. (§ 525-2(a)) The first two of the excepted provisions states that as long as a person with a general power to become the unqualified beneficial owner has that power, the nonvested interest is created when the power terminates. The third of the excepted provisions states that a nonvested property interest, which arises from a transfer to an existing trust, is created when the nonvested property interest in the trust was created. *See also* Unif. Statutory Rule Against Perpetuities § 2, 8B U.L.A. 268 (amended 1990) (explaining that "general principles of property law determine that the time . . . [of creation] is at the decedent's death.")

(explaining that general principles of property law determine that the time [of creation] is at the decedent's death).

See also § 689.225(3)(e) (''if a nongeneral or testamentary power of appointment is exercised to create another nongeneral or testamentary power of appointment, every nonvested property interest or power of appointment created through the exercise of such other nongeneral or testamentary power is considered to have been created at the time of the creation of the first nongeneral or testamentary power of appointment''); Unif. Statutory Rule Against Perpetuities § 2, 8B U.L.A. 268 (amended 1990) (explaining that ''general principles of property law determine that the time . . . [of creation] is at the decedent's death.'')

See generally § 689.225(6)(a) (''For the purposes of this section, a nonvested property interest or a power of appointment created by the exercise of a power of appointment is created when the power is irrevocably exercised or when a revocable exercise becomes irrevocable.'')

A. 268 (amended 1990) (explaining that ''general principles of property law determine that the time . . . [of creation] is at the decedent's death.'')

See generally § 44-6-205(a) (''a nonvested property interest or a power of appointment created by the exercise of a power of appointment is created when the power is irrevocably exercised or when a revocable exercise becomes irrevocable.'')

See generally § 525-5(a) (''a nonvested property interest or a power of appointment created by the exercise of a power of appointment is created when the power is irrevocably exercised or when a revocable exercise becomes irrevocable.'')

Table 10
Rule Against Perpetuities *(continued)*

	FLORIDA	*GEORGIA*	*HAWAII*
14. *Same, but nongeneral testamentary power.*	See # 13.	See # 13.	See # 13.
15. *Same, but general inter vivos power.*	Except as provided in paragraphs (b), (d), and (e) of this subsection and in paragraph (a) of subsection (6), the time of creation of a nonvested property interest or a power of appointment is determined under general principles of property law. (§ 689.225(3)(a)) The first two of the excepted provisions states that as long as a person with a general power to become the unqualified beneficial owner has that power, the nonvested interest is created when the power terminates. The third of the excepted provisions states that a nonvested property interest, which arises from a transfer to an existing trust, is created when the nonvested property interest in the trust was created. *See also* § 689.225(3)(e) ("For purposes of this section, if a nongeneral or testamentary power of appointment is exercised to create another	Except as provided in subsections (b) and (c) of this Code section and in subsection (a) of Code Section 44-6-205, the time of creation of a nonvested property interest or a power of appointment is determined under general principles of property law. (§ 44-6-202(a)) The first two of the excepted provisions states that as long as a person with a general power to become the unqualified beneficial owner has that power, the nonvested interest is created when the power terminates. The third of the excepted provisions states that a nonvested property interest, which arises from a transfer to an existing trust, is created when the nonvested property interest in the trust was created. *See also* Unif. Statutory Rule Against Perpetuities § 2, 8B U.L.A. 268 (amended 1990) (explaining that "the time when	Except as provided in subsections (b) and (c) and in section 525-5(a), the time of creation of a nonvested property interest or a power of appointment is determined under general principles of property law. (§ 525-2(a)) The first two of the excepted provisions states that as long as a person with a general power to become the unqualified beneficial owner has that power, the nonvested interest is created when the power terminates. The third of the excepted provisions states that a nonvested property interest, which arises from a transfer to an existing trust, is created when the nonvested property interest in the trust was created. *See also* Unif. Statutory Rule Against Perpetuities § 2, 8B U.L.A. 268 (amended 1990) (explaining that "the time when the interest or power is created is the date the transfer becomes effective for purposes of property law generally, normally the date of delivery of the

	nongeneral or testamentary power of appointment, every nonvested property interest or power of appointment created through the exercise of such other nongeneral or testamentary power is considered to have been created at the time of the creation of the first nongeneral or testamentary power of appointment''); Unif. Statutory Rule Against Perpetuities § 2, 8B U.L.A. 268 (amended 1990) (explaining that ''the time when the interest or power is created is the date the transfer becomes effective for purposes of property law generally, normally the date of delivery of the deed''); Comment to Unif. Probate Code § 2-902(a) (stating same and adding ''the funding of the trust'' as ''normally'' the time when the interest is created). *See generally* § 689.225(6)(a) (''a nonvested property interest or a power of appointment created by the exercise of a power of appointment is created when the power is irrevocably exercised or when a revocable exercise becomes irrevocable.'')	the interest or power is created is the date the transfer becomes effective for purposes of property law generally, normally the date of delivery of the deed''); Comment to Unif. Probate Code § 2-902(a) (stating same and adding ''the funding of the trust'' as ''normally'' the time when the interest is created). *See generally* § 44-6-205(a) (''a nonvested property interest or a power of appointment created by the exercise of a power of appointment is created when the power is irrevocably exercised or when a revocable exercise becomes irrevocable.'')	deed''); Comment to Unif. Probate Code § 2-902(a) (stating same and adding ''the funding of the trust'' as ''normally'' the time when the interest is created). *See generally* § 525-5(a) (''a nonvested property interest or a power of appointment created by the exercise of a power of appointment is created when the power is irrevocably exercised or when a revocable exercise becomes irrevocable.'')
16. Same, but nongeneral inter vivos power.	See # 15.	See # 15.	See # 15.

Table 10
Rule Against Perpetuities *(continued)*

	FLORIDA	*GEORGIA*	*HAWAII*
17. *When is an interest created if the grantor of a trust has a power to revoke?*	If there is a person who alone can exercise a power created by a governing instrument to become the unqualified beneficial owner of a nonvested property interest or a property interest subject to a power of appointment described in paragraph (b) or paragraph (c) of subsection (2), the nonvested property interest or power of appointment is created when the power to become the unqualified beneficial owner terminates. (§ 689.225(3)(b)) *See also* Unif. Statutory Rule Against Perpetuities § 2, 8B U.L.A. 268 (amended 1990) (explaining that "any nonvested property interest subject to [a power to revoke] is not created . . . until the power terminates (by release, expiration at the death of the donee, or otherwise"); Comment to Unif. Probate Code § 2-902(b) (noting that "nonvested property interest and powers of appointment created in [a revocable inter-vivos trust] are created when	If there is a person who alone can exercise a power created by a governing instrument to become the unqualified beneficial owner of: (1) A nonvested property interest; or (2) A property interest subject to a power of appointment described in subsection (b) or (c) of Code Section 44-6-201, the nonvested property interest or power of appointment is created when the power to become the unqualified beneficial owner terminates. (§ 44-6-202(b)) *See also* Unif. Statutory Rule Against Perpetuities § 2, 8B U.L.A. 268 (amended 1990) (explaining that "any nonvested property interest subject to [a power to revoke] is not created . . . until the power terminates (by release, expiration at the death of the donee, or otherwise"); Comment to Unif. Probate Code § 2-902(b) (noting that "nonvested property interest and powers of	If there is a person who alone can exercise a power created by a governing instrument to become the unqualified beneficial owner of a nonvested property interest or a property interest subject to a power of appointment described in section 525-1(b) or (c), the nonvested property interest or power of appointment is created when the power to become the unqualified beneficial owner terminates. (§ 525-2(b)) *See also* Unif. Statutory Rule Against Perpetuities § 2, 8B U.L.A. 268 (amended 1990) (explaining that "any nonvested property interest subject to [a power to revoke] is not created . . . until the power terminates (by release, expiration at the death of the donee, or otherwise"); Comment to Unif. Probate Code § 2-902(b) (noting that "nonvested property interest and powers of appointment created in [a revocable inter-vivos trust] are created when the power to revoke expires, usually at the settlor's death"). *See generally* § 525-5(a) ("a nonvested property interest or a power

	the power to revoke expires, usually at the settlor's death''). *See generally* § 689.225(6)(a) (''a nonvested property interest or a power of appointment created by the exercise of a power of appointment is created when the power is irrevocably exercised or when a revocable exercisebecomes irrevocable.'')	appointment created in [a revocable inter-vivos trust] are created when the power to revoke expires, usually at the settlor's death''). *See generally* § 44-6-205(a) (''a nonvested property interest or a power of appointment created by the exercise of a power of appointment is created when the power is irrevocably exercised or when a revocable exercise becomes irrevocable.'')	of appointment created by the exercise of a power of appointment is created when the power is irrevocably exercised or when a revocable exercise becomes irrevocable.'')
18. *When does the period of the rule start re an interest contributed to an irrevocable trust? See UPC 2-902(c).*	A nonvested property interest or a power of appointment arising from a transfer of property to a previously funded trust or other existing property arrangement is created when the nonvested property interest or power of appointment in the original contribution was created. (§ 689.225(3)(d))	A nonvested property interest or a power of appointment arising from a transfer of property to a previously funded trust or other existing property arrangement is created when the nonvested property interest or power of appointment in the original contribution was created. (§ 44-6-202(c))	A nonvested property interest or a power of appointment arising from a transfer of property to a previously funded trust or other existing property arrangement is created when the nonvested property interest or power of appointment in the original contribution was created. (§ 525-2(c))
19. *Is there a conclusive presumption of fertility, that is, the ''fertile octogenarian'' rule?*	Yes. Byers v. Beddow, 142 So. 894, 897 (Fla. 1932).[1] *See also* Unif. Statutory Rule Against Perpetuities § 1, 8B U.L.A. 256 (amended 1990) (holding that ''[t]his principle is not superseded by this Act, and in view of new advances in medical science ... [this] is not unrealistic.'')); *but see* C. P. Jhong, Annotation, *Modern Status of*	Yes. Haley v. Regions Bank, 586 S.E.2d 633, 636 (Ga. 2003) (''Georgia law conclusively presumes that the possibility of issue is not extinct until death.'')	No specific state case or statute. *See* Unif. Statutory Rule Against Perpetuities § 1, 8B U.L.A. 256 (amended 1990) (holding that ''[t]his principle is not superseded by this Act, and in view of new advances in medical science ... [this] is not unrealistic.'')); *but see* C. P. Jhong, Annotation, *Modern Status of Presumption of Possibility of Issue Being Extinct*, 98 A.L.R.2d 1285 (2003) (noting ''a trend
	(cont'd)		*(cont'd)*

Table 10
Rule Against Perpetuities *(continued)*

	FLORIDA	*GEORGIA*	*HAWAII*
19. Is there a conclusive presumption of fertility, that is, the "fertile octogenarian" rule? (cont'd)	*Presumption of Possibility of Issue Being Extinct*, 98 A.L.R.2d 1285 (2003) (noting "a trend toward denying the conclusive or absolute nature of the presumption against the possibility of issue being extinct where there is competent evidence to the contrary has developed in the decisions, although some courts still adhere to the traditional view treating the presumption as conclusive or absolute").		toward denying the conclusive or absolute nature of the presumption against the possibility of issue being extinct where there is competent evidence to the contrary has developed in the decisions, although some courts still adhere to the traditional view treating the presumption as conclusive or absolute").
20. What is the earliest age a child is deemed capable of bearing a child? What is the impact of illegitimacy?	Not specifically addressed by USRAP, but the reasoning is the same as set forth in the comment to section 1 of USRAP, 2, Technical Violations of the Common Law Rule. Wait and see will typically result in no violation. Nevertheless, the common law rule ordinarily will be applied initially. Under the rule, courts must presume that living persons are capable of having or fathering children, no matter how young they are. See In re Graite's Will Trusts, [1949] 1 All E.R. 459, 460 (Ch.). Thus, the	Not specifically addressed by USRAP, but the reasoning is the same as set forth in the comment to section 1 of USRAP, 2, Technical Violations of the Common Law Rule. Wait and see will typically result in no violation. Nevertheless, the common law rule ordinarily will be applied initially. Under the rule, courts must presume that living persons are capable of having or fathering children, no matter how young they are. See In re Graite's Will Trusts, [1949] 1 All E.R. 459, 460 (Ch.). Thus, the	Not specifically addressed by USRAP, but the reasoning is the same as set forth in the comment to section 1 of USRAP, 2, Technical Violations of the Common Law Rule. Wait and see will typically result in no violation. Nevertheless, the common law rule ordinarily will be applied initially. Under the rule, courts must presume that living persons are capable of having or fathering children, no matter how young they are. See In re Graite's Will Trusts, [1949] 1 All E.R. 459, 460 (Ch.). Thus, the rule strikes down any interest whose vesting depends

	rule strikes down any interest whose vesting depends on the assertion that, for example, a toddler will not have children. (Keith L. Butler, Notes & Comments, *Long Live the Dead Hand: A Case for the Repeal of the Rule Against Perpetuities in Washington*, 75 Wash. L. Rev. 1237, 1246 n.78 (2000)).	rule strikes down any interest whose vesting depends on the assertion that, for example, a toddler will not have children. (Keith L. Butler, Notes & Comments, *Long Live the Dead Hand: A Case for the Repeal of the Rule Against Perpetuities in Washington*, 75 Wash. L. Rev. 1237, 1246 n.78 (2000)).	on the assertion that, for example, a toddler will not have children. (Keith L. Butler, Notes & Comments, *Long Live the Dead Hand: A Case for the Repeal of the Rule Against Perpetuities in Washington*, 75 Wash. L. Rev. 1237, 1246 n.78 (2000)).
21. *Is the "unborn widow" rule observed?*	No specific state case or statute. *See* Unif. Statutory Rule Against Perpetuities § 1, 8B U.L.A. 246 (amended 1990) (explaining that "[t]he chance that [an] interest will become invalid under the Statutory Rule is small" and so the unborn widow rule would rarely invalidate an interest); *see also* 61 Am Jur 2d *Perpetuities and Restraints on Alienation* § 40 (2003) (noting the same).	Yes. Lanier v. Lanier, 126 S.E.2d 776, 780 (Ga. 1962) *See also* Unif. Statutory Rule Against Perpetuities § 1, 8B U.L.A. 246 (amended 1990) (explaining that "[t]he chance that [an] interest will become invalid under the Statutory Rule is small" and so the unborn widow rule would rarely invalidate an interest); *see also* 61 Am Jur 2d *Perpetuities and Restraints on Alienation* § 40 (2003) (noting the same).	No specific state case or statute. *See* Unif. Statutory Rule Against Perpetuities § 1, 8B U.L.A. 246 (amended 1990) (explaining that "[t]he chance that [an] interest will become invalid under the Statutory Rule is small" and so the unborn widow rule would rarely invalidate an interest); *see also* 61 Am Jur 2d *Perpetuities and Restraints on Alienation* § 40 (2003) (noting the same).
22. *Does the "slothful executor" rule apply, i.e., an administrative contingency clause providing for a "distribution to, e.g., those issue living at the time of the satisfaction of the administrative condition precedent?"*	No specific state case or statute. *See* Unif. Statutory Rule Against Perpetuities § 1, 8B U.L.A. 245 (amended 1990) (Under USRAP an "interest becomes invalid only if it remains in existence and nonvested 90 years after [the testator's] death.	No specific state case or statute. *See* Unif. Statutory Rule Against Perpetuities § 1, 8B U.L.A. 245 (amended 1990) (Under USRAP an "interest becomes invalid only if it remains in existence and nonvested 90 years after [the testator's] death.	No specific state case or statute. *See* Unif. Statutory Rule Against Perpetuities § 1, 8B U.L.A. 245 (amended 1990) (Under USRAP an "interest becomes invalid only if it remains in existence and nonvested 90 years after [the testator's] death. Since it is almost certain that the
	(cont'd)	*(cont'd)*	*(cont'd)*

Table 10
Rule Against Perpetuities *(continued)*

	FLORIDA	*GEORGIA*	*HAWAII*
22. *Does the "slothful executor" rule apply, i.e., an administrative contingency clause providing for a "distribution to, e.g., those issue living at the time of the satisfaction of the administrative condition precedent?" (cont'd)*	Since it is almost certain that the final distribution of [an] estate will occur well within this 90-year period, the chance that [an] interest will be invalid is negligible.")	Since it is almost certain that the final distribution of [an] estate will occur well within this 90-year period, the chance that [an] interest will be invalid is negligible.")	final distribution of [an] estate will occur well within this 90-year period, the chance that [an] interest will be invalid is negligible.")
23. *Does the all-or-nothing rule apply to class gifts?*	No specific state case or statute. *See* Unif. Statutory Rule Against Perpetuities § 1, 8B U.L.A. 257 (amended 1990) ("Although this Act does not supersede the basic idea of the much-maligned 'all-or-nothing' rule, the evils sometimes attributed to it are substantially if not entirely eliminated by the wait-and-see feature of the Statutory Rule and by the availability of reformation under Section 3.")	Yes. Landrum v. Nat'l City Bank, 80 S.E.2d 300, 302 (Ga. 1954) (invalidating a class gift to "nieces" because there were living sisters of the testator and so more nieces could have later been born to the class). *See also* Unif. Statutory Rule Against Perpetuities § 1, 8B U.L.A. 257 (amended 1990) ("Although this Act does not supersede the basic idea of the much-maligned 'all-or-nothing' rule, the evils sometimes attributed to it are substantially if not entirely eliminated by the wait-and-see feature of the Statutory Rule and by the availability of reformation under Section 3.")	No specific state case or statute. *See* Unif. Statutory Rule Against Perpetuities § 1, 8B U.L.A. 257 (amended 1990) ("Although this Act does not supersede the basic idea of the much-maligned 'all-or-nothing' rule, the evils sometimes attributed to it are substantially if not entirely eliminated by the wait-and-see feature of the Statutory Rule and by the availability of reformation under Section 3.")
24. *Is there an exception to the all-or-nothing rule in the case of subclasses or specific sums to each member of the class?*	No specific state case or statute. *See* Unif. Statutory Rule Against Perpetuities § 1, 8B U.L.A. 257 (amended 1990)	No specific state case or statute. *See* Unif. Statutory Rule Against Perpetuities § 1, 8B U.L.A. 257 (amended 1990) ("The	No specific state case or statute. *See* Unif. Statutory Rule Against Perpetuities § 1, 8B U.L.A. 257 (amended 1990) ("The specific-sum

	(''The specific-sum and sub-class doctrines are not superseded by this Act.'')	specific-sum and sub-class doctrines are not superseded by this Act.'')	and sub-class doctrines are not superseded by this Act.'')
25. *Is the infectious invalidity rule followed outside class gifts?*	No specific state case or statute. *See* Unif. Statutory Rule Against Perpetuities § 1, 8B U.L.A. 256 (amended 1990) (explaining that ''[t]he doctrine of infectious invalidity is superseded by this Act by Section 3, under which courts . . . are required to *reform* the disposition to approximate as closely as possible the transferor's . . . plan of distribution.'')	Yes. Walker v. Bogle, 260 S.E.2d 338, 342 (Ga. 1979) (reversing a lower court decision that found a testatrix' dispositive plan void through the doctrine of ''infectious invalidity'' because the court only invalidated two, less important, parts of the will). *But see* Unif. Statutory Rule Against Perpetuities § 1, 8B U.L.A. 256 (amended 1990) (explaining that ''[t]he doctrine of infectious invalidity is superseded by this Act by Section 3, under which courts . . . are required to *reform* the disposition to approximate as closely as possible the transferor's . . . plan of distribution.'')	No specific state case or statute. *See* Unif. Statutory Rule Against Perpetuities § 1, 8B U.L.A. 256 (amended 1990) (explaining that '' [t]he doctrine of infectious invalidity is superseded by this Act by Section 3, under which courts . . . are required to *reform* the disposition to approximate as closely as possible the transferor's . . . plan of distribution.'')
26. *Is there a rule against the suspension of the power of alienation? If so, how is it stated?*	See Harbour Watch Homeowners Ass'n v. Derderian, 618 So. 2d 315, 316 (Fla. Dist. Ct. App. 1993) (discussing the rule against the restraint on alienation as precluding only '' 'only unlimited or absolute restraints on alienation' '')	Yes. Floyd v. Hoover, 141 Ga. App. 588, 234 S.E.2d 89, 92 (Ga. Ct. App. 1977). (''The power of alienation is necessarily incident to every estate in fee simple absolute and no one can create what is intended in law to be a fee simple absolute and at the same time deprive the owner of those rights and privileges which the law attaches to that estate.'')	No specific state case or statute.

Table 10
Rule Against Perpetuities *(continued)*

	FLORIDA	*GEORGIA*	*HAWAII*
27. *Effective date.*	October 1, 1988, (§ 689.225(6)(c)), including powers unexercised on October 1, 1988, though created earlier (§ 689.225(6)(b)), see also # 6, but the extension of the rule to trusts for 360 years only applies to trusts created after December 31, 2000. (§689.225(2)(f)) In Old Port Cove Condominium Assoc. One, Inc. v. Old Port Cove Holdings, Inc., 2007 WL 1264097 (May 2, 2007), the court of appeals held that the current statute is fully retroactive in abrogating the common law rule against perpetuities. *Quaere* as to the 360-year provision for trusts.	May 1, 1990. See also # 6.	June 18, 1992. See also # 6.

1. For questions # 19–25, *see also* § 689.225(7) (noting that "no common-law rule against perpetuities or remoteness in vesting shall exist with respect to any interest or power").

Table 10
Rule Against Perpetuities *(continued)*

	IDAHO	*ILLINOIS*	*INDIANA*
1. *Which rule is in effect: the common law rule, the Uniform Statutory Rule Against Perpetuities (USRAP), other law, or none?*	None. Idaho Code § 55-111 ("[T]here shall be no rule against perpetuities applicable to real or personal property.")	Other. Qualified perpetual trusts (see # 3 (8)) allow for total avoidance of the rule. There are also other exceptions to the common law rule. (765 ILCS §§ 305/1 – 305/6)	USRAP. (§§ 32-17-8-1 – 32-17-8-6)
2. a. *Is the common law rule relevant to any interests?*	N/A	Yes.	Yes, but only as the starting point of the analysis.
b. *What is the relevant rule?*	N/A	The rule against perpetuities as established for many years is that no interest in real estate is good unless it must vest, if at all, not later than twenty-one years and nine months after some life in being at the creation of the interest." (Spicer v. Moss, 100 N.E.2d 761, 771 (Ill. 1951); *see also* 305/2 ("This Act modifies the common law rule of property known as the rule against perpetuities, which, except as modified by statutes in force at the effective date of this Act and by this Act, shall remain in full force and effect.")) As a general matter, a trust containing any limitation which, but for this paragraph (a), would violate the rule against perpetuities (as	A nonvested property interest is invalid unless: (1) When the interest is created, it is certain to vest or terminate no later than 21 years after the death of an individual then alive; or (2) The interest either vests or terminates within 90 years after its creation. (§ 32-17-8-3(a))

(cont'd)

Table 10
Rule Against Perpetuities *(continued)*

	IDAHO	*ILLINOIS*	*INDIANA*
b. *What is the relevant rule? (cont'd)*		modified by statute) shall terminate at the expiration of a period of (A) 21 years after the death of the last to die of all of the beneficiaries of the instrument who were living at the date when the period of the rule against perpetuities commenced to run or (B) 21 years after that date if no beneficiary of the instrument was then living, unless events occur which cause an earlier termination in accordance with the terms of the instrument and then the principal shall be distributed as provided by the instrument. (305/5(a)) The rule does not apply to perpetual trusts. See # 3.	
3. *Does the rule apply to other than private trusts?*	N/A	(a) The rule against perpetuities does not apply: (1) to any disposition of property or interest therein which, at the effective date of this Act, does not violate, or is exempted by statute from the operation of, the common law rule against perpetuities;	Yes. The rule applies except to: (1) A nonvested property interest or a power of appointment arising out of a nondonative transfer, except a nonvested property interest or a power of appointment arising out of any of the following: (A) A premarital or postmarital agreement.

(2) to powers of a trustee to sell, lease or mortgage property or to powers which relate to the administration or management of trust assets, including, without limitation, discretionary powers of a trustee to determine what receipts constitute principal and what receipts constitute income and powers to appoint a successor trustee;

(3) to mandatory powers of a trustee to distribute income, or to discretionary powers of a trustee to distribute principal prior to termination of a trust, to a beneficiary having an interest in the principal which is irrevocably vested in quality and quantity;

(4) to discretionary powers of a trustee to allocate income and principal among beneficiaries, but no exercise of any such power after the expiration of the period of the rule against perpetuities is valid;

(cont'd)

(B) A separation or divorce settlement.

(C) A spouse's election.

(D) A similar arrangement arising out of a prospective, an existing, or a previous marital relationship between the parties.

(E) A contract to make or not to revoke a will or trust.

(F) A contract to exercise or not to exercise a power of appointment.

(G) A transfer in satisfaction of a duty of support.

(H) A reciprocal transfer.

(2) A fiduciary's power relating to the administration or management of assets, including the power of a fiduciary to sell, lease, or mortgage property, and the power of a fiduciary to determine principal and income.

(3) A power to appoint a fiduciary.

(4) A discretionary power of a trustee to distribute principal before termination of a trust to a beneficiary having an indefeasibly vested interest in the income and principal.

(5) A nonvested property interest held by a charity, government, or governmental agency or subdivision, if the nonvested property interest is preceded by

(cont'd)

Table 10
Rule Against Perpetuities *(continued)*

	IDAHO	ILLINOIS	INDIANA
3. *Does the rule apply to other than private trusts? (cont'd)*		(5) to leases to commence in the future or upon the happening of a future event, but no such lease shall be valid unless the term thereof actually commences in possession within 40 years from the date of execution of the lease; (6) to commitments (A) by a lessor to enter into a lease with a subtenant or with the holder of a leasehold mortgage or (B) by a lessee or sublessee to enter into a lease with the holder of a mortgage; (7) to options in gross or to preemptive rights in the nature of a right of first refusal, but no option in gross shall be valid for more than 40 years from the date of its creation; or (8) to qualified perpetual trusts as defined in 765 ILCS 305/3. Qualified	an interest held by another charity, government, or governmental agency or subdivision. (6) A nonvested property interest in or a power of appointment with respect to a trust or other property arrangement forming part of a pension, a profit sharing, a stock bonus, a health, a disability, a death benefit, an income deferral, or other current or deferred benefit plan for one (1) or more employees, independent contractors, or their beneficiaries or spouses, to which contributions are made for the purpose of distributing to or for the benefit of the participants or their beneficiaries or spouses the property, income, or principal in the trust or other property arrangement, except a nonvested property interest or a power of appointment that is created by an election of a participant or a beneficiary or spouse. (7) A property interest, power of appointment, or arrangement

		perpetual trusts are trust created by written instrument executed on or after January 1, 1998, including amendments to a prior-executed instrument or by way of the exercise of a power of appointment granted or amended after that date. The trust, by its terms, provides that the rule does not apply and the trustee or other person has the power to sell property, where the power of sale is not limited by the trust instrument or law for any period of time beyond the period of the rule against perpetuities. (305/4(a))	that was not subject to the common law rule against perpetuities or is excluded by another Indiana statute. (8) A: (a) provision for the accumulation of an amount of the income of a trust estate reasonably necessary for the upkeep, repair, or proper management of the subject of the estate; (b) direction in a trust that provides for the allocation wholly or in part to the principal of the trust of stock dividends or stock rights derived from shares held in a trust; (c) provision for a sinking or reserve fund; or (d) statutory provision directing an accumulation. (§ 32-17-8-2)
4. *Does the rule invalidate the interest at its creation, or is the rule revised by a wait-and-see approach?*	N/A	At its creation for wills (Spicer v. Moss, 100 N.E.2d 761, 771 (Ill. 1951).) Wait-and-see for trusts. (305/5(a))	Wait-and-see. (§ 32-17-8-3(a))
5. *Can the trust be reformed?*	Yes. [N]o trust heretofore or hereafter created, either testamentary or inter vivos, shall be declared void, but shall be so *(cont'd)*	No general reformation, but see # 2b.	Yes, but only if one of the following conditions is met: *(cont'd)*

Table 10
Rule Against Perpetuities *(continued)*

	IDAHO	*ILLINOIS*	*INDIANA*
5. *Can the trust be reformed (cont'd)*	construed as to eliminate parts violating the above provisions [rule against perpetuities or rule against the suspension of power of alienation]. (§ 55-111)		(1) a nonvested property interest or a power of appointment becomes invalid under section 3 of this chapter (see # 2); (2) a class gift is not but might become invalid under section 3 of this chapter and the time has arrived when the share of any class member is to take effect in possession or enjoyment; or (3) a nonvested property interest that is not validated by section 3(a)(1) of this chapter, that is, the traditional common law rule, can vest but not within ninety (90) years after the interest's creation. (§ 32-17-8-6) See also # 27.
6. *If yes to 5., under what theory?*	[I]n such a way that the testators or trustors wishes are carried out to the greatest extent permitted by this act (§ 55-111)	See # 5.	A court shall reform a disposition in the manner that most closely preserves the transferor's plan of distribution and is within the ninety (90) years allowed by section 3(a)(2), 3(b)(2), or 3(c)(2) of this chapter. (§ 32-17-8-6) *See also* § 32-17-8-1(b) ("If a nonvested property interest or a power of appointment was created before May 8, 1991, and:

			(1) is determined in a judicial proceeding commenced on or after May 8, 1991, to violate this state's rule against perpetuities as that rule existed before May 8, 1991; or (2) may violate this state's rule against perpetuities as that rule existed before May 8, 1991; a court upon the petition of an interested person shall reform the disposition by inserting a savings clause that most closely preserves the transferor's plan of distribution and is within the limits of the rule against perpetuities applicable when the nonvested property interest or power of appointment was created.'')
7. *When is a general testamentary power of appointment invalid?*	N/A	With respect to wills, *see* Unif. Statutory Rule Against Perpetuities § 1, 8B U.L.A. 248 (amended 1990) (''Under the Common-law Rule . . . a *nongeneral power* (whether or not presently exercisable) or a *general testamentary power* is invalid as of the time of its creation if it *might* not terminate (by irrevocable exercise or otherwise) within a life in being plus 21 years.'')	A general testamentary power of appointment is invalid unless one of the following conditions is satisfied: (1) When the power is created, it is certain to be irrevocably exercised or otherwise to terminate no later than 21 years after the death of an individual then alive. (2) The power is irrevocably exercised or otherwise terminates within 90 years after its creation. (§ 32-17-8-3(c))
8. *Same, but nongeneral testamentary power.*	N/A	See # 7.	A nongeneral power of appointment . . . is invalid unless one of the following conditions is satisfied:

(cont'd)

Table 10
Rule Against Perpetuities *(continued)*

	IDAHO	*ILLINOIS*	*INDIANA*
8. *Same, but nongeneral testamentary power. (cont'd)*			(1) When the power is created, it is certain to be irrevocably exercised or otherwise to terminate no later than 21 years after the death of an individual then alive. (2) The power is irrevocably exercised or otherwise terminates within 90 years after its creation. (§ 32-17-8-3(c))
9. *Same, but general inter vivos power.*	N/A	*See* Unif. Statutory Rule Against Perpetuities § 1, 8B U.L.A. 248 (amended 1990) ("Under the Common-law Rule, a *general power not presently exercisable because of a condition precedent* is invalid as of the time of its creation if the condition *might* neither be satisfied nor become impossible to satisfy with a life in being plus 21 years.")	A general power of appointment not presently exercisable because of a condition precedent is invalid unless one of the following conditions is satisfied: (1) When the power is created, the condition precedent is certain to be satisfied or become impossible to satisfy no later than 21 years after the death of an individual then alive. (2) The condition precedent either is satisfied or becomes impossible to satisfy within 90 years after its creation. (§ 32-17-8-3(b))
10. *Same, but nongeneral inter vivos power.*	N/A	See # 7.	See # 8.

11. *Is a period of gestation added to the perpetuity period ?*	N/A	Yes. (See # 2a.)	No. The possibility that a child will be born to a person after that person's death is disregarded. (§ 32-17-8-3 (d)) *See also* Unif. Statutory Rule Against Perpetuities § 1, 8B U.L.A. 242-43 (amended 1990) (''[T]he possibility that a child will be born to [a testator] after his death must be disregarded; and the possibility that a child will be born to any of [the testator's] descendants after their deaths must also be disregarded. Note, however, that the rule of sub-section (d) does *not* apply to the question of the entitlement of an after-born child to take a beneficial interest in the trust'').
12. *What is the treatment of a ''later of the traditional rule or 90 years'' clause? See UPC 2-901(e).*	N/A	N/A	Indiana's USRAP applies to clauses that contain that language. § 32-17-8-5(a). *But see* § 32-17-8-5(b) (''[T]he portion of the clause that pertains to the period that exceeds twenty-one (21) years or that might exceed twenty-one (21) years after the death of the survivor of lives in being at the creation of the trust or other property arrangement is not valid. The court shall construe the clause as becoming effective upon: (1) the death of; or (2) the expiration of the period not exceeding twenty-one (21) years after the death of; the survivor of the specified lives in being at the creation of the trust or other property arrangement.''

Table 10
Rule Against Perpetuities *(continued)*

	IDAHO	*ILLINOIS*	*INDIANA*
13. *When is an interest created by the exercise of a general testamentary power deemed created?*	N/A	Northern Trust Co. v. Porter, 13 N.E.2d 487, 491 (Ill. 1938) ("[T]he validity of an appointment, under a general testamentary power, must be determined by considering the donee's appointment as part of the instrument created by the donor. Thus, we must look to see whether or not the remainders will vest in interest (although not necessarily in possession) within the period measured from the time of the creation of the power by the donor.") *See also* comment to Unif. Probate Code § 2-902(a) ("general principles of property law determine that a nonvested property interest or power of appointment created by will is created at the decedent's death"); Unif. Statutory Rule Against Perpetuities § 2, 8B U.L.A. 268 (amended 1990) (stating the same).	Except as provided in subsections (b) and (c) and in section 1(a) of this chapter, the time of creation of a nonvested property interest or a power of appointment is determined under general principles of property law. (§ 32-17-8-4(a)) The first two of the excepted provisions state that as long as a person with a general power to become the unqualified beneficial owner has that power, the nonvested interest is created when the power terminates. The third of the excepted provisions states that a nonvested property interest, which arises from a transfer to an existing trust, is created when the nonvested property interest in the trust was created. *See also* Unif. Statutory Rule Against Perpetuities § 2, 8B U.L.A. 268 (amended 1990) (explaining that "general principles of property law determine that the time . . . [of creation] is at the decedent's death.") *See generally* § 32-17-8-1(a) ("a nonvested property interest or a power of appointment created by the exercise of a power of appointment is created when the power

			is irrevocably exercised or when a revocable exercise becomes irrevocable.'')
14. *Same, but nongeneral testamentary power.*	N/A	See # 13.	See # 13.
15. *Same, but general inter vivos power.*	N/A	*See* comment to Unif. Probate Code § 2-902(a) (''With respect to an inter-vivos transfer, an interest or power is created on the date the transfer becomes effective for purpose of property law generally, normally the date of delivery of the deed or funding of the trust.''); Unif. Statutory Rule Against Perpetuities § 2, 8B U.L.A. 268 (stating the same).	Except as provided in subsections (b) and (c) and in section 1(a) of this chapter, the time of creation of a nonvested property interest or a power of appointment is determined under general principles of property law. (§ 32-17-8-4(a)) The first two of the excepted provisions state that as long as a person with a general power to become the unqualified beneficial owner has that power, the nonvested interest is created when the power terminates. The third of the excepted provisions states that a nonvested property interest, which arises from a transfer to an existing trust, is created when the nonvested property interest in the trust was created. *See also* Unif. Statutory Rule Against Perpetuities § 2, 8B U.L.A. 268 (amended 1990) (explaining that ''the time when the interest or power is created is the date the transfer becomes effective for purposes of property law generally, normally the date of delivery of the deed''); Comment to Unif. Probate Code

(cont'd)

Table 10
Rule Against Perpetuities *(continued)*

	IDAHO	*ILLINOIS*	*INDIANA*
15. Same, but general inter vivos power. (cont'd)			§ 2-902(a) (stating same and adding "the funding of the trust" as "normally" the time when the interest is created). *See generally* § 32-17-8-1(a) ("For the purposes of this section, a nonvested property interest or a power of appointment created by the exercise of a power of appointment is created when the power is irrevocably exercised or when a revocable exercise becomes irrevocable.")
16. Same, but nongeneral inter vivos power.		See # 15.	See # 15.
17. When is an interest created if the grantor of a trust has a power to revoke?	N/A	When the maker of the instrument no longer has the power to revoke or to transfer or direct to be transferred to himself the entire legal or equitable ownership of the property or interest therein. (765 ILCS 305/4(b))	If there is a person who alone can exercise a power created by a governing instrument to become the unqualified beneficial owner of: (1) a nonvested property interest; or (2) a property interest subject to a power of appointment described in section 3(b) or 3(c) of this chapter; the nonvested property interest or power of appointment is created when the power to become the unqualified beneficial owner terminates. (§ 32-17-8-4(b))

			See also Unif. Statutory Rule Against Perpetuities § 2, 8B U.L.A. 268 (amended 1990) (explaining that "any nonvested property interest subject to [a power to revoke] is not created . . . until the power terminates (by release, expiration at the death of the donee, or otherwise"); Comment to Unif. Probate Code § 2-902(b) (noting that "nonvested property interest and powers of appointment created in [a revocable inter-vivos trust] are created when the power to revoke expires, usually at the settlor's death"). *See generally* § 32-17-8-1(a) ("a nonvested property interest or a power of appointment created by the exercise of a power of appointment is created when the power is irrevocably exercised or when a revocable exercise becomes irrevocable.")
18. *When does the period of the rule start re an interest contributed to an irrevocable trust? See UPC 2-902(c).*	N/A	*See* comment to Unif. Probate Code 2-902(c) ("Arguably, at common law, each transfer [to an existing irrevocable inter-vivos trust] starts the period of the Rule running anew as to each transfer.");	A nonvested property interest or a power of appointment arising from a transfer of property to a previously funded trust or other existing property arrangement is created when the nonvested property interest or power of appointment in the original contribution was created. (§ 32-17-8-4(c))

Table 10
Rule Against Perpetuities *(continued)*

	IDAHO	*ILLINOIS*	*INDIANA*
19. *Is there a conclusive presumption of fertility, that is, the "fertile octogenarian" rule?*	[T]here shall be no presumption that a person is capable of having children at any stage of adult life. (§ 55-111)	No. Any person who has attained the age of 65 is deemed not capable of having a child. Evidence is not admissible as to the capacity of having a child by a living person who has attained the age of 65 years. The possibility of adoption is disregarded. (305/4(c)(3)(C))	No specific state case or statute. *See* Unif. Statutory Rule Against Perpetuities § 1, 8B U.L.A. 256 (amended 1990) (holding that "[t]his principle is not superseded by this Act, and in view of new advances in medical science . . . [this] is not unrealistic."); *but see* C. P. Jhong, Annotation, *Modern Status of Presumption of Possibility of Issue Being Extinct*, 98 A.L.R.2d 1285 (2003) (noting "a trend toward denying the conclusive or absolute nature of the presumption against the possibility of issue being extinct where there is competent evidence to the contrary has developed in the decisions, although some courts still adhere to the traditional view treating the presumption as conclusive or absolute").
20. *What is the earliest age a child is deemed capable of bearing a child? What is the impact of illegitimacy?*	Under the rule, courts must presume that living persons are capable of having or fathering children, no matter how young they are. See In re Graite's Will Trusts, [1949] 1 All E.R. 459, 460 (Ch.). Thus, the rule strikes down any interest whose vesting	13 years. (305/4(c)(3)(A))	Not specifically addressed by USRAP, but the reasoning is the same as set forth in the comment to section 1 of USRAP, 2, Technical Violations of the Common Law Rule. Wait and see will typically result in no violation. Nevertheless, the common law rule ordinarily will be

	depends on the assertion that, for example, a toddler will not have children. (Keith L. Butler, Notes & Comments, *Long Live the Dead Hand: A Case for the Repeal of the Rule Against Perpetuities in Washington*, 75 Wash. L. Rev. 1237, 1246 n.78 (2000)).		applied initially. Under the rule, courts must presume that living persons are capable of having or fathering children, no matter how young they are. See In re Graite's Will Trusts, [1949] 1 All E.R. 459, 460 (Ch.). Thus, the rule strikes down any interest whose vesting depends on the assertion that, for example, a toddler will not have children. (Keith L. Butler, Notes & Comments, *Long Live the Dead Hand: A Case for the Repeal of the Rule Against Perpetuities in Washington*, 75 Wash. L. Rev. 1237, 1246 n.78 (2000)).
21. Is the ''unborn widow'' rule observed?	N/A	In determining whether an interest violates the rule against perpetuities: (1) it shall be presumed . . . (C) where the instrument creates an interest in the ''widow,'' ''widower,'' or ''spouse'' of another person, that the maker of the instrument intended to refer to a person who was living at the date that the period of the rule against perpetuities commences to run (305/4(c)(1)(C))	No specific state case or statute. *See* Unif. Statutory Rule Against Perpetuities § 1, 8B U.L.A. 246 (amended 1990) (explaining that '' [t]he chance that [an] interest will become invalid under the Statutory Rule is small'' and so the unborn widow rule would rarely invalidate an interest); *see also* 61 Am Jur 2d *Perpetuities and Restraints on Alienation* § 40 (2003) (noting the same).
22. Does the ''slothful executor'' rule apply, i.e. an administrative contingency clause providing for a ''distribution to, e.g., those issue living at the time of the satisfaction of the administrative condition precedent?''	N/A	In determining whether an interest violates the rule against perpetuities: (1) it shall be presumed . . . (B) in the case of an interest conditioned upon the probate of a will, the *(cont'd)*	No specific state case or statute. *See* Unif. Statutory Rule Against Perpetuities § 1, 8B U.L.A. 245 (amended 1990) (Under USRAP, an ''interest becomes invalid only if it remains in existence and nonvested *(cont'd)*

Table 10
Rule Against Perpetuities *(continued)*

	IDAHO	*ILLINOIS*	*INDIANA*
22. *Does the "slothful executor" rule apply, i.e. an administrative contingency clause providing for a "distribution to, e.g., those issue living at the time of the satisfaction of the administrative condition precedent?"* *(cont'd)*		appointment of an executor, administrator or trustee, the completion of the administration of an estate, the payment of debts, the sale or distribution of property, the determination of federal or state tax liabilities or the happening of any administrative contingency, that the contingency must occur, if at all, within the period of the rule against perpetuities (305/4(c)(1)(B)) *See also* 310/1, providing that vesting of any limitation of property is not deemed deferred for purposes of the rule against perpetuities merely because the limitation is made to the estate of a person or to a personal representative, or to a trustee under a will, or to take effect on the probate of a will. The provision only applies to limitations created after the effective date, 1951.	90 years after [the testator's] death. Since it is almost certain that the final distribution of [an] estate will occur well within this 90-year period, the chance that [an] interest will be invalid is negligible.")
23. *Does the all-or-nothing rule apply to class gifts?*	N/A	Case law unclear. *See generally* Aldendifer v. Wylie, 138 N.E. 143, 146 (Ill. 1923) ("Where a will contains separate	No specific state case or statute. *See* Unif. Statutory Rule Against Perpetuities § 1, 8B U.L.A. 257 (amended 1990) ("Although this

		provisions, some of which are valid and others invalid, the valid ones will be upheld if they can be separated from the invalid and still give effect to the intention of the testator and not interfere with the general testamentary scheme.'')	Act does not supersede the basic idea of the much-maligned 'all-or-nothing' rule, the evils sometimes attributed to it are substantially if not entirely eliminated by the wait-and-see feature of the Statutory Rule and by the availability of reformation under Section 3.'').
24. *Is there an exception to the all-or-nothing rule in the case of subclasses or specific sums to each member of the class?*	N/A	*See* Unif. Statutory Rule Against Perpetuities § 2, 8B U.L.A. 257 (''The common law also recognizes a doctrine called the specific-sum doctrine which is derived from Storrs v. Benbow, 3 De G.M. & G. 390, 43 Eng. Rep 153 (Ch. 1853), and states: If a specified sum of money is to be paid to each member of a class, the interest of each class member is entitled to separate treatment and is valid or invalid under the Rule on its own. The common law also recognizes a doctrine called the sub-class doctrine, which is derived from Cattlin v. Brown, 11 Hare 372, 68 Eng. Rep. 1318 (Ch. 1853), and states: If the ultimate takers are not described as a single class but rather as a group of separate subclasses, and if the share to which each	No specific state case or statute. *See* Unif. Statutory Rule Against Perpetuities § 1, 8B U.L.A. 257 (amended 1990) (''The specific-sum and sub-class doctrines are not superseded by this Act.'')

(cont'd)

Table 10
Rule Against Perpetuities *(continued)*

	IDAHO	*ILLINOIS*	*INDIANA*
24. *Is there an exception to the all-or-nothing rule in the case of subclasses or specific sums to each member of the class? (cont'd)*		separate subclass is entitled will finally be determined within the period of the Rule, the gifts to the different subclasses are separate for the purpose of the Rule.'').	
25. *Is the infectious invalidity rule followed outside class gifts?*	N/A	*See, e.g.*, # 25.	No specific state case or statute. *See* Unif. Statutory Rule Against Perpetuities § 1, 8B U.L.A. 256 (amended 1990) (explaining that ''[t]he doctrine of infectious invalidity is superseded by this Act by Section 3, under which courts . . . are required to *reform* the disposition to approximate as closely as possible the transferor's . . . plan of distribution.'')
26. *Is there a rule against the suspension of the power of alienation? If so, how is it stated?*	Yes. The absolute power of alienation of real property cannot be suspended by any limitation or condition whatever, for a longer period than during the continuance of the lives of the persons in being at the creation of the limitation or condition, and 25 years thereafter . . . nor any rule prohibiting the placing of	Case law unclear. *See* Green v. Gawne, 47 N.E.2d 86, 93 (Ill. 1943) (suggesting that restraints on alienation will be invalidated depending on the circumstances of each particular case or instrument).	Yes. *See* Quilliam v. Union Trust Co., 142 N.E. 214, 216 (Ind. 1924) (invaliding part of a will that suspended the power of alienation of real estate for 50 years).

	restraints on the alienation of personal property . . . (§ 55-111). *But see* Estate of Kirk v. Seideman, 907 P.2d 794, 805 (Idaho 1996) (the rule against the suspension of power of alienation does not apply to charitable trusts).		
27. *Effective date.*	N/A	September 22, 1969.	May 8, 1991 (§ 32-17-8-1(a)) See also # 6.

Table 10
Rule Against Perpetuities *(continued)*

	IOWA	KANSAS	KENTUCKY
1. *Which rule is in effect: the common law rule, the Uniform Statutory Rule Against Perpetuities (USRAP), other law, or none?*	Variation of wait-and-see. (Iowa Code § 558.68)	USRAP. (Kan. Stat. Ann. §§ 59-3401 – 59-3408)	Other. (Ky. Rev. Stat. Ann. §§ 381.215 – 381.217)
2. a. *Is the common law rule relevant to any interests?*	Yes, but only as the starting point of the analysis.	Yes, but only as the starting point of the analysis.	Yes, but only as the starting point of the analysis.
b. *What is the relevant rule?*	(1) A nonvested interest in property is not valid unless it must vest, if at all, within twenty-one years after one or more lives in being at the creation of the interest and any relevant period of gestation. (2) a. In determining whether a nonvested interest would violate the rule against perpetuities in 1, the period of the rule is measured by actual events rather than by possible events, in any case in which that would validate the interest. (§ 558.68)	A nonvested property interest is invalid unless: (1) When the interest is created, it is certain to vest or terminate no later than 21 years after the death of an individual then alive; or (2) The interest either vests or terminates within 90 years after its creation. (§ 59-3401(a))	No interest in real or personal property shall be good unless it must vest, if at all, not later than twenty-one (21) years after some life in being at the creation of the interest. It is the purpose of this section to enact the common law rule against perpetuities, except as hereinafter modified by KRS 381.215 to 381.223. (§ 381.215) Specifically, section 381.216 introduces a wait and-see rule. See #6.
3. *Does the rule apply to other than private trusts?*	No. The rule does not apply to charitable trusts. Kositzky v. Monfore (In re Estate of	Yes. The rule applies except to: (1) A nonvested property interest or a power of appointment arising out of a	No. The rule does not apply to: "A trust created by an employer as part of a stock bonus plan, pension plan, disability or death benefit plan

Keenan), 519 N.W.2d 373 (Iowa 1994).

nondonative transfer, except a nonvested property interest or a power of appointment arising out of (i) a premarital or postmarital agreement, (ii) a separation or divorce settlement, (iii) a spouse's election, (iv) a similar arrangement arising out of a prospective, existing or previous marital relationship between the parties, (v) a contract to make or not to revoke a will or trust, (vi) a contract to exercise or not to exercise a power of appointment, (vii) a transfer in satisfaction of a duty of support, or (viii) a reciprocal transfer;

(2) a fiduciary's power relating to the administration or management of assets, including the power of a fiduciary to sell, lease or mortgage property, and the power of a fiduciary to determine principal and income;

(3) a power to appoint a fiduciary;

(4) a discretionary power of a trustee to distribute principal before termination of a trust to a beneficiary having an indefeasibly vested

(cont'd)

or profit-sharing plan, for the exclusive benefit of some or all of his employees, to which contributions are made by such employer and employees, or both, for the purposes of distributing to such employees the earnings or the principal, or both earnings and principal, of the fund so held in trust, shall not be deemed to be invalid as violating the rule against perpetuities, but such a trust may continue for such time as may be necessary to accomplish the purposes for which it may be created.'' (§ 381.217), or Charitable trusts. Hatcher v. Southern Baptist Theological Seminary, 632 S.W.2d 251, 252 (Ky. 1982)

Table 10
Rule Against Perpetuities *(continued)*

	IOWA	*KANSAS*	*KENTUCKY*
3. Does the rule apply to other than private trusts? (cont'd)		interest in the income and principal; (5) a nonvested property interest held by a charity, government or governmental agency or subdivision, if the nonvested property interest is preceded by an interest held by another charity, government or governmental agency or subdivision; (6) a nonvested property interest in or a power of appointment with respect to a trust or other property arrangement forming part of a pension, profit-sharing, stock bonus, health, disability, death benefit, income deferral or other current or deferred benefit plan for one or more employees, independent contractors or the beneficiaries or spouses, to which contributions are made for the purpose of distributing to or for the benefit of the participants or their beneficiaries or spouses the property, income or principal	

		in the trust or other property arrangement, except a nonvested property interest or a power of appointment that is created by an election of a participant or a beneficiary or spouse; or (7) a property interest, power of appointment or arrangement that was not subject to the common-law rule againt perpetuities or is excluded by another statute of this state. (§ 59-3404)	
4. *Does the rule invalidate the interest at its creation, or is the rule revised by a wait-and-see approach?*	Wait-and-see. (558.68(2)(a))	Wait-and-see. (§ 59-3401(a)(2))	Wait-and-see. (§ 381.216) ("In determining whether an interest would violate the rule against perpetuities the period of perpetuities shall be measured by actual rather than possible events; provided, however, the period shall not be measured by any lives whose continuance does not have a causal relationship to the vesting or failure of the interest.")
5. *Can the trust be reformed?*	Yes. (§ 558.68(3)) See also # 27.	Yes, but only if one of the following conditions applies: (1) A nonvested property interest or a power of appointment becomes invalid under K.S.A. 59-3401, statutory rule against perpetuities;	Yes. (§ 381.216) See also # 27.

(cont'd)

Table 10
Rule Against Perpetuities *(continued)*

	IOWA	*KANSAS*	*KENTUCKY*
5. Can the trust be reformed? (cont'd)		(2) a class gift is not but might become invalid under K.S.A. 59-3401, statutory rule against perpetuities, and the time has arrived when the share of any class member is to take effect in possession or enjoyment; or (3) a nonvested property interest that is not validated by subsection (a)(1)of K.S.A. 59-3401, that is, the traditional common law rule, can vest but not within 90 years after its creation. (§ 59-3403)	
6. *If yes to 5., under what theory?*	[J]udicially reformed to most closely approximate the intention of the creator of the interest in order that the nonvested interest will vest, even though it may not become possessory, within the period of the rule. (§ 558.68(3))	A court shall reform a disposition in the manner that most closely approximates the transferor's manifested plan of distribution and is within the 90 years allowed by subsections (a)(2), (b)(2) or (c)(2) of K.S.A. 59-3401. (§ 59-3403) *See also* § 59-3405(b) (''If a nonvested property interest or a power of appointment was created before the effective	Any interest which would violate said rule as thus modified shall be reformed, within the limits of that rule, to approximate most closely the intention of the creator of the interest. (§ 381.216)

		date of this act and is determined in a judicial proceeding, commenced on or after the effective date of this act, to violate this state's rule against perpetuities as that rule existed before the effective date of this act, a court upon the petition of an interested person may reform the disposition in the manner that most closely approximates the transferor's manifested plan of distribution and is within the limits of the rule against perpetuities applicable when the nonvested property interest or power of appointment was created.'')	
7. *When is a general testamentary power of appointment invalid?*	*See* Unif. Statutory Rule Against Perpetuities § 1, 8B U.L.A. 248 (amended 1990) (''Under the Common-law Rule . . . a *nongeneral power* (whether or not presently exercisable) or a *general testamentary power* is invalid as of the time of its creation if it *might* not terminate (by irrevocable exercise or otherwise) within a life in being plus 21 years.'')	A general testamentary power of appointment is invalid unless one of the following conditions is satisfied: (1) When the power is created, it is certain to be irrevocably exercised or otherwise to terminate no later than 21 years after the death of an individual then alive. (2) The power is irrevocably exercised or otherwise terminates within 90 years after its creation. (§ 59-3401(c))	*See* Unif. Statutory Rule Against Perpetuities § 1, 8B U.L.A. 248 (amended 1990) (''Under the Common-law Rule . . . a *nongeneral power* (whether or not presently exercisable) or a *general testamentary power* is invalid as of the time of its creation if it *might* not terminate (by irrevocable exercise or otherwise) within a life in being plus 21 years.'')

Table 10
Rule Against Perpetuities *(continued)*

	IOWA	KANSAS	KENTUCKY
8. *Same, but nongeneral testamentary power.*	See # 7.	A nongeneral power of appointment . . . is invalid unless one of the following conditions is satisfied: (1) When the power is created, it is certain to be irrevocably exercised or otherwise to terminate no later than 21 years after the death of an individual then alive. (2) The power is irrevocably exercised or otherwise terminates within 90 years after its creation. (§ 59-3401(c))	See # 7.
9. *Same, but general inter vivos power.*	*See* Unif. Statutory Rule Against Perpetuities § 1, 8B U.L.A. 248 (amended 1990) ("Under the Common-law Rule, a *general power not presently exercisable because of a condition precedent* is invalid as of the time of its creation if the condition *might* neither be satisfied nor become impossible to satisfy with a life in being plus 21 years.")	A general power of appointment not presently exercisable because of a condition precedent is invalid unless one of the following conditions is satisfied: (1) When the power is created, the condition precedent is certain to be satisfied or become impossible to satisfy no later than 21 years after the death of an individual then alive. (2) The condition precedent either is satisfied or	*See* Unif. Statutory Rule Against Perpetuities § 1, 8B U.L.A. 248 (amended 1990) ("Under the Common-law Rule, a *general power not presently exercisable because of a condition precedent* is invalid as of the time of its creation if the condition *might* neither be satisfied nor become impossible to satisfy with a life in being plus 21 years.")

		becomes impossible to satisfy within 90 years after its creation. (§ 59-3401(b))	
10. Same, but nongeneral inter vivos power.	See # 7.	See # 8.	See # 7.
11. Is a period of gestation added to the perpetuity period?	Yes, any relevant period of gestation is added. (§ 558.68(1))	No. The possibility that a child will be born to a person after that person's death is disregarded. (§ 59-3401(d)) *See also* Unif. Statutory Rule Against Perpetuities § 1, 8B U.L. A. 242-43 (amended 1990) ("[T]he possibility that a child will be born to [a testator] after his death must be disregarded; and the possibility that a child will be born to any of [the testator's] descendants after their deaths must also be disregarded. Note, however, that the rule of subsection (d) does *not* apply to the question of the entitlement of an after-born child to take a beneficial interest in the trust").	No. (§ 381.215)
12. What is the treatment of a "later of the traditional rule or 90 years" clause? See UPC 2-901(e).	N/A	That language is inoperative to the extent it produces a period of time that exceeds 21 years after the death of the survivor of the specified lives. (§ 59-3401 (e))	N/A

Table 10
Rule Against Perpetuities *(continued)*

	IOWA	KANSAS	KENTUCKY
13. *When is an interest created by the exercise of a general testamentary power deemed created?*	*See* comment to Unif. Probate Code § 2-902(a) (''general principles of property law determine that a nonvested property interest or power of appointment created by will is created at the decedent's death''); Unif. Statutory Rule Against Perpetuities § 2, 8B U.L.A. 268 (amended 1990) (stating the same).	Except as provided in subsections (b) and (c) and in subsection (a) of K.S.A. 59-3405, the time of creation of a nonvested property interest or a power of appointment is determined under general principles of property law (§ 59-3402(a)) The first two of the excepted provisions states that as long as a person with a general power to become the unqualified beneficial owner has that power, the nonvested interest is created when the power terminates. The third of the excepted provisions states that a nonvested property interest, which arises from a transfer to an existing trust, is created when the nonvested property interest in the trust is created. *See also* Unif. Statutory Rule Against Perpetuities § 2, 8B U.L. A. 268 (amended 1990) (explaining that ''general principles of property law determine that the time . . . [of creation] is at the decedent's death.'') *See generally* § 59-3405(a) (''nonvested property interest or	''The learned author, reasoning out the proposition and reviewing the source cases of England, declares that principle as well as weight of authority is that the validity of the appointment must be determined by reference to the death of the creator or donor.'' (De Charette v. De Charette, 94 S.W.2d 1018, 1021 (Ky. 1936)) *See also* comment to Unif. Probate Code § 2-902(a) (''general principles of property law determine that a nonvested property interest or power of appointment created by will is created at the decedent's death''); Unif. Statutory Rule Against Perpetuities § 2, 8B U.L.A. 268 (amended 1990) (stating the same).

		a power of appointment created by the exercise of a power of appointment is created when the power is irrevocably exercised or when a revocable exercise becomes irrevocable.")	
14. *Same, but nongeneral testamentary power.*	See # 13.	See # 13.	See # 13.
15. *Same, but general inter vivos power.*	*See* comment to Unif. Probate Code § 2-902(a) ("With respect to an inter-vivos transfer, an interest or power is created on the date the transfer becomes effective for purpose of property law generally, normally the date of delivery of the deed or funding of the trust."); Unif. Statutory Rule Against Perpetuities § 2, 8B U.L.A. 268 (stating the same).	Except as provided in subsections (b) and (c) and in subsection (a) of K.S.A. 59-3405, the time of creation of a nonvested property interest or a power of appointment is determined under general principles of property law (§ 59-3402(a)) The first two of the excepted provisions states that as long as a person with a general power to become the unqualified beneficial owner has that power, the nonvested interest is created when the power terminates. The third of the excepted provisions states that a nonvested property interest, which arises from a transfer to an existing trust, is created when the nonvested property interest in the trust was created. *See also* Unif. Statutory Rule Against Perpetuities § 2, 8B U.L.A. 268 (amended 1990) (explaining that "the time when the interest or power is created *(cont'd)*	*See* comment to Unif. Probate Code § 2-902(a) ("With respect to an inter-vivos transfer, an interest or power is created on the date the transfer becomes effective for purpose of property law generally, normally the date of delivery of the deed or funding of the trust."); Unif. Statutory Rule Against Perpetuities § 2, 8B U.L.A. 268 (stating the same).

Table 10
Rule Against Perpetuities *(continued)*

	IOWA	*KANSAS*	*KENTUCKY*
15. *Same, but general inter vivos power. (cont'd)*		is the date the transfer becomes effective for purposes of property law generally, normally the date of delivery of the deed''); Comment to Unif. Probate Code § 2-902(a) (stating same and adding ''the funding of the trust'' as ''normally'' the time when the interest is created). *See generally* § 59-3405(a) (''For the purposes of this section, a nonvested property interest or a power of appointment created by the exercise of a power of appointment is created when the power is irrevocably exercised or when a revocable exercise becomes irrevocable.'').	
16. *Same, but nongeneral inter vivos power.*	See # 15.	See # 15.	See # 15.
17. *When is an interest created if the grantor of a trust has a power to revoke?*	*See* comment to Unif. Probate Code § 2-902(b) (noting that ''nonvested property interest and powers of appointment created in [a revocable inter-vivos trust] are created when the power to revoke expires, usually	For purposes of this act, if there is a person who alone can exercise a power created by a governing instrument to become the unqualified beneficial owner of (i) a nonvested property interest or (ii) a property interest subject	*See* comment to Unif. Probate Code § 2-902(b) (noting that ''nonvested property interest and powers of appointment created in [a revocable inter-vivos trust] are created when the power to revoke expires, usually at the settlor's death''); Unif.

at the settlor's death''); Unif. Statutory Rule Against Perpetuities § 2, 8B U.L.A. 268 (amended 1990) (explaining that ''any nonvested property interest subject to [a power to revoke] is not created . . . until the power terminates (by release, expiration at the death of the donee, or otherwise'').	to a power of appointment described in subsection (b) or (c) of K.S.A. 59-3401, the nonvested property interest or power of appointment is created when the power to become the unqualified beneficial owner terminates. For purposes of this act, a joint power with respect to community property or to marital property under the uniform marital property act held by individuals married to each other is a power exercisable by one person alone. (§ 59-3402(b)) *See also* Unif. Statutory Rule Against Perpetuities § 2, 8B U.L.A. 268 (amended 1990) (explaining that ''any nonvested property interest subject to [a power to revoke] is not created . . . until the power terminates (by release, expiration at the death of the donee, or otherwise''); Comment to Unif. Probate Code § 2-902(b) (noting that ''nonvested property interest and powers of appointment created in [a revocable intervivos trust] are created when the power to revoke expires, usually at the settlor's death''). *See generally* § 59-3405(a) (''a nonvested property interest or a power of appointment	Statutory Rule Against Perpetuities § 2, 8B U.L.A. 268 (amended 1990) (explaining that ''any nonvested property interest subject to [a power to revoke] is not created . . . until the power terminates (by release, expiration at the death of the donee, or otherwise'').

(cont'd)

Table 10
Rule Against Perpetuities *(continued)*

	IOWA	*KANSAS*	*KENTUCKY*
17. *When is an interest created if the grantor of a trust has a power to revoke? (cont'd)*		created by the exercise of a power of appointment is created when the power is irrevocably exercised or when a revocable exercise becomes irrevocable.'')	
18. *When does the period of the rule start re an interest contributed to an irrevocable trust? See UPC 2-902(c).*	*See* comment to Unif. Probate Code 2-902(c) (''Arguably, at common law, each transfer [to an existing irrevocable inter-vivos trust] starts the period of the Rule running anew as to each transfer.'');	A nonvested property interest or a power of appointment arising from a transfer of property to a previously funded trust or other existing property arrangement is created when the nonvested property interest or power of appointment in the original contribution was created. (§ 59-3402(c))	*See* comment to Unif. Probate Code 2-902(c) (''Arguably, at common law, each transfer [to an existing irrevocable inter-vivos trust] starts the period of the Rule running a new as to each transfer.'');
19. *Is there a conclusive presumption of fertility that is, the ''fertile octogenarian'' rule?*	*See, e.g.,* Arkansas, question # 19.	No specific state case or statute.[1] *See* Unif. Statutory Rule Against Perpetuities § 1, 8B U.L.A. 256 (amended 1990) (holding that ''[t]his principle is not superseded by this Act, and in view of new advances in medical science . . . [this] is not unrealistic.''); *but see* C. P. Jhong, Annotation, *Modern Status of Presumption of Possibility of Issue Being Extinct*, 98 A.L. R.2d 1285 (2003) (noting ''a	No. Gilbert v. Union College, 343 S. W.2d 829, 830 (Ky. Ct. App. 1961) (The ''unfortunate confusion'' in this field, . . . we believe will be avoided by new Section KRS 381.216, which substitutes actual events as the test for determining the validity of an interest rather than the metaphysical possibilities doctrine which dreamed up the ''fertile octogenarian,'' the ''unborn widow'' and other possibilities as just reasons for invalidating interests in property.)

		trend toward denying the conclusive or absolute nature of the presumption against the possibility of issue being extinct where there is competent evidence to the contrary has developed in the decisions, although some courts still adhere to the traditional view treating the presumption as conclusive or absolute'').	
20. *What is the earliest age a child is deemed capable of bearing a child? What is the impact of illegitimacy?*	Under the rule, courts must presume that living persons are capable of having or fathering children, no matter how young they are. See In re Graite's Will Trusts, [1949] 1 All E.R. 459, 460 (Ch.). Thus, the rule strikes down any interest whose vesting depends on the assertion that, for example, a toddler will not have children. (Keith L. Butler, Notes & Comments, *Long Live the Dead Hand: A Case for the Repeal of the Rule Against Perpetuities in Washington*, 75 Wash. L. Rev. 1237, 1246 n.78 (2000)).	Not specifically addressed by USRAP, but the reasoning is the same as set forth in the comment to section 1 of USRAP, 2, Technical Violations of the Common Law Rule. Wait and see will typically result in no violation. Nevertheless, the common law rule ordinarily will be applied initially. Under the rule, courts must presume that living persons are capable of having or fathering children, no matter how young they are. See In re Graite's Will Trusts, [1949] 1 All E.R. 459, 460 (Ch.). Thus, the rule strikes down any interest whose vesting depends on the assertion that, for example, a toddler will not have children. (Keith L. Butler, Notes & Comments, *Long Live the Dead Hand: A Case for the*	Under the rule, courts must presume that living persons are capable of having or fathering children, no matter how young they are. See In re Graite's Will Trusts, [1949] 1 All E. R. 459, 460 (Ch.). Thus, the rule strikes down any interest whose vesting depends on the assertion that, for example, a toddler will not have children. (Keith L. Butler, Notes & Comments, *Long Live the Dead Hand: A Case for the Repeal of the Rule Against Perpetuities in Washington*, 75 Wash. L. Rev. 1237, 1246 n.78 (2000)).

(cont'd)

Table 10
Rule Against Perpetuities *(continued)*

	IOWA	*KANSAS*	*KENTUCKY*
20. *What is the earliest age a child is deemed capable of bearing a child? What is the impact of illegitimacy? (cont'd)*		*Repeal of the Rule Against Perpetuities in Washington,* 75 Wash. L. Rev. 1237, 1246 n.78 (2000)).	
21. *Is the "unborn widow" rule observed?*	*See, e.g.,* Arkansas, question # 21.	No specific state case or statute. *See* Unif. Statutory Rule Against Perpetuities § 1, 8B U.L.A. 246 (amended 1990) (explaining that "[t]he chance that [an] interest will become invalid under the Statutory Rule is small" and so the unborn widow rule would rarely invalidate an interest); *see also* 61 Am Jur 2d *Perpetuities and Restraints on Alienation* § 40 (2003) (noting the same).	No. Gilbert v. Union College, 343 S. W.2d 829, 830 (Ky. Ct. App. 1961) (The "unfortunate confusion" in this field, . . . we believe will be avoided by new Section KRS 381.216, which substitutes actual events as the test for determining the validity of an interest rather than the metaphysical possibilities doctrine which dreamed up the "fertile octogenarian", the "unborn widow" and other possibilities as just reasons for invalidating interests in property.)
22. *Does the "slothful executor" rule apply, i.e., an administrative contingency clause providing for a "distribution to, e.g., those issue living at the time of the satisfaction of the administrative condition precedent?"*	*See, e.g.,* California, question # 22.	No specific state case or statute. *See* Unif. Statutory Rule Against Perpetuities § 1, 8B U.L.A. 245 (amended 1990) (Under USRAP, an "interest becomes invalid only if it remains in existence and nonvested 90 years after [the testator's] death. Since it is almost certain that	*See, e.g.,* California, question # 22. *But see* # 21 above.

		the final distribution of [an] estate will occur well within this 90-year period, the chance that [an] interest will be invalid is negligible.'')	
23. *Does the all-or-nothing rule apply to class gifts?*	*See, e.g.*, California, question # 22.	Yes. Beverlin v. First Nat'l Bank, 98 P.2d 200, 204 (Kan. 1940) (upholding the principle that ''if the interest of any potential member of a class can by any possibility vest too remotely the entire class gift fails''). *See also* Unif. Statutory Rule Against Perpetuities § 1, 8B U.L. A. 257 (amended 1990) (''Although this Act does not supersede the basic idea of the much-maligned 'all-or-nothing' rule, the evils sometimes attributed to it are substantially if not entirely eliminated by the wait-and-see feature of the Statutory Rule and by the availability of reformation under Section 3.'')	Yes. Taylor v. Dooley, 297 S.W.2d 905, 908 (Ky. 1956) (''When the rule is applied to a gift to a class, the gift must vest in all members of the class within the limited period, and if it is void as to any of the class, it is void as to all.'') *But see* # 21 above.
24. *Is there an exception to the all-or-nothing rule in the case of subclasses or specific sums to each member of the class?*	*See* Unif. Statutory Rule Against Perpetuities § 2, 8B U.L.A. 257 (''The common law also recognizes a doctrine called the specific-sum doctrine which is derived from Storrs v. Benbow, 3 De G.M. & G. 390, 43 Eng. Rep. 153 (Ch. 1853), and *(cont'd)*	*See* Unif. Statutory Rule Against Perpetuities § 1, 8B U.L.A. 257 (amended 1990) (''The specific-sum and sub-class doctrines are not superseded by this Act.'')	*See* Unif. Statutory Rule Against Perpetuities § 2, 8B U.L.A. 257 (''The common law also recognizes a doctrine called the specific-sum doctrine which is derived from Storrs v. Benbow, 3 De G.M. & G. 390, 43 Eng. Rep. 153 (Ch. 1853), and states: If a specified sum of money is *(cont'd)*

Table 10
Rule Against Perpetuities *(continued)*

	IOWA	*KANSAS*	*KENTUCKY*
24. *Is there an exception to the all-or-nothing rule in the case of subclasses or specific sums to each member of the class? (cont'd)*	states: If a specified sum of money is to be paid to each member of a class, the interest of each class member is entitled to separate treatment and is valid or invalid under the Rule on its own. The common law also recognizes a doctrine called the sub-class doctrine, which is derived from Cattlin v. Brown, 11 Hare 372, 68 Eng. Rep. 1318 (Ch. 1853), and states: If the ultimate takers are not described as a single class but rather as a group of separate subclasses, and if the share to which each separate subclass is entitled will finally be determined within the period of the Rule, the gifts to the different subclasses are separate for the purpose of the Rule.'').		to be paid to each member of a class, the interest of each class member is entitled to separate treatment and is valid or invalid under the Rule on its own. The common law also recognizes a doctrine called the sub-class doctrine, which is derived from Cattlin v. Brown, 11 Hare 372, 68 Eng. Rep. 1318 (Ch. 1853), and states: If the ultimate takers are not described as a single class but rather as a group of separate subclasses, and if the share to which each separate subclass is entitled will finally be determined within the period of the Rule, the gifts to the different subclasses are separate for the purpose of the Rule.'').
25. *Is the infectious invalidity rule followed outside class gifts?*	*See, e.g.*, Colorado, question # 25.	Singer Co. v. Makad, Inc. 518 P.2d 493, 497 (Kan. 1973) (noting the Supreme Court of Kansas's ''reluctance to extend the infectious invalidity rule to situations where its use is not	*See, e.g.*, Colorado, question # 25. *But see* # 21 above.

		necessary to prevent a disposition tying up property for a remote period''). *But see* Unif. Statutory Rule Against Perpetuities § 1, 8B U.L.A. 256 (amended 1990) (explaining that ''[t]he doctrine of infectious invalidity is superseded by this Act by Section 3, under which courts . . . are required to *reform* the disposition to approximate as closely as possible the transferor's . . . plan of distribution.'')	
26. *Is there a rule against the suspension of the power of alienation? If so, how is it stated?*	Reasonableness standard. See In re Estate of Claussen, 482 N. W.2d 381, 385 (Iowa 1992) (characterizing the rule as ''the rule against unreasonable restraints on alienation.'')	Case law unclear. *See* Ehrhart v. Spencer, 263 P.2d 246, 250 (Kan. 1953) (explaining that perpetual leases are not violative of the rule against the suspension of the power of alienation). *But see* Metropolitan Life Ins. Co. v. Strnad, 876 P.2d 1362, 1370 (Kan. 1994) (''Kansas courts recognize that restraints on alienation, even indirect restraints, are not favored by the law.'')	§ 381.220, which provided a rule for the duration of restraints on alienation was repealed in 1960.
27. *Effective date.*	July 1, 1983. (§ 558.68(4))	Apparently July 1, 1992. *See also* # 6. The law applies ''on or after the effective date.'' (§ 59-	Instruments taking effect *after* July 1, 1960, including appointments under powers created *before*

(cont'd) *(cont'd)*

Table 10
Rule Against Perpetuities *(continued)*

	IOWA	*KANSAS*	*KENTUCKY*
27. *Effective date. (cont'd)*		3405(a)). Session Laws 1992, ch. 302, § 5, (S.B.624) Section 20 states the law is effective after publication in the statute book. West provides a July 1, 1992 date as does LEXIS.	July 1, 1960. [Note: There seems to be an error in that instruments taking effect on July 1, 1960 are not addressed.]

1. For questions, # 19 - 25, *see also* § 59-3408 (noting that the state's USRAP supersedes the common law rule against perpetuities). The answers to questions # 19–25 are not like to apply in most cases because of the abolition of the rule with respect to the vast majority of trusts.

Table 10
Rule Against Perpetuities *(continued)*

	LOUISIANA	MAINE	MARYLAND
1. *Which rule is in effect: the common law rule, the Uniform Statutory Rule Against Perpetuities (USRAP), other law, or none?*	Other.	Common law rule with major exceptions. In particular, see # 2b for trusts that are exempt much like Illinois Qualified Perpetual Trusts. (Me. Rev. Stat. Ann. 33, §§ 101 – 106)	Common law rule with major exceptions. In particular, see # 2b for trusts that are exempt much like Illinois Qualified Perpetual Trusts. (Md. Code Ann. Est. & Trusts § 11-102)
2. *a. Is the common law rule relevant to any interests?*	La. Rev. Stat. Ann. 9 § 1721 et seq. (sets out the trust code only); Crichton v. Succession of Gredler, 220 So. 2d 714, 719 (La. Ct. App. 1969) (explaining that Louisiana does not follow the common law rule against perpetuities). Rather, a limit on the term of a trust is imposed. (9 § 1833)	Yes, but only as a starting point of the analysis.	Yes, but only as a starting point of the analysis.
b. What is the relevant rule?	If the trust instrument stipulates a term and unless an earlier termination is required by the trust instrument, or by the proper court, a trust shall terminate at: (1) the death of the last surviving income beneficiary or the expiration of twenty years from the death of the settlor last to die, whichever last occurs, of at least one *(cont'd)*	The interest must vest, if at all, within twenty-one years after some life in being at the creation of the interest. (White v. Fleet Bank, 739 A.2d 373, 377 (Me. 1999)) In applying the rule against perpetuities to an interest in real or personal property limited to take effect at or after the termination of one or more life estates in, or lives of, persons in being when *(cont'd)*	[T]he common law rule against perpetuities as now recognized in the State is preserved (§ 11-102) The object of [the] rule is to prevent the future vesting of an estate upon a contingency which is not certain to happen within 21 years, and a fraction of a year beyond to cover the period of gestation, after some life or lives in being at the creation of the estate. (Ringgold v. Carvel, 76 A.2d 327, 330 (Md. 1950)) The statute *(cont'd)*

Table 10
Rule Against Perpetuities *(continued)*

	LOUISIANA	MAINE	MARYLAND
b. *What is the relevant rule? (cont'd)*	settlor and one income beneficiary are natural persons; (2) the death of the last surviving income beneficiary or the expiration of twenty years from the creation of the trust, whichever last occurs, if none of the settlers is a natural person but at least one income beneficiary is a natural person; (3) the expiration of twenty years from the death of the settlor last to die, if at least one settlor is a natural person but none of the income beneficiaries is a natural person; (4) the expiration of fifty years from the creation of the trust, if none of the settlers and none of the income beneficiaries is a natural person. (9 § 1831) If the trust instrument does not stipulate a term, the trust shall terminate (1) upon the death of the last income beneficiary who	the period of said rule commences to run, the validity of the interest shall be determined on the basis of facts existing at the termination of such one or more life estates or lives. In this section an interest which must terminate not later than the death of one or more persons is a "life estate" even though it may terminate at an earlier time. (33 § 101) *See also* 33 § 101-A "The rule against perpetuities does not apply to a trust created after the effective date of this section if: 1. DECLARATION IN INSTRUMENT. The instrument creating the trust states that the rule against perpetuities does not apply to the trust; and 2. POWER TO SELL, LEASE OR MORTGAGE. The trustee or other person to whom the power is properly granted or delegated has the power under the governing instrument, applicable statute or	applies to legal, as well as equitable interests. (§ 11-103(c)) *See* § 11-102(e) ("A trust in which the governing instrument states that the rule against perpetuities does not apply to the trust and under which the trustee, or other person to whom the power is properly granted or delegated, has the power under the governing instrument, applicable statute, or common law to sell, lease, or mortgage property for any period of time beyond the period that is required for an interest created under the governing instrument to vest, so as to be good under the rule against perpetuities.")

	is a natural person; or (2) at the end of the term prescribed in (3) or (4) as if a term had been stipulated. (9 § 1833)	common law to sell or mortgage property or to lease property for any period of time beyond the period that is required for an interest created under the governing instrument to vest in order to be valid under the rule against perpetuities."	
3. *Does the rule apply to other than private trusts?*	No. *See* 9 § 1834 ("The provisions of [§ 1831] shall not apply to class trusts, to trusts by employers for the benefit of employees, or to charitable dispositions contained in trusts for mixed private and charitable purposes.")	No. This rule does not apply to charitable trusts. (Snow v. President & Trustees of Bowdoin College, 175 A. 268, 270 (Me. 1934))	No. The rule does not apply to: (a) A legacy or inter vivos conveyance having a value of $5,000 or less, or of any burial lot of any value, in trust or otherwise, for the purpose of providing for the perpetual care or keeping in good order and condition, or making repairs to, any lot, vault, mausoleum, or other place of sepulture belonging to any individual or several individuals in any cemetery or graveyard, the lots in which are intended for the burial of members of the family, family connections, relatives, or friends of the owners, or their successors in ownership. (b) A legacy or inter vivos conveyance intended to transfer assets from any corporation incorporated for charitable objects, to any other charitable corporation on a contingency or future event.

(cont'd)

Table 10
Rule Against Perpetuities *(continued)*

	LOUISIANA	*MAINE*	*MARYLAND*
3. *Does the rule apply to other than private trusts? (cont'd)*			(c) A trust created by an employer as part of a pension, stock bonus, disability, death benefit, profit-sharing, retirement, welfare, or other plan for the exclusive benefit of some or all of the employees of the employer or their beneficiaries, to which contributions are made by the employer or employees, or both the employer and employees, for the purpose of making distributions to or for the benefit of employees or their beneficiaries out of the income or principal or both the income and principal of the trust, or for any other purposes set out in the plan. (d) A trust for charitable purposes, which shall include all purposes as are within the spirit or letter of the statute of 43 Elizabeth Ch. 4 (1601), commonly known as the statute of charitable uses. (e) A trust in which the governing instrument states that the rule against perpetuities does not apply to the trust and under which the trustee, or other person to whom the power is

			properly granted or delegated, has the power under the governing instrument, applicable statute, or common law to sell, lease, or mortgage property for any period of time beyond the period that is required for an interest created under the governing instrument to vest, so as to be good under the rule against perpetuities. (§ 11-102)
4. *Does the rule invalidate the interest at its creation, or is the rule revised by a wait-and-see approach?*	Wait-and-see. (9 § 1831)	Wait-and-see. (33 § 101; White v. Fleet Bank, 739 A.2d 373, 378 (Me. 1999))	It appears that the rule applies a wait-and-see approach. "In applying the rule against perpetuities to an interest limited to take effect at or after the termination of one or more life estates in, or lives of, persons in being when the period of the rule commences to run, the validity of the interest *shall be determined on the basis of facts existing at the termination of one or more life estates or lives.*" (§ 11-103(a)) (emphasis added)
5. *Can the trust be reformed?*	No specific state case or statute. However, 9 § 1832 provides that if the term is too exclusive, then the trust "shall be enforced as though the maximum allowable term had been stipulated." *See also* 9 § 1898 with respect to "class trusts."	No specific state case or statute.	Yes, but only "[i]f an interest would violate the rule against perpetuities . . . because the interest is contingent upon any person attaining or failing to attain an age in excess of 21." (§ 11-103(b))

Table 10
Rule Against Perpetuities *(continued)*

	LOUISIANA	MAINE	MARYLAND
6. *If yes to 5., under what theory?*	See # 5.	See # 5.	"[T]he age contingency shall be reduced to 21 as to all persons subject to the same age contingency." (§ 11-103(b))
7. *When is a general testamentary power of appointment invalid?*	See # 5.	*See* Unif. Statutory Rule Against Perpetuities § 1, 8B U.L.A. 248 (amended 1990) ("Under the Common-law Rule . . . a *nongeneral power* (whether or not presently exercisable) or a *general testamentary power* is invalid as of the time of its creation if it *might* not terminate (by irrevocable exercise or otherwise) within a life in being plus 21 years.")	*See* Unif. Statutory Rule Against Perpetuities § 1, 8B U.L.A. 248 (amended 1990) ("Under the Common-law Rule . . . a *nongeneral power* (whether or not presently exercisable) or a *general testamentary power* is invalid as of the time of its creation if it *might* not terminate (by irrevocable exercise or otherwise) within a life in being plus 21 years.")
8. *Same, but nongeneral testamentary power.*	See # 5.	See # 7.	See # 7.
9. *Same, but general inter vivos power.*	See # 5.	*See* Unif. Statutory Rule Against Perpetuities § 1, 8B U.L.A. 248 (amended 1990) ("Under the Common-law Rule, a *general power not presently exercisable because of a condition precedent* is invalid as of the time of its creation if the condition *might* neither be satisfied nor become impossible to satisfy	*See* Unif. Statutory Rule Against Perpetuities § 1, 8B U.L.A. 248 (amended 1990) ("Under the Common-law Rule, a *general power not presently exercisable because of a condition precedent* is invalid as of the time of its creation if the condition *might* neither be satisfied nor become impossible to satisfy with a life in being plus 21 years.")

			with a life in being plus 21 years.'')	
10. *Same, but nongeneral inter vivos power.*	See # 5.		See # 7.	See # 7.
11. *Is a period of gestation added to the perpetuity period?*		N/A	Yes. First Portland Nat'l Bank v. Rodriquez, 172 A.2d 107, 114 (Me. 1961) (citing with approval the Model Rule Against perpetuities which holds that '' 'real or personal property shall be good unless it must vest not later than twenty-one years after some life in being at the creation of the interest and any period of gestation involved in the situation to which the limitation applies.' '')	Yes. (See # 2a.)
12. *What is the treatment of a ''later of the traditional rule or 90 years'' clause? See UPC 2-901(e).*		N/A	N/A	N/A
13. *When is an interest created by the exercise of a general testamentary power deemed created?*	See # 5.		*See* comment to Unif. Probate Code § 2-902(a) (''general principles of property law determine that a nonvested property interest or power of appointment created by will is created at the decedent's death''); Unif. Statutory Rule Against Perpetuities § 2, 8B U.L.A. 268 (amended 1990) (stating the same).	It is a settled rule that in order to test the validity of such appointments they must be construed as if they were inserted in the instrument creating the power. (Gambrill v. Gambrill, 89 A. 1094, 1095 (Md. 1914)) *See also* comment to Unif. Probate Code § 2-902(a) (''general principles of property law determine that a nonvested property interest or power of appointment created by will is created at the decedent's death'');

(cont'd)

Table 10
Rule Against Perpetuities *(continued)*

	LOUISIANA	*MAINE*	*MARYLAND*
13. *When is an interest created by the exercise of a general testamentary power deemed created? (cont'd)*			Unif. Statutory Rule Against Perpetuities § 2, 8B U.L.A. 268 (amended 1990) (stating the same).
14. *Same, but nongeneral testamentary power.*	See # 13.	See # 13.	See # 13.
15. *Same, but general inter vivos power.*	See # 5.	*See* comment to Unif. Probate Code § 2-902(a) (''With respect to an inter-vivos transfer, an interest or power is created on the date the transfer becomes effective for purpose of property law generally, normally the date of delivery of the deed or funding of the trust.''); Unif. Statutory Rule Against Perpetuities § 2, 8B U.L.A. 268 (stating the same).	*See* comment to Unif. Probate Code § 2-902(a) (''With respect to an inter-vivos transfer, an interest or power is created on the date the transfer becomes effective for purpose of property law generally, normally the date of delivery of the deed or funding of the trust.''); Unif. Statutory Rule Against Perpetuities § 2, 8B U.L.A. 268 (stating the same).
16. *Same, but nongeneral inter vivos power.*	See # 15.	See # 15.	See # 15.
17. *When is an interest created if the grantor of a trust has a power to revoke?*	See # 5.	*See* comment to Unif. Probate Code § 2-902(b) (noting that ''nonvested property interest and powers of appointment created in [a revocable inter-vivos trust] are created when the power to revoke expires, usually at the settlor's death''); Unif.	*See* comment to Unif. Probate Code § 2-902(b) (noting that ''nonvested property interest and powers of appointment created in [a revocable inter-vivos trust] are created when the power to revoke expires, usually at the settlor's death''); Unif. Statutory Rule Against Perpetuities § 2,

		Statutory Rule Against Perpetuities § 2, 8B U.L.A. 268 (amended 1990) (explaining that "any nonvested property interest subject to [a power to revoke] is not created . . . until the power terminates (by release, expiration at the death of the donee, or otherwise").	8B U.L.A. 268 (amended 1990) (explaining that "any nonvested property interest subject to [a power to revoke] is not created . . . until the power terminates (by release, expiration at the death of the donee, or otherwise").
18. *When does the period of the rule start re an interest contributed to an irrevocable trust? See UPC 2-902(c).*	See # 5.	*See* comment to Unif. Probate Code 2-902(c) ("Arguably, at common law, each transfer [to an existing irrevocable inter-vivos trust] starts the period of the Rule running anew as to each transfer.")	*See* comment to Unif. Probate Code 2-902(c) ("Arguably, at common law, each transfer [to an existing irrevocable inter-vivos trust] starts the period of the Rule running anew as to each transfer.")
19. *Is there a conclusive presumption of fertility, that is, the "fertile octogenarian" rule?*	N/A	*See, e.g.*, Arkansas, question # 19.	Yes. Marty v. First Nat'l Bank, 120 A.2d 841, 845 (Md. 1956) (noting that "it is considered always possible that a living person may have a child.")
20. *What is the earliest age a child is deemed capable of bearing a child? What is the impact of illegitimacy?*	N/A	Under the rule, courts must presume that living persons are capable of having or fathering children, no matter how young they are. See In re Graite's Will Trusts, [1949] 1 All E.R. 459, 460 (Ch.). Thus, the rule strikes down any interest whose vesting depends on the assertion that, for example, a toddler will not have children. (Keith L. Butler, Notes & Comments, *Long Live* *(cont'd)*	Under the rule, courts must presume that living persons are capable of having or fathering children, no matter how young they are. See In re Graite's Will Trusts, [1949] 1 All E. R. 459, 460 (Ch.). Thus, the rule strikes down any interest whose vesting depends on the assertion that, for example, a toddler will not have children. (Keith L. Butler, Notes & Comments, *Long Live the Dead Hand: A Case for the Repeal of the* *(cont'd)*

Table 10
Rule Against Perpetuities *(continued)*

	LOUISIANA	MAINE	MARYLAND
20. *What is the earliest age a child is deemed capable of bearing a child? What is the impact of illegitimacy? (cont'd)*		*the Dead Hand: A Case for the Repeal of the Rule Against Perpetuities in Washington*, 75 Wash. L. Rev. 1237, 1246 n.78 (2000)).	*Rule Against Perpetuities in Washington*, 75 Wash. L. Rev. 1237, 1246 n.78 (2000)).
21. *Is the "unborn widow" rule observed?*	N/A	*See, e.g.*, Arkansas, question # 21.	Yes. Perkins v. Iglehart, 183 Md. 520, 537 (Md. 1944).
22. *Does the "slothful executor" rule apply, i.e., an administrative contingency clause providing in the case of a "distribution to those of issue living at the time of distribution?"*	N/A	*See, e.g.*, California, question # 22.	*See, e.g.*, California, question # 22.
23. *Does the all-or-nothing rule apply to class gifts?*	N/A	*See, e.g.*, Alabama, question # 23.	Yes. Snyder's Estate v. Denitu, 72 A.2d 757, 760 (Md. 1950) ("If [a gift to a class] might not be good as to some members of the class, the entire gift to the class fails.")
24. *Is there an exception to the all-or-nothing rule in the case of subclasses or specific sums to each member of the class?*	N/A	*See* Unif. Statutory Rule Against Perpetuities § 2, 8B U.L.A. 257 ("The common law also recognizes a doctrine called the specific-sum doctrine which is derived from Storrs v. Benbow, 3 De G.M. & G. 390, 43 Eng. Rep 153 (Ch. 1853), and states: If a specified sum of money is to be	*See* Unif. Statutory Rule Against Perpetuities § 2, 8B U.L.A. 257 ("The common law also recognizes a doctrine called the specific-sum doctrine which is derived from Storrs v. Benbow, 3 De G.M. & G. 390, 43 Eng. Rep. 153 (Ch. 1853), and states: If a specified sum of money is to be paid to each member of a

		paid to each member of a class, the interest of each class member is entitled to separate treatment and is valid or invalid under the Rule on its own. The common law also recognizes a doctrine called the sub-class doctrine, which is derived from Cattlin v. Brown, 11 Hare 372, 68 Eng. Rep. 1318 (Ch. 1853), and states: If the ultimate takers are not described as a single class but rather as a group of separate subclasses, and if the share to which each separate subclass is entitled will finally be determined within the period of the Rule, the gifts to the different subclasses are separate for the purpose of the Rule.'').	class, the interest of each class member is entitled to separate treatment and is valid or invalid under the Rule on its own. The common law also recognizes a doctrine called the sub-class doctrine, which is derived from Cattlin v. Brown, 11 Hare 372, 68 Eng. Rep. 1318 (Ch. 1853), and states: If the ultimate takers are not described as a single class but rather as a group of separate subclasses, and if the share to which each separate subclass is entitled will finally be determined within the period of the Rule, the gifts to the different subclasses are separate for the purpose of the Rule.'').
25. *Is the infectious invalidity rule followed outside class gifts?*	N/A	*See, e.g.*, Colorado, question # 25.	*See, e.g.*, Colorado, question # 25.
26. *Is there a rule against the suspension of the power of alienation? If so, how is it stated?*	The trust instrument may provide that the interest of a beneficiary shall not be subject to voluntary or involuntary alienation by a beneficiary. A restraint upon voluntary alienation by a beneficiary is valid. But a restraint upon involuntary alienation by a beneficiary is subject to the limitations prescribed by this sub-part. (9 § 2001)	Reasonableness standard. Estate of Plummer, 666 A.2d 116, 118 (Me. 1995) (''[W]e addressed three factors to be considered in evaluating the reasonableness of a restraint on alienation. Specifically, we considered (1) the method of determining the price;	Standard unclear. With respect to leases, see Julian v. Christopher, 575 A.2d 735, 738–39 (Md. 1990) (noting that ''there is a public policy against restraints on alienation, if a lease is silent on the subject, a tenant may freely sublease or assign. Restraints on alienation are permitted in leases, but are looked upon with disfavor and are strictly construed'').

(cont'd)

Table 10
Rule Against Perpetuities *(continued)*

	LOUISIANA	*MAINE*	*MARYLAND*
26. *Is there a rule against the suspension of the power of alienation? If so, how is it stated? (cont'd)*		(2) the duration of the restraint; and (3) the purpose of the restraint.")	
27. *Effective date.*	The law has prospective and retroactive effect, except if, with respect to a trust created prior to August 1, 1987, a settlor, trustee or beneficiary makes written objection prior to February 1, 1988. *See* Acts of 1987. No. 163, § 3.	Instruments taking effect after August 20, 1955, including appointments after that date by inter vivos instruments or wills under powers created before August 20, 1955. (33 § 106) The revised Maine rule applies only to "inter vivos" instruments taking effect after August 20, 1955, to wills where the testator dies after August 20, 1955, and to appointments made after August 20, 1955, including appointments made by inter vivos instruments or wills under powers created before said August 20. (33 § 106) Prior valid interests are not affected by the law. (33 § 105)	October 1, 1998. *See* Acts 1998, Ch. 694, § 1.

Table 10
Rule Against Perpetuities *(continued)*

	MASSACHUSETTS	*MICHIGAN*	*MINNESOTA*
1. Which rule is in effect: the common law rule, the Uniform Statutory Rule Against Perpetuities (USRAP), other law, or none?	USRAP. (Mass. Gen. Law. Ch. 184A, §§ 1 – 11)	USRAP. (Mich. Comp. Laws §§ 554.71-554.78)	USRAPP. (Minn. Stat. §§ 501A.01-501A.07)
2. a. Is the common law rule relevant to any interests?	Yes, but only as a starting point of the analysis.	Yes, but only as a starting point of the analysis.	Yes, but only as a starting point of the analysis.
b. What is the relevant rule?	A nonvested property interest is invalid unless: (1) When the interest is created, it is certain to vest or terminate no later than 21 years after the death of an individual then alive; or (2) The interest either vests or terminates within 90 years after its creation. (184A, §1(a))	A nonvested property interest is invalid unless 1 or more of the following are applicable to the interest: (a) When the interest is created, it is certain to vest or terminate no later than 21 years after the death of an individual then alive; or (b) The interest either vests or terminates within 90 years after its creation. (§ 554.72(a))	A nonvested property interest is invalid unless: (1) When the interest is created, it is certain to vest or terminate no later than 21 years after the death of an individual then alive; or (2) The interest either vests or terminates within 90 years after its creation. (§ 501A.01(a))
3. Does the rule apply to other than private trusts?	Yes. The rule applies except to: (1) a nonvested property interest or a power of appointment arising out of a nondonative transfer, except a nonvested property interest or a power of appointment arising out of *(cont'd)*	Yes. The rule applies except to: (a) A nonvested property interest or a power of appointment arising out of a nondonative transfer, except a nonvested property interest or a power of appointment arising out of a *(cont'd)*	Yes. The rule applies except to: (1) a nonvested property interest or a power of appointment arising out of a nondonative transfer, except a nonvested property interest or a power of appointment arising out of (i) a premarital or postmarital agreement, *(cont'd)*

Table 10
Rule Against Perpetuities *(continued)*

	MASSACHUSETTS	*MICHIGAN*	*MINNESOTA*
3. *Does the rule apply to other than private trusts? (cont'd)*	(i) a premarital or postmarital agreement, (ii) a separation or divorce settlement, (iii) a spouse's election, (iv) a similar arrangement arising out of a prospective, existing, or previous marital relationship between the parties, (v) a contract to make or not to revoke a will or trust, (vi) a contract to exercise or not to exercise a power of appointment, (vii) a transfer in satisfaction of a duty of support, or (viii) a reciprocal transfer; (2) a fiduciary's power relating to the administration or management of assets, including the power of a fiduciary to sell, lease, or mortgage property, and the power of a fiduciary to determine principal and income; (3) a power to appoint a fiduciary; (4) a discretionary power of a trustee to distribute principal before termination of a	premarital or postmarital agreement; a separation or divorce settlement; a spouse's election; a similar arrangement arising out of a prospective, existing, or previous marital relationship between the parties; a contract to make or not to revoke a will or trust; a contract to exercise or not to exercise a power of appointment; a transfer in satisfaction of a duty of support; or a reciprocal transfer. (b) A fiduciary's power relating to the administration or management of assets, including the power of a fiduciary to sell, lease, or mortgage property, and the power of a fiduciary to determine principal and income. (c) A power to appoint a fiduciary. (d) A discretionary power of a trustee to distribute principal before termination of a trust to a beneficiary having an indefeasibly vested	(ii) a separation or divorce settlement, (iii) a spouse's election, (iv) a similar arrangement arising out of a prospective, existing, or previous marital relationship between the parties, (v) a contract to make or not to revoke a will or trust, (vi) a contract to exercise or not to exercise a power of appointment, (vii) a transfer in satisfaction of a duty of support, or (viii) a reciprocal transfer; (2) a fiduciary's power relating to the administration or management of assets, including the power of a fiduciary to sell, lease, or mortgage property, and the power of a fiduciary to determine principal and income; (3) a power to appoint a fiduciary; (4) a discretionary power of a trustee to distribute principal before termination of a trust to a beneficiary having an indefeasibly vested interest in the income and principal; (5) a nonvested property interest held by a charity, government, or governmental agency or

trust to a beneficiary having an indefeasibly vested interest in the income and principal;

(5) a nonvested property interest held by a charity, government, or governmental agency or subdivision, if the nonvested property interest is preceded by an interest held by another charity, government, or governmental agency or subdivision; (6)

(6) a nonvested property interest in or a power of appointment with respect to a trust or other property arrangement forming part of a pension, profit-sharing, stock bonus, health, disability, death benefit, income deferral, or other current or deferred benefit plan for one or more employees, independent contractors, or their beneficiaries or spouses, to which contributions are made for the purpose of distributing to or for the benefit of the participants or their beneficiaries or spouses the property, income, or principal in the trust or other property arrangement, except a

(cont'd)

interest in the income and principal.

(e) A property interest, power of appointment, or any other arrangement that was not subject to the common-law rule against perpetuities or is excluded by another statute.

(§ 554.75)

See also § 554.381 ("No statutory or common law rule of this state against perpetuities or restraint of alienation shall hereafter invalidate any gift, grant, devise or bequest, in trust or otherwise, for public welfare purposes.")

subdivision, if the nonvested property interest is preceded by an interest held by another charity, government, or governmental agency or subdivision;

(6) a nonvested property interest in or a power of appointment with respect to a trust or other property arrangement forming part of a pension, profit sharing, stock bonus, health, disability, death benefit, income deferral, or other current or deferred benefit plan for one or more employees, independent contractors, or their beneficiaries or spouses, to which contributions are made for the purpose of distributing to or for the benefit of the participants or their beneficiaries or spouses the property, income, or principal in the trust or other property arrangement, except a nonvested property interest or a power of appointment that is created by an election of a participant or a beneficiary or spouse; or

(7) a property interest, power of appointment, or arrangement that was not subject to the common law rule against perpetuities or is excluded by another statute of this state.

(§ 501A.04)

Table 10
Rule Against Perpetuities *(continued)*

	MASSACHUSETTS	*MICHIGAN*	*MINNESOTA*
3. *Does the rule apply to other than private trusts? (cont'd)*	nonvested property interest or a power of appointment that is created by an election of a participant or a beneficiary or spouse; or (7) a property interest, power of appointment, or arrangement that was not subject to the common-law rule against perpetuities or is excluded by another statute of this state. (184A, § 4)		
4. *Does the rule invalidate the interest at its creation, or is the rule revised by a wait-and-see approach?*	Wait-and-see. (184A, § 1(a)(2))	Wait-and-see. (§ 554.72(a))	Wait-and-see. (§ 501A.01(a))
5. *Can the trust be reformed?*	Yes, but only if one of the following conditions is satisfied: (1) a nonvested property interest or power of appointment becomes invalid under Section 1 (see # 2b). (2) a class gift is not, but might become, invalid under Section 1 and the time has arrived when the share of any class member is to take	Yes, but only if one of the following conditions is satisfied: (a) A nonvested property interest or a power of appointment becomes invalid under Section 2 (see # 2b). (b) A class gift is not but might become invalid under Section 2 and the time has arrived when the share of any class member is to take effect in possession or	Yes but only if one of the following conditions is satisfied: (1) a nonvested property interest or a power of appointment becomes invalid under Section 501A.01 (statutory rule against perpetuities); (2) a class gift is not but might become invalid under Section 501A.01 (statutory rule against perpetuities) and the time has arrived when the share of any

	effect in possession or enjoyment; or (3) a nonvested property interest that is not validated by clause (1) of paragraph (a) of Section 1, that is, the traditional common law rule, can vest but not within ninety years after its creation. (184A, § 3)	enjoyment. (c) A nonvested property interest that is not validated by Section 2(1)(a), that is, the traditional common law rule, can vest but not within 90 years after its creation. (§ 554.74)	class member is to take effect in possession or enjoyment; or (3) a nonvested property interest that is not validated by Section 501A.01, subsection (a)(1), that is, the traditional common law rule, can vest but not within 90 years after its creation. (§ 501A.03)
6. *If yes to 5., under what theory?*	[A] court shall reform a disposition that most closely approximates the trans-feror's manifested plan of distribution and is within the ninety years allowed in clause (2) of paragraph (a), clause (2) of paragraph (b), or clause (2) of paragraph (c) of section 1 (184A,§ 3) *See also* ch. 184A, § 6 ("If a nonvested property interest or a power of appointment was created before the effective date of this chapter and is determined in a judicial proceeding, commenced on or after the effective date of this chapter, to violate the commonwealth's rule against perpetuities as that rule existed before the effective date of this chapter, a court upon the petition of an interested person may reform the disposition in the *(cont'd)*	[A] court shall reform a disposition in the manner most closely approximates the transferor's manifested plan of distribution and is within the 90 years allowed by § 554.72 (§ 554.74) *See also* § 555.76(2) ("If a nonvested property interest or a power of appointment was created before the effective date of this act and is determined in a judicial proceeding, commenced on or after the effective date of this act, to violate the rule against perpetuities as it existed before the effective date of this act, a court, upon the petition of an interested person, may reform the disposition in the manner that most closely approximates the transferor's manifested plan of distribution and is within the limits of the rule against perpetuities *(cont'd)*	[A] court shall reform a disposition in the manner most closely approximates the transferor's manifested plan of distribution and is within the 90 years allowed by § 501A.01 (§ 501A.03) *See also* § 501A.5(b) ("If a nonvested property interest or a power of appointment was created before January 1, 1992, and is determined in a judicial proceeding, commenced after December 31, 1991, to violate this state's rule against perpetuities as that rule existed before January 1, 1992, a court upon the petition of an interested person may reform the disposition in the manner that most closely approximates the transferor's manifested plan of distribution and is within the limits of the rule against perpetuities applicable when the nonvested property interest or power of appointment was created.")

Table 10
Rule Against Perpetuities *(continued)*

	MASSACHUSETTS	*MICHIGAN*	*MINNESOTA*
6. *If yes to 5., under what theory? (cont'd)*	manner that most closely approximates the transferor's manifested plan of distribution and is within the limits of the rule against perpetuities applicable when the nonvested property interest or power of appointment was created.'')	applicable when the nonvested property interest or power of appointment was created.'')	
7. *When is a general testamentary power of appointment invalid?*	A general testamentary power of appointment is invalid unless: (1) when the power is created, it is certain to be irrevocably exercised or otherwise to termination no later than 21 years after the death of an individual then alive; or (2) the power is irrevocably exercised or otherwise terminates within 90 years after its creation. (184A, § 1(c))	A general testamentary power of appointment is invalid unless: (a) when the power is created, it is certain to be irrevocably exercised or otherwise to termination no later than 21 years after the death of an individual then alive; or (b) the power is irrevocably exercised or otherwise terminates within 90 years after its creation. (§ 554.72(3))	A general testamentary power of appointment is invalid unless: (1) when the power is created, it is certain to be irrevocably exercised or otherwise to termination no later than 21 years after the death of an individual then alive; or (2) the power is irrevocably exercised or otherwise terminates within 90 years after its creation. (§ 501A.01(c))
8. *Same, but nongeneral testamentary power.*	A nongeneral testamentary power of appointment is invalid unless: (1) when the power is created, it is certain to be irrevocably exercised or otherwise to termination no later than 21	A nongeneral testamentary power of appointment is invalid unless: (a) when the power is created, it is certain to be irrevocably exercised or otherwise to termination no later than 21	A nongeneral testamentary power of appointment is invalid unless: (1) when the power is created, it is certain to be irrevocably exercised or otherwise to termination no later than 21 years after

	years after the death of an individual then alive; or (2) the power is irrevocably exercised or otherwise terminates within 90 years after its creation. (184A, §1(c))	years after the death of an individual then alive; or (b) the power is irrevocably exercised or otherwise terminates within 90 years after its creation. (§ 554.72(3))	the death of an individual then alive; or (2) the power is irrevocably exercised or otherwise terminates within 90 years after its creation. (§ 501A.01(c))
9. *Same, but general inter vivos power.*	A general power of appointment not presently exercisable because of a condition precedent is invalid unless: (1) when the power is created, the condition precedent is certain to be satisfied or becomes impossible to satisfy no later than 21 years after the death of an individual then alive; or (2) the condition precedent either is satisfied or becomes impossible to satisfy within 90 years after its creation. (184A, §1(b))	A general power of appointment not presently exercisable because of a condition precedent is invalid unless: (a) when the power is created, the condition precedent is certain to be satisfied or becomes impossible to satisfy no later than 21 years after the death of an individual then alive; or (b) the condition precedent either is satisfied or becomes impossible to satisfy within 90 years after its creation. (§ 554.72(2))	A general power of appointment not presently exercisable because of a condition precedent is invalid unless: (1) when the power is created, the condition precedent is certain to be satisfied or becomes impossible to satisfy no later than 21 years after the death of an individual then alive; or (2) the condition precedent either is satisfied or becomes impossible to satisfy within 90 years after its creation. (§ 501A.01(b))
10. *Same, but nongeneral inter vivos power.*	See # 8.	See # 8.	See # 8.
11. *Is a period of gestation added to the perpetuity period?*	No. The possibility that a child will be born to a person after that person's death is disregarded. (184A, § 1(d)) *See also* Unif. Statutory Rule Against Perpetuities § 1, 8B *(cont'd)*	No. The possibility that a child will be born to a person after that person's death is disregarded. (§ 554.72(4)) *See also* Unif. Statutory Rule Against Perpetuities § 1, 8B U.L.A. 242-43 *(cont'd)*	No. The possibility that a child will be born to a person after that person's death is disregarded. (§ 501A.01(d)) *See also* Unif. Statutory Rule Against Perpetuities § 1, 8B U.L.A. 242-43 (amended 1990) *(cont'd)*

Table 10
Rule Against Perpetuities *(continued)*

	MASSACHUSETTS	*MICHIGAN*	*MINNESOTA*
11. *Is a period of gestation added to the perpetuity period? (cont'd)*	U.L.A. 242-43 (amended 1990) (''[T]he possibility that a child will be born to [a testator] after his death must be disregarded; and the possibility that a child will be born to any of [the testator's] descendants after their deaths must also be disregarded. Note, however, that the rule of subsection (d) does *not* apply to the question of the entitlement of an after-born child to take a beneficial interest in the trust'').	(amended 1990) (''[T]he possibility that a child will be born to [a testator] after his death must be disregarded; and the possibility that a child will be born to any of [the testator's] descendants after their deaths must also be disregarded. Note, however, that the rule of subsection (d) does *not* apply to the question of the entitlement of an after-born child to take a beneficial interest in the trust'').	(''[T]he possibility that a child will be born to [a testator] after his death must be disregarded; and the possibility that a child will be born to any of [the testator's] descendants after their deaths must also be disregarded. Note, however, that the rule of subsection (d) does *not* apply to the question of the entitlement of an after-born child to take a beneficial interest in the trust'').
12. *What is the treatment of a ''later of the traditional rule or 90 years'' clause? See UPC 2-901(e).*	Massachusetts's USRAP does not specify how it will treat ''later of'' clauses.	Michigan's USRAP does not specify how it will treat ''later of'' clauses.	That language is inoperative to the extent it produces a period of time that exceeds 21 years after the death of the survivor of the specified lives. (§ 501A.01(e))
13. *When is an interest created by the exercise of a general testamentary power deemed created?*	Except as provided in paragraphs (b) and (c) and in paragraph (a) of section five, the time of creation of a nonvested property interest or a power of appointment is determined under general principles of property law. (184A, § 2(a)) The first two of the excepted provisions states that as long as a person	Except as provided in subsections (2), (3), and section 6(1), the time of creation of a nonvested property interest or a power of appointment shall be determined by statutory or common law. (§ 554.73(1)) The first two of the excepted provisions states that as long as a person with a general power to become	Except as provided in subsections (b) and (c) and in section 501A.05, subsection (a), the time of creation of a nonvested property interest or a power of appointment is determined under general principles of property law. (§ 501A.02(a)) The first two of the excepted provisions states that as long as a person with a general power to become the

	with a general power to become the unqualified beneficial owner has that power, the nonvested interest is created when the power terminates. The third of the excepted provisions states that a nonvested property interest, which arises from a transfer to an existing trust, is created when the nonvested property interest in the trust was created. *See also* Unif. Statutory Rule Against Perpetuities § 2, 8B U.L.A. 268 (amended 1990) (explaining that "general principles of property law determine that the time . . . [of creation] is at the decedent's death"). *See generally* § 5(a) ("For the purposes of this section, a nonvested property interest or a power of appointment created by the exercise of a power of appointment is created when the power is irrevocably exercised or when a revocable exercise becomes irrevocable.")	the unqualified beneficial owner has that power, the nonvested interest is created when the power terminates. The third of the excepted provisions states that a nonvested property interest, which arises from a transfer to an existing trust, is created when the nonvested property interest in the trust was created. *See also* Unif. Statutory Rule Against Perpetuities § 2, 8B U.L.A. 268 (amended 1990) (explaining that "general principles of property law determine that the time . . . [of creation] is at the decedent's death"). *See generally* § 554.76(1) ("For the purposes of this section, a nonvested property interest or a power of appointment created by the exercise of a power of appointment is created when the power is irrevocably exercised or when a revocable exercise becomes irrevocable.")	unqualified beneficial owner has that power, the nonvested interest is created when the power terminates. The third of the excepted provisions states that a nonvested property interest, which arises from a transfer to an existing trust, is created when the nonvested property interest in the trust was created. *See also* Unif. Statutory Rule Against Perpetuities § 2, 8B U.L.A. 268 (amended 1990) (explaining that "general principles of property law determine that the time . . . [of creation] is at the decedent's death"). *See generally* § 501A.05(a) ("For the purposes of this section, a nonvested property interest or a power of appointment created by the exercise of a power of appointment is created when the power is irrevocably exercised or when a revocable exercise becomes irrevocable.")
14. *Same, but nongeneral testamentary power.*	See # 13.	See # 13.	See # 13.
15. *Same, but general inter vivos power.*	Except as provided in paragraphs (b) and (c) and in paragraph (a) of section five, the time of creation of a nonvested property interest or a power of *(cont'd)*	Except as provided in subsections (2), (3), and section 6(1), the time of creation of a nonvested property interest or a power of appointment shall be *(cont'd)*	Except as provided in subsections (2), (3), and section 6(1), the time of creation of a nonvested property interest or a power of appointment *(cont'd)*

Table 10
Rule Against Perpetuities *(continued)*

	MASSACHUSETTS	MICHIGAN	MINNESOTA
15. *Same, but general inter vivos power. (cont'd)*	appointment is determined under general principles of property law. (184A, § 2(a)) The first two of the excepted provisions states that as long as a person with a general power to become the unqualified beneficial owner has that power, the nonvested interest is created when the power terminates. The third of the excepted provisions states that a nonvested property interest, which arises from a transfer to an existing trust, is created when the nonvested property interest in the trust was created. *See also* Unif. Statutory Rule Against Perpetuities § 2, 8B U.L.A. 268 (amended 1990) (explaining that "the time when the interest or power is created is the date the transfer becomes effective for purposes of property law generally, normally the date of delivery of the deed"); Comment to Unif. Probate Code § 2-902(a) (stating same and adding "the funding of the trust" as "normally" the time when the interest is created).	determined by statutory or common law. (§ 554.73(1)) The first two of the excepted provisions states that as long as a person with a general power to become the unqualified beneficial owner has that power, the nonvested interest is created when the power terminates. The third of the excepted provisions states that a nonvested property interest, which arises from a transfer to an existing trust, is created when the nonvested property interest in the trust was created. *See also* Unif. Statutory Rule Against Perpetuities § 2, 8B U.L.A. 268 (amended 1990) (explaining that "the time when the interest or power is created is the date the transfer becomes effective for purposes of property law generally, normally the date of delivery of the deed"); Comment to Unif. Probate Code § 2-902(a) (stating same and adding "the funding of the trust" as "normally" the time when the interest is created).	shall be determined by statutory or common law. (§ 554.73(1)) The first two of the excepted provisions states that as long as a person with a general power to become the unqualified beneficial owner has that power, the nonvested interest is created when the power terminates. The third of the excepted provisions states that a nonvested property interest, which arises from a transfer to an existing trust, is created when the nonvested property interest in the trust was created. *See also* Unif. Statutory Rule Against Perpetuities § 2, 8B U.L.A. 268 (amended 1990) (explaining that "the time when the interest or power is created is the date the transfer becomes effective for purposes of property law generally, normally the date of delivery of the deed"); Comment to Unif. Probate Code § 2-902(a) (stating same and adding "the funding of the trust" as "normally" the time when the interest is created). *See generally* § 501A.05(a) ("For the purposes of this section, a

	See generally § 5(a) ("For the purposes of this section, a nonvested property interest or a power of appointment created by the exercise of a power of appointment is created when the power is irrevocably exercised or when a revocable exercise becomes irrevocable.")	*See generally* § 554.76(1) ("For the purposes of this section, a nonvested property interest or a power of appointment created by the exercise of a power of appointment is created when the power is irrevocably exercised or when a revocable exercise becomes irrevocable.")	nonvested property interest or a power of appointment created by the exercise of a power of appointment is created when the power is irrevocably exercised or when a revocable exercise becomes irrevocable.")
16. *Same, but nongeneral inter vivos power.*	See # 15.	See # 15.	See # 15.
17. *When is an interest created if the grantor of a trust has a power to revoke?*	"If there is a person who alone can exercise a power created by a governing instrument to become the unqualified beneficial owner of (i) a nonvested property interest or (ii) a property interest subject to a power of appointment described in paragraph (b) or paragraph (c) of section one, the nonvested property interest or power of appointment is created when the power to become the unqualified beneficial owner terminates." (184A, § 2(b)) *See also* Unif. Statutory Rule Against Perpetuities § 2, 8B U.L.A. 268 (amended 1990) (explaining that "any nonvested property interest subject to [a power to revoke] is not created . . . until the power terminates (by release, expiration at the *(cont'd)*	For purposes of this act, if there is a person who alone can exercise a power created by a governing instrument to become the unqualified beneficial owner of a nonvested property interest or a property interest subject to a power of appointment described in section 2(2) or (3), the nonvested property interest or power of appointment is created when the power to become the unqualified beneficial owner terminates. (§ 554.73(b)) *See also* Unif. Statutory Rule Against Perpetuities § 2, 8B U.L.A. 268 (amended 1990) (explaining that "any nonvested property interest subject to [a power to revoke] is not created . . . until the power terminates (by release, expiration at the death of the donee, or *(cont'd)*	"If there is a person who alone can exercise a power created by a governing instrument to become the unqualified beneficial owner of (i) a nonvested property interest or (ii) a property interest subject to a power of appointment described in section 501A.01, subsection (b) or (c), the nonvested property interest or power of appointment is created when the power to become the unqualified beneficial owner terminates. (§ 501A.02(b)) *See also* Unif. Statutory Rule Against Perpetuities § 2, 8B U.L.A. 268 (amended 1990) (explaining that "any nonvested property interest subject to [a power to revoke] is not created . . . until the power terminates (by release, expiration at the death of the donee, or otherwise"); Comment to Unif. Probate Code § 2-902(b) (noting that "nonvested *(cont'd)*

Table 10
Rule Against Perpetuities *(continued)*

	MASSACHUSETTS	*MICHIGAN*	*MINNESOTA*
17. *When is an interest created if the grantor of a trust has a power to revoke? (cont'd)*	death of the donee, or otherwise''); Comment to Unif. Probate Code § 2-902(b) (noting that ''nonvested property interest and powers of appointment created in [a revocable inter-vivos trust] are created when the power to revoke expires, usually at the settlor's death''). *See generally* § 5(a) (''a nonvested property interest or a power of appointment created by the exercise of a power of appointment is created when the power is irrevocably exercised or when a revocable exercise becomes irrevocable.'')	otherwise''); Comment to Unif. Probate Code § 2-902(b) (noting that ''nonvested property interest and powers of appointment created in [a revocable inter-vivos trust] are created when the power to revoke expires, usually at the settlor's death''). *See generally* § 554.76(1) (''a nonvested property interest or a power of appointment created by the exercise of a power of appointment is created when the power is irrevocably exercised or when a revocable exercise becomes irrevocable.'')	property interest and powers of appointment created in [a revocable inter-vivos trust] are created when the power to revoke expires, usually at the settlor's death''). *See generally* § 501A.05(a) (''a nonvested property interest or a power of appointment created by the exercise of a power of appointment is created when the power is irrevocably exercised or when a revocable exercise becomes irrevocable.'')
18. *When does the period of the rule start re an interest contributed to an irrevocable trust? See UPC 2-902(c).*	A nonvested property interest or power of appointment arising from a transfer of property to a previously funded trust or other existing property arrangement is created when the nonvested property interest or power of appointment in the original contribution was created. (184A, §2(c))	A nonvested property interest or power of appointment arising from a transfer of property to a previously funded trust or other existing arrangement is created when the nonvested property interest or power of appointment in the original contribution was created. (§554.73(c))	A nonvested property interest or power of appointment arising from a transfer of property to a previously funded trust or other existing arrangement is created when the nonvested property interest or power of appointment in the original contribution was created. (§ 501A.02(c))

19. *Is there a conclusive presumption of fertility, that is, the "fertile octogenarian" rule?*	Unclear. *See* Commissioner of Corps. & Taxation v. Bullard, 46 N.E.2d 557, 565 (Mass. 1945) ("It is clear . . . that this court has never laid down expressly or by implication the general proposition applicable to all kinds of cases that there is an "irrebuttable presumption" or rule of substantive law that a woman is capable of bearing children throughout her life.")[1] *See also* Unif. Statutory Rule Against Perpetuities § 1, 8B U.L.A. 256 (amended 1990) (holding that "[t]his principle is not superseded by this Act, and in view of new advances in medical science . . . [this] is not unrealistic.")); *but see* C. P. Jhong, Annotation, *Modern Status of Presumption of Possibility of Issue Being Extinct*, 98 A.L.R.2d 1285 (2003) (noting "a trend toward denying the conclusive or absolute nature of the presumption against the possibility of issue being extinct where there is competent evidence to the contrary has developed in the decisions, although some courts still adhere to the traditional view treating the presumption as conclusive or absolute").	Yes. Gettins v. Grand Rapids Trust Co., 228 N.W. 703, 704 (Mich. 1930). *See also* Unif. Statutory Rule Against Perpetuities § 1, 8B U.L.A. 256 (amended 1990) (holding that "[t]his principle is not superseded by this Act, and in view of new advances in medical science . . . [this] is not unrealistic.")); *but see* C. P. Jhong, Annotation, *Modern Status of Presumption of Possibility of Issue Being Extinct*, 98 A.L.R.2d 1285 (2003) (noting "a trend toward denying the conclusive or absolute nature of the presumption against the possibility of issue being extinct where there is competent evidence to the contrary has developed in the decisions, although some courts still adhere to the traditional view treating the presumption as conclusive or absolute").	No specific state case or statute.[2] *See* Unif. Statutory Rule Against Perpetuities § 1, 8B U.L.A. 256 (amended 1990) (holding that "[t]his principle is not superseded by this Act, and in view of new advances in medical science . . . [this] is not unrealistic.")); *but see* C. P. Jhong, Annotation, *Modern Status of Presumption of Possibility of Issue Being Extinct*, 98 A.L.R.2d 1285 (2003) (noting "a trend toward denying the conclusive or absolute nature of the presumption against the possibility of issue being extinct where there is competent evidence to the contrary has developed in the decisions, although some courts still adhere to the traditional view treating the presumption as conclusive or absolute").

Table 10
Rule Against Perpetuities *(continued)*

	MASSACHUSETTS	*MICHIGAN*	*MINNESOTA*
20. *What is the earliest age a child is deemed capable of bearing a child? What is the impact of illegitimacy?*	Not specifically addressed by USRAP, but the reasoning is the same as set forth in the comment to section 1 of USRAP, 2, Technical Violations of the Common Law Rule. Wait and see will typically result in no violation. Nevertheless, the common law rule ordinarily will be applied initially. Under the rule, courts must presume that living persons are capable of having or fathering children, no matter how young they are. See In re Graite's Will Trusts, [1949] 1 All E.R. 459, 460 (Ch.). Thus, the rule strikes down any interest whose vesting depends on the assertion that, for example, a toddler will not have children. (Keith L. Butler, Notes & Comments, *Long Live the Dead Hand: A Case for the Repeal of the Rule Against Perpetuities in Washington*, 75 Wash. L. Rev. 1237, 1246 n.78 (2000)).	Not specifically addressed by USRAP, but the reasoning is the same as set forth in the comment to section 1 of USRAP, 2, Technical Violations of the Common Law Rule. Wait and see will typically result in no violation. Nevertheless, the common law rule ordinarily will be applied initially. Under the rule, courts must presume that living persons are capable of having or fathering children, no matter how young they are. See In re Graite's Will Trusts, [1949] 1 All E.R. 459, 460 (Ch.). Thus, the rule strikes down any interest whose vesting depends on the assertion that, for example, a toddler will not have children. (Keith L. Butler, Notes & Comments, *Long Live the Dead Hand: A Case for the Repeal of the Rule Against Perpetuities in Washington*, 75 Wash. L. Rev. 1237, 1246 n.78 (2000)).	Not specifically addressed by USRAP, but the reasoning is the same as set forth in the comment to section 1 of USRAP, 2, Technical Violations of the Common Law Rule. Wait and see will typically result in no violation. Nevertheless, the common law rule ordinarily will be applied initially. Under the rule, courts must presume that living persons are capable of having or fathering children, no matter how young they are. See In re Graite's Will Trusts, [1949] 1 All E.R. 459, 460 (Ch.). Thus, the rule strikes down any interest whose vesting depends on the assertion that, for example, a toddler will not have children. (Keith L. Butler, Notes & Comments, *Long Live the Dead Hand: A Case for the Repeal of the Rule Against Perpetuities in Washington*, 75 Wash. L. Rev. 1237, 1246 n.78 (2000)).
21. *Is the "unborn widow" rule observed?*	No specific state case or statute. *See* Unif. Statutory Rule Against Perpetuities § 1, 8B U.L.A. 246 (amended 1990)	No specific state case or statute. *See* Unif. Statutory Rule Against Perpetuities § 1, 8B U.L.A. 246 (amended 1990)	No specific state case or statute. *See* Unif. Statutory Rule Against Perpetuities § 1, 8B U.L.A. 246 (amended 1990) (explaining that

	(explaining that ''[t]he chance that [an] interest will become invalid under the Statutory Rule is small'' and so the unborn widow rule would rarely invalidate an interest); *see also* 61 Am Jur 2d *Perpetuities and Restraints on Alienation* § 40 (2003) (noting the same).	(explaining that ''[t]he chance that [an] interest will become invalid under the Statutory Rule is small'' and so the unborn widow rule would rarely invalidate an interest); *see also* 61 Am Jur 2d *Perpetuities and Restraints on Alienation* § 40 (2003) (noting the same).	''[t]he chance that [an] interest will become invalid under the Statutory Rule is small'' and so the unborn widow rule would rarely invalidate an interest); *see also* 61 Am Jur 2d *Perpetuities and Restraints on Alienation* § 40 (2003) (noting the same).
22. *Does the ''slothful executor'' rule apply, i.e., an administrative contingency clause providing for a ''distribution to, e.g., those issue living at the time of the satisfaction of the administrative condition precedent?''*	No. Brandenburg v. Thorndike, 28 N.E. 575, 576 (Mass. 1885) (explaining that it is not within the ''unlimited discretion of the [executors] to delay the vesting or enjoyment of the estates to such time as they think expedient.'') *See also* Unif. Statutory Rule Against Perpetuities § 1, 8B U.L.A. 245 (amended 1990) (Under USRAP, an ''interest becomes invalid only if it remains in existence and nonvested 90 years after [the testator's] death. Since it is almost certain that the final distribution of [an] estate will occur well within this 90-year period, the chance that [an] interest will be invalid is negligible.'')	No specific state case or statute. *See* Unif. Statutory Rule Against Perpetuities § 1, 8B U.L.A. 245 (amended 1990) (Under USRAP, an ''interest becomes invalid only if it remains in existence and nonvested 90 years after [the testator's] death. Since it is almost certain that the final distribution of [an] estate will occur well within this 90-year period, the chance that [an] interest will be invalid is negligible.'')	No specific state case or statute. *See* Unif. Statutory Rule Against Perpetuities § 1, 8B U.L.A. 245 (amended 1990) (Under USRAP, an ''interest becomes invalid only if it remains in existence and nonvested 90 years after [the testator's] death. Since it is almost certain that the final distribution of [an] estate will occur well within this 90-year period, the chance that [an] interest will be invalid is negligible.'')
23. *Does the all-or-nothing rule apply to class gifts?*	Yes. Springfield Safe Deposit & Trust Co. v. Ireland, 167 N.E. 261, 263 (Mass. 1929) (''When the gift is of the whole estate to a class of persons answering a *(cont'd)*	No specific state case or statute. *See* Unif. Statutory Rule Against Perpetuities § 1, 8B U.L.A. 257 (amended 1990) (''Although this Act does not *(cont'd)*	No specific state case or statute. *See* Unif. Statutory Rule Against Perpetuities § 1, 8B U.L.A. 257 (amended 1990) (''Although this Act does not supersede the basic *(cont'd)*

Table 10
Rule Against Perpetuities *(continued)*

	MASSACHUSETTS	MICHIGAN	MINNESOTA
23. *Does the all-or-nothing rule apply to class gifts? (cont'd)*	given description, and not separately to its members, and any member of that class may have to be ascertained at a period beyond the limit allowed by law, the whole gift is void.'') *See also* Unif. Statutory Rule Against Perpetuities § 1, 8B U.L.A. 257 (amended 1990) (''Although this Act does not supersede the basic idea of the much-maligned 'all-or-nothing' rule, the evils sometimes attributed to it are substantially if not entirely eliminated by the wait-and-see feature of the Statutory Rule and by the availability of reformation under Section 3.'')	supersede the basic idea of the much-maligned 'all-or-nothing' rule, the evils sometimes attributed to it are substantially if not entirely eliminated by the wait-and-see feature of the Statutory Rule and by the availability of reformation under Section 3.'')	idea of the much-maligned 'all-or-nothing' rule, the evils sometimes attributed to it are substantially if not entirely eliminated by the wait-and-see feature of the Statutory Rule and by the availability of reformation under Section 3.'')
24. *Is there an exception to the all-or-nothing rule in the case of subclasses or specific sums to each member of the class?*	No specific state case or statute. *See* Unif. Statutory Rule Against Perpetuities § 1, 8B U.L.A. 257 (amended 1990) (''The specific-sum and sub-class doctrines are not superseded by this Act.'')	No specific state case or statute. *See* Unif. Statutory Rule Against Perpetuities § 1, 8B U.L.A. 257 (amended 1990) (''The specific-sum and sub-class doctrines are not superseded by this Act.'')	No specific state case or statute. *See* Unif. Statutory Rule Against Perpetuities § 1, 8B U.L.A. 257 (amended 1990) (''The specific-sum and sub-class doctrines are not superseded by this Act.'')
25. *Is the infectious invalidity rule followed outside class gifts?*	Yes, but only in ''circumstances where the failure of a gift may so disrupt the dispositive scheme of the settlor or testator that he	No specific state case or statute. *See* Unif. Statutory Rule Against Perpetuities § 1, 8B U.L.A. 256 (amended 1990)	No specific state case or statute. *See* Unif. Statutory Rule Against Perpetuities § 1, 8B U.L.A. 256 (amended 1990) (explaining that

	would prefer that valid prior gifts should also be struck down." England Trust Co. v. Sanger, 149 N.E.2d 598, 605 (Mass. 1958). *But see* Unif. Statutory Rule Against Perpetuities § 1, 8B U.L.A. 256 (amended 1990) (explaining that "[t]he doctrine of infectious invalidity is superseded by this Act by Section 3, under which courts . . . are required to *reform* the disposition to approximate as closely as possible the transferor's . . . plan of distribution.")	(explaining that "[t]he doctrine of infectious invalidity is superseded by this Act by Section 3, under which courts . . . are required to *reform* the disposition to approximate as closely as possible the transferor's . . . plan of distribution.")	"[t]he doctrine of infectious invalidity is superseded by this Act by Section 3, under which courts . . . are required to *reform* the disposition to approximate as closely as possible the transferor's . . . plan of distribution.")
26. Is there a rule against the suspension of the power of alienation? If so, how is it stated?	No specific state statute. *See* Franklin v. Spadafora, 447 N.E.2d 1244, 1346 (Mass. 1983) (explaining that the court will enforce "reasonable restraints on alienation and listing five factors that support the conclusion of reasonableness.")	Michigan's § 554.52, which provided a rule against the suspension of the power of alienation, was repealed.	No specific state statute. *See* Anderson v. Amundson, 126 N.W.2d 250 (Sup. Ct. 1964 "The absolute power of alienation shall not be suspended, by any limitation or condition, for a longer period than during the continuance of two lives in being at the creation of the estate.")
27. Effective date.	June 30, 1990. See also # 6.	December 27, 1998. See also # 6.	January 1, 1992. See also # 6.

1. For questions, # 19-25, *see also* 184A, § 11 (noting that the state's USRAP supersedes the common law rule against perpetuities). The answers to questions # 19–25 are not likely to apply in most cases because of the abolition of the rule with respect to the vast majority of trusts.
2. For questions, # 19-25, *see also* § 501A.06 (noting that the state's USRAP supersedes the common law rule against perpetuities). The answers to questions # 19–25 are not likely to apply in most cases because of the abolition of the rule with respect to the vast majority of trusts.

Table 10
Rule Against Perpetuities *(continued)*

	MISSISSIPPI	*MISSOURI*	*MONTANA*
1. *Which rule is in effect: the common law rule, the Uniform Statutory Rule Against Perpetuities (USRAP), other law, or none?*	Common Law Rule. (C&D Inv. Co. v. Gulf Transport Co., 526 So. 2d 526, 528 (1988))	Common law rule with major exceptions. In particular, see # 2b for trusts that are exempt much like Illinois Qualified Perpetual Trusts. (§ 456.025)	USRAP (Mont. Code Ann. §§ 72-2-1001 – 72-2-1007)
2. a. *Is the common law rule relevant to any interests?*	Yes.	Yes, for some interests.	Yes, but only as the starting point of the analysis.
b. *What is the relevant rule?*	The rule against perpetuities requires that [an interest] must either definitely vest or definitely fail within 21 years of some life in being at the time of the instrument. (C&D Inv. Co. v. Gulf Transport Co., 526 So. 2d 526, 528 (Miss. 1988))	"'The rule against perpetuities is that no interest within its scope is good unless it must vest, if at all, not later than twenty-one years after some life or lives in being at the creation of the interest, to which period is added the period of gestation, if gestation exists.'" (St. Louis Union Trust Co. v. Kelley, 199 S. W.2d 344, 350 (Mo. 1947)) *See also* § 456.025(1) ("The rule against perpetuities shall not apply to and any rule prohibiting unreasonable restraints on or suspension of the power of alienation shall not be violated by a trust if a trustee, or other person or persons to whom the power is properly granted or delegated, has the power	A nonvested property interest is invalid unless: (a) When the interest is created, it is certain to vest or terminate no later than 21 years after the death of an individual then alive; or (b) The interest either vests or terminates within 90 years after its creation. (§ 72-2-1002(1))

		pursuant to the terms of the trust or applicable law to sell the trust property during the period of time the trust continues beyond the period of the rule against perpetuities that would apply to the trust but for this subsection.")	
3. *Does the rule apply to other than private trusts?*	Yes. The rule applies to everything except: § 79-15-21 (inapplicable to investment trusts); § 41-43-51 (inapplicable to cemeteries); *see, e.g.*, Alabama, question # 3 (noting that the Rule generally does not apply to charitable trusts)	Yes. The rule applies except to: – "a trust of real or personal property, or both, created as part of a stock bonus plan, pension plan, disability or death benefit plan, medical benefit plan, profit-sharing plan or retirement plan, for the exclusive benefit of employees or self-employed persons" (§ 456.011) – a trust for charitable purposes. (Mercantile Trust Co. v. Shriners' Hospital, 551 S.W.2d 864, 867 (Mo. Ct. App. 1977) – a qualifying trust. See # 2b. The exception to the rule with respect to qualifying trusts applies to such trusts created by instrument or exercise of a nongeneral power executed or amended on or after August 28, 2001; a trust created by exercise of a general power on or after August 28, 2001; or the laws of Missouri become *(cont'd)*	Yes. The rule applies except to: (1) a nonvested property interest or a power of appointment arising out of a nondonative transfer, except a nonvested property interest or a power of appointment arising out of a: (a) premarital or postmarital agreement; (b) separation or divorce settle-ment; (c) spouse's election; (d) similar arrangement arising out of a prospective, existing, or previous marital relationship between the parties; (e) contract to make or not to revoke a will or trust; (f) contract to exercise or not to exercise a power of appointment; (g) transfer in satisfaction of a duty of support; or (h) reciprocal transfer; *(cont'd)*

Table 10
Rule Against Perpetuities *(continued)*

	MISSISSIPPI	MISSOURI	MONTANA
3. *Does the rule apply to other than private trusts? (cont'd)*		applicable to the trust on or after August 28, 2001, the laws of any other state applied to the trust before August 28, 2001, and the rule did not apply to the trust pursuant to the law of the other state. (§ 456.025(3)(3))	(2) a fiduciary's power relating to the administration or management of assets, including the power of a fiduciary to sell, lease, or mortgage property, and the power of a fiduciary to determine principal and income; (3) the power to appoint a fiduciary; (4) a discretionary power of a trustee to distribute principal before termination of a trust to a beneficiary having an indefeasibly vested interest in the income and principal; (5) a nonvested property interest held by a charity, government, or governmental agency or subdivision if the nonvested property interest is preceded by an interest held by another charity, government, or governmental agency or subdivision; (6) a nonvested property interest in or a power of appointment with respect to a trust or other property arrangement forming part of a pension, profit-sharing, stock bonus, health, disability, death benefit, income deferral, or other current or deferred benefit

			plan for one or more employees or independent contractors, or their beneficiaries or spouses, to which contributions are made for the purpose of distributing to or for the benefit of the participants or their beneficiaries or spouses the property, income, or principal in the trust or other property arrangement, except a nonvested property interest or a power of appointment that is created by an election of a participant or a beneficiary or spouse; or (7) a property interest, power of appointment, or arrangement that was not subject to the common-law rule against perpetuities or is excluded by another statute of this state. (§ 72-2-1005)
4. *Does the rule invalidate the interest at its creation, or is the rule revised by a wait-and-see approach?*	Wait-and-see. (C&D Inv. Co. v. Gulf Transport Co., 526 So. 2d 526, 530 (1988))	At its creation. (Davies v. McDowell, 549 S.W.2d 619, 623 (1977))	Wait-and-see (§ 72-2-1002(1)(b))
5. *Can the trust be reformed?*	N/A	No statutory provision.	Yes but only if one of the following conditions is satisfied: (1) a nonvested property interest or power of appointment becomes invalid under § 72-2-1002 see # 2b; (2) a class gift is not but might become invalid under 72-2-1002 and the time has arrived

(cont'd)

Table 10
Rule Against Perpetuities *(continued)*

	MISSISSIPPI	*MISSOURI*	*MONTANA*
5. *Can the trust be reformed? (cont'd)*			when the share of any class member is to take effect in possession or enjoyment; or (3) a nonvested property interest that is not validated by § 72-2-1002, that is, the traditional common law rule, can vest but not within 90 years after its creation. (§ 72-2-1004)
6. *If yes to 5., under what theory?*	N/A	No statutory provision.	[A] court shall reform a disposition in the manner most closely approximates the transferor's manifested plan of distribution and is within the 90 years allowed by §72-2-1002 (§ 72-2-1004) *See also* § 72-2-1006 ("If a nonvested property interest or a power of appointment was created before October 1, 1989, and is determined in a judicial proceeding commenced on or after October 1, 1989, to violate this state's rule against perpetuities as that rule existed before October 1, 1989, a court, upon the petition of an interested person, may reform the disposition in the manner that most closely approximates the transferor's manifested plan of

			distribution and that is within the limits of the rule against perpetuities applicable when the nonvested property interest or power of appointment was created.")
7. *When is a general testamentary power of appointment invalid?*	*See* Unif. Statutory Rule Against Perpetuities § 1, 8B U.L.A. 248 (amended 1990) ("Under the Common-law Rule . . . a *nongeneral power* (whether or not presently exercisable) or a *general testamentary power* is invalid as of the time of its creation if it *might* not terminate (by irrevocable exercise or otherwise) within a life in being plus 21 years.")	*See* Unif. Statutory Rule Against Perpetuities § 1, 8B U.L.A. 248 (amended 1990) ("Under the Common-law Rule . . . a *nongeneral power* (whether or not presently exercisable) or a *general testamentary power* is invalid as of the time of its creation if it *might* not terminate (by irrevocable exercise or otherwise) within a life in being plus 21 years.")	A general testamentary power of appointment is invalid unless: (a) when the power is created, it is certain to be irrevocably exercised or otherwise to termination no later than 21 years after the death of an individual then alive; or (b) the power is irrevocably exercised or otherwise terminates within 90 years after its creation. (§72-2-1002(3))
8. *Same, but nongeneral testamentary power.*	See # 7.	See # 7.	A nongeneral testamentary power of appointment is invalid unless: (a) when the power is created, it is certain to be irrevocably exercised or otherwise to termination no later than 21 years after the death of an individual then alive; or (b) the power is irrevocably exercised or otherwise terminates within 90 years after its creation. (§72-2-1002(3))

Table 10
Rule Against Perpetuities *(continued)*

	MISSISSIPPI	*MISSOURI*	*MONTANA*
9. *Same, but general inter vivos power.*	*See* Unif. Statutory Rule Against Perpetuities § 1, 8B U.L.A. 248 (amended 1990) ("Under the Common-law Rule, a *general power not presently exercisable because of a condition precedent* is invalid as of the time of its creation if the condition *might* neither be satisfied nor become impossible to satisfy with a life in being plus 21 years.")	*See* Unif. Statutory Rule Against Perpetuities § 1, 8B U.L.A. 248 (amended 1990) ("Under the Common-law Rule, a *general power not presently exercisable because of a condition precedent* is invalid as of the time of its creation if the condition *might* neither be satisfied nor become impossible to satisfy with a life in being plus 21 years.")	A general power of appointment not presently exercisable because of a condition precedent is invalid unless: (a) when the power is created, the condition precedent is certain to be satisfied or becomes impossible to satisfy no later than 21 years after the death of an individual then alive; or (b) the condition precedent either is satisfied or becomes impossible to satisfy within 90 years after its creation. (§72-2-1002(2))
10. *Same, but nongeneral inter vivos power.*	See # 7.	See # 7.	See # 8.
11. *Is a period of gestation added to the perpetuity period?*	Yes. Carter v. Berry, 136 So. 2d 871, 877 (Miss. 1962) (stating that a period of gestation of 9 months may be applied, if necessary.)	Yes. (St. Louis Union Trust Co. v. Kelley, 199 S.W.2d 344, 350 (Mo. 1947))	No. The possibility that a child will be born to a person after that person's death is disregarded. (§ 72-2-1002(4)) *See also* Unif. Statutory Rule Against Perpetuities § 1, 8B U.L.A. 242-43 (amended 1990) ("[T]he possibility that a child will be born to [a testator] after his death must be disregarded; and the possibility that a child will be born to any of [the

			testator's] descendants after their deaths must also be disregarded. Note, however, that the rule of subsection (d) does *not* apply to the question of the entitlement of an after-born child to take a beneficial interest in the trust'').
12. *What is the treatment of a ''later of the traditional rule or 90 years'' clause? See UPC 2-901(e).*	N/A	N/A	That language must be disregarded to the extent it produces a period of time that exceeds 21 years after the death of the survivor of the specified lives. (§ 72-2-1002(5))
13. *When is an interest created by the exercise of a general testamentary power deemed created?*	*See* comment to Unif. Probate Code § 2-902(a) (''general principles of property law determine that a nonvested property interest or power of appointment created by will is created at the decedent's death''); Unif. Statutory Rule Against Perpetuities § 2, 8B U.L.A. 268 (amended 1990) (stating the same).	*See* § 442.557 (''In determining the validity of limitations appointed in the exercise of a general power of appointment exercisable only at the death of the donee of the power by will or other instrument, or of limitations in default of such appointment, the perpetuities period and any similar period shall run from the death of the donee of the power and not from the time of creation of the power.'') *See also* comment to Unif. Probate Code § 2-902(a) (''general principles of property law determine that a nonvested property interest or power of appointment created by will is created at the decedent's death''); Unif. Statutory Rule Against Perpetuities § 2, 8B U.L.A. 268 (amended 1990) (stating the same).	Except as provided in 72-2-1005 and subsections (2) and (3) of this section, the time of creation of a nonvested property interest or a power of appointment is determined under general principles of property law. (§ 72-2-1003(1)) The first two of the excepted provisions states that as long as a person with a general power to become the unqualified beneficial owner has that power, the nonvested interest is created when the power terminates. The third of the excepted provisions states that a nonvested property interest, which arises from a transfer to an existing trust, is created when the nonvested property interest in the trust was created. *See also* Unif. Statutory Rule Against Perpetuities § 2, 8B U.L.A. 268 (amended 1990) (explaining that

(cont'd)

Table 10
Rule Against Perpetuities *(continued)*

	MISSISSIPPI	*MISSOURI*	*MONTANA*
13. *When is an interest created by the exercise of a general testamentary power deemed created? (cont'd)*			''general principles of property law determine that the time . . . [of creation] is at the decedent's death.'') *See generally* § 72-2-1006(a) (''For the purposes of this section, a nonvested property interest or a power of appointment created by the exercise of a power of appointment is created when the power is irrevocably exercised or when a revocable exercise becomes irrevocable.'')
14. *Same, but nongeneral testamentary power.*	See # 13.	*See also* comment to Unif. Probate Code § 2-902(a) (''general principles of property law determine that a nonvested property interest or power of appointment created by will is created at the decedent's death''); Unif. Statutory Rule Against Perpetuities § 2, 8B U.L.A. 268 (amended 1990) (stating the same).	See # 13.
15. *Same, but general inter vivos power.*	*See* comment to Unif. Probate Code § 2-902(a) (''With respect to an inter-vivos transfer, an interest or power is created on the date the transfer becomes effective for purpose of property law generally, normally the date	*See* comment to Unif. Probate Code § 2-902(a) (''With respect to an inter-vivos transfer, an interest or power is created on the date the transfer becomes effective for purpose of property law generally, normally the date	Except as provided in 72-2-1005 and subsections (2) and (3) of this section, the time of creation of a nonvested property interest or a power of appointment is determined under general principles of property law. (§ 72-2-1003(1))

of delivery of the deed or funding of the trust.''); Unif. Statutory Rule Against Perpetuities § 2, 8B U.L.A. 268 (stating the same).	of delivery of the deed or funding of the trust.''); Unif. Statutory Rule Against Perpetuities § 2, 8B U.L.A. 268 (stating the same).	The first two of the excepted provisions states that as long as a person with a general power to become the unqualified beneficial owner has that power, the nonvested interest is created when the power terminates. The third of the excepted provisions states that a nonvested property interest, which arises from a transfer to an existing trust, is created when the nonvested property interest in the trust was created. *See also* Unif. Statutory Rule Against Perpetuities § 2, 8B U.L.A. 268 (amended 1990) (explaining that ''the time when the interest or power is created is the date the transfer becomes effective for purposes of property law generally, normally the date of delivery of the deed''); Comment to Unif. Probate Code § 2-902 (a) (stating same and adding ''the funding of the trust'' as ''normally'' the time when the interest is created). *See generally* § 72-2-1006(a) (''For the purposes of this section, a nonvested property interest or a power of appointment created by the exercise of a power of appointment is created when the power is irrevocably exercised or when a revocable exercise becomes irrevocable.'')

Table 10
Rule Against Perpetuities *(continued)*

	MISSISSIPPI	MISSOURI	MONTANA
16. *Same, but nongeneral inter vivos power.*	See # 15.	See # 15.	See # 15.
17. *When is an interest created if the grantor of a trust has a power to revoke?*	*See* comment to Unif. Probate Code § 2-902(b) (noting that "nonvested property interest and powers of appointment created in [a revocable inter-vivos trust] are created when the power to revoke expires, usually at the settlor's death"); Unif. Statutory Rule Against Perpetuities § 2, 8B U.L.A. 268 (amended 1990) (explaining that "any nonvested property interest subject to [a power to revoke] is not created . . . until the power terminates (by release, expiration at the death of the donee, or otherwise").	*See* comment to Unif. Probate Code § 2-902(b) (noting that "nonvested property interest and powers of appointment created in [a revocable inter-vivos trust] are created when the power to revoke expires, usually at the settlor's death"); Unif. Statutory Rule Against Perpetuities § 2, 8B U.L.A. 268 (amended 1990) (explaining that "any nonvested property interest subject to [a power to revoke] is not created . . . until the power terminates (by release, expiration at the death of the donee, or otherwise").	For purposes of this part, if there is a person who alone can exercise a power created by a governing instrument to become the unqualified beneficial owner of a nonvested property interest or a property interest subject to a power of appointment described in 72-2-1002(2) or (3), the nonvested property interest or power of appointment is created when the power to become the unqualified beneficial owner terminates. (§ 72-2-1003(2)) *See also* Unif. Statutory Rule Against Perpetuities § 2, 8B U.L.A. 268 (amended 1990) (explaining that "any nonvested property interest subject to [a power to revoke] is not created . . . until the power terminates (by release, expiration at the death of the donee, or otherwise"); Comment to Unif. Probate Code § 2-902(b) (noting that "nonvested property interest and powers of appointment created in [a revocable inter-vivos trust] are created when the power to revoke expires, usually at the settlor's death").

			See generally § 72-2-1006(a) (''a nonvested property interest or a power of appointment created by the exercise of a power of appointment is created when the power is irrevocably exercised or when a revocable exercise becomes irrevocable.'')
18. *When does the period of the rule start re an interest contributed to an irrevocable trust? See UPC 2-902(c).*	*See* comment to Unif. Probate Code 2-902(c) (''Arguably, at common law, each transfer [to an existing irrevocable inter-vivos trust] starts the period of the Rule running anew as to each transfer.'')	*See* comment to Unif. Probate Code 2-902(c) (''Arguably, at common law, each transfer [to an existing irrevocable inter-vivos trust] starts the period of the Rule running anew as to each transfer.'')	A nonvested property interest or power of appointment arising from a transfer of property to a previously funded trust or other existing arrangement is created when the nonvested property interest or power of appointment in the original contribution was created. (§ 72-2-1003(3))
19. *Is there a conclusive presumption of fertility, that is, the ''fertile octogenarian'' rule?*	Probably not. *See* Citizens Nat'l Bank v. Longshore, 304 So. 2d 287, 289 (Miss. 1974) (''The common law presumption of the possibility of issue regardless of the age of husband and wife, did not envision modern surgery (e.g., hysterectomy here) rendering procreation impossible.'')	Yes. Loud v. St. Louis Union Trust Co., 249 S.W. 629, 634 (Mo. 1923) (''And in applying the rule it should not be forgotten that a woman is legally presumed to be capable of bearing children so long as she lives.'')	No specific state case or statute. *See* Unif. Statutory Rule Against Perpetuities § 1, 8B U.L.A. 256 (amended 1990) (holding that ''[t]his principle is not superseded by this Act, and in view of new advances in medical science . . . [this] is not unrealistic.'')); *but see* C. P. Jhong, Annotation, *Modern Status of Presumption of Possibility of Issue Being Extinct*, 98 A.L.R.2d 1285 (2003) (noting ''a trend toward denying the conclusive or absolute nature of the presumption against the possibility of issue being extinct where there is competent evidence to the contrary has

(cont'd)

Table 10
Rule Against Perpetuities *(continued)*

	MISSISSIPPI	MISSOURI	MONTANA
19. *Is there a conclusive presumption of fertility, that is, the "fertile octogenarian" rule? (cont'd)*			developed in the decisions, although some courts still adhere to the traditional view treating the presumption as conclusive or absolute").
20. *What is the earliest age a child is deemed capable of bearing a child? What is the impact of illegitimacy?*	Under the rule, courts must presume that living persons are capable of having or fathering children, no matter how young they are. See In re Graite's Will Trusts, [1949] 1 All E.R. 459, 460 (Ch.). Thus, the rule strikes down any interest whose vesting depends on the assertion that, for example, a toddler will not have children. (Keith L. Butler, Notes & Comments, *Long Live the Dead Hand: A Case for the Repeal of the Rule Against Perpetuities in Washington*, 75 Wash. L. Rev. 1237, 1246 n.78 (2000)).	Under the rule, courts must presume that living persons are capable of having or fathering children, no matter how young they are. See In re Graite's Will Trusts, [1949] 1 All E.R. 459, 460 (Ch.). Thus, the rule strikes down any interest whose vesting depends on the assertion that, for example, a toddler will not have children. (Keith L. Butler, Notes & Comments, *Long Live the Dead Hand: A Case for the Repeal of the Rule Against Perpetuities in Washington*, 75 Wash. L. Rev. 1237, 1246 n.78 (2000)).	Not specifically addressed by USRAP, but the reasoning is the same as set forth in the comment to section 1 of USRAP, 2, Technical Violations of the Common Law Rule. Wait and see will typically result in no violation. Nevertheless, the common law rule ordinarily will be applied initially. Under the rule, courts must presume that living persons are capable of having or fathering children, no matter how young they are. See In re Graite's Will Trusts, [1949] 1 All E.R. 459, 460 (Ch.). Thus, the rule strikes down any interest whose vesting depends on the assertion that, for example, a toddler will not have children. (Keith L. Butler, Notes & Comments, *Long Live the Dead Hand: A Case for the Repeal of the Rule Against Perpetuities in Washington*, 75 Wash. L. Rev. 1237, 1246 n.78 (2000)).

21. *Is the "unborn widow" rule observed?*	*See, e.g.,* Arkansas, question # 21.	*See, e.g.,* Arkansas, question # 21.	No specific state case or statute. *See* Unif. Statutory Rule Against Perpetuities § 1, 8B U.L.A. 246 (amended 1990) (explaining that "[t]he chance that [an] interest will become invalid under the Statutory Rule is small" and so the unborn widow rule would rarely invalidate an interest); *see also* 61 Am Jur 2d *Perpetuities and Restraints on Alienation* § 40 (2003) (noting the same).
22. *Does the "slothful executor" rule apply, i.e., an administrative contingency clause providing for a "distribution to, e.g., those issue living at the time of the satisfaction of the administrative condition precedent?"*	*See, e.g.,* California, question # 22.	*See, e.g.,* California, question # 22.	No specific state case or statute. *See* Unif. Statutory Rule Against Perpetuities § 1, 8B U.L.A. 245 (amended 1990) (Under USRAP, an "interest becomes invalid only if it remains in existence and nonvested 90 years after [the testator's] death. Since it is almost certain that the final distribution of [an] estate will occur well within this 90-year period, the chance that [an] interest will be invalid is negligible.")
23. *Does the all-or-nothing rule apply to class gifts?*	Carter v. Berry, 140 So. 2d 843, 848 (Miss. 1962) (appearing to reject the all-or-nothing rule with respect to class gifts; instead favoring a case by case analysis to see if the valid portion of the trust can be separated and saved from the invalid portion of the trust.)	No. § 442.555(1) ("When any limitation or provision violates the rule against perpetuities or a rule or policy corollary thereto and the instrument containing the limitation or provision also contains other limitations or provisions which do not in themselves violate the rule against perpetuities or any such rule or *(cont'd)*	No specific state case or statute. *See* Unif. Statutory Rule Against Perpetuities § 1, 8B U.L.A. 257 (amended 1990) ("Although this Act does not supersede the basic idea of the much-maligned 'all-or-nothing' rule, the evils sometimes attributed to it are substantially if not entirely eliminated by the wait-and-see feature of the Statutory Rule *(cont'd)*

Table 10
Rule Against Perpetuities *(continued)*

	MISSISSIPPI	*MISSOURI*	*MONTANA*
23. *Does the all-or-nothing rule apply to class gifts? (cont'd)*		policy, the other limitations or provisions shall be valid and effective in accordance with their terms unless the limitation or provision which violates the rule against perpetuities or such rule or policy is manifestly so essential to the dispositive scheme of the grantor, settlor or testator that it is inferable that he would not wish the limitations or provisions which do not in themselves violate the rule against perpetuities to stand alone. Doubts as to the probable wishes of the grantor, settlor or testator shall be resolved in favor of the validity of limitations and provisions.'')	and by the availability of reformation under Section 3.'')
24. *Is there an exception to the all-or-nothing rule in the case of subclasses or specific sums to each member of the class?*	*See* Unif. Statutory Rule Against Perpetuities § 2, 8B U.L.A. 257 (''The common law also recognizes a doctrine called the specific-sum doctrine which is derived from Storrs v. Benbow, 3 De G.M. & G. 390, 43 Eng. Rep 153 (Ch. 1853), and states: If a specified sum of money is to be paid to each member of a class,	*See* Unif. Statutory Rule Against Perpetuities § 2, 8B U.L.A. 257 (''The common law also recognizes a doctrine called the specific-sum doctrine which is derived from Storrs v. Benbow, 3 De G.M. & G. 390, 43 Eng. Rep 153 (Ch. 1853), and states: If a specified sum of money is to be paid to each member of a class,	No specific state case or statute. *See* Unif. Statutory Rule Against Perpetuities § 1, 8B U.L.A. 257 (amended 1990) (''The specific-sum and sub-class doctrines are not superseded by this Act.'')

	the interest of each class member is entitled to separate treatment and is valid or invalid under the Rule on its own. The common law also recognizes a doctrine called the sub-class doctrine, which is derived from Cattlin v. Brown, 11 Hare 372, 68 Eng. Rep. 1318 (Ch. 1853), and states: If the ultimate takers are not described as a single class but rather as a group of separate subclasses, and if the share to which each separate subclass is entitled will finally be determined within the period of the Rule, the gifts to the different subclasses are separate for the purpose of the Rule.'').	the interest of each class member is entitled to separate treatment and is valid or invalid under the Rule on its own. The common law also recognizes a doctrine called the sub-class doctrine, which is derived from Cattlin v. Brown, 11 Hare 372, 68 Eng. Rep. 1318 (Ch. 1853), and states: If the ultimate takers are not described as a single class but rather as a group of separate subclasses, and if the share to which each separate subclass is entitled will finally be determined within the period of the Rule, the gifts to the different subclasses are separate for the purpose of the Rule.'').	
25. Is the infectious invalidity rule followed outside class gifts?	Carter v. Berry, 140 So. 2d 843, 850 (Miss. 1962) (''Infectious invalidity is not a universal doctrine, as will be hereinafter noted. Where part of the testator's plan is valid and part invalid, the normal procedure is to examine the total plan of testator, and determine whether that part which is invalid is so integral to the total plan that it can be inferred testator would have preferred all to fail, rather than to have the valid part stand alone. If the valid part actually accomplishes most of testator's desires, then that portion should stand.'')	See # 23 and Cole v. Peters, 3 S. W.3d 846, 851 (Mo. Ct. App. 1999).	No specific state case or statute. *See* Unif. Statutory Rule Against Perpetuities § 1, 8B U.L.A. 256 (amended 1990) (explaining that ''[t]he doctrine of infectious invalidity is superseded by this Act by Section 3, under which courts . . . are required to *reform* the disposition to approximate as closely as possible the transferor's . . . plan of distribution.'')

Table 10
Rule Against Perpetuities *(continued)*

	MISSISSIPPI	*MISSOURI*	*MONTANA*
26. *Is there a rule against the suspension of the power of alienation? If so, how is it stated?*	Reasonableness standard. Sanders v. Hicks, 317 So. 2d 61 (1975) (overruled on other grounds) (finding that restraints will be upheld only if reasonable under the circumstances.) *See also* In re Kelly's Estate, 193 So. 2d 575 (1967)). (''[A] restraint on alienation may not exceed the life of the life tenant or a succession of life tenants living at the time the life estate is created.'')	The rule does not apply with respect to qualifying trusts. See # 2a. (§ 456.025(1)) Reasonableness standard. Cole v. Peters, 3 S.W.3d 846, 850-51 (Mo. Ct. App. 1999)) (considering four factors to determine reasonableness include purpose and duration of restraint).	''Reasonableness'' standard. Edgar v. Hunt, 706 P. 2d 120, 122 (Mont. 1985) (interpreting section 70-1-405, which state ''conditions restraining alienation, when repugnant to the interest created, are void'' as applying ''the majority common law rule that restraints on alienation, when reasonable, are valid.'')
27. *Effective date.*	N/A	August 21, 2001. *See also* # 3.	October 1, 1989. *See also* # 6.

Table 10
Rule Against Perpetuities *(continued)*

	NEBRASKA	NEVADA	NEW HAMPSHIRE
1. *Which rule is in effect: the common law rule, the Uniform Statutory Rule Against Perpetuities (USRAP), other law, or none?*	USRAP. (Neb. Rev. Stat. §§ 76-2001 – § 76-2008) However, note the exception when the trust instrument states that the rule does not apply. See #3.(a).	USRAP. (Nev. Rev. Stat. §§ 111.103 – 111.1039) Attempt to repeal constitutional prohibition of perpetuities, art. 15, §4, was rejected by voters in 2002.	Common law rule with major exceptions. (§ 547:3-K) See #2.b.
2. *a. Is the common law rule relevant to any interests?*	Yes, but only as to the starting point of the analysis.	Yes, but only as to the starting point of the analysis.	Yes, for some interests.
b. What is the relevant rule?	A nonvested property interest is invalid unless: (1) When the interest is created, it is certain to vest or terminate no later than 21 years after the death of an individual then alive; or (2) The interest either vests or terminates within 90 years after its creation. (§ 76-2002(a))	A nonvested property interest is invalid unless: (a) When the interest is created, it is certain to vest or terminate no later than 21 years after the death of an individual then alive; or (b) The interest either vests or terminates within 365 years after its creation. (§ 111.1031(1))	The Rule Against Perpetuities provides that no interest in property is good "'unless it must vest, if at all, not later than twenty-one years after some life in being at the creation of the interest'." (Emerson v. King, 394 A.2d 51, 54 (N.H. 1978)) However the rule does not apply to any disposition of property or interest therein created after January 1, 2004, if (1) the instrument making the disposition or creating the interest contains a provision which expressly exempts the instrument from the application of the rule and (2) the trustee or other person to whom the power is granted or delegated has the power to sell, mortgage, or lease the property for any period of time beyond the period

(cont'd)

Table 10
Rule Against Perpetuities *(continued)*

	NEBRASKA	*NEVADA*	*NEW HAMPSHIRE*
b. *What is the relevant rule? (cont'd)*			required for an interest created under the instrument to be valid under the rule against perpetuities. (§ 547:3-K) This provision is broader than that of a number of other states because it applies to interests in trust as well as otherwise.
3. *Does the rule apply to other than private trusts?*	Yes. The rule applies except to: (1) A nonvested property interest or a power of appointment arising out of a nondonative transfer, except a nonvested property interest or a power of appointment arising out of (i) a premarital or postmarital agreement, (ii) a separation or divorce settlement, (iii) a spouse's election, (iv) a similar arrangement arising out of a prospective, existing, or previous marital relationship between the parties, (v) a contract to make or not to revoke a will or trust, (vi) a contract to exercise or not to exercise a power of appointment, (vii) a transfer in satisfaction of a	Yes. The rule applies except to: (1) A nonvested property interest or a power of appointment arising out of a nondonative transfer, except a nonvested property interest or a power of appointment arising out of: (a) A premarital or postmarital agreement; (b) A separation or divorce settlement; (c) A spouse's election; (d) A similar arrangement arising out of a prospective, existing or previous marital relationship between the parties; (e) A contract to make or not to revoke a will or trust;	Yes. See # 2b. In addition: A trust created by an employer as part of a stock bonus, pension, disability, death benefit or profit sharing plan for the exclusive benefit of some or all of his employees, to which contributions are made by the employer or employees, or both, for the purpose of distributing to the employees the earnings or the principal of the fund held in trust, may continue in perpetuity. (§ 275:48-a) Charitable trusts are not subject to the rule against perpetuities. (Smart v. Town of Durham, 86 A. 821, 823 (N.H. 1913))

duty of support, or (viii) a reciprocal transfer;

(2) A fiduciary's power relating to the administration or management of assets, including the power of a fiduciary to sell, lease, or mortgage property, and the power of a fiduciary to determine principal and income;

(3) A power to appoint a fiduciary;

(4) A discretionary power of a trustee to distribute principal before termination of a trust to a beneficiary having an indefeasibly vested interest in the income and principal;

(5) A nonvested property interest held by a charity, government, or governmental agency or subdivision, if the nonvested property interest is preceded by an interest held by another charity, government, or governmental agency or subdivision;

(6) A nonvested property interest in or a power of appointment with respect to a trust or other property arrangement forming part of a pension, profit-sharing, stock

(cont'd)

(f) A contract to exercise or not to exercise a power of appointment;

(g) A transfer in satisfaction of a duty of support; or

(h) A reciprocal transfer;

(2) A fiduciary's power relating to the administration or management of assets, including the power of a fiduciary to sell, lease or mortgage property, and the power of a fiduciary to determine principal and income;

(3) A power to appoint a fiduciary;

(4) A discretionary power of a trustee to distribute principal before termination of a trust to a beneficiary having an indefeasibly vested interest in the income and principal;

(5) A nonvested property interest held by a charity, government, or governmental agency or subdivision, if the nonvested property interest is preceded by an interest held by another charity, government, or governmental agency or subdivision;

(6) A nonvested property interest in or a power of

(cont'd)

Table 10
Rule Against Perpetuities *(continued)*

	NEBRASKA	*NEVADA*	*NEW HAMPSHIRE*
3. *Does the rule apply to other than private trusts? (cont'd)*	bonus, health, disability, death benefit, income deferral, or other current or deferred benefit plan for one or more employees, independent contractors, or their beneficiaries or spouses, to which contributions are made for the purpose of distributing to or for the benefit of the participants or their beneficiaries or spouses the property, income, or principal in the trust or other property arrangement, except a nonvested property interest or a power of appointment that is created by an election of a participant or a beneficiary or spouse; (7) A property interest, power of appointment, or arrangement that was not subject to the common-law rule against perpetuities or is excluded by another law of this state; (8) A property interest, ownership, or a power of appointment transferred in trust for	appointment with respect to a trust or other property arrangement forming part of a pension, profit-sharing, stock bonus, health, disability, death benefit, income deferral, or other current or deferred benefit plan for one or more employees, independent contractors, or their beneficiaries or spouses, to which contributions are made for the purpose of distributing to or for the benefit of the participants or their beneficiaries or spouses the property, income or principal in the trust or other property arrangement, except a nonvested property interest or a power of appointment that is created by an election of a participant or a beneficiary or spouse; or (7) A property interest, power of appointment or arrangement that was not subject to the common-law rule against perpetuities or is	

charitable purposes by whose terms such trust is to continue for an indefinite or unlimited period or arrangement of like import; or

(9) A trust in which the governing instrument states that the rule against perpetuities does not apply to the trust and under which the trustee or other person to whom the power is properly granted or delegated has power under the governing instrument, any applicable statute, or the common law to sell, lease, or mortgage property for any period of time beyond the period which would otherwise be required for an interest created under the governing instrument to vest. This subdivision shall apply to all trusts created by will or inter vivos agreement executed or amended on or after July 20, 2002, and to all trusts created by exercise of power of appointment granted under instruments executed or amended on or after July 20, 2002.

(§ 76-2005)

expressly excluded by another statute of this state.

(§ 111.1037)

Table 10
Rule Against Perpetuities *(continued)*

		NEBRASKA	*NEVADA*	*NEW HAMPSHIRE*
4.	*Does the rule invalidate the interest at its creation, or is the rule revised by a wait-and-see approach?*	Wait-and-see. (§ 76-2002(a)(2))	Wait-and-see. (§ 111.1031(1)(b))	Wait-and-see. (Merchants Nat'l Bank v. Curtis, 97 A.2d 207, 212 (N.H. 1953))
5.	*Can the trust be reformed?*	Yes, but only if one of the following conditions applies: (1) a nonvested property interest or power of appointment becomes invalid under § 76-2002 (see # 2b); (2) a class gift is not but might become invalid under 76-2002 and the time has arrived when the share of any class member is to take effect in possession or enjoyment; or (3) a nonvested property interest that is not validated by § 76-2002, that is, the traditional common law rule, can vest but not within 90 years after its creation. (§ 76-2004 – only operative after Jan. 1, 2005)	Yes, but only if one of the following conditions applies: (1) a nonvested property interest or power of appointment becomes invalid under § 111.1031 (see # 2b); (2) a class gift is not but might become invalid under 111.1031 and the time has arrived when the share of any class member is to take effect in possession or enjoyment; or (3) a nonvested property interest that is not validated by § 111.1031, that is, the traditional common law rule, can vest but not within 90 years after its creation. (§ 111.1035)	No specific state case or statute.
6.	*If yes to 5., under what theory?*	[A] court shall reform a disposition in the manner that most closely approximates the transferor's manifested plan of	[A] court shall reform a disposition in the manner most closely approximates the transferor's manifested plan of distribution	

		distribution and is within the 90 years allowed by § 76-2002. (§ 76-2004 – only operative after Jan 1, 2005) *See also* § 76-2006(b) – only operative after Jan 1, 2005 (''If a nonvested property interest or a power of appointment was created before August 25, 1989, and is determined in a judicial proceeding, commenced on or after such date, to violate this state's rule against perpetuities as that rule existed before such date, a county court in a proceeding described in section 30-2211 or 30-3812 or a district court upon the petition of an interested person may reform the disposition in the manner that most closely approximates the transferor's manifested plan of distribution and is within the limits of the rule against perpetuities applicable when the nonvested property interest or power of appointment was created.'')	and is within the 90 years allowed by § 111.1031 (§ 111.1035) *See also* § 111.1039 (''With respect to a nonvested property interest or a power of appointment that was created before July 1, 1987, and that violates the rule against perpetuities as that rule existed before that date, a court upon the petition of an interested person may exercise its equitable power to reform the disposition in the manner that most closely approximates the transferor's manifested plan of distribution and is within the limits of the rule against perpetuities applicable when the nonvested property interest or power of appointment was created.'')	
7.	*When is a general testamentary power of appointment invalid?*	A general testamentary power of appointment is invalid unless: (1) when the power is created, it is certain to be irrevocably exercised or otherwise to termination no later than 21 *(cont'd)*	A general testamentary power of appointment is invalid unless: (a) when the power is created, it is certain to be irrevocably exercised or otherwise to termination no later than 21 *(cont'd)*	*See* Unif. Statutory Rule Against Perpetuities § 1, 8B U.L.A. 248 (amended 1990) (''Under the Common-law Rule . . . a *nongeneral power* (whether or not presently exercisable) or a *general testamentary power* *(cont'd)*

Table 10
Rule Against Perpetuities *(continued)*

	NEBRASKA	*NEVADA*	*NEW HAMPSHIRE*
7. *When is a general testamentary power of appointment invalid? (cont'd)*	years after the death of an individual then alive; or (2) the power is irrevocably exercised or otherwise terminates within 90 years after its creation. (§ 76-2002(c))	years after the death of an individual then alive; or (b) the power is irrevocably exercised or otherwise terminates within 90 years after its creation. (§ 111.1031(3))	is invalid as of the time of its creation if it *might* not terminate (by irrevocable exercise or otherwise) within a life in being plus 21 years.'')
8. *Same, but nongeneral testamentary power.*	A nongeneral testamentary power of appointment is invalid unless: (1) when the power is created, it is certain to be irrevocably exercised or otherwise to termination no later than 21 years after the death of an individual then alive; or (2) the power is irrevocably exercised or otherwise terminates within 90 years after its creation. (§ 76-2002(c))	A nongeneral testamentary power of appointment is invalid unless: (a) when the power is created, it is certain to be irrevocably exercised or otherwise to termination no later than 21 years after the death of an individual then alive; or (b) the power is irrevocably exercised or otherwise terminates within 90 years after its creation. (§ 111.1031(3))	See # 7.
9. *Same, but general inter vivos power.*	A general power of appointment not presently exercisable because of a condition precedent is invalid unless: (1) when the power is created, the condition precedent is	A general power of appointment not presently exercisable because of a condition precedent is invalid unless: (a) when the power is created, the condition precedent is	*See* Unif. Statutory Rule Against Perpetuities § 1, 8B U.L.A. 248 (amended 1990) (''Under the Common-law Rule, a *general power not presently exercisable because of a condition precedent* is invalid as of the time of its creation if the

	certain to be satisfied or becomes impossible to satisfy no later than 21 years after the death of an individual then alive; or (2) the condition precedent either is satisfied or becomes impossible to satisfy within 90 years after its creation. (§ 76-2002(b))	certain to be satisfied or becomes impossible to satisfy no later than 21 years after the death of an individual then alive; or (b) the condition precedent either is satisfied or becomes impossible to satisfy within 90 years after its creation. (§ 111.1031(2))	condition *might* neither be satisfied nor become impossible to satisfy with a life in being plus 21 years.'')
10. *Same, but nongeneral inter vivos power.*	See # 8.	See # 8.	See # 7.
11. *Is a period of gestation added to the perpetuity period?*	No. The possibility that a child will be born to a person after that person's death is disregarded. (§ 76-2002(d)) *See also* Unif. Statutory Rule Against Perpetuities § 1, 8B U.L.A. 242-43 (amended 1990) (''[T]he possibility that a child will be born to [a testator] after his death must be disregarded; and the possibility that a child will be born to any of [the testator's] descendants after their deaths must also be disregarded. Note, however, that the rule of subsection (d) does *not* apply to the question of the entitlement of an after-born child to take a beneficial interest in the trust'').	No. The possibility that a child will be born to a person after that person's death is disregarded. (§ 111.1031(4)) *See also* Unif. Statutory Rule Against Perpetuities § 1, 8B U.L.A. 242-43 (amended 1990) (''[T]he possibility that a child will be born to [a testator] after his death must be disregarded; and the possibility that a child will be born to any of [the testator's] descendants after their deaths must also be disregarded. Note, however, that the rule of subsection (d) does *not* apply to the question of the entitlement of an after-born child to take a beneficial interest in the trust'').	There is no explicit mention of a period of gestation in New Hampshire cases. However, *see, e.g.*, Mississippi, Missouri (applying the common law rule which includes a period of gestation).

Table 10
Rule Against Perpetuities *(continued)*

	NEBRASKA	*NEVADA*	*NEW HAMPSHIRE*
12. *What is the treatment of a "later of the traditional rule or 90 years" clause? See UPC 2-901(e).*	Nebraska's USRAP does not specify how it will treat "later of" clauses.	That language is inoperative to the extent it produces a period of time that exceeds 21 years after the death of the survivor of the specified lives. (§ 111.1031(5))	N/A
13. *When is an interest created by the exercise of a general testamentary power deemed created?*	Except as provided in subsections (b) and (c) of this section and subsection (a) of section 76-2006, the time of creation of a nonvested property interest or a power of appointment is determined under general principles of property law. (§ 76-2003(a)) The first two of the excepted provisions states that as long as a person with a general power to become the unqualified beneficial owner has that power, the nonvested interest is created when the power terminates. The third of the excepted provisions states that a nonvested property interest, which arises from a transfer to an existing trust, is created when the nonvested property interest in the trust was created.	Except as provided in subsections 2 and 3 and in subsection 1 of NRS 111.1039, the time of creation of a nonvested property interest or a power of appointment is determined under general principles of property law. (§ 111.1033(1)) The first two of the excepted provisions states that as long as a person with a general power to become the unqualified beneficial owner has that power, the nonvested interest is created when the power terminates. The third of the excepted provisions states that a nonvested property interest, which arises from a transfer to an existing trust, is created when the nonvested property interest in the trust was created. *See also* Unif. Statutory Rule Against Perpetuities § 2, 8B	*See* comment to Unif. Probate Code § 2-902(a) ("general principles of property law determine that a nonvested property interest or power of appointment created by will is created at the decedent's death"); Unif. Statutory Rule Against Perpetuities § 2, 8B U.L.A. 268 (amended 1990) (stating the same).

	See also Unif. Statutory Rule Against Perpetuities § 2, 8B U.L.A. 268 (amended 1990) (explaining that "general principles of property law determine that the time . . . [of creation] is at the decedent's death.") *See generally* § 76-2006(a) (operative date: 1/1/05) ("a nonvested property interest or a power of appointment created by the exercise of a power of appointment is created when the power is irrevocably exercised or when a revocable exercise becomes irrevocable.")	U.L.A. 268 (amended 1990) (explaining that "general principles of property law determine that the time . . . [of creation] is at the decedent's death.") *See generally* § 111.1039(a) ("a nonvested property interest or a power of appointment created by the exercise of a power of appointment is created when the power is irrevocably exercised or when a revocable exercise becomes irrevocable.")	
14. *Same, but nongeneral testamentary power.*	See # 13.	See # 13.	See # 13.
15. *Same, but general inter vivos power.*	Except as provided in subsections (b)and (c) of this section and subsection (a) of section 76-2006, the time of creation of a nonvested property interest or a power of appointment is determined under general principles of property law. (§ 76-2003(a)) The first two of the excepted provisions states that as long as a person with a general power to become the unqualified beneficial owner has that power, the nonvested interest is created when the power terminates. The third of the *(cont'd)*	Except as provided in subsections 2 and 3 and in subsection 1 of NRS 111.1039, the time of creation of a nonvested property interest or a power of appointment is determined under general principles of property law. (§ 111.1033(1)) The first two of the excepted provisions states that as long as a person with a general power to become the unqualified beneficial owner has that power, the nonvested interest is created when the power terminates. The third of the excepted provisions states that *(cont'd)*	*See* comment to Unif. Probate Code § 2-902(a) ("With respect to an inter-vivos transfer, an interest or power is created on the date the transfer becomes effective for purpose of property law generally, normally the date of delivery of the deed or funding of the trust."); Unif. Statutory Rule Against Perpetuities § 2, 8B U.L.A. 268 (stating the same).

Table 10
Rule Against Perpetuities *(continued)*

	NEBRASKA	NEVADA	NEW HAMPSHIRE
15. *Same, but general inter vivos power. (cont'd)*	excepted provisions states that a nonvested property interest, which arises from a transfer to an existing trust, is created when the nonvested property interest in the trust was created. *See also* Unif. Statutory Rule Against Perpetuities § 2, 8B U.L.A. 268 (amended 1990) (explaining that "the time when the interest or power is created is the date the transfer becomes effective for purposes of property law generally, normally the date of delivery of the deed"); Comment to Unif. Probate Code § 2-902(a) (stating same and adding "the funding of the trust" as "normally" the time when the interest is created). *See generally* § 76-2006(a) (operative date: 1/1/05) ("a nonvested property interest or a power of appointment created by the exercise of a power of appointment is created when the power is irrevocably exercised or when a revocable exercise becomes irrevocable.")	a nonvested property interest, which arises from a transfer to an existing trust, is created when the nonvested property interest in the trust was created. *See also* Unif. Statutory Rule Against Perpetuities § 2, 8B U.L.A. 268 (amended 1990) (explaining that "the time when the interest or power is created is the date the transfer becomes effective for purposes of property law generally, normally the date of delivery of the deed"); Comment to Unif. Probate Code § 2-902(a) (stating same and adding "the funding of the trust" as "normally" the time when the interest is created). *See generally* § 111.1039(a) ("a nonvested property interest or a power of appointment created by the exercise of a power of appointment is created when the power is irrevocably exercised or when a revocable exercise becomes irrevocable.")	

16. *Same, but nongeneral inter vivos power.*	See # 16.	See # 16.	See # 16.
17. *When is an interest created if the grantor of a trust has a power to revoke?*	For purposes of the Uniform Statutory Rule Against Perpetuities Act, if there is a person who alone can exercise a power created by a governing instrument to become the unqualified beneficial owner of (i) a nonvested property interest or (ii) a property interest subject to a power of appointment described in subsection (a) or (b) of section 76-2002, the nonvested property interest or power of appointment is created when the power to become the unqualified beneficial owner terminates. (§ 76-2003(b)) *See also* Unif. Statutory Rule Against Perpetuities § 2, 8B U.L.A. 268 (amended 1990) (explaining that "any nonvested property interest subject to [a power to revoke] is not created . . . until the power terminates (by release, expiration at the death of the donee, or otherwise"); Comment to Unif. Probate Code § 2-902(b) (noting that "nonvested property interest and powers of appointment created in [a revocable inter-vivos trust] are created when *(cont'd)*	For purposes of NRS 111.103 to 111.1039, inclusive, if there is a person who alone can exercise a power created by a governing instrument to become the unqualified beneficial owner of: (a) A nonvested property interest; or (b) A property interest subject to a power of appointment described in subsection 2 or 3 of NRS 111.1031, the nonvested property interest or power of appointment is created when the power to become the unqualified beneficial owner terminates. (§ 111.1033(2)) *See also* Unif. Statutory Rule Against Perpetuities § 2, 8B U.L.A. 268 (amended 1990) (explaining that "any nonvested property interest subject to [a power to revoke] is not created . . . until the power terminates (by release, expiration at the death of the donee, or otherwise"); Comment to Unif. Probate Code § 2-902(b) (noting that "nonvested property interest and powers of appointment created in [a revocable inter- *(cont'd)*	*See* comment to Unif. Probate Code § 2-902(b) (noting that "nonvested property interest and powers of appointment created in [a revocable inter-vivos trust] are created when the power to revoke expires, usually at the settlor's death"); Unif. Statutory Rule Against Perpetuities § 2, 8B U.L.A. 268 (amended 1990) (explaining that "any nonvested property interest subject to [a power to revoke] is not created . . . until the power terminates (by release, expiration at the death of the donee, or otherwise").

Table 10
Rule Against Perpetuities *(continued)*

	NEBRASKA	*NEVADA*	*NEW HAMPSHIRE*
17. *When is an interest created if the grantor of a trust has a power to revoke? (cont'd)*	the power to revoke expires, usually at the settlor's death''). *See generally* § 76-2006(a) (operative date: 1/1/05) (''a nonvested property interest or a power of appointment created by the exercise of a power of appointment is created when the power is irrevocably exercised or when a revocable exercise becomes irrevocable.'')	vivos trust] are created when the power to revoke expires, usually at the settlor's death''). *See generally* § 111.1039(a) (''a nonvested property interest or a power of appointment created by the exercise of a power of appointment is created when the power is irrevocably exercised or when a revocable exercise becomes irrevocable.'')	
18. *When does the period of the rule start re an interest contributed to an irrevocable trust? See UPC 2-902(c).*	A nonvested property interest or power of appointment arising from a transfer of property to a previously funded trust or other existing arrangement is created when the nonvested property interest or power of appointment in the original contribution was created. (§ 76-2003(c))	A nonvested property interest or power of appointment arising from a transfer of property to a previously funded trust or other existing arrangement is created when the nonvested property interest or power of appointment in the original contribution was created. (§ 111.1033(3))	*See* comment to Unif. Probate Code 2-902(c) (''Arguably, at common law, each transfer [to an existing irrevocable inter-vivos trust] starts the period of the Rule running anew as to each transfer.'')
19. *Is there a conclusive presumption of fertility, that is, the ''fertile octogenarian'' rule?*	No specific state case or statute.[1] *See* Unif. Statutory Rule Against Perpetuities § 1, 8B U.L.A. 256 (amended 1990) (holding that ''[t]his principle is not superseded by this Act, and in view of new advances in	No specific state case or statute. *See* Unif. Statutory Rule Against Perpetuities § 1, 8B U.L.A. 256 (amended 1990) (holding that ''[t]his principle is not superseded by this Act, and in view of new advances in	No. In re Bassett's Estate, 190 A.2d 415. 417 (N.H. 1963) (rejecting the presumption).

	medical science . . . [this] is not unrealistic.'')); *but see* C. P. Jhong, Annotation, *Modern Status of Presumption of Possibility of Issue Being Extinct*, 98 A.L.R.2d 1285 (2003) (noting ''a trend toward denying the conclusive or absolute nature of the presumption against the possibility of issue being extinct where there is competent evidence to the contrary has developed in the decisions, although some courts still adhere to the traditional view treating the presumption as conclusive or absolute'').	medical science . . . [this] is not unrealistic.'')); *but see* C. P. Jhong, Annotation, *Modern Status of Presumption of Possibility of Issue Being Extinct*, 98 A.L.R.2d 1285 (2003) (noting ''a trend toward denying the conclusive or absolute nature of the presumption against the possibility of issue being extinct where there is competent evidence to the contrary has developed in the decisions, although some courts still adhere to the traditional view treating the presumption as conclusive or absolute'').	
20. *What is the earliest age a child is deemed capable of bearing a child? What is the impact of illegitimacy?*	Not specifically addressed by USRAP, but the reasoning is the same as set forth in the comment to section 1 of USRAP, 2, Technical Violations of the Common Law Rule. Wait and see will typically result in no violation. Nevertheless, the common law rule ordinarily will be applied initially. Under the rule, courts must presume that living persons are capable of having or fathering children, no matter how young they are. See In re Graite's Will Trusts, [1949] 1 All E.R. 459, 460 (Ch.). Thus, the rule strikes down any interest whose vesting depends on the *(cont'd)*	Not specifically addressed by USRAP,, but the reasoning is the same as set forth in the comment to section 1 of USRAP, 2, Technical Violations of the Common Law Rule. Wait and see will typically result in no violation. Nevertheless, the common law rule ordinarily will be applied initially. Under the rule, courts must presume that living persons are capable of having or fathering children, no matter how young they are. See In re Graite's Will Trusts, [1949] 1 All E.R. 459, 460 (Ch.). Thus, the rule strikes down any interest whose vesting depends on the *(cont'd)*	Under the rule, courts must presume that living persons are capable of having or fathering children, no matter how young they are. See In re Graite's Will Trusts, [1949] 1 All E.R. 459, 460 (Ch.). Thus, the rule strikes down any interest whose vesting depends on the assertion that, for example, a toddler will not have children. (Keith L. Butler, Notes & Comments, *Long Live the Dead Hand: A Case for the Repeal of the Rule Against Perpetuities in Washington*, 75 Wash. L. Rev. 1237, 1246 n.78 (2000)).

Table 10
Rule Against Perpetuities *(continued)*

	NEBRASKA	*NEVADA*	*NEW HAMPSHIRE*
20. *What is the earliest age a child is deemed capable of bearing a child? What is the impact of illegitimacy? (cont'd)*	assertion that, for example, a toddler will not have children. (Keith L. Butler, Notes & Comments, *Long Live the Dead Hand: A Case for the Repeal of the Rule Against Perpetuities in Washington*, 75 Wash. L. Rev. 1237, 1246 n.78 (2000)).	assertion that, for example, a toddler will not have children. (Keith L. Butler, Notes & Comments, *Long Live the Dead Hand: A Case for the Repeal of the Rule Against Perpetuities in Washington*, 75 Wash. L. Rev. 1237, 1246 n.78 (2000)).	
21. *Is the "unborn widow" rule observed?*	No specific state case or statute. *See* Unif. Statutory Rule Against Perpetuities § 1, 8B U.L.A. 246 (amended 1990) (explaining that "[t]he chance that [an] interest will become invalid under the Statutory Rule is small" and so the unborn widow rule would rarely invalidate an interest); *see also* 61 Am Jur 2d *Perpetuities and Restraints on Alienation* § 40 (2003) (noting the same).	No specific state case or statute. *See* Unif. Statutory Rule Against Perpetuities § 1, 8B U.L.A. 246 (amended 1990) (explaining that "[t]he chance that [an] interest will become invalid under the Statutory Rule is small" and so the unborn widow rule would rarely invalidate an interest); *see also* 61 Am Jur 2d *Perpetuities and Restraints on Alienation* § 40 (2003) (noting the same).	No explicit mention, *but see* Merchant's Nat'l Bank v. Curtis, 97 A.2d 207, 211 (noting that the rule has never been applied "remorselessly" in New Hampshire and the wait-and-see approach has "the salutary effect of avoiding the punitive and technical aspects of the rule but at the same time confirming the policy and purpose of the rule within reasonable limits"); *compare*, e.g., Arkansas, question # 21 (applying the common law "slothful executor" rule).
22. *Does the "slothful executor" rule apply, i.e., an administrative contingency clause providing for a "distribution to, e.g., those issue living at the time of satisfaction of the administrative condition precedent?"*	No specific state case or statute. *See* Unif. Statutory Rule Against Perpetuities § 1, 8B U.L.A. 245 (amended 1990) (Under USRAP, an "interest becomes invalid only if it remains in existence and	No specific state case or statute. *See* Unif. Statutory Rule Against Perpetuities § 1, 8B U.L.A. 245 (amended 1990) (Under USRAP, an "interest becomes invalid only if it remains in existence and	No explicit mention, *but see* Merchant's Nat'l Bank v. Curtis, 97 A.2d 207, 211 (noting that the rule has never been applied "remorselessly" in New Hampshire and the wait-and-see approach has "the salutary effect of avoiding the punitive and

	nonvested 90 years after [the testator's] death. Since it is almost certain that the final distribution of [an] estate will occur well within this 90-year period, the chance that [an] interest will be invalid is negligible.'')	nonvested 90 years after [the testator's] death. Since it is almost certain that the final distribution of [an] estate will occur well within this 90-year period, the chance that [an] interest will be invalid is negligible.'')	technical aspects of the rule but at the same time confirming the policy and purpose of the rule within reasonable limits''); *compare*, e.g., California, question # 22 (applying the common law ''slothful executor'' rule).
23. *Does the all-or-nothing rule apply to class gifts?*	No specific state case or statute. *See* Unif. Statutory Rule Against Perpetuities § 1, 8B U.L.A. 257 (amended 1990) (''Although this Act does not supersede the basic idea of the much-maligned 'all-or-nothing' rule, the evils sometimes attributed to it are substantially if not entirely eliminated by the wait-and-see feature of the Statutory Rule and by the availability of reformation under Section 3.'')	No specific state case or statute. *See* Unif. Statutory Rule Against Perpetuities § 1, 8B U.L.A. 257 (amended 1990) (''Although this Act does not supersede the basic idea of the much-maligned 'all-or-nothing' rule, the evils sometimes attributed to it are substantially if not entirely eliminated by the wait-and-see feature of the Statutory Rule and by the availability of reformation under Section 3.'')	No explicit mention, *but see* Merchant's Nat'l Bank v. Curtis, 97 A.2d 207, 211 (noting that the rule has never been applied ''remorselessly'' in New Hampshire and the wait-and-see approach has ''the salutary effect of avoiding the punitive and technical aspects of the rule but at the same time confirming the policy and purpose of the rule within reasonable limits''); *compare*, e.g., Alabama, question # 23 (applying the common law ''all-or-nothing'' rule).
24. *Is there an exception to the all-or-nothing rule in the case of subclasses or specific sums to each member of the class?*	No specific state case or statute. *See* Unif. Statutory Rule Against Perpetuities § 1, 8B U.L.A. 257 (amended 1990) (''The specific-sum and subclass doctrines are not superseded by this Act.'')	No specific state case or statute. *See* Unif. Statutory Rule Against Perpetuities § 1, 8B U.L.A. 257 (amended 1990) (''The specific-sum and subclass doctrines are not superseded by this Act.'')	*See* Unif. Statutory Rule Against Perpetuities § 2, 8B U.L.A. 257 (''The common law also recognizes a doctrine called the specific-sum doctrine which is derived from Storrs v. Benbow, 3 De G.M. & G. 390, 43 Eng. Rep 153 (Ch. 1853), and states: If a specified sum of money is to be paid to each member of a class, the interest of each class member is entitled to separate treatment and is valid or invalid under the Rule on its own. The common law also recognizes a doctrine *(cont'd)*

Table 10
Rule Against Perpetuities *(continued)*

	NEBRASKA	*NEVADA*	*NEW HAMPSHIRE*
24. *Is there an exception to the all-or-nothing rule in the case of subclasses or specific sums to each member of the class? (cont'd)*			called the sub-class doctrine, which is derived from Cattlin v. Brown, 11 Hare 372, 68 Eng. Rep. 1318 (Ch. 1853), and states: If the ultimate takers are not described as a single class but rather as a group of separate subclasses, and if the share to which each separate subclass is entitled will finally be determined within the period of the Rule, the gifts to the different subclasses are separate for the purpose of the Rule.'').
25. *Is the infectious invalidity rule followed outside class gifts?*	No specific state case or statute. *See* Unif. Statutory Rule Against Perpetuities § 1, 8B U.L.A. 256 (amended 1990) (explaining that ''[t]he doctrine of infectious invalidity is superseded by this Act by Section 3, under which courts . . . are required to *reform* the disposition to approximate as closely as possible the transferor's . . . plan of distribution.'')	No specific state case or statute. *See* Unif. Statutory Rule Against Perpetuities § 1, 8B U.L.A. 256 (amended 1990) (explaining that ''[t]he doctrine of infectious invalidity is superseded by this Act by Section 3, under which courts . . . are required to *reform* the disposition to approximate as closely as possible the transferor's . . . plan of distribution.'')	No explicit mention, *but see* Merchant's Nat'l Bank v. Curtis, 97 A.2d 207, 211 (noting that the rule has never been applied ''remorselessly'' in New Hampshire and the wait-and-see approach has ''the salutary effect of avoiding the punitive and technical aspects of the rule but at the same time confirming the policy and purpose of the rule within reasonable limits''); *compare*, e.g. Colorado, question # 25 (applying the common law ''all-or-nothing'' rule).
26. *Is there a rule against the suspension of the power of alienation? If so, how is it stated?*	Reasonable standard. Spanish Oaks, Inc. v. Hy-Vee, Inc., 655 N.W.2d 390, 399 (Neb. 2003)	Good faith standard. Waters v. Harper, 250 P. 2d 915, 916-17 (Nev. 1952) (''The general rule	Reasonableness standard. Horse Pond Fish & Game Club v. Cormier, 581 A.2d 478, 480 (N.H. 1990)

	(''Indirect restraints historically have been restricted by the rule against perpetuities and related rules and have not been as harshly struck down as the classical direct restraints. Courts generally have upheld and enforced such nonclassical restraints if they are found reasonably necessary to protect a justifiable or legitimate interest of the parties.'')	relative to the right of alienation in such cases is expressed in 57 Am. Jur. 479, Wills, §710, as follows: 'Whether testators who have executed a joint will, or separate wills, containing mutual and reciprocal provisions are restricted from disposing of the property during their respective lifetimes is a question primarily of the construction of the agreement under which the will or wills were executed. It may be stated generally that the courts do not consider that the parties to a joint and mutual will intended to restrict either party from disposing of property in good faith by transfers effective during his or her lifetime, unless a plain intention to this effect is expressed in the will or in the contract pursuant to which it was executed.' We have no quarrel with the rule as so expressed. The essential question in our view is whether the transfer here considered can be characterized as one in good faith.'')	(To be enforceable, restraints against alienation of property must be reasonable in view of justifiable interests of parties, and unreasonable restraints will be held invalid.)
27. Effective date.	July 20, 2002. See also # 3.	July 1, 1987. See also # 6.	January 1, 2004. However, the exemption only applies to

(cont'd)

Table 10
Rule Against Perpetuities *(continued)*

	NEBRASKA	*NEVADA*	*NEW HAMPSHIRE*
27. Effective date. (cont'd)			dispositions "created after the effective date of this section? . . ." See also # 2b.

1. For questions, # 19–25, *see also* § 76-2008 (noting that the state's USRAP supersedes the common law rule against perpetuities). The answers to questions # 19–25 are not likely to apply in most cases because of the abolition of the rule with respect to the vast majority of many trusts.

Table 10
Rule Against Perpetuities *(continued)*

	NEW JERSEY	NEW MEXICO	NEW YORK
1. *Which rule is in effect: the common law rule, the Uniform Statutory Rule Against Perpetuities (USRAP), other law, or none?*	None. (N.J. Stat. Ann. § 46:2F-9) (''No interest created in real or personal property shall be void by reason of any rule against perpetuities, whether the common law rule or otherwise. The common law rule against perpetuities shall not be in force in this State.''). New Jersey only has a power of alienation provision. See (§ 46:2F-10)	USRAP. (N.M. Stat. Ann. §§ 45-2-901 – 45-2-906)	Common Law Rule. (N.Y. Est. Powers & Trusts Law §§ 9-1.1 – 9.1.8)
2. *a. Is the common law rule relevant to any interests?*	No.	Yes, but only as the starting point of the analysis.	Yes.
b. What is the relevant rule?	N/A	A nonvested property interest is invalid unless: (1) When the interest is created, it is certain to vest or terminate no later than 21 years after the death of an individual then alive; or (2) The interest either vests or terminates within 90 years after its creation. (§ 45-2-901(A))	No estate in property shall be valid unless it must vest, if at all, not later than twenty-one years after one or more lives in being at the creation of the estate and any period of gestation involved. (§ 9-1.1(b))
3. *Does the rule apply to other than private trusts?*	N/A	Yes. The rule applies except to: A. a nonvested property interest or a power of appointment *(cont'd)*	Yes. The rule applies except to: Trusts with transferable certificates (§ 9-1.5) *(cont'd)*

Table 10
Rule Against Perpetuities *(continued)*

	NEW JERSEY	*NEW MEXICO*	*NEW YORK*
3. *Does the rule apply to other than private trusts? (cont'd)*		arising out of a nondonative transfer, except a nonvested property interest or a power of appointment arising out of: (1) a premarital or postmarital agreement; (2) a separation or divorce settlement; (3) spouse's election; (4) a similar arrangement arising out of a prospective, existing or previous marital relationship between the parties; (5) a contract to make or not to revoke a will or trust; (6) a contract to exercise or not to exercise a power of appointment; (7) a transfer in satisfaction of a duty of support; or (8) a reciprocal transfer; B. a fiduciary's power relating to the administration or management of assets, including the power of a fiduciary to sell, lease or mortgage property and the power of a	Trusts for employees (§ 9-1.6) Trusts created by national security exchanges to assist customers of members, member firms, or member corporations (§ 9-1.7) Charitable trusts (In re Estate of Wilson, 452 N.E.2d 1228, 1232 (N. Y. 1983)

fiduciary to determine principal and income;

C. a power to appoint a fiduciary;

D. a discretionary power of a trustee to distribute principal before termination of a trust to a beneficiary having an indefeasibly vested interest in the income and principal;

E. a nonvested property interest held by preceded by an interest held by another charity, government or governmental agency or subdivision;

F. a nonvested property interest in or a power of appointment with respect to a trust or other property arrangement forming part of a pension, profit-sharing, stock bonus, health, disability, death benefit, income deferral or other current or deferred benefit plan for one or more employees, independent contractors or their beneficiaries or spouses, to which contributions are made for the purpose of distributing to or for the benefit of the participants or their beneficiaries or spouses the property, income or principal in the trust or other property arrangement, except a nonvested property interest

(cont'd)

Table 10
Rule Against Perpetuities *(continued)*

	NEW JERSEY	NEW MEXICO	NEW YORK
3. *Does the rule apply to other than private trusts? (cont'd)*		or a power of appointment that is created by an election of a participant or a beneficiary or spouse; G. a property interest, power of appointment or arrangement that was not subject to the common-law rule against perpetuities or that is excluded by another statute of New Mexico; or H. a property interest or arrangement subject to a time limit under the provisions of Section 45-2-907 NMSA 1978 (pertaining to honorary trusts and trusts for pets). (§ 45-2-904)	
4. *Does the rule invalidate the interest at its creation, or is the rule revised by a wait-and-see approach?*	N/A	Wait-and-see. (§ 45-2-901(A)(2))	At its creation. Symphony Space v. Pergola Props., 669 N.E.2d 799, 807 (N.Y. 1996) ("This Court, however, has long refused to 'wait and see' whether a perpetuities violation in fact occurs.")
5. *Can the trust be reformed?*	Yes, but only [w]ith respect to a nonvested property interest or a power of appointment created before the effective date of this	Yes, but only if one of the following conditions applies: (A) a nonvested property interest or power of appointment	N/A

	act, which is determined in a judicial proceeding commenced on or after the effective date of this act, to violate this State's rule against perpetuities as that rule existed before the effective date of this act. (§ 46-2:F-11(b)) Note also that the current law applies to a future property interest or power of appointment in a trust created before the effective date but valid pursuant to the laws of another state that does not have the rule, if the law of New Jersey is made applicable after the effective date by a change in the trusts situs, governing law or otherwise. (§ 46-2:F-11(a)(2))	becomes invalid under § 45-2-901 (see # 2b); (B) a class gift is not but might become invalid under 45-2-901 and the time has arrived when the share of any class member is to take effect in possession or enjoyment; or (C) a nonvested property interest that is not validated by § 45-2-901, that is, the traditional common law rule, can vest but not within 90 years after its creation. (§ 45-2-903)	
6. *If yes to 5., under what theory?*	[A] court upon the petition of an interested person may reform the disposition in the manner that most closely approximates the transferor's manifested plan of distribution and is within the limits of the rule against perpetuities applicable when the nonvested property interest or power of appointment was created. (§ 46-2:F-11(b)). *See also* In re Estate of Passoff, 819 A.2d 26, 31-32 (N.J. 2002)(applying an equitable reformation, where modifying the will is necessary *(cont'd)*	[A] court shall reform a disposition in the manner most closely approximates the transferor's manifested plan of distribution and is within the 90 years allowed by §45-2-901. (§ 45-2-903) *See also* § 45-2-905(B) ("If a nonvested property interest or a power of appointment was created before July 1, 1992 and is determined in a judicial proceeding, commenced on or after July 1, 1992, to violate the New Mexico rule against perpetuities *(cont'd)*	N/A

Table 10
Rule Against Perpetuities *(continued)*

	NEW JERSEY	NEW MEXICO	NEW YORK
6. *If yes to 5., under what theory? (cont'd)*	to give effect to the intent of the decedent).	as that rule existed before July 1, 1992, a court, upon the petition of an interested person, may reform the disposition in the manner that most closely approximates the transferor's manifested plan of distribution and is within the limits of the rule against perpetuities applicable when the nonvested property interest or power of appointment was created.'')	
7. *When is a general testamentary power of appointment invalid?*	N/A	A general testamentary power of appointment is invalid unless: (1) when the power is created, it is certain to be irrevocably exercised or otherwise to termination no later than 21 years after the death of an individual then alive; or (2) the power is irrevocably exercised or otherwise terminates within 90 years after its creation. (§ 45-2-901(C))	*See* Unif. Statutory Rule Against Perpetuities § 1, 8B U.L.A. 248 (amended 1990) (''Under the Common-law Rule . . . a *nongeneral power* (whether or not presently exercisable) or a *general testamentary power is* invalid as of the time of its creation if it might not terminate (by irrevocable exercise or otherwise) within a life in being plus 21 years.'')
8. *Same, but nongeneral testamentary power.*	N/A	A nongeneral testamentary power of appointment is invalid unless:	See # 7.

		(1) when the power is created, it is certain to be irrevocably exercised or otherwise to termination no later than 21 years after the death of an individual then alive; or (2) the power is irrevocably exercised or otherwise terminates within 90 years after its creation. (§ 45-2-901(C))	
9. *Same, but general inter vivospower.*	N/A	A general power of appointment not presently exercisable because of a condition precedent is invalid unless: (1) when the power is created, the condition precedent is certain to be satisfied or becomes impossible to satisfy no later than 21 years after the death of an individual then alive; or (2) the condition precedent either is satisfied or becomes impossible to satisfy within 90 years after its creation. (§ 45-2-901(B))	*See* Unif. Statutory Rule Against Perpetuities § 1, 8B U.L.A. 248 (amended 1990) ("Under the Common-law Rule, a *general power not presently exercisable because of a condition precedent* is invalid as of the time of its creation if the condition *might* neither be satisfied nor become impossible to satisfy with a life in being plus 21 years.")
10. *Same, but nongeneral intervivos power.*	N/A	See # 8.	See # 7.
11. *Is a period of gestation added to the perpetuity period?*	N/A	No. The possibility that a child will be born to a person after that person's death is disregarded.	Yes (§ 9-1.1(b))

(cont'd)

Table 10
Rule Against Perpetuities *(continued)*

	NEW JERSEY	*NEW MEXICO*	*NEW YORK*
11. *Is a period of gestation added to the perpetuity period? (cont'd)*		(§ 45-2-901(D)) *See also* Unif. Statutory Rule Against Perpetuities § 1, 8B U.L.A. 242-43 (amended 1990) (''[T]he possibility that a child will be born to [a testator] after his death must be disregarded; and the possibility that a child will be born to any of [the testator's] descendants after their deaths must also be disregarded. Note, however, that the rule of subsection (d) does not apply to the question of the entitlement of an after-born child to take a beneficial interest in the trust'').	
12. *What is the treatment of a ''later of the traditional rule or 90 years'' clause?*	N/A	That language is inoperative to the extent it produces a period of time that exceeds 21 years after the death of the survivor of the specified lives. (§ 45-2-901(E))	N/A
13. *When is an interest created by the exercise of a general testamentary power deemed created?*	N/A	Except as provided in Subsections B and C of this section and except as provided in Subsection A of Section 45-2-905 NMSA 1978, the time of creation of a nonvested property	Where an estate is created by an instrument exercising a power of appointment, the permissible period of the rule against perpetuities begins: (1) In the case of an instrument exercising a general power

interest or a power of appointment is determined under general principles of property law. (§ 45-2-902(A)) The first two of the excepted provisions states that as long as a person with a general power to become the unqualified beneficial owner has that power, the nonvested interest is created when the power terminates. The third of the excepted provisions states that a nonvested property interest, which arises from a transfer to an existing trust, is created when the nonvested property interest in the trust was created.

See also Unif. Statutory Rule Against Perpetuities § 2, 8B U.L.A. 268 (amended 1990) (explaining that ''general principles of property law determine that the time . . . [of creation] is at the decedent's death.'')

See generally § 45-2-905(A) (''a nonvested property interest or a power of appointment created by the exercise of a power of appointment is created when the power is irrevocably exercised or when a revocable exercise becomes irrevocable.'')

which is presently exercisable, on the effective date of the instrument of exercise.

(§ 10-8.1(a)(1))

Table 10
Rule Against Perpetuities *(continued)*

	NEW JERSEY	*NEW MEXICO*	*NEW YORK*
14. Same, but nongeneral testamentary power.	N/A	See # 13.	See # 13.
15. Same, but general intervivos power.	N/A	Except as provided in Subsections B and C of this section and except as provided in Subsection A of Section 45-2-905 NMSA 1978, the time of creation of a nonvested property interest or a power of appointment is determined under general principles of property law. (§ 45-2-902(A))The first two of the excepted provisions states that as long as a person with a general power to become the unqualified beneficial owner has that power, the nonvested interest is created when the power terminates. The third of the excepted provisions states that a nonvested property interest, which arises from a transfer to an existing trust, is created when the nonvested property interest in the trust was created. *See also* Unif. Statutory Rule Against Perpetuities § 2, 8B U.L.A. 268 (amended 1990) (explaining that "the time when	See # 13.

		the interest or power is created is the date the transfer becomes effective for purposes of property law generally, normally the date of delivery of the deed''); Comment to Unif. Probate Code § 2-902(a) (stating same and adding ''the funding of the trust'' as ''normally'' the time when the interest is created). *See generally* § 45-2-905(A) (''For the purposes of this section, a nonvested property interest or a power of appointment created by the exercise of a power of appointment is created when the power is irrevocably exercised or when a revocable exercise becomes irrevocable.'')	
16. *Same, but nongeneral inter vivos power.*	N/A	See # 15.	See # 13.
17. *When is an interest created if the grantor of a trust has a power to revoke?*	N/A	Under Sections 45-2-901 through 45-2-905 NMSA 1978, if there is a person who alone can exercise a power created by a governing instrument to become the unqualified owner of either a nonvested property interest or a property interest subject to a power of appointment as described in Subsection B or C of Section 45-2-901 NMSA 1978, the nonvested *(cont'd)*	Where the creator of a trust reserves to himself an unqualified power to revoke, the permissible period of the rule against perpetuities begins when the power to revoke terminates by reason of the death of the creator, by a release of such power or otherwise. (§ 10-8.1(b))

Table 10
Rule Against Perpetuities *(continued)*

	NEW JERSEY	*NEW MEXICO*	*NEW YORK*
17. *When is an interest created if the grantor of a trust has a power to revoke? (cont'd)*		property interest or power of appointment is created when the power to become the unqualified beneficial owner terminates. (§ 45-2-902(B)) *See also* Unif. Statutory Rule Against Perpetuities § 2, 8B U.L.A. 268 (amended 1990) (explaining that "any nonvested property interest subject to [a power to revoke] is not created . . . until the power terminates (by release, expiration at the death of the donee, or otherwise"); Comment to Unif. Probate Code § 2-902(b) (noting that "nonvested property interest and powers of appointment created in [a revocable inter-vivos trust] are created when the power to revoke expires, usually at the settlor's death"). *See generally* § 45-2-905(A) ("a nonvested property interest or a power of appointment created by the exercise of a power of appointment is created when the power is irrevocably exercised or when a revocable exercise becomes irrevocable.")	

18. *When does the period of the rule start re an interest contributed to an irrevocable trust? See UPC 2-902(c).*	N/A	A nonvested property interest or power of appointment arising from a transfer of property to a previously funded trust or other existing arrangement is created when the nonvested property interest or power of appointment in the original contribution was created. (§ 45-2-902(C))	*See* comment to Unif. Probate Code 2-902(c) (''Arguably, at common law, each transfer [to an existing irrevocable inter-vivos trust] starts the period of the Rule running anew as to each transfer.'')
19. *Is there a conclusive presumption of fertility, that is, the ''fertile octogenarian'' rule?*	N/A	No specific state case or statute.[1] See Unif. Statutory Rule Against Perpetuities § 1, 8B U.L.A. 256 (amended 1990) (holding that ''[t]his principle is not superseded by this Act, and in view of new advances in medical science . . . [this] is not unrealistic.'')); *but see* C. P. Jhong, Annotation, *Modern Status of Presumption of Possibility of Issue Being Extinct,* 98 A.L.R.2d 1285 (2003) (noting ''a trend toward denying the conclusive or absolute nature of the presumption against the possibility of issue being extinct where there is competent evidence to the contrary has developed in the decisions, although some courts still adhere to the traditional view treating the presumption as conclusive or absolute'').	(2) In the case of a living person, evidence may be given to establish whether he or she is able to have a child at the time in question. (3) Where the validity of a disposition depends upon the ability of a person to have a child at some future time, the possibility that such person may have a child by adoption shall be disregarded. (4) The provisions of subparagraphs (1), (2) and (3) shall not apply for any purpose other than that of determining the validity of a disposition under the rule against perpetuities where such validity depends on the ability of a person to have a child at some future time. A determination of validity or invalidity of a disposition under the rule against perpetuities by the application of subparagraph (1) or (2) or (3) shall not be affected by the later occurrence of facts in contradiction to the facts presumed or determined or the possibility of

(cont'd)

Table 10
Rule Against Perpetuities *(continued)*

	NEW JERSEY	NEW MEXICO	NEW YORK
19. Is there a conclusive presumption of fertility, that is, the "fertile octogenarian" rule? (cont'd)			adoption disregarded under subparagraph (1) or (2) or (3). (§ 9-1.3(e))
20. What is the earliest age a child is deemed capable of bearing a child? What is the impact of illegitimacy?	N/A	Not specifically addressed by USRAP, but the reasoning is the same as set forth in the comment to section 1 of USRAP, 2, Technical Violations of the Common Law Rule. Wait and see will typically result in no violation. Nevertheless, the common law rule ordinarily will be applied initially. Under the rule, courts must presume that living persons are capable of having or fathering children, no matter how young they are. See In re Graite's Will Trusts, [1949] 1 All E.R. 459, 460 (Ch.). Thus, the rule strikes down any interest whose vesting depends on the assertion that, for example, a toddler will not have children. (Keith L. Butler, Notes & Comments, *Long Live the Dead Hand: A Case for the Repeal of the Rule Against Perpetuities in Washington*, 75 Wash. L. Rev. 1237, 1246 n.78 (2000)).	Where the validity of a disposition depends upon the ability of a person to have a child at some future time, it shall be presumed, subject to subparagraph (2), that a male can have a child at fourteen years of age or over, but not under that age, and that a female can have a child at twelve years of age or over, but not under that age or over the age of fifty-five years. (§ 9-1.3(e)(1))

21. *Is the "unborn widow" rule observed?*	N/A		No specific state case or statute. *See* Unif. Statutory Rule Against Perpetuities § 1, 8B U.L.A. 246 (amended 1990) (explaining that "[t]he chance that [an] interest will become invalid under the Statutory Rule is small" and so the unborn widow rule would rarely invalidate an interest); *see also* 61 Am Jur 2d *Perpetuities and Restraints on Alienation* § 40 (2003) (noting the same).	No. (a) Unless a contrary intention appears, the rules of construction provided in this section govern with respect to any matter affecting the rule against perpetuities. (c) Where an estate would, except for this paragraph, be invalid because of the possibility that the person to whom it is given or limited may be a person not in being at the time of the creation of the estate, and such person is referred to in the instrument creating such estate as the spouse of another without other identification, it shall be presumed that such reference is to a person in being on the effective date of the instrument. (§ 9-1.3)
22. *Does the "slothful executor" rule apply, i.e., an administrative contingency clause providing for a "distribution to, e.g., those issue living at the time of the satisfaction of the administrative condition precedent?"*		N/A	No specific state case or statute. *See* Unif. Statutory Rule Against Perpetuities § 1, 8B U.L.A. 245 (amended 1990) (Under USRAP, an "interest becomes invalid only if it remains in existence and nonvested 90 years after [the testator's] death. Since it is almost certain that the final distribution of [an] estate will occur well within this 90-year period, the chance that [an] interest will be invalid is negligible.")	No. (a) Unless a contrary intention appears, the rules of construction provided in this section govern with respect to any matter affecting the rule against perpetuities. (b) Where the duration or vesting of an estate is contingent upon the probate of a will, the appointment of a fiduciary, the location of a distributee, the payment of debts, the sale of assets, the settlement of an estate, the

(cont'd)

Table 10
Rule Against Perpetuities *(continued)*

	NEW JERSEY	NEW MEXICO	NEW YORK
22. *Does the "slothful executor" rule apply, i.e., an administrative contingency clause providing for a "distribution to, e.g., those issue living at the time of the satisfaction of the administrative condition precedent?" (cont'd)*			determination of questions relating to an estate or transfer tax or the occurrence of any specified contingency, it shall be presumed that the creator of such estate intended such contingency to occur, if at all, within twenty-one years from the effective date of the instrument creating such estate. (§ 9-1.3)
23. *Does the all-or-nothing rule apply to class gifts?*	N/A	No specific state case or statute. *See* Unif. Statutory Rule Against Perpetuities § 1, 8B U.L.A. 257 (amended 1990) ("Although this Act does not supersede the basic idea of the much-maligned 'all-or-nothing' rule, the evils sometimes attributed to it are substantially if not entirely eliminated by the wait-and-see feature of the Statutory Rule and by the availability of reformation under Section 3.")	Yes. "In applying the rule against perpetuities to class gifts, class gift must stand or fall as a unit and cannot be split for purposes of determining its viability." (Matter of Estate of Kreuzer, 243 A.D.2d 207, 209 (N.Y. App. Div. 1998))
24. *Is there an exception to the all-or-nothing rule in the case of subclasses or specific sums to each member of the class?*	N/A	No specific state case or statute. *See* Unif. Statutory Rule Against Perpetuities § 1, 8B U.L.A. 257 (amended 1990) ("The specific-sum and sub-	See Unif. Statutory Rule Against Perpetuities § 2, 8B U.L.A. 257 ("The common law also recognizes a doctrine called the specific-sum doctrine which is derived from Storrs

		class doctrines are not superseded by this Act.")	v. Benbow, 3 De G.M. & G. 390, 43 Eng. Rep 153 (Ch. 1853), and states: If a specified sum of money is to be paid to each member of a class, the interest of each class member is entitled to separate treatment and is valid or invalid under the Rule on its own. The common law also recognizes a doctrine called the sub-class doctrine, which is derived from Cattlin v. Brown, 11 Hare 372, 68 Eng. Rep. 1318 (Ch. 1853), and states: If the ultimate takers are not described as a single class but rather as a group of separate subclasses, and if the share to which each separate subclass is entitled will finally be determined within the period of the Rule, the gifts to the different subclasses are separate for the purpose of the Rule.").
25. *Is the infectious invalidity rule followed outside class gifts?*	N/A	No specific state case or statute. *See* Unif. Statutory Rule Against Perpetuities § 1, 8B U.L.A. 256 (amended 1990) (explaining that "[t]he doctrine of infectious invalidity is superseded by this Act by Section 3, under which courts . . . are required to *reform* the disposition to approxi-mate as closely as possible the transferor's . . . plan of distribution.")	*See,* e.g., Colorado, question # 25.

Table 10
Rule Against Perpetuities *(continued)*

	NEW JERSEY	*NEW MEXICO*	*NEW YORK*
26. *Is there a rule against the suspension of the power of alienation? If so, how is it stated?*	A future interest or trust is void if it suspends the power of alienation for longer than the permissible period. The power of alienation is the power to convey to another an absolute fee in possession of land, or full ownership of personalty. The permissible period is within 21 years after the death of an individual or individuals then alive. (§ 46:2F-10(a)(1)) For more detailed rules on calculating the "permissible period," *see* § 46:2F-10(a)(2)-(3). For exceptions to the rule, *see* § 46:2F-10(d).	Reasonableness standard. Gartley v. Ricketts, 760 P.2d 143, 145 (N.M. 1988) ("New Mexico has adopted and interpreted the common law rule against restrictions on alienation to mean that 'reasonable restraints upon the alienation of property are enforceable, but will be construed to operate within their exact limits.'")	(1) The absolute power of alienation is suspended when there are no persons in being by whom an absolute fee or estate in possession can be conveyed or transferred. (2) Every present or future estate shall be void in its creation which shall suspend the absolute power of alienation by any limitation or condition for a longer period than lives in being at the creation of the estate and a term of not more than twenty-one years. Lives in being shall include a child conceived before the creation of the estate but born thereafter. In no case shall the lives measuring the permissible period be so designated or so numerous as to make proof of their end unreasonably difficult. (§ 9-1.1(a))
27. *Effective date.*	The first business day following July 8, 1999. *See* L.1999, Ch. 159, § 17. In general, section 16 applied New Jersey's prior wait-and-see law to interests created prior to July 8, 1999.	July 1, 1992. *See also* # 6.	N/A

1. For questions, # 19–25, see also § 45-2-906 (noting that the state's USRAP supersedes the common law rule against perpetuities). The answers to questions # 19–25 are not likely to apply in most cases because of the abolition of the rule with respect to the vast majority of trusts.

Table 10
Rule Against Perpetuities *(continued)*

	NORTH CAROLINA	*NORTH DAKOTA*	*OHIO*
1. *Which rule is in effect: the common law rule, the Uniform Statutory Rule Against Perpetuities (USRAP), other law, or none?*	USRAP. (N.C. Gen. Stat. §§ 41-15 – 41-22)	USRAP. (N.D. § 47-02-27.1)	Common law rule with major exceptions. In particular, see # 2b for trusts that are exempt much like Illinois Qualified Perpetual Trusts. Ohio Rev. Code Ann. (§§ 2131.08-2131.09)
2. a. *Is the common law rule relevant to any interests?*	Yes, but only as the starting point of the analysis.	Yes, but only as the starting point of the analysis.	Yes, for some interests.
b. *What is the relevant rule?*	A nonvested property interest is invalid unless: (1) When the interest is created, it is certain to vest or terminate no later than 21 years after the death of an individual then alive; or (2) The interest either vests or terminates within 90 years after its creation. (§ 41-15(a))	A contingent property interest is invalid unless: a. When the interest is created, it is certain to vest or terminate no later than twenty-one years after the death of an individual then alive; or b. The interest either vests or terminates within ninety years after its creation. (§ 47-02-27.1(1))	[N]o interest in real or personal property shall be good unless it must vest, if at all, not later than twenty-one years after a life or lives in being at the creation of the interest. (§ 2131.08(A)) *See also* § 2131.09(B)(1) "No rule of law against perpetuities . . . shall apply with respect to any interest in real or personal property held in trust if the instrument creating the trust specifically states that the rule against perpetuities or the provisions of division (B) of section 2131.08 of the Revised Code shall not apply to the trust and if either the trustee of the trust has unlimited power to sell all trust assets or if one or more persons, one of whom may be the trustee, has the unlimited power to terminate the entire trust.")

Table 10
Rule Against Perpetuities *(continued)*

	NORTH CAROLINA	NORTH DAKOTA	OHIO
3. *Does the rule apply to other than private trusts?*	Yes. The rule applies except to: (1) A nonvested property interest or a power of appointment arising out of a nondonative transfer, except a nonvested property interest or a power of appointment arising out of: a. A premarital or postmarital agreement; b. A separation or divorce settlement; c. A spouse's election; d. A similar arrangement arising out of a prospective, existing, or previous marital relationship between the parties; e. A contract to make or not to revoke a will or trust; f. A contract to exercise or not to exercise a power of appointment; g. A transfer in satisfaction of a duty of support; or h. A reciprocal transfer; (2) A fiduciary's power relating to the administration or	Yes. The rule applies except to: 1. A contingent property interest or a power of appointment arising out of a nondonative transfer, except a contingent property interest or a power of appointment arising out of a premarital or postmarital agreement, a separation or divorce settlement, a spouse's election, a similar arrangement arising out of a prospective, existing, or previous marital relationship between the parties, a contract to make or not to revoke a will or trust, a contract to exercise or not to exercise a power of appointment, a transfer in satisfaction of a duty of support, or a reciprocal transfer. 2. A fiduciary's power relating to the administration or management of assets, including the power of a fiduciary to sell, lease, or mortgage property, and the power of a	Yes. The rule applies except to: Business Trusts (§ 1746.14), Real Estate Investment Trusts (§1747.09). A trust created by an employer as part of a stock bonus plan. § 2131.09 (A) Charitable trusts (Schreiner v. Cincinnati Altenheim, 61 Ohio App. 344, 349, 22 N.E.2d 587 (Ohio Ct. App. 1939)) Trusts that qualify under § 2131.09(B)(1). See # 2b.

management of assets, including the power of a fiduciary to sell, lease, or mortgage property, and the power of a fiduciary to determine principal and income;

(3) A power to appoint a fiduciary;

(4) A discretionary power of a trustee to distribute principal before termination of a trust to a beneficiary having an indefeasibly vested interest in the income and principal;

(5) A nonvested property interest held by a charity, government, or governmental agency or subdivision, if the nonvested property interest is preceded by an interest held by another charity, government, or governmental agency or subdivision;

(6) A nonvested property interest in or a power of appointment with respect to a trust or other property arrangement forming part of a pension, profit-sharing, stock bonus, health, disability, death benefit, income deferral, or other current or deferred benefit plan for one or more employees,

(cont'd)

fiduciary to determine principal and income.

3. A power to appoint a fiduciary.
4. A discretionary power of a trustee to distribute principal before termination of a trust to a beneficiary having an indefeasibly vested interest in the income and principal.
5. A contingent property interest held by a charity, government, or governmental agency or subdivision, if the contingent property interest is preceded by an interest held by another charity, government, or governmental agency or subdivision.
6. A property interest, power of appointment, or arrangement that was not subject to the common-law rule against perpetuities or excluded by another statute of this state.

(§ 47-02-27.4)

Table 10
Rule Against Perpetuities *(continued)*

	NORTH CAROLINA	*NORTH DAKOTA*	*OHIO*
3. *Does the rule apply to other than private trusts? (cont'd)*	independent contractors, or their beneficiaries or spouses, to which contributions are made for the purpose of distributing to or for the benefit of the participants or their beneficiaries or spouses the property, income, or principal in the trust or other property arrangement, except a nonvested property interest or a power of appointment that is created by an election of a participant or a beneficiary or spouse; (7) A property interest, power of appointment, or arrangement that was not subject to the common-law rule against perpetuities or is excluded by another statute of this State; (8) A property interest or arrangement subjected to a time limit under Article 14 of Chapter 36A, "Honorary Trusts; Trusts for Pets; Trusts for Cemetery Lots"; or		

	(9) A property interest or arrangement subjected to a time limit under Article 3 of this Chapter, "Time Limits on Options in Gross and Certain Other Interests in Land". (§ 41-18)		
4. *Does the rule invalidate the interest at its creation, or is the rule revised by a wait-and-see approach?*	Wait-and-see. (§ 41-15(a)(2))	Wait-and-see. (§ 47-02-27.1(1)(b))	Wait-and-see. (§ 2131.08(C)) ("In determining whether an interest would violate the rule and in reforming an interest, the period of perpetuities shall be measured by actual rather than possible events.")
5. *Can the trust be reformed?*	Yes, but only if one of the following conditions applies: (1) a nonvested property interest or power of appointment becomes invalid under §41-15 (see # 2b); (2) a class gift is not but might become invalid under 41-15 and the time has arrived when the share of any class member is to take effect in possession or enjoyment; or (3) a nonvested property interest that is not validated by § 41-15, that is, the traditional common law rule, can vest but not within 90 years after its creation. (§ 41-17)	Yes, but only if one of the following conditions applies: (1) a nonvested property interest or power of appointment becomes invalid under §47-02-01.1 (see # 2b); (2) a class gift is not but might become invalid under 47-02-27.1 and the time has arrived when the share of any class member is to take effect in possession or enjoyment; or (3) a nonvested property interest that is not validated by § 47-02-27.1, that is, the traditional common law rule, can vest but not within 90 years after its creation. (§ 47-02-27.3)	Yes. (§ 2131.08(C))

Table 10
Rule Against Perpetuities *(continued)*

	NORTH CAROLINA	NORTH DAKOTA	OHIO
6. *If yes to 5., under what theory?*	[A] court shall reform a disposition in the manner most closely approximates the transferor's manifested plan of distribution and is within the 90 years allowed by § 41-15. (§ 41-17) *See also* § 41-19(b) (''If a nonvested property interest or a power of appointment was created prior to October 1, 1995, and is determined in a judicial proceeding, commenced on or after October 1, 1995, to violate this State's rule against perpetuities as that rule existed before October 1, 1995, a court upon the petition of an interested person may reform the disposition in the manner that most closely approximates the transferor's manifested plan of distribution and is within the limits of the rule against perpetuities applicable when the nonvested property interest or power of appointment was created.'')	[A] court shall reform a disposition in the manner most closely approximates the transferor's manifested plan of distribution and is within the 90 years allowed by § 47-02-27.1. (§ 47-02-27.3) *See also* § 47-02-27.5(2)(''If a contingent property interest or a power of appointment was created before July 1, 1991, and is determined in a judicial proceeding, commenced on or after July 1, 1991, to violate this state's rule against perpetuities as that rule existed before July 1, 1991, a court upon the petition of an interested person may reform the disposition in the manner that most closely approximates the transferor's manifested plan of distribution and is within the limits of the rule against perpetuities applicable when the contingent property interest or power of appointment was created.'')	Any interest in real or personal property that would violate the rule against perpetuities, under division (A) of this section, shall be reformed, within the limits of the rule, to approximate most closely the intention of the creator of the interest. In determining whether an interest would violate the rule and in reforming an interest, the period of perpetuities shall be measured by actual rather than possible events. (§ 2131.08(C)) This provision applies to interests created after December 31, 1967, or powers under instruments created after that date exercising the power, even if the instrument creating the power was itself created prior to 1968. (§ 2131.08(D))
7. *When is a general testamentary power of appointment invalid?*	A general testamentary power of appointment is invalid unless:	A general testamentary power of appointment is invalid unless:	Common law rule. (See Cleveland Trust Co. v. McQuade, 142 N.E.2d

	(1) when the power is created, it is certain to be irrevocably exercised or otherwise to termination no later than 21 years after the death of an individual then alive; or (2) the power is irrevocably exercised or otherwise terminates within 90 years after its creation. (§ 41-15(c))	(a) when the power is created, it is certain to be irrevocably exercised or otherwise to termination no later than 21 years after the death of an individual then alive; or (b) the power is irrevocably exercised or otherwise terminates within 90 years after its creation. (§ 47-02-27.1(3))	249, 257-58 (Ohio Ct. App. 1957); Dollar Sav. & Trust Co. v. First Nat. Bank of Boston, 285 N.E.2d 768, 778 (Ohio Misc. 1972) (applying the rule from *McQuade*); *see also* Unif. Statutory Rule Against Perpetuities § 1, 8B U.L.A. 248 (amended 1990) ("Under the Common-law Rule . . . a nongeneral power (whether or not presently exercisable) or a general testamentary power is invalid as of the time of its creation if it might not terminate (by irrevocable exercise or otherwise) within a life in being plus 21 years.")
8. *Same, but nongeneral testamentary power.*	A nongeneral testamentary power of appointment is invalid unless: (1) when the power is created, it is certain to be irrevocably exercised or otherwise to termination no later than 21 years after the death of an individual then alive; or (2) the power is irrevocably exercised or otherwise terminates within 90 years after its creation. (§ 41-15(c))	A special testamentary power of appointment is invalid unless: (a) when the power is created, it is certain to be irrevocably exercised or otherwise to termination no later than 21 years after the death of an individual then alive; or (b) the power is irrevocably exercised or otherwise terminates within 90 years after its creation." (§ 47-02-27.1(3))	See # 7.
9. *Same, but general inter vivos power.*	A general power of appointment not presently exercisable because of a condition precedent is invalid unless: *(cont'd)*	A general power of appointment not presently exercisable because of a condition precedent is invalid unless: *(cont'd)*	*See* Unif. Statutory Rule Against Perpetuities § 1, 8B U.L.A. 248 (amended 1990) ("Under the Common-law Rule, a *general power not presently exercisable because of a* *(cont'd)*

Table 10
Rule Against Perpetuities *(continued)*

	NORTH CAROLINA	*NORTH DAKOTA*	*OHIO*
9. *Same, but general inter vivos power. (cont'd)*	(1) when the power is created, the condition precedent is certain to be satisfied or becomes impossible to satisfy no later than 21 years after the death of an individual then alive; or (2) the condition precedent either is satisfied or becomes impossible to satisfy within 90 years after its creation. (§41-15(b))	(a) when the power is created, the condition precedent is certain to be satisfied or becomes impossible to satisfy no later than 21 years after the death of an individual then alive; or (b) the condition precedent either is satisfied or becomes impossible to satisfy within 90 years after its creation. (§ 47-02-27.1(2))	*condition precedent* is invalid as of the time of its creation if the condition *might* neither be satisfied nor become impossible to satisfy with a life in being plus 21 years.'')
10. *Same, but nongeneral inter vivos power.*	See # 8.	See # 8.	See # 7.
11. *Is a period of gestation added to the perpetuity period?*	No. The possibility that a child will be born to a person after that person's death is disregarded. (§ 41-15(d)) *See also* comment to § 41-15 (''[T]he possibility that a child will be born to [a testator] after his death must be disregarded; and the possibility that a child will be born to any of [the testator's] descendants after their deaths must also be disregarded. Note, however, that the rule of subsection(d) does *not* apply to the question of the entitlement of an after-born child	No. The possibility that a child will be born to a person after that person's death is disregarded. (§ 47-02-27.1(4)) *See also* Unif. Statutory Rule Against Perpetuities § 1, 8B U.L.A. 242-43 (amended 1990) (''[T]he possibility that a child will be born to [a testator] after his death must be disregarded; and the possibility that a child will be born to any of [the testator's] descendants after their deaths must also be disregarded. Note, however, that the rule of subsection (d) does *not*	Werling v. Sandy, 476 N.E.2d 1053, 1055 (Ohio 1985) (''[A] child in gestation who is subsequently born alive may be considered a life in being throughout the gestation period for purposes of the now statutory rule against perpetuities.'')

	to take a beneficial interest in the trust'').	apply to the question of the entitlement of an after-born child to take a beneficial interest in the trust'').	
12. *What is the treatment of a ''later of the traditional rule or 90 years'' clause? See UPC 2-901(e).*	That language is inoperative to the extent it produces a period of time that exceeds 21 years after the death of the survivor of the specified lives. (§ 41-15(e))	That language is inoperative to the extent it produces a period of time that exceeds 21 years after the death of the survivor of the specified lives. (§ 47-02-27.1(5))	N/A
13. *When is an interest created by the exercise of a general testamentary power deemed created?*	Except as provided in subsections (b) and (c) of this section and in G.S. 41-19(a), the time for creation of a nonvested property interest or a power of appointment is determined under general principles of property law. (§ 41-16(a)) The first two of the excepted provisions states that as long as a person with a general power to become the unqualified beneficial owner has that power, the nonvested interest is created when the power terminates. The third of the excepted provisions states that a nonvested property interest, which arises from a transfer to an existing trust, is created when the nonvested property interest in the trust was created. *See also* comment to § 41-16 (explaining that ''general *(cont'd)*	Except as provided in subsections 2 and 3 of this section and in subsection 1 of section 47-02-27.5, the time of creation of a contingent property interest or a power of appointment is determined under general principles of property law. (§ 47-02-27.2(1)) The first two of the excepted provisions states that as long as a person with a general power to become the unqualified beneficial owner has that power, the nonvested interest is created when the power terminates. The third of the excepted provisions states that a nonvested property interest, which arises from a transfer to an existing trust, is created when the nonvested property interest in the trust was created. *(cont'd)*	[W]e hold that the period for testing the validity of an exercise of a general testamentary power of appointment, under the common-law rule against perpetuities, is measured from the time of the creation of the power and not from its exercise. (Cleveland Trust Co. v. McQuade, 142 N.E.2d 249, 254 (Ohio Ct. App. 1957)) *See also* comment to Unif. Probate Code § 2-902(a) (''general principles of property law determine that a nonvested property interest or power of appointment created by will is created at the decedent's death''); Unif. Statutory Rule Against Perpetuities § 2, 8B U.L.A. 268 (amended 1990) (stating the same).

Table 10
Rule Against Perpetuities *(continued)*

	NORTH CAROLINA	NORTH DAKOTA	OHIO
13. *When is an interest created by the exercise of a general testamentary power deemed created? (cont'd)*	principles of property law determine that the time . . . [of creation] is at the decedent's death.'') *See generally* § 41-19(a) (''a nonvested property interest or a power of appointment created by the exercise of a power of appointment is created when the power is irrevocably exercised or when a revocable exercise becomes irrevocable.'')	*See also* Unif. Statutory Rule Against Perpetuities § 2, 8B U.L.A. 268 (amended 1990) (explaining that ''general principles of property law determine that the time . . . [of creation] is at the decedent's death.'') *See generally* § 47-02-27.5(1) (''a nonvested property interest or a power of appointment created by the exercise of a power of appointment is created when the power is irrevocably exercised or when a revocable exercise becomes irrevocable.'')	
14. *Same, but nongeneral testamentary power.*	See # 13.	See # 13.	See # 13.
15. *Same, but general inter vivos power.*	Except as provided in subsections (b) and (c) of this section and in G.S. 41-19(a), the time for creation of a nonvested property interest or a power of appointment is determined under general principles of property law. (§ 41-16(a)) The first two of the excepted provisions states that as long as a person with a general power to become the unqualified beneficial owner has	Except as provided in subsections 2 and 3 of this section and in subsection 1 of section 47-02-27.5, the time of creation of a contingent property interest or a power of appointment is determined under general principles of property law. (§ 47-02-27.2(1)) The first two of the excepted provisions states that as long as a person with a general power to become	*See* comment to Unif. Probate Code § 2-902(a) (''With respect to an inter-vivos transfer, an interest or power is created on the date the transfer becomes effective for purpose of property law generally, normally the date of delivery of the deed or funding of the trust.''); Unif. Statutory Rule Against Perpetuities § 2, 8B U.L.A. 268 (stating the same).

that power, the nonvested interest is created when the power terminates. The third of the excepted provisions states that a nonvested property interest, which arises from a transfer to an existing trust, is created when the nonvested property interest in the trust was created.

See also comment to § 41-16 (explaining that "the time when the interest or power is created is the date the transfer becomes effective for purposes of property law generally, normally the date of delivery of the deed"); Comment to Unif. Probate Code § 2-902(a) (stating same and adding "the funding of the trust" as "normally" the time when the interest is created).

See generally § 41-19(a) ("For the purposes of this section, a nonvested property interest or a power of appointment created by the exercise of a power of appointment is created when the power is irrevocably exercised or when a revocable exercise becomes irrevocable.")

the unqualified beneficial owner has that power, the nonvested interest is created when the power terminates. The third of the excepted provisions states that a nonvested property interest, which arises from a transfer to an existing trust, is created when the nonvested property interest in the trust was created.

See also Unif. Statutory Rule Against Perpetuities § 2, 8B U.L.A. 268 (amended 1990) (explaining that "the time when the interest or power is created is the date the transfer becomes effective for purposes of property law generally, normally the date of delivery of the deed"); Comment to Unif. Probate Code § 2-902(a) (stating same and adding "the funding of the trust" as "normally" the time when the interest is created).

See generally § 47-02-27.5(1) ("For the purposes of this section, a nonvested property interest or a power of appointment created by the exercise of a power of appointment is created when the power is irrevocably exercised or when a revocable exercise becomes irrevocable.")

Table 10
Rule Against Perpetuities *(continued)*

	NORTH CAROLINA	*NORTH DAKOTA*	*OHIO*
16. *Same, but nongeneral inter vivos power.*	See # 15.	See # 15.	See # 15.
17. *When is an interest created if the grantor of a trust has a power to revoke?*	For purposes of this Article, if there is a person who alone can exercise a power created by a governing instrument to become the unqualified beneficial owner of (i) a nonvested property interest or (ii) a property interest subject to a power of appointment described in G.S. 41-15(b) or (c), the nonvested property interest or power of appointment is created when the power to become the unqualified beneficial owner terminates. (§ 41-16(b)) *See also* comment to § 41-16 (explaining that "any nonvested property interest subject to [a power to revoke] is not created . . . until the power terminates (by release, expiration at the death of the donee, or otherwise"); Comment to Unif. Probate Code § 2-902(b) (noting that "nonvested property interest and powers of appointment created in [a revocable inter-	For purposes of sections 47-02-27.1 through 47-02-27.5, if there is a person who alone can exercise a power created by a governing instrument to become an unqualified beneficial owner of a contingent property interest or a property interest subject to a power of appointment described in subsection 2 or 3 of section 47-02-27.1, the contingent property interest or power of appointment is created when the power to become the unqualified beneficial owner terminates. (§ 47-02-27.2(2)) *See also* Unif. Statutory Rule Against Perpetuities § 2, 8B U.L.A. 268 (amended 1990) (explaining that "any nonvested property interest subject to [a power to revoke] is not created . . . until the power terminates (by release, expiration at the death of the donee, or otherwise"); Comment to Unif. Probate Code § 2-902(b) (noting	The time of the creation of an interest in real or personal property subject to a power reserved by the grantor to revoke or terminate the interest shall be the time at which the reserved power expires by reason of the death of the grantor, by release of the power, or otherwise. (§ 2131.08(b)) *See also* comment to Unif. Probate Code § 2-902(b) (noting that "nonvested property interest and powers of appointment created in [a revocable inter-vivos trust] are created when the power to revoke expires, usually at the settlor's death"); Unif. Statutory Rule Against Perpetuities § 2, 8B U.L.A. 268 (amended 1990) (explaining that "any nonvested property interest subject to [a power to revoke] is not created . . . until the power terminates (by release, expiration at the death of the donee, or otherwise").

	vivos trust] are created when the power to revoke expires, usually at the settlor's death''). *See generally* § 41-19(a) (''a nonvested property interest or a power of appointment created by the exercise of a power of appointment is created when the power is irrevocably exercised or when a revocable exercise becomes irrevocable.'')	that ''nonvested property interest and powers of appointment created in [a revocable inter-vivos trust] are created when the power to revoke expires, usually at the settlor's death''). *See generally* § 47-02-27.5(1) (''a nonvested property interest or a power of appointment created by the exercise of a power of appointment is created when the power is irrevocably exercised or when a revocable exercise becomes irrevocable.'')	
18. When does the period of the rule start re an interest contributed to an irrevocable trust? See UPC 2-902(c).	A nonvested property interest or power of appointment arising from a transfer of property to a previously funded trust or other existing arrangement is created when the nonvested property interest or power of appointment in the original contribution was created. (§ 41-16(c))	A contingent property interest or power of appointment arising from a transfer of property to a previously funded trust or other existing arrangement is created when the nonvested property interest or power of appointment in the original contribution was created. (§ 47-02-27.2(3))	*See* comment to Unif. Probate Code 2-902(c) (''Arguably, at common law, each transfer [to an existing irrevocable inter-vivos trust] starts the period of the Rule running anew as to each transfer.'')
19. Is there a conclusive presumption of fertility, that is, the ''fertile octogenarian'' rule?	Yes. Hicks v. Hicks, 130 S.E.2d 666, 667 (N.C. 1963) (explaining that there is a rebuttable presumption of fertility until death).[1] *See also* comment to § 41-15 (holding that ''[t]his principle is not superseded by this Act, and in view of new advances in *(cont'd)*	No specific state case or statute. *See* Unif. Statutory Rule Against Perpetuities § 1, 8B U.L.A. 256 (amended 1990) (holding that ''[t]his principle is not superseded by this Act, and in view of new advances in medical science . . . [this] is not unrealistic.'')); *but see* C. P. Jhong, Annotation, *Modern* *(cont'd)*	Yes. In re Estate of Herrick, 2003 WL 21361664 (Ohio Ct. App. June 12, 2003) (''Although R.C. 2131.08(C) allows reformation of grants that violate the rule against perpetuities, the legislature has not expressly abrogated certain concepts associated with the rule and applicable in other contexts, among them the 'fertile octogenarian.' *(cont'd)*

Table 10
Rule Against Perpetuities *(continued)*

	NORTH CAROLINA	NORTH DAKOTA	OHIO
19. *Is there a conclusive presumption of fertility, that is, the "fertile octogenarian" rule? (cont'd)*	medical science . . . [this] is not unrealistic.")); *but see* C. P. Jhong, Annotation, *Modern Status of Presumption of Possibility of Issue Being Extinct*, 98 A.L.R.2d 1285 (2003) (noting "a trend toward denying the conclusive or absolute nature of the presumption against the possibility of issue being extinct where there is competent evidence to the contrary has developed in the decisions, although some courts still adhere to the traditional view treating the presumption as conclusive or absolute").	*Status of Presumption of Possibility of Issue Being Extinct*, 98 A.L.R.2d 1285 (2003) (noting "a trend toward denying the conclusive or absolute nature of the presumption against the possibility of issue being extinct where there is competent evidence to the contrary has developed in the decisions, although some courts still adhere to the traditional view treating the presumption as conclusive or absolute").	Therefore, even if [the beneficiaries] established that they were beyond normal child-bearing age, the law would not regard the class of beneficiaries as closed until their deaths.")
20. *What is the earliest age a child is deemed capable of bearing a child? What is the impact of illegitimacy?*	Not specifically addressed by USRAP, but the reasoning is the same as set forth in the comment to section 1 of USRAP, 2, Technical Violations of the Common Law Rule. Wait and see will typically result in no violation. Nevertheless, the common law rule ordinarily will be applied initially. Under the rule, courts must presume that living persons are capable of having or fathering children, no matter	Not specifically addressed by USRAP, but the reasoning is the same as set forth in the comment to section 1 of USRAP, 2, Technical Violations of the Common Law Rule. Wait and see will typically result in no violation. Nevertheless, the common law rule ordinarily will be applied initially. Under the rule, courts must presume that living persons are capable of having or fathering children, no matter	Under the rule, courts must presume that living persons are capable of having or fathering children, no matter how young they are. See In re Graite's Will Trusts, [1949] 1 All E. R. 459, 460 (Ch.). Thus, the rule strikes down any interest whose vesting depends on the assertion that, for example, a toddler will not have children. (Keith L. Butler, Notes & Comments, *Long Live the Dead Hand: A Case for the Repeal of the Rule Against Perpetuities in*

	how young they are. See In re Graite's Will Trusts, [1949] 1 All E.R. 459, 460 (Ch.). Thus, the rule strikes down any interest whose vesting depends on the assertion that, for example, a toddler will not have children. (Keith L. Butler, Notes & Comments, *Long Live the Dead Hand: A Case for the Repeal of the Rule Against Perpetuities in Washington*, 75 Wash. L. Rev. 1237, 1246 n.78 (2000)).	how young they are. See In re Graite's Will Trusts, [1949] 1 All E.R. 459, 460 (Ch.). Thus, the rule strikes down any interest whose vesting depends on the assertion that, for example, a toddler will not have children. (Keith L. Butler, Notes & Comments, *Long Live the Dead Hand: A Case for the Repeal of the Rule Against Perpetuities in Washington*, 75 Wash. L. Rev. 1237, 1246 n.78 (2000)).	*Washington*, 75 Wash. L. Rev. 1237, 1246 n.78 (2000)).
21. Is the ''unborn widow'' rule observed?	No specific state case or statue. *See* comment to § 41-15 (explaining that ''[t]he chance that [an] interest will become invalid under the Statutory Rule is small'' and so the unborn widow rule would rarely invalidate an interest); *see also* 61 Am Jur 2d *Perpetuities and Restraints on Alienation* § 40 (2003) (noting the same).	No specific state case or statue. *See* Unif. Statutory Rule Against Perpetuities § 1, 8B U.L.A. 246 (amended 1990) (explaining that ''[t]he chance that [an] interest will become invalid under the Statutory Rule is small'' and so the unborn widow rule would rarely invalidate an interest); *see also* 61 Am Jur 2d *Perpetuities and Restraints on Alienation* § 40 (2003) (noting the same).	*See, e.g.*, Arkansas, question # 21.
22. Does the ''slothful executor'' rule apply, i.e., an administrative contingency clause providing in the case of a ''distribution to those of issue living at the time of distribution?''	No specific state case or statute. *See* comment to § 41-15 (Under USRAP, an ''interest becomes invalid only if it remains in existence and nonvested 90 years after [the testator's] death. Since it is almost certain that the final distribution *(cont'd)*	No specific state case or statute. *See* Unif. Statutory Rule Against Perpetuities § 1, 8B U.L.A. 245 (amended 1990) (Under USRAP, an ''interest becomes invalid only if it remains in existence and nonvested 90 years after [the *(cont'd)*	*See, e.g.*, California, question # 22.

Table 10
Rule Against Perpetuities *(continued)*

	NORTH CAROLINA	*NORTH DAKOTA*	*OHIO*
22. *Does the "slothful executor" rule apply, i.e., an administrative contingency clause providing in the case of a "distribution to those of issue living at the time of distribution?" (cont'd)*	of [an] estate will occur well within this 90-year period, the chance that [an] interest will be invalid is negligible.")	testator's] death. Since it is almost certain that the final distribution of [an] estate will occur well within this 90-year period, the chance that [an] interest will be invalid is negligible.")	
23. *Does the all-or-nothing rule apply to class gifts?*	No specific state case or statute. *See* comment to § 41-15 ("Although this Act does not supersede the basic idea of the much-maligned 'all-or-nothing' rule, the evils sometimes attributed to it are substantially if not entirely eliminated by the wait-and-see feature of the Statutory Rule and by the availability of reformation under Section 3.")	No specific state case or statute. *See* Unif. Statutory Rule Against Perpetuities § 1, 8B U.L.A. 257 (amended 1990) ("Although this Act does not supersede the basic idea of the much-maligned 'all-or-nothing' rule, the evils sometimes attributed to it are substantially if not entirely eliminated by the wait-and-see feature of the Statutory Rule and by the availability of reformation under Section 3.")	Yes. (Dayton v Phillips, 28 WL Bull. 327, 5 (Ohio Super. Ct. 1892))
24. *Is there an exception to the all-or-nothing rule in the case of subclasses or specific sums to each member of the class?*	No specific state case or statute. *See* comment to § 41-15 ("The specific-sum and subclass doctrines are not superseded by this Act.")	No specific state case or statute. *See* Unif. Statutory Rule Against Perpetuities § 1, 8B U.L.A. 257 (amended 1990) ("The specific-sum and subclass doctrines are not superseded by this Act.")	*See* Unif. Statutory Rule Against Perpetuities § 2, 8B U.L.A. 257 ("The common law . . . recognizes a doctrine called the specific-sum doctrine which is derived from Storrs v. Benbow, 3 De G.M. & G. 390, 43 Eng. Rep 153 (Ch. 1853), and states: If a specified sum of money is to be paid to each member of a class, the interest of each class

			member is entitled to separate treatment and is valid or invalid under the Rule on its own. The common law also recognizes a doctrine called the sub-class doctrine, which is derived from Cattlin v. Brown, 11 Hare 372, 68 Eng. Rep. 1318 (Ch. 1853), and states: If the ultimate takers are not described as a single class but rather as a group of separate subclasses, and if the share to which each separate subclass is entitled will finally be determined within the period of the Rule, the gifts to the different subclasses are separate for the purpose of the Rule.'').
25. Is the infectious invalidity rule followed outside class gifts?	No specific state case or statute. *See* comment to § 41-15 (explaining that ''[t]he doctrine of infectious invalidity is superseded by this Act by Section 3, under which courts . . . are required to *reform* the disposition to approximate as closely as possible the transferor's . . . plan of distribution.'')	No specific state case or statute. *See* Unif. Statutory Rule Against Perpetuities § 1, 8B U.L.A. 256 (amended 1990) (explaining that ''[t]he doctrine of infectious invalidity is superseded by this Act by Section 3, under which courts . . . are required to *reform* the disposition to approximate as closely as possible the transferor's . . . plan of distribution.'')	Unclear. *See* Cleveland Trust Co. v. McQuade, 142 N.E.2d 249, 263 (Ohio Ct. App. 1957) (declining to apply the infectious invalidity rule in this instance but not answering whether the rule is to be applied in any case).
26. Is there a rule against the suspension of the power of alienation? If so, how is it stated?	Reasonableness standard. Smith v. Mitchell, 269 S.E.2d 608, 611 (N.C. 1980) (''A restraint on alienation . . . may be upheld if reasonable.'')	N.D. Cent. Code § 42-02-27, which provided a rule against the suspension of the power of alienation, was repealed in 1991. *See also* N.D. Cent. Code *(cont'd)*	With respect to trusts, *see* § 2131.09(B)(1) (''No . . . suspension of the power of alienation of the title to property, . . . shall apply with respect to any interest in real or *(cont'd)*

Table 10
Rule Against Perpetuities *(continued)*

	NORTH CAROLINA	NORTH DAKOTA	OHIO
26. *Is there a rule against the suspension of the power of alienation? If so, how is it stated? (cont'd)*		§ 42-02-26 ("Conditions restraining alienation, when repugnant to the interest created, are void.")	personal property held in trust if the instrument creating the trust specifically states that the rule against perpetuities or the provisions of division (B) of section 2131.08 of the Revised Code shall not apply to the trust and if either the trustee of the trust has unlimited power to sell all trust assets or if one or more persons, one of whom may be the trustee, has the unlimited power to terminate the entire trust.") With respect to estates in fee, see Baker v. Alexander, 156 N.E. 223, 225 (Ohio App. 1926) ("The only safe rule of decision is to hold, as I understand the common law for ages to have been, that a condition or restriction which would suspend all power of alienation for a single day, is inconsistent with the estate granted, unreasonable and void.")
27. *Effective date.*	October 1, 1995. See also # 6.	July 1, 1991. See also # 6.	January 1, 1968. See also # 6.

1. For questions # 19 – 25, *see also* § 41-22 (noting that the state's USRAP supersedes the common law rule against perpetuities). The answers to questions # 19 – 25 are not likely to apply in most cases because of the abolition of the rule with respect to the vast majority of many trusts.

Table 10
Rule Against Perpetuities *(continued)*

	OKLAHOMA	OREGON	PENNSYLVANIA
1. *Which rule is in effect: the common law rule, the Uniform Statutory Rule Against Perpetuities (USRAP), other law, or none?*	Common Law Rule, with reform elements (Phillips v. Chambers, 51 P.2d 303, 306 (1935))	USRAP. (Or. Rev. Stat. §§ 105.950–105.975)	The rule against perpetuities has been abolished with respect to all interests created after December 31, 2006. (20 Pa. Cons. stat. §6107.1) The Common law rule with wait-and-see addition applies to interests created prior to 2007. (20 § 6107-1(a)(1)) The following analysis applies to interests created before 2007. (20 Pa. Cons. Stat. §§ 6104–6105)
2. *a. Is the common law rule relevant to any interests?*	Yes.	Yes, but only as the starting point of the analysis.	Yes, but only as the starting point of the analysis.
b. What is the relevant rule?	No interest is good *unless it must vest,* if at all, no later than twenty-one years after some life in being at the creation of the interest. (In re Crowl, 737 P.2d 911, 915 (Okla. 1987)) However, reformation is allowed. See # 6.	A nonvested property interest is invalid unless: (a) When the interest is created, it is certain to vest or terminate no later than 21 years after the death of an individual then alive; or (b) The interest either vests or terminates within 90 years after its creation. (§ 105.950(1))	"The rule against perpetuities provides that an interest must vest, if it vests at all, within twenty-one years of a life in being, and is currently codified at Act of June 30, 1972, P.L. 508, No. 164, § 2, 20 Pa.C.S. § 6104." Central Del. County Auth. v. Greyhound Corp., 588 A.2d 485, 486 (Pa. 1991) Upon the expiration of the period allowed by the common law rule against perpetuities as measured by actual rather than possible events, any interest not then vested and any interest in members of a class the membership of which is then

(cont'd)

Table 10
Rule Against Perpetuities *(continued)*

	OKLAHOMA	OREGON	PENNSYLVANIA
b. What is the relevant rule? (cont'd)			subject to increase shall be void. (20 § 6104(b))
3. *Does the rule apply to other than private trusts?*	No. It does not apply to charitable trusts. (Phillips v. Chambers, 51 P.2d 303, 310 (Okla. 1935))	Yes. The rule applies except to: (1) A nonvested property interest or a power of appointment arising out of a nondonative transfer, except a nonvested property interest or a power of appointment arising out of: (a) A premarital or postmarital agreement; (b) A separation or divorce settlement; (c) A spouse's election; (d) A similar arrangement arising out of a prospective existing or previous marital relationship between the parties; (e) A contract to make or not to revoke a will or trust; (f) A contract to exercise or not to exercise a power of appointment; (g) A transfer in satisfaction of a duty of support; or (h) A reciprocal transfer; (2) A fiduciary's power relating to the administration or management of assets,	Yes. The rule applies except to: (1) Interest exempt at common law. Interests which would not have been subject to the common law rule against perpetuities. (2) Cemetery trusts. Interests which are directed to be used for the maintenance, care, or adornment of any cemetery, churchyard, or other place for the burial of the dead, or any portion thereof, or any grave therein or any improvement on or about the same, and which are subject to no condition precedent at the end of the period described in subsection (b). (3) Pension or profit-sharing plans. Interests created by a bona fide trust inter vivos primarily for the benefit of business employees, their families or appointees, under a stock bonus, pension, disability or death benefit, profit-sharing or other employee-benefit plan. (4) Administrative powers. Powers which contribute to the effective management of trust assets, including powers to sell, mortgage, or lease trust assets,

including the power of a fiduciary to sell, lease or mortgage property, and the power of a fiduciary to determine principal and income;

(3) A power to appoint a fiduciary;

(4) A discretionary power of a trustee to distribute principal before termination of a trust to a beneficiary having an inde-feasibly vested interest in the income and principal;

(5) A nonvested property interest held by a charity, government or governmental agency or subdivision, if the nonvested property interest is preceded by an interest held by another charity, government or governmental agency or subdivision;

(6) A nonvested property interest in or a power of appointment with respect to a trust or other property arrangement forming part of a pension, profit sharing, stock bonus, health, disability, death benefit, income deferral or other current or deferred benefit plan for one or more employees,

(cont'd)

powers relating to investment of trust assets, powers to determine what is principal and what is income, and powers to name successor trustees.

(20 § 6104(b))

Table 10
Rule Against Perpetuities *(continued)*

	OKLAHOMA	*OREGON*	*PENNSYLVANIA*
3. *Does the rule apply to other than private trusts? (cont'd)*		independent contractors or their beneficiaries or spouses, to which contributions are made for the purpose of distributing to or for the benefit of the participants or their beneficiaries or spouses the property, income or principal in the trust or other property arrangement, except a nonvested property interest or a power of appointment that is created by an election of a participant or a beneficiary or spouse; or (7) A property interest, power of appointment or arrangement that was not subject to the common-law rule against perpetuities or is excluded by another statute of this state. (§ 105.965)	
4. *Does the rule invalidate the interest at its creation, or is the rule revised by a wait-and-see approach?*	At its creation (See # 2a).	Wait-and-see. (§ 105.950(1)(b))	Wait-and-see. (20 § 6104(b) (using actual events rather than possible events as the measuring device)).
5. *Can the trust be reformed?*	Yes. (60 Okl. St. §§ 75, 77)	Yes, but only if one of the following conditions applies:	No specific provision. However, 20 § 6105 provides how interests

(1) A nonvested property interest or a power of appointment becomes invalid under ORS 105.950, statutory rule against perpetuities;
(2) A class gift is not but might become invalid under ORS 105.950, statutory rule against perpetuities, and the time has arrived when the share of any class member is to take effect in possession or enjoyment; or
(3) A nonvested property interest that is not validated by ORS 105.950(1)(a), that is, the traditional common law rule, can vest but not within 90 years after its creation.

(§ 105.960)

See also § 105.970(2) (''If a nonvested property interest or a power of appointment was created before January 1, 1990, and is determined in a judicial proceeding, commenced on or after January 1, 1990, to violate this state's rule against perpetuities as that rule existed before January 1, 1990, a court may reform the disposition in the manner that most closely approximates the transferor's intent and is within the limits of the applicable rule against perpetuities.'')

are disposed of when invalidity occurs. If a valid interest follows a void income interest, the valid interest is accelerated. (20 § 6105(a)). If a void interest follows a valid interest on condition subsequent or special limitation, it vests in the owner of the valid interest. (20 § 6105(b)) Other void interests vest in the income beneficiary at the end of the permissible period as measured by actual rather than possible events. (20 § 6105(c))

Table 10
Rule Against Perpetuities *(continued)*

	OKLAHOMA	OREGON	PENNSYLVANIA
6. *If yes to 5., under what theory?*	Any interest in real or personal property that would violate the rule against perpetuities shall be reformed, or construed within the limits of the rule, to give effect to the general intent of the creator of that interest whenever that general intent can be ascertained. This provision shall be liberally construed and applied to validate such interest to the fullest extent consistent with such ascertained intent. (60, § 75) If an instrument violates the rule against perpetuities, but can be reformed or construed in accordance with the provisions of this act, it shall not be declared totally invalid. Rather, the provisions thereof that do not offend the rule shall be enforced, and only the provisions thereof that do violate, or might violate, the rule shall be subject to reformation or construction under the doctrine of cy pres within the terms of this act. (60, § 77)	[A] court shall reform a disposition in the manner that most closely approximates the transferor's manifested plan of distribution and is within the ninety years allowed by ORS 105.950 (1)(b), (2)(b) and (3)(b). (§ 105.960)	See # 5.

7. *When is a general testamentary power of appointment invalid?*	*See* Unif. Statutory Rule Against Perpetuities § 1, 8B U.L.A. 248 (amended 1990) (''Under the Common-law Rule . . . a *nongeneral power* (whether or not presently exercisable) or a *general testamentary power* is invalid as of the time of its creation if it *might* not terminate (by irrevocable exercise or otherwise) within a life in being plus 21 years.'')	A general testamentary power of appointment is invalid unless one of the following conditions is satisfied: (a) When the power is created, it is certain to be irrevocably exercised or otherwise to terminate no later than 21 years after the death of an individual then alive. (b) The power is irrevocably exercised or otherwise terminates within 90 years after its creation. (§ 105.950(3))	*See* Unif. Statutory Rule Against Perpetuities § 1, 8B U.L.A. 248 (amended 1990) (''Under the Common-law Rule . . . a *nongeneral power* (whether or not presently exercisable) or a *general testamentary power* is invalid as of the time of its creation if it *might* not terminate (by irrevocable exercise or otherwise) within a life in being plus 21 years.'')
8. *Same, but nongeneral testamentary power.*	See # 7.	A nongeneral power of appointment . . . is invalid unless one of the following conditions is satisfied: (a) When the power is created, it is certain to be irrevocably exercised or otherwise to terminate no later than 21 years after the death of an individual then alive. (b) The power is irrevocably exercised or otherwise terminates within 90 years after its creation. (§ 105.950(3))	See # 7.

Table 10
Rule Against Perpetuities *(continued)*

	OKLAHOMA	*OREGON*	*PENNSYLVANIA*
9. *Same, but general inter vivos power.*	*See* Unif. Statutory Rule Against Perpetuities § 1, 8B U.L.A. 248 (amended 1990) ("Under the Common-law Rule, a *general power not presently exercisable because of a condition precedent* is invalid as of the time of its creation if the condition *might* neither be satisfied nor become impossible to satisfy with a life in being plus 21 years.")	A general power of appointment not presently exercisable because of a condition precedent is invalid unless one of the following conditions is satisfied: (1) When the power is created, the condition precedent is certain to be satisfied or become impossible to satisfy no later than 21 years after the death of an individual then alive. (2) The condition precedent either is satisfied or becomes impossible to satisfy within 90 years after its creation. (§ 105.950(2))	*See* Unif. Statutory Rule Against Perpetuities § 1, 8B U.L.A. 248 (amended 1990) ("Under the Common-law Rule, a *general power not presently exercisable because of a condition precedent* is invalid as of the time of its creation if the condition *might* neither be satisfied nor become impossible to satisfy with a life in being plus 21 years.")
10. *Same, but nongeneral inter vivos power.*	See # 7.	See # 8.	See # 7.
11. *Is a period of gestation added to the perpetuity period ?*	Yes. (Barnes v. Barnes, 280 P.2d 996, 999 (Okla. 1955))	No. The possibility that a child will be born to a person after that person's death is disregarded. (§ 105.950(4)) *See also* Unif. Statutory Rule Against Perpetuities § 1, 8B U.L.A. 242-43 (amended 1990) ("[T]he possibility that a child	Yes. (In re Lewis' Estate, 37 A.2d 482, 484 (Pa. 1944))

		will be born to [a testator] after his death must be disregarded; and the possibility that a child will be born to any of [the testator's] descendants after their deaths must also be disregarded. Note, however, that the rule of subsection (d) does *not* apply to the question of the entitlement of an after-born child to take a beneficial interest in the trust'').	
12. *What is the treatment of a ''later of the traditional rule or 90 years'' clause? See UPC 2-901(e).*	N/A	The language in a governing instrument is inoperative to the extent it produces a period longer than 21 years after lives in being. (§ 105.950(5))	N/A
13. *When is an interest created by the exercise of a general testamentary power deemed created?*	*See* comment to Unif. Probate Code § 2-902(a) (''general principles of property law determine that a nonvested property interest or power of appointment created by will is created at the decedent's death''); Unif. Statutory Rule Against Perpetuities § 2, 8B U.L.A. 268 (amended 1990) (stating the same).	Except as provided in ORS 105.970(1), the time of creation of a nonvested property interest or a power of appointment is determined under general principles of property law. (§ 105.955(1)) The first two of the excepted provisions states that as long as a person with a general power to become the unqualified beneficial owner has that power, the nonvested interest is created when the power terminates. The third of the excepted provisions states that a nonvested property interest, *(cont'd)*	The period allowed by the common law rule against perpetuities under subsection (b) of this section shall be measured from the expiration of any time during which one person while living has the unrestricted power to transfer to himself the entire legal and beneficial interest in the property. (§ 6104(c)) *See also* official comment to § 6104(c) (''The period would begin as of the death of a donee of a power who could appoint by deed or by will (Mifflin's Ap., 121 Pa. 205), but not where the power is to appoint by will *(cont'd)*

Table 10
Rule Against Perpetuities *(continued)*

	OKLAHOMA	*OREGON*	*PENNSYLVANIA*
13. *When is an interest created by the exercise of a general testamentary power deemed created? (cont'd)*		which arises from a transfer to an existing trust, is created when the nonvested property interest in the trust was created. *See also* Unif. Statutory Rule Against Perpetuities § 2, 8B U.L.A. 268 (amended 1990) (explaining that "general principles of property law determine that the time . . . [of creation] is at the decedent's death.") *See generally* § 105.970 ("a nonvested property interest or a power of appointment created by the exercise of a power of appointment is created when the power is irrevocably exercised or when a revocable exercise becomes irrevocable.")	alone: Lawrence's Est., 136 Pa. 354.")
14. *Same, but nongeneral testamentary power.*	See # 13.	See # 13.	See # 13.
15. *Same, but general inter vivos power.*	*See* comment to Unif. Probate Code § 2-902(a) ("With respect to an inter-vivos transfer, an interest or power is created on the date the transfer becomes effective for purpose of property law generally, normally the date of delivery of the deed or funding	Except as provided in ORS 105.970 (1), the time of creation of a nonvested property interest or a power of appointment is determined under general principles of property law. (§ 105.955(1)) The first two of the excepted provisions states	See # 13.

of the trust.''); Unif. Statutory Rule Against Perpetuities § 2, 8B U.L.A. 268 (stating the same).

that as long as a person with a general power to become the unqualified beneficial owner has that power, the nonvested interest is created when the power terminates. The third of the excepted provisions states that a nonvested property interest, which arises from a transfer to an existing trust, is created when the nonvested property interest in the trust was created.

See also Unif. Statutory Rule Against Perpetuities § 2, 8B U.L.A. 268 (amended 1990) (explaining that ''the time when the interest or power is created is the date the transfer becomes effective for purposes of property law generally, normally the date of delivery of the deed''); Comment to Unif. Probate Code § 2-902(a) (stating same and adding ''the funding of the trust'' as ''normally'' the time when the interest is created).

See generally § 105.970 (''a nonvested property interest or a power of appointment created by the exercise of a power of appointment is created when the power is irrevocably exercised or when a revocable exercise becomes irrevocable.'')

Table 10
Rule Against Perpetuities *(continued)*

	OKLAHOMA	OREGON	PENNSYLVANIA
16. *Same, but nongeneral inter vivos power.*	See # 15.	See # 15.	See # 13.
17. *When is an interest created if the grantor of a trust has a power to revoke?*	*See* comment to Unif. Probate Code § 2-902(b) (noting that "nonvested property interest and powers of appointment created in [a revocable inter-vivos trust] are created when the power to revoke expires, usually at the settlor's death"); Unif. Statutory Rule Against Perpetuities § 2, 8B U.L.A. 268 (amended 1990) (explaining that "any nonvested property interest subject to [a power to revoke] is not created . . . until the power terminates (by release, expiration at the death of the donee, or otherwise").	If there is a person who alone can exercise a power created by a governing instrument to become the unqualified beneficial owner of either a nonvested property interest or a property interest subject to a power of appointment described in ORS 105.950(2) or (3), the nonvested property interest or power of appointment is created when the power to become the unqualified beneficial owner terminates. (§ 105.955(2)) *See also* Unif. Statutory Rule Against Perpetuities § 2, 8B U.L.A. 268 (amended 1990) (explaining that "any nonvested property interest subject to [a power to revoke] is not created . . . until the power terminates (by release, expiration at the death of the donee, or otherwise"); Comment to Unif. Probate Code § 2-902(b) (noting that "nonvested property	The period allowed by the common law rule against perpetuities under subsection (b) of this section shall be measured from the expiration of any time during which one person while living has the unrestricted power to transfer to himself the entire legal and beneficial interest in the property. (§ 6104(c)) *See also* official comment to § 6104 (c) ("For revocable trusts the period would begin as of the settlor's death.")

		interest and powers of appointment created in [a revocable inter-vivos trust] are created when the power to revoke expires, usually at the settlor's death''). *See generally* § 105.970 (''a nonvested property interest or a power of appointment created by the exercise of a power of appointment is created when the power is irrevocably exercised or when a revocable exercise becomes irrevocable.'')	
18. *When does the period of the rule start re an interest contributed to an irrevocable trust? See UPC 2-902(c).*	*See* comment to Unif. Probate Code 2-902(c) (''Arguably, at common law, each transfer [to an existing irrevocable inter-vivos trust] starts the period of the Rule running anew as to each transfer.'').	A nonvested property interest or a power of appointment arising from a transfer of property to a previously funded trust or other existing property arrangement is created when the nonvested property interest or power of appointment in the original contribution was created. (§ 105.955(3))	*See* comment to Unif. Probate Code 2-902(c) (''Arguably, at common law, each transfer [to an existing irrevocable inter-vivos trust] starts the period of the Rule running anew as to each transfer.'').
19. *Is there a conclusive presumption of fertility, that is, the ''fertile octogenarian'' rule?*	*See, e.g.*, Arkansas, question # 19.	No specific state case or statute.[1] *See* Unif. Statutory Rule Against Perpetuities § 1, 8B U.L.A. 256 (amended 1990) (holding that ''[t]his principle is not superseded by this Act, and in view of new advances in medical science . . . [this] is not unrealistic.'')); *but see* C. P. Jhong, Annotation, *Modern* *(cont'd)*	No. In re Estate of Weaver, 572 A.2d 1249, 321-322 (Pa. Super. Ct. 1990) (''The new rule required Pennsylvania courts to determine the validity of future interests in accordance with events which actually occurred during the period of the common law rule against perpetuities, . . . eliminated some of the more improbable possibilities that *(cont'd)*

Table 10
Rule Against Perpetuities *(continued)*

	OKLAHOMA	OREGON	PENNSYLVANIA
19. *Is there a conclusive presumption of fertility, that is, the "fertile octogenarian" rule? (cont'd)*		*Status of Presumption of Possibility of Issue Being Extinct*, 98 A.L.R.2d 1285 (2003) (noting "a trend toward denying the conclusive or absolute nature of the presumption against the possibility of issue being extinct where there is competent evidence to the contrary has developed in the decisions, although some courts still adhere to the traditional view treating the presumption as conclusive or absolute").	determined the validity of some future interests under the old rule such as the fertile octogenarian and the unborn widow."); Estate of Weeks, 402 A.2d 657, 659 (Pa. 1979) ("This Court, however, has long held that distribution of trust funds is governed by principles of equity rather than the conclusive common law presumption of 'fertility unto death.' ")
20. *What is the earliest age a child is deemed capable of bearing a child? What is the impact of illegitimacy?*	No answer to either question is provided in case law or statutory law. "In controversies involving heirship and the legitimacy of children, the presumption of law is in favor of legitimacy, and the reason back of this presumption is that the law encourages decency and morality and right living." (Locust et al. v. Caruthers et al., 100 P. 520, 522 (1909))	Not specifically addressed by USRAP, but the reasoning is the same as set forth in the comment to section 1 of USRAP, 2, Technical Violations of the Common Law Rule. Wait and see will typically result in no violation. Nevertheless, the common law rule ordinarily will be applied initially. Under the rule, courts must presume that living persons are capable of having or fathering children, no matter how young they are. See In re Graite's Will	Under the rule, courts must presume that living persons are capable of having or fathering children, no matter how young they are. See In re Graite's Will Trusts, [1949] 1 All E. R. 459, 460 (Ch.). Thus, the rule strikes down any interest whose vesting depends on the assertion that, for example, a toddler will not have children. (Keith L. Butler, Notes & Comments, *Long Live the Dead Hand: A Case for the Repeal of the Rule Against Perpetuities in Washington*, 75 Wash. L. Rev. 1237, 1246 n.78 (2000)).

		Trusts, [1949] 1 All E.R. 459, 460 (Ch.). Thus, the rule strikes down any interest whose vesting depends on the assertion that, for example, a toddler will not have children. (Keith L. Butler, Notes & Comments, *Long Live the Dead Hand: A Case for the Repeal of the Rule Against Perpetuities in Washington*, 75 Wash. L. Rev. 1237, 1246 n.78 (2000)).	
21. *Is the "unborn widow" rule observed?*	*See, e.g.*, Arkansas, question # 21.	No specific state case or statute. *See* Unif. Statutory Rule Against Perpetuities § 1, 8B U.L.A. 246 (amended 1990) (explaining that "[t]he chance that [an] interest will become invalid under the Statutory Rule is small" and so the unborn widow rule would rarely invalidate an interest); *see also* 61 Am Jur 2d *Perpetuities and Restraints on Alienation* § 40 (2003) (noting the same).	No. In re Estate of Weaver, 572 A.2d 1249, 321-322 (Pa. Super. Ct. 1990) ("The new rule required Pennsylvania courts to determine the validity of future interests in accordance with events which actually occurred during the period of the common law rule against perpetuities, . . . eliminated some of the more improbable possibilities that determined the validity of some future interests under the old rule such as the fertile octogenarian and the unborn widow.")
22. *Does the "slothful executor" rule apply, i.e., an administrative contingency clause providing for a "distribution to, e.g., those issue living at the time of the satisfaction of the administrative condition precedent?"*	*See, e.g.*, California, question # 22.	No specific state case or statute. *See* Unif. Statutory Rule Against Perpetuities § 1, 8B U.L.A. 245 (amended 1990) (Under USRAP, an "interest becomes invalid only if it remains in existence and nonvested 90 years after [the	*See*, e.g., California, question # 22.

(cont'd)

Table 10
Rule Against Perpetuities *(continued)*

	OKLAHOMA	OREGON	PENNSYLVANIA
22. *Does the "slothful executor" rule apply, i.e., an administrative contingency clause providing for a "distribution to, e.g., those issue living at the time of the satisfaction of the administrative condition precedent?" (cont'd)*		testator's] death. Since it is almost certain that the final distribution of [an] estate will occur well within this 90-year period, the chance that [an] interest will be invalid is negligible.")	
23. *Does the all-or-nothing rule apply to class gifts?*	Yes. (McLaughlin v. Yingling, 213 P. 552, 562-63 (Okla. 1923))	Yes. Closset v. Burtchaell, 230 P. 554, 561 (Or. 1924) (affirming the all-or-nothing rule as stated in Gray on Perpetuities). *See also* Unif. Statutory Rule Against Perpetuities § 1, 8B U.L.A. 257 (amended 1990) ("Although this Act does not supersede the basic idea of the much-maligned 'all-or-nothing' rule, the evils sometimes attributed to it are substantially if not entirely eliminated by the wait-and-see feature of the Statutory Rule and by the availability of reformation under Section 3.")	Yes. Upon the expiration of the period allowed by the common law rule against perpetuities as measured by actual rather than possible events, . . . any interest in members of a class the membership of which is then subject to increase shall be void. (§ 6104(b)); *see also* In re Lockhart's Estate, 159 A. 874, 876 (Pa. 1932)
24. *Is there an exception to the all-or-nothing rule in the case of subclasses or specific sums to each member of the class?*	*See* Unif. Statutory Rule Against Perpetuities § 2, 8B U.L.A. 257 ("The common law also recognizes a doctrine called the specific-sum doctrine which is derived from Storrs v. Benbow, 3 De G.M. & G. 390, 43 Eng. Rep	No specific state case or statute. *See* Unif. Statutory Rule Against Perpetuities § 1, 8B U.L.A. 257 (amended 1990) ("The specific-sum and subclass doctrines are not superseded by this Act.")	*See* Unif. Statutory Rule Against Perpetuities § 2, 8B U.L.A. 257 ("The common law also recognizes a doctrine called the specific-sum doctrine which is derived from Storrs v. Benbow, 3 De G.M. & G. 390, 43 Eng. Rep 153 (Ch. 1853), and

	153 (Ch. 1853), and states: If a specified sum of money is to be paid to each member of a class, the interest of each class member is entitled to separate treatment and is valid or invalid under the Rule on its own. The common law also recognizes a doctrine called the sub-class doctrine, which is derived from Cattlin v. Brown, 11 Hare 372, 68 Eng. Rep. 1318 (Ch. 1853), and states: If the ultimate takers are not described as a single class but rather as a group of separate subclasses, and if the share to which each separate subclass is entitled will finally be determined within the period of the Rule, the gifts to the different subclasses are separate for the purpose of the Rule.'').		states: If a specified sum of money is to be paid to each member of a class, the interest of each class member is entitled to separate treatment and is valid or invalid under the Rule on its own. The common law also recognizes a doctrine called the sub-class doctrine, which is derived from Cattlin v. Brown, 11 Hare 372, 68 Eng. Rep. 1318 (Ch. 1853), and states: If the ultimate takers are not described as a single class but rather as a group of separate subclasses, and if the share to which each separate subclass is entitled will finally be determined within the period of the Rule, the gifts to the different subclasses are separate for the purpose of the Rule.'').
25. Is the infectious invalidity rule followed outside class gifts?	*See, e.g.*, Colorado, question # 25.	No specific state case or statute. *See* Unif. Statutory Rule Against Perpetuities § 1, 8B U.L.A. 256 (amended 1990) (explaining that ''[t]he doctrine of infectious invalidity is superseded by this Act by Section 3, under which courts . . . are required to *reform* the disposition to approximate as closely as possible the transferor's . . . plan of distribution.'')	Morton Estate, 59 Pa. D. & C.2d 300, 318 (Pa. D. & C. 1972) (striking down provision of testamentary trust using the doctrine of infectious invalidity).

Table 10
Rule Against Perpetuities *(continued)*

	OKLAHOMA	*OREGON*	*PENNSYLVANIA*
26. *Is there a rule against the suspension of the power of alienation? If so, how is it stated?*	Yes. The absolute power of alienation shall not be suspended, by any limitation or condition whatever, for a longer period than during the continuance of the lives of persons in being at the creation of the limitation or condition plus twenty-one (21) years, except as provided in Section 34 of Title 60 of the Oklahoma Statutes (pertaining to a contingent remainder in fee to take effect on death of person to whom first remainder limited before age 21 or otherwise determined before reaching majority). (60, § 31) *See also* tit. 60, § 175.47 (listing exceptions: "when property is given, granted, bequeathed, or devised to: 1. A charitable use; 2. Literary, educational, scientific, religious, or charitable corporations for their sole use and benefit; 3. Any cemetery corporation, society or association; 4. The Department of Mental Health and Substance Abuse Services as provided in Section 1 of this act; or 5. Gifts	Case law unclear. *See* Gange v. Hayes, 237 P.2d 196, 202 (Or. 1951) (finding that an option in a deed without any time limits was an invalid restraint on alienation); Friswold v. United States Nat'l Bank, 257 P. 818, 821 (Or. 1927) ("[A] restriction, . . . against any and all alienation whatever during a limited time, of an estate in fee, is . . . void.")	Reasonableness standard. Rice v. Rice, 359 A.2d 782, 784 (Pa. 1976) ("While the question whether a particular restraint on alienation is unreasonable and so invalid is basically a question of law, the answer depends upon factual considerations, such as the time within which the restraint may be exercised and whether it is supported by consideration.")

	absolute, limited, or in trust, for the advancement of medical science to an incorporated state society of physicians and surgeons.'').		
27. *Effective date.*	October 1, 1971. The law is effective respecting instruments taking effect after the Act becomes effective and this includes appointments afterwards, but by instruments created before the act became effective (60 § 78).	January 1, 1990. *See also* # 5.	All interest and powers, whether created or exercised before or after enactment. (§ 6104(d)). *See also* § 6104(d) (''The provisions of [§ 6104] . . . (relating to rule against perpetuities; disposition when invalidity occurs) shall apply to all interests heretofore or hereafter created.'') However, ## 2-26 only apply to inserts created before 2007. See #1.

1. For questions, # 19 – 25, *see also* § 105.975(3) (noting that the state's USRAP supersedes the common law rule against perpetuities). The answers to questions # 19 – 25 are not likely to apply in most cases because of the abolition of the rule with respect to the vast majority of many trusts.

Table 10
Rule Against Perpetuities *(continued)*

	RHODE ISLAND	*SOUTH CAROLINA*	*SOUTH DAKOTA*
1. *Which rule is in effect: the common law rule, the Uniform Statutory Rule Against Perpetuities (USRAP), other law, or none?*	None. (R.I. Gen. Laws § 34-11-38) ("The common law rule against perpetuities shall no longer be deemed to be in force and/or of any effect in this state, provided, the provisions of this section shall not be construed to invalidate or modify the terms of any interest which would have been valid prior to the effective date of this act, and, provided further, that the provisions of this section shall apply to both legal and equitable interests.")	USRAP. (S.C. Code Ann. §§ 27-6-10 – 27-6-80)	None. (S.D. Codified Laws § 43-5-8) ("The common-law rule against perpetuities is not in force in this state.")
2. *a. Is the common law rule relevant to any interests?*	N/A	Yes, but only as a starting point in the analysis.	N/A
b. What is the relevant rule?	N/A	A nonvested property interest is invalid unless: (1) When the interest is created, it is certain to vest or terminate no later than 21 years after the death of an individual then alive; or (2) The interest either vests or terminates within 90 years after its creation. (§ 27-6-20(A))	N/A

3. *Does the rule apply to other than private trusts?*	N/A	Yes. The rule applies except to: (1) a nonvested property interest or a power of appointment arising out of a nondonative transfer, except a nonvested property interest or a power of appointment arising out of (i) a premarital or postmarital agreement, (ii) a separation or divorce settlement, (iii) a spouse's election, (iv) a similar arrangement arising out of a prospective, existing, or previous marital relationship between the parties, (v) a contract to make or not to revoke a will or trust, (vi) a contract to exercise or not to exercise a power of appointment, (vii) a transfer in satisfaction of a duty of support, or (viii) a reciprocal transfer; (2) a fiduciary's power relating to the administration or management of assets, including the power of a fiduciary to sell, lease, or mortgage property, and the power of a fiduciary to determine principal and income; (3) a power to appoint a fiduciary; *(cont'd)*	N/A

Table 10
Rule Against Perpetuities *(continued)*

	RHODE ISLAND	*SOUTH CAROLINA*	*SOUTH DAKOTA*
3. *Does the rule apply to other than private trusts? (cont'd)*		(4) a discretionary power of a trustee to distribute principal before termination of a trust to a beneficiary having an indefeasibly vested interest in the income and principal; (5) a nonvested property interest held by a charity, government, or governmental agency or subdivision, if the nonvested property interest is preceded by an interest held by another charity, government, or governmental agency or subdivision; (6) a nonvested property interest in or a power of appointment with respect to a trust or other property arrangement forming part of a pension, profit-sharing, stock bonus, and health, disability, death benefit, income deferral, or other current or deferred benefit plan for one or more employees, independent contractors, or their beneficiaries or spouses, to which contributions are made for the purpose of distributing to or for	

		the benefit of the participants or their beneficiaries or spouses the property, income, or principal in the trust or other property arrangement, except a nonvested property interest or a power of appointment that is created by an election of a participant or a beneficiary or spouse; or (7) a property interest, power of appointment, or arrangement that was not subject to the common law rule against perpetuities or is excluded by another statute of this State, including, but not limited to, the interests, powers, and arrangements coming within §§ 13-7-30, 27-5-70, 27-5-80, 33-53-30, 39-55-135, and 62-7-409. (§ 27-6-50) The rule does not apply to business trusts, certain pension plans, and annuity trusts of employers. (§ 27-5-80)	
4. *Does the rule invalidate the interest at its creation, or is the rule revised by a wait-and-see approach?*	N/A	Wait-and-see. (§ 27-6-20(A)(2); Abrams v. Templeton, 465 S.E.2d 117, 120 (S.C. Ct. App. 1995))	N/A

Table 10
Rule Against Perpetuities *(continued)*

	RHODE ISLAND	SOUTH CAROLINA	SOUTH DAKOTA
5. *Can the trust be reformed?*	N/A	Yes, but only if one of the following conditions applies: (1) a nonvested property interest or a power of appointment becomes invalid under § 27-6-20 (see # 2b); (2) a class gift is not but may become invalid under § 27-6-20 and the time has arrived when the share of any class member is to take effect in possession or enjoyment; or (3) a nonvested property interest that is not validated by § 27-6-20(A)(1), that is, the traditional common law rule, can vest but not within ninety years after its creation. (§ 27-6-40)	N/A
6. *If yes to 5., under what theory?*	N/A	A court shall reform a disposition in the manner that most closely approximates the transferor's manifested plan of distribution and is within the ninety years permitted by this chapter. (§ 27-6-40)	N/A

		See also § 27-6-60(B) ("If a nonvested property interest or a power of appointment was created before July 1, 1987, and is determined in a judicial proceeding, co mmenced on or after July 1, 1987, to violate this State's rule against perpetuities as that rule existed before July 1, 1987, a court upon the petition of an interested person shall reform the disposition by inserting a savings clause that preserves most closely the transferor's plan of distribution and that brings that plan within the limits of the rule against perpetuities applicable when the nonvested property interest or power of appointment was created.")	
7. *When is a general testamentary power of appointment invalid?*	N/A	A general testamentary power of appointment is invalid unless one of the following conditions is satisfied: (1) When the power is created, it is certain to be irrevocably exercised or otherwise to terminate no later than 21 years after the death of an individual then alive. (2) The power is irrevocably exercised or otherwise terminates within 90 years after its creation. (§ 27-6-20(C))	N/A

Table 10
Rule Against Perpetuities *(continued)*

	RHODE ISLAND	SOUTH CAROLINA	SOUTH DAKOTA
8. *Same, but nongeneral testamentary power.*	N/A	A nongeneral power of appointment . . . is invalid unless one of the following conditions is satisfied: (1) When the power is created, it is certain to be irrevocably exercised or otherwise to terminate no later than 21 years after the death of an individual then alive. (2) The power is irrevocably exercised or otherwise terminates within 90 years after its creation. (§ 27-6-20(C))	N/A
9. *Same, but general inter vivos power.*	N/A	A general power of appointment not presently exercisable because of a condition precedent is invalid unless one of the following conditions is satisfied: (1) When the power is created, the condition precedent is certain to be satisfied or become impossible to satisfy no later than 21 years after the death of an individual then alive. (2) The condition precedent either is satisfied or	N/A

		becomes impossible to satisfy within 90 years after its creation. (§ 27-6-20(B))	
10. *Same, but nongeneral inter vivos power.*	N/A	See # 8.	N/A
11. *Is a period of gestation added to the perpetuity period ?*	N/A	No. The possibility that a child will be born to a person after that person's death is disregarded. (§ 27-6-20(D)) *See also* Unif. Statutory Rule Against Perpetuities § 1, 8B U.L.A. 242-43 (amended 1990) (''[T]he possibility that a child will be born to [a testator] after his death must be disregarded; and the possibility that a child will be born to any of [the testator's] descendants after their deaths must also be disregarded. Note, however, that the rule of subsection (d) does *not* apply to the question of the entitlement of an after-born child to take a beneficial interest in the trust'').	N/A
12. *What is the treatment of a ''later of the traditional rule or 90 years'' clause? See UPC 2-901(e).*	N/A	South Carolina's USRAP does not specify how it will treat ''later of'' clauses.	N/A
13. *When is an interest created by the exercise of a general testamentary power deemed created?*	N/A	Except as provided in subsections (B) and (C) and in § 27-6-60(A), the time of creation of a *(cont'd)*	N/A

Table 10
Rule Against Perpetuities *(continued)*

	RHODE ISLAND	*SOUTH CAROLINA*	*SOUTH DAKOTA*
13. *When is an interest created by the exercise of a general testamentary power deemed created? (cont'd)*		nonvested property interest or a power of appointment is determined under general principles of property law. (§ 27-6-30(A)) The first two of the excepted provisions states that as long as a person with a general power to become the unqualified beneficial owner has that power, the nonvested interest is created when the power terminates. The third of the excepted provisions states that a nonvested property interest, which arises from a transfer to an existing trust, is created when the nonvested property interest in the trust was created. *See also* Unif. Statutory Rule Against Perpetuities § 2, 8B U.L.A. 268 (amended 1990) (explaining that "general principles of property law determine that the time . . . [of creation] is at the decedent's death.") *See generally* § 27-6-60(A) ("a nonvested property interest or a power of appointment created by the exercise of a power of appointment is created when the power is irrevocably	

		exercised or when a revocable exercise becomes irrevocable.")	
14. *Same, but nongeneral testamentary power.*	N/A	See # 13.	N/A
15. *Same, but general inter vivos power.*	N/A	Except as provided in subsections (B) and (C) and in § 27-6-60(A), the time of creation of a nonvested property interest or a power of appointment is determined under general principles of property law. (§ 27-6-30(A)) The first two of the excepted provisions states that as long as a person with a general power to become the unqualified beneficial owner has that power, the nonvested interest is created when the power terminates. The third of the excepted provisions states that a nonvested property interest, which arises from a transfer to an existing trust, is created when the nonvested property interest in the trust was created. *See also* Unif. Statutory Rule Against Perpetuities § 2, 8B U.L.A. 268 (amended 1990) (explaining that "the time when the interest or power is created is the date the transfer becomes effective for purposes of property law generally, normally the date	N/A

(cont'd)

Table 10
Rule Against Perpetuities *(continued)*

	RHODE ISLAND	SOUTH CAROLINA	SOUTH DAKOTA
15. *Same, but general inter vivos power. (cont'd)*		of delivery of the deed''); Comment to Unif. Probate Code § 2-902(a) (stating same and adding ''the funding of the trust'' as ''normally'' the time when the interest is created). *See generally* § 27-6-60(A) (''a nonvested property interest or a power of appointment created by the exercise of a power of appointment is created when the power is irrevocably exercised or when a revocable exercise becomes irrevocable.'')	
16. *Same, but nongeneral inter vivos power.*	N/A	See # 15.	N/A
17. *When is an interest created if the grantor of a trust has a power to revoke?*	N/A	If there is a person who alone can exercise a power created by a governing instrument to become the unqualified beneficial owner of (i) a nonvested property interest or (ii) a property interest subject to a power of appointment described in § 27-6-20(B) or 27-6-20(C), the nonvested property interest or power of appointment is created when the power to become the unqualified beneficial owner terminates. (§ 27-6-30(B))	N/A

		See also Unif. Statutory Rule Against Perpetuities § 2, 8B U.L.A. 268 (amended 1990) (explaining that "any nonvested property interest subject to [a power to revoke] is not created . . . until the power terminates (by release, expiration at the death of the donee, or otherwise"); Comment to Unif. Probate Code § 2-902(b) (noting that "nonvested property interest and powers of appointment created in [a revocable intervivos trust] are created when the power to revoke expires, usually at the settlor's death"). *See generally* § 27-6-60(A) ("a nonvested property interest or a power of appointment created by the exercise of a power of appointment is created when the power is irrevocably exercised or when a revocable exercise becomes irrevocable.")	
18. *When does the period of the rule start re an interest contributed to an irrevocable trust? See UPC 2-902(c).*	N/A	A nonvested property interest or a power of appointment arising from a transfer of property to a previously funded trust or other existing property arrangement is created when the nonvested property interest or power of appointment in the original contribution was created. (§ 27-6-30(C))	N/A

Table 10
Rule Against Perpetuities *(continued)*

	RHODE ISLAND	SOUTH CAROLINA	SOUTH DAKOTA
19. Is there a conclusive presumption of fertility, that is, the ''fertile octogenarian'' rule?	N/A	No specific state case or statute.[1] *See* Unif. Statutory Rule Against Perpetuities § 1, 8B U.L.A. 256 (amended 1990) (holding that ''[t]his principle is not superseded by this Act, and in view of new advances in medical science . . . [this] is not unrealistic.'')); *but see* C. P. Jhong, Annotation, *Modern Status of Presumption of Possibility of Issue Being Extinct*, 98 A.L.R.2d 1285 (2003) (noting ''a trend toward denying the conclusive or absolute nature of the presumption against the possibility of issue being extinct where there is competent evidence to the contrary has developed in the decisions, although some courts still adhere to the traditional view treating the presumption as conclusive or absolute'').	N/A
20. What is the earliest age a child is deemed capable of bearing a child? What is the impact of illegitimacy?	N/A	Not specifically addressed by USRAP, but the reasoning is the same as set forth in the comment to section 1 of USRAP, 2, Technical Violations of the Common Law Rule. Wait and see will	N/A

		typically result in no violation. Nevertheless, the common law rule ordinarily will be applied initially. Under the rule, courts must presume that living persons are capable of having or fathering children, no matter how young they are. See In re Graite's Will Trusts, [1949] 1 All E.R. 459, 460 (Ch.). Thus, the rule strikes down any interest whose vesting depends on the assertion that, for example, a toddler will not have children. (Keith L. Butler, Notes & Comments, *Long Live the Dead Hand: A Case for the Repeal of the Rule Against Perpetuities in Washington*, 75 Wash. L. Rev. 1237, 1246 n.78 (2000)).	
21. Is the "unborn widow" rule observed?	N/A	No specific state case or statute. *See* Unif. Statutory Rule Against Perpetuities § 1, 8B U.L.A. 246 (amended 1990) (explaining that "[t]he chance that [an] interest will become invalid under the Statutory Rule is small" and so the unborn widow rule would rarely invalidate an interest); *see also* 61 Am Jur 2d *Perpetuities and Restraints on Alienation* § 40 (2003) (noting the same).	N/A

Table 10
Rule Against Perpetuities *(continued)*

	RHODE ISLAND	*SOUTH CAROLINA*	*SOUTH DAKOTA*
22. Does the "slothful executor" rule apply, i.e., an administrative contingency clause providing for a "distribution to, e.g., those issue living at the time of the satisfaction of the administrative condution precedent?"	N/A	No specific state case or statute. *See* Unif. Statutory Rule Against Perpetuities § 1, 8B U.L.A. 245 (amended 1990) (Under USRAP, an "interest becomes invalid only if it remains in existence and nonvested 90 years after [the testator's] death. Since it is almost certain that the final distribution of [an] estate will occur well within this 90-year period, the chance that [an] interest will be invalid is negligible.")	N/A
23. Does the all-or-nothing rule apply to class gifts?	N/A	No specific state case or statute. *See* Unif. Statutory Rule Against Perpetuities § 1, 8B U.L.A. 257 (amended 1990) ("Although this Act does not supersede the basic idea of the much-maligned 'all-or-nothing' rule, the evils sometimes attributed to it are substantially if not entirely eliminated by the wait-and-see feature of the Statutory Rule and by the availability of reformation under Section 3.")	N/A
24. Is there an exception to the all-or-nothing rule in the case of subclasses	N/A	No specific state case or statute. *See* Unif. Statutory Rule	N/A

or specific sums to each member of the class?		Against Perpetuities § 1, 8B U.L.A. 257 (amended 1990) (''The specific-sum and sub-class doctrines are not superseded by this Act.'')	
25. Is the infectious invalidity rule followed outside class gifts?	N/A	No specific state case or statute. *See* Unif. Statutory Rule Against Perpetuities § 1, 8B U.L.A. 256 (amended 1990) (explaining that ''[t]he doctrine of infectious invalidity is superseded by this Act by Section 3, under which courts . . . are required to *reform* the disposition to approximate as closely as possible the transferor's . . . plan of distribution.'')	N/A
26. Is there a rule against the suspension of the power of alienation? If so, how is it stated?	Substantiality test. *See* Chile v. Beck, 452 A.2d 626, 629 (R.I. 1982) (''Limited restraints that do not substantially diminish the whole power of alienation are not necessarily void. Here, our ultimate objective in measuring the scope and effect of the restraints on alienation is to arrive at the intent of the testator.'')	No specific state case or statute. Limited restraints appear to be okay. *See* Lynch v. Lynch, 159 S.E. 26 (S.C. 1991) (''The weight of authority clearly supports the view that a limited restraint upon alienation for a particular purpose is not repugnant to the grant of a fee-simple estate.'')	The absolute power of alienation may not be suspended by any limitation or condition whatever for a longer period than during the continuance of the lives of persons in being plus a period of thirty years at the creation of the limitation or condition, except in the single case mentioned in § 43-9-5 relating to contingent fee remainder on a prior fee remainder. (§ 43-5-1) For more specific rules calculating the period of the rule, *see* § 43-5-5. For additional rules relating to the suspension of the power of alienation, *see* § 43-5-2 – 43-5-9.

Table 10
Rule Against Perpetuities *(continued)*

	RHODE ISLAND	*SOUTH CAROLINA*	*SOUTH DAKOTA*
27. Effective date.	N/A	July 1, 1987. *See also* # 6.	N/A

1. For questions # 19 – 25, *see also* § 27-6-80 (noting that the state's USRAP supersedes the common law rule against perpetuities). The answers to questions # 19 – 25 are not likely to apply in most cases because of the abolition of the rule with respect to the vast majority of many trusts.

Table 10
Rule Against Perpetuities *(continued)*

	TENNESSEE	*TEXAS*	*UTAH*
1. *Which rule is in effect: the common law rule, the Uniform Statutory Rule Against Perpetuities (USRAP), other law, or none?*	USRAP. (Tenn. Code. Ann. §§ 66-1-201 – 66-1-208) For trusts created after June 30, 2007, or that become irrevocable after that date, the perpetuities period is extended to 360 years. However, this only applies to trusts that grant a power of appointment at death to at least one member of each generation of beneficiaries who are beneficiaries more than 90 years after the creation of the interest. The permissible appointees must include all descendants of the beneficiary but may include other persons as well. (§ 66-1-202(a)(3) & (6))	Common Law Rule with possibility of reformation. (Tex. Prop. Code § 112.036)	Modified USRAP. (Utah Code Ann. §§ 75-2-1201 – 75-2-1209)
2. a. *Is the common law rule relevant to any interests?*	Yes, but only as the starting point of the analysis.	Yes, but revised.	Yes, but only as the starting point of the analysis.
b. *What is the relevant rule?*	A nonvested property interest is invalid unless one (1) of the following conditions is satisfied: (1) When the interest is created, it is certain to vest or terminate no later than twenty-one (21) years after *(cont'd)*	The Rule states that no interest is valid unless it must vest, if at all, within twenty-one years after some life in being at the time of the creation of the interest, plus a period of gestation. (§ 112.036) The Rule requires that a challenged conveyance *(cont'd)*	A nonvested property interest is invalid unless within 1,000 years after the interest's creation the interest vests or terminates. (§ 75-2-1203(1))

Table 10
Rule Against Perpetuities *(continued)*

	TENNESSEE	*TEXAS*	*UTAH*
b. What is the relevant rule? (cont'd)	the death of an individual then alive; or (2) The interest either vests or terminates within ninety (90) years after its creation. (§ 66-1-202(a))	be viewed as of the date the instrument is executed, and it is void if by any possible contingency the grant or devise could violate the Rule. (Peveto v. Starkey, 645 S.W.2d 770, 772 (Tex. 1982) (citations omitted))	
3. *Does the rule apply to other than private trusts?*	Yes. The rule applies except to: (1) nonvested property interest or a power of appointment arising out of a nondonative transfer, except a nonvested property interest or a power of appointment arising out of: (A) A premarital or postmarital agreement; (B) A separation or divorce settlement; (C) A spouse's election; (D) A similar arrangement arising out of a prospective, existing, or previous marital relationship between the parties; (E) A contract to make or not to revoke a will or trust; (F) A contract to exercise or not to exercise a power of appointment; (G) A transfer in satisfaction of a duty of support; or	The rule does not apply to charitable trusts. (§ 112.036)	Yes. The rule applies except to: (1) a nonvested property interest or a power of appointment arising out of a nondonative transfer, except a nonvested property interest or a power of appointment arising out of: (a) a premarital or postmarital agreement; (b) a separation or divorce settlement; (c) a spouse's election; (d) a similar arrangement arising out of a prospective, existing, or previous marital relationship between the parties; (e) a contract to make or not to revoke a will or trust; (f) a contract to exercise or not to exercise a power of appointment; (g) a transfer in satisfaction of a duty of support; or (h) a reciprocal transfer; (2) a fiduciary's power relating to the administration or

(H) A reciprocal transfer;

(2) A fiduciary's power relating to the administration or management of assets, including the power of a fiduciary to sell, lease, or mortgage property, and the power of a fiduciary to determine principal and income;

(3) A power to appoint a fiduciary;

(4) A discretionary power of a trustee to distribute principal before termination of a trust to a beneficiary having an indefeasibly vested interest in the income and principal;

(5) A nonvested property interest held by a charity, government, or governmental agency or subdivision, if the nonvested property interest is preceded by an interest held by another charity, government, or governmental agency or subdivision;

(6) A nonvested property interest in or a power of appointment with respect to a trust or other property arrangement forming part of a pension, profit-sharing, stock bonus, health, disability, death benefit, income deferral, or other current or

(cont'd)

management of assets, including the power of a fiduciary to sell, lease, or mortgage property, and the power of a fiduciary to determine principal and income;

(3) a power to appoint a fiduciary;

(4) a discretionary power of a trustee to distribute principal before termination of a trust to a beneficiary having an indefeasibly vested interest in the income and principal;

(5) a nonvested property interest held by a charity, government, or governmental agency or subdivision, if the nonvested property interest is preceded by an interest held by another charity, government, or governmental agency or subdivision;

(6) a nonvested property interest in or a power of appointment with respect to a trust or other property arrangement forming part of a pension, profit-sharing, stock bonus, health, disability, death benefit, income deferral, or other current or deferred benefit plan for one or more employees, independent contractors, or their beneficiaries or spouses, to which contributions are made for the purpose of distributing to or for the benefit of the participants or their beneficiaries or spouses the property, income, or principal in the trust or other

(cont'd)

Table 10
Rule Against Perpetuities *(continued)*

	TENNESSEE	*TEXAS*	*UTAH*
3. *Does the rule apply to other than private trusts? (cont'd)*	deferred benefit plan for one (1) or more employees, independent contractors, or their beneficiaries or spouses, to which contributions are made for the purpose of distributing to or for the benefit of the participants or their beneficiaries or spouses the property, income, or principal in the trust or other property arrangement, except a nonvested property interest or a power of appointment that is created by an election of a participant or a beneficiary or spouse; or (7) A property interest, power of appointment, or arrangement that was not subject to the common law rule against perpetuities or is excluded by another statute of this state. (§ 66-2-605)		property arrangement, except a nonvested property interest or a power of appointment that is created by an election of a participant or a beneficiary or spouse; (7) a property interest, power of appointment, or arrangement that was not subject to the common law rule against perpetuities or is excluded by another statute of this state; or (8) a property interest or arrangement subjected to a time limit under Section 75-2-1001. (§ 75-2-1206)
4. *Does the rule invalidate the interest at its creation, or is the rule revised by a wait-and-see approach?*	Wait-and-see. (§ 66-1-202(a)(2))	At its creation. (See # 2a)	Wait-and-see. (§ 75-2-1203)
5. *Can the trust be reformed?*	Yes, but only if any of the following conditions is satisfied:	Yes. (§§ 112.036; 5.043)	Yes, but only if any of the following conditions is satisfied:

	(1) A nonvested property interest or a power of appointment becomes invalid under the statutory rule against perpetuities provided in § 66-1-202 (see # 2b); (2) A class gift is not but might become invalid under the statutory rule against perpetuities provided in § 66-1-202, and the time has arrived when the share of any class member is to take effect in possession or enjoyment; or (3) A nonvested property interest that is not validated by § 66-1-202(a)(1), that is, the traditional common law rule, can vest but not within ninety (90) years after its creation. (§ 66-1-204).		(1) a nonvested property interest or a power of appointment becomes invalid under Section 75-2-1203 (see # 2b); (2) a class gift is not but might become invalid under Section 75-2-1203 and the time has arrived when the share of any class member is to take effect in possession or enjoyment; or (3) a nonvested property interest that is not validated by Section 75-2-1203, that is, the traditional common law rule, can vest but not within 1,000 years after its creation. (§ 75-2-1205)
6. *If yes to 5., under what theory?*	[A] court shall reform a disposition in the manner that most closely approximates the transferor's manifested plan of distribution and is within the ninety (90) years allowed by §§ 66-1-202(a)(2), (b)(2) or (c)(2). (§ 66-1-204)	Any interest in a trust may, however, be reformed or construed to the extent and as provided by Section 5.043. (§ 112.036) *See* § 5.043(a) ("Within the limits of the rule against perpetuities, a court shall reform or construe an interest in real or personal property that violates the rule to effect the ascertainable general intent of the creator of the interest. A court shall liberally construe and apply this provision to validate an interest to the fullest extent consistent *(cont'd)*	[A] court shall reform a disposition in the manner that most closely approximates the transferor's manifested plan of distribution and is within the 1,000 years allowed by Section 75-2-1203. (§ 75-2-1205) *See also* § 75-2-1207(3) ("If a nonvested property interest or a power of appointment was created before December 31, 2003, and is determined in a judicial proceeding, commenced on or after December 31, 2003, to violate Utah's rule against perpetuities as that rule existed before December 31, 2003, a court *(cont'd)*

Table 10
Rule Against Perpetuities *(continued)*

	TENNESSEE	TEXAS	UTAH
6. *If yes to 5., under what theory? (cont'd)*		with the creator's intent.'') The court may reform or construe an interest according to the doctrine of cy pres by giving effect to the general intent and specific directive of the creator within the limits of the rule against perpetuities. (§ 5.043(b))	upon the petition of an interested person may reform the disposition: (a) in the manner that most closely approximates the transferor's manifested plan of distribution; and (b) that is within the limits of the rule against perpetuities applicable when the nonvested property interest or power of appointment was created.'')
7. *When is a general testamentary power of appointment invalid?*	A general testamentary power of appointment is invalid unless one of the following conditions is satisfied: (1) When the power is created, it is certain to be irrevocably exercised or otherwise to terminate no later than 21 years after the death of an individual then alive. (2) The power is irrevocably exercised or otherwise terminates within 90 years after its creation. (§ 66-1-202(c))	*See* Unif. Statutory Rule Against Perpetuities § 1, 8B U.L.A. 248 (amended 1990) (''Under the Common-law Rule . . . a *nongeneral power* (whether or not presently exercisable) or a *general testamentary power* is invalid as of the time of its creation if it *might* not terminate (by irrevocable exercise or otherwise) within a life in being plus 21 years.'')	A general testamentary power of appointment is invalid unless within 1,000 years after its creation the power of appointment is irrevocably exercised or terminates. (§ 75-2-1203(3))

8. *Same, but nongeneral testamentary power.*	A nongeneral power of appointment . . . is invalid unless one of the following conditions is satisfied: (1) When the power is created, it is certain to be irrevocably exercised or otherwise to terminate no later than 21 years after the death of an individual then alive. (2) The power is irrevocably exercised or otherwise terminates within 90 years after its creation. (§ 66-1-202(c)) *But see* 1. above with respect to a 360-year period as an alternative.	See #7.	A nongeneral power of appointment . . . is invalid unless within 1,000 years after its creation the power of appointment is irrevocably exercised or terminates. (§ 75-2-1203(3))
9. *Same, but general inter vivos power.*	A general power of appointment not presently exercisable because of a condition precedent is invalid unless one of the following conditions is satisfied: (1) When the power is created, the condition precedent is certain to be satisfied or become impossible to satisfy no later than 21 years after the death of an individual then alive. (2) The condition precedent either is satisfied or becomes impossible to satisfy within 90 years after its creation. (§ 66-1-202(b))	*See* Unif. Statutory Rule Against Perpetuities § 1, 8B U.L.A. 248 (amended 1990) ("Under the Common-law Rule, a *general power not presently exercisable because of a condition precedent* is invalid as of the time of its creation if the condition *might* neither be satisfied nor become impossible to satisfy with a life in being plus 21 years.")	A general power of appointment not presently exercisable because of a condition precedent is invalid unless within 1,000 years after the general power of appointment's creation the power of appointment is irrevocably exercised or terminates. (§ 75-2-1203(2))

Table 10
Rule Against Perpetuities *(continued)*

	TENNESSEE	*TEXAS*	*UTAH*
10. *Same, but nongeneral inter vivos power.*	See # 8.	See # 7.	See # 8.
11. *Is a period of gestation added to the perpetuity period?*	No. The possibility that a child will be born to a person after that person's death is disregarded. (§ 66-1-202(d)) *See also* Unif. Statutory Rule Against Perpetuities § 1, 8B U.L.A. 242-43 (amended 1990) (''[T]he possibility that a child will be born to [a testator] after his death must be disregarded; and the possibility that a child will be born to any of [the testator's] descendants after their deaths must also be disregarded. Note, however, that the rule of subsection (d) does *not* apply to the question of the entitlement of an after-born child to take a beneficial interest in the trust'').	Yes. (§ 112.036; Foshee v. Republic Nat'l Bank, 617 S. W.2d 675, 677 (Tex. 1981))	N/A
12. *What is the treatment of a ''later of the traditional rule or 90 years'' clause? See UPC 2-901(e).*	Such language is inoperative to the extent it produces a period of time that exceeds twenty-one (21) years after the death of the survivor of the specified lives. (§ 66-1-202(e))	N/A	Such language is inoperative to the extent it produces a period of time that exceeds twenty-one (21) years after the death of the survivor of the specified lives. (§ 75-2-1203(4))

13. *When is an interest created by the exercise of a general testamentary power deemed created?*	Except as provided in subsections (b) and (c) of this section and in § 66-1-206(a), the time of creation of a nonvested property interest or a power of appointment is determined by other applicable statutes or, if none, under general principles of property law. (§ 66-1-203(a)) The first two of the excepted provisions states that as long as a person with a general power to become the unqualified beneficial owner has that power, the nonvested interest is created when the power terminates. The third of the excepted provisions states that a nonvested property interest, which arises from a transfer to an existing trust, is created when the nonvested property interest in the trust was created. *See also* Unif. Statutory Rule Against Perpetuities § 2, 8B U.L.A. 268 (amended 1990) (explaining that "general principles of property law determine that the time ... [of creation] is at the decedent's death.")	*See* comment to Unif. Probate Code § 2-902(a) ("general principles of property law determine that a nonvested property interest or power of appointment created by will is created at the decedent's death"); Unif. Statutory Rule Against Perpetuities § 2, 8B U.L.A. 268 (amended 1990) (stating the same).	Except as provided in Subsections (2) and (3) and in Section 75-2-1207, the time of creation of a nonvested property interest or a power of appointment is determined under general principles of property law. (§ 75-2-1204(1)) The first two of the excepted provisions states that as long as a person with a general power to become the unqualified beneficial owner has that power, the nonvested interest is created when the power terminates.The third of the excepted provisions states that a nonvested property interest, which arises from a transfer to an existing trust, is created when the nonvested property interest in the trust was created. *See also* Unif. Statutory Rule Against Perpetuities § 2, 8B U.L.A. 268 (amended 1990) (explaining that "general principles of property law determine that the time ... [of creation] is at the decedent's death.") *See generally* § 75-2-1207(b) ("a nonvested property interest or a power of appointment created by the exercise of a power of appointment is created when the power is irrevocably exercised or when a revocable exercise becomes irrevocable.")

Table 10
Rule Against Perpetuities *(continued)*

	TENNESSEE	*TEXAS*	*UTAH*
14. *Same, but nongeneral testamentary power.*	See # 13.	See # 13.	See # 13.
15. *Same, but general inter vivos power.*	Except as provided in subsections (b) and (c) of this section and in § 66-1-206(a), the time of creation of a nonvested property interest or a power of appointment is determined by other applicable statutes or, if none, under general principles of property law. (§ 66-1-203(a)) The first two of the excepted provisions states that as long as a person with a general power to become the unqualified beneficial owner has that power, the nonvested interest is created when the power terminates. The third of the excepted provisions states that a nonvested property interest, which arises from a transfer to an existing trust, is created when the nonvested property interest in the trust was created. *See also* Unif. Statutory Rule Against Perpetuities § 2, 8B	*See* comment to Unif. Probate Code § 2-902(a) ("With respect to an inter-vivos transfer, an interest or power is created on the date the transfer becomes effective for purpose of property law generally, normally the date of delivery of the deed or funding of the trust."); Unif. Statutory Rule Against Perpetuities § 2, 8B U.L.A. 268 (stating the same).	Except as provided in Subsections (2) and (3) and in Section 75-2-1207, the time of creation of a nonvested property interest or a power of appointment is determined under general principles of property law. (§ 75-2-1204(1)) The first two of the excepted provisions states that as long as a person with a general power to become the unqualified beneficial owner has that power, the nonvested interest is created when the power terminates. The third of the excepted provisions states that a nonvested property interest, which arises from a transfer to an existing trust, is created when the nonvested property interest in the trust was created. *See also* Unif. Statutory Rule Against Perpetuities § 2, 8B U.L.A. 268 (amended 1990) (explaining that "the time when the interest or power is created is the date the transfer becomes effective for purposes of property law generally, normally the date of delivery of the deed");

	U.L.A. 268 (amended 1990) (explaining that "the time when the interest or power is created is the date the transfer becomes effective for purposes of property law generally, normally the date of delivery of the deed"); Comment to Unif. Probate Code § 2-902(a) (stating same and adding "the funding of the trust" as "normally" the time when the interest is created).		Comment to Unif. Probate Code § 2-902(a) (stating same and adding "the funding of the trust" as "normally" the time when the interest is created). *See generally* § 75-2-1207(b) ("For the purposes of this section, a nonvested property interest or a power of appointment created by the exercise of a power of appointment is created when the power is irrevocably exercised or when a revocable exercise becomes irrevocable.")
16. *Same, but nongeneral inter vivos power.*	See # 15.	See # 15.	See # 15.
17. *When is an interest created if the grantor of a trust has a power to revoke?*	For purposes of this part, if there is a person who alone can exercise a power created by a governing instrument to become the unqualified beneficial owner of: (1) A nonvested property interest; or (2) A property interest subject to a power of appointment described in §§ 66-1-202(b) or (c); the nonvested property interest or power of appointment is created when the power to become the unqualified beneficial owner terminates. (§ 66-1-203(b))	*See* comment to Unif. Probate Code § 2-902(b) (noting that "nonvested property interest and powers of appointment created in [a revocable inter-vivos trust] are created when the power to revoke expires, usually at the settlor's death"); Unif. Statutory Rule Against Perpetuities § 2, 8B U.L.A. 268 (amended 1990) (explaining that "any nonvested property interest subject to [a power to revoke] is not created . . . until the power terminates (by release, expiration at the death of the donee, or otherwise").	For purposes of this part, if there is a person who alone can exercise a power created by a governing instrument to become the unqualified beneficial owner of: (a) a nonvested property interest; or (b) a property interest subject to a power of appointment described in Subsection 75-2-1203(2)(a) or (b), the nonvested property interest or power of appointment is created when the power to become the unqualified beneficial owner terminates. (§ 75-2-1204(2)) *See also* § 75-2-1207(b) ("a nonvested property interest or a power of appointment created by the

(cont'd)

(cont'd)

Table 10
Rule Against Perpetuities *(continued)*

	TENNESSEE	TEXAS	UTAH
17. *When is an interest created if the grantor of a trust has a power to revoke? (cont'd)*	*See also* Unif. Statutory Rule Against Perpetuities § 2, 8B U.L.A. 268 (amended 1990) (explaining that "any nonvested property interest subject to [a power to revoke] is not created . . . until the power terminates (by release, expiration at the death of the donee, or otherwise"); Comment to Unif. Probate Code § 2-902(b) (noting that "nonvested property interest and powers of appointment created in [a revocable inter-vivos trust] are created when the power to revoke expires, usually at the settlor's death").		exercise of a power of appointment is created when the power is irrevocably exercised or when a revocable exercise becomes irrevocable.") *See generally* Unif. Statutory Rule Against Perpetuities § 2, 8B U.L.A. 268 (amended 1990) (explaining that "any nonvested property interest subject to [a power to revoke] is not created . . . until the power terminates (by release, expiration at the death of the donee, or otherwise"); Comment to Unif. Probate Code § 2-902(b) (noting that "nonvested property interest and powers of appointment created in [a revocable inter-vivos trust] are created when the power to revoke expires, usually at the settlor's death").
18. *When does the period of the rule start re an interest contributed to an irrevocable trust? See UPC 2-902(c).*	A nonvested property interest or a power of appointment arising from a transfer of property to a previously funded trust or other existing property arrangement is created when the nonvested property interest or power of appointment in the original contribution was created. (§ 66-1-203(c))	*See* comment to Unif. Probate Code 2-902(c) ("Arguably, at common law, each transfer [to an existing irrevocable inter-vivos trust] starts the period of the Rule running anew as to each transfer.")	For purposes of this title, a nonvested property interest or a power of appointment arising from a transfer of property to a previously funded trust or other existing property arrangement is created when the nonvested property interest or power of appointment in the original contribution was created. (§ 75-2-1204(3))

19. *Is there a conclusive presumption of fertility, that is, the "fertile octogenarian" rule?*	Yes. McCarley v. McCarley, 360 S.W.2d 27, 29 (Tenn. 1962) (affirming the statement: "'A possibility of issue is always supposed to exist, in law, unless extinguished by the death of the parties . . .' ")[1] *See also* Unif. Statutory Rule Against Perpetuities § 1, 8B U.L.A. 256 (amended 1990) (holding that "[t]his principle is not superseded by this Act, and in view of new advances in medical science . . . [this] is not unrealistic.")); *but see* C. P. Jhong, Annotation, *Modern Status of Presumption of Possibility of Issue Being Extinct*, 98 A.L.R.2d 1285 (2003) (noting "a trend toward denying the conclusive or absolute nature of the presumption against the possibility of issue being extinct where there is competent evidence to the contrary has developed in the decisions, although some courts still adhere to the traditional view treating the presumption as conclusive or absolute").	There is a presumption, but it is rebuttable. Frost Nat'l Bank v. Newton, 554 S.W.2d 149, 156 (Tex. 1977) (holding that there is a "presumption of fertility but recognizes that 'this presumption can be rebutted by relevant evidence as to such person and by past experience concerning births to persons of like age and physical condition.'")	No specific state case or statute. *See* Unif. Statutory Rule Against Perpetuities § 1, 8B U.L.A. 256 (amended 1990) (holding that "[t]his principle is not superseded by this Act, and in view of new advances in medical science . . . [this] is not unrealistic.")); *but see* C. P. Jhong, Annotation, *Modern Status of Presumption of Possibility of Issue Being Extinct*, 98 A.L.R.2d 1285 (2003) (noting "a trend toward denying the conclusive or absolute nature of the presumption against the possibility of issue being extinct where there is competent evidence to the contrary has developed in the decisions, although some courts still adhere to the traditional view treating the presumption as conclusive or absolute").
20. *What is the earliest age a child is deemed capable of bearing a child? What is the impact of illegitimacy?*	Not specifically addressed by USRAP, but the reasoning is the same as set forth in the comment to section 1 of USRAP, 2, Technical Violations of the *(cont'd)*	Under the rule, courts must presume that living persons are capable of having or fathering children, no matter how young they are. See In re Graite's Will *(cont'd)*	Not specifically addressed by USRAP, but the reasoning is the same as set forth in the comment to section 1 of USRAP, 2, Technical Violations of the Common Law Rule. *(cont'd)*

Table 10
Rule Against Perpetuities *(continued)*

	TENNESSEE	TEXAS	UTAH
20. *What is the earliest age a child is deemed capable of bearing a child? What is the impact of illegitimacy? (cont'd)*	Common Law Rule. Wait and see will typically result in no violation. Nevertheless, the common law rule ordinarily will be applied initially. Under the rule, courts must presume that living persons are capable of having or fathering children, no matter how young they are. See In re Graite's Will Trusts, [1949] 1 All E.R. 459, 460 (Ch.). Thus, the rule strikes down any interest whose vesting depends on the assertion that, for example, a toddler will not have children. (Keith L. Butler, Notes & Comments, *Long Live the Dead Hand: A Case for the Repeal of the Rule Against Perpetuities in Washington*, 75 Wash. L. Rev. 1237, 1246 n.78 (2000)).	Trusts, [1949] 1 All E.R. 459, 460 (Ch.). Thus, the rule strikes down any interest whose vesting depends on the assertion that, for example, a toddler will not have children. (Keith L. Butler, Notes & Comments, *Long Live the Dead Hand: A Case for the Repeal of the Rule Against Perpetuities in Washington*, 75 Wash. L. Rev. 1237, 1246 n.78 (2000)).	Wait and see will typically result in no violation. Nevertheless, the common law rule ordinarily will be applied initially. Under the rule, courts must presume that living persons are capable of having or fathering children, no matter how young they are. See In re Graite's Will Trusts, [1949] 1 All E.R. 459, 460 (Ch.). Thus, the rule strikes down any interest whose vesting depends on the assertion that, for example, a toddler will not have children. (Keith L. Butler, Notes & Comments, *Long Live the Dead Hand: A Case for the Repeal of the Rule Against Perpetuities in Washington*, 75 Wash. L. Rev. 1237, 1246 n.78 (2000)).
21. *Is the ''unborn widow'' rule observed?*	No specific state case or statute. *See* Unif. Statutory Rule Against Perpetuities § 1, 8B U.L.A. 246 (amended 1990) (explaining that ''[t]he chance that [an] interest will become invalid under the Statutory Rule is small'' and so the unborn widow rule would rarely invalidate an interest); *see also* 61	*See, e.g.*, Arkansas, question # 21.	No specific state case or statute. *See* Unif. Statutory Rule Against Perpetuities § 1, 8B U.L.A. 246 (amended 1990) (explaining that ''[t]he chance that [an] interest will become invalid under the Statutory Rule is small'' and so the unborn widow rule would rarely invalidate an interest); *see also* 61 Am Jur 2d *Perpetuities and Restraints on*

	Am Jur 2d *Perpetuities and Restraints on Alienation* § 40 (2003) (noting the same).		*Alienation* § 40 (2003) (noting the same). This is even more poignant for Utah's 1000-year rule.
22. *Does the "slothful executor" rule apply, i.e., an administrative contingency clause providing for a "distribution to, e.g., those issue living at the time of the satisfaction of the administrative condition precedent?"*	No specific state case or statute. *See* Unif. Statutory Rule Against Perpetuities § 1, 8B U.L.A. 245 (amended 1990) (Under USRAP, an "interest becomes invalid only if it remains in existence and nonvested 90 years after [the testator's] death. Since it is almost certain that the final distribution of [an] estate will occur well within this 90-year period, the chance that [an] interest will be invalid is negligible.")	*See*, e.g., California, question # 22.	No specific state case or statute. *See* Unif. Statutory Rule Against Perpetuities § 1, 8B U.L.A. 245 (amended 1990) (Under USRAP, an "interest becomes invalid only if it remains in existence and nonvested 90 years after [the testator's] death. Since it is almost certain that the final distribution of [an] estate will occur well within this 90-year period, the chance that [an] interest will be invalid is negligible."). This is even more poignant for Utah's 1000-year rule.
23. *Does the all-or-nothing rule apply to class gifts?*	Yes. Crockett v. Scott, 284 S.W.2d 289, 295 (Tenn. 1955) (affirming the statement that: "'Where the gift is to a class, the class must be such that all the members thereof must necessarily be ascertained and take absolutely vested interests within the period specified by the rule against perpetuities, and if, because of a violation of the rule, a gift or limitation is void as to any of the class to which it is given, it is void as to all.'") *But see* Unif. Statutory Rule Against Perpetuities § 1, 8B	Yes. Henderson v. Moore, 190 S. W.2d 800, 802 (Tex. 1945).	No specific state case or statute. *See* Unif. Statutory Rule Against Perpetuities § 1, 8B U.L.A. 257 (amended 1990) ("Although this Act does not supersede the basic idea of the much-maligned 'all-or-nothing' rule, the evils sometimes attributed to it are substantially if not entirely eliminated by the wait-and-see feature of the Statutory Rule and by the availability of reformation.") This is even more poignant for Utah's 1000-year rule.

(cont'd)

Table 10
Rule Against Perpetuities *(continued)*

	TENNESSEE	*TEXAS*	*UTAH*
23. *Does the all-or-nothing rule apply to class gifts? (cont'd)*	U.L.A. 257 (amended 1990) (''Although this Act does not supersede the basic idea of the much-maligned 'all-or-nothing' rule, the evils sometimes attributed to it are substantially if not entirely eliminated by the wait-and-see feature of the Statutory Rule and by the availability of reformation under Section 3.'')		
24. *Is there an exception to the all-or-nothing rule in the case of subclasses or specific sums to each member of the class?*	No specific state case or statute. *See* Unif. Statutory Rule Against Perpetuities § 1, 8B U.L.A. 257 (amended 1990) (''The specific-sum and sub-class doctrines are not superseded by this Act.'')	*See* Unif. Statutory Rule Against Perpetuities § 2, 8B U.L.A. 257 (''The common law also recognizes a doctrine called the specific-sum doctrine which is derived from Storrs v. Benbow, 3 De G.M. & G. 390, 43 Eng. Rep 153 (Ch. 1853), and states: If a specified sum of money is to be paid to each member of a class, the interest of each class member is entitled to separate treatment and is valid or invalid under the Rule on its own. The common law also recognizes a doctrine called the sub-class doctrine, which is derived from Cattlin v. Brown, 11 Hare 372, 68 Eng. Rep. 1318 (Ch. 1853), and states: If the ultimate takers are not described as a	No specific state case or statute. *See* Unif. Statutory Rule Against Perpetuities § 1, 8B U.L.A. 257 (amended 1990) (''The specific-sum and sub-class doctrines are not superseded by this Act.'')

		single class but rather as a group of separate subclasses, and if the share to which each separate subclass is entitled will finally be determined within the period of the Rule, the gifts to the different subclasses are separate for the purpose of the Rule.'').	
25. *Is the infectious invalidity rule followed outside class gifts?*	No specific state case or statute. *See* Unif. Statutory Rule Against Perpetuities § 1, 8B U.L.A. 256 (amended 1990) (explaining that ''[t]he doctrine of infectious invalidity is superseded by this Act by Section 3, under which courts . . . are required to *reform* the disposition to approximate as closely as possible the transferor's . . . plan of distribution.'')	Not completely. Sellers v. Powers, 426 S.W.2d 533, 536-537 (Tex. 1968) (citations omitted) (explaining that ''the principle of infectious invalidity or inseparability of the valid and invalid interests and the concomitant question'' Is the invalid limitation so essential to the dispositive scheme of the testator . . . that it can be inferred that he would not wish the prior limitation to stand alone? ''The balance of the disposition is not stricken out merely because the limitation is invalid unless additional language or circumstances are present which require an affirmative finding of this intent.''). *See also* § 5.043(c), providing that ''a court shall enforce the provisions of the instrument that do not violate the rule and shall reform or construe under this section a provision that violates or might violate the rule.''	No specific state case or statute. *See* Unif. Statutory Rule Against Perpetuities § 1, 8B U.L.A. 256 (amended 1990) (explaining that ''[t]he doctrine of infectious invalidity is superseded by this Act by Section 3, under which courts . . . are required to *reform* the disposition to approximate as closely as possible the transferor's . . . plan of distribution.'')

Table 10
Rule Against Perpetuities *(continued)*

	TENNESSEE	*TEXAS*	*UTAH*
26. *Is there a rule against the suspension of the power of alienation? If so, how is it stated?*	Absolute prohibition. *See* Hankins v. Mathews, 425 S.W.2d 608, 610 (Tenn. 1968) (affirming the statement that " 'The doctrine of most jurisdictions . . . is that where land is granted or devised in fee, a provision of any sort that the taker shall not alienate, or shall not have power to alienate, is void, whether amounting to a mere naked prohibition or direction, or expressed or construed to be a condition, or conjoined with a limitation over in the event of alienation or attempt to alienate.' ")	Yes. Kelley v. Marlin, 714 S.W.2d 303, 310 (Tex. 1986) ("Probate law protects beneficiaries not only from being forced into unwanted relationships, but also against undue restrictions on their right to maintain and dispose of their property. The United States Supreme Court, as well as courts of this State, have consistently held that restraints on the power of alienation, when incorporated in a deed or will otherwise conveying a fee simple right to the property, are void.")	Redd v. Western Sav. & Loan Co., 646 P.2d 761, 763-64 (Utah 1982) (affirming rule of free alienability, but permitting indirect restraints on alienation if reasonable).
27. *Effective date.*	Effective for all nonvested interests and unexercised powers whenever created. (§ 66-1-206 (a)) However, the law does not apply to interests and powers the validity of which was determined by a final judgment or settlement among interested parties prior to July 1, 1994. (§ 66-1-206(b))	Section 5.043, pertaining to reformation, applies to interests by instruments taking effect on or after September 1, 1969, and an appointment made on or after that date regardless of when the power was created. (§ 5.043(d))	December 31, 2003. *See also* # 6.

1. For questions # 19 – 25, *see also* § 66-1-207 (noting that the state's USRAP supersedes the common law rule against perpetuities). The answers to questions # 19 – 25 are not likely to apply in most cases because of the abolition of the rule with respect to the vast majority of many trusts.

Table 10
Rule Against Perpetuities *(continued)*

		VERMONT	*VIRGINIA*	*WASHINGTON*
1.	*Which rule is in effect: the common law rule, the Uniform Statutory Rule Against Perpetuities (USRAP), other law, or none?*	Variation on USRAP. (27 Vt. Stat. Ann. §§ 501-503)	USRAP. (Va. Code Ann. §§ 55-12.1 – 55-12.6) However, §55-13.3(C) provides that the rule does not apply "to any trust or any interest created in personal property held in such trust, or to any power of appointment over personal property granted under such trust, when the trust instrument, by its terms, provides that the rule against perpetuities shall not apply to such trust."	Other. (Wash. Rev. Code § 11.98.130) Exception for provisions of instruments creating trusts and interests created due to a power of appointment under an instrument creating a trust.
2.	*a. Is the common law rule relevant to any interests?*	Yes, but only as a starting point of the analysis.	Yes, but only as a starting point of the analysis.	Common law rule. In re Estate of Lee, 299 P. 2d 1066, 1068-69 (Wash. 1956) ("The rule against perpetuities prohibits the creation of future estates which, by possibility, may not become vested within a life or lives in being at the time of the testator's death and twenty-one years thereafter.")
	b. What is the relevant rule?	Under the orthodox rule against perpetuities no future interest in property is valid unless it must vest not later than 21 years (and the period of actual gestation) after some life in being at its creation. *(cont'd)*	A nonvested property interest is invalid unless: 1. When the interest is created, it is certain to vest or terminate no later than twenty-one years after the death of an individual then alive; or *(cont'd)*	No provision of an instrument creating a trust, including the provisions of any further trust created, and no other disposition of property made pursuant to exercise of a power of appointment granted in or created through authority under such *(cont'd)*

Table 10
Rule Against Perpetuities *(continued)*

	VERMONT	*VIRGINIA*	*WASHINGTON*
b. What is the relevant rule? (cont'd)	(Ransom v. Bebernitz, 782 A.2d 1155, 1160 n.3 (Vt. 2001)); *but see* questions # 4 – 6 below (wait-and-see and reformation mean that this rule is not strictly applied)	2. The interest either vests or terminates within ninety years after its creation. (§ 55-12.1(A))	instrument is invalid under the rule against perpetuities, or any similar statute or common law, during the one hundred fifty years following the effective date of the instrument. Thereafter, unless the trust assets have previously become distributable or vested, the provision or other disposition of property is deemed to have been rendered invalid under the rule against perpetuities. (§ 11.98.130)
3. Does the rule apply to other than private trusts?	No. The rule does not apply to charitable trusts. (Ball v. Hall, 274 A.2d 516, 523 (Vt. 1971))	Yes. The rule applies except to: 1. A nonvested property interest or a power of appointment arising out of a nondonative transfer, except a nonvested property interest or a power of appointment arising out of (i) a premarital or postmarital agreement; (ii) a separation or divorce settlement; (iii) a spouse's election; (iv) a similar arrangement arising out of a prospective, existing, or previous marital relationship between the parties; (v) a contract to make or not to	Unclear. *See* § 11.98.009 ("Except as provided in this section, this chapter applies to express trusts executed by the trustor after June 10, 1959, and does not apply to resulting trusts, constructive trusts, business trusts where certificates of beneficial interest are issued to the beneficiary, investment trusts, voting trusts, trusts in the nature of mortgages or pledges, trusts created by the judgment or decree of a court not sitting in probate, liquidation trusts, or trusts for the sole purpose of paying dividends, interest, interest coupons, salaries, wages, pensions or profits, trusts

revoke a will or trust; (vi) a contract to exercise or not to exercise a power of appointment; (vii) a transfer in satisfaction of a duty of support; or (viii) a reciprocal transfer;

2. A fiduciary's power relating to the administration or management of assets, including the power of a fiduciary to sell, lease, or mortgage property, and the power of a fiduciary to determine principal and income;
3. A power to appoint a fiduciary;
4. A discretionary power of trustee to distribute principal before termination of a trust to a beneficiary having an indefensibly vested interest in the income and principal;
5. A nonvested property interest held by a charity, government, or governmental agency or subdivision, if the nonvested property interest is preceded by aninterest held by another charity, government, or governmental agency or subdivision;
6. A nonvested property interest in or a power of appointment with respect to a trust or other property arrangement forming part of a pension, profit-sharing, stock bonus, health, disability,

(cont'd)

created in deposits in any financial institution pursuant to chapter 30.22 RCW, unless any such trust which is created in writing incorporates this chapter in whole or in part.")

Table 10
Rule Against Perpetuities *(continued)*

	VERMONT	*VIRGINIA*	*WASHINGTON*
3. *Does the rule apply to other than private trusts? (cont'd)*		death benefit, income deferral, or other current or deferred benefit plan for one or more employees, independent contractors, or their beneficiaries or spouses, to which contributions are made for the purpose of distributing to or for the benefit of the participants or their beneficiaries or spouses the property, income, or principal in the trust or other property arrangement, except a nonvested property interest or a power of appointment that is created by an election of a participant or a beneficiary or spouse; or 7. A property interest, power of appointment, or arrangement that was not subject to the common law rule against perpetuities or is excluded by another statute of this Commonwealth. (§ 55-12.4)	

4. *Does the rule invalidate the interest at its creation, or is the rule revised by a wait-and-see approach?*	Wait-and-see. Colby v. Colby, 596 A.2d 901, 903 (Vt. 1990) ("Vermont has, by passing 27 V.S.A. § 501 [see # 6 below], aligned itself in a group of states adopting what is known as a 'wait and see' rule concerning perpetuities. This rule says that if, at the time of the event, the common law measure given as 'lives in being and twenty-one years' has not been violated, there is no violation of the rule.")	Wait-and-see. (§ 55.12.1(A)(2))	Wait-and-see for trust interests. Specifically, following 150 years after the effective date of the instrument, if the trust assets have not become distributable or vested, the provision or other disposition of property is deemed to have been rendered invalid under the rule against perpetuities. (§ 11.98.130) The common law rule applies for other interests. *See* Robroy Land Co. v. Prather, 622 P.2d 367, 373 (Wa. 1980).
5. *Can the trust be reformed?*	Yes. (27 § 501)	Yes, but only if one of the following conditions is satisfied: 1. A nonvested property interest or a power of appointment becomes invalid under § 55-12.1 (see # 2b); 2. A class gift is not but might become invalid under § 55-12.1 and the time has arrived when the share of any class member is to take effect in possession or enjoyment; or 3. A nonvested property interest that is not validated by subdivision A 1 of § 55-12.1, that is, the traditional common law rule, can vest but not within 90 years after its creation. (§ 55-12.3)	No specific state case or statute.

Table 10
Rule Against Perpetuities *(continued)*

	VERMONT	*VIRGINIA*	*WASHINGTON*
6. *If yes to 5., under what theory?*	Any interest in real or personal property which would violate the rule against perpetuities shall be reformed, within the limits of that rule, to approximate most closely the intention of the creator of the interest. In determining whether an interest would violate said rule and in reforming an interest the period of perpetuities shall be measured by actual rather than possible events. (27 § 501)	[A] court of equity in the county or city wherein the affected property or the greater part thereof is located shall reform a disposition in the manner that most closely approximates the transferor's manifested plan of distribution and is within the ninety years allowed by subdivision A 2, B 2 or C 2 of § 55-12.1. (§ 55-12.3)	See # 5.
7. *When is a general testamentary power of appointment invalid?*	*See* Unif. Statutory Rule Against Perpetuities § 1, 8B U.L.A. 248 (amended 1990) ("Under the Common-law Rule . . . a *nongeneral power* (whether or not presently exercisable) or a *general testamentary power* is invalid as of the time of its creation if it *might* not terminate (by irrevocable exercise or otherwise) within a life in being plus 21 years.")	A general testamentary power of appointment is invalid unless one of the following conditions is satisfied: (1) When the power is created, it is certain to be irrevocably exercised or otherwise to terminate no later than 21 years after the death of an individual then alive. (2) The power is irrevocably exercised or otherwise terminates within 90 years after its creation. (§ 55-12.2(C))	*See* Unif. Statutory Rule Against Perpetuities § 1, 8B U.L.A. 248 (amended 1990) ("Under the Common-law Rule . . . a *nongeneral power* (whether or not presently exercisable) or a *general testamentary power* is invalid as of the time of its creation if it *might* not terminate (by irrevocable exercise or otherwise) within a life in being plus 21 years.")

8. *Same, but nongeneral testamentary power.*	See # 7.	A nongeneral power of appointment . . . is invalid unless one of the following conditions is satisfied: (1) When the power is created, it is certain to be irrevocably exercised or otherwise to terminate no later than 21 years after the death of an individual then alive. (2) The power is irrevocably exercised or otherwise terminates within 90 years after its creation. (§ 55-12.2(C))	See # 7.
9. *Same, but general inter vivos power.*	*See* Unif. Statutory Rule Against Perpetuities § 1, 8B U.L.A. 248 (amended 1990) ("Under the Common-law Rule, a *general power not presently exercisable because of a condition precedent* is invalid as of the time of its creation if the condition *might* neither be satisfied nor become impossible to satisfy with a life in being plus 21 years.")	A general power of appointment not presently exercisable because of a condition precedent is invalid unless one of the following conditions is satisfied: (1) When the power is created, the condition precedent is certain to be satisfied or become impossible to satisfy no later than 21 years after the death of an individual then alive. (2) The condition precedent either is satisfied or becomes impossible to satisfy within 90 years after its creation. (§ 55-12.2(B))	With respect to an inter vivos power, *see* Unif. Statutory Rule Against Perpetuities § 1, 8B U.L.A. 248 (amended 1990) ("Under the Common-law Rule, a *general power not presently exercisable because of a condition precedent* is invalid as of the time of its creation if the condition *might* neither be satisfied nor become impossible to satisfy with a life in being plus 21 years.") One hundred fifty years following the effective date of the instrument if created in a trust, otherwise common law rule. (See # 2b.)

Table 10
Rule Against Perpetuities *(continued)*

	VERMONT	*VIRGINIA*	*WASHINGTON*
10. Same, but nongeneral inter vivos power.	See # 7.	See # 8.	See # 9.
11. Is a period of gestation added to the perpetuity period?	Yes. (See # 2a.)	No. The possibility that a child will be born to a person after that person's death is disregarded. (§ 55-12.2(D)) *See also* comment to § 55-12.2 (''[T]he possibility that a child will be born to [a testator] after his death must be disregarded; and the possibility that a child will be born to any of [the testator's] descendants after their deaths must also be disregarded. Note, however, that the rule of subsection (d) does *not* apply to the question of the entitlement of an after-born child to take a beneficial interest in the trust'').	Yes. Kendall v. Kendall, 261 P. 2d 422, 425 (Wash. 1953)
12. What is the treatment of a ''later of the traditional rule or 90 years'' clause? See UPC 2-901(e).	N/A	That language is inoperative to the extent it produces a period of time that exceeds twenty-one years after the death of the survivor of the specified lives. (§ 55-12.1(E))	N/A

13. *When is an interest created by the exercise of a general testamentary power deemed created?*	*See* comment to Unif. Probate Code § 2-902(a) (''general principles of property law determine that a nonvested property interest or power of appointment created by will is created at the decedent's death''); Unif. Statutory Rule Against Perpetuities § 2, 8B U.L.A. 268 (amended 1990) (stating the same).	Except as provided in subsections B and C and in § 55-12.5, the time of creation of a nonvested property interest or a power of appointment is determined under general principles of property law. (§ 55-12.2(A)) The first two of the excepted provisions states that as long as a person with a general power to become the unqualified beneficial owner has that power, the nonvested interest is created when the power terminates. The third of the excepted provisions states that a nonvested property interest, which arises from a transfer to an existing trust, is created when the nonvested property interest in the trust was created. *See also* comment to §55-12.2 (explaining that ''general principles of property law determine that the time . . . [of creation] is at the decedent's death.'') *See generally* § 55-12.5 (''For the purposes of this section, a nonvested property interest or a power of appointment created by the exercise of a power of appointment is created when the power is irrevocably exercised or when a revocable exercise becomes irrevocable.'')	*See* comment to Unif. Probate Code § 2-902(a) (''general principles of property law determine that a nonvested property interest or power of appointment created by will is created at the decedent's death''); Unif. Statutory Rule Against Perpetuities § 2, 8B U.L.A. 268 (amended 1990) (stating the same).

Table 10
Rule Against Perpetuities *(continued)*

	VERMONT	*VIRGINIA*	*WASHINGTON*
14. *Same, but nongeneral testamentary power.*	See # 13.	See # 13.	See # 13.
15. *Same, but general inter vivos power.*	*See* comment to Unif. Probate Code § 2-902(a) (''With respect to an inter-vivos transfer, an interest or power is created on the date the transfer becomes effective for purpose of property law generally, normally the date of delivery of the deed or funding of the trust.''); Unif. Statutory Rule Against Perpetuities § 2, 8B U.L.A. 268 (stating the same).	Except as provided in subsections B and C and in § 55-12.5, the time of creation of a nonvested property interest or a power of appointment is determined under general principles of property law. (§ 55-12.2(A)) The first two of the excepted provisions states that as long as a person with a general power to become the unqualified beneficial owner has that power, the nonvested interest is created when the power terminates. The third of the excepted provisions states that a nonvested property interest, which arises from a transfer to an existing trust, is created when the nonvested property interest in the trust was created. *See also* comment to § 55-12.2 (explaining that ''the time when the interest or power is created is the date the transfer becomes effective for purposes of property law generally, normally the	*See* comment to Unif. Probate Code § 2-902(a) (''With respect to an inter-vivos transfer, an interest or power is created on the date the transfer becomes effective for purpose of property law generally, normally the date of delivery of the deed or funding of the trust.''); Unif. Statutory Rule Against Perpetuities § 2, 8B U.L.A. 268 (stating the same).

		date of delivery of the deed''); Comment to Unif. Probate Code § 2-902(a) (stating same and adding ''the funding of the trust'' as ''normally'' the time when the interest is created). *See generally* § 55-12.5 (''For the purposes of this section, a nonvested property interest or a power of appointment created by the exercise of a power of appointment is created when the power is irrevocably exercised or when a revocable exercise becomes irrevocable.'')	
16. Same, but nongeneral inter vivos power.	See # 15.	See # 15.	See # 15.
17. When is an interest created if the grantor of a trust has a power to revoke?	*See* comment to Unif. Probate Code § 2-902(b) (noting that ''nonvested property interest and powers of appointment created in [a revocable inter-vivos trust] are created when the power to revoke expires, usually at the settlor's death''); Unif. Statutory Rule Against Perpetuities § 2, 8B U.L.A. 268 (amended 1990) (explaining that ''any nonvested property interest subject to [a power to revoke] is not created . . . until the power terminates (by *(cont'd)*	For the purposes of §§ 55-12.1 through 55-12.6, if there is a person who alone can exercise a power created by a governing instrument to become the unqualified beneficial owner of (i) a nonvested property interest or (ii) a property interest subject to a power of appointment described in subsection B or C in § 55-12.1, the nonvested property interest or power of appointment is created when the power to become the unqualified beneficial owner terminates. *(cont'd)*	Just as for a will, at the time of death. (§ 11.98.160) *See also* comment to Unif. Probate Code § 2-902(b) (noting that ''nonvested property interest and powers of appointment created in [a revocable inter-vivos trust] are created when the power to revoke expires, usually at the settlor's death''); Unif. Statutory Rule Against Perpetuities § 2, 8B U.L.A. 268 (amended 1990) (explaining that ''any nonvested property interest subject to [a power to revoke] is not created . . . until the power terminates (by release, *(cont'd)*

Table 10
Rule Against Perpetuities *(continued)*

	VERMONT	VIRGINIA	WASHINGTON
17. *When is an interest created if the grantor of a trust has a power to revoke? (cont'd)*	release, expiration at the death of the donee, or otherwise'').	(§ 55.12.2(B)) *See also* comment to § 55-12.2 (explaining that ''any nonvested property interest subject to [a power to revoke] is not created . . . until the power terminates (by release, expiration at the death of the donee, or otherwise''); Comment to Unif. Probate Code § 2-902(b) (noting that ''nonvested property interest and powers of appointment created in [a revocable inter-vivos trust] are created when the power to revoke expires, usually at the settlor's death''). *See generally* § 55-12.5 (''For the purposes of this section, a nonvested property interest or a power of appointment created by the exercise of a power of appointment is created when the power is irrevocably exercised or when a revocable exercise becomes irrevocable.'')	expiration at the death of the donee, or otherwise'').
18. *When does the period of the rule start re an interest contributed to an irrevocable trust? See UPC 2-902(c).*	*See* comment to Unif. Probate Code 2-902(c) (''Arguably, at common law, each transfer [to an existing irrevocable	A nonvested property interest or a power of appointment arising from a transfer of property to a previously funded trust or other	*See* comment to Unif. Probate Code 2-902(c) (''Arguably, at common law, each transfer [to an existing irrevocable inter-vivos trust] starts

	inter-vivos trust] starts the period of the Rule running anew as to each transfer.")	existing property arrangement is created when the nonvested property interest or power of appointment in the original contribution was created. (§ 55-12.2(C))	the period of the Rule running anew as to each transfer.")
19. *Is there a conclusive presumption of fertility, that is, the "fertile octogenarian" rule?*	*See, e.g.*, Arkansas, question # 19.	No specific state case or statute. *See also* comment to § 55-12.1 (holding that "[t]his principle is not superseded by this Act, and in view of new advances in medical science . . . [this] is not unrealistic.")); *but see* C. P. Jhong, Annotation, *Modern Status of Presumption of Possibility of Issue Being Extinct*, 98 A.L.R.2d 1285 (2003) (noting "a trend toward denying the conclusive or absolute nature of the presumption against the possibility of issue being extinct where there is competent evidence to the contrary has developed in the decisions, although some courts still adhere to the traditional view treating the presumption as conclusive or absolute").	Yes. Betchard v. Iverson, 212 P. 2d 783, 787 (Wash. 1949) (noting that "the law conclusively presumes that [women] can bear additional children until the day of her death").
20. *What is the earliest age a child is deemed capable of bearing a child? What is the impact of illegitimacy?*	Under the rule, courts must presume that living persons are capable of having or fathering children, no matter how young they are. *See* In re Graite's Will Trusts, [1949] 1 All E.R. 459, *(cont'd)*	Not specifically addressed by USRAP, but the reasoning is the same as set forth in the comment to section 1 of USRAP, 2, Technical Violations of the Common Law Rule. Wait and *(cont'd)*	Under the rule, courts must presume that living persons are capable of having or fathering children, no matter how young they are. See In re Graite's Will Trusts, [1949] 1 All E.R. 459, 460 (Ch.). Thus, the rule *(cont'd)*

Table 10
Rule Against Perpetuities *(continued)*

	VERMONT	*VIRGINIA*	*WASHINGTON*
20. *What is the earliest age a child is deemed capable of bearing a child? What is the impact of illegitimacy? (cont'd)*	460 (Ch.). Thus, the rule strikes down any interest whose vesting depends on the assertion that, for example, a toddler will not have children. (Keith L. Butler, Notes & Comments, *Long Live the Dead Hand: A Case for the Repeal of the Rule Against Perpetuities in Washington*, 75 Wash. L. Rev. 1237, 1246 n.78 (2000)).	see will typically result in no violation. Nevertheless, the common law rule ordinarily will be applied initially. Under the rule, courts must presume that living persons are capable of having or fathering children, no matter how young they are. See In re Graite's Will Trusts, [1949] 1 All E.R. 459, 460 (Ch.). Thus, the rule strikes down any interest whose vesting depends on the assertion that, for example, a toddler will not have children. (Keith L. Butler, Notes & Comments, *Long Live the Dead Hand: A Case for the Repeal of the Rule Against Perpetuities in Washington*, 75 Wash. L. Rev. 1237, 1246 n.78 (2000)).	strikes down any interest whose vesting depends on the assertion that, for example, a toddler will not have children. (Keith L. Butler, Notes & Comments, *Long Live the Dead Hand: A Case for the Repeal of the Rule Against Perpetuities in Washington*, 75 Wash. L. Rev. 1237, 1246 n.78 (2000)).
21. *Is the ''unborn widow'' rule observed?*	*See, e.g.*, Arkansas, question # 21.	No specific state case or statute. *See also* comment to §55-12.1 (explaining that ''[t]he chance that [an] interest will become invalid under the Statutory Rule is small'' and so the unborn widow rule would rarely invalidate an interest); *see also* 61 Am Jur 2d *Perpetuities and*	*See, e.g.*, Arkansas, question # 21.

		Restraints on Alienation § 40 (2003) (noting the same).	
22. *Does the "slothful executor" rule apply, i.e., an administrative contingency clause providing for a "distribution to, e.g., those issue living at the time of the satisfaction of the administrative condition precedent?"*	*See, e.g.*, California, question # 22.	No specific state case or statute. *See also* comment to § 55-12.1 (Under USRAP, an "interest becomes invalid only if it remains in existence and nonvested 90 years after [the testator's] death. Since it is almost certain that the final distribution of [an] estate will occur well within this 90-year period, the chance that [an] interest will be invalid is negligible.")	*See, e.g.*, California, question # 22.
23. *Does the all-or-nothing rule apply to class gifts?*	*See, e.g.*, Alabama, question # 23.	Yes. Rose v. Rose, 60 S.E.2d 45, 48 (Va. 1950) ("For if a contingent gift to a class is rendered void as to one or more members thereof by the rule against perpetuities, then the gift will fail as to all in that class."); Hagemann v. National Bank & Trust Co 237 S.E.2d 388, 391 (Va. 1977) (noting the same). *See also* comment to §55-12.1 ("Although this Act does not supersede the basic idea of the much-maligned 'all-or-nothing' rule, the evils sometimes attributed to it are substantially if not entirely eliminated by the wait-and-see feature of the Statutory Rule and by the availability of reformation under Section 3.")	Yes. Betchard v. Iverson, 212 P. 2d 783, 786 (Wash. 1949) ("If a gift is to a class and it is void as to any member or members of the class, it is void as to all.")

Table 10
Rule Against Perpetuities *(continued)*

	VERMONT	*VIRGINIA*	*WASHINGTON*
24. *Is there an exception to the all-or-nothing rule in the case of subclasses or specific sums to each member of the class?*	*See* Unif. Statutory Rule Against Perpetuities § 2, 8B U.L.A. 257 ("The common law also recognizes a doctrine called the specific-sum doctrine which is derived from Storrs v. Benbow, 3 De G.M. & G. 390, 43 Eng. Rep 153 (Ch. 1853), and states: If a specified sum of money is to be paid to each member of a class, the interest of each class member is entitled to separate treatment and is valid or invalid under the Rule on its own. The common law also recognizes a doctrine called the sub-class doctrine, which is derived from Cattlin v. Brown, 11 Hare 372, 68 Eng. Rep. 1318 (Ch. 1853), and states: If the ultimate takers are not described as a single class but rather as a group of separate subclasses, and if the share to which each separate subclass is entitled will finally be determined within the period of the Rule, the gifts to the different subclasses are separate for the purpose of the Rule.").	No specific state case or statute. *See also* comment to §55-12.1 ("The specific-sum and sub-class doctrines are not superseded by this Act.")	*See* Unif. Statutory Rule Against Perpetuities § 2, 8B U.L.A. 257 ("The common law also recognizes a doctrine called the specific-sum doctrine which is derived from Storrs v. Benbow, 3 De G.M. & G. 390, 43 Eng. Rep 153 (Ch. 1853), and states: If a specified sum of money is to be paid to each member of a class, the interest of each class member is entitled to separate treatment and is valid or invalid under the Rule on its own. The common law also recognizes a doctrine called the sub-class doctrine, which is derived from Cattlin v. Brown, 11 Hare 372, 68 Eng. Rep. 1318 (Ch. 1853), and states: If the ultimate takers are not described as a single class but rather as a group of separate subclasses, and if the share to which each separate subclass is entitled will finally be determined within the period of the Rule, the gifts to the different subclasses are separate for the purpose of the Rule.").

25. *Is the infectious invalidity rule followed outside class gifts?*	*See, e.g.*, Colorado, question # 25.	Yes, but limits the rule. *See* Hageman v. National Bank & Trust Co, 237 S.E.2d 388, 395 (Va. 1977) (noting that "a remainder which is void because in violation of the rule against perpetuities does not necessarily render invalid the prior estate, but that the latter will be sustained notwithstanding the invalidity of the ulterior estate, where the two are not inseparable and dependent parts of a general testamentary scheme, and to uphold the one without the other would not defeat the primary or dominant purpose of the testator. . . ."). *But see* Unif. Statutory Rule Against Perpetuities § 1, 8B U.L.A. 256 (amended 1990) (explaining that "[t]he doctrine of infectious invalidity is superseded by this Act by Section 3, under which courts . . . are required to *reform* the disposition to approximate as closely as possible the transferor's . . . plan of distribution.")	*See, e.g.*, Colorado, question # 25.
26. *Is there a rule against the suspension of the power of alienation? If so, how is it stated?*	No specific state statute. *See* Colby v. Colby, 596 A.2d 901, 902 (1991) ("restraints on alienation are not favored").	Reasonableness standard. *See* Lipps v. First American Service Corp, 286 S.E.2d 215, 218 (Va. 1982) (discussing Virginia's law on restraints on alienation).	Reasonableness standard. *See* McCausland v. Bankers Life Ins. Co., 757 P. 2d 941, 943-44 (Wash. 1988) (discussing whether due-on-sale clauses and prepayment provisions are unreasonable restraints on alienation).

Table 10
Rule Against Perpetuities *(continued)*

	VERMONT	*VIRGINIA*	*WASHINGTON*
27. *Effective date.*	When act "becomes operative," which was not defined. Act was approved, however, May 16, 1957. In Ransom v. Bebernitz, 782 A.2d 1155, 1160 (Vt. 2001), the court stated that the provisions apply to wills and instruments taking effect after the enactment of the statute.	The law applies to a nonvested property interest or a power of appointment created on or after July 1, 2000. An interest or a power created by the exercise of a power of appointment is created when the power is irrevocably exercised or after a revocable exercise becomes irrevocable. (§ 55-12.5)	The act applies to any irrevocable trust with an effective date on or after January 1, 2002, as well as to a prior trust if the instrument so provides. (2001 ch. 60 § 4) It also does not apply to revocable and testamentary trusts if the settlor or testator was incapable since June 1, 2002, to revoke, amend or modify the instrument. (2001 ch. 60 § 4) Generally, an irrevocable trust is created when executed and a revocable trust or will is created at the time of the settlor's or testator's death. (§ 11.98.160)

Table 10
Rule Against Perpetuities *(continued)*

	WEST VIRGINIA	*WISCONSIN*	*WYOMING*
1. *Which rule is in effect: the common law rule, the Uniform Statutory Rule Against Perpetuities (USRAP), other law, or none?*	USRAP. (W. Va. Code §§ 36-1A-1 – 36-1A-8)	None (§ 700.16(5) ("The common-law rule against perpetuities is not in force in this state."))	Common Law Rule, with exception for trusts having a duration of no more than 1,000 years. (Wyo. Stat. Ann. § 34-1-139)
2. *a. Is the common law rule relevant to any interests?*	Yes, but only as a starting point of the analysis.	N/A	Yes, with respect to certain interests.
b. What is the relevant rule?	A nonvested property interest is invalid unless: (1) When the interest is created, it is certain to vest or terminate no later than twenty-one years after the death of an individual then alive; or (2) The interest either vests or terminates within ninety years after its creation. (§ 36-1A-1(a))	N/A	No interest in real or personal property shall be good unless it must vest not later than twenty-one (21) years after some life in being at the creation of the interest and any period of gestation involved in the situation to which the limitation applies. (§ 34-1-139(a)) However, the common law rule does not apply to a trust created after July 1, 2003 if: (b) (i) The instrument creating the trust states that the rule against perpetuities as provided in subsection (a) of this section shall not apply to the trust; (ii) The instrument creating the trust states that the trust shall terminate no later than one thousand (1,000) years after the trust's creation; and

(cont'd)

Table 10
Rule Against Perpetuities *(continued)*

	WEST VIRGINIA	*WISCONSIN*	*WYOMING*
b. What is the relevant rule? (cont'd)			(iii) The trust is governed by the laws of this state and the trustee maintains a place of business, administers the trust in this state or is a resident of this state. (c) The election provided in (b) above is not available for real property owned and held in a trust otherwise making an election under subsection (b) of this section. The common law rule applies to such real property held in a trust making an election under (b), the election under (b) will apply to the remaining personal property assets of the trust. (§ 34-1-139) Note, however, that real property does not include a mineral interest or an interest in a corporation, limited liability company, partnership, business trust or other entity. (§ 34-1-139(d)) Thus, the continued application of the common law rule to real property held in trust can be easily avoided by reassigning the formal ownership of the real property.
3. Does the rule apply to other than private trusts?	Yes. The rule applies except to: (1) A nonvested property interest or a power of	N/A	*See, e.g.*, Vermont, question # 3.

appointment arising out of a nondonative transfer, except a nonvested property interest or a power of appointment arising out of: (A) A premarital or postmarital agreement; (B) a separation or divorce settlement; (C) a spouse's election; (D) a similar arrangement arising out of a prospective, existing, or previous marital relationship between the parties; (E) a contract to make or not to revoke a will or trust; (F) a contract to exercise or not to exercise a power of appointment; (G) a transfer in satisfaction of a duty of support; or (H) a reciprocal transfer;

(2) A fiduciary's power relating to the administration or management of assets, including the power of a fiduciary to sell, lease or mortgage property, and the power of a fiduciary to determine principal and income;

(3) A power to appoint a fiduciary;

(4) A discretionary power of a trustee to distribute principal before termination of a

(cont'd)

Table 10
Rule Against Perpetuities *(continued)*

	WEST VIRGINIA	*WISCONSIN*	*WYOMING*
3. *Does the rule apply to other than private trusts? (cont'd)*	trust to a beneficiary having an indefeasibly vested interest in the income and principal; (5) A nonvested property interest held by a charity, government, or governmental agency or subdivision, if the nonvested property interest is preceded by an interest held by another charity, government, or governmental agency or subdivision; (6) A nonvested property interest in or a power of appointment with respect to a trust or other property arrangement forming part of a pension, profit-sharing, stock bonus, health, disability, death benefit, income deferral, or other current or deferred benefit plan for one or more employees, independent contractors, or their beneficiaries or spouses, to which contributions are made for the purpose of distributing to or for the benefit of the		

		participants or their beneficiaries or spouses the property, income, or principal in the trust or other property arrangement, except a nonvested property interest or a power of appointment that is created by an election of a participant or a beneficiary or spouse; or (2) A property interest, power of appointment, or arrangement that was not subject to the common-law rule against perpetuities or is excluded by another provision of this code. (§ 36-1A-4)		
4.	*Does the rule invalidate the interest at its creation, or is the rule revised by a wait-and-see approach?*	Wait-and-see. (§ 36-1A-1(a)(2))	N/A	At its creation. (See # 2a)
5.	*Can the trust be reformed?*	Yes, but only if one of the following conditions is satisfied: (1) A nonvested property interest or a power of appointment becomes invalid pursuant to the provisions of section one of this article (see # 2b); (2) A class gift is not but might become invalid pursuant to the provisions of section one [§ 36-1A-1] of this article and the time has arrived when the share of any class *(cont'd)*	N/A	N/A

Table 10
Rule Against Perpetuities *(continued)*

	WEST VIRGINIA	*WISCONSIN*	*WYOMING*
5. *Can the trust be reformed? (cont'd)*	member is to take effect in possession or enjoyment; or (3) A nonvested property interest that is not validated by the provisions of subdivision (1), subsection (a), section one [§ 36-1A-1(a)(1)] of this article, that is, the traditional common law rule, can vest but not within ninety years after its creation. (§ 36-1A-3)		
6. *If yes to 5., under what theory?*	[A] court shall reform a disposition in the manner that most closely approximates the transferor's manifested plan of distribution is within the ninety years allowed by the provisions of subdivision (2), subsection (a), or subdivision (2), subsection (b), or subdivision (2), subsection (c), section one of this article. (§ 36-1A-3) *See also* § 36-1A-5(b) ("If a nonvested property interest or a power of appointment was created before the effective date of this article and is determined in a judicial proceeding,	N/A	N/A

	commenced on or after the effective date of this article, to violate this state's rule against perpetuities as that rule existed before the effective date of this article, a court upon the petition of an interested person may reform the disposition in the manner that most closely approximates the transferor's manifested plan of distribution and is within the limits of the rule against perpetuities applicable when the nonvested property interest or power of appointment was created.'')		
7. *When is a general testamentary power of appointment invalid?*	A general testamentary power of appointment is invalid unless one of the following conditions is satisfied: (1) When the power is created, it is certain to be irrevocably exercised or otherwise to terminate no later than 21 years after the death of an individual then alive. (2) The power is irrevocably exercised or otherwise terminates within 90 years after its creation. (§ 36-1A-1(c))	N/A	*See* Unif. Statutory Rule Against Perpetuities § 1, 8B U.L.A. 248 (amended 1990) (''Under the Common-law Rule . . . a *nongeneral power* (whether or not presently exercisable) or a *general testamentary power* is invalid as of the time of its creation if it *might* not terminate (by irrevocable exercise or otherwise) within a life in being plus 21 years.'')

Table 10
Rule Against Perpetuities *(continued)*

	WEST VIRGINIA	WISCONSIN	WYOMING
8. *Same, but nongeneral testamentary power.*	A nongeneral power of appointment . . . is invalid unless one of the following conditions is satisfied: (1) When the power is created, it is certain to be irrevocably exercised or otherwise to terminate no later than 21 years after the death of an individual then alive. (2) The power is irrevocably exercised or otherwise terminates within 90 years after its creation. (§ 36-1A-1(c))	N/A	See # 7.
9. *Same, but general inter vivos power.*	A general power of appointment not presently exercisable because of a condition precedent is invalid unless one of the following conditions is satisfied: (1) When the power is created, the condition precedent is certain to be satisfied or become impossible to satisfy no later than 21 years after the death of an individual then alive. (2) The condition precedent either is satisfied or becomes impossible to	N/A	*See* Unif. Statutory Rule Against Perpetuities § 1, 8B U.L.A. 248 (amended 1990) ("Under the Common-law Rule, a *general power not presently exercisable because of a condition precedent* is invalid as of the time of its creation if the condition *might* neither be satisfied nor become impossible to satisfy with a life in being plus 21 years.")

	satisfy within 90 years after its creation. (§ 36-1A-1(b))		
10. *Same, but nongeneral inter vivos power.*	See # 8.	N/A	See # 7.
11. *Is a period of gestation added to the perpetuity period ?*	No. The possibility that a child will be born to a person after that person's death is disregarded. (§ 36-1A-1(d)) *See also* Unif. Statutory Rule Against Perpetuities § 1, 8B U.L. A. 242-43 (amended 1990) ("[T]he possibility that a child will be born to [a testator] after his death must be disregarded; and the possibility that a child will be born to any of [the testator's] descendants after their deaths must also be disregarded. Note, however, that the rule of subsection (d) does *not* apply to the question of the entitlement of an after-born child to take a beneficial interest in the trust").	N/A	Yes. (See # 2a)
12. *What is the treatment of a "later of the traditional rule or 90 years" clause? See UPC 2-901(e).*	West Virginia's USRAP does not specify how it will treat such clauses.	N/A	N/A
13. *When is an interest created by the exercise of a general testamentary power deemed created?*	Except as provided in subsections (b) and (c) of this section and in subsection (a), section five of this article, the time of	N/A	*See* comment to Unif. Probate Code § 2-902(a) ("general principles of property law determine that a nonvested property interest or power of

	(cont'd)		(cont'd)

Table 10
Rule Against Perpetuities *(continued)*

	WEST VIRGINIA	*WISCONSIN*	*WYOMING*
13. When is an interest created by the exercise of a general testamentary power deemed created? (cont'd)	creation of a nonvested property interest or a power of appointment is determined under general principles of property law. (§ 36-1A-2(a)) *See also* Unif. Statutory Rule Against Perpetuities § 2, 8B U.L.A. 268 (amended 1990) (explaining that "general principles of property law determine that the time .... [of creation] is at the decedent's death.") *See generally* § 36-1A-5(a) ("a nonvested property interest or a power of appointment created by the exercise of a power of appointment is created when the power is irrevocably exercised or when a revocable exercise becomes irrevocable.")		appointment created by will is created at the decedent's death"); Unif. Statutory Rule Against Perpetuities § 2, 8B U.L.A. 268 (amended 1990) (stating the same).
14. Same, but nongeneral testamentary power.	See # 13.	N/A	See # 13.
15. Same, but general inter vivos power.	Except as provided in subsections (b) and (c) of this section and in subsection (a), section five of this article, the time of creation of a nonvested property interest or a power of	N/A	*See* comment to Unif. Probate Code § 2-902(a) ("With respect to an inter-vivos transfer, an interest or power is created on the date the transfer becomes effective for purpose of property law generally,

appointment is determined under general principles of property law. (§ 36-1A-2(a)) The first two of the excepted provisions states that as long as a person with a general power to become the unqualified beneficial owner has that power, the nonvested interest is created when the power terminates. The third of the excepted provisions states that a nonvested property interest, which arises from a transfer to an existing trust, is created when the nonvested property interest in the trust was created.

See also Unif. Statutory Rule Against Perpetuities § 2, 8B U.L.A. 268 (amended 1990) (explaining that "the time when the interest or power is created is the date the transfer becomes effective for purposes of property law generally, normally the date of delivery of the deed"); Comment to Unif. Probate Code § 2-902(a) (stating same and adding "the funding of the trust" as "normally" the time when the interest is created).

See generally § 36-1A-5(a) ("For the purposes of this section, a nonvested property interest or a power of appointment created by the exercise of a power of appointment is created when

(cont'd)

normally the date of delivery of the deed or funding of the trust."); Unif. Statutory Rule Against Perpetuities § 2, 8B U.L.A. 268 (stating the same).

Table 10
Rule Against Perpetuities *(continued)*

	WEST VIRGINIA	*WISCONSIN*	*WYOMING*
15. *Same, but general inter vivos power. (cont'd)*	the power is irrevocably exercised or when a revocable exercise becomes irrevocable.'')		
16. *Same, but nongeneral inter vivos power.*	See # 15.	The permissible period is computed from the time the power is created. (W.S.A. 700.16)	See # 15.
17. *When is an interest created if the grantor of a trust has a power to revoke?*	For purposes of this article, if there is a person who alone can exercise a power created by a governing instrument to become the unqualified beneficial owner of (1) a nonvested property interest or (2) a property interest subject to a power of appointment described in subsection (b) or (c), section one of this article, the nonvested property interest or power of appointment is created when the power to become the unqualified beneficial owner terminates. (§ 36-1A-2(b)) *See also* Unif. Statutory Rule Against Perpetuities § 2, 8B U.L.A. 268 (amended 1990) (explaining that ''any nonvested property interest subject to [a power to revoke] is not created . . . until	N/A	*See* comment to Unif. Probate Code § 2-902(b) (noting that ''nonvested property interest and powers of appointment created in [a revocable inter-vivos trust] are created when the power to revoke expires, usually at the settlor's death''); Unif. Statutory Rule Against Perpetuities § 2, 8B U.L.A. 268 (amended 1990) (explaining that ''any nonvested property interest subject to [a power to revoke] is not created . . . until the power terminates (by release, expiration at the death of the donee, or otherwise'').

	the power terminates (by release, expiration at the death of the donee, or otherwise''); Comment to Unif. Probate Code § 2-902(b) (noting that ''nonvested property interest and powers of appointment created in [a revocable inter-vivos trust] are created when the power to revoke expires, usually at the settlor's death''). *See generally* § 36-1A-5(a) (''a nonvested property interest or a power of appointment created by the exercise of a power of appointment is created when the power is irrevocably exercised or when a revocable exercise becomes irrevocable.'')		
18. When does the period of the rule start re an interest contributed to an irrevocable trust? See UPC 2-902(c).	A nonvested property interest or a power of appointment arising from a transfer of property to a previously funded trust or other existing property arrangement is created when the nonvested property interest or power of appointment in the original contribution was created. (§ 36-1A-2(c))	N/A	*See* comment to Unif. Probate Code 2-902(c) (''Arguably, at common law, each transfer [to an existing irrevocable inter-vivos trust] starts the period of the Rule running anew as to each transfer.'')
19. Is there a conclusive presumption of fertility, that is, the ''fertile octogenarian'' rule?	Yes. Carney v. Kain, 23 S.E. 650, 657 (W. Va. 1895) (noting that the ''law considers that the possibility of issue continues so long as the person lives, no *(cont'd)*	N/A	*See, e.g.*, Arkansas, question # 19.

Table 10
Rule Against Perpetuities *(continued)*

	WEST VIRGINIA	WISCONSIN	WYOMING
19. *Is there a conclusive presumption of fertility, that is, the "fertile octogenarian" rule? (cont'd)*	matter how improbable it may be.")[1] *See also* Unif. Statutory Rule Against Perpetuities § 1, 8B U.L.A. 256 (amended 1990) (holding that "[t]his principle is not superseded by this Act, and in view of new advances in medical science . . . [this] is not unrealistic."); *but see* C. P. Jhong, Annotation, *Modern Status of Presumption of Possibility of Issue Being Extinct*, 98 A.L.R.2d 1285 (2003) (noting "a trend toward denying the conclusive or absolute nature of the presumption against the possibility of issue being extinct where there is competent evidence to the contrary has developed in the decisions, although some courts still adhere to the traditional view treating the presumption as conclusive or absolute").		
20. *What is the earliest age a child is deemed capable of bearing a child? What is the impact of illegitimacy?*	Under the rule, courts must presume that living persons are capable of having or fathering children, no matter how young they are. See In re Graite's Will	N/A	Under the rule, courts must presume that living persons are capable of having or fathering children, no matter how young they are. See In re Graite's Will Trusts, [1949] 1 All

	Trusts, [1949] 1 All E.R. 459, 460 (Ch.). Thus, the rule strikes down any interest whose vesting depends on the assertion that, for example, a toddler will not have children. (Keith L. Butler, Notes & Comments, *Long Live the Dead Hand: A Case for the Repeal of the Rule Against Perpetuities in Washington*, 75 Wash. L. Rev. 1237, 1246 n.78 (2000)).		E.R. 459, 460 (Ch.). Thus, the rule strikes down any interest whose vesting depends on the assertion that, for example, a toddler will not have children. (Keith L. Butler, Notes & Comments, *Long Live the Dead Hand: A Case for the Repeal of the Rule Against Perpetuities in Washington*, 75 Wash. L. Rev. 1237, 1246 n.78 (2000)).
21. *Is the "unborn widow" rule observed?*	Unclear. *See* Berry v. Union Nat'l Bank, 164 W. Va. 258, 266 (W. Va. 1980) (noting that "[o]ther jurisdictions have abolished the fertile octagenarian and unborn widow rules" while not deciding the issue)); *see also* Unif. Statutory Rule Against Perpetuities § 1, 8B U.L.A. 246 (amended 1990) (explaining that "[t]he chance that [an] interest will become invalid under the Statutory Rule is small" and so the unborn widow rule would rarely invalidate an interest); *see also* 61 Am Jur 2d *Perpetuities and Restraints on Alienation* § 40 (2003) (noting the same).	N/A	*See, e.g.*, Arkansas, question # 21.
22. *Does the "slothful executor" rule apply, i.e., an administrative contingency clause providing for a "distribution to, e.g., those issue living at* *(cont'd)*	No specific state case or statute. *See* Unif. Statutory Rule Against Perpetuities § 1, 8B U.L.A. 245 (amended 1990) *(cont'd)*	N/A	*See, e.g.*, California, question # 22.

Table 10
Rule Against Perpetuities *(continued)*

	WEST VIRGINIA	WISCONSIN	WYOMING
the time of satisfaction of the administrative condition precedent?" (cont'd)	(Under USRAP, an "interest becomes invalid only if it remains in existence and nonvested 90 years after [the testator's] death. Since it is almost certain that the final distribution of [an] estate will occur well within this 90-year period, the chance that [an] interest will be invalid is negligible.")		
23. *Does the all-or-nothing rule apply to class gifts?*	No specific state case or statute. *See* Unif. Statutory Rule Against Perpetuities § 1, 8B U.L.A. 257 (amended 1990) ("Although this Act does not supersede the basic idea of the much-maligned 'all-or-nothing' rule, the evils sometimes attributed to it are substantially if not entirely eliminated by the wait-and-see feature of the Statutory Rule and by the availability of reformation under Section 3.")	N/A	*See, e.g.*, Alabama, question # 23.
24. *Is there an exception to the all-or-nothing rule in the case of subclasses or specific sums to each member of the class?*	No specific state case or statute. *See* Unif. Statutory Rule Against Perpetuities § 1, 8B U.L.A. 257 (amended 1990) ("The specific-sum and subclass doctrines are not superseded by this Act.")	N/A	*See* Unif. Statutory Rule Against Perpetuities § 2, 8B U.L.A. 257 ("The common law also recognizes a doctrine called the specific-sum doctrine which is derived from Storrs v. Benbow, 3 De G.M. & G. 390, 43 Eng. Rep. 153 (Ch. 1853), and

			states: If a specified sum of money is to be paid to each member of a class, the interest of each class member is entitled to separate treatment and is valid or invalid under the Rule on its own. The common law also recognizes a doctrine called the sub-class doctrine, which is derived from Cattlin v. Brown, 11 Hare 372, 68 Eng. Rep. 1318 (Ch. 1853), and states: If the ultimate takers are not described as a single class but rather as a group of separate subclasses, and if the share to which each separate subclass is entitled will finally be determined within the period of the Rule, the gifts to the different subclasses are separate for the purpose of the Rule.").
25. *Is the infectious invalidity rule followed outside class gifts?*	Yes. Henderson v. Coombs, 453 S.E.2d 415, 418 (W. Va. 1994) (nothing that "certain equitable rehabilitation methods, either reformation or the doctrine of infectious invalidity, could possibly be used in order to comport with the intentions of the grantor.") *But see* Unif. Statutory Rule Against Perpetuities § 1, 8B U.L.A. 256 (amended 1990) (explaining that "[t]he doctrine of infectious invalidity is superseded by this Act by Section 3, under which courts *(cont'd)*	N/A	*See, e.g.*, Colorado, question # 25.

Table 10
Rule Against Perpetuities *(continued)*

	WEST VIRGINIA	*WISCONSIN*	*WYOMING*
25. *Is the infectious invalidity rule followed outside class gifts? (cont'd)*	. . . are required to *reform* the disposition to approximate as closely as possible the transferor's . . . plan of distribution.'')		
26. *Is there a rule against the suspension of the power of alienation? If so, how is it stated?*	Case law unclear. *See* Wallace v. St. Clair, 127 S.E.2d 742, 751 (W. Va. 1962) (noting that zoning regulations are not a restraint on regulation and will be upheld if reasonable.)	A future interest or trust is void if it suspends the power of alienation for longer than the permissible period. The permissible period is a life or lives in being plus a period of 30 years. (§ 700.16(1)(a)) For more detailed rules on calculating the ''permissible period,'' *see* § 700.16(1)(b)-(c). For exceptions to the rule, *see* § 700.16(4).	McGinnis v. McGinnis, 391 P.2d 927, 932 (Wyo. 1964) (holding that ''there is no effective rule in Wyoming on restraints against alienation unless it be that which was derived from the common law'' and not clearly deciding the common law rule, but finding oil royalties assigned in trust to a bank did not constitute a restraint on alienation.)
27. *Effective date.*	February 22, 1992. *See* W.V. Laws, 1992 Session, ch. 74 (1-1B. No. 2261). See also # 6.	N/A	The special 1,000 year exemption applies in the case of certain trusts created after July 1, 2003. (§ 34-2-139 (b))

Note: Except for North Carolina and Virginia, any comments from the UPC or USRAP have not been officially adopted by the state. Citations to them are for assistance in understanding the basic rules. Note also that much of the language within this Table is quoted directly from state statutes, although quotation marks are often not included.

1. For questions # 19 – 25, *see also* § 36-1A-8 (noting that the state's USRAP supersedes the common law rule against perpetuities). The answers to questions # 19 – 25 are not likely to apply in most cases because of the abolition of the rule with respect to the vast majority of many trusts.

Table 11
Trust Administration: Power to Adjust and Total Return Trusts (current through 5/1/07)

Traditionally, trusts have provided for the payment of the net income and the holding of principal. Effectively, the income beneficiary has been favored by a conservative investment policy and laws that required nothing more than preserving the principal rather than assuring its growth as well. At a time when there was little inflation and the focus was on economic security this may have been justified. However, with changing economic conditions, as well as the validation of financial theories of portfolio investing this became indefensible. Pursuit of a traditional investment policy approach over many years could result in the destruction of real value for the remaindermen. Meanwhile, the position of the income beneficiary was not necessarily secured. The utilization of very conservative financial instruments yielded minimal income. While this may have satisfied the very low requirements of the law, for example, 1-2%, it did not afford a surviving spouse or other income beneficiary with the support needed by such person or persons. Once administration costs and taxes were paid, the trust fund might barely be holding its own or might even be diminishing in real economic terms and very possibly in absolute terms as well.

Another important factor that has contributed to the pressure for reform has been the enhanced awareness and concern regarding the trustee's fiduciary duties, both in terms of the information to be afforded beneficiaries and the duty to treat beneficiaries impartially. With time, the status of the remaindermen has grown, as has the scrutiny of trustee investment management. The emphasis on impartiality has created a conflict with the investment policies traditionally countenanced. On the other hand, the enactment of laws allowing the trustee to be more aggressive in investment policy without incurring liability has nourished a willingness to go beyond traditional investment approaches.These circumstances have led state legislators to enact laws that afford the trustee the power to adjust between income and principal to assure a more equitable allocation based on the year's returns. Trustees are permitted to do so even though the trust agreement is drafted as a traditional "all income" trust and there is no manifestation of intent by the grantor or the instrument to afford the trustee this power.

While statutes affording the trustee a power to adjust have been enacted in the vast majority of states, see column 1 of Table 11.01, they do not resolve the basic conflict inherent in investing for diverse groups of beneficiaries, such as income and remaindermen.

Indeed, the statutes may actually accentuate the problem, since the power to adjust tempts the trustee to alter the traditional and well-established allocation between income and principal, but without clear-cut guidance as to how to do this and without sufficient protection from liability for doing so. As a result much effort has been made over the last decade or so to have states adopt statutes that detail a framework for allowing the trustee, or beneficiaries if the trustee is unwilling, to convert the trust from the traditional "all income" kind to a total return trust, also known as a total return unitrust. Borrowing from the charitable/federal tax area of trust law, these statutes allow conversion of the trust to a unitrust affording the "income" beneficiaries a specified rate of return rather than from the particular source, "income." Essentially, the classic divide between income and principal, and the preoccupation with defining what is income, is demolished. As explained, these statutes specify a specific rate or permissible range of rates of return to which the "income beneficiary or beneficiaries" are entitled. Some statutes allow the rate of return to alter from year to year, but in most of the states that have enacted legislation it must remain in the 3%-5% range. Furthermore, the rate is applied to fair market value, thus making the methodology for calculating fair market value, the assets to be included in the computation, and the process for deciding to exclude certain assets, of exceptional importance.

The crucial point is that artificial distinctions between income and principal no longer exist. An income beneficiary is presumed to expect a certain receipt each year, but the source is no longer crucial. Whereas previously cash returns on investment like interest and dividends were allocated to "income," while unrealized and even realized appreciation to principal, this is downplayed by the conversion statutes. Moreover, the trustee is typically accorded considerable discretion in deciding to convert, but is not liable if the trustee chooses not to do so. In most states, as long as the trustee satisfies a good faith or somewhat comparable standard, the trustee will not face any personal liability for the decision made regarding conversion. Often, similar discretion and protection from liability is given with respect to reconverion to a traditional income trust. However, not as many states have been forthcoming in this regard.

The discretion to convert is not left unchecked. Notice must be given to many, though not all, beneficiaries. They then have a period of time in which to object. A number of states also provide for the trustee and beneficiaries agreeing to the terms of a conversion. If there is no agreement and a beneficiary objects, a process for resolving disputes before a court is also set forth in considerable detail, but varies from statute to statute in details. The issue becomes especially problematic if the beneficiaries are not all sui juris or the trustees are not all independent. Granting the discretion to a trustee to convert or not convert and thereby alter the flow of benefits to particular persons, could generate adverse, income tax, estate tax, gift tax, or generation-skipping transfer taxes at the federal or state level. A number of statutes, thus, limit discretion in these circumstances. This is the case, for example, if the marital deduction or grandfathered generation-skipping transfer tax exemption would be lost. In certain statutes provision is made for the appointment of a disinterested trustee/person to handle those elements of discretion otherwise given to the trustee when they could engender adverse tax consequences or when the power would allow the trustee to abuse the trust fund for the trustee's own direct benefit as a beneficiary or indirect benefit, for example, by satisfying an obligation of support.

One question that is inescapable if beneficiaries are entitled to a certain percentage return on the fair market value of the trust fund is from what sources should the return be paid. Many of the conversion statutes provide a priority, at least when the governing instrument does not provide otherwise. Traditional income comes first, followed by other types of income under the tax law, followed by net realized short and then long-term gains, and then principal. Other statutes simply allow the trustee to exercise largely unrestrained discretion. Just as with the marital deduction and the generation-skipping transfer tax grandfathered exemption, this could generate tax issues. In this regard, the Treasury has been rather forthcoming in adjusting its own definitions in the treasury regulations and rulings in ways that facilitate use of conversion statutes. See, e.g. Treas. Reg. §1.643(b)-1. Ironically, certain state statutes prohibit conversion when there is a risk of negative tax consequences, even though the clarification of the Treasury's position has now ended the exposure to adverse tax consequences.

As the foregoing discussion has indicated the focus has been on the conversion of traditional "all income" trusts to unitrusts. Provision has also been made to varying degrees, and with varying flexibility for reconversion so that an initial decision to convert does not become irrevocable despite changed circumstances. Options with regard to varying the rate of return and the method for calculationg the fair market value of the assets against which the rate of return is multiplied have also been noted. In all this, a large number of states with statutes have failed to address trusts that are drafted as total return unitrusts and do not need to be converted. The same is true for the treasury regulations. It should be added that these original total return unitrusts may require a somewhat different approach from converted trusts. For example, a conversion statute might prescribe a precise rate of return in instances where the grantor has not addressed the matter. However, where the grantor has spoken, there should probably be greater flexibility as to what is permissible.

Table 11.02 delves into the total return unitrust statutes identified in the second and final columns of Table 11.01. It asks a total of 36 questions, one of which is further broken into discrete sub-inquiries. The answers to these questions are explored on a state-by-state basis. The expectation is that over time there will be more state analyses to add as more states adopt some form of total return trust legislation.

Table 11.01
Powers to Adjust

	Does a Statute Explicitly Recognize Total Return Trusts and Adjustments?	*Is There Authorization to Convert an Income Trust to a Total Return Trust?*	*Is There an Express Statutory Framework for a Trust Originally Formed as a Total Return Trust and Not Requiring a Conversion?*
Alabama	Yes. (§ 19-3a-104(a))	No.	No.
Alaska	Yes. (§ 13.38.210)	Yes. (§ 13.38.300)	No.
Arizona	Yes. (§ 14-7403)	No.	No.
Arkansas	Yes. (§ 28-70-104)	No.	No.
California	Yes. (Prob. Code § 16336)	Yes. (§ 16336.4)	No.
Colorado	Yes. (§ 15-1-404)	Yes. (§§ 15-1-404.5)	Yes. (§ 15-1-404.5(13)(b)(III))
Connecticut	Yes. (§ 45a-542c)	No.	No.
Delaware	Yes. (121 § 6113)	Yes. (12 §§ 3527)	Yes. (12§ 3527A)
District of Columbia	Yes. (§ 19-1309.02)	No.	No.
Florida	Yes. (§ 738.104)	Yes. (§ 738.1041)	No.
Georgia	No. (1962 Act)	Yes. (§ 53-12-221)	No.
Hawaii	Yes. (§ 557A-104)	No.	No.
Idaho	Yes. (§ 68-10-104)	No.	No.
Illinois	No provision	Yes. (760 ILCS § 5/5-3)	Yes. (760 ILCS § 5/5-3(m))
Indiana	Yes. (§ 30-2-14-15)	Yes. (§ 30-2-15-1)	Addressed in part. (§ 30-2-15-9(3)
Iowa	No specific provision	Yes. (§ 637.601)	No.
Kansas	Yes. (§ 58-9-104)	No.	No.
Kentucky	Yes. (§ 386.454)	Under limited circumstances (§ 386.454(2) &(4)	No.
Louisiana	Yes. (Rev. Stat. 9:2158)	No.	No.
Maine	Yes. (18 § 7-704)	Yes. (18-A § 7-705)	No.
Maryland	Yes. (Est. & Trusts § 15-502.2)	Yes. (Est. & Tr. § 15-502.1)	No.
Massachusetts	Yes. (203D § 4)	No.	No.
Michigan	Yes. (§ 555.504)	No.	No.
Minnesota	Yes. (§ 5018.705)	No.	No.
Mississippi	No provisions	No.	No.

Missouri	Yes. (§ 469.405)	Yes. (§ 469.411)	Yes. (§ 469.411(5.)(1))
Montana	Yes. (§ 72-34-424)	No.	No.
Nebraska	Yes. (§ 30-3119)	Yes. (§ 30-3119.01)	No.
Nevada	Yes. (§ 164.795)	No.	Yes. (§ 30-3119.01)
New Hampshire	No principal and income provisions	Yes. (§ 564-A:3-c)	No.
New Jersey	Yes. (§ 3B:19B-4)	Under limited circumstances (§ 3B:19B-4)	No.
New Mexico	Yes. (§ 46-3A-104)	Yes. (§ 46-3A-105)	Yes. (§ 46-3A-105)
North Carolina	Yes. (§ 37A-1-104)	Yes. (§ 37A-1-104.1)	Yes. (§ 37A-1-104.2)
North Dakota	Yes. (§ 59-04.2-03)	No.	No.
Ohio	Yes. (§ 1340.42)	Under limited circumstances (§§ 1340,42(G)(3))	No.
Oklahoma	Yes. (§ 175.104)	No.	No.
Oregon	Yes. (§ 129.215)	Yes. (§ 129.225)	No.
Pennsylvania	Yes. (20 § 8104)	Yes. (20 § 8105)	No.
Rhode Island	Yes. (§ 18-4-28)	Yes. (§ 18-4-29)	Yes. (§ 18-4-29)
South Carolina	Yes. (§ 2-7-904)	No.	No.
South Dakota	No statutory provision. (1962 Act)	Yes. (§ 55-15-2)	Yes. (§ 55-15-2(iii))
Tennessee	Yes. (§ 35-6-104)	No.	No.
Texas	Yes. (Prop. § 116.005)	Yes. (Prop. Code § 116.007)	Yes. (Prop. Code § 116.007)
Utah	Yes. (§ 22-3-104)	No.	No.
Vermont	No provision. (older uniform law)	No.	No.
Virginia	Yes. (§ 55-277.4)	Yes. (§ 55-277.4:1)	Yes. (§ 55-277.4:1(B)(iii))
Washington	Yes. (§ 11.104A.020)	Yes. (§ 11.104A.040)	Yes. (§ 11.104A.040(a)(2))
West Virginia	Yes. (§ 448-1-103)	No.	No.
Wisconsin	Yes. (§ 701.20(4))	Yes. (§ 701.20(4g))	No.
Wyoming	Yes. (§ 2-3-804)	No.	No.

Table 11.02
Total Return Trusts
Alaska

1. *Is there a power to convert?*	Yes. (§13.38.300)
2. *Is the statute applicable to new unitrusts?*	No explicit provision.
3. *Is there a required rate of return?*	Yes, 4% in the first three years based on current value. (§13.38.330(b)) Then the rate must be 4% based on an average of the three preceding years. (§ 13.38.330(c))
4. *Can the required rate of return be varied?*	Not in the first three years and then only to the extent a three-year 4% average is maintained.
5. *How can it be varied?*	See #4 above.
6. *Alternatively, does the trustee have discretion within a range?*	See #4.
7. *If so, what is the range?*	See #4.
8. *Must court approval be obtained initially?*	No.
9. *Does the trustee have discretion to:*	
a. *Convert?*	Yes, if certain beneficiaries do not object following notice. (§ 13.38.300)
b. *Reconvert?*	Yes. (§ 13.38.400)
c. *Determine the effective date?*	Yes. (§ 13.38.340(1))
d. *Determine the frequency of payments?*	Yes. (§ 13.38.340(3))
e. *Determine cash or in kind distribution?*	No provision.
f. *Vary the rate?*	See #4 above.
g. *Whether to value annually or less frequently?*	Yes. (§ 13.38.340(5))
h. *What valuation date to use?*	Yes. (§ 13.38.340(6))
i. *Whether to value trust property occupied or used by a beneficiary?*	Yes. (§ 13.38.340(8))
j. *How to prorate in a short year any unitrust payments?*	Yes. (§ 13.38.340(2))
k. *Whether to estimate the value of non-liquid assets?*	Yes. (§ 13.38.3240(8))
l. *The effect of contributions and distributions on valuation?*	Yes. (§ 13.38.340(4))
m. *Other administrative matters?*	Yes. (§ 13.38.340(9))

10. *What standard of conduct is required of the trustee?*	No provision.
11. *What is the remedy for a violation?*	No provision.
12. *If a trustee is interested, must a disinterested trustee be appointed?*	No provision.
13. *If a disinterested trustee is required, who selects him?*	No provision.
14. *Must notice be given before a conversion?*	Yes. (§ 13.38.300)
15. *To whom must notice be given?*	Sui juris beneficiaries who would either get current income or successor income interest as well as remainderman if entitled to principal upon termination of trust immediately before giving of notice. All this assumes no exercise of a power. (§ 13.38.300)
16. *By when must objection be made?*	60 days after mailing of notice. (§ 13.38.300(4))
17. *Can objection be overridden?*	Yes, by petitioning a court. (§ 13.38.310(a)(1))
18. *What if there are not sufficiently competent beneficiaries?*	A court must be petitioned for approval. (§ 13.38.310) The statute requires at least two sui juris beneficiaries to avert the need for court approval—a current income beneficiary and at least one of either a successor income beneficiary or remainderman described in #15 above. (§ 13.38.310(a)(2))
19. *Can a beneficiary petition a court to seek conversion if a trustee refuses?*	Yes. (§ 13.38.310(b)) Thus, the trustee is not obligated to convert upon request. See also §13.38.360, which allows a beneficiary to petition to change rate, period for averaging of rate, or to obtain a greater payout of income in order to preserve a tax benefit.
20. *Is there a duty to convert?*	No. The statute provides that the trustee "may" convert. (§ 13.38.300; see also §13.38.320)
21. *Can a court be petitioned to stop a conversion or reconversion?*	Yes, if income would be higher. This is the only express authorization. See #19.
22. *Is there a statute of limitations?*	No provision.
23. *Is there a mandatory provision for payout of income if greater than the unitrust amount?*	No provision.
24. *If there is an excess payout, is it added to principal?*	No provision.
25. *What is the priority of source of payment of the unitrust amount?*	Net income, net realized short term capital gain, net realized long term capital gain, principal. (§ 13.38.350(b))
26. *Is the priority mandatory?*	Yes (§ 13.38.350(b)), unless specified otherwise in the trust instrument.
27. *How is the fair market value of the trust determined for unitrust purposes?*	No provision. Trust is given discretion. See #9g, h. above.
28. *Are certain items excluded?*	No provision. Trustee is given discretion. See #9i above.

29. *Is the trustee authorized to release his power?*	Yes (§ 13.38.410), but not if it causes adverse tax consequences.
30. *Is there special provision for the marital deduction?*	No conversion allowed if it would result in denial of the marital deduction. (§ 13.38.380(a)(5))
31. *Is there special provision for generation-skipping grandfather preservation?*	No provision.
32. *If the power to convert is utilized must the power to adjust be released?*	Yes. (§ 13.38.300)
33. *Are particular factors presented that the trustee should consider?*	Yes, although the statute says the trustee "may" consider these in deciding whether to convert. (§ 13.38.320)
34. *What standard should a court use?*	Intent of settlor or testator and purposes of the trust. (§ 13.38.310(c))
35. *Must the trust be a locally administered trust?*	No provision.
36. *When does the power to convert not exist?*	If there is an express prohibition in the trust instrument. (§ 13.38.300)

Table 11.02
Total Return Trusts
California

1. *Is there a power to convert?*	Yes. (Prob.§ 16336.4(a), but only if certain conditions regarding power to adjust that are spelled out in § 16336 are satisfied.
2. *Is the statute applicable to new unitrusts?*	No explicit provision.
3. *Is there a required rate of return?*	Generally, the rate is 4% over the lesser of the preceding three years or the shorter existence of the trust. (§ 16336(4)(e)(2))* As an alternative, the trustee can choose a rate in the range of 3%-5%, upon notice and subject to objection by beneficiaries. (§ 16336.5(a))
4. *Can the required rate of return be varied?*	Yes. See #3 above & § 16336.6.
5. *How can it be varied?*	See ##3 & 4 above.
6. *Alternatively, does the trustee have discretion within a range?*	See #3.
7. *If so, what is the range?*	See #3.
8. *Must court approval be obtained initially?*	No.
9. *Does the trustee have discretion to:*	
a. *Convert?*	Yes, if certain beneficiaries do not object following notice. (§ 16336.4(a) (4%) or § 16336.5(a) (3%-5% range))
b. *Reconvert?*	Yes, but not until 3 years after conversion (§ 16336.6), and only if this would enable the trustee to better comply with (§ 16335(b)). See § 16336.6(b).
c. *Determine the effective date?*	Yes. (§ 16336.4(f)(1))
d. *Determine the frequency of payments?*	Yes, in satisfaction of the unitrust amount. (§ 16336.4(f)(2))
e. *Determine cash or in kind distribution?*	No provision.
f. *Vary the rate?*	See #3 above.
g. *Whether to value annually or less frequently?*	Must value at least annually. (§§ 16.336.4(e)(4),* 16336.4(f)(3))
h. *What valuation date to use?*	Yes. (§ 16336.4(f)(4))
i. *Whether to value trust property occupied or used by a beneficiary?*	It must be excluded if residential or tangible personal property, if as of the first business day of the current accounting year the current beneficiary has or had the right to occupy or possess, or to control (§ 16336.4(e)(4)(A)*) The same is true of assets specifically devised to a beneficiary if necessary, in the trustee's judgment, to avoid a material risk of exhausting other trust assets prior to trust termination. Income generated by such asset will be accumulated. (§ 16336.4(e)(4)(B)*) Likewise for an asset in a terminating trust. (§ 16336.4(e)(8)(C)*)

j. How to prorate in a short year any unitrust payments?	Required on a daily basis. (§ 16336.4(e)(6)*)
k. Whether to estimate the value of nonliquid assets?	Yes. (§ 16336.4(f)(5))
l. The effect of contributions and distributions on valuation?	The trustee must make an adjustment if "material," that is, more than 10% of current value. (§ 16336.4(e)(5)*) In other instances where not "material," the trustee can adjust the unitrust amount in the reasonable exercise of the trustee's discretion. *(Id.)*
m. Other administrative matters?	Yes as to any matters the trustee deems appropriate for the proper functioning of the unitrust. (§ 16336.4(f)(7)), including characterization of the unitrust payment for income tax reporting purposes. (§ 16336.4(f)(6))
10. *What standard of conduct is required of the trustee?*	No provision.
11. *What is the remedy for a violation?*	The sole remedy is an order converting, reconverting, changing the rate, or allowing for a necessary and helpful administrative procedure. (§ 16338)
12. *If a trustee is interested, must a disinterested trustee be appointed?*	The key is whether the power has adverse income tax (§ 16336.4(h)(3)), estate or gift tax consequences (§ 16336.4(h)(4)), or the conversion would result in the denial of a marital deduction. (§ 16336.4(h)(5))
13. *If a disinterested trustee is required, who selects him?*	No disinterested trustee is necessary. The interested trustees petition the court. (§§ 16336.4(i), 16336.5(b)(1)(A)(iii)) However, no provision for petition is made if the effect would be disallowance of the marital deduction. See § 16336.4(h)(5).
14. *Must notice be given before a conversion?*	Yes. (§ 16336.4(b)(3))
15. *To whom must notice be given?*	Beneficiaries who would either get current income or are current discretionary income beneficiaries, as well as those entitled to principal upon termination of trust at the time notice is given. Notice can be given to a minor or the minor's guardian. (§ 16336.4(b)(2))
16. *By when must objection be made?*	45 days after mailing of notice. (§§ 16336.4(b)(4), 16502(d))
17. *Can objection be overridden?*	Yes, by petitioning a court. (§ 16336.4(b)(1)(A)(i))
18. *What if there are not sufficiently competent beneficiaries?*	No provision.
19. *Can a beneficiary petition a court to seek conversion if a trustee refuses?*	Yes. (§ 16336.5(b)(2))
20. *Is there a duty to convert?*	No. (§ 16336.7)
21. *Can a court be petitioned to stop a conversion or reconversion?*	No provision.

22. *Is there a special statute of limitations?*	No provision.
23. *Is there a mandatory provision for payout of income if greater than the unitrust amount?*	No provision.
24. *If there is an excess payout, is it added to principal?*	No provision.
25. *What is the priority of source of payment of the unitrust amount?*	Net taxable income as if the trust is not a unitrust, net realized short term capital gain, net realized long term capital gain, tax-exempt and other income, principal. (§ 16336.4(7))
26. *Is the priority mandatory?*	Yes, unless specified otherwise in the governing instrument. (§ 16336.4(e)(7))
27. *How is the fair market value of the trust determined for unitrust purposes?*	No provision. Trust is given discretion. See #9g & #9h above.
28. *Are certain items excluded?*	See #9i above.
29. *Is the trustee authorized to release his power?*	Yes, but not if it causes adverse tax consequences, such as those described in #12 above.
30. *Is there special provision for the marital deduction?*	No conversion allowed if it would result in denial of the marital deduction. (§ 16336.4(h))
31. *Is there special provision for generation-skipping grandfather preservation?*	No provision.
32. *If the power to convert is utilized must the power to adjust be released?*	No provision. Note that a provision in the governing instrument that restricts the power to adjust or to modify the trust does not prevent conversion unless it is clear from the governing instrument that the intent was to deny a power to convert. § 16336.4(a)
33. *Are particular factors presented that the trustee should consider?*	See #1 above.
34. *What standard should a court use?*	Enable the trustee to better comply with § 16335 regarding impartiality and to satisfy factors set forth in § 16336(g): (1) nature, purpose, and expected duration of the trust; (2) the intent of the creator; (3) the identity and circumstances of the beneficiaries; (4) the needs for liquidity, regularity of income, and preservation and appreciation of capital; (5) the assets held in trust, including their nature, use by a beneficiary, and whether acquired by the trustee or received by the beneficiary; (6) the net amount allocated to income and the increase or decrease in value of principal; (7) whether and the extent to which the governing instrument gives the trustee the power to invade principal and accumulate income, as well as the extent to which the power has been exercised; (8) the actual and anticipated effect of economic conditions on principal and income and the effects of inflation and deflation; and (9) the anticipated tax consequences of a unitrust conversion.
35. *Must the trust be a locally administered trust?*	No provision.

36. *When does the power to convert not exist?*	If expressly prohibited by the governing instrument, § 16336.4(a), if the amount payable to a beneficiary as a fixed annuity or fixed fraction would change; if the unitrust amount would be made from an amount permanently set aside for charitable purposes and for which a federal estate or gift tax deduction has been taken, unless both income and principal are set aside; or the conversion would result in disallowance of the federal estate tax or gift tax marital deduction. (§ 16336.4(h); see also § 16336.5(b)(3)-(4))

*This can be deviated from by court order or agreement of parties. (§§ 16336.4(e), 16336.5)

Table 11.02
Total Return Trusts Colorado

1. Is there a power to convert?	Yes. (§ 15-1-404.5)
2. Is the statute applicable to new unitrusts?	Yes. (§ 15-1-404.5(13)(b)(III))
3. Is there a required rate of return?	Yes. It is 4% (§ 15-1-404.5(4)(c)), unless the trust instrument or a court order provides otherwise. *(Id.)* However, the range even then is 3%-5%. (§ 15-1-404.5(7)(a)(I)) Furthermore, the trustee and qualified beneficiaries can agree to a rate between 3% and 5%. (§ 15-1-404.5(2))
4. Can the required rate of return be varied?	Yes. See #3.
5. How can it be varied?	See #3.
6. Alternatively, does the trustee have discretion within a range?	No. See #3.
7. If so, what is the range?	See #3.
8. Must court approval be obtained initially?	No. The trustee can proceed if the beneficiaries do not object or there is an agreement reached with all the "parties." (§ 15-1-404.5(1))
9. Does the trustee have discretion to:	
a. *Convert?*	Yes, if certain beneficiaries do not object following notice. (§ 15-1-404.5(1))
b. *Reconvert?*	No. Either a court order or agreement of the beneficiaries filed with court is needed. (§ 15-1-404.5(3)(b))
c. *Determine the effective date?*	Yes. (§ 15-1-404.5(5)(a))
d. *Determine the frequency of payments?*	No provision.
e. *Determine cash or in kind distribution?*	Yes. (§ 15-1-404.5(5)(c))
f. *Vary the rate?*	See #3 above.
g. *Whether to value annually or less frequently?*	Yes. (§ 15-1-404.5(5)(e))
h. *What valuation date to use?*	No provision.
i. *Whether to value trust property occupied or used by a beneficiary?*	More generally, there is discretion to exclude assets for which there is no readily available market. (§ 15-1-404.5(5)(g)) Regarding tangible property or real property possessed or occupied, the trustee cannot deny use granted under the trust instrument, whether or not treated the trustee treats the property as an excluded asset. (§ 15-1-404.5(5)(g)(III)(B))
j. *How to prorate in a short year any unitrust payments?*	Yes. (§ 15-1-404.5(5)(b))

k. Whether to estimate the value of nonliquid assets?	See #9i; discretion is granted with respect to such assets. (§ 15-1-404.5(5)(g))
l. The effect of contributions and distributions on valuation?	Yes. (§ 15-1-404.5(5)(d))
m. Other administrative matters?	Yes. (§ 15-1-404.5(5)(h))
10. What standard of conduct is required of the trustee?	"Reasonably and in good faith." (§ 15-1-404.5(11)(a)) Actions or omissions are presumed to meet the standard unless a court determines the act or omission was an abuse of discretion. *(Id.)* See also § 15-1-404.5(3)(d)(ii) (protecting trustee except when acting in bad faith).
11. What is the remedy for a violation?	If no violation of the standard set forth in #10 above, the plaintiff must petition court for relief to convert, reconvert, change the distribution percentage, or order administrative procedures. This is the exclusive remedy. (§ 15-1-404.5(11)(b)) The penalty for violation of the standard is not set forth in the statute.
12. If a trustee is interested, must a disinterested trustee be appointed?	The key is whether the power has adverse income tax or estate or gift tax consequences, or the trustee is also a beneficiary and the trustee's decision affects the trustee's beneficial interest. (§ 15-1-404.5(9))
13. If a disinterested trustee is required, who selects him?	No disinterested trustee is necessary. The interested trustees petition the court. (§ 15-1-404.5(10)(a))
14. Must notice be given before a conversion?	Yes. (§ 15-1-404.5(1)(b))
15. To whom must notice be given?	Legally competent beneficiaries who are either (i) distributees or permissible distributees currently of trust income or principal, as well as (ii) legally competent distributees or permissible distributees of trust income or principal if current beneficiary's interest terminated or trust terminated as of date notice is sent. (§ 15-1-404.5(1)(c))
16. By when must objection be made?	60 days after sending of notice. (§ 15-1-404.5(1)(d))
17. Can objection be overridden?	Yes, by petitioning a court. (§ 15-1-404.5(3)(a)(I))
18. What if there are not sufficiently competent beneficiaries?	A court must be petitioned for approval. (§ 15-1-404.5(3)(a)(II)) The statute requires at least two sui juris beneficiaries to avert the need for court approval, that is, one from each of the two categories described in #15 above.
19. Can a beneficiary petition a court to seek conversion if a trustee refuses?	Yes. (§ 15-1-404.5(3)(b)), but only if the trustee has failed to act for 6 months after receipt of a written request to convert, reconvert, or adjust the rate. (§ 15-1-404.5(3)(c))[1]
20. Is there a duty to convert?	No. The matter need not even be addressed unless requested by a beneficiary in writing to do so. (§ 15-1-404.5(11))
21. Can a court be petitioned to stop a conversion or reconversion?	Yes. (§ 15-1-404.5(3)(d)(I)(A) & (B))

22. *Is there a special statute of limitations?*	If a beneficiary received a statement disclosing a matter, a claim must be requested within 6 months of receipt. (§ 15-1-404.5(11)(c)) This is in addition to a standard limitations period or other bar to a claim.
23. *Is there a mandatory provision for payout of income if greater than the unitrust amount?*	Yes, in order to preserve tax benefit. (§ 15-1-404.5(7)(a)(N))
24. *If there is an excess payout, is it added to principal?*	No provision.
25. *What is the priority of source of payment of the unitrust amount?*	Net income, other ordinary income as determined for federal income tax purposes, net realized short term capital gain, net realized long term capital gain, principal for which there is a readily available market, other principal. (§ 15-1-404.5(6)(B))
26. *Is the priority mandatory?*	Yes (§ 15-1-404.5(6)(b)), unless specified otherwise in the trust instrument.
27. *How is the fair market value of the trust determined for unitrust purposes?*	Net fair market value is averaged over the lesser of the 3 preceding years or the period during which the trust has been in existence. (§ 14-1-404.5(4.5)(b)(II))
28. *Are certain items excluded?*	No provision. Trustee is given discretion. See #9i above.
29. *Is the trustee authorized to release his power?*	Yes, if the trustee reasonably believes it is in the best interests of the trust and its beneficiaries. (§ 15-1-404.5(10))
30. *Is there special provision for the marital deduction?*	Yes. The distribution amount cannot be less than net income during the spouse's lifetime. (§ 15-1-404.5(8)(a)(I))
31. *Is there special provision for generation-skipping grandfather preservation?*	Yes. The distribution amount must be no less than net income for a trust exempt from the generation-skipping transfer tax on the effective date of the section, May 22, 2003, by reason of any effective date or transition rule. (§ 15-1-404.5(8)(a)(II))
32. *If the power to convert is utilized must the power to adjust be released?*	Yes. (§ 15-1-404.5(1)(a)))
33. *Are particular factors presented that the trustee should consider?*	Yes, the change will better carry out the purposes of the trust. (§ 15-1-404.5(1)(a))
34. *What standard should a court use?*	The change requested will better carry out the purposes of the trust. (§ 15-1-404.5(3)(e))
35. *Must the trust be a locally administered trust?*	No, if it is governed by Colorado law regarding the meaning and effect of its terms. (§ 15-1-404.5 (13)(b))
36. *When does the power to convert not exist?*	When (i) certain charitable trusts are involved, (ii) the governing instrument prohibits it by reference to one of the provisions of Part 4 of the statutes pertaining to the power to adjust, or (iii) the trust was in existence on May 22, 2003 and the governing instrument incorporates provisions that operate as a total return trust, but can rely on the statute to the extent its provisions are not in conflict with the governing instrument. (§ 15-1-404.5(13)(b)(III))

1. Court action is generally limited to once every 2 years except for good cause. (§ 15-1-404.5(3)(h))

Table 11.02
Total Return Trusts
Delaware

1. *Is there a power to convert?*	Yes. (12 § 3527(b)(1))
2. *Is the statute applicable to new unitrusts?*	Yes. (12 § 3527A) Other than requiring the same 3%-5% payout range permitted for converted unitrusts, it allows the governing instrument of a new unitrust to set the terms and allow or disallow the valuation period of 1 year or an average over a longer period, the right to change the rate, treatment of capital gains, and exclusion of assets the valuing of which are not readily ascertainable or assets used by a trust beneficiary, such as a residence or tangible personal property. (12 § 3527A(i)) If there is no provision on the matter, the default as to the source of funding is the same as for a converted trust. See #25 below; 12 § 3527(h). If the new unitrust agreement does not specifically or by reference to 12 § 3527 deny power to change the rate or convert to an income trust, then the trustee has such powers. (12 § 3527A(e))
3. *Is there a required rate of return?*	A reasonable current return, in the range of 3%-5%. (12 § 3527(f))
4. *Can the required rate of return be varied?*	Yes, but with the requisite notice. (12 § 3527(b)(3))
5. *How can it be varied?*	See #3 above.
6. *Alternatively, does the trustee have discretion within a range?*	See #3.
7. *If so, what is the range?*	See #3.
8. *Must court approval be obtained initially?*	No. (12 § 3527(b))
9. *Does the trustee have discretion to:*	
a. *Convert?*	Yes, if certain beneficiaries do not object following notice. (12 § 3527(b)(3)(d))
b. *Reconvert?*	Yes. (12 § 3527(b)(2))
c. *Determine the effective date?*	Yes. (12 § 3527(i))
d. *Determine the frequency of payments?*	Yes. (12 § 3527(i)(2))
e. *Determine cash or in kind distribution?*	Yes. (12 § 3527(i)(3))
f. *Vary the rate?*	Yes. (12 § 3527(b)(3))
g. *Whether to value annually or less frequently?*	It must be done at least annually. (12 § 3527(e))
h. *What valuation date to use?*	Yes. (12 § 3527(e)) See also #9g above.
i. *Whether to value trust property occupied or used by a beneficiary?*	Generally, the trustee has discretion to determine which assets are excluded. (12 § 3527(e))

j. How to prorate in a short year any unitrust payments?	Yes. (12 § 3527(i)(2))
k. Whether to estimate the value of nonliquid assets?	Use such methods as are reasonable and appropriate. (12 § 3527(e))
l. The effect of contributions and distributions on valuation?	No provision.
m. Other administrative matters?	Yes. (12 § 3527(i)(5))
10. What standard of conduct is required of the trustee?	Good faith. (12 § 3527(m))
11. What is the remedy for a violation?	Good faith conduct insulates the trustee from liability, even if there is lack of notice or the recipient of notice is disabled. However, it does not prevent a petition for a court order to convert, reconvert, or change the percentage. This is, however, the exclusive remedy. (§ 738.104(8))
12. If a trustee is interested, must a disinterested trustee be appointed?	Yes, by the interested trustee. (12 § 3527(c)(3)(b)) An interested trustee is one with a current interest in income or principal, one who can be replaced by an interested distributee as defined in 12 § 3527(a)(3), or one who can satisfy a legal obligation of support of a beneficiary out of the trust fund. (12 § 3527(a)(4))
13. If a disinterested trustee is required, who selects him?	The trustee. See #12 above.
14. Must notice be given before a conversion?	Yes. (12 §§ 3527(b)(3)(b), 3527(c)(3)(c))
15. To whom must notice be given?	(i) The grantor, if living; (ii) all eligible recipients of income; (iii) all persons entitled to principal if the trusts terminates or, if there is no provision for termination, those who would take income or principal if the current income beneficiaries were deceased; and (iv) all advisors and protectors. (12 §§ 3527(b)(3)(b), 3527(c)(3)(c))
16. By when must objection be made?	30 days after serving of notice. (12 §§ 3527(b)(3)(D), 3527 (c)(3)(e))
17. Can objection be overridden?	Yes, by petitioning a court. (12 § 3527(d))
18. What if there are not sufficiently competent beneficiaries?	At least one person in #15 (ii) and (iii) must be competent. (12 §§ 3527(b)(3)(c), 3527(c)(3)(d))
19. Can a beneficiary petition a court to seek conversion if a trustee refuses?	Yes. (12 § 3527(d)) The court can also do so in its own discretion. *(Id.)*
20. Is there a duty to convert?	No, it is in the trustee's sole discretion. (12 § 3527(b))
21. Can a court be petitioned to stop a conversion or reconversion?	No provision.
22. Is there a statute of limitations?	No provision.
23. Is there a mandatory provision for payout of income if greater than the unitrust amount?	No provision.

24. *If there is an excess payout, is it added to principal?*	No provision.
25. *What is the priority of source of payment of the unitrust amount?*	Net accounting income, ordinary income not allocable to net accounting income, net short term capital gain, net long term capital gain, and principal. (12 § 3527(h))
26. *Is the priority mandatory?*	Yes. (12 § 3527(h))
27. *How is the fair market value of the trust determined for unitrust purposes?*	Other than valuing at least annually, any date, dates, or averages are deemed appropriate. (12 § 3527(e))
28. *Are certain items excluded?*	No provision. Trustee is given discretion. See #9i above.
29. *Is the trustee authorized to release his power?*	No provision.
30. *Is there special provision for the marital deduction?*	Yes, the spouse can compel reconversion where a federal gift or estate tax marital deduction has been taken and the spouse would otherwise be entitled to receive the net income of the trust. (12 § 3527(k))
31. *Is there special provision for generation-skipping grandfather preservation?*	No provision.
32. *If the power to convert is utilized must the power to adjust be released?*	No provision.
33. *Are particular factors presented that the trustee should consider?*	With respect to setting the rate, the trustee has to take into account the intentions of the trustor as expressed in the governing instrument, the needs of the beneficiaries, general economic conditions, projected current earnings and appreciation, and projected inflation and its impact on the trust. (12 § 3527(f))
34. *What standard should a court use?*	No provision.
35. *Must the trust be a locally administered trust?*	No. The statute also applies to a trust administered elsewhere whose governing instrument provides that Delaware law governs matters of construction or administration. (12 § 3527(l))
36. *When does the power to convert not exist?*	When (i) the governing instrument reflects an intent that the current beneficiaries are to receive an amount other than a reasonable current return from the trust; (ii) the trust is a pooled income fund or charitable remainder trust; or (iii) the governing instrument expressly prohibits use of this statute by specific reference to the section or expressly states the trustor's intent that net income not be calculated as a unitrust amount. (12 § 3527(l)(1)-(3))

Table 11.02
Total Return Trusts
Florida

1.	*Is there a power to convert?*	Yes. (§ 738.104(2)(a)(1))
2.	*Is the statute applicable to new unitrusts?*	Yes. (§§ 738.1041(11), 738.1041(2)(a)(2))
3.	*Is there a required rate of return?*	3%-5%. (§ 738.1041(b)(1)(a))
4.	*Can the required rate of return be varied?*	Yes. See #3. As an alternative, the rate can be geared to 50% of the § 7520 I.R.C. rate, redetermined each January, but never lower than 3% nor higher than 5%. (§ 738.1041(2)(b)(2)(a))
5.	*How can it be varied?*	See ##3 & 4 above.
6.	*Alternatively, does the trustee have discretion within a range?*	See ##3 & 4.
7.	*If so, what is the range?*	See ##3 & 4.
8.	*Must court approval be obtained initially?*	No.
9.	*Does the trustee have discretion to:*	
	a. *Convert?*	Yes, if certain beneficiaries do not object following notice. (20 § 8105(a)(4))
	b. *Reconvert?*	Yes. (§§ 738.1041(2), 738.1041(6)(d))
	c. *Determine the effective date?*	Yes. (§§ 738.1041(6)(a), 738.1041(6)(d))
	d. *Determine the frequency of payments?*	Yes. (§ 738.1041(6)(b))
	e. *Determine cash or in kind distribution?*	Yes. (§ 738.1041(6)(c))
	f. *Vary the rate?*	See #4 above.
	g. *Whether to value annually or less frequently?*	No provision.
	h. *What valuation date to use?*	No provision.
	i. *Whether to value trust property occupied or used by a beneficiary?*	Generally, the trustee has discretion to determine which assets are excluded. (§§ 738.1041(2)(b)(1)(c), 738.1041(6)(b)) However, if the alternative floating rate in #4 is used, then all assets must be valued annually "reasonably and in good faith." Furthermore, residential or tangible personal property is to be excluded if, on the first business day of the current valuation year, one or more current beneficiaries have or have had the right to occupy, possess, or control the property. In such cases, these rights are deemed to be the unitrust amount. (§ 738.1041(b)(2)(b)) A specifically given asset and return on it is also excluded. *(Id.)*

j. How to prorate in a short year any unitrust payments?	Yes. (§ 738.1041(6)(b))
k. Whether to estimate the value of nonliquid assets?	No provision.
l. The effect of contributions and distributions on valuation?	No provision.
m. Other administrative matters?	Yes. (§ 738.1041(6)(e))
10. What standard of conduct is required of the trustee?	Good faith. (§ 738.1041(8))
11. What is the remedy for a violation?	If the trustee has not acted in good faith, then the remedy is restoration of beneficiaries to prior position, typically through adjustments in trust fund, but if this is inadequate, then the trustee must pay from own funds. (§§ 738.1041(8), 738.105(3)) Good faith conduct insulates the trustee from liability, although it does not prevent a petition for a court order to convert, reconvert, or change the percentage. This is the exclusive remedy. (§ 738.1041(8))
12. If a trustee is interested, must a disinterested trustee be appointed?	Yes, by the interested trustee. (§ 738.1041(b)(1)) An interested trustee is one with a current interest in income or principal, one who can be replaced by a related or subordinate party, or one who can satisfy a legal obligation of support of a beneficiary out of the trust fund. (§ 738.1041(1)(e))
13. If a disinterested trustee is required, who selects him?	The trustee. See #12.
14. Must notice be given before a conversion?	Yes. (§ 738.1041(c)(2))
15. To whom must notice be given?	(i) The grantor, if living; (ii) all eligible recipients of income; (iii) all persons entitled to principal if the trusts terminates or, if there is no provision for termination, those who would take income or principal if the current income beneficiaries were deceased; and (iv) all advisors and protectors. (§ 738.1041(c)(2)(G))
16. By when must objection be made?	60 days after serving of notice. (§ 738.1041(2)(e))
17. Can objection be overridden?	Yes, by petitioning a court. (§ 738.1041(3))
18. What if there are not sufficiently competent beneficiaries?	At least one person in each of #15 (ii) and (iii) must be competent. (§ 738.1041(d))
19. Can a beneficiary petition a court to seek conversion if a trustee refuses?	Yes. A majority in interest of either the income or remainder beneficiaries may do so if no resolution has occurred six months after delivery of objection regarding the amount of income distributions from a regular income trust. (§ 738.1041(9)). "Income trust" is defined in § 738.1041(1)(c). "Majority in interest" is not defined.
20. Is there a duty to convert?	No. The statute provides that the trustee "may" convert. (§ 738.1041(2))
21. Can a court be petitioned to stop a conversion or reconversion?	No provision.

22.	*Is there a special statute of limitations?*	No provision.
23.	*Is there a mandatory provision for payout of income if greater than the unitrust amount?*	No provision.
24.	*If there is an excess payout, is it added to principal?*	No provision.
25.	*What is the priority of source of payment of the unitrust amount?*	None. (§ 738.1041(5)(b))
26.	*Is the priority mandatory?*	N/A
27.	*How is the fair market value of the trust determined for unitrust purposes?*	Trust is given discretion. (§ 738.1041(2)(b)(1)(b))
28.	*Are certain items excluded?*	No provision. Trustee is given discretion. See #9i above.
29.	*Is the trustee authorized to release his power?*	No provision.
30.	*Is there special provision for the marital deduction?*	No provision.
31.	*Is there special provision for generation-skipping grandfather preservation?*	No provision.
32.	*If the power to convert is utilized must the power to adjust be released?*	No express provision, but trustee cannot have both powers. (§ 738.1041(10)(e))
33.	*Are particular factors presented that the trustee should consider?*	No provision.
34.	*What standard should a court use?*	No provision.
35.	*Must the trust be a locally administered trust?*	No. The statute also applies to a trust administered elsewhere under Florida law. (§ 738.1041(10)(a))
36.	*When does not the power exist?*	When (i) the governing instrument reflects an intent that the current beneficiaries are to receive an amount other than a reasonable current return from the trust; (ii) the trust is a charitable trust; (iii) one or more eligible income beneficiaries have a power of withdrawal over the trust not subject to an ascertainable standard and exceeds the "5 or 5" amount, or is a power that can be exercised to discharge a duty of support; (iv) the governing instrument expressly prohibits use of this statute by specific reference to the section; or (v) the trust is one where the trustee currently possesses a power to adjust under § 738.104. (§ 738.1041(10)(a)-(e))

Table 11.02
Total Return Trusts
Georgia

1. *Is there a power to convert?*	Yes. (§ 53-12-221(a))
2. *Is the statute applicable to new unitrusts?*	No explicit provision.
3. *Is there a required rate of return?*	Yes, 4% over the lesser of the average of net fair market value over the preceding three years or the shorter existence of the trust. (§ 53-12-221(d)(3))
4. *Can the required rate of return be varied?*	No. See #3 above.
5. *How can it be varied?*	See #3 above.
6. *Alternatively, does the trustee have discretion within a range?*	No. See #3 above.
7. *If so, what is the range?*	See #3 above.
8. *Must court approval be obtained initially?*	No.
9. *Does the trustee have discretion to:*	
a. *Convert?*	Yes, if certain beneficiaries do not object following notice. (§ 53-12-221(a))
b. *Reconvert?*	No. Court approval is required. (§ 53-12-221(g)(4))
c. *Determine the effective date?*	Yes. (§ 53-12-221(e)(1))
d. *Determine the frequency of payments?*	Yes. (§ 53-12-221(e)(3))
e. *Determine cash or in kind distribution?*	No provision.
f. *Vary the rate?*	See #4 above.
g. *Whether to value annually or less frequently?*	Yes. (§ 53-12-221(e)(5))
h. *What valuation date to use?*	Yes. (§ 53-12-221(e)(6))
i. *Whether to value trust property occupied or used by a beneficiary?*	No provision. See #9k below.
j. *How to prorate in a short year any unitrust payments?*	Yes. (§ 53-12-221 (e)(2))
k. *Whether to estimate the value of nonliquid assets?*	Yes. (§ 53-12-221(e)(7))
l. *The effect of contributions and distributions on valuation?*	Yes. (§ 53-12-221(e)(4))
m. *Other administrative matters?*	Yes. (§ 53-12-221(e)(8))

10. What standard of conduct is required of the trustee?	No provision.
11. What is the remedy for a violation?	No provision.
12. If a trustee is interested, must a disinterested trustee be appointed?	The key is whether the power has adverse income tax (§ 53-12-221(i)(4)), or estate, gift, or generation-skipping transfer tax consequences (§ 53-12-221(i)(5)(A) & (B)).
13. If a disinterested trustee is required, who selects him?	No disinterested trustee is necessary. The interested trustees petition the court. (§ 53-12-221(j)(2)) However, no provision for petition is made if the effect would be disallowance of the marital deduction.
14. Must notice be given before a conversion?	Yes. (§ 53-12-221(a)(2))
15. To whom must notice be given?	Sui juris beneficiaries who would either get current income or successor income interest as well as remainderman if entitled to principal upon termination of trust immediately before giving of notice. All this assumes no exercise of a power. (§ 53-12-221(a)(2)(A) & (B))
16. By when must objection be made?	60 days after mailing of notice. (§ 53-12-221(a)(4))
17. Can objection be overridden?	Yes, by petitioning a court. (§ 53-12-221(b)(1))
18. What if there are not sufficiently competent beneficiaries?	A court must be petitioned for approval. The statute requires at least two sui juris beneficiaries to avert the need for court approval: a current income beneficiary and at least one of either a successor income beneficiary or remainderman described in #15 above. (§ 53-12-221)
19. Can a beneficiary petition a court to seek conversion if a trustee refuses?	Yes. (§ 53-12-221(b)(2)) Thus, the trustee is not obligated to convert upon request. See also § 53-12-221(g), which allows a beneficiary to petition to change rate, period for averaging of rate, to obtain a greater payout of income in order to preserve a tax benefit, or to reconvert.
20. Is there a duty to convert?	No. The statute provides that the trustee "may" convert. (§ 53-12-221(a); see also § 53-12-221(c))
21. Can a court be petitioned to stop a conversion or reconversion?	Yes, if income would be higher. This is the only express authorization. See #19.
22. Is there a special statute of limitations?	No provision.
23. Is there a mandatory provision for payout of income if greater than the unitrust amount?	No provision.
24. If there is an excess payout, is it added to principal?	No provision.
25. What is the priority of source of payment of the unitrust amount?	Net income, net realized short term capital gain, net realized long term capital gain, principal. (§ 53-12-221(f)(3))
26. Is the priority mandatory?	Yes (§ 53-12-221(f)(3)), unless specified otherwise in the trust instrument.

27. *How is the fair market value of the trust determined for unitrust purposes?*	By appraisal or other reasonable method or estimate. (§ 53-12-221(d)(4)). See also #3 above.
28. *Are certain items excluded?*	Yes, residential or tangible personal property that a current beneficiary has or had the right to occupy or possess or control on first business day of valuation year. This is deemed to be the unitrust amount for residential property. No mention of consequence re other tangible property. (§ 53-12-221(d)(5))
29. *Is the trustee authorized to release his power?*	Yes (§ 53-12-221(k)(1)), but not if it causes adverse tax consequences.
30. *Is there special provision for the marital deduction?*	No conversion allowed if it would result in denial of the marital deduction. (§ 53-12-221(i)(1))
31. *Is there special provision for generation-skipping grandfather preservation?*	Only to the extent of #12 above.
32. *If the power to convert is utilized must the power to adjust be released?*	Yes. (§ 53-12-221(a))
33. *Are particular factors presented that the trustee should consider?*	Yes, although the statute says the trustee "may" consider these in deciding whether to convert. (§ 53-12-221 (c))
34. *What standard should a court use?*	Intent of settlor or testator and purposes of the trust. (§ 53-12-221(b)(3))
35. *Must the trust be a locally administered trust?*	No provision.
36. *When does the power to convert not exist?*	If the amount payable to a beneficiary as a fixed annuity or fixed fraction would change; if the unitrust amount would be made from an amount permanently set aside for charitable purposes and for which a federal estate or gift tax deduction has been taken, unless both income and principal are set aside; or the conversion would result in disallowance of the federal estate tax or gift tax marital deduction. (§ 53-12-221(i)(1)-(3)).

Table 11.02
Total Return Trusts
Illinois

1. *Is there a power to convert?*	Yes, by trustee (760 ILCS § 5/5.3(a)), by agreement with primary beneficiaries (760 ILCS § 5/5.3(b)), or by the court (760 ILCS § 5/5.3(c)).
2. *Is the statute applicable to new unitrusts?*	Yes. (760 ILCS § 5/5.3(m))
3. *Is there a required rate of return?*	Yes, 4% if as a result of the trustee's act. (760 ILCS § 5/5.3(d)(3)) No, if by agreement with beneficiaries. It can be anywhere in the range of 3%-5%. (760 ILCS § 5/5.3(b)) There does not seem to be a specific rate or even a range if done on petition by a court. (760 ILCS §§ 5/5.3(c)(5), 5/5.3(g)(1)) Rather, a standard apparently guides the court. See #34 below. If a total return unitrust is new and not converted, the governing instrument can provide for a range from 3%-5% and this presumed conclusively to be a reasonable current return that fairly apportions the total return of the unitrust. (760 ILCS § 5/5.3(m)(3))
4. *Can the required rate of return be varied?*	Yes, in some instances. See #3 above.
5. *How can it be varied?*	See #3 above.
6. *Alternatively, does the trustee have discretion within a range?*	See #3.
7. *If so, what is the range?*	See #3.
8. *Must court approval be obtained initially?*	No.
9. *Does the trustee have discretion to:*	
a. *Convert?*	Yes, if certain beneficiaries do not object following notice. (760 ILCS § 5/5.3(a))
b. *Reconvert?*	No provision.
c. *Determine the effective date?*	Yes. (760 ILCS § 5/5.3(e)(1))
d. *Determine the frequency of payments?*	No provision.
e. *Determine cash or in kind distribution?*	Yes. (760 ILCS § 5/5.3(e)(3))
f. *Vary the rate?*	See #3 above.
g. *Whether to value annually or less frequently?*	Yes. (760 ILCS § 5/5.3(e)(5))
h. *What valuation date to use?*	Yes. Also how many valuation dates. (760 ILCS § 5/5.3(e)(6))
i. *Whether to value trust property occupied or used by a beneficiary?*	No provision.

	j. How to prorate in a short year any unitrust payments?	Yes. (760 ILCS §§ 5/5.3(e)(2), 5/5.3(e)(7)(C))
	k. Whether to estimate the value of nonliquid assets?	All valuation decisions for assets for which there is no readily available market. (760 ILCS § 5/5.3(e)(7))
	l. The effect of contributions and distributions on valuation?	Yes. (760 ILCS § 5/5.3(e)(4))
	m. Other administrative matters?	Yes. (760 ILCS § 5/5.3(e)(8))
10.	*What standard of conduct is required of the trustee?*	Reasonably and in good faith. If the trustee petitions a court to convert under 760 ILCS § 5/5.3(c), the statute states that this is not itself a violation of the duty of impartiality unless the trustee acted in bad faith. (760 ILCS § 5/5.3(c)(4)(C))
11.	*What is the remedy for a violation?*	If the trustee acted or omitted to act reasonably and in good faith, the exclusive remedy is petitioning the court regarding conversion, reconversion, changing the percentage, or ordering administrative procedures. *(Id.)* The presumption is that the trustee acted or omitted to act reasonably and in good faith, unless there is an abuse of discretion. No reference to penalty if the trustee has not acted or omitted to act reasonably and in good faith.
12.	*If a trustee is interested, must a disinterested trustee be appointed?*	Yes, by the interested trustee. (§ 55-15-3) An interested trustee is (i) one who is a beneficiary and conversion or not converting would increase or diminish the trustee's share, (ii) the trustee's power to convert would result in an individual being treated as owner of a part of the trust for income purposes or (ii) property being included in an individual's gross estate. (760 ILCS § 5/5.3(i))
13.	*If a disinterested trustee is required, who selects him?*	There is no provision for a disinterested trustee. The interested trustee may petition the court for conversion. (760 ILCS § 5/5.3(i)(1))
14.	*Must notice be given before a conversion?*	Yes. (760 ILCS § 5/5.3(a)(3))
15.	*To whom must notice be given?*	(i) All legally competent, eligible recipients of income; (ii) all persons who would take income or principal if the current income beneficiaries were deceased. (760 ILCS § 5/5.3(a)(3))
16.	*By when must objection be made?*	60 days after sending notice. (760 ILCS § 5/5.3(a)(5))
17.	*Can objection be overridden?*	Yes, by petitioning a court. (760 ILCS § 5/5.3(c)(1))
18.	*What if there are not sufficiently competent beneficiaries?*	At least one person in #15 (i) and (ii) must be legally competent. (760 ILCS § 5/5.3(a)(4))
19.	*Can a beneficiary petition a court to seek conversion if a trustee refuses?*	Yes, but no sooner than 6 months after the trustee receives a request and declines or fails to honor it. (760 ILCS § 5/5.3(c)(2))
20.	*Is there a duty to convert?*	No, "may" is used in the statute. (760 ILCS § 5/5.3(a)(1))

21. Can a court be petitioned to stop a conversion or reconversion?	Yes. (760 ILCS § 5/5.3(a)(5))
22. Is there a special statute of limitations?	Yes. 2 years from sending the plaintiff a notice or report sufficiently disclosing facts fundamental to the claim such that the person knew or reasonably should have known of the claim. (760 ILCS § 5/5.3(k)) This special limitation period does not apply to a person under a legal disability and who did not have a personal representative.
23. Is there a mandatory provision for payout of income if greater than the unitrust amount?	No provision.
24. If there is an excess payout, is it added to principal?	The trustee is required to recover it and charge interest equal to the distribution percentage. (760 ILCS § 5/5.3(d)(3)) Although not stated, the recovered amount is presumably added to principal. The interest must be "recovered" as well. Quaere whether the trustee can just reduce the next payment or must actually recover it from the beneficiary.
25. What is the priority of source of payment of the unitrust amount?	Net income, ordinary income as defined for federal income tax purposes, net realized short term capital gain, net realized long term capital gain, principal having readily available market value. (760 ILCS § 5/5.3(f)(2))
26. Is the priority mandatory?	Yes (760 ILCS § 5/5.3(f)(2)), unless specified otherwise in the trust instrument. For express unitrusts see 760 ILCS § 5/5.3(m)(4)
27. How is the fair market value of the trust determined for unitrust purposes?	Net fair market value of assets are averaged over the lesser of the 3 preceding years or the period during which the trust has been in existence. (760 ILCS § 5/5.3(d)(2)) However, a court can alter the 3-year period. (760 ILCS § 5/5.3(g)(2)) In the case of express unitrusts the governing instrument can provide for an annual or multiyear average with no cap on the number of years used for averaging as in the case of a converted unitrust. (760 ILCS § 5/5.3(m)(2)(B))
28. Are certain items excluded?	No provision.
29. Is the trustee authorized to release his power?	Yes (760 ILCS § 5/5.3(k)), if the trustee reasonably believes the release is in the best interest of the trust and its beneficiaries. The power can be released by the trustee for some or even all successor trustees. *(Id.)*
30. Is there special provision for the marital deduction?	No provision.
31. Is there special provision for generation-skipping grandfather preservation?	No provision.
32. If the power to convert is utilized must the power to adjust be released?	No provision.
33. Are particular factors presented that the trustee should consider?	Yes: "To better carry out the purposes of the trust and the conversion is in the best interests of the beneficiaries." (760 ILCS § 5/5.3(a)(1))

34. What standard should a court use?	Conversion, reconversion, or adjustment of the distribution percentage will enable the trustee to better carry out the purposes of the trust and the action is in the best interests of the "beneficiaries." (760 ILCS § 5/5.3(c)(5)) There is no indication of how this is addressed if the beneficiaries have conflicting interests.
35. Must the trust be a locally administered trust?	The trust must be (i) administered under Illinois law and be governed by Illinois law or (ii) governed by Illinois law with regard to its meaning and effect of its terms. (760 ILCS § 5/5.3(l))
36. When does the power to convert not exist?	When a charitable remainder trust is involved or when the governing instrument expressly prohibits use of this section by express reference to it. (760 ILCS § 5/5.3(l)(1)-(2))

Table 11.02
Total Return Trusts
Indiana

1.	*Is there a power to convert?*	Yes. (§ 30-2-15-9(1))
2.	*Is the statute applicable to new unitrusts?*	Yes, at least with respect to change of rate. (§ 30-2-15-9(3))
3.	*Is there a required rate of return?*	If the trustee proposes a 4% rate and those entitled to notice do not object, that is the rate. (§ 30-2-15-15(b)) A trust can have a rate between 3%-5% if it represents a reasonable current return and best reflects the goals of the trust and the intent of the settlor or testator if agreed to by the trustee and beneficiaries entitled to notice (§ 30-2-15-15(c)(1)) or if ordered by the court (§ 30-2-15-15(c)(2)).
4.	*Can the required rate of return be varied?*	See #3 above.
5.	*How can it be varied?*	See #3 above.
6.	*Alternatively, does the trustee have discretion within a range?*	No. See #3 above.
7.	*If so, what is the range?*	See #3 above.
8.	*Must court approval be obtained initially?*	No. The trustee can proceed if the beneficiaries entitled to take do not object. (§ 30-2-15-10)
9.	*Does the trustee have discretion to:*	
	a. *Convert?*	Yes, if beneficiaries entitled to notice do not object following notice. (§ 30-2-15-10)
	b. *Reconvert?*	Yes. (§ 30-2-15-9(2))
	c. *Determine the effective date?*	No provision.
	d. *Determine the frequency of payments?*	No. Payments are deemed "income" and distributed as provided in the trust instrument. (§ 30-2-15-24)
	e. *Determine cash or in kind distribution?*	No provision.
	f. *Vary the rate?*	See #3 above.
	g. *Whether to value annually or less frequently?*	No. See #3 above.
	h. *What valuation date to use?*	No provision.
	i. *Whether to value trust property occupied or used by a beneficiary?*	Such residential and tangible personal property for which at least one current income beneficiary has a right to occupy or use, except as a trustee, cannot be included. (§ 30-2-15-8) The right of occupancy or use shall be considered the unitrust amount. (§ 30-2-15-18(1)) Any asset specifically given and the return on investment are also excluded and the return on investment is distributable to the beneficiary. (§ 30-2-15(18)(2)) The trustee "may" exclude other assets without a readily distributable fair market value and they remain governed by the instrument.

j. *How to prorate in a short year any unitrust payments?*	No. Proration on a daily basis is required. (§ 30-2-15-22(b))
k. *Whether to estimate the value of nonliquid assets?*	No provision.
l. *The effect of contributions and distributions on valuation?*	No. Adjustments are required. (§ 30-2-15-21)
m. *Other administrative matters?*	Very broad discretion. (§ 30-2-15-19(b)
10. *What standard of conduct is required of the trustee?*	Good faith (§ 30-2-15-26), regardless whether notice was received by a beneficiary or whether such person had a legal disability. (§ 30-2-15-26(a))
11. *What is the remedy for a violation?*	If the good faith standard has been satisfied, the exclusive remedy is petitioning the court re conversion, reconversion, or changing the percentage. (*Id.*) No reference to penalty if the good faith standard has not been satisfied.
12. *If a trustee is interested, must a disinterested trustee be appointed?*	The key is whether the power has adverse income tax (§ 30-2-14-15(c)(5)), estate tax consequences (§ 30-2-14-15(c)(6)), or the trustee is also a beneficiary. (§ 30-2-14-15(c)(6)) See generally § 30-2-15-11(3).
13. *If a disinterested trustee is required, who selects him?*	No disinterested trustee is necessary. The interested trustees petition the court (§ 30-2-15-11(3))
14. *Must notice be given before a conversion?*	Yes. (§ 30-2-15-10(a))
15. *To whom must notice be given?*	The settlor and their beneficiaries, or their legal or natural guardians, who are either recipients or entitled to trust income or principal, upon termination of trust at the time of giving of notice. (§ 30-2-15-10, 30-2-14-16(b))
16. *By when must objection be made?*	60 days after receiving the notice. (§ 30-2-15-10(c))
17. *Can objection be overridden?*	Yes, by petitioning a court. (§ 30-2-15-11) Note that objection can be raised by the trustor or trust beneficiaries who are current income beneficiaries or beneficiaries entitled to receive income or principal if the trust terminated at the time notice is given. (§ 30-2-14-16(b))
18. *What if there are not sufficiently competent beneficiaries?*	No provision.
19. *Can a beneficiary petition a court to seek conversion if a trustee refuses?*	Yes. (§ 30-2-15-12) Thus, the trustee is not obligated to convert upon request. See also § 11.104A.040(i), which allows a beneficiary to petition to change the rate of the unitrust. (*Id.*; § 30-2-15-13)
20. *Is there a duty to convert?*	No. The statute provides that the trustee "may" convert. (§ 30-2-15-9)
21. *Can a court be petitioned to stop a conversion or reconversion?*	No provision.
22. *Is there a special statute of limitations?*	No provision.

23. *Is there a mandatory provision for payout of income if greater than the unitrust amount?*	Yes, if a marital deduction is involved or the generation-skipping transfer tax does not apply due to an effective date or transition rule. (§ 30-2-15-23(a)) More generally, the unitrust amount cannot be less than trust net income to the extent necessary to satisfy tax law requirements or to preserve a tax benefit. (§ 30-2-15-23(b))
24. *If there is an excess payout, is it added to principal?*	No provision.
25. *What is the priority of source of payment of the unitrust amount?*	Net income, net realized short term capital gain, net realized long term tax capital gain, principal. (§ 30-2-15-25)
26. *Is the priority mandatory?*	Yes (§ 30-2-15-25(a)), unless specified otherwise in the trust instrument.
27. *How is the fair market value of the trust determined for unitrust purposes?*	It is fair market value reduced by debts, regardless whether or not allocable to specific property. (§ 30-2-15-3) In the first two years current, annual valuation on the first business day of the current valuation year is required. Thereafter, the unitrust rate is multiplied by the average of net fair market value of assets on the first business day of the current valuation year as defined in § 30-2-15-1 and each of the two immediately preceding years. (§ 30-2-15-17)
28. *Are certain items excluded?*	See #9i above.
29. *Is the trustee authorized to release his power?*	No provision.
30. *Is there special provision for the marital deduction?*	See #24 above.
31. *Is there special provision for generation-skipping grandfather preservation?*	See #24 above.
32. *If the power to convert is utilized must the power to adjust be released?*	Yes. (§ 30-2-15-9(1))
33. *Are particular factors presented that the trustee should consider?*	No provision.
34. *What standard should a court use?*	Intent of settlor or testator and purposes of the trust. (§ 30-2-15-13)
35. *Must the trust be a locally administered trust?*	No provision.
36. *When does the power to convert not exist?*	The statute provides that a beneficiary cannot obtain a conversion by court order when trustee will not act, if amounts in trust permanently set aside for charitable purposes would be altered, unless both income and principal are set aside. (§ 30-2-15-12)

Table 11.02
Total Return Trusts
Iowa

1.	*Is there a power to convert?*	Yes. (§ 637-602)
2.	*Is the statute applicable to new unitrusts?*	Implied. (§ 637.605(1)(b))
3.	*Is there a required rate of return?*	4%, unless the governing instrument provides a different percentage or the court approves a different percentage between 3%-5% after notice of intent to seek a percentage other than 4%. (§ 637.608) Quaere if the trust instrument can provide for any percentage, even above 5%. As for notice, see #15 below.
4.	*Can the required rate of return be varied?*	See #3 above.
5.	*How can it be varied?*	See #3 above.
6.	*Alternatively, does the trustee have discretion within a range?*	*See #3 above.*
7.	*If so, what is the range?*	See #3 above.
8.	*Must court approval be obtained initially?*	No.
9.	*Does the trustee have discretion to:*	
	a. *Convert?*	Yes, if certain beneficiaries do not object following notice. (§ 637.602(1), 637.603)
	b. *Reconvert?*	Yes (§§ 637.602(2), 637.603), including determining the effective date (§ 637.611(4)).
	c. *Determine the effective date?*	Yes. (§ 637.611(1))
	d. *Determine the frequency of payments?*	Yes. (§ 637.611(2))
	e. *Determine cash or in kind distribution?*	Yes. (§ 637.611(3))
	f. *Vary the rate?*	See #3 above.
	g. *Whether to value annually or less frequently?*	Must be at least annually (§ 637.607) and as deemed appropriate.
	h. *What valuation date to use?*	Yes, if deemed appropriate. (§ 637.607)
	i. *Whether to value trust property occupied or used by a beneficiary?*	No provision.
	j. *How to prorate in a short year any unitrust payments?*	Yes. (§ 637.611(2))
	k. *Whether to estimate the value of nonliquid assets?*	Assets for which a fair market value cannot be readily ascertained shall be valued using valuation methods as are deemed reasonable and appropriate. (§ 637.607)

l. The effect of contributions and distributions on valuation?	No provision.
m. Other administrative matters?	Yes. (§ 637.611(5))
10. What standard of conduct is required of the trustee?	Good faith, regardless whether notice received by beneficiaries or whether such persons had a legal disability. (§ 637.614)
11. What is the remedy for a violation?	If good faith, the exclusive remedy is petitioning the court re conversion or reconversion. *(Id.)* No reference to penalty if the standard of good faith is not observed.
12. If a trustee is interested, must a disinterested trustee be appointed?	Yes, by the interested trustee. (§ 633.605) An interested trustee is one with a current interest in income or principal, one who can be replaced by an interested distributee, or one who can satisfy a legal obligation of support of a beneficiary out of the trust fund. (§ 633.601(4))
13. If a disinterested trustee is required, who selects him?	The trustee. See #12. The interested trustee can still take most actions, but the disinterested person, acting as a fiduciary, determines the method of valuation and which assets may be excluded. (§ 637.605(2)) Notice as per #18 below, must be given and there cannot be objection in order for the trustee to act. See #16 below.
14. Must notice be given before a conversion?	Yes. (§ 637.603(2))
15. To whom must notice be given?	(i) The grantor, if living; (ii) all eligible recipients of income; (iii) all persons entitled to principal if the trusts terminates or, if there is no provision for termination, those who would take income or principal if the current income beneficiaries were deceased; and (iv) all advisors and protectors. (§ 637.603 (2))
16. By when must objection be made?	60 days after receipt of notice. (§ 637.603(4))
17. Can objection be overridden?	Yes, by petitioning a court. (§ 637.606)
18. What if there are not sufficiently competent beneficiaries?	At least one person in #15 (ii) and (iii) must be competent. (§ 637.603(3))
19. Can a beneficiary petition a court to seek conversion if a trustee refuses?	Yes. (§ 637.606) The court then appoints a disinterested person to present the necessary information. *(Id.)*
20. Is there a duty to convert?	No. (§ 637.602) The word "may" is used.
21. Can a court be petitioned to stop a conversion or reconversion?	No provision.
22. Is there a special statute of limitations?	No provision.
23. Is there a mandatory provision for payout of income if greater than the unitrust amount?	Yes, if a marital deduction is involved or the generation-skipping transfer tax does not apply due to an effective date or transition rule. (§ 637.609)
24. If there is an excess payout, is it added to principal?	No provision.

25.	*What is the priority of source of payment of the unitrust amount?*	Net income, other ordinary income as determined for federal income tax purposes, net realized short term capital gain, net realized long term capital gain, principal. (§ 637.610)
26.	*Is the priority mandatory?*	Yes. (§ 637.610)
27.	*How is the fair market value of the trust determined for unitrust purposes?*	The trustee is given discretion to use such averages as are deemed reasonable and appropriate. (§ 637.607) See also #9g, h above.
28.	*Are certain items excluded?*	With regard to assets for which a fair market value cannot readily be ascertained, they may be excluded if all the income is distributed in accordance with the trust instrument. (§ 637.607)
29.	*Is the trustee authorized to release his power?*	No provision.
30.	*Is there special provision for the marital deduction?*	See #23 above.
31.	*Is there special provision for generation-skipping grandfather preservation?*	See #23 above.
32.	*If the power to convert is utilized must the power to adjust be released?*	No provision.
33.	*Are particular factors presented that the trustee should consider?*	No provision.
34.	*What standard should a court use?*	No provision.
35.	*Must the trust be a locally administered trust?*	The trust law applies only to trusts administered locally and under local law. (§ 637.613(1))
36.	*When does the power to convert not exist?*	If the governing instrument reflects an intent that the current beneficiaries are to receive an amount other than a "reasonable current return" from the trustee or the trust is a charitable trust, or an eligible income beneficiary has a power of withdrawal over the trust not limited by an ascertainable standard or which can be exercised to discharge a duty of support, or the governing instrument expressly prohibits use of this subchapter by specific reference to the subchapter. (§ 637.613(4))

Table 11.02
Total Return Trusts
Kentucky

1. *Is there a power to convert?*	There is no comprehensive statute. A unitrust amount may be paid if the statute granting a power to adjust otherwise applies and the trustee cannot otherwise comply with the requirement to act impartially. (§ 386.454(2))
2. *Is the statute applicable to new unitrusts?*	No explicit provision.
3. *Is there a required rate of return?*	Yes, 3%-5% of the value of the trust assets. (*Id.*)
4. *Can the required rate of return be varied?*	Within permissible range. (*Id.*)
5. *How can it be varied?*	By the trustee with court approval. (*Id.*)
6. *Alternatively, does the trustee have discretion within a range?*	See #3 & #4 above.
7. *If so, what is the range?*	See #3 above.
8. *Must court approval be obtained initially?*	Yes. (*Id.*)
9. *Does the trustee have discretion to:*	
a. *Convert?*	Yes, unless it is clear from the terms of the trust or will that the terms are intended to deny the fiduciary the power of adjustment. (§ 386.454(7))
b. *Reconvert?*	Yes, unless it is clear from the terms of the trust or will that the terms are intended to deny the fiduciary the power of adjustment. (*Id.*)
c. *Determine the effective date?*	Yes, unless it is clear from the terms of the trust or will that the terms are intended to deny the fiduciary the power of adjustment. (*Id.*)
d. *Determine the frequency of payments?*	Yes, unless it is clear from the terms of the trust or will that the terms are intended to deny the fiduciary the power of adjustment. (*Id.*)
e. *Determine cash or in kind distribution?*	No provision.
f. *Vary the rate?*	See #3 above.
g. *Whether to value annually or less frequently?*	Valuation must be done annually. (*Id.*)
h. *What valuation date to use?*	No provision.
i. *Whether to value trust property occupied or used by a beneficiary?*	No provision.
j. *How to prorate in a short year any unitrust payments?*	No provision.
k. *Whether to estimate the value of nonliquid assets?*	No provision.

l. The effect of contributions and distributions on valuation?	No provision.
m. Other administrative matters?	No provision.
10. What standard of conduct is required of the trustee?	Impartiality. (*Id.*; see also § 386.452(2))
11. What is the remedy for a violation?	No provision.
12. If a trustee is interested, must a disinterested trustee be appointed?	The key is whether the power has adverse income tax (§ 386.454(4)(e)) or estate tax consequences (§ 386.454 (4)(f)), or the trustee is also a beneficiary (§ 386.454(4)(g)), or, though not a beneficiary, the fiduciary would otherwise be benefited except in terms of reasonable compensation. (§ 386.454(4)(h))
13. If a disinterested trustee is required, who selects him?	No provision is made for adjustment if all of the trustees are interested. Moreover, it appears that if there is an interested fiduciary, no adjustment can be made generally if the effect would be to diminish the income interest for a spouse if by the terms of the trust a marital deduction "would be allowed." (*Id.*; § 386.454(4)(a)) The marital deduction does not actually have to be taken.
14. Must notice be given before a conversion?	Presumably, since court approval must be obtained. (§ 386.454(2))
15. To whom must notice be given?	No provision.
16. By when must objection be made?	No provision.
17. Can objection be overridden?	Yes, in court. (§ 386.454(2))
18. What if there are not sufficiently competent beneficiaries?	No provision.
19. Can a beneficiary petition a court to seek conversion if a trustee refuses?	No provision.
20. Is there a duty to convert?	No. The statute provides that the trustee "may adjust." (§ 386.454(2))
21. Can a court be petitioned to stop a conversion or reconversion?	No provision.
22. Is there a special statute of limitations?	No provision.
23. Is there a mandatory provision for payout of income if greater than the unitrust amount?	No provision.
24. If there is an excess payout, is it added to principal?	No provision.
25. What is the priority of source of payment of the unitrust amount?	No provision.
26. Is the priority mandatory?	No provision.

27. *How is the fair market value of the trust determined for unitrust purposes?*	No provision.
28. *Are certain items excluded?*	No provision.
29. *Is the trustee authorized to release his power?*	Yes (§ 386.454(6)), but not if it causes adverse tax consequences.
30. *Is there special provision for the marital deduction?*	See #13.
31. *Is there special provision for generation-skipping grandfather preservation?*	No provision.
32. *If the power to convert is utilized must the power to adjust be released?*	No, since it is a version of the power to adjust.
33. *Are particular factors presented that the trustee should consider?*	No provision.
34. *What standard should a court use?*	No provision.
35. *Must the trust be a locally administered trust?*	No provision.
36. *When does the power to convert not exist?*	Apart from #12 and #13 (marital deduction) above, (i) if the exercise of the power would change the amount of a fixed annuity or fixed fraction provided for in the governing instrument, (ii) adjustments would be from amounts set aside permanently for charitable purposes; or (iii) a trust income interest qualifying for the annual exclusion would be diminished as a result. (§ 386.454(4)(a)-(c))

Table 11.02
Total Return Trusts
Maine

1.	*Is there a power to convert?*	Yes. (18-A § 7-705(a))
2.	*Is the statute applicable to new unitrusts?*	No explicit provision.
3.	*Is there a required rate of return?*	Yes, 4% over the lesser of the preceding three years or the shorter existence of the trust. (18-A § 7-705(d)(3))
4.	*Can the required rate of return be varied?*	No. See #3 above.
5.	*How can it be varied?*	See #3 above.
6.	*Alternatively, does the trustee have discretion within a range?*	See #3 above.
7.	*If so, what is the range?*	See #3 above.
8.	*Must court approval be obtained initially?*	No.
9.	*Does the trustee have discretion to:*	
a.	*Convert?*	Yes, if certain beneficiaries do not object following notice. (18-A § 7-705(a)(4))
b.	*Reconvert?*	No. Court approval is needed. (18 A § 7-705(g)(4))
c.	*Determine the effective date?*	Yes. (18-A § 7-705(e)(1))
d.	*Determine the frequency of payments?*	Yes. (18-A § 7-705(e)(3))
e.	*Determine cash or in kind distribution?*	No provision.
f.	*Vary the rate?*	See #3 above.
g.	*Whether to value annually or less frequently?*	Yes. (18-A § 7-705(e)(5))
h.	*What valuation date to use?*	Yes. (18-A § 7-705(e)(6))
i.	*Whether to value trust property occupied or used by a beneficiary?*	Yes. (18-A § 7-705(e)(8))
j.	*How to prorate in a short year any unitrust payments?*	Yes. (18-A § 7-705(e)(2))
k.	*Whether to estimate the value of nonliquid assets?*	Yes. (18-A § 7-705(e)(8))
l.	*The effect of contributions and distributions on valuation?*	Yes. (18-A § 7-705(e)(4))
m.	*Other administrative matters?*	Yes. (18-A § 7-705(e)(9))

10. *What standard of conduct is required of the trustee?*	No provision.
11. *What is the remedy for a violation?*	No provision.
12. *If a trustee is interested, must a disinterested trustee be appointed?*	The key is whether the power has adverse income tax (18-A § 7-705(i)(3)), or estate or gift tax consequences (18-A § 7-705(i)(4) & (5)), or the trustee is also a beneficiary. (18-A § 7-705(i)(6))
13. *If a disinterested trustee is required, who selects him?*	No disinterested trustee is necessary. The interested trustees petition the court. (18-A § 7-705(j)) However, no provision for petition is available if the effect would be disallowance of the marital deduction. (18-A § 7-705(i)(5))
14. *Must notice be given before a conversion?*	Yes. (18-A § 7-705(a))
15. *To whom must notice be given?*	Beneficiaries who would are eligible either to receive current income or are entitled to principal upon termination of the trust immediately before giving of notice. All this assumes no exercise of a power. (18-A § 7-705(a)(2))
16. *By when must objection be made?*	60 days after mailing of notice. (18-A § 7-705(a)(4))
17. *Can objection be overridden?*	Yes, by petitioning a court. (18-A § 7-705(b))
18. *What if there are not sufficiently competent beneficiaries?*	No provision as to competency. However, there must be at least one beneficiary eligible to receive current income and one beneficiary who would be entitled to receive principal upon termination of the trust immediately before giving of notice. (18-A § 7-705(a)(2) & (3))
19. *Can a beneficiary petition a court to seek conversion if a trustee refuses?*	Yes. (18-A § 7-705(b)) Thus, the trustee is not obligated to convert upon request. See also 18-A § 7-705(g), which allows a beneficiary to petition to change rate, period for averaging of rate, to obtain a greater payout of income in order to preserve a tax benefit, or to reconvert.
20. *Is there a duty to convert?*	No. The statute provides that the trustee "may" convert. (18-A § 7-705(a); see also 18-A § 7-705(c))
21. *Can a court be petitioned to stop a conversion or reconversion?*	Yes, if income would be higher. This is the only express authorization. See #19.
22. *Is there a special statute of limitations?*	No provision.
23. *Is there a mandatory provision for payout of income if greater than the unitrust amount?*	No provision.
24. *If there is an excess payout, is it added to principal?*	No provision.
25. *What is the priority of source of payment of the unitrust amount?*	Net income, net realized short term capital gain, net realized long term capital gain, principal. (18-A § 7-705(f)(2))
26. *Is the priority mandatory?*	Yes (18-A § 7-705(f)(2)), unless specified otherwise in the trust instrument.

27. *How is the fair market value of the trust determined for unitrust purposes?*	No provision. Trustee is given discretion. See #9g, h above.
28. *Are certain items excluded?*	No provision. Trustee is given discretion. See #9i above.
29. *Is the trustee authorized to release his power?*	Yes (18-A § 7-705(k)), but not if it causes adverse tax consequences.
30. *Is there special provision for the marital deduction?*	No conversion allowed if it would result in denial of the marital deduction. (18-A § 7-705(i)(5))
31. *Is there special provision for generation-skipping grandfather preservation?*	No provision.
32. *If the power to convert is utilized must the power to adjust be released?*	Yes. (18-A § 7-705(a))
33. *Are particular factors presented that the trustee should consider?*	Yes, although the statute says the trustee "may" consider these in deciding whether to convert. (18-A § 7-705(c))
34. *What standard should a court use?*	Intent of settlor or testator and purposes of the trust. (18-A § 7-705(b))
35. *Must the trust be a locally administered trust?*	No provision.
36. *When does the power to convert not exist?*	Apart from #12 and #13 (marital deduction) above, (i) if the exercise of the power would change the amount of a fixed annuity or fixed fraction provided for in the governing instrument or (ii) adjustments would be from amounts set aside permanently for charitable purposes. 18-A § 7-705(i)(1)-(2))

Table 11.02
Total Return Trusts
Maryland

1.	*Is there a power to convert?*	Yes. (Est. & Trusts § 15-502.1(a))
2.	*Is the statute applicable to new unitrusts?*	No provision.
3.	*Is there a required rate of return?*	4% (Est. & Trusts § 15-502.1(c)(1)), unless a court order authorizes otherwise.
4.	*Can the required rate of return be varied?*	Yes, with court approval. (§ 15-502.1(e)(1)) See #3 above.
5.	*How can it be varied?*	See #3 above.
6.	*Alternatively, does the trustee have discretion within a range?*	No.
7.	*If so, what is the range?*	See #6 above.
8.	*Must court approval be obtained initially?*	No. The trustee can proceed upon a beneficiary's request and with notice to the beneficiaries identified in #15 below.
9.	*Does the trustee have discretion to:*	
a.	*Convert?*	No. The trustee must receive a written request from a beneficiary. (Est. & Trusts § 15-502.1(a)(1))
b.	*Reconvert?*	Apparently no, except upon a written request from beneficiary. (Est. & Trusts § 15-502.1(a)(1))
c.	*Determine the effective date?*	No provision.
d.	*Determine the frequency of payments?*	No provision.
e.	*Determine cash or in kind distribution?*	No provision.
f.	*Vary the rate?*	See #3 above.
g.	*Whether to value annually or less frequently?*	No provision.
h.	*What valuation date to use?*	No provision.
i.	*Whether to value trust property occupied or used by a beneficiary?*	Yes. (Est. & Trusts § 15-502.1(d)(3))
j.	*How to prorate in a short year any unitrust payments?*	No provision.
k.	*Whether to estimate the value of nonliquid assets?*	Required to do so; but there is discretion as to how frequently to value such assets. (Est. & Trusts § 15-502.1(d)(2))
l.	*The effect of contributions and distributions on valuation?*	Required to do so. (Est. & Trusts § 15-502.1(d)(1))
m.	*Other administrative matters?*	No provision.

10. *What standard of conduct is required of the trustee?*	If the trust is administered consistent with statute, then the trustee is deemed fair and impartial. (Est. & Trusts § 15-502.1(b))
11. *What is the remedy for a violation?*	There is no remedy other than to direct, deny, or revise the conversion or reconversion. This is apparently the case even if the trustee is guilty of bad faith. (Est. & Trusts § 15-502.3(g)(1)(i)) See also Est. & Trusts § 15-502.3(g)(1)(i), which provides action taken or not taken is binding if done in accordance with statute. Quaere: What if not done in accordance with statute? The trustee cannot be punished under Est. & Trusts § 15-502.3(4)(1), but what was done would presumably not be enforceable.
12. *If a trustee is interested, must a disinterested trustee be appointed?*	The key is whether the power has adverse income tax (Est. & Trusts § 15-502.1(f)(3)), or estate or gift tax consequences (Est. & Trusts § 15-502.1(f)(4)), or the trustee is also a beneficiary. (Est. & Trusts § 15-502.1(f)(6))
13. *If a disinterested trustee is required, who selects him?*	No disinterested trustee is necessary. The interested trustees petition the court if the interested trustees are prohibited due to #36 (iv)-(vi) below. (Est. & Trusts § 15-502.1(g)(2))
14. *Must notice be given before a conversion?*	Yes. (Est. & Trusts § 15-502.1(a)(4)(i))
15. *To whom must notice be given?*	To "qualified beneficiaries", that is, sui juris beneficiaries or guardian of minors or person acting on behalf of disabled person who is either (i) a distributee or permissible distributee of trust income or principal, as well as (ii) a distributee or permissible distributee of trust income or principal upon termination of an interest in (i) on the date of giving of notice or the termination of the trust on that date. (Est. & Trusts §§ 15-502.3(a)(4), 15-502.3(a)(1)) The qualified beneficiaries then all "consent." (Est. & Trusts § 15-502.1(a)(4)(i))
16. *By when must objection be made?*	No provision.
17. *Can objection be overridden?*	Yes, by petitioning a court. (Est. & Trusts § 15-502.3(b))
18. *What if there are not sufficiently competent beneficiaries?*	No provision.
19. *Can a beneficiary petition a court to seek conversion if a trustee refuses?*	Yes. (Est. & Trusts § 15-502.3(b)&(f)) Thus, the trustee is not obligated to convert upon request. The beneficiary can also petition as to reconversion. (Est. & Trusts § 15-502.3(b)(2))
20. *Is there a duty to convert?*	No. it is "discretionary." (Est. & Trusts § 15-502.3(b)(1))
21. *Can a court be petitioned to stop a conversion or reconversion?*	See #19 above.
22. *Is there a statute of limitations?*	No provision.
23. *Is there a mandatory provision for payout of income if greater than the unitrust amount?*	Yes, when "necessary to preserve a tax benefit" and authorized by court order. (Est. & Trusts § 15-502.1(e)(2))

24. *If there is an excess payout, is it added to principal?*	No provision.
25. *What is the priority of source of payment of the unitrust amount?*	Net income and then principal. (Est. & Trusts § 15-502.1(c)(4)) However, the trustee may then determine to account for the unitrust distribution, if net income is insufficient, by paying next from net realized short term gains, then net realized long term gains, and then principal. (Est. & Trusts § 15-502.1(c)(5))
26. *Is the priority mandatory?*	Yes (Est. & Trusts § 15-502.1(c)(4)), unless specified otherwise in the trust instrument.
27. *How is the fair market value of the trust determined for unitrust purposes?*	Averaged over three years unless court order otherwise. (Est. & Trusts § 15-502.1(d)(3))
28. *Are certain items excluded?*	No provision.
29. *Is the trustee authorized to release his power?*	Yes (Est. & Trusts § 15-502.1(h)(1)), if (i) it causes adverse tax consequences; (ii) if the trustee is uncertain whether #36 (iv)-(vi) below apply, (Est. & Trusts § 15-502.1(h)(1)(i)); or (iii) if the trustee determines possessing or exercising the power will or may deprive the trust of a tax benefit or impose a tax burden not described in #36 (iv)-(vi) below. (Est. & Trusts § 15-502.1(h)(1)(ii))
30. *Is there special provision for the marital deduction?*	No conversion allowed if it would result in denial of the marital deduction. (Est. & Trusts § 15-502.1(f)(1))
31. *Is there special provision for generation-skipping grandfather preservation?*	No provision. But see #23 above.
32. *If the power to convert is utilized must the power to adjust be released?*	No provision.
33. *Are particular factors presented that the trustee should consider?*	Yes. The trustee "may" consider whether conversion will enable the trustee to better carry out the intent of the person who created the trust and the purposes of the trust. (Est. & Trusts § 15-502.1(a)(3)) The trustee is *required* to consider the following factors: (1) nature, purpose, and expected duration of the trust; (2) the intent of the creator; (3) the identity and circumstances of the beneficiaries; (4) the needs for liquidity, regularity of income, and preservation and appreciation of capital; (5) the assets held in trust, including their nature, use by a beneficiary, and whether acquired by the trustee or received by the beneficiary; (6) the trustee's power to invade principal or accumulate income and the extent to which the trustee has done so in the past; (7) the actual and anticipated effect of economic conditions on principal and income and the effects of inflation and deflation; and (8) the anticipated tax consequences of a unitrust conversion. (Est. & Trusts § 15-502.1(b))
34. *What standard should a court use?*	No provision.
35. *Must the trust be a locally administered trust?*	No provision.

36. *When does the power to convert not exist?*	(i) If it would result in the disallowance of the marital deduction, see #30 above; (ii) would change a fixed annuity or fixed fraction payable to a beneficiary (iii) would be from amounts permanently set aside for charitable purposes and for which federal estate or gift tax deduction has been taken, unless both income and principal are so set aside; (iv) possessing or exercising the power would cause an individual to be treated as owner of part or all of trust for income tax purposes; (v) would cause the trust assets to be subject to estate or gift tax [no mention of "federal"]; or (vi) the trustee is a beneficiary. (Est. & Trusts § 15-502.1(f)(1)-(6)) If the instrument prohibits conversion, it does not affect this section "[u]nless it is clear from the terms of the trust that the terms are intended to deny the trustee the power conferred" by Est. & Trusts § 15-502.1(a) to convert. But see #23 above.

Table 11.02
Total Return Trusts
Missouri

1. *Is there a power to convert?*	Yes. (§ 469.411(5.)(1)-(2))
2. *Is the statute applicable to new unitrusts?*	Yes, if created after Aug. 28, 2001, and if the terms of the trust clearly manifest an intent that the section apply. (§ 469.411(5.)(1))
3. *Is there a required rate of return?*	No. For the first three accounting periods, it is 3% unless a higher percentage between 3%-5% is specified by the trustee in the trustee's notice of election. (§ 469.411(5.)(2), (§ 469.411(1.)(1)) The same is true for subsequent accounting periods, but it is based on a percentage return on the average of fair market values on the first business day of the current valuation period and *each* prior valuation period. (§ 469.411(1.)(2)) This means the two prior annual periods. (§ 469.411(2.)(2))
4. *Can the required rate of return be varied?*	See #3 above.
5. *How can it be varied?*	See #3 above.
6. *Alternatively, does the trustee have discretion within a range?*	See #3 above.
7. *If so, what is the range?*	See #3 above.
8. *Must court approval be obtained initially?*	No. (§ 469.411(5.)(2))
9. *Does the trustee have discretion to:*	
a. *Convert?*	Yes, with respect to any irrevocable trust. (§ 469.411(5.)(2))
b. *Reconvert?*	No provision.
c. *Determine the effective date?*	No provision.
d. *Determine the frequency of payments?*	No provision.
e. *Determine cash or in kind distribution?*	No provision.
f. *Vary the rate?*	See #3 above.
g. *Whether to value annually or less frequently?*	No less than annually for illiquid assets. (§ 469.411(4.))
h. *What valuation date to use?*	No provision.
i. *Whether to value trust property occupied or used by a beneficiary?*	Residential or tangible personal property is to be excluded if, on the first business day of the current valuation year, one or more current beneficiaries have or have had the right to occupy, possess, or control the property. In such cases, these rights are deemed to be the unitrust amount. (§ 469.411(3.)(1)) A specifically given asset and the return on it is also excluded. *(Id.)*

j. How to prorate in a short year any unitrust payments?	No discretion; must prorate on a daily basis. (§ 469.411(1.)(5))
k. Whether to estimate the value of nonliquid assets?	See #9i above. No other provision.
l. The effect of contributions and distributions on valuation?	No discretion; fair market value must be adjusted to reflect them. (§ 469.411(1.)(3)-(4))
m. Other administrative matters?	No provision.
10. What standard of conduct is required of the trustee?	The only standard set forth relates to nonmarketable assets. See #22 below.
11. What is the remedy for a violation?	No provision.
12. If a trustee is interested, must a disinterested trustee be appointed?	No, but the trustee cannot convert. (§ 469.411(5.)(2)) An interested trustee is (i) one who would be treated as owner of all or part of the trust for income tax purposes, (ii) the trustee possessing or exercising the power would result in estate inclusion for estate tax purposes for the person who has the power to appoint or remove a trustee, (iii) the trustee is a beneficiary, or (iv) the trustee is not a beneficiary but the adjustment would benefit the trustee. (§ 469.405(3.))
13. If a disinterested trustee is required, who selects him?	No provision.
14. Must notice be given before a conversion?	Yes. (§ 469.411(5.)(2))
15. To whom must notice be given?	(i) The grantor, if living; (ii) all qualified beneficiaries or permissible distributes (§ 456.1-103(14., 19.)) of income or principal; (iii) all persons entitled to principal if the permissible distributees' interests terminate on the date the beneficiaries qualify. (§ 469.411(5.)(2))
16. By when must objection be made?	No provision. However, the trustee cannot convert until 60 days of delivering notice. (§ 469.411(5.)(3))
17. Can objection be overridden?	No provision.
18. What if there are not sufficiently competent beneficiaries?	No provision.
19. Can a beneficiary petition a court to seek conversion if a trustee refuses?	No provision.
20. Is there a duty to convert?	No. (§ 469.411(5.)(2))
21. Can a court be petitioned to stop a conversion or reconversion?	No provision.
22. Is there a special statute of limitations?	Three years on the conversion election. (§ 469.411(5.)(3)). However, two years from the time of informing qualified beneficiaries as to valuation. However, there is no such limit if the trustee engaged in fraud as to the valuation report. (§ 469.409(2.)(4))

23. *Is there a mandatory provision for payout of income if greater than the unitrust amount?*	No provision.
24. *If there is an excess payout, is it added to principal?*	No provision.
25. *What is the priority of source of payment of the unitrust amount?*	No provision.
26. *Is the priority mandatory?*	No provision.
27. *How is the fair market value of the trust determined for unitrust purposes?*	The only provision relates to real property and other assets for which there is no active market. (§ 469.411(4.))
28. *Are certain items excluded?*	See #9i above.
29. *Is the trustee authorized to release his power?*	No provision.
30. *Is there special provision for the marital deduction?*	No.
31. *Is there special provision for generation-skipping grandfather preservation?*	No.
32. *If the power to convert is utilized must the power to adjust be released?*	No provision.
33. *Are particular factors presented that the trustee should consider?*	No provision.
34. *What standard should a court use?*	No provision.
35. *Must the trust be a locally administered trust?*	No provision.
36. *When does the power to convert not exist?*	If the trust instrument disallows the conversion. (§ 469.411(5.)) Uniquely, the power may be available with regard to institutional endowment funds. (§ 469.411(5.)(4))

Table 11.02
Total Return Trusts
Nebraska

1.	*Is there a power to convert?*	Yes. (§ 30-3119.01(1))
2.	*Is the statute applicable to new unitrusts?*	No explicit provision.
3.	*Is there a required rate of return?*	Yes. 4%, unless a different percentage is allowed by agreement with the beneficiaries or by court order. (§ 30-3119.01(4)(a)(iii)) In the case of an agreement, the range must be within 3%-5%. (§ 30-3119.01(2)) The same for a court order. (§ 30-3119.01()(a)(1))
4.	*Can the required rate of return be varied?*	No. See #3 above.
5.	*How can it be varied?*	See #3 above.
6.	*Alternatively, does the trustee have discretion within a range?*	See #3 above.
7.	*If so, what is the range?*	See #3 above.
8.	*Must court approval be obtained initially?*	No.
9.	*Does the trustee have discretion to:*	
	a. *Convert?*	Yes, if certain beneficiaries do not object following notice. (§ 30-3119.01(1))
	b. *Reconvert?*	No provision.
	c. *Determine the effective date?*	Yes. (§ 30-3119.01(5)(a))
	d. *Determine the frequency of payments?*	No provision.
	e. *Determine cash or in kind distribution?*	Yes. (§ 30-3119.01(5)(c))
	f. *Vary the rate?*	See #3 above.
	g. *Whether to value annually or less frequently?*	Yes. (§ 30-3119.01(5)(e))
	h. *What valuation date to use?*	Yes, including how many dates. (§ 30-3119.01(5)(f))
	i. *Whether to value trust property occupied or used by a beneficiary?*	The trustee is required not to interfere with use in accordance with the governing instrument whether or not the property is treated as an excluded asset. (§ 30-3119.01(5)(g)(iii)(B))
	j. *How to prorate in a short year any unitrust payments?*	Yes. (§ 30-3119.01(5)(b))
	k. *Whether to estimate the value of nonliquid assets?*	Yes as to how to value and how frequently. Also, whether to exclude the value of such asset. Generally, the trustee is required to exclude unless there are compelling reasons not to do so. (§ 30-3119.01(5)(g)(iii))

l. The effect of contributions and distributions on valuation?	Yes. (§ 30-3119.01(5)(d))
m. Other administrative matters?	Yes. (§ 30-3119.01(5)(h))
10. What standard of conduct is required of the trustee?	A trustee meets the requisite standard if the trustee "reasonably and in good faith" takes action or omits to take action. (§ 30-3119.01(11)(a)) A discretionary act or omission is presumed reasonable and in good faith unless determined by a court to be an abuse of discretion. *(Id.)*
11. What is the remedy for a violation?	The exclusive remedy is a court order as to conversion, reconversion, change in rate, or any administrative procedure "necessary and helpful." (§ 30-3119.01(11)(b))
12. If a trustee is interested, must a disinterested trustee be appointed?	The key is whether the power has adverse income tax or estate tax consequences, or the trustee is also a beneficiary and the exercise or nonexercise of the power would enhance or diminish the trustee's beneficial interest. (§ 30-3119.01(9))
13. If a disinterested trustee is required, who selects him?	No disinterested trustee is necessary. The interested trustees petition the court. (§ 30-3119.01(9)(a))
14. Must notice be given before a conversion?	Yes. (§ 30-3119.01(1)(b))
15. To whom must notice be given?	Legally competent beneficiaries who would are either entitled to (i) current income or (ii) principal upon termination of trust immediately before giving of notice. All this assumes no exercise of a power. (§ 30-3119.01(1)(c))
16. By when must objection be made?	60 days after sending of notice. (§ 30-3119.01(1)(d))
17. Can objection be overridden?	Yes, by petitioning a court. The trustee can also petition to reconvert or change the rate. (§ 30-3119.01(3)(c))
18. What if there are not sufficiently competent beneficiaries?	A court must be petitioned for approval. (§ 30-3119.01(3)(a)(ii)) The statute requires at least two legally competent beneficiaries to avert the need for court approval, one from each of the two categories set forth in #15 above. (§ 30-3119.01(3)(a)(ii)&(iii))
19. Can a beneficiary petition a court to seek conversion if a trustee refuses?	Yes, but the beneficiary must wait first 6 months to determine if the trustee has acted on the beneficiary's request. The beneficiary is allowed to petition to convert or change the rate. (§ 30-3119.01(3)(b))
20. Is there a duty to convert?	No. (§§ 30-3119.01(12), 30-3119.01(1)(a))
21. Can a court be petitioned to stop a conversion or reconversion?	Yes. The trustee can do so. (§ 30-3119.01(3)(d)(i))
22. Is there a special statute of limitations?	Within 6 months after receiving a statement concerning the matter. (§ 30-3119.01(11)(c))
23. Is there a mandatory provision for payout of income if greater than the unitrust amount?	No, but the court can be petitioned so as to preserve a tax benefit. (§ 30-3119.01(7)(a)(iv))

24. *If there is an excess payout, is it added to principal?*	It is recovered by repayment or withholding future distributions from the beneficiary. Interest accrues beginning in the year following the year in which the overpayment occurs. (§ 30-3119.01(4)(a)(iv)(A)-(B)) Recouped amounts are presumably added to the principal, although there is no explicit provision.
25. *What is the priority of source of payment of the unitrust amount?*	Net income, other ordinary income determined for federal income tax purposes, net realized short term capital gain, net realized long term capital gain, principal. (§ 30-3119.01(6)(b))
26. *Is the priority mandatory?*	Yes, unless specified otherwise in the trust instrument. (*Id.*)
27. *How is the fair market value of the trust determined for unitrust purposes?*	Net fair market value averaged over the lesser 3 preceding years or the period during which the trust has been in existence. (§ 30-3119.01(4)(B)(i))
28. *Are certain items excluded?*	See #9i above.
29. *Is the trustee authorized to release his power?*	Yes. (§ 30-3119.01(10)
30. *Is there special provision for the marital deduction?*	Yes, during the spouse's life no less than trust net income must be distributed. (§ 30-3119.01(8)(a)(i))
31. *Is there special provision for generation-skipping grandfather preservation?*	Yes. All net income must be distributed if a trust was exempt from GST tax on Sept. 9, 2000. (§ 30-3119.01(8)(a)(ii)
32. *If the power to convert is utilized must the power to adjust be released?*	Yes. (§ 30-3119.01(3)(g))
33. *Are particular factors presented that the trustee should consider?*	Yes. The trustee must determine that the conversion will enable the trustee to better carry out the intent of the settlor and the purposes of the trust. (§ 30-3119.01(1)(a))
34. *What standard should a court use?*	Whether the proposed relief will enable the trustee to better carry out the purposes of the trust. (§ 30-3119.01(3)(e))
35. *Must the trust be a locally administered trust?*	No, if the governing instrument provides for Nebraska law as to meaning and effect of its terms. (§ 30-3119.01(13)(b))
36. *When does the power to convert not exist?*	When the trust is a charitable trust; conversion is clearly contrary to the manifestation of settlor's intent as expressed in the trust instrument or as established by other admissible evidence; or the trust instrument already provides for a total return trust and its provisions conflict with the statute. In this last case, deference is given to the instrument. (§ 30-3119.01(13)(b)) However, see #3 above.

Table 11.02
Total Return Trusts
New Hampshire

1. *Is there a power to convert?*	Yes. (§ 564-A:3-C(I))
2. *Is the statute applicable to new unitrusts?*	No explicit provision.
3. *Is there a required rate of return?*	Yes, 5% over the lesser of the preceding three years or the shorter existence of the trust. (§ 564-A:3-C(IV)(C))
4. *Can the required rate of return be varied?*	No. See #3 above.
5. *How can it be varied?*	See #4 above.
6. *Alternatively, does the trustee have discretion within a range?*	See ##3 & 4 above.
7. *If so, what is the range?*	See #6 above.
8. *Must court approval be obtained initially?*	No.
9. *Does the trustee have discretion to:*	
a. *Convert?*	Yes, if certain beneficiaries do not object following notice. (§ 564-A-3-C(I)(d))
b. *Reconvert?*	No. Court approval is needed. (§ 564-A:3-C(VII)(d))
c. *Determine the effective date?*	Yes. (§ 564-A:3-C(V)(a))
d. *Determine the frequency of payments?*	Yes. (§ 564-A:3-C(V)(c))
e. *Determine cash or in kind distribution?*	No provision.
f. *Vary the rate?*	See #4 above.
g. *Whether to value annually or less frequently?*	Yes, but only with respect to nonliquid assets. (§ 564-A:3-C(V)(e))
h. *What valuation date to use?*	No provision.
i. *Whether to value trust property occupied or used by a beneficiary?*	Yes. (§ 564-A:3-C(V)(f))
j. *How to prorate in a short year any unitrust payments?*	Yes. (§ 564-A:3-C(V)(b))
k. *Whether to estimate the value of nonliquid assets?*	Yes. (§ 564-A:3-C(V)(e))
l. *The effect of contributions and distributions on valuation?*	Yes. (§ 564-A:3-C(V)(d))
m. *Other administrative matters?*	Yes. (§ 564-A:3-C(V)(g))

10. *What standard of conduct is required of the trustee?*	No provision.
11. *What is the remedy for a violation?*	No provision.
12. *If a trustee is interested, must a disinterested trustee be appointed?*	The key is whether the power has adverse income tax (§ 564-A:3-C(IX)(d)), or estate or gift tax consequences (§ 564-A:3-C(IX)(d)), or the trustee is also a beneficiary. (§ 564-A:3-C(IX)(f))
13. *If a disinterested trustee is required, who selects him?*	No disinterested trustee is necessary. The interested trustees petition the court. (§ 564-A:3-C(X)(b)) However, no provision for petition is made if the effect would be disallowance of the marital deduction.
14. *Must notice be given before a conversion?*	Yes. (§ 564-A:3-C(I)(b))
15. *To whom must notice be given?*	Sui juris beneficiaries who are either (i) currently eligible to receive (§ 564-A:3-C(I)(b)(1)), as well as (ii) beneficiaries entitled to principal upon termination of trust immediately before giving of notice, assuming no exercise of a power. (§ 564-A:3-C(I)(b)(2))
16. *By when must objection be made?*	60 days after mailing of notice. (§ 564-A:3-C(I)(d))
17. *Can objection be overridden?*	Yes, by petitioning a court. (§ 564-A:3-C(II)(a))
18. *What if there are not sufficiently competent beneficiaries?*	A court must be petitioned for approval. (§ 564-A:3-C(II)(a)(2) & (3)) The statute requires at least one beneficiary from each category to avert the need for court approval as described in #15 above. (§ 564-A:3-C(ii)(a)(2) & (3))
19. *Can a beneficiary petition a court to seek conversion if a trustee refuses?*	Yes. (§ 564-A:3-C(II)(b)) Thus, the trustee is not obligated to convert upon request. See also § 564-A:3-C(VII), which allows a beneficiary to petition to change rate, period for averaging of rate, to obtain a greater payout of income in order to preserve a tax benefit, or to reconvert.
20. *Is there a duty to convert?*	No. The statute provides that the trustee "may" convert. (§ 564-A:3-C(III))
21. *Can a court be petitioned to stop a conversion or reconversion?*	Yes, if income would be higher. This is the only express authorization. See #19.
22. *Is there a special statute of limitations?*	No provision.
23. *Is there a mandatory provision for payout of income if greater than the unitrust amount?*	No provision.
24. *If there is an excess payout, is it added to principal?*	No provision.
25. *What is the priority of source of payment of the unitrust amount?*	Net income, net realized short term capital gain, net realized long term capital gain, principal. (§ 564-A:3-C(VI)(b))
26. *Is the priority mandatory?*	Yes (§ 564-A:3-C(VI)(b)), unless specified otherwise in the trust instrument.

27. How is the fair market value of the trust determined for unitrust purposes?	No provision. Trust is given discretion. See #9g, h above.
28. Are certain items excluded?	No provision. Trustee is given discretion. See #9i above.
29. Is the trustee authorized to release his power?	Yes (§ 564-A:3-C(XI)), but not if it causes adverse tax consequences
30. Is there special provision for the marital deduction?	No conversion allowed if it would result in denial of the marital deduction. (§ 564-A:3-C(XI))
31. Is there special provision for generation-skipping grandfather preservation?	No provision.
32. If the power to convert is utilized must the power to adjust be released?	Yes. (§ 564-A:3-C(I))
33. Are particular factors presented that the trustee should consider?	Yes, although the statute says the trustee "may" consider these in deciding whether to convert. (§ 564-A:3-C(III))
34. What standard should a court use?	Intent of settlor or testator and purposes of the trust. (§ 564-A:3-C(II)(c))
35. Must the trust be a locally administered trust?	No provision.
36. When does the power to convert not exist?	(i) If it would result in the disallowance of the marital deduction, see #30 above; (ii) would change a fixed annuity or fixed fraction payable to a beneficiary (iii) would be from amounts permanently set aside for charitable purposes and for which federal estate or gift tax deduction has been taken, unless both income and principal are so set aside. (§ 564-A:3-C(IX))

Table 11.02
Total Return Trusts
New Jersey

1. *Is there a power to convert?*	There is no comprehensive statute. A unitrust amount may be paid if the statute granting a power to adjust otherwise applies and the trustee cannot otherwise comply with the requirement to act impartially. (§ 3B:19B-4(a))
2. *Is the statute applicable to new unitrusts?*	No explicit provision.
3. *Is there a required rate of return?*	No. There are safe harbors. A distribution can be increased in a year to 4% or decreased to 6% of fair market value determined on the first business day of the accounting period. If the trustee observes these percentages, the trustee shall be presumed to be fair and reasonable with respect to all of the beneficiaries (*Id.*)
4. *Can the required rate of return be varied?*	From year to year and in consideration of the permissible floor and cap. (*Id.*)
5. *How can it be varied?*	By the trustee. (*Id.*)
6. *Alternatively, does the trustee have discretion within a range?*	See #3 & #4 above.
7. *If so, what is the range?*	See #3 above.
8. *Must court approval be obtained initially?*	No. (*Id.*)
9. *Does the trustee have discretion to:*	
a. *Convert?*	Yes. See #1 above.
b. *Reconvert?*	No provision.
c. *Determine the effective date?*	No provision.
d. *Determine the frequency of payments?*	No provision.
e. *Determine cash or in kind distribution?*	No provision.
f. *Vary the rate?*	See #3 above.
g. *Whether to value annually or less frequently?*	Valuation must be done annually. See #3 above.
h. *What valuation date to use?*	No provision.
i. *Whether to value trust property occupied or used by a beneficiary?*	No provision.
j. *How to prorate in a short year any unitrust payments?*	No provision.

k. Whether to estimate the value of nonliquid assets?	No provision.
l. The effect of contributions and distributions on valuation?	No provision.
m. Other administrative matters?	No provision.
10. What standard of conduct is required of the trustee?	Impartiality and what is fair and reasonable to all beneficiaries. (§§ 3B:19B-4(a), 3B:19B-3(b))
11. What is the remedy for a violation?	No provision.
12. If a trustee is interested, must a disinterested trustee be appointed?	No provision. If there is a co-trustee, that co-trustee may act, unless the governing instrument provides otherwise. If there is no such co-trustee, then the interested trustee cannot act. (§ 3B:19B-4(d))
13. If a disinterested trustee is required, who selects him?	No provision.
14. Must notice be given before a conversion?	No provision.
15. To whom must notice be given?	No provision.
16. By when must objection be made?	No provision.
17. Can objection be overridden?	No provision.
18. What if there are not sufficiently competent beneficiaries?	No provision.
19. Can a beneficiary petition a court to seek conversion if a trustee refuses?	No provision.
20. Is there a duty to convert?	No. The statute provides that the trustee "may adjust." (§ 3B:19B-4(a))
21. Can a court be petitioned to stop a conversion or reconversion?	No provision.
22. Is there a special statute of limitations?	No provision.
23. Is there a mandatory provision for payout of income if greater than the unitrust amount?	No provision.
24. If there is an excess payout, is it added to principal?	No provision.
25. What is the priority of source of payment of the unitrust amount?	No provision.
26. Is the priority mandatory?	No provision.
27. How is the fair market value of the trust determined for unitrust purposes?	No provision.
28. Are certain items excluded?	No provision.

29. Is the trustee authorized to release his power?	Yes (§ 3B:19B-4(e)), if (i) the trustee is uncertain whether possessing or exercising the power causes adverse tax consequences set forth in #36 (iv)-(vi) below; or (ii) if the trustee determines possessing or exercising the power will or may deprive the trust of a tax benefit or impose a tax burden not described in #36 (iv)-(vi) below. (*Id.*)
30. Is there special provision for the marital deduction?	No provision.
31. Is there special provision for generation-skipping grandfather preservation?	No. provision.
32. If the power to convert is utilized must the power to adjust be released?	No, since it is a version of the power to adjust.
33. Are particular factors presented that the trustee should consider?	Yes. The trustee is *required* to consider the following factors in deciding whether the power of adjustment should be invoked: (1) nature, purpose, and expected duration of the trust; (2) the intent of the settlor; (3) the identity and circumstances of the beneficiaries; (4) the needs for liquidity, regularity of income, and preservation and appreciation of capital; (5) the assets held in trust, including their nature, especially if closely held investments or real property, their use by a beneficiary, and whether acquired by the trustee or received by the beneficiary; (6) the net amount allocated to income under other statutory provisions and the increase or decrease in the value of principal assets; (7) the trustee's power to invade principal or accumulate income and the extent to which the trustee has done so in the past; (8) the actual and anticipated effect of economic conditions on principal and income and the effects of inflation and deflation; and (9) the shifting economic interests or tax benefits between income and remainder beneficiaries as a result of elections and decisions re tax matters; and (10) the anticipated tax consequences of an adjustment. (§ 3B:19B-4(b))
34. What standard should a court use?	No provision.
35. Must the trust be a locally administered trust?	No provision.
36. When does the power to convert not exist?	(i) If the income interest is diminished with respect to a trust requiring income to be paid at least annually to the surviving spouse and the estate or gift tax marital deduction would be allowed, but only if the trustee did not have the power; (ii) if the exercise of the power would change the amount of a fixed annuity or fixed fraction provided for in the governing instrument; (iii) adjustments would be from amounts set aside permanently for charitable purposes, unless both income and principal are set aside; (iv) a trust income interest qualifying for the annual exclusion would have its actuarial value diminished as a result; (v) the trustee is a beneficiary; (vi) although not a beneficiary, the trustee will benefit directly or indirectly from the adjustment; (vii) as a result of possessing or exercising the power to adjust an individual is treated as owner for income tax purposes and would not be if the trustee did not have the power; or (viii) as a result of possessing or exercising the power of adjustment this

causes all or part of the estate assets to be included for estate tax purposes in the estate of a person who has the power to remove or appoint a trustee and the assets would not be so included if the trustee did not possess the power. (§ 3B:19B-4(c)) With respect to (v)-(viii), a co-trustee can act, assuming there is one and the governing instrument does not prohibit this. Generally, terms of a trust that prohibit adjustments between principal and income do not affect the application of the statute unless it is clear form the terms of the trust that the terms were intended to deny the trustee the power of adjustment conferred. (§ 3B:19B-4(f))

Table 11.02
Total Return Trusts
New Mexico

1. *Is there a power to convert?*	Yes. (§ 46-3A-105(A))
2. *Is the statute applicable to new unitrusts?*	No explicit provision.
3. *Is there a required rate of return?*	Yes. 4%, unless a different percentage is allowed by agreement with the beneficiaries or by court order. (§ 46-3A-109(D)) No cap is imposed.
4. *Can the required rate of return be varied?*	Yes. See #3 above.
5. *How can it be varied?*	See #3 above.
6. *Alternatively, does the trustee have discretion within a range?*	See #3 above.
7. *If so, what is the range?*	See #3 above.
8. *Must court approval be obtained initially?*	No.
9. *Does the trustee have discretion to:*	
a. *Convert?*	Yes, if certain beneficiaries do not object following notice. (§ 46-3A-105(A)(4)
b. *Reconvert?*	No provision.
c. *Determine the effective date?*	Yes. (§ 46-3A-107(A)(1))
d. *Determine the frequency of payments?*	No provision.
e. *Determine cash or in kind distribution?*	Yes. (§ 46-3A-107(A)(3))
f. *Vary the rate?*	See #3 above.
g. *Whether to value annually or less frequently?*	Yes. (§ 46-3A-107(5)). However, valuation must occur at least annually.
h. *What valuation date to use?*	Yes, including how many dates. (§ 46-3A-107(6))
i. *Whether to value trust property occupied or used by a beneficiary?*	The trustee is required not to interfere with use in accordance with the governing instrument whether or not the property is treated as an excluded asset. (§ 46-3A-107(B)(2))
j. *How to prorate in a short year any unitrust payments?*	Yes. (§ 46-3A-107(A)(2)
k. *Whether to estimate the value of nonliquid assets?*	Yes as to how to value and how frequently. Also, whether to exclude the value of such asset. Generally, the trustee is required to exclude unless there are compelling reasons not to do so. (§§ 46-3A-107(A)(7), 46-3A-107(B)(1))
l. *The effect of contributions and distributions on valuation?*	Yes. (§ 46-3A-107(A)(4))

m. Other administrative matters?	No provision.
10. What standard of conduct is required of the trustee?	A trustee meets the requisite standard if the trustee "reasonably and in good faith" takes action or omits to take action. (§ 46-3A-112(A))
11. What is the remedy for a violation?	There is some conflict in the law. One provision allows for any remedy provided or available at law as well as a court order as to conversion, reconversion, change in rate, or any administrative procedure "necessary and helpful." (§ 46-3A-112(B)) This would appear not to limit the exposure of the trustee. On the other hand, at least with most conversion and related matters, which are specifically addressed in § 46-3A-105, the trustee is not liable for actions or omissions if the trustee has not acted in bad faith. (§ 46-3A-105(G))
12. If a trustee is interested, must a disinterested trustee be appointed?	The key is whether the power has adverse federal income tax or federal estate tax consequences, or the trustee is also a beneficiary and the exercise or nonexercise of the power would enhance or diminish the trustee's beneficial interest. (§ 46-3A-110)
13. If a disinterested trustee is required, who selects him?	No disinterested trustee is necessary. The interested trustees petition the court. (§ 46-3A-110(A))
14. Must notice be given before a conversion?	Yes. (§ 46-3A-105(A)(2))
15. To whom must notice be given?	Legally competent beneficiaries who are either (i) distributees or permissible distributees of trust income or principal, (ii) would be distributees or permissible distributees of trust income or principal if the interests of those presently entitled terminated on the date qualification of status as a qualified beneficiary is determined, or (ii) would be entitled to trust income or principal upon termination of trust immediately before giving of notice. All this assumes no exercise of a power. (§§ 46-3A-105(A)(3), 46-3A-102(K))
16. By when must objection be made?	60 days after "providing" of notice. (§§ 46-3A-105(A)(2) & 46-3A-105(A)(4))
17. Can objection be overridden?	Yes, by petitioning a court. The trustee can also petition to reconvert or change the rate. (§ 46-3A-105(C)(1))
18. What if there are not sufficiently competent beneficiaries?	A court must be petitioned for approval. (§ 46-3A-105(C)(2)-(3)) The statute requires at least two legally competent beneficiaries to avert the need for court approval, one from each of the two categories set forth in #15 above. (*Id.*)
19. Can a beneficiary petition a court to seek conversion if a trustee refuses?	Yes, but the beneficiary must wait first 6 months to determine if the trustee has acted on the beneficiary's request. The beneficiary is allowed to petition to convert or change the rate. (§ 46-3A-105(D))
20. Is there a duty to convert?	No. The statute provides that the trustee "may" convert. (§ 46-3A-105(A))

21. *Can a court be petitioned to stop a conversion or reconversion?*	Yes, the trustee can. (§ 46-3A-105(F)(1)) With respect to others there is no clear provision. The language is in terms of seeking a conversion, reconversion, or distribution percentage change. (§ 46-3A-105(E))
22. *Is there a special statute of limitations?*	An action must be brought within 6 months after receiving a statement fully disclosing the matter. (§ 46-3A-112(C))
23. *Is there a mandatory provision for payout of income if greater than the unitrust amount?*	No provision.
24. *If there is an excess payout, is it added to principal?*	It is recovered by repayment or withholding future distributions from the beneficiary. Interest accrues beginning in the year following the year in which the overpayment occurs. (§ 46-3A-106(E)) Recouped amounts are presumably added to the principal, although there is no explicit provision.
25. *What is the priority of source of payment of the unitrust amount?*	Net income, other ordinary income determined for federal income tax purposes, net realized short term capital gain, net realized long term capital gain, principal for which there is a readily available market, other principal. (§ 46-3A-108(B))
26. *Is the priority mandatory?*	Yes, unless specified otherwise in the trust instrument. (*Id.*)
27. *How is the fair market value of the trust determined for unitrust purposes?*	Net fair market value averaged over the lesser 3 preceding years or the period during which the trust has been in existence. (§ 46-3A-106(F)(3))
28. *Are certain items excluded?*	See #9i above.
29. *Is the trustee authorized to release his power?*	Yes, if the trustee reasonably believes that it is in the best interests of the trust and the beneficiaries. (§ 46-3A-111) The provision overlooks a possible conflict among beneficiaries.
30. *Is there special provision for the marital deduction?*	No provision.
31. *Is there special provision for generation-skipping grandfather preservation?*	Yes. All net income must be distributed if a trust was exempt from GST tax on July 1, 2005. (§ 46-3A-109(A))
32. *If the power to convert is utilized must the power to adjust be released?*	Yes, by implication. (§ 46-3A-105(J))
33. *Are particular factors presented that the trustee should consider?*	Yes. The trustee must determine that the conversion will enable the trustee to better carry out the intent of the settlor and the purposes of the trust. (§ 46-3A-104(A)(1))
34. *What standard should a court use?*	Whether the proposed relief will enable the trustee to better carry out the purposes of the trust. (§ 46-3A-105(H))
35. *Must the trust be a locally administered trust?*	No, if the governing instrument provides for Nebraska law as to meaning and effect of its terms. (§ 46-3A-113(B))

36. *When does the power to convert not exist?*	When (i) certain charitable trusts are involved, (ii) the governing instrument prohibits it by reference to one of the provisions of the statutes pertaining to total return trusts, or (iii) the trust was in existence on July 1, 2005 and the governing instrument incorporates provisions that operate as a total return trust. In this last case, the statute can be relied upon to the extent its provisions are not in conflict with the governing instrument. (§ 46-3A-113(B)(1)-(3)) Furthermore, the power to convert will not be allowed to affect a provision in the governing instrument that authorizes (i) a distribution of a fixed annuity or fixed fraction payable to a beneficiary; (ii) amounts permanently set aside for charitable purposes, unless both income and principal are so set aside; or (iii) a power to withdraw principal. (§ 46-3A-109(B))

Table 11.02
Total Return Trusts
New York

1. *Is there a power to convert?*	Yes (Est. Powers & Trusts § 11-2.4(a)). For trusts in existence prior to Jan. 1, 2002, the conversion must occur prior to 2006. As for trusts created after 2001, the conversion must occur by the end of the last day of the second full year of the trust after assets first become subject to the trust. (Est. Powers & Trusts § 11-2.4(e)(1)(B)(I)&(II)) No such timing restrictions apply if the trust instrument expressly provides that § 11-2.4 applies. (Est. Powers & Trusts § 11-2.4(e)(1)(A))
2. *Is the statute applicable to new unitrusts?*	No provision, except see #1 as to the trust instrument.
3. *Is there a required rate of return?*	Yes. For the first three accounting periods, it is 4%. (Est. Powers & Trusts § 11-2.4(b)(1)) The same is true for subsequent accounting periods, but it is based on an average of fair market value on the first business day of the current valuation period and *each* prior valuation period. (Est. Powers & Trusts § 11-2.4(b)(2)) This means the two prior annual periods. (Est. Powers & Trusts § 11-2.4(c)(3))
4. *Can the required rate of return be varied?*	See #3 above.
5. *How can it be varied?*	See #3 above.
6. *Alternatively, does the trustee have discretion within a range?*	See #3 above.
7. *If so, what is the range?*	See #3 above.
8. *Must court approval be obtained initially?*	No. (Est. Powers & Trusts § 11-2.4(e)(1)-(2))
9. *Does the trustee have discretion to:*	
a. *Convert?*	Yes. (Est. Powers & Trusts § 11-2.4(a)) The trustee may exercise discretion or seek beneficiary approval. The trust instrument may also provide for conversion. (Est. Powers & Trusts § 11-2.4(c)(1)(A))
b. *Reconvert?*	No provision.
c. *Determine the effective date?*	Yes. (Est. Powers & Trusts § 11-2.4(d)(1)) If no date specified, then the date assets first become subject to the trust. *(Id.)* Thus, the conversion can have retroactive effect.
d. *Determine the frequency of payments?*	No provision.
e. *Determine cash or in kind distribution?*	No provision.
f. *Vary the rate?*	See #3 above.
g. *Whether to value annually or less frequently?*	No provision.

h.	*What valuation date to use?*	No provision.
i.	*Whether to value trust property occupied or used by a beneficiary?*	Residential or tangible personal property is to be excluded if, on the first business day of the current valuation year, one or more current beneficiaries have or have had the right to occupy, possess, or control the property. In such cases, these rights are deemed to the unitrust amount. (Est. Powers & Trusts § 11-2.4(c)(6)(A)) A specifically given asset and any return on it is also excluded, as is any asset held in a testator's estate. (Est. Powers & Trusts § 11-2.4(c)(6)(B))
j.	*How to prorate in a short year any unitrust payments?*	No discretion; must prorate on a daily basis. (Est. Powers & Trusts § 11-2.4(b)(5))
k.	*Whether to estimate the value of nonliquid assets?*	No provision.
l.	*The effect of contributions and distributions on valuation?*	No discretion; fair market value must be adjusted to reflect them. (Est. Powers & Trusts § 11-2.4(b)(3))
m.	*Other administrative matters?*	No provision.
10.	*What standard of conduct is required of the trustee?*	No provision.
11.	*What is the remedy for a violation?*	No provision.
12.	*If a trustee is interested, must a disinterested trustee be appointed?*	No provision.
13.	*If a disinterested trustee is required, who selects him?*	No provision.
14.	*Must notice be given before a conversion?*	Yes. (Est. Powers & Trusts § 11-2.4(e)(1)(B)(III))
15.	*To whom must notice be given?*	Any person interested in the trust, that is, any person requiring notice for settlement of the account of a trustee. See Surr. Ct. Proc. Act § 315. (§ 11-2.4(e)(3)) If a beneficiary under a disability has the same interest as an interested person, then the consent of or notice to a person under disability is not necessary. (*Id.*)
16.	*By when must objection be made?*	No provision, although resort can be had to a court. (Est. Powers & Trusts § 11-2.4(e)(2)(A)-(B))
17.	*Can objection be overridden?*	Yes, by court. (Est. Powers & Trusts § 11-2.4(e)(2)(B))
18.	*What if there are not sufficiently competent beneficiaries?*	No provision.
19.	*Can a beneficiary petition a court to seek conversion if a trustee refuses?*	Yes. (Est. Powers & Trusts § 11-2.4(e)(2)(B))
20.	*Is there a duty to convert?*	No. The statute allows the trustee to elect. (Est. Powers & Trusts § 11-2.4(e)(1)(B))
21.	*Can a court be petitioned to stop a conversion or reconversion?*	Yes as to conversion. See #16 above.
22.	*Is there a special statute of limitations?*	No provision.

23. *Is there a mandatory provision for payout of income if greater than the unitrust amount?*	No provision.
24. *If there is an excess payout, is it added to principal?*	No provision.
25. *What is the priority of source of payment of the unitrust amount?*	No provision.
26. *Is the priority mandatory?*	No provision.
27. *How is the fair market value of the trust determined for unitrust purposes?*	The only provision relates to real property and other assets for which there is no active market. See #9i above.
28. *Are certain items excluded?*	No provision.
29. *Is the trustee authorized to release his power?*	No provision.
30. *Is there special provision for the marital deduction?*	No.
31. *Is there special provision for generation-skipping grandfather preservation?*	No.
32. *If the power to convert is utilized must the power to adjust be released?*	It is implied.
33. *Are particular factors presented that the trustee should consider?*	No provision.
34. *What standard should a court use?*	The court is *required* to consider the following factors in deciding whether the unitrust statute should apply: (1) nature, purpose, and expected duration of the trust; (2) the intent of the creator; (3) the identity and circumstances of the beneficiaries; (4) the needs for liquidity, regularity of income, and preservation and appreciation of capita; (5) the assets held in trust, including their nature, use by a beneficiary, and whether acquired by the trustee or received by the beneficiary; (6) the trustee's power to invade principal or accumulate income and the extent to which the trustee has done so in the past; (7) the actual and anticipated effect of economic conditions on principal and income and the effects of inflation and deflation; and (8) the anticipated tax consequences of a unitrust conversion. (Est. Powers & Trusts § 11-2.4(e)(5))
35. *Must the trust be a locally administered trust?*	No provision.
36. *When does the power to convert not exist*	No provision.

Table 11.02
Total Return Trusts
North Carolina

1. *Is there a power to convert?*	Yes. (§ 37A-1-104.2(a))
2. *Is the statute applicable to new unitrusts?*	Yes. (§ 37A-1-104.21 et seq.)[1]
3. *Is there a required rate of return?*	A reasonable current return in the range 3%-5%. (§ 37A-1-104.2(a))
4. *Can the required rate of return be varied?*	Yes. See #3 above.
5. *How can it be varied?*	See #3 above.
6. *Alternatively, does the trustee have discretion within a range?*	See ##3 & 4 above.
7. *If so, what is the range?*	See #3 and #4 above.
8. *Must court approval be obtained initially?*	No.
9. *Does the trustee have discretion to:*	
a. *Convert?*	Yes, if certain beneficiaries do not object following notice. (§ 37A-1-104.2(a))
b. *Reconvert?*	Yes. (§ 37A-1-104.2(a))
c. *Determine the effective date?*	Yes. (§§ 37A-1-104.5(1), 37A-1-104.5(4) (conversion))
d. *Determine the frequency of payments?*	Yes. (§ 37A-1-104.5(2))
e. *Determine cash or in kind distribution?*	Yes. (§ 37A-1-104.5(3))
f. *Vary the rate?*	See #3 above.
g. *Whether to value annually or less frequently?*	Yes. It must be at least annually. (§ 37A-1-104.4(a))
h. *What valuation date to use?*	No provision.
i. *Whether to value trust property occupied or used by a beneficiary?*	Yes. The trustee has the discretion to exclude them. (§ 37A-1-104.4(a))
j. *How to prorate in a short year any unitrust payments?*	Yes. (§ 37A-1-104.5(2))
k. *Whether to estimate the value of nonliquid assets?*	Yes. Valuation methods, though, must be used as are considered reasonable and appropriate by the trustee. (§ 37A-1-104.4(e))
l. *The effect of contributions and distributions on valuation?*	No provision.
m. *Other administrative matters?*	Yes. (§ 37A-1-104.5(5))

10. *What standard of conduct is required of the trustee?*	Good faith. (§ 37A-1-104.8)
11. *What is the remedy for a violation?*	The exclusive remedy is conversion, reconversion, or change in the percentage. (§ 37A-1-104.8)
12. *If a trustee is interested, must a disinterested trustee be appointed?*	Yes, by the interested trustee. (§ 37A-1-104.2(b)(2)) An interested trustee is (i) one with a current interest in income or principal or would receive it if the trust were terminated, (ii) one who can be replaced by an interested distributee, or (iii) one who can satisfy a legal obligation of support of a beneficiary out of the trust fund. (§ 37A-1-104.1(7)) An interested distributee is a person to whom distributions of income or principal can currently be made and who has the power to remove the existing trustee and designate as successor a person who may be a related or subordinate party with respect to the distributee. (§ 37A-1-104.1(6))
13. *If a disinterested trustee is required, who selects him?*	The trustee. See #12.
14. *Must notice be given before a conversion?*	Yes. (§ 37A-1-104.2(a)(2))
15. *To whom must notice be given?*	(i) The grantor, if living; (ii) all eligible recipients of current income; (iii) all beneficiaries eligible to receive income if the interest of those currently eligible terminated at the time of giving of notice but the trust itself would not terminate; (iv) all persons entitled to principal if the trust were to terminate at the giving of notice; and (v) all advisors and protectors. With respect to (iii) and (iv), it is without regard to the exercise of a general power of appointment. (§ 37A-1-104.2(a)(2))
16. *By when must objection be made?*	60 days after receipt of notice. (§ 37A-1-104.2(a)(4))
17. *Can objection be overridden?*	Yes, by petitioning a court. (§ 37A-1-104.3(a))
18. *What if there are not sufficiently competent beneficiaries?*	At least one person in #15 (ii) and (iii) above must be competent, and at least one person in #15 (iv) must be competent. (§ 37A-1-104.2(a)(3))
19. *Can a beneficiary petition a court to seek conversion if a trustee refuses?*	Yes, after requesting action by the trustee and the latter fails to do so. (§ 37A-1-104.3(b))
20. *Is there a duty to convert?*	No. The statute provides that the trustee "may" convert. (§ 37A-1-104.2(a))
21. *Can a court be petitioned to stop a conversion or reconversion?*	No provision.
22. *Is there a statute of limitations?*	No provision.
23. *Is there a mandatory provision for payout of income if greater than the unitrust amount?*	No provision.
24. *If there is an excess payout, is it added to principal?*	Yes, in the case of express total return unitrusts where the payout is in excess of 5%. (§ 37A-1-104.2(b)) There is no provision for converted trusts.

25. *What is the priority of source of payment of the unitrust amount?*	None.
26. *Is the priority mandatory?*	N/A
27. *How is the fair market value of the trust determined for unitrust purposes?*	The trustee is given discretion but can use an average of the current year and no more than 3 preceding years if it appears desirable to reduce the impact of fluctuations on market value on the unitrust amount. (§ 37A-1-104.4(a))
28. *Are certain items excluded?*	No provision. The trustee is given discretion. See #9i above.
29. *Is the trustee authorized to release his power?*	No provision.
30. *Is there special provision for the marital deduction?*	Yes, if a marital deduction has been taken, the spouse can compel a conversion to a total return unitrust or a reconversion to an income trust. (§ 37A-1-104.7)
31. *Is there special provision for generation-skipping grandfather preservation?*	No provision.
32. *If the power to convert is utilized must the power to adjust be released?*	No provision.
33. *Are particular factors presented that the trustee should consider?*	In setting the rate, the intentions of the grantor as they are expressed in the governing instrument, the needs of the beneficiaries, general economic conditions, projected current earnings and appreciation for the trust, and projected inflation and its impact on the trust. (§ 37A-1-104.4(b))
34. *What standard should a court use?*	No provision.
35. *Must the trust be a locally administered trust?*	No provision.
36. *When does the power to convert not exist?*	When (i) the governing instrument contains a provision clearly expressing an intent that the current beneficiaries are to receive an amount other than a reasonable current return from the trust; (ii) the trust is a charitable trust or one in which any amount is or has been set aside permanently for charitable purposes, unless the income from the trust also is devoted permanently to charitable purposes; or (iii) the governing instrument expressly prohibits use of this statute by specific reference to the section. (§ 37A-1-104.9)

1. Basically, the same rules as for converted trusts apply. However, the fair market value can be based on an unlimited multiple year averaging basis (§ 37A-1-104.22(a)) if so provided in the governing instrument. Also, the return in the 3%-5% range must reasonably apportion between income and remaindermen. (§ 37A-1-104.23) Without a specific authority in the governing instrument to change the rate, it cannot be changed. (§ 37A-1-104.24)) If the governing instrument does not provide for source of payments, it is net accounting income, followed by other ordinary income. The trustee then has discretion to consider paying from net realized short term gains and then net realized long term gains. In either event the final source is principal. (§ 37A-1-104(4)(a))

Table 12.02
Total Return Trusts
Ohio

Ohio has no specific total return statute. However, § 1340.42(G)(3) provides, as part of the power to adjust, a safe harbor. The trustee can adjust net trust accounting income up to 4% of the fair market value of trust assets based on value as of the first business day of the current year. The propriety of the safe-harbor adjustment is "conclusively presumed." This safe-harbor adjustment does not preclude exercise of the power to adjust which the statute otherwise grants the trustee.

Table 11.02
Total Return Trusts
Oregon

1. *Is there a power to convert?*	Yes. (§ 129.225(2)(a))
2. *Is the statute applicable to new unitrusts?*	No explicit provision.
3. *Is there a required rate of return?*	Yes, 4% over the lesser of the preceding three years or the shorter existence of the trust. (§ 129.225(4)(b))
4. *Can the required rate of return be varied?*	No. See #3 above.
5. *How can it be varied?*	See #4 above.
6. *Alternatively, does the trustee have discretion within a range?*	See #4 above.
7. *If so, what is the range?*	See #4 above.
8. *Must court approval be obtained initially?*	No.
9. *Does the trustee have discretion to:*	
a. *Convert?*	Yes, if certain beneficiaries do not object following notice. (§ 129.225(2))
b. *Reconvert?*	No. Court approval is needed. (§ 129.225)(5)(c))
c. *Determine the effective date?*	No provision.
d. *Determine the frequency of payments?*	No provision.
e. *Determine cash or in kind distribution?*	No provision.
f. *Vary the rate?*	See #4 above.
g. *Whether to value annually or less frequently?*	No, valuation must be done annually on the first business day of the calendar year. (§ 129.225(4)(c))
h. *What valuation date to use?*	No provision. See #3 above.
i. *Whether to value trust property occupied or used by a beneficiary?*	Yes. (§ 129.225(4)(c))
j. *How to prorate in a short year any unitrust payments?*	Yes. (§ 129.225(4)(c))
k. *Whether to estimate the value of nonliquid assets?*	Yes. (§ 129.225(4)(c))
l. *The effect of contributions and distributions on valuation?*	Yes. (§ 129.225(4)(c))

m. Other administrative matters?	Yes. (§ 129.225(4)(c))
10. What standard of conduct is required of the trustee?	No provision.
11. What is the remedy for a violation?	No provision.
12. If a trustee is interested, must a disinterested trustee be appointed?	The key is whether the power has adverse income tax consequences (§ 129.225(6)(b)), adverse estate or gift tax consequences (§ 129.225(6)(c)), the marital deduction would be adversely affected (§ 129.325(6)(d)), or the trustee is also a beneficiary. (§ 129.325(6)(e))
13. If a disinterested trustee is required, who selects him?	No disinterested trustee is necessary. An interested trustee may petition the court. (§ 129.325(7)) However, no provision for petition is made if the effect would be disallowance of the marital deduction.
14. Must notice be given before a conversion?	Yes. (§ 129.225(2)(b))
15. To whom must notice be given?	Sui juris beneficiaries who would either get current income or are entitled to principal upon termination of trust immediately before giving of notice. The foregoing assumes no exercise of a power. (§ 129.225(2)(b))
16. By when must objection be made?	60 days after mailing of notice. (§ 129.225(2)(c))
17. Can objection be overridden?	Yes, by petitioning a court. (§ 129.225(3))
18. What if there are not sufficiently competent beneficiaries?	No provision in this statute.
19. Can a beneficiary petition a court to seek conversion if a trustee refuses?	Yes. (§ 129.225(3)) Thus, the trustee is not obligated to convert upon request. See also § 129.225(5), which allows a beneficiary to petition to change the period for averaging of the rate, to obtain a greater payout of income in order to preserve a tax benefit, or to reconvert.
20. Is there a duty to convert?	No. The statute provides that the trustee "may" convert. (§ 129.225(2)(a))
21. Can a court be petitioned to stop a conversion or reconversion?	Yes, if income would be higher. This is the only express authorization. See #19 above.
22. Is there a special statute of limitations?	No provision.
23. Is there a mandatory provision for payout of income if greater than the unitrust amount?	No provision.
24. If there is an excess payout, is it added to principal?	No provision.
25. What is the priority of source of payment of the unitrust amount?	Net income, net realized short term capital gain, net realized long term capital gain, principal. (§ 129.225(4)(e))
26. Is the priority mandatory?	Yes. (§ 129.225(4)(3))

27. *How is the fair market value of the trust determined for unitrust purposes?*	No provision. The trustee is given discretion. See #9g, h above.
28. *Are certain items excluded?*	No provision. Trustee is given discretion. See #9i above.
29. *Is the trustee authorized to release his power?*	No provision.
30. *Is there special provision for the marital deduction?*	No provision.
31. *Is there special provision for generation-skipping grandfather preservation?*	No provision.
32. *If the power to convert is utilized must the power to adjust be released?*	Yes. (§ 129.225(2))
33. *Are particular factors presented that the trustee should consider?*	Yes. Same as #34 below and also § 129.210(2), which requires administration fairly and with impartiality. Quaere: Does this undercut the trustee's freedom to act under the total return unitrust statute?
34. *What standard should a court use?*	Intent of settlor or testator and purposes of the trust. (§ 129.225(3))
35. *Must the trust be a locally administered trust?*	No provision.
36. *When does the power to convert not exist?*	No prohibitions. Even in the case of amounts permanently set aside for charitable purposes, a trustee can petition a court to obtain the relief sought, such as a conversion. (§ 129.225(6))

Table 11.02
Total Return Trusts
Pennsylvania

1. *Is there a power to convert?*	Yes. (20 § 8105(a))
2. *Is the statute applicable to new unitrusts?*	No explicit provision.
3. *Is there a required rate of return?*	Yes, 4% over the lesser of the preceding three years or the shorter existence of the trust. (20 § 8105(d)(3))
4. *Can the required rate of return be varied?*	No. See #3 above.
5. *How can it be varied?*	See #3 above.
6. *Alternatively, does the trustee have discretion within a range?*	See #3 above.
7. *If so, what is the range?*	See #3 above.
8. *Must court approval be obtained initially?*	No.
9. *Does the trustee have discretion to:*	
a. *Convert?*	Yes, if certain beneficiaries do not object following notice. (20 § 8105(a)(4))
b. *Reconvert?*	No. Court approval is needed. (20 § 8105(g)(4))
c. *Determine the effective date?*	Yes. (20 § 8105(e)(1))
d. *Determine the frequency of payments?*	Yes. (20 § 8105(e)(3))
e. *Determine cash or in kind distribution?*	No provision.
f. *Vary the rate?*	See #4 above.
g. *Whether to value annually or less frequently?*	Yes. (20 § 8105(e)(5))
h. *What valuation date to use?*	Yes. (20 § 8105(e)(6))
i. *Whether to value trust property occupied or used by a beneficiary?*	Yes. (20 § 8105(e)(8))
j. *How to prorate in a short year any unitrust payments?*	Yes. (20 § 8105(e)(2))
k. *Whether to estimate the value of nonliquid assets?*	Yes. (20 § 8105(e)(8))
l. *The effect of contributions and distributions on valuation?*	Yes. (20 § 8105(e)(4))
m. *Other administrative matters?*	Yes. (20 § 8105(e)(9))

10. *What standard of conduct is required of the trustee?*	No provision.
11. *What is the remedy for a violation?*	No provision.
12. *If a trustee is interested, must a disinterested trustee be appointed?*	The key is whether the power has adverse income tax (20 consequences § 8105(i)(3)), estate or gift tax consequences (20 § 8105(i)(4) & (5)), or the trustee is also a beneficiary. (20 § 8105(i)(6))
13. *If a disinterested trustee is required, who selects him?*	No disinterested trustee is necessary. The interested trustees petition the court. (20 § 8105(j)) However, no provision for petition is allowed if the effect would be disallowance of the marital deduction.
14. *Must notice be given before a conversion?*	Yes. (20 § 8105(a))
15. *To whom must notice be given?*	Sui juris beneficiaries who (i) are entitled to receive current income, (ii) are entitled to receive a successor income interest, or (iii) are entitled to principal upon termination of the trust immediately before giving of notice. The foregoing assumes no exercise of a power. (20 § 8105(a)(2) & (3))
16. *By when must objection be made?*	60 days after mailing of notice. (20 § 8105(a)(4))
17. *Can objection be overridden?*	Yes, by petitioning a court. (20 § 8105(b)(1)(i))
18. *What if there are not sufficiently competent beneficiaries?*	A court must be petitioned for approval. (20 § 8105(b)(1)(ii) & (iii)) The statute requires at least two sui juris beneficiaries to avert the need for court approval-one from category (i) and one from either category (ii) or (iii) as set forth in #15 above. (20 § 8105(a)(2) & (3))
19. *Can a beneficiary petition a court to seek conversion if a trustee refuses?*	Yes. (20 § 8105(b)(2)) Thus, the trustee is not obligated to convert upon request. See also 20 § 8105(g), which allows a beneficiary to petition to change rate, period for averaging of rate, to obtain a greater payout of income in order to preserve a tax benefit, or to reconvert.
20. *Is there a duty to convert?*	No. The statute provides that the trustee "may" convert. (20 § 8105(a); see also 20 § 8105(c))
21. *Can a court be petitioned to stop a conversion or reconversion?*	Yes, if income would be higher. This is the only express authorization. See #19 above.
22. *Is there a special statute of limitations?*	No provision.
23. *Is there a mandatory provision for payout of income if greater than the unitrust amount?*	No provision.
24. *If there is an excess payout, is it added to principal?*	No provision.
25. *What is the priority of source of payment of the unitrust amount?*	Net income, net realized short term capital gain, net realized long term capital gain, principal. (20 § 8105(f))
26. *Is the priority mandatory?*	Yes (20 § 8105(f)), unless specified otherwise in the trust instrument.

27. *How is the fair market value of the trust determined for unitrust purposes?*	No provision. Trust is given discretion. See #9g, h above.
28. *Are certain items excluded?*	No provision. Trustee is given discretion. See #9i above.
29. *Is the trustee authorized to release his power?*	Yes (20 § 8105(k)), but not if it causes adverse tax consequences
30. *Is there special provision for the marital deduction?*	No conversion allowed if it would result in denial of the marital deduction. (20 § 8105(i)(5))
31. *Is there special provision for generation-skipping grandfather preservation?*	No provision.
32. *If the power to convert is utilized must the power to adjust be released?*	Yes. (20 § 8105(a))
33. *Are particular factors presented that the trustee should consider?*	Yes, although the statute says the trustee "may" consider these in deciding whether to convert. (20 § 8105(c))
34. *What standard should a court use?*	Intent of settlor or testator and purposes of the trust. (20 § 8105(b)(3))
35. *Must the trust be a locally administered trust?*	No provision.
36. *When does the power to convert not exist?*	When (i) it would change the amount payable as a fixed annuity or fixed fraction of the trust assets; (ii) any amount is or has been set aside permanently for charitable purposes and for which a federal estate or gift tax charitable deduction has been taken, unless the income from the trust also is devoted permanently to charitable purposes; or (iii) the conversion would result in the disallowance of the federal estate or gift tax marital deduction and it otherwise would be allowed. (20 § 8105(i)(1)-(3)).

Table 11.02
Total Return Trusts
Rhode Island

1.	*Is there a power to convert?*	Yes. (§ 18-4-29(a))
2.	*Is the statute applicable to new unitrusts?*	Yes. (§ 18-4-29(a))
3.	*Is there a required rate of return?*	A return in the range of 3%-5% is considered "a reasonable apportionment" of the total return of a total return trust. (§ 18-4-29(a)(3))
4.	*Can the required rate of return be varied?*	No, it is "fixed." (§ 18-4-29(a))
5.	*How can it be varied?*	See #4 above.
6.	*Alternatively, does the trustee have discretion within a range?*	See #4.
7.	*If so, what is the range?*	See #4.
8.	*Must court approval be obtained initially?*	A governing trust instrument may provide for a unitrust payout. (§ 18-4-29(a))
9.	*Does the trustee have discretion to:*	
a.	*Convert?*	No provision.
b.	*Reconvert?*	No provision.
c.	*Determine the effective date?*	No provision.
d.	*Determine the frequency of payments?*	No provision.
e.	*Determine cash or in kind distribution?*	No provision.
f.	*Vary the rate?*	No, as the ratio is fixed. See #4 above.
g.	*Whether to value annually or less frequently?*	No provision. However, the statute allows for annual or less frequent valuations, though not addressing trustee discretion in the matter. (§ 18-4-29(a)&(a)(1))
h.	*What valuation date to use?*	No provision.
i.	*Whether to value trust property occupied or used by a beneficiary?*	Generally, the governing instrument (including any changes by court reformation or adjustment by the trustee) may exclude such assets, with use being deemed the equivalent of income. (§ 18-4-29(c))
j.	*How to prorate in a short year any unitrust payments?*	No provision.
k.	*Whether to estimate the value of nonliquid assets?*	No provision.
l.	*The effect of contributions and distributions on valuation?*	No provision.
m.	*Other administrative matters?*	No provision.

10. *What standard of conduct is required of the trustee?*	No provision.
11. *What is the remedy for a violation?*	No provision.
12. *If a trustee is interested, must a disinterested trustee be appointed?*	No provision.
13. *If a disinterested trustee is required, who selects him?*	No provision.
14. *Must notice be given before a conversion?*	No provision.
15. *To whom must notice be given?*	No provision.
16. *By when must objection be made?*	No provision.
17. *Can objection be overridden?*	No provision.
18. *What if there are not sufficiently competent beneficiaries?*	No provision.
19. *Can a beneficiary petition a court to seek conversion if a trustee refuses?*	No provision, other than a general provision for court reformation of a trust into a unitrust. (§ 18-4-29(a))
20. *Is there a duty to convert?*	No provision.
21. *Can a court be petitioned to stop a conversion or reconversion?*	No provision.
22. *Is there a statute of limitations?*	No provision.
23. *Is there a mandatory provision for payout of income if greater than the unitrust amount?*	No provision.
24. *If there is an excess payout, is it added to principal?*	The statute provides that any unitrust payout in excess of 5% is to be treated as a payment of principal. (§ 18-4-29(b)(4))
25. *What is the priority of source of payment of the unitrust amount?*	Ordinary income, ordinary income not allocable to net accounting income, net realized short term capital gain, net realized long term capital gain, and principal. (§ 18-4-29(b))
26. *Is the priority mandatory?*	The governing instrument may provide otherwise or may grant the trustee's discretion. (§ 18-4-29(b))
27. *How is the fair market value of the trust determined for unitrust purposes?*	There is just a general reference to fair market value. (§ 18-4-29(a)(1))
28. *Are certain items excluded?*	No provision. Trustee is given discretion. See #9i above.
29. *Is the trustee authorized to release his power?*	No provision. But see circumstances for releasing the power to adjust. (§ 18-4-28(e))
30. *Is there special provision for the marital deduction?*	No provision.
31. *Is there special provision for generation-skipping grandfather preservation?*	No provision.

32. If the power to convert is utilized must the power to adjust be released?	No provision.
33. Are particular factors presented that the trustee should consider?	No provision.
34. What standard should a court use?	No provision.
35. Must the trust be a locally administered trust?	No provision.
36. When does the power to convert not exist?	No provision. On the other hand, the statute anticipates a conversion in only limited circumstances, (i) by court reformation; (ii) a payout in the 3%-5% range prescribed by a trustee through exercise of the power to adjust provided for in § 18-4-28(a). (§ 18-4-29(a))

Table 11.02
Total Return Trusts
South Dakota

1. *Is there a power to convert?*	Yes. (§ 55-15-2)
2. *Is the statute applicable to new unitrusts?*	Yes. (§ 55-15-2(1)(ii)
3. *Is there a required rate of return?*	No. For the first three accounting periods, it is 3% unless a higher percentage is specified in the instrument, or by the election of the trustee, disinterested person, or the court. (§ 55-15-6(a). The same is true for subsequent accounting periods, but the rate is based on an average of fair market values on the first business day of the current valuation period and *each* prior valuation period. (§ 55-15-6(2)) This means the two prior annual periods. (§ 55-15-1(10)) Various factors must be taken into account when the trustee, disinterested person, or court arrives at a rate, which must be "a reasonable current return." (§ 55-15-6(3))
4. *Can the required rate of return be varied?*	See #3 above.
5. *How can it be varied?*	See #3 above.
6. *Alternatively, does the trustee have discretion within a range?*	See #3 above. Note that there is no cap on the upside.
7. *If so, what is the range?*	See #3 above.
8. *Must court approval be obtained initially?*	No.
9. *Does the trustee have discretion to:*	
a. *Convert?*	Yes, if certain beneficiaries do not object following notice. (§ 55-15-2(4))
b. *Reconvert?*	Yes. (§ 55-15-2)
c. *Determine the effective date?*	No provision.
d. *Determine the frequency of payments?*	No provision.
e. *Determine cash or in kind distribution?*	No provision.
f. *Vary the rate?*	See #3 above.
g. *Whether to value annually or less frequently?*	No provision.
h. *What valuation date to use?*	Annual valuation required. (§ 55-15-5)
i. *Whether to value trust property occupied or used by a beneficiary?*	Residential or tangible personal property is to be excluded if, on the first business day of the current valuation year, one or more current beneficiaries have or have had the right to occupy, possess, or control the property. In such cases, these rights are deemed to be the unitrust amount. (§ 55-15-6(7))

	A specifically given asset and any return on it is also excluded. (*Id.*)
j. How to prorate in a short year any unitrust payments?	No discretion. It must be done on a daily basis. (§ 55-15-6(5))
k. Whether to estimate the value of nonliquid assets?	No provision.
l. The effect of contributions and distributions on valuation?	No discretion. (§ 55-15-6(8))
m. Other administrative matters?	No provision.
10. What standard of conduct is required of the trustee?	Good faith. (§ 55-15-13)
11. What is the remedy for a violation?	If the trustee satisfies the good faith standard, the exclusive remedy is petitioning the court regarding conversion, reconversion, or changing the percentage. (*Id.*) The penalty imposed if the trustee has not acted in good faith is not addressed.
12. If a trustee is interested, must a disinterested trustee be appointed?	Yes, by the interested trustee. (§ 55-15-3) An interested trustee is (i) one with a current interest in income or principal, (ii) one who can be replaced by a related or subordinate party, or (iii) one who can satisfy a legal obligation of support of a beneficiary out of the trust fund. (§ 55-15-1(4)) Generally, by appointing a disinterested trustee, the interested trustee need not petition the court if the action to be taken is determining the percentage return, the method for valuing assets, or the assets to be excluded. (§ 55-15-3)
13. If a disinterested trustee is required, who selects him?	The trustee. See #12 above. If the interested trustee is petitioning a court, the court in the exercise of its discretion may appoint a disinterested trustee. (§ 55-13-4)
14. Must notice be given before a conversion?	Yes. (§ 55-15-2(2))
15. To whom must notice be given?	(i) The grantor, if living; (ii) all eligible recipients of income; (iii) all persons entitled to principal if the trusts terminates or, if there is no provision for termination, those who would take income or principal if the current income beneficiaries were deceased; and (iv) all advisors and protectors. (§ 55-15-2(2))
16. By when must objection be made?	60 days after receipt of notice. (§ 55-15-2(4))
17. Can objection be overridden?	Yes, by petitioning a court. (§ 55-15-4)
18. What if there are not sufficiently competent beneficiaries?	At least one person in each of #15 (ii) and (iii) must be competent. (§ 55-15-2(3))
19. Can a beneficiary petition a court to seek conversion if a trustee refuses?	No provision, except for a surviving spouse. See #30.
20. Is there a duty to convert?	No. (§ 55-15-14)
21. Can a court be petitioned to stop a conversion or reconversion?	No provision.

22. Is there a special statute of limitations?	No provision.
23. Is there a mandatory provision for payout of income if greater than the unitrust amount?	Yes, if a marital deduction is involved or the generation-skipping transfer tax does not apply due to an effective date or transition rule. (§ 55-15-7)
24. If there is an excess payout, is it added to principal?	No provision.
25. What is the priority of source of payment of the unitrust amount?	None. Net short term capital gain and then net long term capital gain may allocated to income to the extent when coupled with other sources does not exceed the unitrust amount for the year or part year. (§ 55-15-8(2))
26. Is the priority mandatory?	No. (*Id.*)
27. How is the fair market value of the trust determined for unitrust purposes?	The trustee is given discretion to use such methods as are deemed reasonable and appropriate. (§ 55-15-5) See #9g, h above.
28. Are certain items excluded?	Assets, with respect to which a fair market value is not readily ascertainable, to the extent that all the income received is distributed to the extent distributable under the governing instrument. (§ 55-15-5) Thus, exclusion or inclusion could change from one year to another.
29. Is the trustee authorized to release his power?	No provision.
30. Is there special provision for the marital deduction?	The spouse has a right to compel a reconversion, if a marital deduction for federal purposes has been claimed. (§ 55-15-11; see also #23 above.)
31. Is there special provision for generation-skipping grandfather preservation?	See #23 above.
32. If the power to convert is utilized must the power to adjust be released?	No provision.
33. Are particular factors presented that the trustee should consider?	No provision.
34. What standard should a court use?	No provision.
35. Must the trust be a locally administered trust?	No provision.
36. When does the power to convert not exist?	When (i) the governing instrument reflects an intent that the current beneficiaries are to receive an amount other than a reasonable current return from the trust; (ii) the trust is a charitable trust; (iii) one or more eligible income beneficiaries have a power of withdrawal over the trust not subject to an ascertainable standard or a power that can be exercised to discharge a duty of support; (iv) the governing instrument expressly prohibits use of this statute by specific reference to the section. (§ 55-15-12)

Table 11.02
Total Return Trusts
Texas

1. *Is there a power to convert?*	No.
2. *Is the statute applicable to new unitrusts?*	Yes. (Tex. Prop. Code § 116.007)
3. *Is there a required rate of return?*	No, but it must be between 3%-5%. (Tex. Prop. Code § 116.007(b)(2))
4. *Can the required rate of return be varied?*	As the statute is written, it does not appear to allow variation once set in the trust instrument.
5. *How can it be varied?*	See #4 above.
6. *Alternatively, does the trustee have discretion within a range?*	No, as the percentage must be set by the trust instrument. (Tex. Prop. Code § 116.007(b)(2))
7. *If so, what is the range?*	See #3 above.
8. *Must court approval be obtained initially?*	No.
9. *Does the trustee have discretion to:*	
a. *Convert?*	No. See #1 above.
b. *Reconvert?*	No provision.
c. *Determine the effective date?*	No provision.
d. *Determine the frequency of payments?*	No provision.
e. *Determine cash or in kind distribution?*	No provision.
f. *Vary the rate?*	See #4 above.
g. *Whether to value annually or less frequently?*	See #4 above.
h. *What valuation date to use?*	No provision.
i. *Whether to value trust property occupied or used by a beneficiary?*	No provision.
j. *How to prorate in a short year any unitrust payments?*	No provision.
k. *Whether to estimate the value of nonliquid assets?*	No provision.
l. *The effect of contributions and distributions on valuation?*	No provision.
m. *Other administrative matters?*	No provision.

10. *What standard of conduct is required of the trustee?*	No provision.
11. *What is the remedy for a violation?*	No provision.
12. *If a trustee is interested, must a disinterested trustee be appointed?*	No provision.
13. *If a disinterested trustee is required, who selects him?*	No provision.
14. *Must notice be given before a conversion?*	No provision.
15. *To whom must notice be given?*	No provision.
16. *By when must objection be made?*	No provision.
17. *Can objection be overridden?*	No provision.
18. *What if there are not sufficiently competent beneficiaries?*	No provision.
19. *Can a beneficiary petition a court to seek conversion if a trustee refuses?*	No provision.
20. *Is there a duty to convert?*	See #4 above.
21. *Can a court be petitioned to stop a conversion or reconversion?*	No provision.
22. *Is there a special statute of limitations?*	No provision.
23. *Is there a mandatory provision for payout of income if greater than the unitrust amount?*	No provision.
24. *If there is an excess payout, is it added to principal?*	No provision.
25. *What is the priority of source of payment of the unitrust amount?*	Net accounting income, ordinary accounting income not allocated to net accounting income, net realized short term capital gain, net realized long term capital gain, principal. (Tex. Prop. Code § 116.007(d))
26. *Is the priority mandatory?*	Not if the trust provides otherwise. (*Id.*)
27. *How is the fair market value of the trust determined for unitrust purposes?*	It may be determined by reference to net fair market value in one year or more than one year. There is ambiguity as to whether this must be addressed in the trust instrument or the trustee has discretion, although most likely the former. (Tex. Prop. Code § 116.007(b)(2))
28. *Are certain items excluded?*	No provision.
29. *Is the trustee authorized to release his power?*	No provision.
30. *Is there special provision for the marital deduction?*	No provision.

31. Is there special provision for generation-skipping grandfather preservation?	No provision.
32. If the power to convert is utilized must the power to adjust be released?	No. See #1 above.
33. Are particular factors presented that the trustee should consider?	No. See #1 above.
34. What standard should a court use?	No. See #1 above.
35. Must the trust be a locally administered trust?	No provision.
36. When does the power to convert not exist?	There is no power to convert. See #1 above.

Table 11.02
Total Return Trusts
Virginia

1. *Is there a power to convert?*	Yes. (§ 55-277.4:1(B))
2. *Is the statute applicable to new unitrusts?*	Yes. (§ 55-277.4:1(B)(iii))
3. *Is there a required rate of return?*	Yes, "a reasonable current return" between 3%-5%. (§ 55-277.4:1(F))
4. *Can the required rate of return be varied?*	See #3 above.
5. *How can it be varied?*	See #3 above.
6. *Alternatively, does the trustee have discretion within a range?*	See #3 above. Note that there is no cap on the upside.
7. *If so, what is the range?*	See #3 above.
8. *Must court approval be obtained initially?*	No.
9. *Does the trustee have discretion to:*	
a. *Convert?*	Yes, if certain beneficiaries do not object following notice. (§ 55-277.4:1(B)(i))
b. *Reconvert?*	Yes. (§§ 55-277.4:1(B)(ii), 55-277.4:1(H)(iv))
c. *Determine the effective date?*	Yes. (§ 55-277.4:1(H)(I))
d. *Determine the frequency of payments?*	Yes. (§ 55-277.4:1(H)(ii))
e. *Determine cash or in kind distribution?*	Yes. (§ 55-277.4:1(H)(iii))
f. *Vary the rate?*	See #3 above.
g. *Whether to value annually or less frequently?*	Valuation must be annually. (§ 55-277.4:1(E))
h. *What valuation date to use?*	Yes. (§ 55-277.4:1(E); see also #9a)
i. *Whether to value trust property occupied or used by a beneficiary?*	No provision.
j. *How to prorate in a short year any unitrust payments?*	Yes. (§ 55-277.4:1(H)(ii))
k. *Whether to estimate the value of non-liquid assets?*	See #28 below.
l. *The effect of contributions and distributions on valuation?*	No provision.
m. *Other administrative matters?*	Yes. (§ 55-277.4:1(H)(v))
10. *What standard of conduct is required of the trustee?*	Good faith. (§ 55-277.4:1(K))

11. *What is the remedy for a violation?*	If the trustee satisfies the good faith standard, the exclusive remedy is petitioning the court regarding conversion, reconversion, or changing the percentage. (*Id.*) There is no reference to the penalty if the good faith standard is not satisfied.
12. *If a trustee is interested, must a disinterested trustee be appointed?*	Yes, by the interested trustee. (§ 55-277.4:1(C)(2)) An interested trustee is (i) one with a current interest in income or principal, (ii) one who can be replaced by a related or subordinate party, or (iii) one who can satisfy a legal obligation of support of a beneficiary out of the trust fund. (§ 55-277.4:1(A)(4))
13. *If a disinterested trustee is required, who selects him?*	The trustee. See #12 above. The disinterested person then has the power to set the percentage return, valuation methodology and which assets are excluded. (§ 55-277.4:1(C)(2))
14. *Must notice be given before a conversion?*	Yes. (§ 55-277.4:1(C))
15. *To whom must notice be given?*	(i) The grantor, if living; (ii) all eligible recipients of income; (iii) all persons entitled to principal if the trusts terminates or, if there is no provision for termination, those who would take income or principal if the current income beneficiaries were deceased; and (iv) all advisors and protectors. (§ 55-277.4:1(B)(2))
16. *By when must objection be made?*	60 days after receipt of notice. (§ 55-277.4:1(B)(4))
17. *Can objection be overridden?*	Yes, by petitioning a court. (§ 55-277.4:1(D))
18. *What if there are not sufficiently competent beneficiaries?*	At least one person in each of #15 (ii) and (iii) must be competent. (§ 55-277.4:1(C)(9))
19. *Can a beneficiary petition a court to seek conversion if a trustee refuses?*	The beneficiary needs to appoint a disinterested person who can petition the court. The court can also do so in the exercise of it own discretion. (*Id.*) See also #30 below.
20. *Is there a duty to convert?*	No. (§ 55-277.4:1(B))
21. *Can a court be petitioned to stop a conversion or reconversion?*	No provision.
22. *Is there a special statute of limitations?*	No provision.
23. *Is there a mandatory provision for payout of income if greater than the unitrust amount?*	No provision.
24. *If there is an excess payout, is it added to principal?*	No provision.
25. *What is the priority of source of payment of the unitrust amount?*	None. Net short term gain and net long term gain can be allocated as long as the percentage return is not exceeded when all other amounts allocated to trust income are also taken into account. (§ 55-277.4:1(G)(2))
26. *Is the priority mandatory?*	No. (*Id.*)

27. How is the fair market value of the trust determined for unitrust purposes?	The trustee is given discretion as to dates and averages of dates as are deemed reasonable and appropriate (§ 55-277.4:1(E)), but there is no provision as to methodology other than "fair market value." But see #28 below.
28. Are certain items excluded?	Assets for which fair market value cannot be readily ascertained shall be valued under a method deemed reasonable and appropriate. Such assets may be excluded, if all the income which is received is distributed to the extent distributable under the terms of the governing instrument. (§ 55-277.4:1(E)) Thus, the exclusion of the asset may change from one year to another.
29. Is the trustee authorized to release his power?	No provision.
30. Is there special provision for the marital deduction?	No provision.
31. Is there special provision for generation-skipping grandfather preservation?	No provision.
32. If the power to convert is utilized must the power to adjust be released?	No provision.
33. Are particular factors presented that the trustee should consider?	Only with respect to setting the rate of return. The factors are: the grantor's intentions as expressed in the trust instrument, the needs of the beneficiaries, general economic conditions, projected current earnings and appreciation for the trust, and projected inflation and its impact on the trust. (§ 55-277.4:1 (F)) No factors are provided for deciding whether to convert, reconvert, change the rate of return, or change the method of valuation.
34. What standard should a court use?	No provision.
35. Must the trust be a locally administered trust?	Yes. (§ 55-277.4:1(J))
36. When does the power to convert not exist?	When the governing instrument reflects an intent that the current beneficiaries are to receive an amount other than a "reasonable current return" from the trust, the trust is a charitable trust, or the governing instrument expressly prohibits it by specific reference to the section or "expressly reflects the grantor's intent that net income not be calculated as a unitrust amount." (§ 55-277.4:1(J)(1)-(3))

Table 11.02
Total Return Trusts
Washington

1. *Is there a power to convert?*	Yes. (§ 11.104A.040(b))
2. *Is the statute applicable to new unitrusts?*	Yes. (§ 11.104A.040(a)(2))
3. *Is there a required rate of return?*	No (§ 11.104A.040(f)(3)), unless the trust instrument expressly prohibits discretion in the trustee.
4. *Can the required rate of return be varied?*	Yes. (§ 11.104A.040(f)(3))
5. *How can it be varied?*	In the trustee's discretion. (§ 11.104A.040(f)(3))
6. *Alternatively, does the trustee have discretion within a range?*	See #5.
7. *If so, what is the range?*	It must be in the range of 3%-5%. If the trustee "makes no determination," it is 4%. (§ 11.104A.040(f)(3)) The fair market value of assets is based on the lesser of the three preceding years or the period the trust has been in existence. (*Id.*)
8. *Must court approval be obtained initially?*	No. The trustee can proceed if the beneficiaries do not object or there is an agreement reached with all the "parties." (§ 11.104A.040(c); see also #17 below)
9. *Does the trustee have discretion to:*	
a. *Convert?*	Yes, if certain beneficiaries do not object following notice. (§ 11.104A.040(b))
b. *Reconvert?*	No. Court approval is needed. (§ 11.104A.040(i)(4))
c. *Determine the effective date?*	Yes. (§ 11.104A.040(g)(1))
d. *Determine the frequency of payments?*	Yes. (§ 11.104A.040(g)(3))
e. *Determine cash or in kind distribution?*	No provision.
f. *Vary the rate?*	See #4 above.
g. *Whether to value annually or less frequently?*	Yes. (§ 11.104A.040(g)(5))
h. *What valuation date to use?*	Yes. (§ 11.104A.040(g)(6))
i. *Whether to value trust property occupied or used by a beneficiary?*	Yes. (§ 11.104A.040(g)(8))
j. *How to prorate in a short year any unitrust payments?*	Yes. (§ 11.104A.040(g)(2))
k. *Whether to estimate the value of nonliquid assets?*	Yes. (§ 11.104A.040(g)(8))
l. *The effect of contributions and distributions on valuation?*	Yes. (§ 11.104A.040(g)(4))

m. Other administrative matters?	Yes. (§ 11.104A.040(g)(9))
10. What standard of conduct is required of the trustee?	No provision.
11. What is the remedy for a violation?	No provision.
12. If a trustee is interested, must a disinterested trustee be appointed?	The key is whether the power has adverse income tax consequences (§ 11.104A.040(l)(2)), adverse estate or gift tax consequences (§ 11.104A.040(l)(3) & (4)), or the trustee is also a beneficiary. (§ 11.104A.040(l)(5))
13. If a disinterested trustee is required, who selects him?	No disinterested trustee is necessary. The interested trustees petition the court. (§ 11.104A.040(m)) However, no provision for petition is made if the effect would be disallowance of the marital deduction.
14. Must notice be given before a conversion?	Yes. (§ 11.104A.040(b))
15. To whom must notice be given?	Sui juris beneficiaries who are either (i) distributees or permissible distributees of trust income or principal, as well as (ii) distributees or permissible distributees of trust principal were there to be a termination of the trust immediately before giving of notice and assuming no exercise of a power. (§ 11.104A.040(b)(2)(ii))
16. By when must objection be made?	60 days after mailing of notice. (§ 11.104A.040(b)(4))
17. Can objection be overridden?	Yes, by petitioning a court. (§ 11.104A.040(d)(1)(i)) Note that objection can be raised by a "party," which includes the trustor, a surviving spouse, and a variety of other persons. (§ 11.96A.030(4))
18. What if there are not sufficiently competent beneficiaries?	A court must be petitioned for approval. (§ 11.104A.040(d)(1)(ii)) The statute requires at least two sui juris beneficiaries to avert the need for court approval, that is, one from (i) and (ii) set forth in #15 above. (§ 11.104A.040(d)(1)(ii))
19. Can a beneficiary petition a court to seek conversion if a trustee refuses?	Yes. (§ 11.104A.040(d)(2)) So can any other "party." Thus, the trustee is not obligated to convert upon request. See also § 11.104A.040(i), which allows a beneficiary to petition to change rate, period for averaging of rate, to obtain a greater payout of income in order to preserve a tax benefit, or to reconvert.
20. Is there a duty to convert?	No. The statute provides that the trustee "may" convert. (§ 11.104A.040(b))
21. Can a court be petitioned to stop a conversion or reconversion?	Yes, if income would be higher. This is the only express authorization. See #19 above.
22. Is there a statute of limitations?	No provision.
23. Is there a mandatory provision for payout of income if greater than the unitrust amount?	No provision.
24. If there is an excess payout, is it added to principal?	No provision.

25. *What is the priority of source of payment of the unitrust amount?*	Net income, net realized short term capital gain, net realized long term capital gain, principal. (§ 11.104A.040(h)(2))
26. *Is the priority mandatory?*	Yes (§ 11.104A.040(h)(2)), unless specified otherwise in the trust instrument.
27. *How is the fair market value of the trust determined for unitrust purposes?*	No provision. Trust is given discretion. See #9g, h above.
28. *Are certain items excluded?*	No provision. Trustee is given discretion. See #9i above.
29. *Is the trustee authorized to release his power?*	Yes (§ 11.104A.040(n)), but not if it causes adverse tax consequences.
30. *Is there special provision for the marital deduction?*	No conversion allowed if it would result in denial of the marital deduction. (§ 11.104A.040(l)(4))
31. *Is there special provision for generation-skipping grandfather preservation?*	No provision.
32. *If the power to convert is utilized must the power to adjust be released?*	Yes. (§ 11.104A.040(b))
33. *Are particular factors presented that the trustee should consider?*	Yes, although the statute says the trustee "may" consider these in deciding whether to convert. (§ 11.104A.040(e))
34. *What standard should a court use?*	Intent of settlor or testator and purposes of the trust. (§ 11.104A.040(d)(3))
35. *Must the trust be a locally administered trust?*	No provision.
36. *When does the power to convert not exist?*	When it would result in the disallowance of the federal estate or gift tax marital deduction that would otherwise be allowed. (§ 11.104A.040(l)(4)). In the case of amounts permanently set aside for charitable purposes as well as those items addressed in #12 above, the trustee can petition the court to convert. (*Id.*)

Table 11.02
Total Return Trusts
West Virginia

1.	*Is there a power to convert?*	Yes. (§44B-1-104a(a)(5))
2.	*Is the statute applicable to new unitrusts?*	Yes, with respect to an "express total return unitrust." (§44B-1-104a(m))[1]
3.	*Is there a required rate of return?*	A reasonable current return in the range 3%-5%. (§44B-1-104a(f))
4.	*Can the required rate of return be varied?*	Yes. See #3 above.
5.	*How can it be varied?*	See #3 above. In the case of an express total return unitrust, see #2 above, the trustee may vary in the absence of an explicit prohibition. (§44B-1-104a(m)(4))
6.	*Alternatively, does the trustee have discretion within a range?*	See ##3 & 4 above.
7.	*If so, what is the range?*	See ##3 & 4 above.
8.	*Must court approval be obtained initially?*	No.
9.	*Does the trustee have discretion to:*	
	a. *Convert?*	Yes, if certain beneficiaries do not object following notice. (§44B-1-104a(b)(2)(D))
	b. *Reconvert?*	Yes. (§44B-1-104a(h)(iv))
	c. *Determine the effective date?*	Yes. (§44B-1-104a(h)(i))
	d. *Determine the frequency of payments?*	Yes. (§44B-1-104a(h)(ii))
	e. *Determine cash or in kind distribution?*	Yes. (§44B-1-104a(h)(iii))
	f. *Vary the rate?*	See ## 3 & 4 above.
	g. *Whether to value annually or less frequently?*	Yes. It must be at least annually. (§44B-104a(e))
	h. *What valuation date to use?*	One deemed appropriate. (§44B-1-104(e))
	i. *Whether to value trust property occupied or used by a beneficiary?*	Yes. The trustee has the discretion to exclude them in the case of an express total return trust. (§44B-1-104(m)(8)(B))
	j. *How to prorate in a short year any unitrust payments?*	Yes. (§44B-1-104a(h)(ii))
	k. *Whether to estimate the value of nonliquid assets?*	Yes. Valuation methods, though, must be used as are considered reasonable and appropriate by the trustee. (§44B-1-104a(e))
	l. *The effect of contributions and distributions on valuation?*	No provision.

	m. Other administrative matters?	Yes. (§44B-1-104a(h)(v))
10.	*What standard of conduct is required of the trustee?*	Good faith. (§44B-1-104a(l))
11.	*What is the remedy for a violation?*	The exclusive remedy is conversion, reconversion, or change in the percentage. (§44B-1-104a(l))
12.	*If a trustee is interested, must a disinterested trustee be appointed?*	Yes, by the interested trustee. (§44B-1-104a(c)(2)) An interested trustee is (i) one with a current interest in income or principal or would receive it if the trust were terminated, (ii) one who can be replaced by an interested distributee, or (iii) one who can satisfy a legal obligation of support of a beneficiary out of the trust fund. (§44B-1-104a(a)(4)) An interested distributee is a person to whom distributions of income or principal can currently be made and who has the power to remove the existing trustee and designate as successor a person who may be a related or subordinate party with respect to the distributee. (§44B-1-104a(a)(3))
13.	*If a disinterested trustee is required, who selects him?*	The trustee. See #12.
14.	*Must notice be given before a conversion?*	Yes. (§44B-1-104a(b)(2))
15.	*To whom must notice be given?*	(i) The grantor, if living; (ii) all eligible recipients of current income; (iii) all beneficiaries eligible to receive income if the interest of those currently eligible terminated at the time of giving of notice but the trust itself would not terminate; (iv) all persons entitled to principal if the trust were to terminate at the giving of notice; and (v) all advisors and protectors. With respect to (iii) and (iv), it is without regard to the exercise of a general power of appointment. (§44B-1-104a(b)(2)(3))
16.	*By when must objection be made?*	30 days after receipt of notice. (§44B-1-104a(b)(2)(B)(iv))
17.	*Can objection be overridden?*	No provision.
18.	*What if there are not sufficiently competent beneficiaries?*	At least one person in #15 (ii) above must be competent, and at least one person in #15 (iii) or (iv) must be competent. (§44B-1-104a(b)(2))
19.	*Can a beneficiary petition a court to seek conversion if a trustee refuses?*	No provision.
20.	*Is there a duty to convert?*	No. The statute provides for situations in which the trustee desires to convert. (§44B-1-104a(d))
21.	*Can a court be petitioned to stop a conversion or reconversion?*	Yes, by the trustee. (§44B-1-104a(1))
22.	*Is there a statute of limitations?*	No provision.
23.	*Is there a mandatory provision for payout of income if greater than the unitrust amount?*	No provision.
24.	*If there is an excess payout, is it added to principal?*	No provision.

25. *What is the priority of source of payment of the unitrust amount?*	Net income, net realized short term capital gain, net realized long term capital and principal. (§44B-1-104a(g))
26. *Is the priority mandatory?*	Yes. (§44B-1-104a(g))
27. *How is the fair market value of the trust determined for unitrust purposes?*	See #9 above.
28. *Are certain items excluded?*	They may be if all income from the asset is distributed to the extent distributable under the terms of the instrument. (§44B-1-104a(e)) See #9i above for express total return trusts.
29. *Is the trustee authorized to release his power?*	No provision.
30. *Is there special provision for the marital deduction?*	Yes, if a marital deduction has been taken, the spouse can compel a conversion to a total return unitrust or a reconversion to an income trust. (§44B-1-104a(i))
31. *Is there special provision for generation-skipping grandfather preservation?*	No provision.
32. *If the power to convert is utilized must the power to adjust be released?*	No provision.
33. *Are particular factors presented that the trustee should consider?*	In setting the rate, the intentions of the grantor as they are expressed in the governing instrument, the needs of the beneficiaries, general economic conditions, projected current earnings and appreciation for the trust, and projected inflation and its impact on the trust. (§44B-1-104a(f))
34. *What standard should a court use?*	No provision.
35. *Must the trust be a locally administered trust?*	The trust must be administered under West Virginia law. (§44B-1-104a(k))
36. *When does the power to convert not exist?*	When (i) the governing instrument contains a provision clearly expressing an intent that the current beneficiaries are to receive an amount other than a reasonable current return from the trust; (ii) the trust is a charitable trust or one in which any amount is or has been set aside permanently for charitable purposes, unless the income from the trust also is devoted permanently to charitable purposes; or (iii) the governing instrument expressly prohibits use of this statute by specific reference to the section. (§44B-1-104a(k)(1)-(3))

1. Basically, the same rules as for converted trusts apply. However, the fair market value can be based on an unlimited multiple year averaging basis (§44B-1-104a(m)(1)) if so provided in the governing instrument. Also, the return in the 3%-5% range must reasonably apportion between income and remaindermen. (§44B-1-104a(m)(5)) Without a specific prohibition in the governing instrument to change the rate, the trustee can change the rate. (§44B-1-104a(m)(4)) If the governing instrument does not provide for source of payments, it is net accounting income, followed by other ordinary income. The trustee then pays from net realized short term gains and then net realized long term gains. The final source is principal. (§44B-1-104a(m)(7)) The trustee can be granted the discretion to treat capital gains as part of the unitrust distribution to the extent the distribution exceeds accounting income and to order classes of income. (§44B-1-104a(m)(6))

Table 11.02
Total Return Trusts
Wisconsin

1. Is there a power to convert?	Yes. (§ 701.20(4g)(a)(1))
2. Is the statute applicable to new unitrusts?	No explicit provision.
3. Is there a required rate of return?	Yes, between 3% and 5%. (§ 701.20(4g)(c)(2)(b))
4. Can the required rate of return be varied?	Yes, with the approval of the sui juris beneficiaries, but always in the 3%-5% range. (§ 701.20(4g)(c)(3)(b))
5. How can it be varied?	See #4 above.
6. Alternatively, does the trustee have discretion within a range?	See #4 above.
7. If so, what is the range?	See #4 above.
8. Must court approval be obtained initially?	No, but beneficiary consent is required. (§ 701.20(4g)(a)(1)) An alternative is for the trustee or a beneficiary to seek court approval. (§ 701.20(4g)(a)(2))
9. Does the trustee have discretion to:[1]	
a. Convert?	Yes, if certain beneficiaries do not object following notice. (§ 701.20(4g)(a)(1))
b. Reconvert?	No. Court approval is needed. See #20 above.
c. Determine the effective date?	No provision.
d. Determine the frequency of payments?	Yes. (§ 701.20(4g)(c)(4)(a))
e. Determine cash or in kind distribution?	No provision.
f. Vary the rate?	See #4 above.
g. Whether to value annually or less frequently?	Yes. (§ 701.20(4g)(c)(4)(d))
h. What valuation date to use?	Yes. (§ 701.20(4g)(c)(4)(e))
i. Whether to value trust property occupied or used by a beneficiary?	Yes. (§ 701.20(4g)(c)(4)(f))
j. How to prorate in a short year any unitrust payments?	Yes. (§ 701.20(4g)(c)(4)(b))
k. Whether to estimate the value of nonliquid assets?	No provision.
l. The effect of contributions and distributions on valuation?	Yes. (§ 701.20(4)(c)(4)(c))
m. Other administrative matters?	Yes. (§ 701.20(4g)(c)(4)(h))

10. What standard of conduct is required of the trustee?	No provision.
11. What is the remedy for a violation?	No provision.
12. If a trustee is interested, must a disinterested trustee be appointed?	The key is whether the power has adverse income tax consequences (§ 701.20(4g)(d)(1)(d)), adverse estate or gift tax consequences (§ 701.20(4g)(d)(1)(e)), adverse effects on the marital deduction (§ 701.20(4g)(d)(1)(b)), or the trustee is also a beneficiary. (§ 701.20(4g)(d)(1)(g))
13. If a disinterested trustee is required, who selects him?	No disinterested trustee is necessary. The court can be petitioned. However, this only works if the issue is that the trustee is a beneficiary. A second trustee, if there is one can petition the court. Otherwise, there can be no conversion with respect to the items referred to in #12 above. (§ 701.20(4g)(d)(2)) This seems a severe result and not consistent with other state statutes.
14. Must notice be given before a conversion?	Yes, but there are certain differences in notice depending on whether a court is being petitioned. (§ 701.20(4g)(a)(1) 7(2))
15. To whom must notice be given?	Sui juris beneficiaries who would either be (i) entitled to receive current income, (ii) entitled to receive a successor income interest, or (iii) entitled to receive principal upon a termination of the trust immediately before giving of notice. All this assumes no exercise of a power. (§§ 701.20(4g)(a)(1)(b), 701.20(4g)(a)(2), 701.20(4c)(b)(3)(a)–(c))
16. By when must objection be made?	60 days after mailing of notice. (§§ 710.20(4c)(b)(1), 701.20(4c)(b)(4)(c))
17. Can objection be overridden?	Yes, by petitioning a court. (§ 710.20(4g)(a)(1)(b))
18. What if there are not sufficiently competent beneficiaries?	The alternative is to petition a court. (§§ 701.20(4g)(a)(1)(c), 701.20(4g)(a)(2)) The statute requires at least two sui juris beneficiaries to avert the need for court approval, one from (i) and one from (ii) or (iii) as set forth in #15 above. (§ 701.20(4g)(a)(1)(c))
19. Can a beneficiary petition a court to seek conversion if a trustee refuses?	Yes. (§ 701.20(4g)(a)(2)) Thus, the trustee is not obligated to convert upon request. See also § 701.20(4g)(c)(7), which allows a beneficiary to petition to change rate, period for averaging of rate, to obtain a greater payout of income in order to preserve a tax benefit, or to reconvert.
20. Is there a duty to convert?	No. The statute provides that the trustee "may" convert. (§ 70.20(4g)(a)(1))
21. Can a court be petitioned to stop a conversion or reconversion?	Yes, since all conversions must be approved by a court if there is lack of consent by all sui juris beneficiaries. (§§ 701.20(4g)(a)(1)(d), 701.20(4g)(a)(2)) A court must also approve a reconversion. (§ 701.20(4g)(c)(7)(d))
22. Is there a special statute of limitations?	No provision.
23. Is there a mandatory provision for payout of income if greater than the unitrust amount?	No provision. However, a greater payout of net income may be approved by a court if necessary to preserve a tax benefit. (§ 701.20(4g)(c)(7)(b))

24. *If there is an excess payout, is it added to principal?*	No provision.
25. *What is the priority of source of payment of the unitrust amount?*	Net income, ordinary income for federal income tax purposes that is not trust net income, net realized short term capital gain, net realized long term capital gain, principal. (§ 701.20(4g)(c)(6))
26. *Is the priority mandatory?*	Yes (§ 701.20(4g)(c)(6)), unless specified otherwise in the trust instrument.
27. *How is the fair market value of the trust determined for unitrust purposes?*	Over 3 to 5 years, or the lesser period of the trust's existence, the precise period determined in the trustee's discretion. (§§ 701.20(4g)(c)(4)(g), 701.20(4g)(c)(1))
28. *Are certain items excluded?*	No provision. Trustee is given discretion. See #9i above.
29. *Is the trustee authorized to release his power?*	Yes (§ 701.20(4g)(e)), if (i) the trustee is uncertain whether possessing or exercising the power causes adverse tax consequences set forth in #12 above and #36 (iv)-(vi) (§ 701.20(4g)(e)); or (ii) if the trustee determines possessing or exercising the power will or may deprive the trust of a tax benefit or impose a tax burden not described in #36 (iv)-(vi). (*Id.*)
30. *Is there special provision for the marital deduction?*	No conversion allowed if it would result in denial of the marital deduction. (§ 701.20(4g)(d)(1)(f))
31. *Is there special provision for generation-skipping grandfather preservation?*	No provision.
32. *If the power to convert is utilized must the power to adjust be released?*	No provision.
33. *Are particular factors presented that the trustee should consider?*	Yes, these factors must be considered. (§§ 701.20(4g)(a)(1), 701.20(4g)(b), 701.20(4b)(1)–(9))
34. *What standard should a court use?*	Whether the relief sought would enable the trustee to better carry out the purposes of the trust. (§ 701.20(4g)(a)(2)(b))
35. *Must the trust be a locally administered trust?*	No provision.
36. *When does the power to convert not exist?*	If the creating instrument specifically prohibits the conversion; the amount payable to a beneficiary as a fixed annuity or fixed fraction would change; the unitrust amount would be satisfied from an amount permanently set aside for charitable purposes and for which an estate or gift tax deduction has been taken, unless both income and principal are set aside; or the conversion would result in the adverse tax consequences set forth in #12 above. (§ 701.20(4g)(d)(1)-(2) If the trustee is a beneficiary this is also a basis for prohibiting conversion, but another trustee, if there is one, is free to petition the court. (*Id.*)

1. All of these require notice and the consent of every sui juris beneficiary.

Table 12
Trust Accounting: Principal and Income (current through 5/1/07)

In the administration of trusts, there are many issues of accounting that must be confronted. The traditional trust typically is divided between income and remainder interests, so that the proper allocation of receipts and expenses between these is a central responsibility of the fiduciary with potentially enormous consequences for the particular beneficiaries.

In many situations, especially involving unique assets, the proper allocation is not apparent. There have been a number of uniform laws proposed that address this matter comprehensively. In particular, the Uniform Principal and Income Act 1997 has been widely enacted by the states. Thus, the answers for each of thirty-four questions are first set forth under the 1997 Act. To the extent a state's law is modeled on the 1997 Act, the answer to a particular question under that state's law affords the statutory cite and then simply refers the reader to the substantive answer in the 1997 Act chart. To the extent the state has deviated from the 1997 Act in some respect, this is indicated in the state chart. For those states that have not enacted the 1997 Act, the substantive answers to the particular questions are set forth directly in the state chart. In some cases, the state statutory and case law simply offer no answers.

Table 12.01
Uniform Principal And Income Act (1997)
Trust Accounting: Principal and Income

1. *Does the trustee have the power to transfer income to principal or to transfer principal to income to meet its duty of impartiality?*	Generally the trustee has the power to adjust between principal and income if the income component is too small or too large based on total return because of investment decisions made under the prudent investor rule to the extent the trustee considers necessary if the following three conditions are satisfied: 1. the trustee invests and manages trust assets as a prudent investor; 2. the terms of the trust describe the amount that may or must be distributed to a beneficiary by referring to the trust's income; and 3. the trustee determines, after applying the rules in § 103 (a) (requiring obserobservance of the Act if the instrument does not direct otherwise or does not give the trustee discretion), that the trustee is unable to comply with § 103(b) pertaining to the requrement of impartiality. In deciding whether and to what extent to exercise the power to adjust, a trustee is to consider all factors relevant to the trust and its beneficiaries, including nine factors enumerated in § 104(b). The trustee also is constrained to adjust based on eight factors listed in § 104(c). (Uniform Principal and Income Act § 104)
2. *What is the effective date for the law? E.g., does it apply to preexisting trusts?*	The effective date is specific to each state that has adopted the Uniform Principal and Income Act.
3. *What percentage is allocated to income and principal from proceeds of:*	
a) *IRA?* b) *Qualified pension or profit-sharing plan?* c) *Other deferred compensation arrangement?*	A trustee must allocate a payment, or any portion of a payment that is characterized as interest or a dividend, or payment in lieu of interest or a dividend to income. The trustee must allocate to principal the balance of the payment and any other payment received in the same accounting period that is not characterized as interest, a dividend or equivalent payment. If no part of the payment is characterized as interest, a dividend or an equivalent payment and all or part of the payment is required to be made, the trustee must allocate ten percent (10%) of the proceeds that are required to be made during the accounting period to income and the balance of the proceeds to principal. If no part of a payment is required to be made or if the payment received by the trustee is the entire amount to which the trustee is entitled, then the trustee must allocate the entire payment to principal. A payment is not "required to be made" to the extent that it is made because the trustee exercises a right of withdrawal. If, in order to obtain an estate tax marital deduction for a trust, the trustee must allocate more of a payment to income than provided by the paragraphs above, the trustee must allocate to income the additional amount necessary to obtain the marital deduction. (Uniform Principal and Income Act § 409)

4. What percentage is allocated to income and principal from proceeds of:	
a) Patents? *b) Copyrights?*	The trustee must allocate ten percent (10%) of the receipts to income and ninety percent (90%) to principal. (Uniform Principal and Income Act § 410(b))
5. What percentage is allocated to income and principal in the event of distributions from:	
a) Corporations? *b) Partnerships?* *c) LLCs?*	The fiduciary must allocate the following receipts from an entity to principal: (1) Property other than money. However, if the trustee makes or continues an election to reinvest cash dividends, the trustee must transfer cash from principal to income in an amount equal to the reinvested dividends. (2) Money received in one distribution or a series of related distributions in exchange for part or all of a trust's interest in the entity; (3) Money received in total or partial liquidation of the entity; and (4) Money received from an entity that is a regulated investment company or a real estate investment trust, if the money distributed is a capital gain dividend for federal income tax purposes. A fiduciary must allocate all other money received from an entity to income. (Uniform Principal and Income Act § 401)
6. What percentage is allocated to income and principal from proceeds of:	
a) Oil and gas? *b) Minerals?* *c) Water?* *d) Other natural resourses (not including timber)?*	The trustee must allocate a receipt received as nominal delay rental or a nominal annual rent on a lease to income. The trustee must allocate a receipt received from a production payment to income if and to the extent that the agreement creating the production payment provides a factor for interest or its equivalent. The balance must be allocated to principal. The trustee must allocate ninety percent (90%) of an amount received as a royalty, shut-in-well payment, take-or-pay payment, bonus, or a delay rental that is more than nominal, to principal and ten percent (10%) to income. The trustee must allocate ninety percent (90%) of the net amount received from a working interest or other interest (not mentioned in the preceding paragraphs) to principal and ten percent (10%) to income. An amount received on account of an interest in water that is renewable must be allocated to income. If the water is not renewable, ninety percent (90%) of the amount must be allocated to principal and ten percent (10%) to income. The rules above apply whether or not a decedent or donor was extracting the minerals, water, or other natural resources before the interest became subject to the trust. (Uniform Principal and Income Act § 411)

e) Timber?	The trustee must allocate the net receipts to income to the extent that the amount of timber removed from the land does not exceed the rate of growth of the timber during the accounting periods in which a beneficiary has a mandatory income interest. The trustee must allocate the net receipts to principal to the extent that 1) the amount of timber removed from the land exceeds the rate of growth of the timber or 2) the net receipts are from the sale of standing timber. The trustee must allocate the net receipts to or between income and principal if the net receipts are from the lease of timberland or from a contract to cut timber from land owned by a trust, by determining the amount of timber removed from the land under the lease or contract and applying the paragraphs above. The trustee must allocate advance payments, bonuses and other payments to principal to the extent that they are not otherwise allocated between income and principal. In determining net receipts to be allocated between income and principal, a trustee must deduct and transfer to principal a reasonable amount for depletion. The rules regarding the allocation of net receipts from timber apply whether or not a decedent or transferor was harvesting timber from the property before it became subject to the trust. (Uniform Principal and Income Act § 412)
f) Rental properties?	Unless the trustee accounts separately for the management of rental properties owned by the trust under § 403, the trustee must allocate to income an amount received as rent of real or personal property, including an amount received for cancellation or renewal of a lease. An amount received as a refundable deposit, including a security deposit or a deposit that is to be applied as rent for future periods, must be added to principal and held subject to the terms of the lease and is not available for distribution to a beneficiary until the trustee's contractual obligations have been satisfied with respect to that amount. (Uniform Principal and Income Act § 405)
7. After a decedent dies, in the case of an estate, or after an income interest ends, when the fiduciary is determining the remaining net income what are the rules regarding payment from income or principal for:	
a) Attorneys fees? *b) Accountants fees?* *c) Fiduciary fees and commissions?* *d) Court costs?* *e) Interest on death taxes*	The fiduciary may pay these fees and costs from income or principal at the fiduciary's discretion, however the fiduciary may pay those expenses from income of property passing to a trust for which the fiduciary claims an estate tax marital or charitable deduction only to the extent that the payment of those expenses from income will not cause the reduction or loss of the deduction. (Uniform Principal and Income Act § 201(2)(B))

f) Debts? *g) Funeral expenses?* *h) Family allowances and similar protections?* *i) Death taxes?* *j) Penalties on death taxes?*	Debts, funeral expenses, disposition of remains, family allowances, and death taxes and related penalties that are apportioned to the estate or terminating income interest by the will, the terms of the trust, or applicable law must be paid from principal. (Uniform Principal and Income Act § 201(2)(C))
8. With respect to trust expenses from the administration of the trust that are not covered by § 201(2)(b-c) [see Question #7]:	
a) Does the trustee have full discretion in allocating between income and principal for expenses incurred in the administration of the trust?	No. (Uniform Principal and Income Act § § 501-502)
b) If not, are there special rules for:	
i) Regular trustee fees? *ii) Advisory or custodial services to the trustee?* *iii) Accountings, judicial proceedings and other matters that involve both the income and remainder interests?*	The Trustee must pay 50% of these expenses from income and 50% from principal. (Uniform Principal and Income Act §§ 501 & 502)
iv) Debts?	The trustee must allocate interest expense on trust debt to income and must allocate payments on principal of trust debt to principal. (Uniform Principal and Income Act § § 501(3) & 502(a)(3))
c) Can the trustee determine what are "transmission" expenses and "management" expenses?	
9. With regard to specific gifts from a trust after an income interest ends or from an estate:	
a) What amounts must be paid from income and principal?	The fiduciary must distribute the net income and the net principal receipts to the beneficiary who is to receive the property. The net income and principal receipts are determined by including all amounts that that the fiduciary receives or pays with respect to the property, whether those amounts accrued or became due before, on, or after the date of the decedent's death or the income interest's terminating event, and by making a reasonable provision for the amounts that the fiduciary believes the estate or terminating income interest may be obligated to pay after the property is distributed. (Uniform Principal and Income Act § 201(1) & § 201(5))
10. With regard to outright pecuniary gifts from an estate or trust?	

a) *Does interest accrue?*	Yes. Interest must be paid from net income and from principal to the extent that net income is insufficient. (Uniform Principal and Income Act § 201(3))
11. *With regard to a gift in trust of a pecuniary amount from an estate or trust?*	
a) *Does interest accrue?*	No. The trust will receive a pro-rata share of the net income determined by the trust's fractional interest in the undistributed principal assets. (Uniform Principal and Income Act § 201(4) & § 202)
12. *With regard to residuary gifts:*	
a) *What amount of income and principal is to be paid to the residuary beneficiary of a trust or an estate?*	The beneficiary will receive a pro-rata share of the beneficiary's fractional interest in the principal assets, as well as, a pro-rata share of net income determined by the beneficiary's fractional interest in the undistributed principal assets. (Uniform Principal and Income Act § 201(4) & § 202)
13. *With regard to "business assets" held in trust:*	
a) *Can the trustee treat them as a separate entity?*	The trustee may maintain separate accounting records for a business or other activity that the trustee is conducting if the trustee determines that it is in the best interest of all the beneficiaries to account separately for the business or other activity instead of accountiung for it as part of the trust's general accounting records, whether or not its assets are segregated from other trust assets. (Uniform Principal and Income Act § 403(a)) Businesses and activities for which the trustee may maintain separate accounts include: 1. Retail, manufacturing, serivce, and other traditional business activities; 2. Farming; 3. Raising and selling livestock and other animals; 4. Managing rental properties; 5. Extracting minerals and other resources; 6. Timber operations; and 7. Transactions in derivative instruments. (Uniform Principal and Income Act § 403(c))
b) *Can the trustee treat distinct assets as separate entities?*	The trustee may account separately for each business or activity for which the trustee determines separate accounting is appropriate. (Uniform Principal and Income Act § 403 and Official Comments)
c) *Can earnings be retained in trust for the reasonable needs of the "business entity", and, if so, to what extent is this permitted?*	Yes. (Uniform Principal and Income Act § 403(b))
14. *With respect to discount bonds:*	

a) *To what extent is the discount added to income or principal upon maturity?*	If the trustee acquires a discount bond with a maturity date of one year or less, the amount received over the purchase price must be allocated to income. Otherwise, the trustee must allocate the entire amount of the proceeds to principal. (Uniform Principal and Income Act § 406(b))
b) *Does the trustee have discretion to allocate discount between income and principal?*	No. (Uniform Principal and Income Act § 406) ***Note***: The trustee has the overriding power to adjust under § 104(a).
c) *Are distinctions drawn between Series E bonds and others?*	No. (Uniform Principal and Income Act § 406)
d) *Are distinctions drawn based on the maturity date of the bond?*	Yes. (Uniform Principal and Income Act § 406(b)) See 14.a) above.
15. *Is there a de minimis rule excusing the trustee from making adjustments in certain cases?*	If a fiduciary determines that an allocation between principal and income required for: 1. Deferred compensation, annuities, and similar payments; 2. Liquidating assets; 3. Minerals, water and other natural resources; 4. Timber; or 5. Asset-backed securities is insubstantial, then the fiduciary may allocate the entire amount to principal unless one of the circumstances in § 104 (c) applies. Additionally, the power may be exercised by a co-trustee under § 104(d) and may be released under § 104(e) under certain circumstances. See the statute for more details. An allocation is presumed to be insubstantial if 1. The amount of the allocation would increase or decrease net income in an accounting period, as determined before the allocation by less than ten percent (10%), or 2. The value of the asset producing the receipt for which the allocation would be made is less than ten percent (10%) of the total value of the trust's assets at the beginning of the accounting period. (Uniform Principal and Income Act § 408)
16. *With respect to derivatives:*	
a) *May income and loss be treated as that of a separate entity?*	Yes. (Uniform Principal and Income Act § § 403, 414(b))
b) *If not, or the trustee chooses not to do so, is income and loss allocated to the income account or to principal?*	To principal. (Uniform Principal and Income Act § 414(b))
17. *To the extent put and call options are not derivatives, how are they allocated in terms of principal and income?*	To principal. (Uniform Principal and Income Act § 414(c))
18. *How are asset-backed securities allocated in terms of principal and income?*	If a trust receives a payment that includes interest or other current return and other proceeds of the collateral financial assets, the trustee must:

1. allocate the portion of the payment which the payer identifies as being from interest or other current return to income, and
2. allocate the balance of the payment to principal.

If a trust receives one or more payments in exchange for the trust's entire interest in an asset-backed security in one accounting period, the trustee must allocate the payments to principal.

If a payment is one of a series of payments that will result in the liquidation of the trust's interest in the security over more than one accounting period, the trustee must allocate ten percent (10%) of the payment to income and ninety percent (90%) to principal.

(Uniform Principal and Income Act § 415(b) & (c))

"Accounting period" means a calendar year unless another 12-month period is selected by a fiduciary. The term includes a portion of a calendar year or other 12-month period that begins when an income interest begins or ends when an income interest ends.

---

19. Are expenses incurred to comply with environmental requirements allocated to income or principal?

Expenses incurred to comply with environmental requirements must be allocated to principal.

(Uniform Principal and Income Act § 502(a)(7))

Note: If a trustee makes or expects to make a principal disbursement described for environmental expenses under § 502 (a)(7), the trustee may transfer an appropriate amount from income to principal in one or more accounting periods to reimburse principal or to provide a reserve for principal disbursements. (See Uniform Principal and Income Act § 504(b)(5))

---

20. Is income tax liability allocated generally to income or principal?

Any tax required to be paid by a fiduciary on the trust's share of an entity's taxable income must be paid proportionately as follows:

1. From income to the extent that receipts from the entity are allocated to income; and
2. From principal to the extent that receipts from the entity are allocated to principal and to the extent that the income taxes owed are greater than the receipts allocable to both income and principal.

The fiduciary must reduce the receipts allocated to principal or income by the amount distributed to a beneficiary from principal or income for which the trust receives a deduction in calculating the tax.

(Uniform Principal and Income Act § 505)

A trustee may make adjustments between principal and income to offset the shifting of economic interests or tax benefits between income beneficiaries and remainder beneficiaries which arise from any of the following:

1. Elections and decisions that the trustee makes from time to time regarding tax matters;
2. An income tax or any other tax that is imposed upon the trustee or a beneficiary as a result of a transaction involving a decedent's estate, a trust, or a distribution from a decedent's estate or a trust; or
3. The ownership by a decedent's estate or trust of an interest in an entity whose taxable income, whether or

	not distributed, is includable in the taxable income of the decedent's estate, trust, or a beneficiary. If the amount of an estate tax marital deduction or charitable contribution deduction is reduced because a fiduciary deducts an amount paid from principal for income tax purposes instead of deducting it for estate tax purposes, and as a result estate taxes paid from principal are increased and income taxes paid by an estate, trust, or beneficiary are decreased, each estate, trust, or beneficiary that benefits from the decrease in income tax shall reimburse the principal from which the increase in estate tax is paid. The total reimbursement must equal the increase in the estate tax to the extent that the principal used to pay the increase would have qualified for a marital deduction or charitable contribution deduction but for the payment. The proportionate share of the reimbursement for each estate, trust, or beneficiary whose income taxes are reduced must be the same as its proportionate share of the total decrease in income tax. An estate or trust shall reimburse principal from income. (Uniform Principal and Income Act § 506)
21. If a Subchapter S shareholder's or partner's portion of tax liability is greater than cash distributed, how is the excess obligation allocated?	From principal. (Uniform Principal and Income Act § 505(c)(2)(B))
22. What is the standard, if any, for making equitable adjustments between income and principal?	In exercising the power to adjust, the fiduciary must administer a trust, or decedent's estate impartially, based on what is fair and reasonable to all of the beneficiaries, except to the extent that the terms of the trust or the will clearly manifest an intention that the fiduciary shall or may favor one or more of the beneficiaries. (Uniform Principal and Income Act § 103(b))
23. Is an income beneficiary entitled to receive income accrued but unpaid when an estate ends?	No. However, when a trustee's obligation to pay a fixed annuity or a fixed fraction of the value of the trust's assets ends, the trustees shall prorate the final payment if and to the extent required by applicable law to accomplish a purpose of the trust or its settlor relating to income, gift, estate, or other tax requirements. (Uniform Principal and Income Act § 303)
24. Is an income beneficiary entitled to receive income accrued but unpaid when a revocable trust ends?	No. However, when a trustee's obligation to pay a fixed annuity or a fixed fraction of the value of the trust's assets ends, the trustees shall prorate the final payment if and to the extent required by applicable law to accomplish a purpose of the trust or its settlor relating to income, gift, estate, or other tax requirements. (Uniform Principal and Income Act § 303)
25. Is an income beneficiary entitled to receive income accrued but unpaid when an irrevocable trust ends?	No. However, when a trustee's obligation to pay a fixed annuity or a fixed fraction of the value of the trust's assets ends, the trustees shall prorate the final payment if and to the extent required by applicable law to accomplish a purpose of the trust or its settlor relating to income, gift, estate, or other tax requirements. (Uniform Principal and Income Act § 303)
26. With regard to mutual funds, how are:	
a) long-term gains allocated between income and principal?	Capital gain dividends are allocated to principal. A capital gain dividend from a mutual fund is the excess of the fund's or trust's net long-term capital gain over its net short-term capital loss. As a result, a capital gain dividend does not include any

	net short-term capital gain. (Uniform Principal and Income Act § 401(c)(4))
b) short-term gains allocated between income and principal?	Net short-term capital gains are allocated to income. A capital gain dividend from a mutual fund is the excess of the fund's or trust's net long-term capital gain over its net short-term capital loss. As a result, a capital gain dividend does not include any net short-term capital gain. (Uniform Principal and Income Act § 401(c)(4))
27. How are distributions from REITs allocated between income and principal?	If a distribution from a REIT is a capital gain dividend for federal income tax purposes, or is in exchange for part or all of the the trust's interest in the REIT, or is received in total or partial liquidation of the REIT, the trustee must allocate the distribution to principal; otherwise, the trustee must allocate the distribution to income. (Uniform Principal and Income Act § 401(c)(4))
28. With respect to underproductive property:	
a) Is an adjustment, e.g., "delayed income," required to be paid to the income beneficiary?	Unless additional income allocations are necessary to qualify a trust for the marital deduction, the trustee must allocate the proceeds of a sale or disposition of property that is not productive of income to principal without regard for the amount of income the asset produces or produced in any accounting period. (Uniform Principal and Income Act § 413)
b) What percentage return makes property underproductive?	The statute only refers to property not productive of income. (Uniform Principal and Income Act § 413)
29. Is the trustee required to increase income so that it is sufficient to qualify for the marital deduction?	Yes. (Uniform Principal and Income Act § 413(a))
30. Is the trustee required to take depreciation?	No. (Uniform Principal and Income Act § 503)
31. Is the trustee's determination on allocations generally presumed to be fair and reasonable?	Yes. (Uniform Principal and Income Act § 103(b))
32. If an item is not addressed in the trust agreement or in the law, must it be allocated to principal or income?	To principal. (Uniform Principal and Income Act § 103(a)(4))
33. When does an asset become subject to a trust:	
a) In the case of transfers during the transferor's life?	The date of transfer. (Uniform Principal and Income Act § 301 (b)(1))
b) In the case of a will?	The date of the testator's death. (Uniform Principal and Income Act § 301(b)(2))
c) In the case of the death of a third party?	The date of the third party's death. (Uniform Principal and Income Act § 301(b)(3))
34. Can a trustee rely on the characterization by an entity as to the source or character of a received distribution?	Yes. (Uniform Principal and Income Act § 401(f))

Table 12.02
Alabama
Trust Accounting: Principal and Income

1. *Does the trustee have the power to transfer income to principal or to transfer principal to income to meet its duty of impartiality?*	See the Uniform Principal and Income Act (1997) chart. (§ 19-3A-104) ***Note***: The terms of the trust must expressly provide for the power to adjust by specific reference to § 19-3A-104(a).
2. *What is the effective date for the law? E.g., does it apply to preexisting trusts?*	The Alabama Principal and Income Act became applicable on January 1, 2001 to every trust and decedent's estate already in existence on January 1, 2001. The Alabama Principal and Income Act became applicable on January 1, 2001 to every testamentary trust to be created on or after January 1, 2001, from a decedent's estate that is already in existence on January 1, 2001. At any time prior to January 1, 2003, any trust and decedent's estate already in existence on January 1, 2001 or testamentary trust to be created on or after January 1, 2001, from a decedent's estate that is already in existence on January 1, 2001 has the right to elect to continue operating under the law in effect prior to the Alabama Principal and Income Act. Any fiduciary, income beneficiary, or presumptive remainder beneficiary of an affected trust or estate shall have the right to make the election to continue operating under the law in effect prior to this chapter, which election shall be made by a written instrument delivered to, or executed by, the fiduciary and placed with the fiduciary's records. The decision of whether to make such election by the fiduciary or by any income beneficiary or presumptive remaindermen shall conclusively bind all persons who may have any interest in the affected trust, including all contingent remaindermen and potential appointees of the affected trust or estate. (§ 19-3A-604) ***Note:*** If a trust owns a interest minerals, water, other natural resources or timber on January 1, 2001, the trustee can continue to allocate the receipts from the interest in the manner used by the trustee before January 1, 2001. (See § 19-3A-411; § 19-3A-412)
3. *What percentage is allocated to income and principal from proceeds of:*	
a) IRA? *b) Qualified pension or profit-sharing plan?* *c) Other deferred compensation arrangement?*	See the Uniform Principal and Income Act (1997) chart. (§ 19-3A-409)
4. *What percentage is allocated to income and principal from proceeds of:*	
a) Patents? *b) Copyrights?*	See the Uniform Principal and Income Act (1997) chart. (§ 19-3A-410(b))

5. *What percentage is allocated to income and principal in the event of distributions from:*	
a) *Corporations?* b) *Partnerships?* c) *LLCs?*	See the Uniform Principal and Income Act (1997) chart. (§ 19-3A-401(b))
6. *What percentage is allocated to income and principal from proceeds of:*	
a) *Oil and gas?* b) *Minerals?* c) *Water?* d) *Other natural resourses (not including timber)?*	See the Uniform Principal and Income Act (1997) chart. (§ 19-3A-411) ***Note***: If a trust owns an interest in minerals, water, or other natural resources on January 1, 2001, the fiduciary may allocate receipts from the interest as provided in the Alabama Principal and Income Act or in the manner used by the fiduciary before January 1, 2001. If the trust acquires an interest in oil and gas or other natural resources after January 1, 2001, then the fiduciary should allocate receipts from the interest as provided the Alabama Principal and Income Act.
e) *Timber*	The fiduciary must allocate the net receipts first to principal, based upon the volume of the timber at the time of transfer to the trust or decedent's estate. The balance shall be allocated eighty percent (80%) to income and twenty percent (20%) to principal. In determining the amount of net receipts from the sale of timber, the fiduciary must deduct the following expenses related to the sale of timber and related products from gross receipts: (1) Management expenses; (2) Legal and accounting expenses and fees; (3) Sales commissions; (4) Reforestation expenses; and (5) Any necessary timber stand improvement expense that is recognized and accepted as good forest management practice at the time of sale. The Alabama Principal and Income Act applies whether or not the decedent or transferor was harvesting timber from the property before it became subject to the trust or decedent's estate. (§ 19-3A-412) If a trust owns an interest in timberland on January 1, 2001, then the fiduciary may allocate net receipts from the sale of timber and related products as provided in the Alabama Principal and Income Act or in the manner used by the fiduciary before January 1, 2001. If the trust acquires an interest in timberland after January 1, 2001, then the fiduciary must allocate net receipts from the sale of timber and related products as provided in the Alabama Principal and Income Act. (§ 19-3A-412)
f) *Rental properties?*	See the Uniform Principal and Income Act (1997) chart. (§ 19-3A-405)
7. *After a decedent dies, in the case of an estate, or after an income interest ends, when the fiduciary is determining the remaining net income, What are the rules regarding payment from income or principal for:*	

a) Attorneys fees? *b) Accountants fees?* *c) Fiduciary fees and expenses?* *d) Court costs?* *e) Interest on death taxes?*	See the Uniform Principal and Income Act (1997) chart. (§ 19-3A-201(c)(2))
f) Debts? *g) Funeral expenses?* *h) Family allowances and similar protections?* *i) Death taxes?* *j) Penalties on death taxes?*	See the Uniform Principal and Income Act (1997) chart. (§ 19-3A-201(c)(3))
8. With respect to trust expenses from the administration of the trust that are not covered by § 19-3A-201(c)(2-3) [see Question #7]:	
a) Does the trustee have full discretion in allocating between income and principal for expenses incurred in the administration of the trust?	No. (§ 19-3A-501; § 19-3A-502)
b) If not, are there special rules for:	
i) Regular trustee fees? *ii) Advisory or cusodial services to the trustee?* *iii) Accountings, judicial proceedings and other matters that involve both the income and remainder interests?*	See the Uniform Principal and Income Act (1997) chart. (§ 19-3A-501(a); § 19-3A-501(b))
iv) Debts?	See the Uniform Principal and Income Act (1997) chart. (§ 19-3A-501(c); § 19-3A-502(a)(3))
c) Can the trustee determine what are "transmission" expenses and "management" expenses?	
9. With regard to specific gifts from a trust after an income interest ends or from an estate:	
a) What amounts must be paid from income and principal?	See the Uniform Principal and Income Act (1997) chart. (§ 19-3A-201(a))
10. With regard to outright pecuniary gifts from an estate or trust?:	
a) Does interest accrue?	Yes. See the Uniform Principal and Income Act (1997) chart. (§ 19-3A-201(b); § 19-3A-201(e))
11. With regard to a gift in trust of a pecuniary amount from an estate or trust?	

a) *Does interest accrue?*	No, but the trust will receive a pro-rata share of the net income determined by the trust's fractional interest in the undistributed principal assets. (§ 19-3A-201(d))
12. *With regard to residuary gifts:*	
a) *What amount of income and principal is to be paid to the residuary beneficiary of a trust or an estate?*	See the Uniform Principal and Income Act (1997) chart. (§ 19-3A-201(d); § 19-3A-202)
13. *With regard to "business assets" held in trust:*	
a) *Can the trustee treat them as a separate entity?*	Yes. (§ 19-3A-403(a); § 19-3A-403(c))
b) *Can the trustee treat distinct assets as separate entities?*	Yes. (§ 19-3A-403)
c) *Can earnings be retained in trust for the reasonable needs of the "business entity," and, if so, to what extent is this permitted?*	Yes. (§ 19-3A-403(b))
14. *With respect to discount bonds:*	
a) *To what extent is the discount added to income or principal upon maturity?*	For zero coupon bonds (bonds that pay zero interest, but not including bonds that pay below market interest that were purchased at a discount), the fiduciary must allocate to income the difference between inventory value or cost, and the amount realized upon sale or maturity, if greater. Otherwise, the fiduciary must allocate to principal any gain realized from the sale or maturity of any bond. (§ 19-3A-406)
b) *Does the trustee have discretion to allocate discount between income and principal?*	No. (§ 19-3A-406) ***Note***: The trustee may still have the overriding power to adjust under § 19-3A-104(a).
c) *Are distinctions drawn between Series E bonds and others?*	No. (§ 19-3A-406)
d) *Are distinctions drawn based on the maturity date of the bond?*	No. (§ 19-3A-406)
15. *Is there a de minimis rule excusing the trustee from making adjustments in certain cases?*	Yes. See the Uniform Principal and Income Act (1997) chart. (§ 19-3A-408) ***Note***: Alabama eliminates the "bright line" test, containing the presumption of insubstantiality, set forth in the Uniform Principal and Income Act § 408.
16. *With respect to derivatives:*	
a) *May income and loss be treated as that of a separate entity?*	Yes. (§ 19-3A-403(a); § 19-3A-403(c)(7); § 19-3A-414(b))
b) *If not, or the trustee chooses not to do so, is income and loss allocated to the income account or to principal?*	To principal. (§ 19-3A-414(b))

17. To the extent put and call options are not derivatives, how are they allocated in terms of principal and income?	To principal. (§ 19-3A-414(c))
18. How are asset-backed securities allocated in terms of principal and income?	See the Uniform Principal and Income Act (1997) chart. (§ 19-3A-415) ***Note***: Alabama uses the term "a twelve month period" instead of the term "one accounting period". See Ala. Code § 19-3A-415 for further details.
19. Are expenses incurred to comply with environmental requirements allocated to income or principal?	A trustee may charge all expenses related to environmental matters to principal or income, as provided by applicable law. Otherwise, all disbursements related to environmental matters should be charged to income. (§ 19-3A-501(e); § 19-3A-502(c))
20. Is income tax liability allocated generally to income or principal?	See the Uniform Principal and Income Act (1997) chart. (§ 19-3A-505; § 19-3A-506)
21. If a Subchapter S shareholder's or partner's portion of tax liability is greater than cash distributed, how is the excess obligation allocated?	The statute does not address how the excess obligation be allocated. (§ 19-3A-505)
22. What is the standard, if any, for making equitable adjustments between income and principal?	See the Uniform Principal and Income Act (1997) chart. (§ 19-3A-103(b))
23. Is an income beneficiary entitled to receive income accrued but unpaid when an estate ends?	No. (§ 19-3A-303)
24. Is an income beneficiary entitled to receive income accrued but unpaid when a revocable trust ends?	Generally no. See the Uniform Principal and Income Act (1997) chart. (§ 19-3A-303)
25. Is an income beneficiary entitled to receive income accrued but unpaid when an irrevocable trust ends?	Generally no. See the Uniform Principal and Income Act (1997) chart. (§ 19-3A-303)
26. With regard to mutual funds, how are:	
a) long-term gains allocated between income and principal?	See the Uniform Principal and Income Act (1997) chart. (§ 19-3A-401(c)(4))
b) short-term gains allocated between income and principal?	See the Uniform Principal and Income Act (1997) chart. (§ 19-3A-401(c)(4))
27. How are distributions from REITs allocated between income and principal?	See the Uniform Principal and Income Act (1997) chart. (§ 19-3A-401(c)(4))
28. With respect to underproductive property:	
a) Is an adjustment, e.g., "delayed income," required to be paid to the income beneficiary?	No. (§ 19-3A-413)

b) *What percentage return makes property underproductive?*	The statute only refers to property not productive of income. (§ 19-3A-413)
29. *Is the trustee required to increase income so that it is sufficient to qualify for the marital deduction?*	Yes. (§ 19-3A-413(a))
30. *Is the trustee required to take depreciation?*	No. (§ 19-3A-503)
31. *Is the trustee's determination on allocations generally presumed to be fair and reasonable?*	Yes. (§ 19-3A-103(b))
32. *If an item is not addressed in the trust agreement or in the law, must it be allocated to principal or income?*	To principal. (§ 19-3A-103(a)(4))
33. *When does an asset become subject to a trust:*	
a) *In the case of transfers during the transferor's life?*	The date the asset is transferred to the trust. (§ 19-3A-301(b)(1))
b) *In the case of a will?*	The death of the testator. (§ 19-3A-301(b)(2))
c) *In the case of the death of a third party?*	The date of the third party's death. (§ 19-3A-301(b)(3))
34. *Can a trustee rely on the characterization by an entity as to the source or character of a received distribution?*	Yes. (§ 19-3A-401(e))

Table 12.02
Alaska
Trust Accounting: Principal and Income

1. *Does the trustee have the power to transfer income to principal or to transfer principal to income to meet its duty of impartiality?*	Yes. (§ 13.38.210)
2. *What is the effective date for the law? E.g., does it apply to preexisting trusts?*	Unless otherwise provided in the governing instrument, the Alaska Principal and Income Act applies to all trusts existing on or after September 1, 2003, and to all estates of a decedent who dies on or after September 1, 2003. (2003 Alaska Sess. Laws 145)
3. *What percentage is allocated to income and principal from proceeds of:*	
a) *IRA?* b) *Qualified pension or profit-sharing plan?* c) *Other deferred compensation arrangement?*	The trustee shall allocate to income the greater of the portion of a payment characterized by the payor: 1. as interest or a dividend, 2. as a remittance in place of interest or a dividend, or 3. as imputed interest for federal income tax purposes. The balance of the payment shall be allocated to principal. If a part of a payment under a contract calling for equal installments over a fixed period of time is not allocable to income under the provisions above, the difference between the trust's acquisition value of the contract and the total expected return shall be considered to be interest. The trustee must allocate to income the portion of each payment equivalent to interest on the then unpaid principal balance at the rate specified in the contract or at a rate necessary to amortize the difference between the expected return and the acquisition value, where that rate is readily ascertainable by the trustee. If there is not a portion of a payment from a separate fund held exclusively for the benefit of the trust that is allocable to income, but the internal net income of the fund determined as if the fund were a separate trust is readily ascertainable by the trustee, the portion of the payment equal to the then undistributed net income of the fund realized since the trust acquired its interest in the fund is considered to be a distribution of income and shall be allocated to the trust income account. The balance of the payment described in this subsection shall be allocated to principal. A trustee shall allocate 10 percent of the part of the payment that is required to be made during the accounting period to income and the balance to principal if there is not a part of the payment that is otherwise allocable to income under the Alaska Principal and Income Act and all or part of the payment is required to be made. The trustee must allocate the entire payment to principal if a part of a payment is not required to be made or the payment received is the entire amount to which the trustee is entitled. Note that a payment is not "required to be made" to the extent that it is made because the trustee exercises a right of withdrawal. If, to obtain a federal estate or gift tax marital deduction for a trust, the trustee must allocate more of a payment to income than provided for by this section, the trustee shall allocate the additional amount necessary to obtain the marital deduction to income. (§ 13.38.690)

4. *What percentage is allocated to income and principal from proceeds of:*	
a) *Patents?* b) *Copyrights?*	See the Uniform Principal and Income Act (1997) chart. (§ 13.38.700)
5. *What percentage is allocated to income and principal in the event of distributions from:*	
a) *Corporations?* b) *Partnerships?* c) *LLCs?*	See the Uniform Principal and Income Act (1997) chart. (§ 13.38.600)
6. *What percentage is allocated to income and principal from proceeds of:*	
a) *Oil and gas?* b) *Minerals?* c) *Water?* d) *Other natural resourses (not including timber)?*	See the Uniform Principal and Income Act (1997) chart. (§ 13.38.710)
e) *Timber*	See the Uniform Principal and Income Act (1997) chart. (§ 13.38.720)
f) *Rental properties?*	See the Uniform Principal and Income Act (1997) chart. (§ 13.38.640)
7. *After a decedent dies, in the case of an estate, or after an income interest ends, when the fiduciary is determining the remaining net income what are the rules regarding payment from income or principal for:*	
a) *Attorneys fees?* b) *Accountants fees?* c) *Fiduciary fees and commissions?* d) *Court costs?* e) *Interest on death taxes*	The Trustee must pay these fees and expenses from principal. (§ 13.38.500(3)(B))
f) *Debts?* g) *Funeral expenses?* h) *Family allowances and similar protections?* i) *Death taxes?* j) *Penalties on death taxes?*	See the Uniform Principal and Income Act (1997) chart. (§ 13.38.500(3)(B))
8. *With respect to trust expenses from the administration of the trust that are not covered by (§ 13.38.500(3)(B) [see Question #7]:*	

a) Does the trustee have full discretion in allocating between income and principal for expenses incurred in the administration of the trust?	No. (§ 13.38.800; § 13.38.810; § 13.38.820)
b) If not, are there special rules for:	
i) Regular trustee fees? *ii) Advisory or cusodial services to the trustee?* *iii) Accountings, judicial proceedings and other matters that involve both the income and remainder interests?*	The trustee must pay for accountings and judicial proceedings or other proceedings, as well as legal services to the trustee from the principal. Otherwise and subject to other exceptions, a trustee may, in the trustee's discretion, allocate to income or principal or partly to each ordinary expenses incurred in connection with the administration, management, or preservation of trust property and the distribution of income, including the compensation of the trustee and of a person providing investment advisory, custodial, or income tax return preparation services to the trustee. (§ 13.38.820) **Note**: See § 13.38.800 and § 13.38.810 for mandatory disbursements.
iv) Debts?	The trustee must allocate interest expense on trust debt to income and must allocate payments on principal of trust debt to principal. (§ 13.38.800(1); § 13.38.810(a)(5))
c) Can the trustee determine what are "transmission" expenses and "management" expenses?	
9. With regard to specific gifts from a trust after an income interest ends or from an estate:	
a) What amounts must be paid from income and principal?	See the Uniform Principal and Income Act (1997) chart. (§ 13.38.500(1))
10. With regard to outright pecuniary gifts from an estate or trust?:	
a) Does interest accrue?	No, but the trust will receive a pro-rata share of the net income determined by the trust's fractional interest in the undistributed principal assets. (§ 13.38.500(2))
11. With regard to a gift in trust of a pecuniary amount from an estate or trust?	
a) Does interest accrue?	No, but the trust will receive a pro-rata share of the net income determined by the trust's fractional interest in the undistributed principal assets. (§ 13.38.500(2))
12. With regard to residuary gifts:	
a) What amount of income and principal is to be paid to the residuary beneficiary of a trust or an estate?	See the Uniform Principal and Income Act (1997) chart. (§ 13.38.500(4); § 13.38.510)

13. With regard to "business assets" held in trust:	
a) Can the trustee treat them as a separate entity?	Yes. See the Uniform Principal and Income Act (1997) chart. (§ 13.38.620)
b) Can the trustee treat distinct assets as separate entities?	Yes. See the Uniform Principal and Income Act (1997) chart. (§ 13.38.620)
c) Can earnings be retained in trust for the reasonable needs of the "business entity", and, if so, to what extent is this permitted?	See the Uniform Principal and Income Act (1997) chart. (§ 13.38.650)
14. With respect to discount bonds:	
a) To what extent is the discount added to income or principal upon maturity?	See the Uniform Principal and Income Act (1997) chart. (§ 13.38.650)
b) Does the trustee have discretion to allocate discount between income and principal?	No. (§ 13.38.650) ***Note***: The trustee has the overriding power to adjust under § 13.38.210.
c) Are distinctions drawn between Series E bonds and others?	No. (§ 13.38.650)
d) Are distinctions drawn based on the maturity date of the bond?	Yes. (§ 13.38.650)
15. Is there a de minimis rule excusing the trustee from making adjustments in certain cases?	Yes. See the Uniform Principal and Income Act (1997) chart. ***Note***: The threshold for an allocation to be presumed insubstantial is five percent (5%) in § 13.38.650 as opposed to ten percent (10%). (§ 13.38.650)
16. With respect to derivatives:	
a) May income and loss be treated as that of a separate entity?	Yes. (§ 13.38.620; § 13.38.740)
b) If not, or the trustee chooses not to do so, is income and loss allocated to the income account or to principal?	To principal. (§ 13.38.740)
17. To the extent put and call options are not derivatives, how are they allocated in terms of principal and income?	To principal. (§ 13.38.740(b))
18. How are asset-backed securities allocated in terms of principal and income?	See the Uniform Principal and Income Act (1997) chart. (§ 13.38.750)
19. Are expenses incurred to comply with environmental requirements allocated to income or principal?	Generally to principal. See the Uniform Principal and Income Act (1997) chart.(§ 13.38.810(a)(8))
20. Is income tax liability allocated generally to income or principal?	See the Uniform Principal and Income Act (1997) chart. (§ 13.38.850; § 13.38.860)

21. *If a Subchapter S shareholder's or partner's portion of tax liability is greater than cash distributed, how is the excess obligation allocated?*	To principal. (§ 13.38.850(c)(2)(B))
22. *What is the standard, if any, for making equitable adjustments between income and principal?*	See the Uniform Principal and Income Act (1997) chart. (§ 13.38.200(b))
23. *Is an income beneficiary entitled to receive income accrued but unpaid when an estate ends?*	No. (§ 13.38.570)
24. *Is an income beneficiary entitled to receive income accrued but unpaid when a revocable trust ends?*	Generally no. See the Uniform Principal and Income Act (1997) chart. (§ 13.38.570)
25. *Is an income beneficiary entitled to receive income accrued but unpaid when an irrevocable trust ends?*	Generally no. See the Uniform Principal and Income Act (1997) chart. (§ 13.38.570)
26. *With regard to mutual funds, how are:*	
a) *long-term gains allocated between income and principal?*	See the Uniform Principal and Income Act (1997) chart. (§ 13.38.600(b)(4))
b) *short-term gains allocated between income and principal?*	See the Uniform Principal and Income Act (1997) chart. (§ 13.38.600(b)(4))
27. *How are distributions from REITs allocated between income and principal?*	See the Uniform Principal and Income Act (1997) chart. (§ 13.38.600(b)(4))
28. *With respect to underproductive property:*	
a) *Is an adjustment, e.g., "delayed income," required to be paid to the income beneficiary?*	No. (§ 13.38.730)
b) *What percentage return makes property underproductive?*	The statute only refers to property not productive of income. (§ 13.38.730)
29. *Is the trustee required to increase income so that it is sufficient to qualify for the marital deduction?*	Yes. (§ 13.38.730)
30. *Is the trustee required to take depreciation?*	No. (§ 13.38.830)
31. *Is the trustee's determination on allocations generally presumed to be fair and reasonable?*	Yes. (§ 13.38.200(b))
32. *If an item is not addressed in the trust agreement or in the law, must it be allocated to principal or income?*	To principal. (§ 13.38.200(a)(4))
33. *When does an asset become subject to a trust:*	

a) *In the case of transfers during the transferor's life?*	The date the asset is transferred to the trust. (§ 13.38.550(b)(1))
b) *In the case of a will?*	The death of the testator. (§ 13.38.550(b)(2))
c) *In the case of the death of a third party?*	The date of the third party's death. (§ 13.38.550(b)(3))
34. *Can a trustee rely on the characterization by an entity as to the source or character of a received distribution?*	Yes. (§ 13.38.600(e))

Table 12.02
Arizona
Trust Accounting: Principal and Income

1. *Does the trustee have the power to transfer income to principal or to transfer principal to income to meet its duty of impartiality?*	Yes. See the Uniform Principal and Income Act (1997) chart. (§ 14-7403(A))
2. *What is the effective date for the law? E.g., does it apply to preexisting trusts?*	An offcode provision gives the effective date as December 31, 2001. However, the Arizona Principal and Income Act does not address its applicability to any preexisting trusts. (2001 Ariz. Sess. Laws 176). ***Note***: If a trust owns a interest minerals, water, other natural resources or timber on December 31, 2001, the trustee can continue to allocate the receipts from the interest in the manner used by the trustee before December 31, 2001. (See, § 14-7420; § 14-7421)
3. *What percentage is allocated to income and principal from proceeds of:*	
a) *IRA?* b) *Qualified pension or profit-sharing plan?* c) *Other deferred compensation arrangement?*	See the Uniform Principal and Income Act (1997) chart. (§ 14-7418)
4. *What percentage is allocated to income and principal from proceeds of:*	
a) *Patents?* b) *Copyrights?*	See the Uniform Principal and Income Act (1997) chart. (§ 14-7419)
5. *What percentage is allocated to income and principal in the event of distributions from:*	
a) *Corporations?* b) *Partnerships?* c) *LLCs?*	See the Uniform Principal and Income Act (1997) chart. (§ 14-7410)
6. *What percentage is allocated to income and principal from proceeds of:*	
a) *Oil and gas?* b) *Minerals?* c) *Water?* d) *Other natural resourses (not including timber)?*	See the Uniform Principal and Income Act (1997) chart. (§ 14-7420) ***Note***: If a trust owns an interest in minerals, water or other natural resources on December 31, 2001, the trustee may allocate receipts from the interest as provided in the Arizona Principal and Income Act or in the manner used by the trustee before December 31, 2001.
e) *Timber*	See the Uniform Principal and Income Act (1997) chart. (§ 14-7421) ***Note***: If a trust owns an interest in timberland on December 31, 2001, the trustee may allocate receipts from the interest as provided in the Arizona Principal and Income Act or in the manner used by the trustee before December 31, 2001.

f) Rental properties?	See the Uniform Principal and Income Act (1997) chart. (§ 14-7414)
7. After a decedent dies, in the case of an estate, or after an income interest ends, when the fiduciary is determining the remaining net income what are the rules regarding payment from income or principal for:	
a) Attorneys fees? *b) Accountants fees?* *c) Fiduciary fees and commissions?* *d) Court costs?* *e) Interest on death taxes*	See the Uniform Principal and Income Act (1997) chart. (§ 14-7405(2)(b))
f) Debts? *g) Funeral expenses?* *h) Family allowances and similar protections?* *i) Death taxes?* *j) Penalties on death taxes?*	See the Uniform Principal and Income Act (1997) chart. (§ 14-7405(2)(c))
8. With respect to trust expenses from the administration of the trust that are not covered by § 14-7405(b-c) [see Question #7]:	
a) Does the trustee have full discretion in allocating between income and principal for expenses incurred in the administration of the trust?	No. See the Uniform Principal and Income Act (1997) chart. (§ 14-7425; § 14-7426)
b) If not, are there special rules for:	
i) Regular trustee fees? *ii) Advisory or cusodial services to the trustee?* *iii) Accountings, judicial proceedings and other matters that involve both the income and remainder interests?*	See the Uniform Principal and Income Act (1997) chart. (§ 14-7425(1); § 14-7425(2))
iv) Debts?	See the Uniform Principal and Income Act (1997) chart. (§ 14-7425(3); § 14-7426(A)(3))
c) Can the trustee determine what are "transmission" expenses and "management" expenses?	
9. With regard to specific gifts from a trust after an income interest ends or from an estate:	
a) What amounts must be paid from income and principal?	See the Uniform Principal and Income Act (1997) chart. (§ 14-7405(1))

10. With regard to outright pecuniary gifts from an estate or trust?:	
a) Does interest accrue?	Yes. See the Uniform Principal and Income Act (1997) chart. (§ 14-7405(3))
11. With regard to a gift in trust of a pecuniary amount from an estate or trust?	
a) Does interest accrue?	No. See the Uniform Principal and Income Act (1997) chart. (§ 14-7405(4); § 14-7406)
12. With regard to residuary gifts:	
a) What amount of income and principal is to be paid to the residuary beneficiary of a trust or an estate?	See the Uniform Principal and Income Act (1997) chart. (§ 14-7405(4); § 14-7406)
13. With regard to "business assets" held in trust:	
a) Can the trustee treat them as a separate entity?	Yes. (§ 14-7412)
b) Can the trustee treat distinct assets as separate entities?	Yes. (§ 14-7412)
c) Can earnings be retained in trust for the reasonable needs of the "business entity," and, if so, to what extent is this permitted?	See the Uniform Principal and Income Act (1997) chart. (§ 14-7412)
14. With respect to discount bonds:	
a) To what extent is the discount added to income or principal upon maturity?	See the Uniform Principal and Income Act (1997) chart. (§ 14-7412(b))
b) Does the trustee have discretion to allocate discount between income and principal?	No. (§ 14-7412(b)) ***Note***: The trustee still has the overriding power to adjust under (§ 14-7403(A))
c) Are distinctions drawn between Series E bonds and others?	No. (§ 14-7412)
d) Are distinctions drawn based on the maturity date of the bond?	Yes. (§ 14-7412)
15. Is there a de minimis rule excusing the trustee from making adjustments in certain cases?	Yes. (§ 14-7417)
16. With respect to derivatives:	
a) May income and loss be treated as that of a separate entity?	Yes. (§ 14-7423; § 14-7412)
b) If not, or the trustee chooses not to do so, is income and loss allocated to the income account or to principal?	To principal. (§ 14-7423(A)).

17. To the extent put and call options are not derivatives, how are they allocated in terms of principal and income?	To principal. (§ 14-7423(B))
18. How are asset-backed securities allocated in terms of principal and income?	See the Uniform Principal and Income Act (1997) chart. (§ 14-7424)
19. Are expenses incurred to comply with environmental requirements allocated to income or principal?	To principal. See the Uniform Principal and Income Act (1997) chart. (§ 14-7426(A)(7))
20. Is income tax liability allocated generally to income or principal?	See the Uniform Principal and Income Act (1997) chart. (§ 14-7429; § 14-7430)
21. If a Subchapter S shareholder's or partner's portion of tax liability is greater than cash distributed, how is the excess obligation allocated?	From principal. (§ 14-7429(C)(2)(B))
22. What is the standard, if any, for making equitable adjustments between income and principal?	See the Uniform Principal and Income Act (1997) chart. (§ 14-7402(B))
23. Is an income beneficiary entitled to receive income accrued but unpaid when an estate ends?	No. (§ 14-7409(C))
24. Is an income beneficiary entitled to receive income accrued but unpaid when a revocable trust ends?	Generally no. See the Uniform Principal and Income Act (1997) chart. (§ 14-7409(C))
25. Is an income beneficiary entitled to receive income accrued but unpaid when an irrevocable trust ends?	Generally no. See the Uniform Principal and Income Act (1997) chart. (§ 14-7409(C))
26. With regard to mutual funds, how are:	
a) long-term gains allocated between income and principal	See the Uniform Principal and Income Act (1997) chart. (§ 14-7410(B)(4))
b) short-term gains allocated between income and principal?	See the Uniform Principal and Income Act (1997) chart. (§ 14-7410(B)(4))
27. How are distributions from REITs allocated between income and principal?	See the Uniform Principal and Income Act (1997) chart. (§ 14-7410(B)(4))
28. With respect to underproductive property:	
a) Is an adjustment, e.g., "delayed income," required to be paid to the income beneficiary?	No. (§ 14-7422)
b) What percentage return makes property underproductive?	The statute only refers to property not productive of income. See the Uniform Principal and Income Act (1997) chart. (§ 14-7422)
29. Is the trustee required to increase income so that it is sufficient to qualify for the marital deduction?	Yes. (§ 14-7422(A))

30. Is the trustee required to take depreciation?	No. (§ 14-7427)
31. Is the trustee's determination on allocations generally presumed to be fair and reasonable?	Yes. (§ 14-7402(B))
32. If an item is not addressed in the trust agreement or in the law, must it be allocated to principal or income?	To principal. (§ 14-7402(A)(4))
33. When does an asset become subject to a trust:	
a) In the case of transfers during the transferor's life?	The date the asset is transferred to the trust. (§ 14-7407(B)(1))
b) In the case of a will?	On the death of the testator. (§ 14-7407(B)(2))
c) In the case of the death of a third party?	The date of the third party's death. (§ 14-7407(B)(3))
34. Can a trustee rely on the characterization by an entity as to the source or character of a received distribution?	Yes. (§ 14-7410(E))

Table 12.02
Arkansas
Trust Accounting: Principal and Income

1. *Does the trustee have the power to transfer income to principal or to transfer principal to income to meet its duty of impartiality?*	Yes. See the Uniform Principal and Income Act (1997) chart. (§ 28-70-104(a))
2. *What is the effective date for the law? E.g., does it apply to preexisting trusts?*	The Arkansas Uniform Principal and Income Act applies to every trust or decedent's estate existing on January 1, 2000 except as otherwise provided in the will or in the Act. (§ 28-70-605) ***Note***: If a trust owns a interest minerals, water, other natural resources or timber on January 1, 2000, the trustee can continue to allocate the receipts from the interest in the manner used by the trustee before January 1, 2000. (See § 28-70-411; § 28-70-412)
3. *What percentage is allocated to income and principal from proceeds of:*	
a) IRA? *b) Qualified pension or profit-sharing plan?* *c) Other deferred compensation arrangement?*	See the Uniform Principal and Income Act (1997) chart. (§ 28-70-409)
4. *What percentage is allocated to income and principal from proceeds of:*	
a) Patents? *b) Copyrights?*	See the Uniform Principal and Income Act (1997) chart. (§ 28-70-410(b))
5. *What percentage is allocated to income and principal in the event of distributions from:*	
a) Corporations? *b) Partnerships?* *c) LLCs?*	See the Uniform Principal and Income Act (1997) chart. (§ 28-70-401)
6. *What percentage is allocated to income and principal from proceeds of:*	
a) Oil and gas? *b) Minerals?* *c) Water?* *d) Other natural resourses (not including timber)?*	See the Uniform Principal and Income Act (1997) chart. (§ 28-70-411) ***Note***: If a trust owns an interest in minerals, water or other natural resources on January 1, 2000, the trustee may allocate receipts from the interest as provided in the Arkansas Principal and Income Act or in the manner used by the trustee before January 1, 2000.
e) Timber	See the Uniform Principal and Income Act (1997) chart. (§ 28-70-412) ***Note:*** If a trust owns an interest in timberland on January 1, 2000, the trustee may allocate receipts from the interest as provided in the Arkansas Principal and Income Act or in the manner used by the trustee before January 1, 2000.

f) Rental properties?	See the Uniform Principal and Income Act (1997) chart. (§ 28-70-405)
7. After a decedent dies, in the case of an estate, or after an income interest ends, when the fiduciary is determining the remaining net income what are the rules regarding payment from income or principal for:	
Attorneys fees? *a) Accountants fees?* *b) Fiduciary fees and commissions?* *c) Court costs?* *d) Interest on death taxes*	See the Uniform Principal and Income Act (1997) chart.(§ 28-70-201(2)(B))
e) Debts? *f) Funeral expenses?* *g) Family allowances and similar protections?* *h) Death taxes?* *i) Penalties on death taxes?*	See the Uniform Principal and Income Act (1997) chart. (§ 28-70-201(2)(C))
8. With respect to trust expenses from the administration of the trust that are not covered by § 201(2)(b-c) [see Question #7]:	
a) Does the trustee have full discretion in allocating between income and principal for expenses incurred in the administration of the trust?	No. (§ 28-70-501; § 28-70-502)
b) If not, are there special rules for:	
i) Regular trustee fees? *ii) Advisory or cusodial services to the trustee?* *iii) Accountings, judicial proceedings and other matters that involve both the income and remainder interests?*	See the Uniform Principal and Income Act (1997) chart. (§ 28-70-501)
iv) Debts?	See the Uniform Principal and Income Act (1997) chart. (§ 28-70-501(3); § 28-70-502(a)(3))
c) Can the trustee determine what are "transmission" expenses and "management" expenses?	
9. With regard to specific gifts from a trust after an income interest ends or from an estate:	
a) What amounts must be paid from income and principal?	See the Uniform Principal and Income Act (1997) chart. (§ 28-70-201(1); § 28-70-201(5))

10. With regard to outright pecuniary gifts from an estate or trust?:	
a) Does interest accrue?	Yes. (§ 28-70-201(3))
11. With regard to a gift in trust of a pecuniary amount from an estate or trust?	
a) Does interest accrue?	No. See the Uniform Principal and Income Act (1997) chart. (§ 28-70-201(4); (§ 28-70-202)
12. With regard to residuary gifts:	
a) What amount of income and principal is to be paid to the residuary beneficiary of a trust or an estate?	See the Uniform Principal and Income Act (1997) chart. (§ 28-70-201(4); § 28-70-202)
13. With regard to "business assets" held in trust:	
a) Can the trustee treat them as a separate entity?	Yes. (§ 28-70-403)
b) Can the trustee treat distinct assets as separate entities?	Yes. (§ 28-70-403)
c) Can earnings be retained in trust for the reasonable needs of the "business entity," and, if so, to what extent is this permitted?	See the Uniform Principal and Income Act (1997) chart. (§ 28-70-403(b))
14. With respect to discount bonds:	
a) To what extent is the discount added to income or principal upon maturity?	See the Uniform Principal and Income Act (1997) chart. (§ 28-70-406(b))
b) Does the trustee have discretion to allocate discount between income and principal?	No. (§ 28-70-406) ***Note***: The trustee has the overriding power to adjust under § 28-70-104(a).
c) Are distinctions drawn between Series E bonds and others?	No. (§ 28-70-406)
d) Are distinctions drawn based on the maturity date of the bond?	Yes. (§ 28-70-406(b))
15. Is there a de minimis rule excusing the trustee from making adjustments in certain cases?	Yes. See the Uniform Principal and Income Act (1997) chart. (§ 28-70-408)
16. With respect to derivatives:	
a) May income and loss be treated as that of a separate entity?	Yes. See the Uniform Principal and Income Act (1997) chart. (§ 28-70-403; § 28-70-414(b))
b) If not, or the trustee chooses not to do so, is income and loss allocated to the income account or to principal?	To principal. (§ 28-70-414(b))

17. To the extent put and call options are not derivatives, how are they allocated in terms of principal and income?	To principal. (§ 28-70-414(c))
18. How are asset-backed securities allocated in terms of principal and income?	See the Uniform Principal and Income Act (1997) chart.(§ 28-70-415)
19. Are expenses incurred to comply with environmental requirements allocated to income or principal?	Generally to principal. See the Uniform Principal and Income Act (1997) chart. (§ 28-70-502(a)(7))
20. Is income tax liability allocated generally to income or principal?	See the Uniform Principal and Income Act (1997) chart. (§ 28-70-505; § 28-70-506)
21. If a Subchapter S shareholder's or partner's portion of tax liability is greater than cash distributed, how is the excess obligation allocated?	To principal. (§ 28-70-505(c)(2)(B))
22. What is the standard, if any, for making equitable adjustments between income and principal?	See the Uniform Principal and Income Act (1997) chart. (§ 28-70-103(b))
23. Is an income beneficiary entitled to receive income accrued but unpaid when an estate ends?	No. (§ 28-70-303)
24. Is an income beneficiary entitled to receive income accrued but unpaid when a revocable trust ends?	Generally no. See the Uniform Principal and Income Act (1997) chart. (§ 28-70-303)
25. Is an income beneficiary entitled to receive income accrued but unpaid when an irrevocable trust ends?	Generally no. See the Uniform Principal and Income Act (1997) chart. (§ 28-70-303)
26. With regard to mutual funds, how are:	
a) long-term gains allocated between income and principal?	See the Uniform Principal and Income Act (1997) chart. (§ 28-70-401(c)(4))
b) short-term gains allocated between income and principal?	See the Uniform Principal and Income Act (1997) chart. (§ 28-70-401(c)(4))
27. How are distributions from REITs allocated between income and principal?	See the Uniform Principal and Income Act (1997) chart. (§ 28-70-401(c)(4))
28. With respect to underproductive property:	
a) Is an adjustment, e.g., "delayed income," required to be paid to the income beneficiary?	No. (§ 28-70-413)
b) What percentage return makes property underproductive?	The statute only addresses unproductive property. (§ 28-70-413)
29. Is the trustee required to increase income so that it is sufficient to qualify for the marital deduction?	Yes. (§ 28-70-413(a))

30. Is the trustee required to take depreciation?	No. (§ 28-70-503)
31. Is the trustee's determination on allocations generally presumed to be fair and reasonable?	Yes. (§ 28-70-103(b))
32. If an item is not addressed in the trust agreement or in the law, must it be allocated to principal or income?	To principal. (§ 28-70-103(a)(4))
33. When does an asset become subject to a trust:	
a) In the case of transfers during the transferor's life?	The date of transfer. See the Uniform Principal and Income Act (1997) chart. (§ 28-70-301(b)(1))
b) In the case of a will?	The date of the testator's death. (§ 28-70-301(b)(2))
c) In the case of the death of a third party?	The date of the thrid party's death. (§ 28-70-301(b)(3))
34. Can a trustee rely on the characterization by an entity as to the source or character of a received distribution?	Yes. (§ 28-70-401(f))

Table 12.02
California
Trust Accounting: Principal and Income

1. *Does the trustee have the power to transfer income to principal or to transfer principal to income to meet its duty of impartiality?*	Yes. See the Uniform Principal and Income Act (1997) chart. (Cal. Prob. Code § 16336)
2. *What is the effective date for the law? E.g., does it apply to preexisting trusts?*	The California Principal and Income Act applies to every trust or decedent's estate existing on or after January 1, 2000 except as provided in the will or trust or in other sections of the California Principal and Income Act. (Cal. Prob. Code § 16339) ***Note***: A trustee may continue using a former allocation method to allocate receipts for water, minerals, other natural resources, and timber under certain circumstances. (See Cal. Prob. Code § 16363(d); Cal. Prob. Code § 16364(d))
3. *What percentage is allocated to income and principal from proceeds of:*	
a) *IRA?* b) *Qualified pension or profit-sharing plan?* c) *Other deferred compensation arrangement?*	A trustee must allocate a payment, or any portion of a payment that is characterized as interest or a dividend, or payment in lieu of interest or a dividend to income. The trustee must allocate to principal the balance of the payment and any other payment received in the same accounting period that is not characterized as interest, a dividend or equivalent payment. If no part of a payment is characterized as interest, a dividend, or an equivalent payment, the trustee must allocate the payment as follows: (1) If the payment is received from an individual account, the trustee must allocate the payment to income to the extent that the payment, when combined with all other payments received from the individual account during that same accounting period, which may be referred to as the "cumulative amount received," does not exceed 4 percent of the account value, which may be referred to as the "income allocation amount." To the extent that any portion of a payment causes the cumulative amount received to exceed the income allocation amount, that portion, together with all further amounts received from the individual account during that accounting period, must be allocated to principal. (2) If the payment is received from a plan, account or other arrangement that is not an individual account, the trustee must allocate the payment as follows: (a) If all or part of the payment is required to be made to the trustee, the trustee must allocate to income 10 percent of the part that is required to be made during the accounting period and the balance to principal. (b) If no part of a payment is required to be made to the trustee or the payment received is the entire amount to which the trustee is entitled, the trustee must allocate the entire payment to principal. ***Note:*** For further information, consult Cal. Prob. Code § 16361.
4. *What percentage is allocated to income and principal from proceeds of:*	

a) *Patents?* b) *Copyrights?*	See the Uniform Principal and Income Act (1997) chart. (Cal. Prob. Code § 16362)
5. *What percentage is allocated to income and principal in the event of distributions from:*	
a) *Corporations?* b) *Partnerships?* c) *LLCs?*	See the Uniform Principal and Income Act (1997) chart. (Cal. Prob. Code § 16350)
6. *What percentage is allocated to income and principal from proceeds of:*	
a) *Oil and gas?* b) *Minerals?* c) *Water?* d) *Other natural resourses (not including timber)?*	See the Uniform Principal and Income Act (1997) chart. (Cal. Prob. Code § 16363) **Note**: If a trust owned an interest in minerals, water, or other natural resources on January 1, 2000, the trustee may at all times allocate receipts from the interest as provided in the California Uniform Principal and Income Act or in the manner reasonably used by the trustee prior to January 1, 2000. Receipts from an interest in minerals, water, or other natural resources acquired after January 1, 2000, must be allocated by the trustee as provided in the California Uniform Principal and Income Act. If the interest was owned by the trust on January 1, 2000, a trustee that allocated receipts from the interest between January 1, 2000, and December 31, 2006, as provided in the California Uniform Principal and Income Act does not have a duty to review that allocation and does not have liability arising from the allocation. (See Cal. Prob. Code § 16363(d))
e) *Timber*	See the Uniform Principal and Income Act (1997) chart. (Cal. Prob. Code § 16364) ***Note***: If a trust owned an interest in timberland on January 1, 2000, the trustee may at all times allocate net receipts from the sale of timber and related products as provided in the California Uniform Principal and Income Act or in the manner reasonably used by the trustee prior to January 1, 2000. Net receipts from an interest in timberland acquired after January 1, 2000, must be allocated by the trustee as provided in the California Uniform Principal and Income Act. If the interest was owned by the trust on January 1, 2000, a trustee that allocated net receipts from the interest between January 1, 2000, and December 31, 2006, as provided in the California Uniform Principal and Income Act must not have a duty to review that allocation and must not have liability arising from the allocation. (See Cal. Prob. Code § 16364(d))
f) *Rental properties?*	See the Uniform Principal and Income Act (1997) chart. (Cal. Prob. Code § 16356)
7. *After a decedent dies, in the case of an estate, or after an income interest ends, when the fiduciary is determining the remaining net income what are the rules regarding payment from income or principal for:*	

a) Attorneys fees? *b) Accountants fees?* *c) Fiduciary fees and commissions?* *d) Court costs?* *e) Interest on death taxes*	See the Uniform Principal and Income Act (1997) chart. (Cal. Prob. Code § 16340(c)(2))
f) Debts? *g) Funeral expenses?* *h) Family allowances and similar protections?* *i) Death taxes?* *j) Penalties on death taxes?*	See the Uniform Principal and Income Act (1997) chart. (Cal. Prob. Code § 16340(c)(3))
8. With respect to trust expenses from the administration of the trust that are not covered by Cal. Prob. Code § 16340(c)(2-3) [see Question #7]:	
a) Does the trustee have full discretion in allocating between income and principal for expenses incurred in the administration of the trust?	No. (Cal. Prob. Code § 16370; Cal. Prob. Code § 16371)
b) If not, are there special rules for:	
i) Regular trustee fees? *ii) Advisory or cusodial services to the trustee?* *iii) Accountings, judicial proceedings and other matters that involve both the income and remainder interests?*	See the Uniform Principal and Income Act (1997) chart. (Cal. Prob. Code § 16370; Cal. Prob. Code § 16371)
iv) Debts?	The trustee must allocate interest expense on trust debt to income and must allocate payments on principal of trust debt to principal. (Cal. Prob. Code § 16370(c); Cal. Prob. Code § 16370(a)(3))
c) Can the trustee determine what are "transmission" expenses and "management" expenses?	
9. With regard to specific gifts from a trust after an income interest ends or from an estate:	
a) What amounts must be paid from income and principal?	See the Uniform Principal and Income Act (1997) chart. (Cal. Prob. Code § 16340(a))
10. With regard to outright pecuniary gifts from an estate or trust?:	
a) Does interest accrue?	Yes. (Cal. Prob. Code § 16340(b))
11. With regard to a gift in trust of a pecuniary amount from an estate or trust?	

a) *Does interest accrue?*	Yes. (Cal. Prob. Code § 16340(b))
12. *With regard to residuary gifts:*	
a) *What amount of income and principal is to be paid to the residuary beneficiary of a trust or an estate?*	See the Uniform Principal and Income Act (1997) chart. (Cal. Prob. Code § 16341)
13. *With regard to "business assets" held in trust:*	
a) *Can the trustee treat them as a separate entity?*	Yes. See the Uniform Principal and Income Act (1997) chart. (Cal. Prob. Code § 16352)
b) *Can the trustee treat distinct assets as separate entities?*	Yes. See the Uniform Principal and Income Act (1997) chart. (Cal. Prob. Code § 16352)
c) *Can earnings be retained in trust for the reasonable needs of the "business entity," and, if so, to what extent is this permitted?*	See the Uniform Principal and Income Act (1997) chart. (Cal. Prob. Code § 16352)
14. *With respect to discount bonds:*	
a) *To what extent is the discount added to income or principal upon maturity?*	See the Uniform Principal and Income Act (1997) chart. (Cal. Prob. Code § 16357)
b) *Does the trustee have discretion to allocate discount between income and principal?*	No. (Cal. Prob. Code § 16352) ***Note***: The trustee has an overriding power to adjust under Cal. Prob. Code § 16336.
c) *Are distinctions drawn between Series E bonds and others?*	No. (Cal. Prob. Code § 16352)
d) *Are distinctions drawn based on the maturity date of the bond?*	Yes. (Cal. Prob. Code § 16352)
15. *Is there a de minimis rule excusing the trustee from making adjustments in certain cases?*	Yes. See the Uniform Principal and Income Act (1997) chart. (Cal. Prob. Code § 16360)
16. *With respect to derivatives:*	
a) *May income and loss be treated as that of a separate entity?*	Yes. (Cal. Prob. Code § 16352(c)(7); Cal. Prob. Code § 16366(b))
b) *If not, or the trustee chooses not to do so, is income and loss allocated to the income account or to principal?*	To principal. (Cal. Prob. Code § 16366(b))
17. *To the extent put and call options are not derivatives, how are they allocated in terms of principal and income?*	To principal. (Cal. Prob. Code § 16366(c))
18. *How are asset-backed securities allocated in terms of principal and income?*	See the Uniform Principal and Income Act (1997) chart. (Cal. Prob. Code § 16367)

19. Are expenses incurred to comply with environmental requirements allocated to income or principal?	Generally to principal. See the Uniform Principal and Income Act (1997) chart. (Cal. Prob. Code § 16371(a)(7))
20. Is income tax liability allocated generally to income or principal?	See the Uniform Principal and Income Act (1997) chart. (Cal. Prob. Code § 16374; Cal. Prob. Code § 16375)
21. If a Subchapter S shareholder's or partner's portion of tax liability is greater than cash distributed, how is the excess obligation allocated?	To principal. (Cal. Prob. Code § 16374(c)(2)(B))
22. What is the standard, if any, for making equitable adjustments between income and principal?	See the Uniform Principal and Income Act (1997) chart. (Cal. Prob. Code § 16335(b))
23. Is an income beneficiary entitled to receive income accrued but unpaid when an estate ends?	No. (Cal. Prob. Code § 16347)
24. Is an income beneficiary entitled to receive income accrued but unpaid when a revocable trust ends?	Generally no. See the Uniform Principal and Income Act (1997) chart. (Cal. Prob. Code § 16347)
25. Is an income beneficiary entitled to receive income accrued but unpaid when an irrevocable trust ends?	Generally no. See the Uniform Principal and Income Act (1997) chart. (Cal. Prob. Code § 16347)
26. With regard to mutual funds, how are:	
a) long-term gains allocated between income and principal?	See the Uniform Principal and Income Act (1997) chart. (Cal. Prob. Code § 16350(c)(4))
b) short-term gains allocated between income and principal?	See the Uniform Principal and Income Act (1997) chart. (Cal. Prob. Code § 16350(c)(4))
27. How are distributions from REITs allocated between income and principal?	See the Uniform Principal and Income Act (1997) chart. (Cal. Prob. Code § 16350(c)(4))
28. With respect to underproductive property:	
a) Is an adjustment, e.g., "delayed income," required to be paid to the income beneficiary?	No. (Cal. Prob. Code § 16365)
b) What percentage return makes property underproductive?	The statute only refers to property not productive of income. (Cal. Prob. Code § 16365)
29. Is the trustee required to increase income so that it is sufficient to qualify for the marital deduction?	Yes. (Cal. Prob. Code § 16365)
30. Is the trustee required to take depreciation?	No. (Cal. Prob. Code § 16372)
31. Is the trustee's determination on allocations generally presumed to be fair and reasonable?	Yes. (Cal. Prob. Code § 16335(b))

32. If an item is not addressed in the trust agreement or in the law, must it be allocated to principal or income?	To principal. (Cal. Prob. Code § 16335(a)(4))
33. When does an asset become subject to a trust:	
a) In the case of transfers during the transferor's life?	The date of transfer. (Cal. Prob. Code § 16345(b)(1))
b) In the case of a will?	The date of the testator's death. (Cal. Prob. Code § 16345(b)(2))
c) In the case of the death of a third party?	The date of the third party's death. (Cal. Prob. Code § 16345(b)(3))
34. Can a trustee rely on the characterization by an entity as to the source or character of a received distribution?	Yes. (Cal. Prob. Code § 16350(e))

Table 12.02
Colorado
Trust Accounting: Principal and Income

1. *Does the trustee have the power to transfer income to principal or to transfer principal to income to meet its duty of impartiality?*

   Yes. See the Uniform Principal and Income Act (1997) chart. (§ 15-1-404)

2. *What is the effective date for the law? E.g., does it apply to preexisting trusts?*

   The effective date for the Colorado Principal and Income Act is July 1, 2001. The Colorado Principal and Income Act applies to every trust or decedent's estate existing on and after July 1, 2001, except as otherwise expressly provided in the will or terms of the trust or in the Colorado Principal and Income Act. For each trust established under a will or trust agreement existing and irrevocable on July 1, 2001, the trustee may elect to apply the Colorado Principal and Income Act in effect on June 30, 2001. However, the trustee must have made such an election by July 1, 2002.

   The Colorado Principal and Income Act does not apply to any trust or decedent's estate existing on July 1, 2001, in which no trustee has the authority to act under § 15-1-404 unless the trustees elect to apply the Colorado Principal and Income Act to the trust. The trustees may make this election at any time. Once an election is made pursuant to this section, the election is irrevocable. (§ 15-1-434)

   Note: A trustee may continue using a former allocation method to allocate receipts for water, minerals, other natural resources, and timber under certain circumstances. See, (§ 15-1-421; § 15-1-422)

3. *What percentage is allocated to income and principal from proceeds of:*

   a) *IRA?*
   b) *Qualified pension or profit-sharing plan?*
   c) *Other deferred compensation arrangement?*

   See the Uniform Principal and Income Act (1997) chart. (§ 15-1-419)

4. *What percentage is allocated to income and principal from proceeds of:*

   a) *Patents?*
   b) *Copyrights?*

   See the Uniform Principal and Income Act (1997) chart. (§ 15-1-420)

5. *What percentage is allocated to income and principal in the event of distributions from:*

   a) *Corporations?*
   b) *Partnerships?*
   c) *LLCs?*

   See the Uniform Principal and Income Act (1997) chart. (§ 15-1-411)

6. *What percentage is allocated to income and principal from proceeds of:*

   a) *Oil and gas?*
   b) *Minerals?*
   c) *Water?*

   See the Uniform Principal and Income Act (1997) chart. (§ 15-1-421)

   Note: If a trust owns an interest in minerals, water, or other natural resources on July 1, 2001, the trustee may allocate

d) *Other natural resourses (not including timber)?*	receipts from the interest as provided in the Colorado Uniform Principal and Income Act or in the manner used by the trustee before July 1, 2001. If the trust acquires an interest in minerals, water, or other natural resources after July 1, 2001, the trustee must allocate receipts from the interest as provided in the Colorado Uniform Principal and Income Act. See, (§ 15-1-421(4))
e) *Timber*	See the Uniform Principal and Income Act (1997) chart. (§ 15-1-422) ***Note***: If a trust owns an interest in timberland on July 1, 2001, the trustee may allocate receipts from the interest as provided in the Colorado Uniform Principal and Income Act or in the manner used by the trustee before July 1, 2001. If the trust acquires an interest in timberland after July 1, 2001, the trustee must allocate receipts from the interest as provided in the Colorado Uniform Principal and Income Act. (See § 15-1-422(4))
f) *Rental properties?*	See the Uniform Principal and Income Act (1997) chart. (§ 15-1-415)
7. *After a decedent dies, in the case of an estate, or after an income interest ends, when the fiduciary is determining the remaining net income what are the rules regarding payment from income or principal for:*	
a) *Attorneys fees?* b) *Accountants fees?* c) *Fiduciary fees and commissions?* d) *Court costs?* e) *Interest on death taxes*	See the Uniform Principal and Income Act (1997) chart. (§ 15-1-406(1)(b)(II))
f) *Debts?* g) *Funeral expenses?* h) *Family allowances and similar protections?* i) *Death taxes?* j) *Penalties on death taxes?*	See the Uniform Principal and Income Act (1997) chart. (§ 15-1-406(1)(b)(III))
8. *With respect to trust expenses from the administration of the trust that are not covered by § 15-1-406(1)(b)(II-III) [see Question #7]:*	
a) *Does the trustee have full discretion in allocating between income and principal for expenses incurred in the administration of the trust?*	No. (§ 15-1-426; § 15-1-427)
b) *If not, are there special rules for:*	
i) *Regular trustee fees?* ii) *Advisory or cusodial services to the trustee?*	See the Uniform Principal and Income Act (1997) chart. (§ 15-1-426(1); § 15-1-427(1))

iii) Accountings, judicial proceedings and other matters that involve both the income and remainder interests?	
iv) Debts?	See the Uniform Principal and Income Act (1997) chart. (§ 15-1-426(1)(c); § 15-1-427(1)(c))
c) Can the trustee determine what are "transmission" expenses and "management" expenses?	
9. With regard to specific gifts from a trust after an income interest ends or from an estate:	
a) What amounts must be paid from income and principal?	See the Uniform Principal and Income Act (1997) chart. (§ 15-1-406(1)(a); § 15-1-406(e))
10. With regard to outright pecuniary gifts from an estate or trust?:	
a) Does interest accrue?	Yes. See the Uniform Principal and Income Act (1997) chart. (§ 15-1-406(1)(c))
11. With regard to a gift in trust of a pecuniary amount from an estate or trust?	
a) Does interest accrue?	No. See the Uniform Principal and Income Act (1997) chart. (§ 15-1-406(1)(d); § 15-1-407)
12. With regard to residuary gifts:	
a) What amount of income and principal is to be paid to the residuary beneficiary of a trust or an estate?	See the Uniform Principal and Income Act (1997) chart. (§ 15-1-406(1)(d); § 15-1-407)
13. With regard to "business assets" held in trust:	
a) Can the trustee treat them as a separate entity?	Yes. See the Uniform Principal and Income Act (1997) chart. (§ 15-1-413)
b) Can the trustee treat distinct assets as separate entities?	Yes. See the Uniform Principal and Income Act (1997) chart. (§ 15-1-413)
c) Can earnings be retained in trust for the reasonable needs of the "business entity," and, if so, to what extent is this permitted?	See the Uniform Principal and Income Act (1997) chart. (§ 15-1-413)
14. With respect to discount bonds:	
a) To what extent is the discount added to income or principal upon maturity?	See the Uniform Principal and Income Act (1997) chart. (§ 15-1-416(2))
b) Does the trustee have discretion to allocate discount between income and principal?	No. (§ 15-1-416) ***Note***: The Trustee has the overriding power to adjust under § 15-1-404.

c) Are distinctions drawn between Series E bonds and others?	No. (§ 15-1-416)
d) Are distinctions drawn based on the maturity date of the bond?	Yes. (§ 15-1-416(2))
15. Is there a de minimis rule excusing the trustee from making adjustments in certain cases?	Yes. See the Uniform Principal and Income Act (1997) chart. (§ 15-1-418)
16. With respect to derivatives:	
a) May income and loss be treated as that of a separate entity?	Yes. (§ 15-1-413(3)(g); § 15-1-424)
b) If not, or the trustee chooses not to do so, is income and loss allocated to the income account or to principal?	To principal. (§ 15-1-424(2))
17. To the extent put and call options are not derivatives, how are they allocated in terms of principal and income?	To principal. (§ 15-1-424(3))
18. How are asset-backed securities allocated in terms of principal and income?	See the Uniform Principal and Income Act (1997) chart. (§ 15-1-425)
19. Are expenses incurred to comply with environmental requirements allocated to income or principal?	Generally, to principal. See the Uniform Principal and Income Act (1997) chart. (§ 15-1-427(1)(g))
20. Is income tax liability allocated generally to income or principal?	See the Uniform Principal and Income Act (1997) chart. (§ 15-1-430; § 15-1-431)
21. If a Subchapter S shareholder's or partner's portion of tax liability is greater than cash distributed, how is the excess obligation allocated?	To principal. (§ 15-1-430(3)(b)(II))
22. What is the standard, if any, for making equitable adjustments between income and principal?	See the Uniform Principal and Income Act (1997) chart. (§ 15-1-403(2))
23. Is an income beneficiary entitled to receive income accrued but unpaid when an estate ends?	No. (§ 15-1-410)
24. Is an income beneficiary entitled to receive income accrued but unpaid when a revocable trust ends?	Generally no. See the Uniform Principal and Income Act (1997) chart. (§ 15-1-403(2))
25. Is an income beneficiary entitled to receive income accrued but unpaid when an irrevocable trust ends?	Generally no. See the Uniform Principal and Income Act (1997) chart. (§ 15-1-403(2))
26. With regard to mutual funds, how are:	
a) long-term gains allocated between income and principal?	See the Uniform Principal and Income Act (1997) chart. (§ 15-1-411(3)(d))

b) short-term gains allocated between income and principal?	See the Uniform Principal and Income Act (1997) chart. (§ 15-1-411(3)(d))
27. How are distributions from REITs allocated between income and principal?	See the Uniform Principal and Income Act (1997) chart. (§ 15-1-411(3)(d))
28. With respect to underproductive property:	
a) Is an adjustment, e.g., "delayed income," required to be paid to the income beneficiary?	No. (§ 15-1-423)
b) What percentage return makes property underproductive?	The statute only refers to property not productive of income. (§ 15-1-423)
29. Is the trustee required to increase income so that it is sufficient to qualify for the marital deduction?	Yes. (§ 15-1-423(1))
30. Is the trustee required to take depreciation?	No. (§ 15-1-428)
31. Is the trustee's determination on allocations generally presumed to be fair and reasonable?	Yes. (§ 15-1-403(2))
32. If an item is not addressed in the trust agreement or in the law, must it be allocated to principal or income?	To principal. (§ 15-1-403(1)(d))
33. When does an asset become subject to a trust:	
a) In the case of transfers during the transferor's life?	The date of transfer. (§ 15-1-408(2)(a))
b) In the case of a will?	The date of the testator's death. (§ 15-1-408(2)(b))
c) In the case of the death of a third party?	The date of the third party's death. (§ 15-1-408(2)(c))
34. Can a trustee rely on the characterization by an entity as to the source or character of a received distribution?	Yes. (§ 15-1-411(6))

Table 12.02
Connecticut
Trust Accounting: Principal and Income

1. *Does the trustee have the power to transfer income to principal or to transfer principal to income to meet its duty of impartiality?*	Yes. See the Uniform Principal and Income Act (1997) chart. (§ 45a-542c(a))
2. *What is the effective date for the law? E.g., does it apply to preexisting trusts?*	The Connecticut Principal and Income Act applies to every decedent's estate existing on or after January 1, 2000, except as otherwise expressly provided in the will or terms of the trust or as provided in the Connecticut Principal and Income Act. (§ 45a-542ff) ***Note:*** A trustee may continue using a former allocation method to allocate receipts for water, minerals, other natural resources, and timber under certain circumstances. (See § 45a-542s; § 45a-542t)
3. *What percentage is allocated to income and principal from proceeds of:*	
a) *IRA?* b) *Qualified pension or profit-sharing plan?* c) *Other deferred compensation arrangement?*	See the Uniform Principal and Income Act (1997) chart. (§ 45a-542q)
4. *What percentage is allocated to income and principal from proceeds of:*	
a) *Patents?* b) *Copyrights?*	See the Uniform Principal and Income Act (1997) chart. (§ 45a-542r)
5. *What percentage is allocated to income and principal in the event of distributions from:*	
a) *Corporations?* b) *Partnerships?* c) *LLCs?*	See the Uniform Principal and Income Act (1997) chart. (§ 45a-542i)
6. *What percentage is allocated to income and principal from proceeds of:*	
a) *Oil and gas* b) *Minerals* c) *Water* d) *Other natural resourses (not including timber)?*	See the Uniform Principal and Income Act (1997) chart. (§ 45a-542s) ***Note***: If a trust owns an interest in minerals, water or other natural resources on January 1, 2000, the trustee may allocate receipts from the interest as provided in the Connecticut Principal and Income Act or in the manner used by the trustee before January 1, 2000.
e) *Timber*	See the Uniform Principal and Income Act (1997) chart. (§ 45a-542t) ***Note:*** If a trust owns an interest in timberland on January 1, 2000, the trustee may allocate receipts from the interest as provided in the Connecticut Principal and Income Act or in the manner used by the trustee before January 1, 2000.

f) Rental properties?	See the Uniform Principal and Income Act (1997) chart. (§ 45a-542m)
7. After a decedent dies, in the case of an estate, or after an income interest ends, when the fiduciary is determining the remaining net income what are the rules regarding payment from income or principal for:	
a) Attorneys fees? *b) Accountants fees?* *c) Fiduciary fees and commissions?* *d) Court costs?* *e) Interest on death taxes*	See the Uniform Principal and Income Act (1997) chart. (§ 45a-542d(2)(B))
f) Debts? *g) Funeral expenses?* *h) Family allowances and similar protections?* *i) Death taxes?* *j) Penalties on death taxes?*	See the Uniform Principal and Income Act (1997) chart. (§ 45a-542d(2)(C))
8. With respect to trust expenses from the administration of the trust that are not covered by § 45a-542d(2)(B-C) [see Question #7]:	
a) Does the trustee have full discretion in allocating between income and principal for expenses incurred in the administration of the trust?	No. (§ 45a-542x; § 45a-542y)
b) If not, are there special rules for:	
i) Regular trustee fees? *ii) Advisory or cusodial services to the trustee?* *iii) Accountings, judicial proceedings and other matters that involve both the income and remainder interests?*	See the Uniform Principal and Income Act (1997) chart. (§ 45a-542x; § 45a-542y)
iv) Debts?	See the Uniform Principal and Income Act (1997) chart. (§ 45a-542x(3); § 45a-542y(3))
c) Can the trustee determine what are "transmission" expenses and "management" expenses?	
9. With regard to specific gifts from a trust after an income interest ends or from an estate:	
a) What amounts must be paid from income and principal?	See the Uniform Principal and Income Act (1997) chart. (§ 45a-542d(1))

10. With regard to outright pecuniary gifts from an estate or trust?:	
a) Does interest accrue?	Yes, interest must be paid from net income and from principal to the extent that net income is insufficient. Unless a will or trust waives such interest or provides for its calculation in a different amount or manner, a pecuniary amount payable outright must bear simple interest at the rate of six percent (6%) per year, beginning one year after the date of death in the case of pecuniary amounts payable under a will, or one year after the day the income interest ends in the case of pecuniary amounts payable from a trust after an income interest ends, and ending on the day the pecuniary amount is paid. (§ 45a-542d(3))
11. With regard to a gift in trust of a pecuniary amount from an estate or trust?	
a) Does interest accrue?	No. See the Uniform Principal and Income Act (1997) chart. (§ 45a-542d(4); § 45a-542e)
12. With regard to residuary gifts:	
a) What amount of income and principal is to be paid to the residuary beneficiary of a trust or an estate?	See the Uniform Principal and Income Act (1997) chart. (§ 45a-542d(4); § 45a-542e)
13. With regard to "business assets" held in trust:	
a) Can the trustee treat them as a separate entity?	Generally yes. See the Uniform Principal and Income Act (1997) chart. (§ 45a-542k)
b) Can the trustee treat distinct assets as separate entities?	Generally yes. See the Uniform Principal and Income Act (1997) chart. (§ 45a-542k)
c) Can earnings be retained in trust for the reasonable needs of the "business entity," and, if so, to what extent is this permitted?	See the Uniform Principal and Income Act (1997) chart. (§ 45a-542k(b))
14. With respect to discount bonds:	
a) To what extent is the discount added to income or principal upon maturity?	See the Uniform Principal and Income Act (1997) chart. (§ 45a-542n(b))
b) Does the trustee have discretion to allocate discount between income and principal?	No. (§ 45a-542n) ***Note:*** The trustee may have overriding power to adjust under § 45a-542c(a).
c) Are distinctions drawn between Series E bonds and others?	No. (§ 45a-542n)
d) Are distinctions drawn based on the maturity date of the bond?	Yes. (§ 45a-542n(b))
15. Is there a de minimis rule excusing the trustee from making adjustments in certain cases?	Yes. (§ 45a-542p)

16. With respect to derivatives:	
a) May income and loss be treated as that of a separate entity?	Yes. (§ 45a-542k(c)(7); § 45a-542v(b))
b) If not, or the trustee chooses not to do so, is income and loss allocated to the income account or to principal?	To principal. (§ 45a-542v(b))
17. To the extent put and call options are not derivatives, how are they allocated in terms of principal and income?	To principal. (§ 45a-542v(c))
18. How are asset-backed securities allocated in terms of principal and income?	See the Uniform Principal and Income Act (1997) chart. (§ 45a-542w)
19. Are expenses incurred to comply with environmental requirements allocated to income or principal?	Generally to principal. See the Uniform Principal and Income Act (1997) chart. (§ 45a-542y(a)(7))
20. Is income tax liability allocated generally to income or principal?	See the Uniform Principal and Income Act (1997) chart. (§ 45a-542bb; § 45a-542cc)
21. If a Subchapter S shareholder's or partner's portion of tax liability is greater than cash distributed, how is the excess obligation allocated?	To principal. (§ 45a-542bb(c)(2)(B))
22. What is the standard, if any, for making equitable adjustments between income and principal?	See the Uniform Principal and Income Act (1997) chart. (§ 45a-542b(b))
23. Is an income beneficiary entitled to receive income accrued but unpaid when an estate ends?	No. (§ 45a-542h)
24. Is an income beneficiary entitled to receive income accrued but unpaid when a revocable trust ends?	Generally no. See the Uniform Principal and Income Act (1997) chart. (§ 45a-542h)
25. Is an income beneficiary entitled to receive income accrued but unpaid when an irrevocable trust ends?	Generally no. See the Uniform Principal and Income Act (1997) chart. (§ 45a-542h)
26. With regard to mutual funds, how are:	
a) long-term gains allocated between income and principal?	See the Uniform Principal and Income Act (1997) chart. (§ 45a-542i(c)(4))
b) short-term gains allocated between income and principal?	See the Uniform Principal and Income Act (1997) chart. (§ 45a-542i(c)(4))
27. How are distributions from REITs allocated between income and principal?	See the Uniform Principal and Income Act (1997) chart. (§ 45a-542i(c)(4))
28. With respect to underproductive property:	

a) *Is an adjustment, e.g., "delayed income," required to be paid to the income beneficiary?*	No. (§ 45a-542u)
b) *What percentage return makes property underproductive?*	The statute only refers to property not productive of income. (§ 45a-542u)
29. *Is the trustee required to increase income so that it is sufficient to qualify for the marital deduction?*	Yes. (§ 45a-542u)
30. *Is the trustee required to take depreciation?*	No. (§ 45a-542h)
31. *Is the trustee's determination on allocations generally presumed to be fair and reasonable?*	Yes. (§ 45a-542b(b))
32. *If an item is not addressed in the trust agreement or in the law, must it be allocated to principal or income?*	To principal. (§ 45a-542b(a)(4))
33. *When does an asset become subject to a trust:*	
a) *In the case of transfers during the transferor's life?*	The date of transfer. (§ 45a-542f(b)(1))
b) *In the case of a will?*	The date of thc testator's death. (§ 45a-542f(b)(2))
c) *In the case of the death of a third party?*	The date of the death of the third party. (§ 45a-542f(b)(3))
34. *Can a trustee rely on the characterization by an entity as to the source or character of a received distribution?*	Yes. (§ 45a-542i(f))

Table 12.02
Delaware
Trust Accounting: Principal and Income

1. *Does the trustee have the power to transfer income to principal or to transfer principal to income to meet its duty of impartiality?*	Yes. See the Uniform Principal and Income Act (1997) chart. (12 § 6113)
2. *What is the effective date for the law? E.g., does it apply to preexisting trusts?*	The provision allowing a trustee to adjust (12 § 6113) became effective on August 1, 2005 apply to trusts and estates whenever created. (75 Del. Laws 97). Other provisions have various effective dates.
3. *What percentage is allocated to income and principal from proceeds of:*	
a) *IRA?* b) *Qualified pension or profit-sharing plan?* c) *Other deferred compensation arrangement?*	The trustee must allocate the proceeds, up to six percent (6%) per year of its inventory value, to income and the balance to principal. (12 § 6109(a))
4. *What percentage is allocated to income and principal from proceeds of:*	
a) *Patents?* b) *Copyrights?*	The trustee must allocate receipts from patents and copyrights in accordance with what is reasonable and equitable in view of the interests of those entitled to income as well as of those entitled to principal, and in view of the manner in which men of ordinary prudence, discretion, and judgment would act in the management of their own affairs. (12 § 6102(a)(3); 12 § 6109(a))
5. *What percentage is allocated to income and principal in the event of distributions from:*	
a) *Corporations?* b) *Partnerships?* c) *LLCs?*	Corporate distributions of shares of the distributing corporation, including distributions in the form of a stock split or stock dividend, are principal. A right to subscribe to shares or other securities issued by the distributing corporation accruing on account of the ownership of shares or other securities in such corporation and the proceeds of any sale of the right are principal. Except to the extent that the corporation indicates that some part of a corporate distribution is a settlement of preferred or guaranteed dividends accrued since the trustee became a stockholder or is in lieu of an ordinary cash dividend, a corporate distribution is principal if the distribution is pursuant to a call of shares; a merger, consolidation or reorganization; a plan by which assets of the corporation are acquired by another corporation; or a total or partial liquidation of the corporation. Distributions made from ordinary income by a regulated investment company or by a trust qualifying and electing to be taxed under federal law as a real estate investment trust are income. All other distributions made by the company or trust, including distributions from capital gains, depreciation or depletion, whether in the form of cash or an option to take new stock or cash or an option to purchase additional shares, are principal.

	Except as provided in the preceding paragraphs, all corporate distributions are income, including cash dividends, distributions of or rights to subscribe to shares or securities or obligations of corporations other than the distributing corporation, and the proceeds of the rights or property distributions. (12 § 6106) ***Note:*** Partnerships and LLC's are not addressed.
6. What percentage is allocated to income and principal from proceeds of:	
a) Oil and gas? *b) Minerals?* *c) Water?* *d) Other natural resourses (not including timber)?*	The trustee must allocate receipts from all natural resources in accordance with what is reasonable and equitable in view of the interests of those entitled to income as well as of those entitled to principal, and in view of the manner in which men of ordinary prudence, discretion, and judgment would act in the management of their own affairs. (12 § 6102(a)(3); 12 § 6109(a))
e) Timber?	The trustee must allocate receipts from the sale of timber in accordance with what is reasonable and equitable in view of the interests of those entitled to income as well as of those entitled to principal, and in view of the manner in which men of ordinary prudence, discretion, and judgment would act in the management of their own affairs. (12 § 6102(a)(3); 12 § 6109(a))
f) Rental properties?	The trustee must include amounts received from renting real or personal property, including sums received for cancellation or renewal of a lease, as income. (12 § 6103(a)(1))
7. After a decedent dies, in the case of an estate, or after an income interest ends, when the fiduciary is determining the remaining net income what are the rules regarding payment from income or principal for:	
a) Attorneys fees? *b) Accountants fees?* *c) Fiduciary fees and commissions?* *d) Court costs?* *e) Interest on death taxes*	The trustee must charge from principal all expenses incurred in connection with the settlement of a decedent's estate, including debts, funeral expenses, estate taxes, interest and penalties concerning taxes, family allowances, fees of attorneys and personal representatives, and court costs. (12 § 6105)
f) Debts? *g) Funeral expenses?* *h) Family allowances and similar protections?* *i) Death taxes?* *j) Penalties on death taxes?*	The trustee must charge from principal all expenses incurred in connection with the settlement of a decedent's estate, including debts, funeral expenses, estate taxes, interest and penalties concerning taxes, family allowances, fees of attorneys and personal representatives, and court costs. (12 § 6105)
8. With respect to trust expenses from the administration of the trust that are not covered by 12 § 6105 [see Question #7]:	
a) Does the trustee have full discretion in allocating between income and	

principal for expenses incurred in the administration of the trust?	No. The trustee does not have full discretion in allocating expenses between income and principal for expenses occurred in the administration of the trust. (12 § 6110)
b) If not, are there special rules for:	
i) Regular trustee fees? *ii) Advisory or custodial services to the trustee?* *iii) Accountings, judicial proceedings and other matters that involve both the income and remainder interests?*	Generally, the following charges must be made against income: 1. one-half of the court costs, attorneys' fees, and other fees on periodic accountings or judicial proceedings, unless the court directs otherwise; 2. court costs, attorneys' fees, and other fees on other accountings or judicial proceedings if the matter primarily concerns the income interest, unless the court directs otherwise; and 3. the ordinary expenses reasonably incurred for the management, administration, and preservation of the trust property. Generally, the following charges must be made against principal: 1. The trustee's regular compensation, court costs and attorneys' fees primarily concerning matters of principal not charged against income; 2. expenses incurred in maintaining or defending any action to construe the trust or protect it or the property or assure the title of any trust property. (12 § 6110) ***Note:*** 12 § 6110 contains many other special rules for allocations and contains many exceptions. Consult the statute.
iv) Debts?	The trustee must allocate interest expense on trust debt to income and must allocate payments on principal of trust debt to principal. (12 § 6110)
c) Can the trustee determine what are "transmission" expenses and "management" expenses?	
9. With regard to specific gifts from a trust after an income interest ends or from an estate:	
a) What amounts must be paid from income and principal?	The fiduciary must distribute to a specific devisee or beneficiary, the income from the property devised or distributed to them less: 1. taxes, ordinary repairs, and other expenses of management and operation of the property, and 2. a portion of interest accrued since the death of the decedent or the after the income interest in a trust terminates; and a portion of taxes imposed on income, excluding taxes on capital gains, that accrue during the period of administration or after an income interest in a trust terminates. (12 § 6105(b)(1))
10. With regard to outright pecuniary gifts from an estate or trust?:	

a) *Does interest accrue?*	No. The Delaware Income and Principal Act does not provide that a beneficiary of an outright pecuniary gift should receive accrued interest on the unpaid amount. (12 § 6105)
11. *With regard to a gift in trust of a pecuniary amount from an estate or trust?*	
a) *Does interest accrue?*	No. The Delaware Income and Principal Act does not provide that a beneficiary of a pecuniary gift in trust should receive accrued interest on the unpaid amount. (12 § 6105)
12. *With regard to residuary gifts:*	
a) *What amount of income and principal is to be paid to the residuary beneficiary of a trust or an estate?*	The fiduciary should distribute to the remainder beneficiaries the balance of the income, less certain expenses that accrue during the period of administration or after an income interest terminates, in proportion to their respective interests in the undistributed assets of the estate or trust. (12 § 6105(b)(2)) Unless otherwise provided in the will creating a trust, the fiduciary must pay any person entitled to the income of a trust of the whole or any part of a residuary estate of a decedent in lieu of any other payments of income or allowances out of the property delivered to the trustee of such trust, interest at the rate of 4% per year until the property is delivered to the trustee. (This section does not apply to real estate, the title to which vests in the trustee immediately upon the death of the decedent.) (12 § 3525)
13. *With regard to "business assets" held in trust:*	
a) *Can the trustee treat them as a separate entity?*	The Delaware Principal and Income Act does not particularly provide for treating distinct assets as separate entities. However, if a trustee uses any part of the principal in the operation of a trade or business or farming operation, the trustee must allocate the proceeds and losses of the trade or business or farming operation in accordance with what is reasonable and equitable in view of the interests of those entitled to income as well as those entitled to principal, and in view of the manner in which people of ordinary prudence, discretion and judgment would act in the management of their own affairs. (12 § 6108)
b) *Can the trustee treat distinct assets as separate entities?*	The Delaware Principal and Income Act does not particularly provide for treating distinct assets as separate entities. However, if a trustee uses any part of the principal in the operation of a trade or business or farming operation, the trustee must allocate the proceeds and losses of the trade or business or farming operation in accordance with what is reasonable and equitable in view of the interests of those entitled to income as well as those entitled to principal, and in view of the manner in which people of ordinary prudence, discretion and judgment would act in the management of their own affairs. (12 § 6108)
c) *Can earnings be retained in trust for the reasonable needs of the "business*	No. The Delaware Principal and Income Act does not provide that the fiduciary may retain earnings for the needs of the business entity.

entity," and, if so, to what extent is this permitted?	
14. With respect to discount bonds:	
a) To what extent is the discount added to income or principal upon maturity?	The appreciation of a bond in accordance with a fixed schedule of appreciation in excess of the price at which it was issued or of a zero coupon bond is income. The increment in value is distributable to the beneficiary who was the income beneficiary at the time of increment from the first principal cash available or, if none is available, when realized by sale, redemption, or other disposition. Whenever unrealized appreciation is distributed as income out of principal, the fiduciary must reimburse principal when the appreciation is realized. Otherwise, any bonds are principal at their inventory value and no provision may be made for amortization of bond premiums or for accumulation for discount, and the proceeds of sale, redemption, or other disposition of bonds are principal. (12 § 6107)
b) Does the trustee have discretion to allocate discount between income and principal?	No. (12 § 6107)
c) Are distinctions drawn between Series E bonds and others?	No. (12 § 6107)
d) Are distinctions drawn based on the maturity date of the bond?	No. (12 § 6107)
15. Is there a de minimis rule excusing the trustee from making adjustments in certain cases?	No.
16. With respect to derivatives:	
a) May income and loss be treated as that of a separate entity?	The Delaware Principal and Income Act does not address derivatives.
b) If not, or the trustee chooses not to do so, is income and loss allocated to the income account or to principal?	The Delaware Principal and Income Act does not address derivatives. Therefore, the trustee must allocate the item in accordance with what is reasonable and equitable in view of the interests of those entitled to income as well as of those entitled to principal, and in view of the manner in which persons of ordinary prudence, discretion, and judgment would act in the management of their own affairs. (12 § 6102(a)(3))
17. To the extent put and call options are not derivatives, how are they allocated in terms of principal and income?	The Delaware Principal and Income Act does not address options. Therefore, the trustee must allocate the item in accordance with what is reasonable and equitable in view of the interests of those entitled to income as well as of those entitled to principal, and in view of the manner in which persons of ordinary prudence, discretion, and judgment would act in the management of their own affairs. (12 § 6102(a)(3))
18. How are asset-backed securities allocated in terms of principal and income?	The Delaware Principal and Income Act does not address asset-backed securities. Therefore, the trustee must allocate the item in accordance with what is reasonable and equitable

	in view of the interests of those entitled to income as well as of those entitled to principal, and in view of the manner in which persons of ordinary prudence, discretion, and judgment would act in the management of their own affairs. (12 § 6102(a)(3))
19. Are expenses incurred to comply with environmental requirements allocated to income or principal?	The Delaware Principal and Income Act does not address expenses for environmental requirements. Therefore, the trustee must allocate the item in accordance with what is reasonable and equitable in view of the interests of those entitled to income as well as of those entitled to principal, and in view of the manner in which persons of ordinary prudence, discretion, and judgment would act in the management of their own affairs. (12 § 6102(a)(3))
20. Is income tax liability allocated generally to income or principal?	Any tax required to be paid by a fiduciary on the trust's share of an entity's taxable income should be paid from income to the extent that receipts from the entity are allocated to income and from principal to the extent that receipts from the entity are allocated to principal. (12 § 6110)
21. If a Subchapter S shareholder's or partner's portion of tax liability is greater than cash distributed, how is the excess obligation allocated?	The Delaware Principal and Income Act does not address this situation. Therefore, the trustee must allocate the item in accordance with what is reasonable and equitable in view of the interests of those entitled to income as well as of those entitled to principal, and in view of the manner in which persons of ordinary prudence, discretion, and judgment would act in the management of their own affairs. (12 § 6102(a)(3))
22. What is the standard, if any, for making equitable adjustments between income and principal?	Any adjustments must be made in a fair and equitable manner with due regard to the respective interests of income beneficiaries and remaindermen. (12 § 6102)
23. Is an income beneficiary entitled to receive income accrued but unpaid when an estate ends?	On termination of an income interest, the income beneficiary whose interest is terminated, or his estate, is entitled to: Income undistributed on the date of termination; income due but not paid to the trustee on the date of termination; and income in the form of periodic payments (other than corporate distributions to stockholders), including rent, interest, or annuities, not due on the date of termination, accrued from day to day. (12 § 6104(d))
24. Is an income beneficiary entitled to receive income accrued but unpaid when a revocable trust ends?	On termination of an income interest, the income beneficiary whose interest is terminated, or his estate, is entitled to: Income undistributed on the date of termination; income due but not paid to the trustee on the date of termination; and income in the form of periodic payments (other than corporate distributions to stockholders), including rent, interest, or annuities, not due on the date of termination, accrued from day to day. (12 § 6104(d))
25. Is an income beneficiary entitled to receive income accrued but unpaid when an irrevocable trust ends?	On termination of an income interest, the income beneficiary whose interest is terminated, or his estate, is entitled to: Income undistributed on the date of termination; income due but not paid to the trustee on the date of termination and income in the form of periodic payments (other than corporate distributions to stockholders), including rent, interest, or annuities, not due on the date of termination, accrued from day to day. (12 § 6104(d))
26. With regard to mutual funds, how are:	

a) *long-term gains allocated between income and principal?*	Distributions made from ordinary income by a regulated investment company are income. All other distributions made by the company or trust, including distributions from capital gains, depreciation, or depletion, whether in the form of cash or an option to take new stock or cash or an option to purchase additional shares, are principal. (12 § 6106(c))
b) *short-term gains allocated between income and principal?*	Distributions made from ordinary income by a regulated investment company are income. All other distributions made by the company, including distributions from capital gains, depreciation, or depletion, whether in the form of cash or an option to take new stock or cash or an option to purchase additional shares, are principal. (12 § 6106(c))
27. *How are distributions from REITs allocated between income and principal?*	Distributions made from ordinary income by a real estate investment trust are income. All other distributions made by the trust, including distributions from capital gains, depreciation, or depletion, whether in the form of cash or an option to take new stock or cash or an option to purchase additional shares, are principal. (12 § 6106(c))
28. *With respect to underproductive property:*	
a) *Is an adjustment, e.g., "delayed income," required to be paid to the income beneficiary?*	No. The Delaware Principal and Income Act does not address underproductive property or delayed income.
b) *What percentage return makes property underproductive?*	The Delaware Principal and Income Act does not address underproductive property.
29. *Is the trustee required to increase income so that it is sufficient to qualify for the marital deduction?*	The Delaware Principal and Income Act does not address the marital deduction.
30. *Is the trustee required to take depreciation?*	Yes. (12 § 6110(a)(2))
31. *Is the trustee's determination on allocations generally presumed to be fair and reasonable?*	The Delaware Principal and Income Act does not have a presumption that allocations are generally presumed to be fair and reasonable.
32. *If an item is not addressed in the trust agreement or in the law, must it be allocated to principal or income?*	If an item is not addressed in the trust agreement or in the law, the trustee must allocate the item in accordance with what is reasonable and equitable in view of the interests of those entitled to income as well as of those entitled to principal, and in view of the manner in which persons of ordinary prudence, discretion, and judgment would act in the management of their own affairs. (12 § 6102(a)(3))
33. *When does an asset become subject to a trust:*	
a) *In the case of transfers during the transferor's life?*	The Delaware Principal and Income Act does not address this issue. (12 § 6104(a))
b) *In the case of a will?*	In the case of an asset becoming subject to a trust by reason of a will, it becomes subject to the trust as of the date of the death of the testator even though there is an intervening period of administration of the testator's estate. (12 § 6104(a))

c) In the case of the death of a third party?	The Delaware Principal and Income Act does not address this issue. (12 § 6104(a))
34. Can a trustee rely on the characterization by an entity as to the source or character of a received distribution?	Yes. (12 § 6106(e))

Table 12.02
District of Columbia
Trust Accounting: Principal and Income

1. *Does the trustee have the power to transfer income to principal or to transfer principal to income to meet its duty of impartiality?*	Yes. See the Uniform Principal and Income Act (1997) chart. (§ 28-4801.04)
2. *What is the effective date for the law? E.g., does it apply to preexisting trusts?*	The District of Columbia Principal and Income Act applies to every trust or decedent's estate existing on April 27, 2001 except as otherwsie expressly provided in the will or the terms of the trust or by the District of Columbia Principal and Income Act. (§ 28-4801.04) ***Note***: A trustee may continue using a former allocation method to allocate receipts for water, minerals, other natural resources, and timber under certain circumstances. (See § 28-4804.11; § 28-4804.12)
3. *What percentage is allocated to income and principal from proceeds of:*	
a) *IRA?* b) *Qualified pension or profit-sharing plan?* c) *Other deferred compensation arrangement?*	See the Uniform Principal and Income Act (1997) chart. (§ 28-4804.09)
4. *What percentage is allocated to income and principal from proceeds of:*	
a) *Patents?* b) *Copyrights?*	See the Uniform Principal and Income Act (1997) chart. (§ 28-4804.10)
5. *What percentage is allocated to income and principal in the event of distributions from:*	
a) *Corporations?* b) *Partnerships?* c) *LLCs?*	See the Uniform Principal and Income Act (1997) chart. (§ 28-4804.01)
6. *What percentage is allocated to income and principal from proceeds of:*	
a) *Oil and gas?* b) *Minerals?* c) *Water?* d) *Other natural resourses (not including timber)?*	See the Uniform Principal and Income Act (1997) chart. (§ 28-4804.11) ***Note:*** If a trust owns an interest in minerals, water, or other natural resources on April 27, 2001, the trustee may allocate net receipts from the interest as provided in the District of Columbia Principal and Income Act or in the manner used by the trustee before April 27, 2001. (See § 28-4804.12(d))
e) *Timber*	See the Uniform Principal and Income Act (1997) chart. (§ 28-4804.12) ***Note:*** If a trust owns an interest in timberland on April 27, 2001, the trustee may allocate net receipts from the sale of timber and related products as provided in the District of Columbia Principal and Income Act or in the manner used by the trustee before April 27, 2001. (See § 28-4804.12(d))

f) Rental properties?	See the Uniform Principal and Income Act (1997) chart. (§ 28-4804.05)
7. After a decedent dies, in the case of an estate, or after an income interest ends, when the fiduciary is determining the remaining net income what are the rules regarding payment from income or principal for:	
a) Attorneys fees? *b) Accountants fees?* *c) Fiduciary fees and commissions?* *d) Court costs?* *e) Interest on death taxes*	See the Uniform Principal and Income Act (1997) chart. (§ 28-4802.01(2)(B))
f) Debts? *g) Funeral expenses?* *h) Family allowances and similar protections?* *i) Death taxes?* *j) Penalties on death taxes?*	See the Uniform Principal and Income Act (1997) chart. (§ 28-4802.01(2)(C)).
8. With respect to trust expenses from the administration of the trust that are not covered by § 28-4802.01(2)(B-C) [see Question #7]:	
a) Does the trustee have full discretion in allocating between income and principal for expenses incurred in the administration of the trust?	No. (§ 28-4805.01; § 28-4805.02)
b) If not, are there special rules for:	
i) Regular trustee fees? *ii) Advisory or cusodial services to the trustee?* *iii) Accountings, judicial proceedings and other matters that involve both the income and remainder interests?*	See the Uniform Principal and Income Act (1997) chart. (§ 28-4805.01; § 28-4805.02)
iv) Debts?	See the Uniform Principal and Income Act (1997) chart. (§ 28-4805.01(3); § 28-4805.02(a)(3))
c) Can the trustee determine what are "transmission" expenses and "management" expenses?	
9. With regard to specific gifts from a trust after an income interest ends or from an estate:	
a) What amounts must be paid from income and principal?	See the Uniform Principal and Income Act (1997) chart. (§ 28-4802.01(1); § 28-4802.01(5))

10. With regard to outright pecuniary gifts from an estate or trust?:	
a) Does interest accrue?	Yes. See the Uniform Principal and Income Act (1997) chart. (§ 28-4802.01(3))
11. With regard to a gift in trust of a pecuniary amount from an estate or trust?	
a) Does interest accrue?	No. See the Uniform Principal and Income Act (1997) chart. (§ 28-4802.01(4); § 28-4802.02)
12. With regard to residuary gifts:	
a) What amount of income and principal is to be paid to the residuary beneficiary of a trust or an estate?	See the Uniform Principal and Income Act (1997) chart. (§ 28-4802.01(4); § 28-4802.02)
13. With regard to "business assets" held in trust:	
a) Can the trustee treat them as a separate entity?	Generally yes. See the Uniform Principal and Income Act (1997) chart. (§ 28-4804.03)
b) Can the trustee treat distinct assets as separate entities?	Generally yes. See the Uniform Principal and Income Act (1997) chart. (§ 28-4804.03)
c) Can earnings be retained in trust for the reasonable needs of the "business entity," and, if so, to what extent is this permitted?	See the Uniform Principal and Income Act (1997) chart. (§ 28-4804.03(b))
14. With respect to discount bonds:	
a) To what extent is the discount added to income or principal upon maturity?	See the Uniform Principal and Income Act (1997) chart. (§ 28-4804.06(b))
b) Does the trustee have discretion to allocate discount between income and principal?	No. (§ 28-4804.06) ***Note:*** The trustee has the overriding power to adjust under § 28-4801.04(a).
c) Are distinctions drawn between Series E bonds and others?	No. (§ 28-4804.06)
d) Are distinctions drawn based on the maturity date of the bond?	Yes. (§ 28-4804.06)
15. Is there a de minimis rule excusing the trustee from making adjustments in certain cases?	Yes. See the Uniform Principal and Income Act (1997) chart. (§ 28-4804.08)
16. With respect to derivatives:	
a) May income and loss be treated as that of a separate entity?	Yes. (§ 28-4804.03(c)(7); § 28-4804.14(b))
b) If not, or the trustee chooses not to do so, is income and loss allocated to the income account or to principal?	To principal. (§ 28-4804.14(b))

17. *To the extent put and call options are not derivatives, how are they allocated in terms of principal and income?*	To principal. (§ 28-4804.14(c))
18. *How are asset-backed securities allocated in terms of principal and income?*	See the Uniform Principal and Income Act (1997) chart. (§ 28-4804.15)
19. *Are expenses incurred to comply with environmental requirements allocated to income or principal?*	Generally to principal. See the Uniform Principal and Income Act (1997) chart. (§ 28-4805.02(a)(7))
20. *Is income tax liability allocated generally to income or principal?*	See the Uniform Principal and Income Act (1997) chart. (§ 28-4805.05; § 28-4805.06)
21. *If a Subchapter S shareholder's or partner's portion of tax liability is greater than cash distributed, how is the excess obligation allocated?*	To principal. (§ 28-4805.05(c)(2)(B))
22. *What is the standard, if any, for making equitable adjustments between income and principal?*	See the Uniform Principal and Income Act (1997) chart. (§ 28-4801.03(b))
23. *Is an income beneficiary entitled to receive income accrued but unpaid when an estate ends?*	No. (§ 28-4803.03)
24. *Is an income beneficiary entitled to receive income accrued but unpaid when a revocable trust ends?*	Generally no. See the Uniform Principal and Income Act (1997) chart. (§ 28-4803.03)
25. *Is an income beneficiary entitled to receive income accrued but unpaid when an irrevocable trust ends?*	Generally no. See the Uniform Principal and Income Act (1997) chart. (§ 28-4803.03)
26. *With regard to mutual funds, how are:*	
a) *long-term gains allocated between income and principal?*	See the Uniform Principal and Income Act (1997) chart. (§ 28-4804.01(c)(4))
b) *short-term gains allocated between income and principal?*	See the Uniform Principal and Income Act (1997) chart. (§ 28-4804.01(c)(4))
27. *How are distributions from REITs allocated between income and principal?*	See the Uniform Principal and Income Act (1997) chart. (§ 28-4804.01(c)(4))
28. *With respect to underproductive property:*	
a) *Is an adjustment, e.g., "delayed income," required to be paid to the income beneficiary?*	No. (§ 28-4804.13)
b) *What percentage return makes property underproductive?*	The statute only refers to property not productive of income. (§ 28-4804.13)
29. *Is the trustee required to increase income so that it is sufficient to qualify for the marital deduction?*	Yes. (§ 28-4804.13(a))

30. Is the trustee required to take depreciation?	No. (§ 28-4805.03)
31. Is the trustee's determination on allocations generally presumed to be fair and reasonable?	Yes. (§ 28-4801.03(b))
32. If an item is not addressed in the trust agreement or in the law, must it be allocated to principal or income?	To principal. (§ 28-4801.03(a)(4))
33. When does an asset become subject to a trust:	
a) In the case of transfers during the transferor's life?	The date of transfer. (§ 28-4803.01(b)(1))
b) In the case of a will?	The date of the testator's death. (§ 28-4803.01(b)(2))
c) In the case of the death of a third party?	The date of the third party's death. (§ 28-4803.01(b)(3))
34. Can a trustee rely on the characterization by an entity as to the source or character of a received distribution?	Yes. (§ 28-4804.01(f))

Table 12.02
Florida
Trust Accounting: Principal and Income

1. *Does the trustee have the power to transfer income to principal or to transfer principal to income to meet its duty of impartiality?*	Yes. See the Uniform Principal and Income Act (1997) chart. (§ 738.104)
2. *What is the effective date for the law? E.g., does it apply to preexisting trusts?*	Except as provided in the trust instrument, the will, or the Florida Principal and Income Act, the Florida Principal and Income Act applies to any receipt or expense received or incurred and any disbursement made after January 1, 2003, by any trust or decedent's estate, whether established before or after January 1, 2003, and whether the asset involved was acquired by the trustee or personal representative before or after January 1, 2003. Receipts or expenses received or incurred and disbursements made before January 1, 2003, shall be governed by Florida law in effect at the time of the event, except as otherwise expressly provided in the will or terms of the trust or in the Florida Principal and Income Act. (§ 738.804) ***Note:*** A trustee may continue using a former allocation method to allocate receipts for water, minerals, other natural resources, and timber under certain circumstances. (See § 738.604; § 738.605)
3. *What percentage is allocated to income and principal from proceeds of:*	
a) *IRA?* b) *Qualified pension or profit-sharing plan?* c) *Other deferred compensation arrangement?*	See the Uniform Principal and Income Act (1997) chart. (§ 738.602) ***Note:*** While § 738.602 has generally the same effect as Uniform Principal and Income Act (1997) § 409, the language of the Florida statute differs.
4. *What percentage is allocated to income and principal from proceeds of:*	
a) *Patents?* b) *Copyrights?*	See the Uniform Principal and Income Act (1997) chart. (§ 738.603)
5. *What percentage is allocated to income and principal in the event of distributions from:*	
a) *Corporations?* b) *Partnerships?* c) *LLCs?*	See the Uniform Principal and Income Act (1997) chart. (§ 738.401(3)) ***Note***: § 738.401(3) contains some additional language not included in Uniform Principal and Income Act § 401. See special rules in § 738.401(7).
6. *What percentage is allocated to income and principal from proceeds of:*	
a) *Oil and gas?* b) *Minerals?* c) *Water?* d) *Other natural resourses (not including timber)?*	See the Uniform Principal and Income Act (1997) chart. (§ 738.604) ***Note***: If a trust owns an interest in minerals, water, or other natural resources on January 1, 2003, the trustee may allocate receipts from the interest as provided in the Florida Principal

	and Income Act or in the manner used by the trustee before January 1, 2003.
e) *Timber*	See the Uniform Principal and Income Act (1997) chart. (§ 738.605) ***Note***: If a trust owns an interest in timberland on January 1, 2003, the trustee may allocate net receipts from the sale of timber and related products as provided in the Florida Uniform Principal and Income Act or in the manner used by the trustee before January 1, 2003.
f) *Rental properties?*	See the Uniform Principal and Income Act (1997) chart. (§ 738.502)
7. *After a decedent dies, in the case of an estate, or after an income interest ends, when the fiduciary is determining the remaining net income what are the rules regarding payment from income or principal for:*	
a) *Attorneys fees?* b) *Accountants fees?* c) *Fiduciary fees and commissions?* d) *Court costs?* e) *Interest on death taxes*	See the Uniform Principal and Income Act (1997) chart. (§ 738.201(2)(b))
f) *Debts?* g) *Funeral expenses?* h) *Family allowances and similar protections?* i) *Death taxes?* j) *Penalties on death taxes?*	See the Uniform Principal and Income Act (1997) chart. (§ 738.201(2)(c))
8. *With respect to trust expenses from the administration of the trust that are not covered by § 738.201(2)(b-c) [see Question #7]:*	
a) *Does the trustee have full discretion in allocating between income and principal for expenses incurred in the administration of the trust?*	No. (§ 738.701; § 738.702)
b) *If not, are there special rules for:*	
i) *Regular trustee fees?* ii) *Advisory or cusodial services to the trustee?* iii) *Accountings, judicial proceedings and other matters that involve both the income and remainder interests?*	See the Uniform Principal and Income Act (1997) chart. (§ 738.701; § 738.702)
iv) *Debts?*	See the Uniform Principal and Income Act (1997) chart. (§ 738.701(1); § 738.702(1)(c))

c) *Can the trustee determine what are "transmission" expenses and "management" expenses?*	
9. *With regard to specific gifts from a trust after an income interest ends or from an estate:*	
a) *What amounts must be paid from income and principal?*	See the Uniform Principal and Income Act (1997) chart. (§ 738.201(1); § 738.201(5))
10. *With regard to outright pecuniary gifts from an estate or trust?:*	
a) *Does interest accrue?*	Yes. See the Uniform Principal and Income Act (1997) chart. (§ 738.201(3))
11. *With regard to a gift in trust of a pecuniary amount from an estate or trust?*	
a) *Does interest accrue?*	No. See the Uniform Principal and Income Act (1997) chart. (§ 738.201(4); § 738.202)
12. *With regard to residuary gifts:*	
a) *What amount of income and principal is to be paid to the residuary beneficiary of a trust or an estate?*	See the Uniform Principal and Income Act (1997) chart. (§ 738.201(4); § 738.202)
13. *With regard to "business assets" held in trust:*	
a) *Can the trustee treat them as a separate entity?*	Yes. See the Uniform Principal and Income Act (1997) chart. (§ 738.403)
b) *Can the trustee treat distinct assets as separate entities?*	Yes. See the Uniform Principal and Income Act (1997) chart. (§ 738.403)
c) *Can earnings be retained in trust for the reasonable needs of the "business entity," and, if so, to what extent is this permitted?*	See the Uniform Principal and Income Act (1997) chart. (§ 738.403(2))
14. *With respect to discount bonds:*	
a) *To what extent is the discount added to income or principal upon maturity?*	The appreciation in value of a bond bearing no stated interest but payable at a future time in excess of the price at which it was issued or purchased, if purchased after issuance, is income. If the increment in value accrues and becomes payable pursuant to a fixed schedule of appreciation, it may be distributed to the income beneficiary from principal or, if no cash is available, when the appreciation is realized by sale, redemption, or other disposition. When unrealized appreciation is distributed as income but out of principal, the principal must be reimbursed for that amount when realized. If, in the reasonable judgment of the trustee, exercised in good faith, the ultimate payment of the bond principal is in doubt, the trustee may

	withhold the payment of incremental interest to the income beneficiary. A trustee must allocate to principal an amount received from the sale, redemption, or other disposition of an interest bearing bond. (§ 738.503)
b) Does the trustee have discretion to allocate discount between income and principal?	No. (§ 738.503) ***Note***: The trustee still has the overriding power to adjust under (§ 738.104)
c) Are distinctions drawn between Series E bonds and others?	No. (§ 738.503)
d) Are distinctions drawn based on the maturity date of the bond?	No. (§ 738.503)
15. Is there a de minimis rule excusing the trustee from making adjustments in certain cases?	Yes. See the Uniform Principal and Income Act (1997) chart. (§ 738.601)
16. With respect to derivatives:	
a) May income and loss be treated as that of a separate entity?	Yes. (§ 738.607; § 738.403(3)(g))
b) If not, or the trustee chooses not to do so, is income and loss allocated to the income account or to principal?	To principal. (§ 738.607(2))
17. To the extent put and call options are not derivatives, how are they allocated in terms of principal and income?	To principal. (§ 738.607(3))
18. How are asset-backed securities allocated in terms of principal and income?	See the Uniform Principal and Income Act (1997) chart. (§ 738.608)
19. Are expenses incurred to comply with environmental requirements allocated to income or principal?	Generally to principal. See the Uniform Principal and Income Act (1997) chart. (§ 738.702(1)(g))
20. Is income tax liability allocated generally to income or principal?	See the Uniform Principal and Income Act (1997) chart. (§ 738.705; § 738.706)
21. If a Subchapter S shareholder's or partner's portion of tax liability is greater than cash distributed, how is the excess obligation allocated?	The excess obligation must be paid from principal. (§ 738.705(3)(b)(2))
22. What is the standard, if any, for making equitable adjustments between income and principal?	See the Uniform Principal and Income Act (1997) chart. (§ 738.103(2))
23. Is an income beneficiary entitled to receive income accrued but unpaid when an estate ends?	No. (§ 738.303)

24. Is an income beneficiary entitled to receive income accrued but unpaid when a revocable trust ends?	Generally no. See the Uniform Principal and Income Act (1997) chart. (§ 738.303)
25. Is an income beneficiary entitled to receive income accrued but unpaid when an irrevocable trust ends?	Generally no. See the Uniform Principal and Income Act (1997) chart. (§ 738.303)
26. With regard to mutual funds, how are:	
a) long-term gains allocated between income and principal?	See the Uniform Principal and Income Act (1997) chart. (§ 738.401(3)(d))
b) short-term gains allocated between income and principal?	See the Uniform Principal and Income Act (1997) chart. (§ 738.401(3)(d))
27. How are distributions from REITs allocated between income and principal?	See the Uniform Principal and Income Act (1997) chart. (§ 738.401(3)(d))
28. With respect to underproductive property:	
a) Is an adjustment, e.g., "delayed income," required to be paid to the income beneficiary?	No. (§ 738.606)
b) What percentage return makes property underproductive?	The statute only refers to property not productive of income. (§ 738.606)
29. Is the trustee required to increase income so that it is sufficient to qualify for the marital deduction?	Yes. (§ 738.606)
30. Is the trustee required to take depreciation?	No. (§ 738.703)
31. Is the trustee's determination on allocations generally presumed to be fair and reasonable?	Yes. (§ 738.103(2))
32. If an item is not addressed in the trust agreement or in the law, must it be allocated to principal or income?	To principal. (§ 738.103(1)(d))
33. When does an asset become subject to a trust:	
a) In the case of transfers during the transferor's life?	The date of transfer. (§ 738.301(2)(a))
b) In the case of a will?	On the death of the testator. (§ 738.301(2)(b))
c) In the case of the death of a third party?	The date of the third party's death. See the Uniform Principal and Income Act (1997) chart. (§ 738.301(2)(c))
34. Can a trustee rely on the characterization by an entity as to the source or character of a received distribution?	Yes. (§ 738.401(8))

Table 12.02
Georgia
Trust Accounting: Principal and Income

1. *Does the trustee have the power to transfer income to principal or to transfer principal to income to meet its duty of impartiality?*	The trustee has the power to adjust between income and principal if: 1. The governing instrument describes what may or must be distributed to a beneficiary by refering to the trust's income. 2. The trustee determines after applying § 53-12-211(a), that the trustee is unable to comply with § 53-12-211(b). (§ 53-12-220)
2. *What is the effective date for the law? E.g., does it apply to preexisting trusts?*	The effective date for the Georgia Principal and Income Act is July 1, 1991. The Georgia Principal and Income Act does not address its application to preexisting trusts. See the Georgia Sessions Laws (1991 Ga. Laws 810). ***Note***: A trustee that, on July 1, 1991, held an item of depletable property of a type specified in § 53-12-217 may allocate receipts from the property in the manner used before July 1, 1991. (§ 53-12-217)
3. *What percentage is allocated to income and principal from proceeds of:*	
a) *IRA?* b) *Qualified pension or profit-sharing plan?* c) *Other deferred compensation arrangement?*	If any part of the principal consists of property subject to depletion, including rights to receive payments on a contract for deferred compensation, the trustee must determine the value and the useful life of the property as of the beginning of each annual accounting period. Receipts shall be allocated to principal to amortize that value; the balance of the receipts shall be allocated to income. (§ 53-12-217) ***Note***: The Georgia Principal and Income Act does not refer to IRA's or pensions specifically. ***Note***: A trustee that, on July 1, 1991, held an item of depletable property of a type specified in § 53-12-217 may allocate receipts from the property in the manner used before July 1, 1991, but as to all depletable property acquired after July 1, 1991, by an existing or new trust, the method of allocation provided in this article shall be used. (§ 53-12-217)
4. *What percentage is allocated to income and principal from proceeds of:*	
a) *Patents?* b) *Copyrights?*	If any part of the principal consists of property subject to depletion, including patents or copyrights, the trustee must determine the value and the useful life of the property as of the beginning of each annual accounting period. Receipts shall be allocated to principal to amortize that value; the balance of the receipts shall be allocated to income. (§ 53-12-217) ***Note***: A trustee that, on July 1, 1991, held an item of depletable property of a type specified in § 53-12-217 may allocate receipts from the property in the manner used before July 1, 1991, but as to all depletable property acquired after July 1, 1991, by an existing or new trust, the method of allocation provided in this article shall be used. (§ 53-12-217)
5. *What percentage is allocated to income and principal in the event of distributions from:*	

a) Corporations? *b) Partnerships?* *c) LLCs?*	Corporate distributions of shares of the distributing corporation, including distributions in the form of a stock split or stock dividend, are principal. A right to subscribe to shares or other securities issued by the distributing corporation accruing on account of the ownership of shares or other securities in such corporation and the proceeds of any sale of the right are principal. Except to the extent that the corporation indicates that some part of a corporate distribution is a settlement of preferred or guaranteed dividends accrued since the trustee became a stockholder or is in lieu of an ordinary cash dividend, a corporate distribution is principal if the distribution is pursuant to a call of shares; a merger, consolidation or reorganization; a plan by which assets of the corporation are acquired by another corporation; or a total or partial liquidation of the corporation. Distributions made from ordinary income by a regulated investment company or by a trust qualifying and electing to be taxed under federal law as a real estate investment trust are income. All other distributions made by the company or trust, including distributions from capital gains, depreciation or depletion, whether in the form of cash or an option to take new stock or cash or an option to purchase additional shares, are principal. Except as provided in the preceding paragraphs, all corporate distributions are income, including cash dividends, distributions of or rights to subscribe to shares or securities or obligations of corporations other than the distributing corporation, and the proceeds of the rights or property distributions. (§ 53-12-214) ***Note***: Partnerships and LLC's are not addressed.
6. What percentage is allocated to income and principal from proceeds of:	
a) Oil and gas? *b) Minerals?* *c) Water?* *d) Other natural resourses (not including timber)?*	Receipts from minerals and other natural resources, but not including timber, must be allocated to principal. (§ 53-12-217) ***Note***: A trustee that, on July 1, 1991, held an item of depletable property of a type specified in § 53-12-217 may allocate receipts from the property in the manner used before July 1, 1991, but as to all depletable property acquired after July 1, 1991, by an existing or new trust, the method of allocation provided in this article shall be used. (§ 53-12-217)
e) Timber?	Unless the governing instrument provides otherwise, receipts from timber must be allocated to principal. (§ 53-12-218)
f) Rental properties?	The trustee must allocate amounts received from renting real or personal property, including sums received for cancellation or renewal of a lease, to income. (§ 53-12-212)
7. After a decedent dies, in the case of an estate, or after an income interest ends, when the fiduciary is determining the remaining net income what are the rules regarding payment from income or principal for:	

a) Attorneys fees? *b) Accountants fees?* *c) Fiduciary fees and commissions?* *d) Court costs?* *e) Interest on death taxes*	Expenses incurred in connection with the settlement of a decedent's estate, including interest and penalties concerning taxes, fees of attorneys and personal representatives, and court costs, may be charged against the principal or income at the discretion of the personal representative. (§ 53-12-219(e))
f) Debts? *g) Funeral expenses?* *h) Family allowances and similar protections?* *i) Death taxes?* *j) Penalties on death taxes?*	Expenses incurred in connection with the settlement of a decedent's estate, including interest and penalties concerning taxes, fees of attorneys and personal representatives, and court costs, may be charged against the principal or income at the discretion of the personal representative. (§ 53-12-219(e))
8. With respect to trust expenses from the administration of the trust that are not covered § 53-12-219(e) [see Question #7]:	
a) Does the trustee have full discretion in allocating between income and principal for expenses incurred in the administration of the trust?	No. (§ 53-12-219)
b) If not, are there special rules for:	
i) Regular trustee fees? *ii) Advisory or custodial services to the trustee?* *iii) Accountings, judicial proceedings and other matters that involve both the income and remainder interests?*	Generally, the following charges must be made against income: 1. one-half of court costs, attorney's fees and other expenses and fees on any judicial accounting, unless the court directs otherwise; 2. court costs, attorney's fees and other expenses and fees on other judicial proceedings if the matter primarily concerns the income interest, unless the court directs otherwise; and 3. one-half of the regular compensation of the trustee. All other charges concerning regular trustee fees; advisory or custodial services to the trustee; and accountings, judicial proceedings and other matters that involve both the income and remainder interests are to generally allocated to principal. ***Note:*** § 53-12-219 contains many other special rules for allocations and contains many exceptions.
iv) Debts?	The trustee must allocate interest expense on trust debt to income and must allocate payments on principal of trust debt to principal. (§ 53-12-219)
c) Can the trustee determine what are "transmission" expenses and "management" expenses?	
9. With regard to specific gifts from a trust after an income interest ends or from an estate:	
a) What amounts must be paid from income and principal?	The income, profit, or increase of specific testamentary gifts, as a general rule, goes with the gift, though the time of enjoyment or vesting may be postponed. (§ 53-4-60)

10. With regard to outright pecuniary gifts from an estate or trust?:	
a) Does interest accrue?	A general or demonstrative testamentary gift usually bears interest at the legal rate after the expiration of 12 months from the death of the testator; provided, however, that when a general or demonstrative testamentary gift is to be paid at a later time or upon a later event, it bears no interest until such time or event. The general rule above yields to the equity and necessity of a particular case if the condition of the estate as to the payment of debts and testamentary gifts is doubtful or if the fund out of which the testamentary gift is to be paid is unavailable for all the charges made upon it or if any other equitable circumstance intervenes. (§ 53-4-61)
11. With regard to a gift in trust of a pecuniary amount from an estate or trust?	
a) Does interest accrue?	A general or demonstrative testamentary gift usually bears interest at the legal rate after the expiration of 12 months from the death of the testator; provided, however, that when a general or demonstrative testamentary gift is to be paid at a later time or upon a later event, it bears no interest until such time or event. The general rule above yields to the equity and necessity of a particular case if the condition of the estate as to the payment of debts and testamentary gifts is doubtful or if the fund out of which the testamentary gift is to be paid is unavailable for all the charges made upon it or if any other equitable circumstance intervenes. (§ 53-4-61)
12. With regard to residuary gifts:	
a) What amount of income and principal is to be paid to the residuary beneficiary of a trust or an estate?	The Georgia Principal and Income Act does not address this issue.
13. With regard to "business assets" held in trust:	
a) Can the trustee treat them as a separate entity?	No. The Georgia Principal and Income Act does not particularly provide for treating business assets as separate entities.
b) Can the trustee treat distinct assets as separate entities?	No. The Georgia Principal and Income Act does not particularly provide for treating distinct assets as separate entities.
c) Can earnings be retained in trust for the reasonable needs of the "business entity," and, if so, to what extent is this permitted?	No. The Georgia Principal and Income Act does not provide that the fiduciary may retain earnings for the needs of the business entity.
14. With respect to discount bonds:	
a) To what extent is the discount added to income or principal upon maturity?	The appreciation of a bond in accordance with a fixed schedule of appreciation in excess of the price at which it was issued is distributable as income. The increment in value is distributable to the beneficiary who was the income beneficiary at the time

	of increment from the first principal cash available or, if none is available, when realized by sale, redemption, or other disposition. Whenever unrealized appreciation is distributed as income out of principal, the fiduciary must reimburse principal when the appreciation is realized. Otherwise, any bonds are principal at their inventory value and no provision may be made for amortization of bond premiums or for accumulation for discount, and the proceeds of sale, redemption, or other disposition of bonds are principal. (§ 53-12-215)
b) Does the trustee have discretion to allocate discount between income and principal?	No. (§ 53-12-215) Note: The trustee has the overriding power to adjust under § 53-12-220.
c) Are distinctions drawn between Series E bonds and others?	No. (§ 53-12-215)
d) Are distinctions drawn based on the maturity date of the bond?	No. (§ 53-12-215)
15. Is there a de minimis rule excusing the trustee from making adjustments in certain cases?	No.
16. With respect to derivatives:	
a) May income and loss be treated as that of a separate entity?	No. The Georgia Principal and Income Act does not address derivatives.
b) If not, or the trustee chooses not to do so, is income and loss allocated to the income account or to principal?	The Georgia Principal and Income Act does not address derivatives. Therefore, unless the governing instrument provides otherwise, the fiduciary must allocate gain and loss from derivatives to principal. (§ 53-12-211(a)(4))
17. To the extent put and call options are not derivatives, how are they allocated in terms of principal and income?	The Georgia Principal and Income Act does not address options. Therefore, unless the governing instrument provides otherwise, the fiduciary must allocate gain and loss from options to principal. (§ 53-12-211(a)(4))
18. How are asset-backed securities allocated in terms of principal and income?	The Georgia Principal and Income Act does not address asset-backed securities. Therefore, unless the governing instrument provides otherwise, the fiduciary must allocate gain and loss from asset-backed securities to principal. (§ 53-12-211(a)(4))
19. Are expenses incurred to comply with environmental requirements allocated to income or principal?	The Georgia Principal and Income Act does not address environmental expenses. Therefore, unless the governing instrument provides otherwise, the fiduciary must allocate environmental expenses to principal. (§ 53-12-219(c))
20. Is income tax liability allocated generally to income or principal?	Any tax required to be paid by a fiduciary on the trust's share of an entity's taxable income should be paid from income to the extent that receipts from the entity are allocated to income and from principal to the extent that receipts from the entity are allocated to principal. (§ 53-12-219)
21. If a Subchapter S shareholder's or partner's portion of tax liability is greater than cash	The Georgia Principal and Income Act does not address this issue. Therefore, unless the governing instrument provides

distributed, how is the excess obligation allocated?	otherwise, the fiduciary must allocate the excess obligation to principal. (§ 53-12-219(c))
22. What is the standard, if any, for making equitable adjustments between income and principal?	In exercising the power to adjust, the fiduciary must administer a trust, or decedent's estate impartially, based on what is fair and reasonable to all of the beneficiaries, except to the extent that the terms of the trust or the will clearly manifest an intention that the fiduciary shall or may favor one or more of the beneficiaries. (§ 53-12-211(b))
23. Is an income beneficiary entitled to receive income accrued but unpaid when an estate ends?	On termination of an income interest, the income beneficiary whose interest is terminated, or his estate, is entitled to income undistributed on the date of termination; income due but not paid to the trustee on the date of termination; and income in the form of periodic payments, other than corporate distribution to stockholders, including rent, interest, or annuities, not due on the date of termination, accrued from day to day. (§ 53-12-213(d))
24. Is an income beneficiary entitled to receive income accrued but unpaid when a revocable trust ends?	On termination of an income interest, the income beneficiary whose interest is terminated, or his estate, is entitled to income undistributed on the date of termination; income due but not paid to the trustee on the date of termination; and income in the form of periodic payments, other than corporate distribution to stockholders, including rent, interest, or annuities, not due on the date of termination, accrued from day to day. (§ 53-12-213(d))
25. Is an income beneficiary entitled to receive income accrued but unpaid when an irrevocable trust ends?	On termination of an income interest, the income beneficiary whose interest is terminated, or his estate, is entitled to income undistributed on the date of termination; income due but not paid to the trustee on the date of termination; and income in the form of periodic payments, other than corporate distribution to stockholders, including rent, interest, or annuities, not due on the date of termination, accrued from day to day. (§ 53-12-213(d))
26. With regard to mutual funds, how are:	
a) long-term gains allocated between income and principal?	Distributions made from ordinary income by a regulated investment company are income. All other distributions made by the company, including distributions from capital gains, depreciation, or depletion, whether in the form of cash or an option to take new stock or cash or an option to purchase additional shares, are principal. (§ 53-12-214(c))
b) short-term gains allocated between income and principal?	Distributions made from ordinary income by a regulated investment company are income. All other distributions made by the company, including distributions from capital gains, depreciation, or depletion, whether in the form of cash or an option to take new stock or cash or an option to purchase additional shares, are principal. (§ 53-12-214(c))
27. How are distributions from REITs allocated between income and principal?	Distributions made from ordinary income by a REIT are income. All other distributions made by a REIT, including distributions from capital gains, depreciation, or depletion, whether in the form of cash or an option to take new stock or cash or an option to purchase additional shares, are principal. (§ 53-12-214(c))

28. With respect to underproductive property:	
a) Is an adjustment, e.g., "delayed income," required to be paid to the income beneficiary?	No. The Georgia Principal and Income Act does not address underproductive property or delayed income.
b) What percentage return makes property underproductive?	The Georgia Principal and Income Act does not address underproductive property.
29. Is the trustee required to increase income so that it is sufficient to qualify for the marital deduction?	The Georgia Principal and Income Act does not address any requirements to increase income to qualify for the marital deduction. Note: The trustee can adjust the allocation of income so as to qualify for the marital deduction. (§ 53-12-220)
30. Is the trustee required to take depreciation?	Yes. (§ 53-12-219(a)(2))
31. Is the trustee's determination on allocations generally presumed to be fair and reasonable?	Yes. (§ 53-12-211(b))
32. If an item is not addressed in the trust agreement or in the law, must it be allocated to principal or income?	To principal. (§ 53-12-211(a)(4))
33. When does an asset become subject to a trust:	
a) In the case of transfers during the transferor's life?	The Georgia Principal and Income Act does not address the issue. (§ 53-12-213)
b) In the case of a will?	In the case of an asset becoming subject to a trust by reason of a will, it becomes subject to the trust as of the date of the death of the testator even though there is an intervening period of administration of the testator's estate. (§ 53-12-213)
c) In the case of the death of a third party?	The Georgia Principal and Income Act does not address the issue. (§ 53-12-213)
34. Can a trustee rely on the characterization by an entity as to the source or character of a received distribution?	Yes. (§ 53-12-214(e))

Table 12.02
Hawaii
Trust Accounting: Principal and Income

1. *Does the trustee have the power to transfer income to principal or to transfer principal to income to meet its duty of impartiality?*	Yes. See the Uniform Principal and Income Act (1997) chart. (§ 557A-104)
2. *What is the effective date for the law? E.g., does it apply to preexisting trusts?*	The Hawaii Principal and Income Act applies to every trust or decedent's estate as of the beginning of an accounting period of the trust or estate after July 1, 2001, except as otherwise expressly provided in the will, terms of the trust, or in the Hawaii Principal and Income Act. (2000 Haw. Sess. Laws Act 191) ***Note***: A trustee may continue using a former allocation method to allocate receipts for water, minerals, other natural resources, and timber under certain circumstances. (See § 557A-411; § 557A-412)
3. *What percentage is allocated to income and principal from proceeds of:*	
a) *IRA?* b) *Qualified pension or profit-sharing plan?* c) *Other deferred compensation arrangement?*	See the Uniform Principal and Income Act (1997) chart. (§ 557A-409)
4. *What percentage is allocated to income and principal from proceeds of:*	
a) *Patents?* b) *Copyrights?*	See the Uniform Principal and Income Act (1997) chart. (§ 557A-410(b))
5. *What percentage is allocated to income and principal in the event of distributions from:*	
a) *Corporations?* b) *Partnerships?* c) *LLCs?*	See the Uniform Principal and Income Act (1997) chart. (§ 557A-401(b))
6. *What percentage is allocated to income and principal from proceeds of:*	
a) *Oil and gas* b) *Minerals* c) *Water* d) *Other natural resourses (not including timber)?*	See the Uniform Principal and Income Act (1997) chart. (§ 557A-411) ***Note:*** If a trust owns an interest in minerals, water or other natural resources on July 1, 2000, the trustee may allocate receipts from the interest as provided in the Hawaii Principal and Income Act or in the manner used by the trustee before July 1, 2000.
e) *Timber*	See the Uniform Principal and Income Act (1997) chart. (§ 557A-412) ***Note:*** If a trust owns an interest in timberland on July 1, 2000, the trustee may allocate receipts from the interest as provided in the Hawaii Principal and Income Act or in the manner used by the trustee before July 1, 2000.

f) Rental properties?	See the Uniform Principal and Income Act (1997) chart. (§ 557A-405)
7. After a decedent dies, in the case of an estate, or after an income interest ends, when the fiduciary is determining the remaining net income what are the rules regarding payment from income or principal for:	
a) Attorneys fees *b) Accountants fees* *c) Fiduciary fees and commissions* *d) Court costs* *e) Interest on death taxes*	See the Uniform Principal and Income Act (1997) chart. (§ 557A-201(2)(B))
f) Debts *g) Funeral expenses* *h) Family allowances and similar protections* *i) Death taxes* *j) Penalties on death taxes?*	See the Uniform Principal and Income Act (1997) chart. (§ 557A-201(2)(C))
8. With respect to trust expenses from the administration of the trust that are not covered by § 557A-201(2)(B-C) [see Question #7]:	
a) Does the trustee have full discretion in allocating between income and principal for expenses incurred in the administration of the trust?	See the Uniform Principal and Income Act (1997) chart. (§ 557A-501; § 557A-502)
b) If not, are there special rules for:	
i) Regular trustee fees? *ii) Advisory or cusodial services to the trustee?* *iii) Accountings, judicial proceedings and other matters that involve both the income and remainder interests?*	See the Uniform Principal and Income Act (1997) chart. (§ 557A-501; § 557A-502)
iv) Debts?	See the Uniform Principal and Income Act (1997) chart. (§ 557A-501(3); § 557A-502(a)(3))
c) Can the trustee determine what are "transmission" expenses and "management" expenses?	
9. With regard to specific gifts from a trust after an income interest ends or from an estate:	
a) What amounts must be paid from income and principal?	See the Uniform Principal and Income Act (1997) chart. (§ 557A-201(1); § 557A-201(5))

10. With regard to outright pecuniary gifts from an estate or trust?:	
a) Does interest accrue?	Yes. See the Uniform Principal and Income Act (1997) chart. (§ 557A-201(3))
11. With regard to a gift in trust of a pecuniary amount from an estate or trust?	
a) Does interest accrue?	No. See the Uniform Principal and Income Act (1997) chart. (§ 557A-201(4); § 557A-202)
12. With regard to residuary gifts:	
a) What amount of income and principal is to be paid to the residuary beneficiary of a trust or an estate?	See the Uniform Principal and Income Act (1997) chart. (§ 557A-201(4); § 557A-202)
13. With regard to "business assets" held in trust:	
a) Can the trustee treat them as a separate entity?	Generally yes. See the Uniform Principal and Income Act (1997) chart. (§ 557A-403)
b) Can the trustee treat distinct assets as separate entities?	Generally yes. See the Uniform Principal and Income Act (1997) chart. (§ 557A-403)
c) Can earnings be retained in trust for the reasonable needs of the "business entity," and, if so, to what extent is this permitted?	See the Uniform Principal and Income Act (1997) chart. (§ 557A-403(b))
14. With respect to discount bonds:	
a) To what extent is the discount added to income or principal upon maturity?	See the Uniform Principal and Income Act (1997) chart. (§ 557A-406(b))
b) Does the trustee have discretion to allocate discount between income and principal?	No. (§ 557A-406) ***Note***: The trustee has overriding power to adjust under § 557A-104.
c) Are distinctions drawn between Series E bonds and others?	No. (§ 557A-406)
d) Are distinctions drawn based on the maturity date of the bond?	Yes. (§ 557A-406(b))
15. Is there a de minimis rule excusing the trustee from making adjustments in certain cases?	Yes. See the Uniform Principal and Income Act (1997) chart. (§ 557A-408)
16. With respect to derivatives:	
a) May income and loss be treated as that of a separate entity?	Yes. (§ 557A-403; § 557A-414(b))
b) If not, or the trustee chooses not to do so, is income and loss allocated to the income account or to principal?	To principal. (§ 557A-414(b))

17. To the extent put and call options are not derivatives, how are they allocated in terms of principal and income?	To principal. (§ 557A-414(c))
18. How are asset-backed securities allocated in terms of principal and income?	See the Uniform Principal and Income Act (1997) chart. (§ 557A-415)
19. Are expenses incurred to comply with environmental requirements allocated to income or principal?	Generally to principal. See the Uniform Principal and Income Act (1997) chart. (§ 557A-502(a)(7))
20. Is income tax liability allocated generally to income or principal?	See the Uniform Principal and Income Act (1997) chart. (§ 557A-505; § 557A-506)
21. If a Subchapter S shareholder's or partner's portion of tax liability is greater than cash distributed, how is the excess obligation allocated?	To principal. (§ 557A-505(c)(2)(B))
22. What is the standard, if any, for making equitable adjustments between income and principal?	See the Uniform Principal and Income Act (1997) chart. (§ 557A-103(b))
23. Is an income beneficiary entitled to receive income accrued but unpaid when an estate ends?	No. (§ 557A-303)
24. Is an income beneficiary entitled to receive income accrued but unpaid when a revocable trust ends?	Generally no. See the Uniform Principal and Income Act (1997) chart. (§ 557A-303)
25. Is an income beneficiary entitled to receive income accrued but unpaid when an irrevocable trust ends?	Generally no. See the Uniform Principal and Income Act (1997) chart. (§ 557A-303)
26. With regard to mutual funds, how are:	
a) long-term gains allocated between income and principal?	See the Uniform Principal and Income Act (1997) chart. (§ 557A-401(c)(4))
b) short-term gains allocated between income and principal?	See the Uniform Principal and Income Act (1997) chart. (§ 557A-401(c)(4))
27. How are distributions from REITs allocated between income and principal?	See the Uniform Principal and Income Act (1997) chart. (§ 557A-401(c)(4))
28. With respect to underproductive property:	
a) Is an adjustment, e.g., "delayed income," required to be paid to the income beneficiary?	No. (§ 557A-413(b))
b) What percentage return makes property underproductive?	The statute only refers to property not productive of income. (§ 557A-413)
29. Is the trustee required to increase income so that it is sufficient to qualify for the marital deduction?	Yes. (§ 557A-413(a))

30. Is the trustee required to take depreciation?	No. (§ 557A-503)
31. Is the trustee's determination on allocations generally presumed to be fair and reasonable?	Yes. (§ 557A-103(b))
32. If an item is not addressed in the trust agreement or in the law, must it be allocated to principal or income?	To principal. (§ 557A-103(a)(4))
33. When does an asset become subject to a trust:	
a) In the case of transfers during the transferor's life?	The date of transfer. (§ 557A-301(b)(1))
b) In the case of a will?	The date of the testator's death. (§ 557A-301(b)(2))
c) In the case of the death of a third party?	The date of the third party's death. (§ 557A-301(b)(3))
34. Can a trustee rely on the characterization by an entity as to the source or character of a received distribution?	Yes. (§ 557A-401(f))

Table 12.02
Idaho
Trust Accounting: Principal and Income

1. *Does the trustee have the power to transfer income to principal or to transfer principal to income to meet its duty of impartiality?*	Yes. See the Uniform Principal and Income Act (1997) chart. (§ 68-10-104)
2. *What is the effective date for the law? E.g., does it apply to preexisting trusts?*	The Idaho Principal and Income Act applies to every trust or decedent's estate existing on July 1, 2001, except as otherwise expressly provided in the will or terms of the trust or in the Idaho Principal and Income Act. (§ 68-10-605) ***Note:*** A trustee may continue using a former allocation method to allocate receipts for water, minerals, other natural resources, and timber under certain circumstances. (See § 68-10-411; § 68-10-412)
3. *What percentage is allocated to income and principal from proceeds of:*	
a) *IRA?* b) *Qualified pension or profit-sharing plan?* c) *Other deferred compensation arrangement?*	See the Uniform Principal and Income Act (1997) chart. (§ 68-10-409(d))
4. *What percentage is allocated to income and principal from proceeds of:*	
a) *Patents?* b) *Copyrights?*	See the Uniform Principal and Income Act (1997) chart. (§ 68-10-410(b))
5. *What percentage is allocated to income and principal in the event of distributions from:*	
a) *Corporations?* b) *Partnerships?* c) *LLCs?*	See the Uniform Principal and Income Act (1997) chart. (§ 68-10-401(b))
6. *What percentage is allocated to income and principal from proceeds of:*	
a) *Oil and gas* b) *Minerals* c) *Water* d) *Other natural resourses (not including timber)?*	See the Uniform Principal and Income Act (1997) chart. (§ 68-10-411) ***Note:*** If a trust owns an interest in minerals, water or other natural resources on July 1, 2001, the trustee may allocate receipts from the interest as provided in the Idaho Principal and Income Act or in the manner used by the trustee before July 1, 2001.
e) *Timber?*	See the Uniform Principal and Income Act (1997) chart. (§ 68-10-412) ***Note:*** If a trust owns an interest in timberland on July 1, 2001, the trustee may allocate receipts from the interest as provided in the Idaho Principal and Income Act or in the manner used by the trustee before July 1, 2001.
f) *Rental properties?*	See the Uniform Principal and Income Act (1997) chart. (§ 68-10-405)

7. After a decedent dies, in the case of an estate, or after an income interest ends, when the fiduciary is determining the remaining net income what are the rules regarding payment from income or principal for:	
a) Attorneys fees *b) Accountants fees* *c) Fiduciary fees and commissions* *d) Court costs* *e) Interest on death taxes*	See the Uniform Principal and Income Act (1997) chart. (§ 68-10-201(2)(B))
f) Debts *g) Funeral expenses* *h) Family allowances and similar protections* *i) Death taxes* *j) Penalties on death taxes?*	See the Uniform Principal and Income Act (1997) chart. (§ 68-10-201(2)(C))
8. With respect to trust expenses from the administration of the trust that are not covered by § 68-10-201(2)(B-C) [see Question #7]:	
a) Does the trustee have full discretion in allocating between income and principal for expenses incurred in the administration of the trust?	No. (§ 68-10-501; § 68-10-502)
b) If not, are there special rules for:	
i) Regular trustee fees? *ii) Advisory or cusodial services to the trustee?* *iii) Accountings, judicial proceedings and other matters that involve both the income and remainder interests?*	See the Uniform Principal and Income Act (1997) chart. (§ 68-10-501; § 68-10-502)
iv) Debts?	See the Uniform Principal and Income Act (1997) chart. (§ 68-10-501(3); § 68-10-502(a)(3))
c) Can the trustee determine what are "transmission" expenses and "management" expenses?	
9. With regard to specific gifts from a trust after an income interest ends or from an estate:	
a) What amounts must be paid from income and principal?	See the Uniform Principal and Income Act (1997) chart. (§ 68-10-201(1); § 68-10-201(5))
10. With regard to outright pecuniary gifts from an estate or trust?:	

a) Does interest accrue?	Yes. See the Uniform Principal and Income Act (1997) chart. (§ 68-10-201(3))
11. With regard to a gift in trust of a pecuniary amount from an estate or trust?	
a) Does interest accrue?	No. See the Uniform Principal and Income Act (1997) chart. (§ 68-10-201(4); § 68-10-202)
12. With regard to residuary gifts:	
a) What amount of income and principal is to be paid to the residuary beneficiary of a trust or an estate?	See the Uniform Principal and Income Act (1997) chart. (§ 68-10-201(4); § 68-10-202)
13. With regard to "business assets" held in trust:	
a) Can the trustee treat them as a separate entity?	Yes. See the Uniform Principal and Income Act (1997) chart. (§ 68-10-403)
b) Can the trustee treat distinct assets as separate entities?	Yes. See the Uniform Principal and Income Act (1997) chart. (§ 68-10-403)
c) Can earnings be retained in trust for the reasonable needs of the "business entity," and, if so, to what extent is this permitted?	Yes. See the Uniform Principal and Income Act (1997) chart. (§ 68-10-403)
14. With respect to discount bonds:	
a) To what extent is the discount added to income or principal upon maturity?	See the Uniform Principal and Income Act (1997) chart. (§ 68-10-406(b))
b) Does the trustee have discretion to allocate discount between income and principal?	No. (§ 68-10-406) ***Note***: The trustee has the overriding power to adjust under § 68-10-104.
c) Are distinctions drawn between Series E bonds and others?	No. (§ 68-10-406)
d) Are distinctions drawn based on the maturity date of the bond?	Yes. (§ 68-10-406(b))
15. Is there a de minimis rule excusing the trustee from making adjustments in certain cases?	Yes. (§ 68-10-408)
16. With respect to derivatives:	
a) May income and loss be treated as that of a separate entity?	Yes. (§ 68-10-403; § 68-10-414(b))
b) If not, or the trustee chooses not to do so, is income and loss allocated to the income account or to principal?	To principal. (§ 68-10- 414(b))

17. To the extent put and call options are not derivatives, how are they allocated in terms of principal and income?	To principal. (§ 68-10-414(c))
18. How are asset-backed securities allocated in terms of principal and income?	See the Uniform Principal and Income Act (1997) chart. (§ 68-10-415)
19. Are expenses incurred to comply with environmental requirements allocated to income or principal?	Generally to principal. See the Uniform Principal and Income Act (1997) chart. (§ 68-10-502(a)(7))
20. Is income tax liability allocated generally to income or principal?	See the Uniform Principal and Income Act (1997) chart. (§ 68-10-505; § 68-10-506)
21. If a Subchapter S shareholder's or partner's portion of tax liability is greater than cash distributed, how is the excess obligation allocated?	From principal. (§ 68-10-505(c)(2)(B))
22. What is the standard, if any, for making equitable adjustments between income and principal?	See the Uniform Principal and Income Act (1997) chart. (§ 68-10-103(b))
23. Is an income beneficiary entitled to receive income accrued but unpaid when an estate ends?	No. (§ 68-10-303)
24. Is an income beneficiary entitled to receive income accrued but unpaid when a revocable trust ends?	Generally no. See the Uniform Principal and Income Act (1997) chart. (§ 68-10-303)
25. Is an income beneficiary entitled to receive income accrued but unpaid when an irrevocable trust ends?	Generally no. See the Uniform Principal and Income Act (1997) chart. (§ 68-10-303).
26. With regard to mutual funds, how are:	
a) long-term gains allocated between income and principal?	See the Uniform Principal and Income Act (1997) chart. (§ 68-10-401(c)(4))
b) short-term gains allocated between income and principal?	See the Uniform Principal and Income Act (1997) chart. (§ 68-10-401(c)(4))
27. How are distributions from REITs allocated between income and principal?	See the Uniform Principal and Income Act (1997) chart. (§ 68-10-401(c)(4))
28. With respect to underproductive property:	
a) Is an adjustment, e.g., "delayed income," required to be paid to the income beneficiary?	See the Uniform Principal and Income Act (1997) chart. (§ 68-10-413)
b) What percentage return makes property underproductive?	The statute only refers to property not productive of income. (§ 68-10-413)
29. Is the trustee required to increase income so that it is sufficient to qualify for the marital deduction?	Yes. (§ 68-10-413(a))

30. Is the trustee required to take depreciation?	No. (§ 68-10-503)
31. Is the trustee's determination on allocations generally presumed to be fair and reasonable?	Yes. (§ 68-10-103(b))
32. If an item is not addressed in the trust agreement or in the law, must it be allocated to principal or income?	To principal. (§ 68-10-103(a)(4))
33. When does an asset become subject to a trust:	
a) In the case of transfers during the transferor's life?	The date of transfer. (§ 68-10-301(b)(1))
b) In the case of a will?	The date of the testator's death. (§ 68-10-301(b)(2))
c) In the case of the death of a third party?	The date of the third party's death. (§ 68-10-301(b)(3))
34. Can a trustee rely on the characterization by an entity as to the source or character of a received distribution?	Yes. (§ 68-10-401(f))

Table 12.02
Illinois
Trust Accounting: Principal and Income

1. *Does the trustee have the power to transfer income to principal or to transfer principal to income to meet its duty of impartiality?*	If the trustee in the trustee's discretion determines that application of the provisions of the Illinois Principal and Income Act would result in a substantial inequity to either the income beneficiaries or the remaindermen, the trustee may allocate receipts and expenses in accordance with what is reasonable and equitable in view of the interests of those entitled to income as well as those entitled to principal. (760 Ill. Comp. Stat. 15/3(b)(2))
2. *What is the effective date for the law? E.g., does it apply to preexisting trusts?*	Except as specifically provided in the governing instrument or in the Illinois Principal and Income Act, the Illinois Principal and Income Act applies to any receipt or expense received or incurred on or after January 1, 1982 by any trust, decedent's estate or legal life estate whether established on, before or after January 1, 1982 and whether the asset involved was acquired by the trustee, personal representative or legal life tenant on, before or after January 1, 1982. (760 Ill. Comp. Stat. 15/16) ***Note:*** If minerals, oil, gas, or other natural resources in, on or under land, except timber, water, soil, sod, dirt, peat, turf or mosses, are held on January 1, 1982, the trustee must allocate all receipts from the property in the manner used before January 1, 1982. (See, 760 Ill. Comp. Stat. 15/10(b))
3. *What percentage is allocated to income and principal from proceeds of:*	
a) *IRA?* b) *Qualified pension or profit-sharing plan?* c) *Other deferred compensation arrangement?*	The receipts from any part of the principal consisting of the right to receive periodic payments under an employment related contract or plan or an individual retirement account or annuity must be allocated to income (i) to the extent designated by the payor as current income for accounting purposes, or (ii) if there is no designation by the payor and if the income is directed by the instrument to be paid to the surviving spouse of the participant under the contract or plan or of the owner of the account or annuity, to the extent of the minimum amount necessary each year to qualify the part in full for the federal estate tax marital deduction on the basis of the interest rate generally applicable for the valuation of annuities at the death of the participant or owner (or, if less, the entire receipts from the part for the year). Otherwise, if any part of the principal consists of the right to receive periodic payments under an employment related contract or plan or an individual retirement account or annuity, the receipts must be allocated to principal. (760 Ill. Comp. Stat. 15/12.1)
4. *What percentage is allocated to income and principal from proceeds of:*	
a) *Patents?* b) *Copyrights?*	The trustee must allocate the entire amount to principal. (760 Ill. Comp. Stat. 15/12)

5. *What percentage is allocated to income and principal in the event of distributions from:*	
a) *Corporations?* b) *Partnerships?* c) *LLCs?*	Corporate distributions of shares of the distributing corporation, including distributions in the form of a stock split or stock dividend, are principal. A right to subscribe to shares or other securities issued by the distributing corporation accruing on account of the ownership of shares or other securities in such corporation and the proceeds of any sale of the right are principal. Except to the extent that the corporation indicates that some part of a corporate distribution is a settlement of preferred or guaranteed dividends accrued since the trustee became a stockholder or is in lieu of an ordinary cash dividend, a corporate distribution is principal if the distribution is pursuant to a call of shares; a merger, consolidation or reorganization; a plan by which assets of the corporation are acquired by another corporation; or a total or partial liquidation of the corporation. Distributions made from ordinary income by a regulated investment company or by a trust qualifying and electing to be taxed under federal law as a real estate investment trust are income. All other distributions made by the company or trust, including distributions from capital gains, depreciation or depletion, whether in the form of cash or an option to take new stock or cash or an option to purchase additional shares, are principal. Except as provided in the preceding paragraphs, all corporate distributions are income, including cash dividends, distributions of or rights to subscribe to shares or securities or obligations of corporations other than the distributing corporation, and the proceeds of the rights or property distributions. (760 Ill. Comp. Stat. 15/7) ***Note:*** Parnerships and LLC's are not addressed.
6. *What percentage is allocated to income and principal from proceeds of:*	
a) *Oil and gas?* b) *Minerals?* c) *Water?* d) *Other natural resourses (not including timber)?*	If any part of the principal consists of a right to receive royalties, overriding or limited royalties, working interests, production payments, net profit interests, or other interest in minerals, oil, gas or other natural resources in, on or under land, except timber, water, soil, sod, dirt, peat, turf or mosses, the trustee must allocate the receipts as follows: (1) if received as rent on a lease or extension payments on a lease, the receipts are income; (2) if received from a production payment, the receipts are income to the extent of any factor for interest or its equivalent provided in the governing instrument. The fiduciary must allocate to principal the fraction of the balance of the receipts which the unrecovered cost of the production payment bears to the balance owed on the production payment, exclusive of any factor for interest or its equivalent. The receipts not allocated to principal are income; (3) if received as a royalty, overriding or limited royalty, or bonus, or from a working, net profit, or any other interest in minerals, oil, gas, or other natural resources, the trustee must

allocate receipts not provided for in the preceding paragraphs on a yearly basis, whether or not any natural resource was being taken from the land at the time the trust was established, as follows: The trustee shall allocate to principal as an allowance for depletion the greater of (i) that portion, if any, of the gross receipts that is allowed as a depletion deduction for federal income tax purposes and (ii) 10% of the gross receipts, except that that allocation shall not exceed 50% of the net receipts remaining after payment of all expenses, direct and indirect, computed without the allowance for depletion. The trustee must allocate the balance of the gross receipts, after payment of all direct and indirect expenses to income.

(760 Ill. Comp. Stat. 15/10)

Note: If minerals, oil, gas or other natural resources in, on or under land, except timber, water, soil, sod, dirt, peat, turf or mosses, are held on January 1, 1982, the trustee must allocate all receipts from the property in the manner used before January 1, 1982. (760 Ill. Comp. Stat. 15/10(b))

The trustee must allocate receipts from water, soil, sod, dirt, peat, turf, or mosses in accordance with what is reasonable and equitable in view of the interests of those entitled to income as well as those entitled to principal. (760 Ill. Comp. Stat. 15/10(c); 760 Ill. Comp. Stat. 15/3)

e) Timber?	The trustee must allocate receipts from timber in accordance with what is reasonable and equitable in view of the interests of those entitled to income as well as those entitled to principal. (760 Ill. Comp. Stat. 15/10(c); 760 Ill. Comp. Stat. 15/3)
f) Rental properties?	The trustee must allocate amounts received from renting real or personal property, including sums received for cancellation or renewal of a lease, to income. (760 Ill. Comp. Stat. 15/4(a)(1))
7. After a decedent dies, in the case of an estate, or after an income interest ends, when the fiduciary is determining the remaining net income what are the rules regarding payment from income or principal for:	
a) Attorneys fees? *b) Accountants fees?* *c) Fiduciary fees and commissions?* *d) Court costs?* *e) Interest on death taxes*	The trustee must charge from principal all expenses incurred in connection with the settlement of a decedent's estate, including debts, funeral expenses, estate taxes, interest and penalties on estate taxes, family allowances, fees of attorneys and personal representatives, and court costs. (760 Ill. Comp. Stat. 15/6)
f) Debts? *g) Funeral expenses?* *h) Family allowances and similar protections?* *i) Death taxes?* *j) Penalties on death taxes?*	The trustee must charge from principal all expenses incurred in connection with the settlement of a decedent's estate, including debts, funeral expenses, estate taxes, interest and penalties on estate taxes, family allowances, fees of attorneys and personal representatives, and court costs. (760 Ill. Comp. Stat. 15/6)

8. *With respect to trust expenses from the administration of the trust that are not covered by 760 Ill. Comp. Stat. 15/6 [see Question #7]:*	
a) *Does the trustee have full discretion in allocating between income and principal for expenses incurred in the administration of the trust?*	No. (760 Ill. Comp. Stat. 15/14)
b) *If not, are there special rules for:*	
i) *Regular trustee fees?* ii) *Advisory or custodial services to the trustee?* iii) *Accountings, judicial proceedings and other matters that involve both the income and remainder interests?*	Generally, the following charges must be made against income: 1. one-half of court costs, attorney's fees and other expenses and fees on any judicial accounting, unless the court directs otherwise; 2. court costs, attorney's fees and other expenses and fees on other judicial proceedings if the matter primarily concerns the income interest, unless the court directs otherwise; and 3. one-half of the regular compensation of the trustee, attorney, investment counsel, custodian or accountant, however, the trustee may have the ability to charge the entire amount to income (see below). Generally, the following charges must be made against principal: 1. one-half of the regular compensation of the trustee, attorney, investment counsel, custodian or accountant shall be paid out of principal, provided that, if in the judgment of the trustee, the charging of a part or all of that portion of such compensation to principal is impracticable because of the lack of sufficient principal cash and readily marketable intangible personal property, or inadvisable because of the nature of the assets, that part or all of such compensation shall be paid out of income. The decision of the trustee to pay a larger portion or all of such compensation out of income shall be conclusive, and the income of the trust shall not be entitled to reimbursement from principal at any subsequent time or times; and 2. court costs, attorney's fees and other expenses and fees in judicial proceedings primarily concerning matters of principal or in any action to construe the trust or protect it or the property or assure the title to any trust property, unless the court directs otherwise. (760 Ill. Comp. Stat. 15/14) ***Note:*** (760 Ill. Comp. Stat. 15/14) contains many other special rules for allocations and contains many exceptions.
iv) *Debts?*	The trustee must allocate interest expense on trust debt to income and must allocate payments on principal of trust debt to principal. (760 Ill. Comp. Stat. 15/14)
c) *Can the trustee determine what are "transmission" expenses and "management" expenses?*	

9. With regard to specific gifts from a trust after an income interest ends or from an estate:	
a) What amounts must be paid from income and principal?	The fiduciary must distribute to a specific devisee or beneficiary, the income from the property devised or distributed to them less property taxes, ordinary repairs, interest, and other expenses of management and protection of the property, and less an appropriate portion of taxes imposed on income, excluding taxes on capital gains, that accrue during the period of administration or after an income interest in a trust terminates, and expenses in excess of income to be charged against the property. (760 Ill. Comp. Stat. 15/6(b)(1))
10. With regard to outright pecuniary gifts from an estate or trust?:	
a) Does interest accrue?	No. The fiduciary must not pay interest or income to a beneficiary (other than the testator's surviving spouse) of an outright pecuniary legacy or gift. However, the fiduciary must pay a proportionate part of the income of the estate to a testator's surviving spouse who receives an outright pecuniary legacy. (760 Ill. Comp. Stat. 15/6)
11. With regard to a gift in trust of a pecuniary amount from an estate or trust?	
a) Does interest accrue?	No. The fiduciary should distribute to any trusts that received a gift of a pecuniary amount and to the remainder beneficiaries and to a surviving spouse that received a pecuniary gift outright the balance of the income, less certain expenses that accrue during the period of administration or after an income interest terminates, in proportion to their respective interests in the undistributed assets of the estate or trust. (760 Ill. Comp. Stat. 15/6)
12. With regard to residuary gifts:	
a) What amount of income and principal is to be paid to the residuary beneficiary of a trust or an estate?	The fiduciary should distribute to any trusts that received a gift of a pecuniary amount and to the remainder beneficiaries and to a surviving spouse that received a pecuniary gift outright the balance of the income, less certain expenses that accrue during the period of administration or after an income interest terminates, in proportion to their respective interests in the undistributed assets of the estate or trust. (760 Ill. Comp. Stat. 15/6)
13. With regard to "business assets" held in trust:	
a) Can the trustee treat them as a separate entity?	No. The Illinois Principal and Income Act does not particularly provide for treating business assets as separate entities.
b) Can the trustee treat distinct assets as separate entities?	No. The Illinois Principal and Income Act does not particularly provide for treating distinct assets as separate entities.
c) Can earnings be retained in trust for the reasonable needs of the "business	No. The Illinois Principal and Income Act does not provide that the fiduciary may retain earnings for the needs of the business entity.

entity," and, if so, to what extent is this permitted?	
14. With respect to discount bonds:	
a) To what extent is the discount added to income or principal upon maturity?	The fiduciary must allocate the appreciation in value of a zero coupon bond (i) that is scheduled to mature not more than one year after its purchase or its otherwise becoming subject to the trust or (ii) that is an issue of the United States and the appreciation in value of which pursuant to a determinable schedule or formula is not required to be included in gross income for federal income tax purposes prior to realization thereof to income at the time the increment is realized. Otherwise, the proceeds of sale, redemption or other disposition of the bond or other obligation are principal. (760 Ill. Comp. Stat. 15/6)
b) Does the trustee have discretion to allocate discount between income and principal?	No. (760 Ill. Comp. Stat. 15/6)
c) Are distinctions drawn between Series E bonds and others?	No. (760 Ill. Comp. Stat. 15/6)
d) Are distinctions drawn based on the maturity date of the bond?	Yes. (760 Ill. Comp. Stat. 15/6)
15. Is there a de minimis rule excusing the trustee from making adjustments in certain cases?	No.
16. With respect to derivatives:	
a) May income and loss be treated as that of a separate entity?	No. The Illinois Principal and Income Act does not address derivatives.
b) If not, or the trustee chooses not to do so, is income and loss allocated to the income account or to principal?	The Illinois Principal and Income Act does not address derivatives. Therefore, the fiduciary must allocate income and loss from derivatives in accordance with what is reasonable and equitable in view of the interests of those entitles to income as well as those entitled to principal. (760 Ill. Comp. Stat. 15/3)
17. To the extent put and call options are not derivatives, how are they allocated in terms of principal and income?	Any amount received or paid for an option and any gain or loss realized from the exercise of an option must be allocated to principal. (760 Ill. Comp. Stat. 15/4; 760 Ill. Comp. Stat. 15/14)
18. How are asset-backed securities allocated in terms of principal and income?	The Illinois Principal and Income Act does not address asset-backed securities. Therefore, the fiduciary must allocate income and loss from asset-backed securities in accordance with what is reasonable and equitable in view of the interests of those entitles to income as well as those entitled to principal. (760 Ill. Comp. Stat. 15/3)
19. Are expenses incurred to comply with environmental requirements allocated to income or principal?	Expenses related to environmental matters must be allocated to principal. (760 Ill. Comp. Stat. 15/14(c)(4.5))

20. Is income tax liability allocated generally to income or principal?	Any tax required to be paid by a fiduciary on the trust's share of an entity's taxable income should be paid from income to the extent that receipts from the entity are allocated to income and from principal to the extent that receipts from the entity are allocated to principal. (760 Ill. Comp. Stat. 15/14)
21. If a Subchapter S shareholder's or partner's portion of tax liability is greater than cash distributed, how is the excess obligation allocated?	The excess obligation is allocated to principal. (760 Ill. Comp. Stat. 15/14(c)(6))
22. What is the standard, if any, for making equitable adjustments between income and principal?	The Illinois Principal and Income Act does not provide for equitable adjustments between principal and income.
23. Is an income beneficiary entitled to receive income accrued but unpaid when an estate ends?	The trustee must pay an amount of income collected by the trustee more than 12 months prior to the termination of an income interest and not disbursed or authorized or directed by the instrument to be added to principal, to an income beneficiary whose interest is terminated. To the extent necessary to qualify an interest for the marital deduction under the federal estate and gift tax laws, the trustee must pay an income beneficiary, whose interest is terminated, on termination of the income interest, income which has been collected by the trustee prior to the date of termination, or which is then earned or accrued but not yet payable, or which is then due but not yet paid. (760 Ill. Comp. Stat. 15/5)
24. Is an income beneficiary entitled to receive income accrued but unpaid when a revocable trust ends?	The trustee must pay an amount of income collected by the trustee more than 12 months prior to the termination of an income interest and not disbursed or authorized or directed by the instrument to be added to principal, to an income beneficiary whose interest is terminated. (760 Ill. Comp. Stat. 15/5)
25. Is an income beneficiary entitled to receive income accrued but unpaid when an irrevocable trust ends?	The trustee must pay an amount of income collected by the trustee more than 12 months prior to the termination of an income interest and not disbursed or authorized or directed by the instrument to be added to principal, to an income beneficiary whose interest is terminated. To the extent necessary to qualify an interest for the marital deduction under the federal estate and gift tax laws, the trustee must pay an income beneficiary, whose interest is terminated, on termination of the income interest, income which has been collected by the trustee prior to the date of termination, or which is then earned or accrued but not yet payable, or which is then due but not yet paid. (760 Ill. Comp. Stat. 15/5)
26. With regard to mutual funds, how are:	
a) long-term gains allocated between income and principal?	Distributions made from ordinary income by a regulated investment company are income. All other distributions made by the company or trust, including distributions from capital gains, depreciation, or depletion, whether in the form of cash or an option to take new stock or cash or an option to purchase additional shares, are principal. (760 Ill. Comp. Stat. 15/7(b)(4))

b) *short-term gains allocated between income and principal?*	Distributions made from ordinary income by a regulated investment company are income. All other distributions made by the company, including distributions from capital gains, depreciation, or depletion, whether in the form of cash or an option to take new stock or cash or an option to purchase additional shares, are principal. (760 Ill. Comp. Stat. 15/7(b)(4))
27. *How are distributions from REITs allocated between income and principal?*	Distributions made from ordinary income by a REIT are income. All other distributions made by a REIT, including distributions from capital gains, depreciation, or depletion, whether in the form of cash or an option to take new stock or cash or an option to purchase additional shares, are principal. (760 Ill. Comp. Stat. 15/7(b)(4))
28. *With respect to underproductive property:*	
a) *Is an adjustment, e.g., "delayed income," required to be paid to the income beneficiary?*	The trustee is not required to pay delayed income to the income beneficiary except under limited circumstances with zero coupon bonds and natural resources. (760 Ill. Comp. Stat. 15/13)
b) *What percentage return makes property underproductive?*	The Illinois Principal and Income Act does not describe the percentage return that makes property underproductive. (760 Ill. Comp. Stat. 15/13)
29. *Is the trustee required to increase income so that it is sufficient to qualify for the marital deduction?*	The Illinois Principal and Income Act does not address the marital deduction except in regards to discount bonds and terminating income interests.
30. *Is the trustee required to take depreciation?*	Yes. (760 Ill. Comp. Stat. 15/14(a-5))
31. *Is the trustee's determination on allocations generally presumed to be fair and reasonable?*	If the instrument or 760 Ill. Comp. Stat. 15/3(b)(2) gives the trustee discretion in crediting a receipt or charging an expense to income or principal or partly to each, no inference of imprudence or partiality arises from the fact that the trustee makes an allocation other than in accordance with the Illinois Principal and Income Act or determines not to do so. (760 Ill. Comp. Stat. 15/3(c))
32. *If an item is not addressed in the trust agreement or in the law, must it be allocated to principal or income?*	If an item is not addressed in the trust agreement or in the law, the trustee must allocate the item in accordance with what is reasonable and equitable in view of the interests of those entitled to income as well as those entitled to principal. (760 Ill. Comp. Stat. 15/3(b)(3))
33. *When does an asset become subject to a trust:*	
a) *In the case of transfers during the transferor's life?*	The Illinois Principal and Income Act does not address the issue. (760 Ill. Comp. Stat. 15/5)
b) *In the case of a will?*	In the case of an asset becoming subject to a trust by reason of a will, it becomes subject to the trust as of the date of the death of the testator even though there is an intervening period of administration of the testator's estate. (760 Ill. Comp. Stat. 15/5)

c) In the case of the death of a third party?	The Illinois Principal and Income Act does not address the issue. (760 Ill. Comp. Stat. 15/5)
34. Can a trustee rely on the characterization by an entity as to the source or character of a received distribution?	Yes. (760 Ill. Comp. Stat. 15/7(e))

Table 12.02
Indiana
Trust Accounting: Principal and Income

1. *Does the trustee have the power to transfer income to principal or to transfer principal to income to meet its duty of impartiality?*	Yes. See the Uniform Principal and Income Act (1997) chart. (§ 30-2-14-15)
2. *What is the effective date for the law? E.g., does it apply to preexisting trusts?*	The Indiana Principal and Income Act applies to every trust or decedent's estate existing on or created after January 1, 2003, except as otherwise expressly provided in the decedent's will; by the terms of the trust; or by the Indiana Principal and Income Act. (2002 Ind. Sess. Laws 84) ***Note***: A trustee may continue using a former allocation method to allocate receipts for water, minerals, other natural resources, and timber under certain circumstances. (See, § 30-2-14-33; § 30-2-14-34)
3. *What percentage is allocated to income and principal from proceeds of:*	
a) *IRA?* b) *Qualified pension or profit-sharing plan?* c) *Other deferred compensation arrangement?*	See the Uniform Principal and Income Act (1997) chart. (§ 30-2-14-31) ***Note:*** The Indiana statute contains additional provisions. (See § 30-2-14-31) If a payment is not characterized as interest or a dividend, and if the payment is made from an individual account corresponding to an original participant, the payment must be allocated between income and principal by: 1. determining the income occurring within the individual account by treating the account as though it were a trust; and 2. considering the income to be distributed as a pro rata portion of all payments made from the individual account during the year. (§ 30-2-14-31(d))
4. *What percentage is allocated to income and principal from proceeds of:*	
a) *Patents?* b) *Copyrights?*	See the Uniform Principal and Income Act (1997) chart. (§ 30-2-14-32(b))
5. *What percentage is allocated to income and principal in the event of distributions from:*	
a) *Corporations?* b) *Partnerships?* c) *LLCs?*	See the Uniform Principal and Income Act (1997) chart. (§ 30-2-14-23)
6. *What percentage is allocated to income and principal from proceeds of:*	
a) *Oil and gas?* b) *Minerals?* c) *Water?*	See the Uniform Principal and Income Act (1997) chart. (§ 30-2-14-33) ***Note***: If a trust owns an interest in minerals, water or other natural resources on January 1, 2003, the trustee may allocate receipts from the interest as provided in the Indiana Principal

d) Other natural resourses (not including timber)?	and Income Act or in the manner used by the trustee before January 1, 2003.
e) Timber	See the Uniform Principal and Income Act (1997) chart. (§ 30-2-14-34) ***Note:*** If a trust owns an interest in timberland on January 1, 2003, the trustee may allocate receipts from the interest as provided in the Indiana Principal and Income Act or in the manner used by the trustee before January 1, 2003.
f) Rental properties?	See the Uniform Principal and Income Act (1997) chart. (§ 30-2-14-27)
7. After a decedent dies, in the case of an estate, or after an income interest ends, when the fiduciary is determining the remaining net income what are the rules regarding payment from income or principal for:	
a) Attorneys fees? *b) Accountants fees?* *c) Fiduciary fees and commissions?* *d) Court costs?* *e) Interest on death taxes*	See the Uniform Principal and Income Act (1997) chart. (§ 30-2-14-18(2)(B))
f) Debts? *g) Funeral expenses?* *h) Family allowances and similar protections?* *i) Death taxes?* *j) Penalties on death taxes?*	See the Uniform Principal and Income Act (1997) chart. (§ 30-2-14-18(2)(C))
8. With respect to trust expenses from the administration of the trust that are not covered by § 30-2-14-18(2)(B-C) [see Question #7]:	
a) Does the trustee have full discretion in allocating between income and principal for expenses incurred in the administration of the trust?	No. See the Uniform Principal and Income Act (1997) chart. (§ 30-2-14-38; § 30-2-14-39)
b) If not, are there special rules for:	
i) Regular trustee fees? *ii) Advisory or cusodial services to the trustee?* *iii) Accountings, judicial proceedings and other matters that involve both the income and remainder interests?*	See the Uniform Principal and Income Act (1997) chart. (§ 30-2-14-38; § 30-2-14-39)
iv) Debts?	See the Uniform Principal and Income Act (1997) chart. (§ 30-2-14-38(3)(A); § 30-2-14-39(a)(3))

c) Can the trustee determine what are "transmission" expenses and "management" expenses?	
9. With regard to specific gifts from a trust after an income interest ends or from an estate:	
a) What amounts must be paid from income and principal?	See the Uniform Principal and Income Act (1997) chart. (§ 30-2-14-18(1); § 30-2-14-18(5))
10. With regard to outright pecuniary gifts from an estate or trust?:	
a) Does interest accrue?	Yes. See the Uniform Principal and Income Act (1997) chart. (§ 30-2-14-18(3))
11. With regard to a gift in trust of a pecuniary amount from an estate or trust?	
a) Does interest accrue?	No. See the Uniform Principal and Income Act (1997) chart. (§ 30-2-14-18(4); § 30-2-14-19)
12. With regard to residuary gifts:	
a) What amount of income and principal is to be paid to the residuary beneficiary of a trust or an estate?	No. See the Uniform Principal and Income Act (1997) chart. (§ 30-2-14-18(4); § 30-2-14-19)
13. With regard to "business assets" held in trust:	
a) Can the trustee treat them as a separate entity?	Generally yes. See the Uniform Principal and Income Act (1997) chart. (§ 30-2-14-25(a))
b) Can the trustee treat distinct assets as separate entities?	Generally yes. See the Uniform Principal and Income Act (1997) chart. (§ 30-2-14-25)
c) Can earnings be retained in trust for the reasonable needs of the "business entity," and, if so, to what extent is this permitted?	See the Uniform Principal and Income Act (1997) chart. (§ 30-2-14-25(b))
14. With respect to discount bonds:	
a) To what extent is the discount added to income or principal upon maturity?	See the Uniform Principal and Income Act (1997) chart. (§ 30-2-14-28)
b) Does the trustee have discretion to allocate discount between income and principal?	No. (§ 30-2-14-28) ***Note:*** The trustee has overriding power to adjust under § 30-2-14-15.
c) Are distinctions drawn between Series E bonds and others?	No. (§ 30-2-14-28)
d) Are distinctions drawn based on the maturity date of the bond?	Yes. (§ 30-2-14-28)

15. *Is there a de minimis rule excusing the trustee from making adjustments in certain cases?*	Yes. (§ 30-2-14-30)
16. *With respect to derivatives:*	
a) *May income and loss be treated as that of a separate entity?*	Yes. (§ 30-2-14-25; § 30-2-14-36(b))
b) *If not, or the trustee chooses not to do so, is income and loss allocated to the income account or to principal?*	To principal. (§ 30-2-14-36(b))
17. *To the extent put and call options are not derivatives, how are they allocated in terms of principal and income?*	To principal. (§ 30-2-14-36(c))
18. *How are asset-backed securities allocated in terms of principal and income?*	See the Uniform Principal and Income Act (1997) chart. (§ 30-2-14-37)
19. *Are expenses incurred to comply with environmental requirements allocated to income or principal?*	Generally to principal. See the Uniform Principal and Income Act (1997) chart. (§ 30-2-14-39(a)(7))
20. *Is income tax liability allocated generally to income or principal?*	See the Uniform Principal and Income Act (1997) chart. (§ 30-2-14-42; § 30-2-14-43)
21. *If a Subchapter S shareholder's or partner's portion of tax liability is greater than cash distributed, how is the excess obligation allocated?*	To principal. (§ 30-2-14-42(c)(2)(b))
22. *What is the standard, if any, for making equitable adjustments between income and principal?*	See the Uniform Principal and Income Act (1997) chart. (§ 30-2-14-14(b))
23. *Is an income beneficiary entitled to receive income accrued but unpaid when an estate ends?*	No. See the Uniform Principal and Income Act (1997) chart. (§ 30-2-14-22)
24. *Is an income beneficiary entitled to receive income accrued but unpaid when a revocable trust ends?*	Generally no. See the Uniform Principal and Income Act (1997) chart. (§ 30-2-14-22)
25. *Is an income beneficiary entitled to receive income accrued but unpaid when an irrevocable trust ends?*	Generally no. See the Uniform Principal and Income Act (1997) chart. (§ 30-2-14-22)
26. *With regard to mutual funds, how are:*	
a) *long-term gains allocated between income and principal?*	See the Uniform Principal and Income Act (1997) chart. (§ 30-2-14-23(c)(4))
b) *short-term gains allocated between income and principal?*	See the Uniform Principal and Income Act (1997) chart. (§ 30-2-14-23(c)(4))
27. *How are distributions from REITs allocated between income and principal?*	See the Uniform Principal and Income Act (1997) chart. (§ 30-2-14-23(c)(4))

28. With respect to underproductive property:	
a) Is an adjustment, e.g., "delayed income," required to be paid to the income beneficiary?	No. (§ 30-2-14-35)
b) What percentage return makes property underproductive?	The statute only refers to property not productive of income. (§ 30-2-14-35)
29. Is the trustee required to increase income so that it is sufficient to qualify for the marital deduction?	Yes. (§ 30-2-14-35)
30. Is the trustee required to take depreciation?	No. (§ 30-2-14-41)
31. Is the trustee's determination on allocations generally presumed to be fair and reasonable?	Yes. (§ 30-2-14-14(b))
32. If an item is not addressed in the trust agreement or in the law, must it be allocated to principal or income?	To principal. (§ 30-2-14-14(a)(4))
33. When does an asset become subject to a trust:	
a) In the case of transfers during the transferor's life?	The date of transfer. (§ 30-2-14-20(b)(1))
b) In the case of a will?	The date of the testor's death. (§ 30-2-14-20(b)(2))
c) In the case of the death of a third party?	The date of the third party's death. (§ 30-2-14-20(b)(3))
34. Can a trustee rely on the characterization by an entity as to the source or character of a received distribution?	Yes. (§ 30-2-14-23(f))

Table 12.02
Iowa
Trust Accounting: Principal and Income

1. *Does the trustee have the power to transfer income to principal or to transfer principal to income to meet its duty of impartiality?*	No. (§ 637.103(b))
2. *What is the effective date for the law? E.g., does it apply to preexisting trusts?*	The Iowa Uniform Principal and Income Act applies to every trust or decedent's estate on and after July 1, 2000, except as otherwise expressly provided in the will, the terms of the trust or in the Iowa Uniform Principal and Income Act. (§ 637.701) ***Note:*** A trustee may continue using a former allocation method to allocate receipts for water, minerals, other natural resources, and timber under certain circumstances. (See § 637.423(4); § 637.424(5))
3. *What percentage is allocated to income and principal from proceeds of:*	
a) IRA? *b) Qualified pension or profit-sharing plan?* *c) Other deferred compensation arrangement?*	See the Uniform Principal and Income Act (1997) chart. (§ 637.421)
4. *What percentage is allocated to income and principal from proceeds of:*	
a) Patents? *b) Copyrights?*	See the Uniform Principal and Income Act (1997) chart. (§ 637.422)
5. *What percentage is allocated to income and principal in the event of distributions from:*	
a) Corporations? *b) Partnerships?* *c) LLCs?*	See the Uniform Principal and Income Act (1997) chart. (§ 637.401) ***Note***: The Iowa Principal and Income Act uses somewhat different language.
6. *What percentage is allocated to income and principal from proceeds of:*	
a) Oil and gas? *b) Minerals?* *c) Water?* *d) Other natural resourses (not including timber)?*	See the Uniform Principal and Income Act (1997) chart. (§ 637.423) ***Note:*** If a trust owns an interest in minerals, water or other natural resources on July 1, 2000, the trustee may allocate receipts from the interest as provided in the Iowa Principal and Income Act or in the manner used by the trustee before July 1, 2000.
e) Timber	See the Uniform Principal and Income Act (1997) chart. (§ 637.424) ***Note:*** If a trust owns an interest in timberland on July 1, 2000, the trustee may allocate receipts from the interest as provided in the Iowa Principal and Income Act or in the manner used by the trustee before July 1, 2000.

f) Rental properties?	See the Uniform Principal and Income Act (1997) chart. (§ 637.411; § 637.403(3)(d))
7. After a decedent dies, in the case of an estate, or after an income interest ends, when the fiduciary is determining the remaining net income what are the rules regarding payment from income or principal for:	
a) Attorneys fees? *b) Accountants fees?* *c) Fiduciary fees and commissions?* *d) Court costs?* *e) Interest on death taxes*	See the Uniform Principal and Income Act (1997) chart. (§ 637.201(2)(b))
f) Debts? *g) Funeral expenses?* *h) Family allowances and similar protections?* *i) Death taxes?* *j) Penalties on death taxes?*	See the Uniform Principal and Income Act (1997) chart. (§ 637.201(2)(c))
8. With respect to trust expenses from the administration of the trust that are not covered by § 637.201(2)(b-c) [see Question #7]:	
a) Does the trustee have full discretion in allocating between income and principal for expenses incurred in the administration of the trust?	No. (§ 637.501; § 637.502)
b) If not, are there special rules for:	
i) Regular trustee fees? *ii) Advisory or cusodial services to the trustee?* *iii) Accountings, judicial proceedings and other matters that involve both the income and remainder interests?*	See the Uniform Principal and Income Act (1997) chart. (§ 637.501; § 637.502)
iv) Debts?	See the Uniform Principal and Income Act (1997) chart. (§ 637.501(3); § 637.502(1)(c))
c) Can the trustee determine what are "transmission" expenses and "management" expenses?	
9. With regard to specific gifts from a trust after an income interest ends or from an estate:	
a) What amounts must be paid from income and principal?	See the Uniform Principal and Income Act (1997) chart. (§ 637.201(1); § 637.201(5))

10. With regard to outright pecuniary gifts from an estate or trust?:	
a) Does interest accrue?	Yes. See the Uniform Principal and Income Act (1997) chart. (§ 637.201(3))
11. With regard to a gift in trust of a pecuniary amount from an estate or trust?	
a) Does interest accrue?	No. See the Uniform Principal and Income Act (1997) chart. (§ 637.201(4); § 637.202)
12. With regard to residuary gifts:	
a) What amount of income and principal is to be paid to the residuary beneficiary of a trust or an estate?	See the Uniform Principal and Income Act (1997) chart. (§ 637.201(4); § 637.202)
13. With regard to "business assets" held in trust:	
a) Can the trustee treat them as a separate entity?	Generally yes. See the Uniform Principal and Income Act (1997) chart. (§ 637.403)
b) Can the trustee treat distinct assets as separate entities?	Generally yes. See the Uniform Principal and Income Act (1997) chart. (§ 637.403)
c) Can earnings be retained in trust for the reasonable needs of the "business entity," and, if so, to what extent is this permitted?	Yes. See the Uniform Principal and Income Act (1997) chart. (§ 637.403(b))
14. With respect to discount bonds:	
a) To what extent is the discount added to income or principal upon maturity?	See the Uniform Principal and Income Act (1997) chart. (§ 637.412)
b) Does the trustee have discretion to allocate discount between income and principal?	No. (§ 637.412)
c) Are distinctions drawn between Series E bonds and others?	No. (§ 637.412)
d) Are distinctions drawn based on the maturity date of the bond?	Yes. (§ 637.412)
15. Is there a de minimis rule excusing the trustee from making adjustments in certain cases?	Yes. See the Uniform Principal and Income Act (1997) chart. (§ 637.420)
16. With respect to derivatives:	
a) May income and loss be treated as that of a separate entity?	Yes. (§ 637.403(3)(f); § 637.426(2))
b) If not, or the trustee chooses not to do so, is income and loss allocated to the income account or to principal?	To principal. (§ 637.426(2))

17. To the extent put and call options are not derivatives, how are they allocated in terms of principal and income?	To principal. (§ 637.426(3))
18. How are asset-backed securities allocated in terms of principal and income?	See the Uniform Principal and Income Act (1997) chart. (§ 637.427)
19. Are expenses incurred to comply with environmental requirements allocated to income or principal?	Generally to principal. See the Uniform Principal and Income Act (1997) chart. (§ 637.502(1)(g))
20. Is income tax liability allocated generally to income or principal?	See the Uniform Principal and Income Act (1997) chart. (§ 637.505; § 637.506)
21. If a Subchapter S shareholder's or partner's portion of tax liability is greater than cash distributed, how is the excess obligation allocated?	From principal. (§ 637.505(3)(b)(2))
22. What is the standard, if any, for making equitable adjustments between income and principal?	Equitable adjustments are not sanctioned by the Iowa Principal and Income Act.
23. Is an income beneficiary entitled to receive income accrued but unpaid when an estate ends?	No. See the Uniform Principal and Income Act (1997) chart. (§ 637.303)
24. Is an income beneficiary entitled to receive income accrued but unpaid when a revocable trust ends?	Generally no. See the Uniform Principal and Income Act (1997) chart. (§ 637.303)
25. Is an income beneficiary entitled to receive income accrued but unpaid when an irrevocable trust ends?	Generally no. See the Uniform Principal and Income Act (1997) chart. (§ 637.303)
26. With regard to mutual funds, how are:	
a) long-term gains allocated between income and principal?	See the Uniform Principal and Income Act (1997) chart. (§ 637.401(3)(d))
b) short-term gains allocated between income and principal?	See the Uniform Principal and Income Act (1997) chart. (§ 637.401(3)(d))
27. How are distributions from REITs allocated between income and principal?	See the Uniform Principal and Income Act (1997) chart. (§ 637.401(3)(d))
28. With respect to underproductive property:	
a) Is an adjustment, e.g., "delayed income," required to be paid to the income beneficiary?	No. (§ 637.425)
b) What percentage return makes property underproductive?	The statute only refers to property not productive of income. (§ 637.425)
29. Is the trustee required to increase income so that it is sufficient to qualify for the marital deduction?	Yes. (§ 637.425)

30. *Is the trustee required to take depreciation?*	No. (§ 637.503)
31. *Is the trustee's determination on allocations generally presumed to be fair and reasonable?*	Yes. (§ 637.103(2))
32. *If an item is not addressed in the trust agreement or in the law, must it be allocated to principal or income?*	To principal. (§ 637.103(1)(d))
33. *When does an asset become subject to a trust:*	
a) *In the case of transfers during the transferor's life?*	The date of transfer. (§ 637.301(2)(a))
b) *In the case of a will?*	The date of the tesator's death. (§ 637.301(2)(b))
c) *In the case of the death of a third party?*	The date of the third party's death. (§ 637.301(2)(c))
34. *Can a trustee rely on the characterization by an entity as to the source or character of a received distribution?*	Yes. (§ 637.401(6))

Table 12.02
Kansas
Trust Accounting: Principal and Income

1. *Does the trustee have the power to transfer income to principal or to transfer principal to income to meet its duty of impartiality?*	Yes. See the Uniform Principal and Income Act (1997) chart. (§ 58-9-104)
2. *What is the effective date for the law? E.g., does it apply to preexisting trusts?*	The Kansas Principal and Income Act applies to every trust or decedent's estate existing July 1, 2000 except as expressly provided in a will, the terms of a trust or in the Kansas Principal and Income Act. (§ 58-9-601) ***Note:*** A trustee may continue using a former allocation method to allocate receipts for water, minerals, other natural resources, and timber under certain circumstances. (§ 58-9-411; § 58-9-412)
3. *What percentage is allocated to income and principal from proceeds of:*	
a) *IRA?* b) *Qualified pension or profit-sharing plan?* c) *Other deferred compensation arrangement?*	See the Uniform Principal and Income Act (1997) chart. (§ 58-9-409)
4. *What percentage is allocated to income and principal from proceeds of:*	
a) *Patents?* b) *Copyrights?*	See the Uniform Principal and Income Act (1997) chart. (§ 58-9-410(b))
5. *What percentage is allocated to income and principal in the event of distributions from:*	
a) *Corporations?* b) *Partnerships?* c) *LLCs?*	See the Uniform Principal and Income Act (1997) chart. (§ 58-9-401(b))
6. *What percentage is allocated to income and principal from proceeds of:*	
a) *Oil and gas?* b) *Minerals?* c) *Water?* d) *Other natural resourses (not including timber)?*	The trustee must allocate a receipt received as nominal delay rental or a nominal annual rent on a lease to income. The trustee must allocate a receipt received from a production payment to income if and to the extent that the agreement creating the production payment provides a factor for interest or its equivalent. The balance must be allocated to principal. The trustee must allocate fifteen percent (15%) of an amount received as a royalty, shut-in-well payment, take-or-pay payment, bonus, or a delay rental that is more than nominal, to principal and eighty-five percent (85%) to income. The trustee must allocate fifteen percent (15%) of the net amount received from a working interest or other interest (not mentioned in the two preceding paragraphs) to principal and eighty-five percent (85%) to income. An amount received on account of an interest in water that is renewable must be allocated to income. If the water is not

	renewable, ninety percent (90%) of the amount must be allocated to principal and ten percent (10%) to income. The rules above apply whether or not a decedent or donor was extracting the minerals, water, or other natural resources before the interest became subject to the trust. If a trust owns an interest in minerals, water, or other natural resources on July 1, 2000, the trustee may allocate receipts from the interest as provided in the Kansas Principal and Income Act or in the manner used by the trustee before July 1, 2000. (§ 58-9-411)
e) Timber	See the Uniform Principal and Income Act (1997) chart. (§ 58-9-412) Note: If a trust owns an interest in timberland on July 1, 2000, the trustee may allocate receipts from the interest as provided in the Kansas Principal and Income Act or in the manner used by the trustee before July 1, 2000.
f) Rental properties?	See the Uniform Principal and Income Act (1997) chart. (§ 58-9-405)
7. After a decedent dies, in the case of an estate, or after an income interest ends, when the fiduciary is determining the remaining net income what are the rules regarding payment from income or principal for:	
a) Attorneys fees? *b) Accountants fees?* *c) Fiduciary fees and commissions?* *d) Court costs?* *e) Interest on death taxes*	See the Uniform Principal and Income Act (1997) chart. (§ 58-9-201(2)(B))
f) Debts? *g) Funeral expenses?* *h) Family allowances and similar protections?* *i) Death taxes?* *j) Penalties on death taxes?*	See the Uniform Principal and Income Act (1997) chart. (§ 58-9-201(2)(C))
8. With respect to trust expenses from the administration of the trust that are not covered by § 201(2)(b-c) [see Question #7]:	
a) Does the trustee have full discretion in allocating between income and principal for expenses incurred in the administration of the trust?	No. (§ 58-9-501; § 58-9-502)
b) If not, are there special rules for:	
i) Regular trustee fees? *ii) Advisory or cusodial services to the trustee?*	See the Uniform Principal and Income Act (1997) chart. (§ 58-9-501; § 58-9-502)

iii) Accountings, judicial proceedings and other matters that involve both the income and remainder interests?	
iv) Debts?	See the Uniform Principal and Income Act (1997) chart. (§ 58-9-501(3); § 58-9-502(a)(3))
c) Can the trustee determine what are "transmission" expenses and "management" expenses?	
9. With regard to specific gifts from a trust after an income interest ends or from an estate:	
a) What amounts must be paid from income and principal?	See the Uniform Principal and Income Act (1997) chart. (§ 58-9-201(1); § 58-9-201(5))
10. With regard to outright pecuniary gifts from an estate or trust?:	
a) Does interest accrue?	Yes. See the Uniform Principal and Income Act (1997) chart. (§ 58-9-201(3))
11. With regard to a gift in trust of a pecuniary amount from an estate or trust?	
a) Does interest accrue?	No. See the Uniform Principal and Income Act (1997) chart. (§ 58-9-201(4); § 58-9-202)
12. With regard to residuary gifts:	
a) What amount of income and principal is to be paid to the residuary beneficiary of a trust or an estate?	See the Uniform Principal and Income Act (1997) chart. (§ 58-9-201(4); § 58-9-202)
13. With regard to "business assets" held in trust:	
a) Can the trustee treat them as a separate entity?	Generally yes. See the Uniform Principal and Income Act (1997) chart. (§ 58-9-403)
b) Can the trustee treat distinct assets as separate entities?	Generally yes. See the Uniform Principal and Income Act (1997) chart. (§ 58-9-403)
c) Can earnings be retained in trust for the reasonable needs of the "business entity," and, if so, to what extent is this permitted?	Yes. See the Uniform Principal and Income Act (1997) chart. (§ 58-9-403(b))
14. With respect to discount bonds:	
a) To what extent is the discount added to income or principal upon maturity?	See the Uniform Principal and Income Act (1997) chart. (§ 58-9-406(b))
b) Does the trustee have discretion to allocate discount between income and principal?	No. (§ 58-9-406) Note: The trustee has overriding power to adjust under (§ 58-9-104(a))

c) *Are distinctions drawn between Series E bonds and others?*	No. (§ 58-9-406)
d) *Are distinctions drawn based on the maturity date of the bond?*	Yes. (§ 58-9-406(b))
15. *Is there a de minimis rule excusing the trustee from making adjustments in certain cases?*	Yes. (§ 58-9-408)
16. *With respect to derivatives:*	
a) *May income and loss be treated as that of a separate entity?*	Yes. (§ 58-9-403; § 58-9-414(b))
b) *If not, or the trustee chooses not to do so, is income and loss allocated to the income account or to principal?*	To principal. (§ 58-9-414(b))
17. *To the extent put and call options are not derivatives, how are they allocated in terms of principal and income?*	To principal. (§ 58-9-414(c))
18. *How are asset-backed securities allocated in terms of principal and income?*	See the Uniform Principal and Income Act (1997) chart. (§ 58-9-415)
19. *Are expenses incurred to comply with environmental requirements allocated to income or principal?*	To principal. (§ 58-9-502(a)(7))
20. *Is income tax liability allocated generally to income or principal?*	See the Uniform Principal and Income Act (1997) chart. (§ 58-9-505; § 58-9-506)
21. *If a Subchapter S shareholder's or partner's portion of tax liability is greater than cash distributed, how is the excess obligation allocated?*	To principal. (§ 58-9-505(c)(2)(B))
22. *What is the standard, if any, for making equitable adjustments between income and principal?*	See the Uniform Principal and Income Act (1997) chart. (§ 58-9-103(b))
23. *Is an income beneficiary entitled to receive income accrued but unpaid when an estate ends?*	No. (§ 58-9-303)
24. *Is an income beneficiary entitled to receive income accrued but unpaid when a revocable trust ends?*	Generally no. See the Uniform Principal and Income Act (1997) chart. (§ 58-9-303)
25. *Is an income beneficiary entitled to receive income accrued but unpaid when an irrevocable trust ends?*	Generally no. See the Uniform Principal and Income Act (1997) chart. (§ 58-9-303)
26. *With regard to mutual funds, how are:*	
a) *long-term gains allocated between income and principal?*	See the Uniform Principal and Income Act (1997) chart. (§ 58-9-401(c)(4))

b) short-term gains allocated between income and principal?	See the Uniform Principal and Income Act (1997) chart. (§ 58-9-401(c)(4))
27. How are distributions from REITs allocated between income and principal?	See the Uniform Principal and Income Act (1997) chart. (§ 58-9-401(c)(4))
28. With respect to underproductive property:	
a) Is an adjustment, e.g., "delayed income," required to be paid to the income beneficiary?	No. (§ 58-9-413)
b) What percentage return makes property underproductive?	The statute only refers to property not productive of income. (§ 58-9-413)
29. Is the trustee required to increase income so that it is sufficient to qualify for the marital deduction?	Yes. (§ 58-9-413(a))
30. Is the trustee required to take depreciation?	No. (§ 58-9-503)
31. Is the trustee's determination on allocations generally presumed to be fair and reasonable?	Yes. (§ 58-9-103(b))
32. If an item is not addressed in the trust agreement or in the law, must it be allocated to principal or income?	To principal. (§ 58-9-103(a)(4))
33. When does an asset become subject to a trust:	
a) In the case of transfers during the transferor's life?	The date of transfer. (§ 58-9-301(b)(1))
b) In the case of a will?	The date of the testator's death. (§ 58-9-301(b)(2))
c) In the case of the death of a third party?	The date of the third party's death. (§ 58-9-301(b)(3))
34. Can a trustee rely on the characterization by an entity as to the source or character of a received distribution?	Yes. (§ 58-9-401(f))

Table 12.02
Kentucky
Trust Accounting: Principal and Income

1. *Does the trustee have the power to transfer income to principal or to transfer principal to income to meet its duty of impartiality?*	Note: § 286.3-277 deals with fiduciary standards required for a bank or trust company acting as fiduciary. A trustee may adjust between principal and income to the extent the trustee considers necessary if 1. § 286.3-277 applies by law or by election that is approved by a District Court, 2. the terms of the trust describe the amount that may or shall be distributed to a beneficiary by referring to the trust's income, 3. the trustee determines, after applying the rules in § 386.452(1) that the trustee is unable to comply with § 386.452(2), and 4. the adjustment, including an adjustment method such as an annual percentage distribution if the percentage is not less than three percent (3%) nor more than five percent (5%) of the fair market value of the trust assets determined annually, is approved by the District Court. The trustee of a trust to which § 286.3-277 does not apply by law may elect to have such provisions apply to the administration of the trust with approval of the District Court. A personal representative may adjust between principal and income in the same manner as a trustee if 1. § 286.3-277 applies to the personal representative by law or if the personal representative elects to have § 286.3-277 apply to the administration of the estate, upon approval of the District Court, which approval may be an adjustment method such as an annual percentage distribution if the percentage is not less than three percent (3%) nor more than five percent (5%) of the fair market value of the trust assets determined annually, and 2. The amount distributable to a beneficiary of the estate is determined by reference to the income of the estate; and 3. the personal representative determines, and after applying the rules of 386.452(1), that the personal representative is unable to comply with § 386.452(2). (§ 386.454) The provisions of § 386.454 that allow a trustee to adopt the prudent investor rule and make allocations to income will not apply to any trust without District Court approval. ((§ 386.502(1))
2. *What is the effective date for the law? E.g., does it apply to preexisting trusts?*	The Kentucky Principal and Income Act, other than § 386.454, applies to all trusts administered under Kentucky law, except as otherwise specifically provided in the instrument creating the trust, regardless of when created. (§ 386.502(2)) ***Note:*** A trustee may continue using a former allocation method to allocate receipts for water, minerals, other natural resources, and timber under certain circumstances. (See § 386.484; § 386.486)
3. *What percentage is allocated to income and principal from proceeds of:*	

a) *IRA?* b) *Qualified pension or profit-sharing plan?* c) *Other deferred compensation arrangement?*	See the Uniform Principal and Income Act (1997) chart. (§ 386.480)
4. *What percentage is allocated to income and principal from proceeds of:*	
a) *Patents?* b) *Copyrights?*	See the Uniform Principal and Income Act (1997) chart. (§ 386.482)
5. *What percentage is allocated to income and principal in the event of distributions from:*	
a) *Corporations?* b) *Partnerships?* c) *LLCs?*	See the Uniform Principal and Income Act (1997) chart. (§ 386.466)
6. *What percentage is allocated to income and principal from proceeds of:*	
a) *Oil and gas?* b) *Minerals?* c) *Water?* d) *Other natural resourses (not including timber)?*	See the Uniform Principal and Income Act (1997) chart. (§ 386.484) ***Note:*** If a trust owns an interest in minerals, water or other natural resources on January 1, 2005, the trustee may allocate receipts from the interest as provided in the Kentucky Principal and Income Act or in the manner used by the trustee before January 1, 2005.
e) *Timber?*	See the Uniform Principal and Income Act (1997) chart. (§ 386.486) ***Note:*** If a trust owns an interest in timberland on January 1, 2005, the trustee may allocate receipts from the interest as provided in the Kentucky Principal and Income Act or in the manner used by the trustee before January 1, 2005.
f) *Rental properties?*	See the Uniform Principal and Income Act (1997) chart. (§ 386.486)
7. *After a decedent dies, in the case of an estate, or after an income interest ends, when the fiduciary is determining the remaining net income what are the rules regarding payment from income or principal for:*	
a) *Attorneys fees?* b) *Accountants fees?* c) *Fiduciary fees and commissions?* d) *Court costs?* e) *Interest on death taxes*	See the Uniform Principal and Income Act (1997) chart. (§ 386.456(2)(b))
f) *Debts?* g) *Funeral expenses?*	See the Uniform Principal and Income Act (1997) chart. (§ 386.456(2)(c))

h) Family allowances and similar protections? *i) Death taxes?* *j) Penalties on death taxes?*	
8. With respect to trust expenses from the administration of the trust that are not covered by § 386.456(2)(b-c) [see Question #7]:	
a) Does the trustee have full discretion in allocating between income and principal for expenses incurred in the administration of the trust?	No. (§ 386.490; § 386.492).
b) If not, are there special rules for:	
i) Regular trustee fees? *ii) Advisory or cusodial services to the trustee?* *iii) Accountings, judicial proceedings and other matters that involve both the income and remainder interests?*	See the Uniform Principal and Income Act (1997) chart. (§ 386.490; § 386.492)
iv) Debts?	See the Uniform Principal and Income Act (1997) chart. (§ 386.490(3); § 386.492(1)(d))
c) Can the trustee determine what are "transmission" expenses and "management" expenses?	
9. With regard to specific gifts from a trust after an income interest ends or from an estate:	
a) What amounts must be paid from income and principal?	See the Uniform Principal and Income Act (1997) chart. (§ 386.456(1); § 386.456(5))
10. With regard to outright pecuniary gifts from an estate or trust?:	
a) Does interest accrue?	Yes. See the Uniform Principal and Income Act (1997) chart. (§ 386.456(3))
11. With regard to a gift in trust of a pecuniary amount from an estate or trust?	
a) Does interest accrue?	No. See the Uniform Principal and Income Act (1997) chart. (§ 386.456(4); § 386.458)
12. With regard to residuary gifts:	
a) What amount of income and principal is to be paid to the residuary beneficiary of a trust or an estate?	See the Uniform Principal and Income Act (1997) chart. (§ 386.456(4); § 386.458)
13. With regard to "business assets" held in trust:	

a) Can the trustee treat them as a separate entity?	The Kentucky Principal and Income Act does not contain a provision that expressly allows the trustee to treat certain businesses or activities as a separate entity.
b) Can the trustee treat distinct assets as separate entities?	The Kentucky Principal and Income Act does not contain a provision that expressly allows the trustee to separately account for certain businesses or activities.
c) Can earnings be retained in trust for the reasonable needs of the "business entity," and, if so, to what extent is this permitted?	The Kentucky Principal and Income Act does not contain a provision that expressly allows earnings to be retained for the reasonable needs of a business entity.
14. With respect to discount bonds:	
a) To what extent is the discount added to income or principal upon maturity?	See the Uniform Principal and Income Act (1997) chart. (§ 386.474(b))
b) Does the trustee have discretion to allocate discount between income and principal?	No. (§ 386.474) ***Note:*** The trustee might have the overriding power to adjust under (§ 386.454)
c) Are distinctions drawn between Series E bonds and others?	No. (§ 386.474)
d) Are distinctions drawn based on the maturity date of the bond?	Yes. (§ 386.474(b))
15. Is there a de minimis rule excusing the trustee from making adjustments in certain cases?	Yes. (§ 386.478)
16. With respect to derivatives:	
a) May income and loss be treated as that of a separate entity?	The Kentucky Principal and Income Act does not contain any specific provisions for derivatives.
b) If not, or the trustee chooses not to do so, is income and loss allocated to the income account or to principal?	The Kentucky Principal and Income Act does not contain any specific provisions for derivatives. Therefore, any items should be allocated to principal. (§ 386.452(d))
17. To the extent put and call options are not derivatives, how are they allocated in terms of principal and income?	To principal. (§ 386.470(6))
18. How are asset-backed securities allocated in terms of principal and income?	The Kentucky Principal and Income Act does not contain any specific provisions for asset-backed securities. Therefore, any items should be allocated to principal. (§ 386.452(d))
19. Are expenses incurred to comply with environmental requirements allocated to income or principal?	Generally to principal. See the Uniform Principal and Income Act (1997) chart. (§ 386.492(1)(h))
20. Is income tax liability allocated generally to income or principal?	See the Uniform Principal and Income Act (1997) chart. (§ 386.498; § 386.500) ***Note:*** The District Court must approve any adjustement under (§ 386.500(1)).

21. If a Subchapter S shareholder's or partner's portion of tax liability is greater than cash distributed, how is the excess obligation allocated?	To principal. (§ 386.498(3)(b)(2))
22. What is the standard, if any, for making equitable adjustments between income and principal?	See the Uniform Principal and Income Act (1997) chart. (§ 386.452(2))
23. Is an income beneficiary entitled to receive income accrued but unpaid when an estate ends?	No. (§ 386.464)
24. Is an income beneficiary entitled to receive income accrued but unpaid when a revocable trust ends?	Generally no. See the Uniform Principal and Income Act (1997) chart. (§ 386.464).
25. Is an income beneficiary entitled to receive income accrued but unpaid when an irrevocable trust ends?	Generally no. See the Uniform Principal and Income Act (1997) chart. (§ 386.464).
26. With regard to mutual funds, how are:	
a) long-term gains allocated between income and principal?	See the Uniform Principal and Income Act (1997) chart. (§ 386.466(3)(d))
b) short-term gains allocated between income and principal?	See the Uniform Principal and Income Act (1997) chart. (§ 386.466(3)(d))
27. How are distributions from REITs allocated between income and principal?	See the Uniform Principal and Income Act (1997) chart. (§ 386.466(3)(d))
28. With respect to underproductive property:	
a) Is an adjustment, e.g., "delayed income," required to be paid to the income beneficiary?	No. (§ 386.488)
b) What percentage return makes property underproductive?	The statute only refers to property not productive of income. (§ 386.488)
29. Is the trustee required to increase income so that it is sufficient to qualify for the marital deduction?	Yes. (§ 386.488(1))
30. Is the trustee required to take depreciation?	No. (§ 386.494)
31. Is the trustee's determination on allocations generally presumed to be fair and reasonable?	Yes. (§ 386.452(2))
32. If an item is not addressed in the trust agreement or in the law, must it be allocated to principal or income?	To principal. (§ 386.452(1)(d))
33. When does an asset become subject to a trust:	

a) In the case of transfers during the transferor's life?	The date of transfer. (§ 386.460(2)(a))
b) In the case of a will?	The date of the testator's death. (§ 386.460(2)(b))
c) In the case of the death of a third party?	The date of the third party's death. (§ 386.460(2)(c))
34. Can a trustee rely on the characterization by an entity as to the source or character of a received distribution?	Yes. (§ 386.466(6))

Table 12.02
Louisiana
Trust Accounting: Principal and Income

1. *Does the trustee have the power to transfer income to principal or to transfer principal to income to meet its duty of impartiality?*	Yes. Subject to the limitations set forth in § § 9:2159-9:2163, a trustee may make an adjustment between principal and income when the interest of one or more beneficiaries is defined by reference to the "income" of a trust, and the trustee determines, after taking into account the allocations for the year under the Louisiana provisions for Allocation to Principal and Income (§ § 9:2141-9:2157), that the adjustment is necessary in order for the trustee to satisfy his duty to be fair and reasonable to all the beneficiaries, taking into account the purposes of the trust. (§ 9:2158)
2. *What is the effective date for the law? E.g., does it apply to preexisting trusts?*	The Louisiana Trust Code, which includes the provisions on allocating principal and income, became effective July 29, 1964. (1964 La. Acts 338) The provisions for allocating principal and income in the Louisiana Trust Code do not address the applicability of the provisions to preexisting trusts.
3. *What percentage is allocated to income and principal from proceeds of:*	
a) IRA? *b) Qualified pension or profit-sharing plan?* *c) Other deferred compensation arrangement?*	The trustee must allocate the receipts from rights to receive payments on a contract for deferred compensation, up to five percent (5%) per year of its inventory value, to income and the balance to principal. (§ 9:2154)
4. *What percentage is allocated to income and principal from proceeds of:*	
a) Patents? *b) Copyrights?*	The trustee must allocate the receipts from patents and copyrights, up to five percent (5%) per year of its inventory value, to income and the balance to principal. (§ 9:2154)
5. *What percentage is allocated to income and principal in the event of distributions from:*	
a) Corporations? *b) Partnerships?* *c) LLCs?*	Corporate distributions of shares of the distributing corporation, including distributions in the form of a stock split or stock dividend, are principal. A right to subscribe to shares or other securities issued by the distributing corporation accruing on account of the ownership of shares or other securities in such corporation and the proceeds of any sale of the right are principal. Except to the extent that the corporation indicates that some part of a corporate distribution is a settlement of preferred or guaranteed dividends accrued since the trustee became a stockholder or is in lieu of an ordinary cash dividend, a corporate distribution is principal if the distribution is pursuant to a call of shares; a merger, consolidation or reorganization; a plan by which assets of the corporation are acquired by another corporation; or a total or partial liquidation of the corporation. Distributions made from ordinary income by a regulated investment company or by a trust qualifying and electing to be taxed under federal law as a real estate investment trust are income.

	All other distributions made by the company or trust, including distributions from capital gains, depreciation or depletion, whether in the form of cash or an option to take new stock or cash or an option to purchase additional shares, are principal. Except as provided in the preceding paragraphs, all corporate distributions are income, including cash dividends, distributions of or rights to subscribe to shares or securities or obligations of corporations other than the distributing corporation, and the proceeds of the rights or property distributions. (§ 9:2149) ***Note:*** Parnerships and LLC's are not addressed.
6. What percentage is allocated to income and principal from proceeds of:	
a) Oil and gas? *b) Minerals?* *c) Water?* *d) Other natural resourses (not including timber)?*	Receipts for rent on a lease or extension payments on a lease are income. Receipts from a production payment are income to the extent of any factor for interest or its equivalent provided in the governing instrument. The fiduciary must allocate to principal the fraction of the balance of the receipts which the unrecovered cost of the production payments bears to the balance owed on the production payment, exclusive of any factor for interest or its equivalent. The receipts not allocated to principal are income. If received as a royalty, overriding or limited royalty, or bonus, or from a working, net profit, or any other interest in minerals or other natural resources, receipts (not provided for in the two preceding paragraphs) must be apportioned on a yearly basis, whether or not any natural resource was being taken from the land at the time the trust was established. Twenty-seven and one-half per cent (27 1/2%) of the gross receipts (but not to exceed fifty per cent (50%) of the net receipts remaining after payment of all expenses, direct and indirect, computed without allowance for depletion) must be added to principal as an allowance for depletion. The balance of the gross receipts, after payment of all expenses, direct and indirect, is income. (§ 9:2152) ***Note***: These rules are not applicable to proceeds from water.
e) Timber?	The trustee must allocate receipts from the sale of timber in accordance with what is reasonable and equitable in view of the interests of those entitled to income as well as of those entitled to principal, and in view of the manner in which men of ordinary prudence, discretion, and judgment would act in the management of their own affairs. (§ 9:2153)
f) Rental properties?	The trustee must include amounts received from renting real or personal property, including sums received for cancellation or renewal of a lease, as income. (§ 9:2144)
7. After a decedent dies, in the case of an estate, or after an income interest ends, when the fiduciary is determining the remaining net income what are the rules regarding payment from income or principal for:	

a) Attorneys fees? *b) Accountants fees?* *c) Fiduciary fees and commissions?* *d) Court costs?* *e) Interest on death taxes*	The provisions for allocating principal and income in the Louisiana Trust Code do not address these expenses and costs. 1997 La. Acts 1421, art. 1415 defines "administrative expenses" as "obligations incurred in the collection, preservation, management, and distribution of the estate of the decedent." Debts of the decedent are defined as obligations of the decedent or those that arise as a result of his death, such as the cost of his funeral and burial. The official comment says administrative expenses "is broadly defined to include expenses that are incurred after death in preserving, safeguarding, and operating the property of the estate, such as repairs, costs of maintenance and upkeep, interest attributable to a debt, and custodial fees." The fees of the executor and attorney are omitted from the list of examples of administrative expenses, but since the term is "broadly defined," it presumably includes them. (1997 La. Acts 1421, art. 1415)
f) Debts? *g) Funeral expenses?* *h) Family allowances and similar protections?* *i) Death taxes?* *j) Penalties on death taxes?*	The provisions for allocating principal and income in the Louisiana Trust Code do not address these expenses and costs. 1997 La. Acts 1421, art. 1415 defines "administrative expenses" as "obligations incurred in the collection, preservation, management, and distribution of the estate of the decedent." Debts of the decedent are defined as obligations of the decedent or those that arise as a result of his death, such as the cost of his funeral and burial. The official comment says administrative expenses "is broadly defined to include expenses that are incurred after death in preserving, safeguarding, and operating the property of the estate, such as repairs, costs of maintenance and upkeep, interest attributable to a debt, and custodial fees." The fees of the executor and attorney are omitted from the list of examples of administrative expenses, but since the term is "broadly defined," it presumably includes them. (1997 La. Acts 1421, art. 1415)
8. With respect to trust expenses from the administration of the trust:	
a) Does the trustee have full discretion in allocating between income and principal for expenses incurred in the administration of the trust?	No. (§ 9:2156)
b) If not, are there special rules for:	
i) Regular trustee fees? *ii) Advisory or custodial services to the trustee?* *iii) Accountings, judicial proceedings and other matters that involve both the income and remainder interests?*	Generally, the following charges must be made against income: 1. one-half of the court costs, attorneys' fees, and other fees on periodic accountings or judicial proceedings, unless the court directs otherwise; 2. court costs, attorneys' fees, and other fees on other accountings or judicial proceedings if the matter primarily concerns the income interest, unless the court directs otherwise; and 3. one-half of the trustee's regular compensation whether based on a percentage of principal or income.

	Generally, the following charges must be made against principal: 1. one-half of the trustee's regular compensation, court costs and attorneys' fees primarily concerning matters of principal; 2. expenses incurred in maintaining or defending any action to construe the trust or protect it or the property or assure the title of any trust property. (§ 9:2156) ***Note:*** § 9:2156 contains many other special rules for allocations and contains many exceptions.
iv) Debts?	The trustee must allocate interest expense on trust debt to income and must allocate payments on principal of trust debt to principal. (§ 9:2156)
c) Can the trustee determine what are "transmission" expenses and "management" expenses?	
9. With regard to specific gifts from a trust after an income interest ends or from an estate:	
a) What amounts must be paid from income and principal?	All legacies, whether particular, general, or universal, include the fruits and products attributable to the object of the legacy from the date of death, but the right of any legatee to distribution under this Article is subject to administration of the succession. (1997 La. Acts 1421, art. 1598. In the accounting between successors, the particular legatee will be charged from the day of death with the debts of the decedent and the administrative expenses that are attributable to identifiable property bequeathed or to the production of its fruits and products. (1997 La. Acts 1421, art. 1422)
10. With regard to outright pecuniary gifts from an estate or trust?:	
a) Does interest accrue?	The legatee of a specified amount of money is entitled to interest on it, at a reasonable rate, beginning one year after the testator's death, but the executor may, by contradictory proceedings with the legatee and upon good cause shown, obtain an extension of time for such interest to begin to accrue and for such other modification with regard to payment of interest as the court deems appropriate. If, however, the legacy is subject to a usufruct for life of a surviving spouse or is held in trust subject to an income interest for life, to or for the benefit of a surviving spouse, the spouse shall be entitled to interest on the money from the date of death at a reasonable rate. (1997 La. Acts 1421, art. 1598)
11. With regard to a gift in trust of a pecuniary amount from an estate or trust?	
a) Does interest accrue?	The legatee of a specified amount of money is entitled to interest on it, at a reasonable rate, beginning one year after the testator's death, but the executor may, by contradictory proceedings with the legatee and upon good cause shown,

	obtain an extension of time for such interest to begin to accrue and for such other modification with regard to payment of interest as the court deems appropriate. If, however, the legacy is subject to a usufruct for life of a surviving spouse or is held in trust subject to an income interest for life, to or for the benefit of a surviving spouse, the spouse shall be entitled to interest on the money from the date of death at a reasonable rate. (1997 La. Acts 1421, art. 1598)
12. With regard to residuary gifts:	
a) What amount of income and principal is to be paid to the residuary beneficiary of a trust or an estate?	All legacies, whether particular, general, or universal, include the fruits and products attributable to the object of the legacy from the date of death, but the right of any legatee to distribution under this Article is subject to administration of the succession. (1997 La. Acts 1421, art. 1598) In the accounting between successors, the particular legatee will be charged from the day of death with the debts of the decedent and the administrative expenses that are attributable to identifiable property bequeathed or to the production of its fruits and products. Therefore, the fruits of the entire estate will no longer belong to the universal successor to help him pay the general debts and charges; however, the universal successor will not have to shoulder any of the debts or expenses in connection with legacies of identifiable property either. (1997 La. Acts 1421, art. 1422)
13. With regard to "business assets" held in trust:	
a) Can the trustee treat them as a separate entity?	The Louisiana Trust Code, which includes the provisions on allocating principal and income, does not particularly provide for treating business assets as a separate entity. However, if a trustee uses any part of the principal in the operation of a business of which, as trustee, he is a proprietor or a partner, the proceeds and losses of the business shall be allocated in accordance with what is reasonable and equitable in view of the interests of those entitled to income as well as of those entitled to principal, and in view of the manner in which men of ordinary prudence, discretion, and intelligence would act in the management of their own affairs. (§ 9:2151)
b) Can the trustee treat distinct assets as separate entities?	The Louisiana Trust Code, which includes the provisions on allocating principal and income, does not particularly provide for treating distinct assets as separate entities. However, if a trustee uses any part of the principal in the operation of a business of which, as trustee, he is a proprietor or a partner, the proceeds and losses of the business shall be allocated in accordance with what is reasonable and equitable in view of the interests of those entitled to income as well as of those entitled to principal, and in view of the manner in which men of ordinary prudence, discretion, and intelligence would act in the management of their own affairs. (§ 9:2151)
c) Can earnings be retained in trust for the reasonable needs of the "business entity," and, if so, to what extent is this permitted?	No. The Louisiana Trust Code, which includes the provisions on allocating principal and income, does not provide that the fiduciary may retain earnings for the needs of the business entity.

14. With respect to discount bonds:	
a) To what extent is the discount added to income or principal upon maturity?	The appreciation of a bond or obligation in accordance with a fixed schedule of appreciation in excess of the price at which it was issued is distributable is income. (§ 9:2150)
b) Does the trustee have discretion to allocate discount between income and principal?	No. (§ 9:2150) Note: The trustee has the overriding power to adjust under § 9:2158.
c) Are distinctions drawn between Series E bonds and others?	No. (§ 9:2150)
d) Are distinctions drawn based on the maturity date of the bond?	No. (§ 9:2150)
15. Is there a de minimis rule excusing the trustee from making adjustments in certain cases?	No.
16. With respect to derivatives:	
a) May income and loss be treated as that of a separate entity?	No. The Louisiana Trust Code, which includes the provisions on allocating principal and income, does not address derivatives being treated as separate entities.
b) If not, or the trustee chooses not to do so, is income and loss allocated to the income account or to principal?	The Louisiana Trust Code, which includes the provisions on allocating principal and income, does not address derivatives. Therefore, unless the governing instrument provides otherwise, the fiduciary must allocate gain and loss from derivatives to principal. (§ 9:2142(2))
17. To the extent put and call options are not derivatives, how are they allocated in terms of principal and income?	The Louisiana Trust Code, which includes the provisions on allocating principal and income, does not address options. Therefore, unless the governing instrument provides otherwise, the fiduciary must allocate gain and loss from options to principal. (§ 9:2142(2))
18. How are asset-backed securities allocated in terms of principal and income?	The Louisiana Trust Code, which includes the provisions on allocating principal and income, does not address asset-backed securities. Therefore, unless the governing instrument provides otherwise, the fiduciary must allocate gain and loss from asset-backed securities to principal. (§ 9:2142(2))
19. Are expenses incurred to comply with environmental requirements allocated to income or principal?	The Louisiana Trust Code, which includes the provisions on allocating principal and income, does not address environmental requirements. (See § 9:2156)
20. Is income tax liability allocated generally to income or principal?	Any tax required to be paid by a fiduciary on the trust's share of an entity's taxable income should be paid from income to the extent that receipts from the entity are allocated to income and from principal to the extent that receipts from the entity are allocated to principal. (§ 9:2156)
21. If a Subchapter S shareholder's or partner's portion of tax liability is greater than cash distributed, how is the excess obligation allocated?	The Louisiana Trust Code, which includes the provisions on allocating principal and income, does not address this situation.

22. What is the standard, if any, for making equitable adjustments between income and principal?	The trustee must decide that an adjustment is necessary in order for the trustee to satisfy his duty to be fair and reasonable to all the beneficiaries, taking into account the purposes of the trust. (§ 9:2158)
23. Is an income beneficiary entitled to receive income accrued but unpaid when an estate ends?	On termination of an income interest, the income beneficiary whose interest is terminated, or his estate, is entitled to: Income undistributed on the date of termination; income due but not paid to the trustee on the date of termination and income in the form of periodic payments (other than corporate distributions to stockholders), including rent, interest, or annuities, not due on the date of termination, accrued from day to day. (§ 9:2147)
24. Is an income beneficiary entitled to receive income accrued but unpaid when a revocable trust ends?	On termination of an income interest, the income beneficiary whose interest is terminated, or his estate, is entitled to: Income undistributed on the date of termination; income due but not paid to the trustee on the date of termination and income in the form of periodic payments (other than corporate distributions to stockholders), including rent, interest, or annuities, not due on the date of termination, accrued from day to day. (§ 9:2147)
25. Is an income beneficiary entitled to receive income accrued but unpaid when an irrevocable trust ends?	On termination of an income interest, the income beneficiary whose interest is terminated, or his estate, is entitled to: Income undistributed on the date of termination; income due but not paid to the trustee on the date of termination and income in the form of periodic payments (other than corporate distributions to stockholders), including rent, interest, or annuities, not due on the date of termination, accrued from day to day. (§ 9:2147)
26. With regard to mutual funds, how are:	
a) long-term gains allocated between income and principal?	Distributions made from ordinary income by a regulated investment company are income. All other distributions made by the company, including distributions from capital gains, depreciation, or depletion, whether in the form of cash or an option to take new stock or cash or an option to purchase additional shares, are principal. (§ 9:2149(C))
b) short-term gains allocated between income and principal?	Distributions made from ordinary income by a regulated investment company are income. All other distributions made by the company, including distributions from capital gains, depreciation, or depletion, whether in the form of cash or an option to take new stock or cash or an option to purchase additional shares, are principal. (§ 9:2149(C))
27. How are distributions from REITs allocated between income and principal?	Distributions made from ordinary income by a REIT are income. All other distributions made by the REIT, including distributions from capital gains, depreciation, or depletion, whether in the form of cash or an option to take new stock or cash or an option to purchase additional shares, are principal. (§ 9:2149(C))
28. With respect to underproductive property:	

a) Is an adjustment, e.g., "delayed income," required to be paid to the income beneficiary?	Yes. Generally, a portion of the net proceeds of sale of any part of principal which has not produced an average net income of at least one per cent (1%) per year of its inventory value for more than a year (including as income the value of any beneficial use of the property by the income beneficiary) must be treated as delayed income to which the income beneficiary is entitled. (§ 9:2155) For a calculation of the delayed income and for exceptions to the rule, see § 9:2155.
b) What percentage return makes property underproductive?	Property is not considered productive of income if the property has not produced an average net income of at least one per cent (1%) per year of its inventory value for more than a year (including as income the value of any beneficial use of the property by the income beneficiary). (§ 9:2155)
29. Is the trustee required to increase income so that it is sufficient to qualify for the marital deduction?	The Louisiana Trust Code, which includes the provisions on allocating principal and income, does not address the marital deduction.
30. Is the trustee required to take depreciation?	Yes. (§ 9:2156)
31. Is the trustee's determination on allocations generally presumed to be fair and reasonable?	The Louisiana Trust Code, which includes the provisions on allocating principal and income, not have a presumption that allocations are generally presumed to be fair and reasonable. (§ 9:2158)
32. If an item is not addressed in the trust agreement or in the law, must it be allocated to principal or income?	If an item is not addressed in the trust agreement or in the law, the trustee must allocate the item to principal. (§ 9:2142(3))
33. When does an asset become subject to a trust:	
a) In the case of transfers during the transferor's life?	The Louisiana Trust Code, which includes the provisions on allocating principal and income, does not address this issue. (§ 9:2145)
b) In the case of a will?	The Louisiana Trust Code, which includes the provisions on allocating principal and income, does not address this issue. (§ 9:2145)
c) In the case of the death of a third party?	The Louisiana Trust Code, which includes the provisions on allocating principal and income, does not address this issue. (§ 9:2145)
34. Can a trustee rely on the characterization by an entity as to the source or character of a received distribution?	Yes. (§ 9:2149(F))

Table 12.02
Maine
Trust Accounting: Principal and Income

1. *Does the trustee have the power to transfer income to principal or to transfer principal to income to meet its duty of impartiality?*	A trustee has the power to adjust between principal and income to the extent the trustee considers necessary if: 1. the terms of the trust describe the amount that may or must be distributed to a beneficiary by referring to the trust's income; and 2. the trustee determines, after applying the rules in 18-A § 7-703(a), that the trustee is unable to comply with 18-A § 7-703(b). (18-A § 7-704) ***Note:*** 18-A § 7-704 does not mention that the trustee must manage and invest the trustee assets as a prudent investor.
2. *What is the effective date for the law? E.g., does it apply to preexisting trusts?*	The Maine Principal and Income Act applies to every trust or decedent's estate, including those in existence on January 1, 2003, beginning with the first fiscal year of the trust or decedent's estate that begins on or after January 1, 2003, except as otherwise expressly provided in the will or terms of the trust or in the Maine Principal and Income Act. (18-A § 7-773) ***Note:*** A trustee may continue using a former allocation method to allocate receipts for water, minerals, other natural resources, and timber under certain circumstances. (See 18-A § 7-751; 18-A § 7-752)
3. *What percentage is allocated to income and principal from proceeds of:*	
a) *IRA?* b) *Qualified pension or profit-sharing plan?* c) *Other deferred compensation arrangement?*	See the Uniform Principal and Income Act (1997) chart. (18-A § 7-749)
4. *What percentage is allocated to income and principal from proceeds of:*	
a) *Patents?* b) *Copyrights?*	See the Uniform Principal and Income Act (1997) chart. (18-A § 7-750)
5. *What percentage is allocated to income and principal in the event of distributions from:*	
a) *Corporations?* b) *Partnerships?* c) *LLCs?*	See the Uniform Principal and Income Act (1997) chart. (18-A § 7-741)
6. *What percentage is allocated to income and principal from proceeds of:*	
a) *Oil and gas?* b) *Minerals?* c) *Water?* d) *Other natural resourses (not including timber)?*	See the Uniform Principal and Income Act (1997) chart. (18-A § 7-751) ***Note***: If a trust owns an interest in minerals, water or other natural resources on January 1, 2002, the trustee may allocate receipts from the interest as provided in the Maine Principal

	and Income Act or in the manner used by the trustee before January 1, 2002.
e) Timber	The Maine Principal and Income Act contains a different formula than the Uniform Principal and Income Act (1997). Although the results of the formulas will likely be the same, one should consult the language in (18-A § 7-752) See the Uniform Principal and Income Act (1997) chart. (18-A § 7-752) ***Note:*** If a trust owns an interest in timberland on January 1, 2002, the trustee may allocate receipts from the interest as provided in the Maine Principal and Income Act or in the manner used by the trustee before January 1, 2002.
f) Rental properties?	See the Uniform Principal and Income Act (1997) chart. (18-A § 7-745)
7. After a decedent dies, in the case of an estate, or after an income interest ends, when the fiduciary is determining the remaining net income what are the rules regarding payment from income or principal for:	
a) Attorneys fees? *b) Accountants fees?* *c) Fiduciary fees and commissions?* *d) Court costs?* *e) Interest on death taxes*	See the Uniform Principal and Income Act (1997) chart. (18-A § 7-721(b)(2))
f) Debts? *g) Funeral expenses?* *h) Family allowances and similar protections?* *i) Death taxes?* *j) Penalties on death taxes?*	See the Uniform Principal and Income Act (1997) chart. (18-A § 7-721(b)(3))
8. With respect to trust expenses from the administration of the trust that are not covered 18-A § 7-721(b)(2-3) [see Question #7]:	
a) Does the trustee have full discretion in allocating between income and principal for expenses incurred in the administration of the trust?	No. (18-A § 7-761; 18-A § 7-762)
b) If not, are there special rules for:	
i) Regular trustee fees? *ii) Advisory or cusodial services to the trustee?* *iii) Accountings, judicial proceedings and other matters that involve both the income and remainder interests?*	See the Uniform Principal and Income Act (1997) chart. (18-A § 7-761; 18-A § 7-762)

iv) Debts?	See the Uniform Principal and Income Act (1997) chart. (18-A § 7-761(c); 18-A § 7-762(a)(3))
c) Can the trustee determine what are "transmission" expenses and "management" expenses?	
9. With regard to specific gifts from a trust after an income interest ends or from an estate:	
a) What amounts must be paid from income and principal?	See the Uniform Principal and Income Act (1997) chart. (18-A § 7-721(a); 18-A § 7-721(e))
10. With regard to outright pecuniary gifts from an estate or trust?:	
a) Does interest accrue?	Yes. See the Uniform Principal and Income Act (1997) chart. (18-A § 7-721(c))
11. With regard to a gift in trust of a pecuniary amount from an estate or trust?	
a) Does interest accrue?	No. See the Uniform Principal and Income Act (1997) chart. (18-A § 7-721(d); 18-A § 7-722)
12. With regard to residuary gifts:	
a) What amount of income and principal is to be paid to the residuary beneficiary of a trust or an estate?	See the Uniform Principal and Income Act (1997) chart. (18-A § 7-721(d); 18-A § 7-722)
13. With regard to "business assets" held in trust:	
a) Can the trustee treat them as a separate entity?	Generally yes. See the Uniform Principal and Income Act (1997) chart. (18-A § 7-743)
b) Can the trustee treat distinct assets as separate entities?	Generally yes. See the Uniform Principal and Income Act (1997) chart. (18-A § 7-743)
c) Can earnings be retained in trust for the reasonable needs of the "business entity," and, if so, to what extent is this permitted?	See the Uniform Principal and Income Act (1997) chart. (18-A § 7-743(b))
14. With respect to discount bonds:	
a) To what extent is the discount added to income or principal upon maturity?	See the Uniform Principal and Income Act (1997) chart. (18-A § 7-746(b))
b) Does the trustee have discretion to allocate discount between income and principal?	No. (18-A § 7-746) ***Note:*** The trustee has overriding power to adjust under 18-A § 7-704.
c) Are distinctions drawn between Series E bonds and others?	No. (18-A § 7-746)

d) Are distinctions drawn based on the maturity date of the bond?	Yes. (18-A § 7-746)
15. Is there a de minimis rule excusing the trustee from making adjustments in certain cases?	Yes. (18-A § 7-748)
16. With respect to derivatives:	
a) May income and loss be treated as that of a separate entity?	Yes. (18-A § 7-754; 18-A § 7-743)
b) If not, or the trustee chooses not to do so, is income and loss allocated to the income account or to principal?	To principal. (18-A § 7-754(b))
17. To the extent put and call options are not derivatives, how are they allocated in terms of principal and income?	To principal. (18-A § 7-754(c))
18. How are asset-backed securities allocated in terms of principal and income?	See the Uniform Principal and Income Act (1997) chart. (18-A § 7-755)
19. Are expenses incurred to comply with environmental requirements allocated to income or principal?	Generally to principal. See the Uniform Principal and Income Act (1997) chart. (18-A § 7-762(a)(7))
20. Is income tax liability allocated generally to income or principal?	See the Uniform Principal and Income Act (1997) chart. (18-A § 7-765; 18-A § 7-766)
21. If a Subchapter S shareholder's or partner's portion of tax liability is greater than cash distributed, how is the excess obligation allocated?	From principal. (18-A § 7-765(c)(2)(ii))
22. What is the standard, if any, for making equitable adjustments between income and principal?	See the Uniform Principal and Income Act (1997) chart. (18-A § 7-703(b))
23. Is an income beneficiary entitled to receive income accrued but unpaid when an estate ends?	No. (18-A § 7-733)
24. Is an income beneficiary entitled to receive income accrued but unpaid when a revocable trust ends?	Generally no. See the Uniform Principal and Income Act (1997) chart. (18-A § 7-733)
25. Is an income beneficiary entitled to receive income accrued but unpaid when an irrevocable trust ends?	Generally no. See the Uniform Principal and Income Act (1997) chart. (18-A § 7-733)
26. With regard to mutual funds, how are:	
a) long-term gains allocated between income and principal?	See the Uniform Principal and Income Act (1997) chart. (18-A § 7-741(c)(4))
b) short-term gains allocated between income and principal?	See the Uniform Principal and Income Act (1997) chart. (18-A § 7-741(c)(4))

27. How are distributions from REITs allocated between income and principal?	See the Uniform Principal and Income Act (1997) chart. (18-A § 7-741(c)(4))
28. With respect to underproductive property:	
a) Is an adjustment, e.g., "delayed income," required to be paid to the income beneficiary?	No. (18-A § 7-753)
b) What percentage return makes property underproductive?	The statute only refers to property not productive of income. (18-A § 7-753)
29. Is the trustee required to increase income so that it is sufficient to qualify for the marital deduction?	Yes. (18-A § 7-753)
30. Is the trustee required to take depreciation?	No. (18-A § 7-763)
31. Is the trustee's determination on allocations generally presumed to be fair and reasonable?	Yes. (18-A § 7-703(b))
32. If an item is not addressed in the trust agreement or in the law, must it be allocated to principal or income?	To principal. (18-A § 7-703(a)(4))
33. When does an asset become subject to a trust:	
a) In the case of transfers during the transferor's life?	The date of transfer. (18-A § 7-731(b)(1))
b) In the case of a will?	The date of the testator's death. (18-A § 7-731(b)(2))
c) In the case of the death of a third party?	The date of the third party's death. (18-A § 7-731(b)(3))
34. Can a trustee rely on the characterization by an entity as to the source or character of a received distribution?	Yes. (18-A § 7-741(f))

Table 12.02
Maryland
Trust Accounting: Principal and Income

1. *Does the trustee have the power to transfer income to principal or to transfer principal to income to meet its duty of impartiality?*	The Maryland Principal and Income Act does not have a provision that grants the trustee the power to transfer income to principal or to transfer from principal to income to meet its duty of impartiality.
2. *What is the effective date for the law? E.g., does it apply to preexisting trusts?*	The Maryland Principal and Income Act applies to each trust or decedent's estate existing on October 1, 2000, except as otherwise expressly provided in the will or terms of the trust or under the Maryland Principal and Income Act. (2000 Md. Sess. Laws 292) ***Note:*** A trustee may continue using a former allocation method to allocate receipts for water, minerals, other natural resources, and timber under certain circumstances. (See Est. & Trusts § 15-518; Est. & Trusts § 15-519)
3. *What percentage is allocated to income and principal from proceeds of:*	
a) *IRA?* b) *Qualified pension or profit-sharing plan?* c) *Other deferred compensation arrangement?*	See the Uniform Principal and Income Act (1997) chart. (Est. & Trusts § 15-516)
4. *What percentage is allocated to income and principal from proceeds of:*	
a) *Patents?* b) *Copyrights?*	See the Uniform Principal and Income Act (1997) chart. (Est. & Trusts § 15-517)
5. *What percentage is allocated to income and principal in the event of distributions from:*	
a) *Corporations?* b) *Partnerships?* c) *LLCs?*	See the Uniform Principal and Income Act (1997) chart. (Est. & Trusts § 15-508) ***Note***: Est. & Trusts § 15-508(f) contains additional language concerning regulated investment companies and investment funds. This provision allows the trustee to make an irrevocable election under which the trustee will pay an amount, determined by a formula, to income. This provision is similar in character to a unitrust.
6. *What percentage is allocated to income and principal from proceeds of:*	
a) *Oil and gas?* b) *Minerals?* c) *Water?* d) *Other natural resourses (not including timber)?*	See the Uniform Principal and Income Act (1997) chart. (Est. & Trusts § 15-518) ***Note***: If a trust owns an interest in minerals, water or other natural resources on October 1, 2000, the trustee may allocate receipts from the interest as provided in the Maryland Principal and Income Act or in the manner used by the trustee before October 1, 2000.
e) *Timber?*	See the Uniform Principal and Income Act (1997) chart. (Est. & Trusts § 15-519)

	Note: If a trust owns an interest in timberland on October 1, 2000, the trustee may allocate receipts from the interest as provided in the Maryland Principal and Income Act or in the manner used by the trustee before October 1, 2000.
f) Rental properties?	See the Uniform Principal and Income Act (1997) chart. (Est. & Trusts § 15-512)
7. After a decedent dies, in the case of an estate, or after an income interest ends, when the fiduciary is determining the remaining net income what are the rules regarding payment from income or principal for:	
a) Attorneys fees? *b) Accountants fees?* *c) Fiduciary fees and commissions?* *d) Court costs?* *e) Interest on death taxes*	See the Uniform Principal and Income Act (1997) chart. (Est. & Trusts § 15-503(2)(ii))
f) Debts? *g) Funeral expenses?* *h) Family allowances and similar protections?* *i) Death taxes?* *j) Penalties on death taxes?*	See the Uniform Principal and Income Act (1997) chart. (Est. & Trusts § 15-503(2)(iii))
8. With respect to trust expenses from the administration of the trust that are not covered by Est. & Trusts § 15-503(2)(ii-iii) [see Question #7]:	
a) Does the trustee have full discretion in allocating between income and principal for expenses incurred in the administration of the trust?	No. (Est. & Trusts § 15-523; Est. & Trusts § 15-524)
b) If not, are there special rules for:	
i) Regular trustee fees? *ii) Advisory or cusodial services to the trustee?* *iii) Accountings, judicial proceedings and other matters that involve both the income and remainder interests?*	See Est. & Trusts § 15-523 & Est. & Trusts § 15-524 regarding the portion of trustee fees that are to be paid from principal and income. The trustee has discretion on whether to pay for custodial and advisory services from income or principal. (Est. & Trusts § 15-523; Est. & Trusts § 15-524) All expenses for accountings, judicial proceedings and other matters that involve both the income and remainder interests must be paid one half from income and one half from principal. (Est. & Trusts § 15-523; Est. & Trusts § 15-524)
iv) Debts?	See the Uniform Principal and Income Act (1997) chart. (Est. & Trusts § 15-523(4); Est. & Trusts § 15-524(a)(5))
c) Can the trustee determine what are "transmission" expenses and "management" expenses?	

9. *With regard to specific gifts from a trust after an income interest ends or from an estate:*	
a) *What amounts must be paid from income and principal?*	See the Uniform Principal and Income Act (1997) chart. (Est. & Trusts § 15-503(1); Est. & Trusts § 15-503(4)) Est. & Trusts § 15-503(1) contains additional provisions: If the income and principal receipts from the specific property are not sufficient to pay the taxes, ordinary repairs, and other expenses of management and operation relating to the property, or if there are no income or principal receipts, then expenses in excess of income and principal receipts must be charged to the beneficiary.
10. *With regard to outright pecuniary gifts from an estate or trust?:*	
a) *Does interest accrue?*	The Maryland Principal and Income Act does not specifically address whether interest accrues with regard to an outright pecuniary gift. (Est. & Trusts § 15-503)
11. *With regard to a gift in trust of a pecuniary amount from an estate or trust?*	
a) *Does interest accrue?*	No. See the Uniform Principal and Income Act (1997) chart. (Est. & Trusts § 15-503(3); Est. & Trusts § 15-504)
12. *With regard to residuary gifts:*	
a) *What amount of income and principal is to be paid to the residuary beneficiary of a trust or an estate?*	See the Uniform Principal and Income Act (1997) chart. (Est. & Trusts § 15-503(3); Est. & Trusts § 15-504)
13. *With regard to "business assets" held in trust:*	
a) *Can the trustee treat them as a separate entity?*	Generally yes. See the Uniform Principal and Income Act (1997) chart. (Est. & Trusts § 15-510)
b) *Can the trustee treat distinct assets as separate entities?*	Generally yes. See the Uniform Principal and Income Act (1997) chart. (Est. & Trusts § 15-510)
c) *Can earnings be retained in trust for the reasonable needs of the "business entity," and, if so, to what extent is this permitted?*	Yes. See the Uniform Principal and Income Act (1997) chart. (Est. & Trusts § 15-510).
14. *With respect to discount bonds:*	
a) *To what extent is the discount added to income or principal upon maturity?*	See the Uniform Principal and Income Act (1997) chart. (Est. & Trusts § 15-513)
b) *Does the trustee have discretion to allocate discount between income and principal?*	No. (Est. & Trusts § 15-513)
c) *Are distinctions drawn between Series E bonds and others?*	No. (Est. & Trusts § 15-513)

d) *Are distinctions drawn based on the maturity date of the bond?*	Yes. (Est. & Trusts § 15-513)
15. *Is there a de minimis rule excusing the trustee from making adjustments in certain cases?*	Yes. (Est. & Trusts § 15-515)
16. *With respect to derivatives:*	
a) *May income and loss be treated as that of a separate entity?*	Yes. (Est. & Trusts § 15-521(b); Est. & Trusts § 15-510)
b) *If not, or the trustee chooses not to do so, is income and loss allocated to the income account or to principal?*	To principal. (Est. & Trusts § 15-521(b))
17. *To the extent put and call options are not derivatives, how are they allocated in terms of principal and income?*	To principal. (Est. & Trusts § 15-521(c))
18. *How are asset-backed securities allocated in terms of principal and income?*	See the Uniform Principal and Income Act (1997) chart. (Est. & Trusts § 15-522)
19. *Are expenses incurred to comply with environmental requirements allocated to income or principal?*	Generally to principal. See the Uniform Principal and Income Act (1997) chart. (Est. & Trusts § 15-524(a)(9))
20. *Is income tax liability allocated generally to income or principal?*	See the Uniform Principal and Income Act (1997) chart. (Est. & Trusts § 15-527; Est. & Trusts § 15-528)
21. *If a Subchapter S shareholder's or partner's portion of tax liability is greater than cash distributed, how is the excess obligation allocated?*	To principal. (Est. & Trusts § 15-527(c)(2)(ii))
22. *What is the standard, if any, for making equitable adjustments between income and principal?*	The Maryland Principal and Income Act does not permit equitable adjustment between income and principal.
23. *Is an income beneficiary entitled to receive income accrued but unpaid when an estate ends?*	No. (Est. & Trusts § 15-507)
24. *Is an income beneficiary entitled to receive income accrued but unpaid when a revocable trust ends?*	Generally no. See the Uniform Principal and Income Act (1997) chart. (Est. & Trusts § 15-507)
25. *Is an income beneficiary entitled to receive income accrued but unpaid when an irrevocable trust ends?*	Generally no. See the Uniform Principal and Income Act (1997) chart. (Est. & Trusts § 15-507)
26. *With regard to mutual funds, how are:*	
a) *long-term gains allocated between income and principal?*	See the Uniform Principal and Income Act (1997) chart. (Est. & Trusts § 15-508(c)(4))
b) *short-term gains allocated between income and principal?*	See the Uniform Principal and Income Act (1997) chart. (Est. & Trusts § 15-508(c)(4))

27. How are distributions from REITs allocated between income and principal?	See the Uniform Principal and Income Act (1997) chart. (Est. & Trusts § 15-508(c)(4))
28. With respect to underproductive property:	
a) Is an adjustment, e.g., "delayed income," required to be paid to the income beneficiary?	See the Uniform Principal and Income Act (1997) chart. (Est. & Trusts § 15-520)
b) What percentage return makes property underproductive?	The statute only refers to property not productive of income. (Est. & Trusts § 15-520)
29. Is the trustee required to increase income so that it is sufficient to qualify for the marital deduction?	Yes. (Est. & Trusts § 15-520(a))
30. Is the trustee required to take depreciation?	No. (Est. & Trusts § 15-525)
31. Is the trustee's determination on allocations generally presumed to be fair and reasonable?	Yes. (Est. & Trusts § 15-502(b))
32. If an item is not addressed in the trust agreement or in the law, must it be allocated to principal or income?	To principal. (Est. & Trusts § 15-502(a)(4))
33. When does an asset become subject to a trust:	
a) In the case of transfers during the transferor's life?	The date of transfer. (Est. & Trusts § 15-505(b)(1))
b) In the case of a will?	The date of the testator's death. (Est. & Trusts § 15-505(b)(2))
c) In the case of the death of a third party?	The date of the third party's death. (Est. & Trusts § 15-505(b)(3))
34. Can a trustee rely on the characterization by an entity as to the source or character of a received distribution?	Yes. (Est. & Trusts § 15-508(g))

Table 12.02
Massachusetts
Trust Accounting: Principal and Income

1. *Does the trustee have the power to transfer income to principal or to transfer principal to income to meet its duty of impartiality?*	See the Uniform Principal and Income Act (1997) chart. (203D § 4)
2. *What is the effective date for the law? E.g., does it apply to preexisting trusts?*	The Massachusetts Principal and Income Act applies to every trust or decedent's estate existing on January 1, 2006 except as otherwise expressly provided in the will or terms of the trust or in the Massachusetts Principal and Income Act. (2005 Mass. Acts 129) ***Note:*** A trustee may continue using a former allocation method to allocate receipts for water, minerals, other natural resources, and timber under certain circumstances. (See, 203D § 20; 203D § 21)
3. *What percentage is allocated to income and principal from proceeds of:*	
a) *IRA?* b) *Qualified pension or profit-sharing plan?* c) *Other deferred compensation arrangement?*	See the Uniform Principal and Income Act (1997) chart. (203D § 18)
4. *What percentage is allocated to income and principal from proceeds of:*	
a) *Patents?* b) *Copyrights?*	See the Uniform Principal and Income Act (1997) chart. (203D § 19)
5. *What percentage is allocated to income and principal in the event of distributions from:*	
a) *Corporations?* b) *Partnerships?* c) *LLCs?*	See the Uniform Principal and Income Act (1997) chart. (203D § 10)
6. *What percentage is allocated to income and principal from proceeds of:*	
a) *Oil and gas?* b) *Minerals?* c) *Water?* d) *Other natural resourses (not including timber)?*	See the Uniform Principal and Income Act (1997) chart. (203D § 20) ***Note:*** If a trust owns an interest in minerals, water or other natural resources on January 1, 2006, the trustee may allocate receipts from the interest as provided in the Massachusetts Principal and Income Act or in the manner used by the trustee before January 1, 2006.
e) *Timber?*	See the Uniform Principal and Income Act (1997) chart. (203D § 21) ***Note:*** If a trust owns an interest in timberland on January 1, 2006, the trustee may allocate receipts from the interest as provided in the Massachusetts Principal and Income Act or in the manner used by the trustee before January 1, 2006.

f) Rental properties?	See the Uniform Principal and Income Act (1997) chart. (203D § 14)
7. After a decedent dies, in the case of an estate, or after an income interest ends, when the fiduciary is determining the remaining net income what are the rules regarding payment from income or principal for:	
a) Attorneys fees? *b) Accountants fees?* *c) Fiduciary fees and commissions?* *d) Court costs?* *e) Interest on death taxes*	See the Uniform Principal and Income Act (1997) chart. (203D § 6(2)(ii))
f) Debts? *g) Funeral expenses?* *h) Family allowances and similar protections?* *i) Death taxes?* *j) Penalties on death taxes?*	See the Uniform Principal and Income Act (1997) chart. (203D § 6(2)(iii))
8. With respect to trust expenses from the administration of the trust that are not covered by 203D § 6(2)(ii-iii) [see Question #7]:	
a) Does the trustee have full discretion in allocating between income and principal for expenses incurred in the administration of the trust?	No. (203D § 25; 203D § 26)
b) If not, are there special rules for:	
i) Regular trustee fees? *ii) Advisory or cusodial services to the trustee?* *iii) Accountings, judicial proceedings and other matters that involve both the income and remainder interests?*	The Trustee has discretion on whether to disburse from income or principal amounts paid for the regular compensation of the trustee, amounts paid to any person providing investment advisory or custodial services, and expenses for accountings, judicial proceedings or other matters that involve both the income and remainder interests as shall be determined by the trustee. (203D § 25; 203D § 26)
iv) Debts?	The trustee must allocate interest expense on trust debt to income and must allocate payments on principal of trust debt to principal. (203D § 25(2); 203D § 26(a)(3))
c) Can the trustee determine what are "transmission" expenses and "management" expenses?	
9. With regard to specific gifts from a trust after an income interest ends or from an estate:	

a) What amounts must be paid from income and principal?	See the Uniform Principal and Income Act (1997) chart. (203D § 6(1); 203D § 6(5))
10. With regard to outright pecuniary gifts from an estate or trust?:	
a) Does interest accrue?	Yes. See the Uniform Principal and Income Act (1997) chart. (203D § 6(3))
11. With regard to a gift in trust of a pecuniary amount from an estate or trust?	
a) Does interest accrue?	No. See the Uniform Principal and Income Act (1997) chart. (203D § 6(4). 203D § 7)
12. With regard to residuary gifts:	
a) What amount of income and principal is to be paid to the residuary beneficiary of a trust or an estate?	See the Uniform Principal and Income Act (1997) chart. (203D § 6(4). 203D § 7)
13. With regard to "business assets" held in trust:	
a) Can the trustee treat them as a separate entity?	Yes. See the Uniform Principal and Income Act (1997) chart. (203D § 12(a))
b) Can the trustee treat distinct assets as separate entities?	Yes. See the Uniform Principal and Income Act (1997) chart. (203D § 12(a))
c) Can earnings be retained in trust for the reasonable needs of the "business entity," and, if so, to what extent is this permitted?	See the Uniform Principal and Income Act (1997) chart. (203D § 12(b))
14. With respect to discount bonds:	
a) To what extent is the discount added to income or principal upon maturity?	The Massachusetts Principal and Income Act does not discuss discount bonds or other obligations to pay money. Therefore, the discount should be added to principal. (203D § 15; 203D § 3(a)(4))
b) Does the trustee have discretion to allocate discount between income and principal?	No. (203D § 15). *Note:* The trustee has the overriding power to adjust under (203D § 4(a))
c) Are distinctions drawn between Series E bonds and others?	No. (203D § 15)
d) Are distinctions drawn based on the maturity date of the bond?	No. (203D § 15)
15. Is there a de minimis rule excusing the trustee from making adjustments in certain cases?	Yes. See the Uniform Principal and Income Act (1997) chart. (203D § 17)
16. With respect to derivatives:	

a) May income and loss be treated as that of a separate entity?	Yes. (203D § 23(a); 203D § 12)
b) If not, or the trustee chooses not to do so, is income and loss allocated to the income account or to principal?	To principal. (203D § 23(a))
17. To the extent put and call options are not derivatives, how are they allocated in terms of principal and income?	To principal. (203D § 23(b))
18. How are asset-backed securities allocated in terms of principal and income?	See the Uniform Principal and Income Act (1997) chart. (203D § 24)
19. Are expenses incurred to comply with environmental requirements allocated to income or principal?	Generally to principal. See the Uniform Principal and Income Act (1997) chart. (203D § 26(a)(7))
20. Is income tax liability allocated generally to income or principal?	See the Uniform Principal and Income Act (1997) chart. (203D § 29) ***Note***: The Massachusetts Principal and Income Act does not have a section similar to Uniform Principal and Income Act § 506, which allows for adjustments between principal and income because of taxes.
21. If a Subchapter S shareholder's or partner's portion of tax liability is greater than cash distributed, how is the excess obligation allocated?	From principal. (203D § 29(c)(2)(ii))
22. What is the standard, if any, for making equitable adjustments between income and principal?	See the Uniform Principal and Income Act (1997) chart. (203D § 3(b))
23. Is an income beneficiary entitled to receive income accrued but unpaid when an estate ends?	No. See the Uniform Principal and Income Act (1997) chart. (203D § 9; 203D § 2 ("undistributed income"))
24. Is an income beneficiary entitled to receive income accrued but unpaid when a revocable trust ends?	Generally no. See the Uniform Principal and Income Act (1997) chart. (203D § 9; 203D § 2 ("undistributed income"))
25. Is an income beneficiary entitled to receive income accrued but unpaid when an irrevocable trust ends?	Generally no. See the Uniform Principal and Income Act (1997) chart. (203D § 9; 203D § 2 ("undistributed income"))
26. With regard to mutual funds, how are:	
a) long-term gains allocated between income and principal?	See the Uniform Principal and Income Act (1997) chart. (203D § 10(b)(4))
b) short-term gains allocated between income and principal?	See the Uniform Principal and Income Act (1997) chart. (203D § 10(b)(4))
27. How are distributions from REITs allocated between income and principal?	See the Uniform Principal and Income Act (1997) chart. (203D § 10(b)(4))

28. With respect to underproductive property:	
a) Is an adjustment, e.g., "delayed income," required to be paid to the income beneficiary?	No. (203D § 22)
b) What percentage return makes property underproductive?	The statute only refers to property not productive of income. (203D § 22)
29. Is the trustee required to increase income so that it is sufficient to qualify for the marital deduction?	Yes. (203D § 22(a))
30. Is the trustee required to take depreciation?	No. (203D § 27)
31. Is the trustee's determination on allocations generally presumed to be fair and reasonable?	Yes. (203D § 3(b))
32. If an item is not addressed in the trust agreement or in the law, must it be allocated to principal or income?	To principal. (203D § 3(a)(4))
33. When does an asset become subject to a trust:	
a) In the case of transfers during the transferor's life?	The date of transfer. (203D § 8(b)(1))
b) In the case of a will?	The date of the testator's death. (203D § 8(b)(2))
c) In the case of the death of a third party?	The date of the third party's death. (203D § 8(b)(3))
34. Can a trustee rely on the characterization by an entity as to the source or character of a received distribution?	Yes. (203D § 10(c))

Table 12.02
Michigan
Trust Accounting: Principal and Income

1. *Does the trustee have the power to transfer income to principal or to transfer principal to income to meet its duty of impartiality?*	Yes. See the Uniform Principal and Income Act (1997) chart. (§ 555.504(1))
2. *What is the effective date for the law? E.g., does it apply to preexisting trusts?*	The Michigan Principal and Income Act applies to each trust or decedent's estate existing on September 1, 2004 except as otherwise expressly provided in the will or terms of the trust or by the Michigan Principal and Income Act. (§ 555.1005) ***Note:*** A trustee may continue using a former allocation method to allocate receipts for water, minerals, other natural resources, and timber under certain circumstances. (See, § 555.811; § 555.812)
3. *What percentage is allocated to income and principal from proceeds of:*	
a) IRA? *b) Qualified pension or profit-sharing plan?* *c) Other deferred compensation arrangement?*	See the Uniform Principal and Income Act (1997) chart. (§ 555.809)
4. *What percentage is allocated to income and principal from proceeds of:*	
a) Patents? *b) Copyrights?*	See the Uniform Principal and Income Act (1997) chart. (§ 555.810)
5. *What percentage is allocated to income and principal in the event of distributions from:*	
a) Corporations? *b) Partnerships?* *c) LLCs?*	See the Uniform Principal and Income Act (1997) chart. (§ 555.801)
6. *What percentage is allocated to income and principal from proceeds of:*	
a) Oil and gas? *b) Minerals?* *c) Water?* *d) Other natural resourses (not including timber)?*	See the Uniform Principal and Income Act (1997) chart. (§ 555.811) ***Note:*** If a trust owns an interest in minerals, water or other natural resources on September 1, 2004, the trustee may allocate receipts from the interest as provided in the Michigan Principal and Income Act or in the manner used by the trustee before September 1, 2004.
e) Timber?	See the Uniform Principal and Income Act (1997) chart. (§ 555.812) ***Note:*** If a trust owns an interest in timberland on September 1, 2004, the trustee may allocate receipts from the interest as provided in the Michigan Principal and Income Act or in the manner used by the trustee before September 1, 2004.
f) Rental properties?	See the Uniform Principal and Income Act (1997) chart. (§ 555.805)

7. *After a decedent dies, in the case of an estate, or after an income interest ends, when the fiduciary is determining the remaining net income what are the rules regarding payment from income or principal for:*	
a) *Attorneys fees?* b) *Accountants fees?* c) *Fiduciary fees and commissions?* d) *Court costs?* e) *Interest on death taxes*	See the Uniform Principal and Income Act (1997) chart. (§ 555.601(b)(ii))
f) *Debts?* g) *Funeral expenses?* h) *Family allowances and similar protections?* i) *Death taxes?* j) *Penalties on death taxes?*	See the Uniform Principal and Income Act (1997) chart. (§ 555.601(b)(iii))
8. *With respect to trust expenses from the administration of the trust that are not covered by (§ 555.601(b)(ii-iii) [see Question #7]:*	
a) *Does the trustee have full discretion in allocating between income and principal for expenses incurred in the administration of the trust?*	No. (§ 555.901; § 555.902)
b) *If not, are there special rules for:*	
i) *Regular trustee fees?* ii) *Advisory or cusodial services to the trustee?* iii) *Accountings, judicial proceedings and other matters that involve both the income and remainder interests?*	See the Uniform Principal and Income Act (1997) chart. (§ 555.901; § 555.902)
iv) *Debts?*	See the Uniform Principal and Income Act (1997) chart. (§ 555.901(c); § 555.902(1)(c))
c) *Can the trustee determine what are "transmission" expenses and "management" expenses?*	
9. *With regard to specific gifts from a trust after an income interest ends or from an estate:*	
a) *What amounts must be paid from income and principal?*	See the Uniform Principal and Income Act (1997) chart. (§ 555.601(a); § 555.601(e))
10. *With regard to outright pecuniary gifts from an estate or trust?:*	

a) Does interest accrue?	Yes. See the Uniform Principal and Income Act (1997) chart. (§ 555.601(c))
11. With regard to a gift in trust of a pecuniary amount from an estate or trust?	
a) Does interest accrue?	No. See the Uniform Principal and Income Act (1997) chart. (§ 555.601(d); § 555.602)
12. With regard to residuary gifts:	
a) What amount of income and principal is to be paid to the residuary beneficiary of a trust or an estate?	See the Uniform Principal and Income Act (1997) chart. (§ 555.601(d); § 555.602)
13. With regard to "business assets" held in trust:	
a) Can the trustee treat them as a separate entity?	Generally yes. See the Uniform Principal and Income Act (1997) chart. (§ 555.803)
b) Can the trustee treat distinct assets as separate entities?	Generally yes. See the Uniform Principal and Income Act (1997) chart. (§ 555.803)
c) Can earnings be retained in trust for the reasonable needs of the "business entity," and, if so, to what extent is this permitted?	See the Uniform Principal and Income Act (1997) chart. (§ 555.803)
14. With respect to discount bonds:	
a) To what extent is the discount added to income or principal upon maturity?	See the Uniform Principal and Income Act (1997) chart. (§ 555.806(2))
b) Does the trustee have discretion to allocate discount between income and principal?	No. (§ 555.806) ***Note:*** The trustee has overriding power to adjust under § 555.504.
c) Are distinctions drawn between Series E bonds and others?	No. (§ 555.806)
d) Are distinctions drawn based on the maturity date of the bond?	Yes. (§ 555.806(b))
15. Is there a de minimis rule excusing the trustee from making adjustments in certain cases?	Yes. See the Uniform Principal and Income Act (1997) chart. (§ 555.808)
16. With respect to derivatives:	
a) May income and loss be treated as that of a separate entity?	Yes. (§ 555.803; § 555.814)
b) If not, or the trustee chooses not to do so, is income and loss allocated to the income account or to principal?	To principal. (§ 555.814(2))

17. To the extent put and call options are not derivatives, how are they allocated in terms of principal and income?	To principal. (§ 555.814(3))
18. How are asset-backed securities allocated in terms of principal and income?	See the Uniform Principal and Income Act (1997) chart. (§ 555.815)
19. Are expenses incurred to comply with environmental requirements allocated to income or principal?	Generally to principal. See the Uniform Principal and Income Act (1997) chart. (§ 555.902(1)(g))
20. Is income tax liability allocated generally to income or principal?	See the Uniform Principal and Income Act (1997) chart. (§ 555.905; § 555.906)
21. If a Subchapter S shareholder's or partner's portion of tax liability is greater than cash distributed, how is the excess obligation allocated?	From principal. (§ 555.905(3)(b)(ii))
22. What is the standard, if any, for making equitable adjustments between income and principal?	See the Uniform Principal and Income Act (1997) chart. (§ 555.503(3))
23. Is an income beneficiary entitled to receive income accrued but unpaid when an estate ends?	No. (§ 555.703)
24. Is an income beneficiary entitled to receive income accrued but unpaid when a revocable trust ends?	Generally no. See the Uniform Principal and Income Act (1997) chart. (§ 555.703)
25. Is an income beneficiary entitled to receive income accrued but unpaid when an irrevocable trust ends?	Generally no. See the Uniform Principal and Income Act (1997) chart. (§ 555.703)
26. With regard to mutual funds, how are:	
a) long-term gains allocated between income and principal?	See the Uniform Principal and Income Act (1997) chart. (§ 555.801(3)(d))
b) short-term gains allocated between income and principal?	See the Uniform Principal and Income Act (1997) chart. (§ 555.801(3)(d))
27. How are distributions from REITs allocated between income and principal?	See the Uniform Principal and Income Act (1997) chart. (§ 555.801(3)(d))
28. With respect to underproductive property:	
a) Is an adjustment, e.g., "delayed income," required to be paid to the income beneficiary?	No. (§ 555.813)
b) What percentage return makes property underproductive?	The statute only refers to property not productive of income. (§ 555.813)
29. Is the trustee required to increase income so that it is sufficient to qualify for the marital deduction?	Yes. (§ 555.813)

30. Is the trustee required to take depreciation?	No. (§ 555.903)
31. Is the trustee's determination on allocations generally presumed to be fair and reasonable?	Yes. (§ 555.503(3))
32. If an item is not addressed in the trust agreement or in the law, must it be allocated to principal or income?	To principal. (§ 555.503(1)(c))
33. When does an asset become subject to a trust:	
a) In the case of transfers during the transferor's life?	The date of transfer. (§ 555.701(2)(a))
b) In the case of a will?	The date of the testator's death. (§ 555.701(2)(b)).
c) In the case of the death of a third party?	The date of the third party's death. (§ 555.701(2)(c)).
34. Can a trustee rely on the characterization by an entity as to the source or character of a received distribution?	Yes. (§ 555.801(6)).

Table 12.02
Minnesota
Trust Accounting: Principal and Income

1. *Does the trustee have the power to transfer income to principal or to transfer principal to income to meet its duty of impartiality?*	See the Uniform Principal and Income Act (1997) chart. (§ 501B.705)
2. *What is the effective date for the law? E.g., does it apply to preexisting trusts?*	Except as specifically provided in the governing instrument, § 501.48 through § 501.63, apply to a receipt or expense received or incurred after January 1, 1970, and before January 1, 1990, by any trust or decedent's estate whether established before or after January 1, 1970, and whether the asset involved was acquired by the trustee before or after January 1, 1970. Except as specifically provided in the governing instrument, § 501B.59 through § 501B.76 apply to a receipt or expense received or incurred after December 31, 1989, by a trust or decedent's estate whether established before, on, or after January 1, 1990, and whether the asset involved or legal estate was acquired by the trustee, personal representative, legal life tenant, or remainderperson before, on, or after January 1, 1990. (§ 501B.73)
3. *What percentage is allocated to income and principal from proceeds of:*	
a) *IRA?* b) *Qualified pension or profit-sharing plan?* c) *Other deferred compensation arrangement?*	The trustee must allocate the receipts from the property in accordance with what is reasonable and equitable in view of the interests of those entitled to income and those entitled to principal. To the extent that a payment is characterized by the payer as interest or a dividend or a payment made in lieu of interest or a dividend, a trustee must allocate it to income. The amount allocated to principal is presumed to be reasonable and equitable if it is neither substantially more nor less than the amount allowable as a deduction for depletion, amortization, depreciation, or similar costs under the Internal Revenue Code of 1986. (§ 501B.69)
4. *What percentage is allocated to income and principal from proceeds of:*	
a) *Patents?* b) *Copyrights?*	The trustee must allocate the receipts from the property in accordance with what is reasonable and equitable in view of the interests of those entitled to income and those entitled to principal. To the extent that a payment is characterized by the payer as interest or a dividend or a payment made in lieu of interest or a dividend, a trustee must allocate it to income. The amount allocated to principal is presumed to be reasonable and equitable if it is neither substantially more nor less than the amount allowable as a deduction for depletion, amortization, depreciation, or similar costs under the Internal Revenue Code of 1986. (§ 501B.69)
5. *What percentage is allocated to income and principal in the event of distributions from:*	

a) Corporations? *b) Partnerships?* *c) LLCs?*	Distributions of shares of a distributing corporation or similar equity ownership interests in noncorporate entities, including distributions in the form of or equivalent to a stock split or stock dividend, are principal. An entity owner's right to subscribe to shares, ownership interests, or other securities of the distributing entity and the proceeds of any sale of that right are principal. Except for distributions from regulated investment companies, real estate investment trusts, and pass through entities, and except to the extent that the entity indicates that some part of an entity distribution is a settlement of preferred or guaranteed corporate dividends or distribution preferences based upon a return on invested capital accrued under the governing instrument since the trustee acquired the related ownership interest or is in lieu of an ordinary cash dividend or similar distribution from current earnings of the entity, an entity distribution is principal if the distribution is pursuant to: (0) redemption of the ownership interest or a call of shares; (1) a merger, consolidation, reorganization, or other plan by which assets of the entity are acquired by another entity; or (2) a total or partial liquidation of the entity, including a distribution the entity indicates is a distribution in total or partial liquidation or distribution of assets, other than cash, pursuant to a court decree or final administrative order by a government agency ordering distribution of the particular assets. Distributions made from ordinary income by a regulated investment company or by real estate investment trust are income. All other distributions made by the company or trust, including distributions from capital gains, depreciation, or depletion, whether in the form of cash or an option to take new stock or cash or an option to purchase additional shares, are principal. Distributions from pass-through entities must be allocated between income and principal as reasonably and equitably determined by the trustee for any accounting period during which an entity is a pass-through entity for all or any portion of the accounting period. Except as provided in the preceding paragraphs, all distributions from entities are income. (§ 501B.64)
6. What percentage is allocated to income and principal from proceeds of:	
a) Oil and gas? *b) Minerals?* *c) Water?* *d) Other natural resourses (not including timber)?*	If a part of the principal consists of a right to receive royalties, overriding or limited royalties, working interests, production payments, net profit interests, or other interests in minerals or other natural resources in, on, or under land, the receipts from taking the natural resources from the land must be allocated as follows: (a) If receipts are for rent on a lease or extension payments on a lease, the receipts are income. (b) If receipts are from a production payment carved out of a mineral property, the receipts are income to the extent of a factor for interest or its equivalent provided

	in the governing instrument or a greater amount determined by the trustee to be reasonable and equitable in view of the interests of those entitled to income as well as those entitled to principal. The receipts not allocated to income are principal. (c) If received as a royalty, overriding or limited royalty, or bonus or from a working, net profit, or other interest in minerals or other natural resources, receipts not provided for in the two preceding paragraphs [paragraphs (a) & (b)] must be apportioned on a yearly basis in accordance with this paragraph whether or not any natural resource was being taken from the land at the time the trust was established. The receipts from these properties must be allocated in accordance with what is reasonable and equitable in view of the interests of those entitled to income as well as of those entitled to principal. The amount allocated to principal must be presumed to be reasonable and equitable if it is neither substantially more nor less than the amount allowable as a deduction for depletion, amortization, depreciation, or similar costs under the Internal Revenue Code of 1986. Any allocated amount must be added to principal as an allowance for depletion of the asset. The balance of the gross receipts, after payment from the receipts of all direct and indirect expenses, is income. (§ 501B.67)
e) Timber?	See the Uniform Principal and Income Act (1997) chart. (§ 501B.68)
f) Rental properties?	The trustee must include amounts received from renting real or personal property, including sums received for cancellation or renewal of a lease, as income. (§ 501B.61(1))
7. After a decedent dies, in the case of an estate, or after an income interest ends, when the fiduciary is determining the remaining net income what are the rules regarding payment from income or principal for:	
a) Attorneys fees? *b) Accountants fees?* *c) Fiduciary fees and commissions?* *d) Court costs?* *e) Interest on death taxes*	All expenses incurred in connection with the settlement of a decedent's estate, including debts, funeral expenses, estate taxes, interest and penalties concerning taxes, family allowances, fees of attorneys and personal representatives, and court costs must be charged against the principal of the estate. (§ 501B.63(1))
f) Debts? *g) Funeral expenses?* *h) Family allowances and similar protections?* *i) Death taxes?* *j) Penalties on death taxes?*	All expenses incurred in connection with the settlement of a decedent's estate, including debts, funeral expenses, estate taxes, interest and penalties concerning taxes, family allowances, fees of attorneys and personal representatives, and court costs must be charged against the principal of the estate. (§ 501B.63(1))

8. *With respect to trust expenses from the administration of the trust that are not covered § 501B.63(1) [see Question #7]:*	
a) *Does the trustee have full discretion in allocating between income and principal for expenses incurred in the administration of the trust?*	No. (§ 501B.71)
b) *If not, are there special rules for:*	
i) *Regular trustee fees?* ii) *Advisory or custodial services to the trustee?* iii) *Accountings, judicial proceedings and other matters that involve both the income and remainder interests?*	Generally, the following charges must be made against income: 1. one-half of the court costs, attorneys' fees, and other fees on periodic accountings or judicial proceedings, unless the court directs otherwise; 2. court costs, attorneys' fees, and other fees on other accountings or judicial proceedings if the matter primarily concerns the income interest, unless the court directs otherwise; and 3. one-half of the trustee's regular compensation for services performed for the income beneficiary or in the production of income whether based on a percentage of principal or income, and all expenses reasonably incurred for current management of principal and application of income. The following charges must be made against principal: 1. one-half of the trustee's regular compensation, court costs and attorneys' fees primarily concerning matters of principal; 2. expenses incurred in maintaining or defending any action to construe the trust or protect it or the property or assure the title of any trust property. (§ 501B.71) ***Note:*** § 501B.71 contains many other special rules for allocations and contains many exceptions. Consult the statute.
iv) *Debts?*	The trustee must allocate interest expense on trust debt to income and must allocate payments on principal of trust debt to principal. (§ 501B.71)
c) *Can the trustee determine what are "transmission" expenses and "management" expenses?*	
9. *With regard to specific gifts from a trust after an income interest ends or from an estate:*	
a) *What amounts must be paid from income and principal?*	The fiduciary must distribute to a specific devisee or beneficiary, the income from the property devised or distributed to them less property taxes, ordinary repairs, interest, and other expenses of management and operation of the property, and less an appropriate portion of taxes imposed on income, excluding taxes on capital gains, that accrue during the period of administration or after an income interest in a trust terminates. (§ 501B.63)

10. With regard to outright pecuniary gifts from an estate or trust?:	
a) Does interest accrue?	Yes. The fiduciary must pay a beneficiary who receives a pecuniary amount outright, the interest or any other amount provided by the will, the terms of the trust instrument or applicable law from income determined in accordance with the rules applicable to a trustee or, to the extent income is insufficient, from principal. If a beneficiary is to receive a pecuniary amount outright from a trust after an income interest ends and no interest or other amount is provided for by the terms of the trust instrument or applicable law, the trustee shall distribute the interest or other amount to which the beneficiary would be entitled under applicable law if the pecuniary amount were required to be paid under a will. (§ 501B.63)
11. With regard to a gift in trust of a pecuniary amount from an estate or trust?	
a) Does interest accrue?	No. The fiduciary should distribute to any trusts that received a gift of a pecuniary amount and to the remainder beneficiaries the balance of the income, less certain expenses that accrue during the period of administration or after an income interest terminates, in proportion to their respective interests in the undistributed assets of the estate or trust. (§ 501B.63)
12. With regard to residuary gifts:	
a) What amount of income and principal is to be paid to the residuary beneficiary of a trust or an estate?	The fiduciary should distribute to any trusts that received a gift of a pecuniary amount and to the remainder beneficiaries the balance of the income, less certain expenses that accrue during the period of administration or after an income interest terminates, in proportion to their respective interests in the undistributed assets of the estate or trust. (§ 501B.63)
13. With regard to "business assets" held in trust:	
a) Can the trustee treat them as a separate entity?	Yes. A trustee who conducts a business or other activity as a sole proprietor may establish and maintain a separate account for the transactions of the business or other activity, whether or not its assets are segregated from other trust assets, if the trustee determines that it is in the best interest of all the beneficiaries to establish a separate account instead of accounting for the business or other activity as part of the trust's general accounting records. (§ 501B.665)
b) Can the trustee treat distinct assets as separate entities?	Yes. A trustee who conducts a business or other activity as a sole proprietor may establish and maintain a separate account for the transactions of the business or other activity, whether or not its assets are segregated from other trust assets, if the trustee determines that it is in the best interest of all the beneficiaries to establish a separate account instead of accounting for the business or other activity as part of the trust's general accounting records. (§ 501B.665)

c) *Can earnings be retained in trust for the reasonable needs of the "business entity," and, if so, to what extent is this permitted?*	Yes. A trustee who accounts separately for a business or other activity may determine the extent to which cash receipts must be retained for working capital, the acquisition or replacement of fixed assets and the other reasonably forseeable needs of the business or other activity, and the extent to which the remaining cash receipts are accounted for as principal or income in the trust's general accounting records. (§ 501B.665)
14. *With respect to discount bonds:*	
a) *To what extent is the discount added to income or principal upon maturity?*	Any non-zero coupon bonds are principal at their inventory value and no provision may be made for amortization of bond premiums or for accumulation for discount. The proceeds of sale, redemption, or other disposition of non-zero coupon bonds are principal. The increment in value realized upon sale or redemption of a zero coupon bond must be allocated to income. (§ 501B.65)
b) *Does the trustee have discretion to allocate discount between income and principal?*	No. (§ 501B.65) ***Note:*** The trustee has the overriding power to adjust under § 501B.705.
c) *Are distinctions drawn between Series E bonds and others?*	No. (§ 501B.65)
d) *Are distinctions drawn based on the maturity date of the bond?*	No. (§ 501B.65)
15. *Is there a de minimis rule excusing the trustee from making adjustments in certain cases?*	No.
16. *With respect to derivatives:*	
a) *May income and loss be treated as that of a separate entity?*	The Minnesota Principal and Income Act does not address derivatives. (See, § 501B.60(1)(3))
b) *If not, or the trustee chooses not to do so, is income and loss allocated to the income account or to principal?*	The Minnesota Principal and Income Act does not address derivatives. (See § 501B.60(1)(3))
17. *To the extent put and call options are not derivatives, how are they allocated in terms of principal and income?*	The trustee must allocate any amount received or paid for an option and any gain or loss realized from the exercise of an option to principal. (§ 501B.61(2)(10))
18. *How are asset-backed securities allocated in terms of principal and income?*	The Minnesota Principal and Income Act does not address asset-backed securities. (See § 501B.60(1)(3))
19. *Are expenses incurred to comply with environmental requirements allocated to income or principal?*	The Minnesota Principal and Income Act does not address environmental expenses. (See § 501B.60(1)(3))
20. *Is income tax liability allocated generally to income or principal?*	Any tax required to be paid by a fiduciary on the trust's share of an entity's taxable income should be paid from income to the extent that receipts from the entity are allocated to income and from principal to the extent that receipts from the entity are allocated to principal. (§ 501B.71)

21. If a Subchapter S shareholder's or partner's portion of tax liability is greater than cash distributed, how is the excess obligation allocated?	The Minnesota Principal and Income Act does not address this issue.
22. What is the standard, if any, for making equitable adjustments between income and principal?	In exercising the power to adjust, the fiduciary must administer a trust, or decedent's estate impartially, based on what is fair and reasonable to all of the beneficiaries, except to the extent that the terms of the trust or the will clearly manifest an intention that the fiduciary shall or may favor one or more of the beneficiaries. See the Uniform Principal and Income Act (1997) chart. (§ 501B.60)
23. Is an income beneficiary entitled to receive income accrued but unpaid when an estate ends?	On termination of an income interest, the income beneficiary whose interest is terminated, or his estate, is entitled to: Income undistributed on the date of termination; income due but not paid to the trustee on the date of termination and income in the form of periodic payments (other than corporate distributions to stockholders), including rent, interest, or annuities, not due on the date of termination, accrued from day to day. (§ 501B.62)
24. Is an income beneficiary entitled to receive income accrued but unpaid when a revocable trust ends?	On termination of an income interest, the income beneficiary whose interest is terminated, or his estate, is entitled to: Income undistributed on the date of termination; income due but not paid to the trustee on the date of termination and income in the form of periodic payments (other than corporate distributions to stockholders), including rent, interest, or annuities, not due on the date of termination, accrued from day to day. (§ 501B.62)
25. Is an income beneficiary entitled to receive income accrued but unpaid when an irrevocable trust ends?	On termination of an income interest, the income beneficiary whose interest is terminated, or his estate, is entitled to: Income undistributed on the date of termination; income due but not paid to the trustee on the date of termination and income in the form of periodic payments (other than corporate distributions to stockholders), including rent, interest, or annuities, not due on the date of termination, accrued from day to day. (§ 501B.62)
26. With regard to mutual funds, how are:	
a) long-term gains allocated between income and principal?	Distributions made from ordinary income by a regulated investment company are income. All other distributions made by the company, including distributions from capital gains, depreciation, or depletion, whether in the form of cash or an option to take new stock or cash or an option to purchase additional shares, are principal. (§ 501B.64)
b) short-term gains allocated between income and principal?	Distributions made from ordinary income by a regulated investment company are income. All other distributions made by the company, including distributions from capital gains, depreciation, or depletion, whether in the form of cash or an option to take new stock or cash or an option to purchase additional shares, are principal. (§ 501B.64)
27. How are distributions from REITs allocated between income and principal?	Distributions made from ordinary income by a REIT are income. All other distributions made by the REIT, including distributions

	from capital gains, depreciation, or depletion, whether in the form of cash or an option to take new stock or cash or an option to purchase additional shares, are principal. (§ 501B.64)
28. With respect to underproductive property:	
a) Is an adjustment, e.g., "delayed income," required to be paid to the income beneficiary?	The Minnesota Principal and Income Act does not address underproductive property.
b) What percentage return makes property underproductive?	The Minnesota Principal and Income Act does not address underproductive property.
29. Is the trustee required to increase income so that it is sufficient to qualify for the marital deduction?	The Minnesota Principal and Income Act does not address the marital deduction.
30. Is the trustee required to take depreciation?	Yes. (§ 501B.71(1)(2))
31. Is the trustee's determination on allocations generally presumed to be fair and reasonable?	Yes. (§ 501B.60(3))
32. If an item is not addressed in the trust agreement or in the law, must it be allocated to principal or income?	If an item is not addressed in the trust agreement or in the law, the trustee must allocate the item in accordance with what is reasonable and equitable in view of the interests of those entitled to income as well as of those entitled to principal, and in view of the manner in which persons of ordinary prudence, discretion, and judgment would act in the management of their own affairs. (§ 501B.60(1)(3))
33. When does an asset become subject to a trust:	
a) In the case of transfers during the transferor's life?	The asset becomes subject to the trust on the date the asset is transferred to the trust. (§ 501B.62)
b) In the case of a will?	In the case of an asset that becomes subject to a trust because of the death of any person, the asset becomes subject to the trust as of the date of the death of the person or, if later, the date the estate or trust becomes entitled to the asset if acquired after the death of the person, even though there is an intervening period of administration of an estate or trust during which the beneficiary may have no right to a distribution of the income. (§ 501B.62)
c) In the case of the death of a third party?	In the case of an asset that becomes subject to a trust because of the death of any person, the asset becomes subject to the trust as of the date of the death of the person or, if later, the date the estate or trust becomes entitled to the asset if acquired after the death of the person, even though there is an intervening period of administration of an estate or trust during which the beneficiary may have no right to a distribution of the income. (§ 501B.62)
34. Can a trustee rely on the characterization by an entity as to the source or character of a received distribution?	Yes. (§ 501B.64(6))

Table 12.02
Mississippi
Trust Accounting: Principal and Income

1. *Does the trustee have the power to transfer income to principal or to transfer principal to income to meet its duty of impartiality?*	No.
2. *What is the effective date for the law? E.g., does it apply to preexisting trusts?*	Except as specifically provided in the trust instrument or the will or the Mississippi Principal and Income Act, the Mississippi Principal and Income Act applies to any receipt or expense received or incurred after January 1, 1967, by any trust or decedent's estate. The date of the creation of the trust or of the decedent's estate and the acquisition date of any trust assets are immaterial. (§ 91-17-29) However, if the trustee holds a natural resource specified in § 91-17-19 on January 1, 1967, the trustee must allocate the receipts from the property in the same manner as the trustee did before January 1, 1967. (§ 91-17-19(c)(2))
3. *What percentage is allocated to income and principal from proceeds of:*	
a) *IRA?* b) *Qualified pension or profit-sharing plan?* c) *Other deferred compensation arrangement?*	The trustee must allocate the proceeds, up to five percent (5%) per year of its inventory value, to income and the balance to principal. (§ 91-17-23)
4. *What percentage is allocated to income and principal from proceeds of:*	
a) *Patents?* b) *Copyrights?*	The trustee must allocate the proceeds, up to five percent (5%) per year of its inventory value, to income and the balance to principal. (§ 91-17-23)
5. *What percentage is allocated to income and principal in the event of distributions from:*	
a) *Corporations?* b) *Partnerships?* c) *LLCs?*	Corporate distributions of shares of the distributing corporation, including distributions in the form of a stock split or stock dividend, are principal. A right to subscribe to shares or other securities issued by the distributing corporation accruing on account of the ownership of shares or other securities in such corporation and the proceeds of any sale of the right are principal. Except to the extent that the corporation indicates that some part of a corporate distribution is a settlement of preferred or guaranteed dividends accrued since the trustee became a stockholder or is in lieu of an ordinary cash dividend, a corporate distribution is principal if the distribution is pursuant to a call of shares; a merger, consolidation or reorganization; a plan by which assets of the corporation are acquired by another corporation; or a total or partial liquidation of the corporation. Distributions made from ordinary income by a regulated investment company or by a trust qualifying and electing to be taxed under federal law as a real estate investment trust are income. All other distributions made by the company or trust, including

	distributions from capital gains, depreciation or depletion, whether in the form of cash or an option to take new stock or cash or an option to purchase additional shares, are principal. Except as provided in the preceding paragraphs, all corporate distributions are income, including cash dividends, distributions of or rights to subscribe to shares or securities or obligations of corporations other than the distributing corporation, and the proceeds of the rights or property distributions. (§ 91-17-13) ***Note:*** Parnerships and LLC's are not addressed.
6. What percentage is allocated to income and principal from proceeds of:	
a) Oil and gas? *b) Minerals?* *c) Water?* *d) Other natural resourses (not including timber)?*	Receipts for rent on a lease or extension payments on a lease are income. Receipts from a production payment are income to the extent of any factor for interest or its equivalent provided in the governing instrument. The fiduciary must allocate to principal the fraction of the balance of the receipts which the unrecovered cost of the production payments bears to the balance owed on the production payment, exclusive of any factor for interest or its equivalent. The receipts not allocated to principal are income. If received as a royalty, overriding or limited royalty, or bonus, or from a working, net profit, or any other interest in minerals or other natural resources, receipts (not provided for in the two preceding paragraphs) must be apportioned on a yearly basis, whether or not any natural resource was being taken from the land at the time the trust was established. Twenty-seven and one-half per cent (27 1/2%) of the gross receipts (but not to exceed fifty per cent (50%) of the net receipts remaining after payment of all expenses, direct and indirect, computed without allowance for depletion) must be added to principal as an allowance for depletion. The balance of the gross receipts, after payment of all expenses, direct and indirect, is income. If a trustee, on January 1, 1967, held minerals or other natural resources, the trustee must allocate receipts from the property in the manner used before January 1, 1967, but as to all depletable property acquired after January 1, 1967 by an existing or new trust, the method of allocation provided the Mississippi Principal and Income act must be used. (§ 91-17-19) *Note:* These rules are not applicable to proceeds from water.
e) Timber?	The trustee must allocate receipts from the sale of timber in accordance with what is reasonable and equitable in view of the interests of those entitled to income as well as of those entitled to principal, and in view of the manner in which men of ordinary prudence, discretion, and judgment would act in the management of their own affairs. (§ 91-17-21)
f) Rental properties?	The trustee must include amounts received from renting real or personal property, including sums received for cancellation or renewal of a lease, as income. (§ 91-17-7(1)(a))
7. After a decedent dies, in the case of an estate, or after an income interest ends,	

when the fiduciary is determining the remaining net income what are the rules regarding payment from income or principal for:	
a) Attorneys fees? *b) Accountants fees?* *c) Fiduciary fees and commissions?* *d) Court costs?* *e) Interest on death taxes*	The trustee must charge from principal all expenses incurred in connection with the settlement of a decedent's estate, including debts, funeral expenses, estate taxes, interest and penalties concerning taxes, family allowances, fees of attorneys and personal representatives, and court costs. (§ 91-17-11(1))
f) Debts? *g) Funeral expenses?* *h) Family allowances and similar protections?* *i) Death taxes?* *j) Penalties on death taxes?*	The trustee must charge from principal all expenses incurred in connection with the settlement of a decedent's estate, including debts, funeral expenses, estate taxes, interest and penalties concerning taxes, family allowances, fees of attorneys and personal representatives, and court costs. (§ 91-17-11(1))
8. *With respect to trust expenses from the administration of the trust that are not covered by § 91-17-11(1) [see Question #7]:*	
a) Does the trustee have full discretion in allocating between income and principal for expenses incurred in the administration of the trust?	No. (§ 91-17-27)
b) If not, are there special rules for:	
i) Regular trustee fees? *ii) Advisory or custodial services to the trustee?* *iii) Accountings, judicial proceedings and other matters that involve both the income and remainder interests?*	The following charges must be made against income: 1. one-half of the court costs, attorneys' fees, and other fees on periodic accountings or judicial proceedings, unless the court directs otherwise; 2. court costs, attorneys' fees, and other fees on other accountings or judicial proceedings if the matter primarily concerns the income interest, unless the court directs otherwise; and 3. one-half of the trustee's regular compensation for services performed for the income beneficiary or in the production of income whether based on a percentage of principal or income, and all expenses reasonably incurred for current management of principal and application of income. The following charges must be made against principal: 1. one-half of the trustee's regular compensation, court costs and attorneys' fees primarily concerning matters of principal; 2. expenses incurred in maintaining or defending any action to construe the trust or protect it or the property or assure the title of any trust property. (§ 91-17-27) ***Note:*** § 91-17-27 contains many other special rules for allocations and contains many exceptions.
iv) Debts?	The trustee must allocate interest expense on trust debt to income and must allocate payments on principal of trust debt to principal. (§ 91-17-27)

c) *Can the trustee determine what are "transmission" expenses and "management" expenses?*	
9. *With regard to specific gifts from a trust after an income interest ends or from an estate:*	
a) *What amounts must be paid from income and principal?*	The fiduciary must distribute to a specific devisee or beneficiary, the income from the property devised or distributed to them less property taxes, ordinary repairs, interest, and other expenses of management and operation of the property, and less an appropriate portion of taxes imposed on income, excluding taxes on capital gains, that accrue during the period of administration or after an income interest in a trust terminates. (§ 91-17-11(2)(b))
10. *With regard to outright pecuniary gifts from an estate or trust?:*	
a) *Does interest accrue?*	The Mississippi Income and Principal Act does not provide that a beneficiary of an outright pecuniary gift should receive accrued interest on the unpaid amount.
11. *With regard to a gift in trust of a pecuniary amount from an estate or trust?*	
a) *Does interest accrue?*	No. The fiduciary should distribute to any trusts that received a gift of a pecuniary amount and to the remainder beneficiaries the balance of the income, less certain expenses that accrue during the period of administration or after an income interest terminates, in proportion to their respective interests in the undistributed assets of the estate or trust. (§ 91-17-11(2)(b))
12. *With regard to residuary gifts:*	
a) *What amount of income and principal is to be paid to the residuary beneficiary of a trust or an estate?*	The fiduciary should distribute to any trusts that received a gift of a pecuniary amount and to the remainder beneficiaries the balance of the income, less certain expenses that accrue during the period of administration or after an income interest terminates, in proportion to their respective interests in the undistributed assets of the estate or trust. (§ 91-17-11(2)(b))
13. *With regard to "business assets" held in trust:*	
a) *Can the trustee treat them as a separate entity?*	The Mississippi Principal and Income Act does not particularly provide for treating distinct assets as separate entities. However, if a trustee uses any part of the principal in the continuance of a business of which the settlor was a sole proprietor or a partner, the net profits of the business are income. If a loss results in any fiscal or calendar year, the loss to principal. Any net loss must not be carried into any other fiscal or calendar year for purposes of calculating net income. (§ 91-17-17)
b) *Can the trustee treat distinct assets as separate entities?*	The Mississippi Principal and Income Act does not particularly provide for treating distinct assets as separate entities. However, If a trustee uses any part of the principal in the continuance of a business of which the settlor was a sole

	proprietor or a partner, the net profits of the business are income. If a loss results in any fiscal or calendar year, the loss to principal. Any net loss must not be carried into any other fiscal or calendar year for purposes of calculating net income. (§ 91-17-17)
c) *Can earnings be retained in trust for the reasonable needs of the "business entity," and, if so, to what extent is this permitted?*	No. The Mississippi Principal and Income Act does not provide that the fiduciary may retain earnings for the needs of the business entity.
14. With respect to discount bonds:	
a) *To what extent is the discount added to income or principal upon maturity?*	The appreciation of a bond in accordance with a fixed schedule of appreciation in excess of the price at which it was issued is distributable as income. The increment in value is distributable to the beneficiary who was the income beneficiary at the time of increment from the first principal cash available or, if none is available, when realized by sale, redemption, or other disposition. Whenever unrealized appreciation is distributed as income out of principal, the fiduciary must reimburse principal when the appreciation is realized. Otherwise, any bonds are principal at their inventory value and no provision may be made for amortization of bond premiums or for accumulation for discount, and the proceeds of sale, redemption, or other disposition of bonds are principal. (§ 91-17-15)
b) *Does the trustee have discretion to allocate discount between income and principal?*	No. (§ 91-17-15)
c) *Are distinctions drawn between Series E bonds and others?*	No. (§ 91-17-15)
d) *Are distinctions drawn based on the maturity date of the bond?*	No. (§ 91-17-15)
15. Is there a de minimis rule excusing the trustee from making adjustments in certain cases?	No.
16. With respect to derivatives:	
a) *May income and loss be treated as that of a separate entity?*	The Mississippi Principal and Income Act does not address derivatives. (§ 91-17-5(c))
b) *If not, or the trustee chooses not to do so, is income and loss allocated to the income account or to principal?*	The Mississippi Principal and Income Act does not address derivatives. Therefore, the trustee must allocate income, gain, and loss from derivatives in accordance with what is reasonable and equitable in view of the interests of those entitled to income as well as of those entitled to principal, and in view of the manner in which persons of ordinary prudence, discretion, and judgment would act in the management of their own affairs. (§ 91-17-5(c))
17. To the extent put and call options are not derivatives, how are they allocated in terms of principal and income?	The Mississippi Principal and Income Act does not address options. Therefore, the trustee must allocate gain or loss from options in accordance with what is reasonable and equitable in

	view of the interests of those entitled to income as well as of those entitled to principal, and in view of the manner in which persons of ordinary prudence, discretion, and judgment would act in the management of their own affairs. (§ 91-17-5(c))
18. How are asset-backed securities allocated in terms of principal and income?	The Mississippi Principal and Income Act does not address asset-backed securities. Therefore, the trustee must allocate asset-backed securities in accordance with what is reasonable and equitable in view of the interests of those entitled to income as well as of those entitled to principal, and in view of the manner in which persons of ordinary prudence, discretion, and judgment would act in the management of their own affairs. (§ 91-17-5(c))
19. Are expenses incurred to comply with environmental requirements allocated to income or principal?	The Mississippi Principal and Income Act does not address environmental expenses. (See § 91-17-5(c); § 91-17-27)
20. Is income tax liability allocated generally to income or principal?	Any tax required to be paid by a fiduciary on the trust's share of an entity's taxable income should be paid from income to the extent that receipts from the entity are allocated to income and from principal to the extent that receipts from the entity are allocated to principal. (§ 91-17-27)
21. If a Subchapter S shareholder's or partner's portion of tax liability is greater than cash distributed, how is the excess obligation allocated?	The Mississippi Principal and Income Act does not address this situation. (See § 91-17-5(c); § 91-17-27)
22. What is the standard, if any, for making equitable adjustments between income and principal?	The Mississippi Principal and Income Act does not provide for equitable adjustments between principal and income.
23. Is an income beneficiary entitled to receive income accrued but unpaid when an estate ends?	On termination of an income interest, the income beneficiary whose interest is terminated, or his estate, is entitled to: Income undistributed on the date of termination; income due but not paid to the trustee on the date of termination and income in the form of periodic payments (other than corporate distributions to stockholders), including rent, interest, or annuities, not due on the date of termination, accrued from day to day. (§ 91-17-9(4))
24. Is an income beneficiary entitled to receive income accrued but unpaid when a revocable trust ends?	On termination of an income interest, the income beneficiary whose interest is terminated, or his estate, is entitled to: Income undistributed on the date of termination; income due but not paid to the trustee on the date of termination and income in the form of periodic payments (other than corporate distributions to stockholders), including rent, interest, or annuities, not due on the date of termination, accrued from day to day. (§ 91-17-9(4))
25. Is an income beneficiary entitled to receive income accrued but unpaid when an irrevocable trust ends?	On termination of an income interest, the income beneficiary whose interest is terminated, or his estate, is entitled to: Income undistributed on the date of termination; income due but not paid to the trustee on the date of termination and income in the form of periodic payments (other than corporate distributions to stockholders), including rent, interest, or annuities, not due on the date of termination, accrued from day to day. (§ 91-17-9(4))

26. With regard to mutual funds, how are:	
a) long-term gains allocated between income and principal?	Distributions made from ordinary income by a regulated investment company are income. All other distributions made by the company, including distributions from capital gains, depreciation, or depletion, whether in the form of cash or an option to take new stock or cash or an option to purchase additional shares, are principal. (§ 91-17-13)
b) short-term gains allocated between income and principal?	Distributions made from ordinary income by a regulated investment company are income. All other distributions made by the company, including distributions from capital gains, depreciation, or depletion, whether in the form of cash or an option to take new stock or cash or an option to purchase additional shares, are principal. (§ 91-17-13)
27. How are distributions from REITs allocated between income and principal?	Distributions made from ordinary income by a REIT are income. All other distributions made by a REIT, including distributions from capital gains, depreciation, or depletion, whether in the form of cash or an option to take new stock or cash or an option to purchase additional shares, are principal. (§ 91-17-13)
28. With respect to underproductive property:	
a) Is an adjustment, e.g., "delayed income," required to be paid to the income beneficiary?	Generally yes. Generally, a portion of the net proceeds of sale of any part of principal which has not produced an average net income of at least one per cent (1%) per year of its inventory value for more than a year (including as income the value of any beneficial use of the property by the income beneficiary) must be treated as delayed income to which the income beneficiary is entitled. (§ 91-17-25)
b) What percentage return makes property underproductive?	Property is not considered productive of income if the property has not produced an average net income of at least one per cent (1%) per year of its inventory value for more than a year (including as income the value of any beneficial use of the property by the income beneficiary). (§ 91-17-25)
29. Is the trustee required to increase income so that it is sufficient to qualify for the marital deduction?	The Mississippi Principal and Income Act does not address the marital deduction.
30. Is the trustee required to take depreciation?	Yes. The trustee must charge against income a reasonable allowance for depreciation on property subject to depreciation under generally accepted accounting principles, but no allowance may be made for depreciation of that portion of real property used by a beneficiary as a residence or for depreciation of property held by the trustee on January 1, 1967, for which the trustee is not then making an allowance for depreciation. (§ 91-17-27(1)(b))
31. Is the trustee's determination on allocations generally presumed to be fair and reasonable?	The Mississippi Principal and Income Act does not have a presumption that allocations are generally presumed to be fair and reasonable.

32. *If an item is not addressed in the trust agreement or in the law, must it be allocated to principal or income?*	If an item is not addressed in the trust agreement or in the law, the trustee must allocate the item in accordance with what is reasonable and equitable in view of the interests of those entitled to income as well as of those entitled to principal, and in view of the manner in which persons of ordinary prudence, discretion, and judgment would act in the management of their own affairs. (§ 91-17-5(c))
33. *When does an asset become subject to a trust:*	
a) *In the case of transfers during the transferor's life?*	The Mississippi Principal and Income Act does not address this issue. (§ 91-17-9)
b) *In the case of a will?*	In the case of an asset becoming subject to a trust by reason of a will, it becomes subject to the trust as of the date of the death of the testator even though there is an intervening period of administration of the testator's estate. (§ 91-17-9)
c) *In the case of the death of a third party?*	The Mississippi Principal and Income Act does not address this issue. (§ 91-17-9)
34. *Can a trustee rely on the characterization by an entity as to the source or character of a received distribution?*	Yes. (§ 91-17-13(5))

Table 12.02
Missouri
Trust Accounting: Principal and Income

1. *Does the trustee have the power to transfer income to principal or to transfer principal to income to meet its duty of impartiality?*	See the Uniform Principal and Income Act (1997) chart. (§ 469.405(1))
2. *What is the effective date for the law? E.g., does it apply to preexisting trusts?*	The Missouri Principal and Income Act applies to every trust or decedent's estate existing on August 28, 2001, except as otherwise expressly provided in the will or terms of the trust or in the Missouri Principal and Income Act. (§ 469.467) **Note:** A trustee may continue using a former allocation method to allocate receipts for water, minerals, other natural resources, and timber under certain circumstances. (See § 469.441; § 469.443)
3. *What percentage is allocated to income and principal from proceeds of:*	
a) IRA? *b) Qualified pension or profit-sharing plan?* *c) Other deferred compensation arrangement?*	If any portion of a payment is characterized as a distribution to the trustee of interest, dividends or a dividend equivalent, the trustee must allocate the portion so characterized to income. The trustee shall allocate the balance of that payment to principal. (§ 469.437) If no part of a payment is allocated to income, consult § 469.437 for the allocation scheme.
4. *What percentage is allocated to income and principal from proceeds of:*	
a) Patents? *b) Copyrights?*	See the Uniform Principal and Income Act (1997) chart. (§ 469.439)
5. *What percentage is allocated to income and principal in the event of distributions from:*	
a) Corporations? *b) Partnerships?* *c) LLCs?*	See the Uniform Principal and Income Act (1997) chart. (§ 469.423)
6. *What percentage is allocated to income and principal from proceeds of:*	
a) Oil and gas? *b) Minerals?* *c) Water?* *d) Other natural resourses (not including timber)?*	See the Uniform Principal and Income Act (1997) chart. (§ 469.441) **Note:** If a trust owns an interest in minerals, water or other natural resources on August 28, 2001, the trustee may allocate receipts from the interest as provided in the Missouri Principal and Income Act or in the manner used by the trustee before August 28, 2001.
e) Timber?	See the Uniform Principal and Income Act (1997) chart. (§ 469.443) **Note:** If a trust owns an interest in timberland on August 28, 2001, the trustee may allocate receipts from the interest as provided in the Missouri Principal and Income Act or in the manner used by the trustee before August 28, 2001.

f) Rental properties?	See the Uniform Principal and Income Act (1997) chart. (§ 469.431)
7. After a decedent dies, in the case of an estate, or after an income interest ends, when the fiduciary is determining the remaining net income what are the rules regarding payment from income or principal for:	
a) Attorneys fees? *b) Accountants fees?* *c) Fiduciary fees and commissions?* *d) Court costs?* *e) Interest on death taxes*	See the Uniform Principal and Income Act (1997) chart. (§ 469.413(2)(b))
f) Debts? *g) Funeral expenses?* *h) Family allowances and similar protections?* *i) Death taxes?* *j) Penalties on death taxes?*	See the Uniform Principal and Income Act (1997) chart. (§ 469.413(2)(c))
8. With respect to trust expenses from the administration of the trust that are not covered by (§ 469.413(2)(b-c)) [see Question #7]:	
a) Does the trustee have full discretion in allocating between income and principal for expenses incurred in the administration of the trust?	No. See the Uniform Principal and Income Act (1997) chart. (§ 469.451; § 469.453)
b) If not, are there special rules for:	
i) Regular trustee fees? *ii) Advisory or cusodial services to the trustee?* *iii) Accountings, judicial proceedings and other matters that involve both the income and remainder interests?*	See the Uniform Principal and Income Act (1997) chart. (§ 469.451; § 469.453)
iv) Debts?	See the Uniform Principal and Income Act (1997) chart. (§ 469.451(3); § 469.453(1)(3))
c) Can the trustee determine what are "transmission" expenses and "management" expenses?	
9. With regard to specific gifts from a trust after an income interest ends or from an estate:	
a) What amounts must be paid from income and principal?	See the Uniform Principal and Income Act (1997) chart. (§ 469.413(1); (§ 469.413(5))

10. With regard to outright pecuniary gifts from an estate or trust?:	
a) Does interest accrue?	Yes. See the Uniform Principal and Income Act (1997) chart. (§ 469.413(3))
11. With regard to a gift in trust of a pecuniary amount from an estate or trust?	
a) Does interest accrue?	No. See the Uniform Principal and Income Act (1997) chart. (§ 469.413(4); § 469.415)
12. With regard to residuary gifts:	
a) What amount of income and principal is to be paid to the residuary beneficiary of a trust or an estate?	See the Uniform Principal and Income Act (1997) chart. (§ 469.413(4); § 469.415)
13. With regard to "business assets" held in trust:	
a) Can the trustee treat them as a separate entity?	Generally yes. See the Uniform Principal and Income Act (1997) chart. (§ 469.427)
b) Can the trustee treat distinct assets as separate entities?	Generally yes. See the Uniform Principal and Income Act (1997) chart. (§ 469.427)
c) Can earnings be retained in trust for the reasonable needs of the "business entity," and, if so, to what extent is this permitted?	Yes. See the Uniform Principal and Income Act (1997) chart. (§ 469.427)
14. With respect to discount bonds:	
a) To what extent is the discount added to income or principal upon maturity?	See the Uniform Principal and Income Act (1997) chart. (§ 469.432)
b) Does the trustee have discretion to allocate discount between income and principal?	No. (§ 469.432). ***Note***: The trustee has overriding power to adjust under § 469.405(1).
c) Are distinctions drawn between Series E bonds and others?	No. (§ 469.432)
d) Are distinctions drawn based on the maturity date of the bond?	Yes. (§ 469.432)
15. Is there a de minimis rule excusing the trustee from making adjustments in certain cases?	Yes. See the Uniform Principal and Income Act (1997) chart. (§ 469.435)
16. With respect to derivatives:	
a) May income and loss be treated as that of a separate entity?	Yes. (§ 469.427; § 469.447(2))
b) If not, or the trustee chooses not to do so, is income and loss allocated to the income account or to principal?	To principal. (§ 469.447(2))

17. To the extent put and call options are not derivatives, how are they allocated in terms of principal and income?	To principal. (§ 469.447(3))
18. How are asset-backed securities allocated in terms of principal and income?	See the Uniform Principal and Income Act (1997) chart. (§ 469.449)
19. Are expenses incurred to comply with environmental requirements allocated to income or principal?	Generally to principal. See the Uniform Principal and Income Act (1997) chart. (§ 469.453(1)(9))
20. Is income tax liability allocated generally to income or principal?	See the Uniform Principal and Income Act (1997) chart. (§ 469.459; § 469.461)
21. If a Subchapter S shareholder's or partner's portion of tax liability is greater than cash distributed, how is the excess obligation allocated?	From principal. (§ 469.459(3)(2)(b))
22. What is the standard, if any, for making equitable adjustments between income and principal?	See the Uniform Principal and Income Act (1997) chart. (§ 469.403(2))
23. Is an income beneficiary entitled to receive income accrued but unpaid when an estate ends?	No. See the Uniform Principal and Income Act (1997) chart. (§ 469.421)
24. Is an income beneficiary entitled to receive income accrued but unpaid when a revocable trust ends?	Generally no. See the Uniform Principal and Income Act (1997) chart. (§ 469.421)
25. Is an income beneficiary entitled to receive income accrued but unpaid when an irrevocable trust ends?	Generally no. See the Uniform Principal and Income Act (1997) chart. (§ 469.421)
26. With regard to mutual funds, how are:	
a) long-term gains allocated between income and principal?	See the Uniform Principal and Income Act (1997) chart. (§ 469.423(3)(4))
b) short-term gains allocated between income and principal?	See the Uniform Principal and Income Act (1997) chart. (§ 469.423(3)(4))
27. How are distributions from REITs allocated between income and principal?	See the Uniform Principal and Income Act (1997) chart. (§ 469.423(3)(4))
28. With respect to underproductive property:	
a) Is an adjustment, e.g., "delayed income," required to be paid to the income beneficiary?	No. (§ 469.445(2))
b) What percentage return makes property underproductive?	The statute only refers to property not productive of income. (§ 469.445)
29. Is the trustee required to increase income so that it is sufficient to qualify for the marital deduction?	Yes. (§ 469.445(1))

30. Is the trustee required to take depreciation?	No. (§ 469.455)
31. Is the trustee's determination on allocations generally presumed to be fair and reasonable?	Yes. (§ 469.403(2))
32. If an item is not addressed in the trust agreement or in the law, must it be allocated to principal or income?	To principal. (§ 469.403(1)(4))
33. When does an asset become subject to a trust:	
a) In the case of transfers during the transferor's life?	The date of transfer. (§ 469.417(2)(1))
b) In the case of a will?	The date of the testator's death. (§ 469.417(2)(2))
c) In the case of the death of a third party?	The date of the third party's death. (§ 469.417(2)(3))
34. Can a trustee rely on the characterization by an entity as to the source or character of a received distribution?	Yes. (§ 469.423(6))

Table 12.02
Montana
Trust Accounting: Principal and Income

1. *Does the trustee have the power to transfer income to principal or to transfer principal to income to meet its duty of impartiality?*	Yes. See the Uniform Principal and Income Act (1997) chart. (§ 72-34-424)
2. *What is the effective date for the law? E.g., does it apply to preexisting trusts?*	The Montana Principal and Income Act applies to every trust or decedent's estate existing on or after October 1, 2003, except as otherwise expressly provided in the trust or will or in the Montana Principal and Income Act. (§ 72-34-427)
3. *What percentage is allocated to income and principal from proceeds of:*	
a) IRA? *b) Qualified pension or profit-sharing plan?* *c) Other deferred compensation arrangement?*	See the Uniform Principal and Income Act (1997) chart. (§ 72-34-441)
4. *What percentage is allocated to income and principal from proceeds of:*	
a) Patents? *b) Copyrights?*	The trustee must allocate eighty-five percent (85%) of the receipts to income and fifteen percent (15%) to principal. (§ 72-34-442)
5. *What percentage is allocated to income and principal in the event of distributions from:*	
a) Corporations? *b) Partnerships?* *c) LLCs?*	See the Uniform Principal and Income Act (1997) chart. (§ 72-34-433)
6. *What percentage is allocated to income and principal from proceeds of:*	
a) Oil and gas? *b) Minerals?* *c) Water?* *d) Other natural resourses (not including timber)?*	The trustee must allocate a receipt received as nominal delay rental or a nominal annual rent on a lease to income. The trustee must allocate a receipt received from a production payment to income if and to the extent that the agreement creating the production payment provides a factor for interest or its equivalent. The balance must be allocated to principal. The trustee must allocate fifteen percent (15%) of an amount received as a royalty, shut-in-well payment, take-or-pay payment, bonus, or a delay rental that is more than nominal, to principal and eighty-five percent (85%) to income. The trustee must allocate fifteen percent (15%) of the net amount received from a working interest or other interest (not mentioned in the two preceding paragraphs) to principal and eighty-five percent (85%) to income. An amount received on account of an interest in water that is renewable must be allocated to income. If the water is not renewable, fifteen percent (15%) of the amount must be allocated to principal and eighty-five percent (85%) to income.

	The rules above apply whether or not a decedent or donor was extracting the minerals, water, or other natural resources before the interest became subject to the trust. (§ 72-34-443)
e) Timber?	See the Uniform Principal and Income Act (1997) chart. (§ 72-34-444)
f) Rental properties?	See the Uniform Principal and Income Act (1997) chart. (§ 72-34-437)
7. After a decedent dies, in the case of an estate, or after an income interest ends, when the fiduciary is determining the remaining net income what are the rules regarding payment from income or principal for:	
a) Attorneys fees? *b) Accountants fees?* *c) Fiduciary fees and commissions?* *d) Court costs?* *e) Interest on death taxes*	See the Uniform Principal and Income Act (1997) chart. (§ 72-34-428(3)(b))
f) Debts? *g) Funeral expenses?* *h) Family allowances and similar protections?* *i) Death taxes?* *j) Penalties on death taxes?*	See the Uniform Principal and Income Act (1997) chart. (§ 72-34-428(3)(c))
8. With respect to trust expenses from the administration of the trust that are not covered by § 72-34-428(3)(b-c) [see Question #7]:	
a) Does the trustee have full discretion in allocating between income and principal for expenses incurred in the administration of the trust?	No. See the Uniform Principal and Income Act (1997) chart. (§ 72-34-448; § 72-34-449)
b) If not, are there special rules for:	
i) Regular trustee fees? *ii) Advisory or cusodial services to the trustee?* *iii) Accountings, judicial proceedings and other matters that involve both the income and remainder interests?*	See the Uniform Principal and Income Act (1997) chart. (§ 72-34-448; § 72-34-449) ***Note:*** The mandatory allocation is subject to alteration by the courts.
iv) Debts?	See the Uniform Principal and Income Act (1997) chart. (§ 72-34-448(3); § 72-34-449(1)(c))
c) Can the trustee determine what are "transmission" expenses and "management" expenses?	

9. *With regard to specific gifts from a trust after an income interest ends or from an estate:*	
a) *What amounts must be paid from income and principal?*	See the Uniform Principal and Income Act (1997) chart. (§ 72-34-428(1))
10. *With regard to outright pecuniary gifts from an estate or trust?:*	
a) *Does interest accrue?*	Yes. See the Uniform Principal and Income Act (1997) chart. (§ 72-34-428(2))
11. *With regard to a gift in trust of a pecuniary amount from an estate or trust?*	
a) *Does interest accrue?*	Yes. (§ 72-34-428(2))
12. *With regard to residuary gifts:*	
a) *What amount of income and principal is to be paid to the residuary beneficiary of a trust or an estate?*	See the Uniform Principal and Income Act (1997) chart. (§ 72-34-428(4); § 72-34-429)
13. *With regard to "business assets" held in trust:*	
a) *Can the trustee treat them as a separate entity?*	Generally yes. See the Uniform Principal and Income Act (1997) chart. (§ 72-34-435)
b) *Can the trustee treat distinct assets as separate entities?*	Generally yes. See the Uniform Principal and Income Act (1997) chart. (§ 72-34-435)
c) *Can earnings be retained in trust for the reasonable needs of the "business entity," and, if so, to what extent is this permitted?*	See the Uniform Principal and Income Act (1997) chart. (§ 72-34-435)
14. *With respect to discount bonds:*	
a) *To what extent is the discount added to income or principal upon maturity?*	See the Uniform Principal and Income Act (1997) chart. (§ 72-34-438)
b) *Does the trustee have discretion to allocate discount between income and principal?*	No. (§ 72-34-438) Note: The trustee has overriding power to adjust under (§ 72-34-424)
c) *Are distinctions drawn between Series E bonds and others?*	No. (§ 72-34-438)
d) *Are distinctions drawn based on the maturity date of the bond?*	Yes. (§ 72-34-438)
15. *Is there a de minimis rule excusing the trustee from making adjustments in certain cases?*	Yes. See the Uniform Principal and Income Act (1997) chart. (§ 72-34-440)
16. *With respect to derivatives:*	

a) *May income and loss be treated as that of a separate entity?*	Yes. (§ 72-34-446(2); § 72-34-435)
b) *If not, or the trustee chooses not to do so, is income and loss allocated to the income account or to principal?*	To principal. (§ 72-34-446(2))
17. *To the extent put and call options are not derivatives, how are they allocated in terms of principal and income?*	To principal. (§ 72-34-446(3))
18. *How are asset-backed securities allocated in terms of principal and income?*	See the Uniform Principal and Income Act (1997) chart. (§ 72-34-447)
19. *Are expenses incurred to comply with environmental requirements allocated to income or principal?*	Generally to principal. See the Uniform Principal and Income Act (1997) chart. (§ 72-34-449(1)(g))
20. *Is income tax liability allocated generally to income or principal?*	See the Uniform Principal and Income Act (1997) chart. (§ 72-34-452; § 72-34-453)
21. *If a Subchapter S shareholder's or partner's portion of tax liability is greater than cash distributed, how is the excess obligation allocated?*	From principal. (§ 72-34-452(3)(b)(ii))
22. *What is the standard, if any, for making equitable adjustments between income and principal?*	In exercising the power to adjust, the fiduciary must administer a trust, or decedent's estate impartially, except to the extent that the terms of the trust or the will clearly manifest an intention that the fiduciary shall or may favor one or more of the beneficiaries. (§ 72-34-423(2))
23. *Is an income beneficiary entitled to receive income accrued but unpaid when an estate ends?*	No. (§ 72-34-432)
24. *Is an income beneficiary entitled to receive income accrued but unpaid when a revocable trust ends?*	Generally no. See the Uniform Principal and Income Act (1997) chart. (§ 72-34-432)
25. *Is an income beneficiary entitled to receive income accrued but unpaid when an irrevocable trust ends?*	Generally no. See the Uniform Principal and Income Act (1997) chart. (§ 72-34-432)
26. *With regard to mutual funds, how are:*	
a) *long-term gains allocated between income and principal?*	See the Uniform Principal and Income Act (1997) chart. (§ 72-34-433(3)(d))
b) *short-term gains allocated between income and principal?*	See the Uniform Principal and Income Act (1997) chart. (§ 72-34-433(3)(d))
27. *How are distributions from REITs allocated between income and principal?*	See the Uniform Principal and Income Act (1997) chart. (§ 72-34-433(3)(d))
28. *With respect to underproductive property:*	

a) Is an adjustment, e.g., "delayed income," required to be paid to the income beneficiary?	No. (§ 72-34-445)
b) What percentage return makes property underproductive?	The statute only refers to property not productive of income. (§ 72-34-445)
29. Is the trustee required to increase income so that it is sufficient to qualify for the marital deduction?	Yes. (§ 72-34-445)
30. Is the trustee required to take depreciation?	No. (§ 72-34-450)
31. Is the trustee's determination on allocations generally presumed to be fair and reasonable?	Yes. (§ 72-34-423(2))
32. If an item is not addressed in the trust agreement or in the law, must it be allocated to principal or income?	To principal. (§ 72-34-450)
33. When does an asset become subject to a trust:	
a) In the case of transfers during the transferor's life?	The date of transfer. (§ 72-34-430(2)(a)).
b) In the case of a will?	The date of the testator's death. (§ 72-34-430(2)(b))
c) In the case of the death of a third party?	The date of the third party's death. (§ 72-34-430(2)(c))
34. Can a trustee rely on the characterization by an entity as to the source or character of a received distribution?	Yes. (§ 72-34-433(5))

Table 12.02
Nebraska
Trust Accounting: Principal and Income

1. *Does the trustee have the power to transfer income to principal or to transfer principal to income to meet its duty of impartiality?*	Yes. See the Uniform Principal and Income Act (1997) chart. (§ 30-3119)
2. *What is the effective date for the law? E.g., does it apply to preexisting trusts?*	The Nebraska Principal and Income Act applies to every trust or decedent's estate existing on or after September 1, 2001, except as otherwise expressly provided in the will or terms of the trust or in the Nebraska Principal and Income Act. (§ 30-3149) ***Note:*** A trustee may continue using a former allocation method to allocate receipts for water, minerals, other natural resources, and timber under certain circumstances. (See, § 30-3137; § 30-3138)
3. *What percentage is allocated to income and principal from proceeds of:*	
a) *IRA?* b) *Qualified pension or profit-sharing plan?* c) *Other deferred compensation arrangement?*	See the Uniform Principal and Income Act (1997) chart. (§ 30-3135)
4. *What percentage is allocated to income and principal from proceeds of:*	
a) *Patents?* b) *Copyrights?*	See the Uniform Principal and Income Act (1997) chart. (§ 30-3136)
5. *What percentage is allocated to income and principal in the event of distributions from:*	
a) *Corporations?* b) *Partnerships?* c) *LLCs?*	See the Uniform Principal and Income Act (1997) chart. (§ 30-3127)
6. *What percentage is allocated to income and principal from proceeds of:*	
a) *Oil and gas?* b) *Minerals?* c) *Water?* d) *Other natural resourses (not including timber)?*	See the Uniform Principal and Income Act (1997) chart. (§ 30-3137) ***Note:*** If a trust owns an interest in minerals, water or other natural resources on September 1, 2001, the trustee may allocate receipts from the interest as provided in the Nebraska Principal and Income Act or in the manner used by the trustee before September 1, 2001.
e) *Timber?*	See the Uniform Principal and Income Act (1997) chart. (§ 30-3138) ***Note:*** If a trust owns an interest in timberland on September 1, 2001, the trustee may allocate receipts from the interest as provided in the Nebraska Principal and Income Act or in the manner used by the trustee before September 1, 2001.

f) Rental properties?	See the Uniform Principal and Income Act (1997) chart. (§ 30-3131)
7. After a decedent dies, in the case of an estate, or after an income interest ends, when the fiduciary is determining the remaining net income what are the rules regarding payment from income or principal for:	
a) Attorneys fees? *b) Accountants fees?* *c) Fiduciary fees and commissions?* *d) Court costs?* *e) Interest on death taxes*	See the Uniform Principal and Income Act (1997) chart. (§ 30-3122(2)(B))
f) Debts? *g) Funeral expenses?* *h) Family allowances and similar protections?* *i) Death taxes?* *j) Penalties on death taxes?*	See the Uniform Principal and Income Act (1997) chart. (§ 30-3122(2)(C))
8. With respect to trust expenses from the administration of the trust that are not covered by § 30-3122(2)(B-C) [see Question #7]:	
a) Does the trustee have full discretion in allocating between income and principal for expenses incurred in the administration of the trust?	No. (§ 30-3142; § 30-3143)
b) If not, are there special rules for:	
i) Regular trustee fees? *ii) Advisory or cusodial services to the trustee?* *iii) Accountings, judicial proceedings and other matters that involve both the income and remainder interests?*	See the Uniform Principal and Income Act (1997) chart. (§ 30-3142; § 30-3143)
iv) Debts?	See the Uniform Principal and Income Act (1997) chart. (§ 30-3142(3); § 30-3143(a)(3))
c) Can the trustee determine what are "transmission" expenses and "management" expenses?	
9. With regard to specific gifts from a trust after an income interest ends or from an estate:	
a) What amounts must be paid from income and principal?	See the Uniform Principal and Income Act (1997) chart. (§ 30-3122(1); § 30-3122(5))

10. With regard to outright pecuniary gifts from an estate or trust?:	
a) Does interest accrue?	Yes. See the Uniform Principal and Income Act (1997) chart. (§ 30-3122(3))
11. With regard to a gift in trust of a pecuniary amount from an estate or trust?	
a) Does interest accrue?	No. See the Uniform Principal and Income Act (1997) chart. (§ 30-3122(4); § 30-3123)
12. With regard to residuary gifts:	
a) What amount of income and principal is to be paid to the residuary beneficiary of a trust or an estate?	See the Uniform Principal and Income Act (1997) chart. (§ 30-3122(4); § 30-3123)
13. With regard to "business assets" held in trust:	
a) Can the trustee treat them as a separate entity?	Generally yes. See the Uniform Principal and Income Act (1997) chart. (§ 30-3129)
b) Can the trustee treat distinct assets as separate entities?	Generally yes. See the Uniform Principal and Income Act (1997) chart. (§ 30-3129)
c) Can earnings be retained in trust for the reasonable needs of the "business entity," and, if so, to what extent is this permitted?	Yes. See the Uniform Principal and Income Act (1997) chart. (§ 30-3129)
14. With respect to discount bonds:	
a) To what extent is the discount added to income or principal upon maturity?	See the Uniform Principal and Income Act (1997) chart. (§ 30-3132)
b) Does the trustee have discretion to allocate discount between income and principal?	No. (§ 30-3132) ***Note:*** The trustee has the overriding power to adjust under § 30-3119.
c) Are distinctions drawn between Series E bonds and others?	No. (§ 30-3132)
d) Are distinctions drawn based on the maturity date of the bond?	Yes. (§ 30-3132)
15. Is there a de minimis rule excusing the trustee from making adjustments in certain cases?	Yes. See the Uniform Principal and Income Act (1997) chart. (§ 30-3134)
16. With respect to derivatives:	
a) May income and loss be treated as that of a separate entity?	Yes. (§ 30-3140(b); § 30-3129)
b) If not, or the trustee chooses not to do so, is income and loss allocated to the income account or to principal?	To principal. (§ 30-3140(b))

17. *To the extent put and call options are not derivatives, how are they allocated in terms of principal and income?*	To principal. (§ 30-3140(c))
18. *How are asset-backed securities allocated in terms of principal and income?*	See the Uniform Principal and Income Act (1997) chart. (§ 30-3141)
19. *Are expenses incurred to comply with environmental requirements allocated to income or principal?*	Generally to principal. See the Uniform Principal and Income Act (1997) chart. (§ 30-3143(a)(7))
20. *Is income tax liability allocated generally to income or principal?*	See the Uniform Principal and Income Act (1997) chart. (§ 30-3146; § 30-3147)
21. *If a Subchapter S shareholder's or partner's portion of tax liability is greater than cash distributed, how is the excess obligation allocated?*	To principal. (§ 30-3146(c)(2)(B))
22. *What is the standard, if any, for making equitable adjustments between income and principal?*	See the Uniform Principal and Income Act (1997) chart. (§ 30-3118(b))
23. *Is an income beneficiary entitled to receive income accrued but unpaid when an estate ends?*	No. (§ 30-3126)
24. *Is an income beneficiary entitled to receive income accrued but unpaid when a revocable trust ends?*	Generally no. See the Uniform Principal and Income Act (1997) chart. (§ 30-3126)
25. *Is an income beneficiary entitled to receive income accrued but unpaid when an irrevocable trust ends?*	Generally no. See the Uniform Principal and Income Act (1997) chart. (§ 30-3126)
26. *With regard to mutual funds, how are:*	
a) *long-term gains allocated between income and principal?*	See the Uniform Principal and Income Act (1997) chart. (§ 30-3127(f))
b) *short-term gains allocated between income and principal?*	See the Uniform Principal and Income Act (1997) chart. (§ 30-3127(f)).
27. *How are distributions from REITs allocated between income and principal?*	See the Uniform Principal and Income Act (1997) chart. (§ 30-3127(f))
28. *With respect to underproductive property:*	
a) *Is an adjustment, e.g., "delayed income," required to be paid to the income beneficiary?*	No. (§ 30-3139)
b) *What percentage return makes property underproductive?*	The statute only refers to property not productive of income. (§ 30-3139)
29. *Is the trustee required to increase income so that it is sufficient to qualify for the marital deduction?*	Yes. (§ 30-3139(a))

30. Is the trustee required to take depreciation?	No. (§ 30-3144)
31. Is the trustee's determination on allocations generally presumed to be fair and reasonable?	Yes. (§ 30-3118(b))
32. If an item is not addressed in the trust agreement or in the law, must it be allocated to principal or income?	To principal. (§ 30-3118(a)(4))
33. When does an asset become subject to a trust:	
a) In the case of transfers during the transferor's life?	The date of transfer. (§ 30-3124(b)(1))
b) In the case of a will?	The date of the testator's death. (§ 30-3124(b)(2))
c) In the case of the death of a third party?	The date of the third party's death. (§ 30-3124(b)(3))
34. Can a trustee rely on the characterization by an entity as to the source or character of a received distribution?	Yes. (§ 30-3127(f))

Table 12.02
Nevada
Trust Accounting: Principal and Income

1. *Does the trustee have the power to transfer income to principal or to transfer principal to income to meet its duty of impartiality?*	See the Uniform Principal and Income Act (1997) chart. (§ 164.795(1))
2. *What is the effective date for the law? E.g., does it apply to preexisting trusts?*	The Nevada Principal and Income Act does not address its application to preexisting trusts. However, the effective date of the Act is October 1, 2003. ***Note:*** A trustee may continue using a former allocation method to allocate receipts for water, minerals, other natural resources, and timber under certain circumstances. (See § 164.875; § 164.880)
3. *What percentage is allocated to income and principal from proceeds of:*	
a) *IRA?* b) *Qualified pension or profit-sharing plan?* c) *Other deferred compensation arrangement?*	See the Uniform Principal and Income Act (1997) chart. (§ 164.865)
4. *What percentage is allocated to income and principal from proceeds of:*	
a) *Patents?* b) *Copyrights?*	See the Uniform Principal and Income Act (1997) chart. (§ 164.870)
5. *What percentage is allocated to income and principal in the event of distributions from:*	
a) *Corporations?* b) *Partnerships?* c) *LLCs?*	See the Uniform Principal and Income Act (1997) chart. (§ 164.825)
6. *What percentage is allocated to income and principal from proceeds of:*	
a) *Oil and gas?* b) *Minerals?* c) *Water?* d) *Other natural resourses (not including timber)?*	See the Uniform Principal and Income Act (1997) chart. (§ 164.875) ***Note:*** If a trust owns an interest in minerals, water or other natural resources on October 1, 2003, the trustee may allocate receipts from the interest as provided in the Nevada Principal and Income Act or in the manner used by the trustee before October 1, 2003.
e) *Timber?*	See the Uniform Principal and Income Act (1997) chart. (§ 164.880) ***Note:*** If a trust owns an interest in timberland on October 1, 2003, the trustee may allocate receipts from the interest as provided in the Nevada Principal and Income Act or in the manner used by the trustee before October 1, 2003.
f) *Rental properties?*	See the Uniform Principal and Income Act (1997) chart. (§ 164.845)

7. After a decedent dies, in the case of an estate, or after an income interest ends, when the fiduciary is determining the remaining net income what are the rules regarding payment from income or principal for:	
a) Attorneys fees? *b) Accountants fees?* *c) Fiduciary fees and commissions?* *d) Court costs?* *e) Interest on death taxes*	See the Uniform Principal and Income Act (1997) chart. (§ 164.800(2)(b))
f) Debts? *g) Funeral expenses?* *h) Family allowances and similar protections?* *i) Death taxes?* *j) Penalties on death taxes?*	See the Uniform Principal and Income Act (1997) chart. (§ 164.800(2)(c))
8. With respect to trust expenses from the administration of the trust that are not covered by § 164.800(2)(b-c) [see Question #7]:	
a) Does the trustee have full discretion in allocating between income and principal for expenses incurred in the administration of the trust?	No. (§ 164.900; § 164.905)
b) If not, are there special rules for:	
i) Regular trustee fees? *ii) Advisory or cusodial services to the trustee?* *iii) Accountings, judicial proceedings and other matters that involve both the income and remainder interests?*	See the Uniform Principal and Income Act (1997) chart. (§ 164.900; § 164.905)
iv) Debts?	See the Uniform Principal and Income Act (1997) chart. (§ 164.900(3); § 164.905(1)(c))
c) Can the trustee determine what are "transmission" expenses and "management" expenses?	
9. With regard to specific gifts from a trust after an income interest ends or from an estate:	
a) What amounts must be paid from income and principal?	See the Uniform Principal and Income Act (1997) chart. (§ 164.800(1); § 164.800(5))
10. With regard to outright pecuniary gifts from an estate or trust?:	

a) Does interest accrue?	Yes. See the Uniform Principal and Income Act (1997) chart. (§ 164.800(3))
11. With regard to a gift in trust of a pecuniary amount from an estate or trust?	
a) Does interest accrue?	No. See the Uniform Principal and Income Act (1997) chart. (§ 164.800(4); § 164.805)
12. With regard to residuary gifts:	
a) What amount of income and principal is to be paid to the residuary beneficiary of a trust or an estate?	See the Uniform Principal and Income Act (1997) chart. (§ 164.800(4); § 164.805)
13. With regard to "business assets" held in trust:	
a) Can the trustee treat them as a separate entity?	Generally yes. See the Uniform Principal and Income Act (1997) chart. (§ 164.835(1))
b) Can the trustee treat distinct assets as separate entities?	Generally yes. See the Uniform Principal and Income Act (1997) chart. (§ 164.835(1))
c) Can earnings be retained in trust for the reasonable needs of the "business entity," and, if so, to what extent is this permitted?	Yes. See the Uniform Principal and Income Act (1997) chart. (§ 164.835(2))
14. With respect to discount bonds:	
a) To what extent is the discount added to income or principal upon maturity?	See the Uniform Principal and Income Act (1997) chart. (§ 164.850)
b) Does the trustee have discretion to allocate discount between income and principal?	No. (§ 164.850) ***Note:*** The trustee has the overriding power to adjust under § 164.795.
c) Are distinctions drawn between Series E bonds and others?	No. (§ 164.850)
d) Are distinctions drawn based on the maturity date of the bond?	Yes. (§ 164.850)
15. Is there a de minimis rule excusing the trustee from making adjustments in certain cases?	Yes. See the Uniform Principal and Income Act (1997) chart. (§ 164.860).
16. With respect to derivatives:	
a) May income and loss be treated as that of a separate entity?	Yes. (§ 164.835(3)(g); § 164.890(b))
b) If not, or the trustee chooses not to do so, is income and loss allocated to the income account or to principal?	To principal. (§ 164.890(b))

17. To the extent put and call options are not derivatives, how are they allocated in terms of principal and income?	To principal. (§ 164.890(c))
18. How are asset-backed securities allocated in terms of principal and income?	See the Uniform Principal and Income Act (1997) chart. (§ 164.895)
19. Are expenses incurred to comply with environmental requirements allocated to income or principal?	Generally to principal. See the Uniform Principal and Income Act (1997) chart. (§ 164.905(1)(g))
20. Is income tax liability allocated generally to income or principal?	See the Uniform Principal and Income Act (1997) chart. (§ 164.920; § 164.925)
21. If a Subchapter S shareholder's or partner's portion of tax liability is greater than cash distributed, how is the excess obligation allocated?	From principal. (§ 164.920(3)(b)(2))
22. What is the standard, if any, for making equitable adjustments between income and principal?	See the Uniform Principal and Income Act (1997) chart. (§ 164.720(2))
23. Is an income beneficiary entitled to receive income accrued but unpaid when an estate ends?	No. (§ 164.820)
24. Is an income beneficiary entitled to receive income accrued but unpaid when a revocable trust ends?	Generally no. See the Uniform Principal and Income Act (1997) chart. (§ 164.820)
25. Is an income beneficiary entitled to receive income accrued but unpaid when an irrevocable trust ends?	Generally no. See the Uniform Principal and Income Act (1997) chart. (§ 164.820)
26. With regard to mutual funds, how are:	
a) long-term gains allocated between income and principal?	See the Uniform Principal and Income Act (1997) chart. (§ 164.825(3)(d))
b) short-term gains allocated between income and principal?	See the Uniform Principal and Income Act (1997) chart. (§ 164.825(3)(d))
27. How are distributions from REITs allocated between income and principal?	See the Uniform Principal and Income Act (1997) chart. (§ 164.825(3)(d))
28. With respect to underproductive property:	
a) Is an adjustment, e.g., "delayed income," required to be paid to the income beneficiary?	No. (§ 164.885)
b) What percentage return makes property underproductive?	The statute only refers to property not productive of income. (§ 164.885)
29. Is the trustee required to increase income so that it is sufficient to qualify for the marital deduction?	Yes. (§ 164.885(1))

30. Is the trustee required to take depreciation?	No. (§ 164.910)
31. Is the trustee's determination on allocations generally presumed to be fair and reasonable?	Yes. (§ 164.720(2))
32. If an item is not addressed in the trust agreement or in the law, must it be allocated to principal or income?	To principal. (§ 164.790)
33. When does an asset become subject to a trust:	
a) In the case of transfers during the transferor's life?	The date of transfer. (§ 164.810(2)(a))
b) In the case of a will?	The date of the testator's death. (§ 164.810(2)(b))
c) In the case of the death of a third party?	The date of the third party's death. (§ 164.810(2)(c))
34. Can a trustee rely on the characterization by an entity as to the source or character of a received distribution?	Yes. (§ 164.825(6))

Table 12.02
New Hampshire
Trust Accounting: Principal and Income

1. *Does the trustee have the power to transfer income to principal or to transfer principal to income to meet its duty of impartiality?*	Yes. See the Uniform Principal and Income Act (1997) chart. (564-C:1-104(a))
2. *What is the effective date for the law? E.g., does it apply to preexisting trusts?*	Except as otherwise provided in the New Hampshire Principal and Income Act, the New Hampshire Principal and Income Act applies to (1) to every inter vivos trust created on or after January 1, 2007 except as otherwise expressly provided in the terms of the trust or in the New Hampshire Principal and Income Act; (2) to any inter vivos trust created before January 1, 2007 upon the election of the trustee to apply this chapter made in writing and delivered to the beneficiaries then entitled to receive income and principal from the trust; (3) to any estate existing or testamentary trust of a decedent who dies on or after January 1, 2007; (4) to any estate or testamentary trust upon the approval by a court of competent jurisdiction, upon either (A) a petition filed by an interested person or (B) the court on its own motion. (564-C:6-602) ***Note:*** A trustee may continue using a former allocation method to allocate receipts for water, minerals, other natural resources, and timber under certain circumstances. (See 564-C:4-411; 564-C:4-412)
3. *What percentage is allocated to income and principal from proceeds of:*	
a) IRA? *b) Qualified pension or profit-sharing plan?* *c) Other deferred compensation arrangement?*	See the Uniform Principal and Income Act (1997) chart. (564-C:4-409)
4. *What percentage is allocated to income and principal from proceeds of:*	
a) Patents? *b) Copyrights?*	See the Uniform Principal and Income Act (1997) chart. (564-C:4-410(b))
5. *What percentage is allocated to income and principal in the event of distributions from:*	
a) Corporations? *b) Partnerships?* *c) LLCs?*	See the Uniform Principal and Income Act (1997) chart. (564-C:4-401)
6. *What percentage is allocated to income and principal from proceeds of:*	
a) Oil and gas? *b) Minerals?* *c) Water?*	See the Uniform Principal and Income Act (1997) chart. (564-C:4-411) ***Note***: If a trust owns an interest in minerals, water or other natural resources on January 1, 2007, the trustee may allocate

d) *Other natural resourses (not including timber)?*	receipts from the interest as provided in the New Hampshire Principal and Income Act or in the manner used by the trustee before January 1, 2007.
e) *Timber?*	See the Uniform Principal and Income Act (1997) chart. (564-C:4-412) **Note:** If a trust owns an interest in timberland on January 1, 2007, the trustee may allocate receipts from the interest as provided in the New Hampshire Principal and Income Act or in the manner used by the trustee before January 1, 2007.
f) *Rental properties?*	See the Uniform Principal and Income Act (1997) chart. (564-C:4-405)
7. *After a decedent dies, in the case of an estate, or after an income interest ends, when the fiduciary is determining the remaining net income what are the rules regarding payment from income or principal for:*	
a) *Attorneys fees?* b) *Accountants fees?* c) *Fiduciary fees and commissions?* d) *Court costs?* e) *Interest on death taxes*	See the Uniform Principal and Income Act (1997) chart. (564-C:2-201(2)(B))
f) *Debts?* g) *Funeral expenses?* h) *Family allowances and similar protections?* i) *Death taxes?* j) *Penalties on death taxes?*	See the Uniform Principal and Income Act (1997) chart. (564-C:2-201(2)(C))
8. *With respect to trust expenses from the administration of the trust that are not covered 564-C:2-201(2)(B-C) [see Question #7]:*	
a) *Does the trustee have full discretion in allocating between income and principal for expenses incurred in the administration of the trust?*	No. (564-C:5-501; 564-C:5-502)
b) *If not, are there special rules for:*	
i) *Regular trustee fees?* ii) *Advisory or custodial services to the trustee?* iii) *Accountings, judicial proceedings and other matters that involve both the income and remainder interests?*	The trustee must allocate these expenses based on the trustee's determination of the amount of these expenses that involve the income and remainder interests. See the statutory language for more details. (564-C:5-501(a); 564-C:5-502(a)(1))
iv) *Debts?*	See the Uniform Principal and Income Act (1997) chart. (564-C:5-501(b); 564-C:5-502(a)(3))

c) Can the trustee determine what are "transmission" expenses and "management" expenses?	
9. With regard to specific gifts from a trust after an income interest ends or from an estate:	
a) What amounts must be paid from income and principal?	See the Uniform Principal and Income Act (1997) chart. (564-C:2-201(1); 564-C:2-201(5))
10. With regard to outright pecuniary gifts from an estate or trust?:	
a) Does interest accrue?	Yes. See the Uniform Principal and Income Act (1997) chart. (564-C:2-201(3))
11. With regard to a gift in trust of a pecuniary amount from an estate or trust?	
a) Does interest accrue?	No. See the Uniform Principal and Income Act (1997) chart. (564-C:2-201(4); 564-C:2-202)
12. With regard to residuary gifts:	
a) What amount of income and principal is to be paid to the residuary beneficiary of a trust or an estate?	See the Uniform Principal and Income Act (1997) chart. (564-C:2-201(4); 564-C:2-202)
13. With regard to "business assets" held in trust:	
a) Can the trustee treat them as a separate entity?	Generally yes. See the Uniform Principal and Income Act (1997) chart. (564-C:4-403)
b) Can the trustee treat distinct assets as separate entities?	Generally yes. See the Uniform Principal and Income Act (1997) chart. (564-C:4-403)
c) Can earnings be retained in trust for the reasonable needs of the "business entity," and, if so, to what extent is this permitted?	Yes. See the Uniform Principal and Income Act (1997) chart. (564-C:4-403(b))
14. With respect to discount bonds:	
a) To what extent is the discount added to income or principal upon maturity?	See the Uniform Principal and Income Act (1997) chart. (564-C:4-406(b))
b) Does the trustee have discretion to allocate discount between income and principal?	No. (564-C:4-406(b)) Note: The trustee has overriding power to adjust under 564-C:1-104(a).
c) Are distinctions drawn between Series E bonds and others?	No. (564-C:4-406(b))
d) Are distinctions drawn based on the maturity date of the bond?	Yes. (564-C:4-406(b))

15. Is there a de minimis rule excusing the trustee from making adjustments in certain cases?	Yes. See the Uniform Principal and Income Act (1997) chart. (564-C:4-408)
16. With respect to derivatives:	
a) May income and loss be treated as that of a separate entity?	Yes. (564-C:4-403; 564-C:4-414(b))
b) If not, or the trustee chooses not to do so, is income and loss allocated to the income account or to principal?	To principal. (564-C:4-414(b))
17. To the extent put and call options are not derivatives, how are they allocated in terms of principal and income?	To principal. (564-C:4-414(c))
18. How are asset-backed securities allocated in terms of principal and income?	See the Uniform Principal and Income Act (1997) chart. (564-C:4-415)
19. Are expenses incurred to comply with environmental requirements allocated to income or principal?	Generally to principal. See the Uniform Principal and Income Act (1997) chart. (564-C:5-502(a)(7))
20. Is income tax liability allocated generally to income or principal?	See the Uniform Principal and Income Act (1997) chart. (564-C:5-505; 564-C:5-506)
21. If a Subchapter S shareholder's or partner's portion of tax liability is greater than cash distributed, how is the excess obligation allocated?	From principal. (564-C:5-505(c)(2)(B))
22. What is the standard, if any, for making equitable adjustments between income and principal?	See the Uniform Principal and Income Act (1997) chart. (564-C:1-103(b))
23. Is an income beneficiary entitled to receive income accrued but unpaid when an estate ends?	No. See the Uniform Principal and Income Act (1997) chart. (564-C:3-303)
24. Is an income beneficiary entitled to receive income accrued but unpaid when a revocable trust ends?	Generally no. See the Uniform Principal and Income Act (1997) chart. (564-C:3-303)
25. Is an income beneficiary entitled to receive income accrued but unpaid when an irrevocable trust ends?	Generally no. See the Uniform Principal and Income Act (1997) chart. (564-C:3-303)
26. With regard to mutual funds, how are:	
a) long-term gains allocated between income and principal?	See the Uniform Principal and Income Act (1997) chart. (564-C:4-401(c)(4))
b) short-term gains allocated between income and principal?	See the Uniform Principal and Income Act (1997) chart. (564-C:4-401(c)(4))
27. How are distributions from REITs allocated between income and principal?	See the Uniform Principal and Income Act (1997) chart. (564-C:4-401(c)(4))

28. *With respect to underproductive property:*	
a) *Is an adjustment, e.g., "delayed income," required to be paid to the income beneficiary?*	No. (564-C:4-413)
b) *What percentage return makes property underproductive?*	The statute only refers to property not productive of income. (564-C:4-413)
29. *Is the trustee required to increase income so that it is sufficient to qualify for the marital deduction?*	Yes. (564-C:4-413(a))
30. *Is the trustee required to take depreciation?*	No. (564-C:5-503)
31. *Is the trustee's determination on allocations generally presumed to be fair and reasonable?*	Yes. (564-C:1-103(b))
32. *If an item is not addressed in the trust agreement or in the law, must it be allocated to principal or income?*	To principal. (564-C:1-103(a)(4))
33. *When does an asset become subject to a trust:*	
a) *In the case of transfers during the transferor's life?*	The date of transfer. (564-C:3-301(b)(1))
b) *In the case of a will?*	The date of the testator's death. (564-C:3-301(b)(2))
c) *In the case of the death of a third party?*	The date of the third party's death. (564-C:3-301(b)(3))
34. *Can a trustee rely on the characterization by an entity as to the source or character of a received distribution?*	Yes. (564-C:4-401(e))

Table 12.02
New Jersey
Trust Accounting: Principal and Income

1. *Does the trustee have the power to transfer income to principal or to transfer principal to income to meet its duty of impartiality?*	A trustee may adjust between principal and income if 1. the terms of the trust describe the amount that may or shall be distributed to a beneficiary by referring to the trust's income and 2. the trustee determines, after applying the rules in (§ 3B:19B-3(a)) that the trustee is unable to comply with (§ 3B:19B-3(b)) A decision by a trustee to increase the distribution to the income beneficiary or beneficiaries in any accounting period will be presumed to be fair and reasonable to all of the beneficiaries if the total income distribution does not exceed four percent of the net fair market value of the trust assets on the first business day of that accounting period. A decision by a trustee to decrease the distribution to the income beneficiary or beneficiaries in any accounting period will be presumed to be fair and reasonable to all of the beneficiaries if the total income distribution is at least six percent of the net fair market value of the trust assets on the first business day of that accounting period. Any adjustment by a trustee between income and principal with respect to any accounting period must be made during that accounting period or within 65 days after the end of that period. (§ 3B:19B-4)
2. *What is the effective date for the law? E.g., does it apply to preexisting trusts?*	The New Jersey Principal and Income Act applies to every trust or decedent's estate existing on or after January 1, 2002, except as otherwise expressly provided in the will or terms of the trust or in the New Jersey Principal and Income Act. (§ 3B:19B-30) ***Note:*** A trustee may continue using a former allocation method to allocate receipts for water, minerals, other natural resources, and timber under certain circumstances. (See § 3B:19B-19(d); § 3B:19B-20(d))
3. *What percentage is allocated to income and principal from proceeds of:*	
a) *IRA?* b) *Qualified pension or profit-sharing plan?* c) *Other deferred compensation arrangement?*	See the Uniform Principal and Income Act (1997) chart. (§ 3B:19B-17) ***Note***: § 3B:19B-17 uses language that differs from the Uniform Principal and Income Act (1997) § 409.
4. *What percentage is allocated to income and principal from proceeds of:*	
a) *Patents?* b) *Copyrights?*	See the Uniform Principal and Income Act (1997) chart. (§ 3B:19B-18)
5. *What percentage is allocated to income and principal in the event of distributions from:*	
a) *Corporations?* b) *Partnerships?* c) *LLCs?*	See the Uniform Principal and Income Act (1997) chart. (§ 3B:19B-10)

6. *What percentage is allocated to income and principal from proceeds of:*	
a) *Oil and gas?* b) *Minerals?* c) *Water?* d) *Other natural resourses (not including timber)?*	See the Uniform Principal and Income Act (1997) chart. (§ 3B:19B-19) ***Note:*** If a trust owns an interest in minerals, water or other natural resources on January 1, 2002, the trustee may allocate receipts from the interest as provided in the New Jersey Principal and Income Act or in the manner used by the trustee before January 1, 2002.
e) *Timber?*	See the Uniform Principal and Income Act (1997) chart. (§ 3B:19B-20) ***Note:*** If a trust owns an interest in timberland on January 1, 2002, the trustee may allocate receipts from the interest as provided in the New Jersey Principal and Income Act or in the manner used by the trustee before January 1, 2002.
f) *Rental properties?*	See the Uniform Principal and Income Act (1997) chart. (§ 3B:19B-14)
7. *After a decedent dies, in the case of an estate, or after an income interest ends, when the fiduciary is determining the remaining net income what are the rules regarding payment from income or principal for:*	
a) *Attorneys fees?* b) *Accountants fees?* c) *Fiduciary fees and commissions?* d) *Court costs?* e) *Interest on death taxes*	Fees for attorneys and accountants, fees for fiduciaries and commissions, court costs, and interest on death taxes that are apportioned to the estate or terminating income interest by the will, the terms of the trust, or applicable law must be paid from principal. (§ 3B:19B-5(b)(2))
f) *Debts?* g) *Funeral expenses?* h) *Family allowances and similar protections?* i) *Death taxes?* j) *Penalties on death taxes?*	Debts, funeral expenses, disposition of remains, family allowances, and death taxes and related penalties that are apportioned to the estate or terminating income interest by the will, the terms of the trust, or applicable law must be paid from principal. See the Uniform Principal and Income Act (1997) chart. (§ 3B:19B-5(b)(2))
8. *With respect to trust expenses from the administration of the trust that are not covered (§ 3B:19B-5(b)(2) [see Question #7]:*	
a) *Does the trustee have full discretion in allocating between income and principal for expenses incurred in the administration of the trust?*	No. See the Uniform Principal and Income Act (1997) chart. (§ 3B:19B-24; § 3B:19B-25)
b) *If not, are there special rules for:*	
i) *Regular trustee fees?* ii) *Advisory or custodial services to the trustee?*	The Trustee must pay from income commissions that are legally allowed to be paid to a trustee on income receipts and that are properly chargeable to the trust. The Trustee must pay

iii) Accountings, judicial proceedings and other matters that involve both the income and remainder interests?	from principal commissions that are legally allowed to be paid to a trustee on principal receipts and that are properly chargeable to the trust. Advisory and custodial services are to be allocated fifty percent to income and fifty percent to principal. Expenses for accounting, judicial proceedings, and other matters that involve both the income and remainder interests are to be allocated from principal or as the court otherwise directs. ***Note:*** This only applies if these expenses do not primarily concern the income interest. See § 3B:19B-24(c) and § 3B:19B-25(a)(6) for more details. (§ 3B:19B-24; § 3B:19B-25)
iv) Debts?	See the Uniform Principal and Income Act (1997) chart. (§ 3B:19B-24(c); § 3B:19B-25(a)(4))
c) Can the trustee determine what are "transmission" expenses and "management" expenses?	
9. With regard to specific gifts from a trust after an income interest ends or from an estate:	
a) What amounts must be paid from income and principal?	See the Uniform Principal and Income Act (1997) chart. (§ 3B:19B-5(a))
10. With regard to outright pecuniary gifts from an estate or trust?:	
a) Does interest accrue?	Yes. See the Uniform Principal and Income Act (1997) chart. (§ 3B:19B-5(c))
11. With regard to a gift in trust of a pecuniary amount from an estate or trust?	
a) Does interest accrue?	Yes. See the Uniform Principal and Income Act (1997) chart. (§ 3B:19B-5(c); § 3B:19B-5(d))
12. With regard to residuary gifts:	
a) What amount of income and principal is to be paid to the residuary beneficiary of a trust or an estate?	See the Uniform Principal and Income Act (1997) chart. (§ 3B:19B-5(d); § 3B:19B-6)
13. With regard to "business assets" held in trust:	
a) Can the trustee treat them as a separate entity?	Generally yes. See the Uniform Principal and Income Act (1997) chart. (§ 3B:19B-12)
b) Can the trustee treat distinct assets as separate entities?	Generally yes. See the Uniform Principal and Income Act (1997) chart. (§ 3B:19B-12(a))
c) Can earnings be retained in trust for the reasonable needs of the "business entity," and, if so, to what extent is this permitted?	Yes. See the Uniform Principal and Income Act (1997) chart. (§ 3B:19B-12(b))

14. With respect to discount bonds:	
a) To what extent is the discount added to income or principal upon maturity?	See the Uniform Principal and Income Act (1997) chart. (§ 3B:19B-15(b))
b) Does the trustee have discretion to allocate discount between income and principal?	No. (§ 3B:19B-15) ***Note:*** The trustee has overriding power to adjust under § 3B:19B-15(b).
c) Are distinctions drawn between Series E bonds and others?	No. (§ 3B:19B-15)
d) Are distinctions drawn based on the maturity date of the bond?	Yes. (§ 3B:19B-15(b)).
15. Is there a de minimis rule excusing the trustee from making adjustments in certain cases?	No.
16. With respect to derivatives:	
a) May income and loss be treated as that of a separate entity?	Yes. (§ 3B:19B-12(c)(7); § 3B:19B-22)
b) If not, or the trustee chooses not to do so, is income and loss allocated to the income account or to principal?	To principal. (§ 3B:19B-22(b))
17. To the extent put and call options are not derivatives, how are they allocated in terms of principal and income?	To principal. (§ 3B:19B-22(c))
18. How are asset-backed securities allocated in terms of principal and income?	See the Uniform Principal and Income Act (1997) chart. (§ 3B:19B-23(c))
19. Are expenses incurred to comply with environmental requirements allocated to income or principal?	To principal. (§ 3B:19B-25(a)(9))
20. Is income tax liability allocated generally to income or principal?	See the Uniform Principal and Income Act (1997) chart. (§ 3B:19B-28) ***Note:*** The New Jersey Principal and Income Act does not contain provisions allowing adjustments to offset the shifting of tax benefits as does the Uniform Principal and Income Act (1997) § 506.
21. If a Subchapter S shareholder's or partner's portion of tax liability is greater than cash distributed, how is the excess obligation allocated?	From principal. (§ 3B:19B-28(c)(2)(b))
22. What is the standard, if any, for making equitable adjustments between income and principal?	See the Uniform Principal and Income Act (1997) chart. (§ 3B:19B-3(b))
23. Is an income beneficiary entitled to receive income accrued but unpaid when an estate ends?	No. (§ 3B:19B-9)

24. Is an income beneficiary entitled to receive income accrued but unpaid when a revocable trust ends?	Generally no. See the Uniform Principal and Income Act (1997) chart. (§ 3B:19B-9)
25. Is an income beneficiary entitled to receive income accrued but unpaid when an irrevocable trust ends?	Generally no. See the Uniform Principal and Income Act (1997) chart. (§ 3B:19B-9)
26. With regard to mutual funds, how are:	
a) long-term gains allocated between income and principal?	See the Uniform Principal and Income Act (1997) chart. (§ 3B:19B-10(c)(4))
b) short-term gains allocated between income and principal?	See the Uniform Principal and Income Act (1997) chart. (§ 3B:19B-10(c)(4))
27. How are distributions from REITs allocated between income and principal?	See the Uniform Principal and Income Act (1997) chart. (§ 3B:19B-10(c)(4))
28. With respect to underproductive property:	
a) Is an adjustment, e.g., "delayed income," required to be paid to the income beneficiary?	No. (§ 3B:19B-21)
b) What percentage return makes property underproductive?	The statute only refers to property not productive of income. (§ 3B:19B-21)
29. Is the trustee required to increase income so that it is sufficient to qualify for the marital deduction?	Yes. (§ 3B:19B-21(a))
30. Is the trustee required to take depreciation?	No. (§ 3B:19B-26)
31. Is the trustee's determination on allocations generally presumed to be fair and reasonable?	Yes. (§ 3B:19B-3(b))
32. If an item is not addressed in the trust agreement or in the law, must it be allocated to principal or income?	To principal. (§ 3B:19B-3(a)(4))
33. When does an asset become subject to a trust:	
a) In the case of transfers during the transferor's life?	The date of transfer. (§ 3B:19B-7(b)(1))
b) In the case of a will?	The date of the testator's death. (§ 3B:19B-7(b)(2))
c) In the case of the death of a third party?	The date of the third party's death. (§ 3B:19B-7(b)(3))
34. Can a trustee rely on the characterization by an entity as to the source or character of a received distribution?	Yes. (§ 3B:19B-10(f))

Table 12.02
New Mexico
Trust Accounting: Principal and Income

1. *Does the trustee have the power to transfer income to principal or to transfer principal to income to meet its duty of impartiality?*	Yes. See the Uniform Principal and Income Act (1997) chart. (§ 46-3A-104)
2. *What is the effective date for the law? E.g., does it apply to preexisting trusts?*	The New Mexico Principal and Income Act applies to every trust or decedent's estate existing on July 1, 2001, except as otherwise expressly provided in the will or terms of the trust or in the New Mexico Principal and Income Act. (§ 46-3A-603) ***Note:*** A trustee may continue using a former allocation method to allocate receipts for water, minerals, other natural resources, and timber under certain circumstances. (See § 46-3A-411; § 46-3A-412)
3. *What percentage is allocated to income and principal from proceeds of:*	
a) *IRA?* b) *Qualified pension or profit-sharing plan?* c) *Other deferred compensation arrangement?*	See the Uniform Principal and Income Act (1997) chart. (§ 46-3A-409)
4. *What percentage is allocated to income and principal from proceeds of:*	
a) *Patents?* b) *Copyrights?*	See the Uniform Principal and Income Act (1997) chart. (§ 46-3A-410(b))
5. *What percentage is allocated to income and principal in the event of distributions from:*	
a) *Corporations?* b) *Partnerships?* c) *LLCs?*	See the Uniform Principal and Income Act (1997) chart. (§ 46-3A-401)
6. *What percentage is allocated to income and principal from proceeds of:*	
a) *Oil and gas?* b) *Minerals?* c) *Water?* d) *Other natural resourses (not including timber)?*	The trustee must allocate a receipt received as nominal delay rental or a nominal annual rent on a lease to income. The trustee must allocate a receipt received from a production payment to income if and to the extent that the agreement creating the production payment provides a factor for interest or its equivalent. The balance must be allocated to principal. If a trustee receives an amount from a working interest, royalty payment, shut-in well payment, take-or-pay payment, bonus or delay rental or any other interest not provided for in the two preceding paragraphs, the trustee should allocate to principal an amount that is equivalent to the amount allowable as a deduction from gross income for depletion purposes under the federal income tax law in effect at the time of severance. The trustee should allocate the balance to income. If the

	amount that is allowed as a deduction is less than fifteen percent of gross income for depletion purposes, or if depletion is not allowed, then the amount to be allocated to principal and the amount to be allocated to income must be determined in accordance with § 46-3A-104 (dealing with adjustments between income and principal). An amount received on account of an interest in water that is renewable must be allocated to income. If the water is not renewable, ninety percent (90%) of the amount must be allocated to principal and ten percent (10%) to income. (§ 46-3A-411) ***Note***: If a trust owns an interest in minerals, water or other natural resources on July 1, 2001, the trustee may allocate receipts from the interest as provided in the New Mexico Principal and Income Act or in the manner used by the trustee before July 1, 2001.
e) Timber?	See the Uniform Principal and Income Act (1997) chart. (§ 46-3A-412) ***Note:*** If a trust owns an interest in timberland on July 1, 2001, the trustee may allocate receipts from the interest as provided in the New Mexico Principal and Income Act or in the manner used by the trustee before July 1, 2001.
f) Rental properties?	See the Uniform Principal and Income Act (1997) chart. (§ 46-3A-405)
7. After a decedent dies, in the case of an estate, or after an income interest ends, when the fiduciary is determining the remaining net income what are the rules regarding payment from income or principal for:	
a) Attorneys fees? *b) Accountants fees?* *c) Fiduciary fees and commissions?* *d) Court costs?* *e) Interest on death taxes*	See the Uniform Principal and Income Act (1997) chart. (§ 46-3A-201(2)(B))
f) Debts? *g) Funeral expenses?* *h) Family allowances and similar protections?* *i) Death taxes?* *j) Penalties on death taxes?*	See the Uniform Principal and Income Act (1997) chart. (§ 46-3A-201(2)(C))
8. With respect to trust expenses from the administration of the trust that are not covered by § 46-3A-201(2)(B-C) [see Question #7]:	
a) Does the trustee have full discretion in allocating between income and principal for expenses incurred in the administration of the trust?	No. See the Uniform Principal and Income Act (1997) chart. (§ 46-3A-501; § 46-3A-502)

b) If not, are there special rules for:	
i) Regular trustee fees? *ii) Advisory or custodial services to the trustee?* *iii) Accountings, judicial proceedings and other matters that involve both the income and remainder interests?*	See the Uniform Principal and Income Act (1997) chart. (§ 46-3A-501; § 46-3A-502)
iv) Debts?	See the Uniform Principal and Income Act (1997) chart. (§ 46-3A-501(3); § 46-3A-502(a)(3))
c) Can the trustee determine what are "transmission" expenses and "management" expenses?	
9. With regard to specific gifts from a trust after an income interest ends or from an estate:	
a) What amounts must be paid from income and principal?	See the Uniform Principal and Income Act (1997) chart. (§ 46-3A-201(1); § 46-3A-201(5))
10. With regard to outright pecuniary gifts from an estate or trust?:	
a) Does interest accrue?	Yes. See the Uniform Principal and Income Act (1997) chart. (§ 46-3A-201(3))
11. With regard to a gift in trust of a pecuniary amount from an estate or trust?	
a) Does interest accrue?	No. See the Uniform Principal and Income Act (1997) chart. (§ 46-3A-201(4); § 46-3A-202)
12. With regard to residuary gifts:	
a) What amount of income and principal is to be paid to the residuary beneficiary of a trust or an estate?	See the Uniform Principal and Income Act (1997) chart. (§ 46-3A-201(4); § 46-3A-202)
13. With regard to "business assets" held in trust:	
a) Can the trustee treat them as a separate entity?	Generally yes. See the Uniform Principal and Income Act (1997) chart. (§ 46-3A-403)
b) Can the trustee treat distinct assets as separate entities?	Generally yes. See the Uniform Principal and Income Act (1997) chart. (§ 46-3A-403)
c) Can earnings be retained in trust for the reasonable needs of the "business entity," and, if so, to what extent is this permitted?	See the Uniform Principal and Income Act (1997) chart. (§ 46-3A-403(b))
14. With respect to discount bonds:	

a) *To what extent is the discount added to income or principal upon maturity?*	See the Uniform Principal and Income Act (1997) chart. (§ 46-3A-406(b))
b) *Does the trustee have discretion to allocate discount between income and principal?*	No. (§ 46-3A-406) **Note:** The trustee has the overriding power to adjust under (§ 46-3A-104(a)
c) *Are distinctions drawn between Series E bonds and others?*	No. (§ 46-3A-406)
d) *Are distinctions drawn based on the maturity date of the bond?*	Yes. (§ 46-3A-406(b))
15. *Is there a de minimis rule excusing the trustee from making adjustments in certain cases?*	Yes. See the Uniform Principal and Income Act (1997) chart. (§ 46-3A-408)
16. *With respect to derivatives:*	
a) *May income and loss be treated as that of a separate entity?*	Yes. See the Uniform Principal and Income Act (1997) chart. (§ 46-3A-403; § 46-3A-414(b))
b) *If not, or the trustee chooses not to do so, is income and loss allocated to the income account or to principal?*	To principal. (§ 46-3A-414(b))
17. *To the extent put and call options are not derivatives, how are they allocated in terms of principal and income?*	To principal. (§ 46-3A-414(b))
18. *How are asset-backed securities allocated in terms of principal and income?*	See the Uniform Principal and Income Act (1997) chart. (§ 46-3A-415)
19. *Are expenses incurred to comply with environmental requirements allocated to income or principal?*	Generally to principal. See the Uniform Principal and Income Act (1997) chart. (§ 46-3A-502(a)(7))
20. *Is income tax liability allocated generally to income or principal?*	See the Uniform Principal and Income Act (1997) chart. (§ 46-3A-505; § 46-3A-506)
21. *If a Subchapter S shareholder's or partner's portion of tax liability is greater than cash distributed, how is the excess obligation allocated?*	To principal. (§ 46-3A-505(c)(2)(B))
22. *What is the standard, if any, for making equitable adjustments between income and principal?*	See the Uniform Principal and Income Act (1997) chart. (§ 46-3A-103(b))
23. *Is an income beneficiary entitled to receive income accrued but unpaid when an estate ends?*	No. (§ 46-3A-303)
24. *Is an income beneficiary entitled to receive income accrued but unpaid when a revocable trust ends?*	Generally no. See the Uniform Principal and Income Act (1997) chart. (§ 46-3A-303)

25. Is an income beneficiary entitled to receive income accrued but unpaid when an irrevocable trust ends?	Generally no. See the Uniform Principal and Income Act (1997) chart. (§ 46-3A-303)
26. With regard to mutual funds, how are:	
a) long-term gains allocated between income and principal?	See the Uniform Principal and Income Act (1997) chart. (§ 46-3A-401(c)(4))
b) short-term gains allocated between income and principal?	See the Uniform Principal and Income Act (1997) chart. (§ 46-3A-401(c)(4))
27. How are distributions from REITs allocated between income and principal?	See the Uniform Principal and Income Act (1997) chart. (§ 46-3A-401(c)(4))
28. With respect to underproductive property:	
a) Is an adjustment, e.g., "delayed income," required to be paid to the income beneficiary?	No. (§ 46-3A-413)
b) What percentage return makes property underproductive?	The statute only refers to property not productive of income. (§ 46-3A-413)
29. Is the trustee required to increase income so that it is sufficient to qualify for the marital deduction?	Yes. (§ 46-3A-413(a))
30. Is the trustee required to take depreciation?	No. (§ 46-3A-503)
31. Is the trustee's determination on allocations generally presumed to be fair and reasonable?	Yes. (§ 46-3A-103(b))
32. If an item is not addressed in the trust agreement or in the law, must it be allocated to principal or income?	To principal. (§ 46-3A-103(a)(4))
33. When does an asset become subject to a trust:	
a) In the case of transfers during the transferor's life?	The date of transfer. (§ 46-3A-301(b)(1))
b) In the case of a will?	The date of the testator's death. (§ 46-3A-301(b)(2))
c) In the case of the death of a third party?	The date of the third party's death. (§ 46-3A-301(b)(3))
34. Can a trustee rely on the characterization by an entity as to the source or character of a received distribution?	Yes. (§ 46-3A-401(f))

Table 12.02
New York
Trust Accounting: Principal and Income

1. *Does the trustee have the power to transfer income to principal or to transfer principal to income to meet its duty of impartiality?*	The New York Principal and Income Act does not contain a provision that would allow a trustee to adjust principal and income to meet its duty of impartiality.
2. *What is the effective date for the law? E.g., does it apply to preexisting trusts?*	The New York Principal and Income Act applies to every trust or decedent's estate existing on January 1, 2002, except as otherwise expressly provided in the will or terms of the trust or in the New York Principal and Income Act. (Est. Powers & Trusts § 11-A-6.4) ***Note:*** A trustee may continue using a former allocation method to allocate receipts for water, minerals, other natural resources, and timber under certain circumstances. (See Est. Powers & Trusts § 11-A-4.11; Est. Powers & Trusts § 11-A-4.12)
3. *What percentage is allocated to income and principal from proceeds of:*	
a) *IRA?* b) *Qualified pension or profit-sharing plan?* c) *Other deferred compensation arrangement?*	See the Uniform Principal and Income Act (1997) chart. (Est. Powers & Trusts § 11-A-4.9)
4. *What percentage is allocated to income and principal from proceeds of:*	
a) *Patents?* b) *Copyrights?*	See the Uniform Principal and Income Act (1997) chart. (Est. Powers & Trusts § 11-A-4.11)
5. *What percentage is allocated to income and principal in the event of distributions from:*	
a) *Corporations?* b) *Partnerships?* c) *LLCs?*	See the Uniform Principal and Income Act (1997) chart. (Est. Powers & Trusts § 11-A-4.1)
6. *What percentage is allocated to income and principal from proceeds of:*	
a) *Oil and gas?* b) *Minerals?* c) *Water?* d) *Other natural resourses (not including timber)?*	See the Uniform Principal and Income Act (1997) chart. (Est. Powers & Trusts § 11-A-4.11) ***Note:*** If a trust owns an interest in minerals, water or other natural resources on January 1, 2002, the trustee may allocate receipts from the interest as provided in the New York Principal and Income Act or in the manner used by the trustee before January 1, 2002.
e) *Timber?*	See the Uniform Principal and Income Act (1997) chart. (Est. Powers & Trusts § 11-A-4.12 ***Note:*** If a trust owns an interest in timberland on January 1, 2002, the trustee may allocate receipts from the interest as provided in the New York Principal and Income Act or in the manner used by the trustee before January 1, 2002.

f) Rental properties?	See the Uniform Principal and Income Act (1997) chart. (Est. Powers & Trusts § 11-A-4.5)
7. After a decedent dies, in the case of an estate, or after an income interest ends, when the fiduciary is determining the remaining net income what are the rules regarding payment from income or principal for:	
a) Attorneys fees? *b) Accountants fees?* *c) Fiduciary fees and commissions?* *d) Court costs?* *e) Interest on death taxes*	See the Uniform Principal and Income Act (1997) chart. (Est. Powers & Trusts § 11-A-2.1(2)(B))
f) Debts? *g) Funeral expenses?* *h) Family allowances and similar protections?* *i) Death taxes?* *j) Penalties on death taxes?*	See the Uniform Principal and Income Act (1997) chart. (Est. Powers & Trusts § 11-A-2.1(2)(C))
8. With respect to trust expenses from the administration of the trust that are not covered by Est. Powers & Trusts § 11-A-2.1(2) (B-C) [see Question #7]:	
a) Does the trustee have full discretion in allocating between income and principal for expenses incurred in the administration of the trust?	No. (Est. Powers & Trusts § 11-A-5.1; Est. Powers & Trusts § 11-A-5.2)
b) If not, are there special rules for:	
i) Regular trustee fees? *ii) Advisory or custodial services to the trustee?* *iii) Accountings, judicial proceedings and other matters that involve both the income and remainder interests?*	The New York Principal and Income Act does not address the regular compensation of the trustee directly; however, because regular trustee fees are ordinary expenses incurred in connection with adminstration and management or trust property, all regular trustee fees should be paid from income. (Est. Powers & Trusts § 11-A-5.1(3)) The trustee must allocate one-third (1/3) of the regular compensation of any person providing investment advisory or custodial services to the trustee to income. The balance should be allocated to principal. Unless a court finds that any judicial proceeding primarily concerns income and that it is equitable to charge all or part of the expense of such proceeding to income, the trustee must allocate expenses for accountings, judicial proceedings, or any other matter to principal. (Est. Powers & Trusts § 11-A-5.1; Est. Powers & Trusts § 11-A-5.2)
iv) Debts?	See the Uniform Principal and Income Act (1997) chart. (Est. Powers & Trusts § 11-A-5.1(3); (Est. Powers & Trusts § 11-A-5.2(a)(3))

c) *Can the trustee determine what are "transmission" expenses and "management" expenses?*	
9. *With regard to specific gifts from a trust after an income interest ends or from an estate:*	
a) *What amounts must be paid from income and principal?*	See the Uniform Principal and Income Act (1997) chart. (Est. Powers & Trusts § 11-A-2.1(1); Est. Powers & Trusts § 11-A-2.1(5))
10. *With regard to outright pecuniary gifts from an estate or trust?:*	
a) *Does interest accrue?*	Yes. See the Uniform Principal and Income Act (1997) chart. (Est. Powers & Trusts § 11-A-2.1(3))
11. *With regard to a gift in trust of a pecuniary amount from an estate or trust?*	
a) *Does interest accrue?*	No. See the Uniform Principal and Income Act (1997) chart. (Est. Powers & Trusts § 11-A-2.1(4); Est. Powers & Trusts § 11-A-2.2)
12. *With regard to residuary gifts:*	
a) *What amount of income and principal is to be paid to the residuary beneficiary of a trust or an estate?*	See the Uniform Principal and Income Act (1997) chart. (Est. Powers & Trusts § 11-A-2.1(4); Est. Powers & Trusts § 11-A-2.2)
13. *With regard to "business assets" held in trust:*	
a) *Can the trustee treat them as a separate entity?*	Generally yes. See the Uniform Principal and Income Act (1997) chart. (Est. Powers & Trusts § 11-A-4.3)
b) *Can the trustee treat distinct assets as separate entities?*	Generally yes. See the Uniform Principal and Income Act (1997) chart. (Est. Powers & Trusts § 11-A-4.3)
c) *Can earnings be retained in trust for the reasonable needs of the "business entity," and, if so, to what extent is this permitted?*	Yes. See the Uniform Principal and Income Act (1997) chart. (Est. Powers & Trusts § 11-A-4.3(b))
14. *With respect to discount bonds:*	
a) *To what extent is the discount added to income or principal upon maturity?*	A trustee must allocate to principal an amount received from the sale, redemption, or other disposition of bond. The increment in value of a zero coupon bond is income. If the income accrues pursuant to a fixed schedule of appreciation, the trustee may distribute the income as it accrues, and the trustee may transfer the appropriate amount from principal to income on each such date. When unrealized appreciation is distributed as income but out of principal, the trustee must reimburse the principal from income whenever the appreciation is realized. (Est. Powers & Trusts § 11-A-4.6(b))

b) *Does the trustee have discretion to allocate discount between income and principal?*	No. (Est. Powers & Trusts § 11-A-4.6(b))
c) *Are distinctions drawn between Series E bonds and others?*	No. (Est. Powers & Trusts § 11-A-4.6(b))
d) *Are distinctions drawn based on the maturity date of the bond?*	No. (Est. Powers & Trusts § 11-A-4.6(b))
15. *Is there a de minimis rule excusing the trustee from making adjustments in certain cases?*	Yes. See the Uniform Principal and Income Act (1997) chart. (Est. Powers & Trusts § 11-A-4.8)
16. *With respect to derivatives:*	
a) *May income and loss be treated as that of a separate entity?*	Yes. See the Uniform Principal and Income Act (1997) chart. (Est. Powers & Trusts § 11-A-4.14(b); Est. Powers & Trusts § 11-A-4.3(c)(7))
b) *If not, or the trustee chooses not to do so, is income and loss allocated to the income account or to principal?*	To principal. (Est. Powers & Trusts § 11-A-4.14(b))
17. *To the extent put and call options are not derivatives, how are they allocated in terms of principal and income?*	To principal. (Est. Powers & Trusts § 11-A-4.14(c))
18. *How are asset-backed securities allocated in terms of principal and income?*	See the Uniform Principal and Income Act (1997) chart. (Est. Powers & Trusts § 11-A-4.15)
19. *Are expenses incurred to comply with environmental requirements allocated to income or principal?*	To principal. See the Uniform Principal and Income Act (1997) chart. (Est. Powers & Trusts § 11-A-5.2(a)(7))
20. *Is income tax liability allocated generally to income or principal?*	See the Uniform Principal and Income Act (1997) chart. (Est. Powers & Trusts § 11-A-5.5; Est. Powers & Trusts § 11-A-5.6)
21. *If a Subchapter S shareholder's or partner's portion of tax liability is greater than cash distributed, how is the excess obligation allocated?*	From principal. (Est. Powers & Trusts § 11-A-5.5(c)(2)(B))
22. *What is the standard, if any, for making equitable adjustments between income and principal?*	The New York Principal and Income Act does not contain a provision that would allow a trustee to adjust principal and income to meet its duty of impartiality.
23. *Is an income beneficiary entitled to receive income accrued but unpaid when an estate ends?*	No. (Est. Powers & Trusts § 11-A-3.3)
24. *Is an income beneficiary entitled to receive income accrued but unpaid when a revocable trust ends?*	Generally no. See the Uniform Principal and Income Act (1997) chart. (Est. Powers & Trusts § 11-A-3.3)
25. *Is an income beneficiary entitled to receive income accrued but unpaid when an irrevocable trust ends?*	Generally no. See the Uniform Principal and Income Act (1997) chart. (Est. Powers & Trusts § 11-A-3.3)

26. With regard to mutual funds, how are:	
a) long-term gains allocated between income and principal?	See the Uniform Principal and Income Act (1997) chart. (Est. Powers & Trusts § 11-A-4.1(c)(4))
b) short-term gains allocated between income and principal?	See the Uniform Principal and Income Act (1997) chart. (Est. Powers & Trusts § 11-A-4.1(c)(4))
27. How are distributions from REITs allocated between income and principal?	See the Uniform Principal and Income Act (1997) chart. (Est. Powers & Trusts § 11-A-4.1(c)(4))
28. With respect to underproductive property:	
a) Is an adjustment, e.g., "delayed income," required to be paid to the income beneficiary?	No. (Est. Powers & Trusts § 11-A-4.13)
b) What percentage return makes property underproductive?	The statute only refers to property not productive of income. (Est. Powers & Trusts § 11-A-4.13)
29. Is the trustee required to increase income so that it is sufficient to qualify for the marital deduction?	Yes. (Est. Powers & Trusts § 11-A-4.13(a))
30. Is the trustee required to take depreciation?	No. (Est. Powers & Trusts § 11-A-5.3)
31. Is the trustee's determination on allocations generally presumed to be fair and reasonable?	Yes. (Est. Powers & Trusts § 11-A-1.3(b))
32. If an item is not addressed in the trust agreement or in the law, must it be allocated to principal or income?	To principal. (Est. Powers & Trusts § 11-A-1.3(a)(4))
33. When does an asset become subject to a trust:	
a) In the case of transfers during the transferor's life?	The date of transfer. (Est. Powers & Trusts § 11-A-3.1(b)(1))
b) In the case of a will?	The date of the testator's death. (Est. Powers & Trusts § 11-A-3.1(b)(2))
c) In the case of the death of a third party?	The date of the third party's death. (Est. Powers & Trusts § 11-A-3.1(b)(3))
34. Can a trustee rely on the characterization by an entity as to the source or character of a received distribution?	Yes. (Est. Powers & Trusts § 11-A-4.1(f))

Table 12.02
North Carolina
Trust Accounting: Principal and Income

1. *Does the trustee have the power to transfer income to principal or to transfer principal to income to meet its duty of impartiality?*	Yes. See the Uniform Principal and Income Act (1997) chart. (§ 37A-1-104(a))
2. *What is the effective date for the law? E.g., does it apply to preexisting trusts?*	The North Carolina Principal and Income Act applies to every trust or decedent's estate existing on January 1, 2004, except as otherwise expressly provided in the will or terms of the trust or in the North Carolina Principal and Income Act. (2003 N.C. Sess. Laws 232) ***Note:*** A trustee may continue using a former allocation method to allocate receipts for water, minerals, other natural resources, and timber under certain circumstances. (See § 37A-4-411; § 37A-4-412)
3. *What percentage is allocated to income and principal from proceeds of:*	
a) IRA? *b) Qualified pension or profit-sharing plan?* *c) Other deferred compensation arrangement?*	See the Uniform Principal and Income Act (1997) chart. (§ 37A-4-409)
4. *What percentage is allocated to income and principal from proceeds of:*	
a) Patents? *b) Copyrights?*	See the Uniform Principal and Income Act (1997) chart. (§ 37A-4-410(b))
5. *What percentage is allocated to income and principal in the event of distributions from:*	
a) Corporations? *b) Partnerships?* *c) LLCs?*	See the Uniform Principal and Income Act (1997) chart. (§ 37A-4-401)
6. *What percentage is allocated to income and principal from proceeds of:*	
a) Oil and gas? *b) Minerals?* *c) Water?* *d) Other natural resourses (not including timber)?*	See the Uniform Principal and Income Act (1997) chart. (§ 37A-4-411) ***Note:*** If a trust owns an interest in minerals, water or other natural resources on January 1, 2004, the trustee may allocate receipts from the interest as provided in the North Carolina Principal and Income Act or in the manner used by the trustee before January 1, 2004.
e) Timber?	See the Uniform Principal and Income Act (1997) chart. (§ 37A-4-412) ***Note:*** If a trust owns an interest in timberland on January 1, 2004, the trustee may allocate receipts from the interest as provided in the North Carolina Principal and Income Act or in the manner used by the trustee before January 1, 2004.

f) Rental properties?	See the Uniform Principal and Income Act (1997) chart. (§ 37A-4-405)
7. After a decedent dies, in the case of an estate, or after an income interest ends, when the fiduciary is determining the remaining net income what are the rules regarding payment from income or principal for:	
a) Attorneys fees? *b) Accountants fees?* *c) Fiduciary fees and commissions?* *d) Court costs?* *e) Interest on death taxes*	See the Uniform Principal and Income Act (1997) chart. (§ 37A-2-201(2)(b))
f) Debts? *g) Funeral expenses?* *h) Family allowances and similar protections?* *i) Death taxes?* *j) Penalties on death taxes?*	See the Uniform Principal and Income Act (1997) chart. (§ 37A-2-201(2)(c))
8. With respect to trust expenses from the administration of the trust that are not covered by § 37A-2-201(2)(b-c) [see Question #7]:	
a) Does the trustee have full discretion in allocating between income and principal for expenses incurred in the administration of the trust?	No. See the Uniform Principal and Income Act (1997) chart. (§ 37A-5-501; § 37A-5-502)
b) If not, are there special rules for:	
i) Regular trustee fees? *ii) Advisory or custodial services to the trustee?* *iii) Accountings, judicial proceedings and other matters that involve both the income and remainder interests?*	See the Uniform Principal and Income Act (1997) chart. (§ 37A-5-501; § 37A-5-502)
iv) Debts?	See the Uniform Principal and Income Act (1997) chart. (§ 37A-5-501(3); § 37A-5-502(a)(3))
c) Can the trustee determine what are "transmission" expenses and "management" expenses?	
9. With regard to specific gifts from a trust after an income interest ends or from an estate:	
a) What amounts must be paid from income and principal?	See the Uniform Principal and Income Act (1997) chart. (§ 37A-2-201(1); § 37A-2-201(5).

10. With regard to outright pecuniary gifts from an estate or trust?:	
a) Does interest accrue?	Yes. Interest accrues beginning a year after 1. the date of death of the person whose death gives rise to the payment of the pecuniary gift or 2. the happening of a contingency that causes the income interest to end. (§ 37A-2-201(3))
11. With regard to a gift in trust of a pecuniary amount from an estate or trust?	
a) Does interest accrue?	No. See the Uniform Principal and Income Act (1997) chart. (§ 37A-2-201(4); § 37A-2-202)
12. With regard to residuary gifts:	
a) What amount of income and principal is to be paid to the residuary beneficiary of a trust or an estate?	See the Uniform Principal and Income Act (1997) chart. (§ 37A-2-201(4); § 37A-2-202)
13. With regard to "business assets" held in trust:	
a) Can the trustee treat them as a separate entity?	Generally yes. See the Uniform Principal and Income Act (1997) chart. (§ 37A-4-403)
b) Can the trustee treat distinct assets as separate entities?	Generally yes. See the Uniform Principal and Income Act (1997) chart. (§ 37A-4-403)
c) Can earnings be retained in trust for the reasonable needs of the "business entity," and, if so, to what extent is this permitted?	Yes. See the Uniform Principal and Income Act (1997) chart. (§ 37A-4-403)
14. With respect to discount bonds:	
a) To what extent is the discount added to income or principal upon maturity?	See the Uniform Principal and Income Act (1997) chart. (§ 37A-4-406(b))
b) Does the trustee have discretion to allocate discount between income and principal?	No. (§ 37A-4-406) ***Note:*** The trustee has the overriding power to adjust under § 37A-1-104(a).
c) Are distinctions drawn between Series E bonds and others?	No. (§ 37A-4-406)
d) Are distinctions drawn based on the maturity date of the bond?	Yes. (§ 37A-4-406(b))
15. Is there a de minimis rule excusing the trustee from making adjustments in certain cases?	Yes. See the Uniform Principal and Income Act (1997) chart. (§ 37A-4-408)
16. With respect to derivatives:	
a) May income and loss be treated as that of a separate entity?	Yes. (§ 37A-4-403(c)(7); § 37A-4-414(b))

b) *If not, or the trustee chooses not to do so, is income and loss allocated to the income account or to principal?*	To principal. (§ 37A-4-414(b))
17. *To the extent put and call options are not derivatives, how are they allocated in terms of principal and income?*	To principal. (§ 37A-4-414(c))
18. *How are asset-backed securities allocated in terms of principal and income?*	See the Uniform Principal and Income Act (1997) chart. (§ 37A-4-415)
19. *Are expenses incurred to comply with environmental requirements allocated to income or principal?*	Generally to principal. See the Uniform Principal and Income Act (1997) chart. (§ 37A-5-502(a)(7))
20. *Is income tax liability allocated generally to income or principal?*	See the Uniform Principal and Income Act (1997) chart. (§ 37A-5-505; § 37A-5-506)
21. *If a Subchapter S shareholder's or partner's portion of tax liability is greater than cash distributed, how is the excess obligation allocated?*	From principal. (§ 37A-5-505(c)(2)(b))
22. *What is the standard, if any, for making equitable adjustments between income and principal?*	See the Uniform Principal and Income Act (1997) chart. (§ 37A-1-103(b))
23. *Is an income beneficiary entitled to receive income accrued but unpaid when an estate ends?*	No. (§ 37A-3-303)
24. *Is an income beneficiary entitled to receive income accrued but unpaid when a revocable trust ends?*	Generally no. See the Uniform Principal and Income Act (1997) chart. (§ 37A-3-303)
25. *Is an income beneficiary entitled to receive income accrued but unpaid when an irrevocable trust ends?*	Generally no. See the Uniform Principal and Income Act (1997) chart. (§ 37A-3-303)
26. *With regard to mutual funds, how are:*	
a) *long-term gains allocated between income and principal?*	See the Uniform Principal and Income Act (1997) chart. (§ 37A-4-401(c)(4))
b) *short-term gains allocated between income and principal?*	See the Uniform Principal and Income Act (1997) chart. (§ 37A-4-401(c)(4))
27. *How are distributions from REITs allocated between income and principal?*	See the Uniform Principal and Income Act (1997) chart. (§ 37A-4-401(c)(4))
28. *With respect to underproductive property:*	
a) *Is an adjustment, e.g., "delayed income," required to be paid to the income beneficiary?*	No. (§ 37A-4-413)
b) *What percentage return makes property underproductive?*	The statute only refers to property not productive of income. (§ 37A-4-413)

29. Is the trustee required to increase income so that it is sufficient to qualify for the marital deduction?	Yes. (§ 37A-4-413(a))
30. Is the trustee required to take depreciation?	No. (§ 37A-5-503)
31. Is the trustee's determination on allocations generally presumed to be fair and reasonable?	Yes. (§ 37A-1-103(b))
32. If an item is not addressed in the trust agreement or in the law, must it be allocated to principal or income?	To principal. (§ 37A-1-103(a)(4))
33. When does an asset become subject to a trust:	
a) In the case of transfers during the transferor's life?	The date of transfer. (37A-3-301(b)(1))
b) In the case of a will?	The date of the testator's death. (§ 37A-3-301(b)(2))
c) In the case of the death of a third party?	The date of the third party's death. (§ 37A-3-301(b)(3))
34. Can a trustee rely on the characterization by an entity as to the source or character of a received distribution?	Yes. (§ 37A-4-401(f))

Table 12.02
North Dakota
Trust Accounting: Principal and Income

1. *Does the trustee have the power to transfer income to principal or to transfer principal to income to meet its duty of impartiality?*	No. (§ 59-04.2-03)
2. *What is the effective date for the law? E.g., does it apply to preexisting trusts?*	The North DakotaUniform Principal and Income Act does not specify whether or not it applies to preexisting trusts. ***Note:*** A trustee may continue using a former allocation method to allocate receipts for water, minerals, other natural resources, and timber under certain circumstances. (See § 59-04.2-19; § 59-04.2-20)
3. *What percentage is allocated to income and principal from proceeds of:*	
a) *IRA?* b) *Qualified pension or profit-sharing plan?* c) *Other deferred compensation arrangement?*	See the Uniform Principal and Income Act (1997) chart. (§ 59-04.2-17)
4. *What percentage is allocated to income and principal from proceeds of:*	
a) *Patents?* b) *Copyrights?*	See the Uniform Principal and Income Act (1997) chart. (§ 59-04.2-18)
5. *What percentage is allocated to income and principal in the event of distributions from:*	
a) *Corporations?* b) *Partnerships?* c) *LLCs?*	See the Uniform Principal and Income Act (1997) chart. (§ 59-04.2-09)
6. *What percentage is allocated to income and principal from proceeds of:*	
a) *Oil and gas?* b) *Minerals?* c) *Water?* d) *Other natural resourses (not including timber)?*	See the Uniform Principal and Income Act (1997) chart. (§ 59-04.2-19) ***Note:*** If a trust owns an interest in minerals, water or other natural resources on August 1, 1999, the trustee may allocate receipts from the interest as provided in the North Dakota Principal and Income Act or in the manner used by the trustee before August 1, 1999.
e) *Timber?*	See the Uniform Principal and Income Act (1997) chart. (§ 59-04.2-20) ***Note***: If a trust owns an interest in timberland on August 1, 1999, the trustee may allocate receipts from the interest as provided in the North Dakota Principal and Income Act or in the manner used by the trustee before August 1, 1999.
f) *Rental properties?*	See the Uniform Principal and Income Act (1997) chart. (§ 59-04.2-13)

7. After a decedent dies, in the case of an estate, or after an income interest ends, when the fiduciary is determining the remaining net income what are the rules regarding payment from income or principal for:	
a) Attorneys fees? *b) Accountants fees?* *c) Fiduciary fees and commissions?* *d) Court costs?* *e) Interest on death taxes*	See the Uniform Principal and Income Act (1997) chart. (§ 59-04.2-04(2)(b))
f) Debts? *g) Funeral expenses?* *h) Family allowances and similar protections?* *i) Death taxes?* *j) Penalties on death taxes?*	See the Uniform Principal and Income Act (1997) chart. (§ 59-04.2-04(2)(c))
8. With respect to trust expenses from the administration of the trust that are not covered by § 59-04.2-04(2)(b-c) [see Question #7]:	
a) Does the trustee have full discretion in allocating between income and principal for expenses incurred in the administration of the trust?	No. (§ 59-04.2-24; § 59-04.2-25)
b) If not, are there special rules for:	
i) Regular trustee fees? *ii) Advisory or custodial services to the trustee?* *iii) Accountings, judicial proceedings and other matters that involve both the income and remainder interests?*	See the Uniform Principal and Income Act (1997) chart. (§ 59-04.2-24; § 59-04.2-25)
iv) Debts?	See the Uniform Principal and Income Act (1997) chart. (§ 59-04.2-24(3); § 59-04.2-25(1)(c))
c) Can the trustee determine what are "transmission" expenses and "management" expenses?	
9. With regard to specific gifts from a trust after an income interest ends or from an estate:	
a) What amounts must be paid from income and principal?	See the Uniform Principal and Income Act (1997) chart. (§ 59-04.2-04(1); § 59-04.2-04(5))
10. With regard to outright pecuniary gifts from an estate or trust?:	

a) *Does interest accrue?*	Yes. See the Uniform Principal and Income Act (1997) chart. (§ 59-04.2-04(3))
11. *With regard to a gift in trust of a pecuniary amount from an estate or trust?*	
a) *Does interest accrue?*	No. See the Uniform Principal and Income Act (1997) chart. (§ 59-04.2-04(4); § 59-04.2-05)
12. *With regard to residuary gifts:*	
a) *What amount of income and principal is to be paid to the residuary beneficiary of a trust or an estate?*	See the Uniform Principal and Income Act (1997) chart. (§ 59-04.2-04(4); § 59-04.2-05)
13. *With regard to "business assets" held in trust:*	
a) *Can the trustee treat them as a separate entity?*	Generally yes. See the Uniform Principal and Income Act (1997) chart. (§ 59-04.2-11)
b) *Can the trustee treat distinct assets as separate entities?*	Generally yes. See the Uniform Principal and Income Act (1997) chart. (§ 59-04.2-11)
c) *Can earnings be retained in trust for the reasonable needs of the "business entity," and, if so, to what extent is this permitted?*	Yes. See the Uniform Principal and Income Act (1997) chart. (§ 59-04.2-11(2))
14. *With respect to discount bonds:*	
a) *To what extent is the discount added to income or principal upon maturity?*	See the Uniform Principal and Income Act (1997) chart. (§ 59-04.2-14)
b) *Does the trustee have discretion to allocate discount between income and principal?*	No. (§ 59-04.2-14)
c) *Are distinctions drawn between Series E bonds and others?*	No. (§ 59-04.2-14)
d) *Are distinctions drawn based on the maturity date of the bond?*	Yes. (§ 59-04.2-14(2))
15. *Is there a de minimis rule excusing the trustee from making adjustments in certain cases?*	No. (§ 59-04.2-16)
16. *With respect to derivatives:*	
a) *May income and loss be treated as that of a separate entity?*	Yes. (§ 59-04.2-11(3); § 59-04.2-22(2))
b) *If not, or the trustee chooses not to do so, is income and loss allocated to the income account or to principal?*	To principal. (§ 59-04.2-22(2))

17. To the extent put and call options are not derivatives, how are they allocated in terms of principal and income?	To principal. (§ 59-04.2-22(3))
18. How are asset-backed securities allocated in terms of principal and income?	See the Uniform Principal and Income Act (1997) chart. (§ 59-04.2-23)
19. Are expenses incurred to comply with environmental requirements allocated to income or principal?	Generally to principal. See the Uniform Principal and Income Act (1997) chart. (§ 59-04.2-25(1)(g))
20. Is income tax liability allocated generally to income or principal?	See the Uniform Principal and Income Act (1997) chart. (§ 59-04.2-28; § 59-04.2-29)
21. If a Subchapter S shareholder's or partner's portion of tax liability is greater than cash distributed, how is the excess obligation allocated?	From principal. (§ 59-04.2-28(3)(b)(2))
22. What is the standard, if any, for making equitable adjustments between income and principal?	The trustee does not have the power to transfer income to principal or to transfer from principal to income. (§ 59-04.2-02 (2); § 59-04.2-03)
23. Is an income beneficiary entitled to receive income accrued but unpaid when an estate ends?	No. See the Uniform Principal and Income Act (1997) chart. (§ 59-04.2-08)
24. Is an income beneficiary entitled to receive income accrued but unpaid when a revocable trust ends?	Generally no. See the Uniform Principal and Income Act (1997) chart. (§ 59-04.2-08)
25. Is an income beneficiary entitled to receive income accrued but unpaid when an irrevocable trust ends?	Generally no. See the Uniform Principal and Income Act (1997) chart. (§ 59-04.2-08)
26. With regard to mutual funds, how are:	
a) long-term gains allocated between income and principal?	See the Uniform Principal and Income Act (1997) chart. (§ 59-04.2-09(3)(d))
b) short-term gains allocated between income and principal?	See the Uniform Principal and Income Act (1997) chart. (§ 59-04.2-09(3)(d))
27. How are distributions from REITs allocated between income and principal?	See the Uniform Principal and Income Act (1997) chart. (§ 59-04.2-09(3)(d))
28. With respect to underproductive property:	
a) Is an adjustment, e.g., "delayed income," required to be paid to the income beneficiary?	The North Dakota Principal and Income Act does not provide any guidance for unproductive or underproductive property. (§ 59-04.2-21)
b) What percentage return makes property underproductive?	The North Dakota Principal and Income Act does not provide any guidance for unproductive or underproductive property. (§ 59-04.2-21)
29. Is the trustee required to increase income so that it is sufficient to qualify for the marital deduction?	The North Dakota Principal and Income Act does not provide any guidance for increasing income in order to qualify for the marital deduction. (§ 59-04.2-21)

30. Is the trustee required to take depreciation?	No. (§ 59-04.2-26)
31. Is the trustee's determination on allocations generally presumed to be fair and reasonable?	Yes. (§ 59-04.2-02(2))
32. If an item is not addressed in the trust agreement or in the law, must it be allocated to principal or income?	To principal. (§ 59-04.2-02(1)(d))
33. When does an asset become subject to a trust:	
a) In the case of transfers during the transferor's life?	The date of transfer. (§ 59-04.2-06(2)(a))
b) In the case of a will?	The date of the testator's death. (§ 59-04.2-06(2)(b))
c) In the case of the death of a third party?	The date of the third party's death. (§ 59-04.2-06(2)(c))
34. Can a trustee rely on the characterization by an entity as to the source or character of a received distribution?	Yes. (§ 59-04.2-09(6))

Table 12.02
Ohio
Trust Accounting: Principal and Income

1. *Does the trustee have the power to transfer income to principal or to transfer principal to income to meet its duty of impartiality?*	See the Uniform Principal and Income Act (1997) chart. (§ 5812.03)
2. *What is the effective date for the law? E.g., does it apply to preexisting trusts?*	The Ohio Principal and Income Act applies to every trust or decedent's estate existing on January 1, 2003, except as otherwise expressly provided in the will or terms of the trust or in the Ohio Principal and Income Act. (§ 5812.52) ***Note:*** A trustee may continue using a former allocation method to allocate receipts for water, minerals, other natural resources, and timber under certain circumstances. (See § 5812.34; § 5812.35)
3. *What percentage is allocated to income and principal from proceeds of:*	
a) *IRA?* b) *Qualified pension or profit-sharing plan?* c) *Other deferred compensation arrangement?*	See the Uniform Principal and Income Act (1997) chart. (§ 5812.32)
4. *What percentage is allocated to income and principal from proceeds of:*	
a) *Patents?* b) *Copyrights?*	See the Uniform Principal and Income Act (1997) chart. (§ 5812.33)
5. *What percentage is allocated to income and principal in the event of distributions from:*	
a) *Corporations?* b) *Partnerships?* c) *LLCs?*	See the Uniform Principal and Income Act (1997) chart. (§ 5812.18)
6. *What percentage is allocated to income and principal from proceeds of:*	
a) *Oil and gas?* b) *Minerals?* c) *Water?* d) *Other natural resourses (not including timber)?*	See the Uniform Principal and Income Act (1997) chart. (§ 5812.34) ***Note:*** If a trust owns an interest in minerals, water or other natural resources on January 1, 2003, the trustee may allocate receipts from the interest as provided in the Ohio Principal and Income Act or in the manner used by the trustee before January 1, 2003.
e) *Timber?*	See the Uniform Principal and Income Act (1997) chart. (§ 5812.35) ***Note***: If a trust owns an interest in timberland on January 1, 2003, the trustee may allocate receipts from the interest as provided in the Ohio Principal and Income Act or in the manner used by the trustee before January 1, 2003.
f) *Rental properties?*	See the Uniform Principal and Income Act (1997) chart. (§ 5812.25)

7. *After a decedent dies, in the case of an estate, or after an income interest ends, when the fiduciary is determining the remaining net income what are the rules regarding payment from income or principal for:*	
a) *Attorneys fees?* b) *Accountants fees?* c) *Fiduciary fees and commissions?* d) *Court costs?* e) *Interest on death taxes*	See the Uniform Principal and Income Act (1997) chart. (§ 5812.07(B)(2))
f) *Debts?* g) *Funeral expenses?* h) *Family allowances and similar protections?* i) *Death taxes?* j) *Penalties on death taxes?*	See the Uniform Principal and Income Act (1997) chart. (§ 5812.07(B)(3))
8. *With respect to trust expenses from the administration of the trust that are not covered by § 5812.07(B)(2-3) [see Question #7]:*	
a) *Does the trustee have full discretion in allocating between income and principal for expenses incurred in the administration of the trust?*	No. (§ 5812.42; § 5812.43)
b) *If not, are there special rules for:*	
i) *Regular trustee fees?* ii) *Advisory or custodial services to the trustee?* iii) *Accountings, judicial proceedings and other matters that involve both the income and remainder interests?*	See the Uniform Principal and Income Act (1997) chart. (§ 5812.42; § 5812.43)
iv) *Debts?*	See the Uniform Principal and Income Act (1997) chart. (§ 5812.42(C); § 5812.43(A)(3))
c) *Can the trustee determine what are "transmission" expenses and "management" expenses?*	
9. *With regard to specific gifts from a trust after an income interest ends or from an estate:*	
a) *What amounts must be paid from income and principal?*	See the Uniform Principal and Income Act (1997) chart. (§ 5812.07(A); § 5812.07(E))
10. *With regard to outright pecuniary gifts from an estate or trust?:*	

a) *Does interest accrue?*	Yes. See the Uniform Principal and Income Act (1997) chart. (§ 5812.07(C))
11. *With regard to a gift in trust of a pecuniary amount from an estate or trust?*	
a) *Does interest accrue?*	No. See the Uniform Principal and Income Act (1997) chart. (§ 5812.07(D); § 5812.08)
12. *With regard to residuary gifts:*	
a) *What amount of income and principal is to be paid to the residuary beneficiary of a trust or an estate?*	See the Uniform Principal and Income Act (1997) chart. (§ 5812.07(D); § 5812.08)
13. *With regard to "business assets" held in trust:*	
a) *Can the trustee treat them as a separate entity?*	Generally yes. See the Uniform Principal and Income Act (1997) chart. (§ 5812.20)
b) *Can the trustee treat distinct assets as separate entities?*	Generally yes. See the Uniform Principal and Income Act (1997) chart. (§ 5812.20)
c) *Can earnings be retained in trust for the reasonable needs of the "business entity," and, if so, to what extent is this permitted?*	Yes. See the Uniform Principal and Income Act (1997) chart. (§ 5812.20)
14. *With respect to discount bonds:*	
a) *To what extent is the discount added to income or principal upon maturity?*	See the Uniform Principal and Income Act (1997) chart. (§ 5812.26)
b) *Does the trustee have discretion to allocate discount between income and principal?*	No. (§ 5812.26). ***Note:*** The trustee has the overriding power to adjust under § 5812.03.
c) *Are distinctions drawn between Series E bonds and others?*	No. (§ 5812.26)
d) *Are distinctions drawn based on the maturity date of the bond?*	Yes. (§ 5812.26)
15. *Is there a de minimis rule excusing the trustee from making adjustments in certain cases?*	Yes. See the Uniform Principal and Income Act (1997) chart. (§ 5812.31)
16. *With respect to derivatives:*	
a) *May income and loss be treated as that of a separate entity?*	Yes. (§ 5812.20(C)(7); § 5812.37(B))
b) *If not, or the trustee chooses not to do so, is income and loss allocated to the income account or to principal?*	To principal. (§ 5812.37(B))

17. To the extent put and call options are not derivatives, how are they allocated in terms of principal and income?	To principal. (§ 5812.37(C))
18. How are asset-backed securities allocated in terms of principal and income?	See the Uniform Principal and Income Act (1997) chart. (§ 5812.38)
19. Are expenses incurred to comply with environmental requirements allocated to income or principal?	Generally to principal. See the Uniform Principal and Income Act (1997) chart. (§ 5812.47(A)(7))
20. Is income tax liability allocated generally to income or principal?	See the Uniform Principal and Income Act (1997) chart. (§ 5812.46; § 5812.47)
21. If a Subchapter S shareholder's or partner's portion of tax liability is greater than cash distributed, how is the excess obligation allocated?	From principal. (§ 5812.46(C)(2)(b))
22. What is the standard, if any, for making equitable adjustments between income and principal?	See the Uniform Principal and Income Act (1997) chart. (§ 5812.02(B))
23. Is an income beneficiary entitled to receive income accrued but unpaid when an estate ends?	No. (§ 5812.14)
24. Is an income beneficiary entitled to receive income accrued but unpaid when a revocable trust ends?	Generally no. See the Uniform Principal and Income Act (1997) chart. (§ 5812.14)
25. Is an income beneficiary entitled to receive income accrued but unpaid when an irrevocable trust ends?	Generally no. See the Uniform Principal and Income Act (1997) chart. (§ 5812.14)
26. With regard to mutual funds, how are:	
a) long-term gains allocated between income and principal?	See the Uniform Principal and Income Act (1997) chart. (§ 5812.18(C)(4))
b) short-term gains allocated between income and principal?	See the Uniform Principal and Income Act (1997) chart. (§ 5812.18(C)(4))
27. How are distributions from REITs allocated between income and principal?	See the Uniform Principal and Income Act (1997) chart. (§ 5812.18(C)(4))
28. With respect to underproductive property:	
a) Is an adjustment, e.g., "delayed income," required to be paid to the income beneficiary?	No. (§ 5812.36)
b) What percentage return makes property underproductive?	The statute only refers to property not productive of income. (§ 5812.36)
29. Is the trustee required to increase income so that it is sufficient to qualify for the marital deduction?	Yes. (§ 5812.36)

30. Is the trustee required to take depreciation?	No. (§ 5812.44)
31. Is the trustee's determination on allocations generally presumed to be fair and reasonable?	Yes. (§ 5812.02(B))
32. If an item is not addressed in the trust agreement or in the law, must it be allocated to principal or income?	To principal. (§ 5812.02(A)(4)).
33. When does an asset become subject to a trust:	
a) In the case of transfers during the transferor's life?	The date of transfer. (§ 5812.12(B)(1))
b) In the case of a will?	The date of the testator's death. (§ 5812.12(B)(2))
c) In the case of the death of a third party?	The date of the third party's death. (§ 5812.12(B)(3))
34. Can a trustee rely on the characterization by an entity as to the source or character of a received distribution?	Yes. (§ 5812.18(F))

Table 12.02
Oklahoma
Trust Accounting: Principal and Income

1. *Does the trustee have the power to transfer income to principal or to transfer principal to income to meet its duty of impartiality?*	Yes. See the Uniform Principal and Income Act (1997) chart. (60 § 175.104(A))
2. *What is the effective date for the law? E.g., does it apply to preexisting trusts?*	The Oklahoma Principal and Income Act applies to every trust or decedent's estate existing on November 1, 1998, except as otherwise expressly provided in the will or the terms of the trust or in the Oklahoma Principal and Income Act. (60 § 175.602) ***Note:*** A trustee may continue using a former allocation method to allocate receipts for water, minerals, other natural resources, and timber under certain circumstances. (See 60 § 175.411; 60 § 175.412)
3. *What percentage is allocated to income and principal from proceeds of:*	
a) *IRA?* b) *Qualified pension or profit-sharing plan?* c) *Other deferred compensation arrangement?*	See the Uniform Principal and Income Act (1997) chart. (60 § 175.409)
4. *What percentage is allocated to income and principal from proceeds of:*	
a) *Patents?* b) *Copyrights?*	See the Uniform Principal and Income Act (1997) chart. (60 § 175.410(B))
5. *What percentage is allocated to income and principal in the event of distributions from:*	
a) *Corporations?* b) *Partnerships?* c) *LLCs?*	See the Uniform Principal and Income Act (1997) chart. (60 § 175.401)
6. *What percentage is allocated to income and principal from proceeds of:*	
a) *Oil and gas?* b) *Minerals?* c) *Water?* d) *Other natural resourses (not including timber)?*	The trustee must allocate a receipt of less than One Thousand Dollars ($1,000) that is received as nominal delay rental or a nominal annual rent on a lease to income. The trustee must allocate a receipt of One Thousand Dollars ($1,000) or more that is received as nominal delay rental or a nominal annual rent fifteen percent (15%) to principal and eighty-five percent (85%) to income. The trustee must allocate a receipt received from a production payment to income if and to the extent that the agreement creating the production payment provides a factor for interest or its equivalent. The balance must be allocated to principal. The trustee must allocate fifteen percent (15%) of an amount received as a royalty, shut-in-well payment, take-or-pay payment, bonus, or a delay rental that is more than nominal, to principal and eighty-five percent (85%) to income.

	The trustee must allocate fifteen percent (15%) of the net amount received from a working interest or other interest (not mentioned in the two preceding paragraphs) to principal and eighty-five percent (85%) to income. An amount received on account of an interest in water that is renewable must be allocated to income. If the water is not renewable, ninety percent (90%) of the amount must be allocated to principal and ten percent (10%) to income. The rules above apply whether or not a decedent or donor was extracting the minerals, water, or other natural resources before the interest became subject to the trust. (60 § 175.411) ***Note:*** If a trust owns an interest in minerals, water or other natural resources on November 1, 1998, the trustee may allocate receipts from the interest as provided in the Oklahoma Principal and Income Act or in the manner used by the trustee before November 1, 1998.
e) Timber?	See the Uniform Principal and Income Act (1997) chart. (60 § 175.412) ***Note:*** If a trust owns an interest in timberland on November 1, 1998, the trustee may allocate receipts from the interest as provided in the Oklahoma Principal and Income Act or in the manner used by the trustee before November 1, 1998.
f) Rental properties?	See the Uniform Principal and Income Act (1997) chart. (60 § 175.405)
7. After a decedent dies, in the case of an estate, or after an income interest ends, when the fiduciary is determining the remaining net income what are the rules regarding payment from income or principal for:	
a) Attorneys fees? *b) Accountants fees?* *c) Fiduciary fees and commissions?* *d) Court costs?* *e) Interest on death taxes*	See the Uniform Principal and Income Act (1997) chart. (60 § 175.201(2)(b))
f) Debts? *g) Funeral expenses?* *h) Family allowances and similar protections?* *i) Death taxes?* *j) Penalties on death taxes?*	See the Uniform Principal and Income Act (1997) chart. (60 § 175.201(2)(c))
8. With respect to trust expenses from the administration of the trust that are not covered by 60 § 175.201(2)(b-c) [see Question #7]:	
a) Does the trustee have full discretion in allocating between income and	No. (60 § 175.501; 60 § 175.502)

principal for expenses incurred in the administration of the trust?	
b) If not, are there special rules for:	
i) Regular trustee fees? *ii) Advisory or custodial services to the trustee?* *iii) Accountings, judicial proceedings and other matters that involve both the income and remainder interests?*	See the Uniform Principal and Income Act (1997) chart. (60 § 175.501; 60 § 175.502)
iv) Debts?	See the Uniform Principal and Income Act (1997) chart. (60 § 175.501(3); 60 § 175.502(A)(3))
c) Can the trustee determine what are "transmission" expenses and "management" expenses?	
9. With regard to specific gifts from a trust after an income interest ends or from an estate:	
a) What amounts must be paid from income and principal?	See the Uniform Principal and Income Act (1997) chart. (60 § 175.201(1); 60 § 175.201(5))
10. With regard to outright pecuniary gifts from an estate or trust?:	
a) Does interest accrue?	Yes. See the Uniform Principal and Income Act (1997) chart. (60 § 175.201(3))
11. With regard to a gift in trust of a pecuniary amount from an estate or trust?	
a) Does interest accrue?	No. See the Uniform Principal and Income Act (1997) chart. (60 § 175.201(4); 60 § 175.202)
12. With regard to residuary gifts:	
a) What amount of income and principal is to be paid to the residuary beneficiary of a trust or an estate?	See the Uniform Principal and Income Act (1997) chart. (60 § 175.201(4); 60 § 175.202)
13. With regard to "business assets" held in trust:	
a) Can the trustee treat them as a separate entity?	Generally yes. (60 § 175.403)
b) Can the trustee treat distinct assets as separate entities?	Generally yes. (60 § 175.403)
c) Can earnings be retained in trust for the reasonable needs of the "business entity," and, if so, to what extent is this permitted?	Yes. See the Uniform Principal and Income Act (1997) chart. (60 § 175.403(B))

14. With respect to discount bonds:	
a) To what extent is the discount added to income or principal upon maturity?	See the Uniform Principal and Income Act (1997) chart. (60 § 175.406(B))
b) Does the trustee have discretion to allocate discount between income and principal?	No. (60 § 175.406) ***Note:*** The trustee has the overriding power to adjust under 60 § 175.104(A).
c) Are distinctions drawn between Series E bonds and others?	No. (60 § 175.406)
d) Are distinctions drawn based on the maturity date of the bond?	Yes. (60 § 175.406(B))
15. Is there a de minimis rule excusing the trustee from making adjustments in certain cases?	Yes. See the Uniform Principal and Income Act (1997) chart. (60 § 175.408)
16. With respect to derivatives:	
a) May income and loss be treated as that of a separate entity?	Yes. (60 § 175.403(C)(7); 60 § 175.414(B))
b) If not, or the trustee chooses not to do so, is income and loss allocated to the income account or to principal?	To principal. (60 § 175.414(B))
17. To the extent put and call options are not derivatives, how are they allocated in terms of principal and income?	To principal. (60 § 175.414(C))
18. How are asset-backed securities allocated in terms of principal and income?	See the Uniform Principal and Income Act (1997) chart. (60 § 175.415)
19. Are expenses incurred to comply with environmental requirements allocated to income or principal?	Generally to principal. See the Uniform Principal and Income Act (1997) chart. (60 § 175.502(A)(7))
20. Is income tax liability allocated generally to income or principal?	See the Uniform Principal and Income Act (1997) chart. (60 § 175.505; 60 § 175.506)
21. If a Subchapter S shareholder's or partner's portion of tax liability is greater than cash distributed, how is the excess obligation allocated?	From principal. (60 § 175.505(C)(2)(b))
22. What is the standard, if any, for making equitable adjustments between income and principal?	See the Uniform Principal and Income Act (1997) chart. (60 § 175.103(B)
23. Is an income beneficiary entitled to receive income accrued but unpaid when an estate ends?	No. (60 § 175.303)
24. Is an income beneficiary entitled to receive income accrued but unpaid when a revocable trust ends?	Generally no. See the Uniform Principal and Income Act (1997) chart. (60 § 175.303)

25. Is an income beneficiary entitled to receive income accrued but unpaid when an irrevocable trust ends?	Generally no. See the Uniform Principal and Income Act (1997) chart. (60 § 175.303)
26. With regard to mutual funds, how are:	
a) long-term gains allocated between income and principal?	See the Uniform Principal and Income Act (1997) chart. (60 § 175.401(C)(4))
b) short-term gains allocated between income and principal?	See the Uniform Principal and Income Act (1997) chart. (60 § 175.401(C)(4))
27. How are distributions from REITs allocated between income and principal?	See the Uniform Principal and Income Act (1997) chart. (60 § 175.401(C)(4))
28. With respect to underproductive property:	
a) Is an adjustment, e.g., "delayed income," required to be paid to the income beneficiary?	No. (60 § 175.413)
b) What percentage return makes property underproductive?	The statute only refers to property not productive of income. (60 § 175.413)
29. Is the trustee required to increase income so that it is sufficient to qualify for the marital deduction?	Yes. (60 § 175.413(A))
30. Is the trustee required to take depreciation?	No. (60 § 175.503)
31. Is the trustee's determination on allocations generally presumed to be fair and reasonable?	Yes. (60 § 175.103(B))
32. If an item is not addressed in the trust agreement or in the law, must it be allocated to principal or income?	To principal. (60 § 175.103(A)(4))
33. When does an asset become subject to a trust:	
a) In the case of transfers during the transferor's life?	The date of transfer. (60 § 175.301(B)(1))
b) In the case of a will?	The date of the testator's death. (60 § 175.301(B)(2))
c) In the case of the death of a third party?	The date of the third party's death. (60 § 175.301(B)(3))
34. Can a trustee rely on the characterization by an entity as to the source or character of a received distribution?	Yes. (60 § 175.401(F))

Table 12.02
Oregon
Trust Accounting: Principal and Income

1. *Does the trustee have the power to transfer income to principal or to transfer principal to income to meet its duty of impartiality?*	See the Uniform Principal and Income Act (1997) chart. (§ 129.215)
2. *What is the effective date for the law? E.g., does it apply to preexisting trusts?*	Except as expressly provided in a will or in the terms of a trust or in the Oregon Principal and Income Act, the Oregon Principal and Income Act applies to the administration of all trusts and estates, whether coming into existence before, on or after January 1, 2004. (2003 Or. Laws 279) ***Note:*** A trustee may continue using a former allocation method to allocate receipts for water, minerals, other natural resources, and timber under certain circumstances. (See § 129.365; § 129.370)
3. *What percentage is allocated to income and principal from proceeds of:*	
a) *IRA?* b) *Qualified pension or profit-sharing plan?* c) *Other deferred compensation arrangement?*	See the Uniform Principal and Income Act (1997) chart. (§ 129.355)
4. *What percentage is allocated to income and principal from proceeds of:*	
a) *Patents?* b) *Copyrights?*	See the Uniform Principal and Income Act (1997) chart. (§ 129.360)
5. *What percentage is allocated to income and principal in the event of distributions from:*	
a) *Corporations?* b) *Partnerships?* c) *LLCs?*	See the Uniform Principal and Income Act (1997) chart. (§ 129.300)
6. *What percentage is allocated to income and principal from proceeds of:*	
a) *Oil and gas?* b) *Minerals?* c) *Water?* d) *Other natural resourses (not including timber)?*	See the Uniform Principal and Income Act (1997) chart. (§ 129.365) ***Note***: If a trust owns an interest in minerals, water or other natural resources on January 1, 2004, the trustee may allocate receipts from the interest as provided in the Oregon Principal and Income Act or in the manner used by the trustee before January 1, 2004.
e) *Timber?*	See the Uniform Principal and Income Act (1997) chart. (§ 129.370) ***Note:*** If a trust owns an interest in timberland on January 1, 2004, the trustee may allocate receipts from the interest as provided in the Oregon Principal and Income Act or in the manner used by the trustee before January 1, 2004.

f) Rental properties?	See the Uniform Principal and Income Act (1997) chart. (§ 129.315)
7. After a decedent dies, in the case of an estate, or after an income interest ends, when the fiduciary is determining the remaining net income what are the rules regarding payment from income or principal for:	
a) Attorneys fees? *b) Accountants fees?* *c) Fiduciary fees and commissions?* *d) Court costs?* *e) Interest on death taxes*	See the Uniform Principal and Income Act (1997) chart. (§ 129.250(2)(b))
f) Debts? *g) Funeral expenses?* *h) Family allowances and similar protections?* *i) Death taxes?* *j) Penalties on death taxes?*	See the Uniform Principal and Income Act (1997) chart. (§ 129.250(2)(c))
8. With respect to trust expenses from the administration of the trust that are not covered by § 129.250(2)(b-c) [see Question #7]:	
a) Does the trustee have full discretion in allocating between income and principal for expenses incurred in the administration of the trust?	No. (§ 129.400; § 129.405)
b) If not, are there special rules for:	
i) Regular trustee fees? *ii) Advisory or custodial services to the trustee?* *iii) Accountings, judicial proceedings and other matters that involve both the income and remainder interests?*	See the Uniform Principal and Income Act (1997) chart. (§ 129.400; § 129.405)
iv) Debts?	See the Uniform Principal and Income Act (1997) chart. (§ 129.400(3); § 129.405(1)(c))
c) Can the trustee determine what are "transmission" expenses and "management" expenses?	
9. With regard to specific gifts from a trust after an income interest ends or from an estate:	
a) What amounts must be paid from income and principal?	See the Uniform Principal and Income Act (1997) chart. (§ 129.250(1); § 129.250(5))

10. With regard to outright pecuniary gifts from an estate or trust?:	
a) Does interest accrue?	Yes. See the Uniform Principal and Income Act (1997) chart. (§ 129.250(3))
11. With regard to a gift in trust of a pecuniary amount from an estate or trust?	
a) Does interest accrue?	No. See the Uniform Principal and Income Act (1997) chart. (§ 129.250(4); § 129.255)
12. With regard to residuary gifts:	
a) What amount of income and principal is to be paid to the residuary beneficiary of a trust or an estate?	See the Uniform Principal and Income Act (1997) chart. (§ 129.250(4); § 129.255)
13. With regard to "business assets" held in trust:	
a) Can the trustee treat them as a separate entity?	Generally yes. See the Uniform Principal and Income Act (1997) chart. (§ 129.308)
b) Can the trustee treat distinct assets as separate entities?	Generally yes. See the Uniform Principal and Income Act (1997) chart. (§ 129.308)
c) Can earnings be retained in trust for the reasonable needs of the "business entity," and, if so, to what extent is this permitted?	Yes. See the Uniform Principal and Income Act (1997) chart. (§ 129.308(2))
14. With respect to discount bonds:	
a) To what extent is the discount added to income or principal upon maturity?	See the Uniform Principal and Income Act (1997) chart. (§ 129.320(2))
b) Does the trustee have discretion to allocate discount between income and principal?	No. (§ 129.320) ***Note:*** The trustee has the overriding power to adjust under § 129.215.
c) Are distinctions drawn between Series E bonds and others?	No. (§ 129.320)
d) Are distinctions drawn based on the maturity date of the bond?	Yes. (§ 129.320(2))
15. Is there a de minimis rule excusing the trustee from making adjustments in certain cases?	Yes. See the Uniform Principal and Income Act (1997) chart. (§ 129.350)
16. With respect to derivatives:	
a) May income and loss be treated as that of a separate entity?	Yes. (§ 129.308(3)(g); § 129.380)
b) If not, or the trustee chooses not to do so, is income and loss allocated to the income account or to principal?	To principal. (§ 129.380(2))

17. *To the extent put and call options are not derivatives, how are they allocated in terms of principal and income?*	To principal. (§ 129.380(3))
18. *How are asset-backed securities allocated in terms of principal and income?*	See the Uniform Principal and Income Act (1997) chart. (§ 129.385)
19. *Are expenses incurred to comply with environmental requirements allocated to income or principal?*	Generally to principal. See the Uniform Principal and Income Act (1997) chart. (§ 129.405(1)(g))
20. *Is income tax liability allocated generally to income or principal?*	See the Uniform Principal and Income Act (1997) chart. (§ 129.420; § 129.425)
21. *If a Subchapter S shareholder's or partner's portion of tax liability is greater than cash distributed, how is the excess obligation allocated?*	From principal. (§ 129.420(3)(b)(B))
22. *What is the standard, if any, for making equitable adjustments between income and principal?*	See the Uniform Principal and Income Act (1997) chart. (§ 129.210(2))
23. *Is an income beneficiary entitled to receive income accrued but unpaid when an estate ends?*	No. See the Uniform Principal and Income Act (1997) chart. (§ 129.280)
24. *Is an income beneficiary entitled to receive income accrued but unpaid when a revocable trust ends?*	Generally no. See the Uniform Principal and Income Act (1997) chart. (§ 129.280)
25. *Is an income beneficiary entitled to receive income accrued but unpaid when an irrevocable trust ends?*	Generally no. See the Uniform Principal and Income Act (1997) chart. (§ 129.280)
26. *With regard to mutual funds, how are:*	
a) long-term gains allocated between income and principal?	See the Uniform Principal and Income Act (1997) chart. (§ 129.300(3)(d))
b) short-term gains allocated between income and principal?	See the Uniform Principal and Income Act (1997) chart. (§ 129.300(3)(d))
27. *How are distributions from REITs allocated between income and principal?*	See the Uniform Principal and Income Act (1997) chart. (§ 129.300(3)(d))
28. *With respect to underproductive property:*	
a) Is an adjustment, e.g., "delayed income," required to be paid to the income beneficiary?	No. (§ 129.375)
b) What percentage return makes property underproductive?	The statute only refers to property not productive of income. (§ 129.375)
29. *Is the trustee required to increase income so that it is sufficient to qualify for the marital deduction?*	Yes. (§ 129.375(1))

30. Is the trustee required to take depreciation?	No. (§ 129.375)
31. Is the trustee's determination on allocations generally presumed to be fair and reasonable?	Yes. (§ 129.210(2))
32. If an item is not addressed in the trust agreement or in the law, must it be allocated to principal or income?	To principal. (§ 129.210(1)(d))
33. When does an asset become subject to a trust:	
a) In the case of transfers during the transferor's life?	The date of transfer. (§ 129.270(2)(a))
b) In the case of a will?	The date of the testator's death. (§ 129.270(2)(b))
c) In the case of the death of a third party?	The date of the third party's death. (§ 129.270(2)(c))
34. Can a trustee rely on the characterization by an entity as to the source or character of a received distribution?	Yes. (§ 129.300(6))

Table 12.02
Pennsylvania
Trust Accounting: Principal and Income

1. *Does the trustee have the power to transfer income to principal or to transfer principal to income to meet its duty of impartiality?*	Yes. (20 § 8104(a))
2. *What is the effective date for the law? E.g., does it apply to preexisting trusts?*	The Pennsylvania Uniform Principal and Income Act does not contain any language addressing its applicability to preexisting trusts.
3. *What percentage is allocated to income and principal from proceeds of:*	
a) *IRA?* b) *Qualified pension or profit-sharing plan?* c) *Other deferred compensation arrangement?*	The general rule is that the trustee must allocate to income the greater of: 1. the portion of a payment characterized by the payor as interest or a dividend or a remittance in lieu of interest or a dividend; or 2. the portion of the payment characterized as imputed interest for Federal income tax purposes. The general rule is that the balance is allocable to principal. (20 § 8149)
4. *What percentage is allocated to income and principal from proceeds of:*	
a) *Patents?* b) *Copyrights?*	See the Uniform Principal and Income Act (1997) chart. (20 § 8150)
5. *What percentage is allocated to income and principal in the event of distributions from:*	
a) *Corporations?* b) *Partnerships?* c) *LLCs?*	See the Uniform Principal and Income Act (1997) chart. (20 § 8141)
6. *What percentage is allocated to income and principal from proceeds of:*	
a) *Oil and gas?* b) *Minerals?* c) *Water?* d) *Other natural resourses (not including timber)?*	The trustee must allocate a receipt received as nominal delay rental or a nominal annual rent on a lease to income. The trustee must allocate a receipt received from a production payment to income if and to the extent that the agreement creating the production payment provides a factor for interest or its equivalent. The balance must be allocated to principal. The trustee must allocate two-thirds of an amount received as a royalty, shut-in-well payment, take-or-pay payment, bonus, or a delay rental that is more than nominal, to principal and one-third to income. The trustee must allocate two-thirds of the net amount received from a working interest or other interest (not mentioned in the two preceding paragraphs) to principal and one-third to income. An amount received on account of an interest in water that is renewable must be allocated to income. If the water is not renewable, two-thirds of the amount must be allocated to principal and one-third to income.

	The rules above apply whether or not a decedent or donor was extracting the minerals, water, or other natural resources before the interest became subject to the trust. (20 § 8151)
e) Timber?	See the Uniform Principal and Income Act (1997) chart. (20 § 8152)
f) Rental properties?	See the Uniform Principal and Income Act (1997) chart. (20 § 8145)
7. After a decedent dies, in the case of an estate, or after an income interest ends, when the fiduciary is determining the remaining net income what are the rules regarding payment from income or principal for:	
a) Attorneys fees? *b) Accountants fees?* *c) Fiduciary fees and commissions?* *d) Court costs?* *e) Interest on death taxes*	These expenses must be paid from principal. (20 § 8121(3)(ii))
f) Debts? *g) Funeral expenses?* *h) Family allowances and similar protections?* *i) Death taxes?* *j) Penalties on death taxes?*	The expenses must be paid from principal. (20 § 8121(3)(ii))
8. With respect to trust expenses from the administration of the trust that are not covered by 20 § 8121(3)(ii) [see Question #7]:	
a) Does the trustee have full discretion in allocating between income and principal for expenses incurred in the administration of the trust?	No. (20 § 8161; 20 § 8162; 20 § 8163)
b) If not, are there special rules for:	
i) Regular trustee fees? *ii) Advisory or custodial services to the trustee?* *iii) Accountings, judicial proceedings and other matters that involve both the income and remainder interests?*	The trustee has discretion in allocating regular trustee fees and advisory and custodial fees between income and principal. (20 § 8163) The trustee must pay expenses for accountings, expenses for judicial or other proceedings and fees for legal services to the trustee from principal. (20 § 8162)
iv) Debts?	See the Uniform Principal and Income Act (1997) chart. (20 § 8161(1); 20 § 8162(a)(5))
c) Can the trustee determine what are "transmission" expenses and "management" expenses?	

9. With regard to specific gifts from a trust after an income interest ends or from an estate:	
a) What amounts must be paid from income and principal?	See the Uniform Principal and Income Act (1997) chart. (20 § 8121(1); 20 § 8121(5)) ***Note:*** The language in 20 § 8121(5) differs from the Uniform Principal and Income Act (1997).
10. With regard to outright pecuniary gifts from an estate or trust?:	
a) Does interest accrue?	Yes. See the Uniform Principal and Income Act (1997) chart. (20 § 8121(2))
11. With regard to a gift in trust of a pecuniary amount from an estate or trust?	
a) Does interest accrue?	Yes. See the Uniform Principal and Income Act (1997) chart. (20 § 8121(2))
12. With regard to residuary gifts:	
a) What amount of income and principal is to be paid to the residuary beneficiary of a trust or an estate?	See the Uniform Principal and Income Act (1997) chart. (20 § 8121(4); 20 § 8122)
13. With regard to "business assets" held in trust:	
a) Can the trustee treat them as a separate entity?	Generally yes. See the Uniform Principal and Income Act (1997) chart. (20 § 8143)
b) Can the trustee treat distinct assets as separate entities?	Generally yes. See the Uniform Principal and Income Act (1997) chart. (20 § 8143)
c) Can earnings be retained in trust for the reasonable needs of the "business entity," and, if so, to what extent is this permitted?	Yes. See the Uniform Principal and Income Act (1997) chart. (20 § 8143)
14. With respect to discount bonds:	
a) To what extent is the discount added to income or principal upon maturity?	See the Uniform Principal and Income Act (1997) chart. (20 § 8146)
b) Does the trustee have discretion to allocate discount between income and principal?	No. (20 § 8146) ***Note:*** The trustee has the overriding power to adjust under 20 § 8104(a).
c) Are distinctions drawn between Series E bonds and others?	No. (20 § 8146)
d) Are distinctions drawn based on the maturity date of the bond?	Yes. (20 § 8146)

15. Is there a de minimis rule excusing the trustee from making adjustments in certain cases?	See the Uniform Principal and Income Act (1997) chart. ***Note:*** The insubstantiality presumption threshold is 5% in Pennsylavania and not 10% as in the Uniform Principal and Income Act (1997) § 408. An allocation is presumed to be insubstantial if 1. The amount of the allocation would increase or decrease net income in an accounting period, as determined before the allocation by less than five percent (5%), or 2. The value of the asset producing the receipt for which the allocation would be made is less than five percent (5%) of the total value of the trust's assets at the beginning of the accounting period. (20 § 8148)
16. With respect to derivatives:	
a) May income and loss be treated as that of a separate entity?	Yes. (20 § 8143; 20 § 8154(a))
b) If not, or the trustee chooses not to do so, is income and loss allocated to the income account or to principal?	To principal. (20 § 8154(a))
17. To the extent put and call options are not derivatives, how are they allocated in terms of principal and income?	To principal. (20 § 8154(b))
18. How are asset-backed securities allocated in terms of principal and income?	See the Uniform Principal and Income Act (1997) chart. (20 § 8155)
19. Are expenses incurred to comply with environmental requirements allocated to income or principal?	Generally to principal. (20 § 8162(a)(8))
20. Is income tax liability allocated generally to income or principal?	See the Uniform Principal and Income Act (1997) chart. (20 § 8166) ***Note:*** The Pennsylvania Principal and Income Act does not contain a section similar to Uniform Principal and Income Act § 506.
21. If a Subchapter S shareholder's or partner's portion of tax liability is greater than cash distributed, how is the excess obligation allocated?	From principal. (20 § 8166(c)(2)(ii))
22. What is the standard, if any, for making equi-table adjustments between income and principal?	See the Uniform Principal and Income Act (1997) chart. (20 § 8103(b))
23. Is an income beneficiary entitled to receive income accrued but unpaid when an estate ends?	No. See the Uniform Principal and Income Act (1997) chart. (20 § 8133)
24. Is an income beneficiary entitled to receive income accrued but unpaid when a revocable trust ends?	Generally no. See the Uniform Principal and Income Act (1997) chart. (20 § 8133)
25. Is an income beneficiary entitled to receive income accrued but unpaid when an irrevocable trust ends?	Generally no. See the Uniform Principal and Income Act (1997) chart. (20 § 8133)

26. With regard to mutual funds, how are:	
a) long-term gains allocated between income and principal?	See the Uniform Principal and Income Act (1997) chart. (20 § 8141(b)(4))
b) short-term gains allocated between income and principal?	See the Uniform Principal and Income Act (1997) chart. (20 § 8141(b)(4))
27. How are distributions from REITs allocated between income and principal?	See the Uniform Principal and Income Act (1997) chart. (20 § 8141(b)(4))
28. With respect to underproductive property:	
a) Is an adjustment, e.g., "delayed income," required to be paid to the income beneficiary?	No. (20 § 8153)
b) What percentage return makes property underproductive?	The statute only refers to property not productive of income. (20 § 8153)
29. Is the trustee required to increase income so that it is sufficient to qualify for the marital deduction?	Yes. (20 § 8153)
30. Is the trustee required to take depreciation?	No. (20 § 8164)
31. Is the trustee's determination on allocations generally presumed to be fair and reasonable?	Yes. (20 § 8103(b))
32. If an item is not addressed in the trust agreement or in the law, must it be allocated to principal or income?	To principal. (20 § 8103(a)(4))
33. When does an asset become subject to a trust:	
a) In the case of transfers during the transferor's life?	The date of transfer. (20 § 8131(b)(1))
b) In the case of a will?	The date of the testator's death. (20 § 8131(b)(2))
c) In the case of the death of a third party?	The date of the third party's death. (20 § 8131(b)(3))
34. Can a trustee rely on the characterization by an entity as to the source or character of a received distribution?	Yes. (20 § 8141(e))

Table 12.02
Rhode island
Trust Accounting: Principal and Income

1. *Does the trustee have the power to transfer income to principal or to transfer principal to income to meet its duty of impartiality?*	Yes. A trustee may adjust between principal and income to the extent the trustee considers it to be advisable if the trustee invests and manages trust assets as a prudent investor and the terms of the trust describe the amount that may or must be distributed to a beneficiary by referring to the trust's income. (§ 18-4-28)
2. *What is the effective date for the law? E.g. does it apply to preexisting trusts?*	Rhode Island does not have a Principal and Income Act.
3. *What percentage is allocated to income and principal from proceeds of:*	
a) *IRA?* b) *Qualified pension or profit-sharing plan?* c) *Other deferred compensation arrangement?*	Rhode Island law does not address the allocation of principal and income from receipts from IRA's, pensions, profit sharing plans, or other deferred compensation arrangements.
4. *What percentage is allocated to income and principal from proceeds of:*	
a) *Patents?* b) *Copyrights?*	Rhode Island law does not address the allocation of principal and income from receipts from patents or copyrights.
5. *What percentage is allocated to income and principal in the event of distributions from:*	
a) *Corporations?* b) *Partnerships?* c) *LLCs?*	Rhode Island law does not address the allocation of principal and income from receipts from corporate, partnership or LLC distributions.
6. *What percentage is allocated to income and principal from proceeds of:*	
a) *Oil and gas?* b) *Minerals?* c) *Water?* d) *Other natural resourses (not including timber)?*	Rhode Island law does not address the allocation of principal and income from receipts from any natural resources.
e) *Timber?*	Rhode Island law does not address the allocation of principal and income from receipts from timber
f) *Rental properties?*	Rhode Island law does not address the allocation of principal and income from receipts from rental property
7. *After a decedent dies, in the case of an estate, or after an income interest ends, when the fiduciary is determining the remaining net income what are the rules regarding payment from income or principal for:*	

a) Attorneys fees? *b) Accountants fees?* *c) Fiduciary fees and commissions?* *d) Court costs?* *e) Interest on death taxes*	Rhode Island law does not address the allocation of these expenses.
f) Debts? *g) Funeral expenses?* *h) Family allowances and similar protections?* *i) Death taxes?* *j) Penalties on death taxes?*	Rhode Island law does not address the allocation of these expenses.
8. With respect to trust expenses from the administration of the trust that are not covered Question #8:	
a) Does the trustee have full discretion in allocating between income and principal for expenses incurred in the administration of the trust?	Rhode Island law does not address the allocation of all these expenses.
b) If not, are there special rules for:	
i) Regular trustee fees? *ii) Advisory or custodial services to the trustee?* *iii) Accountings, judicial proceedings and other matters that involve both the income and remainder interests?*	Reasonable expenses and costs incurred in the execution of the trust and reasonable compensation for services rendered as trustee may be equitably apportioned between principal and income in a manner that the trustee determines. (§ 18-6-1).
iv) Debts?	Rhode Island law does not address the allocation of debt payments between income and principal.
c) Can the trustee determine what are "transmission" expenses and "management" expenses?	
9. With regard to specific gifts from a trust after an income interest ends or from an estate:	
a) What amounts must be paid from income and principal?	Rhode Island law does not address the allocation of income to specific gifts.
10. With regard to outright pecuniary gifts from an estate or trust?:	

a) Does interest accrue?	Unless otherwise provided in the will, a general pecuniary legatee is not entitled to interest on his or her legacy for the period of one year from and after the death of the testator. After the one year period the executor or administrator with the will annexed, unless otherwise provided by the testator, shall not be chargeable for more interest on any pecuniary legacy than the entire net income actually earned by the legacy if and when left in the investment as made by the testator, or actually invested in notes secured by mortgage upon real estate situated in this state, or in the bonds of any city or town in this state, or deposited in any savings bank in this state, or in the participation account of any trust company in this state, or invested in any other manner specially ordered by the probate court. But if otherwise invested, the legacy shall bear interest at the rate of six percent (6%) per annum or such larger rate as the same may have earned; provided, however, that nothing herein contained shall authorize executors or administrators to make investments other than trustees are allowed to make, unless specially authorized by the will to do so. (§ 33-6-15)
11. With regard to a gift in trust of a pecuniary amount from an estate or trust?	
a) Does interest accrue?	Unless otherwise provided in the will, a general pecuniary legatee is not entitled to interest on his or her legacy for the period of one year from and after the death of the testator. After the one year period the executor or administrator with the will annexed, unless otherwise provided by the testator, shall not be chargeable for more interest on any pecuniary legacy than the entire net income actually earned by the legacy if and when left in the investment as made by the testator, or actually invested in notes secured by mortgage upon real estate situated in this state, or in the bonds of any city or town in this state, or deposited in any savings bank in this state, or in the participation account of any trust company in this state, or invested in any other manner specially ordered by the probate court. But if otherwise invested, the legacy shall bear interest at the rate of six percent (6%) per annum or such larger rate as the same may have earned; provided, however, that nothing herein contained shall authorize executors or administrators to make investments other than trustees are allowed to make, unless specially authorized by the will to do so. (§ 33-6-15)
12. With regard to residuary gifts:	
a) What amount of income and principal is to be paid to the residuary beneficiary of a trust or an estate?	Rhode Island law does not address the allocation of income to residuary gifts.
13. With regard to "business assets" held in trust:	

a) *Can the trustee treat them as a separate entity?*	Rhode Island law does not provide that the trustee can treat "business assets" as a separate entity. However, executors and administrators may be authorized by the probate court before which the estate is in settlement to work up and complete any stock and materials in an unfinished state, or to continue any business of the decedent so far as may be expedient for the prudent winding up of the business, if the court shall find that it will be for the interest of the estate. (§ 33-9-7)
b) *Can the trustee treat distinct assets as separate entities?*	Rhode Island law does not provide that the trustee can treat distinct assets as a separate entities.
c) *Can earnings be retained in trust for the reasonable needs of the "business entity," and, if so, to what extent is this permitted?*	No. Rhode Island law does not provide that the fiduciary may retain earnings for the needs of the business entity.
14. With respect to discount bonds:	
a) *To what extent is the discount added to income or principal upon maturity?*	Rhode Island law does not address the allocation of discount bonds to income and principal.
b) *Does the trustee have discretion to allocate discount between income and principal?*	Rhode Island law does not address the allocation of discount bonds to income and principal.
c) *Are distinctions drawn between Series E bonds and others?*	Rhode Island law does not address the allocation of discount bonds to income and principal.
d) *Are distinctions drawn based on the maturity date of the bond?*	Rhode Island law does not address the allocation of discount bonds to income and principal.
15. Is there a de minimis rule excusing the trustee from making adjustments in certain cases?	No.
16. With respect to derivatives:	
a) *May income and loss be treated as that of a separate entity?*	Rhode Island law does not address whether income or loss from derivatives can be treated as that of a separate entity.
b) *If not, or the trustee chooses not to do so, is income and loss allocated to the income account or to principal?*	Rhode Island law does not address the allocation of receipts from derivatives to income and principal.
17. To the extent put and call options are not derivatives, how are they allocated in terms of principal and income?	Rhode Island law does not address the allocation of receipts from options to income and principal.
18. How are asset-backed securities allocated in terms of principal and income?	Rhode Island law does not address the allocation of receipts from asset-backed securities to income and principal.

19. Are expenses incurred to comply with environmental requirements allocated to income or principal?	The fiduciary may charge the reasonable cost of any inspection, insurance, review, abatement, response, or cleanup, or any other remedial action, as authorized, against the income or principal of the estate, trust, personal estate, or business assets and is not be personally responsible for those costs. The fiduciary is not personally liable to any beneficiary or any other party for any decrease in value or exhaustion of assets by reason of the fiduciary's reasonable compliance with any environmental laws, specifically including any reporting requirements under those laws. (§ 18-4-26)
20. Is income tax liability allocated generally to income or principal?	Rhode Island law does not address the allocation of income tax liability in between income and principal.
21. If a Subchapter S shareholder's or partner's portion of tax liability is greater than cash distributed, how is the excess obligation allocated?	Rhode Island law does not address the allocation of income tax liability in between income and principal.
22. What is the standard, if any, for making equitable adjustments between income and principal?	Rhode Island law does not have a standard for making equitable adjustments (§ 18-4-28)
23. Is an income beneficiary entitled to receive income accrued but unpaid when an estate ends?	Rhode Island law does not address accrued income that is unpaid when a trust ends.
24. Is an income beneficiary entitled to receive income accrued but unpaid when a revocable trust ends?	Rhode Island law does not address accrued income that is unpaid when a trust ends.
25. Is an income beneficiary entitled to receive income accrued but unpaid when an irrevocable trust ends?	Rhode Island law does not address accrued income that is unpaid when a trust ends.
26. With regard to mutual funds, how are:	
a) long-term gains allocated between income and principal?	Rhode Island law does not address the allocation of receipts from mutual funds between income and principal.
b) short-term gains allocated between income and principal?	Rhode Island law does not address the allocation of receipts from mutual funds between income and principal.
27. How are distributions from REITs allocated between income and principal?	Rhode Island law does not address the allocation of receipts from REITs between income and principal.
28. With respect to underproductive property:	
a) Is an adjustment, e.g., "delayed income," required to be paid to the income beneficiary?	Rhode Island law does not address underproductive property.
b) What percentage return makes property underproductive?	Rhode Island law does not address underproductive property.

29. Is the trustee required to increase income so that it is sufficient to qualify for the marital deduction?	Rhode Island law does not specifically address increasing income to qualify for the marital deduction. However, a trustee may not make an adjustment that diminishes the income interest in a trust that requires all of the income to be used at least annually to a surviving spouse and for which an estate tax or gift tax marital deduction would be allowed, in whole or in part, if the trustee did not have the power to make the adjustment. (§ 18-4-28(c))
30. Is the trustee required to take depreciation?	Rhode Island law does not address whether a trustee is required to take depreciation.
31. Is the trustee's determination on allocations generally presumed to be fair and reasonable?	Rhode Island law does not have a presumption that allocations are generally presumed to be fair and reasonable.
32. If an item is not addressed in the trust agreement or in the law, must it be allocated to principal or income?	Rhode Island law does not have a default setting.
33. When does an asset become subject to a trust:	
a) In the case of transfers during the transferor's life?	Rhode Island law does not address when an asset becomes subject to a trust.
b) In the case of a will?	Rhode Island law does not address when an asset becomes subject to a trust.
c) In the case of the death of a third party?	Rhode Island law does not address when an asset becomes subject to a trust.
34. Can a trustee rely on the characterization by an entity as to the source or character of a received distribution?	Rhode Island law does not address whether a trustee can rely on the characterization by an entity as to the source or character of a received distribution.

Table 12.02
South Carolina
Trust Accounting: Principal and Income

1. *Does the trustee have the power to transfer income to principal or to transfer principal to income to meet its duty of impartiality?*	Yes. See the Uniform Principal and Income Act (1997) chart. (§ 62-7-904(A))
2. *What is the effective date for the law? E.g., does it apply to preexisting trusts?*	The South Carolina Principal and Income Act does not contain any language addressing its applicability to preexisting trusts.
3. *What percentage is allocated to income and principal from proceeds of:*	
a) IRA? *b) Qualified pension or profit-sharing plan?* *c) Other deferred compensation arrangement?*	See the Uniform Principal and Income Act (1997) chart. (§ 62-7-918)
4. *What percentage is allocated to income and principal from proceeds of:*	
a) Patents? *b) Copyrights?*	See the Uniform Principal and Income Act (1997) chart. (§ 62-7-919)
5. *What percentage is allocated to income and principal in the event of distributions from:*	
a) Corporations? *b) Partnerships?* *c) LLCs?*	See the Uniform Principal and Income Act (1997) chart. (§ 62-7-910)
6. *What percentage is allocated to income and principal from proceeds of:*	
a) Oil and gas? *b) Minerals?* *c) Water?* *d) Other natural resourses (not including timber)?*	See the Uniform Principal and Income Act (1997) chart. (§ 62-7-920) ***Note***: If a trust owns an interest in minerals, water or other natural resources on January 1, 2006, the trustee may allocate receipts from the interest as provided in the South Carolina Principal and Income Act or in the manner used by the trustee before January 1, 2006.
e) Timber?	See the Uniform Principal and Income Act (1997) chart. (§ 62-7-921) ***Note***: If a trust owns an interest in timberland on January 1, 2006, the trustee may allocate receipts from the interest as provided in the South Carolina Principal and Income Act or in the manner used by the trustee before January 1, 2006.
f) Rental properties?	See the Uniform Principal and Income Act (1997) chart. (§ 62-7-914)
7. *After a decedent dies, in the case of an estate, or after an income interest ends, when the fiduciary is determining the remaining net income what are the rules*	

regarding payment from income or principal for:	
a) Attorneys fees? *b) Accountants fees?* *c) Fiduciary fees and commissions?* *d) Court costs?* *e) Interest on death taxes*	See the Uniform Principal and Income Act (1997) chart. (§ 62-7-905(2)(b))
f) Debts? *g) Funeral expenses?* *h) Family allowances and similar protections?* *i) Death taxes?* *j) Penalties on death taxes?*	See the Uniform Principal and Income Act (1997) chart. (§ 62-7-905(2)(c))
8. With respect to trust expenses from the administration of the trust that are not covered by § 62-7-905(2)(b-c) [see Question #7]:	
a) Does the trustee have full discretion in allocating between income and principal for expenses incurred in the administration of the trust?	No. (§ 62-7-925; § 62-7-926)
b) If not, are there special rules for:	
i) Regular trustee fees? *ii) Advisory or custodial services to the trustee?* *iii) Accountings, judicial proceedings and other matters that involve both the income and remainder interests?*	See the Uniform Principal and Income Act (1997) chart. (§ 62-7-925; § 62-7-926)
iv) Debts?	See the Uniform Principal and Income Act (1997) chart. (§ 62-7-925(3); § 62-7-926(A)(3))
c) Can the trustee determine what are "transmission" expenses and "management" expenses?	
9. With regard to specific gifts from a trust after an income interest ends or from an estate:	
a) What amounts must be paid from income and principal?	See the Uniform Principal and Income Act (1997) chart. (§ 62-7-905(1); § 62-7-905(5))
10. With regard to outright pecuniary gifts from an estate or trust?:	
a) Does interest accrue?	A fiduciary must distribute to an outright pecuniary beneficiary the interest or other amount provided by the will or the terms of the trust. If the will or the terms of the trust provide no interest amount, the trustee must not pay any interest or other income

	on the outright pecuniary gift for one year after the first appointment of a personal representative. Beginning one year after the first appointment of a personal representative, the fiduciary must treat an outright pecuniary beneficiary as a remainder beneficiary. The trustee may not pay interest to a remainder beneficiary. If a beneficiary is to receive a pecuniary amount outright from a trust after an income interest ends and no interest or other amount is provided for by the terms of the trust, the fiduciary must treat the pecuniary amount as if it were required to be paid under a will and as if the payment were being made beginning one year after the first appointment of a personal representative. (§ 62-7-905(4))
11. With regard to a gift in trust of a pecuniary amount from an estate or trust?	
a) Does interest accrue?	No. See the Uniform Principal and Income Act (1997) chart. (§ 62-7-905; § 62-7-906)
12. With regard to residuary gifts:	
a) What amount of income and principal is to be paid to the residuary beneficiary of a trust or an estate?	See the Uniform Principal and Income Act (1997) chart. (§ 62-7-905; § 62-7-906)
13. With regard to "business assets" held in trust:	
a) Can the trustee treat them as a separate entity?	Generally yes. See the Uniform Principal and Income Act (1997) chart. (§ 62-7-912(A))
b) Can the trustee treat distinct assets as separate entities?	Generally yes. See the Uniform Principal and Income Act (1997) chart. (§ 62-7-912(A))
c) Can earnings be retained in trust for the reasonable needs of the "business entity," and, if so, to what extent is this permitted?	Yes. See the Uniform Principal and Income Act (1997) chart. (§ 62-7-912(B))
14. With respect to discount bonds:	
a) To what extent is the discount added to income or principal upon maturity?	See the Uniform Principal and Income Act (1997) chart. (§ 62-7-915(B))
b) Does the trustee have discretion to allocate discount between income and principal?	No. (§ 62-7-915(B)) Note: The trustee has the overriding power to adjust under (§ 62-7-904(A))
c) Are distinctions drawn between Series E bonds and others?	No. (§ 62-7-904)
d) Are distinctions drawn based on the maturity date of the bond?	Yes. (§ 62-7-904(B))
15. Is there a de minimis rule excusing the trustee from making adjustments in certain cases?	Yes. See the Uniform Principal and Income Act (1997) chart. (§ 62-7-917)

16. With respect to derivatives:	
a) May income and loss be treated as that of a separate entity?	Yes. (§ 62-7-912(C)(7). § 62-7-923(B))
b) If not, or the trustee chooses not to do so, is income and loss allocated to the income account or to principal?	To principal. (§ 62-7-923(B))
17. To the extent put and call options are not derivatives, how are they allocated in terms of principal and income?	To principal. (§ 62-7-923(C))
18. How are asset-backed securities allocated in terms of principal and income?	See the Uniform Principal and Income Act (1997) chart. (§ 62-7-924)
19. Are expenses incurred to comply with environmental requirements allocated to income or principal?	Generally to principal. See the Uniform Principal and Income Act (1997) chart. (§ 62-7-926(A)(7))
20. Is income tax liability allocated generally to income or principal?	See the Uniform Principal and Income Act (1997) chart. (§ 62-7-929; § 62-7-930)
21. If a Subchapter S shareholder's or partner's portion of tax liability is greater than cash distributed, how is the excess obligation allocated?	From principal. (§ 62-7-929(C)(2)(b))
22. What is the standard, if any, for making equitable adjustments between income and principal?	See the Uniform Principal and Income Act (1997) chart. (§ 62-7-903(B))
23. Is an income beneficiary entitled to receive income accrued but unpaid when an estate ends?	No. (§ 62-7-909)
24. Is an income beneficiary entitled to receive income accrued but unpaid when a revocable trust ends?	Generally no. See the Uniform Principal and Income Act (1997) chart. (§ 62-7-909)
25. Is an income beneficiary entitled to receive income accrued but unpaid when an irrevocable trust ends?	Generally no. See the Uniform Principal and Income Act (1997) chart. (§ 62-7-909)
26. With regard to mutual funds, how are:	
a) long-term gains allocated between income and principal?	See the Uniform Principal and Income Act (1997) chart. (§ 62-7-910(B)(4))
b) short-term gains allocated between income and principal?	See the Uniform Principal and Income Act (1997) chart. (§ 62-7-910(B)(4))
27. How are distributions from REITs allocated between income and principal?	See the Uniform Principal and Income Act (1997) chart. (§ 62-7-910(B)(4))
28. With respect to underproductive property:	

a) *Is an adjustment, e.g., "delayed income," required to be paid to the income beneficiary?*	No. (§ 62-7-922)
b) *What percentage return makes property underproductive?*	The statute only refers to property not productive of income. (§ 62-7-922)
29. *Is the trustee required to increase income so that it is sufficient to qualify for the marital deduction?*	Yes. (§ 62-7-922)
30. *Is the trustee required to take depreciation?*	No. (§ 62-7-927)
31. *Is the trustee's determination on allocations generally presumed to be fair and reasonable?*	Yes. (§ 62-7-903(B))
32. *If an item is not addressed in the trust agreement or in the law, must it be allocated to principal or income?*	To principal. (§ 62-7-903(A)(4))
33. *When does an asset become subject to a trust:*	
a) *In the case of transfers during the transferor's life?*	The date of transfer. (§ 62-7-907(B)(1))
b) *In the case of a will?*	The date of the testator's death. (§ 62-7-907(B)(2))
c) *In the case of the death of a third party?*	The date of the third party's death. (§ 62-7-907(B)(3))
34. *Can a trustee rely on the characterization by an entity as to the source or character of a received distribution?*	Yes. (§ 62-7-910(F))

Table 12.02
South Dakota
Trust Accounting: Principal and Income

1. *Does the trustee have the power to transfer income to principal or to transfer principal to income to meet its duty of impartiality?*	No.
2. *What is the effective date for the law? E.g., does it apply to preexisting trusts?*	Except as specifically provided in the trust instrument, the will, or the South Dakota Principal and Income Act, the South Dakota Principal and Income Act applies to any receipt or expense received or incurred after July 1, 1984, by any trust executed or the estate of any decedent dying on or after July 1, 1984. (§ 55-13-14)
3. *What percentage is allocated to income and principal from proceeds of:*	
a) *IRA?* b) *Qualified pension or profit-sharing plan?* c) *Other deferred compensation arrangement?*	The trustee must allocate the receipts from rights to receive payments on a contract for deferred compensation, up to five percent (5%) per year of its inventory value, to income and the balance to principal. (§ 55-13-11)
4. *What percentage is allocated to income and principal from proceeds of:*	
a) *Patents?* b) *Copyrights?*	The trustee must allocate the receipts from patents and copyrights, up to five percent (5%) per year of its inventory value, to income and the balance to principal. (§ 55-13-11)
5. *What percentage is allocated to income and principal in the event of distributions from:*	
a) *Corporations?* b) *Partnerships?* c) *LLCs?*	Corporate distributions of shares of the distributing corporation, including distributions in the form of a stock split or stock dividend, are principal. A right to subscribe to shares or other securities issued by the distributing corporation accruing on account of the ownership of shares or other securities in such corporation and the proceeds of any sale of the right are principal. Except to the extent that the corporation indicates that some part of a corporate distribution is a settlement of preferred or guaranteed dividends accrued since the trustee became a stockholder or is in lieu of an ordinary cash dividend, a corporate distribution is principal if the distribution is pursuant to a call of shares; a merger, consolidation or reorganization; a plan by which assets of the corporation are acquired by another corporation; or a total or partial liquidation of the corporation. Distributions made from ordinary income by a regulated investment company or by a trust qualifying and electing to be taxed under federal law as a real estate investment trust are income. All other distributions made by the company or trust, including distributions from capital gains, depreciation or depletion, whether in the form of cash or an option to take new stock or cash or an option to purchase additional shares, are principal.

	Except as provided in the preceding paragraphs, all corporate distributions are income, including cash dividends, distributions of or rights to subscribe to shares or securities or obligations of corporations other than the distributing corporation, and the proceeds of the rights or property distributions. (§ 55-13-6) ***Note:*** Parnerships and LLC's are not addressed.
6. *What percentage is allocated to income and principal from proceeds of:*	
a) *Oil and gas?* b) *Minerals?* c) *Water?* d) *Other natural resourses (not including timber)?*	Receipts for rent on a lease or extension payments on a lease are income. Receipts from a production payment are income to the extent of any factor for interest or its equivalent provided in the governing instrument. The fiduciary must allocate to principal the fraction of the balance of the receipts which the unrecovered cost of the production payments bears to the balance owed on the production payment, exclusive of any factor for interest or its equivalent. The receipts not allocated to principal are income. If received as a royalty, overriding or limited royalty, or bonus, or from a working, net profit, or any other interest in minerals or other natural resources, receipts (not provided for in the two preceding paragraphs) must be apportioned on a yearly basis, whether or not any natural resource was being taken from the land at the time the trust was established. Twenty-seven and one-half per cent (27 1/2%) of the gross receipts (but not to exceed fifty per cent (50%) of the net receipts remaining after payment of all expenses, direct and indirect, computed without allowance for depletion) must be added to principal as an allowance for depletion. The balance of the gross receipts, after payment of all expenses, direct and indirect, is income. If a trustee, on July 1, 1984, held minerals or other natural resources, the trustee must allocate receipts from the property in the manner used before July 1, 1984, but as to all depletable property acquired after July 1, 1984 by an existing or new trust, the method of allocation provided the South Dakota Principal and Income act must be used. (§ 55-13-9) ***Note:*** These rules are not applicable to proceeds from water.
e) *Timber?*	The trustee must allocate receipts from the sale of timber in accordance with what is reasonable and equitable in view of the interests of those entitled to income as well as of those entitled to principal, and in view of the manner in which men of ordinary prudence, discretion, and judgment would act in the management of their own affairs. (§ 55-13-10)
f) *Rental properties?*	The trustee must include amounts received from renting real or personal property, including sums received for cancellation or renewal of a lease, as income. (§ 55-13-3(a)(1))
7. *After a decedent dies, in the case of an estate, or after an income interest ends, when the fiduciary is determining the*	

remaining net income what are the rules regarding payment from income or principal for:	
a) Attorneys fees? *b) Accountants fees?* *c) Fiduciary fees and commissions?* *d) Court costs?* *e) Interest on death taxes*	The trustee must charge from principal all expenses incurred in connection with the settlement of a decedent's estate, including debts, funeral expenses, estate taxes, interest and penalties concerning taxes, family allowances, fees of attorneys and personal representatives, and court costs. (§ 55-13-5(a))
f) Debts? *g) Funeral expenses?* *h) Family allowances and similar protections?* *i) Death taxes?* *j) Penalties on death taxes?*	The trustee must charge from principal all expenses incurred in connection with the settlement of a decedent's estate, including debts, funeral expenses, estate taxes, interest and penalties concerning taxes, family allowances, fees of attorneys and personal representatives, and court costs. (§ 55-13-5(a))
8. With respect to trust expenses from the administration of the trust that are not covered by § 55-13-5(a) [see Question #7]:	
a) Does the trustee have full discretion in allocating between income and principal for expenses incurred in the administration of the trust?	No. (§ 55-13-13)
b) If not, are there special rules for:	
i) Regular trustee fees? *ii) Advisory or custodial services to the trustee?* *iii) Accountings, judicial proceedings and other matters that involve both the income and remainder interests?*	Generally, the following charges must be made against income: 1. one-half of the court costs, attorneys' fees, and other fees on periodic accountings or judicial proceedings, unless the court directs otherwise; 2. court costs, attorneys' fees, and other fees on other accountings or judicial proceedings if the matter primarily concerns the income interest, unless the court directs otherwise; and 3. one-half of the trustee's regular compensation for services performed for the income beneficiary or in the production of income whether based on a percentage of principal or income, and all expenses reasonably incurred for current management of principal and application of income. Generally, the following charges must be made against principal: 1. one-half of the trustee's regular compensation, court costs and attorneys' fees primarily concerning matters of principal; 2. expenses incurred in maintaining or defending any action to construe the trust or protect it or the property or assure the title of any trust property. (§ 55-13-13) ***Note:*** § 55-13-13 contains many other special rules for allocations and contains many exceptions.
iv) Debts?	The trustee must allocate interest expense on trust debt to income and must allocate payments on principal of trust debt to principal. (§ 55-13-13).

c) *Can the trustee determine what are "transmission" expenses and "management" expenses?*	
9. *With regard to specific gifts from a trust after an income interest ends or from an estate:*	
a) *What amounts must be paid from income and principal?*	The fiduciary must distribute to a specific devisee or beneficiary, the income from the property devised or distributed to them less property taxes, ordinary repairs, interest, and other expenses of management and operation of the property, and less an appropriate portion of taxes imposed on income, excluding taxes on capital gains, that accrue during the period of administration or after an income interest in a trust terminates. (§ 55-13-5(b)(1))
10. *With regard to outright pecuniary gifts from an estate or trust?:*	
a) *Does interest accrue?*	The South Dakota Income and Principal Act does not provide that a beneficiary of an outright pecuniary gift should receive accrued interest on the unpaid amount.
11. *With regard to a gift in trust of a pecuniary amount from an estate or trust?*	
a) *Does interest accrue?*	No. The fiduciary should distribute to any trusts that received a gift of a pecuniary amount and to the remainder beneficiaries the balance of the income, less certain expenses that accrue during the period of administration or after an income interest terminates, in proportion to their respective interests in the undistributed assets of the estate or trust. (§ 55-13-5(b)(2))
12. *With regard to residuary gifts:*	
a) *What amount of income and principal is to be paid to the residuary beneficiary of a trust or an estate?*	The fiduciary should distribute to any trusts that received a gift of a pecuniary amount and to the remainder beneficiaries the balance of the income, less certain expenses that accrue during the period of administration or after an income interest terminates, in proportion to their respective interests in the undistributed assets of the estate or trust. (§ 55-13-5(b)(2))
13. *With regard to "business assets" held in trust:*	
a) *Can the trustee treat them as a separate entity?*	The South Dakota Principal and Income Act does not particularly provide for treating business assets as a separate entity. However, If a trustee uses any part of the principal in the continuance of a business of which the settlor was a sole proprietor or a partner, the net profits of the business are income. (§ 55-13-8)
b) *Can the trustee treat distinct assets as separate entities?*	The South Dakota Principal and Income Act does not particularly provide for treating distinct assets as separate entities. However, If a trustee uses any part of the principal in the continuance of a business of which the settlor was a sole proprietor or a partner, the net profits of the business are income. (§ 55-13-8).

c) Can earnings be retained in trust for the reasonable needs of the "business entity," and, if so, to what extent is this permitted?	No. The South Dakota Principal and Income Act does not provide that the fiduciary may retain earnings for the needs of the business entity.
14. With respect to discount bonds:	
a) To what extent is the discount added to income or principal upon maturity?	The appreciation of a bond or obligation in accordance with a fixed schedule of appreciation in excess of the price at which it was issued is distributable as income. The increment in value is distributable to the beneficiary who was the income beneficiary at the time of increment from the first principal cash available or, if none is available, when realized by sale, redemption, or other disposition. Whenever unrealized appreciation is distributed as income out of principal, the fiduciary must reimburse principal when the appreciation is realized. (§ 55-13-7)
b) Does the trustee have discretion to allocate discount between income and principal?	No. (§ 55-13-7)
c) Are distinctions drawn between Series E bonds and others?	No. (§ 55-13-7)
d) Are distinctions drawn based on the maturity date of the bond?	No. (§ 55-13-7)
15. Is there a de minimis rule excusing the trustee from making adjustments in certain cases?	No.
16. With respect to derivatives:	
a) May income and loss be treated as that of a separate entity?	No. The South Dakota Principal and Income Act does not address derivatives being treated as separate entities.
b) If not, or the trustee chooses not to do so, is income and loss allocated to the income account or to principal?	The South Dakota Principal and Income Act does not address derivatives. Therefore, unless the governing instrument provides otherwise, the fiduciary must allocate gain and loss from derivatives in accordance with what is reasonable and equitable in view of the interests of those entitled to income as well as of those entitled to principal, and in view of the manner in which persons of ordinary prudence, discretion, and judgment would act in the management of their own affairs. (§ 55-13-2(a)(3))
17. To the extent put and call options are not derivatives, how are they allocated in terms of principal and income?	The South Dakota Principal and Income Act does not address options. Therefore, unless the governing instrument provides otherwise, the fiduciary must allocate gain and loss from options in accordance with what is reasonable and equitable in view of the interests of those entitled to income as well as of those entitled to principal, and in view of the manner in which persons of ordinary prudence, discretion, and judgment would act in the management of their own affairs. (§ 55-13-2(a)(3))
18. How are asset-backed securities allocated in terms of principal and income?	The South Dakota Principal and Income Act does not address asset-backed securities. Therefore, unless the governing instrument provides otherwise, the fiduciary must allocate

	gain and loss from asset-backed securities in accordance with what is reasonable and equitable in view of the interests of those entitled to income as well as of those entitled to principal, and in view of the manner in which persons of ordinary prudence, discretion, and judgment would act in the management of their own affairs. (§ 55-13-2(a)(3))
19. Are expenses incurred to comply with environmental requirements allocated to income or principal?	The South Dakota Principal and Income Act does not address environmental requirements. Therefore, unless the governing instrument provides otherwise, the fiduciary must allocate expenses from complying with environmental requirements in accordance with what is reasonable and equitable in view of the interests of those entitled to income as well as of those entitled to principal, and in view of the manner in which persons of ordinary prudence, discretion, and judgment would act in the management of their own affairs. (§ 55-13-2(a)(3))
20. Is income tax liability allocated generally to income or principal?	Any tax required to be paid by a fiduciary on the trust's share of an entity's taxable income should be paid from income to the extent that receipts from the entity are allocated to income and from principal to the extent that receipts from the entity are allocated to principal. (§ 55-13-13)
21. If a Subchapter S shareholder's or partner's portion of tax liability is greater than cash distributed, how is the excess obligation allocated?	The South Dakota Principal and Income Act does not address this situation.
22. What is the standard, if any, for making equitable adjustments between income and principal?	The South Dakota Principal and Income Act does not provide for equitable adjustments between principal and income.
23. Is an income beneficiary entitled to receive income accrued but unpaid when an estate ends?	On termination of an income interest, the income beneficiary whose interest is terminated, or his estate, is entitled to: Income undistributed on the date of termination; income due but not paid to the trustee on the date of termination and income in the form of periodic payments (other than corporate distributions to stockholders), including rent, interest, or annuities, not due on the date of termination, accrued from day to day. (§ 55-13-4(d))
24. Is an income beneficiary entitled to receive income accrued but unpaid when a revocable trust ends?	On termination of an income interest, the income beneficiary whose interest is terminated, or his estate, is entitled to: Income undistributed on the date of termination; income due but not paid to the trustee on the date of termination and income in the form of periodic payments (other than corporate distributions to stockholders), including rent, interest, or annuities, not due on the date of termination, accrued from day to day. (§ 55-13-4(d))
25. Is an income beneficiary entitled to receive income accrued but unpaid when an irrevocable trust ends?	On termination of an income interest, the income beneficiary whose interest is terminated, or his estate, is entitled to: Income undistributed on the date of termination; income due but not paid to the trustee on the date of termination and income in the form of periodic payments (other than corporate distributions to stockholders), including rent, interest, or annuities, not due on the date of termination, accrued from day to day. (§ 55-13-4(d))
26. With regard to mutual funds, how are:	

a) long-term gains allocated between income and principal?	Distributions made from ordinary income by a regulated investment company are income. All other distributions made by the company, including distributions from capital gains, depreciation, or depletion, whether in the form of cash or an option to take new stock or cash or an option to purchase additional shares, are principal. (§ 55-13-6(c))
b) short-term gains allocated between income and principal?	Distributions made from ordinary income by a regulated investment company are income. All other distributions made by the company, including distributions from capital gains, depreciation, or depletion, whether in the form of cash or an option to take new stock or cash or an option to purchase additional shares, are principal. (§ 55-13-6(c))
27. How are distributions from REITs allocated between income and principal?	Distributions made from ordinary income by a REIT are income. All other distributions made by a REIT, including distributions from capital gains, depreciation, or depletion, whether in the form of cash or an option to take new stock or cash or an option to purchase additional shares, are principal. (§ 55-13-6(c))
28. With respect to underproductive property:	
a) Is an adjustment, e.g., "delayed income," required to be paid to the income beneficiary?	No. The South Dakota Principal and Income Act does not address underproductive property. Note: South Dakota has repealed § 55-13-12 dealing which dealt with underproductive property.
b) What percentage return makes property underproductive?	The South Dakota Principal and Income Act does not address underproductive property. Note: South Dakota has repealed § 55-13-12 dealing which dealt with underproductive property.
29. Is the trustee required to increase income so that it is sufficient to qualify for the marital deduction?	The South Dakota Principal and Income Act does not address the marital deduction.
30. Is the trustee required to take depreciation?	Yes. The trustee must charge against income a reasonable allowance for depreciation on property subject to depreciation under generally accepted accounting principles, but no allowance may be made for depreciation of that portion of real property used by a beneficiary as a residence or for depreciation of property held by the trustee on July 1, 1984, for which the trustee is not then making an allowance for depreciation. (§ 55-13-13(a)(2))
31. Is the trustee's determination on allocations generally presumed to be fair and reasonable?	The South Dakota Principal and Income Act does not have a presumption that allocations are generally presumed to be fair and reasonable. (§ 55-13-2(b))
32. If an item is not addressed in the trust agreement or in the law, must it be allocated to principal or income?	If an item is not addressed in the trust agreement or in the law, the trustee must allocate the item in accordance with what is reasonable and equitable in view of the interests of those entitled to income as well as of those entitled to principal, and in view of the manner in which persons of ordinary prudence, discretion, and judgment would act in the management of their own affairs. (§ 55-13-2(a)(3))

33. When does an asset become subject to a trust:	
a) In the case of transfers during the transferor's life?	The South Dakota Principal and Income Act does not address this issue. (§ 55-13-4(a))
b) In the case of a will?	In the case of an asset becoming subject to a trust by reason of a will, it becomes subject to the trust as of the date of the death of the testator even though there is an intervening period of administration of the testator's estate. (§ 55-13-4(a))
c) In the case of the death of a third party?	The South Dakota Principal and Income Act does not address this issue. (§ 55-13-4(a))
34. Can a trustee rely on the characterization by an entity as to the source or character of a received distribution?	Yes. (§ 55-13-6(e))

Table 12.02
Tennessee
Trust Accounting: Principal and Income

1. *Does the trustee have the power to transfer income to principal or to transfer principal to income to meet its duty of impartiality?*	See the Uniform Principal and Income Act (1997) chart. (§ 35-6-104)
2. *What is the effective date for the law? E.g., does it apply to preexisting trusts?*	The Tennessee Principal and Income Act applies to every trust or decedent's estate existing on or after July 1, 2000, except as otherwise expressly provided in the will or terms of the trust or in the Tennessee Principal and Income Act. (§ 35-6-602) ***Note:*** A trustee may continue using a former allocation method to allocate receipts for water, minerals, other natural resources, and timber under certain circumstances. (See § 35-6-411; § 35-6-412)
3. *What percentage is allocated to income and principal from proceeds of:*	
a) IRA? *b) Qualified pension or profit-sharing plan?* *c) Other deferred compensation arrangement?*	See the Uniform Principal and Income Act (1997) chart. (§ 35-6-409)
4. *What percentage is allocated to income and principal from proceeds of:*	
a) Patents? *b) Copyrights?*	See the Uniform Principal and Income Act (1997) chart. (§ 35-6-410(b))
5. *What percentage is allocated to income and principal in the event of distributions from:*	
a) Corporations? *b) Partnerships?* *c) LLCs?*	See the Uniform Principal and Income Act (1997) chart. (§ 35-6-401)
6. *What percentage is allocated to income and principal from proceeds of:*	
a) Oil and gas? *b) Minerals?* *c) Water?* *d) Other natural resourses (not including timber)?*	See the Uniform Principal and Income Act (1997) chart. (§ 35-6-411) ***Note***: If a trust owns an interest in minerals, water or other natural resources on June 30, 1999, the trustee may allocate receipts from the interest as provided in the Tennessee Principal and Income Act or in the manner used by the trustee before July 1, 1999.
e) Timber?	See the Uniform Principal and Income Act (1997) chart. (§ 35-6-412) ***Note:*** If a trust owns an interest in timberland on June 30, 1999, the trustee may allocate receipts from the interest as provided in the Tennessee Principal and Income Act or in the manner used by the trustee before July 1, 1999.
f) Rental properties?	See the Uniform Principal and Income Act (1997) chart. (§ 35-6-405)

7. After a decedent dies, in the case of an estate, or after an income interest ends, when the fiduciary is determining the remaining net income what are the rules regarding payment from income or principal for:	
a) Attorneys fees? *b) Accountants fees?* *c) Fiduciary fees and commissions?* *d) Court costs?* *e) Interest on death taxes*	See the Uniform Principal and Income Act (1997) chart. (§ 35-6-201(2)(B))
f) Debts? *g) Funeral expenses?* *h) Family allowances and similar protections?* *i) Death taxes?* *j) Penalties on death taxes?*	See the Uniform Principal and Income Act (1997) chart. (§ 35-6-201(2)(C))
8. With respect to trust expenses from the administration of the trust that are not covered by § 35-6-201(2)(B-C) [see Question #7]:	
a) Does the trustee have full discretion in allocating between income and principal for expenses incurred in the administration of the trust?	No. (§ 35-6-501; § 35-6-502)
b) If not, are there special rules for:	
i) Regular trustee fees? *ii) Advisory or custodial services to the trustee?* *iii) Accountings, judicial proceedings and other matters that involve both the income and remainder interests?*	See the Uniform Principal and Income Act (1997) chart. (§ 35-6-501; § 35-6-502)
iv) Debts?	See the Uniform Principal and Income Act (1997) chart. (§ 35-6-501(3); § 35-6-502(a)(3))
c) Can the trustee determine what are "transmission" expenses and "management" expenses?	
9. With regard to specific gifts from a trust after an income interest ends or from an estate:	
a) What amounts must be paid from income and principal?	See the Uniform Principal and Income Act (1997) chart. (§ 35-6-201(1); § 35-6-201(5))
10. With regard to outright pecuniary gifts from an estate or trust?:	

a) Does interest accrue?	Yes. See the Uniform Principal and Income Act (1997) chart. (§ 35-6-201(3))
11. With regard to a gift in trust of a pecuniary amount from an estate or trust?	
a) Does interest accrue?	No. See the Uniform Principal and Income Act (1997) chart. (§ 35-6-201(4); § 35-6-202)
12. With regard to residuary gifts:	
a) What amount of income and principal is to be paid to the residuary beneficiary of a trust or an estate?	See the Uniform Principal and Income Act (1997) chart. (§ 35-6-201(4); § 35-6-202)
13. With regard to "business assets" held in trust:	
a) Can the trustee treat them as a separate entity?	Generally yes. See the Uniform Principal and Income Act (1997) chart. (§ 35-6-403)
b) Can the trustee treat distinct assets as separate entities?	Generally yes. See the Uniform Principal and Income Act (1997) chart. (§ 35-6-403)
c) Can earnings be retained in trust for the reasonable needs of the "business entity," and, if so, to what extent is this permitted?	Yes. See the Uniform Principal and Income Act (1997) chart. (§ 35-6-403(b))
14. With respect to discount bonds:	
a) To what extent is the discount added to income or principal upon maturity?	See the Uniform Principal and Income Act (1997) chart. (§ 35-6-406(b))
b) Does the trustee have discretion to allocate discount between income and principal?	No. (§ 35-6-406) ***Note:*** The trustee has the overriding power to adjust under § 35-6-104(a).
c) Are distinctions drawn between Series E bonds and others?	No. (§ 35-6-406)
d) Are distinctions drawn based on the maturity date of the bond?	Yes. (§ 35-6-406(b))
15. Is there a de minimis rule excusing the trustee from making adjustments in certain cases?	Yes. See the Uniform Principal and Income Act (1997) chart. (§ 35-6-408)
16. With respect to derivatives:	
a) May income and loss be treated as that of a separate entity?	Yes. (§ 35-6-403(c)(7); § 35-6-414(b))
b) If not, or the trustee chooses not to do so, is income and loss allocated to the income account or to principal?	To principal. (§ 35-6-414(b))

17. To the extent put and call options are not derivatives, how are they allocated in terms of principal and income?	To principal. (§ 35-6-414(c))
18. How are asset-backed securities allocated in terms of principal and income?	See the Uniform Principal and Income Act (1997) chart. (§ 35-6-415)
19. Are expenses incurred to comply with environmental requirements allocated to income or principal?	Generally to principal. See the Uniform Principal and Income Act (1997) chart. (§ 35-6-502(a)(7))
20. Is income tax liability allocated generally to income or principal?	See the Uniform Principal and Income Act (1997) chart. (§ 35-6-505; § 35-6-506)
21. If a Subchapter S shareholder's or partner's portion of tax liability is greater than cash distributed, how is the excess obligation allocated?	From principal. (§ 35-6-505(c)(2)(B))
22. What is the standard, if any, for making equitable adjustments between income and principal?	See the Uniform Principal and Income Act (1997) chart. (§ 35-6-103(b))
23. Is an income beneficiary entitled to receive income accrued but unpaid when an estate ends?	No. See the Uniform Principal and Income Act (1997) chart. (§ 35-6-303)
24. Is an income beneficiary entitled to receive income accrued but unpaid when a revocable trust ends?	Generally no. See the Uniform Principal and Income Act (1997) chart. (§ 35-6-303)
25. Is an income beneficiary entitled to receive income accrued but unpaid when an irrevocable trust ends?	Generally no. See the Uniform Principal and Income Act (1997) chart. (§ 35-6-303)
26. With regard to mutual funds, how are:	
a) long-term gains allocated between income and principal?	See the Uniform Principal and Income Act (1997) chart. (§ 35-6-401(c)(4))
b) short-term gains allocated between income and principal?	See the Uniform Principal and Income Act (1997) chart. (§ 35-6-401(c)(4))
27. How are distributions from REITs allocated between income and principal?	See the Uniform Principal and Income Act (1997) chart. (§ 35-6-401(c)(4))
28. With respect to underproductive property:	
a) Is an adjustment, e.g., "delayed income," required to be paid to the income beneficiary?	No. (§ 35-6-413)
b) What percentage return makes property underproductive?	The statute only refers to property not productive of income. (§ 35-6-413)
29. Is the trustee required to increase income so that it is sufficient to qualify for the marital deduction?	Yes. (§ 35-6-413(a))

30. Is the trustee required to take depreciation?	No. (§ 35-6-503)
31. Is the trustee's determination on allocations generally presumed to be fair and reasonable?	Yes. (§ 35-6-103(b))
32. If an item is not addressed in the trust agreement or in the law, must it be allocated to principal or income?	To principal. (§ 35-6-103(a)(4))
33. When does an asset become subject to a trust:	
a) In the case of transfers during the transferor's life?	The date of transfer. (§ 35-6-301(b)(1))
b) In the case of a will?	The date of the testator's death. (§ 35-6-301(b)(2))
c) In the case of the death of a third party?	The date of the third party's death. (§ 35-6-301(b)(3))
34. Can a trustee rely on the characterization by an entity as to the source or character of a received distribution?	Yes. (§ 35-6-401(f))

Table 12.02
Texas
Trust Accounting: Principal and Income

1. *Does the trustee have the power to transfer income to principal or to transfer principal to income to meet its duty of impartiality?*	See the Uniform Principal and Income Act (1997) chart. (Prop. § 116.005(a))
2. *What is the effective date for the law? E.g., does it apply to preexisting trusts?*	Except as otherwise expressly provided by the will, the terms of the trust, or this Act, the Texas Principal and Income Act applies only to: 1. a trust existing or created on or after January 1, 2004; 2. the estate of a decedent who dies before January 1, 2004, if the probate or administration of the estate is pending as of January 1, 2004; and 3. the estate of a decedent who dies on or after January 1, 2004. (2003 Tex. Gen. Laws 659) ***Note***: A trustee may continue using a former allocation method to allocate receipts for liquidating assets; water, minerals, other natural resources; and timber under certain circumstances. (See Prop. § 116.173, Prop. § 116.174; Prop. § 116.175)
3. *What percentage is allocated to income and principal from proceeds of:*	
a) *IRA?* b) *Qualified pension or profit-sharing plan?* c) *Other deferred compensation arrangement?*	A trustee must allocate a payment, or any portion of a payment that is characterized as interest or a dividend, or payment in lieu of interest or a dividend to income. The trustee must allocate to principal the balance of the payment and any other payment received in the same accounting period that is not characterized as interest, a dividend or equivalent payment. If no part of the payment is characterized as interest, a dividend or an equivalent payment and all or part of the payment is required to be made, the trustee must allocate to income the part of the payment that does not exceed an amount equal to four percent of the fair market value of the future payment asset over the total amount that the trustee has allocated to income for all previous payments received from the future payment asset during the same accounting period in which the payment is made. The trustee must then allocate the balance to principal. The determination of the fair market value of a future payment asset is made on the later of the date on which the future payment asset first becomes subject to the trust or the last day of the accounting period of the trust that immediately precedes the accounting period during which the payment is received. If no part of a payment is required to be made or if the payment received by the trustee is the entire amount to which the trustee is entitled, then the trustee must allocate the entire payment to principal. A payment is not "required to be made" to the extent that it is made because the trustee exercises a right of withdrawal. If, in order to obtain an estate tax marital deduction for a trust, the trustee must allocate more of a payment to income than provided by the paragraphs above, the trustee must allocate to

	income the additional amount necessary to obtain the marital deduction. (Prop. § 116.172)
4. What percentage is allocated to income and principal from proceeds of:	
a) Patents? *b) Copyrights?*	See the Uniform Principal and Income Act (1997) chart. (Prop. § 116.173) ***Note:*** If a trust owns an interest in a liquidating asset on January 1, 2004, the trustee may allocate receipts from the interest as provided in the Texas Principal and Income Act or in the manner used by the trustee before January 1, 2004.
5. What percentage is allocated to income and principal in the event of distributions from:	
a) Corporations? *b) Partnerships?* *c) LLCs?*	See the Uniform Principal and Income Act (1997) chart. (Prop. § 116.151)
6. What percentage is allocated to income and principal from proceeds of:	
a) Oil and gas? *b) Minerals?* *c) Water?* *d) Other natural resourses (not including timber)?*	The trustee must allocate a receipt received as nominal delay rental or a nominal annual rent on a lease to income. The trustee must allocate a receipt received from a production payment to income if and to the extent that the agreement creating the production payment provides a factor for interest or its equivalent. The balance must be allocated to principal. The trustee must equitably allocate an amount received as a royalty, shut-in-well payment, take-or-pay payment, bonus, or a delay rental that is more than nominal. The trustee must equitably allocate the net amount received from a working interest or other interest (not mentioned in the three preceding paragraphs). An amount received on account of an interest in water that is renewable must be allocated to income. If the water is not renewable, the trustee must allocate an amount equitably The rules above apply whether or not a decedent or donor was extracting the minerals, water, or other natural resources before the interest became subject to the trust. An allocation of an amount is presumed to be equitable if the amount allocated to principal is equal to the amount allowed by the I.R.C. of 1986 as a deduction for depletion of the interest. (Prop. § 116.174) ***Note:*** If a trust owns an interest in minerals, water or other natural resources on January 1, 2004, the trustee may allocate receipts from the interest as provided in the Texas Principal and Income Act or in the manner used by the trustee before January 1, 2004.
e) Timber?	See the Uniform Principal and Income Act (1997) chart. (Prop. § 116.175)

	Note: If a trust owns an interest in timberland on January 1, 2004, the trustee may allocate receipts from the interest as provided in the Texas Principal and Income Act or in the manner used by the trustee before January 1, 2004.
f) *Rental properties?*	See the Uniform Principal and Income Act (1997) chart. (Prop. § 116.162)
7. *After a decedent dies, in the case of an estate, or after an income interest ends, when the fiduciary is determining the remaining net income what are the rules regarding payment from income or principal for:*	
a) *Attorneys fees?* b) *Accountants fees?* c) *Fiduciary fees and commissions?* d) *Court costs?* e) *Interest on death taxes*	See the Uniform Principal and Income Act (1997) chart. (Prop. § 116.051(2)(B))
f) *Debts?* g) *Funeral expenses?* h) *Family allowances and similar protections?* i) *Death taxes?* j) *Penalties on death taxes?*	See the Uniform Principal and Income Act (1997) chart. (Prop. § 116.051(2)(C))
8. *With respect to trust expenses from the administration of the trust that are not covered by Prop. § 116.051(2)(B-C) [see Question #7]:*	
a) *Does the trustee have full discretion in allocating between income and principal for expenses incurred in the administration of the trust?*	No. (Prop. § 116.201; Prop. § 116.202)
b) *If not, are there special rules for:*	
i) *Regular trustee fees?* ii) *Advisory or custodial services to the trustee?* iii) *Accountings, judicial proceedings and other matters that involve both the income and remainder interests?*	See the Uniform Principal and Income Act (1997) chart. (Prop. § 116.201; Prop. § 116.202)
iv) *Debts?*	See the Uniform Principal and Income Act (1997) chart. (Prop. § 116.201(3); Prop. § 116.202(a)(3))
c) *Can the trustee determine what are "transmission" expenses and "management" expenses?*	

9. With regard to specific gifts from a trust after an income interest ends or from an estate:	
a) What amounts must be paid from income and principal?	See the Uniform Principal and Income Act (1997) chart. (Prop. § 116.051(1); Prop. § 116.051(5))
10. With regard to outright pecuniary gifts from an estate or trust?:	
a) Does interest accrue?	Yes. See the Uniform Principal and Income Act (1997) chart. (Prop. § 116.051(3))
11. With regard to a gift in trust of a pecuniary amount from an estate or trust?	
a) Does interest accrue?	No. See the Uniform Principal and Income Act (1997) chart. (Prop. § 116.051(4); Prop. § 116.052)
12. With regard to residuary gifts:	
a) What amount of income and principal is to be paid to the residuary beneficiary of a trust or an estate?	See the Uniform Principal and Income Act (1997) chart. (Prop. § 116.051(4); Prop. § 116.052)
13. With regard to "business assets" held in trust:	
a) Can the trustee treat them as a separate entity?	Generally yes. See the Uniform Principal and Income Act (1997) chart. (Prop. § 116.153)
b) Can the trustee treat distinct assets as separate entities?	Generally yes. See the Uniform Principal and Income Act (1997) chart. (Prop. § 116.153)
c) Can earnings be retained in trust for the reasonable needs of the "business entity," and, if so, to what extent is this permitted?	Yes. See the Uniform Principal and Income Act (1997) chart. (Prop. § 116.153(b))
14. With respect to discount bonds:	
a) To what extent is the discount added to income or principal upon maturity?	See the Uniform Principal and Income Act (1997) chart. (Prop. § 116.163)
b) Does the trustee have discretion to allocate discount between income and principal?	No. (Prop. § 116.163) ***Note:*** The trustee has the overriding power to adjust under Prop. § 116.005.
c) Are distinctions drawn between Series E bonds and others?	No. (Prop. § 116.163)
d) Are distinctions drawn based on the maturity date of the bond?	Yes. (Prop. § 116.163)
15. Is there a de minimis rule excusing the trustee from making adjustments in certain cases?	Yes. See the Uniform Principal and Income Act (1997) chart. (Prop. § 116.171) ***Note:*** The Texas Principal and Income Act does not contain a "presumption of insubstantiality" provision.

16. With respect to derivatives:	
a) May income and loss be treated as that of a separate entity?	Yes. (Prop. § 116.153(c)(7); Prop. § 116.177(b))
b) If not, or the trustee chooses not to do so, is income and loss allocated to the income account or to principal?	To principal. (Prop. § 116.177(b))
17. To the extent put and call options are not derivatives, how are they allocated in terms of principal and income?	To principal. (Prop. § 116.177(c))
18. How are asset-backed securities allocated in terms of principal and income?	See the Uniform Principal and Income Act (1997) chart. (Prop. § 116.178)
19. Are expenses incurred to comply with environmental requirements allocated to income or principal?	Generally to principal. See the Uniform Principal and Income Act (1997) chart. (Prop. § 116.202(a)(7))
20. Is income tax liability allocated generally to income or principal?	See the Uniform Principal and Income Act (1997) chart. (Prop. § 116.205; Prop. § 116.206)
21. If a Subchapter S shareholder's or partner's portion of tax liability is greater than cash distributed, how is the excess obligation allocated?	From principal. (Prop. § 116.205(c)(2)(B))
22. What is the standard, if any, for making equitable adjustments between income and principal?	See the Uniform Principal and Income Act (1997) chart. (Prop. § 116.104(b))
23. Is an income beneficiary entitled to receive income accrued but unpaid when an estate ends?	No. See the Uniform Principal and Income Act (1997) chart. (Prop. § 116.103)
24. Is an income beneficiary entitled to receive income accrued but unpaid when a revocable trust ends?	Generally no. See the Uniform Principal and Income Act (1997) chart. (Prop. § 116.103)
25. Is an income beneficiary entitled to receive income accrued but unpaid when an irrevocable trust ends?	Generally no. See the Uniform Principal and Income Act (1997) chart. (Prop. § 116.103)
26. With regard to mutual funds, how are:	
a) long-term gains allocated between income and principal?	See the Uniform Principal and Income Act (1997) chart. (Prop. § 116.151(c)(4))
b) short-term gains allocated between income and principal?	See the Uniform Principal and Income Act (1997) chart. (Prop. § 116.151(c)(4))
27. How are distributions from REITs allocated between income and principal?	See the Uniform Principal and Income Act (1997) chart. (Prop. § 116.151(c)(4))
28. With respect to underproductive property:	
a) Is an adjustment, e.g., "delayed income," required to be paid to the income beneficiary?	No. (Prop. § 116.176)

b) What percentage return makes property underproductive?	The statute only refers to property not productive of income. (Prop. § 116.176)
29. Is the trustee required to increase income so that it is sufficient to qualify for the marital deduction?	Yes. (Prop. § 116.176(a))
30. Is the trustee required to take depreciation?	No. (Prop. § 116.203)
31. Is the trustee's determination on allocations generally presumed to be fair and reasonable?	Yes. (Prop. § 116.004(b))
32. If an item is not addressed in the trust agreement or in the law, must it be allocated to principal or income?	To principal. (Prop. § 116.004(a)(4))
33. When does an asset become subject to a trust:	
a) In the case of transfers during the transferor's life?	The date of transfer. (Prop. § 116.101(b)(1))
b) In the case of a will?	The date of the testator's death. (Prop. § 116.101(b)(2))
c) In the case of the death of a third party?	The date of the third party's death. (Prop. § 116.101(b)(3))
34. Can a trustee rely on the characterization by an entity as to the source or character of a received distribution?	Yes. (Prop. § 116.151(f))

Table 12.02
Utah
Trust Accounting: Principal and Income

1. *Does the trustee have the power to transfer income to principal or to transfer principal to income to meet its duty of impartiality?*	See the Uniform Principal and Income Act (1997) chart. (§ 22-3-104)
2. *What is the effective date for the law? E.g., does it apply to preexisting trusts?*	The Utah Principal and Income Act applies to every trust or decedent's estate existing on May 3, 2004 except as otherwise expressly provided in the will or terms of the trust or in the Utah Principal and Income Act. (§ 22-3-603) ***Note:*** A trustee may continue using a former allocation method to allocate receipts for water, minerals, other natural resources, and timber under certain circumstances. (See § 22-3-411; § 22-3-412)
3. *What percentage is allocated to income and principal from proceeds of:*	
a) *IRA?* b) *Qualified pension or profit-sharing plan?* c) *Other deferred compensation arrangement?*	See the Uniform Principal and Income Act (1997) chart. (§ 22-3-409)
4. *What percentage is allocated to income and principal from proceeds of:*	
a) *Patents?* b) *Copyrights?*	See the Uniform Principal and Income Act (1997) chart. (§ 22-3-410(2))
5. *What percentage is allocated to income and principal in the event of distributions from:*	
a) *Corporations?* b) *Partnerships?* c) *LLCs?*	See the Uniform Principal and Income Act (1997) chart. (§ 22-3-401)
6. *What percentage is allocated to income and principal from proceeds of:*	
a) *Oil and gas?* b) *Minerals?* c) *Water?* d) *Other natural resourses (not including timber)?*	See the Uniform Principal and Income Act (1997) chart. (§ 22-3-411) ***Note:*** If a trust owns an interest in minerals, water or other natural resources on May 3, 2004, the trustee may allocate receipts from the interest as provided in the Utah Principal and Income Act or in the manner used by the trustee before May 3, 2004.
e) *Timber?*	See the Uniform Principal and Income Act (1997) chart. (§ 22-3-412) ***Note:*** If a trust owns an interest in timberland on May 3, 2004, the trustee may allocate receipts from the interest as provided in the Utah Principal and Income Act or in the manner used by the trustee before May 3, 2004.
f) *Rental properties?*	See the Uniform Principal and Income Act (1997) chart. (§ 22-3-405)

7. After a decedent dies, in the case of an estate, or after an income interest ends, when the fiduciary is determining the remaining net income what are the rules regarding payment from income or principal for:	
a) Attorneys fees? *b) Accountants fees?* *c) Fiduciary fees and commissions?* *d) Court costs?* *e) Interest on death taxes*	See the Uniform Principal and Income Act (1997) chart. (§ 22-3-201(2)(b))
f) Debts? *g) Funeral expenses?* *h) Family allowances and similar protections?* *i) Death taxes?* *j) Penalties on death taxes?*	See the Uniform Principal and Income Act (1997) chart. (§ 22-3-201(2)(c))
8. With respect to trust expenses from the administration of the trust that are not covered by § 22-3-201(2)(b-c) [see Question #7]:	
a) Does the trustee have full discretion in allocating between income and principal for expenses incurred in the administration of the trust?	No. (§ 22-3-501; § 22-3-502)
b) If not, are there special rules for:	
i) Regular trustee fees? *ii) Advisory or custodial services to the trustee?* *iii) Accountings, judicial proceedings and other matters that involve both the income and remainder interests?*	See the Uniform Principal and Income Act (1997) chart. (§ 22-3-501; § 22-3-502)
iv) Debts?	See the Uniform Principal and Income Act (1997) chart. (§ 22-3-501(3); § 22-3-502(1)(c))
c) Can the trustee determine what are "transmission" expenses and "management" expenses?	
9. With regard to specific gifts from a trust after an income interest ends or from an estate:	
a) What amounts must be paid from income and principal?	See the Uniform Principal and Income Act (1997) chart. (§ 22-3-201(1); § 22-3-201(5))
10. With regard to outright pecuniary gifts from an estate or trust?:	

a) *Does interest accrue?*	Yes. See the Uniform Principal and Income Act (1997) chart. (§ 22-3-201(3))
11. *With regard to a gift in trust of a pecuniary amount from an estate or trust?*	
a) *Does interest accrue?*	No. See the Uniform Principal and Income Act (1997) chart. (§ 22-3-201(4); § 22-3-202)
12. *With regard to residuary gifts:*	
a) *What amount of income and principal is to be paid to the residuary beneficiary of a trust or an estate?*	See the Uniform Principal and Income Act (1997) chart. (§ 22-3-201(4); § 22-3-202)
13. *With regard to "business assets" held in trust:*	
a) *Can the trustee treat them as a separate entity?*	Generally yes. See the Uniform Principal and Income Act (1997) chart. (§ 22-3-403)
b) *Can the trustee treat distinct assets as separate entities?*	Generally yes. See the Uniform Principal and Income Act (1997) chart. (§ 22-3-403)
c) *Can earnings be retained in trust for the reasonable needs of the "business entity," and, if so, to what extent is this permitted?*	Yes. See the Uniform Principal and Income Act (1997) chart. (§ 22-3-403(2))
14. *With respect to discount bonds:*	
a) *To what extent is the discount added to income or principal upon maturity?*	See the Uniform Principal and Income Act (1997) chart. (§ 22-3-406(2))
b) *Does the trustee have discretion to allocate discount between income and principal?*	No. (§ 22-3-406) ***Note:*** The trustee has the overriding power to adjust under § 22-3-104(1).
c) *Are distinctions drawn between Series E bonds and others?*	No. (§ 22-3-406)
d) *Are distinctions drawn based on the maturity date of the bond?*	Yes. (§ 22-3-406(2))
15. *Is there a de minimis rule excusing the trustee from making adjustments in certain cases?*	Yes. See the Uniform Principal and Income Act (1997) chart. (§ 22-3-408)
16. *With respect to derivatives:*	
a) *May income and loss be treated as that of a separate entity?*	Yes. (§ 22-3-403(3)(g); § 22-3-414(2))
b) *If not, or the trustee chooses not to do so, is income and loss allocated to the income account or to principal?*	To principal. (§ 22-3-414(2))

17. To the extent put and call options are not derivatives, how are they allocated in terms of principal and income?	To principal. (§ 22-3-414(3))
18. How are asset-backed securities allocated in terms of principal and income?	See the Uniform Principal and Income Act (1997) chart. (§ 22-3-415)
19. Are expenses incurred to comply with environmental requirements allocated to income or principal?	Generally to principal. See the Uniform Principal and Income Act (1997) chart. (§ 22-3-502(1)(g))
20. Is income tax liability allocated generally to income or principal?	See the Uniform Principal and Income Act (1997) chart. (§ 22-3-505; § 22-3-506)
21. If a Subchapter S shareholder's or partner's portion of tax liability is greater than cash distributed, how is the excess obligation allocated?	From principal. (§ 22-3-505(3)(b)(ii))
22. What is the standard, if any, for making equitable adjustments between income and principal?	See the Uniform Principal and Income Act (1997) chart. (§ 22-3-103(2))
23. Is an income beneficiary entitled to receive income accrued but unpaid when an estate ends?	No. (§ 22-3-303)
24. Is an income beneficiary entitled to receive income accrued but unpaid when a revocable trust ends?	Generally no. See the Uniform Principal and Income Act (1997) chart. (§ 22-3-303)
25. Is an income beneficiary entitled to receive income accrued but unpaid when an irrevocable trust ends?	Generally no. See the Uniform Principal and Income Act (1997) chart. (§ 22-3-303)
26. With regard to mutual funds, how are:	
a) long-term gains allocated between income and principal?	See the Uniform Principal and Income Act (1997) chart. (§ 22-3-401(3)(d))
b) short-term gains allocated between income and principal?	See the Uniform Principal and Income Act (1997) chart. (§ 22-3-401(3)(d))
27. How are distributions from REITs allocated between income and principal?	See the Uniform Principal and Income Act (1997) chart. (§ 22-3-401(3)(d))
28. With respect to underproductive property:	
a) Is an adjustment, e.g., "delayed income," required to be paid to the income beneficiary?	No. (§ 22-3-413)
b) What percentage return makes property underproductive?	The statute only refers to property not productive of income. (§ 22-3-413)
29. Is the trustee required to increase income so that it is sufficient to qualify for the marital deduction?	Yes. (§ 22-3-413(1))

30. Is the trustee required to take depreciation?	No. (§ 22-3-503)
31. Is the trustee's determination on allocations generally presumed to be fair and reasonable?	Yes. (§ 22-3-103(2))
32. If an item is not addressed in the trust agreement or in the law, must it be allocated to principal or income?	To principal. (§ 22-3-103(1)(d))
33. When does an asset become subject to a trust:	
a) In the case of transfers during the transferor's life?	The date of transfer. (§ 22-3-301(2)(a))
b) In the case of a will?	The date of the testator's death. (§ 22-3-301(2)(b))
c) In the case of the death of a third party?	The date of the third party's death. (§ 22-3-301(2)(c))
34. Can a trustee rely on the characterization by an entity as to the source or character of a received distribution?	Yes. (§ 22-3-401(6))

Table 12.02
Vermont
Trust Accounting: Principal and Income

1. *Does the trustee have the power to transfer income to principal or to transfer principal to income to meet its duty of impartiality?*	No.
2. *What is the effective date for the law? E.g., does it apply to preexisting trusts?*	The Vermont Principal and Income Act applies to all estates of tenants or remaindermen which became legally effective after June 1, 1957. (1957 Vt. Acts & Resolves 171)
3. *What percentage is allocated to income and principal from proceeds of:*	
a) *IRA?* b) *Qualified pension or profit-sharing plan?* c) *Other deferred compensation arrangement?*	If the principal consists of property subject to depletion, such as leaseholds, patents, copyrights and royalty rights, and the trustee or tenant in possession is not under a duty to change the form of the investment of the principal, the trustee must allocate the full amount of rents, royalties or return from the property to income. When the trustee or tenant is under a duty, arising either by law or by the terms of the transaction by which the principal was established, to change the form of the investment, either at once or as soon as it may be done without loss, then the trustee must allocate the return from such property, not in excess of 5% per year of its fair inventory value or in default thereof its market value at the time the principal was established, or at its cost where purchased later, to income and the remainder to principal. (14 § 3311)
4. *What percentage is allocated to income and principal from proceeds of:*	
a) *Patents?* b) *Copyrights?*	If the principal consists of property subject to depletion, such as leaseholds, patents, copyrights and royalty rights, and the trustee or tenant in possession is not under a duty to change the form of the investment of the principal, the trustee must allocate the full amount of rents, royalties or return from the property to income. When the trustee or tenant is under a duty, arising either by law or by the terms of the transaction by which the principal was established, to change the form of the investment, either at once or as soon as it may be done without loss, then the trustee must allocate the return from such property, not in excess of 5% per year of its fair inventory value or in default thereof its market value at the time the principal was established, or at its cost where purchased later, to income and the remainder to principal. (14 § 3311)
5. *What percentage is allocated to income and principal in the event of distributions from:*	
a) *Corporations?* b) *Partnerships?* c) *LLCs?*	All dividends on shares of a corporation forming a part of the principal which are payable in the shares of the corporation are principal. Subject to the provisions the Vermont Principal and Income Act, all dividends payable otherwise than in the shares of the corporation itself, including ordinary and extraordinary dividends and dividends payable in shares or other securities or obligations of corporations other than the declaring corporation, are income.

All rights to subscribe to the shares or other securities or obligations of a corporation accruing on account of the ownership of shares or other securities in such corporation, and the proceeds of any sale of such rights, are principal. All rights to subscribe to the shares or other securities or obligations of a corporation accruing on account of the ownership of shares or other securities in another corporation, and the proceeds of any sale of such rights, are income.

If the assets of a corporation are liquidated, amounts paid as cash dividends but declared before such liquidation occurs or as arrears of preferred or guaranteed dividends are deemed income. All other amounts paid upon corporate shares on disbursement of the corporate assets to the stockholders are principal. All disbursements of corporate assets to the stockholders, whenever made, which are designated by the corporation as a return of capital or division of corporate property are principal.

If a corporation succeeds another by merger, consolidation or reorganization or otherwise acquires its assets, and the corporate shares of the succeeding corporation are issued to the shareholders of the original corporation in like proportion to, or in substitution for, their shares of the original corporation, the two corporations are be considered a single corporation in applying the Vermont Principal and Income Act. But two corporations are not be considered a single corporation under this section merely because one owns corporate shares of or otherwise controls or directs the other.

In applying the Vermont Principal and Income Act, the date when a dividend accrues to the person who is entitled to it is the date specified by the corporation as the one on which the stockholders entitled thereto are determined, or in default thereof the date of declaration of the dividend. (14 § 3306).

6. What percentage is allocated to income and principal from proceeds of:	
a) Oil and gas? *b) Minerals?* *c) Water?* *d) Other natural resourses (not including timber)?*	When part of the principal consists of any interest in lands, including royalties, overriding royalties, and working interests, that contains timber, minerals, oil, gas, or other natural resources and the trustee or tenant is authorized by law or by the terms of the transaction by which the principal or trust was established to sell, lease, or otherwise develop such natural resources, and no provision is made for the disposition of the net proceeds thereof after the payment of expenses and carrying charges on such property, such proceeds: 1. If received as extension payments on a lease or bonus for the execution of the same, are income. 2. If received as consideration whether as royalties or otherwise, for the permanent severance of such natural resources from the lands, the trustee must allocate an amount equal to the percentage of allowable depletion for federal tax purposes to principal and to income. However, if no federal tax deduction exists at the time, the trustee must allocate twenty percent (20%) of the net proceeds to principal and the balance to income. (14 § 3310)

e) Timber?	When part of the principal consists of any interest in lands, including royalties, overriding royalties, and working interests, that contains timber, minerals, oil, gas, or other natural resources and the trustee or tenant is authorized by law or by the terms of the transaction by which the principal or trust was established to sell, lease, or otherwise develop such natural resources, and no provision is made for the disposition of the net proceeds thereof after the payment of expenses and carrying charges on such property, such proceeds: 1. If received as extension payments on a lease or bonus for the execution of the same, are income. 2. If received as consideration whether as royalties or otherwise, for the permanent severance of such natural resources from the lands, the trustee must allocate an amount equal to the percentage of allowable depletion for federal tax purposes to principal and to income. However, if no federal tax deduction exists at the time, the trustee must allocate twenty percent (20%) of the net proceeds to principal and the balance to income. (14 § 3310)
f) Rental properties?	All receipts from the rental of realty or personalty are income. (14 § 3303)
7. After a decedent dies, in the case of an estate, or after an income interest ends, when the fiduciary is determining the remaining net income what are the rules regarding payment from income or principal for:	
a) Attorneys fees? *b) Accountants fees?* *c) Fiduciary fees and commissions?* *d) Court costs?* *e) Interest on death taxes*	The Vermont Principal and Income Act does not address the allocation of these expenses. (14 § 3304; 14 § 3313)
f) Debts? *g) Funeral expenses?* *h) Family allowances and similar protections?* *i) Death taxes?* *j) Penalties on death taxes?*	The Vermont Principal and Income Act does not address the allocation of these expenses. (14 § 3304; 14 § 3313)
8. With respect to trust expenses from the administration of the trust:	
a) Does the trustee have full discretion in allocating between income and principal for expenses incurred in the administration of the trust?	No. The trustee does not have full discretion in allocating expenses between income and principal for expenses occurred in the administration of the trust. (14 § 3313)
b) If not, are there special rules for:	
i) Regular trustee fees? *ii) Advisory or custodial services to the trustee?*	The trustee must pay regular trustee compensation, court costs, attorneys' fees, other fees for regular accountings, from income. (14 § 3313)

iii) Accountings, judicial proceedings and other matters that involve both the income and remainder interests?	
iv) Debts?	The trustee must allocate interest expense on trust debt to income and must allocate payments on principal of trust debt to principal. (14 § 3313)
c) Can the trustee determine what are "transmission" expenses and "management" expenses?	
9. With regard to specific gifts from a trust after an income interest ends or from an estate:	
a) What amounts must be paid from income and principal?	The fiduciary must distribute to a beneficiary of a specific gift, the net income from the property specifically given to the benficiary. (14 § 3304)
10. With regard to outright pecuniary gifts from an estate or trust?:	
a) Does interest accrue?	The fiduciary must distribute to the pecuniary beneficiaries (including trusts) and remainder beneficiaries, the net income from the property in proportion to their interests in the property. (14 § 3304)
11. With regard to a gift in trust of a pecuniary amount from an estate or trust?	
a) Does interest accrue?	The fiduciary must distribute to the pecuniary beneficiaries (including trusts) and remainder beneficiaries, the net income from the property in proportion to their interests in the property. (14 § 3304)
12. With regard to residuary gifts:	
a) What amount of income and principal is to be paid to the residuary beneficiary of a trust or an estate?	The fiduciary must distribute to the pecuniary beneficiaries (including trusts) and remainder beneficiaries, the net income from the property in proportion to their interests in the property. (14 § 3304)
13. With regard to "business assets" held in trust:	
a) Can the trustee treat them as a separate entity?	The Vermont Principal and Income Act does not particularly provide for treating distinct assets as separate entities. However, If a trustee uses any part of the principal in the continuance of a business of which the settlor was a sole proprietor or a partner, the net profits of the business are income. If a loss results in any fiscal or calendar year, the loss to principal. Any net loss must not be carried into any other fiscal or calendar year for purposes of calculating net income. (14 § 3308)
b) Can the trustee treat distinct assets as separate entities?	The Vermont Principal and Income Act does not particularly provide for treating distinct assets as separate entities.

	However, If a trustee uses any part of the principal in the continuance of a business of which the settlor was a sole proprietor or a partner, the net profits of the business are income. If a loss results in any fiscal or calendar year, the loss to principal. Any net loss must not be carried into any other fiscal or calendar year for purposes of calculating net income. (14 § 3308)
c) Can earnings be retained in trust for the reasonable needs of the "business entity," and, if so, to what extent is this permitted?	No. The Vermont Principal and Income Act does not provide that the fiduciary may retain earnings for the needs of the business entity. (14 § 3308)
14. With respect to discount bonds:	
a) To what extent is the discount added to income or principal upon maturity?	The trustee must allocate any gain or loss on the sale or maturity of bonds to principal regardless of whether the bond was purchased at a discount. (14 § 3307)
b) Does the trustee have discretion to allocate discount between income and principal?	No. (14 § 3307)
c) Are distinctions drawn between Series E bonds and others?	No. (14 § 3307)
d) Are distinctions drawn based on the maturity date of the bond?	No. (14 § 3307)
15. Is there a de minimis rule excusing the trustee from making adjustments in certain cases?	No.
16. With respect to derivatives:	
a) May income and loss be treated as that of a separate entity?	The Vermont Principal and Income Act does not address derivatives.
b) If not, or the trustee chooses not to do so, is income and loss allocated to the income account or to principal?	The Vermont Principal and Income Act does not address derivatives. However, under 14 § 3303, gain or loss should be allocated to principal. (14 § 3303)
17. To the extent put and call options are not derivatives, how are they allocated in terms of principal and income?	The Vermont Principal and Income Act does not address options. However, under 14 § 3303, gain or loss should be allocated to principal. (14 § 3303)
18. How are asset-backed securities allocated in terms of principal and income?	The Vermont Principal and Income Act does not address asset-backed securities. See 14 § 3303 for further details on allocating receipts from asset-backed securities. (14 § 3303)
19. Are expenses incurred to comply with environmental requirements allocated to income or principal?	The Vermont Principal and Income Act does not address environmental requirements. However, under 14 § 3313, expenses for environmental requirements should be allocated to principal. (14 § 3313)
20. Is income tax liability allocated generally to income or principal?	Any tax required to be paid by a fiduciary on the trust's share of an entity's taxable income should be paid from income to the extent that receipts from the entity are allocated to income and from principal to the extent that receipts from the entity are allocated to principal. (14 § 3313)

21. If a Subchapter S shareholder's or partner's portion of tax liability is greater than cash distributed, how is the excess obligation allocated?	The Vermont Principal and Income Act does not address this situation. (14 § 3313)
22. What is the standard, if any, for making equitable adjustments between income and principal?	The Vermont Principal and Income Act does not provide for equitable adjustments between principal and income.
23. Is an income beneficiary entitled to receive income accrued but unpaid when an estate ends?	If an income beneficiary dies, the decedent's estate is entitled to the portion income from periodic payments, including rent, interest, and annuities, but not including corporate dividends that accrued before the decedent's death. (14 § 3305)
24. Is an income beneficiary entitled to receive income accrued but unpaid when a revocable trust ends?	If an income interest ends, the income beneficiary is entitled to the portion income from periodic payments, including rent, interest, and annuities, but not including corporate dividends that accrued before the income interest ended. (14 § 3305)
25. Is an income beneficiary entitled to receive income accrued but unpaid when an irrevocable trust ends?	If an income interest ends, the income beneficiary is entitled to the portion income from periodic payments, including rent, interest, and annuities, but not including corporate dividends that accrued before the income interest ended. (14 § 3305)
26. With regard to mutual funds, how are:	
a) long-term gains allocated between income and principal?	The Vermont Principal and Income Act does not address distributions from registered investment companies (mutual funds). (14 § 3306)
b) short-term gains allocated between income and principal?	The Vermont Principal and Income Act does not address distributions from registered investment companies (mutual funds). (14 § 3306)
27. How are distributions from REITs allocated between income and principal?	The Vermont Principal and Income Act does not address distributions from real estate investment trusts. (14 § 3306)
28. With respect to underproductive property:	
a) Is an adjustment, e.g., "delayed income," required to be paid to the income beneficiary?	Yes. Generally, a portion of the net proceeds of sale of any part of principal which has not produced an average net income of at least one per cent (1%) per year of its inventory value for more than a year (including as income the value of any beneficial use of the property by the income beneficiary) must be treated as delayed income to which the income beneficiary is entitled. (14 § 3312) For a calculation of the delayed income and for exceptions to the rule, see 14 § 3312.
b) What percentage return makes property underproductive?	Property is not considered productive of income if the property has not produced an average net income of at least one per cent (1%) per year of its inventory value for more than a year (including as income the value of any beneficial use of the property by the income beneficiary). (14 § 3312)
29. Is the trustee required to increase income so that it is sufficient to qualify for the marital deduction?	The Vermont Principal and Income Act does not address the marital deduction.

30. Is the trustee required to take depreciation?	The Vermont Principal and Income Act does not address depreciation.
31. Is the trustee's determination on allocations generally presumed to be fair and reasonable?	The Vermont Principal and Income Act does not have a presumption that allocations are generally presumed to be fair and reasonable.
32. If an item is not addressed in the trust agreement or in the law, must it be allocated to principal or income?	The Vermont Principal and Income Act has no clear default settings for allocating items to principal or income. However, it appears that these items should be allocated to principal. (14 § 3303; 14 § 3313)
33. When does an asset become subject to a trust:	
a) In the case of transfers during the transferor's life?	The Vermont Principal and Income Act does not address this issue.
b) In the case of a will?	The Vermont Principal and Income Act does not address this issue.
c) In the case of the death of a third party?	The Vermont Principal and Income Act does not address this issue.
34. Can a trustee rely on the characterization by an entity as to the source or character of a received distribution?	The Vermont Principal and Income Act does not address this issue.

Table 12.02
Virginia
Trust Accounting: Principal and Income

1. *Does the trustee have the power to transfer income to principal or to transfer principal to income to meet its duty of impartiality?*	See the Uniform Principal and Income Act (1997) chart. (§ 55-277.4(A))
2. *What is the effective date for the law? E.g., does it apply to preexisting trusts?*	The Virginia Principal and Income Act applies to every trust or decedent's estate or nontrust estate existing on or after January 1, 2000, except as otherwise expressly provided in the will or terms of the trust, any other governing document or in the Virginia Principal and Income Act. (§ 55-277.33)
3. *What percentage is allocated to income and principal from proceeds of:*	
a) *IRA?* b) *Qualified pension or profit-sharing plan?* c) *Other deferred compensation arrangement?*	See the Uniform Principal and Income Act (1997) chart. (§ 55-277.18)
4. *What percentage is allocated to income and principal from proceeds of:*	
a) *Patents?* b) *Copyrights?*	See the Uniform Principal and Income Act (1997) chart. (§ 55-277.19)
5. *What percentage is allocated to income and principal in the event of distributions from:*	
a) *Corporations?* b) *Partnerships?* c) *LLCs?*	See the Uniform Principal and Income Act (1997) chart. (§ 55-277.10)
6. *What percentage is allocated to income and principal from proceeds of:*	
a) *Oil and gas?* b) *Minerals?* c) *Water?* d) *Other natural resourses (not including timber)?*	See the Uniform Principal and Income Act (1997) chart. (§ 55-277.20) ***Note:*** If a trust owns an interest in minerals, water or other natural resources on January 1, 2000, the trustee may allocate receipts from the interest as provided in the Virginia Principal and Income Act or in the manner used by the trustee before January 1, 2000.
e) *Timber?*	See the Uniform Principal and Income Act (1997) chart. (§ 55-277.21) ***Note:*** If a trust owns an interest in timberland on January 1, 2000, the trustee may allocate receipts from the interest as provided in the Virginia Principal and Income Act or in the manner used by the trustee before January 1, 2000.
f) *Rental properties?*	See the Uniform Principal and Income Act (1997) chart. (§ 55-277.14)
7. *After a decedent dies, in the case of an estate, or after an income interest ends, when the fiduciary is determining the*	

remaining net income what are the rules regarding payment from income or principal for:	
a) Attorneys fees? *b) Accountants fees?* *c) Fiduciary fees and commissions?* *d) Court costs?* *e) Interest on death taxes*	See the Uniform Principal and Income Act (1997) chart. (§ 55-277.5(2)(b))
f) Debts? *g) Funeral expenses?* *h) Family allowances and similar protections?* *i) Death taxes?* *j) Penalties on death taxes?*	See the Uniform Principal and Income Act (1997) chart. (§ 55-277.5(2)(c))
8. With respect to trust expenses from the administration of the trust that are not covered by § 55-277.5(2)(b-c) [see Question #7]:	
a) Does the trustee have full discretion in allocating between income and principal for expenses incurred in the administration of the trust?	No. See the Uniform Principal and Income Act (1997) chart. (§ 55-277.25; § 55-277.26)
b) If not, are there special rules for:	
i) Regular trustee fees? *ii) Advisory or custodial services to the trustee?* *iii) Accountings, judicial proceedings and other matters that involve both the income and remainder interests?*	See the Uniform Principal and Income Act (1997) chart. (§ 55-277.25; § 55-277.26)
iv) Debts?	See the Uniform Principal and Income Act (1997) chart. (§ 55-277.25(3); § 55-277.26(A)(3))
c) Can the trustee determine what are "transmission" expenses and "management" expenses?	
9. With regard to specific gifts from a trust after an income interest ends or from an estate:	
a) What amounts must be paid from income and principal?	See the Uniform Principal and Income Act (1997) chart. (§ 55-277.5(1); § 55-277.5(5))
10. With regard to outright pecuniary gifts from an estate or trust?:	
a) Does interest accrue?	Yes. See the Uniform Principal and Income Act (1997) chart. (§ 55-277.5(3))

11. With regard to a gift in trust of a pecuniary amount from an estate or trust?	
a) Does interest accrue?	No. See the Uniform Principal and Income Act (1997) chart. (§ 55-277.5(4); § 55-277.6)
12. With regard to residuary gifts:	
a) What amount of income and principal is to be paid to the residuary beneficiary of a trust or an estate?	See the Uniform Principal and Income Act (1997) chart. (§ 55-277.5(4); § 55-277.6)
13. With regard to "business assets" held in trust:	
a) Can the trustee treat them as a separate entity?	Generally yes. See the Uniform Principal and Income Act (1997) chart. (§ 55-277.12)
b) Can the trustee treat distinct assets as separate entities?	Generally yes. See the Uniform Principal and Income Act (1997) chart. (§ 55-277.12)
c) Can earnings be retained in trust for the reasonable needs of the "business entity," and, if so, to what extent is this permitted?	Yes. See the Uniform Principal and Income Act (1997) chart. (§ 55-277.12(B)
14. With respect to discount bonds:	
a) To what extent is the discount added to income or principal upon maturity?	See the Uniform Principal and Income Act (1997) chart. (§ 55-277.15)
b) Does the trustee have discretion to allocate discount between income and principal?	No. (§ 55-277.15) ***Note:*** The trustee has the overriding power to adjust under § 55-277.4(A).
c) Are distinctions drawn between Series E bonds and others?	No. (§ 55-277.15)
d) Are distinctions drawn based on the maturity date of the bond?	Yes. (§ 55-277.15)
15. Is there a de minimis rule excusing the trustee from making adjustments in certain cases?	Yes. See the Uniform Principal and Income Act (1997) chart. (§ 55-277.17)
16. With respect to derivatives:	
a) May income and loss be treated as that of a separate entity?	Yes. (§ 55-277.12(C)(7); § 55-277.23(B))
b) If not, or the trustee chooses not to do so, is income and loss allocated to the income account or to principal?	To principal. (§ 55-277.23(B))
17. To the extent put and call options are not derivatives, how are they allocated in terms of principal and income?	To principal. (§ 55-277.23(C))

18. *How are asset-backed securities allocated in terms of principal and income?*	See the Uniform Principal and Income Act (1997) chart. (§ 55-277.24)
19. *Are expenses incurred to comply with environmental requirements allocated to income or principal?*	Generally to principal. See the Uniform Principal and Income Act (1997) chart. (§ 55-277.26(A)(7))
20. *Is income tax liability allocated generally to income or principal?*	See the Uniform Principal and Income Act (1997) chart. (§ 55-277.29; § 55-277.30)
21. *If a Subchapter S shareholder's or partner's portion of tax liability is greater than cash distributed, how is the excess obligation allocated?*	From principal. (§ 55-277.29(C)(2)(b))
22. *What is the standard, if any, for making equitable adjustments between income and principal?*	See the Uniform Principal and Income Act (1997) chart. (§ 55-277.3(B))
23. *Is an income beneficiary entitled to receive income accrued but unpaid when an estate ends?*	No. (§ 55-277.9)
24. *Is an income beneficiary entitled to receive income accrued but unpaid when a revocable trust ends?*	Generally no. See the Uniform Principal and Income Act (1997) chart. (§ 55-277.9)
25. *Is an income beneficiary entitled to receive income accrued but unpaid when an irrevocable trust ends?*	Generally no. See the Uniform Principal and Income Act (1997) chart. (§ 55-277.9)
26. *With regard to mutual funds, how are:*	
a) *long-term gains allocated between income and principal?*	See the Uniform Principal and Income Act (1997) chart. (§ 55-277.10(C)(4))
b) *short-term gains allocated between income and principal?*	See the Uniform Principal and Income Act (1997) chart. (§ 55-277.10(C)(4))
27. *How are distributions from REITs allocated between income and principal?*	See the Uniform Principal and Income Act (1997) chart. (§ 55-277.10(C)(4))
28. *With respect to underproductive property:*	
a) *Is an adjustment, e.g., "delayed income," required to be paid to the income beneficiary?*	No. (§ 55-277.22)
b) *What percentage return makes property underproductive?*	The statute only refers to property not productive of income. (§ 55-277.22)
29. *Is the trustee required to increase income so that it is sufficient to qualify for the marital deduction?*	Yes. (§ 55-277.22(A))
30. *Is the trustee required to take depreciation?*	No. (§ 55-277.27)

31. Is the trustee's determination on allocations generally presumed to be fair and reasonable?	Yes. (§ 55-277.3(B))
32. If an item is not addressed in the trust agreement or in the law, must it be allocated to principal or income?	To principal. (§ 55-277.3(A)(4))
33. When does an asset become subject to a trust:	
a) In the case of transfers during the transferor's life?	The date of transfer. (§ 55-277.7(B)(1))
b) In the case of a will?	The date of the testator's death. (§ 55-277.7(B)(2))
c) In the case of the death of a third party?	The date of the third party's death. (§ 55-277.7(B)(3))
34. Can a trustee rely on the characterization by an entity as to the source or character of a received distribution?	Yes. (§ 55-277.10(F))

Table 12.02
Washington
Trust Accounting: Principal and Income

1. *Does the trustee have the power to transfer income to principal or to transfer principal to income to meet its duty of impartiality?*	Yes. See the Uniform Principal and Income Act (1997) chart. (§ 11.104A.020)
2. *What is the effective date for the law? E.g., does it apply to preexisting trusts?*	Except as specifically provided otherwise in the terms of a trust or a will, the Washington Principal and Income Act applies to any receipt or expense received or incurred on or after January 1, 2003, by any trust or decedent's estate, whether established before, on, or after January 1, 2003, and whether the asset involved was acquired by the fiduciary before, on, or after January 1, 2003. (§ 11.104A.905) ***Note:*** A trustee may continue using a former allocation method to allocate receipts for water, minerals, other natural resources, and timber under certain circumstances. (See § 11.104A.200; § 11.104A.210)
3. *What percentage is allocated to income and principal from proceeds of:*	
a) *IRA?* b) *Qualified pension or profit-sharing plan?* c) *Other deferred compensation arrangement?*	A trustee must allocate a payment, or any portion of a payment that is characterized as interest or a dividend, or payment in lieu of interest or a dividend to income. The trustee must allocate to principal the balance of the payment and any other payment received in the same accounting period that is not characterized as interest, a dividend or equivalent payment. If no part of the payment is characterized as interest, a dividend or an equivalent payment, the trustee must allocate to income four percent (4%) of the total value of the interests of the trustee in the plan, annuity, or similar payment as of the first business day of the accounting period and the balance to principal. (§ 11.104A.180)
4. *What percentage is allocated to income and principal from proceeds of:*	
a) *Patents?* b) *Copyrights?*	See the Uniform Principal and Income Act (1997) chart. (§ 11.104A.190)
5. *What percentage is allocated to income and principal in the event of distributions from:*	
a) *Corporations?* b) *Partnerships?* c) *LLCs?*	See the Uniform Principal and Income Act (1997) chart. (§ 11.104A.100)
6. *What percentage is allocated to income and principal from proceeds of:*	
a) *Oil and gas?* b) *Minerals?* c) *Water?* d) *Other natural resourses (not including timber)?*	See the Uniform Principal and Income Act (1997) chart. (§ 11.104A.200) ***Note***: If a trust owns an interest in minerals, water or other natural resources on January 1, 2003, the trustee may allocate receipts from the interest as provided in the Washington Principal and Income Act or in the manner used by the trustee before January 1, 2003.

e) *Timber?*	See the Uniform Principal and Income Act (1997) chart. (§ 11.104A.210) ***Note:*** If a trust owns an interest in timberland on January 1, 2003, the trustee may allocate receipts from the interest as provided in the Washington Principal and Income Act or in the manner used by the trustee before January 1, 2003.
f) *Rental properties?*	See the Uniform Principal and Income Act (1997) chart. (§ 11.104A.140)
7. *After a decedent dies, in the case of an estate, or after an income interest ends, when the fiduciary is determining the remaining net income what are the rules regarding payment from income or principal for:*	
a) *Attorneys fees?* b) *Accountants fees?* c) *Fiduciary fees and commissions?* d) *Court costs?* e) *Interest on death taxes*	See the Uniform Principal and Income Act (1997) chart. (§ 11.104A.050(2)(ii))
f) *Debts?* g) *Funeral expenses?* h) *Family allowances and similar protections?* i) *Death taxes?* j) *Penalties on death taxes?*	See the Uniform Principal and Income Act (1997) chart. (§ 11.104A.050(2)(iii))
8. *With respect to trust expenses from the administration of the trust that are not covered by § 11.104A.050(2)(ii-iii) [see Question #7]:*	
a) *Does the trustee have full discretion in allocating between income and principal for expenses incurred in the administration of the trust?*	No. (§ 11.104A.250; § 11.104A.260)
b) *If not, are there special rules for:*	
i) *Regular trustee fees?* ii) *Advisory or custodial services to the trustee?* iii) *Accountings, judicial proceedings and other matters that involve both the income and remainder interests?*	See the Uniform Principal and Income Act (1997) chart. (§ 11.104A.250; § 11.104A.260)
iv) *Debts?*	See the Uniform Principal and Income Act (1997) chart. (§ 11.104A.250(3); § 11.104A.260(a)(3))
c) *Can the trustee determine what are "transmission" expenses and "management" expenses?*	

9. With regard to specific gifts from a trust after an income interest ends or from an estate:	
a) What amounts must be paid from income and principal?	See the Uniform Principal and Income Act (1997) chart. (§ 11.104A.050(1); § 11.104A.050(5))
10. With regard to outright pecuniary gifts from an estate or trust?:	
a) Does interest accrue?	A fiduciary must distribute to a beneficiary who receives a pecuniary amount outright the interest or any other amount provided by the will, the terms of a trust, or applicable law from net income or from principal to the extent that net income is insufficient. Otherwise, a beneficiary of an outright pecuniary gift will not receive any interest or other income. (§ 11.104A.050(3))
11. With regard to a gift in trust of a pecuniary amount from an estate or trust?	
a) Does interest accrue?	No. See the Uniform Principal and Income Act (1997) chart. (§ 11.104A.050(4); § 11.104A.060)
12. With regard to residuary gifts:	
a) What amount of income and principal is to be paid to the residuary beneficiary of a trust or an estate?	See the Uniform Principal and Income Act (1997) chart. (§ 11.104A.050(4); § 11.104A.060)
13. With regard to "business assets" held in trust:	
a) Can the trustee treat them as a separate entity?	Generally yes. See the Uniform Principal and Income Act (1997) chart. (§ 11.104A.120)
b) Can the trustee treat distinct assets as separate entities?	Generally yes. See the Uniform Principal and Income Act (1997) chart. (§ 11.104A.120)
c) Can earnings be retained in trust for the reasonable needs of the "business entity," and, if so, to what extent is this permitted?	Yes. See the Uniform Principal and Income Act (1997) chart. (§ 11.104A.120(b))
14. With respect to discount bonds:	
a) To what extent is the discount added to income or principal upon maturity?	See the Uniform Principal and Income Act (1997) chart. (§ 11.104A.150(b))
b) Does the trustee have discretion to allocate discount between income and principal?	No. (§ 11.104A.150) ***Note:*** The trustee has the overriding power to adjust under § 11.104A.020.
c) Are distinctions drawn between Series E bonds and others?	No. (§ 11.104A.150)
d) Are distinctions drawn based on the maturity date of the bond?	Yes. See the Uniform Principal and Income Act (1997) chart. (§ 11.104A.150(b))

15. Is there a de minimis rule excusing the trustee from making adjustments in certain cases?	Yes. See the Uniform Principal and Income Act (1997) chart. (§ 11.104A.170)
16. With respect to derivatives:	
a) May income and loss be treated as that of a separate entity?	Yes. (§ 11.104A.120(c)(7); § 11.104A.230(b))
b) If not, or the trustee chooses not to do so, is income and loss allocated to the income account or to principal?	To principal. (§ 11.104A.230(b))
17. To the extent put and call options are not derivatives, how are they allocated in terms of principal and income?	To principal. (§ 11.104A.230(c))
18. How are asset-backed securities allocated in terms of principal and income?	See the Uniform Principal and Income Act (1997) chart. (§ 11.104A.240)
19. Are expenses incurred to comply with environmental requirements allocated to income or principal?	Generally to principal. See the Uniform Principal and Income Act (1997) chart. (§ 11.104A.260(a)(7))
20. Is income tax liability allocated generally to income or principal?	See the Uniform Principal and Income Act (1997) chart. (§ 11.104A.290; § 11.104A.300)
21. If a Subchapter S shareholder's or partner's portion of tax liability is greater than cash distributed, how is the excess obligation allocated?	From principal. (§ 11.104A.290(c)(2)(ii))
22. What is the standard, if any, for making equitable adjustments between income and principal?	See the Uniform Principal and Income Act (1997) chart. (§ 11.104A.010(b))
23. Is an income beneficiary entitled to receive income accrued but unpaid when an estate ends?	No. (§ 11.104A.090)
24. Is an income beneficiary entitled to receive income accrued but unpaid when a revocable trust ends?	Generally no. See the Uniform Principal and Income Act (1997) chart. (§ 11.104A.090)
25. Is an income beneficiary entitled to receive income accrued but unpaid when an irrevocable trust ends?	Generally no. See the Uniform Principal and Income Act (1997) chart. (§ 11.104A.090)
26. With regard to mutual funds, how are:	
a) long-term gains allocated between income and principal?	See the Uniform Principal and Income Act (1997) chart. (§ 11.104A.100(c)(4))
b) short-term gains allocated between income and principal?	See the Uniform Principal and Income Act (1997) chart. (§ 11.104A.100(c)(4))
27. How are distributions from REITs allocated between income and principal?	See the Uniform Principal and Income Act (1997) chart. (§ 11.104A.100(c)(4))

28. With respect to underproductive property:	
a) Is an adjustment, e.g., "delayed income," required to be paid to the income beneficiary?	No. (§ 11.104A.220)
b) What percentage return makes property underproductive?	The statute only refers to property not productive of income. (§ 11.104A.220).
29. Is the trustee required to increase income so that it is sufficient to qualify for the marital deduction?	Yes. (§ 11.104A.220(a)).
30. Is the trustee required to take depreciation?	No. (§ 11.104A.270)
31. Is the trustee's determination on allocations generally presumed to be fair and reasonable?	Yes. (§ 11.104A.010)
32. If an item is not addressed in the trust agreement or in the law, must it be allocated to principal or income?	To principal. (§ 11.104A.010(a)(4))
33. When does an asset become subject to a trust:	
a) In the case of transfers during the transferor's life?	The date of transfer. (§ 11.104A.070(b)(1))
b) In the case of a will?	The date of the testator's death. (§ 11.104A.070(b)(2))
c) In the case of the death of a third party?	The date of the third party's death. (§ 11.104A.070(b)(3))
34. Can a trustee rely on the characterization by an entity as to the source or character of a received distribution?	Yes. (§ 11.104A.100(f))

Table 12.02
West Virginia
Trust Accounting: Principal and Income

1. *Does the trustee have the power to transfer income to principal or to transfer principal to income to meet its duty of impartiality?*	See the Uniform Principal and Income Act (1997) chart. (§ 44B-1-104)
2. *What is the effective date for the law? E.g., does it apply to preexisting trusts?*	The West Virginia Principal and Income Act applies, to any will or trust established under an instrument executed on or after July 1, 2000 except as otherwise expressly provided in the will or terms of the trust or in this chapter, or if the trustee or personal representative elects in either's sole discretion to administer the trust or will under this chapter. With respect to any will or trust established under an instrument executed prior to July 1, 2000, The West Virginia Principal and Income Act applies if the trustee or personal representative elects, in either's sole discretion, to administer the trust or will under this chapter. (§ 44B-6-604) ***Note:*** A trustee may continue using a former allocation method to allocate receipts for water, minerals, other natural resources, and timber under certain circumstances. (See § 44B-4-411; § 44B-4-412)
3. *What percentage is allocated to income and principal from proceeds of:*	
a) *IRA?* b) *Qualified pension or profit-sharing plan?* c) *Other deferred compensation arrangement?*	See the Uniform Principal and Income Act (1997) chart. (§ 44B-4-409)
4. *What percentage is allocated to income and principal from proceeds of:*	
a) *Patents?* b) *Copyrights?*	See the Uniform Principal and Income Act (1997) chart. (§ 44B-4-410)
5. *What percentage is allocated to income and principal in the event of distributions from:*	
a) *Corporations?* b) *Partnerships?* c) *LLCs?*	See the Uniform Principal and Income Act (1997) chart. (§ 44B-4-401)
6. *What percentage is allocated to income and principal from proceeds of:*	
a) *Oil and gas?* b) *Minerals?* c) *Water?* d) *Other natural resourses (not including timber)?*	See the Uniform Principal and Income Act (1997) chart. (§ 44B-4-411) ***Note:*** If a trust owns an interest in minerals, water or other natural resources on July 1, 2000, the trustee may allocate receipts from the interest as provided in the West Virginia Principal and Income Act or in the manner used by the trustee before July 1, 2000.
e) *Timber?*	See the Uniform Principal and Income Act (1997) chart. (§ 44B-4-412)

	Note: If a trust owns an interest in timberland on July 1, 2000, the trustee may allocate receipts from the interest as provided in the West Virginia Principal and Income Act or in the manner used by the trustee before July 1, 2000.
f) Rental properties?	See the Uniform Principal and Income Act (1997) chart. (§ 44B-4-405)
7. After a decedent dies, in the case of an estate, or after an income interest ends, when the fiduciary is determining the remaining net income what are the rules regarding payment from income or principal for:	
a) Attorneys fees? *b) Accountants fees?* *c) Fiduciary fees and commissions?* *d) Court costs?* *e) Interest on death taxes*	See the Uniform Principal and Income Act (1997) chart. (§ 44B-2-201(2)(B))
f) Debts? *g) Funeral expenses?* *h) Family allowances and similar protections?* *i) Death taxes?* *j) Penalties on death taxes?*	See the Uniform Principal and Income Act (1997) chart. (§ 44B-2-201(2)(C))
8. With respect to trust expenses from the administration of the trust that are not covered by § 44B-2-201(2)(B-C) [see Question #7]:	
a) Does the trustee have full discretion in allocating between income and principal for expenses incurred in the administration of the trust?	No. (§ 44B-5-501; § 44B-5-502)
b) If not, are there special rules for:	
i) Regular trustee fees? *ii) Advisory or custodial services to the trustee?* *iii) Accountings, judicial proceedings and other matters that involve both the income and remainder interests?*	See the Uniform Principal and Income Act (1997) chart. (§ 44B-5-501; § 44B-5-502) ***Note:*** The statute infers that a court can change the percentage disbursements from income and principal.
iv) Debts?	See the Uniform Principal and Income Act (1997) chart. (§ 44B-5-501(3); § 44B-5-502(a)(3))
c) Can the trustee determine what are "transmission" expenses and "management" expenses?	

9. With regard to specific gifts from a trust after an income interest ends or from an estate:	
a) What amounts must be paid from income and principal?	See the Uniform Principal and Income Act (1997) chart. (§ 44B-2-201(1); § 44B-2-201(5))
10. With regard to outright pecuniary gifts from an estate or trust?:	
a) Does interest accrue?	Yes. See the Uniform Principal and Income Act (1997) chart. (§ 44B-2-201(3))
11. With regard to a gift in trust of a pecuniary amount from an estate or trust?	
a) Does interest accrue?	No. See the Uniform Principal and Income Act (1997) chart. (§ 44B-2-201(4); § 44B-2-202)
12. With regard to residuary gifts:	
a) What amount of income and principal is to be paid to the residuary beneficiary of a trust or an estate?	See the Uniform Principal and Income Act (1997) chart. (§ 44B-2-201(4); § 44B-2-202)
13. With regard to "business assets" held in trust:	
a) Can the trustee treat them as a separate entity?	Generally yes. See the Uniform Principal and Income Act (1997) chart. (§ 44B-4-403)
b) Can the trustee treat distinct assets as separate entities?	Generally yes. See the Uniform Principal and Income Act (1997) chart. (§ 44B-4-403)
c) Can earnings be retained in trust for the reasonable needs of the "business entity," and, if so, to what extent is this permitted?	Yes. See the Uniform Principal and Income Act (1997) chart. (§ 44B-4-403(b))
14. With respect to discount bonds:	
a) To what extent is the discount added to income or principal upon maturity?	See the Uniform Principal and Income Act (1997) chart. (§ 44B-4-406(b))
b) Does the trustee have discretion to allocate discount between income and principal?	No. (§ 44B-4-406) *Note:* The trustee has the overriding power to adjust under § 44B-1-104(a).
c) Are distinctions drawn between Series E bonds and others?	No. (§ 44B-4-406)
d) Are distinctions drawn based on the maturity date of the bond?	Yes. (§ 44B-4-406(b))
15. Is there a de minimis rule excusing the trustee from making adjustments in certain cases?	Yes. See the Uniform Principal and Income Act (1997) chart. (§ 44B-4-408)

16. With respect to derivatives:	
a) May income and loss be treated as that of a separate entity?	Yes. (§ 44B-4-403(c)(7); § 44B-4-414(b))
b) If not, or the trustee chooses not to do so, is income and loss allocated to the income account or to principal?	To principal. (§ 44B-4-414(b))
17. To the extent put and call options are not derivatives, how are they allocated in terms of principal and income?	To principal. (§ 44B-4-414(c))
18. How are asset-backed securities allocated in terms of principal and income?	See the Uniform Principal and Income Act (1997) chart. (§ 44B-4-415)
19. Are expenses incurred to comply with environmental requirements allocated to income or principal?	Generally to principal. See the Uniform Principal and Income Act (1997) chart. (§ 44B-5-502(a)(7))
20. Is income tax liability allocated generally to income or principal?	See the Uniform Principal and Income Act (1997) chart. (§ 44B-5-505; § 44B-5-506.
21. If a Subchapter S shareholder's or partner's portion of tax liability is greater than cash distributed, how is the excess obligation allocated?	From principal. (§ 44B-5-505(c)(2)(B))
22. What is the standard, if any, for making equitable adjustments between income and principal?	See the Uniform Principal and Income Act (1997) chart. (§ 44B-1-103(b))
23. Is an income beneficiary entitled to receive income accrued but unpaid when an estate ends?	No. See the Uniform Principal and Income Act (1997) chart. (§ 44B-3-303)
24. Is an income beneficiary entitled to receive income accrued but unpaid when a revocable trust ends?	Generally no. See the Uniform Principal and Income Act (1997) chart. (§ 44B-3-303)
25. Is an income beneficiary entitled to receive income accrued but unpaid when an irrevocable trust ends?	Generally no. See the Uniform Principal and Income Act (1997) chart. (§ 44B-3-303)
26. With regard to mutual funds, how are:	
a) long-term gains allocated between income and principal?	See the Uniform Principal and Income Act (1997) chart. (§ 44B-4-401(c)(4))
b) short-term gains allocated between income and principal?	See the Uniform Principal and Income Act (1997) chart. (§ 44B-4-401(c)(4))
27. How are distributions from REITs allocated between income and principal?	See the Uniform Principal and Income Act (1997) chart. (§ 44B-4-401(c)(4))
28. With respect to underproductive property:	

a) Is an adjustment, e.g., "delayed income," required to be paid to the income beneficiary?	No. (§ 44B-4-413)
b) What percentage return makes property underproductive?	The statute only refers to property not productive of income. (§ 44B-4-413)
29. Is the trustee required to increase income so that it is sufficient to qualify for the marital deduction?	Yes. See the Uniform Principal and Income Act (1997) chart. (§ 44B-4-413(a))
30. Is the trustee required to take depreciation?	No. See the Uniform Principal and Income Act (1997) chart. (§ 44B-5-503)
31. Is the trustee's determination on allocations generally presumed to be fair and reasonable?	Yes. See the Uniform Principal and Income Act (1997) chart. (§ 44B-1-103(b))
32. If an item is not addressed in the trust agreement or in the law, must it be allocated to principal or income?	To principal. (§ 44B-1-103(a)(4))
33. When does an asset become subject to a trust:	
a) In the case of transfers during the transferor's life?	The date of transfer. (§ 44B-3-301(b)(1))
b) In the case of a will?	The date of the testator's death. (§ 44B-3-301(b)(2))
c) In the case of the death of a third party?	The date of the third party's death. (§ 44B-3-301(b)(3))
34. Can a trustee rely on the characterization by an entity as to the source or character of a received distribution?	Yes. (§ 44B-4-401(f))

Table 12.02
Wisconsin
Trust Accounting: Principal and Income

1. *Does the trustee have the power to transfer income to principal or to transfer principal to income to meet its duty of impartiality?*	See the Uniform Principal and Income Act (1997) chart. (§ 701.20(4)(a))
2. *What is the effective date for the law? E.g., does it apply to preexisting trusts?*	The Wisconsin Principal and Income Act does not contain any language addressing its applicability to preexisting trusts. ***Note:*** A trustee may continue using a former allocation method to allocate receipts for water, minerals, other natural resources, and timber under certain circumstances. (See, § 701.20(20); (§ 701.20(21))
3. *What percentage is allocated to income and principal from proceeds of:*	
a) *IRA?* b) *Qualified pension or profit-sharing plan?* c) *Other deferred compensation arrangement?*	***Note:*** The provision in the Wisconsin Principal and Income Act addressing deferred compensation, annuities, and similar payments is lengthy; therefore, one should examine § 701.20 (18) when dealing with these issues. A trustee must allocate a payment, or any portion of a payment that is characterized as interest or a dividend, or payment in lieu of interest or a dividend to income. The trustee must allocate to principal the balance of the payment and any other payment received in the same accounting period that is not characterized as interest, a dividend or equivalent payment. For each accounting period of a trust in which the trust receives a payment but no part of any payment is allocated to income under the paragraph above, the trustee must allocate to income the portion of the aggregate value of all payments received by the trustee in the accounting period that is equal to the amount of "plan income" that is attributable to the trust's interest in the plan from which payment is received for that accounting period. The trustee shall allocate the balance of any payments to principal. "Plan income" is defined in § 701.20(18)(c)(1). If, in order to obtain an estate tax marital deduction for a trust, the trustee must allocate more of a payment to income than provided by the two paragraphs above, the trustee must allocate to income the additional amount necessary to obtain the marital deduction. (§ 701.20(18))
4. *What percentage is allocated to income and principal from proceeds of:*	
a) *Patents?* b) *Copyrights?*	See the Uniform Principal and Income Act (1997) chart. (§ 701.20(19))
5. *What percentage is allocated to income and principal in the event of distributions from:*	
a) *Corporations?* b) *Partnerships?* c) *LLCs?*	See the Uniform Principal and Income Act (1997) chart. (§ 701.20(10))

6. *What percentage is allocated to income and principal from proceeds of:*	
a) *Oil and gas?* b) *Minerals?* c) *Water?* d) *Other natural resourses (not including timber)?*	See the Uniform Principal and Income Act (1997) chart. (§ 701.20(20))
e) *Timber?*	See the Uniform Principal and Income Act (1997) chart. (§ 701.20(21))
f) *Rental properties?*	See the Uniform Principal and Income Act (1997) chart. (§ 701.20(14))
7. *After a decedent dies, in the case of an estate, or after an income interest ends, when the fiduciary is determining the remaining net income what are the rules regarding payment from income or principal for:*	
a) *Attorneys fees?* b) *Accountants fees?* c) *Fiduciary fees and commissions?* d) *Court costs?* e) *Interest on death taxes*	See the Uniform Principal and Income Act (1997) chart. (§ 701.20(5)(b)(2))
f) *Debts?* g) *Funeral expenses?* h) *Family allowances and similar protections?* i) *Death taxes?* j) *Penalties on death taxes?*	See the Uniform Principal and Income Act (1997) chart. (§ 701.20(5)(b)(3))
8. *With respect to trust expenses from the administration of the trust that are not covered by § 701.20(5)(b)(2-3) [see Question #7]:*	
a) *Does the trustee have full discretion in allocating between income and principal for expenses incurred in the administration of the trust?*	No. (§ 701.20(25); § 701.20(26))
b) *If not, are there special rules for:*	
i) *Regular trustee fees?* ii) *Advisory or custodial services to the trustee?* iii) *Accountings, judicial proceedings and other matters that involve both the income and remainder interests?*	See the Uniform Principal and Income Act (1997) chart. (§ 701.20(25); § 701.20(26))

iv) Debts?	See the Uniform Principal and Income Act (1997) chart. (§ 701.20(25)(c); § 701.20(26)(a)(3))
c) Can the trustee determine what are "transmission" expenses and "management" expenses?	
9. With regard to specific gifts from a trust after an income interest ends or from an estate:	
a) What amounts must be paid from income and principal?	See the Uniform Principal and Income Act (1997) chart. (§ 701.20(5)(a); § 701.20(5)(e))
10. With regard to outright pecuniary gifts from an estate or trust?:	
a) Does interest accrue?	A fiduciary must distribute to a beneficiary or a trust for a beneficiary that receives a pecuniary amount, not determined by a pecuniary formula, the legal rate of interest provided in § 138.04 on any unpaid portion of the pecuniary amount. The interest begins to accrue one year after the decedent's death or after the income interest in the trust ends. The interest must be distributed from net income or from principal to the extent that net income is insufficient. A fiduciary must distribute the net income remaining after the distributions in the paragraph above to all other beneficiaries, including a beneficiary who receives a pecuniary amount determined by a pecuniary formula, in the same manner as residuary and remainder beneficiaries. (§ 701.20(5); § 701.20(6))
11. With regard to a gift in trust of a pecuniary amount from an estate or trust?	
a) Does interest accrue?	A fiduciary must distribute to a beneficiary or a trust for a beneficiary that receives a pecuniary amount, not determined by a pecuniary formula, the legal rate of interest provided in § 138.04 on any unpaid portion of the pecuniary amount. The interest begins to accrue one year after the decedent's death or after the income interest in the trust ends. The interest must be distributed from net income or from principal to the extent that net income is insufficient. A fiduciary must distribute the net income remaining after the distributions in the paragraph above to all other beneficiaries, including a beneficiary who receives a pecuniary amount determined by a pecuniary formula, in the same manner as residuary and remainder beneficiaries. (§ 701.20(5); § 701.20(6))
12. With regard to residuary gifts:	
a) What amount of income and principal is to be paid to the residuary beneficiary of a trust or an estate?	See the Uniform Principal and Income Act (1997) chart. (§ 701.20(5)(d); § 701.20(6))
13. With regard to "business assets" held in trust:	

a) *Can the trustee treat them as a separate entity?*	Generally yes. See the Uniform Principal and Income Act (1997) chart. (§ 701.20(12))
b) *Can the trustee treat distinct assets as separate entities?*	Generally yes. See the Uniform Principal and Income Act (1997) chart. (§ 701.20(12))
c) *Can earnings be retained in trust for the reasonable needs of the "business entity," and, if so, to what extent is this permitted?*	Yes. See the Uniform Principal and Income Act (1997) chart. (§ 701.20(12)(b))
14. *With respect to discount bonds:*	
a) *To what extent is the discount added to income or principal upon maturity?*	See the Uniform Principal and Income Act (1997) chart. (§ 701.20(15))
b) *Does the trustee have discretion to allocate discount between income and principal?*	No. (§ 701.20(15)) **Note:** The trustee has the overriding power to adjust under § 701.20(4)(a).
c) *Are distinctions drawn between Series E bonds and others?*	No. (§ 701.20(15))
d) *Are distinctions drawn based on the maturity date of the bond?*	Yes. (§ 701.20(15)(b))
15. *Is there a de minimis rule excusing the trustee from making adjustments in certain cases?*	Yes. See the Uniform Principal and Income Act (1997) chart. (§ 701.20(17))
16. *With respect to derivatives:*	
a) *May income and loss be treated as that of a separate entity?*	Yes. (§ 701.20(12)(c)(7); § 701.20(23))
b) *If not, or the trustee chooses not to do so, is income and loss allocated to the income account or to principal?*	To principal. (§ 701.20(23)(b))
17. *To the extent put and call options are not derivatives, how are they allocated in terms of principal and income?*	To principal. (§ 701.20(23)(c))
18. *How are asset-backed securities allocated in terms of principal and income?*	See the Uniform Principal and Income Act (1997) chart. (§ 701.20(24))
19. *Are expenses incurred to comply with environmental requirements allocated to income or principal?*	Generally to principal. See the Uniform Principal and Income Act (1997) chart. (§ 701.20(26)(a)(7))
20. *Is income tax liability allocated generally to income or principal?*	See the Uniform Principal and Income Act (1997) chart. (§ 701.20(29); § 701.20(30))
21. *If a Subchapter S shareholder's or partner's portion of tax liability is greater than cash distributed, how is the excess obligation allocated?*	From principal. (§ 701.20(29)(c)(2)(b))

22. *What is the standard, if any, for making equitable adjustments between income and principal?*	See the Uniform Principal and Income Act (1997) chart. (§ 701.20(3)(b))
23. *Is an income beneficiary entitled to receive income accrued but unpaid when an estate ends?*	No. See the Uniform Principal and Income Act (1997) chart. (§ 701.20(9))
24. *Is an income beneficiary entitled to receive income accrued but unpaid when a revocable trust ends?*	See the Uniform Principal and Income Act (1997) chart. (§ 701.20(9))
25. *Is an income beneficiary entitled to receive income accrued but unpaid when an irrevocable trust ends?*	See the Uniform Principal and Income Act (1997) chart. (§ 701.20(9))
26. *With regard to mutual funds, how are:*	
a) *long-term gains allocated between income and principal?*	See the Uniform Principal and Income Act (1997) chart. (§ 701.20(10)(c)(4))
b) *short-term gains allocated between income and principal?*	See the Uniform Principal and Income Act (1997) chart. (§ 701.20(10)(c)(4))
27. *How are distributions from REITs allocated between income and principal?*	See the Uniform Principal and Income Act (1997) chart. (§ 701.20(10)(c)(4))
28. *With respect to underproductive property:*	
a) *Is an adjustment, e.g., "delayed income," required to be paid to the income beneficiary?*	No. (§ 701.20(22))
b) *What percentage return makes property underproductive?*	The statute only refers to property not productive of income. (§ 701.20(22))
29. *Is the trustee required to increase income so that it is sufficient to qualify for the marital deduction?*	Yes. (§ 701.20(22)(a))
30. *Is the trustee required to take depreciation?*	No. (§ 701.20(27)
31. *Is the trustee's determination on allocations generally presumed to be fair and reasonable?*	Yes. (§ 701.20(3)(b))
32. *If an item is not addressed in the trust agreement or in the law, must it be allocated to principal or income?*	To principal. (§ 701.20(3)(a)(4))
33. *When does an asset become subject to a trust:*	
a) *In the case of transfers during the transferor's life?*	The date of transfer. (§ 701.20(7)(b)(1))
b) *In the case of a will?*	The date of the testator's death. (§ 701.20(7)(b)(2))

c) *In the case of the death of a third party?*	The date of the third party's death. (§ 701.20(7)(b)(3))
34. *Can a trustee rely on the characterization by an entity as to the source or character of a received distribution?*	Yes. (§ 701.20(10)(f))

Table 12.02
Wyoming
Trust Accounting: Principal and Income

1. *Does the trustee have the power to transfer income to principal or to transfer principal to income to meet its duty of impartiality?*	Yes. See the Uniform Principal and Income Act (1997) chart. (§ 2-3-804(a))
2. *What is the effective date for the law? E.g., does it apply to preexisting trusts?*	The Wyoming Principal and Income Act applies to every trust or decedent's estate existing on July 1, 2001 except as otherwise expressly provided in the will or terms of the trust or in the Wyoming Principal and Income Act. (§ 2-3-834) ***Note:*** A trustee may continue using a former allocation method to allocate receipts for water, minerals, other natural resources, and timber under certain circumstances. (See § 2-3-821; § 2-3-822)
3. *What percentage is allocated to income and principal from proceeds of:*	
a) IRA? *b) Qualified pension or profit-sharing plan?* *c) Other deferred compensation arrangement?*	See the Uniform Principal and Income Act (1997) chart. (§ 2-3-819)
4. *What percentage is allocated to income and principal from proceeds of:*	
a) Patents? *b) Copyrights?*	See the Uniform Principal and Income Act (1997) chart. (§ 2-3-820(b))
5. *What percentage is allocated to income and principal in the event of distributions from:*	
a) Corporations? *b) Partnerships?* *c) LLCs?*	See the Uniform Principal and Income Act (1997) chart. (§ 2-3-811)
6. *What percentage is allocated to income and principal from proceeds of:*	
a) Oil and gas? *b) Minerals?* *c) Water?* *d) Other natural resourses (not including timber)?*	The trustee must allocate a receipt received as nominal delay rental or a nominal annual rent on a lease to income. The trustee must allocate a receipt received from a production payment to income if and to the extent that the agreement creating the production payment provides a factor for interest or its equivalent. The balance must be allocated to principal. The trustee must allocate 27.5% of an amount received as a royalty, shut-in-well payment, take-or-pay payment, bonus, or a delay rental that is more than nominal, to principal and 72.5% to income. The trustee must allocate 27.5% of the net amount received from a working interest or other interest (not mentioned in the two preceding paragraphs) to principal and 72.5% to income. An amount received on account of an interest in water that is renewable must be allocated to income. If the water is not

	renewable, 27.5% of the amount must be allocated to principal and 72.5% to income. The rules above apply whether or not a decedent or donor was extracting the minerals, water, or other natural resources before the interest became subject to the trust. (§ 2-3-821) ***Note:*** If a trust owns an interest in minerals, water or other natural resources on July 1, 2001, the trustee may allocate receipts from the interest as provided in the Wyoming Principal and Income Act or in the manner used by the trustee before July 1, 2001.
e) Timber?	See the Uniform Principal and Income Act (1997) chart. (§ 2-3-822) ***Note:*** If a trust owns an interest in timberland on July 1, 2001, the trustee may allocate receipts from the interest as provided in the Wyoming Principal and Income Act or in the manner used by the trustee before July 1, 2001.
f) Rental properties?	See the Uniform Principal and Income Act (1997) chart. (§ 2-3-815)
7. After a decedent dies, in the case of an estate, or after an income interest ends, when the fiduciary is determining the remaining net income what are the rules regarding payment from income or principal for:	
a) Attorneys fees? *b) Accountants fees?* *c) Fiduciary fees and commissions?* *d) Court costs?* *e) Interest on death taxes*	See the Uniform Principal and Income Act (1997) chart. (§ 2-3-806(a)(ii)(B))
f) Debts? *g) Funeral expenses?* *h) Family allowances and similar protections?* *i) Death taxes?* *j) Penalties on death taxes?*	See the Uniform Principal and Income Act (1997) chart. (§ 2-3-806(a)(ii)(C))
8. With respect to trust expenses from the administration of the trust that are not covered by § 2-3-806(a)(ii)(B-C) [see Question #7]:	
a) Does the trustee have full discretion in allocating between income and principal for expenses incurred in the administration of the trust?	No. See the Uniform Principal and Income Act (1997) chart. (§ 2-3-826; § 2-3-827)
b) If not, are there special rules for:	
i) Regular trustee fees?	See the Uniform Principal and Income Act (1997) chart. (§ 2-3-826; § 2-3-827)

ii) Advisory or custodial services to the trustee? *iii) Accountings, judicial proceedings and other matters that involve both the income and remainder interests?*	
iv) Debts?	See the Uniform Principal and Income Act (1997) chart. (§ 2-3-826(a)(iii); § 2-3-827(a)(iii))
c) Can the trustee determine what are "transmission" expenses and "management" expenses?	
9. With regard to specific gifts from a trust after an income interest ends or from an estate:	
a) What amounts must be paid from income and principal?	See the Uniform Principal and Income Act (1997) chart. (§ 2-3-806(a)(i); § 2-3-806(a)(v))
10. With regard to outright pecuniary gifts from an estate or trust?:	
a) Does interest accrue?	Yes. See the Uniform Principal and Income Act (1997) chart. (§ 2-3-806(a)(iii))
11. With regard to a gift in trust of a pecuniary amount from an estate or trust?	
a) Does interest accrue?	No. See the Uniform Principal and Income Act (1997) chart. (§ 2-3-806(a)(iv); § 2-3-807)
12. With regard to residuary gifts:	
a) What amount of income and principal is to be paid to the residuary beneficiary of a trust or an estate?	See the Uniform Principal and Income Act (1997) chart. (§ 2-3-806(a)(iv); § 2-3-807)
13. With regard to "business assets" held in trust:	
a) Can the trustee treat them as a separate entity?	Generally yes. See the Uniform Principal and Income Act (1997) chart. (§ 2-3-813)
b) Can the trustee treat distinct assets as separate entities?	Generally yes. See the Uniform Principal and Income Act (1997) chart. (§ 2-3-813)
c) Can earnings be retained in trust for the reasonable needs of the "business entity," and, if so, to what extent is this permitted?	Yes. See the Uniform Principal and Income Act (1997) chart. (§ 2-3-813(b))
14. With respect to discount bonds:	
a) To what extent is the discount added to income or principal upon maturity?	See the Uniform Principal and Income Act (1997) chart. (§ 2-3-816(b))

b) *Does the trustee have discretion to allocate discount between income and principal?*	No. (§ 2-3-816) ***Note:*** The trustee has the overriding power to adjust under § 2-3-804(a).
c) *Are distinctions drawn between Series E bonds and others?*	No. (§ 2-3-816)
d) *Are distinctions drawn based on the maturity date of the bond?*	Yes. (§ 2-3-816)
15. *Is there a de minimis rule excusing the trustee from making adjustments in certain cases?*	Yes. See the Uniform Principal and Income Act (1997) chart. (§ 2-3-818)
16. *With respect to derivatives:*	
a) *May income and loss be treated as that of a separate entity?*	Yes. (§ 2-3-813(c)(vii); § 2-3-824(b))
b) *If not, or the trustee chooses not to do so, is income and loss allocated to the income account or to principal?*	To principal. (§ 2-3-824(b))
17. *To the extent put and call options are not derivatives, how are they allocated in terms of principal and income?*	To principal. (§ 2-3-824(c))
18. *How are asset-backed securities allocated in terms of principal and income?*	See the Uniform Principal and Income Act (1997) chart. (§ 2-3-825)
19. *Are expenses incurred to comply with environmental requirements allocated to income or principal?*	Generally to principal. See the Uniform Principal and Income Act (1997) chart. (§ 2-3-827(a)(vii))
20. *Is income tax liability allocated generally to income or principal?*	See the Uniform Principal and Income Act (1997) chart. (§ 2-3-830; § 2-3-831)
21. *If a Subchapter S shareholder's or partner's portion of tax liability is greater than cash distributed, how is the excess obligation allocated?*	From principal. (§ 2-3-830(c)(ii)(B))
22. *What is the standard, if any, for making equitable adjustments between income and principal?*	See the Uniform Principal and Income Act (1997) chart. (§ 2-3-803(b))
23. *Is an income beneficiary entitled to receive income accrued but unpaid when an estate ends?*	No. See the Uniform Principal and Income Act (1997) chart. (§ 2-3-810).
24. *Is an income beneficiary entitled to receive income accrued but unpaid when a revocable trust ends?*	Generally no. See the Uniform Principal and Income Act (1997) chart. (§ 2-3-810)
25. *Is an income beneficiary entitled to receive income accrued but unpaid when an irrevocable trust ends?*	Generally no. See the Uniform Principal and Income Act (1997) chart. (§ 2-3-810)

26. With regard to mutual funds, how are:	
a) long-term gains allocated between income and principal?	See the Uniform Principal and Income Act (1997) chart. (§ 2-3-811(c)(iv))
b) short-term gains allocated between income and principal?	See the Uniform Principal and Income Act (1997) chart. (§ 2-3-811(c)(iv))
27. How are distributions from REITs allocated between income and principal?	See the Uniform Principal and Income Act (1997) chart. (§ 2-3-811(c)(iv))
28. With respect to underproductive property:	
a) Is an adjustment, e.g., "delayed income," required to be paid to the income beneficiary?	No. (§ 2-3-823)
b) What percentage return makes property underproductive?	The statute only refers to property not productive of income. See the Uniform Principal and Income Act (1997) chart. (§ 2-3-823)
29. Is the trustee required to increase income so that it is sufficient to qualify for the marital deduction?	Yes. (§ 2-3-823)
30. Is the trustee required to take depreciation?	No. (§ 2-3-828)
31. Is the trustee's determination on allocations generally presumed to be fair and reasonable?	Yes. (§ 2-3-803(b))
32. If an item is not addressed in the trust agreement or in the law, must it be allocated to principal or income?	To principal. See the Uniform Principal and Income Act (1997) chart. (§ 2-3-803(a)(iv))
33. When does an asset become subject to a trust:	
a) In the case of transfers during the transferor's life?	The date of transfer. (§ 2-3-808(b)(i))
b) In the case of a will?	The date of the testator's death. (§ 2-3-808(b)(ii))
c) In the case of the death of a third party?	The date of the third party's death. (§ 2-3-808(b)(iii))
34. Can a trustee rely on the characterization by an entity as to the source or character of a received distribution?	Yes. (§ 2-3-811(f))

Table 13
Contacts Resulting in State Taxation of a Trust's or Estate's Income (current through 5/1/07)

Subject to due process concerns, states are free to tax trust and estate income. There is a risk that a trust's or estate's income will be exposed to multiple state income taxation, thereby reducing, perhaps significantly, the income available either for accumulation in a trust or for distribution to the beneficiaries of the trust or the devisees of the estate.

Each state has its own unique matrix of statutory rules as to the contacts justifying state income taxation of the trust or estate. In the case of a trust, Table 13.01 explores the topic first from the standpoint of which contacts entitle the state to tax the trust on all of its income. Consideration is next given to whether the particular state taxes income from sources within the state, even if the contacts previously considered are not present. A similar two-stage analysis is then pursued with respect to estates in Table 13.02, in which different contacts than those relevant to trusts may be at issue, and different rules as to taxability of source-based income may apply.

Tax savings can be achieved and multiple state taxation avoided by appropriate location of the relevant contacts through the estate planning process. To the extent that this flexibility in the planning process is not available, the reader should be aware of foreign tax credit provisions that are provided for, in varying degree, in many states. In other words, certain states will credit a portion of taxes paid to other states.

Note also that the particular contacts identified in the tables are the ones ordinarily employed by statute or case law to justify income taxation. In the case of trusts, this would include the residence or domicile of the settlor, the residence of the trustee, the situs of administration, the residence of the beneficiary, and the state of a court appointing the trustee. Consideration is also given to the authority to tax when the property in an inter vivos trust comes from a transferor who was domiciled or resident in the state at the time of the transfer, but the trust is being administered from and by a trustee in another state. With respect to testamentary trusts, the additional contact of the testator's domicile or residence at death is considered.

Table 13.02 explores the jurisdiction to impose an income tax with respect to estates. Contacts similar to those reviewed in the context of testamentary trusts are set forth. The results for testamentary trusts and estates are quite similar, although in certain states there may be occasional differences.

Table 13.01, Part 1
Trusts

	A Trust Is Taxed on Its Entire Income[*] If:					
	The Creator of the Trust in the Current Year Is a Resident of the State	*The Creator of the Trust in the Current Year Is Domiciled in the State*	*The Trustee in the Current Year Is a Resident of the State*	*The Trust in the Current Year Is Administered in the State*	*The Trustee Was Appointed by a Court in the State*	*The Beneficiary in the Current Year Is a Resident of the State*
Alabama	Yes. (§§ 40-18-25,[1] 40-18-2(a)(5), 40-18-2(a)(7))	Yes. (§§ 40-18-2(7), 40-18-25, 40-18-2(5))	Yes. (Admin. Code 810-3-2.03(2)). See also Admin Code 810-3-14-.05(5); 810-3-25-.05.	No.	No.	No.
Alaska	*No income tax on trusts*	—	—	—	—	—
Arizona	No. (§ 43-1311)	No. (§ 43-1311)	Yes. (§§ 43-1311(A), 43-1301(5)). If trust has more than one fiduciary, at least one of the fiduciaries must be a resident of Arizona. (§ 43-1301(5))	Yes, but only if a corporation is the sole fiduciary or is a cofiduciary with a nonresident, engaged in inter-state trust administration, and conducts the administration of the trust in Arizona. (§ 43-1301(5))	No.	Maybe.[2] (§ 43-1315)
Arkansas	Yes. (§§ 26-51-201(a) & (b), 26-51-102(9))	Yes. (§§ 26-51-102 (9), 26-51-201(a) & (b))	No.	No.	No.	Yes. (§ 26-51-201(b) &(c))
California	No.	No.	Yes, regardless of the residence of the set-tlor. (Rev. & Tax. § 17742(a))[3]	No.	No.	Yes, regardless of the residence of the settlor. (Rev. & Tax. § 17742(a))[4]

Colorado	No.	No.	No.	Yes. (§§ 39-22-103 (10), 39-22-104(1))	No.	No.
Connecticut	No.	No.	No.	No.	No.	No.[5]
Delaware	No.	Yes. (30 §§ 1601(8), 1631)	Yes, under certain circumstances.[6]	No.	No.	No.[7]
District of Columbia[8]	No.	No. (§§ 47-1809.01, 47-1809.03)	No.[9] (§ 47-1809.02)	No.	No.	No.
Florida	*No income tax on trusts.* There was a personal property tax, but it was repealed by ch. 2006-312, H.B. No. 209, eff. Jan. 1, 2007.					
Georgia[10]	No.	No.	Yes.[11] (§ 48-7-22(a)(1))	No.	No.	Yes.[12] (§ 48-7-22(a)(1)(C))
Hawaii	No.	No.	Yes.[13] (§§ 235-1, 235-4(e)(1))	Yes. (§§ 235-1, 235-4)	No.	Yes.[14] (§§ 235-4(a), 235-4(e)(2), 235-1[14])
Idaho	No.	No.	No.	No.	No.	No.
Illinois	No.	Yes.[15] (35 ILCS §§ 5/201(a), 5/1501(a)(20)(D))	No.	No.	No.	No.
Indiana[16]	No.	No.	No.	No.	No.	No.
Iowa[17]	No.	No.	No.	No.	No.	No.
Kansas	No.	No.	No.	Yes.[18] (§§ 79-32,109(d), 79-32,134)	No.	No.
Kentucky[19]	No.	No.	No.	No.	No.	Yes.[20] (103 KY ADC 19:010, § 5)
Louisiana[21]	No.	No.	No.	Yes.[22]	No.	No.

Table 13.01, Part 1
Trusts *(continued)*

	A Trust Is Taxed on Its Entire Income If:*					
	The Creator of the Trust in the Current Year Is a Resident of the State	*The Creator of the Trust in the Current Year Is Domiciled in the State*	*The Trustee in the Current Year Is a Resident of the State*	*The Trust in the Current Year Is Administered in the State*	*The Trustee Was Appointed by a Court in the State*	*The Beneficiary in the Current Year Is a Resident of the State*
Maine	No.	Yes. (36 §§ 5102(4)(C), 5160)	No.	No. (36 § 5102(4)(D) Repealed)	No.	No.
Maryland[23]	Yes. (Tax-Gen. § 10-101(k)(1)(iii)(2))	Yes. (Tax-Gen. § 10-101(k)(1)(i)(1))	No.	Yes, if "principally" administered. (Tax-Gen. § 10-101(k)(1)(iii)(3))	No.	No.
Massachusetts	Yes. (62 §§ 10(c) & 1(f))	Yes. (62 §§ 10(c) & 1(f))	Yes. (62 § 10(c))	No.	No.	Yes. (62 § 10(a))
Michigan	Yes.[24] (§§ 206.18(a) & (c), 206.110(1))	Yes.[25] (§§ 206.18(c), 206.110(1))	No.	No.	No.	No.
Minnesota	No.	No.	No.	No.	No.	No.
Mississippi[26]	No.	No.	No.	No.	No.	No.
Missouri	No.	Yes[27] (§§ 143.331(3), 143.341), assuming at least one income beneficiary is a resident on the last day of the taxable year. (§ 143.331(3)(b))	No.	No.	No.	No.

Montana	No.	No.	Yes, if a domicile or nexus with Montana. (Form F103 Fiduciary Income Tax Return)	No.	No.	Yes.[28] (§ 15-30-135(1) & (3))
Nebraska	No.	No.	No.	No.	No.	No.
Nevada	*No income tax on trusts*	—	—	—	—	—
New Hampshire	No.	No.	Yes.[29] (§ 77:10)	No.	Yes. (§ 77:10)	Yes. (§ 77:10)
New Jersey	No.	No.	No.	No.	No.	No.
New Mexico[30]	No.	No.	Yes.[31] 6 (§§ 7-2-2(B), (I),(N); 7-2-3)	No.	No.	No.
New York	No.	No.	No.	No.	No.	No.
North Carolina	No.	No.	No.	No.	No.	Yes. (§ 105-160.2)
North Dakota[32]	Yes.[33] (Admin. Code § 81-03-02.1-04.(2)(f))	Yes.[34] (Admin. Code § 81-03-02.1-04.(2)(f))	Yes.[35] (Admin. Code § 81-03-02.1-04.(2)(b))	Yes.[36] (Admin. Code § 81-03-02.1-04.(2)(d))	No.	Yes.[37] (Admin. Code § 81-03-02.1-04.(2)(a))
Ohio	No.	No.	No.	No.	No.	Yes in certain circumstances. (§ 5747.01(I)(3)(a)(ii) & iii)) The beneficiary must be a qualifying beneficiary, which is same as a potential current beneficiary in I.R.C. § 1361(e)(2). (§ 5747.01(I)(3)(c)) See Table 10.01, Part 2.
Oklahoma	No.	No.	No.	No.	No.	No.
Oregon	No.	No.	Yes.[38] (§§ 316.267, 316.282(1)(d))	Yes. (§§ 316.267, 316.282(1)(d))	No.	No.

Table 13.01, Part 1
Trusts *(continued)*

	A Trust Is Taxed on Its Entire Income If:*					
	The Creator of the Trust in the Current Year Is a Resident of the State	*The Creator of the Trust in the Current Year Is Domiciled in the State*	*The Trustee in the Current Year Is a Resident of the State*	*The Trust in the Current Year Is Administered in the State*	*The Trustee Was Appointed by a Court in the State*	*The Beneficiary in the Current Year Is a Resident of the State*
Pennsylvania	No.[39] (72 §§ 7301(s)(2), 7302(a))	No. (72 §§ 7301(p) & (s)(2), 7302(a))	No.	No.	No.	No.
Rhode Island	No.[40] (§§ 44-30-5(a)(2), 44-30-5(c)(2) & (4), 44-30-1)	No. (§§ 44-30-5(c)(2) & (4), 44-30-1)	No.	No.	No.	No.[41] (§§ 44-30-5(a)(1) & (2), 44-30-5(c)(5), 44-30-1)
South Carolina	No.	No.	No.	Yes. (§§ 12-6-30(5), 12-6-610)	No.	No.
South Dakota	*No income tax on trusts*	—	—	—	—	—
Tennessee	No.	No.	No.	No.	No.	Yes. (§§ 67-2-110, 67-2-111(a); also § 67-2-101(5))
Texas	*No income tax on trusts*	—	—	—	—	—
Utah	No.	No.	No.	Yes. (§§ 59-10-103(1)(w), 75-7-103(1)(i)(iii), 59-10-201)	No.	No.
Vermont	No.	No.	No.	No.	No.	No.
Virginia	No.	Yes. (§§ 58.1-302, 58.1-361(A))	No.	Yes. (§§ 58.1-302, 58.1-361(A))	No.	No.
Washington	*No income tax on trusts*	—	—	—	—	—
West Virginia	No.	Yes. (§§ 11-21-7(c)(3), 11-21-18)	No.	No.	No.	No.

Wisconsin	Yes.[42] (§ 71.14(2))	No.	No.	Maybe.[43] (§ 71.14(3m)(a)-(b)	No.	No.
Wyoming	*No income tax on trusts*	—	—	—	—	—

* The reference to "income" typically refers to "taxable income." However, careful consideration needs to be given to the calculation of the figure against which the tax rate is multiplied.

1. "Every estate and trust resident in Alabama" is taxed on all taxable income. (§ 40-18-2(5)) However, there is no definition of this phrase. Under § 40-18-25(c), an estate or trust created by a person not a resident and an estate of a person not a resident of Alabama are subject to tax only to the extent individuals other than residents are liable for tax. By negative implication this subjects estates and trusts created by persons who are residents of Alabama to taxation. A nonresident individual's gross income includes only income "from property owned or business transacted in Alabama." (§ 40-18-14(4)) Note that the cross-reference in § 40-18-25(c) seems incorrectly to refer to § 40-18-14(3). In Rev. Rul. 97-007 (July 11, 1997), the Department of Revenue stated that a "'resident trust' is generally considered to be a trust either created by an Alabama resident or the estate of an Alabama resident." Note that there are filing requirements independent of tax liability. Section 40-18-29, which imposes a filing requirement on "[e]very fiduciary" is limited by the Revenue Ruling to situations where either the trust or the beneficiary is subject to Alabama income tax. Thus, the trust may be nonresident but, nevertheless, required to file.

2. If for any reason the taxes imposed on income of a trust are not paid when due and remain unpaid when such income is distributable to the beneficiaries, or if the income is distributable to the beneficiaries before the taxes are due and the taxes are not paid when due, such income is taxable to the beneficiaries when distributable to them, except that in the case of nonresident beneficiaries such income is taxable only to the extent it is derived from sources within the state of Arizona. (§ 43-1315)

3. "The residence of a corporate fiduciary of a trust means the place where the corporation transacts the major portion of its administration of the trust." (Rev. & Tax. § 17742(b)) If there are two or more fiduciaries for a trust, the income taxable under § 17742 is apportioned according to the number of fiduciaries resident in California pursuant to rules and regulations prescribed by the Franchise Tax Board. (Rev. & Tax. § 17743)

4. If the beneficiary has only a contingent interest in the trust, the beneficiary's residence is not a basis for trust income taxation. (Rev. & Tax. § 17742(a)) If there are two or more beneficiaries for a trust, the income taxable under § 17742 is apportioned according to the number of beneficiaries resident in California pursuant to rules and regulations prescribed by the Franchise Tax Board. (Rev. & Tax. § 17744)

5. However, when other than a testamentary trust is involved, the presence of nonresident, noncontingent beneficiaries will result in no taxation of the portion of allocable property apportioned to them. (§ 12-701(a)(4))

6. Section 1601(8), in addition to other bases, defines resident trusts subject to income taxation as "a trust with respect to which the conditions of 1 of the following paragraphs are met during more than one half of any taxable year: (1) The trust has only 1 trustee who or which is (i) a resident individual of this State; (ii) a corporation, partnership or other organization having an office for the conduct of trust business in this State; (2) The trust has more than 1 trustee, and 1 of such trustees is a corporation, partnership or other organization having an office for the conduct of trust business in this state; or (3) The trust has more than 1 trustee, all of whom are individuals and one half or more of whom are resident individuals of this State." Thus, there are circumstances in which the income of a trust will be taxed if the trustee is a resident of the state.

7. Note that resident trusts and estates are allowed a deduction for the portion of income set aside for future distribution to nonresident beneficiaries. (§ 1636(a))

8. If the creator was not domiciled in D.C. at the creation of the trust it is a nonresident trust not subject to taxation on its entire income. However, the provision is contradictory, since it is a resident trust "if the trust consists of property of a person domiciled in the District . . ."

9. The residence or situs of the fiduciary does not control the classification of estates and trusts as resident or nonresident. (§ 47-1809.02).

10. "Resident" includes: (1) every individual who is a legal resident of Georgia on income tax day; (2) every individual who, though not necessarily a legal resident of Georgia, nevertheless resides within the state of Georgia on a more or less regular or permanent basis and not on the temporary or transitory basis of a visitor or sojourner and who so resides within the state of Georgia on income tax day; and (3) every individual who on income tax day has been residing within the state of Georgia for 183 days or part-days or longer, in the aggregate, of the immediately preceding 365 day period. (§ 48-7-1(10)(A))

11. Tax is imposed upon resident fiduciaries and upon nonresident fiduciaries: receiving income from business done in Georgia, managing funds or property located in Georgia, or managing funds or property for the benefit of a resident of Georgia. (§ 48-7-22(a)(1)(A)-(C)) If trust income is accumulated for, is distributed, or becomes distributable during the taxable year to a nonresident and the income was not from a source in Georgia, the income is not taxed even though the trustee is a resident of the state. There is also no tax on income received by a resident fiduciary from business done outside the state, property held outside the state, or intangible property, other than licensing for use of the property. No return of income exempt under the law is required. (§ 48-7-22(a)(3)(A))

12. Tax is imposed upon resident fiduciaries and upon nonresident fiduciaries managing funds or property for the benefit of a resident of Georgia. (§ 48-7-22(a)(1)(C))

13. In the case of a trust, it is a resident if the fiduciary is a resident or the administration is carried on in the state. (§§ 235-1, 235-4) If there is more than one fiduciary and they are all residents, the trust is resident, even if administered out of state. (Haw. Reg. § 18-235-1.17(2)) If there is more than one fiduciary and they are all residents, the trust is resident even if administered out of state (Haw. Reg. § 18-235-1.17(2)) If the administration of the trust is partly carried out in the state, the trust is resident if at least one-half of the fiduciaries are resident. (Haw. Reg. § 18-235-1.17(3))

14. A resident beneficiary is taxed on income whether or not the trust is taxed. (§ 235-4(e)(2)) The key question is whether the beneficiary would have been taxed if the income had been received directly. *(Id.)* Residents are taxed on all their income regardless of source. (§ 235-4(a)) A resident beneficiary is entitled to a credit for taxes paid by a nonresident trust to the other state. Although the wording is ambiguous, the credit is based on income allocated to the resident beneficiary. (§ 235-4.5(c)) *See also* Haw. Reg. § 18-235-4-06.
15. According to 36 ILCS § 5/1501(a)(2)(D), a "resident" includes "an irrevocable trust, the grantor of which was domiciled in this State at the time such trust became irrevocable."
16. The trust is subject to taxation if it has a situs in the state. (§§ 6-3-1-12(d), § 6-3-1-13) The meaning of trust "situs" is not defined in the statute, case law, or administrative regulations. However, 45 Ind. Admin. Code 3.1-1-12 defines the residence of a trust as "the place where it is administered."
17. An estate or trust is taxed like an individual. A nonresident is taxed on what is essentially Iowa-source income. A resident is taxed "on all taxable income." (§ 422.5) Only an individual can be a resident. (§ 422.4(15)) Nevertheless, the differences between residents and nonresidents are made applicable to estates and trusts by the reference in § 422.6 to § 422.5. The problem is that the statute, case law, and administrative regulations fail to indicate what makes an estate or trust resident or nonresident.
18. "Resident trust" means a trust which is administered in Kansas. A trust is not deemed to be administered in Kansas solely because it is subject to the jurisdiction of a district court within Kansas. (§ 79-32, 109(d))
19. Section 141.030(1) makes trusts and estates taxable like individuals. Under § 141.020(4), a nonresident individual is taxed on his Kentucky-source income. However, the statute, case law, and administrative regulations do not establish what makes an estate or trust resident or nonresident. However, 103 KY ADC 19:010, § 4 provides that a resident estate or trust must report and pay tax on all taxable income except that portion of net income distributable or distributed during the taxable year, and that portion of the net income from intangible personal property attributable to a nonresident beneficiary.
20. The Administrative Code provides that a resident beneficiary must report and pay tax on his share of the distributed or distributable income from a resident or nonresident estate or trust. (103 KY ADC 19:010, § 5).
21. Pursuant to 47:181, the taxes imposed on individuals apply to estates and trusts. Pursuant to 47:182, the net income of an estate or trust is computed in the same manner as for individuals, subject to certain adjustments. Pursuant to 47:241, a nonresident individual is taxed primarily on income from sources within Louisiana. However, the statute, case law, and administrative regulations fail to indicate what makes an estate or trust resident or nonresident. However, all of the foregoing provisions are superseded to the extent inconsistent with §§ 47:300.1-300.11. See § 47:300.11. Thus, the latter provisions are the primary authority. A resident trust is a trust or a portion of a trust created by last will and testament of a decedent who at his death was domiciled in Louisiana. (§ 47:300.10(3)(a)) If it is not this type of trust, the trust is a resident trust if the trust instrument provides that the trust shall be governed by the laws of the state of Louisiana. If the trust instrument provides that the trust is governed by the laws of any state other than the state of Louisiana, then the trust shall not be considered a resident trust. If the trust instrument is silent with regard to the designation of the governing law, then the trust shall be considered a resident trust only if the trust is administered in Louisiana. (§ 47:300.10(3)(b))
22. *Id.*
23. Section 10-102 states that a "Tax is imposed on the Maryland taxable income of each individual and of each corporation." The Code then defines individual as "...a natural person or a fiduciary" in § 10-101(e). Under § 10-210, a nonresident individual is essentially taxed on his Maryland-source income. Accordingly, the same would be true of a nonresident trust or estate, as these terms are defined in § 10-101(h)(1).
24. "Domicile" means a place where a person has his true, fixed and permanent home and principal establishment to which, whenever absent therefrom he intends to return, and domicile continues until another permanent establishment is established. (§ 206.18(a)) If a person lives in Michigan at least 183 days during the tax year or more than half the days during a taxable year of less than 12 months, that person is a resident individual domicilied in the state of Michigan. *Id.* Note that the Michigan statute has been held unconstitutional, on the ground that the domicile of the grantor at the creation is not a sufficient nexus alone to justify taxation by the state in later years. (Blue v. Dep't of Treasury, 185 Mich. App. 406, 462 N.W.2d 762 (1990))
25. The trust must be created by or consist of property of a person domiciled in the state at the time the trust becomes irrevocable. (§ 206.18(c))
26. A "nonresident" trust or estate is subject to taxation on what is essentially its Mississippi-source income. (§ 27-7-23) A "resident" trust or estate is taxed on "its entire net income." (§ 27-7-5) The statutes, case law, and administrative regulations fail to indicate what makes a trust or estate resident or nonresident.
27. A trust created by, or consisting of property of, a person domiciled in the state on the date the trust or portion of the trust became irrevocable. (§ 143.331(3))
28. A tax is imposed upon either the fiduciaries or the beneficiaries of estates and trusts, except to the extent such estates and trusts is held for educational, charitable, or religious purposes, and the tax is levied, collected, and paid annually with respect to the income of estates or of any kind of property held in trust, including: income received by estates of deceased persons during the period of administration or settlement of the estate; income accumulated in trust for the benefit of unborn or unascertained persons or persons with contingent interests; income held for future distribution under the terms of the will or trust; and income which is to be distributed to the beneficiaries periodically, whether or not at regular intervals, and the income collected by a guardian of a minor, to be held or distributed as the court may direct. The fiduciary is responsible for making the return of income for the estate or trust for which he acts, whether the fiduciary or the beneficiaries are taxable with reference to the income of such estate or trust. (§ 15-30-135(1)-(2))
29. Income received by estates held by trustees, any one of whom is an inhabitant of New Hampshire, or has derived his appointment from a court of New Hampshire, is subject to tax to the extent that the persons to whom the income from such trust is payable or for whose benefit it is accumulated, are inhabitants of New Hampshire. (§ 77:10)

30. An ''individual'' includes an estate, a trust, or a fiduciary acting for a trust or estate. (§ 7-2-2(I)) The estate or trust, as an ''individual,'' would be subject to tax on what is essentially New Mexico-source income if it is a ''nonresident individual.'' (§ 7-2-2(N)) It is subject to tax on its ''net income'' if it is a ''resident individual.'' The statute and case law fail to indicate when a trust is resident or nonresident. The statute does provide that ''resident'' means an individual who is domiciled in New Mexico during any part of the taxable year or an individual who is physically present in New Mexico for one hundred eighty-five days or more during the taxable year; but any individual, other than someone who was physically present in New Mexico for one hundred eighty-five days or more during the taxable year, who, on or before the last day of the taxable year, changed his place of abode to a place without New Mexico with the bona fide intention of continuing actually to abide permanently without New Mexico is not a resident for the purposes of the Income Tax Act for periods after that change of abode. (§ 7-2-2(S)) The regulation, §3.3.3.7, defines a nonresident trust as a trust in which the trustee responsible for the funds and for distribution of the funds is a resident of another state. A nonresident trust is still subject to New Mexico income tax if it is engaged in the transaction of business in, into or from the state or is deriving income from any property located in the state. See also Fiduciary Income Tax Instructions Form FID-1, which adds income from compensation as subject to tax in New Mexico.

31. *Id.*

32. The tax imposed on individuals generally applies to estates and trusts. (§ 57-38-07) Individuals who are nonresidents are taxed on only certain types of North Dakota-source income. The administrative regulations instruct that a trust or estate is a resident trust or estate when it has a relationship to the state sufficient to create nexus. This includes, but is not limited to, the following contacts: (a) a beneficiary of the trust or estate is a domiciliary or resident of the state of North Dakota; (b) the trustee or executor is a domiciliary or resident of the state of North Dakota; (c) assets making up any part of the trust or estate have situs in the state of North Dakota; (d) any or all of the administration or income production of the trust or estate takes place within the state of North Dakota; (e) the laws of the state of North Dakota are specifically made applicable to the trust or estate or to the opposite parties with respect to their fiduciary relationship; (f) the trust is a revocable trust, and the grantor is a domiciliary or resident of the state of North Dakota. (Admin. Code § 81-03-02.1-04.(2)(a)-(f))

33. *Id.*

34. *Id.*

35. *Id.*

36. *Id.*

37. *Id.*

38. Section 316.282(1)(d) defines resident trust as ''. . . a trust of which the fiduciary is resident of Oregon, or a trust the administration of which is carried on in Oregon.''

39. Resident includes those who are domiciled in the state unless he/she maintains no permanent place of abode in the state and does maintain a permanent place of abode elsewhere and spends in the aggregate not more than thirty days of the taxable year in the State, and Resident includes those who are not domiciled in the state but who have a permanent abode in the state and who spend more than 183 days of the taxable year in the state. (72 § 7301(p))

40. Under § 44-30-5(c)(2) a revocable trust which becomes irrevocable upon the occurrence of any event (including death) which terminates a person's power to revoke, but only after the event, and only if the person having the power to revoke was a Rhode Island resident individual at the time of the event, is taxed on its entire income. Under § 44-30-5(c)(4) an irrevocable trust created by or consisting of property contributed by a person who is a resident individual at the time the trust was created or the property contributed while the person is alive and a resident individual in the state and after the person's death if the person died a resident individual of the state is taxed on its income to the extent that the beneficiaries are Rhode Island resident individuals, subject to regulations promulgated by the tax administrator. (§ 44-30-5(c)(5)) Resident individual includes those who are domiciled in the state. In determining the domicile of an individual, the geographic location of professional advisors selected by an individual, including without limitation advisors who render medical, financial, legal, insurance, fiduciary or investment services, shall not be taken into consideration. (§ 44-30-5(a)(1)) Resident also includes those who are not domiciled in the state but who have a permanent abode in the state and who spend more than 183 days of the taxable year in the state, unless the individual is in the armed forces of the United States. (§ 44-30-5(a)(2))

41. Positive responses for imposition of the income tax are positive only to the extent that the beneficiaries are Rhode Island resident individuals. (§ 44-30-5(c)(5))

42. Under § 71.14(2) a trust created by a decedent, by will, contract, declaration of trust or implication of law, who at the time of death was a resident of Wisconsin is considered resident (and fully taxable) at the domicile of the decedent at death, until transferred by the court having jurisdiction to another court's jurisdiction.

43. Only two types of trusts, or portions of trusts, that become irrevocable on or after October 29, 1999, or that became irrevocable before October 29, 1999, and are first administered in the state of Wisconsin on or after October 29, 1999, are resident of Wisconsin. This includes trusts, or portions of trusts, the assets of which consist of property placed in the trust by a person who is either (1) a resident of Wisconsin at the time that the property was placed in the trust if, at the time that the assets were placed in the trust, the trust was irrevocable, or (2) a resident of Wisconsin at the time that the trust became irrevocable if, at the time that the property was placed in the trust, the trust was revocable. (§ 71.14(3m)(a)) A trust is revocable if the person whose property constitutes the trust may revest title to the property in that person, and s irrevocable if the power to revest title, does not exist. (§ 71.14(3m)(b))

Table 13.01, Part 2
Trusts

A Trust Is Taxed on Its Entire Income If:*

	The Testamentary Trust Is Created By Will of a Decedent Who At Death Was a Resident of the State	*The Testamentary Trust Is Created By Will of a Decedent Who At Death Was Domiciled in the State*	*The Inter Vivos Trust Consists of Property of a Person Who, At the Time of Transfer, Was a Resident of the State*	*The Inter Vivos Trust Consists of Property of a Person Who, At the Time of Transfer, Was Domiciled in the State*	*The Trust Is Registered in the State*	*The Trust Is a Resident or Has a Situs in the State, But Residence or Situs Is Not Defined*	*Other Basis for Trust Income Taxation (Such as for ''Nonresident Trust'') Income From a Source in the State*
Alabama	No.	No.	No.	No.	No.	Yes.[1]	Yes, property owned or business transacted in the state. (§§ 40-18-2(a)(4), 40-18-25(b) & (c), 40-18-14(3))
Alaska	*No income tax on trusts*	—	—	—	—	—	—
Arizona	No. (§§ 43-1311, 43-1011, 43-1301(5))	No.	No.	No.	No.	No.	Yes, with respect to a non-resident trust.[2] (§ 43-1301(1)(a))
Arkansas	Yes. (§ 26-51-201(a) & (b)); 26-51-102(a)	Yes. (§ 26-51-201(a)); 26-51-102(a)	No.	No.	No.	Yes.[3]	Yes. (§ 26-51-202)
California	No.	No.	No.	No.	No.	No.	No. However, a non-resident beneficiary is taxed on income from a trust to the extent derived from sources in the state. (Rev. & Tax. § 17734)
Colorado	No.	No.	No.	No.	No.	No.	Yes. (§ 39-22-404)

Connecticut	Yes. (§ 12-701(a)(4)(C))	Yes, since definition of resident is someone who is domiciled in this state. (§§ 12-701(a)(i)(A), 12-701(a)(4)(C)) Note that certain domiciliaries with limited physical presence in the state may avoid taxation. (Id.)	Yes.[4] (§ 12-701(a)(4) (D)(i))	Yes.	No.	No.	Yes. (§§ 12-701(a)(b); 12-713(a))
Delaware	No.	Yes. (30 § 1601(8)(a))	No.	Yes. (30 § 1601(8)(b))	No.	No.	Yes.[5] (30 § 1639)
District of Columbia	No.	Yes. (§§ 47-1809.01, 47-1809.03)	No.	Yes. (§§ 47-1809.01, 47-1809.03)	No.	No.	No.
Florida	*No income tax on trusts.* (§ 220.02)	—	—	—	—	—	—
Georgia	No.	No.	No.	No.	No.	No.	Yes.[6] (§§ 48-7-22, 48-7-30)
Hawaii	No.	No.	No.	No.	No.	No.	Yes. (§ 235-4(e)(1))
Idaho	No.	No.	No.	No.	No.	Yes.[7]	Yes.[8] (§§ 63-3030(a)(8); 63-3026A(3))
Illinois	No.	Yes. (35 ILCS §§ 5/201(a), 5/1501(a)(20)(C))	No.	No.	No.	No.	Yes. (35 ILCS §§ 5/306, 5/301(c)(1)) But see § 5/301(c)(2)(A))
Indiana[9]	No.	No.	No.	No.	No.	Yes.[10]	Yes. (§ 6-3-2-1(a))

Table 13.01, Part 2
Trusts *(continued)*

	A Trust Is Taxed on Its Entire Income If:*						
	The Testamentary Trust Is Created By Will of a Decedent Who At Death Was a Resident of the State	*The Testamentary Trust Is Created By Will of a Decedent Who At Death Was Domiciled in the State*	*The Inter Vivos Trust Consists of Property of a Person Who, At the Time of Transfer, Was a Resident of the State*	*The Inter Vivos Trust Consists of Property of a Person Who, At the Time of Transfer, Was Domiciled in the State*	*The Trust Is Registered in the State*	*The Trust Is a Resident or Has a Situs in the State, But Residence or Situs Is Not Defined*	*Other Basis for Trust Income Taxation (Such as for "Nonresident Trust") Income From a Source in the State*
Iowa[11]	Yes. (Admin. Code § 701-89.3(1))	No.	No.	No.	No.	Yes.[12]	Yes, with respect to a nonresident trust. (§ 422.8(2)(a) & (3))
Kansas	No.	No.	No.	No.	No.	No.	Yes. (§ 79-32,137)
Kentucky[13]	No.	No.	No.	No.	No.	Yes.[14]	Yes.[15] (§§ 141.020(4), 141.030(1))
Louisiana[16]	No.	Yes.[17]	No.	No.	No.	No.	Yes. (§§ 47:300.3(2), 47:300.7)
Maine	No.	Yes. (36 §§ 5102(4)(B), 5160)	No.	Yes. (36 §§ 5102(4)(C), 5160)	No. (36 § 5102(4)(D) Repealed)	No.	Yes. (36 § 5175)
Maryland[18]	No.	Yes. (Tax-Gen. § 10-101(K)(1)(iii)(1))	No.	No.	No.	No.	No. (Tax-Gen. § 10-206)
Massachusetts	Yes. (62 §§ 10(c) & 1(f))	Yes. (62 §§ 10(c) & 1(f))	No.	No.	No.	No.	Yes. (62 §§ 5A, 10(a))

Michigan	Yes. (§§ 206.18(a) & (c), 206.110(1))	Yes.[19] (§§ 206.18(c), 206.110(1))	Yes. (§§ 206.18(a) & (c), 206.110(1))	Yes. (§§ 206.18(a) & (c), 206.110(1))	No.	No.	Yes. (§§ 206.51 (4), 206.110(2))
Minnesota	No.	Yes.[20] (§§ 290.01(7b), 290.22)	No.	Yes.[21] (§§ 290.01(7b), 290.22)	No.	No.	Yes. (§ 290.014 sub div. (3))
Mississippi[22]	No.	No.	No.	No.	No.	Yes.[23]	Yes. (§§ 27-7-5(3), 27-7-23(b))
Missouri	No.	Yes.[24] (§§ 143.331(2), 143.341), assuming at least one income beneficiary is a resident on the last day of the taxable year. (§ 143.331(2)(b))	No.	Yes. (§§ 143.331 (3), 143.341), assuming at least one income beneficiary is a resident on the last day of the taxable year. (§ 143.331(3)(b))	No.	No.	Yes. (§ 143.381)
Montana	No.	No.	No.	No.	No.	No.	Yes. (§ 15-30-105(1))
Nebraska	No.	Yes. (§§ 77-2714.01(6)(b), 77-2717)	No.	Yes.[25] (§§ 77-2714.01 (6)(c), 77-2717)	No.	No.	Yes.[26] (§§ 77-2717(b), 77-2724)
Nevada	*No income tax on trusts*	—	—	—	—	—	—
New Hampshire	No.	No.	No.	No.	No.	No.	Yes.[27] (§ 77:12)
New Jersey	No.	Yes.[28] (§§ 54A:1-2(o)(2), 54A:2-1)	No.	Yes.[29] (§§ 54A:1-2(o)(3), 54A:2-1-1, 54A:5-8	No.	No.	Yes. (§ 54A:5-8)
New Mexico[30]	No.	No.	No.	No.	No.	Yes.[31] (§§ 7-2-2, 7-2-3)	Yes. (§§ 7-2-2(I)& (N); 7-2-3)
New York[32]	No.	Yes. (Tax §§ 605(b)(3)(B), 618)	No.	Yes.[33] (Tax §§ 605(b)(3)(C), 618)	No.	No.	Yes.[34] (Tax §§ 601(e)(1), 633(a))
North Carolina	No.	No.	No.	No.	No.	No.	Yes. (17 ADC § 6B.3716(b)(1))

(cont'd)

Table 13.01, Part 2
Trusts *(continued)*

A Trust Is Taxed on Its Entire Income If:*

	The Testamentary Trust Is Created By Will of a Decedent Who At Death Was a Resident of the State	*The Testamentary Trust Is Created By Will of a Decedent Who At Death Was Domiciled in the State*	*The Inter Vivos Trust Consists of Property of a Person Who, At the Time of Transfer, Was a Resident of the State*	*The Inter Vivos Trust Consists of Property of a Person Who, At the Time of Transfer, Was Domiciled in the State*	*The Trust Is Registered in the State*	*The Trust Is a Resident or Has a Situs in the State, But Residence or Situs Is Not Defined*	*Other Basis for Trust Income Taxation (Such as for "Nonresident Trust") Income From a Source in the State*
North Corolina *(cont'd)*							Also, a nonresident beneficiary is taxed on income from a trust to the extent derived from sources in the state.[35] (§ 105-160.2)
North Dakota[36]	No.	No.	No.	No.	No.	No. Residence is defined, but situs has not been defined.[37]	Yes. However, restricted in the caseof income from intangibles.[38] (§§ 57-38-07, 57-38-05) In the case of income from tangible property, it is limited to property with a situs in the state.[39] (§ 57-38-04(3))

Ohio[40]	No.	Yes. (§ 5747.01(I)(3)(a)(i)&(3)(e)(i))	No.	Yes.[41] (§ 5747.01(I)(3)(a) (ii))	No.	No.	Yes, if nexus with the state under the U.S. Constitution. (§ 5747.02(A))
Oklahoma	No.	Yes. (68 §§ 2353(6)(a), 2355(E))	No.	Yes.[42] (68 §§ 2353(6)(a)& (b), 2355(E))	No.	No.	Yes. (68 § 2362)
Oregon	No.	No.	No.	No.	No.	No.	Yes. (§§ 316.307(3)&(4), 316.312(1))
Pennsylvania	Yes.[43] (72 §§ 7301(s)(1), 7302(a))	Yes. (72 §§ 7301(p) & (s)(1), 7302(a))	Yes.[44] (72 §§ 7301(s)(2), 7302(a))	Yes. (72 §§ 7301(p) & (s)(2), 7302(a))	No.	No.	Yes. (72 § 7302(b))
Rhode Island[45]	Yes. (§§ 44-30-5(c)(3), 44-30-1) Note that § 44-30-5(c)(5) provides that a trust is resident only to the extent that the beneficiaries are Rhode Island resident individuals.[46]	Yes. (§§ 44-30-5(a)(1) & (2), 44-30-5(c)(3), 44-30-1) Note that § 44-30-5(c)(5) provides that a trust is resident only to the extent that the beneficiaries are Rhode Island resident individuals.[47]	Yes. (§§ 44-30-5(a)(2), 44-30-5(c)(4), 44-30-1) Note that § 44-30-5(c)(5) provides that a trust is resident only to the extent that the beneficiaries are Rhode Island resident individuals.[48]	Yes. (§§ 44-30-5(a)(1), 44-30-5(c)(4), 44-30-1) Note that § 44-30-5(c)(5) provides that a trust is resident only to the extent that the beneficiaries are Rhode Island resident individuals.[49]	No.	No.	Yes. (§§ 44-30-1, 44-30-35)
South Carolina	No.	No.	No.	No.	No.	No.	Yes. (§§ 12-6-1720, 12-6-620)
South Dakota	*No income tax on trusts*	—	—	—	—	—	—
Tennessee	No.	No.	No.	No.	No.	No.	No.
Texas	*No income tax on trusts*	—	—	—	—	—	—

Table 13.01, Part 2
Trusts *(continued)*

A Trust Is Taxed on Its Entire Income If:*

	The Testamentary Trust Is Created By Will of a Decedent Who At Death Was a Resident of the State	*The Testamentary Trust Is Created By Will of a Decedent Who At Death Was Domiciled in the State*	*The Inter Vivos Trust Consists of Property of a Person Who, At the Time of Transfer, Was a Resident of the State*	*The Inter Vivos Trust Consists of Property of a Person Who, At the Time of Transfer, Was Domiciled in the State*	*The Trust Is Registered in the State*	*The Trust Is a Resident or Has a Situs in the State, But Residence or Situs Is Not Defined*	*Other Basis for Trust Income Taxation (Such as for "Nonresident Trust") Income From a Source in the State*
Utah	No.	Yes. (§§ 59-10-103(1)(w) 75-7-103)(ii); 59-10-201)	No.	No.	No.	No.	Yes. (§ 59-10-204)
Vermont	No.	Yes.[50] (32 §§ 5811(11)(B) (i), 5822)	No.	Yes.[51] (32 §§ 5811(11)(B) (ii), 5822)	No.	No.	Yes.(32 § 5823(b)&(c), 5811 (9)&(11)(B))
Virginia	No.	Yes. (§§ 58.1-302, 58.1-361(A))	No.	Yes. (§§ 58.1-302, 58.1-361(A))	No.	No.	Yes.[52] (§ 58.1-362)
Washington	*No income tax on trusts*	—	—	—	—	—	—
West Virginia	No.	Yes. (§§ 11-21-7(c)(2), 11-21-18)	No.	Yes. (§§ 11-21-7(c)(3), 11-21-18)	No.	No.	Yes. (§§ 11-21-38, 11-21-39)
Wisconsin	Yes.[53] (§ 71.14(2)	No.	No.	No.	No.	No.	Yes.[54] (§§ 71.02, 71.04(4))
Wyoming	*No income tax on trusts*	—	—	—	—	—	—

* The reference to "income " typically refers to "taxable income." However careful consideration needs to be given to the calculation of the figure against which the tax rate is multiplied.

1. "Every estate and trust resident in Alabama" is taxed on all taxable income. (§ 40-18-2) However, there is no definition of this phrase. Under § 40-18-25(c), a trust created by a person not a resident and an estate of a person not a resident of Alabama are subject to tax only to the extent individuals other than residents are liable for tax. By negative implication this subjects estates and trusts created by persons who are residents of Alabama to taxation. However, a resident estate or trust that has gross income taxable in Alabama and another state will be allowed a credit for net income taxes paid to the other state on such income as provided in § 40-18-21. (AL ADC 810-3-25-.04(2))

2. If for any reason the taxes imposed on income of a trust are not paid when due and remain unpaid when such income is distributable to the beneficiaries, or if the income is distributable to the beneficiaries before the taxes are due and the taxes are not paid when due, such income is taxable to the beneficiaries when distributable to them, except that in the case of nonresident beneficiaries such income is taxable only to the extent it is derived from sources within the state of Arizona. (§ 43-1315)

3. Income tax is imposed on the entire income of every resident trust and estate. (§ 26-51-201(a)) However, the terms are not defined in the Code. Under § 26-51-201(b) and (c), trusts and estates created by a nonresident trustor, donor, settlor, or a nonresident testator, even though administered by a resident trustee or personal representative, or trusts being administered by a resident trustee of which the beneficiaries are nonresidents are taxed only on income from real or tangible personal property and unincorporated businesses in Arkansas. The same limitation applies to estates administered by resident personal representatives of which the beneficiaries are nonresidents. (§ 26-51-202) By negative implication this suggests that trusts and estates created by a resident trustor, donor, settlor, or a resident testator would be taxed on their entire income. It also appears that if the beneficiaries of the estate or trust are residents of Arkansas, the trust or estate may be taxed on its entire income.

4. If the transfer is to a revocable trust that later becomes irrevocable, then the relevant time will be when the trust becomes irrevocable. However, if the trust remains revocable until the settlor's death, then the relevant time is the date of transfer to the trust. (§ 12-701(a)(4)(D)(ii)&(iii))

5. In the case of a nonresident estate or nonresident trust:(1) Items of income, gain, loss and deduction mean those derived from, or connected with, sources in this State; (2) Items of income, gain, loss and deduction entering into the definition of federal distributable net income include such items from another estate or trust of which the first estate or trust is a beneficiary; (3) The source of items of income, gain, loss or deduction shall be determined under rules or regulations prescribed by the Director in accordance with the rules of 30 § 1124, as if the estate or trust were a nonresident individual. (30 § 1639)

6. Tax is imposed upon resident fiduciaries and upon nonresident fiduciaries: receiving income from business done in Georgia, managing funds or property located in Georgia, or managing funds or property for the benefit of a resident of Georgia. (§ 48-7-22(a)(1)(A)-(C))

7. A trust, "the residence of which trust is in Idaho, having gross income of $100 or more for the current taxable year," is subject to taxation. (§ 63-3030(a)(7)) The statute and case law fail to indicate when a trust has a residence in Idaho. However, Admin. Code 35.01.01.035.01(a)-(e) provides that a trust other than a qualified funderal trust is treated as a resident trust if three or more of the following condiitions exist: the domicile or residency of the grantor is in Idaho; the trust is governed by Idaho law; the trust has real or tangible personal property located in Idaho; the trustee has a domicile or residency in Idaho; or administration takes place in Idaho. Administration of the trust includes conducting trust business, investing assets of the trust, making administrative decisions, record keeping and filing of tax returns. (ID ADC 35.01.01.035.01(e)) Also, in determining the residency status of a trust, no distinction is made between inter vivos trusts and testamentary trusts, or between revocable trusts and irrevocable trusts. (ID ADC 35.01.01.035.04)

8. "Every trust required to file a federal return under the Internal Revenue Code, the residence of which is in a state other than Idaho, having a gross income from Idaho sources in excess of $100," is subject to taxation. (§ 63-3030(a)(8))

9. The trust is subject to taxation if it has a situs in the state. (§§ 6-3-1-12(d), 6-3-2-1(a)) The meaning of trust "situs" is not defined in the statute, case law, or administrative regulations.

10. *Id.*

11. An estate or trust is taxed like an individual. A nonresident is taxed on what is essentially Iowa-source income. A resident is taxed "on all taxable income." (§ 422.5) Only an individual can be a resident. (§ 422.4(15)) Nevertheless, the differences between residents and nonresidents are made applicable to estates and trusts by the reference in § 422.6 to § 422.5. The situs of a testamentary trust for tax purposes is the state of the decedent's residence at the time of death until the jurisdiction of the court in which the trust proceedings are pending is terminated. In the event of termination and the trust remains open, the situs of the trust is governed by the same rules as pertain to the situs of inter vivos trusts. (IA ADC § 701-89.3(422) If an inter vivos trust is created by a court or makes an accounting to it, then that state has taxing jurisdiction until jurisdiction is terminated. If an inter vivos trust is a grantor trust or is deemed owned by a person, then the state of the residence of the grantor or owner is determinative. If an inter vivos trust is neither of the above, then tax situs depends on the relevant facts of the particular case. The relevant facts include, but are not limited to the residence of the trustee or a majority of them, the location of the principal office where the trust is administered and the location of the evidence of the intangible assets of the trust. The following factors are not relevant: the residence of the grantor, a statement in the trust instrument as to situs of administration, and the residence of the beneficiaries. (IA ADC § 701-89.3(422)

12. *Id.*

13. Section 141.030(1) makes trusts and estates taxable like individuals. Under § 141.020(4), a nonresident individual is taxed on his Kentucky-source income. However, the statute, case law, and administrative regulations do not establish what makes an estate or trust resident or nonresident. However, 103 KY ADC 19:010, § 4 provides that a resident estate or trust must report and pay tax on all taxable income except that portion of net income distributable or distributed during the taxable year, and that portion of the net income from intangible personal property attributable to a nonresident beneficiary. Also, a resident beneficiary must report and pay tax on his share of the distributed or distributable income from a resident or nonresident estate or trust. (103 KY ADC 19:010, § 5) In addition, a nonresident estate, trust, or beneficiary is subject to tax only on income received from real or tangible personal property located in Kentucky. (103 KY ADC 19:010, § 6)

14. *Id.*

15. The administrative code provides that a nonresident estate, trust, or beneficiary is Subject to tax only on income received from real or tangible personal property located in Kentucky. (103 KY ADC 19:010, § 6)

16. Pursuant to § 47:181, the taxes imposed on individuals apply to estates and trusts. Pursuant to § 47:182, the net income of an estate or trust is computed in the same manner as for individuals, subject to certain adjustments. Pursuant to § 47:241, a nonresident individual is taxed primarily on income from sources within Louisiana. However, the statute, case law, and administrative regulations fail to indicate what makes an estate or trust resident or nonresident. However, all of the foregoing provisions are superseded to the extent inconsistent with §§ 47:300.1-300.11. See § 47:300.11. Thus, the latter provisions are the primary authority. A resident trust is a trust or a portion of a trust created by last will and testament of a decedent who at his death was domiciled in Louisiana. (§ 47:300.10(3)(a)) If it is not this type of trust, the trust is a resident trust if the trust instrument provides that the trust shall be governed by the laws of the state of Louisiana. If the trust instrument provides that the trust is governed by the laws of any state other than the state of Louisiana, then the trust shall not be considered a resident trust. If the trust instrument is silent with regard to the designation of the governing law, then the trust shall be considered a resident trust only if the trust is administered in Louisiana. (§ 47:300.10(3)(b))

17. *Id.*
18. Section 10-102 states that a "Tax is imposed on the Maryland taxable income of each individual and of each corporation." The code then defines Individual as "... a natural person or a fiduciary" in § 10-101(e). Under § 10-210, a nonresident individual is essentially taxed on his Maryland-source income. Accordingly, the same would be true of a nonresident trust or estate, as these terms are defined in § 10-101(g).
19. "Domicile" means a place where a person has his true, fixed and permanent home and principal establishment to which, whenever absent therefrom he intends to return, and domicile continues until another permanent establishment is established. (§ 206.18(a)). If a person is domiciledlives in Michigan at least 183 days during the tax year or more than half the days during a taxable year of less than 12 months, that person is a resident individual domicilied in the statet of Michigan. Id.
20. A "resident trust" is a trust, except a grantor type trust, which either (1) was created by a will of a decedent who at death was domiciled in Minnesota or (2) is an irrevocable trust, the grantor of which was domiciled in this state at the time the trust became irrevocable. A trust is considered irrevocable to the extent the grantor is not treated as the owner thereof under sections 671 to 678 of the Internal Revenue Code. The term "grantor type trust" means a trust where the income or gains of the trust are taxable to the grantor or others treated as substantial owners under sections 671 to 678 of the Internal Revenue Code. This applies to trusts, except grantor type trusts, that became irrevocable after December 31, 1995, or are first administered in Minnesota after December 31, 1995. (§ 290.01(7b))
21. *Id.*
22. A "nonresident" trust or estate is subject to taxation on what is essentially its Mississippi-source income. (§ 27-7-23) A "resident" trust or estate is taxed on "its entire net income." (§ 27-7-5) The statutes, case law, and administrative regulations fail to indicate what makes a trust or estate resident or nonresident.
23. *Id.*
24. A trust created by, or consisting of property of, a person domiciled in the state on the date the trust or portion of the trust became irrevocable. (§ 143.331(3))
25. A trust is fully taxed if the trust or portion of the trust consists of property of an individual domiciled in Nebraska at the time such individual may no longer exercise the power to revest title to the property in himself. (§ 77-2714.01(6)(c))
26. The tax imposed on all nonresident estates and trusts is the portion of the tax imposed on resident estates and trusts which is attributable to the income derived from sources within Nebraska. The tax which is attributable to income derived from sources within Nebraska is determined by multiplying the liability to Nebraska for a resident estate or trust with the same total income by a fraction, the numerator of which is the nonresident estate's or trust's Nebraska income as determined by sections 77-2724 and 77-2725 and the denominator of which is its total federal income after first adjusting each by the amounts provided in section 77-2716. (§ 77-2717(b))
27. Section 77:12 reads "If an inhabitant of this state receives income from one or more trustees, none of whom is an inhabitant of this state or has derived his appointment from a court of this state, such income shall be subject to the taxes imposed by this chapter if it would be taxable to such inhabitant if received by him from its source."
28. A trust, or a portion of a trust, consisting of property transferred by will of a decedent who at his death was domiciled in New Jersey. (§ 54A:1-2(o)(2))
29. A trust, or portion of a trust, consisting of the property of: a person domiciled in New Jersey at the time such property was transferred to the trust, if such trust or portion of a trust was then irrevocable, or if it was then revocable and has not subsequently become irrevocable; or a person domiciled in New Jersey at the time such trust, or portion of a trust, became irrevocable, if it was revocable when such property was transferred to the trust but has subsequently become irrevocable. For the purposes of the foregoing, a trust or portion of a trust is revocable if it is subject to a power, exercisable immediately or at any future time, to revest title in the person whose property constitutes such trust or portion of a trust, and a trust or portion of a trust becomes irrevocable when the possibility that such power may be exercised has been terminated. (§ 54A:1-2(o)(3)). Under § 54A:1-2 a trust or portion of a trust, consisting of property of a person domiciled in New Jersey at the time the property was transferred to the trust, if the trust was then revocable, or if it was then irrevocable and has not subsequently become irrevocable or of a person domiciled in the state at the time the trust became irrevocable, if it was revocable when such property was transferred to the trust but has subsequently become irrevocable.
30. An "individual" includes an estate, a trust, or a fiduciary acting for a trust or estate. (§ 7-2-2(I)) The estate or trust, as an "individual," would be subject to tax on what is essentially New Mexico-source income if it is a "nonresident individual." (§ 7-2-2(N)) It is subject to tax on its "net income" if it is a "resident individual." The statute does provide that "resident" means an individual who is domiciled in New Mexico during any part of the taxable year or an individual who is physically present in New Mexico for one hundred eighty-five days or more during the taxable year; but any individual, other than someone who was physically present in New Mexico for one hundred eighty-five days or more during the taxable year, who, on or before the last day of the taxable year, changed his place of abode to a place without New Mexico with the bona fide intention of continuing actually to abide permanently without New Mexico is not a resident for the purposes of the Income Tax Act for periods after that change of abode. (§ 7-2-2(S)) The regulation, §3.3.3.7, defines a nonresident trust as a trust in which the trustee responsible for the funds and for distributions of the funds is a resident of another state. A nonresident trust is still subject to New Mexico income tax if it is engaged in the transaction of business in, into or from the state or is deriving income from any property located in the state. See also Fiduciary Income Tax Instructions Form FID-1, which adds income from compensation as subject to tax in New Mexico.
31. *Id.*
32. Note that a resident trust is not subject to tax if all of the following conditions are satisfied: all the trustees are domiciled in a state other than New York; the entire corpus of the trusts, including real and tangible property, is located outside the state of New York; and all income and gains of the trust are derived from or connected with sources outside of the state of New York, determined as if the trust were a non-resident trust. Intangible property is located in the state of New York if one or more of the trustees are domiciled in the state of New York. Also, a trustee which is a banking and which is domiciled outside the state of New York at the time it becomes a trustee of the trust is deemed to continue to be a trustee domiciled outside the state of New York notwithstanding that it

thereafter otherwise becomes a trustee domiciled in the state of New York by virtue of being acquired by, or becoming an office or branch of, a corporate trustee domiciled within the state of New York. (§ 605(b)(3)(D))

33. Under § 605(b)(3)(C) a trust or portion of a trust, consisting of property of a person domiciled in New York at the time the property was transferred to the trust, if the trust was then revocable, or if it was then irrevocable and has not subsequently become irrevocable or of a person domiciled in the state at the time the trust became irrevocable, if it was revocable when such property was transferred to the trust but has subsequently become irrevocable. For the purposes of the foregoing, a trust or portion of a trust is revocable if it is subject to a power, exercisable immediately or at any future time, to revest title in the person whose property constitutes such trust or portion of a trust, and a trust or portion of a trust becomes irrevocable when the possibility that such power may be exercised has been terminated.

34. Note that a resident trust is not subject to tax if all of the following conditions are satisfied: all the trustees are domiciled in a state other than New York; the entire corpus of the trusts, including real and tangible property, is located outside the state of New York; and all income and gains of the trust are derived from or connected with sources outside of the state of New York, determined as if the trust were a non-resident trust. Intangible property is located in the state of New York if one or more of the trustees are domiciled in the state of New York. Also, a trustee which is a banking and which is domiciled outside the state of New York at the time it becomes a trustee of the trust is deemed to continue to be a trustee domiciled outside the state of New York notwithstanding that it thereafter otherwise becomes a trustee domiciled in the state of New York by virtue of being acquired by, or becoming an office or branch of, a corporate trustee domiciled within the state of New York. (§ 605(b)(3)(D))

35. A nonresident beneficiary is taxed on income from an estate or trust to the extent that the income (i) is derived from North Carolina sources and is attributable to the ownership of any interest in real or tangible personal property in the state of North Carolina or (ii) is derived from a business, trade, profession, or occupation carried on in the state of North Carolina. (§ 105-160.2). If an estate or trust has income from sources outside of North Carolina and if any of the beneficiaries are nonresidents of North Carolina, the portion of federal taxable income of the Fiduciary that is subject to North Carolina tax must be determined. The determination of the amount of undistributed income from intangible property which is for the benefit of a resident is based on the beneficiary's state of residence on the last day of the taxable year of the trust. In the case of both resident and nonresident beneficiaries, the determination of the amount of undistributed income from intangible property which is for the benefit of a resident is made on the basis that the resident beneficiary's interest for the taxable year relates to the interest of both resident and nonresident income beneficiaries for the taxable year. (17 ADC § 6B.3724)

36. The tax imposed on individuals generally applies to estates and trusts. (§ 57-38-07) Individuals who are nonresidents are taxed on only certain types of North Dakota-source income. The administrative regulations instruct that a trust or estate is a resident trust or estate when it has a relationship to the state sufficient to create nexus. This includes, but is not limited to, the following contacts: (a) a beneficiary of the trust or estate is a domiciliary or resident of the state of North Dakota; (b) the trustee or executor is a domiciliary or resident of the state of North Dakota; (c) assets making up any part of the trust or estate have situs in the state of North Dakota; (d) any or all of the administration or income production of the trust or estate takes place within the state of North Dakota; (e) the laws of the state of North Dakota are specifically made applicable to the trust or estate or to the opposite parties with respect to their fiduciary relationship; (f) the trust is a revocable trust, and the grantor is a domiciliary or resident of the state of North Dakota. (Admin. Code § 81-03-02.1-04(2)(a)-(f))

37. *Id.*

38. Income from intangibles subject to tax: Income and gains derived from transactions in the regular course of the taxpayer's trade or business carried on in this state, or the acquisition, management, and disposition of intangible personal property to the extent it constitutes a trade or business in the state. (§ 57-38-05)

39. The determination of when property has a situs in the state is not always easy to determine under the law.

40. Effective only for trust taxable years beginning in 2003 or 2004.

41. The provision only applies to the extent that the trust is irrevocable. "Irrevocability" exists if the transferor is not deemed the owner under I.R.C. §§ 671-678. (§ 5747.01(I)(3)(b)) Thus, the trust may be only partially resident in the state. A formula is prescribed for determining the extent of residence. (§ 5747.01(I)(3)(d)) Taxing jurisdiction, whether in whole or in part, only applies if there is a "qualifying beneficiary" who is at least domiciled in the state for part of the current year. Taxing jurisdiction also exists, whether in whole or in part, if assets were transferred by a person domiciled in Ohio when the trust document or instrument became irrevocable, but again only if there is a qualifying beneficiary. (§ 5747.01(I)(3)(a)(iii)) Finally, a pourover trust may be subject to tax if a transfer is made to a trust created by the decedent while domiciled in the state or to which the decedent transferred assets during life, assuming the trust became irrevocable while the decedent was domiciled in the state and there is in the current tax period a qualifying beneficiary. (§§ 5747.01(I)(3)(a)(1), (3)(e)(ii), & (3)(f)(i)-(iv). Nevertheless, in this instance, at least one trust qualifying beneficiary must be a "resident domiciled in the state . . ." (emphasis added). A qualifying beneficiary has the same meaning as "potential current beneficiary" under I.R.C. § 1361(e)(2). Essentially, it means a beneficiary who is entitled to receive or may receive income or principal during the current tax period. Certain contractually-imposed transfers to trusts could also lead to taxing jurisdiction. (§ 5747.01(I)(3)(f)(iii)-(iv).

42. A trust or portion of a trust is subject to tax, if it consists of property of a person domiciled in Oklahoma at the time the property was transferred to the trust if the trust or portion of the trust is not irrevocable, or a trust or portion of a trust consists of property of a person domiciled in Oklahoma at the time of the transfer and the trust was then revocable, or a trust or portion of a trust consists of property of a person domiciled in Oklahoma when the trust or portion thereof became irrevocable. (68 § 2353(6)(a) & (b))

43. Resident includes those who are domiciled in the state unless he/she maintains no permanent place of abode in the state and does maintain a permanent place of abode elsewhere and spends in the aggregate not more than thirty days of the taxable year in the State, and Resident includes those who are not domiciled in the state but who have a permanent abode in the state and who spend more than 183 days of the taxable year in the state. (72 § 7301(p))

44. The term "resident trust" for this purpose does not include charitable trusts or pension or profit sharing trusts. (72 § 7301(s)(2)) Resident includes those who are domiciled in the state unless he/she maintains no permanent place of abode in the state and does maintain a permanent place of abode elsewhere and spends in the aggregate not more than thirty days of the taxable year in the State, and Resident includes those who are not domiciled in the state but who have a permanent abode in the state and who spend more than 183 days of the taxable year in the state. (72 § 7301(p)).

45. Resident individual includes those who are domiciled in the state. In determining the domicile of an individual, the geographic location of professional advisors selected by an individual, including without limitation advisors who render medical, financial, legal, insurance, fiduciary or investment services, shall not be taken into consideration. (§ 44-30-5(a)(1)) Resident also includes those who are

not domiciled in the state but who have a permanent abode in the state and who spend more than 183 days of the taxable year in the state, unless the individual is in the armed forces of the United States. (§ 44-30-5(a)(2))

46. *Id.*

47. *Id.*

48. *Id.*

49. *Id.*

50. A trust, or portion of a trust. (32 § 5811(11)(B)(i))

51. A trust is taxable on its entire income if a trust or portion of a trust consisting of property of a person domiciled in Vermont at the time the property was transferred to the trust, if the trust was then irrevocable or if it was then revocable and has not subsequently become irrevocable or of a person domiciled in Vermont at the time the trust or portion of the trust became irrevocable, if it was revocable when the property was transferred to the trust but has subsequently become irrevocable. (§ 5811(11)(B)(ii)(I)-(II)) A trust or a portion of a trust is revocable if it is subject to a power, exercisable immediately or at any future time, to revest title in the person whose property constitutes such trust or portion of a trust, and a trust or portion of a trust becomes irrevocable when the possibility that such power may be exercised has been terminated. *Id.*

52. The Virginia taxable income of a nonresident estate or trust is its share of income, gain, loss and deduction attributable to Virginia sources as determined under § 58.1-363 increased or reduced, as the case may be, by: (1) The amount derived from or connected with Virginia sources of any income, gain, loss and deduction recognized for federal income tax purposes but excluded from the computation of distributable net income of the estate or trust; and (2) The net amount of any modifications as provided for in § 58.1-322 with respect to the income or gain as referred to above. (§ 58.1-362(1)-(2))

53. Under § 71.14(2) a trust created by a decedent, by will, contract, declaration of trust or implication of law, who at the time of death was a resident of Wisconsin is considered resident (and fully taxable) at the domicile of the decedent at death, until transferred by the court having jurisdiction to another court's jurisdiction.

54. Nonresident individuals and nonresident estates and trusts engaged in business within and without the state of Wisconsin are taxed only on such income as is derived from business transacted and property located within the state of Wisconsin. (§ 71.04(4))

Table 13.02
Estates

	An Estate Is Taxed on Its Entire Income If:							
	The Decedent Was At Death a Resident of the State	*The Decedent Was At Death Domiciled in the State*	*The Fiduciary Is a Resident of the State*	*The Estate Is Administered in the State*	*The Fiduciary Was Appointed By a Court in the State*	*The Beneficiary Is a Resident of the State*	*The Estate Is a Resident or Has a Situs in the State, But Residence or Situs Is Not Defined*	*Other Estates Taxed on Income From a Source in the State*
Alabama[1]	Yes. (§§ 40-18-25, 40-18-2(5), 40-18-2(7))	Yes. (§§ 40-18-2(7), 40-18-25)	No.	No.	No.	No.	Yes.[2]	Yes. (§ 40-18-25(c))
Alaska	*No income tax on estates*	—	—	—	—	—	—	—
Arizona	Yes. (§ 43-1301(4))	No.	No.	No.	No.	No.	No.	Yes, with respect to a nonresident estate. (§ 43-1301(1)(a))
Arkansas	Yes. (§§ 26-51-201(a) & (b), 26-51-102(9))	Yes. (§§ 26-51-102 (9), 26-51-201 (a) & (b))	No.	No.	No.	Yes. (§ 26-51-201 (b) & (c))	Yes.[3]	Yes. (§ 26-51-202)
California	Yes, regardless of the residence of the fiduciary or beneficiary. (Rev. & Tax. § 17742(a))[4]	Yes.[5] (Rev. & Tax. § 17014(a))	No.	No.	No.	No.	No.	No, however, a non-resident beneficiary is taxed on income from a trust to the extent derived from sources in the state. (Rev. & Tax. § 17734)

Table 13.02
Estates *(continued)*

An Estate Is Taxed on Its Entire Income If:

	The Decedent Was At Death a Resident of the State	*The Decedent Was At Death Domiciled in the State*	*The Fiduciary Is a Resident of the State*	*The Estate Is Administered in the State*	*The Fiduciary Was Appointed By a Court in the State*	*The Beneficiary Is a Resident of the State*	*The Estate Is a Resident or Has a Situs in the State, But Residence or Situs Is Not Defined*	*Other Estates Taxed on Income From a Source in the State*
Colorado	No.	No.	No.	Yes. (§§ 39-22-103(7), 39-22-104(1.7))	No.	No.	No.	Yes. (§ 39-22-404)
Connecticut	Yes. (§ 12-701 (a)(4)(A))	No. (§ 12-701 (a) (4))	No.	No.	No.	No.	No.	Yes. (§§ 12-713, 12-714(a)(1))
Delaware	No.	Yes. (30 §§ 1601(7), 1632)	No.	No.	No.	No.	No.	Yes.[6] (30 § 1639)
District of Columbia	No.	Yes. (§§ 47-1809.01, 47-1809.3)	No.[7] (§ 47-1809.02)	No.	No.	No.	No.	No.
Florida	*No income tax on estates.* (§ 220.02)	—	—	—	—	—	—	—
Georgia	No.	No.	Yes.[8] (§ 48-7-22 (a)(1))	No.	No.	Yes.[9] (§ 48-7-22(a) (1) & (c))	No.	Yes.[10] (§§ 48-7-22, 48-7-30)
Hawaii	Yes. (§§ 235-1, 235-4(e)(1))	Yes. (§§ 235-1, 235-4(e)(1))	No.	Yes. (§§ 235-1, 235-4(e)(1))	Yes. (§§ 235-1, 235-4(e)(1))	Yes.[11] (§ 235-4(e)(2))	No.	Yes. (§ 235-4(e)(1))
Idaho	No.	Yes. (Admin. Code §35.01.01.034)	No.	No.	No.	No.	Yes.[12] (§ 63-3030 (a)(5))	Yes.[13] (§ 63-3030 (a)(6))

Illinois	No.	Yes. (35 ILCS §§ 5/1501(a) (20) (B), 5/201(a))	No.	No.	No.	No.	No.	Yes. (35 ILCS §§ 5/301(c) (1), 5/306)
Indiana	Yes.[14] (§§ 6-3-1-12(c), 6-3-2-1(a))	Yes. (§§ 6-3-1-12(c), 6-3-2-1(a))	No.	No.	No.	No.	No.	Yes. (§ 6-3-2-1(a))
Iowa	No.	No.	No.	No.	No.	No.	Yes.[15]	Yes. (§ 422.8)
Kansas	No.	Yes. (§§ 79-32,109(c), 79-32,134)	No.	No.	No.	No.	No.	Yes. (§ 79-32,137)
Kentucky[16]	No.	No.	No.	No.	No.	Yes.[17]	Yes.[18]	Yes.[19] (§§ 141.020(4), 141.030(1))
Louisiana[20]	No.	Yes. (§ 47:300.10(2))	No.	No.	No.	No.	No.	Yes. (§§ 47:300.3 (2), 47:300.7)
Maine	No.	Yes. (36 § 5102 (4)(A), 5160)	No.	No.	No.	No.	No.	Yes. (36 § 5175)
Maryland[21]	No.	Yes. (Tax-Gen. § 10-101(K)(1) (ii))	No.	No.	No.	No.	No.	Yes. (Tax-Gen. § 10-210)
Massachusetts	Yes. (62 §§ 9, 1(f))	Yes. (62 §§ 9, 1(f))	No.	No.	No.	Yes. (62 § 9)	No.	Yes. (62 §§ 5A, 9)
Michigan	Yes. (§§ 206.18 (a) & (c), 206.110(1))	Yes.[22] (§§ 206.18(b), 206.110(1))	No.	No.	No.	No.	No.	Yes. (§§ 206.51(4), 206.110(2))
Minnesota	No.	Yes. (§§ 290.01 (7a), 290.22)	No.	Yes. (§§ 290.01 (7a), 290.22)	Yes.[23] (§§ 290.01 (7a), 290.22)	No.	No.	Yes. (§ 290.014 subdiv. 3(1))

Table 13.02
Estates *(continued)*

An Estate Is Taxed on Its Entire Income If:

	The Decedent Was At Death a Resident of the State	*The Decedent Was At Death Domiciled in the State*	*The Fiduciary Is a Resident of the State*	*The Estate Is Administered in the State*	*The Fiduciary Was Appointed By a Court in the State*	*The Beneficiary Is a Resident of the State*	*The Estate Is a Resident or Has a Situs in the State, But Residence or Situs Is Not Defined*	*Other Estates Taxed on Income From a Source in the State*
Mississippi	No.	No.	No.	No.	No.	No.	Yes.[24]	Yes. (§§ 27-7-5(3), 27-7-23(b))
Missouri	No.	Yes. (§§ 143.331(1), 143.341)	No.	No.	No.	No.	No.	Yes. (§ 143.381)
Montana	No.	No.	Yes.[25]	No.	No.	Yes.[26] (§ 15-30-135(1) & (2))	No.	Yes. (§ 15-30-105(1))
Nebraska	No.	Yes. (§§ 77-2714.01 (6)(a), 77-2717)	No.	No.	No.	No.	No.	Yes.[27] (§§ 77-2717(b),77-2724)
Nevada	*No income tax on estates*	—	—	—	—	—	—	—
New Hampshire	Maybe.[28] (§ 77:9)	Yes.[29]	No.	No.	No.	No.	No.	No.
New Jersey	No.	Yes. (§§ 54A: 1-2(o)(1), 54A:2-1)	No.	No.	No.	No.	No.	Yes. (§ 54A:5-8)
New Mexico	No.	No.	No.	No.	No.	No.	Yes.[30] (§§ 7-2-2, 7-2-3)	Yes. (§§ 7-2-2(I), 7-2-3)
New York	No.	Yes. (Tax §§ 605(b)(3) (A), 618)	No.	No.	No.	No.	No.	Yes. (Tax §§ 601(e), 633)

North Carolina	No.	No.	No.	No.	No.	Yes. (§ 105-160.2, 17 ADC § 6B.3716(b) (2))	No.	Yes. (17 ADC § 6B.3716(b)(1)) Also, a nonresident beneficiary is taxed on income from a trust to the extent derived from sources in the state.[31] (§ 105-160.2)
North Dakota[32]	No.	No.	Yes, or domiciliary.[33] (Admin. Code § 81-03-02.1-04.(2)(b))	Yes.[34] (Admin. Code § 81-03-02.1-04.(2)(d))	No.	Yes, or domiciliary.[35] (Admin. Code § 81-03-02.1-04.(2)(b))	No. Residence is defined, but situs has not been defined[36]	Yes. However, restricted in thecase of income from intangibles.[37](§§ 57-38-07, 57-38-05) In the case of income from tangible property, it is limited to property with a situs in the state.[38] (§ 57-38-04(3))
Ohio	No.	Yes. (§§ 5747.01(I) (2), 5747.02(A))	No.	No.	No.	No.	No.	Yes. (§ 5747.02(A))
Oklahoma	No.	Yes. (68 §§ 2353(5), 2355)	No.	No.	No.	No.	No.	Yes. (68 § 2362)
Oregon	No.	No.	No.	Yes.[39] (§§ 316.282(1) (b), 316.267)	Yes.[40] (§§ 316.282(1) (b), 316.267)	No.	No.	Yes. (§§ 316.307(3) & (4), 316.312(1))

Table 13.02
Estates *(continued)*

An Estate Is Taxed on Its Entire Income If:

	The Decedent Was At Death a Resident of the State	*The Decedent Was At Death Domiciled in the State*	*The Fiduciary Is a Resident of the State*	*The Estate Is Administered in the State*	*The Fiduciary Was Appointed By a Court in the State*	*The Beneficiary Is a Resident of the State*	*The Estate Is a Resident or Has a Situs in the State, But Residence or Situs Is Not Defined*	*Other Estates Taxed on Income From a Source in the State*
Pennsylvania	Yes.[41] §§ 7301(p) & (r), 7302(a))	Yes. (72 §§ 7301(p) & (r), 7302(a))	No.	No.	No.	No.	No.	Yes. (72 § 7302(b))
Rhode Island	Yes.[42] (§§ 44-30-5(c)(1), 44-30-5(a)(2), 44-30-1)	Yes. (§§ 44-30-5(a) & (c)(1), 44-30-5(a)(1), 44-30-1)	No.	No.	No.	No.	No.	Yes. (§§ 44-30-1, 44-30-35)
South Carolina	No.	Yes. (§§ 12-6-30(4), 12-6-610)	No.	No.	No.	No.	No.	Yes. (§§ 12-6-1720, 12-6-620)
South Dakota	*No income tax on estates*	—	—	—	—	—	—	—
Tennessee	Yes. (§§ 67-2-101(5), 67-2-110)	Yes. (§§ 67-2-101(5), 67-2-110)	No.	No.	No.	Yes. (§ 67-2-110)	No.	No.
Texas	*No income tax on estates*	—	—	—	—	—	—	—
Utah	No.	Yes. (§§ 59-10-103(1)(w), 59-10-201, 75-7-103(1)(i)(i))	No.	No.	No.	No.	No.	Yes. (§ 59-10-204)
Vermont	No.	Yes. (32 §§ 5811 (12), 5822)	No.	No.	No.	No.	No.	Yes. (32 § 5823(b))

Virginia	No.	Yes. (§§ 58.1-302, 58.1-361(A))	No.	Yes. (§§ 58.1-302, 58.1-361(A))	No.	No.	No.	Yes.[43] (§ 58.1-362)
Washington	*No income tax on estates*	—	—	—	—	—	—	—
West Virginia	No.	Yes. (§§ 11-21-7(c)(1), 11-21-18)	No.	No.	No.	No.	No.	Yes. (§§ 11-21-38, 11-21-39)
Wisconsin	No.	Yes. (§§ 71.02, 71.14(1))	No.	No.	No.	No.	No.	Yes.[44] (§§ 71.02, 71.04(4))
Wyoming	*No income tax on estates*	—	—	—	—	—	—	—

1. "Every estate and trust resident in Alabama" is taxed on all taxable income. (§ 40-18-2(a)(5)) A resident estate is the estate of any person who was a resident of Alabama at death. (§ 40-18-1(20)) A resident trust is resident in a particular year if it was created by will of a person who died a resident, or became irrevocable when the settlor was a resident, and for more than 7 months in the year a person who resided in Alabama or is domiciled there is a fiduciary or a beneficiary to whom distributions are currently being made. (§ 40-18-1(21)) Quaere whether a single resident beneficiary can trigger taxation of all of the trust's income.
2. *Id.* However, a resident estate or trust that has gross income taxable in Alabama and another state will be allowed a credit for net income taxes paid to the other state on such income as provided in § 40-18-21. (AL ADC 810-3-25-.04(2))
3. Income tax is imposed on the entire income of every resident trust and estate. (§ 26-51-201(a)) However, the terms are not defined in the Code. Under § 26-51-201(b) and (c), trusts and estates created by a nonresident trustor, donor, settlor, or a nonresident testator, even though administered by a resident trustee or personal representative, or trusts being administered by a resident trustee of which the beneficiaries are nonresidents are taxed only on income from real or tangible personal property and unincorporated businesses domiciled in Arkansas. The same limitation applies to estates administered by resident personal representatives of which the beneficiaries are nonresidents. (§ 26-51-202) By negative implication this suggests that trusts and estates created by a resident trustor, donor, settlor, or a resident testator would be taxed on their entire income. It also appears that if the beneficiaries of the estate or trust are residents of Arkansas, the trust or estate may be taxed on its entire income.
4. An individual who is not domiciled in the state may still be a resident if in the state for other than a "temporary or transitory purpose." (Rev. & Tax § 17014(a)(1)) Though temporarily absent from the state, a person does not lose his residency. (*Id.* § 17014(c))
5. An individual who is domiciled in the state is deemed a resident and thus subject to tax. Domicile, as distinct from residence, is relevant if the person is outside the state "for a temporary or transitory purpose." (Rev. & Tax § 17014(a)(2)) Certain domiciliaries may be treated as not being outside for a temporary or transitory purpose and, thus, being a nonresident, if absent from the state for at least 546 consecutive days under an employment-related contract, but subject to certain other restrictions as well. (*Id.* § 17014(b)&(d))
6. In the case of a nonresident estate or nonresident trust:(1) Items of income, gain, loss and deduction mean those derived from, or connected with, sources in this State; (2) Items of income, gain, loss and deduction entering into the definition of federal distributable net income include such items from another estate or trust of which the first estate or trust is a beneficiary; (3) The source of items of income, gain, loss or deduction shall be determined under rules or regulations prescribed by the Director in accordance with the rules of 30 § 1124, as if the estate or trust were a nonresident individual. (30 § 1639)
7. The residence or situs of the fiduciary does not control the classification of estates and trusts as resident or nonresident. (§ 47-1809.02)
8. Tax is imposed upon resident fiduciaries and upon nonresident fiduciaries: receiving income from business done in Georgia, managing funds or property located in Georgia, or managing funds or property for the benefit of a resident of Georgia. (§ 48-7-22(a)(1)(A)-(C))
9. Tax is imposed upon resident fiduciaries and upon nonresident fiduciaries managing funds or property for the benefit of a resident of Georgia. (§ 48-7-22(a)(1)(C))
10. Tax is imposed upon resident fiduciaries and upon nonresident fiduciaries receiving income from business done in Georgia or managing funds or property located in Georgia. (§ 48-7-22(a)(1)(A)-(B))
11. A resident beneficiary is taxed on income whether or not the estate is taxed. (§ 235-4(e)(2)) The key question is whether the beneficiary would have been taxed if the income had been received directly. *(Id.)* Residents are taxed on all their income regardless of source. (§ 235-4(a))

12. "Every estate, the residence of which estate is in Idaho, having gross income of $600 or more for the current taxable year" is subject to taxation. (§ 63-3030(a)(5)) Although no statutory provision or case indicates when an estate has a residence in the state, the Admin. Code § 35.01.01.034 indicates that it is when the decedent died domiciled in Idaho, and if the estate is other than an estate of a decedent, it is treated as a resident estate if the person for whom the estate was created is a resident of Idaho.
13. "Every estate, the residence of which is in a state other than Idaho, having a gross income from Idaho sources in excess of $600" is subject to taxation. (§ 60-3030(a)(6))
14. The term "resident" means that the decedent was domiciled in Indiana during the taxable year or had maintained a permanent place of residence in Indiana and spent more than 183 days within the taxable year there.
15. An estate or trust is taxed like an individual. A nonresident is taxed on what is essentially Iowa-source income. A resident is taxed "on all taxable income." (§ 422.5) Only an individual can be a resident. (§ 422.4(15)) Nevertheless, the differences between residents and nonresidents are made applicable to estates and trusts by the reference in § 422.6 to § 422.5. The problem is that the statute, case law, and administrative regulations fail to indicate what makes an estate or trust resident or nonresident.
16. Section 141.030(1) makes trusts and estates taxable like individuals. Under § 141.020(4), a nonresident individual is taxed on his Kentucky-source income. However, the statute, case law, and administrative regulations do not establish what makes an estate resident or nonresident. However, 103 KY ADC 19:010, § 4 provides that a resident estate or trust must report and pay tax on all taxable income except that portion of net income distributable or distributed during the taxable year, and that portion of the net income from intangible personal property attributable to a nonresident beneficiary. Also, a resident beneficiary must report and pay tax on his share of the distributed or distributable income from a resident or nonresident estate or trust. (103 KY ADC 19:010, § 5) In addition, a nonresident estate, trust, or beneficiary is subject to tax only on income received from real or tangible personal property located in Kentucky. (103 KY ADC 19:010, § 6)
17. *Id.*
18. *Id.*
19. Also, the Administrative Code provides that a nonresident estate, trust, or beneficiary is subject to tax only on income received from real or tangible personal property located in Kentucky. (103 KY ADC 19:010, § 6)
20. Pursuant to 47:181, the taxes imposed on individuals apply to estates and trusts. Pursuant to 47:182, the net income of an estate or trust is computed in the same manner as for individuals, subject to certain adjustments. Pursuant to 47:241, a nonresident individual is taxed primarily on income from sources within Louisiana. However, the statute, case law, and administrative regulations fail to indicate what makes an estate or trust resident or nonresident. However, all of the foregoing provisions are superseded to the extent inconsistent with §§ 47:300.1-300.11. See § 47:300.11. Thus, the latter provisions are the primary authority. A resident estate is an estate of a decedent who was domiciled in Louisiana at the time of his death. (§ 47:300.10(2)) Non-U.S. estates have the alternative to elect to be taxed at a flat 5% of total gross income from Louisiana sources. (§ 47:300.3(3))
21. Section 10-102 states that a "Tax is imposed on the Maryland taxable income of each individual and of each corporation." The Code then defines Individual as ". . . a natural person or a fiduciary" in § 10-101(e). Under § 10-210, a nonresident individual is essentially taxed on his Maryland-source income. Accordingly, the same would be true of a nonresident trust or estate, as these terms are defined in § 10-101(h)(1)(ii) & (iii).
22. "Domicile" means a place where a person has his true, fixed and permanent home and principal establishment to which, whenever absent therefrom he intends to return, and domicile continues until another permanent establishment is established. (§ 206.18(a)) If a person is domiciled in Michigan at least 183 days during the tax year or more than half the days during a taxable year of less than 12 months, that person is a resident individual domicilied in the state of Michigan. Id.
23. The administration of the estate carried on in Minnesota must be in a proceeding other than an ancillary proceeding. (§ 290.01(7a))
24. A "nonresident" trust or estate is subject to taxation on what is essentially its Mississippi-source income. (§ 27-7-23) A "resident" trust or estate is taxed on "its entire net income." (§ 27-7-5) The statutes, case law, and administrative regulations fail to indicate what makes a trust or estate resident or nonresident.
25. A tax is imposed upon either the fiduciaries or the beneficiaries of estates and trusts, except to the extent such estates and trusts is held for educational, charitable, or religious purposes, and the tax is levied, collected, and paid annually with respect to the income of estates or of any kind of property held in trust, including: income received by estates of deceased persons during the period of administration or settlement of the estate; income accumulated in trust for the benefit of unborn or unascertained persons or persons with contingent interests; income held for future distribution under the terms of the will or trust; and income which is to be distributed to the beneficiaries periodically, whether or not at regular intervals, and the income collected by a guardian of a minor, to be held or distributed as the court may direct. The fiduciary is responsible for making the return of income for the estate or trust for which he acts, whether the fiduciary or the beneficiaries are taxable with reference to the income of such estate or trust. (§ 15-30-135(1)-(2))
26. *Id.*
27. The tax imposed on all nonresident estates and trusts is the portion of the tax imposed on resident estates and trusts which is attributable to the income derived from sources within Nebraska. The tax which is attributable to income derived from sources within Nebraska is determined by multiplying the liability to Nebraska for a resident estate or trust with the same total income by a fraction, the numerator of which is the nonresident estate's or trust's Nebraska income as determined by sections 77-2724 and 77-2725 and the denominator of which is its total federal income after first adjusting each by the amounts provided in section 77-2716. (§ 77-2717(b))
28. The statute uses the term "dwelt"; however, a definition of "dwelt" is not provided. One case, Stark v. Parker, 56 N.H. 481 (Sup. Ct. 1876), indicates "dwelt" is actually synonymous with domicile and not residence.
29. *Id.*
30. An "individual" includes an estate or a fiduciary acting for an estate. (§ 7-2-2(I)) This suggests that the fiduciary may provide a separate nexus for taxation, than the estate itself. The estate as an "individual," would be subject to tax on what is essentially New Mexico-source income if it is a "nonresident individual." It is subject to tax on its "net income" if it is a "resident individual." The statute, case law, and administrative regulations fail to indicate when an estate is resident or nonresident. The statute does provide that "resident" means an individual who is domiciled in New Mexico during any part of the taxable year or an individual who is physically present in New Mexico for one hundred eighty-five days or more during the taxable year; but any individual, other than someone who was physically

present in New Mexico for one hundred eighty-five days or more during the taxable year, who, on or before the last day of the taxable year, changed his place of abode to a place without New Mexico with the bona fide intention of continuing actually to abide permanently without New Mexico is not a resident for the purposes of the Income Tax Act for periods after that change of abode. (§ 7-2-2(S)) Fiduciary Income Tax Instructions Form FID-1 states that an estate must file a return if the decedent was a resident of New Mexico or the estate had income from transactions of business into or from New Mexico, or property in New Mexico, or compensation in New Mexico.

31. A nonresident beneficiary is taxed on income from an estate or trust to the extent that the income (i) is derived from North Carolina sources and is attributable to the ownership of any interest in real or tangible personal property in the state of North Carolina or (ii) is derived from a business, trade, profession, or occupation carried on in the state of North Carolina. (§ 105-160.2) If an estate or trust has income from sources outside of North Carolina and if any of the beneficiaries are nonresidents of North Carolina, the portion of federal taxable income of the Fiduciary that is subject to North Carolina tax must be determined. The determination of the amount of undistributed income from intangible property which is for the benefit of a resident is based on the beneficiary's state of residence on the last day of the taxable year of the trust. In the case of both resident and nonresident beneficiaries, the determination of the amount of undistributed income from intangible property which is for the benefit of a resident is made on the basis that the resident beneficiary's interest for the taxable year relates to the interest of both resident and nonresident income beneficiaries for the taxable year. (17 ADC § 6B.3724)

32. The tax imposed on individuals generally applies to estates and trusts. (§ 57-38-07) Individuals who are nonresidents are taxed on only certain types of North Dakota-source income. The administrative regulations instruct that a trust or estate is a resident trust or estate when it has a relationship to the state sufficient to create nexus. This includes, but is not limited to, the following contacts: (a) a beneficiary of the trust or estate is a domiciliary or resident of the state of North Dakota; (b) the trustee or executor is a domiciliary or resident of the state of North Dakota; (c) assets making up any part of the trust or estate have situs in the state of North Dakota; (d) any or all of the administration or income production of the trust or estate takes place within the state of North Dakota; (e) the laws of the state of North Dakota are specifically made applicable to the trust or estate or to the opposite parties with respect to their fiduciary relationship; (f) the trust is a revocable trust, and the grantor is a domiciliary or resident of the state of North Dakota. (Admin. Code § 81-03-02.1-04.(2)(a)-(f))

33. *Id.*

34. *Id.*

35. *Id.*

36. *Id.*

37. Income from intangibles subject to tax: Income and gains derived from transactions in the regular course of the taxpayer's trade or business carried on in this state, or the acquisition, management, and disposition of intangible personal property to the extent it constitutes a trade or business in the state. (§ 57-38-05)

38. The determination of when property has a situs in the state is not always easy to determine under the law.

39. A resident estate subject to tax is defined in § 316.282(1)(b) as "... an estate of which the fiduciary was appointed by an Oregon court or the administration of which is carried on in Oregon."

40. *Id.*

41. Resident includes those who are domiciled in the state unless he/she maintains no permanent place of abode in the state and does maintain a permanent place of abode elsewhere and spends in the aggregate not more than thirty days of the taxable year in the State, and those who are not domiciled in the state but who have a permanent abode in the state and who spend more than 183 days of the taxable year in the state. (72 § 7301(p))

42. Resident individual includes those who are domiciled in the state. In determining the domicile of an individual, the geographic location of professional advisors selected by an individual, including without limitation advisors who render medical, financial, legal, insurance, fiduciary or investment services, shall not be taken into consideration. (§ 44-30-5(a)(1)) Resident also includes those who are not domiciled in the state but who have a permanent abode in the state and who spend more than 183 days of the taxable year in the state, unless the individual is in the armed forces of the United States. (§ 44-30-5(a)(2))

43. The Virginia taxable income of a nonresident estate or trust is its share of income, gain, loss and deduction attributable to Virginia sources as determined under § 58.1-363 increased or reduced, as the case may be, by: (1) The amount derived from or connected with Virginia sources of any income, gain, loss and deduction recognized for federal income tax purposes but excluded from the computation of distributable net income of the estate or trust; and (2) The net amount of any modifications as provided for in § 58.1-322 with respect to the income or gain as referred to above. (§ 58.1-362(1)-(2))

44. Nonresident individuals and nonresident estates and trusts engaged in business within and without the state of Wisconsin are taxed only on such income as is derived from business transacted and property located within the state of Wisconsin. (§ 71.04(4))

Table 14
Income Tax Rates for Trusts and Estates (current through 5/1/07)

This table indicates the actual rates of taxation on trust and estate taxation. The table should be considered along with Tables 11.01 and 11.02, which detail the circumstances under which a state will exercise its jurisdiction to tax a trust's or estate's income.

As is apparent from the state-by-state analysis, there is a considerable range of rates from state to state. Thus, even if a trust or estate does have the necessary contacts for a particular state to tax the income, the rates are still important in terms of just how onerous the anticipated or actual tax will be. However, this table is only intended to provide a snapshot of the maximum tax based on gross income, since no consideration is given to the exclusions, deductions, and credits that may affect taxable income and the ultimate tax payable to the state. The table also does not set forth the principles under the particular state's law for determining how much income is to be allocated to the trust or estate and how much to the grantor or the beneficiaries. Finally, rates of *individual* taxation are not provided, even though this could prove helpful in deciding whether accumulation or distribution to beneficiaries in the case of a discretionary trust would be most tax-advantageous.

The reader should also be aware of the deduction allowed at the federal level for state income taxes paid. The value of this deduction will increase, and, thus, the burden of the state tax will decline, as the taxpayer moves into a higher federal tax bracket. Indeed, federal tax law will drive many decisions relating to the income taxation of trusts and estates. Still, this table will afford an important indication of the maximum exposure to income tax at the state level.

Table 14
Income Tax Rates for Trusts and Estates

	Comments	*Chart*
Alabama	The tax rate imposed on trusts and estates is the same tax rate as individuals who are single persons.[1] (§§ 40-18-25(a)–(c), 40-18-5(1); AL ADC 810-3-25-.04(1)) However, a resident estate or trust that has gross income taxable in Alabama and another state will be allowed a credit for net income taxes paid to the other state on such income as provided in § 40-18-21. (AL ADC 810-3-25-.04(2))	a. Two percent of taxable income not in excess of five hundred dollars ($500). b. Four percent of taxable income in excess of five hundred dollars ($500) and not in excess of three thousand dollars ($3,000). c. Five percent of taxable income in excess of three thousand dollars ($3,000).
Alaska		*No income tax on trusts and estates.*
Arizona	The tax rate imposed on trusts and estates is the same tax rate as "individuals," except for trusts that are taxable as partnerships or corporations under the Internal Revenue Code. However, individual is not defined. Arizona Administrative Code R15-5-2215(3)(d) defines an individual taxpayer filing as a "single" person as including trusts and estates. (§ 43-1311)	*If taxable income is:* — *The tax is:* $0–$10,000 — 2.87% of taxable income $10,001–$25,000 — $287, plus 3.20% of the excess over $10,000 $25,001–$50,000 — $767, plus 3.74% of the excess over $25,000 $50,001–$150,000 — $1,702, plus 4.72% of the excess over $50,000 $150,001 and over — $6,422, plus 5.04% of the excess over $150,000 (§ 43-1011(3)(a))
Arkansas	No tax due from a trust or estate of a nonresident settlor or trustee, even if a resident trustee or personal representative is serving, except if the income is derived from (a) land in Arkansas, as well as gains from sale; (b) interests in land and gains from the sale thereof; (c) tangible personal property, including gains from the sale thereof; and (d) unincorporated businesses domiciled in Arkansas. (§ 26-51-201(b)) Similar limitations apply with respect to income received by a nonresident beneficiary. (§ 26-51-201(b))	(1) On the first two thousand nine hundred ninety-nine dollars ($2,999) of net income or any part thereof, one percent (1%); (2) On the next three thousand dollars ($3,000) of net income or any part thereof, two and one-half percent (2.5%); (3) On the next three thousand dollars ($3,000) of net income or any part thereof, three and one-half percent (3.5%); (4) On the next six thousand dollars ($6,000) of net income or any part thereof, four and one-half percent (4.5%); (5) On the next ten thousand dollars ($10,000) of net income or any part thereof, six percent (6%); (6) On net income of twentyfive thousand dollars ($25,000) and above, seven percent (7%). (§ 26-51-201(a)(1)–(6))

California	The tax is imposed on federal taxable income, as modified and at rates for an individual. (Rev. & Tax §§ 17041(a)(1) & (e), 17731)	*If taxable income is:*	*The tax is:*
		Not over $3,650	1% of the taxable income
		Over $3,650 but not over $8,650	$36.50 plus 2% of excess over $3,650
		Over $8,650 but not over $13,650	$136.50 plus 4% of excess over $8,650
		Over $13,650 but not over $18,950	$336.50 plus 6% of excess over $13,650
		Over $18,950 but not over $23,950	$654.50 plus 8% of excess over $18,950
		Over $23,950	$1,054.50 plus 9.3% of excess over $23,950
		(Rev. & Tax. § 17041)	
Colorado	4.63% of federal taxable income, with certain modifications. (§ 39-22-104(1.7))		
Connecticut	For trusts or estates, the rate of tax is 4.5% of their Connecticut taxable income for taxable years commencing on or after January 1, 2003. (§ 12-700(a)(6)(D))		
Delaware	The trust or estate is taxed like an individual. (30 §§ 1631, 1632). However, the following trusts are not subject to tax: trusts taxable as corporations, tax-exempt trusts, and real estate investment trusts. (30 § 1633). There is also a separate tax on the ordinary income portion of a lump-sum distribution received by every resident estate or trust. (30 § 1102(b))	*If taxable income is:*	*The tax is:*
		Over $2,000	2.20%
		Over $5,000	3.90%
		Over $10,000	4.80%
		Over $20,000	5.20%
		Over $25,000	5.55%
		Over $60,000	5.95%
		(30 § 1102(a)(10) & (11))	
	Caution: 30 § 1636(a) permits a deduction to be taken by a resident estate or trust to the extent its federal taxable income is "set aside for future distribution to nonresident beneficiaries.		

Table 14
Income Tax Rates for Trusts and Estates *(continued)*

	Comments	Chart	
District of Columbia	The tax rate imposed on "residents" applies to the income of resident estates, and income from any kind of property held in trusts, including: (1) Income accumulated in trust for the benefit of unborn or unascertained person or persons with contingent interests, and income accumulated or held for future distribution under the terms of the will or trust; (2) income which is to be distributed currently by the fiduciary to the beneficiaries, and income collected by a guardian of any infant or incompetent person which is to be held or distributed as the court may direct; (3) income received by estates of deceased persons during the period of administration or settlement of the estate; and (4) income which, in the discretion of the fiduciary, may be either distributed to the beneficiaries or accumulated. (§ 47-1809.03)	For taxable years beginning after December 31, 2000 (§ 47-1806.03(a)(4)(A))	
		If taxable income is:	*The tax is:*
		Not over $10,000	5% of the taxable income
		Over $10,000 but not over $30,000	$500, plus 7.5% of the excess over $10,000
		Over $30,000	$2,000, plus 9.3% of the excess over $30,000
		For taxable years beginning after December 31, 2003 (§ 47-1806.03(a)(5)(A))	
		If taxable income is:	*The tax is:*
		Not over $10,000	5.0% of the taxable income
		Over $10,000 but not over $30,000	$500, plus 7.5% of the excess over $10,000
		Over $30,000	$2,000, plus 9.0% of the excess over $30,000
		For taxable years beginning after December 31, 2004 (§ 47-1806.03(a)(6)(A))	
		If taxable income is:	*The tax is:*
		Not over $10,000	4.5% of the taxable income
		Over $10,000 but not over $40,000	$450, plus 7% of the excess over $10,000
		Over $40,000	$2,550, plus 8.7% of the excess over $40,000
		For taxable years beginning after December 31, 2005 (§ 47-1806.03(a)(7)(A))	
		If taxable income is:	*The tax is:*
		Not over $10,000	4% of the taxable income
		Over $10,000 but not over $40,000	$400, plus 6% of the excess over $10,000
		Over $40,000	$2,200, plus 8.5% of the excess over $40,000

Florida		*No income tax on trusts and estates.* (§ 220.02)	
Georgia	The tax rate imposed on trusts and estates is the same tax rate as individuals. (§§ 48-7-22(b), 48-7-20(d))	*If Georgia taxable income is:*	*The tax is:*
		Not over $750.00	1%
		Over $750.00 but not over $2,250.00	$7.50 plus 2% of amount over $750.00
		Over $2,250.00 but not over $3,750.00	$37.50 plus 3% of amount over $2,250.00
		Over $3,750.00 but not over $5,250.00	$82.50 plus 4% of amount over $3,750.00
		Over $5,250.00 but not over $7,000.00	$142.50 plus 5% of amount over $5,250.00
		Over $7,000.00	$230.00 plus 6% of the amount over $7,000
		(§ 48-7-22(b))	
Hawaii		For taxable years beginning after December 31, 2001	
		If the taxable income is:	*The tax shall be:*
		Not over $2,000	1.40% of taxable income
		Over $2,000 but not over $4,000	$28.00 plus 3.20% of excess over $2,000
		Over $4,000 but not over $8,000	$92.00 plus 5.50% of excess over $4,000
		Over $8,000 but not over $12,000	$312.00 plus 6.40% of excess over $8,000
		Over $12,000 but not over $16,000	$568.00 plus 6.80% of excess over $12,000
		Over $16,000 but not over $20,000	$840.00 plus 7.20% of excess over $16,000
		Over $20,000 but not over $30,000	$1,128.00 plus 7.60% of excess over $20,000
		Over $30,000 but not over $40,000	$1,888.00 plus 7.90% of excess over $30,000
		Over $40,000	$2,678.00 plus 8.25% of excess over $40,000
		(§ 235-51(d))	
Idaho		*When Idaho taxable income is:*	*The rate is:*
		Less than $1,000	1.6%
		$1,000 but less than $2,000	$16, plus 3.6% of the amount over $1,000
		(cont'd)	*(cont'd)*

Table 14
Income Tax Rates for Trusts and Estates *(continued)*

State	Comments	Chart	
Idaho *(cont'd)*		$2,000 but less than $3,000	$52, plus 4.1% of the amount over $2,000
		$3,000 but less than $4,000	$93, plus 5.1% of the amount over $3,000
		$4,000 but less than $5,000	$144, plus 6.1% of the amount over $4,000
		$5,000 but less than $7,500	$205, plus 7.1% of the amount over $5,000
		$7,500 but less than $20,000	$383, plus 7.4% of the amount over $7,500
		Over $20,000	$1308, plus 7.8% of the amount over $20,000
		(§ 63-3024(a))	
Illinois		(1) In the case of an individual, trust or estate, for taxable years ending prior to July 1, 1989, an amount equal to 2.5% of the taxpayer's net income for the taxable year. (2) In the case of an individual, trust or estate, for taxable years beginning prior to July 1, 1989, and ending after June 30, 1989, an amount equal to the sum of (i) 2.5% of the taxpayer's net income for the period prior to July 1, 1989, as calculated under Section 202.3, and (ii) 3% of the taxpayer's net income for the period after June 30, 1989, as calculated under Section 202.3. (3) In the case of an individual, trust or estate, for taxable years beginning after June 30, 1989, an amount equal to 3% of the taxpayer's net income for the taxable year. (35 ILCS 5/201(b))	
Indiana	The tax rate imposed on trusts and estates is the same tax rate as residents. (§ 6-3-1-12) The tax rate is 3.4% of adjusted gross income of every resident, and on the adjusted gross income derived from sources within Indiana of every nonresident. (§ 6-3-2-1)		
Iowa	The tax rate imposed on individuals applies as well to trusts and estates. (§ 422.6)	a. On all taxable income from zero through one thousand dollars, thirtysix hundredths of one percent. b. On all taxable income exceeding one thousand dollars but not exceeding two thousand dollars, seventy-two hundredths of one percent.	

		c. On all taxable income exceeding two thousand dollars but not exceeding four thousand dollars, two and forty-three hundredths percent. d. On all taxable income exceeding four thousand dollars but not exceeding nine thousand dollars, four and one-half percent. e. On all taxable income exceeding nine thousand dollars but not exceeding fifteen thousand dollars, six and twelve hundredths percent. f. On all taxable income exceeding fifteen thousand dollars but not exceeding twenty thousand dollars, six and forty-eight hundredths percent. g. On all taxable income exceeding twenty thousand dollars but not exceeding thirty thousand dollars, six and eight-tenths percent. h. On all taxable income exceeding thirty thousand dollars but not exceeding forty-five thousand dollars, seven and ninety-two hundredths percent. i. On all taxable income exceeding forty-five thousand dollars, eight and ninety-eight hundredths percent. (§ 422.5(1)(a)-(i)) There is imposed upon every resident and nonresident of Iowa, including estates and trusts, the greater of the tax determined in "a" through "i" above or the state alternative minimum tax equal to seventy-five percent of the maximum state individual income tax rate for the tax year, rounded to the nearest one-tenth of one percent, of the state alternative minimum taxable income of the taxpayer (§ 422.5(1)(k)), which also sets forth the computation of the alternative minimum tax.
Kansas	The tax rate imposed on the Kansas taxable income of trusts and estates is the same rates as imposed on unmarried resident individuals. (§§ 79-32,110(d), 79-32,110(a)(2)(B))	For tax year 1998, and all tax years thereafter *If the taxable income is:* — *The tax is:* Not over $15,000 — 3.5% of Kansas taxable income Over $15,000 but not over $30,000 — $525 plus 6.25% of excess over $15,000 Over $30,000 — $1,462.50 plus 6.45% of excess over $30,000
Kentucky	The tax rate imposed on trusts and estates is the same tax rate as imposed on individuals. (§§ 141.030(1), 141.020))	For taxable years beginning before January 1, 2005: (1) Two percent (2%) of the amount of net income not exceeding three thousand dollars ($3,000); (2) Three percent (3%) of the amount of net income in excess of three thousand dollars ($3,000) but not in excess of four thousand dollars ($4,000); (3) Four percent (4%) of the amount of net income in excess of four thousand dollars ($4,000) but not in excess of five thousand dollars ($5,000); (4) Five percent (5%) of the amount of net income in excess of five thousand dollars ($5,000) but not in excess of eight thousand dollars ($8,000);

(cont'd)

Table 14
Income Tax Rates for Trusts and Estates *(continued)*

	Comments	Chart
Kentucky *(cont'd)*		(5) Six percent (6%) of the amount of net income in excess of eight thousand dollars ($8,000). (§ 141.020(2)(a)) For taxable years beginning after December 31, 2004: (1) Two percent (2%) of the amount of net income not exceeding three thousand dollars ($3,000); (2) Three percent (3%) of the amount of net income in excess of three thousand dollars ($3,000) but not in excess of four thousand dollars ($4,000); (3) Four percent (4%) of the amount of net income in excess of four thousand dollars ($4,000) but not in excess of five thousand dollars ($5,000); (4) Five percent (5%) of the amount of net income in excess of five thousand dollars ($5,000) but not in excess of eight thousand dollars ($8,000); (5) Five and eight-tenths percent (5.8%) of the amount of net income in excess of eight thousand dollars ($8,000) but not in excess of seventy-five thousand dollars ($75,000); (6) Six percent (6%) of the amount of net income in excess of seventy-five thousand dollars ($75,000). (§ 141.020(2)(b))
Louisiana	An income tax is imposed for each taxable year upon the Louisiana taxable income of every estate or trust, whether resident or nonresident. (§ 47:300.1) The taxes imposed apply to the income of estates or of any kind of property held in trust including: (1) Income accumulated in trust for the benefit of unborn or unascertained persons or persons with contingent interests and income accumulated or held for future distribution under the terms of the will or trust. (2) Income that is to be distributed currently by the fiduciary to the beneficiaries and income collected by a guardian of an infant that is to be held or distributed as the court may direct.	The tax to be assessed, levied, collected, and paid upon the Louisiana taxable income of an estate or trust is computed at the following rates: (1) Two percent on the first ten thousand dollars of Louisiana taxable income. (2) Four percent on the next forty thousand dollars of Louisiana taxable income. (3) Six percent on Louisiana taxable income in excess of fifty thousand dollars. (§ 47:300.1)

	(3) Income received by the estates of deceased persons during the period of administration or settlement of the estate. (4) Income that, in the discretion of the fiduciary, may be either distributed to the beneficiaries or accumulated. (§ 47:300.2)		
Maine	The rates are imposed as for resident individuals. (36 §§ 5160, 5111(1-B))	*Maine Taxable Income* Less than $4,200 At least $4,200 but less than $8,350 At least $8,350 but less than $16,700 $16,700 or more (§ 5111(1-B))	*The tax is:* 2.0% $84 plus 4.5% of excess over $4,200 $271 plus 7.0% of excess over $8,360 $856 plus 8.5% of excess over $16,700
Maryland	The tax rate imposed on trusts and estates is the same tax rate as individuals (Tax-Gen. §§ 10-101(g), 10-105(a)) in that the term "individual" is defined to include a fiduciary.	(1) 2% of Maryland taxable income of $1 through $1,000; (2) 3% of Maryland taxable income of $1,001 through $2,000; (3) 4% of Maryland taxable income of $2,001 through $3,000; and (4) for Maryland taxable income in excess of $3,000: (i) 4.875% for a taxable year beginning after December 31, 1997 but before January 1, 1999; (ii) 4.85% for a taxable year beginning after December 31, 1998 but before January 1, 2000; (iii) 4.85% for a taxable year beginning after December 31, 1999 but before January 1, 2001; (iv) 4.8% for a taxable year beginning after December 31, 2000 but before January 1, 2002;and (v) 4.75% for a taxable year beginning after December 31, 2001. (§ 10-105(a))	
Massachusetts	Trusts and estates are taxed at the same rates as individuals. (62 § 10(a)&(c)) Massachusetts gross income is divided into three parts. Part A gross income consists of certain interest that is not exempted, such as bank account interest (62 § 2(b)(1)(A)) dividends, and short-term capital gains. (62 § 2(b)(1)(C)) Part B gross income is the rest of Massachusetts gross income that is not Part A or Part C. (62 § 2(b)(2)) Part C gross income is capital gain income of capital assets held for more than one year. (62 § 2(b)(3))	*Class* A, short-term capital gain A, interest and dividends B C (62 § 4)	*Rate* 12.0% 5.95% 5.3% 5.3%

Table 14
Income Tax Rates for Trusts and Estates *(continued)*

	Comments	*Chart*
Michigan	The tax rate imposed on trusts and estates is the tax rate "levied and imposed upon the taxable income of every person other than a corporation." (§§ 206.51(8)(a)(iii), 206.51(1))	(a) On and after January 1, 2004 and before July 1, 2004, 4.0%. (b) On and after July 1, 2004, 3.9%. (§ 206.51e) (c) For tax years that begin on or after January 1, 2003 and before January 1, 2004—4.0% (§ 206.51d)
Minnesota	Estates and trusts must compute their income tax by applying the rates imposed upon married individuals filing joint returns and surviving spouses to their taxable income, except that the income brackets will be one half of the amounts listed on the chart given. (§290.06 Subd. 2c(a))	(1) On the first $25,680, 5.35 percent; (2) On all over $25,680, but not over $102,030, 7.05 percent; (3) On all over $102,030, 7.85 percent. (§290.06 Subd. 2c(a))
Mississippi		On the first five thousand dollars ($5,000.00) of taxable income, or any part thereof, at the rate of three percent (3%); On the next five thousand dollars ($5,000.00) of taxable income, or any part thereof, at the rate of four percent (4%); and On all taxable income in excess of ten thousand dollars ($10,000.00), at the rate of five percent (5%). (§ 27-7-5)
Missouri	The tax rate imposed on trusts and estates is the same as is imposed on resident individuals, with some modifications. Rate tables are actually provided for "resident individuals." (§§ 143.311, 143.061, 143.011)	*If the Missouri taxable income is:* — *The tax is:* Not over $1,000.00 — 1.5% of the Missouri taxable income Over $1,000 but not over $2,000 — $15 plus 2% of excess over $1,000 Over $2,000 but not over $3,000 — $35 plus 2.5% of excess over $2,000 Over $3,000 but not over $4,000 — $60 plus 3% of excess over $3,000 Over $4,000 but not over $5,000 — $90 plus 3.5% of excess over $4,000 Over $5,000 but not over $6,000 — $125 plus 4% of excess over $5,000 Over $6,000 but not over $7,000 — $165 plus 4.5% of excess over $6,000 Over $7,000 but not over $8,000 — $210 plus 5% of excess over $7,000 Over $8,000 but not over $9,000 — $260 plus 5.5% of excess over $8,000 Over $9,000 — $315 plus 6% of excess over $9,000 (§ 143.011)
Montana	The tax rate imposed on trusts and estates is the same tax rate as is imposed on individuals. (§§ 15-30-137, 15-30-103(1) &	(1) (a) on the first $2,300 of taxable income or any part of that income, 1%;

	(2)) Credits allowed individuals under Title 15, chapter 30, also apply to estates and trusts when applicable. (§ 15-30-137)	(b) on the next $1,800 of taxable income or any part of that income, 2%; (c) on the next $2,100 of taxable income or any part of that income, 3%; (d) on the next $2,200 of taxable income or any part of that income, 4%; (e) on the next $2,400 of taxable income or any part of that income, 5%; (f) on the next $3,100 of taxable income or any part of that income, 6%; (g) on any taxable income in excess of $13,900 or any part of that income, 6.9%. (§ 15-30-103(1)) (2) By November 1 of each year, the department will multiply the bracket amount contained in subsection (1) above by the inflation factor for that taxable year and round the cumulative brackets to the nearest $100. The resulting adjusted brackets are effective for that taxable year and are used as the basis for imposition of the tax in subsection (1). (§ 15-30-103(2))
Nebraska	Trusts and estates are taxed at the same rates as individuals. (§§ 77-2715(4), 77-2717(1)(a)(iii)) (The primary rate of tax is 3.7% (§ 77-2701.01) In the case of taxable years beginning on or after January 1, 2003, the primary rate is multiplied by the following factors from the lowest to highest brackets: .6932, .9646, 1.3846, and 1.848 (§ 77-2715.02(e)), with rounding to hundredths of one percent. (§ 77-2715.02(b))	*Taxable Income Over* / *But Not Over* / *Rate* 0 / $500 / 2.56% $500 / $4,700 / 3.57% $4,700 / $15,150 / 5.12% $15,150 / / 6.84% (§ 77-2715.02(2)(a) & (e))
Nevada		*No income tax on trusts and estates.*
New Hampshire		5% tax rate on income from interest and dividends. (§§ 77:1, 77:3, 77:9, 77:10)
New Jersey	A tax is imposed for each taxable year on the New Jersey gross income of every estate or trust (other than a charitable trust or a trust forming part of a pension or profit-sharing plan). (§ 54A:2-1)	*If the taxable income is:* — *The tax is:* Not over $20,000 — 1.400% of taxable income Over $20,000 but not over $35,000 — $280.00 plus 1.750% of the excess over $20,000 Over $35,000 but not over $40,000 — $542.50 plus 3.500% of the excess over $35,000 Over $40,000 but not over $75,000 — $717.50 plus 5.525% of the excess over $40,000 Over $75,000 but not over $500,000 — $2,651.25 plus 6.370% of excess over $75,000 Over $500,000 — $29,723.75 plus 8.970% of the excess over $500,000 (§ 54A:2-1(b)(4))

Table 14
Income Tax Rates for Trusts and Estates *(continued)*

	Comments	Chart	
New Mexico	The tax rate imposed on estates and trusts is the same tax rate imposed on single individuals. (§ 7-2-2(I))	For any taxable year beginning in 2006:	*The tax shall be:*
		If the taxable income is:	
		Not over $5,500	1.7% of taxable income
		Over $5,500 but not over $11,000	$93.50 plus 3.2% of excess over $5,500
		Over $11,000 but not over $16,000	$269.50 plus 4.7% of excess over $11,000
		Over $16,000 (§ 7-2-7)	$504.50 plus 6.0% of excess over $16,000
		For any taxable year beginning on or after January 1, 2007:	*The tax shall be:*
		If the taxable income is:	
		Not over $5,500	1.7% of taxable income
		Over $5,500 but not over $11,000	$93.50 plus 3.2% of excess over $5,500
		Over $11,000 but not over $16,000	$269.50 plus 4.7% of excess over $11,000
		Over $16,000	$504.50 plus 5.3% of excess over $16,000 (§ 7-2-7)
		For any taxable year beginning on or after January 1, 2008:	*The tax shall be:*
		If the taxable income is:	
		Not over $5,500	1.7% of taxable income
		Over $5,500 but not over $11,000	$93.50 plus 3.2% of excess over $5,500
		Over $11,000 but not over $16,000	$269.50 plus 4.7% of excess over $11,000
		Over $16,000	$504.50 plus 4.9% of excess over $16,000 (§ 7-2-7)
New York	In addition to the personal income tax, individuals, estates or trusts are subject to a 6% tax on minimum taxable income. (Tax Law §§ 602, 622, 636)	(Tax Law § 601(c)(1)) For taxable years beginning after 2005:	
		If the New York taxable income is:	*The tax is:*
		Not over $8,000	4% of the New York taxable income
		Over $8,000 but not over $11,000	$320 plus 4.5% of excess over $8,000

Over $11,000 but not over $13,000	$455 plus 5.25% of excess over $11,000
Over $13,000 but not over $20,000	$560 plus 5.9% of excess over $13,000
Over $20,000	$973 plus 6.85% of excess over $20,000

(2)(added, L 2003) For taxable years beginning in 2005:

If the New York taxable income is:	*The tax is:*
Not over $8,000	4% of the New York taxable income
Over $8,000 but not over $11,000	$320 plus 4.5% of excess over $8,000
Over $11,000 but not over $13,000	$455 plus 5.25% of excess over $11,000
Over $13,000 but not over $20,000	$560 plus 5.9% of excess over $13,000
Over $20,000 but not over $100,000	$973 plus 6.85% of excess over $20,000
Over $100,000 but not over $500,000	$6,453 plus 7.25% of excess over $100,000
Over $500,000	$35,453 plus 7.7% of excess over $500,000

(Tax Law § 601(c)(2)) For taxable years beginning in 2004:

If the New York taxable income is:	*The tax is:*
Not over $8,000	4% of the New York taxable income
Over $8,000 but not over $11,000	$320 plus 4.5% of excess over $8,000
Over $11,000 but not over $13,000	$455 plus 5.25% of excess over $11,000
Over $13,000 but not over $20,000	$560 plus 5.9% of excess over $13,000
Over $20,000 but not over $100,000	$973 plus 6.85% of excess over $20,000
Over $100,000 but not over $500,000	$6,453 plus 7.375% of excess over $100,000
Over $500,000	$35,953 plus 7.7% of excess over $500,000

(Tax Law § 601(c)(3)) For taxable years beginning in 2003:

If the New York taxable income is:	*The tax is:*
Not over $8,000	4% of the New York taxable income

(cont'd) *(cont'd)*

Table 14
Income Tax Rates for Trusts and Estates *(continued)*

	Comments	*Chart*	
New York *(cont'd)*		Over $8,000 but not over $11,000	$320 plus 4.5% of excess over $8,000
		Over $11,000 but not over $13,000	$455 plus 5.25% of excess over $11,000
		Over $13,000 but not over $20,000	$560 plus 5.9% of excess over $13,000
		Over $20,000 but not over $100,000	$973 plus 6.85% of excess over $20,000
		Over $100,000 but not over $500,000	$6,453 plus 7.5% of excess over $100,000
		Over $500,000	$36,453 plus 7.7% of excess over $500,000
		(Tax Law § 601(c)(4))	
New York City	Note that there is some uncertainty whether higher rates will be imposed. Compare N.Y. Tax Law §§ 1301-A, 1302, 1304(a)(3)(A) & (B)(3), which is set forth in the tables herein, and N.Y.C. Admin. Code § 11-1701, 11-1702, & 11-1704.1. See also St. Dep't of Tax and Fin., TSB-M-04(1)I, Revised Summary of Personal Income Tax Legislative Changes Enacted in 2003 (Feb. 25, 2004).	For taxable years beginning in 2005:	
		If City taxable income is:	*The tax is:*
		Not over $12,000	2.907% of the city taxable income
		Over $12,000 but not over $25,000	$349 plus 3.534% of excess over $12,000
		Over $25,000 but not over $50,000	$808 plus 3.591% of excess over $25,000
		Over $50,000 but not over $100,000	$1,706 plus 3.648% of excess over $50,000
		Over $100,000 but not over $500,000	$3,530 plus 4.05% of excess over $100,000
		Over $500,000	$19,730 plus 4.45% of excess over $500,000 (§ 1304-D(a)(3)(A))
		For taxable years beginning after 2008:	
		If the city taxable income is:	*The tax is:*
		Not over $12,000	1.18% of the city taxable income

		Over $12,000 but not over $25,000	$142 plus 1.435% of excess over $12,000
		Over $25,000 but not over $50,000	$692 plus 1.48% of excess over $50,000
		Over $50,000	$328 plus 1.455% of excess over $50,000
		(§ 1304(b)(3))	
North Carolina		Until January 1, 2008:	

North Carolina

Until January 1, 2008:

Taxable income Over	*Up To*	*Rate*
$0	$12,750	6%
$12,750	$60,000	7%
$60,000	$120,000	7.75%
Over $120,000	NA	8.25%

Beginning January 1, 2008

Taxable income Over	*Up To*	*Rate*
$0	$12,750	6%
$12,750	$60,000	7%
$60,000	NA	7.75%

(§§105-160.2,105-134.2(a)(3))

North Dakota

The tax rate imposed on trusts and estates is the same tax rate as individuals. (§§ 57-38-07, 57-38-29)

1. On taxable income in excess of three thousand dollars, a tax of two and sixty-seven hundredths percent
2. On taxable income in excess of three thousand dollars and not in excess of five thousand dollars, a tax of four percent.
3. On taxable income in excess of five thousand dollars and not in excess of eight thousand dollars, a tax of five and thirty-three hundredths percent.
4. On taxable income in excess of eight thousand dollars and not in excess of fifteen thousand dollars, a tax of six and sixty-seven hundredths percent.
5. On taxable income in excess of fifteen thousand dollars and not in excess of twenty-five thousand dollars, a tax of eight percent.
6. On taxable income in excess of twenty-five thousand dollars and not in excess of thirty-five thousand dollars, a tax of nine and thirty-three hundredths percent.
7. On taxable income in excess of thirty-five thousand dollars and not in excess of fifty thousand dollars, a tax of ten and sixty-seven hundredths percent.
8. On taxable income in excess of fifty thousand dollars, a tax of twelve percent.

(§ 57-38-29)

Table 14
Income Tax Rates for Trusts and Estates *(continued)*

	Comments	*Chart*	
Ohio	The tax rate imposed on the taxable income of trusts and estates is the same as is imposed on the adjusted gross income of individuals, less exemptions. (§ 5747.02)	(1) For taxable years beginning in 2004:	
		Taxable Income	*Tax*
		$5,000 or less	.743%
		More than $5,000 but not more than $10,000	$37.15 plus 1.486% of the amount in excess of $5,000
		More than $10,000 but not more than $15,000	$111.45 plus 2.972% of the amount in excess of $10,000
		More than $15,000 but not more than $20,000	$260.05 plus 3.715% of the amount in excess of $15,000
		More than $20,000 but not more than $40,000	$445.80 plus 4.457% of the amount in excess of $20,000
		More than $40,000 but not more than $80,000	$1,337.20 plus 5.201% of the amount in excess of $40,000
		More than $80,000 but not more than $100,000	$3,417.60 plus 5.943% of the amount in excess of $80,000
		More than $100,000 but not more than $200,000	$4,606.20 plus 6.9% of the amount in excess of $100,000
		More than $200,000	$11,506.20 plus 7.5% of the amount in excess of $200,000
		(§ 5747.02(1))	
		(2) For taxable years beginning in 2005:	*Tax*
		Taxable Income	
		$5,000 or less	.712%
		More than $5,000 but not more than $10,000	$35.60 plus 1.424% of the amount in excess of $5,000
		More than $10,000 but not more than $15,000	$106.80 plus 2.847% of the amount in excess of $10,000
		More than $15,000 but not more than $20,000	$249.15 plus 3.559% of the amount in excess of $15,000
		More than $20,000 but not more than $40,000	$427.10 plus 4.27% of the amount in excess of $20,000
		More than $40,000 but not more than $80,000	$1,281.10 plus 4.983% of the amount in excess of $40,000
		More than $80,000 but not more than $100,000	$3,274.30 plus 5.693% of the amount in excess of $80,000

More than $100,000 but not more than $200,000	$4,412.90 plus 6.61% of the amount in excess of $100,000
More than $200,000	$11,022.90 plus 7.185% of the amount in excess of $200,000

(§ 5747.02(2))

(3) For taxable years beginning in 2006:

Taxable Income	*Tax*
$5,000 or less	.681%
More than $5,000 but not more than $10,000	$34.05 plus 1.361% of the amount in excess of $5,000
More than $10,000 but not more than $15,000	$102.10 plus 2.722% of the amount in excess of $10,000
More than $15,000 but not more than $20,000	$238.20 plus 3.403% of the amount in excess of $15,000
More than $20,000 but not more than $40,000	$408.35 plus 4.083% of the amount in excess of $20,000
More than $40,000 but not more than $80,000	$1,224.95 plus 4.764% of the amount in excess of $40,000
More than $80,000 but not more than $100,000	$3,130.55 plus 5.444% of the amount in excess of $80,000
More than $100,000 but not more than $200,000	$4,219.35 plus 6.32% of the amount in excess of $100,000
More than $200,000	$10,539.35 plus 6.87% of the amount in excess of $200,000

(§ 5747.02(3))

(4) For taxable years beginning in 2007:

Taxable Income	*Tax*
$5,000 or less	.649%
More than $5,000 but not more than $10,000	$32.45 plus 1.299% of the amount in excess of $5,000
More than $10,000 but not more than $15,000	$97.40 plus 2.598% of the amount in excess of $10,000
More than $15,000 but not more than $20,000	$227.30 plus 3.247% of the amount in excess of $15,000
More than $20,000 but not more than $40,000	$389.65 plus 3.895% of the amount in excess of $20,000
More than $40,000 but not more than $80,000	$1,168,65 plus 4.546% of the amount in excess of $40,000
More than $80,000 but not more than $100,000	$2,987.05 plus 5.194% of the amount in excess of $80,000
More than $100,000 but not more than $200,000	$4,025.85 plus 6.031% of the amount
(cont'd)	*(cont'd)*

Table 14
Income Tax Rates for Trusts and Estates *(continued)*

	Comments	*Chart*	
Ohio *(cont'd)*			in excess of $100,000
		More than $200,000	$10,056.8555 plus 6.5% of the amount in excess of $200,000
		(§ 5747.02(4))	
		(5) For taxable years beginning in 2008:	
		Taxable Income	*Tax*
		$5,000 or less	.618%
		More than $5,000 but not more than $10,000	$30.90 plus 1.236% of the amount in excess of $5,000
		More than $10,000 but not more than $15,000	$92.70 plus 2.473% of the amount in excess of $10,000
		More than $15,000 but not more than $20,000	$216.35 plus 3.091% of the amount in excess of $15,000
		More than $20,000 but not more than $40,000	$370.90 plus 3.708% of the amount in excess of $20,000
		More than $40,000 but not more than $80,000	$1,112.50 plus 4.327% of the amount in excess of $40,000
		More than $80,000 but not more than $100,000	$2,843.30 plus 4.945% of the amount in excess of $80,000
		More than $100,000 but not more than $200,000	$3,832.30 plus 5.741% of the amount in excess of $100,000
		More than $200,000	$9,573.30 plus 6.24% of the amount in excess of $200,000
		(§ 5747.02(5))	
		(6) For taxable years beginning in 2009 or thereafter:	
		Taxable Income	*Tax*
		$5,000 or less	.587%
		More than $5,000 but not more than $10,000	$29.35 plus 1.174% of the amount in excess of $5,000
		More than $10,000 but not more than $15,000	$88.05 plus 2.348% of the amount in excess of $10,000
		More than $15,000 but not more than $20,000	$205.45 plus 2.935% of the amount in excess of $15,000
		More than $20,000 but not more than $40,000	$352.20 plus 3.521% of the amount in excess of $20,000
		More than $40,000 but not more than $80,000	$1,056.40 plus 4.109% of the amount in excess of $40,000
		More than $80,000 but not more than $100,000	$2,700.00 plus 4.695% of the amount in excess of $80,000

		More than $100,000 but not more than $200,000	$3,639.00 plus 5.451% of the amount in excess of $100,000
		More than $200,000 (§ 5747.02(6))	$9,090.00 plus 5.925% of the amount in excess of $200,000
Oklahoma	The tax rate imposed on trusts and estates for tax years beginning on or after Jan. 1, 2006 is the same tax rate as single individuals, (68 § 2355(B)(1) & (F))	Rate Schedule for Method 1 (Not deducting federal income tax) (1) 0.5% tax on first $1,000.00 or part thereof (2) 1% tax on next $1,500.00 or part thereof (3) 2% tax on next $1,250.00 or part thereof (4) 3% tax on next $1,150.00 or part thereof (5) 4% tax on next $1,300.00 or part thereof (6) 5% tax on next $1,500.00 or part thereof (7) 6.5 % tax on remainder for 2006 tax year (8) 5.65% on remainder for 2007 tax year (9) 5.55% tax on remainder for 2008 tax year (10) 5.50% tax on remainder for 2009 tax year and thereafter (11) If State Bd. of Equalizations determines, then 5.25% tax on remainder for 2010 and thereafter ((68 § 2355(B)(1))	
Oregon	The tax rate imposed on trusts and estates is the same tax rate as individuals. (§§ 316.267, 316.272) The rate tables are adjusted for inflation. (§ 316.037(1)(b)) The income tax brackets are adjusted through 1999.	*Taxes and Rates* Not over $2,000 Over $2,000 but not over $5,000 Over $5,000 (§ 316.037(1)(a))	*Taxable Income (Single Taxpayers)* 5% of taxable income $100 plus 7% of the excess over $2,000 $310 plus 9% of the excess over $5,000
Pennsylvania	Tax rate is 3.07%. (72 § 7302(a))		
Rhode Island		(ix) For the period January 1, 1999 through December 31, 1999 the rate shall be equal to twenty six and five-tenths percent (26.5%) of the tax payer's federal income tax liability. (x) For the period January 1, 2000 through December 31, 2000 the rate shall be equal to twenty six percent (26%) of the taxpayer's federal income tax liability. (xi) For the period January 1, 2001 through December 31, 2001 the rate shall be equal to twenty five and five-tenths percent (25.5%) of the taxpayer's federal income tax liability. (xii) For the period January 1, 2002 and thereafter the rate shall be twenty five percent (25%) of the taxpayer's federal income tax liability. (§ 44-30-2(a)(1)(ix)(xii))	

Table 14
Income Tax Rates for Trusts and Estates *(continued)*

	Comments	Chart	
South Carolina		Not over $2,220	2.5% of taxable income
		Over $2,220 but not over $4,440	$56 plus 3 percent of the excess over $2,220;
		Over $4,440 but not over $6,660	$123 plus 4 percent of the excess over $4,440;
		Over $6,660 but not over $8,880	$212 plus 5 percent of the excess over $6,660;
		Over $8,880 but not over $11,100	$323 plus 6 percent of the excess over $8,880;
		Over $11,100	$456 plus 7 percent of the excess over $11,100
		(§ 12-6-510(A))	
South Dakota		*No income tax on trusts or estates.*	
Tennessee	Tax rate is 6% on dividends and interest. (§§ 67-2-102, 67-2-101(5))		
Texas		*No income tax on trusts or estates.*	
Utah	The tax rate imposed on trusts and estates is the same tax rate as is imposed on individuals filing separately. (§§ 59-10-201(1), 59-10-201.1, 59-10-104(2)) A resident estate or trust is allowed the credit provided in § 59-10-1003, relating to an income tax imposed by another state, or D.C., or a possession of the U.S.	*If the state taxable income is:*	*The tax is:*
		Less than or equal to $1,000	2.3% of the state taxable income
		Greater than $1,000 but less than or equal to $2,000	$23, plus 3.3% of state taxable income greater than $1,000
		Greater than $2,000 but less than or equal to $3,000	$56, plus 4.2% of state taxable income greater than $2,000
		Greater than $3,000 but less than or equal to $4,000	$98, plus 5.2% of state taxable income greater than $3,000
		Greater than $4,000 but less than or equal to $5,500	$150, plus 6% of state taxable income greater than $4,000
		Greater than $5,500	$240, plus 6.98% of state taxable income greater than $5,500
		(§ 59-10-104(2))	
Vermont	A special tax rate is imposed on the taxable income of estates and trusts. (32 § 5822(a)(5)) However, further adjustments are presented. (32 § 5822(c)). In	*If taxable income is:*	*The tax is:*
		$1,850 or less	3.6% of taxable income
		Over $1,850 but not over $4,400	$67 plus 7.2% of taxable income over $1,850

	particular, the amount of tax is increased by 24% of the federal tax liability for additional taxes on qualified retirement plans, recapture of federal investment tax credit, tax on qualified lump-sum distributions of pension income not included in federal taxable income, and decreased by 24% of the reduction in tax liability due to farm income averaging. There are also credits of 24% of the retirement income credit, investment tax credit, child care and dependent care credits. (32 § 5822(d)) The brackets are adjusted for inflation beginning with 2003. (32 § 5822(b))	Over $4,400 but not over $6,750	$250 plus 8.5% of taxable income over $4,400
		Over $6,750 but not over $9,200	$450 plus 9.0% of taxable income over $6,750
		Over $9,200	$670 plus 9.5% of taxable income over $9,200
		(32 § 5822(a)(5))	
Virginia	The tax rate imposed on trusts and estates is the same tax rate as individuals. (§§ 58.1-360, 58.1-320)	Two percent on income not in excess of $3,000. Three percent on income in excess of $3,000 but not in excess of $5,000. Five percent on income in excess of $5,000 but not in excess of $17,000. Five and three-quarters percent on income in excess of $17,000 for taxable years beginning on and after January 1, 1990. (§ 58.1-320)	
Washington	No income tax on trusts or estates. However, they may be subject to the Business and Occupation Tax at rates applied to gross proceeds of sales or gross income of the business that vary with the business activity. (§§ 82.04.220 et seq.) To the extent profits are in the form of return on investments, they are not subject to the tax. See John H. Sellen Const. Co. v. State Dep't Rev., 558 P.2d 1342 (1976).		
West Virginia		*If the West Virginia taxable income is:*	*The tax is:*
		Not over $10,000	3% of the taxable income
		Over $10,000 but not over $25,000	$300.00 plus 4% of excess over $10,000
		Over $25,000 but not over $40,000	$900.00 plus 4.5% of excess over $25,000
		(cont'd)	*(cont'd)*

Table 14
Income Tax Rates for Trusts and Estates *(continued)*

	Comments	*Chart*	
West Virginia *(cont'd)*		Over $40,000 but not over $60,000	$1,575.00 plus 6% of excess over $40,000
		Over $60,000	$2,775.00 plus 6.5% of excess over $60,000
		(§ 11-21-4e)	
Wisconsin	The tax rate imposed on trusts and estates is the same tax rate as individuals. (§ 71.125(1))	For taxable years beginning after December 31, 2000 (a) On all taxable income from $0 to $7,500, 4.6%. (b) On all taxable income exceeding $7,500 but not exceeding $15,000, 6.15%. (c) On all taxable income exceeding $15,000 but not exceeding $112,500, 6.5%. (d) On all taxable income exceeding $112,500, 6.75% (§ 71.06(1p))	
Wyoming		*No income tax on trusts or estates.*	

1. However, there is a deduction for amounts paid or permanently put aside for a charitable purpose to the extent specified in 26 U.S.C. § 642(c). (§ 40-18-25(b); AL ADC 810-3-25-.01). Also, certain trusts qualifying under the Internal Revenue Code are exempt from taxation under § 40-18-25 including: (a) any qualified trust relating to qualified pension, profit sharing, or stock bonus plans; (b) a custodial account, an annuity contract, or a contract issued by an insurance company; (c) an individual retirement account, an individual retirement annuity, or any custodial account; (d) a retirement bond; (e) corporations organized for the exclusive purpose of holding title to property, collecting income thereform, and remitting the proceeds, less expenses, to an organization that is exempt under § 40-18-25; (f) voluntary employee's beneficiary associations; (g) local teacher's retirement fund associations; (h) a trust or trusts forming part of a plan providing for the payment of supplemental unemployment compenstion benefits; (i) an organization or trust created exclusively to form part of a quafified group legal services plan or plans; (j) a trust created exclusively to pay liability insurance premiums for, pay administrative and other expenses of, and pay claims for liability for disability or death due to black lung; (k) a charitable remainder annuity trust or charitable remainder unitrust. (AL ADC 810-3-25-.06)

Table 15
State Inheritance, Estate, Generation-Skipping Transfer, and Gift Taxes (current through 5/1/07)

Under Section 2011 of the Internal Revenue Code, the federal government was prepared to avoid the collection of double death taxes at both the federal and state level by allowing the state to keep a specified amount. This was accomplished by a credit for state taxes. See Table 15.08. In view of the availability of this credit, state legislation was drafted in every state so as to soak up the maximum amount of the credit but in most states not to impose a tax liability in excess of the federal credit. Nevertheless, there might still have been actual tax liability in excess of the maximum credit amount if more than one state sought to claim in death taxes the maximum amount of the federal credit. Moreover, not every state limited itself to a death tax based on the federal credit. In a number of states an independent inheritance or succession tax was imposed on the beneficiaries or an independent estate or succession tax was imposed on the estate of the decedent. A separate tax geared to the credit was generally imposed in these states when the independent tax yielded an amount that was less than the available federal credit amount.

While the independent taxes remain unaffected, the "soak-up" tax has been affected by the total elimination of the credit in 2005. The effect is to repeal the state soak-up tax. **When referring to Table 15.02, this fact must not be ignored, since most of the states with soak-up tax systems will no longer collect any tax from them.** A number of states have enacted legislation to deem the I.R.C. § 2011 credit still in force as of a particular date prior to its repeal. The general cut-off date for the present Table 15.02 is April 30, 2007. The reader should try to keep current regarding changes in states after April 30, 2007, as there is still a great deal of ongoing legislative activity in this area. Note also that the sharing of revenues between states will likely be altered with more going to states that have frozen the credit in place if the other state has not done so. Table 15.09 is a State-by-State Summary of the Current (as of April 30, 2007) State Estate Tax Situation.

Table 15.01 reviews, for each state, whether a tax not dependent on the federal § 2011 credit is imposed. Although often imposed on the beneficiaries in the nature of an inheritance tax, with different levels of taxation often based on relationship to the decedent, the question still remains what property is subject to tax. The table indicates fair uniformity among states in taxing all sorts of interests in property, as well as allowing for exemptions, such as for transfers to a spouse or a charity. In terms of a key concern of this work, Table 15.01 reviews precisely what property is subject to tax, depending on whether the decedent was a domiciliary or nondomiciliary. The taxation of nondomiciliaries is often considerably less expansive in its scope. But while nondomiciliary status is obviously preferable, it does not mean there is no tax. The attorney must be aware that states other than the domiciliary state may also be taxing certain interests in property. There are also substantial traps, since a state like New York may impose tax based on the maximum credit amount prior to reduction or repeal of I.R.C § 2011. It may then reduce this amount only by the lesser of the tax imposed by the residence state or the proportion of the total gross estate value represented by the local property of the non-resident. If the residence state no longer has a tax or defers to another state so as to pick up only whatever is left of the former credit, e.g., Florida, there may be a disproportionate tax paid to the nonresidence state. As can be seen, reference simply to the tax law of the domicile is insufficient for obtaining a true picture of the potential tax burden during the estate planning process or in determining to which states tax must be paid once the individual has died.

Table 15.02 continues the analysis with regard to the estate tax. The estate tax, which is imposed on the estate rather than the beneficiaries, typically was capped in an amount equal to the maximum federal credit. This table indicates whether the state imposes an estate tax, when payment is to be made, and whether the tax is linked to the federal credit, and as of what date if relevant. The table explains for each state which property is subject to tax in the case of a domiciliary and a nondomiciliary, as is done in Table 15.01 with regard to any tax not dependent on the federal credit for state death taxes.

In addition, the table indicates how each state addresses the problem of other states also claiming the federal credit amount. As was previously indicated, certain states, like New York, have a problematic formula. In many cases, but not all, a state will claim only a pro rata portion of the credit amount, based on the fraction of the total gross estate that the property being taxed by the particular state represents. Furthermore, in some cases, the estate tax will be imposed, as noted, only if the independent inheritance, succession, or estate tax is less than the federal credit amount.

Of course, caution must be exercised. With the repeal of the federal credit for state death taxes, there may not be an actual estate tax imposed, even though the statutory framework is still on the books and is analyzed in Table 15.02. Table 15.09 Alt. #3 indicates those states with regard to which the estate tax has been effectively repealed along with the repeal of I.R.C. § 2011.

Table 15.03 proceeds with a similar analysis with respect to state generation-skipping transfer taxes. Many, but by no means all, states impose this tax. Those that do so, however, rely exclusively on the federal credit for state generation-skipping transfer taxes set forth in I.R.C. § 2604. The federal credit, which is pegged at a maximum 5 percent of the federal generation-skipping transfer tax, is available for generation-skipping transfers other than direct skips. However, some states do not explicitly exclude direct skips from their tax, thus raising the prospect of both federal and state taxation.

The § 2604 credit is repealed effective January 1, 2005. Unlike the case of the § 2011 state death tax credit, few states have enacted legislation to deem this credit still in effect. Consequently, the repeal of the federal credit will have the effect of repealing almost all state generation-skipping transfer taxes.

As with the estate tax, a major issue is which property is subject to tax by a particular state. This is an especially difficult topic because links that existed when a trust was created may no longer exist when the generation-skipping transfer occurs. Moreover, the property itself may no longer be located in the state. Depending on domiciliary or nondomiciliary status at a particular point in time specified in the statute, the taxing state is likely to seek a prorated portion of tax based on the maximum federal credit, at least when another state is also claiming some or all of the maximum credit amount with respect to the same property.

Table 15.04 addresses the imposition of gift tax by the states. Very few states impose this tax. With regard to each of these states, the date for payment of the tax is set forth. In addition, the property subject to taxation in the cases of a domiciliary and nondomiciliary is also addressed.

Table 15.05 explores the matter of waivers, that is, the state requirement for a formal release by the government, often based on payment of taxes, before assets can be transferred after the death of the decedent. This information should be especially helpful when there is a tax liability in another state as well as at the domicile. The table indicates the appropriate person from whom waivers must be obtained for each state imposing the requirement. It also indicates those states that do not require waivers. In some states, waivers are not required, but the fiduciary is not permitted to make any transfer or distribution until all taxes are paid. A liability for taxes may be imposed by statute on a fiduciary who makes a prior transfer or distribution.

Table 15.06 addresses how states resolve conflicts over death taxation. In particular, many states have adopted the Uniform Act on Interstate Compromise of Death Taxes and/or the Uniform Act on Arbitration of Inheritance Taxes. These acts set forth a procedure whereby states can resolve disputes over the domicile of the decedent. Domicile is critical, since it affords a constitutionally sound basis for taxing all of the decedent's assets. Moreover, the Supreme Court has held that as long as there is a reasonable basis, more than one state can claim to be the domicile. Thus, state resolution of the conflict is vital to avoid multiple taxation of the same property. The attorney must, therefore, be aware of these relief procedures.

Likewise, the attorney must be aware of the reciprocal exemption provisions of many state statutes. These statutes often provide that a state will not tax a nondomiciliary with regard to certain property, usually intangible personal property, if the nondomiciliary's state of domicile affords a reciprocal exemption to the taxing state's domiciliaries. Thus, a careful analysis of these provisions can result in an avoidance of multiple state tax exposure with respect to substantial assets. The earlier tables detailing tax liability need to be considered in light of Table 15.06, which may eliminate the liability that those tables indicate would otherwise be imposed.

The foregoing tables should prove helpful for estate planning as well as postmortem tax compliance. The estate planner will be able to evaluate the jurisdictional bases of different states to tax and the likely tax to be imposed. If necessary, links of the client or the property with certain states can be terminated. After death, the attorney can use the tables to determine readily the exposure to tax in the various states, the need for waivers, and the availability of conflict resolution and reciprocal exemption provisions to reduce the tax burden.

To facilitate the determination of the actual tax exposure, Table 15.07 sets forth the rate schedules of state inheritance, succession, estate, generation-skipping transfer, and gift taxes for those states with such independent rate schedules. The rate schedules are organized on a state-by-state basis. Brief consideration is given to the availability of key deductions/exemptions and various credits and exclusions. Since many states rely on the federal credit for state death taxes in determining the state tax, the relevant portions of I.R.C. § 2011 are set forth for quick reference in Table 15.08.

One final note on terminology is in order. Many states utilize the terms "resident" and "nonresident." In the transfer tax area, these terms, for federal constitutional reasons, ordinarily mean "domiciliary" and "nondomiciliary." This definitional approach should be contrasted with the income taxation of trusts and estates, see Tables 11.01 and 11.02, where "residence" means actual residence and not domicile. Of course, as those tables demonstrate, states may well have different concepts of when a trust or estate is an actual "resident" of the state.

Table 15.01
Inheritance and Succession Tax

	Is There an Inheritance, Estate, or Succession Tax Not Based on the § 2011 Federal Credit?	*When Must Payment Be Made?*	*Are Interests Other Than Outright Ownership Subject to Tax?*	*Are Broad Deductions for Charitable and Marital Transfers, as Well as Administrative Expenses, Allowed?*	*With Regard to a Domiciliary,* * *What Property Is Subject to Tax?*	*With Respect to a Nondomiciliary,* * *What Property Is Subject to Tax?*
Alabama	No.	N/A	N/A	N/A	N/A	N/A
Alaska	No.	N/A	N/A	N/A	N/A	N/A
Arizona	No.	N/A	N/A	N/A	N/A	N/A
Arkansas	No.	N/A	N/A	N/A	N/A	N/A
California	No. (Rev. & Tax. § 13301)	N/A	N/A	N/A	N/A	N/A
Colorado	No.	N/A	N/A	N/A	N/A	N/A
Connecticut**	Effective 1/1/05, there is an estate tax on the Connecticut taxable estate. (§ 12-391, Public Act No. 05-251, § 69 (June 8, 2005)) For the rate, see Table 15.07.	The estate tax is due 9 months after the date of death. (§ 12-392)	Yes. (§ 12-391)	Yes. (§ 12-391)	The property includes real property in this state, tangible personal property that does not have an actual situs in another state, and all intangible property. (§ 12-391(d))	Same as domiciliary, except the tax does not apply to the transfer of intangible personal property. (§ 12-391(d))
Delaware	No.	N/A	N/A	N/A	N/A	N/A
District of Columbia	No.	N/A	N/A	N/A	N/A	N/A
Florida	No.	N/A	N/A	N/A	N/A	N/A
Georgia	No.	N/A	N/A	N/A	N/A	N/A
Hawaii	No.	N/A	N/A	N/A	N/A	N/A
Idaho	No.	N/A	N/A	N/A	N/A	N/A
Illinois	No.	N/A	N/A	N/A	N/A	N/A

Indiana	Yes. (§ 6-4.1-2-1(a)) For the rate, see Table 15.07.	Payment of the inheritance tax is due 12 months after death. (§ 6-4.1-9-1)	Yes. (§ 6-4.1-2-2 et seq.)	Yes. (§§ 6-4.1-3-13–6.4.1-3-15) There are also exemptions to the inheritance tax: the first $100,000 of property interests transferred to a Class A transferee; the first $500 of property interests transferred to a Class B transferee; the first $100 of property interests transferred to a Class C transferee. (§§ 6-4.1-3-10–6-4.1-3-12)	The property includes real property in this state, tangible personal property that does not have an actual situs in another state, and all intangible property. (§ 6-4.1-2-2)	Same as domiciliary, except that the tax applies to real property in Indiana, whether or not held in trust, and whether or not the property is required to be distributed in kind. However, the tax does not apply if the transfer was to an "irrevocable trust" during the decedent's lifetime, not made in contemplation of death, and the decedent did not have a retained interest. The tax also applies to tangible personal property with a situs in Indiana. (§ 6-4.1-2-3)
Iowa	Yes. (§ 450.2) For the rate, See Table 15.07.	The inheritance tax is due nine months after the decedent's death. (§ 450.6)	Yes. (§ 450.3)	Yes. (§§ 450.9, 450.12)	The property includes real property in this state, tangible personal property that does not have an actual situs in another state, and all intangible property. (§ 450.2) (the wording is unclear as to whether the fee requirement actually applies). (§ 450.2)	Same as for a domiciliary, except the tax only applies to real estate and tangible personal property in the state, subject to the jurisdiction of Iowa courts, or thereafter brought into the state and subject to court jurisdiction. (§ 450.2)
Kansas	Yes. (§79-15, 203) However, the tax is repealed eff. Jan. 1, 2010. (S.365 § 55) *(cont'd)*	Nine months after death. (§ 79-15,226) However, return must be filed if the gross *(cont'd)*	Yes. (§§ 79-15, 209-79-15,217)	Yes. (§§ 79-15, 218-79-15,223)	The taxable estate. (§ 79-15,203) Note that the gross estate includes transfers *(cont'd)*	Property with a Kansas situs, including real property, tangible *(cont'd)*

Table 15.01
Inheritance and Succession Tax *(continued)*

	Is There an Inheritance, Estate, or Succession Tax Not Based on the § 2011 Federal Credit?	*When Must Payment Be Made?*	*Are Interests Other Than Outright Ownership Subject to Tax?*	*Are Broad Deductions for Charitable and Marital Transfers, as Well as Administrative Expenses, Allowed?*	*With Regard to a Domiciliary,* What Property Is Subject to Tax?*	*With Respect to a Nondomiciliary,* What Property Is Subject to Tax?*
Kansas *(cont'd)*	For the rate, See Table 15.07.	estate is in excess of $1,000,000, even if Kansas-situs property is $1 and there is no tax liability. (§79-15,225(a))			within one year of death, other than transfers of life insurance policies for which no federal gift tax return was due and in the case of a bona fide transaction for an adequate considera-tion in money or money's worth. (§ 79-15,209)	personal property, and *intangible* personal property. (§ 79-15,203((a)) The tax on the taxable estate is determined by multiplying the tax on the total taxable estate by the percen-tage determined by dividing the value of all property included in the gross estate that is within the jurisdiction of Kansas by the value of all property included in the gross estate (§79-15,204)
Kentucky	Yes. (§ 140.010) For the rate of taxation, See Table 15.07.	The inheritance tax is due at death and is delinquent if not paid within 18 months. If paid within 18 months, there is no interest charge. There is, on the other hand, a discount of 5% if the taxes are paid within nine months. (§ 140.210(1)) If the tax liability on a bene-ficiary's net distribu-tive share exceeds $5,000, payments may be paid in 10	Yes. (§ 140.010) For the rate taxation, See Table 15.07.	In part, with respect to exemption of trans-fers to educational, religious, and charita-ble institutions, and to cities and public insti-tutions (§ 140.060) and with respect to certain pay ments under employee's trusts (§ 140.063).	The property includes any interest of an "inhabitant" in real or personal property in the state, all tangible personal property "wherever situated" if it has "not acquired a situs for tax pur-poses of taxation outside this state," and all intangibles belonging to a Ken-tucky domiciliary, except partnership property located in another state and	Intangible property with a "business situs" in the state, all real property in the state and interest therein, and all tangi-ble personal property witha situs in this state if "not taxable elsewhere." (§ 140.010)

		annual installments, with interest beginning with the date of filing the return. (§ 140.222)			subject to an inheritance or estate tax there. (§ 140.010)	
Louisiana	Yes. (§ 47:2401) For the rate, see Table 15.07.	Inheritance taxes must be paid within nine months after the death of the decedent. (§ 47:2420) Interest begins to accrue on unpaid inheritance tax after nine months. (§ 47:2420(A))	Yes. (§ 47:2404(A))	Yes. (§ 47:2402)	The property subject to tax includes property of any kind and wherever located. (§ 47:2404(A))	Nonresidents are technically taxed on all property included in any inheritance or gift made in contemplation of death, including all immovable property located in the state and all tangible movable property located in the state. However, intangible property is specifically not subject to tax. (§ 47:2404(A)) This tax is subject to the exemptions set forth in § 47:2402, such as transfers to a spouse and charities. Constitutionally, Louisiana cannot tax non residents on real property and tangible personal property not situated in Louisiana.
Maine	No. (36 § 3461 repealed, effective April 2, 1998)	N/A	N/A	N/A	N/A	N/A

Table 15.01
Inheritance and Succession Tax *(continued)*

	Is There an Inheritance, Estate, or Succession Tax Not Based on the § 2011 Federal Credit?	*When Must Payment Be Made?*	*Are Interests Other Than Outright Ownership Subject to Tax?*	*Are Broad Deductions for Charitable and Marital Transfers, as Well as Administrative Expenses, Allowed?*	*With Regard to a Domiciliary,* What Property Is Subject to Tax?*	*With Respect to a Nondomiciliary,* What Property Is Subject to Tax?*
Maryland	Yes. (Tax-Gen. § 7-202) For the rate, see Table 15.07.	The inheritance tax is due at the time of accounting for the distribution. (Tax-Gen. § 7-217(a)) An information report, however, is due within three months of the appointment of a personal representative. (Tax-Gen. § 7-224)	Yes. (Tax-Gen. § 7-202)	Yes. (Tax-Gen. § 7-203)	Property with a "taxable situs" in the state is subject to the tax. (Tax-Gen. § 7-202)	Same as for a domiciliary (Tax-Gen. § 7-203), with the exception of no tax on the receipt of personal property from a nonresident decedent if the state or country of decedent's residence at death does not impose death tax on such property or affords a reciprocal exemption similar to Maryland's provision. (Tax-Gen. § 7-203(f))
Massachusetts	No. (65A § 1)	N/A	N/A	N/A	N/A	N/A
Michigan	No.	N/A	N/A	N/A	N/A	N/A
Minnesota	No.	N/A	N/A	N/A	N/A	N/A
Mississippi	No.	N/A	N/A	N/A	N/A	N/A
Missouri	No.	N/A	N/A	N/A	N/A	N/A
Montana	No.	N/A	N/A	N/A	N/A	N/A
Nebraska	Yes. (§ 77-2001) For the rate, see Table 15.07.	The inheritance tax is due 12 months after the decedent's death. (§ 77-2010) Interest is charged from date the tax became	Yes. (§ 77-2002)	The inheritance tax does not apply to transfers to the surviving spouse. (§ 77-2004) Property transferred to the United	All property is subject to tax. (§ 77-2001)	Same as for a domiciliary, but only with respect to property "within the state." (§ 77-2001)

		payable if the tax is not paid within 12 months of death. (*Id.*)		States or to any state, or any political subdivision of either, is exempt from the inheritance tax. (§ 77-2007.03) The inheritance tax does not apply to transfers for religious, charitable or educational purposes provided that the recipient is located in Nebraska or in a state with a reciprocal exemption. (§ 77-2007.04)		
Nevada	No.	N/A	N/A	N/A	N/A	N/A
New Hampshire	The tax, Chapter 86, was repealed, effective January 1, 2003.	N/A	N/A	N/A	N/A	N/A
New Jersey	Yes. (§ 54:34-1) For the rate, see Table 15.07.	Inheritance taxes are due at the death of the decedent. (§ 54:35-1) All taxes not paid within eight months thereafter accrue interest at 10% per annum. (§ 54:35-3)	Yes. (§ 54:34-1)	Yes. (§ 54:34-4)	The property on which the tax is imposed is real or tangible personal property, whether in trust or not within the state, and all intangible personal property. (§ 54:34-1)	All real and tangible personal property "within" the state exceeding the value of $500 (§ 54:34-1), and not specifically exempted by § 54:34-4, is taxed according to the beneficiary's relation to the decedent and the value of the property.
New Mexico	No.	N/A	N/A	N/A	N/A	N/A
New York	No. Tax §§ 220 to 245 repealed by L. 2004, ch.	N/A	N/A	N/A	N/A	N/A

(cont'd)

Table 15.01
Inheritance and Succession Tax *(continued)*

	Is There an Inheritance, Estate, or Succession Tax Not Based on the § 2011 Federal Credit?	*When Must Payment Be Made?*	*Are Interests Other Than Outright Ownership Subject to Tax?*	*Are Broad Deductions for Charitable and Marital Transfers, as Well as Administrative Expenses, Allowed?*	*With Regard to a Domiciliary,* What Property Is Subject to Tax?*	*With Respect to a Nondomiciliary,* What Property Is Subject to Tax?*
New York *(cont'd)*	60, Pt. I, § 1, effective Aug. 20, 2004.					
North Carolina	No.	N/A	N/A	N/A	N/A	N/A
North Dakota	No.	N/A	N/A	N/A	N/A	N/A
Ohio	Yes. (§ 5731.02) For the rate, see Table 15.07.	The tax is due within nine months after the decedent's death. (§ 5731.23)	Yes. (§§ 5731.03–5731.131)	Yes. (§§ 5731.15–5731.17)	All property in which the decedent had an interest, very much along the lines of the federal gross estate. (§§ 5731.03–5731.131)	The tax is computed based upon the transfer of real property "in this state," tangible personal property "having an actual situs in this state," and intangible personal property "employed in carrying on a business in this state" unless the state of domicile afforded a reciprocal exemption. (§§ 5731.19, 5731.34) The tax is computed by calculating the tax as if the decedent were a domiciliary of Ohio with all his property located in the state and then multiplying the tax by a fraction the numerator of which is the property taxable by Ohio in the case of a

						nondomiciliary and the denominator of which is the worldwide gross estate. (§ 5731.19)
Oklahoma	Yes. (68 § 802) For the rate, see Table 15.07.	The tax is due within nine months of death. Interest thereafter accrues at 1¼% per month. (68 § 806)	Yes. (68 § 807)	Yes. (68 §§ 808, 809)	Property "within the jurisdiction of this state." (68§ 807(A)(1))	Apparently same as domiciliary except intangible property is excluded, unless the intangible property is generally required to be included in the gross estate, the transferor was a domiciliary or another jurisdiction and either (a) the other jurisdiction imposed no death or transfer tax on personal property of domiciliaries of Oklahoma, except tangible personal property with an actual situs in the other jurisdiction or (b) with regard to the kind of property referred to in (a) the other jurisdiction granted a reciprocal exemption to domiciliaries *and* allowed a similar exemption to domiciliaries from the

(cont'd)

Table 15.01
Inheritance and Succession Tax *(continued)*

	Is There an Inheritance, Estate, or Succession Tax Not Based on the § 2011 Federal Credit?	*When Must Payment Be Made?*	*Are Interests Other Than Outright Ownership Subject to Tax?*	*Are Broad Deductions for Charitable and Marital Transfers, as Well as Administrative Expenses, Allowed?*	*With Regard to a Domiciliary,* What Property Is Subject to Tax?*	*With Respect to a Nondomiciliary,* What Property Is Subject to Tax?*
Oklahoma *(cont'd)*						jurisdiction of the transferor. (68 § 807(A)(1))
Oregon	No.	N/A	N/A	N/A	N/A	N/A
Pennsylvania	Yes. (72 § 9116) For the rate, see Table 15.07.	The inheritance tax is due at the date of the decedent's death and is delinquent if not paid after nine months. There is a 5% discount if paid within three months of the death. (72 § 9142)	Yes. (72 § 9107)	Yes. (72 § 9111 et seq.)	All real and tangible personal property with a situs in Pennsylvania, as well as intangible personal property. All real and tangible personal property with a situs outside Pennsylvania is taxed if the decedent had contracted to sell it and the state of situs of the property does not subject it to death tax. (72 § 9102, definition of "Property" or "Estate")	The tax is computed upon the value of real property and tangible personal property located in Pennsylvania, in excess of unpaid property taxes assessed on the property and any indebtedness for which it is liened, mortgaged, or pledged. (72 §§ 9116(b)(2); 9102)
Rhode Island	No.	N/A	N/A	N/A	N/A	N/A
South Carolina	No.	N/A	N/A	N/A	N/A	N/A
South Dakota	No. (§ ON-11-15) The former Inheritance Tax was abolished by Amendment C, voted on by the public	N/A	N/A	N/A	N/A	N/A

	November 7, 2000. However, the statute remains on the books at ch. 10-40.					
Tennessee	Yes. (§ 67-8-303) For the rate, see Table 15.07.	Inheritance taxes must be paid nine months after the death of the decedent. (§ 67-8-419)	Yes. (§ 67-8-303)	Yes. (§§ 67-8-315, 67-8-316)	Property subject to tax includes real property within the state, tangible personal property that does not have an "actual situs" outside the state, all intangible property. (§ 67-8-303(a)(1))	Nonresidents are taxed only on the transfer of real property situated within the state and tangible personal property that has "an actual situs within this state." (§ 67-8-303(a)(2))
Texas	No. (Tax § 211.051)	N/A	N/A	N/A	N/A	N/A
Utah	No.	N/A	N/A	N/A	N/A	N/A
Vermont	No.	N/A	N/A	N/A	N/A	N/A
Virginia	No. However, there is a minor tax on the probate of wills and grant of administration. See Table 15.07 and § 58.1-1712.	N/A	N/A	N/A	N/A	N/A
Washington	Yes, with respect to decedents dying on or after May 17, 2005. (§ 83.100.040) For the rate, see Table 15.07.	Payment due 9 months after date of death. (§§ 83.100.050, 83.100.060)	Yes, just as under federal tax law determination of the gross estate. (§ 83.100.020(5))	Yes, closely resembles the federal taxable estate. Instead of a unified credit, there is a deduction of $1,500,000 in 2005 and $2,000,000 thereafter. (§ 83.100.020(14))	Every transfer of property located in Washington is subject to tax. This inclsudes any intangible property of a resident, wherever located. (§ 83.100.040(1))	Property located in Washington is subject to tax. (§ 83.100.040)

Table 15.01
Inheritance and Succession Tax *(continued)*

	Is There an Inheritance, Estate, or Succession Tax Not Based on the § 2011 Federal Credit?	*When Must Payment Be Made?*	*Are Interests Other Than Outright Ownership Subject to Tax?*	*Are Broad Deductions for Charitable and Marital Transfers, as Well as Administrative Expenses, Allowed?*	*With Regard to a Domiciliary,* What Property Is Subject to Tax?*	*With Respect to a Nondomiciliary,* What Property Is Subject to Tax?*
West Virginia	No.	N/A	N/A	N/A	N/A	N/A
Wisconsin	No.	N/A	N/A	N/A	N/A	N/A
Wyoming	No.	N/A	N/A	N/A	N/A	N/A

* The terms domiciliary and nondomiciliary are used herein. Many statutes use the terms "resident" or "nonresident." However, the case law makes clear "domiciliary" and "nondomiciliary" are intended. Still, caution is advised.

Table 15.02
Estate Tax

	Is There an Estate Tax?	*When Must Payment of Tax Be Made?*	*In the Case of an Estate Tax, How Is It Computed for a Domiciliary?*	*In the Case of an Estate Tax, How Is It Computed for a Nondomiciliary, U.S. Resident?*
Alabama	Yes. (§ 40-15-2) However, with the phase-out of the federal credit, no tax or filing of a return is presently due.	Estate tax must be paid on or before nine months after the decedent's death (§§ 40-15-4, 40-15-7(g)) (same for nondomiciliaries).	The tax equals the full amount of state tax permissible as a credit or deduction in computing the federal estate tax. (§ 40-15-2) The tax is the proportion that the value of the estate within or subject to the jurisdiction of Alabama bears to the value of the gross estate. (§ 40-15-17)	The tax is imposed on real property or tangible personal property "located" in Alabama and other items "lawfully subject to the imposition of an estate tax by the state of Alabama." (§ 40-15-7(a)) It is also imposed on real property and tangible personal property in Alabama or such property transferred in contemplation of death or, e.g., held in trust and intended to pass in possession or enjoyment at or after the death are taxed. (§ 40-15-7(h)) Moneys, credits, securities, and other intangible personal property in Alabama, but not employed by the owner in carrying on a business in the state are deemed located at the domicile of the owner. If held in trust, they shall not be deemed to be located in Alabama simply because the owner was domiciled in the state, except if no other state subjects this property to death taxation. (§ 40-15-8) The tax due is the proportion of the federal estate tax available as a credit or deduction as would be leviable upon an estate of similar taxable net value, less the proportion of any exemption to which the estate is entitled, which the actual value of the real estate and tangible personal property located in Alabama bears to the actual value of the gross estate wherever situated. (§ 40-15-7(b))

Table 15.02
Estate Tax *(continued)*

	Is There an Estate Tax?	*When Must Payment of Tax Be Made?*	*In the Case of an Estate Tax, How Is It Computed for a Domiciliary?*	*In the Case of an Estate Tax, How Is It Computed for a Nondomiciliary, U.S. Resident?*
Alaska	Yes. (§ 43.31.011)	The tax is payable 15 months after decedent's death. (§ 43.31.141)	The tax is the amount of the federal estate tax credit for taxes paid to states reduced by the amount of the credit allocable to those "constitutional" estate, inheritance, legacy and succession taxes actually paid to other states. With respect to the property located in another state that is owned or subject to tax, a portion of the credit is allocated to that state based on the value of the property taxed by the state as a fraction of the value of the total gross estate. The Alaska tax is the allowable credit less the lower of actual "constitutional" taxes paid each other state or the value determined by the fraction discussed above. The proportion allocable to other states is the ratio of the value of property taxed in the other states to the entire gross estate. (§ 43.31.011) With the repeal of the federal credit, no tax is currently imposed.	The tax is the amount of the credit allowable under the federal estate tax laws for taxes actually paid to the states, as the value of Alaska real and tangible personal property, intangible personal property with a business situs in Alaska, and the securities and obligations of corporations organized under Alaska's laws in Alaska bears to the entire gross estate. (§ 43.31.021) In the case of a nonresident *alien*, the property included is real, tangible personal, and "intangible personal property physically present" in Alaska. (§ 43.31.031(a)) The tax equals the proportion of the state death tax credit "actually paid to the several states" as the value of the aforesaid property taxable in Alaska bears to the value of the estate taxable by the U.S. wherever situated. (*Id.*) With the repeal of the federal credit, no tax is currently imposed.
Arizona	No. Repealed by Laws 2006, ch. 262, § 3, eff. Sept. 21, 2006.	N/A	N/A	N/A
Arkansas	No. (§25-59-103)	N/A	N/A	N/A
California	Yes. (Rev. & Tax. § 13302) However, the tax paid to California and at the federal level cannot exceed the death tax liability to	The tax is due at the date of the decedent's death and is delinquent if not paid within nine months of	The tax is the maximum allowable amount of the federal tax credit allocable to California situs property. This is determined by multiplying the credit by the percentage that the gross value of the property located in	Same as for a domiciliary. (Rev. & Tax. §§ 13302–13304) With the repeal of the federal credit, no tax is currently imposed.

	the U.S. if this section were not in effect. (*Id.*)	the death. (Rev. & Tax. §§ 13531–13532)	California bears to the gross value of the entire estate subject to the federal estate tax. (Rev. & Tax. §§ 13302–13304) With the repeal of the federal credit, no tax is currently imposed.	
Colorado	Yes. (§ 39-23.5-103)	The estate tax must be paid at the time for filing the federal estate tax return. (§§ 39-23.5-108(1), 39-23.5-107(1))	The tax is the amount of the federal credit. (§ 39-23.5-103(1)) The Colorado estate tax is reduced by the lesser of (1) the amount of the death tax paid to the other state which is allowed as a credit against the federal estate taxor (2) the amount which is determined by multiplying the federal credit by a fraction with the numerator equal to the value of the gross estate less the value of the property located in Colorado and with the denominator equal to the value of the gross estate. (§ 39-23.5-103(2)) With the repeal of the federal credit, no tax is currently imposed.	The tax is the amount determined by multiplying the federal credit by a fraction, with the numerator equal to the value of the property located in Colorado which is included in the gross estate and with the denominator equal to the value of the gross estate for purposes of the federal estate tax. (§ 39-23.5-104(2)) Property of a nondomiciliary that is located in Colorado includes real property situated in Colorado held in trust, and tangible property in the state, but intangibles that have acquired an actual or business situs in this state are not taxable. (§ 39-23.5-104(3)) With the repeal of the federal credit, no tax is currently imposed.
Connecticut	Yes. (§ 12-391)	The tax becomes due at the date of the decedent's death and is delinquent if not paid within nine months of death. (§ 12-392(a)(1))	The tax is imposed on the Connecticut taxable estate determined as under the federal estate tax with this amount taxed under the rates set forth in § 12-391(g). The Connecticut taxable estate includes taxable gifts since 2005. A credit is allowed for taxes paid on these gifts to the state. (§§ 12-391(c)(1), (d)(1)) See Table 15.07 and § 12-391(g) for the actual rates of tax. Taxable gifts are the same as for federal purposes, but not including transfers of real property and tangible personal property situated outside of the state. (§ 12-643(c))	Property subject to the tax includes real property in the state and tangible personal property having an actual situs in the state. The amount of the tax is computed by multiplying the tax determined under the rate schedule in § 12-391 by a fraction, the numerator of which is the value of the gross estate over which the state has jurisdiction, including taxable gifts since 2005, and the denominator of which is the value of the gross estate. A credit is allowed for gift tax paid to the state beginning in 2005. § 12-391(e)(1) Taxable gifts are the same as for federal purposes, but only pertains to transfers of real property and tangible personal property

(cont'd)

Table 15.02
Estate Tax *(continued)*

	Is There an Estate Tax?	*When Must Payment of Tax Be Made?*	*In the Case of an Estate Tax, How Is It Computed for a Domiciliary?*	*In the Case of an Estate Tax, How Is It Computed for a Nondomiciliary, U.S. Resident?*
Connecticut *(cont'd)*				situated in the state. (§ 12-643(c)) As for the actual rate of tax, see Table 15.07 and (§ 12-391(g))
Delaware	Yes. (30 § 1502)	Payment is due on or before the date for filing the return, which is due on the date for the federal estate tax return, with extensions. (30§ 1505)	The tax is equal to the federal credit (30 § 1502) The amount equal to death taxes paid to other state is subtracted from this amount. However, it cannot reduce the tax below the credit multiplied by a fraction, the numerator of which is the Delaware real and tangible personal property, as well as all intangible personal property, forming part of the taxable estate and the denominator being the taxable estate for federal estate tax purposes, excluding real and tangible personal property not located in any state. (30 § 1503) With the repeal of the federal credit, no tax is currently imposed.	The federal credit based on real property and tangible personal property in the state is multiplied by a fraction the numerator of which is real property and tangible personal property located in the state and the denominator of which is the decedent's federal taxable estate, not including real and tangible personal property not located in any state. (30 § 1504) With the repeal of the federal credit, no tax is currently imposed.
District of Columbia	Yes. (§ 47-3702(a))	Payment within 10 months of death. (§ 47-3705(a) & (c))	The tax is the amount of the federal credit, as in effect on January 1, 2001. (§ 47-3701; 47-3702(a)) The amount of estate tax due is reduced in the case of real or tangible personal property located outside D.C. by the lesser of the amount of the death tax paid to the other state or the amount computed by multiplying the federal credit by a fraction with a numerator of the value of the gross estate taxed by the other state and with a denominator of the value of the gross estate. (§ 47-3702(b))	The tax is the amount of the federal credit as in effect on January 1, 2001, (§§ 47-3701; 47-3702(a)) multiplied by a fraction with the numerator equal to the value of the gross estate over which the District of Columbia has jurisdiction and with the denominator equal to the value of the entire gross estate. (§ 47-3703(b))

Florida	Yes. (§ 198.02)	Payment of the estate tax must be made at the time for filing the federal estate tax return. (§ 198.15) This is required even if there is no Florida tax liability. Tax Information and Publication, No. 06C03-01, Fla. Dep't Rev., Feb. 15, 2006.	The tax is the amount of the federal credit. (§ 198.02) The tax is the amount by which the federal credit exceeds the aggregate amount of all constitutionally valid death taxes actually paid to other states in connection with the decedent's estate. (§ 198.02) With the repeal of the federal credit, no tax is currently imposed.	The tax is imposed on "every person who at the time of death was not a resident of this state but was a resident of the United States. . . ." The tax is the sum equal to the proportion of the amount of the federal credit, as the value of the real and tangible personal property with a situs in Florida, the intangible personal property having a business situs in the state, and the securities and obligations of corporations organized under Florida law bears to the value of the gross estate. (§ 198.03) In the case of a nonresident alien, the denominator of the fraction is the estate taxable by the U.S. wherever situated, life insurance on a nonresident alien, and deposits in a bank not engaged in a business in the U.S. are not deemed physically situated in Florida. (§ 198.04) With the repeal of the federal credit, no tax is currently imposed.
Georgia	No. (§ 48-12-1.1) Repealed by Laws 2005, Act 31, §26, effective April 12, 2005.	N/A	N/A	N/A
Hawaii	Yes. (§ 236D-3)	The payment of the estate tax is due at the time that the federal estate tax return must be filed. (§ 236D-6)	The tax is the amount of the federal credit. (§ 236D-3(a)) The tax is reduced by the lesser of the amount of tax paid to the other state or the amount computed by multiplying the federal credit by a fraction with a numerator equal to the value of the property subject to the death tax paid to the other state and with a denominator equal to the value of the gross estate. (§ 236D-3(b)) With the repeal of the federal credit, no tax is currently imposed.	The tax is computed by multiplying the federal credit by a fraction with the numerator equal to the value of the property situated in Hawaii and with the denominator equal to the value of the gross estate. (§ 236D-4(b)) Generally, Hawaii will not tax if the resident state also does not tax the property, except for real property with a situs in Hawaii and whether or not in a trust the corpus of which is part of the gross estate, a beneficial interest in a land trust owning real property in the state, and tangible personal property with a situs in the state. (§ 235D-4(c)) With the repeal of the federal credit, no tax is currently imposed.

Table 15.02
Estate Tax *(continued)*

	Is There an Estate Tax?	*When Must Payment of Tax Be Made?*	*In the Case of an Estate Tax, How Is It Computed for a Domiciliary?*	*In the Case of an Estate Tax, How Is It Computed for a Nondomiciliary, U.S. Resident?*
Idaho	Yes. (§ 14-403)	Payment is due on or before the federal estate tax return filing deadline. (§ 14-406(1))	The starting point is the "property of a resident," which includes Idaho real property, tangible personal property with a situs in Idaho, and all intangible personal property owned by the resident, regardless of where it is located. (§ 14-403(3)) The tax is the amount of the federal credit. (§ 14-403(1)) The tax is reduced by the lesser of: (a) the amount of tax paid to the other state or (b) the amount computed by multiplying the federal credit by a fraction with a numerator equal to the value of the property subject to the death tax paid to the other state and with a denominator equal to the value of the gross estate. (§ 14-403(2)) With the repeal of the federal credit, no tax is currently imposed.	The tax is computed by multiplying the federal credit by a fraction with the numerator equal to the value of the property "located in Idaho" and with the denominator equal to the value of the gross estate. (§ 14-404(2)) Property is exempt from tax to the extent that the same types of property of a resident are exempt from taxation under the nondomicilary's state. (§ 14-404(3)) With the repeal of the federal credit, no tax is currently imposed.
Illinois	Yes. (35 ILCS § 405/3(a)) Note: The Illinois estate tax is still computed with respect to the federal taxable estate, which includes the § 2058 deduction for state death taxes. As a result, this has to be removed from the computation of the Illinois estate tax. An interrelated computation is involved. The attorney general's office will make the computation. See 2006 Important Notice Regarding Illinois Estate Tax and Fact	The payment of the estate tax is due at the same time as the dead line for paying the federal estate tax. (35 ILCS § 405/6(a))	For decedents dying on or after January 1, 2003 and on or before December 31, 2005, the tax is the amount of the federal credit as of December 31, 2001. (35 ILCS § 405/2 "State Tax Credit" (a)) For decedents dying on or after January 1, 2006 and on or before December 31, 2009, the tax is the amount of the federal credit as of December 31, 2001. However, the exclusion amount is fixed at $2,000,000 through 2009. (*Id.* (b)) For decedents dying after December 31, 2009, the tax is equal to the amount of the credit allowable under § 2011 or § 2604 of the Code. (*Id.* (c)). The tax is reduced by the lesser of the amount of the federal credit paid to another state and the amount computed by multiplying the federal credit by	Same as for a domiciliary. (35 ILCS § 405/3(b)) However, the property subject to tax is Illinois-situs real property and tangible personal property, including only such property held in trust. (35 ICLS § 405/5 (a))

	Sheet. See www.illinoisattorneygeneral.gov/publications/pdf/Estate_Tax_Notice_2006.pdf.		the fraction with the numerator equal to the gross value of the transferred property having a tax situs in another state and with the denominator equal to the gross value of all the transferred property. (35 ILCS § 405/3(b))	
Indiana	Yes. (§ 6-4.1-11-1)	The tax must be paid within 12 months after the date of the decedent's death. (§ 6-4.1-11-3(a))	The tax is the amount in step four. Step one: Divide (a) the value of the real and tangible personal property located in Indiana and the value of intangible personal property wherever located by (b) the value of the total gross estate for federal tax purposes. Step two: Multiply (a) the quotient from step one by (b) the federal credit for state death taxes paid. Step three: Subtract (a) the amount of all Indiana inheritance taxes actually paid from (b) the product from step two. Step four: Determine the greater of (a) the remainder from step three or (b) zero. (§ 6-4.1-11-2(a)) With the repeal of the federal credit, no tax is currently imposed.	Same as for a domiciliary, except intangible personal property is not included in (a) of step one. (§ 6-4.1-11-2(b)) With the repeal of the federal credit, no tax is currently imposed.
Iowa	Yes. (§ 451.2)	The estate tax is due nine months after the decedent's death. (§ 451.6)	The tax is the amount of the federal estate tax credit for state death taxes if all the property "is located in Iowa, or is subject to the jurisdiction of the courts of Iowa." If there is property "located outside" Iowa, the credit for state death taxes is prorated on the basis that the "Iowa property" bears to the gross estate for purposes of the federal tax. (§ 451.2(1)) The estate tax is credited with the amount of any inheritance tax due to Iowa. (§ 451.2(2)) With the repeal of the federal credit, no tax is currently imposed.	Same as for a domiciliary when proration is used. (§ 451.2) With the repeal of the federal credit, no tax is currently imposed.
Kansas	See Tables 15.01 & 15.07.	See Table 15.01.	See Table 15.01.	See Table 15.01.

Table 15.02
Estate Tax *(continued)*

	Is There an Estate Tax?	*When Must Payment of Tax Be Made?*	*In the Case of an Estate Tax, How Is It Computed for a Domiciliary?*	*In the Case of an Estate Tax, How Is It Computed for a Nondomiciliary, U.S. Resident?*
Kentucky	Yes. (§ 140.130)	The estate tax is due at death and is delinquent if not paid within 18 months. There is a discount of 5% if the taxes are paid within nine months. (§ 140.210(1))	The tax is computed by multiplying the federal credit for state death taxes by the ratio that the portion of the net estate over which Kentucky has jurisdiction bears to the total net estate. The total amount of inheritance taxes paid, less any discount taken, is credited against the estate tax. (§ 140.130) With the repeal of the federal credit, no tax is currently imposed.	Same as for a domiciliary. (§ 140.130(2)) With the repeal of the federal credit, no tax is currently imposed.
Louisiana	Yes. (§ 47:2431)	Estate taxes must be paid prior to the filing of the federal estate tax return or nine months after the death of the decedent, whichever comes first. (§ 47:2432(B)) Interest begins to accrue on unpaid estate taxes after nine months. (§ 47:2420(A))	The tax is the amount of the federal credit less Louisiana inheritance taxes until July 1, 2004. On or after July 1, 2004, the tax is the amount of federal credit. (§ 47:2432(A)) Louisiana does not provide for the accommodation of other states. The maximum amount of the credit for the state death taxes must be paid to the state. (§ 47:2432) The tax is not explicitly limited as to individuals or property and is, thus, apparently, limited only by federal constitutional constraints. With the repeal of the federal credit, no tax is currently imposed.	Same as for domiciliary to the extent Louisiana has jurisdiction over some of estate property. (§ 47:2432(A)) With the repeal of the federal credit, no tax is currently imposed.
Maine	Yes. (36 § 4063)	Estate taxes are due nine months from the date of the testator. (36 § 4068)	Imposed with respect to every person who dies on or after Jan. 1, 2002, and was a domiciliary at the time of death. The amount is equal to the federal credit multiplied by a fraction, the numerator of which consists of Maine real and personal tangible property, as well as all intangible property. Denominator consists of the decedent's gross estate. This is modified by Maine qualified terminable interest property and Maine elective property. (36 § 4063) See also 36 § 4062 (1-A) for	A tax is imposed upon the transfer of real property situated in the state and upon tangible personal property located in the state. This applies whether or not the property is held in trust or via a pass-through entity. The amount of the tax is a sum equal to proportion of the federal credit for state death taxes which the value of Maine real and tangible personal property taxed in the state which qualifies for the federal credit bears to the value of the

			Maine qualified terminable interest property and Maine elective property. The first reduces the gross estate and the second increases it comparable to I.R.C. § 2044. "Federal credit" means the maximum credit as determined as of December 31, 2002. (§ 4062) In addition, for purposes of calculating the state death tax credit, the unified credit amount is determined as of December 31, 2000. (§ 4062)	decedent's total federal gross estate. (36 § 4064)
Maryland	Yes. (Tax-Gen. § 7-302)	Generally, the payment must be made nine months after the decedent's death. (Tax-Gen. §§ 7-305, 7-306)	The tax is the difference between the inheritance tax and any greater amount of the federal credit allocable to Maryland, which is the amount of the federal credit reduced by the proportion that the amount of the estate not included in the Maryland estate bears to the amount of the entire estate. (Tax-Gen. § 7-304) Notwithstanding a reduction upon repeal of the federal credit, the Maryland estate tax will remain in force without reduction as if there had been no reduction or repeal in the federal credit. (§ 7-309) The federal credit should be determined as in effect on December 31, 2001. (§ 7-309(b)) The federal credit used to determine the Maryland estate tax may not exceed 16% of the amount by which the decendent's taxable estate, as defined under I.R.C. § 2051, exceeds $ 1,000,000. (§ 7-309 (b)(2)(iii))	Same as for a domiciliary. (Tax-Gen. § 7-304) The tax is imposed on the transfer of the Maryland estate of each decedent who was a nonresident whose estate includes any interest in real or tangible personal property located in Maryland. (Tax-Gen. § 7-302(2)) A provision indicates that Maryland will tax the out-of-state tangible personal property of a nonresident otherwise being taxed, if its state does not accord a reciprocal benefit to Maryland residents. The provision is meaningless, since there is a federal constitutional prohibition against taxing the out-of-state tangible personal property of a nonresident decedent. (Tax-Gen. § 7-303(a))
Massachusetts	Yes. (65C § 2A)	The estate tax is due and payable 9 months from the date of death.	The tax is the amount by which the federal estate tax credit (as in effect on December 31, 2000) exceeds the lesser of (a) the aggregate amount of constitutionally valid estate, legacy and succession taxes actually paid to the several states or (b) an amount equal to such proportion of such allowable credit as the value of properties taxable by other states bears to the value of the entire federal gross estate wherever situated. (65C § 2A(a))	A tax is imposed on real and tangible personal property located in Massachusetts. The amount of the tax is the sum equal to the proportion of the credit which the value of Massachusetts real and tangible personal property taxed in Massachusetts which qualifies for such credit bears to the value of the decedent's total federal gross estate. (65C § 2A(b))

Table 15.02
Estate Tax *(continued)*

	Is There an Estate Tax?	*When Must Payment of Tax Be Made?*	*In the Case of an Estate Tax, How Is It Computed for a Domiciliary?*	*In the Case of an Estate Tax, How Is It Computed for a Nondomiciliary, U.S. Resident?*
Michigan	Yes. (§ 205.232) Because a taxpayer can choose the maximum allowable federal credit now in effect, zero, the tax has been effectively repealed.	Taxes are due and payable on or before the last day prescribed by law for paying the corresponding federal transfer taxes, pursuant to the federal return, excluding extensions. (§ 205.236)	Tax is equal to the maximum allowable federal credit for state death taxes, I.R.C. § 2011, in effect on January 1, 1998 or, at the option of the personal representative, in effect on the date of the decedent's death. (§ 205:256(g)) The personal representative has the option of choosing the federal credit in effect on January 1, 1998 or at the date of the decedent's death. (§ 205.256(g)) The tax is reduced by the amount of all estate, inheritance, legacy and succession taxes paid to states other than Michigan, which amount is not to exceed an amount equal to the proportionate share of that maximum allowable federal credit that the gross value of all real and tangible personal property located in states other than Michigan bears to the gross value of all property included in the decedent's gross estate wherever located. (§ 205.232(1)) With the repeal of the federal credit, no tax is currently imposed.	Tax is an amount equal to the proportionate share of the maximum allowable federal credit that the gross value of all real and tangible personal property located in Michigan bears to the gross value of all property included in the decedent's gross estate wherever located. (§ 205.232(2)) Nonresidents may be entitled to an exemption for personal property located in Michigan. (§ 205.253) The allowable federal credit means the federal credit for state death taxes, I.R.C. § 2011, in effect on January 1, 1998 or, at the option of the personal representative, in effect on the date of the decedent's death. (§ 205:256(g)) With the repeal of the federal credit, no tax is currently imposed.
Minnesota	Yes. (§ 291.01)	The tax is due nine months after the decedent's death. (§ 289A.20(3))	The tax is the proportion of the maximum federal credit, as amended through December 31, 2000, for state death taxes that the "Minnesota gross estate" bears to the value of the federal gross estate. (§ 291.03(1)) The Minnesota gross estate is equal to the federal gross estate, but does not include any property with a situs outside Minnesota. (§ 291.005(2)) For purposes of calculating the state estate tax, the federal unified credit amount determined as of December 31, 2000 is used. (§ 291.03(1))	The tax is the proportion of the federal credit for state death taxes that the "Minnesota gross estate" bears to the value of the federal gross estate. (§ 291.03(1))

Mississippi	Yes. (§ 27-9-5)	Taxes are due nine months after the decedent's death. (§ 27-9-27)	The tax is the maximum amount of state death tax credit or deduction. The tax imposed should not exceed the aggregate amounts which may be credited against or deducted for federal estate tax. The tax imposed should be in the proportion that the Mississippi estate bears to the entire estate wherever located. (§ 27-9-5) With the repeal of the federal credit, no tax is currently imposed.	Same as for domiciliary. (§ 27-9-5) With the repeal of the federal credit, no tax is currently imposed.
Missouri	Yes. (§ 145.011)	The estate tax must be paid when the return is filed (i.e., within nine months of the death). (§ 145.511)	The tax is the amount of the federal credit, reduced by an amount computed by multiplying the tax by a fraction with the numerator equal to the gross estate excluding all property having a "tax situs" outside of Missouri and with the denominator equal to the value of the gross estate for federal tax purposes. (§§ 145.011, 145.041) With the repeal of the federal credit, no tax is currently imposed.	Same as for a domiciliary. (§§ 145.011, 145.041) With the repeal of the federal credit, no tax is currently imposed.
Montana	Yes. (§ 72-16-904)	Estate taxes are due 18 months from the death of the decedent. (§ 72-16-909)	The tax is equal to the maximum federal credit allowable against the federal estate tax imposed with respect to the portion of the decedent's estate having a taxable situs in Montana, less the inheritance taxes due the state. If only a portion of the estate has a tax situs in Montana, the credit is determined by multiplying the federal credit by the percentage that the value of the estate property having a tax situs in Montana bears to the value of the entire estate. (§ 72-16-905) With the repeal of the federal credit, no tax is currently imposed.	Same as for domiciliary. (§ 72-16-905) With the repeal of the federal credit, no tax is currently imposed.
Nebraska	Yes. (§ 77-2101.01)	The tax must be paid within 12 months of the decedent's death. (§ 77-2102)	The tax should be calculated according to the schedule in § 77-2101.03, reduced by the lesser of (1) the aggregate amount of all taxes paid to other states, or (2) the sum of	The tax is only imposed on real and tangible personal property in Nebraska. The amount of the tax and its proration is determined as with a domiciliary. (§§ 77-2101.01 & 77-2101.03)

(cont'd)

Table 15.02
Estate Tax *(continued)*

	Is There an Estate Tax?	*When Must Payment of Tax Be Made?*	*In the Case of an Estate Tax, How Is It Computed for a Domiciliary?*	*In the Case of an Estate Tax, How Is It Computed for a Nondomiciliary, U.S. Resident?*
Nebraska *(cont'd)*			(a) the amount determined by multiplying the amount calculated in § 77-2101.03 (see Table 13.07) by the percentage which the gross value of the property not situated in Nebraska bears to the total gross estate, and (b) the amount of Nebraska inheritance taxes paid. (§§ 77-2101.01 & 77-2101.03).	
Nevada	Yes. (§ 375A.100)	The estate tax payment is due at the date of death and is delinquent if not paid within nine months. (§ 375A.200(3))	The tax is imposed on real and tangible personal property with a situs in Nevada, as well as all intangible personal property. (§ 375A.100(1)) The tax is the amount of the federal credit allocable to Nevada property. (§ 375A.100(1)) The allocable portion of the credit is determined by multiplying the federal credit by the percentage that the gross value of the property taxable by Nevada bears to the gross value of the total estate subject to federal estate tax. (§ 375A.105) With the repeal of the federal credit, no tax is currently imposed.	Same as for domiciliaries, except that the tax is imposed only on Nevada situs real property, tangible personal property, and intangible personal property in Nevada, including stock of a corporation recognized or having its principal place of business in Nevada or doing a "major part of its business in Nevada" or a federal corporation or national bank with its principal place of its business or a major part of its business in Nevada. However, savings accounts in S&Ls, and bank deposits not used in connection with a business conducted or operating in Nevada are excluded. (§ 375A.100(2)) With the repeal of the federal credit, no tax is currently imposed.
New Hampshire	Yes. (§ 87:1)	The estate tax is due at the same time the federal estate tax is payable. (§ 87:2)	Tax equals the maximum federal credit allowable with respect to property subject to New Hampshire state tax. The tax is imposed in every case in which the credit for state death taxes paid is available as a credit on the decedent's federal estate tax return. (§ 87:1) With the repeal of the federal credit, no tax is currently imposed.	Same as for domiciliary. (§ 87:1) With the repeal of the federal credit, no tax is currently imposed.

New Jersey	Yes. (§ 54:38-1)	Estate taxes are due nine months from the death of the decedent. All taxes not paid at the expiration of nine months accrue interest at 10% per annum. (§ 54:38-5)	The amount of the tax is, at the election of the person liable for the payment, either the maximum amount of the federal credit as in effect on December 31, 2001, or an amount determined pursuant to the simplified tax (computation) system to produce a similar liability. (§ 54:38-1(a)(2)(a)) The amount of the tax is the excess, if any, of the federal credit over the aggregate amount of all estate, inheritance, succession or legacy taxes actually paid to any and all states and territories, including New Jersey. (§ 54:38-1(b))	Estate tax is levied only on residents. (§ 54:38-1)
New Mexico	Yes. (§ 7-7-3(A))	The tax must be paid at the time that the federal return is filed. (§ 7-7-6)	The tax is the amount of the federal credit. (§ 7-7-3(A)) The tax is credited with the lesser of the amount of the death tax paid to another state and credited against the federal estate tax or of the amount determined by multiplying the federal credit by a fraction with the numerator equal to the value of the property subject to the death tax of another state and with the denominator equal to the value of the gross estate for federal tax purposes. (§ 7-7-3(B)) With the repeal of the federal credit, no tax is currently imposed.	The tax is determined by multiplying the federal credit by the fraction with the numerator equal to the value of the property located in New Mexico and with the denominator equal to the value of the gross estate for federal tax purposes. (§ 7-7-4(B)) With the repeal of the federal credit, no tax is currently imposed.
New York	Yes. (Tax § 952)	Estate taxes are due within nine months after the date of death. (Tax §§ 972 & 974)	The tax is the maximum amount of the federal credit calculated under the Internal Revenue Code as in effect on July 22, 1998. (Tax § 951(a)) The unified credit amount used for the calculation is the amount in effect at death, but not greater than $1,000,000. (*Id.*) However, if the transfer is subject to tax by another state regarding *(cont'd)*	Nonresidents are taxed on the transfer of real and tangible personal property that is located in the state and that would be includible in the decedent's federal estate or New York gross estate if the decedent were a resident of the state. The tax otherwise is generally computed the same as for domiciliaries. However, the "New York gross estate" in the numerator *(cont'd)*

Table 15.02
Estate Tax *(continued)*

	Is There an Estate Tax?	*When Must Payment of Tax Be Made?*	*In the Case of an Estate Tax, How Is It Computed for a Domiciliary?*	*In the Case of an Estate Tax, How Is It Computed for a Nondomiciliary, U.S. Resident?*
New York *(cont'd)*			which the credit is allowed, then the N.Y. state tax is reduced by the lesser of the death taxes paid to other states and allowable as the credit or an amount determined by multiplying the maximum amount of the credit by a fraction, the numerator of which is the decedent's federal gross estate reduced by his New York gross estate and the denominator of which is his federal gross estate. (Tax § 952) The N.Y. gross estate is the federal gross estate reduced by the value of real or tangible personal property with "an actual situs outside New York state." (Tax § 954)	does not include intangible personal property. (Tax§ 960) This can lead to a major New York liability as the state death tax credit is phased out since it allows New York to keep taxes equal to the former allowable state death tax credit and determined under the harsher federal tax law as in effect in 1998. This can lead to a major New York liability as the state death tax credit is phased out since it allows New York to keep taxes equal to the former allowable state death tax credit and determined under the harsher federal tax law as in effect in 1998.
North Carolina	Yes. (§ 105-32.2)	Taxes are due when a federal estate tax return is due. (§ 105-32.4) If there is a correction at the federal level in the tax due or the amount of the state death tax credit, the personal representative must file a corrected state tax return. (§ 105-32.8)	The tax is the amount of the federal credit as in effect on December 31, 2001. The tax is reduced by the lesser of the death tax paid another state or an amount equal to the credit amount multiplied by a fraction, the numerator of which is the "North Carolina percentage." This is the value of the estate that has a tax situs in another state and the denominator of which is the decedent's federal gross estate.	The tax is the amount of the federal credit as in effect on December 31, 2001, multiplied by a fraction, the numerator of which is the value of real property and tangible personal property located in North Carolina and intangible personal property having a "tax situs" there and the denominator of which is the value of the federal gross estate. (§ 105-32.2).
North Dakota	Yes. (§ 57-37.1-02)	The tax is due at the death of the	The tax is the amount of the federal credit that is allocable for the portion of the estate	

		decedent and is late if not paid within 15 months. (§ 57-37.1-07)	having a "taxable situs" in North Dakota, which is determined by multiplying the credit by the percentage that the value of the estate having a "taxable situs" in North Dakota bears to the entire federal gross estate. (§ 57-37.1-04(1)) Situs rules are set forth in § 57-37.1-01(6). In the case of tangible personal property, its situs is where "it was normally kept or located at the time of the decedent's death." For intangible property, it is the state of residence. With the repeal of the federal credit, no tax is currently imposed.	Same as for a domiciliary. (§ 57-37.1-04) With the repeal of the federal credit, no tax is currently imposed.
Ohio	Yes. (§ 5731.02)	The estate tax payment is due nine months after the decedent's death. (§ 5731.23)	A regular estate tax is imposed independent of the federal credit. (§ 5731.02) It is imposed on all property wherever situated, other than out of state real property and tangible personal property having an "actual situs" out of state. (§ 5731.01(A)) An additional estate tax in the amount of the federal credit is also imposed on residents. This additional tax is credited with the amount of any death taxes paid under the regular Ohio estate tax (§ 5731.02) as well as to any state or the District of Columbia. (§ 5731.18) Since the pickup tax is based on the death taxes and references to the Internal Revenue Code are to the Code on December 28, 2006, a time when the credit was repealed, there is no pick-up tax any longer. (§ 5701.11(A), enacted by 2006 H699, eff. Dec. 28, 2006)	The tax is computed by determining the amount of tax that would be payable if the decedent was a domiciliary. This amount is then multiplied by a fraction with the numerator equal to the value of the real property situated in Ohio and tangible personal property with an "actual situs" in the state, as well as intangible personal property used in carrying on a business in the state, and with the denominator equal to the value of the gross estate, wherever the property is situated. (§ 5731.19(B)) An additional estate tax is also imposed. The tax is the amount of the additional estate tax that would be levied if the decedent was a resident multiplied by a fraction with the numerator equal to the value of the real and tangible personal property located in Ohio and intangible property used in carrying on a business in Ohio and with the denominator equal to the value of the gross estate, wherever the property is situated. The amount of the estate tax already imposed is

(cont'd)

Table 15.02
Estate Tax *(continued)*

	Is There an Estate Tax?	*When Must Payment of Tax Be Made?*	*In the Case of an Estate Tax, How Is It Computed for a Domiciliary?*	*In the Case of an Estate Tax, How Is It Computed for a Nondomiciliary, U.S. Resident?*
Ohio *(cont'd)*				credited against the additional estate tax. (§ 5731.19(C))
Oklahoma	Yes. (68 § 802)	The tax is due at the time of death and is delinquent if not paid within nine months of the death. (68 § 806(a))	There is an estate tax independent of the federal credit. (68 § 803) It probably applies to property "in" Oklahoma, although this is not certain. If the estate tax is less than the allowable federal credit for state death taxes paid, an additional tax equal to the difference between the estate tax and the federal credit is also imposed. The federal credit for death taxes is the percentage of the credit that bears the same percentage as the value of the property of the estate "in" Oklahoma bears to the total value of the estate. (68 § 804) Note that the federal credit has been repealed so there is no longer a pick-up tax.	Same as for a domiciliary. However, intangible personal property is not included in the gross estate, unless (a) the jurisdiction or residence did not impose a death tax regarding personal property, other than tangible personal property having "an actual situs" in the jurisdiction, or (b) the jurisdiction granted a reciprocal exemption to nonresidents for personal property other than tangible personal property having an actual situs there and the exemption is afforded to residents of the jurisdiction of the residence of the transferor. (68 §§ 804, 807)
Oregon	Yes. (§ 118.010)	Tax is due at same time the federal estate tax is payable. (§ 118.100(1))	The tax is the maximum federal credit. If the domiciliary owns property outside Oregon's jurisdiction, then the tax is equal to the credit multiplied by a fraction, the numerator of which is real and tangible personal property located in Oregon and intangible personal property located everywhere, and the denominator of which is the total appraised value of the decedent's gross estate. (§ 118.010(3)) With the repeal of the federal credit, no tax is currently imposed.	The tax is the maximum federal credit multiplied by a ratio. The numerator is the sum of appraised value of real, tangible personal property and intangible property located in Oregon. The denominator is the total appraised value of the decedent's gross estate. (§ 118.010(4)(a)) Intangible personal property is exempted if Oregon domiciliaries are given a similar exemption by the state or country of domicile. (§ 118.010(4)(b)) With the repeal of the federal credit, no tax is currently imposed.
Pennsylvania	Yes. (72 § 9117)	The tax is due nine months after the	If the inheritance tax paid is less than the federal state death tax credit, then an estate	The tax is computed by multiplying the maximum federal credit for state death taxes by a

		decedent's death. (72 § 9145(c))	tax for the difference is imposed. (72 § 9117) The tax is reduced by the greater of: (a) the amount of death taxes actually paid to other states except for any death tax expressly imposed to receive the benefit of the federal credit; or (b) the amount determined by multiplying the federal credit by a fraction with the numerator equal to the value of the real property and tangible personal property located in another state and with the denominator equal to the value of the decedent's gross estate for federal estate tax purposes. (72 § 9117) With the repeal of the federal credit, no tax is currently imposed.	fraction with the numerator equal to the value of the real or tangible personal property having a situs in Pennsylvania and with the denominator equal to the value of the gross estate for purposes of the federal estate tax. The tax is reduced by the amount of any inheritance tax paid. (72 § 9117) With the repeal of the federal credit, no tax is currently imposed.
Rhode Island	Yes. (§ 44-22-1.1)	Taxes due nine months from the death of the decedent. (§ 44-23-16)	The tax is equal to the maximum credit for state death taxes allowed by § 2011 as in effect on January 1, 2001. (§ 44-22-1.1(a)(2)). State tax is reduced to an amount determined by multiplying the tax by a fraction whose numerator is the gross estate excluding all property not having a "tax situs" in the state and whose denominator is the gross estate. (§ 44-22-1.1(b)) Property has a tax situs in Rhode Island if it is real or tangible personal property with an actual situs in the state or any intangible personal property of a decedent who was a resident. (§ 44-22-1.1(e)) For purposes of calculating the state death tax credit, the unified credit amount is determined as of December 31, 2000. (§ 44-22-1.1(a)(2))	The provision is the same as for residents, except that nonresidents are not subject to estate tax for intangible personal property. (§ 44-22-1.1)
South Carolina	Yes. (§ 12-16-510)	The estate tax is due nine months after the death. (§ 12-16-1110)	The tax is the amount of the federal credit based on the Internal Revenue Code on December 31, 2005. Since on that same date the Code did not provide for a federal credit for state death taxes, there is no actual tax imposed by South Carolina.	The federal credit is multiplied by a fraction with the numerator equal to the portion of the gross estate over which South Carolina has jurisdiction for estate tax purposes and with the denominator equal to the value of the

(cont'd) *(cont'd)*

Table 15.02
Estate Tax *(continued)*

	Is There an Estate Tax?	*When Must Payment of Tax Be Made?*	*In the Case of an Estate Tax, How Is It Computed for a Domiciliary?*	*In the Case of an Estate Tax, How Is It Computed for a Nondomiciliary, U.S. Resident?*
South Carolina *(cont'd)*			(§§ 12-16-510(A); 12-16-20(5); 12-6-40(A)) If real or tangible property is located out of state, the tax due is credited with the lesser of: (a) the amount of the death tax paid to another state that is credited against the federal tax; or (b) the amount computed by multiplying the credit by a fraction with the numerator equal to the value of the gross estate over which another state has jurisdiction but only to the same extent South Carolina would exert jurisdiction to tax a resident of the other state(s) and with the denominator equal to the value of the gross estate. (§ 12-16-510)	gross estate. Intangible personal property is not included. (§ 12-16-520)
South Dakota	Yes. (§ 10-40A-2)	The estate tax is due at death and is payable as soon as the amount of tax is determined. (§ 10-41-61)	The tax is imposed on the transfer of the estate and is the difference between the federal credit and any lesser state death taxes imposed by South Dakota. The tax is reduced by any state death taxes other than pick-up state death taxes imposed by another state on property included in the gross estate. (§ 10-40A-3) With the repeal of the federal credit, no tax is currently imposed.	Same as for domiciliaries, except the tax applies only to tangible personal property or real property in South Dakota. (§ 10-40A-2) With the repeal of the federal credit, no tax is currently imposed.
Tennessee	Yes. (§ 67-8-204)	Estate taxes are payable at the same time at which the federal estate tax is payable. (§ 67-8-207)	The tax is equal to the amount of the excess of the federal credit over the aggregate of Tennessee inheritance and other state taxes payable out of the "Tennessee estate." (§ 67-8-204) The Tennessee estate is the property the transfer of which Tennessee has	Same as for domiciliaries if owned real property situated within the state or tangible personal property having an actual situs in the state. (§§ 67-8-202(2), 67-8-204)

			the power to tax. (§ 67-8-202(8)) The estate tax is a pick-up tax and does not yield additional tax because of the repeal of the federal credit.	
Texas	Yes. (Tax § 211.051)	Payment is due nine months after the decedent's death. (Tax § 211.102)	The estate tax is equal to the amount of the federal credit. However, the tax is reduced by the lesser of: (a) the amount of the death tax paid to another state that is allowable as a federal credit; or (b) the amount computed by multiplying the credit by a fraction with the numerator equal to the value of the federal gross estate less the value of the real and tangible personal property located in Texas and less the value of the intangible personal property wherever located and with the denominator equal to the value of the federal gross estate. (Tax § 211.051) The physical location of evidence of intangible property is not relevant. Real property in a personal trust is not taxed if the real property has an actual situs outside Texas. (Tax § 211.051(c)) With the repeal of the federal credit, no tax is currently imposed.	The tax is determined by multiplying the federal credit by a fraction, the numerator of which is the value of property located in Texas and included in the gross estate, and the denominator of which is the gross estate. (Tax § 211.052(b)) Property located in Texas includes real property having an actual situs in Texas, whether or not held in trust, and tangible personal property having an actual situs in the state. (Tax § 211.052(b) & (c)) In the case of a nonresident alien, property located in Texas includes real property in Texas whether or not held in trust and tangible personal property in Texas. However, intangibles in Texas are *not* taxable. In the case of a nonresident alien, any intangible property located in the state or directly or indirectly subject to the protection, preservation, or regulation under state law is taken into account, to the extent includable in the gross estate. In other respects, the calculation is the same as for domiciliaries of other states. (Tax § 211.053) With the repeal of the federal credit, no tax is currently imposed.
Utah	Yes. (§ 59-11-103)	Payment is due on or before the date that the federal return is	The tax is imposed on the taxable estate in an amount equal to the federal credit. If another state is taxing "property of a	The tax is equal to an amount computed by multiplying the federal credit by a fraction, the numerator of which is the value of "property

(cont'd) *(cont'd)*

Table 15.02
Estate Tax *(continued)*

	Is There an Estate Tax?	*When Must Payment of Tax Be Made?*	*In the Case of an Estate Tax, How Is It Computed for a Domiciliary?*	*In the Case of an Estate Tax, How Is It Computed for a Nondomiciliary, U.S. Resident?*
Utah *(cont'd)*		due, including extensions. (§§ 59-11-106(1), 59-11-105(1))	resident," then the Utah tax is reduced by the lesser of the amount of the death tax paid to another state or of the amount computed by multiplying the federal credit by a fraction with the numerator equal to the value of the property subject to the death tax of another state and with the denominator equal to the value of the gross estate. (§ 59-11-103) The "property of a resident" includes real property located in the state, tangible personal property having an "actual situs" in the state, and all intangible personal property owned by the resident. (§ 59-11-103(3)) With the repeal of the federal credit, no tax is currently imposed.	located in this state," and the denominator of which is the value of the gross estate. The "property located in this state" includes (a) real property and interests such as mineral interests, royalties, production payments, leasehold interests, or working interests in minerals; (b)tangible personal property with an actual situs in Utah, including money; (c) intangible personal property having a trade or business situs in Utah; and (d) the securities of a corporation organized in Utah. (§ 59-11-104(3)) With the repeal of the federal credit, no tax is currently imposed.
Vermont	Yes. (32 § 7442a)	The tax is due at the time the federal estate tax return must be filed. (32 §§ 7447 & 7446)	The tax is imposed on the "Vermont estate," which term is not defined by statute. The tax is the amount of the federal credit as in effect on January 1, 2001 that exceeds the lesser of (a)the amount of all constitutionally valid state death taxes actually paid to other states, or (b)the amount equal to the proportion of the federal credit which the property taxed by other states bears to the value of the gross estate for federal tax purposes. (32 § 7442a)	The tax is the amount equal to the proportion of the federal credit that the value of the Vermont real and tangible personal property taxed in Vermont bears to the value of the total gross estate for federal estate tax purposes. (32 § 7442a)
Virginia	Yes. (§ 58.1-902) However, there is no tax for estates of decedents dying on or after July 1, 2007, because the tax is based on the repealed IRC §	The estate tax is due at the time the federal estate tax return must be filed. (§ 58.1-905)	The tax is imposed on the taxable estate, which is determined as per I.R.C. § 2051. (§ 58.1-901) Apparently, the "property of a resident" subject to tax includes real property in Virginia, tangible personal property with an "actual situs" there, and all	The tax is the amount determined by multiplying the federal credit by a fraction with the numerator equal to the value of the gross estate over which Virginia has jurisdiction and with the denominator equal to the value of the gross estate for federal estate tax purposes.

	2011 credit for state death taxes. (§58.1-901) See ch. 4, H.B. No. 5019, §§ 1, 6. (Aug. 28, 2006)		intangible property regardless of where it is located. The tax is equal to the amount of the federal credit. (§ 58.1-902) If the Virginia resident had real and tangible personal property located outside the state and subject to a death tax for which the I.R.C. § 2011 federal credit is allowed, then the tax due will be credited with an amount equal to the lesser of (a) the amount of the death tax paid to another state and credited against the federal credit or (b) the amount computed by multi plying the federal credit by a fraction the numerator of which is equal to the value of the property over which another state has jurisdiction and the denominator of which is equal to the value of the gross estate. (§ 58.1-902)	(§ 58.1-903) The tax does not apply to intangible personal property. (§ 58.1-903)
Washington	Yes. (§ 83.100.040)	The payment of the estate tax coincides with the filing requirements for the federal tax return not including any extensions for filing, generally within 9 months of decedent's date of death. (§ 83.100.050)	Every transfer of property located in Washington is subject to tax. This includes any intangible property of a resident, wherever located. (§ 83.100.040)	Property located in Washington is subject to tax. (§ 83.100.040(b)) The tax is calculated on the basis of the property located in Washington, which is the numerator of the fraction and the gross estate of the decedent is the denominator of the fraction. The fraction is multiplied by the value of the Washington taxable estate, which is the same as the value of the federal taxable estate. *Id.* Also, intangibles are presumably not Washington property of a nondomiciliary of Washington. (§ 83.100.040(l))
West Virginia	Yes. (§ 11-11-3)	The tax is due on the date of the decedent's death and is delinquent if the tax is unpaid nine months after the *(cont'd)*	The tax is imposed on the net taxable estate, (§ 11-11-2) which is determined as per IRC § 2051. Apparently, the "property of a resident" subject to tax includes real property in West Virginia, taxable personal property with an "actual situs" there, and all intangible *(cont'd)*	The tax is computed by multiplying the federal credit by a fraction with the numerator equal to the value of the property over which West Virginia exerts jurisdiction for purposes of the estate tax and with the denominator equal to the value of the gross estate for purposes of *(cont'd)*

Table 15.02
Estate Tax *(continued)*

	Is There an Estate Tax?	*When Must Payment of Tax Be Made?*	*In the Case of an Estate Tax, How Is It Computed for a Domiciliary?*	*In the Case of an Estate Tax, How Is It Computed for a Nondomiciliary, U.S. Resident?*
West Virginia *(cont'd)*		payment due date. (§ 11-11-13)	property. The tax is the amount of the federal credit. The tax is reduced by the lesser of (a) the amount of the death tax paid to another state and credited against the federal estate tax and the federal generation-skipping tax, or (b) the amount computed by multiplying the federal credit by a fraction the numerator of which is equal to the value of the property over which the other state has jurisdiction "to the same extent to which West Virginia would exert jurisdiction . . . with respect to residents of such other state (or states)," and the denominator of which is equal to the value of the gross estate for federal tax purposes. (§ 11-11-4) With the repeal of the federal credit, no tax is currently imposed.	the federal estate tax. The estate tax of a nondomiciliary applies to real and tangible personal property located in West Virginia, but it does not apply to the intangible personal property. (§ 11-11-5) With the repeal of the federal credit, no tax is currently imposed.
Wisconsin	Yes. (§ 72.02)	The payment is due nine months after the death. (§ 72.22)	The tax is equal to the amount of the federal credit. "Federal credit" means, for deaths occurring after September 30, 2002, and before January 1, 2008, the credit as in effect on December 31, 2000. (§ 72.01 (11m)) The tax is imposed on all transfers by the decedent of any property with a "taxable situs" in the state (§ 72.02), although another provision refers to taxing "any transfers of property" (§ 72.11(1)(a)). Transfer is simply defined as "the passing of property." (§ 72.01(2)) If only a portion of the decedent's property is located in Wisconsin, the tax is determined by multiplying the credit by a fraction the numerator of	Same as for a domiciliary. Property having a "taxable situs" in the case of a nonresident would, presumably, not include intangible personal property. (§ 72.11(2))

			which equals the value of the property with a taxable situs in Wisconsin and the denominator of which equals the value of the estate that qualifies for the federal credit. (§ 72.02) For persons dying in 2008 and there after the reference is to the current federal credit, which has been repealed, so there is no estate tax liability.	
Wyoming	Yes. (§ 39-19-103)	The payment of the tax must be made whenever the federal tax return is due. (§ 39-19-107(b))	The tax is imposed on the transfer of the "Wyoming gross estate" and equals the maximum federal tax credit. The tax is the greater of an amount equal to the credit multiplied by a fraction, the numerator of which is the value of the Wyoming gross estate, and the denominator of which is the federal gross estate, or the actual credit allowable to the Wyoming gross estate. (§ 39-19-103(b)) The Wyoming gross estate is the value of the federal gross estate, except for real or tangible personal property having an "actual situs" outside Wyoming. (§ 39-19-101(a)(v)) With the repeal of the federal credit, no tax is currently imposed.	Same as domiciliary, but the Wyoming estate does not include intangible personal property. (§§ 39-19-101(a)(v), 39-19-103(c)) With the repeal of the federal credit, no tax is currently imposed.

Table 15.03
Generation-Skipping Transfer Tax

	Is There a Generation-Skipping Transfer Tax?	*Is the Generation-Skipping Transfer Tax Limited to the § 2604 Credit?**	*When Must Payment of Tax Be Made?*	*In the Case of a Generation-Skipping Transfer Tax, How Is It Computed for a Domiciliary?**	*In the Case of a Generation-Skipping Transfer Tax, How Is It Computed for a Nondomiciliary,* U.S. Resident?*
Alabama	Yes. (§ 40-15A-2)	Yes. (§ 40-15A-2)	This tax is due and payable at the same time as the federal tax on generation-skipping transfers. (§ 40-15A-5)	It applies to intangible property of a person domiciled in the state as of the date of transfer or death, if the transfer occurs after death, as well as real and tangible personal property in Alabama at the time of the generation-skipping transfer. (§ 40-15A-3) The tax equals the full amount of state tax permissible as a credit in computing any federal generation-skipping transfer tax. (§ 40-15A-2)	Same as for a domiciliary, but limited to real and tangible personal property in the state at the time of the generation-skipping transfer. (§§ 40-15A-3, 40-15A-2)
Alaska	No.	N/A	N/A	N/A	N/A
Arizona	No. (Laws 2006, ch. 262 § 3, beginning with 2006)	N/A	N/A	N/A	N/A
Arkansas	No.	N/A	N/A	N/A	N/A
California	Yes. (Rev. & Tax. § 16710)	Yes. (Rev. & Tax. § 16710)	On or before the same date as the last date for filing the federal generation-skipping transfer return. (Rev. & Tax. § 16752)	The tax is the amount of the federal credit for state generation-skipping transfer taxes. If transferred property is real property located out side of California or personal property having a "business situs" out of the state and is taxable by another state, the tax is reduced by an amount that bears the same ratio to the total federal credit as the value of the property tax able in another state bears to the value of the gross	The tax applies to "generation-skipping transfers." This term is defined as under federal law, but only applies if the original transferor was a resident of California at the date of the original transfer or the property transferred is real or

				generation-skipping transfer for federal tax purposes. (Rev. & Tax. § 16710)	personal property in California. (Rev. & Tax. § 16702)
Colorado	Yes. (§ 39-23.5-106)	Yes. (§ 39-23.5-106)	Generation-skipping transfer taxes must be paid at the time for filing the federal generation-skipping transfer return. (§§ 39-23.5-108(1), 39-23.5-107(1))	The tax is the amount of the federal credit multiplied by a fraction with the numerator equal to the value of the property located in Colorado which is included in the generation-skipping transfer and with the denominator equal to the value of the entire generation-skipping transfer for purposes of the federal tax. (§ 39-23.5-106(2)) Property located in Colorado includes real property held in trust or other wise, tangible personal property in the state, and intangible personal property owned by a trust with its principal place of administration in the state at the time of the generation-skipping transfer. (§ 39-23.5-106(3))	Same as for a domiciliary. (§ 39-23.5-106)
Connecticut	Yes. (§ 12-390b)	Yes. (§ 12-390b)	Upon a taxable distribution or termination on the day for filing a return (§ 12-390c(a)(1)), which is due at the time for filing the federal return. (§ 12-390c(b)(1))	The tax equals the federal credit except if real or tangible personal property located out of the state is subject to the tax by another state. In that case, the tax is reduced by the lesser of (a) the taxes paid the other state(s), or (b) an amount computed by multiplying the credit by a fraction, the numerator of which is the value of transferred real and tangible personal property over which the other state(s) has jurisdiction to the same extent Connecticut would exert jurisdiction and the denominator of which is the value of all transferred property subject to the generation-skipping transfer tax wherever located. A transferor is a resident if one *(cont'd)*	A tax is imposed if real or tangible personal property located in the state is the subject of the generation-skipping transfer. To determine the tax, the credit is multiplied by a fraction, the numerator of which is the property located in Connecticut subject to the tax and over which Connecticut has taxing jurisdiction and the denominator of which *(cont'd)*

Table 15.03
Generation-Skipping Transfer Tax *(continued)*

	Is There a Generation-Skipping Transfer Tax?	*Is the Generation-Skipping Transfer Tax Limited to the § 2604 Credit?**	*When Must Payment of Tax Be Made?*	*In the Case of a Generation-Skipping Transfer Tax, How Is It Computed for a Domiciliary?**	*In the Case of a Generation-Skipping Transfer Tax, How Is It Computed for a Nondomiciliary,* U.S. Resident?*
Connecticut *(cont'd)*				at the time of the original transfer. (§ 12-390b(a))	is the value of all transferred property "subject to generation-skipping transfer taxes, wherever located." (§ 12-390b(b))
Delaware	No.	N/A	N/A	N/A	N/A
District of Columbia	No.	N/A	N/A	N/A	N/A
Florida	Yes. (§ 198.021)	Yes. (§ 198.021)	The generation-skipping transfer tax must be paid at the time for filing the federal generation-skipping transfer tax return. (§§ 198.15, 198.155)	The tax is the amount of the federal credit, to the extent that the credit exceeds the aggregate amount of all "constitutionally valid" taxes on the same transfer actually paid to other states. The tax only applies if the original transferor was a resident at the date of the original transfer. (§ 198.021)	The tax applies to real or personal property in the state. The tax is the amount allowable as a federal credit reduced by the amount which bears the same ratio to the federal credit as the value of the generation-skipping transfer property taxable by other states bears to the gross generation-skipping transfer property. (§ 198.031)

Georgia	No.	N/A	N/A	N/A	N/A
Hawaii	Yes. (§ 236D-3.5)	Yes. (§ 236D-3.5(a))	The generation-skipping transfer tax is due at the time that the federal generation-skipping transfer tax return must be filed. (§ 236D-6(a))	The tax is the amount of the federal credit if the transfer is of "[p]roperty located in [Hawaii]" or of "[p]roperty from a resident trust." If another state taxes the transfer under a state law that also qualifies for the federal credit, the tax is reduced by the lesser of the amount of tax paid to the other state or the amount computed by multiplying the federal credit by a fraction with a numerator equal to the value of the property subject to the tax paid to the other state and with a denominator equal to the value of all property subject to the federal generation-skipping tax. (§ 236D-3.5) For purposes of the tax, a resident trust is a trust of which is carried on in Hawaii or, if carried on partly outside the state, a trust of which one-half or more of the fiduciaries reside in Hawaii. (§ 236D-2)	Same as for a domiciliary. (§ 236D-4)
Idaho	Yes. (§§ 14-403, 14-404)	Yes. (§§ 14-402-14-404)	The generation-skipping transfer tax is due on or before the date the federal return is due. (§§ 14-406, 14-405)	Although the term "federal credit" is defined as referring to the generation-skipping transfer tax, no provision actually addresses the calculation of the tax, e.g., which property is taken into account when more than one state is imposing the tax. (§ 14-403)	Yes. (§ 14-404)
Illinois	Yes. (35 ILCS § 405/4)	Yes. (35 ILCS § 405/4(b)) For decedents dying on or after January 1, 2003 and on or before December 31, 2005, the tax is the amount of the federal credit as of December 31, 2001. (35 ILCS § 405/2 "state tax credit" *(cont'd)*	The payment of the generation-skipping transfer tax is due at the same time as the deadline for filing the federal generation-skipping transfer tax return. (35 ILCS § 405/6(a))	The tax is imposed on every generation-skipping transfer involving "transferred property" having a "tax situs" in Illinois. (35 ILCS § 405/4(a)) The time when the tax situs must exist and whether the original or later generation-skipping "transfer" is being referred to are unclear. The tax is the amount of the federal credit reduced by the lesser of the amount of the federal credit paid to any other state and the amount computed by multiplying the federal credit by the fraction with the *(cont'd)*	Same as for a domiciliary. (35 ILCS § 405/4(b))

Table 15.03
Generation-Skipping Transfer Tax *(continued)*

	Is There a Generation-Skipping Transfer Tax?	*Is the Generation-Skipping Transfer Tax Limited to the § 2604 Credit?**	*When Must Payment of Tax Be Made?*	*In the Case of a Generation-Skipping Transfer Tax, How Is It Computed for a Domiciliary?**	*In the Case of a Generation-Skipping Transfer Tax, How Is It Computed for a Nondomiciliary,* U.S. Resident?*
Illinois *(cont'd)*		(a)) For decedents dying on or after January 1, 2006 and on or before December 31, 2009, the tax is the amount of credit as of December 31, 2001. However, the exclusion amount is only $2,000,000 (*Id.* (b)) For decedents dying after December 31, 2009, the amount of the credit allowable under § 2011 or § 2604 of the Code. (*Id.* (c))		numerator equal to the gross value of the transferred property located in another state and with the denominator equal to the gross value of all the transferred property. (35 ILCS § 405/4(b))	
Indiana	Yes. (§ 6-4.1-11.5-7)	Yes. (§ 6-4.1-11.5-8(a))	Payment of the generation-skipping transfer tax is due 12 months after the death of the person whose death resulted in the generation-skipping transfer. (§ 6-4.1-11.5-9) Quaere if a lifetime transfer, such as a direct skip, is subject to tax.	The tax is the amount in step four. Step one: Divide (a) the value of the transferred property legally located in Indiana by (b) the total value of the transferred property. Step two: Multiply (a) the quotient from step one by (b) the federal generation-skipping transfer tax credit. Step three: Determine the remainder of (a) the federal generation-skipping transfer tax credit minus (b) the generation-skipping transfer taxes paid to other states. Step four: Determine the greater of (a) the step two amount or (b) the step three amount. (§ 6-4.1-11.5-8(a))	Same as for a domiciliary, except intangible personal property is not included in (a) of step one. (§ 6-4.1-11.5-3)

Iowa	Yes. (§ 450A.2)	Yes. (§ 450A.2)	The generation-skipping transfer tax is due nine months after the person's death that causes the generation-skipping transfer. (§ 450A.4)	The tax is the amount of the total federal credit. If property included in the generation-skipping transfer is located outside of Iowa and is not subject to the jurisdiction of Iowa courts, the tax is prorated on the basis that the value of Iowa property included in the transfer bears to the total value of the property included in the generation-skipping transfer. (§ 450A.2) The tax only applies to those transfers as a result of the death of an individual and does not include direct skips. (*Id.*)	Same as for a domiciliary. (§ 450A.2)
Kansas	N/A	N/A	N/A	N/A	N/A
Kentucky	No.	N/A	N/A	N/A	N/A
Louisiana	No	N/A	N/A	N/A	N/A
Maine	No.	N/A	N/A	N/A	N/A
Maryland	Yes. (Tax-Gen. § 7-402)	Yes. (Tax-Gen. § 7-403)	The payment must be made no later than the date for filing the return (Tax-Gen. § 7-406), which is the same date as required for filing the federal return (Tax-Gen. § 7-405).	The tax is only imposed on a generation-skipping transfer due to death. The original transferor must have been a resident on the date of the original transfer. If not, the generation-skipping transfer must involve Maryland-situs property. The tax does not apply to a direct skip. (Tax-Gen. § 7-402) The tax is the amount of the federal credit. (Tax-Gen. § 7-403)	Same as for a domiciliary. (Tax-Gen. § 7-403)
Massachusetts	Yes. (65C § 4A)	Yes. (65C § 4A)	The federal law requirements for payment in the case of a taxable termination or distribution apply. (65C § 4A(e))	The tax applies to every generation-skipping transfer if the original transferor was a resident at the time of the original transfer or the property "transferred" is "in" the state. (§ 65C § 4A(a)(1)) The tax is the amount allowable as a federal credit for state death taxes under I.R.C. § 2604. (65C § 4A(b)) Note that the Massachusetts statute mistakenly refers to I.R.C. § 2602. Importantly, the tax is currently preserved due to the reference to the credit as in effect on December 31, 1981. (65C § 4A(c))	The tax is only applied to transferred real or personal property that is located in the state. The tax is the amount allowable as a federal credit. (65C § 4A(c))

Table 15.03
Generation-Skipping Transfer Tax *(continued)*

	Is There a Generation-Skipping Transfer Tax?	*Is the Generation-Skipping Transfer Tax Limited to the § 2604 Credit?**	*When Must Payment of Tax Be Made?*	*In the Case of a Generation-Skipping Transfer Tax, How Is It Computed for a Domiciliary?**	*In the Case of a Generation-Skipping Transfer Tax, How Is It Computed for a Nondomiciliary,* U.S. Resident?*
Michigan	Yes. (§ 205.233)	Yes. (§ 205.233)	Tax is due and payable on or before the last day prescribed by law for paying the corresponding federal transfer tax, pursuant to the federal return, excluding extensions. (§ 205.236)	The tax is equal to the maximum allowable federal credit reduced by the amount of all generation-skipping transfer taxes paid to other states, which amount is not to exceed an amount equal to the proportional share of the maximum allowable federal credit that the gross value of all real and tangible personal property located outside Michigan bears to the gross value of all estate property wherever located. (§ 205.233(1)) The allowable federal credit means the federal credit for state generation-skipping transfer tax, I.R.C. § 2604, in effect on January 1, 1998, or, at the option of the personal representative, in effect on the date of the decedent's death. (§ 205.256(g)) Note that this optimal date appears to have been addressing the estate tax rather than the generation-skipping transfer tax.	The tax is an amount equal to the proportional share of the maximum allowable federal credit that the gross value of all transferred real and tangible personal property located in Michigan bears to the gross value of all transferred property subject to generation-skipping transfer taxes wherever located. (§ 205.233(2)) The allowable federal credit means the federal credit for state generation-skipping transfer tax, I.R.C. § 2604, in effect on January 1, 1998, or, at the option of the personal representative, in effect on the date of the decedent's death. (§ 205:256(g)) Note that this optimal date

					appears to have been addressing the estate tax rather than the generation-skipping transfer tax.
Minnesota	No.	N/A	N/A	N/A	N/A
Mississippi	No.	N/A	N/A	N/A	N/A
Missouri	Yes. (§ 145.995)	Yes. (§ 145.995)	The generation-skipping transfer tax must be paid when the return is filed, as provided by the director of revenue. (§§ 145.511, 145.995)	The tax is the amount of the I.R.C. § 2604 credit, reduced by the amount computed by multiplying the tax by a fraction with the numerator equal to the property included in the generation-skipping transfer, excluding all property not having a "tax situs" in Missouri, and with the denominator equal to the value of the property included in the generation-skipping transfer for federal tax purposes. (§§ 145.995 & 145.011)	Same as for a domiciliary. (§§ 145.995 & 145.011)
Montana	Yes. (§ 72-16-1002)	Yes. (§ 72-16-1002(1))	The generation-skipping transfer tax must be paid on or before the deadline for filing the federal generation-skipping transfer tax return. (§ 72-16-1003(2))	Tax is imposed on all generation-skipping transfers, other than direct skips, occurring as a result of the decedent's death, in an amount equal to the maximum federal credit. If any of the property transferred is located in another state, the tax is reduced by an amount that bears the same ratio to the federal credit as the value of the property taxed in the other state bears to the value of the gross transfer. (§ 72-16-1002)	Same as for domiciliary. (§ 72-16-1002)
Nebraska	Yes. (§ 77-2101.02)	No. (§ 77-2101.02)	The tax must be paid within 12 months of the date of transfer. (§ 77-2102)	All property of resident is taxed if part of a "generation-skipping transfer or distribution."[1] Taxable generation-skipping transfers are taxed at a rate of 16 percent of the Nebraska taxable transfer. (§ 77-2101.03) This amount should be reduced by the lesser of (1) generation-skipping transfer taxes paid to other states, or (2) the amount determined by multiplying the tax determined by § 77- *(cont'd)*	The tax applies to the "generation-skipping transfer"[2] of Nebraska real property and tangible personal property. (§ 77-2101.02) The amount of the tax and the offset for any taxes by other states *(cont'd)*

Table 15.03
Generation-Skipping Transfer Tax *(continued)*

	Is There a Generation-Skipping Transfer Tax?	*Is the Generation-Skipping Transfer Tax Limited to the § 2604 Credit?**	*When Must Payment of Tax Be Made?*	*In the Case of a Generation-Skipping Transfer Tax, How Is It Computed for a Domiciliary?**	*In the Case of a Generation-Skipping Transfer Tax, How Is It Computed for a Nondomiciliary,* U.S. Resident?*
Nebraska *(cont'd)*				2101.03 by the percentage which the gross value that the transferred property situated elsewhere bears to the gross value of the transferred property. (§ 77-2101.02)	is the same as for domiciliaries. (§ 77-2101.02, referring to § 77-2101.03)
Nevada	Yes. (§ 375B.100)	Yes. (§ 375B.100(1))	The tax is due on or before the date the federal generation-skipping transfer tax is due. (§ 375B.240)	The tax is limited to generation-skipping transfers due to a death and does include direct skips. (§ 375B.100) The tax is the amount determined by multiplying the federal credit by the percentage which the gross value of the transferred property located in Nevada bears to the gross value of the entire property transferred for purposes of the federal generation-skipping tax. (§ 375B.110(2))	Same as for a domiciliary. (§ 375B.110)
New Hampshire	No.	N/A	N/A	N/A	N/A
New Jersey	No.	N/A	N/A	N/A	N/A
New Mexico	No.	N/A	N/A	N/A	N/A
New York	Yes. (Tax § 1022)	Yes. (Tax § 1022) However, the credit is determined with all amendments enacted on or before July 22, 1998. (Tax § 1020(a))	Generation-skipping transfer taxes are due on April 15 of the year after the transfer. (Tax § 1023)	Tax is imposed on every generation-skipping transfer which includes "New York property" in an amount computed by multiplying the maximum allowable I.R.C. § 2604 credit by a fraction, the numerator of which is the value of New York property included in the generation-skipping transfer and the denominator of which is the value of all property included in the generation-skipping transfer. (Tax § 1022) "New York property" means real and tangible personal property in New York, intangible personal property in New York employed	The calculation is the same as for state residents, except that intangible personal property not employed in an occupation, trade, or business of the nonresident is not included in "New York Property," as defined in Tax § 1021(b). (Tax § 1022)

				in carrying on a trade, business, or occupation in the state, and intangible personal property where the original transferor was a resident of the state at the time of the original transfer. (§ 1021(b)) The tax is currently preserved due to reference to the law in effect on July 22, 1998. (Tax § 951(a))	
North Carolina	Yes. (§ 105-32.7)	Yes. (§ 105-32.7(b))	The tax is due when the federal tax is due. (§ 105-32.7(c))	The tax applies to all generation-skipping transfers if (a) the original transferor was a resident at the time of the original transfer (§ 105-32.7(a)(1)) or if (b) the transferor was not then a resident, then only real or personal property with a North Carolina situs and intangible property that has a tax situs in North Carolina (§ 105.32.7(a)(2)) are subject to the tax. The amount of the tax is the maximum federal credit. If property is located in another state, the amount of the tax is the North Carolina percentage. If the original transferor at the time of the original transfer was a "resident," then the North Carolina percentage is the net value of the property that does not have a tax situs in another state, divided by the net value of all property transferred. (§ 105-32.7(b))	In the case of an original transferor who was not a "resident" of North Carolina at the time of the original transfer, the North Carolina percentage is the net value of real property in North Carolina plus the net value of any personal property having a tax situs in the state, divided by the net value of all property transferred, "unless the original transferor's state of residence uses a different formula to determine that state's percentage." If so, then North Carolina's percentage is determined by the other state's law. (§ 105-32.7(b)) *Quaere* whether the other state's law at the time of the original transfer or the taxable event is relevant.
North Dakota	No.	N/A	N/A	N/A	N/A

Table 15.03
Generation-Skipping Transfer Tax *(continued)*

	Is There a Generation-Skipping Transfer Tax?	*Is the Generation-Skipping Transfer Tax Limited to the § 2604 Credit?**	*When Must Payment of Tax Be Made?*	*In the Case of a Generation-Skipping Transfer Tax, How Is It Computed for a Domiciliary?**	*In the Case of a Generation-Skipping Transfer Tax, How Is It Computed for a Nondomiciliary,* U.S. Resident?*
Ohio	Yes. (§ 5731.181)	Yes. (§ 5731.181(B))	The taxes must be paid when the return is due, which is the same time as for federal tax law. (§ 5731.181(C) & (D))	The tax is imposed on property with a situs in Ohio and involving a transfer as a result of the death of an individual. (§ 5731.181(B)) Such property includes real and tangible personal property in the state, intangible personal property employed in carrying on a business in the state, intangible personal property owned by a trust where the trustee resides or has its principal place of business in the state, or if more than one trustee, then the trust's principal place of administration is in Ohio. (*Id.*) The tax is the amount of the federal credit. If another state imposes a generation-skipping transfer tax, the tax commissioner may enter into a compromise. (§ 5731.181(e))	Same as for a domiciliary. (§ 5731.181)
Oklahoma	No.	N/A	N/A	N/A	N/A
Oregon	No.	N/A	N/A	N/A	N/A
Pennsylvania	No.	N/A	N/A	N/A	N/A
Rhode Island	Yes. (§ 44-40-3)	Yes. (§ 44-40-3)	The payment is due at the same time as under the federal tax law. (§ 44-40-13) Provision is only made for a payment of tax in the case of a taxable distribution or termination, although the tax would	The tax is imposed with regard to "every" generation-skipping transfer. (§ 44-40-3(a)) A generation-skipping transfer is the same as for federal tax purposes, but only if the original transferor was a resident of Rhode Island at the time of the original transfer, "and" the deemed transferor is a resident at the time of his death, "and" the property transferred is real or personal property "in" Rhode Island. (§ 44-40-2(4)) However, if another state is	Same as for resident.

			appear to apply to direct skips as well.	taxing real property or personal property in another state, then the Rhode Island tax is reduced by an amount which is determined by multiplying the federal credit by a fraction, the numerator of which is the value of the property taxable in the other state and the denominator of which is the gross generation-skipping transfer. (§ 44-40-3(b))	
South Carolina	Yes. (§ 12-16-720)	Yes. (§ 12-16-720)	The tax is due as determined pursuant to federal tax law on a taxable distribution or termination. (§ 12-16-730) No mention is made of direct skips, although they are not excluded from the meaning of generation-skipping transfer.	The tax is imposed where the original transferor was a resident of South Carolina at the time of the original transfer or, if not then resident, the tax is imposed with respect to transfers of property with a situs in South Carolina. The tax is the maximum federal credit for state generation-skipping transfer taxes reduced by the aggregate amount of all taxes on the same transfer actually paid to other states. (§ 12-16-720)	The tax is the maximum federal credit for state generation-skipping taxes reduced by the amount which bears the same ratio to the federal credit as the value of the transferred property taxable by other states bears to the value of the gross generation-skipping transfer for purposes of the federal generation-skipping tax. Intangible personal property is not included. (§ 12-16-720)
South Dakota	No.	N/A	N/A	N/A	N/A
Tennessee	Yes. (§ 67-8-603)	Yes. (§ 67-8-603)	The tax must be paid at the time required under the federal law. (§ 67-8-604(a))	Tax is imposed on every generation-skipping transfer in an amount equal to the amount allowable as a credit for state taxes under I.R.C. § 2604. If any of the property transferred is real property located in another state or tangible personal property located in another state which requires the payment of a tax for which credit is received against the federal generation-skipping transfer tax, any tax otherwise due shall be reduced by an	Same as for a domiciliary.

(cont'd)

Table 15.03
Generation-Skipping Transfer Tax *(continued)*

	Is There a Generation-Skipping Transfer Tax?	*Is the Generation-Skipping Transfer Tax Limited to the § 2604 Credit?**	*When Must Payment of Tax Be Made?*	*In the Case of a Generation-Skipping Transfer Tax, How Is It Computed for a Domiciliary?**	*In the Case of a Generation-Skipping Transfer Tax, How Is It Computed for a Nondomiciliary,* U.S. Resident?*
Tennessee *(cont'd)*				amount which bears the same ratio to the total state tax credit allowable for federal generation-skipping transfer tax purposes as the value of such property taxable in such other states bears to the value of the gross generation-skipping transfer for generation-skipping transfer tax purposes. (§ 67-8-603)	
Texas	Yes. (Tax § 211.054)	Yes. (Tax § 211.054)	The tax is due at the same time as the federal tax. (Tax § 211.105)	The tax is the amount computed by multiplying the federal generation-skipping transfer tax credit by a fraction, with the numerator equal to the value of the "[p]roperty located in Texas" that is included in the generation-skipping transfer and with the denominator equal to the value of the generation-skipping transfer. (Tax § 211.054) "Property located in Texas" includes real property with an actual situs in Texas and even if held in trust, tangible personal property having an actual situs in Texas, and tangible personal property owned by a trust and having its principal place of administration in Texas at the time of the generation-skipping transfer. (Tax § 211.054(c))	Same as for a domiciliary.
Utah	No.	N/A	N/A	N/A	N/A
Vermont	Yes. (32 § 7460)	Yes as it was in effect on January 1, 2001. (32 § 7460(b))	On or before the last day prescribed for filing the federal return. (32 § 7460(d))	The tax is imposed on all transfers subject to the federal generation-skipping transfer tax if the original transferor was a resident at the time of the original transfer. The amount is	Same as in the case of domiciliary, except only to the extent of real or tangible

				equal to the amount allowable as a credit for state death taxes under IRC § 2604. (32 § 7460(b)) The tax is currently preserved due to reference to the credit in effect on January 1, 2001. (32 § 7460(b))	personal property in Vermont. (32 § 7460(c))
Virginia	Yes. (§ 58.1-936)	Yes. (§ 58.1-936)	The payment of the tax is due when a federal tax would be due for a taxable distribution or taxable termination. (§ 58.1-937(B))	The tax is imposed on all property where the original transferor was a resident of Virginia at the time of the original transfer or, if not, then on the generation-skipping transfer of real or personal property having a situs in Virginia. (§ 58.1-936) In the first case, the tax is the amount that the federal credit exceeds the aggregate amount of all taxes paid to other states on the same transfer. (§ 58.1-936) In the second situation, the tax is the amount equal to the amount of the federal credit reduced by the amount which bears the same ratio to the federal credit as the value of the transferred property taxable by other states bears to the value of the gross transfer for federal generation-skipping transfer tax purposes. (§ 58.1-936)	Same as in the case of domiciliary.
Washington	No. Repealed. (§ 83.100.045), L. 2005, ch. 516, § 17, effective May 17, 2005. Effective 5/17/05: No.	N/A	N/A	N/A	N/A
West Virginia	No.	N/A	N/A	N/A	N/A
Wisconsin	No.	N/A	N/A	N/A	N/A
Wyoming	No.	N/A	N/A	N/A	N/A

Table 15.03
Generation-Skipping Transfer Tax *(continued)*

	Is There a Generation-Skipping Transfer Tax?	*Is the Generation-Skipping Transfer Tax Limited to the § 2604 Credit?**	*When Must Payment of Tax Be Made?*	*In the Case of a Generation-Skipping Transfer Tax, How Is It Computed for a Domiciliary?**	*In the Case of a Generation-Skipping Transfer Tax, How Is It Computed for a Nondomiciliary,* U.S. Resident?*

*** The federal credit for state generation-skipping transfer taxes terminated at the end of 2004. (Pub.L. No. 107-16, § 532(d) (June 7, 2001)) As a result, if a state tax is based on the credit and the state law does not grandfather in the credit, the state generation-skipping transfer tax will no longer be in effect. Unless expressly indicated in this Table, the credit has not been grandfathered.**

1. Under §77-2101(2), a generation-skipping transfer tax is imposed on taxable transfers that give rise to federal tax liability. Federal tax law, however, does not have separate categories for transfers *or* distributions.
2. Note that there is no reference to distributions, as in the case of domiciliaries.

Table 15.04
Gift Tax

	Is There a Gift Tax?	*If So, When Is Payment Due?*	*In the Case of a Gift Tax, How Is It Computed for a Domiciliary?*	*In the Case of a Gift Tax, How Is It Computed for a Non-domiciliary, U.S. Resident?*
Connecticut	Yes. (§ 12-640) For the rate, see Table 15.07.	The tax is payable by April 15 following the close of the calendar year in which the gift was made. (§ 12-647)	The tax is imposed on the transfers by gift which are included as taxable gifts for federal gift tax purposes. The deductions allowed under I.R.C. §§ 2522 to 2524 are available. (§ 12-643(a)) "Connecticut tax able gifts" does not apply to the transfer of real property and tangible personal property having a situs outside the state. (§ 12-641) No reference is made to intangible property in the statute. But see Dept. Rev. Services, Conn. Informational Publication, IP 2004 (24) (Sept. 13, 2004), 2004 WL 2294152, 2004 Conn. Tax LEXIS 43, stating that gifts of intangible property are subject to tax.	Same as for domiciliary. (§ 12-643(a)) However, the "Connecticut taxable gifts" in the case of a non domiciliary only includes the transfer of real property and tangible personal property situated in the state. (§ 12-643(c)) (see also Dept. Rev. Services, Conn. Informational Publication, IP 2004(24), (Sept. 13, 2004), 2004 WL 2294152, 2004 Conn. Tax LEXIS 43)
Louisiana	Yes. (§ 47:1201) For the rate, see Table 15.07.	The tax must be paid on or before the 15th day of April of the calendar year immediately following the year in which the gifts are made. (§ 47:1208(C)(1))	Residents are taxed on all property transferred if the property is located within the state. Intangible property is deemed to be located in the state. (§ 47:1203(B)) This tax is subject to the exclusions and exemptions set forth in §§ 47:1204 and 47:1205. Exempt transfers are gifts made to charitable, religious, or educational institutions in Louisiana; gifts made to the United States, Louisiana, or any of its political subdivisions; and gifts made to a spouse. (§ 47:1204) There is also a $10,000 annual exclusion, a $30,000 lifetime exemption, and provisions for gifts by spouses to third parties. (§ 47:1205)The gift taxis based on the aggregate sum of gifts in excess of the annual exclusion and lifetime exemption. (§ 47:1207)	Nonresidents are taxed on all property transferred if the property has a situs in the state (§ 47:1203(C)), but, by implication, not including intangible personal property. The tax is subject to the exclusions and exemptions set forth in §§ 47:1204 and 47:1205.

Table 15.04
Gift Tax *(continued)*

	Is There a Gift Tax?	*If So, When Is Payment Due?*	*In the Case of a Gift Tax, How Is It Computed for a Domiciliary?*	*In the Case of a Gift Tax, How Is It Computed for a Non-domiciliary, U.S. Resident?*
North Carolina	Yes. (§ 105-188) For the rate, see Table 15.07.	The tax is due on April 15 following the end of the calendar year. (§ 105-197)	The gift tax is imposed on all property "within the jurisdiction" of North Carolina. There is an annual exclusion equal to the federal inflation-adjusted exclusion amount provided in § 2503(b) of the Internal Revenue Code. (§ 105-188(d)) There is a total exemption of $100,000 for transfers to the donor's lineal issue, lineal ancestor, adopted child or step child. (§ 105-188(g)) Property passing to a surviving spouse, including qualified terminable interest property, is exempt from the gift tax. (§ 105-188(h)(4)) Transfers for religious, charitable or educational purposes are also exempt if the recipient is located in North Carolina or in a state with a reciprocal exemption. (§ 105-188(h)(2)&(3)) The tax is based on the aggregate sum of the net gifts made to the same donee and is computed by applying the gift tax rates to the aggregate sum of the net gifts for all calendar years since January 1, 1948. (§ 105-188(e))	Same as for a domiciliary. (§ 105-188(b)) There is some uncertainty why this statement is made: "In the case of a gift made by a nonresident, the taxes shall apply only if the property is within the jurisdiction of this State." The same limitation already is imposed on residents (i.e., domiciliaries). (§ 105-188(a))
Tennessee	Yes. (§ 67-8-101) For the rate, see Table 15.07.	Tax must be paid on or before April 15 following the close of the calendar year of the gift. (§ 67-8-111)	Residents are taxed on gifts of: (a) real property located in the state; (b) tangible personal property located in the state; and (c) all intangible personal property. (§ 67-8-101) The taxable gifts are then reduced by deductible gifts, standard exemptions, and gifts between spouses, as set forth in §§ 67-8-103, 67-8-104, and 67-8-105, respectively. The net taxable gifts are	Nonresidents are taxed on gifts of real property located in the state and tangible personal property located in the state. (§ 67-8-101) The taxable gifts are then reduced by deductible gifts, standard exemptions, and gifts between spouses, as set forth in §§ 67-8-103, 67-8-104, and

		then multiplied by the tax rates set forth in § 67-8-106. The unified credit amount does *not* apply to gifts as it does to estates.	67-8-105, respectively. The net taxable gifts are then multiplied by the tax rates set forth in § 67-8-106. The unified credit amount does not apply to gifts as it does to estates.
Texas through Wyoming do not impose a state gift tax.			

Table 15.05
Waivers

	Are Waivers Required for Transfer of Assets or Payment Required Before Transfer?	*From Whom Are Waivers Obtained?*
Alabama	Only with respect to nonresident decedents. With respect to delivery of property to a foreign legal representative, the tax must first be paid or security posted. (§ 40-15-7(d))	The Department of Revenue. (§ 40-15-7(d))
Alaska	No. However, executor is liable for tax if property is distributed to heirs, next of kin, distributees, legatees, or devisees without having paid or secured the tax due to the state, or obtained the release of the property from the lien of the tax. (§ 43.31.221)	N/A
Arizona	N/A	N/A
Arkansas	N/A	N/A
California	No. However, see Rev. & Tax § 13530.	N/A
Colorado	No. (§ 39-23.5-107(5))	N/A
Connecticut	No. However, "[n]o executor, administrator or other person acting in a fiduciary capacity shall be required to transfer, pay over or distribute any property . . . until the amount of such tax or taxes due . . . is paid or, if the apportionment of tax has not been determined, until adequate security is furnished by the transferee for such payment." (§ 12-403)	N/A
Delaware	No. However, the executor, administrator or other fiduciary is not required to pay or distribute any fund or property until the taxes are paid and, if the apportionment has not been determined, until adequate security is furnished by the transferee. (12 § 2904)	N/A
District of Columbia	No. However, "[t]he personal representative of every decedent subject to the tax imposed by this chapter *shall*, before distribution of the estate, pay to the mayor any taxes, penalties, and interest due under this chapter." (§ 47-3713). The personal representative	The Mayor will certify payment. (§ 47-3710)

	is liable if the estate is distributed before payment. (§ 47-3712) A certificate of payment may be obtained from the Mayor. (§ 47-3710)	
Florida	No. However, "[i]f any personal representative shall make distribution either in whole or part of any of the property of an estate to the heirs, next of kin, distributes, legatees, or devisees without having paid or secured the tax due . . . he or she shall become personally liable for the tax so due the state . . ." (§ 198.23)	N/A
Georgia	No.	N/A
Hawaii	A release gives the personal representative the authority to transfer all property composing the decedent's estate. (§ 236D-8(b)) Although this language appears mandatory, the Department of Revenue simply makes a release available as the only way to be certain of no tax liability before distribution of the estate. The personal representative is liable for tax on property distributed before payment. (§ 236D-12(a))	The Department of Taxation. (§ 236D-8(a))
Idaho	No. However, "[a]ny personal representative who distributes any portion of the property without first paying the tax imposed . . . is personally liable for the tax." (§ 14-410(2)) Also, a receipt, a certificate of transfer, and any other appropriate instrument is issued upon payment of amounts due. (§ 14-409(2))	Tax Commission. (§ 14-409(2))
Illinois	No.	N/A
Indiana	No transfer is permissible until the tax has been paid. (§ 6-4.1-8-2(a)) For the transfer of personal property in possession of another, the Department of State Revenue or the county assessor must give written consent. (§ 6-4.1-8-4) Notice must also be given when money is transferred or life insurance paid, or other types of assets transferred primarily in the case of a resident decedent, without obtaining consent. (§§ 6-4.1-8-4–6-4.1-8-5) If a person violates the consent or notice requirements of § 6-4.1-8-4 or	Department of State Revenue or in certain instances the county assessor for the county in which the decedent was domiciled may give written consent to the transfer of personal property. (§§ 6-4.1-8-4–6-4.1-8-5)

(cont'd)

Table 15.05
Waivers *(continued)*

	Are Waivers Required for Transfer of Assets or Payment Required Before Transfer?	*From Whom Are Waivers Obtained?*
Indiana *(cont'd)*	§ 6-4.1-8-5, that person is liable for the taxes and is subject to an additional penalty not to exceed $1,000. (§§ 6-4.1-8-7)	
Iowa	A foreign personal representative cannot transfer Iowa stock before the tax is paid to the Department of Revenue and Finance. Otherwise, the corporation permitting its stock to be transferred is liable to pay the tax, interest, and costs. (§ 450.87) No withdrawal of funds from a joint account is permitted unless the Department of Revenue and Finance receives notice. (§ 450.97 (repealed effective 7/1/2005))	N/A
Kansas	No.	N/A
Kentucky	No.	N/A
Louisiana	Banks, depositories, or other custodians are not allowed to deliver or transfer property to heirs or legatees unless the tax has been paid or it is judicially determined that no tax is due. (§ 47:2413(B))	N/A
Maine	No.	N/A
Maryland	Tax must be paid before property is distributed. (Tax-Gen. § 7-216(a)(1)) The person distributing the property is liable for the tax until the tax is paid. (Tax-Gen. § 7-216(a)(2))	N/A
Massachusetts	No. However, the executor is liable for the tax. (65C § 6)	N/A
Michigan	No. The personal representative must obtain a release from the tax lien or pay the tax before distribution to avoid personal liability. (§ 205.244)	N/A
Minnesota	No. No personal representative shall be required to transfer property unless all taxes are paid. (§ 291.12)	N/A

Mississippi	No. However, every executor or administrator who pays any debts due by the estate before he satisfies and pays the tax due is personally liable. (§ 27-9-37)	N/A
Missouri	No.	N/A
Montana	No. However, administrators, executors, trustees, and grantees are liable for the tax with interest until it has been paid. (§ 72-16-908)	N/A
Nebraska	An administrator, executor, or trustee may not deliver or be compelled to deliver any specific legacy or property subject to tax until he has collected the tax thereon. (§ 77-2011)	N/A
Nevada	No.	N/A
New Hampshire	No.	N/A
New Jersey	No property owned by the decedent as of the date of death may be transferred without the written [consent of the director of the Division of Taxation in the Department of the Treasury]. (§ 54:38-6) No corporation of the state can transfer any of its stock belonging to a resident decedent unless notice of the time of the intended transfer is served upon the State Tax Commissioner at least 10 days prior to the transfer, nor until the Commissioner consents thereto in writing. (§ 54:35-21) No executor or trustee shall turn over any property until payment of tax. To do so, incurs personal liability. (§ 54:36-7) A fiduciary is not required to transfer funds or property until tax is paid. (§ 3B:24-7)	The State Tax Commissioner must consent. (§ 54:35-21) The State Tax Commissioner shall issue a statement of payment or exemption upon determination of such. (§ 54:35-9)
New Mexico	The tax must be paid before property is transferred or the transferor becomes liable for the tax. (§ 7-7-12)	N/A
New York	An executor who distributes any asset of the estate prior to payment in full of the tax shall be personally liable. (Tax § 975(b))	N/A
North Carolina	No.	N/A
North Dakota	No.	N/A

Table 15.05
Waivers *(continued)*

	Are Waivers Required for Transfer of Assets or Payment Required Before Transfer?	*From Whom Are Waivers Obtained?*
Ohio	Waivers are required in resident estates for transfer of stock in a domestic corporation. (§ 5731.39(A)) No waiver is necessary in the case of a nonresident decedent for the transfer of intangible personal property. (§ 5731.40) An administrator, executor, or trustee may not deliver or be compelled to deliver any property, the transfer of which is subject to taxes until the taxes have been collected. If the property is transferred before payment of the tax, the executor will be personally liable. (§ 5731.37(B))	The Tax Commissioner. (§ 5731.39(G)(1))
Oklahoma	If the ownership of a corporation, association, joint-stock company, or trust doing business within Oklahoma is held in shares, the entity must secure a waiver before a transfer or payment is made. (68 § 813)	The Oklahoma Tax Commissioner. (68 § 813)
Oregon	If a foreign executor, administrator or trustee assigns or transfers any stock in the state standing in the name of the decedent liable for any such tax, the tax shall be paid to the Department of Revenue on or before the transfer thereof. No such transfer is valid until the tax is paid. (§ 118.310) The personal representative shall not deliver any property until the tax has been collected on such property. (§ 118.240)	The Oregon Tax Court. (§ 118.410)
Pennsylvania	No. However, no personal representative may be compelled to pay or deliver property to the transferee except upon payment of the tax due. If the property is delivered before payment of the tax, the personal representative will be personally liable. (72 § 9146)	N/A
Rhode Island	No person having possession of property forming a part of the estate of a resident decedent may deliver or transfer the property unless the transferor furnishes the tax administrator with a statement under oath describing the property and the person to whom the	Waivers must be obtained from the Tax Administrator. (§ 44-23-34)

	property is being delivered. If a statement is not provided, the transferor is liable for the tax. (§ 44-23-35) A permit is required for the transfer of securities of a corporation incorporated in the state or doing business in the state. (§ 44-23-34) With respect to other property, the executor is personally liable until tax is paid. (§ 44-23-9)	
South Carolina	Upon payment of tax a certificate releasing all property from a tax lien is issued. (§ 12-16-1510(D)) The tax on transfers of in-state stocks or obligations must be paid "on transfer" by foreign executors, administrators, or trustees. (§ 12-16-1210) If a personal representative distributes property without having paid the tax, he is personally liable. (§ 12-16-1150)	Department of Revenue. (§ 12-16-1510(D))
South Dakota	Tax payment or agreement is required before transfer of property in a nonresident estate. (§ 10-41-58) No personal representative may deliver or be compelled to deliver any property subject to taxation until he has collected the tax thereon. (§ 10-41-65)	The Department of Revenue. (§ 10-41-55)
Tennessee	Yes, in the case of stocks, bonds, and real estate. Property subject to taxation shall not be transferred unless the Commissioner consents in writing. (§ 67-8-417(e)(1)) The law provides that no part of the property should be distributed until the tax thereon is paid. (§ 67-8-417(a)(1))	Commissioner of Revenue. (§ 67-8-417(a)(2) & (e)(1))
Texas	No. The personal representative is liable for the tax on any property transferred before the tax is paid. (Tax § 211.201(a))	N/A
Utah	No. However, the personal representative is liable for tax on property transferred before payment. (§ 59-11-111(2))	N/A
Vermont	No. However, the transferor is liable for tax on property transferred before payment. (32 § 7452)	N/A
Virginia	No. However, if a personal representative distributes any property without paying or securing payment of the tax thereon, he is personally liable for the tax due. (§ 58.1-909)	N/A
Washington	No. However, any person who transfers property before payment is liable for the tax. (§ 83.100.120 (1) & (2))	N/A

Table 15.05
Waivers *(continued)*

	Are Waivers Required for Transfer of Assets or Payment Required Before Transfer?	*From Whom Are Waivers Obtained?*
West Virginia	No. However, any person exercising control who transfers property before payment is liable for the tax. (§ 11-11-20(b))	N/A
Wisconsin	No.	N/A
Wyoming	No. However, the court shall not issue a decree of final distribution until tax is paid. (§ 39-19-107(c)(ii)(B))	N/A

Table 15.06
Conflicts Between States

	Are There Compromise or Arbitration Provisions for Disputes over the Decedent's Domicile?	*Is There a Provision for the Reciprocal Exemption of Taxes?*
Alabama	No provision.	There is a reciprocal exemption for the intangible personal property of a nonresident if the property is not employed in carrying on business within Alabama and if the property is subject to a death tax in another state. (§ 40-15-8) This is true even if the trustee is domiciled in this state. (*Id.*) These provisions apply only if the decedent's state of residence has similar reciprocal provisions. (§ 40-15-9)
Alaska	There is a general provision for compromise of the tax if the liability of the taxpayer is in doubt. (§ 43.05.070) The Department of Revenue may compromise the tax if there is doubt as to the liability of the tax payer for the collectibility of the tax. (*Id.*) To facilitate estate settlement and distribution, the Department and executor may agree to a compromise amount of tax in full satisfaction of the tax due. (§ 43.31.260).	Personal property of a nonresident, other than tangible personal property located in Alaska, is not taxed if the state of residence of the decedent allowed a reciprocal exemption as to all personal property, except tangible personal property having an actual situs therein and allowed a similar exemption to residents of the state of residence of the decedent. (§ 43.31.410(2))
Arizona	There is a general provision that allows the Department of Revenue to enter into a closing agreement to satisfy a taxpayer's tax liability. (§ 42-1113)	No.
Arkansas	The Director of Finance and Administration may compromise any controversy relating to a state tax. (§ 26-18-705)	With respect to property of a nonresident located in Arkansas, Arkansas will not tax if the other state has a reciprocal provision regarding Arkansas residents. (§ 26-59-107(c))
California	California has adopted both the Uniform Act on Interstate Compromise of Death Taxes and the Uniform Act on Interstate Arbitration of Death Taxes. (Rev. & Tax. §§ 13810, 13820)	No.
Colorado	Colorado has adopted both the Uniform Act on Interstate Compromise of Death Taxes and the Uniform Act on Interstate Arbitration of Death Taxes. (§ 39-24-101)	No.
Connecticut	The Commissioner of Revenue Services has the authority to make a written agreement with other taxing authorities to compromise the controversy or submit the controversy to arbitration. (§§ 12-372, 12-395(a))	No.

Table 15.06
Conflicts Between States *(continued)*

	Are There Compromise or Arbitration Provisions for Disputes over the Decedent's Domicile?	*Is There a Provision for the Reciprocal Exemption of Taxes?*
Delaware	Delaware has adopted both the Uniform Act on Interstate Compromise of Death Taxes and the Uniform Act on Interstate Arbitration of Death Taxes. (30 §§ 1703, 1704)	No.
District of Columbia	Yes. The Mayor has the authority to compromise. (§ 47-3704)	No.
Florida	No. Presumption of domiciliary status. Determined solely under Ch. 198 proceeding. (§ 198.015)	There is an exemption from all transfer taxes if the nonresident was a resident of a state that did not tax Floridians, except on tangible personal property in the state, or if there is a reciprocal exemption Provision regarding death taxes on personal property, other than tangible personal property with an actual situs in the state and permitted a similar exemption to residents of the state. (§ 198.44)
Georgia	There is a provision allowing for a compromise agreement when a dispute over the collection of taxes exists. (§ 48-2-18.1)	No.
Hawaii	No provision.	The estate tax exempts the property of a resident taxed by another state if that state has a reciprocal provision allowing the property to be taxed in the state of domicile. (§ 236D-3(b)) The estate tax exempts the property of a nonresident to the extent that the decedent's state of residence exempts the property of Hawaii residents except for real and tangible personal property having an actual situs in Hawaii. (§ 236D-4(c)) See also § 236D-15.
Idaho	No provision.	The estate tax exempts the property of a resident taxed by another state if that state has a reciprocal provision allowing the property to be taxed in the state of domicile. (§ 14-403(2)) The estate tax exempts the property of a nonresident to the extent that the decedent's state of residence exempts the same types of property of a resident of Idaho. (§ 14-404(3))

Illinois	The Attorney General may enter into a written compromise agreement with the taxing authorities of another state or states. The person required to file the Illinois state tax return or pay the Illinois tax also has full power and authority to enter into the written compromise agreement with the taxing authorities of another state or states. (35 ILCS § 405/17)	No.
Indiana	The Department of State Revenue may, with the approval of the attorney general, enter into a compromise agreement concerning the amount of the inheritance tax. (§ 6-4.1-12-5(a)) The department may enter into a compromise agreement if there is substantial doubt as to whether the decedent was a resident of Indiana. (§ 6-4.1-12-5(b)(6))	No.
Iowa	No provision.	No.
Kansas	No provision.	No. The Kansas reciprocal exemption of death taxes has been repealed effective July 1, 1998.
Kentucky	The Secretary of Revenue may enter into a written compromise agreement. (§ 140.285(1))	The intangible personal property of a nonresident decedent held in trust by a Kentucky trustee is exempt from taxation if the decedent's state of residence has a reciprocal provision (§ 140.275(1)) and if the personal representative presents evidence the tax has been or will be paid in the other state.
Louisiana	No provision.	No general reciprocity provision. However, donations to charitable institutions located in another state are exempt if the other state has a reciprocal provision. (Rev. Stat. § 47:2402(6))
Maine	Maine has adopted both the Uniform Interstate Arbitration of Death Taxes Act and the Uniform Interstate Compromise of Death Taxes Act. (36 §§ 3911, 3981)	Yes. A reciprocal exemption will apply to any state where Maine is given reasonable assurance of the collection of death taxes when a Maine domiciliary's estate is administered in that other state. The statute should be construed to ensure that the state of domicile receives all death taxes due it. (36 § 4045)
Maryland	Maryland has adopted both the Uniform Act on Interstate Compromise of Death Taxes and the Uniform Act on Interstate Arbitration of Death Taxes. (Tax-Gen. §§ 7-115, 7-118)	The inheritance and estate taxes do not apply to the personal property of a nonresident, except for tangible personal property located in Maryland, if the decedent's state or country of residence does not tax "the receipt of similar personal property of a resident of this State" or

(cont'd)

Table 15.06
Conflicts Between States *(continued)*

	Are There Compromise or Arbitration Provisions for Disputes over the Decedent's Domicile?	*Is There a Provision for the Reciprocal Exemption of Taxes?*
Maryland *(cont'd)*		has a reciprocal exemption provision "similar to" the Maryland provision. (Tax-Gen. §§ 7-203(f), 7-303)
Massachusetts	Massachusetts has adopted both the Uniform Act on Interstate Arbitration of Death Taxes and the Uniform Interstate Compromise of Death Taxes Act. (65B §§ 1-7)	No.
Michigan	Michigan has adopted both the Uniform Act on Interstate Compromise of Death Taxes and the Uniform Act on Interstate Arbitration of Death Taxes. (§ 205.601, *et seq.*)	There is an exemption from all transfer taxes if the nonresident was a resident of a state that did not tax residents of Michigan, except on tangible personal property in the state, or if there is a reciprocal exemption provision regarding death taxes on personal property, other than tangible personal property with an actual situs in the state and permitted a similar exemption to residents of the state. (§ 205.201(2)(b))
Minnesota	Minnesota has adopted both the Uniform Act on Interstate Compromise of Death Taxes and the Uniform Act on Interstate Arbitration of Death Taxes. (§ 291.41, *et seq.*)	No.
Mississippi	The commissioner, with the approval of the attorney general may agree upon the amount of taxes at any time due or to become due. (§ 27-9-41)	There is an exemption from all transfer taxes if the nonresident was a resident of a state that did not tax residents of Mississippi, except on tangible personal property in the state, or if there is a reciprocal exemption provision regarding death taxes on personal property, other than tangible personal property with an actual situs in the state and permitted a similar exemption to residents of the state. (§ 27-9-13(b))
Missouri	The Director of Revenue may make a written agreement of Compromise with the taxing authorities of another state. (§ 145.201)	No.
Montana	No provision.	No.

Nebraska	Nebraska has adopted both the Uniform Act on Interstate Compromise of Death Taxes and the Uniform Act on Interstate Arbitration of Death Taxes. (§ 77-3301)	There is an exemption from all transfer taxes if the nonresident was a resident of a state that did not tax residents of Nebraska, except on tangible personal property in the state, or if there is a reciprocal exemption provision regarding death taxes on personal property, other than tangible personal property with an actual situs in the state and permitted a similar exemption to residents of the state. (§ 77-2007.01)
Nevada	Nevada has adopted both the Uniform Act on Interstate Compromise of Death Taxes and the Uniform Act on Interstate Arbitration of Death Taxes. (§§ 375A.410, 375A.460)	No.
New Hampshire	The Department of Revenue has the power to enter into written agreements with taxing authorities of other states if there is a conflict over the decedent's domicile. If an agreement cannot be reached, the Department of Revenue can enter arbitration. (§§ 90:1–90:4)	No.
New Jersey	New Jersey has adopted the Uniform Interstate Compromise of Death Taxes Act. The Director of the Division of Taxation has the power to compromise and enter into agreements with other states claiming the domicile of the decedent. (§ 54:38A-1)	No.
New Mexico	No provision.	The transfer of the property of a nonresident is exempt to the extent that the decedent's state of residence exempts the property of New Mexico residents from death taxes. (§ 7-7-4(D))
New York	New York has adopted the Uniform Interstate Compromise of Death Taxes Act. The Commissioner of Taxation and Finance has the power to enter into written agreements with taxing authorities of other states if there is a conflict over the decedent's domicile. (Tax § 978(a))	Taxes imposed by the state on personal property (except tangible personal property located in the state) are not payable if the transferor is a resident of a state or territory of the United States, the laws of which contain a reciprocal provision under which nonresidents are exempted from death and transfer taxes on all personal property other than tangible personal property located in the state. (Tax § 960-a)
North Carolina	The Secretary of Revenue has authority to make agreements with the taxing officials of other states or with taxpayers in cases of disputes as to the domicile of the decedent. (§ 105-240.1)	No.
North Dakota	No provision.	No.
Ohio	Yes. The Tax Commissioner, with the permission of the probate court, may enter into a compromise with the taxing authorities of *(cont'd)*	Intangible personal property of a nonresident is not taxed if the state of residence of the decedent allowed a reciprocal exemption as to all *(cont'd)*

Table 15.06
Conflicts Between States *(continued)*

	Are There Compromise or Arbitration Provisions for Disputes over the Decedent's Domicile?	*Is There a Provision for the Reciprocal Exemption of Taxes?*
Ohio *(cont'd)*	another state claiming that the decedent was domiciled in that state. (§ 5731.35)	personal property, except tangible personal property having an actual situs therein and allowed a similar exemption to residents of the state. (§ 5731.34)
Oklahoma	No provision.	There is an exemption from all transfer taxes if the nonresident was a resident of a state that did not tax Oklahomans, except on tangible personal property in that state, or if there is a reciprocal exemption provision regarding transfer or death taxes on personal property, other than tangible personal property with an actual situs in the state, and the state permitted a similar exemption to residents of the state. (68 § 807(A)(1)(b))
Oregon	The Department of Revenue may enter into written agreements with other taxing officials if there is a dispute as to the decedent's domicile. (§ 118.865) If no agreement can be reached, the Director of the Department of Revenue can appoint a person to a board of arbitration to resolve the dispute. (§ 118.870)	Intangible personal property of a nonresident is not included in the numerator of the ratio for determining tax liability, if a "similar exemption" is provided by the laws of the state or country of decedent's residence in favor of residents of Oregon. (§ 118.010(4)(b))
Pennsylvania	Yes, Pennsylvania has adopted both the Uniform Act on Interstate Compromise of Death Taxes and the Uniform Act on Interstate Arbitration of Death Taxes. (72 §§ 9157, 9158)	No. However intangibles of non-residents are specifically exempt from inheritance tax. (72 § 9111)
Rhode Island	The State Tax Administrator can enter into agreements with other taxing officials claiming the domicile of the decedent. (§ 44-23-29) If an agreement cannot be reached, the taxing administrator can enter into arbitration. (§ 44-23-30)	No.
South Carolina	South Carolina has adopted both the Uniform Act on Interstate Compromise of Death Taxes and the Uniform Act on Interstate Arbitration of Death Taxes. (§§ 12-16-210 through 12-16-320)	No.
South Dakota	No provision.	No.

Tennessee	The Commissioner of Revenue may enter into written agreements with other taxing officials if there is a dispute as to the decedent's domicile. (§ 67-8-503) If no agreement can be reached, the Commissioner of Revenue can appoint a person to a board of arbitration to resolve the dispute. (§ 67-8-504)	No.
Texas	The comptroller may enter into a written compromise agreement which must be approved by the Attorney General. (Tax § 211.109)	No.
Utah	No provision.	Transfers of intangible personal property having a situs in the state and of securities of any corporation or entity organized under the laws of the state are exempt from taxation, to the extent that the same types of property of a Utah resident are exempt in the nonresident's state. (§ 59-11-104(4))
Vermont	Vermont has adopted both the Uniform Act on Interstate Compromise of Death Taxes and the Uniform Act on Interstate Arbitration of Death Taxes. (32 §§ 7202, 7102)	No.
Virginia	Virginia has adopted both the Uniform Act on Interstate Compromise of Death Taxes and the Uniform Act on Interstate Arbitration of Death Taxes. (§§ 58.1-922, 58.1-923)	No.
Washington	The department may enter into an agreement in writing with any person relating to the liability of such person in respect of any tax imposed by any of the preceding chapters of this title for any taxable period or periods. (§ 82.32.350)	No. Repealed L. 200, Ch. 516, § 17 (§ 83.100.040(3)). Effective 5/17/2005.
West Virginia	West Virginia has adopted both the Uniform Act on Interstate Compromise of Death Taxes and the Uniform Act on Interstate Arbitration of Death Taxes. (§§ 11-11A-1, 11-11B-1)	No.
Wisconsin	The Department of Revenue may enter into a written agreement with the taxing authority of another state to settle the dispute before a panel of arbitrators. (§ 72.35(1))	The estate tax does not apply to the intangible personal property of a nonresident if the decedent's state of residence has a reciprocal provision. (§ 72.11(2))
Wyoming	No provision.	No.

Table 15.07
Inheritance, Estate, Succession, Transfer, and Gift Tax Rates
Connecticut

Estate Tax (§ 12-391(g)), effective January 1, 2005	
Amount of Connecticut Taxable Estate	*Tax Rate*
Not over $2,000,000	None
Over $2,000,000 but not over $2,100,000	5.085% of the excess over $0
Over $2,100,000 but not over $2,600,000	$106,800 plus 8% of the excess over $2,100,000
Over $2,600,000 but not over $3,100,000	$146,800 plus 8.8% of the excess over $2,600,000
Over $3,100,000 but not over $3,600,000	$190,800 plus 9.6% of the excess over $3,100,000
Over $3,600,000 but not over $4,100,000	$238,800 plus 10.4% of the excess over $3,600,000
Over $4,100,000 but not over $5,100,000	$290,800 plus 11.2% of the excess over $4,100,000
Over $5,100,000 but not over $6,100,000	$402,800 plus 12% of the excess over $5,100,000
Over $6,100,000 but not over $7,100,000	$522,800 plus 12.8% of the excess over $6,100,000
Over $7,100,000 but not over $8,100,000	$650,800 plus 13.6% of the excess over $7,100,000
Over $8,100,000 but not over $9,100,000	$786,800 plus 14.4% of the excess over $8,100,000
Over $9,100,000 but not over $10,100,000	$930,800 plus 15.2% of the excess over $9,100,000
Over $10,100,000	$1,082,800 plus 16% of the excess over $10,100,000

Gift Tax (§ 12-642(a)(3)), effective January 1, 2005

Amount of Taxable Gifts	*Tax Rate*
Not over $2,000,000	None
Over $2,000,000 but not over $2,100,000	5.085% of the excess over $0
Over $2,100,000 but not over $2,600,000	$106,800 plus 8% of the excess over $2,100,000
Over $2,600,000 but not over $3,100,000	$146,800 plus 8.8% of the excess over $2,600,000
Over $3,100,000 but not over $3,600,000	$190,800 plus 9.6% of the excess over $3,100,000
Over $3,600,000 but not over $4,100,000	$238,800 plus 10.4% of the excess over $3,600,000
Over $4,100,000 but not over $5,100,000	$290,800 plus 11.2% of the excess over $4,100,000
Over $5,100,000 but not over $6,100,000	$402,800 plus 12% of the excess over $5,100,000
Over $6,100,000 but not over $7,100,000	$522,800 plus 12.8% of the excess over $6,100,000
Over $7,100,000 but not over $8,100,000	$650,800 plus 13.6% of the excess over $7,100,000
Over $8,100,000 but not over $9,100,000	$786,800 plus 14.4% of the excess over $8,100,000
Over $9,100,000 but not over $10,100,000	$930,800 plus 15.2% of the excess over $9,100,000
Over $10,100,000	$1,082,800 plus 16% of the excess over $10,100,000

Table 15.07
Inheritance, Estate, Succession, Transfer, and Gift Tax Rates
Indiana

Inheritance Tax (§§ 6-4.1-1-3, 6-4.1-5-1)

Class A transferee—transferee is a lineal ancestor or lineal descendant of the transferor, including stepchildren and their lineal descendants, regardless if they were adopted:

Net Taxable Value of Property Transferred	Inheritance Tax
$25,000 or less	1% of net taxable value
$25,001–50,000	$250, plus 2% on amount over $25,000
$50,001–200,000	$750, plus 3% on amount over $50,000
$200,001–300,000	$5,250, plus 4% on amount over $200,000
$300,001–500,000	$9,250, plus 5% on amount over $300,000
$500,001–700,000	$19,250, plus 6% on amount over $500,000
$700,001–1,000,000	$31,250, plus 7% on amount over $700,000
$1,000,001–1,500,000	$52,250, plus 8% on amount over $1,000,000
Over $1,500,000	$92,250, plus 10% on amount over $1,500,000

(§ 6-4.1-5-1(b))

Class B transferee—transferee is a brother or sister of the transferor, or a descendant of a brother or sister of the transferor, or a spouse, widow, or widower of a child of a transferor:

$100,000 or less	7% of net taxable value
$100,001–500,000	$7,000, plus 10% on amount over $100,000
$500,001–1,000,000	$47,000, plus 12% on amount over $500,000
Over $1,000,000	$107,000, plus 15% on amount over $1,000,000

(§ 6-4.1-5-1(c))

Class C transferee—transferee, except a surviving spouse, who is neither a Class A nor a Class B transferee:

$100,000 or less	10% of net taxable value
$100,001–1,000,000	$10,000, plus 15% on amount over $100,000
Over $1,000,000	$145,000, plus 20% on amount over $1,000,000

(§ 6-4.1-5-1(d))

Transfers to a surviving spouse are exempt from tax. (§ 6-4.1-3-7) The first $100,000 transferred to a Class A transferee is exempt from tax. (§ 6-4.1-3-10) The first $500 transferred to a Class B transferee is exempt from tax. (§ 6-4.1-3-11) The first $100 transferred to a Class C transferee is exempt from tax. (§ 6-4.1-3-12)

Table 15.07
Inheritance, Estate, Succession, Transfer, and Gift Tax Rates
Iowa

Inheritance Tax (§ 450.10)

(1) For transfers to the brother or sister, son-in-law, or daughter-in-law, the tax rate is:

Taxable Property	Tax Rate
$0–12,500	5%
$12,501–25,000	6%
$25,001–75,000	7%
$75,001–100,000	8%
$100,001–150,000	9%
Over $150,000	10%

(2) For transfers to persons not included in subsections 1 and 6, the tax rate is:

Taxable	Tax Rate
$0–50,000	10%
$50,001–100,000	12%
(§ 77-2006) Over $100,000	15%

(3) For transfers to societies, institutions or associations incorporated or organized under the laws of another state, territory, province or country for charitable, educational or religious purposes or to cemetery associations not organized under Iowa laws or to resident trustees for uses outside of Iowa, the tax rate is 10% on the entire amount so transferred.

(4) For transfers to any firm, corporation or society organized for profit, or fraternal or social organizations which do not qualify for exemption under Sections 170(c) and 2055 of the Internal Revenue Code, the tax rate is 15% on the entire amount so transferred.

(5) For transfers to persons included under subsection (1), there is a credit applied to the tax imposed on the individual share an amount equal to the tax imposed by Iowa on the decedent on any property or the proportionate share on property passing to the person taxed, which is identifiable as having been received by the decedent as a share in the estate of another decedent who died within two years of the death of the decedent or which is identifiable as having been acquired by the decedent in exchange for property so received.

(6) For transfers to the surviving spouse, and parents, grandparents, great-grandparents, and other lineal ascendants, children, stepchildren, grandchildren, great-grandchildren, and other lineal descendants, there is no tax.

Table 15.07
Inheritance, Estate, Succession, Transfer, and Gift Tax Rates
Kansas

Estate Tax (§ 79-15,221)	
2007	
Amount of Taxable Estate	Rate
Not over $1,000,000	Zero
Over $1,000,000 but not over $2,000,000	3.0% of excess over $1,000,000
Over $2,000,000 but not over $5,000,000	$30,000 plus 6.0% of excess over $2,000,000
Over $5,000,000 but not over $10,000,000	$210,000 plus 8.0% of excess over $5,000,000
Over $10,000,000	$610,000 plus 10.0% of excess over $10,000,000
2008	
Amount of Taxable Estate	Rate
Not over $1,000,000	Zero
Over $1,000,000 but not over $2,000,000	1% of excess over $1,000,000
Over $2,000,000 but not over $5,000,000	$10,000 plus 2.0% of excess over $2,000,000
Over $5,000,000 but not over $10,000,000	$70,000 plus 5.0% of excess over $5,000,000
Over $10,000,000Rate	$320,000 plus 7.0% of excess over $10,000,000
2009	
Amount of Taxable Estate	Rate
Not over $1,000,000	Zero
Over $1,000,000 but not over $2,000,000	0.5% of excess over $1,000,000
Over $2,000,000 but not over $5,000,000	$5,000 plus 1.0% of excess over $2,000,000
Over $5,000,000 but not over $10,000,000	$35,000 plus 2.0% of excess over $5,000,000
Over $10,000,000	$135,000 plus 3.0% of excess over $10,000,000

Table 15.07
Inheritance, Estate, Succession, Transfer, and Gift Tax Rates
Kentucky

Inheritance tax (§ 140.070)

Transfer to Class A Beneficiary	Tax Rate
$0–20,000	2%
$20,001–30,000	3%
$30,001–45,000	4%
$45,001–60,000	5%
$60,001–100,000	6%
$100,001–200,000	7%
$200,001–500,000	8%
Over $500,000	10%

Class A beneficiary includes decedent's parent, surviving spouse, child by blood, stepchild, child adopted during infancy, child adopted during adulthood who was reared by the decedent during infancy or a grandchild who is the issue of a child by blood, the issue of a stepchild, the issue of a child adopted during adulthood who was reared by the decedent during infancy, the issue of a child adopted during infancy, brother, sister, or brother or sister of the half blood. (§ 140.070(1))

Transfer to Class B Beneficiary	Tax Rate
$0–10,000	4%
$10,001–20,000	5%
$20,001–30,000	6%
$30,001–45,000	8%
$45,001–60,000	10%
$60,001–100,000	12%
$100,001–200,000	14%
Over $200,000	16%

Class B beneficiary consists of decedent's nephew, niece, or a nephew or niece of the half-blood, daughter-in-law, son-in-law, aunt or uncle, or a great-grandchild who is the grandchild of a child by blood, of a stepchild or of a child adopted during infancy. (§ 140.070(2))

Transfer to Class C Beneficiary	Tax Rate
$0–10,000	6%
$10,001–20,000	8%
$20,001–30,000	10%
$30,001–45,000	12%
$45,001–60,000	14%
Over $60,000	16%

Class C beneficiary includes any educational, religious, or other institutions, societies, or associations, or any cities, towns, or public institutions not exempted by § 140.060, or to any person not included in either Class A or Class B. (§ 140.070(3))

Table 15.07
Inheritance, Estate, Succession, Transfer, and Gift Tax Rates
Louisiana

Inheritance Tax (§ 47:2403)

A. Transfers to direct descendants by blood or affinity, ascendants, or surviving spouse:

Amount of Transfer Over the Amount Exempt under § 47:2402(1), currently $25,000.	Tax Rate
$0–20,000	2%
Over $20,000	3%

B. Collateral relations including brother or sister by affinity and their descendants:

Amount of Transfer	Tax Rate
$1,001–21,000	5%
Over $21,000	7%

C. Transfers to strangers:

Amount of Transfer	Tax Rate
$501–5,500	5%
Over $5,500	10%

. . .

E. Notwithstanding any provision of this section to the contrary, for deaths occurring after June 30, 1998, the tax rate as provided in this section shall be as follows:

(1) For deaths occurring after June 30, 1998, and before July 1, 2001, the tax rates provided in this section shall be reduced by 18%. (§ 47:2403(E)(1))

(2) For deaths occurring after June 30, 2001, and before July 1, 2002, the tax rates provided in this section shall be reduced by 40%. (§ 47:2403(E)(2))

(3) For deaths occurring after June 30, 2002, and before July 1, 2003, the tax rates provided in this section shall be reduced by 60%. (§ 47:2403(E)(3))

(4) For deaths occurring after June 30, 2003, the tax rates provided in this section shall be reduced by 80%. (§ 47:2403(E)(4))

Gift Tax (§ 47:1206)

Amount of Gift (cumulative excess over annual exclusion and lifetime exemptions)	Tax Rate
$0–15,000	2%
Over $15,000	3%

Table 15.07
Inheritance, Estate, Succession, Transfer, and Gift Tax Rates
Maryland

Inheritance Tax Rate (Tax-Gen. § 7-204)
Collateral tax rate: The inheritance tax rate is 10% of the "clear value" of the property that passes from a decedent. (Tax-Gen. § 7-204(b)) "Clear value" is fair market value minus expenses (Tax-Gen. § 7-204(a)).
A family allowance bars application of the inheritance tax to ancestors of the decedent up to the grandparent generational level, lineal descendants, the spouse of the decedent, a spouse of a lineal descendant, a sibling, a stepparent or stepchild, or a corporation if all the stockholders "consist of the surviving spouse, parents, stepparents, stepchildren, brother, sisters, and lineal descendants of the decedent and spouses of the lineal descendants." (Tax-Gen. § 7-203(b))

Table 15.07
Inheritance, Estate, Succession, Transfer, and Gift Tax Rates
Nebraska

Inheritance Tax (§§ 77-2001–77-2006)

For transfers to any parent, lineal descendant, grandparent, sibling, child or adopted child, lineal descendant born in lawful wedlock, lineal descendant legally adopted, person to whom the decedent stood for not less than 10 years prior to death in the acknowledged relation of a parent, or the spouse or surviving spouse of any such persons, married to the decedent at the time of the former spouse's prior death, and persons having any of these relationships to a spouse who is married to the decedent at the time of his death, the tax is 1% of the value of the property received in excess of $10,000. (§§ 77-2004, 77-2005.01)[1]

For transfers to any aunt, uncle, niece or nephew related by blood or adoption, or other lineal descendant of the same, or the spouse or surviving spouse of any such persons, or the same relatives of a former spouse who was married to the decedent at the time of the former spouse's prior death, and persons having any of these relations to a spouse who is married to the decedent at the time of the decedent's death, the tax is 6% of the value of the property received by each person in excess of $2,000 and not exceeding $60,000, and 9% on the excess over $60,000. (§§ 77-2005, 77-2005-01)[2]

For all other transfers, the tax is:

Value of Transfer	Tax Rate
$0–5,000	6%
$5,001–10,000	9%
$10,001–20,000	12%
$20,001–50,000	15%
Over $50,000	18%

If the clear market value of the beneficial interest is five hundred dollars or less, it shall not be subject to any tax. (§ 77-2006)

1. Persons fitting within these categories are any parent, grandparent, sibling, child or adopted child, lineal descendant born in lawful wedlock, lineal descendant legally adopted, decedent stood for not less than 10 years prior to death in the acknowledged relation of a parent, or the spouse or surviving spouse of any such persons married to the decedent at the time of the former spouse's prior death, and persons having any of these relationships to a spouse who is married to the decedent at the time of his death. (§ 77-2005.01)
2. Persons fitting within these categories are any aunt, uncle, niece or nephew related by blood or adoption, or other lineal descendant of a former spouse who was married to the decedent at the time of the former spouse's prior death, and persons having any of these relations to a spouse who is married to the decedent at the time of the decedent's death. (§ 77-2005.01)

Estate Tax (§ 77-2101.03(2))

For decedents dying on or after July 1, 2003, the tax on the Nebraska taxable estate is:

Nebraska taxable estate				
At least	But less than	Tax =	+ %	Of Excess Over
$ 0	$100,000	$ 0	5.6	$ 0
100,000	500,000	5,600	6.4	100,000
1,000,000	1,500,000	67,200	8.0	1,000,000
1,500,000	2,000,000	107,200	8.8	1,500,000
2,000,000	2,500,000	151,200	9.6	2,000,000
2,500,000	3,000,000	199,200	10.4	2,500,000
3,000,000	3,500,000	251,200	11.2	3,000,000
3,500,000	4,000,000	307,200	12.0	3,500,000
4,000,000	5,000,000	367,200	12.8	4,000,000
5,000,000	6,000,000	495,200	13.6	5,000,000
6,000,000	7,000,000	631,200	14.4	6,000,000
7,000,000	8,000,000	775,200	15.2	7,000,000
8,000,000	9,000,000	927,200	16.0	8,000,000
9,000,000	—	1,087,200	16.8	9,000,000

Generation-Skipping Transfer Tax (§ 77-2101.03(3))

A taxable generation-skipping transfer is taxable at a rate of 16% of the Nebraska taxable transfer, but then reduced as specified in Table 15.03, Nebraska.

Table 15.07
Inheritance, Estate, Succession, Transfer, and Gift Tax Rates
New Jersey

Inheritance Tax (§ 54:34-2)

No tax is imposed on transfers to spouses after January 1, 1985 or domestic partners (as defined in Section 3 of Pub. L. No. 2003, C. 246, (§ 26:8A-3) effective 180 days after its enactment on January 12, 2004), or transfers to parents, grandparents, children, or grandchildren after July 1, 1988. (§ 54:34-2(a)(1) & (a)(2))

Transfers made after July 1, 1988 to brother, sister, wife, or widow of son of decedent, or husband or widower of a daughter of decedent:

Amount of Transfer	Tax Rate
$0–25,000	0%
$25,001–1,100,000	11%
$1,100,001–1,400,000	13%
$1,400,001–1,700,000	14%
Over $1,700,000	16%

(§ 54:34-2(c)(2))

Transfers to all transferees not listed above:

Amount of Transfer	Tax Rate
$0–700,000	15%
Over $700,000	16%

(§ 54:34-2(d))

Table 15.07
Inheritance, Estate, Succession, Transfer, and Gift Tax Rates
North Carolina

Gift Tax (§ 105-188(f))

For transfers where the donee is the lineal issue, lineal ancestor, stepchild, or adopted child of the donor (for each $100 or fraction thereof):

Net Taxable Estate	Rate of Tax
First $10,000 above the exemption	1%
$10,001–25,000	2%
$25,001–50,000	3%
$50,001–100,000	4%
$100,001–200,000	5%
$200,001–500,000	6%
$500,001–1,000,000	7%
$1,000,001–1,500,000	8%
$1,500,001–2,000,000	9%
$2,000,001–2,500,000	10%
$2,500,001–3,000,000	11%
Over $3,000,000	12%

Transfers where the donee is the brother or sister or descendant of the brother or sister, or the uncle or aunt by blood of the donor (for each $100 or fraction thereof):

Net Taxable Estate	Rate of Tax
First $5,000	4%
$5,001–10,000	5%
$10,001–25,000	6%
$25,001–50,000	7%
$50,001–100,000	8%
$100,001–250,000	10%
$250,001–500,000	11%
$500,001–1,000,000	12%
$1,000,001–1,500,000	13%
$1,500,001–2,000,000	14%
$2,000,001–3,000,000	15%
Over $3,000,000	16%

For transfers where the donee is in any other degree of relationship, or a stranger in blood to the donor, or a body politic or corporate (for each $100 or fraction thereof):

Net Taxable Estate	Rate of Tax
First $10,000	8%
$10,001–25,000	9%
$25,001–50,000	10%
$50,001–100,000	11%
$100,001–250,000	12%
$250,001–500,000	13%
$500,001–1,000,000	14%
$1,000,001–1,500,000	15%
$1,500,001–2,500,000	16%
Over $2,500,000	17%

The tax is determined on a grossed-up basis, with a tentative tax first being determined on all gifts from the donor to the *particular* donee since January 1, 1948. A tentative tax computed on all gifts to this donee for all prior years is then subtracted from the initial tentative tax. (§ 105-188(e)) There is an annual exclusion. The tax is imposed on gifts of property within the state. (§ 105-188(a) & (b))

Table 15.07
Inheritance, Estate, Succession, Transfer, and Gift Tax Rates
Ohio

Estate Tax Rates (§ 5731.02)

Taxable Estate	The Tax Is:
$0–40,000	2% of the taxable estate
$40,001–100,000	$800 plus 3% of the excess over $40,000
$100,001–200,000	$2,600 plus 4% of the excess over $100,000
$200,001–300,000	$6,600 plus 5% of the excess over $200,000
$300,001–500,000	$11,600 plus 6% of the excess over $300,000
Over $500,000	$23,600 plus 7% of the excess over $500,000

A credit is allowed equal to the lesser of $500 or the amount of the tax for persons dying on or after July 1, 1968, but before January 1, 2001; the lesser of $6,600 or the amount of the tax for persons dying on or after January 1, 2001, but before January 1, 2002; or the lesser of $13,900 or the amount of the tax for persons dying on or after January 1, 2002. (§ 5731.02(B))

Table 15.07
Inheritance, Estate, Succession, Transfer, and Gift Tax Rates
Oklahoma

Estate Tax Rates (68 §§ 803, 825)

Upon the passing of the net estate of any decedent effective Jan. 1, 2007 and, prior to that date, the passing of the net estate to the father, mother, child, child of husband or wife, adopted child, or any lineal descendants of decedent or of such adopted child, the tax is:

Taxable Estate Equal to or More Than	Taxable Estate Less Than	Tax on Amount in Column 1	Rate of Tax on Excess Over Amount in Column 1
$0	$10,000	$0	0.5%
$10,000	$20,000	$50	1%
$20,000	$40,000	$150	1.5%
$40,000	$60,000	$450	2%
$60,000	$100,000	$850	2.5%
$100,000	$250,000	$1,850	3%
$250,000	$500,000	$6,350	6.5%
$500,000	$750,000	$22,600	7%
$750,000	$1,000,000	$40,100	7.5%
$1,000,000	$3,000,000	$58,850	8%
$3,000,000	$5,000,000	$218,850	8.5%
$5,000,000	$10,000,000	$388,850	9%
$10,000,000	—	$838,850	10%

Upon the passing of the net estate for all other transfers, with respect to decedent's dying prior to Jan. 1, 2007, the tax is:

Taxable Estate Equal to or More Than	Taxable Estate Less Than	Tax on Amount in Column 1	Rate of Tax on Excess Over Amount in Column 1
$0	$10,000	$0	1%
$10,000	$20,000	$100	2%
$20,000	$40,000	$300	3%
$40,000	$60,000	$900	4%
$60,000	$100,000	$1,700	5%
$100,000	$250,000	$3,700	6%
$250,000	$500,000	$12,700	13%
$500,000	$1,000,000	$45,200	14%
$1,000,000	—	$115,200	15%

Substantial exemptions apply. For example, the exemption for 2006 and 2007 is $1,000,000. For 2008 it is $2,000,000. (68 § 809(A)(9)) For 2009, it is $3,000,000. (68 § 809(A)(10)) **Beginning in 2010, the tax is repealed altogether. See ch. 42, H.B. 1172, § 6 (June 27, 2006).**

Table 15.07
Inheritance, Estate, Succession, Transfer, and Gift Tax Rates
Pennsylvania

Inheritance Tax Rate (72 § 9116)	
(1)	The inheritance tax rate is 4.5% for transfers of property to the (a) grandfather, grandmother, father, mother and lineal descendants or (b) wife or widow and husband or widower of a child.
(1.1)	The inheritance tax rate for transfers to the surviving spouse is 0% for decedents dying on or after January 1, 1995.
(1.2)	The inheritance tax upon the transfer of property from a child 21 years of age or younger to or for the use of a natural or adoptive parent, or stepparent, is taxed at a rate of 0%.
(1.3)	The inheritance tax upon the transfer of property passing to or for the use of a sibling is taxed at a rate of 12%.
(2)	The inheritance tax rate for transfers for all persons other than those designated in subclauses (1), (1.1), (1.2), or (1.3) is 15%.
(3)	When property passes to or for the use of a husband and wife with right of survivorship, one of whom is taxable at a rate lower than the other, the lower rate of tax shall be applied to the entire interest.

Table 15.07
Inheritance, Estate, Succession, Transfer, and Gift Tax Rates
Tennessee

Inheritance Tax (§ 67-8-314)

Class A—Husband, wife, son, daughter, lineal ancestor, lineal descendant, brother, sister, stepchild, son-in-law or daughter-in-law, person related to decedent through legal adoption. A marital deduction, consistent with federal law, however, is allowed. (§ 67-8-315(a)(6))

Net Taxable Estate Over	Tax	Rate on Excess Over Amount in Column 1
$0	$—	5.5%
$40,000	$2,200	6.5%
$240,000	$15,200	7.5%
$440,000	$30,200	9.5%

Class B—All others. A charitable deduction is allowed, if to the U.S., Tennessee, a Tennessee charity, or to an institution in another state that treats transfers to Tennessee institutions similarly. (§ 67-8-315(a)(1))

Net Taxable Estate Over	Tax	Rate on Excess Over Amount in Column 1
$0	$—	5.5%
$40,000	$2,200	6.5%
$240,000	$15,200	7.5%
$440,000	$30,200	9.5%

Gift Tax (§ 67-8-106)[4]

Class A—Husband, wife, son, daughter, lineal ancestor, lineal descendant, brother, sister, stepchild, son-in-law or daughter-in-law, person related to decedent through legal adoption.

Amount of Transfer	Tax Rate
$0–40,000	5.5%
$40,001–240,000	6.5%
$240,001–440,000	7.5%
over $440,000	9.5%

Class B—All others.

Amount of Transfer	Tax Rate
$0–50,000	6.5%
$50,001–100,000	9.5%
$100,001–150,000	1.2%
$150,001–200,000	13.5%
over $200,000	16%

4. A charitable deduction as described for the inheritance tax (§ 67-8-103(b)), a marital deduction (§ 67-8-105), and an annual exclusion which is limited to an aggregate total of $10,000 for all Class A donees in a year. The limit is $5,000 for all Class B donees. (§ 67-8-104) In the event that the net single exemption for gifts for Class A is exceeded, then a gift to each Class A donee is exempted up to $42,000 per donee, if a present interest. The same rule applies to Class B donees but is limited to $3,000. The standard exemption amount applicable to gifts to Class A donees increases with the federal exclusion. (§ 67-8-104(c)) There is no unified credit available for gifts, although there is one for the inheritance tax. It is an exemption equal to the I.R.C. § 2010 applicable exclusion amount, but not to exceed $850,000 in 2004, $950,000 in 2005, and $1,000,000 in 2006 and thereafter. This exemption is apportioned for nonresidents based on the ratio that the value of property included in the gross estate bears to the value of all property that would have been included if the person had been a Tennessee resident. (§ 67-8-316(c))

Table 15.07
Inheritance, Estate, Succession, Transfer, and Gift Tax Rates
Virginia

Tax on the probate of wills: A tax equal to 10 cents for every $100 of value, or fraction of $100, is imposed on estates with a value over $15,000. (§ 58.1-1712)

Table 15.07
Inheritance, Estate, Succession, Transfer, and Gift Tax Rates
Washington

Estate Tax Rates (§ 83.100-040(2)(a))				
If Washington Taxable Estate is at least	But Less Than	The amount of Tax Equals	Plus Tax Rate %	Of Washington Taxable Rate
		Initial Tax Amount		Value Greater Than
$0	$1,000,000	$0	10.00%	$0
$1,000,000	$2,000,000	$100,000	14.00%	$1,000,000
$2,000,000	$3,000,000	$240,000	15.00%	$2,000,000
$3,000,000	$4,000,000	$390,000	16.00%	$3,000,000
$4,000,000	$6,000,000	$550,000	17.00%	$4,000,000
$6,000,000	$7,000,000	$890,000	18.00%	$6,000,000
$7,000,000	$9,000,000	$1,070,000	18.50%	$7,000,000
Above $9,000,000		$1,440,000	19.00%	Above $9,000,000

Table 15.08
I.R.C. § 2011 Federal Credit for State Death Taxes

The credit terminates with respect to estates of decedents dying after December 31, 2004. A deduction, IRC § 2058, replaces the credit for estates of decedents dying on or after January 1, 2005. (Pub. L. No. 107-16, § 532(b), June 7, 2001)

I.R.C. § 2604 Federal Credit for State Generation-Skipping Transfer Taxes

The credit terminates for transfers made on or after January 1 2005. (Pub. L. No. 107-16, § 532(d), June 7, 2001)

Table 15.09
State-by-State Summary of Current State Inheritance and Estate Tax Situation

State	Alt. #1: State Estate Tax is the Federal Credit Frozen at a Certain Date	Alt. #2: State Tax Independent of Federal Credit	Alt. #3: State Estate Tax Repealed with Federal Credit in 2005
Alabama	N/A	N/A	§ 40-15-2
Alaska	N/A	N/A	§ 43.31.011
Arizona	N/A	N/A	§ 42-4051*
Arkansas	N/A	N/A	§ 26-59-103
California	N/A	N/A	§§ 13301 & 13302
Colorado	N/A	N/A	§§ 39-23.5-103
Connecticut	N/A	§12-391(d)	N/A
Delaware	N/A	N/A	30 §1502
District of Columbia	§ 47-3701 January 1, 2001	N/A	N/A
Florida	N/A	N/A	§§ 198.02 & 198.41
Georgia	N/A	N/A	§ 48-12-1.1
Hawaii	N/A	N/A	§ 236D-3
Idaho	N/A	N/A	§ 14-403
Illinois	35 §§ 405/2 & 405/3 December 31, 2001, but also a $2,000,000 applic-able exclusion amount	N/A	N/A
Indiana	N/A	§ 6-4.1-1-3	§ 6-4.1-11-5
Iowa	N/A	§ 450.10	§§ 451.2 & 451.13
Kansas	N/A	§79-15, 221	N/A
Kentucky	N/A	§ 140.070	§ 140.130
Louisiana	N/A	§ 47:2403	§ 47:2432
Maine	§ 4062-63 December 31, 2002	N/A	N/A
Maryland	Tax-Gen. § 7-302 December 31, 2001	N/A	N/A
Massachusetts**	65C § 2A December 31, 2000	N/A	N/A
Michigan	§ 205.256(g) The credit as in effect on January 1, 1998 or, at the option of the personal	N/A	§ 205.256(g) The credit as in effect on January 1, 1998 or, at the option of the personal

	representative, at time of death of decedent. This means that the state's estate tax is effectively repealed.		representative, at the time of death of decedent. This means that the state's estate tax is effectively repealed.
Minnesota	§ 291.03 December 31, 2000	N/A	N/A
Mississippi	N/A	N/A	§ 27-9-5
Missouri	N/A	N/A	§ 145.011 & § 145.1000
Montana	N/A	N/A	§ 72-16-905
Nebraska	N/A	§§ 77-2001 & 77-2101.03	N/A
Nevada	N/A	N/A	§ 375A.100
New Hampshire	N/A	N/A	§§ 87:1 & 87:9
New Jersey	§§ 54:38-1(2)(a) December 31, 2001	§ 54:34-1	N/A
New Mexico	N/A	N/A	§ 7-7-3
New York***	Tax § 951 July 22, 1998	N/A	N/A
North Carolina	§ 105-32.2 December 31, 2001	N/A	N/A
North Dakota	N/A	N/A	§ 57-37.1-04
Ohio	N/A	§ 5731.02	§ 5701.11(A)
Oklahoma	N/A	68 §803	68 §804
Oregon	N/A	N/A	§ 118.010(2)
Pennsylvania	N/A	N/A	72 § 9117
Rhode Island	§ 44-22-1.1 January 1, 2001	N/A	N/A
South Carolina	N/A	N/A	§§12-16-20(s) & 12-6-40(A)
South Dakota	N/A		§ 10-40A-3
Tennessee	N/A	§ 67-8-314	§ 67-8-204
Texas	N/A	N/A	Tax § 211.051
Utah	N/A	N/A	§ 59-11-103
Vermont****	32 §§ 7442a, 7475 January 1, 2001	N/A	N/A
Virginia	N/A	N/A	§ 58.1-901, eff. July 1, 2007

Washington	N/A	§ 83.100.040	N/A
West Virginia	N/A	N/A	§ 11-11-4
Wisconsin	§§ 72.02 & 72.01(11m) December 31, 2000 for deaths during 2007	N/A	§§ 72.02 & 72.01 for deaths occurring in 2008 and thereafter
Wyoming	N/A	N/A	§§ 39-19-103 & 39-19-104

* The tax was repealed independent of the federal credit by Laws 2006, Ch. 262, § 3, eff. Sep't 21, 2006.

** The generation skipping transfer tax is also preserved by reference to the I.R.C. § 2602 credit in effect on December 31, 1981. (65C § 4A(c))

*** The generation skipping transfer tax is also preserved by reference to the I.R.C. in effect on or before July 22, 1998 (Tax § 951(a))

**** The generation skipping transfer tax is also preserved by reference to the I.R.C. § 2604 credit in effect on January 1, 2001 (32 § 7460(b))

Table 15.10
Internal Revenue Code Section 2011(b): State Death Tax Credit Before Repeal

(b) Amount of credit.

(1) In general. Except as provided in paragraph (2), the credit allowed by this section shall not exceed the appropriate amount stated in the following table:

If the adjusted taxable estate is:	The maximum tax credit shall be:
Not over $90,000	8/10ths of 1% of the amount by which the adjusted taxable estate exceeds $40,000
Over $90,000 but not over $140,000	$400 plus 1.6% of the excess over $90,000
Over $140,000 but not over $240,000	$1,200 plus 2.4% of the excess over $140,000
Over $240,000 but not over $440,000	$3,600 plus 3.2% of the excess over $240,000
Over $440,000 but not over $640,000	$10,000 plus 4% of the excess over $440,000
Over $640,000 but not over $840,000	$18,000 plus 4.8% of the excess over $640,000
Over $840,000 but not over $1,040,000	$27,600 plus 5.6% of the excess over $840,000
Over $1,040,000 but not over $1,540,000	$38,800 plus 6.4% of the excess over $1, 040,000
Over $1,540,000 but not over $2,040,000	$70,800 plus 7.2% of the excess over $1,540,000
Over $2,040,000 but not over $2,540,000	$106,800 plus 8% of the excess over $2,040,000
Over $2,540,000 but not over $3,040,000	$146,800 plus 8.8% of the excess over $2,540,000
Over $3,040,000 but not over $3,540,000	$190,800 plus 9.6% of the excess over $3,040,000
Over $3,540,000 but not over $4,040,000	$238,800 plus 10.4% of the excess over $3,540,000
Over $4,040,000 but not over $5,040,000	$290,800 plus 11.2% of the excess over $4,040,000
Over $5,040,000 but not over $6,040,000	$402,800 plus 12% of the excess over $5,040,000
Over $6,040,000 but not over $7,040,000	$522,800 plus 12.8% of the excess over $6,040,000
Over $7,040,000 but not over $8,040,000	$650,800 plus 13.6% of the excess over $7,040,000
Over $8,040,000 but not over $9,040,000	$786,800 plus 14.4% of the excess over $8,040,000
Over $9,040,000 but not over $10,040,000	$930,800 plus 15.2% of the excess over $9,040,000
Over $10,040,000	$1,082,800 plus 16% of the excess over $10,040,000

(2) Reduction of maximum credit.

(A) In general. In the case of estates of decedents dying after December 31, 2001, the credit allowed by this section shall not exceed the applicable percentage of the credit otherwise determined under paragraph (1).

(B) Applicable percentage.

In the case of estates of decedents dying during:	The applicable percentage is:
2002	75 percent
2003	50 percent
2004	25 percent

(3) Adjusted taxable estate. For purposes of this section, the term "adjusted taxable estate" means the taxable estate reduced by $ 60,000.

Using the CD-ROM

SYSTEM REQUIREMENTS

- IBM PC or compatible computer with CD-ROM drive
- Windows 95 or higher
- Microsoft® Word 7.0 for Windows™ or compatible word processor
- 10 MB available on hard drive

The *Multistate Guide to Estate Planning* contains files of the Advance Directives of the fifty states, along with more than 50 forms that can be used in conjunction with this book.

Subject to the conditions in the license agreement and the limited warranty, which are reproduced at the end of this book, you may duplicate the files on this disc, modify them as necessary, and create your own customized versions. Using the disc in any way indicates that you accept the terms of the license agreement.

USING THE CD-ROM

The disc data is intended for use with your word processing software. Each document is provided in Rich Text Format. These files can be read by all compatible word processors, including Microsoft Word for Windows and WordPerfect 7 or above. Check your owner's manual for information on the conversion of the documents as required.

USING THE DOCUMENTS

The list of the Disc Contents is available on your disc in a file called _contents.rtf. The listing includes each individual form (both with and without practice notes (comments)). You can open this file and view it on your screen and use it to link to the documents you're interested in, or print a hard copy to use for reference.

1. Open the file _contents.rtf in your word processor.
2. Locate the file you wish to access, and click on the hyperlinked file name. Your word processor will then open the file.
3. You may copy files from the CD-ROM to your hard disk. To edit files you have copied, remember to clear the read-only attribute from the file. To do this, select the name of the file in My Computer, right-click the filename, then choose Properties, and clear the Read-only checkbox.

SOFTWARE SUPPORT

If you experience any difficulties installing or running the electronic files and cannot resolve the problem using the information presented here, call our toll-free software support hotline at 800 835 0105 or visit our website at http://support.cch.com.

CD-ROM Contents

Form	Form Name	File Name	File Type
AK Form 01	Alaska Directives	AKFM01	RTF
AL Form 01	Alabama Directives	ALFM01	RTF
AR Form 01	Arkansas Directives	ARFM01	RTF
AZ Form 01	Arizona Directives	AZFM01	RTF
CA Form 01	California Directive/California Probate Code	CAFM01	RTF
CO Form 01	Colorado Directives	COFM01	RTF
CT Form 01	Connecticut Directives	CTFM01	RTF
DC Form 01	District of Columbia Directives	DCFM01	RTF
FL Form 01	Florida Directives	FLFM01	RTF
GA Form 01	Georgia Directives	GAFM01	RTF
GM Form 01	Guam Directives	GMFM01	RTF
HI Form 01	Hawaii Directives	HIFM01	RTF
IA Form 01	Iowa Directives	IAFM01	RTF
ID Form 01	Idaho Directives	IDFM01	RTF
IL Form 01	Illinois Directives	ILFM01	RTF
IN Form 01	Indiana Directives	INFM01	RTF
KS Form 01	Kansas Directives	KSFM01	RTF
KY Form 01	Kentucky Directives	KYFM01	RTF
LA Form 01	Louisiana Directives	LAFM01	RTF
MA Form 01	Massachusetts Directives	MAFM01	RTF
MD Form 01	Maryland Directives	MDFM01	RTF
ME Form 01	Maine Directives	MEFM01	RTF
MI Form 01	Michigan Directives	MIFM01	RTF
MN Form 01	Minnesota Directives	MNFM01	RTF
MO Form 01	Missouri Directives	MOFM01	RTF
MS Form 01	Mississippi Directives	MSFM01	RTF
MT Form 01	Montana Directives	MTFM01	RTF
NC Form 01	North Carolina Directives	NCFM01	RTF
ND Form 01	North Dakota Directives	NDFM01	RTF
NE Form 01	Nebraska Directives	NEFM01	RTF
NH Form 01	New Hampshire Directives	NHFM01	RTF
NJ Form 01	New Jersey Directives	NJFM01	RTF
NM Form 01	New Mexico Directives	NMFM01	RTF
NV Form 01	Nevada Directives	NVFM01	RTF
NY Form 01	New York Directives	NYFM01	RTF

Form	Form Name	File Name	File Type
OH Form 01	Ohio Directives	**OHFM01**	**RTF**
OK Form 01	Oklahoma Directives	**OKFM01**	**RTF**
OR Form 01	Oregon Directives	**ORFM01**	**RTF**
PA Form 01	Pennsylvania Directives	**PAFM01**	**RTF**
RI Form 01	Rhode Island Directives	**RIFM01**	**RTF**
SC Form 01	South Carolina Directives	**SCFM01**	**RTF**
SD Form 01	South Dakota Directives	**SDFM01**	**RTF**
TN Form 01	Tennessee Directives	**TNFM01**	**RTF**
TX Form 01	Texas Directives	**TXFM01**	**RTF**
UT Form 01	Utah Directives	**UTFM01**	**RTF**
VA Form 01	Virginia Directives	**VAFM01**	**RTF**
VT Form 01	Vermont Directives	**VTFM01**	**RTF**
WA Form 01	Washington Directives	**WAFM01**	**RTF**
WI Form 01	Wisconsin Directives	**WIFM01**	**RTF**
WV Form 01	West Virginia Directives	**WVFM01**	**RTF**
WY Form 01	Wyoming Directives	**WYFM01**	**RTF**

SOFTWARE LICENSE AGREEMENT FOR ELECTRONIC FILES TO ACCOMPANY 2008 MULTISTATE GUIDE TO ESTATE PLANNING (THE "BOOK").

PLEASE READ THE TERMS AND CONDITIONS OF THIS LICENSE AGREEMENT CAREFULLY BEFORE INSTALLING THE FILES FROM THE CD-ROM.

THE ELECTRONIC FILES ARE COPYRIGHTED AND LICENSED (NOT SOLD). BY INSTALLING THE ELECTRONIC FILES ("THE SOFTWARE"), YOU ARE ACCEPTING AND AGREEING TO THE TERMS OF THIS LICENSE AGREEMENT. IF YOU ARE NOT WILLING TO BE BOUND BY THE TERMS OF THIS LICENSE AGREEMENT, YOU SHOULD REMOVE THE SOFTWARE FROM YOUR COMPUTER AT THIS TIME AND PROMPTLY RETURN THE PACKAGE IN RESELLABLE CONDITION AND YOU WILL RECEIVE A REFUND OF YOUR MONEY. THIS LICENSE AGREEMENT REPRESENTS THE ENTIRE AGREEMENT CONCERNING THE SOFTWARE BETWEEN YOU AND CCH (REFERRED TO AS "LICENSOR"), AND IT SUPERSEDES ANY PRIOR PROPOSAL, REPRESENTATION, OR UNDERSTANDING BETWEEN THE PARTIES.

1. License Grant. Licensor hereby grants to you, and you accept, a nonexclusive license to use the Software, and any computer programs contained therein in machine-readable, object code form only, and the accompanying User Documentation, only as authorized in this License Agreement. The Software may be used only on a single computer owned, leased, or otherwise controlled by you, or in the event of the inoperability of that computer, on a backup computer selected by you. Neither concurrent use on two or more computers nor use in a local area network or other network is permitted without separate authorization and the possible payment of other license fees. You agree that you will not assign, sublease, transfer, pledge, lease, rent, or share your rights under the License Agreement. You agree that you may not reverse engineer, decompile, disassemble, or otherwise adapt, modify, or translate the Software.

Upon loading the Software into your computer, you may retain the Software CD-ROM for backup purposes. In addition, you may make one copy of the Software on a set of diskettes (or other storage medium) for the purpose of backup in the event the Software files are damaged or destroyed. You may make one copy of any additional User Documentation (such as the README.TXT file or the "About the Computer Disc" section of the Book) for backup purposes. Any such copies of the Software or the User Documentation shall include the Licensor's copyright and other proprietary notices. Except as authorized under this paragraph, no copies of the Software or any portions thereof may be made by you or any person under your authority or control.

2. Licensor's Rights. You acknowledge and agree that the Software and the User Documentation are proprietary products of Licensor protected under U.S. copyright law. You further acknowledge and agree that all right, title, and interest in and to the Software, including associated intellectual property rights, are and shall remain with Licensor. This License Agreement does not convey to you an interest in or to the Software, including associated intellectual property rights, which are and shall remain with Licensor. This License Agreement does not convey to you an interest in or to the Software, but only a limited right of use revocable in accordance with the terms of this License Agreement.

3. License Fees. The license fees paid by you are paid in consideration of the licenses granted under this License Agreement.

4. Term. This License Agreement is effective upon your installing this software and shall continue until terminated. You may terminate this License Agreement at any time by removing all copies of the Software and returning the CD-ROM to Licensor. Licensor may terminate this License Agreement upon the breach by you of any term hereof. Upon such termination by Licensor, you agree to return to Licensor the Software and all copies and portions thereof.

5. Limited Warranty. Licensor warrants, for our benefit alone, for a period of 90 days from the date of commencement of this License Agreement (referred to as the "Warranty Period") that the Program CD-ROM in which the software is contained is free from defects in material and workmanship. If during the Warranty Period, a defect appears in the Program CD-ROM, you may return the Program to Licensor for either replacement or, at Licensor's option, refund of amounts paid by you under this License Agreement. You agree that the foregoing constitutes your sole and exclusive remedy for breach by Licensor of any warranties made under this Agreement. EXCEPT FOR THE WARRANTIES SET FORTH ABOVE, THE PROGRAM CD-ROM, AND THE SOFTWARE CONTAINED THEREIN, ARE LICENSED "AS-IS," AND LICENSOR DISCLAIMS ANY AND ALL OTHER WARRANTIES, WHETHER EXPRESS OR IMPLIED, INCLUDING, WITHOUT LIMITATION, ANY IMPLIED WARRANTIES OF MERCHANTABILITY OR FITNESS FOR A PARTICULAR PURPOSE.

6. Limitation of Liability. Licensor's cumulative liability to you or any other party for any loss or damages resulting from any claims, demands, or actions arising out of or relating to this Agreement shall not exceed the license fee paid to Licensor for the use of the Software. IN NO EVENT SHALL LICENSOR BE LIABLE FOR ANY INDIRECT, INCIDENTAL, CONSEQUENTIAL, SPECIAL OR EXEMPLARY DAMAGES (INCLUDING, BUT NOT LIMITED TO, LOSS OF DATA, BUSINESS INTERRUPTION, OR LOST PROFITS) EVEN IF LICENSOR HAS BEEN ADVISED OF THE POSSIBILITY OF SUCH DAMAGES.

7. Miscellaneous. The License Agreement shall be construed and governed in accordance with the laws of the State of Delaware. Should any term of this License Agreement be declared void or unenforceable by any court of competent jurisdiction, such declaration shall have no effect on the remaining terms hereof. The failure of either party to enforce any rights granted hereunder or to take action against the other party in the event of any breach hereunder shall not be deemed a waiver by that party as to subsequent enforcement of rights or subsequent actions in the event of future breaches.